HENRY SIDGWICK: EYE OF THE UNIVERSE

Henry Sidgwick is one of the great intellectual figures of nineteenth-century Britain. He was first and foremost a great moral philosopher, whose master-work, *The Methods of Ethics*, is still widely studied today. But he was many other things besides, writing on religion, economics, politics, education, and literature. He was deeply involved in the founding of the first college for women at the University of Cambridge, and he was a leading figure in para-psychology. He was also much concerned with the sexual politics of his close friend John Addington Symonds, a pioneer of gay studies. Through his famous student G. E. Moore, a direct line can be traced from Sidgwick and his circle to the Bloomsbury group.

Bart Schultz has written a magisterial overview of this great Victorian sage – the first comprehensive study, offering provocative new critical perspectives on the life and the work. Sidgwick's ethical work is situated in the context of his theological and political commitments and is revealed as a necessarily guarded statement of his deepest philosophical convictions and doubts. All other areas of his writings are covered and presented in the context of the late Victorian culture of imperialism.

This biography, or "Goethean reconstruction," will be eagerly sought out by readers interested in philosophy, Victorian studies, political theory, the history of ideas, educational theory, the history of psychology, and gender and gay studies.

Bart Schultz is Fellow and Lecturer in the Division of the Humanities and Special Programs Coordinator in the Graham School of General Studies at the University of Chicago.

Henry Sidgwick:
Eye of the Universe
An Intellectual Biography

Bart Schultz
University of Chicago

CAMBRIDGE
UNIVERSITY PRESS

PUBLISHED BY THE PRESS SYNDICATE OF THE UNIVERSITY OF CAMBRIDGE
The Pitt Building, Trumpington Street, Cambridge, United Kingdom

CAMBRIDGE UNIVERSITY PRESS
The Edinburgh Building, Cambridge CB2 2RU, UK
40 West 20th Street, New York, NY 10011-4211, USA
477 Williamstown Road, Port Melbourne, VIC 3207, Australia
Ruiz de Alarcón 13, 28014 Madrid, Spain
Dock House, The Waterfront, Cape Town 8001, South Africa

http://www.cambridge.org

First published 2004

Printed in the United States of America

Typeface Ehrhardt 10.5/13 pt.   *System* LaTeX 2$_\varepsilon$ [TB]

A catalog record for this book is available from the British Library.

Library of Congress Cataloging in Publication data
Schultz, Bart.
Henry Sidgwick, eye of the universe : an intellectual biography / Bart Schultz.
p.   cm.
Includes bibliographical references and index.
ISBN 0-521-82967-4
1. Sidgwick, Henry, 1838–1900.   1. Title.
BJ604.S5S38   2004
192–dc21
[B]   2003055354

ISBN 0 521 82967 4 hardback

FOR MARTY AND MADELEINE

"We learn only from people we love."

— Goethe

Remember me when I am gone away,
Gone far away into the silent land;
When you can no more hold me by the hand,
Nor I half turn to go yet turning stay.
Remember me when no more day by day
You tell me of our future that you planned:
Only remember me; you understand
It will be late to counsel then or pray.
Yet if you should forget me for a while
And afterwards remember, do not grieve:
For if the darkness and corruption leave
A vestige of the thoughts that once I had,
Better by far you should forget and smile
Than that you should remember and be sad.

> "Remember," by Christina Rossetti,
> described by Henry Sidgwick as
> "perhaps the most perfect thing
> that any living poet has written"

I ask for life – for life Divine
Where man's true self may move
In one harmonious cord to twine
The threads of *Knowledge* and of Love

> Henry Sidgwick, circa 1859

Contents

Acknowledgments

Henry Sidgwick: Eye of the Universe reflects a very long, very strange trip. It is quite possible that my thinking about Henry Sidgwick (and John Addington Symonds) began longer ago than I can actually recall, at some point in the 1960s when I was reading various works in which their names figured – works that, befitting the times, had to do with religion, ethics, art, psychology, and cosmic consciousness. My sixties vision of a new age resonated happily, at least on some counts, with the visions of a new age that animated the late Victorians – visions that rebelled against the limitations of a perversely hypocritical commonsense morality. What curious forces led to my intense, continuing engagement with these figures and themes into and beyond 2001 can only make for much speculation. At any rate, circa 1967, I would not have been at all likely to prophesy that this scholarly tome was the form that my artwork would take.

I console myself with the thought that I have at least had a most unorthodox academic career and wound up marrying an art historian and adopting a beautiful little girl. It is to Marty and Madeleine that I owe everything that is good, in this book and in such life as has existed outside of it, and it is to them that I dedicate it.

My parents, Reynolds and Marian Schultz, now deceased, and my three sisters, their husbands and children, were and are a source of loving support, whatever qualms they might have about my stubborn waywardness, on display in the material that follows.

And who could forget dear Churchill, the world's largest miniature Schnauzer?

I would like to express my gratitude to the many friends who contributed to this project. Their support – and, of course, criticism – has been vital and generous. First thanks must again go to Marty, her critical reading having been so crucial to my efforts. Next thanks must go to Jerry

Schneewind, the rightly acknowledged dean of Sidgwick studies, who has been a model and a marvel, showing just how open-minded a senior scholar can be, even while being absolutely unstinting in his (much-needed) critical input. Mark Singer, another friend from the Sidgwick Society, has also, for all our differences, provided much welcome help and stimulus, as has Russell Hardin, to whom I owe far more than I can convey. In more recent days, my long-distance collegial friendship and collaboration with Roger Crisp has been a source of great pleasure and intellectual value; my work with him on "Sidgwick 2000" (*Utilitas* 12, November 2000) did much to inspire me to complete *Henry Sidgwick: Eye of the Universe*. Closer to home, I have benefited from Charles Larmore's erudite company, our exchanges invariably proving most thought-provoking. Very importantly, both John Skorupski and Tom Hurka have been exceedingly generous with their time and input, providing me with a wealth of detailed critical commentary that is reflected in the following pages time and again. Finally, exchanges with Rob Shaver, Brad Hooker, David Weinstein, Sissela Bok, and Stephen Darwall, during the assemblage of "Sidgwick 2000," also proved most fruitful. In fact, the journals *Ethics* and *Utilitas* ought to be included in this list, given how much they have meant to my work. Cambridge University Press and my editor, Terence Moore, belong here as well. The Press also supplied me with an excellent and congenial copy editor, Russell Hahn, whose efforts are reflected on nearly every page.

Some old teachers – some of whom are, alas, now gone – will always have my enduring gratitude; the late Alan Donagan, the late David Greenstone, Shirley Castelnuovo, John Murphy, Jon Elster, Stephen Toulmin, and Brian Barry stand out in my memory. I owe them much, even if my interests and thinking have always remained rather apart. The late William Frankena, although never one of my formal teachers, went out of his way to help me, and my correspondence with him was a great source of inspiration. The late John Rawls was similarly generous, as was the late Edward Said.

Of course, alongside these names, I must mention my students in the College at the University of Chicago, from whom it has been my pleasure to learn for the past fifteen years. Insofar as I have been able to "remain a boy" – that is, like Sidgwick's friend John Grote, excited but undecided about all the great questions, including the question of whether there are any great questions – it is thanks to them. I am also truly grateful

to the talented scholar-administators who make Chicago such an excit-
ing community, including Dan Garber, Geof Stone, John Boyer, Richard
Saller, Bernie Silberman, Bill Brown, Janel Mueller, Joel Snyder, Dan
Shannon, and Jeff Rosen.

I am also aware of very real debts to Barbara Donagan, David Brink,
John Deigh, Donald Davidson, Dale Miller, Ian Jarvie, Peter Nicholson,
Alan Gauld, Chris Stray, Robert Todd, David Tracy, Stuart Michaels,
Martha Nussbaum, Phyllis Grosskurth, George Chauncey, David Phillips,
Georgios Varouxakis, Dick Arneson, Monique Canto-Sperber, Louis
Crompton, John Gibbins, Bill Lubenow, Chris Parsons, Richard Stern,
Julian Baggini, Jennifer Welchman, Alan Ryan, Onora O'Neil, Richard
Flathman, Wendy Donner, Maria Morales, Ray Monk, Stefan Collini,
Ross Harrison, Evelyn Perry, Dave Coxall, Charlene Haddock Seigfried,
John Pemble, Noam Chomsky, and Isabelle Richet.

Two further scholarly projects have turned out to be quite useful for my
work on this book. Assembling *The Complete Works and Select Scholarly
Correspondence of Henry Sidgwick* (Charlottesville, VA: InteLex Corporation, 1997; 2nd ed. 1999), the first such collection of Sidgwick's works, for
the InteLex Corporation's Past Masters series of electronic databases was a
time-consuming but valuable undertaking. My thanks to Mark Rooks and
Brad Lamb, who invited me to take on the project and who also devoted a
great deal of time to it. It is courtesy of them that so much Sidgwickian text
has been transferred to this electronic format and made readily available
for scholarly work.

Work on the InteLex project brought me into collaboration with the historian Jean Wilkins, who not only did a fine job of transcribing Sidgwick's
journal, but was also instrumental in tracking down various obscure works
in the Cambridge libraries and thus helped with the overall assembly of
the database as well. And it was at an early stage of that project that I also
recruited the aid of the historian Janet Oppenheim, who supplied valuable
advice and material relating to Sidgwick's parapsychological research. Her
premature death, from cancer, was a terrible loss to the scholarly community. A friend of Janet Oppenheim's from the British Society for Psychical
Research, Eleanor O'Keeffe, was also extremely helpful, doing everything
that she could to ensure that we had a complete record of Sidgwick's
publications for the Society.

With the second edition of the *Complete Works*, I was brought into
collaboration with Andrew Dakyns and Belinda Robinson. Andrew, the

xii   Acknowledgments

descendant of Sidgwick's dear friend Henry Graham Dakyns, turned out
to be as enjoyable and erudite a companion as his ancestor was reputed to
have been, and my work with him and Belinda – first on the Sidgwick–
Dakyns correspondence included in the database, and then on the volume
Strange Audacious Life: The Construction of John Addington Symonds – has
been a delight. I was also led in this connection to make contact with
Herbert Schueller and Bob Peters, the heroic editors of the pathbreaking,
three-volume *Letters of John Addington Symonds* (Detroit: Wayne State
University Press, 1967–69), a complementary copy of which Bob generously sent to me.

Andrew, Belinda, and I first got together at a conference, John
Addington Symonds: The Public and Private Faces of Victorian Culture,
sponsored by the Department of the History of Art and the Department of Historical Studies and held at Bristol University in the spring
of 1998. My visit to Bristol was enchanting, thanks especially to John
Pemble and Annie Burnside, the latter being the warden of Clifton Hill
House, Symonds's old home, in which the conference was held, and where
I also had the pleasure of meeting Vikky and Chris Furse, the latter one
of Symonds's descendants. The conference papers were revised and published as *John Addington Symonds: Culture and the Demon Desire*, ed. John
Pemble (London: Macmillan, 2000). My paper on that occasion, "Truth
and Its Consequences: The Friendship of Symonds and Henry Sidgwick,"
was a distillation of much of my work following an earlier conference,
Henry Sidgwick as Philosopher and Historian, organized by me and held
at the University of Chicago in May of 1990 – work that later appeared in
revised, extended form as my collection *Essays on Henry Sidgwick* (New
York: Cambridge University Press, 1992). A special thanks to the many
reviewers of this last volume.

Much of the preparatory work for this project was conducted at
Cambridge University, Sidgwick's home for most of his adult life. My visits
there always involved trips to the beautiful Wren Library, Trinity College,
to consult the Sidgwick Papers. Working in the shadow of Lord Byron
proved inspirational, and it is a great pleasure to thank David McKitterick,
the librarian; Ronald Milne, the former sublibrarian; Jonathan Smith, the
archivist; and former archivist Diana Chardin for making these visits so
enjoyable and productive. Without their help – and without the generous assistance of many other staff members as well, notably Andrew
Lambert – my work could not have prospered. A special thanks goes to

Diana Chardin for tracking down one of Sidgwick's (all-too-few) lecture manuscripts and to Jonathan Smith for vital aid with my references and the cover photo. My most grateful acknowledgment goes to the Master and Fellows of Trinity College for allowing the reproduction of various manuscript materials from the Sidgwick Papers.

The Modern Record Centre at King's College, Cambridge, also proved to be an invaluable resource. It contains a great quantity of important correspondence and manuscript material, including the correspondence with Oscar Browning and eight volumes of student notes taken from Sidgwick's lectures on the history of ethics. Jacqueline Cox, the archivist, has been extraordinarily helpful and efficient, along with her assistant, Elizabeth Stratton. I am very pleased to thank the Master and Fellows of King's College for allowing the reproduction of various letters.

My visits to Newnham College were also inspirational; Newnham simply lives and breathes the spirit of the Sidgwicks, what they stood for practically and philosophically. It was during my first visit to Cambridge, while meditating by the Sidgwick fountain at Newnham, that the resolution to write this book formed in my mind. My thanks go to the Newnham College Library and Archives, especially to Elisabeth van Houts, the former archivist; Anne Thompson, the current archivist; and Deborah Hodder, the librarian, who have been unfailingly pleasant and helpful. I happily acknowledge the Principal and Fellows of Newnham College for allowing reproduction of certain materials herein.

At University Library, Cambridge, which also holds a significant body of Sidgwick material, I received much aid and information from Mark Nichols and Godfrey Waller, for which I am most grateful; my thanks go to that remarkable institution for allowing the reproduction of various materials herein.

Thanks also go to the staff members at Darwin College Library, the Philosophy Library, the Library at Gonville and Caius College, the Social and Political Library, the Library at Downing College, the Marshall Library, and the Library at Girton College (where Kate Perry was especially helpful). Special thanks go to the people at Clare Hall, particularly Dacea Smith, for their hospitality during some of my visits to Cambridge.

At Oxford University, the Bodleian's Helen Langley, in Modern Political Papers, very generously gave of her time and expertise, doing much to expedite my work. Thanks also go to Colin Harris, in Modern Papers, for his valuable assistance. Grateful acknowledgment goes to the Bodleian Library for supplying microfilm copies of the Bryce correspondence (especially valuable for analyzing Sidgwick's handwriting) and the correspondence between Symonds and Roden Noel and for allowing various reproductions of their materials.

Katharine Thompson, the modern manuscripts assistant at Balliol College Library, was quite helpful in fielding my inquiries about Sidgwick holdings. And I would like to thank the library at Harris Manchester College for supplying me with a missing Metaphysical Society paper and graciously allowing the reproduction of various parts of Sidgwick's papers for the Society. Ms. Pauline Adams, at the Amelia B. Edwards Archive, Somerville College, also supplied me with some most helpful information about their archival holdings.

The London Library, which holds the original manuscript of the Symonds memoirs, is a remarkable institution, and I am most grateful to the staff there for welcoming me and providing expert help with my research.

I am also delighted to thank the Department of Manuscripts at the University of St. Andrews, especially Norman Reid, who was a wonderful fund of helpful information and of crucial importance in allowing the reproduction of Sidgwick's letters to Wilfrid Ward in the InteLex database. Thanks also go to Paul Johnson for his help with the final check of the transcriptions of that correspondence. It is a pleasure to acknowledge the University of St. Andrews for allowing me to use this material.

A warm thank-you goes to Richard Freeman, the owner of the Foxwell Papers, for graciously allowing their reproduction in my database and aiding my research in other ways as well.

Liz Waxdoff, the archivist at Knebworth, and the staff at the Hertfordshire Record Office, especially Kathryn Thompson, helped track down some important correspondence and were most generous in lending their efforts to this project. I am of course delighted to express my thanks to Lord Cobbold for kind permission to reproduce Sidgwick's letter to Robert Lytton, from the Knebworth House Collection.

Sincerest thanks also go to Michael Richardson, in Manuscripts at the University of Bristol Library, for expertly and enthusiastically fielding any number of inquiries about the Sidgwick and Symonds material held in the collection there and supplying me with some very important material. It is a pleasure to thank the University of Bristol Library for permission to reproduce the letters from Sidgwick to Symonds.

And another sincerest thanks goes to Brian Dyson, the university archivist, in Archives and Special Collections at the Brynmoor Jones Library, University of Hull; his help, and that of his assistant, Angela Quinby, in dealing with the Roden Noel letters to Sidgwick was invaluable, as was his aid in contacting Desmond Heath, the author of *Roden Noel: A Wide Angle* and the husband of Sylvia Putterill, one of Noel's descendants. I am delighted to thank the library at the University of Hull for allowing me to use some of this material. And I am delighted to thank Desmond Heath for supplying me with a complementary copy of his book and valuable – very rare – additional correspondence from Sidgwick to Noel, not only granting me permission to use it, but gifting it to me. I eagerly look forward to continuing work with him to bring to light more Sidgwick–Noel correspondence.

The British Library has been another happy and rewarding retreat, with particular thanks going to C. J. Wright, J. Conway, Zoë Stansell, and Michael Boggan, of the Department of Manuscripts, for helping me in various ways, notably by expediting receipt of a microfilm copy of the Sidgwick–Balfour correspondence. I am grateful to the British Library for permission to reprint selected letters from this collection, and to Lord Balfour, who has always been very cordial and helpful in responding to my inquiries. Jane Hill and the staff at the Historical Search Room of the Scottish Records Office, Edinburgh, where most of the Whittingehame Balfour papers are now held, were also singularly patient and helpful in responding to my many questions.

The staff at the Sheffield Archives, Sheffield City Libraries, have also been a valuable resource, supplying me with important material from the Carpenter manuscripts in their possession; I gratefully acknowledge their permission to use some of the letters of Edward Carpenter and Horatio Brown in their possession. A sincere thanks goes to François Lafitte, the literary heir to Havelock Ellis, for graciously and helpfully responding to my inquiries.

Naturally, the Historical Manuscripts Commission, UK National Register of Archives, was a most useful resource, and I have often availed myself of it; warm thanks go to the many staff members there who have aided my efforts, particularly Dr. A. P. Lewis, in the Curatorial Office, who supplied me with much information about Horatio Brown's manuscripts and correspondence.

The staff at the Harry Ransom Humanities Research Center at the University of Texas, Austin, has been a rich resource, both personally and electronically.

Grateful acknowledgment also goes to the staff in Special Collections and Archives at the Milton S. Eisenhower Library at The Johns Hopkins University, particularly to Joan Grattan, who helped discover the (presumed lost) letter from Sidgwick to John Stuart Mill. It is a pleasure to thank the Milton S. Eisenhower Library for allowing the reproduction of this important document.

And it is a special pleasure to express my indebtedness to Harvard University, the vast scholarly resources of which have been invaluable to my work. I am especially grateful to the Houghton Library, particularly to Leslie Morris, and to Bay James, the James heir, for permission to reproduce parts of Henry and Eleanor Sidgwick's letters to William James.

Thanks, too, go to the Beinecke Rare Book and Manuscript Library at Yale University, for their helpful reception while researching Sidgwick's letters to George Eliot.

I am also delighted to thank the Library at the University of Wales, Aberystwyth, especially Jackie Woollam, for help with my inquiries and for generously and speedily supplying me with a copy of the unabridged version of "The Pursuit of Culture."

Over the years, many other institutions and individuals have been very generous in furthering my research. With apologies to those I may inadvertently omit, I would like to record my thanks to the staff in Special Collections at the University of Edinburgh and the staff in Special Collections at the University of Glasgow. In the United States, I have also been helped by the staffs in Special Collections at the Joseph Regenstein Library at the University of Chicago, the Bancroft Library at the University of California–Berkeley, the Sterling Memorial Library at Stanford University, the Butler Library at Columbia University, the New York Public Library, and numerous others. The Regenstein Library, I should add, has been a source and second home to me for more than twenty-five years.

The Theosophical Society, with its U.S. national headquarters in Wheaton, Illinois, responded to some of my inquiries.

Lord Rayleigh and the Rt. Honorable Guy Strutt were most gracious in allowing me to visit Terling Place, where the Sidgwicks spent so much of their time (and are buried), and to do research on the estate. Their aid and hospitality was and is deeply appreciated, and I gratefully acknowledge their efforts and generosity. My feeling for the atmosphere in which the Sidgwicks lived gained much from this truly memorable visit.

A visit to the Sidgwicks' house in Cambridge, "Hillside," was also fascinating, and my thanks go to the students who now inhabit it for allowing me to look around, wandering and wondering in incomprehensible reverie.

Last, but very, very far from least, my research and travels have benefited immeasurably from the aid and sympathy generously given by Ms. Ann Baer, Sidgwick's great-niece, a descendant of Arthur Sidgwick, who supplied me with much useful information about the Sidgwick family tree. My profound thanks go to her and to the other members of the Sidgwick family – especially the philosopher Andrew Belsey – for being so supportive of my research and encouraging the publication of the fruits thereof. Ann Baer was also kind enough to put me in touch with Roberta Blanshard, who was eager to aid my search for various Sidgwick materials that had once been in the possession of her late husband, Brand Blanshard, a founder of the Sidgwick Society.

As this record should suggest, the voyage producing *Henry Sidgwick: Eye of the Universe* has been a long one. And it could well go on forever, given how much research remains to be done. Sympathetic understanding, contemporary or historical, is hard work.

Abbreviations

References to and citations of Sidgwick's major works are given parenthetically in the text using the following abbreviations. All works were
published by Macmillan and Co., London, except for the pamphlet "The
Ethics of Conformity and Subscription" (London: Williams and Norgate)
and *Practical Ethics* (London: Swan Sonnenschein). A space separates abbreviation and page number. If the reference is to an edition other than the
last, the number of the edition is placed immediately after the abbreviation
and before the space. Thus, (ME1 7) refers to *The Methods of Ethics*, first
edition, p. 7.

ECS   "The Ethics of Conformity and Subscription," 1870.

ME   *The Methods of Ethics*, 1st ed., 1874; 2nd ed., 1877; 3rd ed., 1884;
4th ed., 1890; 5th ed., 1893; 6th ed., 1901; 7th ed., 1907; Japanese
translation, 1898; German translation, 1909; Italian translation,
1995; French translation, 2003. Sidgwick also published *A Supplement to the First Edition of the Methods of Ethics* (1878) and *A
Supplement to the Second Edition of the Methods of Ethics* (1884),
containing the changes made to each of those editions.

PPE   *The Principles of Political Economy*, 1st ed., 1883; 2nd ed., 1887;
3rd ed., 1901.

OHE   *Outlines of the History of Ethics for English Readers*, 1st ed., 1886;
2nd ed., 1888; 3rd ed., 1892; 4th ed., 1896; 5th ed., 1902; Italian
translation, 1902.

EP   *The Elements of Politics*, 1st ed., 1891; 2nd ed., 1897; 3rd ed., 1908;
4th ed., 1919.

PE   *Practical Ethics: A Collection of Addresses and Essays*, 1st ed., 1898;
2nd ed., 1909.

Posthumous Books

GSM   *Lectures on the Ethics of T. H. Green, H. Spencer, and J. Martineau*, ed. E. E. Constance Jones, 1902.

PSR   *Philosophy, Its Scope and Relations: An Introductory Course of Lectures*, ed. James Ward, 1902.

DEP   *The Development of European Polity*, ed. Eleanor Mildred Sidgwick, 1903.

MEA   *Miscellaneous Essays and Addresses*, ed. Eleanor Mildred Sidgwick and Arthur Sidgwick, 1904.

LPK   *Lectures on the Philosophy of Kant and Other Philosophical Lectures and Essays*, ed. James Ward, 1905.

M   *Henry Sidgwick, A Memoir*, ed. Eleanor Mildred Sidgwick and Arthur Sidgwick, 1906.

For a complete bibliography, covering all of Sidgwick's many essays, articles, and reviews, as well as the archival resources and reviews of his major works, see the entry on him by J. B. Schneewind and Bart Schultz in *The Cambridge Bibliography of English Literature, Vol. 4, 1800–1900*, 3rd ed., ed. Joanne Shattock (Cambridge: Cambridge University Press, 1999). The only complete collection of Sidgwick's writings is *The Complete Works and Select Correspondence of Henry Sidgwick*, ed. Bart Schultz et al. (Charlottesville, VA: InteLex Corporation, 1997; 2nd ed. 1999), an electronic database to which frequent reference is made in the text. This collection is referred to in the text by the abbreviation CWC; because of the electronic format, no page references to it are given, though the original print or archival references are often provided or simply used instead. However, much of the material in the database – such as the complete, matched Sidgwick–Dakyns correspondence – has been transcribed and reproduced for the first time, and the originals are from private collections without archival or other reference numbers. Please note that the translations of Greek terms and expressions are reserved for the notes, though, unless otherwise indicated, these are simply the translations given in the work being cited.

Overture

My aim in what I am about to say now is to give such an account of my life – mainly my inner intellectual life – as shall render the central and fundamental aims that partially at least determined its course when apparently most fitful and erratic, as clear and intelligible as I can. That aim is very simply stated. It has been the solution, or contribution to the solution, of the deepest problems of human life. The peculiarity of my career has been that I have sought light on these problems, and that not casually but systematically and laboriously, from very various sources and by very diverse methods.

Henry Sidgwick, "Autobiographical Fragment" dictated from his deathbed[1]

Stranger lives than Henry Sidgwick's have resulted from the philosophical quest for the ultimate truth about the Universe, but his is nonetheless a source of considerable fascination. As a Victorian philosopher, social scientist, literary critic, educator, reformer, and parapsychologist, an academic who spent nearly his entire adult life teaching at and reforming Cambridge University, Sidgwick was at the philosophical heart of England when England was at the height of its worldly power. He was friendly with everyone from William Gladstone to George Eliot, had in one brother-in-law a future prime minister and in another a future archbishop of Canterbury, and served as a leading figure in that most famous of elite secret discussion societies, the Cambridge "Apostles," which would go on to give the world the Bloomsbury circle and the Cambridge spies. And, after the publication of his masterpiece, *The Methods of Ethics* (1874), he was often regarded as the most philosophically sophisticated defender of the utilitarianism of John Stuart Mill, who had been perhaps the single most influential intellectual figure of the mid-Victorian period.

Sidgwick represented a form of philosophical life that held on to many of the reformist Millian hopes for an open, educating society rich in social experimentation and cultural vanguards, a society that would represent a progressively expanding circle of human sympathy and the flourishing of social intelligence. Like other academic liberals, notably his friend T. H. Green, he helped open the way for such developments as the ethical culture movement and the settlement movement. In fact, Sidgwick battled in a brilliant series of culture wars about the fate of religion, morals, art, and education, proving himself a forceful critic of Matthew Arnold's claims about "the best that has been thought and said." Significant portions of the modern university curriculum now being fought over were shaped by Sidgwick, the classicist who opposed mandatory Greek and Latin, who helped to establish philosophy as an independent professional discipline, who worried about the scientific illiteracy of the graduates in the humanities, and who fought to extend educational opportunities to women and the working class. Cambridge University's Newnham College stands today as a vivid reminder of Sidgwick's life and work, or at least of one of the more public parts of it. His influence often worked behind the scenes.

Yet Sidgwick always remained rather distanced, even alienated, from a good many of his cultural contexts; his life, like Mill's, was punctuated by mental and moral crises. An exceptionally self-critical, reflective voice, his brilliance shone through more in his perpetual doubt about the proposed solutions to "the deepest problems of human life" than in the defense of one. One formative event, personally and philosophically, was his agonized decision in 1869 to resign his position at Cambridge because he could no longer in good conscience subscribe to the Thirty-Nine Articles of the Church of England, as legally required. This drama would replay itself over and again in his life, his detailed casuistical reflections on it extending from his early publications and to his last, since even after subscription was no longer required he would question whether someone as skeptical as himself ought to be teaching ethics.[2] Ironically, given how recent critics of utilitarianism have urged that it cannot effectively handle the matter of integrity, Sidgwick's life and work were entangled from beginning to end with precisely this issue, which was of a piece with his struggle with hypocrisy, both his own and that of the larger culture.

Sidgwick thus represented the classic mid-Victorian, post-Darwinian struggle between the "emancipated head and the traditional heart."[3] However, to paint his deepest concerns in such broad strokes is scarcely to do justice to the richer, more intriguing, and more troubling elements of his legacy. Unlike Nietzsche, who died at nearly the same historical moment,

Sidgwick was an eminently sane person much loved for his sympathetic and beneficent character, with a certain genius for intimate friendship and conversation, albeit of a seriously philosophical sort. But like Nietzsche, and unlike Bentham or Mill, he regarded the "death of God" as of monumental significance for Western civilization, a potential cataclysm. This was where the deepest problems were to be found, the ones most demanding of serious reflection and self-scrutiny, of all the rigors of the Socratic quest. Sidgwick's various inquiries and reformist efforts were infused with a sense of urgency and anxiety that finds no clear parallel in the earlier utilitarians, energetic reformers though they were; this urgency and anxiety had everything to do with the fate of civilization in a post-Christian era and with the need for a new cultural synthesis.

My aim in this book is to convey some sense of just what Sidgwick's self-assessment actually involved, and of how his "inner intellectual life" ultimately evolved, how he became what he was. But the Sidgwick who emerges in the following pages is quite different from the one featured in most twentieth-century readings of him, framed when his legacy was often rather cloudy.

As a once-popular line of interpretation had it, the utilitarian tradition of promoting the greatest happiness for the greatest number began, in its modern, secular form, with Jeremy Bentham's fanatical legal and political reformism, culminating in Britain's Reform Act of 1832, which movement was then philosophically and politically developed and qualified mainly by the younger Mill, with whom it crested. Sidgwick is then cast as a kind of bookish, academicized remnant of this legacy, holding out against the wave of philosophical idealism that swept such figures as Green and F. H. Bradley into the forefront of British philosophy, until with the new century G. E. Moore and Bertrand Russell shifted the current, and contemporary analytical philosophy was launched. "The last surviving representative of the Utilitarians" is how Russell depicted and dispatched his teacher, "Old Sidg."[4]

Indeed, during the twentieth century, Sidgwick was all too often viewed as merely an "eminent Victorian," an erudite but dull read, what with all that tedious Victorian earnestness. By the time Russell, Moore, Lytton Strachey, J. M. Keynes, and Ludwig Wittgenstein were designing the Cambridge scene, in the early decades of the twentieth century, Sidgwick was deemed the dead hand of a pre-philosophical, hypocritical, sexually warped era. It was a lonely C. D. Broad, a later successor to Sidgwick's chair at Cambridge, who would write that "Sidgwick's *Methods of Ethics* seems to me to be on the whole the best treatise on moral theory that has ever been written, and to be one of the English philosophical classics."[5] For the most part, the aesthetic vanguards of Bloomsbury, along with the logical positivists and empiricists and those under the spell of the magnetic Wittgenstein or of ordinary language philosophy, found Sidgwick's substantive ethical theorizing a quaint relic of Cambridge's dim past, better forgotten. And the (long) enduring elements of the earlier, idealistic school were not exactly given to recalling the importance of Sidgwick, even when they criticized what they saw as the simplistic formalism of the new analytical movement. F. H. Bradley went from being a youthful critic of Sidgwick to being an older critic of Russell and Moore.

Ironically, it was the remarkably pervasive Bloomsbury mentality that, as much as anything, clouded the reception of Sidgwick during the first half of the twentieth century. "He never did anything but wonder whether Christianity was true and prove it wasn't and hope that it was" – this was the famous pronouncement of J. M. Keynes, after reading *Henry Sidgwick, A Memoir* (1906), assembled by Eleanor Sidgwick and Arthur Sidgwick.[6] The Bloomsbury letters, especially those between Keynes and Strachey, are littered with disparaging remarks about Sidgwick, his life, his times, and his philosophy.[7] Strachey called it "an appalling time to have lived" and "the Glass Case Age":

Themselves as well as their ornaments, were left under glass cases. Their refusal to face any fundamental question fairly – either about people or God – looks at first sight like cowardice; but I believe it was simply the result of an innate incapacity for penetration – for getting either out of themselves or into anything or anybody else. They were enclosed in glass. How intolerable! Have you noticed, too, that they were nearly all physically impotent? – Sidgwick himself, Matthew Arnold, Jowett, Leighton, Ruskin, Watts. It's damned difficult to copulate through a glass case.[8]

Strachey had in fact seriously considered using Sidgwick as one of the featured figures in his wickedly sarcastic *Eminent Victorians* (1918), but he contented himself with pronouncing him a "shocking wobbler," and a dishonest one at that, someone whose lamentations over his lost faith were suspiciously prolonged. Moreover, the leading Bloomsberries, mostly bred by the Apostles, were none too pleased with the light shed on them by the *Memoir*, which told of Sidgwick's involvement with the group.

Even those who lamented the ascendance of Bloomsbury tended, in the very act, to concede its importance. F. R. Leavis, the famous literary critic who directed much of his criticism at both Bloomsbury and the cult of Wittgenstein, expostulated, "Can we imagine Sidgwick or Leslie Stephen or Maitland being influenced by, or interested in, the equivalent of Lytton Strachey? By what steps, and by the operation of what causes, did so great a change come over Cambridge in so comparatively short a time?"[9] That the change was great was something that few cared to deny, whatever their stance on its quality. But in any event, the younger generations of Apostles were scarcely prone to casting nostalgic backward glances, even at one of their "Popes" who had profoundly shaped their own order.

Given the social and intellectual positioning of the Bloomsbury group, it is perhaps not surprising that their judgments on cultural matters carried such punch, though in the case of Sidgwick, the disparagement was exacerbated by the constant flow of invidious comparisons to Moore, whose *Principia Ethica* (1903) was virtually an object of worship. Strachey effused to Moore:

I think your book has not only wrecked and shattered all writers on Ethics from Aristotle and Christ to Herbert Spencer and Mr Bradley, it has not only laid the true foundations of Ethics, it has not only left all modern philosophy *bafouee* – these seem to me small achievements compared to the establishment of that Method which shines like a sword between the lines. It is the scientific method deliberately applied, for the first time, to Reasoning. Is that true? You perhaps shake your head, but henceforward who will be able to tell lies one thousand times as easily as before? The truth, there can be no doubt, is really now upon the march. I date from Oct. 1903 the beginning of the Age of Reason.[10]

Echoes of this can still be found in some philosophers of a metaethical bent. An influential recent work, "Toward *Fin de siècle* Ethics: Some Trends," coauthored by Stephen Darwall, Allan Gibbard, and Peter Railton," takes Moore's *Principia* as setting the agenda for twentieth-century ethical philosophizing: "However readily we now reject as antiquated his views in semantics and epistemology, it seems impossible to deny that Moore was on to something."[11]

But of course, despite his own Bloomsbury-style rhetoric, most of what Moore was "on to" was already there in Sidgwick, his teacher in the 1890s, whose *Methods* is the most heavily cited work in the *Principia*. Moore had attended the Sidgwick lectures that were posthumously published as *Lectures on the Ethics of T. H. Green, H. Spencer, and J. Martineau*, and many of the more philosophical reviewers of the first edition of *Principia*, such as Bernard Bosanquet, noted how deeply indebted he was to Sidgwick's work.[12] Moore's *Principia* in fact shared much of its philosophical orientation with earlier work by Sidgwick and Hastings Rashdall and with developing work by H. A. Prichard, David Ross, A. C. Ewing, and Broad.[13] In later years, Russell, at least, readily admitted how unfairly Sidgwick had been treated during this dawning of "the Age of Reason," though his own noncognitivist approach to ethics scarcely served to renew interest in the *Methods*, however indebted to that work he may have been.[14]

Getting beyond the caricatures of Sidgwick floating through the first half of the twentieth century has been no easy task. If few commentaries on Sidgwick have quite succeeded in doing this, perhaps part of the reason is that they have failed to grasp how, ironically enough, Sidgwick was so profoundly important in shaping the Bloomsbury circle itself, or at least the better, more philosophical parts of it, those reflecting its Apostolic origins. This latter refers to more than the academic commonalities binding, say, Moore, Broad, and Ross, or what Keynes acknowledged as "the foot" Moore had in Sidgwick. It refers, more comprehensively, to the Apostolic ethic, linked to the Victorian Platonic revival, of molding character for the wholehearted, high-minded, disinterested fellowship committed to the pursuit of truth via intimate conversation – a dialogical ethic that in Sidgwick, as in Moore, often resulted in creative tensions with elements of the utilitarian tradition, though the utilitarian tradition itself has often been much too narrowly read on this score. Of the Bloomsberries, Leonard Woolf, at least, recognized this:

I am writing today just over a century after the year in which Sidgwick was elected an Apostle, and looking back to the year 1903 I can say that our beliefs, our discussions, our intellectual behaviour in 1903 were in every conceivable way exactly the same as those described by Sidgwick. The beliefs 'fantastically idealistic and remote from reality and real life', the absurd arguments, 'the extravagantly scholastic' method were not as simple or silly as they seemed.

For Woolf, what became Bloomsbury was shaped by Strachey's generation of Apostles, who were all given over to Moorism and "the purification of that divinely cathartic question which echoed through the Cambridge

Courts of my youth as it had 2,300 years before echoed through the streets of Socratic Athens: 'What do you mean by that?' "[15] But Moore's Platonism was but another reflection of that Apostolic ethic by which Sidgwick had been philosophically turned, the one he would carry into innumerable discussion societies and friendships devoted to the deepest problems. This was education with the personal touch, putting one's life on the line and challenging convention and the common wisdom – the form of education Sidgwick valued most.

At any rate, had he lived another decade, Sidgwick would have viewed Bloomsbury as but one more vanguard Apostolic experiment – albeit a rather naive and apolitical one – testing the limits of the human potential and the horizons of happiness through unorthodox art and unorthodox sex. Moore, Russell, Strachey, Keynes, and Virginia Woolf may have mocked their Victorian predecessors, but to a surprising degree, in their unconventional explorations of the potential of friendship and art for building a post-Christian ethic, they simply realized some – by no means all – of Sidgwick's hopes for future generations.

Yet if Bloomsbury would have carried little shock value for Sidgwick, it might have dismayed him in some respects. For Sidgwick had a more encompassing intellectual vision – a wider, deeper, more troubled, and ultimately more troubling vision of things to come. Oddly enough, to understand this more fully, it is necessary to challenge not only his detractors, but also many of his admirers.

Admittedly, despite lingering Bloomsbury prejudice, Sidgwick is today a much-prized member of the philosophical canon, perhaps more highly regarded among Anglo–American philosophers than at any time since his death. The second half of the twentieth century was considerably kinder to his reputation than the first half, albeit in a somewhat blinkered way. Consider Alan Donagan's instructive exaggeration, expressing something of the outlook during the late 1970s:

Most of Sidgwick's contemporary rivals, Herbert Spencer and James Martineau, for example, have long been unread. And those who are still referred to – T. H. Green, F. H. Bradley, perhaps Bernard Bosanquet now and then – may safely be neglected by a young philosopher aspiring to contribute to the main current of analytic moral philosophy. Nor need he expend much labor even on Sidgwick's predecessor and master, John Stuart Mill, or on his pupil and critic, G. E. Moore. Yet he cannot, in the principate of Rawls, omit to address himself to *The Methods of Ethics*.[16]

Donagan's estimation is, of course, a product of the Rawlsian revolution, sparked by John Rawls's hugely influential work *A Theory of Justice* (1971) and, more recently, by *Political Liberalism* (1996).[17] Rawls long insisted on the importance of Sidgwick's *Methods* both as a seminal model of how to do moral theory in general and as a fundamental challenge to his own particular theory of "justice as fairness." According to Rawls, classical utilitarianism was a profoundly important theory of enduring relevance, and Sidgwick was the most philosophically profound and insightful representative of it; more philosophically acute than Bentham or James Mill and more consistent than John Stuart Mill, he went beyond all of them in providing an impartial, scholarly defense of the view that individual actions and social institutions ought ultimately to be judged by how well they serve the greatest happiness.[18] Not only did Sidgwick powerfully articulate just what was involved in the classical utilitarian approach to ethics, economics, and politics, but he did so by using a method that avoided the dead ends of premature metaethics: careful, comprehensive, historically informed comparisons of the best of the competing substantive views about how to determine what one ought to do – that is, the different ways of plausibly systematizing the core ethical concepts of right, good, and virtue. Sidgwick's exhaustive comparison of the "methods" of utilitarianism, egoism, and commonsense or dogmatic intuitional morality – seeking to reconcile these views or at least to clarify their differences, while pointing up the weak spots even in his own favored positions – was a far cry from Bentham's thunderous denunciations of natural rights as "nonsense upon stilts." Sidgwick worked assiduously to do justice to the alternative views, and he went well beyond Mill in showing how utilitarianism could do justice to many of our commonsense moral rules.[19]

Such claims on Sidgwick's behalf no doubt reflected Rawls's own early struggles to shake free of both the positivistic and Wittgensteinian hostility to substantive "theory" in ethics and appeals to the history of philosophy. Clearly, Rawls himself brilliantly succeeded in doing this, playing a central role in what has been called the "Great Expansion" of substantive ethical theorizing in recent decades, as well as in the revitalization of historical work by philosophers. Of course, one of his weighty allies in bolstering the history of philosophy was J. B. Schneewind, whose brilliant book *Sidgwick's Ethics and Victorian Moral Philosophy*[20] was by far the most important twentieth-century commentary on Sidgwick. On the more analytical side, Derek Parfit's extraordinary *Reasons and Persons*[21] was clearly a direct outgrowth of the renewed interest in Sidgwick's work. In certain respects, this book began life as an effort to come to terms with the ways in which Sidgwick figured in the conflicting arguments of, on the one side, such neo-Kantian philosophers as Rawls and Schneewind and, on the other, such neo-utilitarian philosophers as Parfit.[22] Of special importance here has been the issue of just how to interpret Sidgwick's methodology and his views on the meaning and justification of moral claims, his metaethics. Oddly, Sidgwick has been praised both for his Rawlsian avoidance of metaethical worries and for doing substantive ethical theory from a developed metaethical standpoint, the theory of knowledge called "philosophical" or "rational" intuitionism (which he contrasted with William Whewell's "dogmatic" intuitionist defense of the self-evidence of commonsense moral rules).

However, this effort to reconcile the different readings of Sidgwick led only to a warmer appreciation for Sidgwick's original and very sophisticated position, a complex, fallibilistic intuitionism that also finds a place for coherence and consensus as criteria for reducing the probability of error. His intuitionism dovetailed with his Apostolic, dialogical inquiry, and he wielded it in a decidedly skeptical fashion, deploying it in ways that, far from endorsing the ethical status quo, tended to undermine the notion of certain ethical truth – though without lapsing into relativism or subjectivism – and avoided most of the metaphysical and metaethical entanglements usually associated with intuitionism.[23]

Some suggestions along these lines have been made by James Kloppenberg, in *Uncertain Victory*, but unfortunately his effort to link Sidgwick to pragmatist and progressivist movements fails to capture the tensions and shifts within Sidgwick's epistemological trajectory, or to deal with the particulars of the history of intuitionism.[24] Sidgwick came to have a vivid appreciation for the social nature of inquiry and the disappointments of the philosophical "quest for certainty," the quest for the ultimate, final truth about the universe shared by Plato and Descartes, but he learned the hard way. His Apostolic conscience remained highly Platonic, however frustrated.

Furthermore, like the works of Rawls, Parfit, Schneewind, and others, Kloppenberg's account is silent on, among other things, all questions of sexuality and race, questions so central to both the late Victorians and Bloomsbury, and so relevant to matters epistemological. Despite various abstract concerns with the nature of the knowing self and personal identity, recent authors concerned with Sidgwick have been largely oblivious to these proto-Bloomsbury priorities of Sidgwick and his circle. Perversely, the positive academic reception of Sidgwick's work still reflects various prejudicial Bloomsbury readings of him.

Indeed, curiously enough, Sidgwick's Bloomsbury critics and analytical admirers have all tended to be blinded by a too-narrow view of the classical utilitarian backdrop to Sidgwick's work.[25] Utilitarianism has, of course, come in for an extraordinary amount of criticism from a great many quarters during the past century, much of it astonishingly dim. Even Rawls's generous acknowledgment of the significance of this tradition was part of a sustained effort to demonstrate its inferiority to the theory of justice as fairness. But all too often the historical reading of this tradition has suffered from a too-hasty equation of it with classical and neoclassical economic theory and practice, or with rational choice theory generally, or, worse, some vision of purely administrative rationality.

Thus, in some disciplines, Bentham and his followers, the Philosophical Radicals of the early nineteenth century, continue to go down in history as the zealous champions of classical liberal reformism, the authors of endless proclamations on behalf of institutions productive of the greatest happiness of the greatest number. Panoptical prisons run by invisible authorities, a market economy guided by an invisible hand, subterranean sewers flushing away microscopic germs, a trim and efficient political and legal system kept in line by an omnipresent public eye, and Lancastrian schools drilling the scrutinizing conscience of Dickens's Mr. Gradgrind into ever-improving pupils – these were the means by which humanity would progress and flourish, find happiness as well as pursue it. Facts, free markets, self-help, and clear law – yes; lawyers, politicians, and priests – no, or at least in sharply limited numbers. Poets were also dispensable, being mere purveyors of falsehood. Hard facts to unmask sinister interests – that was the war cry. The cultivation of one's soul did not signify.

But as both a philosophy and a fighting creed, utilitarianism was a wild, conflicted current of history, figuring in everything from early women's liberation to the attempt to decriminalize same-sex behavior. The actual history of utilitarianism was a strange affair, absorbing and assimilating everything from the Platonic revival to Romanticism to Darwinism to parapsychology. It deserves to be reread from some different perspectives, both positive and negative, that bring out the complexity of its reformism and of the psychological analyses grounding its reformism. After all, Bentham allowed that by

the natural constitution of the human frame, on most occasions of their lives men in general embrace this principle, without thinking of it: if not for the ordering of their own actions, yet for the trying of their own actions, as well as of those of other men. . . . There are even few who have not taken some occasion or other to quarrel with it, either on account of their not understanding always how to apply it, or on account of some prejudice or other which they were afraid to examine into, or could not bear to part with. For such is the stuff that man is made of: in principle and in practice, in a right track and in a wrong one, the rarest of all human qualities is consistency.[26]

The effort to show how ordinary practical reasoning is often inconsistent, incoherent, or hypocritical, masking the true sources of the self, would seem to be one that animated Mill and Sidgwick as well, even if they were less iconoclastic than Bentham.

Of particular importance here is the way in which the utilitarian tradition of Bentham and Mill was much more concerned with – and quite radical about – matters of sex and gender than has typically been recognized. Bentham produced, though he did not publish, the very first call for the decriminalization of "paederasty" in the English language. And his "Offenses Against One's Self: Paederasty" was remarkably eloquent in condemning the (often unconscious) "hatred of pleasure and horror of singularity." In this, he sounded the note of toleration for difference more often associated with the younger Mill, though Mill could scarcely have written the line "It is wonderful that nobody has ever yet fancied it to be sinful to scratch where it itches, and that it has never been determined that the only natural way of scratching is with such or such a finger and that it is unnatural to scratch with any other."[27] As Louis Crompton has demonstrated,

Bentham made himself the spokesman of a silent and invisible minority. First, he rejects the silence taboo. 'It seems rather too much,' he remarks with dry irony, 'to subscribe to men's being hanged to save the indecency of enquiring whether they deserve it.' Then . . . he pleads from a more rational mode of debate, which would scrutinize the purported social evils of forbidden sexual conduct rather than give rise to fervid rhetoric. . . . But, most of all, he insists that we should establish that an act really does cause social harm before we criminalize it.[28]

Although John Stuart Mill did not apply his eloquence to this particular Benthamite cause, he did of course advance the cause of feminism in ways that were also concerned with countering the psychology of bigotry and the unconscious hatred of pleasure, recognizing that legal reform was only one element of reform. As Mary Lyndon Shanley has suggested:

> Mill's plea for an end to the subjection of women was not made, as critics such as Gertrude Himmelfarb assert, in the name of "the absolute nature of the principle of liberty, the exaltation of individuality whatever its particular form," but in the name of the need of both men and women for community. . . . *The Subjection of Women* was an eloquent brief for men and women and a devastating critique of the corruption of marital inequality. Beyond that it also expressed Mill's profoundly held belief that any "liberal" regime must promote the conditions under which friendship, not only in marriage but in other associations as well, will take root and flourish.[29]

As Mill famously put it, when

> each of two persons, instead of being a nothing, is a something; when they are attached to one another, and are not too much unlike to begin with; the constant partaking in the same things, assisted by their sympathy, draws out the latent capacities of each for being interested in the things which were at first interesting only to the other; and works a gradual assimilation of the tastes and characters to one another, partly by the insensible modifications of each, but more by a real enriching of the two natures, each acquiring the tastes and capacities of the other in addition to its own.

This, he observes, often happens "between two friends of the same sex, who are much associated in daily life," and it would be common in marriage, did not the lopsided socialization process render it "next to an impossibility to form a really well-assorted union."[30] No reform was more urgent than that of rendering the family a school of sympathy rather than a school of despotism. The capacity for authentic friendship was a core element of the happiness to be maximized.

To be sure, Mill famously distanced himself from his Benthamite inheritance, proclaiming it "one-eyed" and insufficiently sensitive to the internal culture of the individual, the feeling and caring side highlighted by the Romantic movement, which could and should be stimulated by poetry and art. Wendy Donner has urged that

Mill's utilitarian commitments require him to maintain that feelings are pivotal to morality and that if we are to take pleasure in intellectual pursuits or in the good of others we must be persons who feel deeply, who are in touch with our emotions, and who are motivated by our concern for others. Cultivation of sympathy with others is the foundation of moral development, and two widely held tenets of feminism – a stress on the importance of feelings and of sympathetic attachments to others – flow from this.[31]

Indeed, Mill's politics of friendship, which also reflected his debt to the Platonic revival during the Victorian era, also put him at odds with the earlier Benthamite views about laissez-faire. Mill and Harriet Taylor grew increasingly committed to exploring decentralized socialist alternatives to capitalism, forms of economic organization less hostile to the cultivation of sympathy and civic friendship. Happiness, for them, was not a known quantity but something the frontiers of which needed to be explored through practical social experiments testing the human potential – "experiments in living."

Thus, it is astonishing how often the earlier, secular utilitarian tradition was in fact busily engaging the very concerns that Keynes and Strachey (not to mention Russell and Moore) thought it had entirely neglected: the exploration of states of consciousness (or higher pleasures) defining ultimate good, the cultivation of these and the sympathetic self through friendship (and art), the perversities of the social intolerance of heterodox sexual relations, hetero- and homo-, and, indeed, the challenges posed by the unconscious roots of motivation.[32] For both Bentham and Mill, the deeper appeal of utilitarianism, and the deeper forms of resistance to it, worked themselves out below the level of the conscious calculating ego. And the cause of Greek love had been better served by Bentham than by Byron and Shelley, and it would be better served still by Sidgwick and his friends, for whom friendship, in many different varieties, was both a crucial element of the happiness to be aimed at and a vital aspect of the inquiries needed to explore the human potential for happiness.

At any rate, the hidden history of utilitarianism – especially in relation to and in contrast with visions of human nature as basically (and narrowly) self-interested or egoistic – forms another broad theme of this book, for Sidgwick's contributions on this matter are of singular importance. To be sure, Sidgwick was rather uncannily in line with many of the more compelling features of Mill's moral and social philosophy, and it is useful to read him as carrying on that eclectic legacy (even more useful than to link him, as Rawls does, to the more purely hedonistic Benthamite one). On a great raft of issues, he picked up where Mill – the real Mill – left off. Thus, Mill reworked utilitarianism: to reconcile it somewhat with commonsense moral rules and traditions; to recognize the complexity of individual psychology and the force of Romantic notions of human emotions, character, and happiness; to appraise the potential utility of religious belief; to explore the possibilities for some form of socialism (ethical if not economic); to make it a force for the liberation of women and the vitality and progress of a truly open society; and even (very tentatively, and despite his antipathy to Whewell) to suggest grounding it on intuition. On all of these counts and others, Sidgwick took his point of departure from Mill, the Mill who was at once a great liberal, a great reformer, a great socialist, and a great utilitarian. And behind the particular concerns, there was always the overriding obsession with the growth of "sympathy," of "friendship," so crucial for the future post-Christian era, so crucial for experiments in living. Sidgwick's feminism, evident in the work for women's higher education that he undertook in collaboration with his wife, Eleanor, effectively continued the efforts of Mill and Taylor. And this sheds further light on the continuity of their conceptions of reform and social equality, culture and civilization.[33]

Thus, if Sidgwick was a type of utilitarian, he was one who reflected the real complexity of that tradition rather than the stock view of it, so much so that later opponents of utilitarianism often look mild in comparison. As his friend James Bryce remarked:

Sidgwick's attitude toward the Benthamite system of Utilitarianism illustrates the cautiously discriminative habit of mind I have sought to describe. If he had been required to call himself by any name, he would not have refused that of Utilitarian, just as in mental philosophy he leaned to the type of thought represented by the two Mills rather than to the Kantian idealism of his friend and school contemporary, the Oxford professor T. H. Green. But the system of Utility takes in his hands a form so much more refined and delicate than was given to it by Bentham and James Mill, and is expounded with so many qualifications unknown to them, that it has become a very different thing, and is scarcely, if at all, assailable by the arguments which moralists of the idealistic type have brought against the older doctrine.[34]

Indeed, in seeking to ground the "Great Hap" principle on an intuitionist epistemology more often associated with the critics of utilitarianism (such as Whewell), Sidgwick, as Moore admitted, remained quite free
of any taint of the "naturalistic fallacy" that supposedly undercut Mill's
justificatory efforts. Moreover, Sidgwick sought to appropriate Kantian
universalizability for his own purposes, and if he criticized idealism at
length, he also brought out many of the problems involved in trying to defend utilitarianism against commonsense and other objections, clarifying
such matters as the difference between total and average utility calculations, in connection with the question of optimal population growth. Most
important, however, Sidgwick did not think that utilitarianism could be
reconciled with egoism or self-interest; without a theistic postulate that the
universe has a friendly moral order, there was ever the potential for a basic
conflict between acting for one's own greatest happiness and acting for
the greatest happiness of all, each option presenting itself as what one has
most reason to do. The gloomy last line of the first edition of the *Methods*
rang out like an English version of the "crisis of the Enlightenment,"
warning that practical reason might be reduced to a "chaos."[35]

This was the infamous "dualism of practical reason," and the attempt
to get beyond it – to effect some form of "harmonization" – was for
Sidgwick another element of the deepest problems of human life, one that
arose with special urgency with the decline of orthodox religion. He had
none of that Humean insouciance that could take up skepticism toward
such matters as the coincidence of duty and interest – or the worth of theistic claims – with imperturbible good cheer. Sidgwick could not bear the
thought of a universe so fundamentally perverse as to allow that the wages
of virtue might "be dust," and he endlessly explored every possible means
of harmonization, including the perfectionist path of achieving reconciliation via cultivation of the self. In this, he was also more sophisticated
than his predecessors on the problems involved in defining happiness,
the limitations of construing it in terms of pleasure or desirable consciousness, and the uncertainties involved in seeking to maximize it. With
him, Benthamite clarity had an extremely ironic denouement, highlighting the vast realm of the incalculable in human affairs, how much had to be
left to uncertain judgment, and how deeply problematic egoistic reasons
could be.[36]

Clearly, as much as Sidgwick was obsessed with egoism, he had nothing like the confidence of past or present libertarians in the ability of

markets and governmental institutions to mobilize self-interest to further the general happiness. A society cannot long hold together with such weak cement, and in society as it stood, egoistic concern was too apt to take a narrow and singularly self-defeating form. Indeed, Sidgwick thought that it was crucial to foster, among other things, the "spirit of justice," and "to develop the elements from which the moral habit of justice springs – on the one hand, sympathy, and the readiness to imagine oneself in another's place and look at things from his point of view; and on the other hand, the intelligent apprehension of common interests" (PE 61).[37] And when it came to praising attempts to build more cooperative, beneficent social relations, in which work is its own reward or done for the sake of the community, he could sound like his mentor Mill on socialism.

But Sidgwick carried these concerns to new limits, places the older utilitarians had never envisioned. Fretful about the viability of traditional religious belief, and about the conclusiveness of the reasons for acting to advance the greatest happiness, he was intensely interested in the possibility that psychical research might provide some new evidence for the moral order of the universe, for the reality of the afterlife. Thus, the aggressive secular utilitarianism of Bentham, who was morbidly afraid of ghosts, eventually produced the eclectic utilitarianism of Sidgwick, who chased ghosts with a passion, convinced that they might reveal to him the "secret of the Universe."

Moreover, Sidgwick's explorations of the Other World were inextricably linked to his explorations of the Inner World, the world of depth psychology that Freud would shortly be entering, partly courtesy of Sidgwick's Society for Psychical Research. In his dealings with psychics and mediums, or with ordinary people who had had extraordinary experiences, he was exposed to the vast range of unconscious mental processes: trance states, premonitions, hallucinations, dreams, visions, channelling, split and multiple personalities. This was unlike anything Mill had ever dealt with, in his efforts to marry utilitarianism to Romantic celebrations of individual genius and powerful emotion. If Mill had called for a new science of individual psychology – ethology – Sidgwick answered the call by delving into depth psychology and parapsychology, playing a key role in what has misleadingly been called the "discovery of the unconscious." Studied religious introspection, the Platonic revival, Romantic self-expression, Apostolic friendship, parapsychology, and the utilitarian investigation of the nature of pleasure all ended up pushing Sidgwick in the same direction – to make of himself an experiment in living, to test the limits defining his "true self," when the true self was turning out to be difficult to decipher. Should psychical research fail to provide evidence for the afterlife, much would depend on how far sentiment could be reshaped to foster sympathy without such foundations.

What is more, this search for the truth about self-identity was often tied to questions of sexual identity. It is a remarkable and revealing fact that nearly all of Sidgwick's closest friends were champions of male love: H. G. Dakyns, Roden Noel, Oscar Browning, F. W. Myers, Arthur Sidgwick (his brother), and, of course, John Addington Symonds. Sidgwick and his friends were not of Mill's formative period; they were admirers not only of Wordsworth's Romanticism, but also of the penetrating intellectuality of Arthur Hugh Clough's "Dipsychus," the ambivalences of Tennyson's "In Memoriam," and the vitality of Whitman's *Leaves of Grass* – the poetic voices that spoke to the deep homoerotic divisions of the self, and from whom they took their deepest inspiration in their struggles to frame a new science of the self. They too were analysts of the twin-souled, like James and DuBois.[38]

Sidgwick's relationship with Symonds is of special significance. Symonds, the son of a physician who positively personified the medicalization of discourse surrounding sexuality,[39] was early on persuaded that his homosexuality was an inherent disposition, and in due course he became equally convinced that it was not a morbid condition, that the culture of ancient Greece had demonstrated that homosexuality could be a healthy aspect of high cultural life, and that the poetry of Whitman pointed the way to a new synthesis of the best of ancient and modern. It was to be a New Age, with Millian sympathy extended to include that very Hellenic Whitmanian comradeship.[40] For Sidgwick, Symonds's Hellenism and Whitmania represented further experiments, alternative ways of revitalizing and edifying a culture that all good Millians agreed needed revitalizing and edifying.[41] And his letters and journal exchanges with this remarkable friend would prove to be the most passionate and revealing of all his writings, intensely debating the fate of ethics in a godless world and everything else under the sun and over the rainbow.

Sidgwick was, however, a very cautious reformer when it came to such explosive issues, and he worked assiduously to keep Symonds from being ruined by public scandal. No history of utilitarianism has yet captured this side of the story – how Sidgwick's intuitionism inexorably led on to an epistemology of the closet.[42] A dual-source theory of practical reason, a longstanding concern over hypocrisy, and a dipsychical moral psychology produced a very sensitive rethinking of the public and the private. An esoteric morality? Sidgwick, at least, worked very hard to keep it esoteric, effectively constructing the standard biographical treatment of Symonds that spun his sexual angst into religious angst. Quite possibly the issue of hypocrisy loomed so large for him because he was, in so many ways, perpetually caught up in trying to elude certain forms of public reaction.

Thus, despite a reputation for saintly honesty, won in part by his 1869 resignation, Sidgwick was quite given to behind-the-scenes efforts betraying a highly qualified belief in the value of veracity. And of course, he has often been criticized in more abstract philosophical terms for advancing a doubly indirect approach to happiness, both individual and social, countenancing the possibility of justifying on utilitarian grounds an "esoteric morality" in which the true (utilitarian) principles of ethics were known to and practiced by an elite group of philosophical sophisticates only. This seems in flat contradiction to the Kantian insistence – evident in Rawls's theory of justice – on "publicity" as a basic criterion of moral principles, a criterion usually supposed to be much in accord with common sense.[43]

Such accusations, sometimes provocatively framed in terms of the possibility of Sidgwick's ethics supporting colonial paternalism or "Government House" utilitarianism, have never been formulated in a clear and historically informed way.[44] That is, not only has Sidgwick's sexual politics been glossed over in his critical reception, but remarkably little attention has been devoted even to his political theory and practice, which is odd indeed, given how often the classical utilitarians are celebrated – or derided – for having produced comprehensive works covering politics, law, economics, ethics, and so on.[45] In Sidgwick's case, however, it means that his ethics has been treated only in an isolated and abstract way, without reference to his economic and political views and entanglements (much less his sexual ones). To read his *Methods* without benefit of these contexts is, alas, to dangerously decontextualize his *Methods*. His ethical work appears in a different light when connected with his claims about, say, home rule for Ireland or the duty to advance the cause of civilization across the globe. As with Mill, many of the most profoundly troubling questions arise when one considers Sidgwick's work outside of the domestic context. Just how were Millian friendship and sympathy supposed to figure in imperial rule?[46]

Sidgwick was a friend and colleague of such imperialist luminaries as Sir John Seeley and Charles Henry Pearson, and it is natural to wonder to what extent he shared their influential views of England's "civilizing" imperial mission – and their worries over the "lower" classes and races, race "degradation," and so forth. Sidgwick's invocations of such things as "common sense," the "consensus of experts," and the direction of "civilised opinion" read quite differently if read as tacit or possible affirmations of racial superiority. Just who, it may well be asked, concretely represented the "spirit of justice" and the "consensus of experts"? The Millian inheritance, although pre-Darwinian and emphasizing nurture over nature, was nonetheless deeply involved in British rule in India.[47] Sidgwick's work was post-Darwinian and the product of an environment that was often both more crudely racist and more enamored of empire. And these changing historical contexts made themselves felt in Sidgwick's life and work: he took seriously views that he should have dismissed with the full force of his skeptical intellect and was guilty of some very serious lapses of judgment, amounting to a form of racism.[48]

Indeed, the great outstanding paradox of Sidgwick's life and work is how he could have been so soberly critical of all the philosophizing that went into the ethical and political vision of the gentlemanly imperialists while remaining so complacent, even enthusiastic, about England's civilizing mission, its role in educating the world.[49] The Platonic, idealistic, and utilitarian ideals afloat in the Victorian world in general and Oxbridge in particular could be all too unreflective.[50]

That these matters have been treated with a method of avoidance for the past century is singularly unfortunate and philosophically distorting, of a piece with the distortions resulting from the neglect of Sidgwick's sexual politics, practical ethics, and casuistry. Admittedly, some will find this line of interpretation disturbing – the issues of racism and pederasty are disturbing. If some come away from this book agreeing with Moore that Sidgwick was a "wicked edifactious person," that cannot be helped, though Moore and Bloomsbury shared many of Sidgwick's failings. On my Goethean reconstruction of Sidgwick's quest, Sidgwick ends up being a much harder philosopher to come to terms with – better than the familiar depictions in some respects, worse in others.[51] Perhaps he ends up being a more interesting philosopher simply because he ends up being a more complex and conflicted person, his own mix of light and shade.

So much for thematics and problematics. My general pragmatist orientation spares me any undue worries about eclecticism, or about the somewhat unorthodox organization of this book. The treatment is only roughly chronological; the chapters often recapitulate earlier material from a new angle; and the argument is often indirect and allusive. The following two chapters deal with Sidgwick's early intellectual life, before the publication of the *Methods*, and the formative influences on him; although many of the basic facts rehearsed may be familiar, the focus on his Apostolic ideals and the context of the Platonic revival is somewhat novel, and opens the way to the emphasis in later chapters on the social dimensions of Sidgwick's epistemology. The fourth chapter deliberately changes voice and approaches the *Methods* through the interpretive controversies of Sidgwick's more narrowly philosophical commentators, past and present. The purpose of this is twofold: to convey some sense of the most significant philosophical readings of the *Methods* and the content of Sidgwick's philosophical ethics in more analytical terms, but also to suggest in a preliminary way some of the limitations of analytical efforts to treat Sidgwick's work so innocently, as though it were simply that of a slightly senior contemporary. Just how different Sidgwick's world was becomes increasingly evident in the following chapters, which deal with his parapsychology, his views on sex and gender, and his elaborate, often offensive positions on economic and political issues, including imperialism and race. Again, these dimensions of Sidgwick's inquiries do illuminate his philosophical work, and the way he interpreted his social epistemology of Apostolic fellowship and Millian friendship. The Sidgwickian ascent to abstraction, in the perpetual hope of winning the prized consensus of experts, may strike some as in effect another mask of conquest, papering over legitimate concrete conflict with high principle and tacit elitism. At any rate, it is hard to deny that the life can in some ways reveal the thought and stimulate rethinking.

Ironically, in the end, it may well seem that I have agreed with Sidgwick's self-assessment concerning the symmetry and continuity of his life – at least his inner life – even if much of my gloss of it may appear highly destructive. But as Sidgwick once said, "I think my present *formule de la vie* is from Walt Whitman. 'I have urged you forward, and still urge you, without the slightest idea of our destination.'" (M 514).

First Words

But in the English universities no thought can find place, except that which can reconcile itself with orthodoxy. They are ecclesiastical institutions; and it is the essence of all churches to vow adherence to a set of opinions made up and prescribed, it matters little whether three or thirteen centuries ago. Men will some day open their eyes, and perceive how fatal a thing it is that the instruction of those who are intended to be the guides and governors of mankind should be confided to a collection of persons thus pledged. If the opinions they are pledged to were every one as true as any fact in physical science, and had been adopted, not as they almost always are, on trust and authority, but as the result of the most diligent and impartial examination of which the mind of the recipient was capable; even then, the engagement under penalties always to adhere to the opinions once assented to, would debilitate and lame the mind, and unfit it for progress, still more for assisting the progress of others. The person who has to think more of what an opinion leads to, than of what is the evidence of it, cannot be a philosopher, or a teacher of philosophers.

John Stuart Mill, "Whewell on Moral Philosophy"[1]

I. Sidgwick and the Talking Cure

When Henry Sidgwick died of cancer, on August 28, 1900, he was even less at home in the world than Bentham or Mill had been when they passed on. He was buried in the quiet family corner of the village churchyard at Terling Place, the spacious Essex estate of the Rayleighs, to whom he was related by marriage. Although he had prepared a brief, minimally religious statement to be read at his funeral, he was given the Church of England ceremony, and thus in death maintained something of the tolerant facade to which he had become accustomed in life. His brother-in-law, the famous Tory politician Arthur Balfour, wrote of him to Lady Elcho: "He was ardently desirous of finishing some literary and philosophic designs, so

far only sketched in outline: and I am sorry that it was otherwise ordained –
not merely because it was a disappointment to him but because, though I
never was a disciple of his, I do believe that he had something valuable to
say which he has left unsaid." By contrast, Mill's dying words were "You
know that I have done my work."[2]

There is more than a little irony in the idea that Sidgwick died leaving
much unsaid, for he was by all accounts a most expressive man, albeit one
whose books did not do him justice. *The Methods of Ethics*, first published
in 1874, may well be his great philosophical masterpiece, but those who
knew him best were unanimous in thinking that it was his talk, and the profoundly sympathetic character that the talk expressed, that made Sidgwick
what he was. The Millian struggle to come to terms with imagination and
intimacy, friendship and fellow feeling, had found a new champion, a
philosopher of interiority for whom intimate talk, and its role in inquiry
into personal and philosophical truth, would become a guiding concern.
The pursuit of truth involved the pursuit of unity, and the pursuit of
unity involved intimate talk, even poetic talk. As Frank Podmore, one of
Sidgwick's younger colleagues in parapsychological research, flatly put it:
"No one who knew Sidgwick only from his most important philosophical
works could form any fair idea of the man. . . . His talk was always alive
with sympathy and humour."[3]

That Sidgwick was devoted to talk may not seem terribly surprising,
given that he spent his entire adult life in the academic setting of Cambridge
University – from 1883 as Knightbridge Professor of Moral Philosophy –
and was every bit as much the philosopher-educator as Plato, Rousseau,
or Dewey. But like such illustrious counterparts, he was also highly critical of the educational system as he found it. He agreed with Mill that
Oxbridge was more church than university, often a fount of the "higher
ignorance." The talk at which he excelled was neither Victorian sermoniz-
ing, nor political oratory, nor donnish lecturing, which last he deemed a
relic from the pre-Gutenberg era.[4] His conversation was not in the mode of
Carlyle's peremptory holding forth, or, except reluctantly, along the lines
of the German professorial model. His was very much the "new school"
of professional academics, whose reforms virtually created modern
Cambridge and changed the face of higher education in general. He stood
for modern languages, modern literature, modern biblical criticism, modern science, and the attitudes toward intellectual freedom that such inquiries manifested – which may be part of the reason why his views are

proving uncannily relevant to current debates over multiculturalism, post-modernism, and the fate of the university.

Still, for Sidgwick the ultimate meaning of education ran deeper than any canon or curriculum, and reflected his conversational virtues. In line with recent sentiment, he would have agreed that although it is important which books one has read, more important still is how one has read the books. Sidgwickian inquiry, like Socratic inquiry, demanded critical thinking, not displays of barren erudition or fawning invocations of great thinkers and great books. As Balfour, who had been his student before becoming his brother-in-law, observed: "Of all the men I have known he was the readiest to consider every controversy and every controversialist on their merits. He never claimed authority; he never sought to impose his views; he never argued for victory; he never evaded an issue." In an afterthought richly suggestive of the tensions in Sidgwick's life, Balfour adds: "Whether these are the qualities which best fit their possessor to found a 'school' may well be doubted." (M 311)

Sidgwick regarded this as the meaning of education, even of culture, which he rarely missed an opportunity to advance. In a later essay on "The Pursuit of Culture," filled with the reflections of a lifetime, he explained that

since the most essential function of the mind is to think and know, a man of culti-vated mind must be essentially concerned for knowledge: but it is not knowledge merely that gives culture. A man may be learned and yet lack culture: for he may be a pedant, and the characteristic of a pedant is that he has knowledge without culture. So again, a load of facts retained in the memory, a mass of reasonings got up merely for examination, these are not, they do not give culture. It is the love of knowledge, the ardour of scientific curiosity, driving us continually to absorb new facts and ideas, to make them our own and fit them into the living and growing system of our thought; and the trained faculty of doing this, the alert and supple intelligence exercised and continually developed in doing this, – it is in these that culture essentially lies. (PE 121)

Perhaps, in the end, it was the promotion of culture in this sense that de-fined Sidgwick's reformism and his efforts to "elevate and purify" social life. Like both Mill and Dewey, he had before his mind a vision of an *educating* society, not simply an educated society.[5] But his endeavors followed a certain pattern. Although, in one capacity or another, he often found himself participating in the more conventional forms of public and private address, the one project to which he was unstintingly devoted, for which he never seemed to want energy, was the discussion group. Not only did he always remain faithful to his first and formative such group, the famous Cambridge Apostles, but he became a mainstay of any number of other discussion societies as well: the "Grote Club," the Eranus, the Metaphysical Society, the Political Economy Club, the Ad Eundem Society, and Synthetic Society all received years of commitment from him, and these are only the better known of the groups to which he lent his skills. Such interaction provided him with his model for critical inquiry – be it philosophical, theological, or scientific – and thus for both his academic work and his work for academic reform – for example, his work for philosophy as an academic discipline, for universities open to women and extending their resources to all classes, and for a curriculum less preoccupied with rote learning of the classics and more attuned to modern methods and topics. Pluralistic and interdisciplinary, drawing from academic and nonacademic worlds, these were vehicles for cultivating humanity that went beyond narrow institutional reformism. And the traces of his participation in these groups are visible in *The Methods of Ethics*, even if it was in person that Sidgwick struck others as the true *lumen siccum*, or "pure white light."[6]

The lure of discussion was always the same: free and open inquiry into issues of deep concern, usually involving religious or moral questions, and this as a search for unity in a conflictual world and an antidote to the dogma and dogmatism of school and church. If the Enlightenment project were to be realized, it would have to be realized in this context, with the sincere pursuit of truth and no authority but the better argument. What Sidgwick brought to these discussions, however, was genuinely exceptional, and reflective of the character that he brought to his friendships. As his student and colleague F. W. Maitland put it, in a review of *Henry Sidgwick, A Memoir*:

Sidgwick was a wonderful talker; a better I have never heard. . . . Sidgwick's talk never became, and never tended to become, a monologue. He seemed at least as desirous to hear as to be heard, and gave you the impression that he would rather be led than lead. Even more than the wit and the wisdom, the grace and the humour, it was the wide range of sympathy that excited admiration when the talk was over. To see with your eyes, to find interest in your interests, seemed to be one of his main objects, while he was amusing and instructing and delighting you. As a compliment that was pleasant; but I cannot think that it was a display of mere urbanity. Sidgwick genuinely wished to know what all sorts of people thought and felt about all sorts of things. His irony never hurt, it was so kindly; and, of all known forms of wickedness, 'Sidgwickedness' was the least wicked. Good as are the letters in this book, I cannot honestly say that they are as good, or nearly as good, as their writer's talk. A letter, being a monologue, cannot represent just what seemed most to distinguish him from some other brilliant talkers.[7]

Maitland allowed that Sidgwick was a "most unegotistical talker, and a most unegotistical man," whose singular virtue was "truthfulness."

Relatives, friends, colleagues, former pupils, acquaintances were all in agreement about the singular attractiveness of Sidgwick as a conversational partner: he impressed everyone from Gladstone to Madame Blavatsky. Again, this did not necessarily refer to his lecture style, which, though it had the merits of careful, many-sided argument, could be something of a strain for those not truly engaged with the relevant subject. Many students found his lecturing admirable – W. R. Sorley called his teaching "a training in the philosophical temper – in candor, self-criticism, and regard for truth"[8] – but even some of the good ones, such as Bertrand Russell and G. E. Moore, found him dull. Russell observed that Sidgwick always told precisely one joke per lecture, and that after the suspense of awaiting its appearance had passed, attention flagged.[9] But Russell would also in due course confess that he and Moore had not given Sidgwick anything like the respect that he deserved, even as both of them more or less unconsciously absorbed a great deal of Sidgwick's outlook.

According to James Bryce, who knew Sidgwick well and joined him in many discussion societies:

Sidgwick did not write swiftly or easily, because he weighed carefully everything he wrote. But his mind was alert and nimble in the highest degree. Thus he was an admirable talker, seeing in a moment the point of an argument, seizing on distinctions which others had failed to perceive, suggesting new aspects from which a question might be regarded, and enlivening every topic by a keen yet sweet and kindly wit. Wit, seldom allowed to have play in his books, was one of the characteristics which made his company charming. Its effect was heightened by a hestation in his speech which often forced him to pause before the critical word or phrase of the sentence had been reached. When that word or phrase came, it was sure to be the right one. Though fond of arguing, he was so candid and fair, admitting all that there was in his opponent's case, and obviously trying to see the point from his opponent's side, that nobody felt annoyed at having come off second best, while everybody who cared for good talk went away feeling not only that he knew more about the matter than he did before, but that he had enjoyed an intellectual pleasure of a rare and high kind. The keenness of his penetration was not formidable, because it was joined to an indulgent judgment: the ceaseless activity of his intellect was softened rather than reduced by the gaiety of his manner. His talk was conversation, not discourse, for though he naturally became the centre of nearly every company in which he found himself, he took no more than his share. It was like the sparkling of a brook whose ripples seem to give out sunshine.[10]

"A first-rate talker," "a brilliant talker," "the best talker I ever heard" – such phrases are littered throughout the reminiscences of Sidgwick. In his younger days, as an undergraduate and junior Fellow, he was apparently more aloof, striking some as cold or priggish, with a chilly Socratic wit. When F. W. H. Myers praised a mediocre religious writer, exclaiming "Of such is the Kingdom of Heaven!," Sidgwick sneered, "H-h-h-ave you been there?"[11] And even some of his later friends, such as his prize student and literary executor E. E. Constance Jones, could paint Sidgwickedness in this cooler light, complaining that the *Memoir* failed to catch the "Socratic irony, that Horatian satire, that *malice* (in the French, not the English, sense of the word) which gave a peculiar zest and charm to Sidgwick's conversation."[12] When Balfour exclaimed that he would follow the Church of England through thick and thin, Sidgwick dryly replied that he would follow it through thin.

On Myers's account, the reserve and preoccupation of Sidgwick's youth, when he was professedly "cased in a bark of selfish habit," gave way because "by sheer meditation, by high resolve, he made himself such as we all know him."[13] Whether this was quite the case may be doubted – it rather smacks of the Victorian worship of self-command and character building. But Myers would come to know Sidgwick very well, as a long-standing member of the "Sidgwick Group" of psychical researchers. What is surely correct is that Sidgwick regarded himself as a kind of psychological experiment – or "experiment in living," to use the Millian expression. He did think of his life in terms of a test of the human potential, of the possibility of a more sympathetic and conversational culture, one less dependent on orthodox religion. The "New Woman" whom he did so much to encourage was to be accompanied by a "New Man," and both would enter a "New Age." Such was the distillation of Sidgwick's quest to solve the "deepest problems" of human life.

Tracing the vicissitudes of this experiment, of how Sidgwick became what he was, is no small task. The multitude of respects in which he remained a creature of his time will become plain enough. Certainly, he was not immune to talk of character and self-control, or civilization and progress, or race and rule. And he felt, to varying degrees, the three great anxieties of modern liberalism. As sketched by Alan Ryan, these are: "fear of the culturally estranged condition of what has been variously called the 'underclass,' the 'unwashed mob,' the *lumpenproletariat*, or (by Hegel) the *Pöbel* . . . unease about 'disenchantment,' the loss of a belief that the world possesses a religious and spiritual meaning . . . [and] fear that the degeneration of the French Revolution between 1789 and 1794 into a regime of pure terrorism was only the harbinger of revolutions to come."[14] These anxieties have often congealed into something resembling the Platonic dread of genuine democracy (as apt to degenerate into mob rule, demagoguery, etc.) or have resulted in a kind of "self-inflicted wound," since liberals "want the emancipation that leads to disenchantment, but want the process that emancipates us to relocate us in the world as well."[15] This last, as we shall see, was what produced the most troubled Sidgwickian dreams.

But if Sidgwick felt these anxieties, so did Mill, James, Dewey, and a host of others whose works remain highly relevant and contested today, and it is vital to achieve some comparable understanding of just how he negotiated these matters, so crucial to the development of the public sphere.

Clearly, Sidgwick's experiment was filled with unresolved tensions. It was Sidgwick the philosopher who chastened a nephew for dismissing a scientific heretic for having no claim to be heard: "He asks for attention, not to his authority, but to his arguments." An admirable position, but it was also Sidgwick the philosopher who held that "those who could hope to advance the study of philosophy, or even could profit by the study, were few" (M 305). How did he construe the role of the philosopher in the educating society? What were his hopes for the democratic potential of the more open, more sympathetic, more utilitarian society of the future? How might the conversational norms of the private discussion group be translated into a larger cultural sphere? Between Mill's belief in a cultural elite or vanguard, the Coleridgean clerisy, and Dewey's Whitmanian faith in radical democracy and social intelligence, where does one find Sidgwick? Did quantity of participation stand in inverse relation to quality of participation? Was he the apostle of the democratic Socrates, or the

elitist Plato? Whose voices mattered, and why? And what did all this talk
have to do with utilitarianism?

II. Sidgwick the Apostle

> I still think the best motto for a true Metaphysic are those two lines of
>   Shelley: –
> I am the eye with which the Universe
> Beholds itself and knows itself divine.
>
> Sidgwick to Roden Noel (M 151)

It is not too much to say that Cambridge University destroyed the
young Henry Sidgwick, and as a result the mature Henry Sidgwick fell in
love with the place. For when Sidgwick arrived at Trinity College in the
autumn of 1855, he was as fortified in Anglican orthodoxy as any young,
rising member of the bourgeoisie could be, thanks in large measure to his
first mentor, Edward White Benson, the future archbishop of Canterbury.
But by the time of his graduation in 1859, wreathed in every possible
honor, he was in a state of religious, moral, and philosophical turmoil
that took ten years to work out – his years, as he explained to Benson, of
"Storm and Stress." The ongoing crisis culminated in the resignation of
his Fellowship because he could no longer in good conscience subscribe
to the Thirty-nine Articles of the Church of England.

In external respects, his life had been an unbroken success story. As at
Rugby, he distinguished himself in both classics and mathematics, and he
was reading voraciously in literature, poetry, philosophy, political economy, and many other areas.[16] He had won the Bell scholarship in his
second term, and the Craven in 1857, when he was also made a scholar of
Trinity College. In 1858, he added Sir William Browne's prize for Latin
and Greek epigrams. Although he took both the classical and the mathematical Triposes, he had been advised to focus more heavily on his classics,
which he did. He took a First Class in both and was First Chancellor's
Medallist, but he was Thirty-third Wrangler in mathematics and Senior
Classic in his chosen study – the very top classical scholar. With surprise
to none, he was elected a Fellow of Trinity College in October of 1859.
His first lectureship was in classics, and it was in that area that his teaching had its beginning, with the normal mix of formal duties and private
tutoring.

But the most important development in Sidgwick's life was not quite so visible to the public eye: it had come in the shape of the Cambridge Conversazione Society, better known as the Cambridge Apostles. Founded in 1820 by a number of St. John's undergraduates – including George Tomlinson, later bishop of Gibralter – the Society quickly evolved into a secret, select discussion group for Cambridge's best and brightest, drawn primarily from Trinity and King's. Before Sidgwick's time, it had had such notable and influential members as Alfred Lord Tennyson, Arthur Hallam, Erasmus Darwin, John Frederick Denison Maurice, John Sterling, James Fitzjames Stephen, Henry Sumner Maine, William George Harcourt, Richard Monckton Milnes, and Edward Henry Stanley. After Sidgwick's active membership, it became perhaps the best-known secret society in England, celebrated for honing the philosophical abilities of Russell and Moore and for fortifying the gay propensities of the Bloomsbury set, especially Keynes and Strachey.[17]

Sidgwick found the Society irresistible:

I have noted the great change that took place about the middle of my undergraduate time. Up to that point I cannot remember that I had formed any ambition beyond success in my examinations and the attainment of a Trinity Fellowship; but in the Michaelmas term of my second year an event occurred which had more effect on my intellectual life than any one thing that happened to me afterwards: I became a member of a discussion society – old and possessing historical traditions – which went by the name of "The Apostles." A good description of it as it existed in his time is to be found in the late Dean Merivale's autobiography. When I joined it the number of members was not large, and there is an exuberant vitality in Merivale's description to which I recall nothing corresponding. But the spirit, I think, remained the same, and gradually this spirit – at least as I apprehended it – absorbed and dominated me. I can only describe it as the spirit of the pursuit of truth with absolute devotion and unreserve by a group of intimate friends who were perfectly frank with each other, and indulged in any amount of humorous sarcasm and playful banter, and yet each respects the other, and when he discourses tries to learn from him and see what he sees. Absolute candour was the only duty that the tradition of the society enforced. No consistency was demanded with opinions previously held – truth as we saw it then and there was what we had to embrace and maintain, and there were no propositions so well established that an Apostle had not the right to deny or question, if he did so sincerely and not from mere love of paradox. The gravest subjects were continually debated, but gravity of treatment, as I have said, was not imposed, though sincerity was. In fact it was rather a point of the apostolic mind to understand how much suggestion and instruction may be derived from what is in form a jest – even in dealing with the gravest matters.

I had at first been reluctant to enter this society when I was asked to join it. I thought that a standing weekly engagement for a whole evening would interfere with my work for my two Triposes. But after I had gradually apprehended the spirit as I have described it, it came to seem to me that no part of my life at Cambridge was so real to me as the Saturday evening on which the apostolic debates were held; and the tie of attachment to the society is much the strongest corporate bond which I have known in life. I think, then, that my admission into this society and the enthusiastic way in which I came to idealise it really determined or revealed that the deepest bent of my nature was towards the life of thought – thought exercised on the central problems of human life. (M 34–35)

Here, then, against all the forces of Sidgwick's youth, was a powerful counterforce: the Saturday evening Apostolic meetings over "whales" (anchovy toast), with papers given and discussed by luminaries and friends, faculty and students, sharing the Apostolic spirit. In this "school of mind and heart," as a later Apostle would explain, one "mastered the art of reconciling by a phrase the most divergent of hypotheses, the most fundamentally antagonistic of antinomies" and grew accustomed to differ from one's comrades in "nothing but opinion." Like so many others, Sidgwick, "upbourne by the ethereal atmosphere of free and audacious enquiry," could discover "to his delight that, towards midnight on a Saturday, he too could soar."[18]

And small wonder, given the intellectual ferment of that time and place. Sheldon Rothblatt has noted how Sidgwick's first decade at Cambridge "coincided with one of the most exciting intellectual periods of the nineteenth century, and he was soon completely absorbed in the writings of Mill, Comte, Spencer, Strauss, Renan, Carlyle, Matthew Arnold, George Eliot and Darwin, wandering freely from biological science to biblical scholarship, ethics and problems of proof."[19] Of course, the ferment was sometimes quite foul-smelling, especially in the aftermath of the Indian Mutiny of 1857, when racist pseudoscience increasingly entered the debates. And the overly orthodox young Sidgwick was not always as receptive as he should have been to such things as, say, Mill's case against the subjection of women.[20]

By Sidgwick's day, the Apostles were not just a model for the life of the mind. Members were elected for life, and even after they became "Angels," ceasing to participate on a regular weekly basis, they often maintained strong ties to the Society and its past and present members – a habit encouraged by the Society's annual dinner, at which old and new "Brethren" had a chance to meet and mingle. Indeed, the Society was caught up in the London literary scene, via such means as the brief interest of Sterling and Maurice in the literary paper the *Athenaeum*, and it would be increasingly active, behind the scenes, in various reform movements, particularly in education. Thus, it provided a powerful support group for its members, support that would be of special value to those seeking academic careers. As later chapters will show, the Society was, in effect, a powerful tool for challenging the Church of England's domination of education.

Election to the Apostles was no little accomplishment, even for someone like Sidgwick, who seemed the virtual embodiment of the virtues of the rising middle and professional class. But surpassing expectations was a habit of his. The son of an Anglican clergyman of modest means, Henry's entire life fell within the reign of Queen Victoria, but by the end of it he was about as well connected as any nonaristocrat could be. His two brothers, William and Arthur, would both become Oxford classicists, and his sister Mary would wind up marrying Benson and living in Lambeth Palace. The upward trajectory of the family, courtesy of Rugby, Oxbridge, and the church, was spectacular. And this is not to mention his future brothers-in-law Arthur Balfour and Lord Rayleigh, the latter of whom would win the Nobel Prize for discovering argon. Thus, Sidgwick found himself belonging to some of the most influential cultural and political circles in England, at a time when England was the greatest imperial power on earth.

Yet if the Sidgwicks ended up on a lofty plateau of cultural accomplishment, their path was not untypical, inauspicious as the beginnings may seem. Henry set out like many a middle-class clergyman's son; he simply went further.

What little is known of Sidgwick's early life has mostly been reported in the *Memoir*.[21] He was the son of Mary Crofts and the Rev. William Sidgwick, who at the time of Henry's birth, on May 31, 1838, was headmaster of the grammar school at Skipton, near Leeds in Yorkshire. William Sidgwick's father was another William; he had arrived in Skipton from Leeds in 1784 and owned a water-powered cotton-spinning mill, a business most of his sons followed him in. But it is hard to go much further back. In the *Memoir*, Sidgwick records a visit to the "Raikes," his uncle Robert's house in Skipton, and the light this shed on the Sidgwick genealogy:

My uncle is still meditating the problem of our genealogy; he gave me a copy of the stamp which the tobacconist at Leeds – believed to be 'Honest James' and my great-great-grandfather – used for his packets of Virginia. But we do not seem able to trace back the tobacconist to our ancestral hill-valley on the Cumbrian border. So we must be content to *begin* with Tobacco. One might start from a worse thing. (M 423)

The allusion here is to "a persistent tradition in the family that they had originally migrated from Dent, a picturesque dale in the far north-west of the county. . . . At Dent there have been for the last four centuries at least, as the parish registers show, 'sidesmen' (or small farmers owning their own land) of the name of Sidgwick or Sidgswick. The only one of the clan who was at all widely known was Adam Sedgwick of Cambridge." (M 1)[22] The altered spelling of the name of the famous geologist and philosopher was apparently an error from the mid eighteenth century. At any rate, as one of Henry's American obituaries would note, the "district will best be recognized by Americans as the Brontë country, and Sidgwick's family were 'dalesmen,' – an acute, hard-headed, and never-tiring race."[23] But in some of his correspondence, Sidgwick would remark on how his own family afforded many excellent examples of the problem of finding appropriate employment for solid but not terribly ambitious middle-class types.

Henry's father did not go into the cotton-spinning business, but was sent to Trinity College, Cambridge, graduating in 1829. The *Memoir* reports that after his graduation, he apparently made a grand tour of the Continent, and that he counted among his friends W. M. Thackeray and Perronet Thompson, the second of whom would figure in the development of utilitarianism. Sidgwick's mother, Mary Crofts, had come from East Riding, Yorkshire. She had been orphaned at an early age and had been raised, along with three brothers and two sisters, by her bachelor uncle, the Rev. William Carr, whose family had for generations held the living at Bolton Abbey. She married William Sidgwick in 1833.

Henry's older brother, William Carr Sidgwick, had been born in 1834, but the next two siblings, Henrietta Rose and Edward Plunket, both died in childhood, despite efforts to relocate to healthier environs. The boy died in 1840, and the girl in 1841, not long after the death of the father, when

Henry was only three. This was an alarming and quick succession of losses, and it must have left a painful mark on the family. Perhaps Henry was seeing ghosts from a very early age. At any rate, even his earliest correspondence would refer to his "ghost-seeing" tendencies, and he would always have members of his family collect ghost stories for him.

He was not of particularly robust health himself. Though not exactly unhealthy, he was never positively athletic or vigorous, and was variously plagued over the course of his life by hay fever, stuttering, insomnia, depression, impotence, and dyspepsia, with one very serious bout of this last as a Cambridge undergraduate, when he seemed near death. As a five-year-old he was forced on doctor's orders to give up chess because the game was said to "overexcite" him, possibly contributing to his later stammer (though as an adult he continued to enjoy playing). In all, though Sidgwick's body would be a source of physical and metaphysical consternation to him for his entire life, he managed to compensate for many of his infirmities, and as an adult pursued serious walking, jogging (fully clothed, and through the middle of Cambridge), lawn tennis, and garden golf. These concessions to health were somewhat compromised by a sedentary, academic lifestyle and an addiction to cigarettes.

With William, Henry, and the two younger siblings, Arthur and Mary, it was a fairly full Sidgwick household that in 1844 settled in Redland, on the outskirts of Bristol. Mary Sidgwick built a happy and comfortable life for them, though no doubt their impressive upward trajectory was smoothed by the prosperity and proximity of the larger family. In 1873, upon hearing of the death of his uncle, J. B. Sidgwick, Henry wrote to his mother: "I was much startled and grieved, having no idea that he was in any danger. I remember well the last time that I saw him at the mill, little thinking that it was the last time. I seem to remember all my childish feelings about him as the Head of the family, and it makes me sad to think that I shall never see his fine impressive old face again." (M 279)

Once the family was settled, Henry proved to be a rather precocious child, with marked Apostolic tendencies:

After the move to Redland the boy lived at home for four years under a governess (Miss Green), with Latin lessons from his mother, and then for two years more he went to a day school in Bristol known as the Bishop's College. . . . The younger brother and sister remember chiefly the earlier years, when Henry was the inventive genius of the nursery. Nearly all the games which the three children most relished were either devised by him, or greatly improved by his additions, and amongst them was a special language whereby the children believed they might safely discuss their secrets in the presence of the cold world of elders. The tedium of Sunday, when games (unless constructively religious) were forbidden, was beguiled, under his direction, not only by an extended secular use of the animals of Noah's ark, but for a while by the preaching of actual sermons written with all seriousness, on which the children bestowed remarkable pains. (M 4)

This inventiveness was in fact kept up in later life. A mysterious piece entitled "The Ural Mountains: A New Parlour Game" appeared in *Macmillan's Magazine* in early 1862, signed with the initials E.E.B. and H.S. It described a game in which one person would be elected judge and the rest of the company would be divided into two sides, each side electing a captain. "The game is begun by the captains, one of whom accuses the other of some imaginary crime, – the more absurd the better. He is then subject to an examination from his antagonist as to the circumstances of the charge, his means of knowing it, the supposed motives, and anything in heaven or earth that may be considered to be in any way connected with it."[24] The interrogation and counterinterrogation are carried on by each team member in turn, each being responsible for elaborating the charge or defense in a consistent way. Any inconsistencies are challenged as "blots" and referred to the judge; the side that ends up with the fewest blots wins.

In a letter to his close friend Graham Dakyns from March of 1862, Sidgwick explains that he had nothing to do with the *Macmillan's* article, though he "assuredly" did invent the game. His close friend and fellow Apostle Earnest Bowen was the one responsible for the published account, though Bowen apparently thought it right to give Sidgwick his share of the credit. Such inventiveness and creativity were also evident in Sidgwick's talent for improvising stories for children, who generally liked him, and in this connection it is also important to note his love of poetry as a creative outlet. According to the *Memoir*, although Sidgwick published only a few of his poems, "he had in his early years, like many others, higher hopes and ambitions in this line" (M 64).[25]

In 1850, Sidgwick was sent off to a school in Blackheath, run by the Thucydides scholar H. Dale, where his brother William was also a student. William later recalled "the gaiety and vivacity of his disposition, which made him a general favourite," the "unusual cleverness which he showed from the first in his studies," and his nearly being killed by an accidental blow from a golf club (M 5). But the school closed the following year, and after a brief return to the Bristol day school, Henry was off to Rugby – a somewhat surprising development, since his father "had always held the strongest objections to the old public schools, from a rooted belief in their low moral tone" (M 6). His view, however accurate, had been formed before Thomas Arnold's reformism improved the reputation of Rugby, producing the image of it as inspiring in students a high sense of duty and social responsibility.[26]

Sidgwick made many lifelong friends at Rugby – most notably Henry Graham Dakyns, Charles Bowen, T. H. Green, F. E. Kitchener, Charles Bernard, and C. H. Tawney – and he succeeded brilliantly in his studies, working mainly under the classical scholars Charles Evans and Thomas Evans. Bowen would later produce a charming and vivid reminiscence of the young Sidgwick that serves as something of a corrective to Myers's recollections:

[W]ithin his first few years after leaving school there were but few branches of knowledge and of human interest into which he had not plunged, and in many with good results. Perhaps I should except the world of sport, which he regarded not indeed for a moment with contempt, but with an amused and large-hearted tolerance quite his own. In intellectual matters I should put down, as his first and supreme characteristic, candour. It seemed to me then, as it does now, something morally beautiful and surprising; it dominated and coloured his other great qualities, those of subtlety, memory, boldness, and the tolerance of which I have just spoken was in the next degree his most striking attribute. Perhaps pure laziness was the shortcoming for which he had least sympathy; but he seemed to make, as a very great mind does, allowances for everything; he was considerate and large-hearted because he saw so much.

A younger generation cannot well realise how bright and cheerful a companion he was in early years. In the spring of life he could be versatile and gay with the rest: abundant in quiet humour: not boisterous, as many or most, but full of playful thoughts and ready for the mirthful side of things as well as the serious. He was small and not very strong; I doubt whether he excelled in any physical game, but he could walk fairly, and I have a delightful recollection of a short knapsack tour that we had together in South Wales.[27]

The decision to allow Henry, and then Arthur, to attend Rugby was by all accounts the result of a new force in the Sidgwick household: Benson. Benson was actually a cousin of the Rev. William Sidgwick, and another product of Cambridge. In 1850, when still an undergraduate, he had been stunned by the unexpected deaths of his mother and older sister, which turn of events left him in charge of the family, which he in turn discovered had not been provided for. Relief came from friends and relatives, among them Mary Sidgwick, and Benson formed a close bond with her family. Shortly after persuading her that Rugby under E. M. Goulburn had undergone a great improvement in morals, and that Henry could safely attend, Benson himself was offered a mastership there, so that he and Henry headed to Rugby together. Benson would become, in succession, Sidgwick's first mentor, his occasional teacher, his brother-in-law, and, ultimately, archbishop. He nurtured Henry from the start, especially during some unhappy times at Rugby, and the mentoring was made all the more complete after June of 1853, when Mary Sidgwick moved the family to the "Blue House" on Newbold Road in Rugby. For the next two years, Sidgwick could live at home, thus avoiding the "low morals" associated with school life, and Benson also came to live there, with the result that their contact was greater than ever. In Sidgwick's words, "through his talk in home life, his readings aloud, etc., his advice and stimulus abundantly given *tête-à-tête*, his intellectual influence over me was completely maintained."[28] All other influences paled beside that of Benson: "The points in which Sidgwick differed from other boys – his unusual ability and intellectual curiosity, his passion for reading, and his lack of interest or aptitude for some of the more active pursuits of the ordinary boy – all tended to make natural the close tie with one only a few years older, to whom he owed much, whom he deeply admired, and whom it was his strong ambition and hope, at this time, to follow and resemble" (M 15). As he wrote to his sister, Mary:

No one knows, my dearest Minnie, I do not think even you could tell, what Edward has been to me – it is not merely that he has been my hero ever since I knew him, and that my hero-worship of him has grown even as my admiration for goodness & beauty & truth has grown – it is not merely that he has come to be as one of ourselves, a sharer of the firm & deep household affection that nothing else can ever resemble – a deeper debt still than these and more than I can tell you now I owe him. There is only one bond that could knit him closer to us, and I need not say what that one is.[29]

Henry was close to his sister, and to his younger brother Arthur, and would forever be dispensing elder brotherly advice to them. The bond referred to in this letter was of course the marital one, but it must be said that, to judge from *Mother*, the memoir of Mary Benson assembled by her son Fred, this bit of brotherly advice may have reflected an excessive deference to the hero rather than to his sister's interests. Mary's gentle and sympathetic nature was fairly quashed by her marriage to the much older Benson, who had apparently decided that Mary was to be his wife long before Mary herself was mature enough to so much as consider the matter in a serious way. The marriage was not a happy one, and Mary, who was often depressed, and even suffered something of a breakdown, apparently found some relief from her autocratic husband in intimate female friendships.[30]

What was the precise content of Benson's influence on Henry? Decidedly non-Apostolic. The model that Benson afforded Sidgwick was one that, after having first thoroughly assimilated it, would serve as the object of rebellion for him for the rest of his life. Benson was a moderate High Churchman, with few genuinely liberalizing tendencies. With later hindsight, Sidgwick would describe his position thus:

For him, the only hope of effective and complete social reform lay in the increased vitality and increased influence of the Christian Church: useful work might be done by those outside – his recognition of the value of such work was always ample and cordial – but it could only be of limited and partial utility. The healing of the nations could only come from one source; and any social science that failed to recognize this must be proceeding on a wrong track. And the struggle for perfect impartiality of view, which seemed to me an imperative duty, presented itself to him – as I came to understand – as a perverse and futile effort to get rid of the inevitable conditions of intellectual and spiritual life. I remember he once said to me in those years that my generation seemed to be possessed by an insane desire to jump off its own shadow: but the image was not adequate, for in the spiritual region he regarded the effort to get rid of the bias given by early training and unconsciously imbibed tradition, as not only futile but profoundly dangerous.

I do not mean that he failed to do justice to the motives of free-thinkers. Even in the sixties – when it was not uncommon for orthodox persons to hint, or even openly say, that no man could fail to admit the overwhelming evidence for Christianity, unless his reason was perverted by carnal appetites or wordly ambitions – I never remember his uttering a word of this kind: and I remember many instances of his cordial recognition of the disinterested aims and moral rectitude of particular free-thinkers. Still, the paralysis of religious life, naturally resulting from the systematic and prolonged maintenance of this attitude of 'unbiassed' inquiry, seemed to him fraught with the gravest spiritual perils; however well-intentioned in its origin, it could hardly fail to be seconded by the baser elements of human nature, the flesh desiring to shake off the yoke of the spirit.[31]

Of course, such insights and distance were a Cambridge development, and could hardly have been manifest in the years when Benson was Sidgwick's ego ideal, providing the (male) intellectual and moral guidance that had been missing from his home life. Benson provided the willing, earnest pupil, and the "extraordinary intellectual diet" of Cambridge provided the conflict. As Rothblatt explains, the Apostles must have "both stimulated and depressed" Sidgwick, "since the questions raised by his reading could never be purely academic. Rugby had sent him into the world to be useful, but as he turned over in his mind the implications of higher criticism, neo-epicureanism, positivism and Darwinian science, little seemed left of the Rugby world of service, responsibility and certainty."[32] The Apostles were no respecters of orthodoxy. At the least, what they tended to seek was some ideal union of Jesus and Socrates. The conflict was complete; the whole manner of conversation was in contrast. As Sidgwick perceptively observed of Benson:

I think he had little taste for arguing out methodically points of fundamental disagreement where the issues were large and vital. At any rate I think he would rather do this with comparative strangers than with intimate friends: in the case of the latter, the sense of profound divergence, which such discussions inevitably intensify, was painful to him. The disposition to avoid such discussions was, indeed, only the negative side of the sympathetic quality that constituted the peculiar charm of his conversation, – the quickness and tact with which he found topics on which his interlocutor's mind was in general harmony with his own, and the spontaneous buoyancy and force of sympathy with which he threw himself into full and frank discussion of these topics.[33]

Any such attitude was in marked contrast to the Apostolic demand for sympathetic intimacy *and* truth, for the conversation that put everything on the line. Consequently, and not surprisingly, Benson could be of little intellectual help to Sidgwick during his years of religious doubt. The most intimate friends of Sidgwick's adult life would also be, in Apostolic fashion, the most intellectually significant and demanding ones. Admirably, his wife would count among them.

Ironically enough, Benson himself would set Sidgwick on the very path that would lead to their doctrinal – though never personal – alienation from each other. With Benson's aid, Sidgwick's Rugby career flourished. Goulburn wanted him to try for the Balliol scholarship, for which promising Rugby students traditionally competed. But Sidgwick knew that

Benson, without directly saying as much, wanted him to go to his own Cambridge. Even an unexpressed Benson wish was sufficient, of course, and in October of 1855, Sidgwick began his life at Trinity College. Until the year 1900, when the cancer that would end his life forced him to resign, he would be present there every single term save one.

III. Little Systems

> Our little systems have their day;
> They have their day and cease to be:
> They are but broken lights of thee,
> And thou, O Lord, are more than they.
> Alfred Lord Tennyson,
> *In Memoriam*

Sidgwick tells another story about his Cambridge self-creation, in addition to the one about joining the Apostles. It was not a whimsical letter to Minnie in which he recounted how "he had always been rather a selfish being," until in 1857 he was taken seriously ill: "Suddenly my attention was concentrated on *My Digestion*." With this, he realized how selfish he was, meaning not that he was absorbed in his "own pleasures and pains," but in his "own notions and dreams." At first he tried to shape himself directly, "by conscientious struggles, efforts of Will," but eventually he came to a very Millian insight about the indirect pursuit of happiness, realizing that direct effort "does not answer for an invalid; one has not to fight oneself in open battles, but to circumvent oneself by quietly encouraging all the various interests that take one out of self." And for him, "the *great* artifice was the direct and sympathetic observation of others. I used to try and think how they were feeling, and sometimes to prophesy what they would say. I think most of my little knowledge of my fellow-creatures comes from that period of my life." (M 271)

That Sidgwick's indigestion may have thus contributed to his Apostolic conversational abilities may seem a silly, low-minded gloss on such high-minded activity, but the significance of such invalidism – or of the body generally – cannot be lightly dismissed.[34] Recall Maitland's observation that Sidgwick's "range of sympathy was astonishingly wide. He seemed to delight in divining what other people were thinking, or were about to think, in order that he might bring his mind near to theirs, learn from them what could be learnt, and then, if argument was desirable, argue at close quarters."[35]

As will become increasingly evident, Sidgwick's construction of the fleshly body in relation to sympathetic understanding played an exceedingly important role in his religious, ethical, and parapsychological struggles. Some would also try to situate this obsession with figurative and literal forms of telepathic empathizing, mingling of minds, and so on, in the context of the fascination with mesmerism that first became marked during the earlier Victorian period, and that itself represented a response to anxiety over social conflict and the growth of democracy, with new forms of political leadership seeking to understand and achieve crowd control and consensus in novel ways.[36] This line of interpretation, not heretofore developed in connection with Sidgwick, will be more fully addressed in Chapter 5, but it is suggestive of just how emblematic of social currents the seemingly more eccentric side of Sidgwickian sympathy may actually have been, of just how much his parapsychological interests reflected what was "in the air."

Moreover, Sidgwick's friendship with John Addington Symonds, the source of some of the most intense intellectual and emotional exchanges of his life, was very much shaped by Symonds's chronic invalidism and the way this affected his philosophical outlook. Symonds shared many of Sidgwick's interests, especially in forms of depth psychology, and his own explorations of Platonic eros provided further forms of struggle with bodily existence and how it related to the intimacy of minds. Sidgwick was positively robust compared to Symonds, and in the only times he ever experienced anything close to Symonds's tubercular physical weakness were during this undergraduate bout and in the last months of his life.

It appears that he did make the most of such experiences. Evident in the foregoing remarks is the struggle with egoism and the body, via sympathetic talk, that would color the rest of his life, especially during his times of intellectual crisis. His diary and commonplace book, from his early years at Cambridge, are filled with records of his battle with self and flesh. Consider this earnest prayer, recorded in his diary:

> Before the Sacrament. I confess my errors to
> Jesus Christ in whom I humbly hope & pray
> that I believe with a saving faith –
> 1. My selfishness – This I feel is my great evil

combined with my self-consciousness & my
occasional reactionary asceticism it leads to
acts of great folly as well as wrong-doing.
O God deliver me from this make it
my sole aim primarily to do thy will,
secondarily to further my own health
& self-improvement intellectually morally
& physically; but always relatively if
not subordinately to the welfare of
others – give me a complete devotion
to Jesus Christ & a desire to imitate
him in his utter abandonment of self
in the cause of those whose nature He
took – grant me to realize so as to
feel these great realities; that I may
not merely prate about but acknowledge
from my heart the superiority of heavenly things
to earthly.
2. Pride of Intellect – O God grant me neither
to exalt too high nor to despise this
gloriously capable part of my nature.[37]

The "reactionary asceticism" leading to "acts of great folly as well as wrong-doing" was apparently quite real, and this may be a reference back to his earlier abstemiousness, his habit of drinking only water, which his physicians claimed contributed to his digestive problem. But his somewhat compulsive battling with his own constitution took other forms as well, such as his efforts to overcome his insomnia and stammering.[38] Indeed, it is intriguing that his celebrated conversation involved just such a struggle on the very surface, as it were, in that he was often complimented for deploying his stammer to enhance the effect of his wit, turning a kind of physical resistance into a triumph of intellect. As he wrote to Dakyns, in August of 1864, "Strive not to let your spirit be clouded by your flesh: in every *disease* this is the worst danger. I mean what is called hypochondria, the state when one's thoughts are enslaved to one's clay."[39] It is not at all far-fetched to read these things as symptomatic portents or manifestations of the battles against materialism characteristic of his parapsychology and his own self-experimentation. But then, one had to watch out for the intellect as well.

It should be remarked that Sidgwick apparently had quite extraordinary powers of mental concentration, no doubt related to that absorption in thought that often kept him from recognizing friends and acquaintances when he passed them in the street. Oscar Browning recorded his observations of Sidgwick during the University Scholarship exam, noting how while everyone else was scribbling away at their Latin verses, Sidgwick simply sat there motionlessly meditating for nearly the entire period. With only minutes to go, he came out of his spell and wrote out his entire exam perfectly.[40]

Absorption in self and pride of intellect – such were the sins of the young Sidgwick. And sins they were, to his mind, even after the influence of Benson started to fade. The commonplace book records:

> But I desire only studies that however abstract in . . . reasonings have for their end human happiness. Thus Political Economy to make men happier and better en masse: Theology, to know, not what conduces to *my* eternal weal, but to *our* &c. The strongest conviction I have is a belief in what Comte calls "altruisme": the cardinal doctrine, it seems to me, of Jesus of Nazareth. I do not penetrate into my innermost feelings: it may be that my philanthropy has it's root in selfishness: I may be convinced that the only means of securing my own happiness is to pursue that of my fellow-creatures: but surely if this profound and enlightened selfishness be a vice, and I sometimes fear that it is, in me, no better regimen could be applied to it than that suggested by itself, namely, devotion to Society. Whether Comtist or not I feel as if I never should swerve from my cardinal maxim, wh is also his "L'amour pur principe. Le progres pour but."[41]

Such remarks, linking Christianity to Comte, should suggest the thoroughly religious context (even without Benson) of Sidgwick's early dabblings with utilitarianism. His reluctance to penetrate his innermost feelings was not at all like that of the eighteenth-century skeptics – say, Hume, who asked, "Why rake into those corners of nature which spread a nuisance all around?" Nor, at this early stage, did he show any great confidence in Bentham's artificial harmony of interests, as so often construed, however misleadingly, as simply a matter-of-fact acceptance of the prevalence of self-interested motives. Even in his later sympathy with Bentham, he was apt to regard the prevalence of self-interest as akin to the prevalence of sin, something that had to be recognized and dealt with realistically, though certainly not applauded. He was bent on disciplining himself to altruism, always suspecting, however, that his deeper nature could be betraying him.

His consolation was that perhaps he could satisfy his true self by altruistic action.

And of course, the truth is that Sidgwick did seek to penetrate his innermost feelings, and his gloriously capable intellect was largely employed in doing precisely that. After all, that was his Apostolic quest. Again, although during his first year or so at Cambridge he was still under Benson's sway, the next year saw him "fall under different influences, which went on increasing" until he was "definitely enlisted as an 'Academic Liberal.'" And it was the "rapidity and completeness of his transfer of allegiances" that would later strike him, and the way in which it was effected by groups like the Apostles and by his own independent studies, rather than by his formal schooling, about which he hardly ever spoke with any enthusiasm (rather the opposite). But the transformation was not like that of, say, Bertrand Russell, who would speedily abandon the religion of his youth under similar Apostolic circumstances, but then turn a scornful eye on the entire Christian tradition. Sidgwick would always regard insouciant atheism or agnosticism as shallow, insensitive to the religious experience and the demands of the human heart.

Sidgwick's account of his transition is of the first importance, and neatly outlines the different sides of his quest.

To explain more precisely the 'contrast' of which I have spoken, I will begin by sketching briefly the ideal which, under the influence primarily of J. S. Mill, but partly of Comte seen through Mill's spectacles, gradually became dominant in my mind in the early sixties: – I say 'in my mind,' but you will understand that it was largely derived from intercourse with others of my generation, and that at the time it seemed to me the only possible ideal for all adequately enlightened minds. It had two aspects, one social and the other philosophical or theological. What we aimed at from a social point of view was a complete revision of human relations, political, moral and economic, in the light of science directed by comprehensive and impartial sympathy; and an unsparing reform of whatever, in the judgment of science, was pronounced to be not conducive to the general happiness. This social science must of course have historical knowledge as a basis: but, being science, it must regard the unscientific beliefs, moral or political, of past ages as altogether wrong, – at least in respect of the method of their attainment, and the grounds on which they were accepted. History, in short, was conceived as supplying the material on which we had to work, but not the ideal which we aimed at realizing; except so far as history properly understood showed that the time had come for the scientific treatment of political and moral problems.

As regards theology, those with whom I sympathised had no close agreement in conclusions, – their views varied from pure positivism to the 'Neochristianity' of the Essayists and Reviewers: and my own opinions were for many years unsettled and widely fluctuating. What was fixed and unalterable and accepted by us all was the necessity and duty of examining the evidence for historical Christianity with strict scientific impartiality; placing ourselves as far as possible outside traditional sentiments and opinions, and endeavouring to weigh the pros and cons on all theological questions as a duly instructed rational being from another planet – or let us say from China – would naturally weigh them.[42]

This account comports well with the better-known one affixed to the sixth edition of the *Methods*, in which Sidgwick alludes to the suffocating orthodoxy of both Benson and the formal Cambridge curriculum: "My first adhesion to a definite Ethical system was to the Utilitarianism of Mill: I found in this relief from the apparently external and arbitrary pressure of moral rules which I had been educated to obey, and which presented themselves to me as to some extent doubtful and confused; and sometimes, even when clear, as merely dogmatic, unreasoned, incoherent." (ME xvii) But it also indicates the larger historical currents that Sidgwick was caught up in. Utilitarianism was but one possible form for this enthusiasm, and it did not in itself define the complex of religious questions and controversies, the general innovativeness, of the era. In fact, as will be shown, it did not represent the direction of the times at all, but was in some respects a more old-fashioned creed. The academic liberals were a much more diverse and divided group than the term "Millian" would suggest.

The academic liberals of these years, the many university figures who went in for reformism and public service, certainly cherished ambitious hopes for the revamping of all that was sectarian, and they expected to play a leading role in preparing the nation for greater democratization, better and broader education, increased professionalization, and more progressive, less superstitious and dogmatic forms of worship and morality. The Apostles were of course much identified with this movement, as were several other vanguard groups around Oxbridge, though as a movement it could shelter philosophies as diverse as Sidgwick's utilitarianism, Huxley's Darwinism, T. H. Green's idealism, and the Oxford Hellenism of Pater and the early Symonds.

Theologically, the *Essays and Reviews* proved to be a turning point, when published in 1860. The book was a collection of critical and latitudinarian or Broad Church pieces, designed to encourage open discussion of biblical questions by figures of eminence – Benjamin Jowett, Frederick Temple, Baden Powell, Mark Pattison, H. B. Wilson, Rowland Williams, and C. W. Goodwin. Of these, only Goodwin, of Cambridge, was a layperson. The heated controversy that followed its appearance predictably pointed up the differences that now existed between Sidgwick and Benson. Sidgwick was disgusted by the reaction of the church and sent a harsh letter to the *Times*, stating: "What we all want is, briefly, not a condemnation, but a refutation. The age when ecclesiastical censures were sufficient in such cases has passed away. . . . For philosophy and history alike have taught them [the laity] to seek not what is 'safe,' but what is true." (M 64–65) This was what Benson had in mind when he complained about the insane desire to jump off one's own shadow. Some years later, after the book had been condemned by the Convocation of Canterbury, Benson would defend the promotion of Temple to the see of Exeter, but he would do so on the grounds that Temple did not share the views of the other contributors.

To seek not what is safe but what is true, and to do so with strict scientific impartiality, even on questions of religion and morality – these were convictions that Sidgwick absorbed as his own, the convictions of his generation. How could one go out, in good Rugby fashion, to do one's Duty, when all was doubtful, even Duty itself?

The content of Sidgwick's theological transformation will be addressed in subsequent chapters. First, however, it is necessary to consider at greater length a more fundamental transformation, the transformation reverberating throughout Sidgwick's talk about talk and self-creation – namely, his Apostolic vision of the pursuit of truth. This is the key to his theological and ethical development, and even to his talk itself. However playful the Apostolic banter may have been, it had a very real effect on Sidgwick and the growth of his utilitarian orientation. Lurking within his utilitarianism, one always finds a poetic Apostolic soul.

IV. Pursuit of Truth

Truth, I hold, not to be that which every man troweth, but to be that which lies at the bottom of all men's trowings, that in which these trowings have their only meeting point.

Frederick Denison Maurice, in *Towards Unity*

Now, though there were different roads to this end, and though each teacher believed himself, and induced his disciples to believe, that his was the shortest, yet one method was common to them all; all sought to acquire power by means of *words*. The mastery over words was the great art which the Athenian youth was to cultivate; his own feelings, and an observation of what was passing every day in his city, told him that there was a charm and fascination in these which the physical force of an Oriental tyrant might vainly try to compete with. It seems to have been the first observation of Socrates when he began earnestly to meditate on the condition of his countrymen, that in this case, as in most others, the tyrants were slaves; that those who wished to rule the world by the help of words were themselves in the most ignominious bondage to words. The wish to break this spell seems to have taken strong possession of his mind. . . . As he reflected, he began more and more clearly to perceive that words, besides being the instruments by which we govern others, are means by which we may become acquainted with ourselves.

Frederick Denison Maurice, Moral and Metaphysical Philosophy[43]

Important as it surely is to understand the Benthamite and Millian influences on Sidgwick, it should be clear, by this point, that it is more important still to understand the influence of the Apostles on him, since they were the ones who liberated his mind in the first place, kindling his passion for truth, for the life of thought, for mastering the "deepest problems of human life." But to understand the Apostles, one must begin by shedding light on the mysterious figure of F. D. Maurice, a man who, though virtually unread today, was a gigantic force during the Victorian period and in many ways stood behind both Sidgwick and Mill, as a powerful voice pleading the limitations of utilitarianism.

John Frederick Denison Maurice was Apostle number thirty, vetted in 1823. But as Arthur Hallam would write to his Oxford friend Gladstone, the effect that Maurice "has produced on the minds of many at Cambridge by the single creation of that society, the Apostles, (for the spirit though not the form *was* created by him) is far greater than I can dare to calculate, and will be felt both directly and indirectly in the age that is before us."[44] Tennyson, too, admired Maurice, making him godfather of his own son (named after Hallam), and Maurice would in turn establish the long Apostolic tradition of worshipping the Tennyson and Arthur Hallam relationship, at the heart of *In Memoriam*.

Born in 1805, Maurice was the son of a very liberal-minded Unitarian clergyman, and it has often been suggested that his lifelong opposition to doctrinaire religion and admiration of the search for unity in practical ethical conduct was the result of witnessing his happy family life torn apart by the conversion of his mother and older sisters to Calvinism. In any event, his liberal Unitarian background certainly had an enduring effect on him, even after his conversion to Anglicanism.

After an unusual undergraduate career at both Cambridge and (following a journalistic stint in London) Oxford, when his religious heterodoxy had pushed him in directions allowing him to avoid subscription, he eventually quelled his doubts sufficiently to be ordained and became chaplain of Guy's Hospital and Lincoln's Inn, and then a professor of English literature, later theology, at King's College, London. His reluctance to believe that a benevolent God could decree eternal damnation in any literal sense led to his dismissal from King's in 1853, but he had nonetheless become one of the most influential Broad Church theologians of the day, a founding father of Christian Socialism, and a champion, like Mill, of higher education for women. In 1866, after the death of John Grote, he would return to Cambridge as the Knightbridge Professor.

Quite prolific, Maurice published such works as *The Kingdom of Christ* (1838), *Theological Essays* (1853), and a novel, *Eustace Conway* (1834). It was he who would directly or indirectly lead a number of younger-generation Apostles – including Apostle number 138, Sidgwick – into involvement with such causes as the Working Men's Colleges and women's higher education. Sidgwick knew Maurice personally from the annual Apostolic dinners, which Maurice always attended, and, after the latter's return to Cambridge, from their joint participation in the "Grote club," the philosophical discussion group for dons that had originally met at the home of the previous Knightbridge Professor, John Grote.[45] Sidgwick in fact drew the elder Maurice into the club, at a time when the former's struggles with subscription were coming to resemble those of the latter's earlier self. The *Memoir* records how he would stimulate his older colleague's recollections of "English social and political life in the thirties, forties, and fifties" (M 137).[46]

But Maurice's influence was more encompassing, vaster, than such concrete institutional connections would suggest. His work, like Mill's, spanned the transition from the age of the First Reform Bill and the bourgeois reformism of the Benthamites and Whigs against the Tories, through the radical working-class protests of the Chartists, all the way into the era of the Second Reform Bill and the dominance of Gladstone's Liberal Party. The means by which he navigated these demands for greater democracy were bound to appeal to certain kinds of academic liberals. As Richter has observed of Sidgwick's friend T. H. Green, there was an

orthodox unorthodoxy about the faith he constructed, like so many others in his age, out of Wordsworth and Coleridge, Dr Arnold, Carlyle, F. D. Maurice and Kingsley. . . . Disparate in detail, they were united in their Romantic, Broad Church, or Christian Socialist opposition to what they regarded as undesirable characteristics of the eighteenth century which had persevered as the cardinal errors of their own time. Among these were the previous century's mocking spirit, or lack of reverence, its atheism, materialism, hedonism, its mechanical model of the universe, its psychology based upon the association of ideas, and its egoistic individualism.[47]

For Maurice, by contrast with "Benthamism," societies hold together "through the trust of men in each other and through trust in someone whom they could not see and could not name, but who, they felt, was not far from any one of them."[48] The Christian socialists allowed that the working class had been treated brutally by capitalism, but thought the cure was fostering Christian fellowship rather than revolution.[49] Maurice, however, abjured any claim to found a theological or philosophical school; dogma, doctrine, system, party – all were the selfish and blinding forces working against unity, the recognition of "Christ in you." He held that the righteousness of God speaks "in Christ directly to that in each man which God has created to recognize His voice. . . . the conscience with its mysterious duplicity is the very self in each man; that which is feeling after God haply it may find him, that which, if it does not find him, must sink into selfishness and brutality and make gods after its own likeness."[50] He even disliked the label "Broad Church." The Anglican "Church" was *not* a "System," with an official point of view, but rather an attempt to embrace all warring factions: "Let us make Spaniards, Frenchmen, Italians, understand that we do not ask them to leave their churches for ours, to accept any single English tradition which is not also theirs."[51] As he put it in later life, "I was sent into the world that I might persuade men to recognize Christ as the centre of their fellowship with each other, that so they might be united in their families, their countries, and as men, not in schools and factions."[52]

It was this faith that led Mill to complain that

there was more intellectual power wasted in Maurice than in any other of my contemporaries. . . . Great powers of generalization, rare ingenuity and subtlety, and a wide perception of important and unobvious truths, served him not for putting something better into the place of the worthless heap of received opinions on the great subjects of thought, but for proving to his own mind that the Church of England had known everything from the first, and that all the truths on the ground of which the Church and orthodoxy have been attacked (many of which he saw as clearly as any one) are not only consistent with the Thirty-nine Articles, but are better understood and expressed in those Articles than by any one who rejects them.[53]

Mill had gotten to know Maurice and his friend John Sterling at the London Debating Society during the late 1820s, at just about the time Maurice was shaping the Apostles, and despite his exasperation with his Anglicanism, learned a tremendous amount from him, becoming in effect an Apostle in absentia.

Sidgwick, for the most part, did not think any too highly of Maurice's theology or biblical scholarship either. But it was not on such elements that the influence depended. Maurice was a source for Sidgwick in other ways – for example, in the fear of premature system building, and the effect that it might have on the pursuit of truth. It is well to bear in mind the title of Sidgwick's masterwork, when considering Maurice's insistence that "[w]hen once a man begins to build a system the very gifts and qualities which might serve in the investigation of truth, become the greatest hindrances to it. He must make the different parts of the scheme fit into each other: his dexterity is shown, not in detecting facts, but in cutting them square." The terms "system" and "method" are "the greatest contraries imaginable: the one indicating that which is most opposed to life, freedom, variety; and the other that without which they cannot exist."[54]

Method, for Maurice, was truth, or the dialogical pursuit of it, anyway. But truth, as Chadwick remarks of him, "was to be found only in hints and shadows." To Maurice's mind, "direct knowledge and experience of God was beyond language and could allow no substitute in the religious catchwords of the sects. . . . He reached towards the indefinable while he struggled to avoid defining it."[55] And thus, as Schneewind has argued, "Maurice is a true Coleridgean in his insistence that there is something of value to be learned from the deepest views of any thinker on religious matters. Each in his own way has seen a part or an aspect of the truth. So far as each has done so, each is right: it is only their denials, Maurice teaches, that are wrong."[56]

The reference here is, of course, to Samuel Taylor Coleridge, the poet and critic whom Mill himself had set against Bentham as representing the opposing spirit of the age. If Bentham had always inspired one to ask of "any ancient or received opinion, Is it true?," Coleridge inspired one to ask "What is the meaning of it?" Thus, the

one took his stand outside the received opinion, and surveyed it as an entire stranger to it: the other looked at it from within, and endeavoured to see it with the eyes of a believer in it; to discover by what apparent facts it was at first suggested, and by what appearances it has ever since been rendered continually credible – has seemed, to a succession of persons, to be a faithful interpretation of their experience.[57]

The Coleridgean orientation is certainly evident throughout Maurice's work, but, as Mill notes in another context, if Maurice was a Coleridgean, he was "far superior" in intellect to Coleridge, who in fact had little philosophical originality and merely plagiarized vast tracts of German philosophy. In reality, much of the Romanticism that led Mill to qualify and humanize the utilitarian doctrines that he had inherited from his father and Bentham came to him via Maurice. And it was just such allegiances that defined Maurice as one of the "Mystics," when it came to his participation in the Apostles during their early years. The Benthamites, Whigs, and Tories might dominate such vehicles as the Cambridge Union, but when it came to the Saturday evening discussions, the Mystics set the tone, and Maurice chief among them. They appropriated Coleridge's notion of a clerisy, a set of opinion leaders who could substitute for the traditional clergy and lead the work of spiritual regeneration. It was a regeneration to be won through such things as modern literature – the works of Wordsworth, Shelley, and Keats – rather than through mere political reform. Thus, Wordsworth was useful because his poetry could "make men look within for those things in which they agree, instead of looking without for those in which they differ."[58]

As Allen has maintained, this kind of work called for Apostles, for a set of the spiritually awakened, or at least of the soul-searching. "This aspect of the Apostolic spirit encouraged the choice of new members on the basis of their potential for spiritual growth. Once elected, a new member found himself a part of an intimate, exclusive group which invited, expected, but did not normally compel him to confess his deepest thoughts and to share with others the experience of self-examination." And this was indeed an alternative to traditional Cambridge, of which John Sterling complained that "God is called upon to erect his tabernacle among the crumbling and weed-clad ruins of a wasted mind." Thus,

Whatever one may think of Maurice's early beliefs as a guide to political behaviour (or for that matter as a guide to Coleridgean principles), there is no doubt of their value as educational theory, for they are based on a profound sense of the psychological needs of young men like himself. In place of the self-denying accumulation of factual knowledge demanded by the Honours degree system, in place of the self-indulgent idleness encouraged by the Ordinary degree system, in place of the self-assertive rant enforced by the Union's traditions, Maurice offered his fellow-Apostles a justification for personal growth through contemplation, a process based on the individual's own assessment of his needs yet shared with others pursuing the same ideal. The Society did not merely fill a gap in the University's curriculum by providing informal discussion of contemporary culture. Its more essential educational role was to promote the individual's sense of his identity and personal worth through exploration and definition of his most deeply held beliefs. Again, one notes the Society's similarity to . . . the confessional group, in which soul-searching and public confession of belief are the group's main business.[59]

It is also surely no coincidence that the growth of such alternative educational resources would overlap and mutually interact with the Tractarian movement, which has been credited with revitalizing and personalizing the tutorial method in ways that proved useful to Jowett and the Oxford Hellenists.[60] However different their orientations toward religion, they shared a strong sense of the moral bankruptcy of the educational status quo.

When it came to the "art of reconciling by a phrase," and of soaring, Maurice knew no peer. But when it came to penetrating innermost feelings, and being separated by nothing but opinion, the "Brethren" worked together. They descended from Maurice like a spiritual family, inheriting his drive to seek "a deeper, unifying level, one of active sympathy for other people and their personal beliefs."[61] Here, then, was the mission of true education, of a culture fit for an educating society. Unity and sympathy, but without Millian naturalism.

Quite plainly, mystic Apostledom shared much with old Socratic method.[62] As Rothblatt has suggested, Maurice's use of paradox, of avoiding system and synthesis by a "logical sleight of hand," was a "way of finding unity," and for his admirers, it made him "a supremely socratic figure . . . singularly successful in defining terms and devising meanings which furthered his own argument, at the same time conveying to his listeners an appreciation of their own careless reasoning and the argument which had been concealed from them."[63] Maurice himself would have been happy to allow that this was so. Indeed, his ascendance coincided with the revival of Platonism in England, one figure in which had been Maurice's own revered classics teacher, Julius Hare. As he remembered Hare's dialectical approach:

One could not get the handy phrase one wished about Greek ideals and poetical unity; but, by some means or other, one rose to the apprehension that the poem *had* a unity in it, and that the poet *was* pursuing an ideal, and that the unity was not created by him, but perceived by him, and that the ideal was not a phantom, but something which must have had a most real effect upon himself, his age, and his country. I cannot the least tell how Hare imparted this conviction to me; I only know that I acquired it, and could trace it very directly to his method of teaching. . . . we were reading the Gorgia of Plato. But here, again, the lecturer was not tempted for an instant to spoil us of the good which Plato could do us, by talking to us about him, instead of reading him with us. There was no *résumé* of his philosophy, no elaborate comparison of him with Aristotle, or with any of the moderns. Our business was with a single dialogue; we were to follow that through its windings, and to find out by degrees, if we could, what the writer was driving at, instead of being told beforehand. . . . to give us second-hand reports, though they were ever so excellent – to save us the trouble of thinking – to supply us with a moral, instead of showing us how we might find it, not only in the book but in our hearts, this was clearly not his intention.[64]

Perhaps, despite his Christianity, Maurice was more Socratic than Platonic, as the designation "Broad Church" might suggest. That is, assuming (with Vlastos, Nussbaum, and many other classical scholars) that the claims of Socrates really were quite distinct from those of Plato, it appears that the tension between these different approaches to inquiry runs through much of the debate in these early culture wars. In Nussbaum's words, the

historical Socrates is committed to awakening each and every person to self-scrutiny. He relies on no sources of knowledge external to the beliefs of the citizens he encounters, and he regards democracy as the best of the available forms of government, though not above criticism. Plato, by contrast, argues for the restriction of Socratic questioning to a small, elite group of citizens, who will eventually gain access to timeless, metaphysical sources of knowledge; these few should rule over the many.[65]

As we shall see, the Apostolic legacy certainly had its share of Platonic elitism, and of other forms of elitism as well. But the better, more enduring legacy of Maurice came from the Socratic temperament that he passed on, a temperament that Sidgwick, a later "Pope" among the Apostles, would manifest with special clarity. Moreover, even the Socratic side of the Apostolic story was refined and complicated. It is notorious that Socrates himself was cold, ironic, strange, not a model of compassion or even justice.[66] What marked out Apostolic conversation, however, as it was realized in such figures as Maurice and Sidgwick, was the determined, sympathetic effort at unity, the empathic, kindly entering into the perspectives of others. Whether Christian or Romantic, the aim of the confessional group or the encounter group, this imaginative effort was tinged by Platonic eros, the philosophical friendship celebrated in the *Symposium*. *In Memoriam*, something of an Apostolic bible, was after all a celebration of homoerotic friendship, and profoundly suggestive of the Apostolic vision of insight achieved and expressed intimately and poetically.

In truth, the lessons of the leading lights of the Apostles cannot be happily reconstructed in terms of many of the familiar battle lines of recent debates over ancients versus moderns. Neither Maurice nor Sidgwick regarded Socratic inquiry as in some kind of basic conflict with modern methods of (genuine) critical inquiry. Maurice attributed to Hare

the setting before his pupils of an ideal not for a few 'religious' people, but for all mankind, which can lift men out of the sin which 'assumes selfishness as the basis of all actions and life,' and secondly, the teaching them that 'there is a way out of party opinions which is not a compromise between them, but which is implied in both, and of which each is bearing witness.' 'Hare did not tell us this. . . . Plato himself does not say it; he makes us feel it.'

And by this means, the spirit of Bacon was also present: "we were, just as much as the student of natural philosophy, feeling our way from particulars to universals, from facts to principles."[67]

Debates over the canon in English-speaking universities often betray a remarkable ignorance of the fact that Plato only entered it during the early Victorian period, that he had such champions as Mill and Maurice, and that he proved a most controversial innovation, being widely regarded as a "misleader of youth." In 1837, Macaulay complained in the pages of the *Edinburgh Review* that while the Baconian philosophy sought simply "to provide man with what he requires while he continues to be man," the "aim of the Platonic philosopy was to exalt man into a god." Thus, "Plato drew a good bow: but, like Acestes in Virgil, he aimed at the stars. . . . The philosophy of Plato began in words and ended in words – noble words, indeed – words such as were to be expected from the finest of human intellects exercising boundless dominion over the finest of human languages."[68]

Yet Maurice's assimilation of Bacon and Wordsworth, Socrates and Plato was sincere. He was not one to admire the Greeks for despising what human experience might teach. His "whole sympathies had been with the scientific men when they were asserting what they had humbly, patiently investigated, and found out to be true. He was never tired to quoting the spirit of Mr. Darwin's investigations as a lesson and a model for Churchmen."[69] And in this, Sidgwick was truly his spiritual heir, though as Richard Deacon has noted, against "Sidgwick's claim that the Apostles 'absorbed and dominated' him, Leonard Woolf made the point that this was 'not quite the end of the story . . . every now and again an Apostle has dominated and left an impression . . . upon the Society. Sidgwick himself was one of these . . . refertilising and revivifying its spirit and traditions.' "[70] For it was Sidgwick who "paved the way to the Apostles becoming a society of total doubters, if not atheists."

Just words – but what else did one need to go soaring on a Saturday night?

V. Dialogue

If I say that it is impossible for me to keep quiet because that means disobeying the god, you will not believe me and will think I am being ironical. On the other hand, if I say that it is the greatest good for a man to discuss virtue every day and those other things about which you hear me conversing and testing myself and others, for the unexamined life is not worth living for men, you will believe me even less.

Socrates, *Apology*

When he [Socrates] speaks of the dignity of the philosopher, he means us to understand the dignity of a man who does not exalt himself, who does not put himself in the way of the thing which he is examining, who has the simplest, most open eye for receiving light, whencesoever it shall come. That there is a source of light from whence it does come, and that this light is connected with man, is a principle assumed, if it is ever so imperfectly developed, in all his words and acts.

F. D. Maurice, *Moral and Metaphysical Philosophy*

In the sweep of the Platonic revival that so marked the Victorian era, Socrates was to be catapulted into a new prominence in cultural debates. Maurice and the Apostles, Mill and the utilitarians, and a host of Anglican theologians took Socrates as a figure whose importance was surpassed only by that of Jesus. This was how he figured in Mill's *On Liberty*, a work the Apostles eagerly devoured.

Of course, as later chapters will detail, the Platonic Revival was also a sexually loaded affair, and Sidgwick and his friends played no little role in demonstrating how subversive an appeal to the ancients could be. But it is also important simply to situate Sidgwick's Apostolic notions of sympathetic conversation in this context in a preliminary way, the better to bring out the full significance of Maurice and Mill for his vision of philosophy. This is a social and intellectual context that merits independent treatment, such was its importance to the Victorian world.

On the surface, at least, Plato and the Greeks were supposed to help revitalize a flagging, self-doubting culture, and an extraordinary range of thinkers would try to appropriate this inheritance for their own purposes. Of these, Sidgwick was one of the more acute, and it is instructive that the 1860s, which are so often identified as his years of religious "storm and stress," were also the years during which his Apostolic sense of dialogue matured, as he evolved from classicist to philosopher. And in hammering out his own interpretive stance, he could again draw on Mill and his disciples, who, as much as Maurice, regarded themselves as bold innovators in reviving the study of Socrates and Plato in the thirties. Indeed, one of Mill's chief philosophical and political allies, George Grote, was perhaps the leading figure in the Platonic revival, and an avowed Benthamite.[71] Of his monumental *History of Greece* and *Plato*, T. H. Irwin has observed: "Grote's work constitutes a contribution of the first rank both to the study of Greek history and to the study of Greek philosophy. None of his English contemporaries equalled his contribution to either area of study; and no one at all has equalled his contribution to both areas."[72]

Much of what Mill wrote on Plato was, in fact, by way of enthusiastic reviews of Grote. For Mill, Grote had succeeded in setting out the best side of Socrates, his role as a critic and skeptic. Sidgwick, too, would align himself with Grote's work, though in a somewhat different way. Still, one's views on Grote served as something of a political touchstone. When Mill and Sidgwick linked themselves to Grote on Greece, they were self-consciously allying themselves with the chief liberal alternative to and critique of the conservative, Tory interpretation of the failings of Greek democracy. Grote was simply the most formidable to those who, like Connop Thirwall, Hare, Jowett, and Maurice, sought to liberate Greek history from the conservative opponents of democracy, from such figures as William Mitford. Mill the empiricist and Maurice the mystic may have differed on epistemology, but both passionately believed that the lesson of ancient Athens was *not* the impossibility – or viciousness – of democratic self-rule and the necessity of a paternalistic aristocracy.

Just how Sidgwick fell in with Grote's program is a complex matter. Frank Turner, in *The Greek Heritage in Victorian Britain*, cites him in connection with some comments by James Bryce, his close friend, to the effect that so great were the differences between the direct democracy of Athens and the representative democracy of nineteenth-century Britain that "no arguments drawn from their experience are of any value as enabling us to predict its possible results here."[73] And there is much to such a reading, which highlights the characteristic Sidgwickian caution about the lessons of history.

Still, it is illuminating to try to situate Sidgwick a little more precisely in the context of these debates, which were so vital for the Millians, the Apostles, and the academic liberals in general. The method that went into the *Methods* owed an enormous amount to his developing views, during the 1860s, on the meaning of the Greeks, especially Socrates, Plato, and Aristotle. What Sidgwick called his years of storm and stress had more turbulence in them than his account of religious struggles suggests.

To be sure, there were profound differences between Jowett's Hellenizing Oxford and Sidgwick's less humanistic Cambridge. Robert

Todd has even argued that Sidgwick was responsible for diminishing the role of the classics in the study of philosophy at Cambridge, doing so out of his general analytical aversion to the history of philosophy. Although there is some truth in the claim that Sidgwick's notion of the Moral Sciences Tripos made the classics less significant in the undergraduate philosophy curriculum, this does not do justice to the extraordinary importance of Plato and Aristotle in Sidgwick's own philosophical work, or to the way they shaped his larger Apostolic vision of the educational enterprise.[74]

Indeed, during the sixties and even the seventies, Sidgwick would identify himself as one of Grote's disciples. As always, he took scrupulous care in framing his arguments, but he was not wholly averse to trying to draw some lessons from the fate of Socrates. In his review of Thomas Maguire's *Essays on the Platonic Ethics*, for example, he made it plain that if the battle was between the Academy and modern positivism – which is to say, between philosophers like Maguire and Grote, respectively – then he would side with the latter:

Mr. Grote was a historian, and a philosopher, and a philosophical historian: but he was not exactly a historical philosopher, and had nothing better to do, after expounding the views of an author, than to try and condemn them by the standard of the latest empiricism. Such a procedure naturally provokes a rejoinder 'from the Academy.' But Mr. Grote's results had attractions which the answer inevitably lacks. In the first place, the modern adversary has much less temptation to blur the outlines of ancient thought than the modern apologist. Further, Mr. Grote's manner of direct and simple controversy enhanced the fresh and vivid presentation of the Athenian world which is the great charm of his work. We had the English Benthamite in the market with Socrates, and in the garden with Plato: and the result, though incongruous, was enlivening, and stimulative to the historical imagination. Dr. Maguire's commentation has no compensating interest: and we cannot but regret that he has not devoted his scholarship and ability to a work more adapted to the age in which he lives.[75]

To give a somewhat tangled, but still useful, illustration of Sidgwick's position on the Socratic method, consider how he goes about explaining, in his seminal essays on "The Sophists," that although the Socrates of the *Gorgias* tries to identify sophistical argument with rhetoric, he also insists that the self-styled teachers of the art of conduct – many taken to be sophists – are merely too superficial, rather than subversives promoting "a speculative moral scepticism leading to pure egoism in practice" (LPK 56).[76] At a time when popular opinion had become overtly hostile to all such "experts," who were blamed for the decline of Athenian democracy, Plato

has no sympathy whatever with the prevalent fury against the Professors of Conduct, the blind selfish impulse of the Athenian public to find some scapegoat to punish for the general demoralisation which had produced such disastrous consequences. He does not say – as posterity generally have understood him to say – "It is not Socrates who has done the mischief, but other teachers of virtue with whom you confound him." On the contrary, he is anxious to show that the mischief is not attributable to Professors of Conduct at all. It is with this view that he introduces Callicles, the 'practical man' who despised professors, and thinks that the art of private and public life is to be learnt from men of the world. This is the sort of man who is likely to hold egoistic and sensual maxims of conduct. His unaided reflection easily penetrates the incoherences and superficialities of the popular morality: his immoral principles are weeds that spring up naturally in the social soil, without any professional planting and watering, so long as the sun of philosophy is not risen. (LPK 368–69)

The same worry, he continues, is evident in the *Republic*, which is eloquent on "the *naturalness* of the evolution of audacious unrestrained egoism from conventional morality." This is a worry that would loom very large in Sidgwick's *Methods*.

At any rate, the Platonic Socrates is not obsessed with the "Professors of the Art of Conduct," or with "shielding morality from their destructive analysis, and reaffirming the objectivity of duty in opposition to their 'Absolute Subjektivität'." "Sophistik" is a "scarecrow" put together by German commentators on Plato, including the illustrious Zeller.[77] In fact, in "one of the most brilliant and effective passages that Plato ever wrote," he "rings forth" that "You, the Public," are the "Arch-Sophist, it is your Public Opinion that corrupts youth" (LPK 347). As Sidgwick recasts it, to the charge of the demos against Socrates that he corrupts youth, who then "make oligarchical revolutions," the disciple of Socrates may respond, in effect, "it is you who cause the demoralisation, by your low views of virtue and of the gods. An acute and spirited youth pushes these to their logical conclusions: he decides that consummate Injustice is one of the καλά which the proverb declares to be χαλεπά: and thus inspired he enters clubs and plots revolutions." (LPK 370)

It was not quite in Sidgwick to think that the degeneration of Athenian politics into oligarchy was the result of the sun of philosophy having risen, of youth being exposed to too much by way of the "art of words."

He rejected the view of German classicists that "the earliest professional teaching of morality in Greece *must have been* egoistic and anti-social" (LPK 371). More problematic was the low state of popular morality, the mocking irreverence toward religion, which led the brighter (and better-off) youth not to take it seriously.[78] This was a lesson, congenial to his estimate of the state of Christian faith, that he would carry forth into many departments of theory and practice. If, in 1862, his friend Green could chide him for being a "kind of mild Positivist," this may have been in part because, although he could not "swallow" Comte's Religion of Humanity, he did allow that Comte's "arguments as to the necessity of Religion of some sort have great weight with me" (M 87, 76). To Sidgwick's mind, the Socratic street evangelist might too readily be supplied with a cross for his troubles; popular morality was not to be trusted, which was one of the things that made the dualism of practical reason that much more disturbing.

But the moral Sidgwick drew here was not one congenial to landed aristocrats. Although he allowed that the public could be dangerous, the attitude of Callicles was only a potential problem. Sidgwick never held that the "tyranny of the majority" was a concern applicable to ancient Athens, which showed "a remarkable maintenance of liberty in the strict sense of individual liberty – power of doing what one likes, without dangerous disorder." Indeed, the end of Greece's cultural greatness had nothing to do with democracy, but was the result of the Macedonian conquest of 336 B.C. And besides, speaking of the great Greek philosophers, "while agreeing that unbridled democracy is bad, our writers all seem to agree that ordinary selfish oligarchy – the government of the rich minority in their own interest – is worse."[79] All classes needed educating, all needed the benefit of clerisy. And still more importantly, even the philosopher could go only so far in rejecting common sense.

Indeed, Sidgwick was concerned, more than Mill or Grote, to draw out a positive, constructive Socrates. At the least, he argues, "there was a time at which Plato attacked as Sophists rhetorical moralists and politicians, a later time at which he defined a Sophist as a perverse disputer, and a time between the two at which he contended against the same sort of perverse disputations without identifying it with Sophistry." And this "seems strongly confirmatory" of the view "that this kind of disputatious Sophistry is post-Socratic and a degenerative offshoot of Socratic method" (LPK 350). The true Socrates, as he would later put it, had a positive side, combining an ardent, skeptical search for knowledge of ultimate good with a "provisional adhesion to the commonly received view of good and evil, in all its incoherent complexity" and a "personal firmness, apparently as easy as it was actually invincible, in carrying out consistently such practical convictions as he had attained." Thus,

it is really essential to the Socratic method that the perpetual particular scepticism it develops should be combined with a permanent general faith in the common sense of mankind. For while he is always attacking common opinion, and showing it, from its inconsistencies, not to be knowledge, still the premises of his arguments are always taken from the common thought which he shares with his interlocutors, and the knowledge which he seeks is implicitly assumed to be something that will harmonise and not overthrow these common beliefs. This is manifested in the essential place which dialogue holds in his pursuit of truth: it is only through discourse that he hopes to come to knowledge. (OHE 31, 29)

This was a vision of the Socratic method that fell midway between the more destructive side emphasized by Mill and Grote and the positive, even mystical unity emphasized by Maurice. And it fits well with recent readings of the Socratic elenchus. Thus, for Gregory Vlastos, Socrates is less interested in propositions than in lives, for that is the test of seriousness:

One can put on a solemn face, a grave voice, shamming an earnestness one does not feel. But if one puts oneself on record as saying what one believes, one has given one's opinion the weight of one's life. Since people consider their opinions more expendable than their life, Socrates wants them to tie their opinions to their life as a pledge that what they say is what they mean.

Thus, there is a double objective: "to discover how every human being ought to live *and* to test that single human being who is doing the answering – to find out if *he* is living as he ought to live."[80] Philosophy and therapy are mixed, often in potent poetic form, and there is a personal risk in asking "What is justice?" or "What is love?" when in such company.

This much the Apostles well knew – it was practically the foundation of their faith, the new faith that shaped and was shaped by Henry Sidgwick. Words were the way to the "true self."

3

Unity

(1) We may be over-conscientious about using words which do not to us convey what we believe: we must remember that our ideas are more or less incommunicable to uneducated minds and that what we have out-grown is actually not only 'best for them' but perhaps brings them as near as they can be brought to the truth. (2) We may often clothe new ideas in old words: the uneducated will not feel the inconsistency, and will imbibe the new teaching unconsciously: Mr Maurice is an excellent pattern in this species of useful ingenuity, though he carries it I think too far. (3) We *must* sometimes sacrifice our *individuality* to a *system*: if the teaching we are forced to give is better than what would otherwise be given, we must be satisfied with having chosen the lesser evil.

I must say a word as to my phrase 'Regulative Beliefs'. I did not mean by this *moral rules* only but such parts of our creed as we believe to influence conduct: if we are only *sceptical* as to any of these beliefs, we should still, I think, teach them, if teaching be our duty: if we have rejected any of such beliefs, generally held, we should *not*, except in a very urgent case – alluded to in (3) – As to speculative beliefs the Athanasian creed offers an excellent example of what I would avoid teaching. If I had to teach a moral duty such as obedience I think I should teach the broad rule at one time, and the limitations at another, as a suitable opportunity arose for introducing them. They would be more likely, I imagine, thus to combine in due proportions in the rustic brain.

Henry Sidgwick, "Instructions for the 'Initial Society'"[1]

I. Serious Thought

The Initial Society was a very curious group. Formed around 1860, it included not only Sidgwick and such intimate Rugby friends as Henry Graham Dakyns, but also such young women as Elisabeth Rhodes and Sidgwick's sister Mary. It was, that is, a rare co-ed venture and, rather paradoxically, a "discussion by correspondence" society, meant to duplicate to some degree the virtues of live, candid discussion, in part by having the members contribute their thoughts on various questions via letters signed only with their initials. Protective anonymity for what might prove to be embarrassing statements.

As the instructions just quoted suggest, Sidgwick was the ringleader of this particular unit of the liberal clerisy. Especially noteworthy is the direct invocation of Maurice, who had not yet returned to Cambridge, and the various Mauricean themes – the painful necessity of sometimes sacrificing individuality to system, the need to formulate educational strategies for the "rustic brain," and so forth. The Platonic note is sounded throughout. Very earnest, very reforming, and very secure in the superiority that comes through educational achievement of the right sort – such was the creed of the academic liberal, who sought to liberalize academics and academicize everyone else. The road to an ounce of humility would be a long and difficult one, especially when it led through other cultures.

In some respects, Sidgwick's baldly elitist instructions represent a distillation of the attitude that he would bring to his many reforming efforts, and should be kept in mind when trying to reconstruct these. However, also important is the recognition that the reforming activities themselves sometimes proved better than the attitudes that set them in motion – attitudes that, at least occasionally, changed in consequence.

Much depended on context. Although Sidgwick would certainly be an avid participant in any number of larger efforts at cultural reform, with groups ranging from the Initial Society to the Metaphysical Society to the Cambridge Cabinetmakers Cooperative, his special concern was academic reform, the field that he knew best and in which he felt he could make a serious difference. Of course, his Apostolic vision of Socratic searching was more or less destined to put him at odds not only with family and such old friends as Benson, but also with the academic establishment that had established him. If the Apostles had taught him that his true bent was the investigation of the "deepest problems of human life," they had also taught him that such investigations were often unwelcome in the ancient universities. Both the older Apostles and the newer academic liberals recognized this unpleasant fact. Donnishness was not thought.

Thus, it is not surprising that some of Sidgwick's earlier efforts at reformism had to do with reforming classics, the very field in which he lectured. He went public with what would prove to be a lifelong cause in the mid-sixties, agitating for the reform of the Classical Tripos to lay more stress on philosophizing and less on memorization and versification:

[T]here are but few undergraduates who 'generalize, classify and combine' for themselves or 'collect into rules and principles' the results of their own observation. But I do believe they learn close attention, accurate observation, subtlety of discrimination, and the power of applying the generalizations of others with judgment and tact, and moreover their verbal memory is cultivated to a considerable extent. But the habits of reading reflectively and intelligently, of combining isolated facts into an organized whole, of following and appreciating a subtle and continuous argument, of grasping new ideas with facility and just apprehension, are at least equally valuable: and if they are more difficult to acquire, that is precisely the reason why the highest education in the country ought to make vigorous efforts to impart them. Strong powers of abstract and discursive thought must be always rare: but I lament that we do so little to stimulate and direct them. Nor must we forget that it is much more important for ordinary men to learn to think correctly about historical and philosophical subjects than about philological: and that each study requires to a certain extent a special training; which men who do not receive it from others have to acquire for themselves (except in the case of a gifted few) by gradually finding out their mistakes and deficiencies in a prolonged process of self-education.[2]

Such thoughts were given fuller expression in "The Theory of Classical Education," which Sidgwick published in 1867.[3] There he pointedly observed that "the advocates of classical education, while they rightly insist that educational studies should be capable of disciplining the mind, forget that it is equally desirable that they should be capable of stimulating it." With true Socratic irony, he cites a Mr. Clark's claim that "it is a strong recommendation to any subject to affirm that it is dry and distasteful," commenting that one "cannot help thinking that there is some confusion here between 'dry' and 'hard'" (MEA 314–15).

These may not seem like democratic sentiments, given the concern with elite philosophical education, but the message is at least the broadly Millian one about making education more relevant and thereby improving the quality of public deliberation. When Sidgwick trained his critical acumen on his own time and place, he was concerned with both the state of popular morality and the inadequate reflectiveness of elite morality, as this was molded by elite education.

Much could be made of Sidgwick's reform of classics at Cambridge. Again, the influence of classical authors on his philosophical vision has sometimes been underestimated out of an exaggerated sense of how Sidgwick's Cambridge differed from T. H. Green's Oxford. As Christopher Brooke has observed, the

history of Oxford and Cambridge is a saga of mutual imitation; and yet there have been some things which Cambridge has failed to copy from Oxford, to its loss. By linking philosophy to classics in Mods and Greats the Oxford tutors ensured that numerous undergraduates studied history and philosophy as well as classical literature; and although no Oxford moral philosopher of the age now seems to us to hold a candle to Sidgwick, far more Oxford students studied philosophy than sat at Sidgwick's feet.[4]

Thus, the suggestion is that despite Sidgwick's debts to Socrates, Plato, and Aristotle, and his feeling that the classics should not be an exercise in rote learning, he failed to turn Cambridge into the equivalent of Jowett's Oxford, the hotbed of the Platonic revival, when he had the chance to do so by working more of the classics into the Moral Sciences Tripos. Robert Todd, quoting Sidgwick's exasperated confession that he hated "the history of philosophy even more than any other history; it is so hard to know what any particular man thought, and so worthless when you do know it," argues that it was just this analytical attitude that contributed to his downplaying of classical education at Cambridge.[5] According to Todd:

This larger need to understand the contemporary world was clearly one that Sidgwick satisfied philosophically in a Moral Sciences Tripos freed from any extensive historical studies. It helps explain why he was content to leave the study of ancient philosophy to the Classical Tripos, after he had found it unsuitable for an undergraduate curriculum in philosophy. In his own work Sidgwick of course made constructive use of the history of philosophy, ancient as well as modern. He also held general views about the nature and historical evolution of Greek ethical thought, and formulated a sound conception of the procedures to be followed in dealing with the history of philosophy. But none of this either significantly influenced him in the teaching of philosophy, or led him to emphasize the study of ancient philosophy in the Cambridge Moral Sciences Tripos. He placed limited value on historical studies in philosophy generally in the context of an undergraduate curriculum.[6]

As Todd observes, in "The Theory of Classical Education," Sidgwick emphasized not only science but also modern literature, the branch of literature "which explains to us (as far as possible) the intellectual life of our own age; which teaches us the antecedents of the ideas and feelings among which, and in which, we shall live and move." This, as we shall see, would prove to be of fundamental importance: Sidgwick would devoutly carry on the Apostolic tradition of using modern literature, particularly poetry, to explore, express, and refine the human emotional fabric. Again, he was himself a poet and critic of some talent.

And yet, in some respects, what Todd demonstrates is just how relevant Sidgwick found the classics to his ethical work. Todd notes that in his essay on "Liberal Education," for example, in which Sidgwick posed the question of whether philosophy ought "to be studied, to the extent that it is at Oxford, through the medium of Plato and Aristotle," he allowed that this would be appropriate for the history of ethics, since "the principles of ethics lie still involved in doubt and conflict" and hence might be better confronted via problems from a more remote period.[7] This effort to achieve impartiality through greater historical distance would often serve as a counterweight to his view that progress had rendered historical example largely irrelevant, and it would be evident in such works as *The Elements of Politics*. But in any event, Sidgwick, in this essay, took the opportunity largely to endorse Mill's recent lecture at St. Andrews on the nature of education, noting that he and Mill agreed that "there should be *some* literary element in general education" and that "classical literature," including Plato and Aristotle, is "best adapted for this purpose," though the superiority is only a matter of degree and study of it should not preclude interest in other literatures. This is not quite the stock Cambridge emphasis on Newton, Locke, and mathematics, but a more balanced view, though Oxford is criticized for its "exaggerated neglect of the more definite branches of study in favour of the less definite." For the Sidgwickian student: "Before he attempts the problems with which the human mind is still militant, he should understand the processes by which it had been triumphant."[8]

Furthermore, by Sidgwick's lights, much of the deeper educational enterprise took place more or less outside of the formal institutional context. When it came to the discussion societies, for example, the differences between Cambridge and Hellenizing Oxford were less marked; education could be a very personal affair at both of the ancient universities.[9] Indeed, it had to be. Like Mill and the early Apostles, Sidgwick was not enamoured with the educational quality of formal Oxbridge: "the warmest admirer of these ancient seats of learning is forced to speak of their intellectual aspect in much colder terms; and the comparatively meagre results of the large sums spent upon liberal studies there, has become a commonplace with the critics who undertake the ungrateful task of making periodic inroads on our national self-complacency."[10]

To be sure, Sidgwick did have a rather different vision of professional philosophy from that of Hellenzing (or idealizing) Oxford, one that was more analytical and less historical.[11] But that should not be taken to mean that he disparaged the value of this philosophical inheritance in the fashion of later (or even Comtean) positivists. In an early paper, probably delivered to the Apostles, Sidgwick struggled with the question, as his title put it, "Is Philosophy *the Germ* or the Crown of Science?" He was keenly aware that "the great philosophers each has made a system, and his system has made a noise and filled a considerable space in the horizon of thought for a time but ultimately it has collapsed, dwindled, and vanished, leaving behind it what? Why some particular discovery some luminiferous and fructiferous ideas in some special department of study." But he could not rest content with this reduction of philosophy to the "germ" of science, or with the disparaging views of the ongoing philosophical quest it could support:

Many would say that man is now mature: his time for the stimulating dreams of youth is over: he is deeply impressed with the vanity of attempting ever anew the solution of the insoluble: and he has been impressed with this in time, because the incidental profit of these vain attempts has ceased.

I confess that to me to argue this seems a flagrant abandonment of just the basis of experience on which the arguer plants his feet. How can we tell that the function of Philosophy is over? Even if we attribute to it no more than this Germinal function? If a man says to me that he and his friends have really no interest in solving the Universe, I have nothing to answer but 'Then in heaven's name leave the universe alone.' But if he tries to prove that any one else ought to leave it alone, I ask by what empirical arguments he proves that this crisis in the history of thought has been reached: that the endeavour to grasp the Golden robe of complete Wisdom will no longer as of old leave even a fragment thereof in our hands.

But more: it may be said that it is impossible that Philosophy should perform this germinal function, as long as we have made up our minds that this is it's only function. The supreme effort from which alone any partial discovery of the kind described can come, cannot be made without a hope of the supreme attainment that transcends all partial discoveries. Therefore in this as in other matters just from the most practical point of view, for the winning of just the most definitely measurable results we must pursue the ideal: and that though the face of the ideal is "evermore unseen/and fixed upon the far sea line." (CWC)[12]

These last lines, a bit of Tennyson's "The Voyager" that Sidgwick would frequently quote, are perhaps a little too bleak to capture his early vision of philosophy. Consider, by contrast, how he responded to his friend Roden Noel in a letter of 1871:

> You say that "we do not use terms in the same way" and there is one which we certainly do not – Absolute. *I* do not mean by it total complete: all that can be known about the objects. But I oppose it to relative in the sense in which you generally but not always use the word: i.e. implying that two contradictory opinions about the same object – say a planet – held by two persons may both be true.
> It is this latter opinion, and all that hangs on it, which I feel it important to refute. As to the unknowable, I admit that I have a faith that nothing is intrinsically unknowable: that if one thing is true, true today yesterday and for ever, true for all men; then is the Spirit of Truth come who will guide us into all truth. Or, (to parody Archimedes,) 'Give me but a locus Standi and I will *prove* the Universe. (CWC)

To deny the larger philosophical impulse, then, would be self-defeating and contrary to his faith in "things in general."[13] And after all, if Mill could join in the Platonic revival, so could Sidgwick, and all the more easily. Both thought that they were being truer to the Greek spirit than their critics:

> And if there be any who believe that the summit of a liberal education, the crown of the highest culture, is Philosophy – meaning by Philosophy the sustained effort, if it be no more than an effort, to frame a complete and reasoned synthesis of the facts of the universe – on them it may be especially urged how poorly equipped a man comes to such a study, however competent he may be to interpret the thoughts of ancient thinkers, if he has not qualified himself to examine, comprehensively and closely, the wonderful scale of methods by which the human mind has achieved its various degrees of conquest over the world of sense. When the most fascinating of ancient philosophers taught, but the first step of this conquest had been attained. We are told that Plato wrote over the door of his school, 'Let no one who is without geometry enter here.' In all seriousness we may ask the thoughtful men, who believe that Philosophy can still be best learnt by the study of the Greek masters, to consider what the inscription over the door should be in the nineteenth century of the Christian era. (MEA 316–17)

In effect, the classicists had abandoned the actual spirit of Greek philosophy, had become a church of sorts, requiring submersion in scripture. Everything vital was missing. And of course, this was in perfect parallel to Sidgwick's thoughts about orthodox religion. The two were scarcely separable – the question of the role of philosophy could not be separated from the question of the role of religion. By Sidgwick's time, to promote the one was to demote the other, and this was a heavy responsibility, one that bore especially heavily on an academic liberal out to improve cultural life. Given the fragility of goodness, the precariousness of ordinary decency, the philosopher's position was fraught, even if it was not the main causal factor involved in the degeneration of a society's morals. For Sidgwick, it was crucial to understand how the sun of philosophy might rise, in his own era, and what this would mean for a popular morality that was often as confused and incoherent as that of the ancient Athenians. Indeed, materialism and mocking irreverence had never had so much corrosive power, and this courtesy of science itself. And this was not to mention sexual matters.

What was a philosopher to do? What was the larger cultural project, beyond improving the institutional apparatus of philosophical education? Just how important was it not to "be over-conscientious about using words which do not to us convey what we believe"? And what kind of Millian reformer could insist that "our ideas are more or less incommunicable to uneducated minds and that what we have out-grown is actually not only 'best for them' but perhaps brings them as near as they can be brought to the truth"?

II. After the Way of Heresy

He who begins by loving Christianity better than truth, will proceed by loving his own sect or church better than Christianity, and end in loving himself better than all.

Samual Taylor Coleridge, *Aids to Reflection*

The more a man feels the value, the true import, of the moral and religious teaching which passes amongst us by the name of Christianity, the more will he hesitate to base it upon those foundations which, as a scholar, he feels to be unstable. Manuscripts are doubtful, records may be unauthentic, criticism is feeble, historical facts must be left uncertain. Even in like manner my own personal experience is most limited, perhaps even most delusive: what have I seen, what do

I know? Nor is my personal judgement a thing which I feel any great satisfaction in trusting. My reasoning powers are weak; my memory doubtful and confused; my conscience, it may be, callous or vitiated. . . . I see not what other alternative any sane and humble-minded man can have but to throw himself upon the great religious tradition. But I see not either how any upright and strict dealer with himself – how any man not merely a slave to spiritual appetites, affections and wants – any man of intellectual as well as moral honesty – and without the former the latter is but a vain thing – I see not how anyone who will not tell lies to himself, can dare to affirm that the narrative of the four Gospels is an essential integral part of that tradition.

Arthur Hugh Clough, *The Religious Tradition*

This Socratic prelude to the discussion of Sidgwick's struggles with religious faith is important because, after all, as Sidgwick agonized over the corrosive effects of religious doubt and skepticism in his own time, his chief anthropological and sociological sources for thinking about the role and meaning of religious belief were derived from his classical training. Socrates and the fate of Athenian democracy were ever before his mind, much more so than any other historical precedent – say, the period of the Reformation or the Enlightenment, or even the French Revolution, important though that undoubtedly was. And both Mill and the Apostles would have inspired him to deploy this historical material for the cause of reason and reform, however acute his historical sensibilities might have been. And they were very acute.

It is very helpful to think of Sidgwick as taking his point of departure in ethics from the (Apostolic) Socratic method, while trying to develop the more constructive side of it, just as Plato and Aristotle had done. Unlike Plato and Aristotle, however, Sidgwick was never able to convince himself that philosophy could deliver ultimate and final ethical truth. Progress, yes, but clear and certain truth, no. This led to considerable worrying on his part, since he seemed always in danger of lapsing back into a naive Socratic acceptance of common sense in the large, while treating it to merciless critical dissection in the small. And science itself, the chief evidence of intellectual progress, often seemed to threaten rather than to buttress the claims for ethical progress. In short, he was often on the verge of doubting the meaning of progress altogether, which was a most heretical thought for an era so apt to confuse evolution with progress, and a most painful one for an individual whose mission was to impart truth to the rustic brain.

In fact, Sidgwick's entire classical orientation also came in for something of a jolt during the sixties, when he both expanded his linguistic interests considerably and developed a keen sense of the questions raised by textual criticism. Or rather, one could say that in struggling with the historical Socrates, he was also brought to struggle with the historical Jesus, and to employ many of the very same scholarly techniques. After all, did not the problem of determining just what measure of inspiration one might take from the historically distant Socrates translate into a similar problem with the historically distant Jesus?

In the "Autobiographical Fragment," Sidgwick recounts how in 1862 he

was powerfully impressed by Renan's *Etudes d'Histoire Religieuse*, and derived from Renan's eloquent persuasions the conviction that it was impossible really to understand at first hand Christianity as a historical religion without penetrating more deeply the mind of the Hebrews and of the Semitic stock from which they sprang. This led to a very important and engrossing employment of a great part of my spare time in the study of Arabic and Hebrew. I may say that the provisional conclusions I had formed with regard to Christianity are expressed in an article on "Ecce Homo." . . . My studies, aimed directly at a solution of the great issues between Christianity and Scepticism or Agnosticism, had not, as I knew, led to a really decisive result, and I think it was partly from weariness of a continual internal debate which seemed likely to be interminable that I found the relief, which I certainly did find, in my renewal of linguistic studies. (M 36–37)

The effort was a daunting one, for from September of 1862, when he "devoted every day and the whole day for five weeks in Dresden to the study of Arabic with a private tutor," until 1865, he gave over the "greater part" of his spare time "to the study of Arabic and Hebrew literature and history" and even considered putting in for one of the Cambridge professorships in Arabic. This latter seemed an attractive plan because, although he was still lecturing in classics, his interests had shifted, and the more appealing alternative seemed closed: the sole chair in moral philosophy at Cambridge also included moral theology, and "it seemed most probable that a layman would not be appointed to it – still less a layman known to be unorthodox." No such difficulty would attend an Arabic professorship.

To his credit, Sidgwick came to see that "the study of Arabic, pursued as it ought to be pursued by one who aimed at representing it in the University, would absorb too much time" – drawing him "inevitably away from the central problems which constituted my deepest interest" (M 37).[14] That those problems, religious and metaphysical, did constitute his deepest interest had been forcibly brought home to him by another employment opportunity, an 1861 offer of a position at Rugby. Despite the enthusiasm of his family, and his own initially positive response to this warm tribute from his alma mater, Sidgwick was blocked by "one plain fact" – namely, that he *knew* his "vocation in life to be not teaching but study" (M 71). True, he would often deny that he was sufficiently pious to believe that "destiny has placed me among modern monkery to do in it whatever the nineteenth century, acting through me, will" (M 118). But it was a rather Apostolic thought.

Although Sidgwick's projected "comparison of the Hebrew development of religion with Arabic Mohammedanism" never saw the light, the intensive linguistic study (which also included German, the better to read the latest biblical criticism) was clearly of great importance to his intellectual growth. In the *Essays and Reviews*, Jowett had confidently urged that the Bible be read in just the same way as any other book; its value would withstand the effort. But figures such as Renan, and the even more formidably erudite David Friedrich Strauss,[15] had done just that, treating scripture to textual and historical criticism that raised serious scholarly questions about its historicity, consistency, accuracy, and coherency.[16] The results were extremely discomfiting to orthodox Christians.

Earnest Renan was a renowned scholar and linguist, and it is not surprising that his work made a deep impression on Sidgwick, who had been trained by both Benson and Cambridge to appreciate the minute and careful study of language. Renan was born in a small village in Brittany in 1823, and rose from these very humble origins to become one of the most controversial and provocative of French scholars, with such productions as his *Vie de Jésus* (1863). His early education had been at Catholic seminaries, with the expectation that he would go into the priesthood, but as with Sidgwick, a corrosive intelligence and love of free inquiry led him astray. In one of his autobiographical writings, he recalled how a so-so teacher of metaphysics turned out to be a good judge of Renan:

My argumentations in Latin, given with a firm and emphatic air, astonished and disquieted him.... That evening he took me aside. He pointed out to me eloquently what was anti-Christian in the commitment to reason and the harm that rationalism did to faith. In strange agitation, he reproached me with my passion for study. Research! What good was that? Everything essential for us is known. Science saves no souls. And, his excitement rising more and more, he said to me with a deeply felt emphasis: "You are not a Christian."[17]

In the end, most French Catholics would probably have agreed with Renan's hapless instructor, though Renan, like Sidgwick, always remained a model of personal rectitude. He rejected all claims to the supernatural, to the miraculous, and sought to show how the life of Jesus might inspire even if he were regarded as no more than human. He accepted a fully scientific worldview, in which all of nature works in accordance with causal laws, and he regarded history and criticism as working within just such an understanding. His own contributions were primarily linguistic. As Blanshard has explained, Renan "was not a genius in philosophy; he was a genius in language." That is,

He read the book of Isaiah, and saw that there was not one Isaiah, as the church had taught, but two. He read the book of Daniel, whose prophecies were accepted by the church as inspired, and concluded that it was too unreliable to have a place in Scripture at all. He read the Pentateuch, which was accepted by the church as written by Moses, though Moses could hardly have written the account of his own death. It was thus not the metaphysical difficulties of two worlds of truth that finally settled the balance; it was rather the drip, drip on the soil of his mind of hundreds of these incidents of contradiction, of the histori-cally incredible, of parallels with pagan religion, that wore his creed away by their attrition.[18]

Such was his scholarship, but his life of Jesus sought more. Written mostly while he was on a tour of Palestine, and without any scholarly apparatus, it was a sustained attempt to present a demystified Jesus who, while he did not work miracles, was an ethical teacher of such force and greatness that it was perfectly understandable how he could have altered the course of the world. Jesus had founded religion just as Socrates had founded ethical philosophy; if he was mistaken about a supernatural King-dom of Heaven or God, he was nevertheless right about universal love as the absolute ethical ideal. Such an expression of faith and hope was im-mortality enough.

However, as Edward Said has emphasized, Renan's philological mission was fundamentally orientalizing. Renan "did not really speak as one man to all men but rather as a reflective, specialized voice that took . . . the inequality of races and the necessary domination of the many by the few for granted as an antidemocratic law of nature and society." This vision of philology, opening the way to Nietzsche and certainly relevant for understanding the larger dimensions of Sidgwick's religious and linguistic struggles, may seem puzzling:

[H]ow was it possible for Renan to hold himself and what he was saying in such a paradoxical position? For what was philology on the one hand if not a science of all humanity, a science premised on the unity of the human species and the worth of every human detail, and yet what was the philologist on the other hand if not – as Renan himself proved with his notorious race prejudice against the very Oriental Semites whose study had made his professional name – a harsh divider of men into superior and inferior races, a liberal critic whose work harbored the most esoteric notions of temporality, origins, development, relationship, and human worth. . . . Renan had a strong guild sense as a professional scholar, a professional Orientalist, in fact, a sense that put distance between himself and the masses. But more important . . . is Renan's own conception of his role as an Oriental philologist within philology's larger history, development, and objectives as he saw them. In other words, what may to us seem like paradox was the expected result of how Renan perceived his dynastic position within philology, its history and inaugural discoveries, and what he, Renan, did within it. Therefore Renan should be characterized, not as speaking *about* philology, but rather as *speaking philologically* with all the force of an initiate using the encoded language of a new prestigious science none of whose pronouncements about language itself could be construed either directly or naively.[19]

The idea of spelling out the direction of history, be it progress or decay, through the esoteric and elite (not to mention Eurocentric) analysis of language was scarcely a foreign one to Sidgwick and his Apostolic circle. Naturally, his positivist, Comtean tendencies – shared and stimulated by his intimate friend Dakyns – would incline him to hunt for laws of religious and moral historical development. Interestingly, however, another particularly close friend from this period, Noel, did a great deal to stimulate his orientalist interests. The aristocratic Noel, who was the fourth son of the earl of Gainsborough and whose godmother was none other than Queen Victoria, was four years older than Sidgwick, though he had joined the Apostles a year later, in 1857. Upon graduation, as Desmond Heath has observed, "Roden went to Egypt with another friend, Cyril Graham – in fact they reckoned they were the first Europeans to reach the oasis of Kur-Kur, in the Libyan desert, with its forests of petrified palms. For two long years, he continued in the East . . . visiting Nubia and the Holy Land, Palmyra, then Lebanon, Greece and Turkey."[20] Noel's accounts inflamed Sidgwick's imagination:

You take me through a number of dream-like scenes and experiences, investing them with a reality that they did not before possess, as clustering round you, whom I have actually seen and known and talked to and shared anchovy toast with!... Your account of Palestine and Palmyra almost recalled the old feeling of half-pleasant, half-painful longing (like a hungry man's reading about a feast) with which I used to devour *Eothen* and *The Crescent and the Cross*.... Well, I wish you freedom from fevers, conquest over bronchitis, and that you may quarry countless treasures of learning from the neglected mines of the Royal tombs. If you throw any light on Platonic mysticism, bring out any esoteric doctrines that our uninitiated eyes are now blind to, why, we shall be proud of you as a man and a brother. (M 48)

Curiously, though, Noel tended to be less unorthodox than Sidgwick at this time, much less in the grip of the new criticism:

I confess I know nothing of the processes of historic criticism by which all our beliefs in any past events are so skilfully hocus-pocused away. Of course I am aware it must be a valuable science.

But I have not yet had occasion or interest for the mastery of it. So that I fear you would think me quite out of court if I were to attempt to testify what I think of that great problem – which certainly is a *historical one*. Indeed you know what I think. The Gospel History you have ascertained to be legend. Then of course Jesus was not Son of God and Man – for there never was such a person, *or* we know nothing of him who was so called for centuries.

It may be the effect of sheer prejudice. *I* cannot help believing the main body of the history as I read it. True, I have not minutely analysed the various accounts and found all the constituent elements evaporating and leaving a sorry residuum. But as a whole it commends itself to me as the most solid, substantial history of all – as the central history, throwing light on all other. Who conceived the character of Christ? – fluctuating and heterogeneous from Renan's point of view, no doubt, but from one which I shall call profounder and more spiritual, (and that *partly* because the profoundest and most spiritual men in successive ages have taken it), homogeneous and consistent. This is not a mere Art-creation. And if a profound spiritual harmony and homogeneity underlies the character, it is not an accretion of myths – No, look at all other myths. There is not the flesh and blood life-look about them that there is here.

Besides, if some History be resolvable into Myth, is not Myth often resolvable into History?

For Noel, the figure of Christ – who *"both proclaimed* and *acted upon* the purest and most exalted morality, who was at all events the most loving and unselfish of men, the most self-renouncing and self-sacrificing" and "by the force of His life and death, as well as His words" made "the principle of Love the most honoured of all, giving it a new energising force in society, teaching men, in short, to feel that God is Love" – quite transcends biblical criticism: "Now cut away passage after passage with criticism, still you must destroy the whole conception of the character in the Gospels before you get rid of this distinct impression." Thus,

I must believe *that His consciousness simply mirrored the Truth.* I do not say that God has not given us other less spiritual kinds of light – intellectual, e.g. from other sources – other old-world civilisations, such as the Roman, and Greek. Let us fully acknowledge it. But such a God-saturated *human life* is the profoundest and most vital of all influences on the human spirit, and therefore indirectly acts upon all our systems of thought.

I do not wish to isolate Him. I know I am most unorthodox. If I isolate Him He is no use to me. But I cannot agree with you that whether He *was* all this, or not, is of no religious importance. To me it is of the very highest. For *here* . . . God has manifested Himself as He has not done elsewhere, and if so, we cannot dispense with the contemplation of this biography without lowering our standard and our idea of God. Comparing ourselves with Christ, we feel infinitely dwarfed, and yet (as His is our own proper human nature of which we have all the elements) there is that in us which responds to the virtue in Him, and draws us up to His level. We learn then both about God and about man. He reveals in His person the fact of our Sonship to God – He opens up in our Nature the choked spring of Deity within it – and He leads the way to the full realisation, in the consciousness of all men, of their relationship to God, and their full enjoyment of the privileges of it. He has triumphed over selfishness. . . . Without that life as a beacon, I should have thought it *im*possible that the Ideal should so triumph in me or my race.[21]

Noel admits that he has left Sidgwick a "loophole," since he could urge that Christ's ideal was a mistaken one, not the highest. But there "we should differ in toto. Goethe, I suppose, could hardly think His Life the highest. But if you say 'we cannot *know* what is the highest kind of life,' you then cut away all possible hope of progress. You must have an ideal, and strive to live more and more up to that." Indeed, the "ideal" is more than mere argument. Sidgwick seems to "undervalue history – fact – example – the love and worship of an external noble object." But "[t]heories and metaphysics won't do alone to teach us all about the 'eternal and spiritual part of our nature'. *And Christ truly is a man*, not the dried-up part of one, a philosopher or metaphysician, (that is why most of *them* object to Him)." To such an ideal, one must subordinate one's own judgment.

This is fine Apostolic soaring, though one would never guess from Noel's religious arguments that he was to prove to be one of Sidgwick's most licentious bisexual friends, one who was once photographed naked as Bacchus. But their discussions of religious matters rather overshadowed their exchanges on sexual matters, such as the advisability of marriage, which will be considered in later chapters. For the present, what is of interest is the way in which Noel, more than such friends as Dakyns, was impressing upon Sidgwick the importance of both orientalist studies and the figure of Christ as an ideal of perfect love and altruism. Here was an Apostolic intimate pushing a case that resembled in some respects that of Renan – who retained a vivid appreciation of Christ as a moral exemplar – but who was perhaps even more in line with other forces attempting in unorthodox ways to revitalize the image of Christ's greatness. At a later date, Noel would be more mystical, more Hegelian, more pantheistic, and more apt to put forth Whitman as an exemplar of greatness. But in the years of storm and stress, he, like so many others, was obsessed with the personality of Jesus, and he found in Sidgwick a most disturbing doubter. For Noel, "Manhood reverences noble example and experience, and profits by them" – or ought to. And the example of Goethe is not the right one: "Intellect is the Deity of Goethe. But to furnish food for intellect he sees the fullest experience to be necessary. Yet both the practical and the etherial Goethe is radically wrong, Intellect is not the most Divine element. In my creed, it is Love. Therefore Christ and not Goethe is the ideal of Humanity."[22] This would prove to be, for Sidgwick, the all-important contrast, capturing the contest between Christian sympathy and Greek perfection in more modern form. His theological vacillations met his ethical vacillations just here.

Of course, given the battering that religion was receiving at this time, from biblical criticism and Darwinian and geological science, it is not to be wondered at that such revisionary readings of the Gospels as Renan's should find a wide audience, or that he was hardly alone in providing provocative new interpretations of the life of Jesus. In England, a book that shared this emphasis on the character and ethics of Jesus was published anonymously in 1866. This was *Ecce Homo*, which, as it transpired, was authored by Sidgwick's longtime Cambridge colleague, the historian John Seeley – not coincidentally, another profoundly orientalizing influence, one of the leading theorists of British imperialism.[23] It was Sidgwick's review of Seeley's volume that summed up the results of his linguistic turn, the fruit of his visits to Germany. The review was published in the *Westminster Review* in 1866, and it included some trenchant remarks on Renan:

The defect of Renan's *Vie de Jésus* was not its historical fidelity but its want of that quality. It was not in so far as he had realised the manner in which the idea of Jesus was conditioned by the circumstances of time and place and the laws of human development, but in so far as he had failed to do so, that his work proved inefficacious to stir the feelings of Englishmen. We felt that he had looked at his subject through Parisian spectacles; and taken up too ostentatiously the position of a spectator – a great artistic error in a historian. His most orthodox assailants in England felt for the most part that their strength lay in showing not that the Jesus of Renan was a mere man and ought to have been more, but that he was not the right man. (MEA 22–23)

As is clear from other sources as well, Sidgwick had some sympathy with such critics. Renan's type of history is a "system of ingenious guesses," and if Darwin's great champion T. H. Huxley would "have us worship ('chiefly silently') a Subject without Predicates," Renan would "have us adore . . . Predicates without a Subject." Strauss is "better than many Renans." (M 105, 147). Perhaps Sidgwick even had in mind Maurice's view that Renan's Jesus "is a charming Galilean with a certain sympathy for beautiful scenery and an affectionate tenderness for the peasants who follow him; but he is provoked to violence, impatience, base trickery, as soon as he finds his mission as a reformer unsuccessful. . . . We in England should say he was a horrible liar and audacious blasphemer." For Maurice, "the book is detestable, morally as well as theologically. It brought to my mind . . . that wonderful dream of Richter's in which Jesus tells the universe, 'Children, you have no Father.'"[24]

For all that, when it comes to addressing the vision of *Ecce Homo*, Sidgwick's indebtedness to the more critical, historical sides of both Strauss and Renan is manifest; his views contrast with Seeley's in much the same way they did with Noel's:

Considering that we derive our knowledge of the facts from a limited number of documents, handed down to us from an obscure period, and containing matter which in any other history we should regard as legendary: considering that in consequence these documents have been subjected for many years to an elaborate, minute, and searching investigation: that hundreds of scholars have spent their lives in canvassing such questions as the date of their composition, their authorship, the conscious objects or unconscious tendency of each author, his means of information, and his fidelity to fact, the probability of their being compiled or translated from previous works in whole or part, or of their having undergone revisions since the original publication, the contradictions elicited by careful examination of each or close comparison of them together, the methods of reconciling these contradictions or deciding between conflicting evidence, and many other similar points, – it might seem natural that the author of such a work as this should carefully explain to his readers his plan and principles for settling or avoiding these important preliminary questions. (MEA 2)

Sidgwick, in other words, was not impressed by the historical consciousness of *Ecce Homo* – the method is "radically wrong" and the conclusions "only roughly and partially right" (MEA 39).

In fact, the criticisms directed at Seeley are withering, and often developed by way of invidious comparison with the historical school. Unlike the historical school, Seeley believes that the compelling, "incontrovertible" evidence regarding the character and thought of Jesus might in itself be so suggestive of his uniqueness that it could lend credence to the miracle stories. But to follow Seeley and speak "of miracles 'provisionally as real' is the one thing that no one will do. The question of their reality stands at the threshold of the subject, and can by no device be conjured away." The new criticism accepts the principle applied elsewhere in history – namely, that nothing happens in violation of the laws of nature – and does "not regard the reality of miracles as a question of more or less evidence, to be decided by presumptions with regard to the veracity of witnesses." (MEA 4, 5) The very question of which evidence is acceptable requires taking a position on the miraculous, and in fact the evidence that Seeley adduces is anything but incontrovertible. As Owen Chadwick has observed, for Renan, "to believe in the supernatural was like believing in ghosts."[25] Sidgwick, as we shall shortly see, thought that this was just the right challenge.

Characteristically, however, and in line with his Socratic anxieties, Sidgwick could not rest content with mere negative criticism. Sound history may require unstinting criticism and controversy, but

it is good to be reminded from time to time to drop the glass of criticism, and let the dust-clouds of controversy settle. Many students who cannot patiently lend their minds to our author's teaching may be stimulated by it to do as he has done: may be led to contemplate in the best outline that each for himself can frame, with unwonted clearness of vision and unwonted force of sympathy, the features of a conception, a life, a character which the world might reverence more wisely, but can never love too well. (MEA 39)

As he put it to Dakyns:

I have had the work of Christ put before me by a powerful hand, and been made to recognise its extraordinary excellence as I have never before done; and though I do not for a moment relinquish my right to judge it by the ideal, and estimate its defects, partialities, etc., yet I do feel the great need that mankind have of a pattern, and I have none that I could propose to substitute. Hence I feel that I should call myself a Christian if I were in a country where [text missing]. Now, as long as the views I hold on religion and morality are such as I should think only desirable to publish to the educated, it seems to me it is not my social duty to dissent. (M 145–46)[26]

Seeley is "diffuse," but he is not "turgid," and he has stirred Sidgwick "with real eloquence." There is much in his vision of Jesus that, as with Renan's or Noel's, would appeal to someone with utilitarian sympathies, since he is presented as a teacher of love, whose view of religion as a positive, warm, emotional matter contrasted with the older Hebrew conception of religion in terms of a legalistic set of "Thou shalt nots." Still, Sidgwick's vision of Jesus and the Christian religion is subtler and far more historical than Seeley's. He even accuses Seeley of going too far in making Jesus out to be a utilitarian, objecting to his central claims about Jesus' placing happiness in a political constitution and requiring "a disinterested sacrifice of self to the interests of the whole society." This, Sidgwick urges, is an overstatement, making Jesus too nearly akin to Bentham. It is better to say that "Jesus taught philanthropy more from the point of view of the individual than from that of society" (MEA 19). Ultimately, according to Sidgwick,

The truth seems to be that in the simple and grand conception that Jesus formed of man's position and value in the universe, all the subsequent development of

Christianity is implicitly contained: but that the evolution of this conception was gradual, and was not completed at his death. The one thing important to Jesus in man was a principle so general that faith, love, and moral energy seem only different sides of it. It was the ultimate coincidence, or rather, if we may use a Coleridgean word, *indifference* of religion and morality. It was "the single eye," the *rightness*, of a man's heart before God. It was faith in the conflict with baser and narrower impulses, love when it became emotion, moral energy as it took effect on the will. It was that which living in a man filled his whole body with a light, purified him completely, so that nothing external could defile him. (MEA 23)

This principle carries several further consequences. Jesus' work "intensified or deepened all moral obligations," for the "inner light could not produce right outward acts, except through the medium of right inward impulses," and the man who had it "could acquiesce in no compromises, but must aim at perfection." It is this inner rightness of heart that fixes one's place in the Kingdom of God – not birth, wealth, etc. – and the Kingdom is thus open to all of Adam's seed. With this development, "the ceremonial law must fall. This elaborate system of minute observances was needless, and if needless it was burdensome." (MEA 25) But not all of this work was done by Jesus; clearly, Saint Paul was crucial in explicitly drawing out these implications, and indeed, the historical progress of ethics and civilization suggests how much was yet to come after Jesus, great as his ethical example was. Seeley's account could not accommodate the growth, the progress, of doctrine, though such a view of history was an element common to Coleridge, Maurice, Whewell, Newman, Comte, Mill, and perhaps most of the notable moral theorists of Darwin's century. "Here and there we feel that if Jesus planted, Jean Jacques and Comte have watered" (MEA 19). Progress was real, whether or not it was the result of divine intervention.

Thus, Sidgwick's (rather ironic) appeal to Comte and Mill as representing the best in the Christian tradition allowed that that tradition had grown and progressed, and that it contained various elements that were difficult to reconcile. To Noel, Sidgwick explained, with reference to his criticisms of Seeley and others,

I have counted the cost, and am content to go on exciting the disgust of enthusiasts – that is, of the people whose sympathy I value most – in defence of (what seems to me) historic truth and sound criticism. It seems to me that ultimate religious agreement is ideally possible on my method, and not even ideally possible on yours – as each sect and party will go on making a particular view of history a test of spirituality and thus feel itself at liberty to dispense . . . with other arguments. (M 150)

One could scarcely hope for a plainer statement of Sidgwick's own quest for unity, of how critical inquiry, for him, held out the hope of both truth and reconciliation. The Socratic search was a very personal business.

And in this pursuit of truth, there is a profound sense in which Sidgwick took up directly the challenge, not of Seeley, but of Renan. One could not, with Seeley, deduce the miracles from the morality of Jesus – Renan was right. But perhaps Renan was wrong in too hastily assuming that modern science could not recognize the existence of ghosts. Although the gospels should not receive a special dispensation to ignore the laws of nature, perhaps the laws of nature might allow that the "miraculous" does occur, today as much as two thousand years ago. But that is not a question to be settled by books.

III. Rational Faith

I pass by a kind of eager impulse from one Drama or Heart-Tragedy or Comedy as the case may be to another: and when I begin to take stock as it were on my account, my prudential instincts being awakened, I wonder what it all means, and whether there is any higher or lower, better or worse in human life, except so far as sympathy and a kind of rude philosophy go.

Sidgwick to Dakyns, April 29, 1862 (M 78)

The sixties were undoubtedly some of Sidgwick's most turbulent years, but in many respects, the overall direction of his thought during this time was a painfully consistent one:

I want to earn my freedom from the Church of England. What a hideous compromise between baseness and heroism! Yet I do not see anything else in this strange age of transition for a man who feels bitterly the *Drück* of hypocrisy, yet cannot reconcile himself to cut the Gordian knot. My feeling is that emotional Theism will shine in more and more upon mankind through the veil of history and life; that all religions are good in so far as they approximate to it, and that formulae are necessary for the mass of mankind in their present state: and that the task of substituting a purer for a crasser formula is a grand one, but I must leave it to a man who has more belief in himself than I have. In short I feel with regard to the Church of England δοῦλος ἐκλήθης; μὴ σοὶ μελέτω ἀλλ᾽ εἰ καὶ δύναεαι ἐλεύθερος γενέσ θαι, μᾶλλον χρῆσαι, & I mean to put it if possible in my power. (M 122–23)[27]

In 1862, he had declared that "one ought to begin by being a Theist – to contemplate, I mean, a Heart and Mind behind phenomena" and allowed that if, at that point, he was "only a Theist," it would not be "for want of profound and devoted study" if he did not "become a Christian" (M 81–82). No one could deny that he gave himself over to profound and devoted study, avoiding any open break with his church, but the effort never got him beyond the above formulation of historical theism, at least for any length of time. He was determined not to barter his "intellectual birthright for a mess of mystical pottage." By 1866, after much linguistic study, he could still complain that he had "discovered nothing and settled nothing. Is Theism to be the background or the light of the picture of life?" (M 141) And by 1870, he is concluding,

I do not feel called or able to preach religion except as far as it is involved in fidelity to one's true self. I firmly believe that religion is normal to mankind, and therefore take part unhesitatingly in any social action to adapt and sustain it (as far as a layman may). I know also that my true self is a Theist, but I believe that many persons are really faithful to themselves in being irreligious, and I do not feel able to prophesy to them. (M 228)

His complaint with the irreligious is not their disbelief, but "that they are content with, happy in, a universe where there is no *God*" (M 228). Sidgwick could entertain the thought that there was no God; what he could not entertain was the thought of being happily content in such a cold, uncaring, unjust universe.[28]

The essence of Sidgwick's position was nicely expressed in an 1870 letter that he sent to the *Times* concerning "Clerical Engagements." He delineated three different theological orientations: that of "Simple Scripturalism," holding that the errors of the Bible are insignificant and that "all the more important historical statements, and absolutely all the statements on moral and theological subjects in the Bible, are true"; that of "Historical Scripturalists," who agree that the theology of the Bible is final, but who "hold that only its theological and moral statements have this peculiar claim on our acceptance, and that on all other subjects a Biblical writer is just as likely to err as any other equally honest and conscientious person," and that even the theology of the Bible should be read historically; and finally, that of the "Rationalist," who holds that although the "most important part of religious truth (what may be fairly called the true religion) was discovered or revealed before the first century of Christianity was closed" and "no sound developments of later thought are likely to deviate from the main lines laid down in the Bible," nevertheless, "no expression, even of these truths, by the Biblical writers is to be regarded as authoritative." According to this last view, with which Sidgwick identifies himself, the

theology of the Bible has, and always will have, a unique interest for mankind, but unique only as the interest of Greek philosophy is unique, because it is the fountain from which the main stream of thought upon the subject is derived; so that not only must it always be presupposed and referred to by religious thinkers, but must always possess for them what M. Renan calls the 'charme des origines.'

However, the Rationalist believes that

the process of development which the historical scripturalist traces between the earlier and later of them has continued since, and will continue, and that we cannot forecast its limits; and that even where the doctrine of the Bible, taken as a whole, is clear, an appeal lies always open to the common sense, common reason, and combined experience of the religious portion of mankind. (CWC)[29]

It is, of course, the Rationalist view that Sidgwick takes to be the direction of history. He is confident "that the thought of civilised Europe is moving rapidly in its direction, and that it must inevitably spread and prevail," but he also wishes "as heartily as any broad Churchman can, that it may spread with the least possible disruption and disorganization of existing institutions, the least possible disruption of old sympathies and associations."

Hence, the three-way current of Sidgwick's storm and stress. He cannot, intellectually, ignore the possibility of atheism and materialism, though he cannot accept such a worldview as emotionally satisfying and does not think humanity at large capable of this either. Yet the crude superstition and ahistoricism of most orthodox Christianity is hardly something that he can accept intellectually, though he recognizes its sociological and political importance and is determined not to abandon orthodoxy lightly. He hopes to be able (eventually, at least) to vindicate a minimal, theistic conception of the universe and to work for gradual social reforms that will duly install this view in place of the older ones.

What was the precise content of Sidgwick's critique of orthodox Christianity? How did it accord with or differ from the views of Renan, Noel, and Strauss?

Sidgwick's views on various points of doctrine certainly did fluctuate a great deal, but in retrospect, he was fairly consistent in singling out certain key difficulties. In the manuscript of the "Autobiographical Fragment," the text breaks off into a number of scattered remarks that include his confession that of all the miracle tales in the Bible, the one that struck him as simply unbelievable was the doctrine of the Virgin Birth of Jesus. His testimony on this score must have struck his wife, Eleanor Mildred Sidgwick, as accurate and unsuspect, since she was taking the dictation and never in public or private registered any objection to this point. And in his 1870 pamphlet on "The Ethics of Conformity and Subscription" (actually composed around 1867), he singled out the Virgin Birth as one of the most problematic issues dividing Anglicans, since a sincere Christian could certainly believe that Jesus was God and that miracles could occur, yet also hold that "legends may have been mixed up with the evangelical narrations, and that some probably have been. A man who holds this general view is very likely to reject the miraculous conception of Jesus, as the narrative of it has a very legendary aspect, and the evidence which supports it is exceptionally weak." (CS 33)

However, a later friend, Canon Charles Gore, would record that Sidgwick had confessed to him that his chief difficulty with orthodoxy had to do with Jesus' apparent belief in his immediate return as the glorified Christ; this difficulty would have been especially hard to overcome, since it involved an error by Jesus on a matter of great theological and ethical significance, and the historical, textual evidence for attributing this false belief to him was overwhelming.[30]

Evident as it may be that such objections are bound up with the results of historical biblical criticism, Sidgwick could, in some humors, speak rather disparagingly of the additional value of such historical work. Thus, even in the midst of his "orientalist" studies, he could complain that

I have the secret conviction that the great use of learning Hebrew is to ascertain how little depends on it, and, with regard to Biblical criticism, that it is impossible to demonstrate from themselves the non-infallibility of the Hebrew writings: just as it would be to demonstrate the non-infallibility of Livy if there was any desire to uphold it. It all depends on the scientific sense, and antiquarianism will never overthrow superstition except in a few intellects who would probably have got rid of it anyway.[31]

In 1863, he wrote to Dakyns: "My own views do not alter; you know I attach less and less value to criticism the more time I spend over it. How can a close knowledge of Hebrew help us to convince a man who after reading the English Version believes that God Almighty wrote the account of Noah's flood?" (M 99) The year 1864 finds him sarcastically observing that it "was probably an erroneous idea of my relations to the infinite" to suppose that "it was all-important to have a view on the historical question. As if after dying I were likely to meet God and He to say, Well, are you a Christian? 'No,' I say, 'but I have a theory on the origin of the Gospels which is really the best I could form on the evidence; and please, this ought to do as well.'" (M 123–24) And at length, in 1865, he complains "How I wish I had employed my leisure which I have so wasted, in studying philosophy and art!" (M 122)

As the "Autobiographical Fragment" records:

I began also to think that the comparative historical study which I had planned would not really give any important aid in answering the great questions raised by the orthodox Christianity from which my view of the Universe had been derived. Was Jesus incarnate God, miraculously brought into the world as a man? Were his utterances of divine authority? Did he actually rise from the grave with a human body glorified, and therewith ascend into heaven? Or if the answers to these questions could not strictly be affirmative in the ordinary sense of the term, what element of truth, vital for mankind, could be disengaged from the husk of legend, or symbolised by the legend, supposing the truth itself capable of being established by human reasoning? Study of Philosophy and Theology, which I had never abandoned, began again to occupy more of my time. (M 37–38)

Because Sidgwick's somewhat exaggerated reaction against historical study in some ways carried over to the history of philosophy, and even to the teaching of such, it should be stressed that his considered complaint was *not* that historical criticism was valueless (though he sometimes made it sound that way), but that it was insufficient by itself to solve the "deepest problems of human life." The exasperation that he vented over his inconclusive results scarcely conveyed just how indebted he was and would remain to Strauss and Renan. After all, Seeley's shortcomings were shared by many more orthodox figures, such as Bishop Mansel, another object of Sidgwick's critical talents. Of Mansel's Bampton Lectures, he wrote: "He really is a well-meaning man, and *il a raison* for the most part against Metaphysicians. But he talks of Revelation as if the Bible had dropped from the skies ready translated into English; he ignores all historical criticism utterly." (M 81) And in a review of 1873, in which he anticipates a number of arguments he would later marshall against the idealists, he challenges Mansel's apparent claim that, theological beliefs being designed to guide practice rather than to satisfy reason, the contradiction between two such beliefs is no argument against them:

> It is no use to say that it is restricted to the interpretation of Revelation: for the deduction of dogma from Scripture is a process of reasoning, which has always been guided by the maxim that different texts of Scripture must be made mutually consistent. Now either this maxim is invalid, in which case the creeds must crumble again into a chaos of texts: or if it is valid, we require some criterion to distinguish the contradictions that we ought to embrace. Such a criterion Mansel never offers: and he seems to deal in a perfectly arbitrary manner with the antinomies which beset the exercise of our reason when it strives to attain the absolute.[32]

This hardly seems like a profession of the uselessness of historical criticism, and it is in fact more in keeping with Sidgwick's general attitude, evident in many other works, than the impatience expressed in some of his letters. Before embarking on his biblical criticism, he could complacently say that a man "impressed with the Divine Government and the Divine sympathy" by "reading simply and candidly the New Testament, will end by being more orthodox than at first one thinks possible when one feels one's indignation kindled against Persecuting Bishops" (M 79). No such claim could have passed his pen after his exposure to Renan and Strauss.

Although Sidgwick did at one time or another toy with going wholeheartedly with "Maurice and Broad Church," his fundamental objections to that position formed a more conspicuous feature of his theological twists and turns. They were given cogent expression in an 1871 review of a book by one of Maurice's disciples:

> [T]he key to Mr. Hutton's theology, as it is to that of his master, Mr. Maurice . . . may be expressed thus: 'God is immediately or intuitively, but not adequately, made known to us: and what is made known of Him is more than can be expressed in propositions, or communicated from one man to another.' This seems to me an appropriate account of our apprehension of Divine, as of much other, fact: but I am unable to see how it furnishes the barrier against scepticism which

Mr. Maurice and Mr. Hutton seem to find in it. The 'sources of our faith' may be indefinitely wider than that 'evidences of our convictions': but when the diversities of faith cause any one to enquire into the truth or falsehood of his own, a rational answer must indicate 'evidences' and not 'sources.' Mr. Hutton sees this, and offers 'really universal reasons' for believing the Incarnation. These are the old combination of psychological and historical premisses: only miracles are omitted from the latter. 'We have need of believing in a Filial God: and Jesus claimed to be and was recognised as such.' In explaining the former premiss Mr. Hutton rather confounds emotional want with intellectual anticipation: even if it be true that our spiritual yearnings cannot be satisfied without this belief, the presumption thus obtained cannot be compared with the presumption that a friend or a chemical substance will act in a given way. The exposition of these spiritual needs, as Mr. Hutton apprehends them, is highly interesting: but they seem to me too idiosyncratic to constitute 'really universal reasons.' Who, except him, 'knows' that the 'free will of all men (except Jesus) is intrinsically indifferent,' and that 'self-sacrifice is not indigenous in man'? If we long to institute a complete comparison of the spiritual effects of pure theism and Christianity, we find the materials too scanty: so that Mr. Hutton's method of psychological proof, even if cogent, is as yet inapplicable.[33]

Much as Sidgwick admired the Mauricean passion for unity, he was too sharply aware of conflict and difference to go along with that version of Platonized Christianity. For what if what is being apprehended is only the God of theism, rather than that of Christianity in its more proper forms? Perhaps the unifying intuition was more Platonic than Christian. Or perhaps it was more Socratic than Platonic, something simpler and even less amenable to articulation than Plato's eternal forms. Maurice's appeal to conscience was a wonderfully sophisticated and liberal-minded one, but for all that, it was still an appeal to conscience, and for practical purposes useless. Sidgwick, who found that his conscience "was more utilitarian than most," sought a way of actually reconciling conflicting "evidences" (M 228). Sympathetic, conversational soul searching required more tools with which to work. Jesus was no more above criticism than Socrates, and the criticism often ran on parallel tracks.

He even sticks up for Goethe, against Hutton's account. In a most revealing passage, he urges that Hutton is

even betrayed here and there into phrases which have a touch of impatient Philistinism. To talk of Goethe's "sickly pottering" about the "pyramid of his existence" is surely an inadequate manner of speaking of the apostle of self-culture.

And on the whole the critic seems to lean too much to the common error, which in one passage he resists, of taking the Goethe of the autobiography for the real Goethe. No one was ever fascinated by the hero of *Wahrheit und Dichtung*. The charm of Goethe depends on the rare harmony of strikingly contrasted qualities, the poise and balance of strongly conflicting impulses: the intellect of driest light, yet with perpetual vision of a radiantly coloured world: the nature responsive to all gales of emotion and breezes of sentiment, yet using all as forces to carry it in its "unhasting unresting" course – which we only see by comprehensive comparison of his studied and unstudied utterances, and his life as seen and felt by his contemporaries.[34]

Of this essay, Noel wrote to Sidgwick, "It is wonderfully terse, pregnant, to the point. I suppose nothing has ever been said about Goethe more to the point than the last sentences."[35]

The criticisms of the Mauricean vision were telling, and profoundly suggestive of the course of Sidgwick's theological probing. Even in 1864, impatient with his historical work, he had urged that what is "required is psychological experiments in ethics and intuitive Theism: that is what on the whole the human race has got to do for some years" (M 124). The call for such experiments was serious: he had long held that more work needed to be done on the psychology of religious belief – indeed, on psychology generally[36] – if one were to argue with any plausibility as to just what kind of religious belief humanity might require. After all, there "is no proof against there being a Mind & Heart behind phenomena," and, Sidgwick confessed, "the contemplation of this hypothesis answers to a need now existing in my nature, and the experience of thousands testifies that such contemplation generates an abiding ἐνθουσιασμός, with all its attendant noblenesses and raptures."[37] But what was the meaning of this need and this effect? Was the human condition one of abject superstition, demanding totem and taboo? Was it less superstitious but nonetheless inherently prone to some minimal faith in a just universe, such that the suffering of innocents was only apparent and righteousness would in the long run receive its reward? Was some sort of faith, even if incapable of rational demonstration, essential to human flourishing or functioning? How far away from earlier religions might civilization progress? What if Socrates, for example, turned out to be simply a schizoid combination of critical acumen and primitive idolatry? One could not make either Mauricean or Comtean claims until such issues were sorted out.

In his early Apostolic days, Sidgwick had read a paper entitled "Is Prayer a Permanent Function of Humanity?" – it was a question that epitomized much of his thinking, during the sixties and beyond, and one to which he would return at the very end of his life.[38] He wondered whether there were not some psychological natures so "healthy, finely moulded, well nerved, symmetrical" that they could do without the practice of supplication and all that went with it. Moreover, he suspected that such natures "might feel in reading history as if mankind had gone to sleep after the bright sunny days of Athenian life and were just waking up again after the long nightmare of mediaeval superstition." Sidgwick predictably goes on to confess that he feels the opposing case "with much more force," since one could argue from "the virtue and happiness that religion has produced in the unsymmetrical and weak to the still greater effects of the same kind, it might produce in the symmetrical and strong." (CWC)[39] And the religious have an edge over the symmetrical people in facing the trials of old age and death. Yet even so, the doubts were there, and had been watered by the example of the ancient Athenians.[40] And by that of Goethe and those of Sidgwick's friends who followed him.

These issues, with their psychological, sociological, and anthropological orientations, were coming at Sidgwick from all sides – from Darwin, Maurice, Mill, Renan, Comte, and others – and they would continue to haunt him for the rest of his life. But he gave them a novel twist, carrying them in directions never quite anticipated by his predecessors.

For Sidgwick, psychology meant, in large part, parapsychology.[41] The crucial questions could not be fully addressed without consideration of a much wider range of evidence than had previously been treated of. Perhaps personal survival of death was one of the elements of truth in Christianity, to be separated from the husk of legend. Perhaps Maurice was at least right in thinking that one must address sympathetically the evidences of all the world religions, including, of course, the Socratic. Maurice, however, thought that "disembodied spirits" belonged "to the realm of fancy and not of fact. Our Lord took all pains while He was on earth to show how much He cared for bodies." Here he was in an odd accord with Renan, who also had no time for ghosts. But for Sidgwick, the natural reply was that it was just as dogmatic to go along uncritically with materialistic science as it was to go along with orthodox religion. What evidence was there for ghosts? For the miraculous as a permanent function of the universe? Just possibly, Maurice did not take the Socratic Daimon seriously enough.

In 1867, in a singularly illuminating letter to his friend Roden Noel, Sidgwick explained:

Only I happened to read Lecky in the Long. You know the book – *History of Rationalism*. With the perverseness that sometimes characterises me I took up the subject from entirely the opposite point of view to Lecky, and determined to investigate the *evidence* for medieval miracles, as he insists it is *not* an investigation of this evidence, but merely the progress of events, march of mind, etc. which has brought about our present disbelief in them. The results have, I confess, astonished myself. I keep silence at present even from good words, but I dimly foresee that I shall have to entirely alter my whole view of the universe and admit the "miraculous," as we call it, as a *permanent* element in human history and experience. You know my "Spiritualistic" ghost-seeing tendencies. These all link on, and the Origins of all religions find themselves explained. However, as I say, I keep silence at present; I am only in the middle of my inquiries. (M 160)

Curiously enough, this venture was in part an inheritance from Benson. Among the discussion societies that Sidgwick had joined as an undergraduate, there was also the Ghost Society, devoted to the collection and critical examination of ghost stories. It had been founded by Benson and some friends during his undergraduate tenure, and thus Sidgwick had been steadily accumulating the results of collective research on the subject for a decade prior to the 1867 letter. A letter to his sister in 1858 explains that "my ghostological investigations are flourishing; I have taken unto myself associates here, and am prosecuting my researches with vigour; meeting with failures and vexatious exaggerations but still getting a good deal of real matter."[42]

As his diary reveals, the theological relevance of this subject – something Benson ultimately rejected – had come home to him early on: "Why should not God be willing to give us a few glimpses of the unseen worlds which we all believe exist." This was an interest that apparently endured intact through all his theological wanderings. In 1863, he wrote to Dakyns: "In Theology I am much as ever: I have not yet investigated Spiritualism, but I am still bent upon doing so as soon as I have the opportunity" (M 94). And again, in 1864, "As to Spiritualism, do not speak of it: I have not progressed, but am in painful doubt; still, I have some personal experiences and much testimony, and I find it hard to believe that I shall not discover some unknown laws, psychological or other" (M 106). T. H. Green may have "sniffed" at the project, but Sidgwick was unmoved.

Interestingly, though not surprisingly, Sidgwick's ghostological investigations tended to mirror the Apostolic mode of inquiry. This is not merely because a number of the associates he had taken on were in fact also Apostles – for instance, Oscar Browning and J. J. Cowell, the latter of whom collaborated with Sidgwick in experiments in automatic or "spirit" writing. More important was the overall mission and method; in Janet Oppenheim's view, the Apostolic "idea of a group of men meeting regularly to discuss, with utter frankness and without restrictions, questions of religious, philosophical, and ethical import" would inspire a number of those who went on to form the the Society for Psychical Research, in 1882, especially the smaller "Sidgwick Group" that worked as an intimate cohort within the larger organization.[43] The characteristic tone was caught in a letter from Sidgwick to Myers in the late seventies: "My dear Fred, My brother William is not coming to me, so that I could probably pursue Truth *before* Christmas, 23rd or 24th."[44]

For Sidgwick, the aim of the Ghost Society, and then the SPR, was not dramatically different from that of the Apostles or of other philosophical groups. If anything, it was even more directly addressed to the "deepest problems of human life." Here was the rare opportunity to employ free, open scientific inquiry to reenchant the world, rather than to deprive it of significance. As Eleanor later recounted, in the "Autobiographical Fragment," the "whole subject" of psychical research "connected itself with his philosophical and theological studies. . . . comparative thaumatology required its investigation; and, further, the possibility of direct proof of continued individual existence after death could not be neglected either from a theological or an ethical point of view." (M 43) Later retrospect also confirmed what he had feared all along, namely, that this was not a path likely to lead him back to his childhood faith:

It is now a long time since I could even imagine myself believing in Christianity after the orthodox fashion; not that I have any abstract objection to miracles, but because I cannot see any rational ground for treating the marvellous stories of the Gospels differently from the many other marvellous narratives which we meet with in history and biography, ancient and modern. While, if I were to believe all these marvellous narratives, I should have to suppose a continual communication between an "unseen universe" and our planet; and this would prevent the Gospel story from having anything like the unique character that it has for Christians. I do not make this latter supposition merely for the sake of argument; I am not inclined to oppose to this series of marvellous narratives (outside the Gospels) the sort of unhesitating {dis}belief that most of my orthodox friends do. In fact, I have spent a good deal of my leisure for some years in investigating ghost stories, spiritualistic phenomena, etc., etc., and I have not yet abandoned the hope of finding some residuum of truth in them. . . . Meanwhile the dilemma is clear and certain to me. *Either* one must believe in ghosts, modern miracles, etc., *or* there can be no ground for giving credence to the Gospel story: and as I have not yet decided to do the former, I am provisionally incredulous as to the latter – and in fact for many years I have not thought of Christianity except as the creed of my friends and fellow-countrymen, etc. (M 347)

In other words, the progress of genuine science, free and open inquiry, might just usher in the religion of the future, even if it worked rather destructively on the religions of the past. At any rate, what was the alternative, if one insisted on giving an account of the built-in features of human credulity and human hope? Both theology and biblical criticism needed fresh facts. Indeed, the peculiarities of parapsychology – "psychical research" – with its focus on unseen worlds, unconscious voices, telepathic communication, the communications of mediums, and so forth, proved extremely conducive to the Apostolic mission of bearing witness to one's inner life. Was it not a thoroughly Socratic question, to inquire to what extent this inner life was in fact more than inner? Or was it, possibly, something akin to that impulse that had led Plato to press beyond Socrates, seeking the final proof that the soul exists and is eternal, but doing so now with the methods furnished by Bacon, Mill, and Darwin?

Sidgwick's psychical research was, therefore, a continuation of his theological and philosophical search and anything but a gullible diversion from his "real" work – though to be sure, reconciling his claims about the importance of the world unseen with the particulars of his arguments about ethics, politics, epistemology, and intuition will prove to be an intricate and demanding task. His search for a meaningful but not mystical, progressive but not presumptuous, perennial philosophy was more or less bound to touch all other parts of his life, even if different parts were differently affected. His search for sympathetic understanding and unity may have been common to his Millian and Apostolic tendencies, and in part symptomatic of the pervasive fear of social conflict and otherness at home and abroad in the empire. For the discussions of such psychological evolution could not help but be entangled, at one level or another, in discussions of race and rule, democracy and decadence. But to carry such matters into parapsychology (often inaugurating the discourse, as it were) was a risky business, hinting at a form of scientific esotericism very different from philology or Comtism.

Myers, an early student of Sidgwick's, who would become one of the stalwarts of the Sidgwick Group and one of Sidgwick's closest friends, would often recall how in 1868, when they had taken "a star-light walk," he asked Sidgwick

almost with trembling, whether he thought that when Tradition, Intuition, Metaphysic, had failed to solve the riddle of the Universe, there was still a chance that from any actual observable phenomena – ghosts, spirits, whatsoever there might be – some valid knowledge might be drawn as to a World Unseen. Already, it seemed, he had thought that this was possible; steadily, though in no sanguine fashion, he indicated some last grounds of hope; and from that night onwards I resolved to pursue this quest, if it might be, at his side.[45]

Myers did, of course, along with such luminaries as Edmund Gurney, Walter Leaf, Lord Rayleigh, William James, Arthur and Gerald Balfour, and Sidgwick's future wife, Eleanor Mildred Balfour.

It should be observed that in some ways, Sidgwick's commitment to psychical research represented a continuation of his Apostolic efforts that would also put him at odds with the later Apostles. And his friendship with Myers had a good deal to do with this. As Richard Deacon has explained, when the SPR was formally founded, Sidgwick

was by then an 'Angel' and no longer the dominant figure in the Apostles. His interest in psychic phenomena only attracted a very few of the younger Apostles. When one of them proposed the question 'Can we communicate with the departed?' as a subject for debate, he was almost unanimously rejected. Alfred Whitehead . . . is said to have caustically commented on this proposal that 'such matters are best left to Myers, or his paramour, Eusapia Palladino.'

Antagonism to Myers rather than disloyalty to Sidgwick would seem to be one reason why discussions on psychic matters were avoided by the Society. Myers was not very popular in some circles at Cambridge, and the Apostolic grapevine did not miss much gossip about outsiders. Members of the Society had learned that Myers was reputed to have stolen the work of another Cambridge man and claimed the product as his own. But, apart from such tittle-tattle, Myers was suspected of all manner of sexual quirks and it was alleged that he looked upon psychical research as giving him opportunities for voyeurism. However, this was probably an unjust accusation for a man who, until he became absorbed by his studies of spiritualism and mesmerism, was best known as a poet and essayist. Whether he actually knew Eusapia Palladino is irrelevant; she had acquired a reputation as a medium, but was also notorious for introducing eroticism into séances. Myers was sufficiently odd in his behaviour, nonetheless, to insist on accompanying young Edmund Gurney and his bride on their honeymoon to Switzerland, even against the most vehement protests from the bride.[46]

What Virginia Woolf would later say of the Apostles – that they were a "society of equals enjoying each other's foibles" – would no doubt strike many as more aptly said of the Sidgwick Group. But for Sidgwick, at least, it represented the most serious side of his quest, the continuation of his earlier Apostolic interests and religious struggles, albeit one that he did not wish to impose on his more unreceptive friends.

Chapter 5 will explore these matters more fully, including Sidgwick's controversial friendship with Myers. The point to stress here, as a prelude to the following chapter on *The Methods of Ethics*, is simply that Sidgwick and Myers were in deep accord on the most fundamental issues. For Myers, the deepest question of human life was the theistic one: "Is the Universe friendly?" Sidgwick's intellect and philosophical analyses were infinitely subtler than Myers's, but in the end he devoted himself to much the same question. Throughout his adult life, he would always keep a bit of scripture before his mind, as a sort of working motto. Of all the lines that served in this capacity, none was more revealing than that for the years 1861–65: "After the way which they call heresy, so worship I the God of my fathers."

V. Fire and Light

Perhaps you would like to hear the present phase of the "Apostolic" Succession. We are: Brandreth, Sidgwick, Tawney, Browning, Cowell, Trevelyn, Jebb . . . Trevelyan you may know by report, a Harrow man and the nephew of Macaulay. He will be my chief friend when this last wave shall have burst, sweeping off Tawney, Browning, Cowell. The vicissitudes of human things affect even The Society slightly: at least I think our discussions are less vigorous now than usual; but the great Idea, which sits invisible among us, has I trust, as potent a magic as ever to elevate and unite. . . .

Sidgwick to Noel, February 18, 1860 (M 47–48)

Cowell maintained "The end justifies the means" I assent assuming the words used in a popular sense – Brandreth judging acts morally by their consequences alone denied that bad means *could* lead to a good end. This is practically useless – All our rules are imperfect, we express our perception of this by principles like the

above – As to "Great Happ" theory I am softened to it: it is perhaps only a philosophico-logico-practical representation of "Love is the fulfilling of the law" – But (1) we must take care to consider the soul's happiness and (2) we must not discard the props which we have in our conceptions, imperfect tho' they be of Truth, Justice &c. (Purity, Rectitude &c are parts of the ideal which Love will teach us to mold others to) –
Jebb rigid & moral, Tawney? but *earnest*. What is the duty of Religious Faith? Am I to Let the clouds come and pass trusting to be ultimately brighter for the tempest & only praying for Truth – Alas! I do not love her enough.

Sidgwick's diary from 1860[47]

Sidgwick's diary from the spring of 1860 gives a vivid impression of his interaction with his fellow Apostles, and of the nascent utilitarianism that would eventually blossom into *The Methods of Ethics*. The compelling thought that all our moral rules are imperfect, coupled with the question concerning the duty of religious faith and the fear of not loving truth quite enough, were natural companions to the progressive, rationalistic theism that he would fight so hard to vindicate. It was no simple matter to keep apart the two aspects of his Apostolic conversion – the social, on the one side, and the philosophical or theological, on the other. The prospects for the "complete revision of human relations" in the "light of science directed by comprehensive and impartial sympathy" would depend on, among other things, the outcome of the "psychological experiments in ethics and intuitive Theism" carried out in conjunction with psychical research. Perhaps parapsychology would be able to unify the Apostolic mystics and the utilitarian skeptics, the idealists and the naturalists, labor and capital, England and the rest of the world. The conquest of the "Other World" carried the hope of the conquest of otherness generally, the flip side of the quest for sympathetic unity. It would be a brilliant synthesis, and a rather literally Platonic one at that, the coronation of capital "P" Philosophy.

What Sidgwick increasingly came to realize, however, over the course of the sixties, was that cracking the "secret of the Universe" was going to be a rather time-consuming business, and that he had better cultivate the patience of a Darwin when it came to accumulating evidence. Thus, in 1863, he confessed to Dakyns: "I think a hundred times of what the British public are ripe for, for once that I think of what I believe. Perhaps the conviction is growing on me that the Truth about the studies I've set my heart on (Theology & Moral Philosophy) will not be found out for a generation or two." (M 97) The exact nature of his experiments in automatic writing and telepathy will be considered in a later chapter; for the present, it is sufficient to note that he was quite early on convinced that at least some of the evidence for paranormal phenomena must be sound. But the world of parapsychology loomed before him with all the vastness of an unexplored continent, even universe, and he was no more inclined to make hasty speculations about this than about any other department of thought.

But of course, the world did go on, and his practical commitments prevented any complete retreat into the deepest problems. As always, he was reading political economy "as a ballast to my necessarily busy selfishness which would otherwise be intolerable to my real self" (M 66). He hated the thought of growing too introspective and self-absorbed, and had a "golden rule" never to think about himself for more than half an hour a day. He would not allow any such thing, being firmly opposed to the tendency, encouraged by speculative thinking, to grow "antipractical." Interestingly, at the end of his life he would be urging that people – particularly the younger generation of Apostles – needed to be more introspective, even prayerful.[48] But that was not his concern during the sixties, when painful introspective meditation came all too easily. Admittedly, however, he would have had some difficulty going all the way with any such tendency, at his particular time and place, for he was swept up in currents of history both great and small, always, it seemed, moving rapidly.

Cambridge proved a congenial headquarters, at least in the midst of his storm and stress. In 1865, he was invited to examine for the Moral Sciences Tripos, which was also to be agreeably revamped in 1867, at which time the College also arranged for him to exchange his classical lectureship for a more suitable one in moral sciences. Sidgwick did not hesitate, and the change allowed him a greater concentration of his energies: "I took the post offered me, determined to throw myself into the work of making, if possible, a philosophical school in Cambridge" (M 38). By 1868, he was lecturing on moral and mental philosophy and, as noted earlier, busily defining the Cambridge school by contrasting it with Oxford's *Literae Humaniores*. Ultimately, he would expand the role of Lecturer to encompass more individual teaching.

With the return of Maurice, as Knightbridge Professor, it looked as though Cambridge philosophy would have a decidedly reformist bent. As Rothblatt has argued, Maurice "was an Apostle who had returned to Cambridge especially to guide the new generation." Whether it was Maurice or Sidgwick who did the guiding is unclear, but in any event they worked together at close quarters – notably in the discussion society known as the Grote Club – until Maurice's death, in 1872.

The Grote Club, it should be added, was a singularly important venue for this work. Its origins are somewhat hazy, but it seems to have included from the start at least John Grote, Sidgwick, J. B. Mayor, and Aldis Wright, and to have been a faculty discussion group largely devoted to philosophy. Grote, who was both Knightbridge Professor and vicar at the parish at Trumpington, was the senior member and host, once the meetings ceased being held in various members' rooms and were moved to his vicarage. As a (slightly) later member, John Venn, noted, Grote was an admirable moderator: "Nothing escaped his keen and critical judgment, and he asserted himself just sufficiently to draw out the thoughts of those who were shy in expressing themselves, and to keep the conversation from straggling into side issues." He also had an "extreme aversion to any dogmatic statement," and Sidgwick found this most Apostolic, as he explained in an 1865 letter to Dakyns:

The kind of talk we have at Trumpington, my "Apostolic" training makes me in some respects appreciate peculiarly. Consequently, I am a sort of Thaliarchus at that feast of reason, i.e. other men may be truer βάκχοι, in fact, I know they are, but I am a genial θυρσοφόρος. But at Cambridge there is a good deal of the feast of reason if you know where to look for it, and if you evade shams. But there is very little of the flow of soul. We communicate in one kind (this is not a ribald joke, but a profound allegory).
Distinguished names – but 'tis, somehow,
As if they played at being names
Still more distinguished.
     This is becoming a motto of mine, not of course with regard to Cambridge, but to our age. (M 133)[49]

Apparently, the Apostles and the Grote Club were for Sidgwick the two speculative societies at Cambridge that especially encouraged the flow of soul. According to John Gibbins, "Grote trained Sidgwick in impartiality, fair-mindedness, and the rigorous enquiring style that is generally held to be the most characteristic and praiseworthy feature of *The Methods of Ethics* of 1874, and of George Moore's *Principia Ethica* of 1903. He also helped reform Trinity College, the Knightbridge Chair of Moral Philosophy and the Moral Science Tripos significantly, before Sidgwick."[50] For his part, Sidgwick would sometimes wonder just what he had got from Grote; as he put it to Dakyns, in a letter of 1866:

I have less of a creed, philosophically speaking. I think I have more knowledge of what the thoughts of men have been, and a less conscious faculty of choosing the true and refusing the false among them.

I wonder whether I shall remain a boy all my life in this respect. I do not say this paradoxically, but having John Grote in my mind, who certainly retained, with the freshness, the indecisiveness of youth till the day of his death [sic]. I wonder whether we are coming to an age of general indecisiveness; I do not mean the frivolous scepticism of modern Philistines (I almost prefer the frivolous dogmatism of ancient ditto), but the feeling of a man who will not make up his mind till mankind has. I feel that this standpoint is ultimately indefensible, because mankind have never made up their mind except in consequence of some individual having done so. Still there seems to me to be a dilemma. In the present age an educated man must either be prophet or persistent sceptic – there seems no *media via*. (M 157–58)

As the following chapter will suggest, this emphasis on doubt and consensus was given formal expression in the epistemology of the *Methods*. In any event, Grote powerfully reinforced the Apostolic and Mauricean elements in Sidgwick's work, and the Grote Club, along with the Apostles, oiled the machinery for the further reform of Cambridge and Cambridge philosophy, what with Grote being succeeded by Maurice. Although some of their work was visible to the (educated) public eye, much would take place behind the scenes or appear only in that guarded, masked form that Maurice had done so much to perfect. Indeed, Apostolic secrecy had at this point become formal Apostolic policy. As Lubenow records:

[I]n the 1860s, the question had been addressed when a quarrel broke out amongst the Brethren about the extent to which secrecy was binding in the apostolic tradition. John Jermyn Cowell, the future barrister and sometime secretary of the Alpine Club, wrote to the greatest living Angel, Lord Houghton, about 'the traditions of the Elders', to settle the dispute. Houghton thought little good would come from talking about the Society 'to the general world who are more likely to mistake its objects & misunderstand its principles', and urged a policy of secrecy. Concluding with a suitable apostolic salutation, Houghton authorized Cowell to use his letter in discussions about the question.[51]

In any event, now many of Sidgwick's practical reformist concerns would take definite shape: educational reform, higher education for women, the Charity Organization Society, the working men's colleges, the Free Christian Union, the cabinetmakers cooperative – these were matters of common cause with the older, more experienced Maurice. Sidgwick the social and educational reformer was not, however, lingering in the background. According to Rothblatt, Sidgwick "must be considered a central figure in any account of the generation of the 1860s. His hand, sometimes his inspiration, was in every major administrative or teaching reform in that critical period in which modern Cambridge was born."[52]

But again, as important as the reform of Sidgwick's home base surely was, it was but one battle in a much larger war. Even in 1861, he had presciently explained to Dakyns that "[i]f I stay at Cambridge I should like to divide my time between general scepticism as free as air, and inductive 'Politik' as practical & detailed as I can get it, to secure me from being a dreamer," and that he wanted to "form a Liberal Mediative party on the principles of J. S. Mill" (M 69). Once he awoke from "the thralldom" of his historical investigations, he was apt to "agree with Mill against Comte" as to the impossibility of history standing on its own as a science, and to think that "Politick, besides, is so infinitely more important just now" (M 124). This it would have been hard to deny. After all, the era in question was that leading up to the Second Reform Bill, the great reform act of 1867, which marked the first real extension of the franchise to the working class and hence the first real move to something like representative democracy. The great battles between Palmerston, Russell, Derby, Gladstone, and Disraeli kept the public fascinated and frightened – no one was sure quite what to expect. Nor would the economic setbacks of the seventies and such upheavals as the French Commune do much to reassure those who worried about the winds of political change. As Eric Hobsbawm has framed the dilemma of nineteenth-century liberals:

What indeed, would happen in politics when the masses of the people, ignorant and brutalized, unable to understand the elegant and salutary logic of Adam Smith's free market, controlled the political fate of states? They would, as likely as not, pursue a road which led to that social revolution whose brief reappearance in 1871 had so terrified the respectable. In its ancient insurrectional form, revolution might no longer seem imminent, but was it not concealed behind any major extension of the franchise beyond the ranks of the propertied and educated? Would this not, as the future Lord Salisbury feared in 1866, inevitably lead to communism?[53]

And J. S. Mill, whose *Logic* and *Principles of Political Economy* had become the textbooks of the nation, was increasingly being revealed as a voice for radicalism; as MP for Westminster, he dared to propose granting the vote to women, the first such effort ever made in Parliament. But even Mill worried about what would happen when political empowerment came to a class that was largely illiterate and subject to a wide array of evils. True, he did not share the contempt for the working class expressed by Robert Lowe, in 1866: "If you want venality," Lowe asked, "if you want drunkenness and facility for being intimidated . . . if . . . you want impulsive, unreflecting and violent people . . . do you go to the top or the bottom?"[54] Still, Mill himself had warned the workers that strong drink and weak morals did not make for healthy political participation, and his *Considerations on Representative Government* urged that one's ballot power be proportional to one's education.[55] His socialism, he later explained, made him less sympathetic to democracy, under the circumstances.

Sidgwick, as we shall see, for all his candor and sympathy, was not capable of this degree of Millian forthrightness, and he fell rather short of Mill in his radicalism. He wrote to Oscar Browning, in November of 1865:

As for Rent, I for one do not mind the Ricardo-rent of land getting accumulated in large masses, provided care is taken (by giving long leases, etc.) that this does not interfere with the amelioration of the soil: and then you have your ἀρχαιόπλουτοι at once. What I want to do is to put an end to the existing and threatening strife between Labour and Capital by any possible means.

Browning had worried that Sidgwick and political economy generally were hostile to the "families of ancient wealth" supposedly necessary for a high degree of culture. Sidgwick assured him that this was not so, in his own case at least, though he notes that

of course people who make the lucky hits are uneducated generally, but that is just the point; if you could get all classes properly educated in the highest sense of the term, a man who came into a fortune by 'striking ile' would not waste it: and if he did not become a patron of Art himself, he might bring up his children to be so. (M 132–33)[56]

Education was the indispensable key, according to both Mill and Sidgwick. Both could not help but admire, whatever their theological qualms, Maurice's work for Christian socialism, workingmen's colleges, and so on – efforts to reach out to and culturally encompass the alienated workers. But the issue here was first and foremost the educational quality of the larger cultural sphere of society, rather than institutional or curricular changes. One inevitably colored the other; school and society were never quite distinct (as Dewey would go on to spend a career arguing). Consider Sidgwick's explanation of why he wanted to join the Freemasons: "My reasons for joining the fraternity are partly general, for, though I do not at all know what the object of it is and am aware that the 'Great Secret' must be humbug, I am still desirous of helping the mingling of classes, wh. I conceive freemasonry does." He admits, however, that his main hope is that it will give him "at least a slight additional means of penetrating the life of foreign countries: for Freemasonry is all over the world."[57] Although it is not known just what became of this particular strategy, Sidgwick's reasoning is extremely revealing of his quest to conquer otherness, at home and abroad. As with the Apostles, it was through the work of a society famous for shrouding its workings in secrecy that understanding and reform were supposed to come.

Some sense of the complex web of Millian educational reformism can be gleaned from Alan Ryan's comparison of Mill with another great culture critic of the period, Matthew Arnold, author of the famous *Culture and Anarchy*, published in 1869. As Ryan rightly insists, there are some interesting allegiances between Mill the utilitarian and Arnold the perfectionist champion of literary culture:

Both, evidently, think of the ideals of liberal education as even more important for an industrial and commercially minded society than for its simpler predecessors. Against the critics of liberal education in nineteenth-century America, who thought a more utilitarian, practical, and vocational education should replace traditional liberal education, their reply is that just because the society offers so many incentives to acquire the vocational and practical skills we require, it is all the more important to balance these pressures by disinterested, non-instrumental, and in that sense impractical instruction.[58]

This is quite accurate, and suggests how in order even to begin to think sensibly about Mill's utilitarianism (and Sidgwick's), one must forget the image of soulless, antipoetical utilitarianism popularized in Dickens's *Hard Times*. The call for a clerisy, common to Arnold, Mill, and Sidgwick, was not a celebration of the virtues of Mr. Gradgrind.[59]

But the differences between the two are still more important:

Mill's ideal of a liberal education was firmly rooted in an attachment to the classics, as his rectorial address to St. Andrews University insisted. What the classics were to teach was another matter. Mill admired the Athenians for their politics, for the vitality of their citizens' lives, and for their democratic aspirations. Athenians did not confine their interests to a literary education, and they were not superstitious about the wisdom of their ancestors. In short, a concern for the classics was to feed a concern for a lively democratic politics, and for a kind of political and intellectual ambition that Mill thought Victorian Englishmen lacked. It followed that when Mill asked the question whether we should seek an education for citizenship or an education in the classical tradition, he inevitably answered Both, and when he asked whether such an education ought to be a scientific or a literary education he unhesitatingly answered Both once more. These were not Arnold's politics, nor Arnold's educational ideals.[60]

Ryan suggests that we might take away from Mill v. Arnold the "*half-comforting* thought that our anxieties and uncertainties are not new," that our educational situation today is not "an especially fallen one," and that even in the midst of "culture wars" we can still "do a great deal of good."

Missing from Ryan's account, however, is the further comfort, or insight, to be gained by considering Sidgwick v. Arnold. For, in keeping with the themes developed in the previous chapter, it should be clear that the confrontation with Arnold is merely one more manifestation – though an extremely important one – of the attempt by the Millians to recapture and rethink the Platonic legacy, turning it into their own usable history at a time when history seemed rather desperate for political precedent. Arnold was no unthinking Tory, no defender of what Mill famously termed the "stupid party." His challenge was the more important precisely because he shared so much of the liberal progressivism of his critics, of their recognition that a cultural revolution was required, in conjunction with the political one. As Ryan notes, Arnold was as earnest as Mill in wishing "the blessings of a literary high culture to be extended to the working class."[61]

As in the case of Mill, one can get a very good feel for Sidgwick's priorities by closely comparing him to Arnold. Sidgwick himself recognized this, and he devoted considerable effort to defining himself against "The Prophet of Culture," as he entitled his first essay on the subject, published in *Macmillan's*. His life was in fact framed by two such essays – "The Prophet of Culture," from 1867, and the "The Pursuit of Culture as an Ideal," from 1897. Arnold took Sidgwick seriously and responded to him in one of the essays included in *Culture and Anarchy*, in which he insinuated that Sidgwick was puritanical. Sidgwick did not seem terribly annoyed by the charge.

Sidgwick's take on Arnold is often quite Millian, but it also highlights his own special concerns. The first essay condemns Arnold mostly for being effete and self-indulgent when it comes to religious enthusiasm and calls to action; the second, curiously more Millian, takes more direct aim at the excessively literary notion of culture favored by Arnold and reaffirms, after long reflection, the views expressed in various of Sidgwick's earlier works to the effect that no notion of culture that neglects the scientific attitude could possibly be relevant to the nineteenth century. Thus, in a line quoted earlier (one that he could have written at nearly any point in his adult life),

It is the love of knowledge, the ardour of scientific curiosity, driving us continually to absorb new facts and ideas, to make them our own and fit them into the living and growing system of our thought; and the trained faculty of doing this, the alert and supple intelligence exercised and continually developed in doing this, – it is in these that culture essentially lies. (PE 121)

In any event, both essays suggest how "culture" needs to be construed in the modern age, and how it should be complimented by such things as an ethic of self-sacrifice. This search for a new synthesis was a defining one.

It is worth dwelling some on the first essay precisely because of the religious questions addressed, the way in which it fills out the story of Sidgwick's storm and stress and expresses his vision of what modernity demands. Sidgwick dryly marvels at "the imperturbable cheerfulness with which Mr. Arnold seems to sustain himself on the fragment of culture that is left him, amid the deluge of Philistinism that he sees submerging our age and country" (MEA 41). He allows that "the impulse toward perfection in a man of culture is not practically limited to himself, but tends to expand in infinitely increasing circles. It is the wish of culture, taking ever wider and wider sweeps, to carry the whole race, the whole universe, harmoniously towards perfection." (MEA 44) But it is all too rarely that this "paradisaical state of culture" exists, such that there "is no conflict, no antagonism, between the full development of the individual and the progress of the world." Thus,

We dwell in it a little space, and then it vanishes into the ideal. Life shows us the conflict and the discord: on one side are the claims of harmonious self-development, on the other the cries of struggling humanity: we have hitherto let our sympathies expand along with our other refined instincts, but now they threaten to sweep us into regions from which those refined instincts shrink. Not that harmonious self-development calls on us to *crush* our sympathies; it asks only that they should be a little repressed, a little kept under: we may become (as Mr. Arnold delicately words it) philanthropists 'tempered by renouncement.' There is much useful and important work to be done, which may be done harmoniously: still we cannot honestly say that this seems to us the most useful, the most important work, or what in the interests of the world is most pressingly entreated and demanded. This latter, if done at all, must be done as self-sacrifice, not as self-development. And so we are brought face to face with the most momentous and profound problem of ethics. (MEA 44–45)

This, as we have seen, is very much what Sidgwick was forever lamenting as the most momentous and profound problem of ethics, his own and society's – recall his youthful remarks about selfishness. But it is not what Mill would have said, being far too much a vision of the rationalist fruit out of the Christian seed. According to Sidgwick, the very essence of religion is self-sacrifice; not so, culture.

The religious man tells himself that in obeying the instinct of self-sacrifice he has chosen true culture, and the man of culture tells himself that by seeking self-development he is really taking the best course to 'make reason and the will of God prevail.' But I do not think either is quite convinced. I think each dimly feels that it is necessary for the world that the other line of life should be chosen by some, and each and all look forward with yearning to a time when circumstances shall have become kinder and more pliable to our desires, and when the complex impulses of humanity that we share shall have been chastened and purified into something more easy to harmonise. And sometimes the human race seems to the eye of enthusiasm so very near this consummation: it seems that if just a few simple things were done it would reach it. But these simple things prove mountains of difficulty; and the end is far off. I remember saying to a friend once – a man of deep culture – that his was a 'fair-weather theory of life.' He answered with much earnestness, 'We mean it to be fair weather henceforth.' And I hope the skies are growing clearer every century; but meanwhile there is much storm and darkness yet, and we want – the world wants – all the self-sacrifice that religion can stimulate. Culture diffuses 'sweetness and light'; I do not undervalue these blessings; but religion gives fire and strength, and the world wants fire and strength even more than sweetness and light. Mr. Arnold feels this when he says that culture must 'borrow a devout energy' from religion; but devout energy, as Dr. Newman somewhere says, is not to be borrowed. At the same time, I trust that the ideal of culture and the ideal of religion will continually approach one another: that culture will keep developing its sympathy, and gain in fire and strength; that religion will teach that unnecessary self-sacrifice is folly, and that whatever tends to make life harsh and gloomy cometh of evil. And if we may allow that the progress of culture is clearly in this direction, surely we may say the same of religion. . . . To me the ultimate and ideal relation of culture and religion is imaged like the union of the golden and silver sides of the famous shield – each leading to the same 'orbed perfection' of actions and results, but shining with a diverse splendour in the light of its different principle. (MEA 45–47)

Small wonder that those who embrace what critics take to be the excessive "demandingness" of utilitarianism – for example, Peter Singer – look to Sidgwick as their spiritual godfather, or that those who (misguidedly) think of perfectionism as more high-minded or idealistic than utilitarianism should find him so baffling. For Sidgwick was, in a plain sense, searching for a new religion, a new synthesis combining the best of the classical and the Christian. Mill himself had recognized the enervating state of society, the sickening Philistinism and conformity that called for strong medicine. But Mill had also stressed in no uncertain terms that the foundation of utilitarianism lay in "the social feelings of mankind; the desire to be in unity with our fellow creatures," such that not "only does all strengthening of social ties, and all healthy growth of society, give to each individual a stronger personal interest in practically consulting the welfare of others; it also leads him to identify his *feelings* more and more with their good" and to come "as though instinctively, to be conscious of himself as a being who *of course* pays regard to others." And Mill could be so upbeat in his conviction that in

an improving state of the human mind, the influences are constantly on the increase, which tend to generate in each individual a feeling of unity with all the rest; which feeling, if perfect, would make him never think of, or desire, any beneficial condition for himself, in the benefits of which they are not included. If we now suppose this feeling of unity to be taught as a religion, and the whole force of education, of institutions, and of opinion, directed, as it once was in the case of religion, to make every person grow up from infancy surrounded on all sides both by the profession and by the practice of it, I think that no one, who can realize this conception, will feel any misgiving about the sufficiency of the ultimate sanction for the Happiness morality.[62]

Such statements, depicting an end Sidgwick himself felt deeply drawn to, nonetheless sounded the note of sweetness and light, rather than the fire and strength needed for the shorter run, the enthusiasm of Seeley or Noel.

Arnold's not unworthy response to this Sidgwickian flourish was to suggest that whether or not the world needed fire and strength more than sweetness and light would depend, as Sidgwick allowed, on the historical situation. But "any glance at the world around us shows that with us, with the most respectable and strongest part of us, the ruling force is now, and long has been, a Puritan force, – the care for fire and strength, strictness of conscience, Hebraism, rather than the care for sweetness and light, spontaneity of consciousness, Hellenism."[63]

Once again, therefore, the ancient Greek world came back to challenge and bend Sidgwick, as it would yet again, and still more formidably, in the views of his close friend John Addington Symonds, with whom, ironically enough, he was forming a close relationship at just this time. Rival efforts to co-opt the Platonic legacy were everywhere. And the Goethean ideal would find champions far more formidable than Arnold.

Still, there was real force in Sidgwick's objections to Arnold, beyond the obvious point that it was difficult to cheerfully wave aside the impact of the various scientific revolutions. For Sidgwick, Arnold has not probed the intellectual or emotional sources of religion. He allows that they "subdue the obvious faults of our animality," but in fact he only judges "of religious organisations as a dog judges of human beings, chiefly by scent." By contrast, for Sidgwick, who in this proves himself a true forefather of James and Dewey,

every man of deep culture ought to have a conception of the importance and intricacy of the religious problem, a sense of the kind and amount of study that is required for it, a tact to discriminate worthy and unworthy treatment of it, an instinct which, if he has to touch on it, will guide him round the lacunae of apprehension that the limits of his nature and leisure have rendered inevitable. (MEA 49)

Arnold allows that culture is, in the main, a matter of curiosity, but he has no curiosity about or sympathy for the roots of religion. He shows no appreciation for experiments in ethics and intuitive theism. Yet even Mill, anticipating James's "will to believe," had allowed that as long as reason is not impaired, "the indulgence of hope with regard to the government of the universe and the destiny of man after death," although it can be no more than hope, "is legitimate and philosophically defensible. Such hope "makes life and human nature a far greater thing to the feelings, and gives greater strength as well as greater solemnity to all the sentiments which are awakened in us by our fellow-creatures and by mankind at large," affording that "enlargement of the general scale of the feelings" such that the "loftier aspirations" might no longer be "in the same degree checked and kept down by a sense of the insignificance of human life – the disastrous feeling of 'not worth while.'"[64] Perhaps Mill, too, harbored some doubts about the age of transition.

What is more, Sidgwick is only too happy to voice the more democratic side of his puritanism. If any culture really has the

noblest element, the passion for propagating itself, for making itself prevail, then let it learn 'to call nothing common or unclean.' It can only propagate itself by shedding the light of its sympathy liberally; by learning to love common people and common things, to feel common interests. Make people feel that their own poor life is ever so little beautiful and poetical; then they will begin to turn and seek after the treasures of beauty and poetry outside and above it. (MEA 53)

Again, the task of education, in the broad as well as the narrow sense, is to stimulate the mind, not merely to discipline it. For purposes of illustration, Sidgwick turns, not to Mill, but to the old antagonist of the Benthamites, Thomas Macaulay. Macaulay, "though he loved literature, loved also common people and common things, and therefore he can make the common people who live among common things love literature" (MEA 53). One should not despise popularizers or those they serve.[65] And Sidgwick's Apostolic mind could not help but emphasize the importance of literature for the culture of the future, albeit literature of a certain type. Ironically, as we shall see, some of his friends identified him with the art for art's sake aesthetic vision of Swinburne, the poet and critic, a product of Oxford Hellenism who found Arnold rigid and humorless. The power of poeticizing life was surely not a concern to which he was deaf.

However, given their partisan angle, Sidgwick's initial attacks on Arnold were in some ways less revealing of his overall, enduring perspective on these matters than his later reflections. During the sixties, he was especially perturbed by the Arnoldian tendency to drop "from the prophet of an ideal culture into a more or less prejudiced advocate of the actual." Perfectionism of this sort could too easily become a counsel of complacency when it came to social reform, "always hinting at a convenient season, that rarely seems to arrive." It remains effete and elite: "For what does action, social action, really mean? It means losing oneself in a mass of disagreeable, hard, mechanical details, and trying to influence many dull or careless or bigoted people for the sake of ends that were at first of doubtful brilliancy, and are continually being dimmed and dwarfed by the clouds of conflict." (MEA 58, 56)

When he returned to the subject in the nineties, his recollections of the old controversies were more seasoned and judicious. True, as the man himself admitted, Arnold was "not a systematic thinker with philosophical principles duly coherent and interdependent." Consequently, "it is not surprising that he did not always mean the same thing by culture . . . his conception expanding and contracting elastically, as he passes from phase to phase of a long controversey." Thus, from an earlier and more narrowly construed account of culture as literary culture – the "Greek and Roman learning" of Lord Chesterfield – Arnold had swung wildly, expanding his conception to cover religion and science as modes of inquiry, efforts at "seeing things as they really are" but inflated to deal with all dimensions of human perfection. And this is confusing.

It was evident that Arnold had changed his idea; at the same time, he had not changed it altogether. For in subsequent essays, and even in the same essay, it is made clear that the method of culture is still, for Arnold, purely literary: it is attained by reading the best books. Now even in the latter half of the nineteenth century the desire to cultivate the intellect and taste by reading the best books, and the passion for social improvement, are not, if we look at actual facts, always found together; or even if we grant that the one can hardly exist without some degree of the others, at any rate they co-exist in different minds in very varying proportions. And when Arnold tells us that the Greeks had arrived, in theory at least, at a harmonious adjustment of the claims of both, we feel that his admiration for Hellenism has led him to idealise it; for we cannot but remember how Plato politely but firmly conducts the poets out of his republic, and how the Stoics sneered at Aristotle's praises of pure speculation. In short, we might allow Arnold to define the aim of culture either as the pursuit of sweetness and light or, more comprehensively, as the pursuit of complete spiritual perfection, including the aim of making reason and the will of God prevail: but, in the name of culture itself, we must refuse to use the same word for two such different things; since the resulting confusion of thought will certainly impede our efforts to see things as they are.

And when the alternatives are thus presented, it seems clear that usage is on the side of the narrower meaning. For what philanthropy is now increasingly eager to diffuse, under the name of culture, is something different from religion and morality; it is not these goods that have been withheld from the poor, nor of which the promotion excuses the luxurious expenditure of the rich. Poverty – except so far as it excludes even adequate moral instruction – is no bar to morality, as it is happily in men's power to do their duty in all relations of life, under any pressure of outward circumstances; and it is the rich, not the poor, that the gospel warns of their special difficulty in entering the kingdom of heaven. Again, if the pursuit of culture is taken to transcend and include the aim of promoting religion and morality, these sublimer goods cannot but claim by far the larger share of attention. Indeed, Arnold himself told us, in a later essay, that at least three-fourths of human life belong to morality, and religion as supplying motive force to morality: art and science together can at most claim the remaining fourth. But if so, any discussion of the principles that should guide our effort after the improvement of the three-fourths of life that morality claims, of the difficulties that such effort encounters, of the methods which it has to apply – all this must inevitably lead us far away from the consideration of culture in the ordinary sense.[66]

The more encompassing vision of perfection was more in accord with Sidgwick's own efforts to define "culture," of course, but he thought that he was more in touch with the spirit of the age than Arnold, who, for all his elasticity, had never really managed the scientific attitude: "His method of 'seeing things as they are' is simply to read the best books of all ages and countries, and let the unimpeded play of his consciousness combine the results." These were to be the "Great Books," needless to say – the works of "Plato, Cicero, Machiavelli, Shakespeare, Voltaire, Goethe." But

imagine a man learning physical science in this way. . . . imagine a learner, desirious of seeing the starry universe as it is, set down to read the treatises of Ptoloemy, Copernicus, Galileo, Kepler, and so on, and let his consciousness play about them in an untrammelled manner; instead of learning astronomical theory from the latest books, and the actual method of astronomical observation in a modern observatory![67]

Moreover,

Man, whatever else he is, is part of the world of nature, and modern science is more and more resolutely claiming him as an object of investigation. . . . the intuitions of literary genius will not avail to reduce to scientific order the complicated facts of psychical experience, any more than the facts of the physical world. And this is no less true of those special branches of the study of social man which have attained a somewhat more advanced condition than the general science of society which, in idea, comprehends them – e.g., economics, political science, archaelogy, philology.[68]

Nor can literature of itself "establish a relation between the results of science and our sense of conduct and our sense of beauty," important as that function is for it.

For when we try to satisfy completely the demand I have just indicated, to bring into true and clear intellectual relations the fundamental notions of studies, so diverse as positive science, ethics, and the theory of the fine arts, order, coherence, system must be the special objects aimed at; and this result can only be attained by philosophy, whose peculiar task, indeed, it is to bring into clear, orderly, harmonious relations, the fundamental notions and methods of all special sciences and studies. But it is not a task which philosophy can as yet be said to have satisfactorily accomplished; the height from which all normal human aims and activities can be clearly and fully contemplated in true and harmonious relations, is a height not yet surmounted by the human mind – perhaps it never will be surmounted – perhaps (to change the metaphor) the face of this ideal

> "Is evermore unseen
> And fixed upon the far sea-line,"

which changes with every advance in the endless voyaging of man's intellect.[69]

Yet Sidgwick is willing to make

a very substantial concession – that literature of the thoughtful kind, the poetry and eloquence that really deserves to be called a criticism of life, gives even to philosophers a most important part of the matter of philosophy, though it does not give philosophical form and order; and it gives a provisional substitute for philosophy to the many who do not philosophise. It gives, or helps to give, the kind of wide interest in, the versatile sympathy with, the whole complex manifestation of the human spirit in time, which is required – even if we are considering merely the intellectual element of culture – as a correction to the specialisation which the growth of science inexorably imposes.

For Sidgwick, the specialist is not by virtue of expertise a person of culture; the "habit of taking delight in the best literature" is a crucial corrective, with the function of maintaining "our intellectual interests and sympathies

in due breadth and versatility, while at the same time gratifying and exercising our sense of beauty." In this respect, literature is special. In addition
to being widely available – unlike Greek sculpture – it is "the most *altruistic*
of the fine arts" in that "it is an important part of its function to develop
the sensibility for other forms of beauty besides its own."[70]

And Sidgwick takes the occasion to issue some very Apostolic words
about how to acquire culture, understood as "the love of knowledge, the
ardour of scientific curiosity," and how "to acquire along with it the refinement of sensibility, the trained and developed taste for all manifestations
of beauty which no less belongs to culture." Culture, like virtue, can only
be taught in a certain way:

Virtue can be taught by a teacher who loves virtue, and so can culture, but not
otherwise; since, as Goethe sings: – 'Speech that is to stir the heart must from the
heart have sprung.' Experience shows that the love of knowledge and beauty can
be communicated through intellectual sympathy: there is a beneficent contagion
in the possession of it; but it must be admitted that its acquistion cannot be secured
by any formal system of lessons. No recipe for it can be enclosed in a syllabus, nor
can it be tested by the best regulated examinations.[71]

True education, in fine, has the personal touch. Nor is this necessarily
a matter of the relationship between teacher and student, in the formal
sense:

So far I have spoken of culture as something to be communicated by teachers or
acquired by solitary study. But when men of my age look back on their University
life, and ask themselves from what sources they learnt such culture as they did
learn, I think that most would give a high place – and some the chief place –
to a third educational factor, the converse with fellow-students. Even if we did
not learn most from this source, what we so learnt was learnt with most ease
and delight; and especially the value of this converse in broadening intellectual
interests, and keeping alive the flame of eager desire to know truth and feel beauty,
is difficult to over-estimate. Indeed, this always appears to me one great reason
why we have Universities at all, as at presented constituted.[72]

Perhaps many of these remarks did reflect Sidgwick's more mature
appreciation of what culture and education were all about. But surely
many, many elements were consistent features of his Apostolic mind:
the visions of inquiry, education, art, culture, and philosophy were in
their essence the fixed points of his mental universe. There was a distinct, continuous effort on his part to have it all – science and religion,

self-sacrifice and self-development, philosophy and literature, aristocracy and democracy, quality of education and quantity of education.

To be sure, the younger Sidgwick was more conflicted, less happily reconciled to the ongoing search for ever-receding truth. And he was clearly of a divided mind when it came to entering into the common mind, the "rustic" brain. How strange that the same person could have written to Symonds in 1867, the very same year as "The Prophet of Culture": "my best never comes out except when I am played upon & stirred by affection and subtle sympathy combined: when I do not get this, I become lethargic. Among the 'dim' common populations I seem to change and become common." (CWC)[73] And in that early, Apostolic paper on "Prayer," he had explained that "religion will always be beneficial and often of vital necessity on the one hand to natures where the emotional and passionate elements preponderate over the rational and active: and again to those whom constitution or fortune have depressed and saddened," adding breezily that he is not going to "speak of the sensual herd of whom Religion will ever be the only real elevator." Even his dear friend Noel, an aristocrat after all, though one with a decidedly radical bent, could during the sixties tease Sidgwick for tending toward a "Pseudo-Philosophy . . . that opposes itself to the vulgar opinion out of a kind of esoteric pride, which perchance we of 'the Brotherhood' may be peculiarly liable to."[74] Among other things, Sidgwick had wondered about the advisability of marriage, which, though valuable for the "inferior man," was perhaps a drag on the "superior man" in his effort to identify with the "universal heart of humanity." The just-married Noel's advice ran:

Let the mere student be content to be a mere student, all well. But let him not hope to acquire a fuller sympathy with the 'universal heart of humanity' than the practical man, by the process of placing himself above or outside of humanity and contemplating it, (or rather contemplating his idea of it formed a priori and from books.) A curious sympathy will result.[75]

Such remarks were telling indeed, as was Noel's advice that, if it is "not always by any means our duty to take 'our largest cut' of pleasure," still "this pleasant course *may* be duty sometimes."

As later chapters will elaborate, this form of elitism was something that Sidgwick would strain to moderate in the years to follow, not always successfully. But it is instructive in suggesting the nature of his point of departure and the tensions that would define his struggles. And after

all, Macaulay rather notoriously had no love at all for the literature of
Hinduism; his "love" for the common people of India demanded that
they be taught English and the love of *Western* literature.[76] To invoke him
as Sidgwick did raises the spectre of England's "civilizing" mission in
India and other parts of the globe.

In any event, these various points, even when qualified in recognition
of Sidgwick's imperial context, do also suggest the significance of Ryan's
plea for the ongoing relevance of the Victorian debates. That the general
cultural atmosphere is vital to the educational and democratic potential
of society, that this culture must value critical inquiry in a way capacious
enough to recognize the worth of both science and religion, philosophy
and literature, in addition to the Hellenistic legacy – these were not revelations that awaited the twentieth century.[77] And some might even be a little
nostalgic for the eloquence and passion shown by a Mill or a Sidgwick
on the subject of encouraging the mingling of classes and stimulating the
educational potential of all citizens, even if they did grotesquely underestimate what they stood to learn from other classes and other cultures,
tending to think of intellectual stimulation as proceeding from themselves
downward, particularly when it came to the larger world. After all, they
did help pave the way for better strategies, such as those of Jane Addams
and the settlement movement.[78]

Moreover, the foregoing remarks ought also to help us appreciate just
what Sidgwick's assessment of the importance of traditional Christianity
amounted to, and why he was so nervous about advancing the new rationalism, always hoping for a minimum of disruption to the old orthodoxy.
Perhaps they also shed some further light on his complex attitude toward
the Platonic revival and the uses to which it could be put. Sidgwick shared
much with Mill, but he had his own worries as well, and the central one
was that audacious egoism, that selfishness, that he so feared in both self
and society, even as he found its high-minded Goethean version difficult to resist. His was a most difficult balancing act: without wanting to
cause pain by disrupting the old, he nevertheless realized that the culture, morals, and education appropriate to the democratic society of the
future would be in many respects new. He wanted to preserve, even foster
respect for, quasi-religious fire and strength, while reviving the study of
Plato, adding Bentham and Mill to the curriculum along with modern
science in general and much modern literature, and inviting women and
workers to join him in Apostolic-style classroom discussions as well as in

the larger world of the educated public. In the end, his lessons, like Mill's, were directed at all classes and all peoples, however arrogantly. Rich as well as poor were expected to attend the school of sympathy and doubt, and they were even expected to learn from each other. Rather amazingly, they were apparently also expected, in due course, to learn from the "other world."

But at this point, in the late sixties, Sidgwick was led into some of his most productive doubting of all. To call for fire and strength, self-sacrifice, was all very well, but given his doubts about the larger fabric of the cosmos, it was often unclear, to say the least, just what duty actually demanded, beyond the familiar demand for "more research." Worse, it was unclear what duty demanded of him. Even Mill had come around to thinking that the universities might be made to harbor genuine thought after all, and the struggle was on. But the reformers, as much as those they planned on reforming, found it very hard to escape the atmosphere of hypocrisy that they so bitterly condemned.

VI. The Poetry of Hypocrisy

The intellectual function, then, which Clough naturally assumed was scepticism of the Socratic sort – scepticism occupied about problems on which grave practical issues depended. The fundamental assumptions involved in men's habitual lines of endeavour, which determined their ends and guided the formation of their rules, he was continually endeavouring to clear from error, and fix upon a sound basis. He would not accept either false solutions or no solutions, nor, unless very relectantly, provisional solutions. At the same time, he saw just as clearly as other men that the continued contemplation of insoluble problems is not merely unpractical, but anti-practical; and that a healthy and natural instinct forces most men, after a few years of feverish youthful agitation, resolutely to turn away from it. But with this instinct Clough's fine passion for absolute truth conflicted; if he saw two sides of a question, he must keep seeking a point of view from which they might be harmonised. In one of the most impressive of the poems . . . he describes his disposition
To finger idly some old Gordian knot,
Unskilled to sunder, and too weak to cleave;
but the reluctance to cleave knots, in the speculative sphere, does not proceed from weakness.

> Sidgwick, "The Poems and Prose Remains of Arthur Hugh Clough" (MEA 65–66)

Oddly enough, just as Sidgwick's position at Cambridge seemed more conducive than ever to his inquiries into the "deepest problems," an old guilt that had been kept in partial abeyance by his linguistic studies returned to haunt him with renewed force. In a recollection of singular significance, he explained:

Meanwhile I had been led back to philosophy by a quite different line of thought from a practical point of view – that is, by the question that seemed to continually to press with more urgency for a definite answer – whether I had a right to keep my Fellowship. I did my very best to decide the question methodically on general principles, but I found it very difficult, and I may say that it was while struggling with the difficulty thence arising that I went through a good deal of the thought that was ultimately systematised in the *Methods of Ethics*. (M 38)

This was a practical problem of the first importance, and one that in many ways encapsulated a good many of the larger practical political problems that engaged Sidgwick during the sixties. Conscientious objection to subscription to the Thirty-nine Articles of the Church of England was for Sidgwick and his time what conscientious objection to the draft was to the students in the 1960s who opposed the war in Vietnam, or what objection to loyalty oaths was in the 1950s. The *Methods* was a work loaded with political relevance, in much the same way that Rawls's *A Theory of Justice* was when it appeared in 1971. And rightly so. How many capable persons were lost to the English academic world, and to the social world it underwrote, because of the demand that one swear such allegiance? Agnostics, Jews, Unitarians, Catholics, Methodists, and countless others were all beyond the pale of officially sanctioned higher education until the educational tests were abolished in 1871. Small wonder that the youthful Mill and the earlier utilitarians should have had such withering contempt for Oxford and Cambridge, regarding them as imposter universities, ecclesiastical institutions all.

Nor was Mill the only one of Sidgwick's mentors to take up the cause. The young Maurice had also confronted the issue, and in a very personal way, since he had, as the Cambridge system allowed, largely and successfully completed his course of studies, taking a first in civil law. It was a proud Unitarian father who wrote, after his son had opted not to subscribe, and thus not to graduate:

Fred has left Cambridge, and has preserved his principles at the sacrifice of his interests. With this I am more satisfied than if he had taken a degree, and had been immediately presented with a fellowship. He was willing to state that he was a full believer in Christianity, and would conform to all the rules of the Gospel; but subscribe he must, if he would retain his scholarships. . . . This he could not do, and therefore was not permitted to take his degree, though he had passed all his examinations with credit.[79]

Eventually, Maurice would come around to the view expressed in one of his book titles, *Subscription No Bondage*, but that would be after some intellectual reconfiguration; and even then, he generally held that although subscription could be a good thing, in practice it often was not. After all, he knew that his own students, "if they think,"

must pass, some more, some less, consciously through phases of Arianism, Sabellianism, Tritheism, through Pantheism in many shapes. I know that they will be often on the borders of Atheism. I deliberately stir up the thoughts which will be drawn in these directions; I give them the pledge and hope of a home and resting-place after their toil; I say it is night, not afar off. You are living, moving, having your being in this God; but you may traverse many lonely deserts, and ford many rivers, and scale many mountains before you discover how near He is. Spinozism, Hegelism, Comtism – all may offer themselves to you on your pilgrimage; you may turn in for a while and rest in any of them; and God, not we, must, if our faith is true, teach you that there is any larger and freer dwelling-place than that which they afford.

'What then is subscription? I answer, it expresses the consent of the students to be taught according to certain conditions of thought.[80]

But the reality, Maurice agreed, was that although "subscription *might* make University teaching and learning more honest," it in fact "*does* make both less honest." Such was the view of a great many intelligent commentators, and even those sympathetic to subscription often took the more flexible line that subscription involved only a general conformity, not belief in the detailed phrases of the Articles. As Arthur Stanley nicely put it, if the question of what was actually being subscribed to were pressed on the details, there was not "one clergyman in the church" who could "cast a stone at another – they must all go out, from the greatest to the least, from the archbishop in his palace at Lambeth to the humblest curate in the wilds of Cumberland."[81] Such views had led to a royal commission being appointed in 1864 to consider the terms of subscription, and then to the Clerical Subscription Act of 1865, officially legitimating what was understood to be the more general form of assent: "I assent to the thirty-nine articles of religion, and to the Book of Common Prayer. . . . I believe the doctrine . . . as therein set forth, to be agreeable to the word of God."

It was on this score that Sidgwick was especially dismayed with the state of his country's morals. Nothing provoked him like the taint of hypocrisy. In a heated letter of 1862, he launched into a tirade in response to some of Dakyns's worries about the confidentiality of their letters:

But I do not agree with you as to the duty of concealment: I am certain the duty is all the other way: it is a spurious philanthropy that suppresses earnest convictions to avoid offence: why the very antagonism deepens the spiritual life of those who are {merely} really orthodox tho' it makes the formalist blacker. Don't think I want to preach to you: but your letter alarms just a little: there is just a breath in it of the miserable semi-hypocrisy that is paralysing the intellectual religion of England. My only motive for not speaking out now is scepticism: I am not *sure* I am *right* & so I keep silence even from good words, but it is pain & grief to me & hence my present hunger to get to the bottom of all the detailed & technical controversy & see if a stable defence of orthodoxy is lurking under any of the dry leaves.

I told J. B. Mayor last term my perplexity about holding Fellowship and he anwered wisely I think that 'when the views that were at present negative became positive in me I ought to resign not till then.' (CWC)[82]

This last bit of advice comported well with the guidelines of the Initial Society – in effect, the motto of Davy Crockett, "Always be sure you're right, then go ahead." Yet Sidgwick was bridling at the very constraints that largely defined his life, whether it be with the Initial Society, the Apostles, the Grote Club, the psychical researchers, or, as we shall see, Symonds and his circle. Neither Mill nor Maurice was quite the ideal that the young Sidgwick most admired when it came to this burning issue. Mill was too much the hostile critic from outside, Maurice too much the friendly conciliator from within (after all, Sidgwick was hardly being drawn through doubt to belief). Rather, Sidgwick looked to another source for guidance, one that would prove to be as influential as any: the poet Arthur Hugh Clough.

Clough, who died prematurely in 1861, was one of the most popular poets of the later Victorian period, and the struggles of his life served Sidgwick as a veritable mirror of his own trials. He had been a star pupil of Thomas Arnold's at Rugby, after which he had gone to Balliol College,

Oxford, where he also attended Newman's services and lectures, making such friends as W. G. "Ideal" Ward, and joined the progressive Oxford debating society. Although he achieved only a second-class degree – and walked back to Rugby to announce to Arnold, "I have failed" – he nonetheless became a Fellow of Oriel College and eventually Subdean there. During that time, he brought Emerson to Oxford, and then traveled with him in revolutionary France. He resigned his Fellowship at Oriel in 1848, and a number of his most highly regarded poems were composed around the period of his resignation crisis: "The Bothie of Tober-Na-Vuolich," "Ambarvalia," and "Amours De Voyage." Not surprisingly, these were the pieces that Sidgwick liked best, and his 1869 essay on "The Poems and Prose Remains of Arthur Hugh Clough" perhaps affords, all in all, the single best window onto Sidgwick's soul of any of his publications. Ironically, Clough was a friend of Matthew Arnold's, though there was considerable critical distance between them.

During the 1860s, especially, Clough was of unsurpassed emotional importance to Sidgwick – he was the "wine of life" (M 141–42). Thus it was that in 1866 he could write to Clough's widow to thank her for sending him a copy of her edition of the poet's works:

I ventured to ask Lushington's advocacy to procure me the book, because I felt that to no one, out of the range of his personal friendships, could Clough be an object of more intense individual interest than to myself. I suppose every one has some one book of poems to which he turns in any solitary mood that demands special sympathy: such a book, in these latter years I have had in Clough's poems. They are so dear to me in this peculiar way, that I should find it difficult to judge impartially their literary merit: yet I cannot but think that there are few poets – only two, it seems to me – of the present age whom the world would less willingly let die. He was the one true disciple of Wordsworth, with a far deeper interest than Wordsworth in the fundamental problems of human life, and a more subtle, more cultivated intellect. But – as with Wordsworth – every ornament, every melody in his poems seems the natural spontaneous utterance of his thought and feeling: with him thought seems always to glow with feeling and the two to run into simple music.

His rarest excellence seems to me his singular comprehensive complex sympathy. Many poets have treated the problems of life sometimes with bitter irony, sometimes with vehement oscillation of passion: but with him irony and sympathy – for *all* that is not base – seem indissolubly blended, and he never loses that judicial fairness in balancing conflicting influences, which we demand of a philosopher, but hardly expect from a poet. (CWC)

Here, then, was the poet who could serve Sidgwick in his time of crisis, in much the same way that Wordsworth had served Mill during his mental crisis, when Mill came to realize that the Benthamism (as he understood it) into which he had been born was emotionally flat and lifeless. Clough was Socratic, and ironic, but his skepticism was matched with that singular comprehensive sympathy that spoke to the Christian: he was the "agnostic who couldn't have cared more, to whom religion was a matter of life or death."[83] Tennyson as a poet may have moved Sidgwick more, but his intellect was not as sharp, his ambivalence not as perfect.[84] Clough better represented Sidgwick's "individual habits of thought and sentiment" (M 538).

"He clings to the 'beauty of his dreams;' but – two and two make four" – that is, what Sidgwick loved in Clough was

the painfulness, and yet inevitableness of this conflict, the childlike simplicity and submissiveness with which he yields himself up to it; the patient tenacity with which he refuses to quit his hold of any of the conflicting elements; the consistency with which it is carried into every department of life; the strange mixture of sympathy and want of sympathy with his fellow-creatures that necessarily accompanies it. (MEA 66)

Clough was truly philosophical in his "horror of illusions and deceptions of all kinds" and his "passionate devotion not to search after truth, but to truth itself – absolute, exact truth." His skill

lay in balancing assertions, comparing points of view, sifting gold from dross in the intellectual products presented to him, rejecting the rhetorical, defining the vague, paring away the exaggerative, reducing theory and argument to their simplest form, their 'lowest terms.' 'Lumen siccum,' as he calls it in one of his poems, is the object of his painful search, his eager hope, his anxious loyalty. (MEA 65)

Here, then, was one who could truly speak to the depths of an Apostolic soul. The expression "*lumen siccum*" became a permanent fixture of Sidgwick's vocabulary.

The truth is – if Clough had not lived and written, I should probably be now exactly where he was. I have not solved in any way the Gordian Knot which he fingered. I can neither adequately rationalise faith, nor reconcile faith and reason, nor suppress reason. But this is just the benefit of an utterly veracious man like Clough, that it is impossible for any one, however sympathetic, to remain where he was. He exposes the ragged edges of himself. One sees that in an irreligious age one must not let oneself drift, or else the rational element of oneself is disproportionately expressed and developed by the influence of environment, and one loses fidelity to one's true self. (M 228)

One's "true self" – for Sidgwick this was of course the issue, and his was a theistic one, longing for a friendly universe, a Heart and Mind behind phenomena. Clough, he felt, was "in a very literal sense before his age." His "point of view and habit of mind" were "less singular in England in the year 1869 than they were in 1859, and much less than they were in 1849." Clough, not Wordsworth or Arnold, was the prophet of their culture, someone who understood how

We are growing year by year more introspective and self-conscious: the current philosophy leads us to a close, patient, and impartial observation and analysis of our mental processes: and the current philosophy is partly the effect and partly the cause of a more widespread tendency. We are growing at the same time more unreserved and unveiled in our expression: in conversations, in journals and books, we more and more say and write what we actually do think and feel, and not what we intend to think or should desire to feel. We are growing also more sceptical in the proper sense of the word: we suspend our judgment much more than our predecessors, and much more contentedly: we see that there are many sides to many questions: the opinions that we do hold we hold if not more loosely, at least more at arm's length: we can imagine how they appear to others, and can conceive ourselves not holding them. We are losing in faith and confidence: if we are not failing in hope, our hopes at least are becoming more indefinite; and we are gaining in impartiality and comprehensiveness of sympathy. In each of these respects, Clough, if he were still alive, would find himself gradually more and more at home in the changing world. (MEA 60)

This was a mind in which Sidgwick could find himself: bearing witness to the true self, scrupulously pursuing truth, saying what you believe, growing more comprehensive in sympathy and impartiality. Clough's world had been indulgent of pious deception and hypocrisy. But not Clough. "Lax subscription to articles," Sidgwick observed, "was the way of Clough's world: and it belonged to his balanced temper to follow the way of his world for a time, not approving, but provisionally submitting and experimentalising." To do this, following the way of the world "till its unsatisfactoriness has been thoroughly proved" and then "suddenly to refuse to do it any longer," was neither heroic nor pleasant, but "as a *via media* between fanaticism and worldliness, it would naturally commend itself to a mind like Clough's" (MEA 68). And, to be sure, to a mind like Sidgwick's. All of his poetic friends – Noel and Symonds, for example – recognized that this was "Sidgwick's poet."

For Sidgwick had followed Clough's example. He had provisionally submitted for quite some time. As early as 1860, he could write to Browning that

I see that there is a great gulf between my views and the views once held by those who framed the Articles: and now held by at least a portion of the Church of England; I think I could juggle myself into signing the Articles as well as any one else: but I really feel that it may at least be the duty of some – if so ἐμοῦ γε – to avoid the best-motivated perjury. (M 62)

And again, Mayor had advised him in 1862 that "when the views that were at present negative became positive in me, I ought to resign, not till then" (M 83). In the aftermath of his immersion in historical biblical studies, this was precisely what happened.

VII. Fully Persuaded in His Own Mind

During most of his adult life Sidgwick had some text – a different one at different periods – which ran in his head, representing the keynote, so to speak, of his thought about his own life. From about 1861 to about 1865 the text was, "After the way which they call heresy, so worship I the God of my fathers." From about 1865 to October 1869 it was, "Are not Abana and Pharpar, rivers of Damascus, better than all the waters of Israel? may I not wash in them, and be clean? . . . And his servants . . . said, My father, if the prophet had bid thee do some great thing, wouldest thou not have done it?" From October 1869 to about 1875 the text was, "Let every man be fully persuaded in his own mind." From about 1875 to about 1890, "But this one thing I do, forgetting those things that are behind, and stretching forth unto those that are before, I press towards the mark." And finally from about 1890, "Gather up the fragments that are left, that nothing be lost."

Memoir, p. 125

Matthew Arnold might have taken a certain satisfaction in knowing how utterly Sidgwick adored Clough. For it was Arnold who argued that religion had become culture, and culture had become poetry – the wars of religion were soon to be culture wars. Sidgwick's rejoinder would have been that with Clough, poetry had become philosophy, at least in some degree. But in any event, both Sidgwick and Arnold appreciated the need for some sort of clerisy, some vanguard of genuine educators, to teach the public the Socratic method and the merits of Clough and to blow away all the "semi-hypocrisy" poisoning the air.

Clough set him a rather stern example, the more so since Clough's resignation, like Maurice's, took place at a time when such an act carried the very real risk of an extreme diminution of one's prospects. By Sidgwick's day, change was in the air; even the self-promoting littérateur Leslie Stephen, a star of the intellectual aristocracy but no one's model of moral courage, had resigned, claiming that he could not believe in the Universal Flood. The prospect of being Saint Lawrence on "a cold grid-iron," as C. D. Broad wittily remarked, must have made Sidgwick all the more miserable, all the more apt to regard himself as a failure in the practical sphere.

Stephen did, however, give what was probably a nastily accurate picture of the situation:

The average Cambridge don of my day was (as I thought and think) a sensible and honest man who wished to be both rational and Christian. He was rational enough to see that the old orthodox position was untenable. He did not believe in Hell, or in 'verbal inspiration' or the 'real presence.' He thought that the controversies upon such matters were silly and antiquated, and spoke of them with indifference, if not with contempt. But he also thought that religious belief of some kind was necessary or valuable, and considered himself to be a genuine believer. He assumed that somehow or other the old dogmas could be explained away or 'rationalised' or 'spiritualised.' He could accept them in some sense or other, but did not ask too closely in what sense. Still less did he go into ultimate questions of philosophy. He shut his eyes to the great difficulties or took the answer for granted.[85]

This was exactly what a Cloughian could not do.

It is perhaps suggestive of Sidgwick's vacillating views during the sixties that he could announce to Dakyns in 1866 that he had "finally parted from Mill and Comte – not without tears and wailings and cuttings of the hair," and that he was an "eclectic" who believed in the "possibility of pursuing conflicting methods of mental philosophy side by side" (M 158), and then, within the space of a year, write directly to Mill, for the first time, asking his advice about subscription because "there is no one living whose opinion would be more valuable to me and to many others than yours" (CWC).[86] On the whole, of course, the latter sentiment was the more reliable, and therefore, it is all the more indicative of the importance of the subscription issue to Sidgwick that he should choose to write to Mill about this matter, above all others.

As Sidgwick puts it, in a letter dated July 28, 1867, the "subject is the position which liberals (speculatively I mean, "Aufgehlärte" of various shades) ought to take-up with regard to the traditional (in England the established) religion of the country." Sidgwick actually introduces himself as a "Cambridge Liberal," who had been urged to write to Mill by Professor Fawcett, and explains that he has a personal interest in the question, though it is also of "great social importance." The subject is also one, Sidgwick complains, on which it is "next to impossible to obtain a full and open discussion on generally accepted principles," though he would like to solve it "on principles of pure ethics, without any reference to the truth or falsity of any particular religion." This admittedly poses some difficulty, since the "orthodox cannot be brought to give any other answer than that a man should believe the truth." Sidgwick also desires "to solve it according to principles of objective, social ('utilitarian') morality," especially since

the majority of unprejudiced persons with whom I have broached the subject are satisfied to say that a man ought to act according to his conscience: whereas to me there seems to be just the same futility in referring an individual to his subjective standard, the resultant of his moral instincts and habits, on this, as on any other question of social duty.

To ask that the problem be solved may, of course, be asking too much, and Sidgwick will be happy enough if matters get more fully argued out and there is at least a clearer line between "expedient conformity and inexpedient hypocrisy."

Put more precisely, the problem concerns the varying degrees of conformity expected of clergymen or "actual teachers of religion," all other persons "who have taken definite religious tests," the general run of educators "at schools or universities belonging to particular churches whose professional career depends upon their being believed to adhere more or less stringently to a certain creed," and finally, "persons who simply take part in a form of worship." There are, Sidgwick observes, people in all of these classes in the Church of England "who do not believe in the distinctive (what would be generally called the fundamental) doctrines of that Church – but who still, from other than selfish motives, conform and conceal their opinions." The arguments on their behalf are manifold: more or less unbelieving clergymen may believe that "they are having a better influence on their flocks" than their orthodox counterparts. On the other side, more rigorist clergy may insist that their flocks should believe the prayers and creeds every bit as wholly and sincerely as they do. The related legal arguments do not actually solve anything, as long as the moral ones remain so unclear – for instance, what it would be honorable for someone not subject to legal punishment to do.

Sidgwick identified himself as being in the second group, of those who have taken definite tests, and he asked Mill to discuss the issue personally, or at least to read a statement of his on it, if possible. Mill in turn declined the invitation to meet personally, but he was generous and encouraging, and agreed to read Sidgwick's longer statement of the problem.[87] That would of course turn out to be a draft of the pamphlet on "The Ethics of Conformity and Subscription," Sidgwick's prelude to the *Methods*. As in the case of his essays on Arnold, Sidgwick bracketed his life with works on this subject; two of the central contributions to *Practical Ethics*, the last book he published during his lifetime, returned to it, and this in itself might indicate the inestimable importance of this theme in his life.

When the first pamphlet finally appeared in print, in 1870, it was rather after the fact, and after a good deal of Sidgwickian agitation. In 1867 and 1868 there had been a movement for various university reforms, including "a proposal to omit the words in the oath sworn by fellows on their election, promising conformity to the Church of England" (M 172). Sidgwick and J. Lamprière Hammond had been among the ringleaders, but their efforts were defeated at the annual meeting in December of 1868. Consequently, in June of 1869, Sidgwick at last resigned his assistant tutorship and his Fellowship, writing to his mother that "[w]hatever happens I am happy and know that I have done what was right. In fact, though I had some struggle before doing it, it now appears not the least bit of sacrifice, but simply the natural and inevitable thing to do." (M 197) He explained the case more fully to Mrs. Clough, in a letter from July of 1869:

As for my resignation and consequent prospects, you are very good to think about them. Personally I feel no doubt that I have done right. For long I have had no doubt except what arose from the fact that most of the persons whose opinion I most regard think differently. But one must at last act on one's own view. It is my painful conviction that the prevailing lax subscription is not perfectly conscientious in the case of many subscribers: and that those who subscribe laxly from the highest motives are responsible for the degradation of moral and religious feeling that others suffer. It would require very clear and evident gain of some other kind to induce me to undergo this responsibility. And such gain I do not see. Even if I make the extreme supposition that all heretics avow themselves such and are driven away from the universities, some harm would no doubt be done, but not so much as is supposed. A reaction must come soon and the universities be thrown open; meanwhile there are plenty of excellent teachers on all subjects who are genuinely orthodox; and even as regards religious speculation the passion for truth in young minds would be stimulated by such an event, and they would find plenty of sources for "illumination" even if our rushlights were put out.

All this is, of course, an unpractical supposition. I make it to show myself that I am obeying a sound general rule – I feel very strongly the importance of "providing things honest in the sight of all men." It is surely a great good that one's moral position should be one that simple-minded people can understand. I happen to care very little what men in general think of me individually: but I care very much about what they think of human nature. I dread doing anything to support the plausible suspicion that men in general, even those who profess lofty aspirations, are secretly swayed by material interests.

After all, it is odd to be finding subtle reasons for an act of mere honesty: but I am reduced to that by the refusal of my friends to recognise it as such. (M 201)

Thus, as always, Sidgwick is concerned about the general state of public morals, worrying away about egoistic hypocrisy – for why is it a "plausible suspicion" that "men in general, even those who profess lofty aspirations, are secretly swayed by material interests"? Is that not at least part of the "degradation of moral and religious feeling" that even high-minded laxity aggravates? Is he not still worried about "fire and strength" and cultivating a humanity that knows and values self-sacrifice and sympathy?

Even so, Sidgwick refrained from being too unctuous about his course. As he wrote to Dakyns, the "great, vital, productive, joy-giving qualities that I admire in others I cannot attain to: I can only lay on the altar of humanity as an offering this miserable bit of legal observance." In fact, he simply hates being "forced to condemn others . . . for not acting in the same way," although he admits that "a moral impulse must be universally-legislative: the notion of 'gratifying my own conscience' is to me self-contradictory." Even his positivism is "half-against" him – the "effect on society of maintaining the standard of veracity is sometimes so shadowy that I feel as if I was conforming to a mere 'metaphysical' formula." He has, he feels, been "under water in the depths of abstract-ethical egoistic debate," and he longs to "emerge; perhaps I shall recover the calm outward gaze, the quick helpful hand, of the lover and child of nature." (M 199–200).

Hardly a likely outcome, for a Sidgwick. Noel wrote to him: "You must feel fish-out-of-watery?"[88]

But things did turn out tolerably well. Once again, Cambridge proved to be Sidgwick's salvation. As he explained to his mother, in a letter dated June 14, 1869:

Everything is settled. The "Seniority" have offered me the post of Lecturer on Moral Sciences on 200£ a year, with the understanding that I am going to repudiate all dogmatic obligations, – I mean to resign my fellowship *because* it is held on terms of such obligations. I have also had a conversation with *Lightfoot* (whom I name *orthodox causâ*) who is very kind and understands the step as I mean it – regretting it, of course. I have been partly determined by his advice not to secede from the Church of England. I have no wish to do that, as long as orthodox persons of a reasonable sort – I mean persons who really do accept the "Apostles Creed" and yet are not bigots – have no wish that I should secede from it. I think that as "*Apostles Creed*" is used in Baptism and Confirmation, I am *primâ facie* supposed to accept it, and ought not to claim the social privileges of a member of the Church against the wish of the mass of reasonable persons in it. At the same time I do not think one is bound to regard the creed that is necessary for admission as meaning for *bonâ fide membership* afterwards, if reasonable orthodox persons do not so regard it. And my wish is to show myself as sympathetic as possible to the national religion, while declining to profess agreement with it's doctrines. (CWC)

This decision on the part of the "Seniority," which must have included Maurice, allowed Sidgwick to carry on in his familiar life, though with some reduction in income. And the counsel of Bishop Lightfoot allowed him to carry on some semblance of his church affiliation. Here, of course, one sees the careful gradations of duty according to role. The standard of veracity for laity and that for clergy or those taking definite tests are not necessarily the same thing. If Lightfoot held that the Apostles' Creed was "not dogmatically obligatory on laymen," then that was the reasonable view (M 198). The balance of considerations involved in showing his sympathy for the national religion while declining to profess it is perhaps what would have been expected, given his rationalist tendencies hedged by skepticism. Some lines from Tennyson apparently caught his mood: "Yet pull not down my minster towers, that were / So gravely, gloriously

wrought; / Perchance I may return with others there / When I have
cleared my thought" (M 202).

VIII. The Ethics of Conformity and Subscription

I have written a pamphlet... which will perhaps be printed – on the text, 'Let
every man be fully persuaded in his own mind.' That is really the gist of the
pamphlet – that if the preachers of religion wish to retain their hold over educated
men they must show in their utterances on sacred occasions the same sincerity,
exactness, unreserve, that men of science show in expounding the laws of nature.
I do not think that much good is to be done by saying this, but I want to liberate
my soul, and then ever after hold my peace.

                              Sidgwick to his sister, Mary, April 1870 (M 226)

What were the actual consequences of Sidgwick's resignation? How
accurate was his assessment of the situation? How, exactly, did his struggle with the question of subscription lead him through the thinking expounded in *The Methods of Ethics*? Was this episode really as significant
as he seemed to think? Was it the culmination of his years of storm and
stress?

These are difficult questions, but in the final analysis, there appears to
be little reason to doubt the veracity of Sidgwick's estimate of these matters. The themes and problematics of his resignation crisis, the anxieties
over egoism and hypocrisy, would reverberate and replay themselves in his
later life and work, forming a turbulent subcurrent running beneath his
cautious reformism and weighty academic efforts to gauge just what the
British public might be ripe for. Once one reads such works as the *Methods*
and the *Elements of Politics* bearing in mind Sidgwick's profound commitment to avoiding the rupture of common sense and common religion –
the importance, for him, of instigating social change only from a platform
firmly planted in the realities of the present (or of at least masking the call
for change by an appeal to what we all think) – it becomes very difficult
to resist the thought that his formative period formed him for a very long
time to come. The Apostolic virtues of the discussion group must allow
the interplay of speaker and hearer, proceeding (ideally, anyway) from
an empathetic grasp of the views of one's partners. In a very real sense,
Sidgwick wanted to regard the larger public as a conversational partner, albeit one he could come to understand and guide, educate, without
offending.[89]

A good way to appreciate the position Sidgwick had reached in the late sixties is by attending closely to his pamphlet on "The Ethics of Conformity and Subscription." It was a profoundly Cloughian piece of work, replete with all the anxieties of an anxious age, but also with a certain fearless zest – the liberation of a soul that had been long pent up.

"Conformity and Subscription" certainly conveys Sidgwick's sense that the Cloughian age had come. He is impressed by the "large strides" that have been made "towards complete civil and social equality of creeds" and thinks the "secular disadvantages that religious dissidences formerly entailed, have been so rapidly diminishing, that we may look forward confidently to their speedy exinction." Thus, we "have abolished church rates; we are inaugurating a system of primary education, which is, at any rate, designed to place all sects, as far as possible, on a par; and it is obvious that the ecclesiastical restrictions on the higher education cannot be much longer maintained." (CS 10)

Most importantly, Sidgwick is persuaded that "on the whole, the recognition of the necessity of free inquiry, and of the possibility of conscientious difference of opinion, almost without limit, is so general, that most of my readers will be prepared to discuss the question on the neutral ground of ethics." Indeed, the "effort to unite cordially with Dissenters, wherever such union is possible, has ceased to be the differencing characteristic of one party in the Church of England; and it is but rarely that a conformist dares to avow in public any sentiment but respect for conscientious non-conformity." Even those fighting "for the relics of Anglican privilege" have given up grave admonitions concerning schism, offering instead "voluble and pathetic appeals to 'our common Christianity'." (CS 6, 7) All this toleration is not "the mere drapery of enlightened unbelief" or a mere "external compromise," but is in fact deeply rooted in

the present tendencies of religious thought; and not of religious thought only, but of all thought on subjects where first principles and method are as yet indeterminate, and where therefore persons of equal intelligence, sincerity, and application, are continually led to the most profoundly diverse conclusions. Controversies on such subjects are carried on, not perhaps less keenly than before, but more fairly, temperately, and dispassionately, with more mutual understanding, and, we may almost say, mutual interest, in the conflicting opinions. This tempered dogmatism must be carefully distinguished from the superficial eclecticism that sometimes results from the same causes, the state of mind that prides itself on holding no form of creed in particular, but combining the best parts of all: this latter is not, I think, peculiarly characteristic of the present age; what I am noticing is the habit of holding opinions firmly and earnestly, and yet, as it were, at arm's length, of seeing how they look when viewed on the outside, and divining by analogy how the opinions of others look when viewed on the inside. A dogmatist of this temper has a natural respect for, even a spontaneous sympathy with, any one who holds any creed with consistency, clearness, and sincerity. Accordingly, one result of this increase of real internal toleration on the part of dogmatists, is to encourage much greater openness and unreserve on the part of heretics of all kinds and degrees. This openness is sometimes deplored by ecclesiastical writers and speakers, but in the present strained relations of intellectual culture and religious faith, the most fatal mistake that can be made in the interests of the latter, next to that of discouraging theological inquiry as sinful, is to discourage the expression of theological disagreement as unedifying. It would be a great gain to religion if preachers would abandon all idea of restricting inquiry and discussion, and confine themselves entirely (in so far as they deal with the question) to improving the method of inquiry, and elevating the manner of the discussion. (CS 12–13)

All this was profoundly heartfelt, of course, though it strikes a slightly more optimistic note than the earlier letter to Mill. The direction of the times is here made to sound highly Apostolic, as the flowering of Socratic discussion conjoined with sympathy. But of course, unlike Arnold, Sidgwick gives this cultural change a certain modernist cast: "this frankness, even audacity, in theological investigation and discussion, is rendered especially necessary by a fact, the influence of which upon theology is often noticed, although not quite from this point of view – I mean the increasing predominance of positive science as an element of our highest intellectual culture." Sidgwick does not agree with those who hold that for those of a scientific bent, "theology must inevitably become more and more shadowy and unreal, and its interminable debates more and more distasteful." Perhaps he had psychical research in mind, as well as Darwin, when he continued by suggesting "that the scientific inquiries which are most eagerly pursued, and excite the keenest interest in lookers-on, are precisely those where the method is least determinate, the reasonings most hypothetical, and the conclusions most disputable." But the crucial point is that

What theology has to learn from the predominant studies of the age is something very different from advice as to its method or estimates of its utility; it is the imperative necessity of accepting unreservedly the conditions of life under which these studies live and flourish. It is sometimes said that we live in an age that rejects authority. The statement, thus qualified, seems misleading; probably there never was a time when the number of beliefs held by each individual, undemonstrated and unverified by himself, was greater. But it is true that we only accept authority of a particular sort; the authority, namely, that is formed and maintained by the unconstrained agreement of individual thinkers, each of whom we believe to be seeking truth with single-mindedness and sincerity, and declaring what he has found with scrupulous veracity, and the greatest attainable exactness and precision. (CS 14–15)

This careful statement, at once so sensitive to the complexities of large-scale modern societies and so insistent on the Socratic virtues at work in scientific practice and public debate, beautifully encapsulates Sidgwick's hopes for the direction of modern culture.[90] The tone irresistibly recalls Dewey's claim that the "the traits of good method are straightforwardness, flexible intellectual interest or open-minded will to learn, integrity of purpose, and acceptance of responsibility for the consequences of one's activities including thought."[91] For Sidgwick, it is pointless for theologians to dwell "on the imbecility of the inquisitive intellect" or "the inadequacy of language to express profound mysteries" – for clearly, "the exceptional protection that has been claimed for theological truth is a fatal privilege." It is a plain fact that "the divergence of religious beliefs, conscientiously entertained by educated persons, is great, is increasing, and shows no symptom of diminution."[92] The (highly Apostolic) question, then, is how to feel that same security that we feel with respect to science in connection with religious inquiry: namely, "that our teacher is declaring to us truth precisely as it appears to him, without reserve or qualification." And from this, to ask: how are we to organize "religious instruction, and combine in a common formula of worship?" (CS 15–16)

Here, of course, we confront the specific problem of subscription, the different grades of expected conformity, and so on, a problem made all the more poignant by the demand for free and open inquiry. After all, Sidgwick argues, consider the potentially excruciating position of an "intelligent and promising young clergyman." Suppose, in keeping with the standard of modern inquiry, "we impress on him the need which the Church has of a learned clergy; we bid him read, study, investigate; we encourage him (as his better nature prompts him) to respect learning and sincerity wherever he finds them, and to weigh arguments with the single desire to be convinced of the truth." But then, of course, we inform him, that if Truth should appear to him to lie anywhere below a certain line drawn rather high up in the scale, honour and duty call upon him to withdraw from his ministerial functions, resign the prospects of his career, uproot himself from a position where he may feel that his means of exercising good are daily growing, allow his acquired faculties of special work to become useless, and, amid the distress of his friends and kindred, with his abandoned profession hanging like a weight round his neck, endeavour, late in life, to learn some new work by which he may live.

Even if such a person was quite thoroughly orthodox when ordained, how could he be confident that further study would raise no doubts? Who would go into the business on such conditions? As Sidgwick pointedly remarks, "No one will venture to be ordained except those who are too fanatical or too stupid to doubt that they will always believe exactly what they believed at twenty-three" (CS 37–38). And how much good will they do the church or, for that matter, society? How can education be translated into an ongoing process of educating?

Here lies the more specific difficulty that especially troubles Sidgwick: what is

the duty which the persons who form the progressive – or, to use a neutral term, the deviating – element in a religious community owe to the rest of that community; the extent to which, and the manner in which, they ought to give expression and effect to their opinions within the community; and the point at which the higher interests of truth force them to the disruption of old ties and cherished associations. (CS 5)

How, given his sympathetic portrayal of the plight of the intelligent young clergyman, could Sidgwick take such a rigorist line concerning the evils of hypocrisy and the degradation of popular religious and moral feeling? After all, he had insisted that even those in his own position, those taking definite religious oaths, ought to resign rather than serve under such conditions. Would not the same standard, or an even more stringent one, apply to the actual teachers of religion?

The firm Cloughian was clear that it did, hard as such self-sacrifice was to live with. His main point is that it is damaging in the extreme to pretend that the clergy should maintain an esoteric standard, different from the common understandings, that would leave them open to the charge of "solemn imposture." Thus, "we look to the clergy to maintain the standard of, at any rate, the peaceful virtues; and . . . it is a serious blow to the spiritual interests of the country, that any considerable and respectable section of them should be charged with habitual unveracity and be unable to refute the charge." Admittedly, given the state of society, it would be painful to always insist on such veracity, but the solution is to proceed "by openly relaxing the engagements, not by secretly tampering with their obligation" – and it is essential to do this openly, since no one will "take a strong interest in grievances by which no one will declare himself aggrieved." (CS 37, 9) Still, the clergy must meet a higher standard than the laity. Consider again the problem of the Virgin Birth:

A man may certainly be a sincere Christian in the strictest sense – that is, he may believe that Jesus was God – without holding this belief. Many persons now take an intermediate view of miracles between accepting and rejecting them *en bloc*. They hold that miracles may occur, and that some recorded in the Gospels undoubtedly did occur; but that also legends may have been mixed up with the evangelical narrations, and that some probably have been. A man who holds this general view is very likely to reject the miraculous conception of Jesus. . . . Now, to him, this rejection may appear of no religious importance; it may even seem to him unreasonable that men should make their view of Christ's character and function to depend upon the nature of his conception. Still, to the majority of Christians, the belief is so important – the gulf that divides those who hold it from those who reject it seems so great, that the confidence of a congregation in the veracity of their minister would be entirely ruined, if he avowed his disbelief in this doctrine and still continued to recite the Creed. And it seems to me, that a man who acts thus, can only justify himself by proving the most grave and urgent social necessity for his conduct. (CS 33)

Clearly, this is what Sidgwick had in mind by way of the dangerous degradation of moral and religious feeling that lax subscription fostered – even the lax subscription of someone such as himself, a mere taker of definite oaths. In fact, even as regards the laity, he goes so far as to suggest that it is important to strive to approximate the ideal of a national ministry and form of genuine worship, and that the only way this could possibly be accomplished is through "the frank and firm avowal, on all proper occasions, on the part of the laity, of all serious and deliberate doctrinal disagreement with any portion of the service" (CS 24–25). This, however, seems to have been a standard from which he exempted himself, as we shall see in due course.

One might forgive Sidgwick for worrying, as he did, that the calculation of consequences that he carried out in the case of subscription was indeed rather "shadowy." (As it would transpire, the vast uncertainty attending such calculations would be another major theme of the *Methods*, much to Sidgwick's chagrin.) But in a famous article, "Sidgwick and Whewellian Intuitionism: Some Dilemmas," Alan Donagan went so far as to deny that Sidgwick's words and deeds were at all genuinely utilitarian, or even effective on behalf of his cause. Thus,

> In none of these transactions is there the slightest breath of utilitarianism. In *The Ethics of Conformity and Subscription*, Sidgwick closely followed Whewell's application of the nonutilitarian principle of truth. And, to judge by the reasons he gave in his correspondence, he likewise acted on Whewellian grounds in resigning his fellowship. Both in acting, and in defending his action, utilitarian considerations appear to have entered his mind only to be dismissed. Yet of none of this are there any traces in *The Methods of Ethics*.[93]

Donagan was himself a true Whewellian, and one is tempted to say that that may help to explain why he was wrong on all counts. Sidgwick himself was quite clear, in writing to Mill, that he wanted to solve the problem of subscription in a utilitarian way, and if one misses the way in which his solution is in keeping with his utilitarianism, that may be because one is working with an inadequate notion of utilitarianism – as, it seems, was Donagan.[94] For as Schneewind has explained, Sidgwick's pamphlet anticipates his later views in several ways. First, he "insists on answering questions about practice in terms of realistic appraisals of the facts and the probabilities. He does not sketch an ideal church or an ideal society and ask how we can obtain guidance from considering it." Second, he "fails to find any clear common-sense maxims which both relate specifically to the ethical issue concerning him and direct us to a definite solution to it. There is a duty of veracity; there are duties of fidelity to one's chosen church; but there is no principle of similar scope which tells us what to do when these two sets of duties conflict." And finally, the "difficulties are resolved, in each case, by an appeal to what is expedient or useful or least harmful – by an appeal, in short, to some form of the utilitarian principle."[95]

This seems right. Schneewind is of course happy to concede – indeed, even to argue at length – that Sidgwick learned a tremendous amount from Whewell, who was the master of Trinity when Sidgwick arrived there, and whose work on moral philosophy was – much to Sidgwick's dismay – part of the established curriculum. But the dual conviction that all "our rules are imperfect" and that even so "we must not discard the props which we have in our conceptions . . . of Truth, Justice &c." had been, through the sixties, as close to a constant as Sidgwick could muster. Sidgwick would have been the first to agree that the calculation of consequences in cases such as this is a very hard thing to carry off with any plausibility; but, as with Mill, he would have denied that there was any real alternative to trying, or that Whewell himself had effectively circumvented the problem.

However, these are arguments that quickly lead to the heart of Sidgwick's ethical theory, and they are better considered in connection with the *Methods*, the subject of the following chapter. At this juncture, the foregoing sketch of the common ground between Sidgwick's pamphlet and his magnum opus should be sufficient to suggest how he could have worked out the lines of the latter in connection with the problem posed in the former. Those who doubt the connection between these works, or the utilitarian nature of that connection, ought to be given some pause by the fact that Mill himself weighed in on Sidgwick's side, and this even though he was well known for advising dissenting young clergymen to reform the church from within, rather than leaving it in the hands of the more reactionary elements. Although Sidgwick expressed a certain disappointment with Mill's response to his pamphlet, apparently thinking it a little too perfunctory in light of his great crisis, the truth is that Mill was warmly appreciative of Sidgwick's efforts, even giving him a bit of sage advice that tacitly suggested considerable confidence in Sidgwick's utilitarian potential:

What ought to be the exceptions (for that there ought to be some, however few, exceptions seems to be admitted) to the general duty of truth? This large question has never yet been treated in a way at once rational and comprehensive, partly because people have been afraid to meddle with it, and partly because mankind have never yet generally admitted that the effect which actions tend to produce on human happiness is what constitutes them right or wrong. I would suggest that you should turn your thoughts to this more comprehensive subject.[96]

This Sidgwick did, and the result was *The Methods of Ethics* and what would turn out to be a lifelong engagement with matters of hypocrisy and integrity. The destiny that awaited him was an eternal struggle with the problems of this turbulent decade: self-cultivation versus self-sacrifice, skepticism versus belief, sympathetic unity versus conflictual difference, and the private versus the public.

Before moving on to the *Methods*, however, mention should be made of a few other consequences that flowed from the Cloughian act of Sidgwick's utilitarian conscience. Against Donagan, it must be said that there are excellent reasons for sharing the view of so many of Sidgwick's peers – that his resignation, the action of a high-minded man of spotless reputation and academic credentials, did have an important effect in speeding the abolition of the educational tests. Donagan too hastily follows the somewhat dismissive account in Winstanley's *Later Victorian Cambridge*, suggesting that, as Sidgwick himself insisted, change was already very much in the air and the elimination of the tests inevitable.[97] But what Sidgwick's more knowing champions appear to have recognized was that Sidgwick's act had a disproportionate impact on Prime Minister Gladstone, who, although he had already unsuccessfully opposed the tests, would have been given a considerable boost in his efforts by Sidgwick's example. Gladstone had for some time held Sidgwick in very high esteem.[98]

Another, somewhat personalized consequence of Sidgwick's resignation is recorded in the *Memoir*:

Sidgwick threw himself heartily into the establishment by the University of an examination for women. The examination was first held in the summer of 1869, and he was one of the examiners. The establishment of this examination was an outcome of the active movement going on at the time in different parts of the country for providing women with improved educational opportunities – a movement the crying need for which was emphasised by the report of the Schools Inquiry Commission in 1869, and the very unsatisfactory state of girls' and women's education therein revealed. The demand was not for examination only, and schemes for instruction by course of lectures and classes were being tried in various places. Sidgwick had had his thoughts turned in a general way to the subject of the education of women by the writings of J. S. Mill, and doubtless also by F. D. Maurice, whose interest in it is well known, and who was . . . at this time Professor of Moral Philosophy at Cambridge. But his taking it up actively at this particular moment was partly due to a need which he felt of doing some practically useful work. What he did in giving up his Fellowship was negative, and he wanted to do something positive. (M 204–5)

This play of negative and positive action, or at least Sidgwick's sense of it, was destined to become one of the major aftereffects of his resignation crisis, figuring time and again, in one guise or another, in his theoretical and practical ethics. He would continue to worry about the duties incumbent on him in his academic role, especially when it seemed that his experiments in ethics and intuitive theism were driving him to decidedly uncomfortable conclusions. And his casuistical doubts concerning hypocrisy would influence and intertwine with those of many of his friends.[99] He would continue to strive to balance the active and the passive tendencies in his life, refusing, like a good Rugbyean, to become "antipractical" even when it was obscure in the extreme just what practicality demanded. After all, nothing we have considered so far suggests that he had answered that most fundamental of questions: why be moral at all? It may well be that Sidgwick did go further than any previous utilitarian in assimilating Kantian considerations – positive versus negative actions, acts versus omissions – within a broadly utilitarian framework, and that this is the reason why critics such as Donagan have found it so hard to make sense of him. But there was much more to him than closet Kantianism.

Truth to tell, although what follows will be much taken up with the details of Sidgwick's past and present philosophical reception, his philosophical reception, both past and present, leaves a lot out of the picture. The year 1867 was a singular one for Sidgwick not only because he then made direct contact with Mill, but also because that year brought him into an intimate friendship with Symonds, who would eventually prove to be the most intellectually probing and emotionally troubling of all his closest friends. Although he had known Symonds distantly for quite a few years, he had not been part of his inner circle, of which, however, his younger brother Arthur was a fixture. But in a letter of July 7, 1867, Symonds wrote to Dakyns: "Henry Sidgwick has been with me a week. He is numbered among mine."[100]

Now Sidgwick would have to contend with a prophet of culture who was as critical as Mill, as contemplative as Clough, and as classical as Arnold and Jowett, but who actually had something important to say about sex. The problem of hypocrisy now wore a new mask. With the private life of John Addington Symonds, the public sphere would never be the same. And neither would the Platonic revival.

But the discussion of Sidgwick and Symonds must come after discussion of philosophical ethics and ghosts – two Sidgwickian priorities that were more highly visible to the educated public.

4

Consensus versus Chaos

Part I. Consensus

But just as the scientific discoverer must not follow his own whims and fancies but earnestly seek truth, so it is not the man who abandons himself to impulse, but the man who, against mere impulse and mere convention alike, seeks and does what is Right who will really lead mankind to the truer way, to richer and fuller and more profoundly harmonious life. My ideal is a law infinitely constraining and yet infinitely flexible, not prescribing perhaps for any two men the same conduct, and yet the same law, because recognised by all as objective, and always varying on rational and therefore general grounds, 'the same,' as Cicero says, 'for you and for me, here and at Athens, now and for ever.'

Sidgwick to Roden Noel, 1871 (M 243)

Or would it not be absurd to strain every nerve to attain to the utmost precision and clarity of knowledge about other things of trifling moment and not to demand the greatest precision for the greatest matters?

Plato, Republic, 504 E (the epigraph to The Methods of Ethics)

Mr. Henry Sidgwick has recently published a book which, apart from its intrinsic value, is an interesting display of rare intellectual virtues. He almost seems to illustrate a paradox which would be after his own heart, that a man may be too reasonable.

Leslie Stephen, "Sidgwick's Methods of Ethics"[1]

I. A Great Work

Clearly, Sidgwick counted the problems of ethics, especially the problem of egoistic self-regard, among the "deepest problems of human life." And to his dismay, what his years of storm and stress had brought home to him was not only the intractability of the theological questions he had set himself, but also, relatedly, the potential insolubility of the fundamental problems of ethics. "Self-sacrifice" was the deepest of deep problems. Was his utilitarian conscience too demanding?

As we have seen, it had been a most difficult period, during which his private, Apostolic soul searching had ultimately led to a very public engagement with the problem of saying what one meant and backing it up with deeds – in effect, a self-sacrificing attempt to inject more conversational Socratic candor into the formulas of public discourse. Educational institutions, potentially so important for social change, ought not to require systematic dishonesty, rendering public morality a contemptible sham in the eyes of earnest and intelligent youth. Again, laxness, not philosophy, was the corrupting force, and self-sacrifice, not self-perfection, was the answer.

But this was modern England, not ancient Athens. In so many ways, Sidgwick was obviously a child of his times, obsessed with the crisis of religious faith and the correlative problem of hypocrisy. From Maurice and Clough to Stephen and Sidgwick, the spirit of the age had been inexorably working toward the day of Darwin and doubt, of democracy and – it was feared – decadence. If Sidgwick struggled harder and thought more critically than most, he was nonetheless within the current that would in due course be producing Nietzschean reverberations throughout the modernist worldview.[2] And indeed, many have wondered just how positive Sidgwick's views had become, following his turbulent decade.

True, he had acted with resolve and straightforwardness in resigning his position. But this had come after years of experimentalizing and hesitation, when he had been more inclined to say: "I sometimes think again of resigning. I am so bankrupt of most things men desire, I would at least have a sort of savings bank pittance of honesty. But perhaps this very impulse is only another form of Protean vacillation and purposelessness." (M 142) And besides, his action admittedly sprang from a religious and ethical stance that was largely agnostic, a suspension of final judgment until the process of inquiry had been carried much further than he had been able to carry it. He did, to be sure, want to show that doubt did not necessitate a falling off of moral standards. And, as Chadwick has put it, he

was also sure that in a land where religion and morality were inseparable, the decline of the one was certain to lead to the decline of the other. He would never attack religion lest he injure the society in which he lived. It even became a delicate question of conscience for him how far it could be right to speak out; he must say what he thought if he were asked, and yet he must not trample upon the scruples of others.[3]

But in none of this is there a demonstration that the best account of morality is utilitarianism and that there are conclusive reasons for acting according to its dictates.

Consequently, if one turns to *The Methods of Ethics* hoping to find the big answers to the big questions, one will probably come away disappointed. Better to expect from Sidgwick only that judiciousness that his "true" self could wrest from his highly Socratic, skeptical intellect. To be sure, this skepticism is not merely critical or destructive, much less Cartesian, but more of a pervasive sense of fallibilism, admitting both the limitations of human knowledge and the demands of practical action. Curiously enough, this turn of mind was very happily captured in Sidgwick's presidential address to the Economic Section of the British Association, in 1885:

Really, in this as in other departments, my tendency is to scepticism, but scepticism of a humble, empirical, and more or less hopeful kind. I do not argue, or even think, that nothing is known, still less that nothing can be known by the received methods, but that of what is most important to know we, as yet, know much less than most people suppose. (CWC)

Or, as he would often put it, he had a terrific faith in "Things in General," even if not much faith in any belief in particular. This was a very Socratic faith indeed, by his very own account. But it was, to Sidgwick's mind, more of a "working philosophy" than a "fighting faith."

If one turns to the *Methods* in this spirit, one can hardly come away disappointed, though it is perhaps by now evident that for his part, Sidgwick threw himself into the work with higher expectations. His wild mood swings during the sixties, when he would soar high and then sink low, reflected the vastness of the task he had set himself. As he wrote to Dakyns, in 1865: "I have kept silence even from good words because I have found out nothing yet, either ἰδίᾳ or κοινῇ συμφέρον. I seem on the verge ever of discovering the secret of life, but perhaps I am like the rustic of Horace and the turbid stream of doubt & debate flows & will flow." (M 127)[4] One might say that he was reduced to "scepticism of a humble, empirical, and more or less hopeful kind," after having given himself over to a much grander hope – one that would periodically return to haunt him in later life, even after he had cultivated a more becoming sense of patience. The epigraph from Plato is telling, as is the fact that he had originally planned to use a second epigraph, drawn from Descartes: "Ils élevent fort haut la vertu, mais ils n'enseignent pas assez à la connaître" (CWC).[5]

This pairing of Plato and Descartes, the two finest examples of what Dewey termed the philosophical quest for certainty, ought to suggest the degree of ambition that the younger Sidgwick brought to the "deepest problems," in ethics as in theology. Perhaps, too, it was frustrated ambition that led him to retain the more moderate passage from Plato while dropping the one from Descartes. Sidgwick, at least, was only too ready to pronounce his work a failure. In a famous story, related to F. H. Hayward by Oscar Browning, Browning told of his encounter with Sidgwick shortly after he had completed the *Methods*; pointing to his manuscript, Sidgwick sadly observed: "I have long wished and intended to write a work on Ethics. Now it is written. I have adhered to a plan I laid out for myself; its first word was to be 'Ethics,' its last word 'Failure.'" As Hayward comments, the "word 'Failure' disappeared from the second and succeeding editions, but I doubt whether Sidgwick ever acquired a faith in the possibility of a perfectly satisfactory ethical system."[6]

But this sense of failure was only the inevitable result of having aimed at the stars. One can scarcely resist the thought that he considered himself on a mission from Mill, and as a potential heir to Mill's role. How odd that the *Methods* should finally see the light just after Mill's death. Of the latter, Sidgwick had written to Charles Henry Pearson, in a letter dated May 10, 1873:

> I cannot go on – Mill is dead! – I wonder if this news will have affected you at all as it does me. . . . 'Vive le roi' – but I do not know who it is to be: most of my friends say Herbert Spencer – if so I am a rebel. At Oxford I hear much of Hegelians, but they have not made up their minds to say anything yet.[7]

Sidgwick also had some instructive reflections on the spirit of the age, thoughts that, in more guarded form, he also put into a short obituary notice of Mill.[8] He recognized that "Mill's prestige has been declining lately: partly from the cause to which most people attribute it – the public exhibition of his Radicalism, but partly to the natural termination of his philosophical reign, which was of the kind to be naturally early and brief." At Oxford, the reaction was "going too far," but still, the change had come: "from 1860–1865 or thereabouts he ruled England in the region of thought as very few men ever did: I do not expect to see anything like it again."[9] Still, one detects in such remarks certain aspirations, a sense that the reaction must be kept from going too far, though also that this cause may be ill served by public exhibitions of one's radicalism. Among the academic liberals, Sidgwick was a likely claimant to the Millian mantle, though such rivals as Leslie Stephen – a mere littérateur, according to Sidgwick – might have disputed this. But of course, *the Book* had yet to appear, and as Jowett had once nastily observed, "One man is as good as another until he has written a book."[10]

Certainly, as we have seen, Sidgwick's book was long in the making. His interest in utilitarianism – encompassing ethics, politics, and political economy – dated back to his Apostolic days. The record of his ethical doubts is as long as the record of his theological ones, with which it was intertwined. His diary and commonplace book are replete with accounts of his struggle to find in Mill and Comte the culmination of the Christian moral vision, and his correspondence from the sixties suggests that however powerfully he was distracted by his forays into historical biblical criticism or by the urgency of sorting out his duty, the questions of ethics were at no point absent from his mind. Much as he vacillated, and much as he was intermittently smitten with the ancient Greeks or with the "Selfish Philosophy," the trend of his thought was clear enough – toward altruism and self-sacrifice.

Thus, in 1862, he informs Dakyns that he is "revolving a Theory of Ethics" and that he thinks he sees "a reconciliation between the moral sense and utilitarian theories" (M 75). He also starts telling people, only half-facetiously, that he is "engaged on a Great Work," though he confesses to Dakyns that he has not "advanced much" in his "Reconciliation of Ethical Systems." Not surprisingly, the big stumbling block is egoistic self-regard, or, on the other side, how to justify self-sacrifice. He complains that "Bain is the only thoroughly honest Utilitarian philosopher I know, and he allows self-sacrifice and τὰ ἐχόμενα to constitute a 'glorious paradox,' whereas Comte and all practical Utilitarians exalt the same sentiments into the supreme Rule of life" (M 77–78).[11] Thus he writes, in a letter forecasting much of what was to come:

You know I want intuitions for Morality; at least one (of Love) is required to supplement the utilitarian morality, and I do not see why, if we are to have one, we may not have others. I have worked away vigorously at the selfish morality, but I cannot persuade myself, except by trusting intuition, that Christian self-sacrifice is really a happier life than classical insouciance. . . . That is, the question seems to me an open one. The effort to attain the Christian ideal may be a life-long painful struggle; and therefore, though I may believe this ideal when realised productive of greater happiness, yet individually (if it is not a question of life or death) my laxness would induce me to prefer a lower, more attainable Goethean ideal. Intuitions turn the scale. I shall probably fall away from Mill and Co. for a phase. (M 90)

By 1864, Sidgwick's Great Work is tentatively entitled "Eudaemonism Restated," but it is causing him no end of problems. Haunted by his Mauricean conscience, he writes: "I will hope for any amount of religious and moral development, but I will not stir a finger to compress the world into a system, and it does not at present seem as if it was going to harmonize itself without compression" (M 108). Soon he is calling for the experiments in ethics and intuitive theism – often of a highly personal nature – that the world must fall back on, and even avowing that "life is more than any study. . . . Every soul has a right to live; let *das Individuum* 'get its sop and hold its noise'; you see, I believe that enlightened egoism will always put a limit to itself." (M 124) In November of 1865, he writes to Dakyns: "The hard shell of Epicureanism (in the best sense, I hope) has grown round me. I feel sometimes as if it were an extraneous adjunct – but I could not live without it now probably. I believe in Selfish Ethics; and politics founded on self-interest well-understood – and more and more I believe in nothing else." (CWC) But he does not believe it long.

In February of 1867, he reads a paper to the Grote Club – the faculty discussion group organized around the person of John Grote, Maurice's immediate predecessor as Knightbridge Professor – in which he sketches out his division of ethical methods. According to the notes of fellow Grote Club member Alfred Marshall,

S read a long & general sketch of the various systems of morality. I. Absolute right II Make yourself noble III Make yourself happy IV Increase the general happiness. In the course of it he committed himself to the statement that without appreciating the effect of our action on the happiness of ourselves or of others we could have no idea of right & wrong.

Other notes from various of these meetings report how Sidgwick identified himself as a utilitarian, fought to get Bentham and Mill included in the curriculum, and attacked Whewell's "dogmatism & freespokenness" – that is, the way in which he would "put down whatever came into his head without troubling himself to connect it with what came before or give reasons first."[12]

Such remarks are more instructive than one would initially suspect. An excellent way to approach the *Methods* is by reading it, as Schneewind has done, in the light of the great conflicts between Mill, the romanticized utilitarian, and Whewell, the intuitionist defender of orthodoxy whom Mill himself singled out as representing just about everything that utilitarianism should oppose. Bring to this Sidgwick's anxieties about self-sacrifice and the varieties of egoism – including the classical Greek variant, "make yourself noble" – and one has the main conflicting elements that Sidgwick struggled to harmonize in the *Methods*. In fact, for the rest of his life, through the five (and a half) editions of the book that he completed, Sidgwick would be rethinking his short list of the going "methods," mainly by showing how some new contender – say, Idealism – could be assimilated to his architectonic. The *Methods* represented not only a rearguard defense of the Millian legacy against the old intuitionist opponents, but also some preemptive maneuvers against the emerging Idealist and evolutionist perspectives.

On this score, it is also important to reiterate that, great as the influence of Mill was on both Sidgwick's times and Sidgwick, the disciple had always harbored certain misgivings about the master. This was true from the very start. Again, as the "Autobiographical Fragment" records, even when Sidgwick, the newly minted Fellow, began the "more or less systematic study of philosophy, in the form of a study of J. S. Mill's works," he was aware that

the nature of his philosophy – the attitude it took up towards the fundamental questions as to the nature of man and his relation to God and the universe – was not such as to encourage me to expect from philosophy decisive positive answers to these questions, and I was by no means then disposed to acquiesce in negative or agnostic answers. In fact I had not in any way broken with the orthodox Christianity in which I had been brought up, though I had become sceptical with regard to many of its conclusions, and generally with regard to its methods of proof. (M 36)

Hence, of course, the years of storm and stress, biblical criticism, and so forth. When Sidgwick joined in founding the (short-lived) Free Christian

Union, in June of 1868, the express object of the society was to recognize how Christians "in vain pursuit of Orthodoxy, have parted into rival Churches, and lost the bond of common work and love" and to invite "to common action all who deem men responsible, not for the attainment of Divine truth, but only for the serious search for it," relying "for the religious improvement of human life, on filial Piety and brotherly Charity, with or without more particular agreement in matters of doctrinal theology" (M 190).

On this count, the master, it must be said, would also have had serious misgivings about the disciple. However much Sidgwick's evolution was in the direction of Millian agnostic hope, and however much he appreciated Mill's guarded respect for the religious impulse, he was always more troubled than Mill by certain possibilities for the "religion of the future." In his brilliant essays on "The Utility of Religion" and "Theism," Mill had poured buckets of cold water on the idea that religion as such, as opposed to early education and public opinion generally, plays anything like the key social role that many (figures such as Sidgwick) were apt to attribute to it. Mill even went so far as to suggest that it was

not only possible but probable, that in a higher, and, above all, a happier condition of human life, not annihilation but immortality may be the burdensome idea; and that human nature, though pleased with the present, and by no means impatient to quit it, would find comfort and not sadness in the thought that it is not chained through eternity to a conscious existence which it cannot be assured that it will always wish to preserve.[13]

This line of criticism – which Sidgwick found nearly impossible to assimilate, try as he might – will be developed more fully in connection with Sidgwick's parapsychology and the account of Symonds, who shared Mill's view, but it is an important qualification to keep in mind when thinking of Sidgwick as a Millian.

Still, by way of anticipation, it should be said that Sidgwick was as much fascinated with the supposed "religion of the future" as he was frightened by it, and in his struggles with his true self versus his Millian conscience one finds a thousand intimations of what was to come, with Symonds and Carpenter, Russell and Moore, and Bloomsbury. For between Mill, Maurice, and the Apostles, Sidgwick had learned the ethical and epistemological significance of intimate friendship – the school of sympathy that was to take the place of orthodox Christianity even if theism were vindicated, but especially if it were not. Indeed, friendship was the great sustaining element, philosophically and personally, as he struggled to finish the *Methods*. In a letter of March 7, 1872, he wrote to Dakyns: "I feel often as unrelated and unadapted to my universe as man can feel: except on the one side of friendship: and there, in my deepest gloom all seems strangely good: and you among the best. . . . But 'golden news' expect none unless I light perchance on the Secret of the Universe, in which case I will let you know." (M 259)[14] And in a most moving bit of introspection, concerning the painful period of December 1867, when, among other calamities, his close friend Cowell had died, Sidgwick wrote to Oscar Browning: "How such a loss makes the days seem irrevocable when we made friendships without knowing what they were worth. Well, if life teaches one that it is some compensation for other losses." (M 178)[15]

Thought and feeling, the universal and the particular, humanity in general and one's own circle of attachments, self-sacrifice and self-perfection – these were apparent conflicts that fueled the search for reconciliation and unity, generative tensions that held out prospects for a future in which comradeship would, at least to some degree, fill the void left by orthodox religion. The years of storm and stress were also years of intense fellowship that would put an Apostolic stamp on the *Methods* that even Sidgwick's dry judicious style could not cover up. Needless to say, reconciliation was not always forthcoming, and the esoteric pursuit of truth often sat uneasily with the real world of politics, the more so given how Sidgwick always managed to turn supposedly tough-minded utilitarian calculation into studied reflectiveness, uncertain judgment, and agnosticism.

To be sure, as we have seen, Sidgwick was emphatic in claiming that his "first adhesion to a definite Ethical system was to the utilitarianism of Mill." And he even remarked that one of the things he found so attractive about this was the relief it afforded him from the moral rules – "external and arbitrary" – that he had been raised upon, which were given a philosophical gloss in Whewell's *Elements of Morality*, the undergraduate text that left him with the abiding impression that "[i]ntuitional moralists were hopelessly loose (as compared to mathematicians) in their definitions and axioms" (ME xvii). Yet what Mill's ethics did not help him with was the big problem that his Christian inheritance had so impressed upon him: self-sacrifice. Thus, in a key statement, he writes:

The two elements of Mill's view which I am accustomed to distinguish as Psychological Hedonism [that each man does seek his own Happiness] and Ethical Hedonism [that each man ought to seek the general Happiness] both attracted me, and I did not at first perceive their incoherence.

Psychological Hedonism – the law of universal pleasure-seeking – attracted me by its frank naturalness. Ethical Hedonism, as expounded by Mill, was morally inspiring by its dictate of readiness for absolute self-sacrifice. They appealed to different elements of my nature, but they brought these into apparent harmony: they both used the same words "pleasure," "happiness," and the persuasiveness of Mill's exposition veiled for a time the profound discrepancy between the natural end of action – private happiness, and the end of duty – general happiness. Or if a doubt assailed me as to the coincidence of private and general happiness, I was inclined to hold that it ought to be cast to the winds by a generous resolution.

But a sense grew upon me that this method of dealing with the conflict between Interest and Duty, though perhaps proper for practice could not be final for philosophy. For practical men who do not philosophise, the maxim of subordinating self-interest, as commonly conceived, to "altruistic" impulses and sentiments which they feel to be higher and nobler is, I doubt not, a commendable maxim; but it is surely the business of Ethical Philosophy to find and make explicit the rational ground of such action.

I therefore set myself to examine methodically the relation of Interest and Duty. This involved a careful study of Egoistic Method, to get the relation of Interest and Duty clear. Let us suppose that my own Interest is paramount. What really is my Interest, how far can acts conducive to it be known, how far does the result correspond with Duty (or Wellbeing of Mankind)? This investigation led me to feel very strongly *this* opposition, rather than that which Mill and the earlier Utilitarians felt between so-called Intuitions or Moral Sense Perceptions, and Hedonism, whether Epicurean or Utilitarian. Hence the arrangement of my book – ii., iii., iv. [Book ii. Egoism, Book iii. Intuitionism, Book iv. Utilitarianism]. (ME xvi–xvii)

This investigation led Sidgwick to conclude that "no complete solution of the conflict between my happiness and the general happiness was possible on the basis of mundane experience," that the problem of the "moral choice of the general happiness or acquiescence in self-interest as ultimate" was therefore real and that solving it was a "practical necessity," and, despite his aversion to Whewell, that there was need of "a fundamental ethical intuition," since the utilitarian method could not "be made coherent and harmonious without this fundamental intuition" (ME xvii–xix).

That is, he rejected the claim, associated with psychological hedonism, that as a matter of fact people invariably do pursue their own individual pleasure, but he nonetheless appreciated the need to supply a rational justification for self-sacrifice or disinterested action generally. John Skorupski has described at length just how Sidgwick parted company with both Mill and Green when it came to the claim that a desired object is always desired "under the idea that it will contribute to one's good," and how expert he was at insinuating doubt that the good of the individual part and that of the societal whole were always coincident.[16] But it is also important to bear in mind just how sensitive Sidgwick was to the charge that utilitarianism lacked justificatory grounds and metaphysical weight – Green's point of departure in seeking a new, Idealist ground for ethics in the face of religious crisis.

With this statement about the need for a fundamental intuition, one witnesses, as it were, both the birth and the death of the *Methods*: the conflict between the happiness of the individual and the happiness of society – the "dualism of practical reason," as Sidgwick called it – both inspired the work and proved to be too much for it, indeed was the chief reason for Sidgwick's postpartum sense of failure. Although it is certainly correct that he worked through many of the arguments of the *Methods* in connection with his resignation crisis, the larger conflict looming in the background of that casuistical exercise was, after all, the familiar one of self-sacrifice versus self-interest – or better, how far self-interest could be expanded to cover self-sacrifice, reconciling the two. Here was a clearcut case of the uselessness of mundane experience in harmonizing the discordant elements of human life. Here, too, was the main reason for the distance that he felt from the earlier utilitarians, even from Mill.

What is missing from Sidgwick's explications of how the *Methods* came to be is not so much the core philosophical matter as its social significance, and the personal side of its social significance. For the self-sacrifice of "practical men who do not philosophise" was, to Sidgwick's mind, bound up with religion, and the future of religion was highly insecure. Besides, even if the sentiments of humanity grew increasingly sympathetic as a matter of sociology, this was not sufficient to rationally legitimate the cultural changes that he had worked so diligently to further. Everything he sought to advance, with his educational and cultural reformism, was built around the hope that the sun of philosophy might rise without going immediately into eclipse.

II. *The Methods of Ethics*: Method, Good, Pleasure

The *Methods* departs from classical utilitarianism in a number of ways. It centers on an examination of the accepted moral opinions and modes of thought of common sense. It involves a rejection of empiricism and dismisses the issue of determinism as irrelevant. It emphasizes an attempt to reconcile positions seen by utilitarians as deeply opposed to each other. It finds ethical egoism as reasonable a utilitarianism; and it concludes with arguments to show that, because of this, no full reconciliation of the various rational methods for reaching moral decisions is possible and therefore that the realm of practical reason is probably incoherent.

J. B. Schneewind, "Sidgwick and the Cambridge Moralists"[17]

Among other things I am altered: and have a terror of time and change. I feel that my Theism is rather like that of Beranger's Epicurean: God has been so good to me, or (as Clough says) "thank somebody." But I certainly ought in one respect to get the sympathy of the orthodox: as I do not much believe in my own practical reason. I think that with great trouble one may come to calculate the sources of such happiness as may then be found to be nearly valueless to us. Or better, in the development of human nature, the incalculable element increases at a more rapid ratio than the calculable, so that though the latter is always increasing it is (after a certain advance in intellect) always getting comparatively less.

And I am to lecture on Ethics next term! just when I am inclined to say to Philosophy "malim cum poetis insanire, quam cum istis hominibus rationaliter sentire."

Sidgwick to H. G. Dakyns, 1868 (CWC)

The architectonic of the *Methods* is not user-friendly. Given the complex composition and dense argument of Sidgwick's masterpiece, the hermeneutic circle of interpretation can quickly come to feel like a surreal treadmill, with the parts melting into wholes and the wholes melting into parts in an endless ordeal that never seems to involve forward movement.

The Preface to the first edition of the *Methods* begins rather disarmingly: "In offering to the public a new book upon a subject so trite as Ethics, it seems desirable to indicate clearly at the outset its plan and purpose." Sidgwick then proposes to sketch its distinctive characteristics "negatively," by saying what the book is not:

It is not, in the main, metaphysical or psychological: at the same time it is not dogmatic or directly practical: it does not deal, except by way of illustration, with the history of ethical thought: in a sense it might be said to be not even critical, since it is only quite incidentally that it offers any criticism of the systems of individual moralists (ME vii).

On the positive side, the book claims

to be an examination, at once expository and critical, of the different methods of obtaining reasoned convictions as to what ought to be done which are to be found – either explicit or implicit – in the moral consciousness of mankind generally: and which, from time to time, have been developed, either singly or in combination, by individual thinkers, and worked up into the systems now historical. (ME vii)

In pursuing this examination, Sidgwick avoids the venerable task of in-quiring "into the Origin of the Moral Faculty" by appealing to the "simple assumption (which seems to be made implicitly in all ethical reasoning) that there is something under any given circumstances which it is right or reasonable to do, and that this may be known." The moral faculty he will leave to psychology; moreover, he will make "no further assumption as to the nature of the object of ethical knowledge," so that his "treatise is not dogmatic: all the different methods developed in it are expounded and criticised from a neutral position, and as impartially as possible." (ME vii–viii) Indeed, this by now familiar phrasing is absolutely central to how he conceives his task:

[T]hus, though my treatment of the subject is, in a sense, more practical than that of many moralists, since I am occupied from first to last in considering how conclusions are to be rationally reached in the familiar matter of our common daily life and actual practice; still, my immediate object – to invert Aristotle's phrase – is not Practice but Knowledge. I have thought that the predominance in the minds of moralists of a desire to edify has impeded the real progress of ethical science: and that this would be benefited by an application to it of the same disinterested curiosity to which we chiefly owe the great discoveries of physics. It is in this spirit that I have endeavoured to compose the present work: and with this view I have desired to concentrate the reader's attention, from first to last, not on the practical results to which our methods lead, but on the methods themselves. I have wished to put aside temporarily the urgent need which we all feel of finding and adopting the true method of determining what we ought to do; and to consider simply what conclusions will be rationally reached if we start with certain ethical premises, and with what degree of certainty and precision. (ME viii)

Such statements of purpose have been much admired by prominent twentieth-century ethical theorists, notably by John Rawls. In his Foreword to the Hackett edition of the *Methods*, and elsewhere, Rawls praised the work not only for its philosophically sophisticated presentation of classical utilitarianism, but also for being "the first truly academic work in moral philosophy which undertakes to provide a systematic comparative study of moral conceptions, starting with those which historically and by present assessment are the most significant."[18] But some caution must be exercised in drawing such comparisons between the *Methods* and more recent moral theory. If it is true that Sidgwick does in proto–Rawlsian fashion seek to set aside many tangled metaphysical issues, appealing only to a "minimal metaethics,"[19] it is also true that he often conceives his project in quite different terms from those of philosophers working in the "great expansion" of substantive ethical theorizing in the late twentieth century.

For example, by a "method" Sidgwick means something rather different from a "theory" or a "principle." A method is a rational procedure "for determining right conduct in any particular case," which is to say, for determining the rightness of one's act by determining in a reasoned way whether it has those right-making properties singled out by what is taken to be justifiable principle. Just as an ultimate principle does not in and of itself show how to determine whether some particular act is right, so a method does not in and of itself vindicate the ultimate principle to which reasoned appeal is made. One might think that the universe is the work of a benevolent, utilitarian God, with everything tending to the greatest happiness, but also hold that one's own lot, practically speaking, is to follow God's commandments absolutely rather than try to second-guess the Divine calculation of consequences – thus, one's method would be deontological, but this would rest on a (theological) utilitarian axiom. Similarly, one might hold an egoistic ultimate principle, but think that one's own good is best secured not by empirical calculation of probable benefits but by acting in strict accordance with certain evolutionary or psychological directives (a case Sidgwick describes as "deductive hedonism").

At any rate, this distinction is evident when Sidgwick explains that his object is

to expound as clearly and as fully as my limits will allow the different methods of Ethics that I find implicit in our common moral reasoning; to point out their mutual relations; and where they seem to conflict, to define the issue as much as possible. In the course of this endeavour I am led to discuss the considerations which should, in my opinion, be decisive in determining the adoption of ethical first principles: but it is not my primary aim to establish such principles; nor, again, is it my primary aim to supply a set of practical directions for conduct. (ME 14)

He is, as it turns out, more concerned about ultimate principles than such remarks let on, but it is nonetheless important to appreciate that he does not simply collapse together the notions of method, theory, and principle.[20] Although a "method" is more abstract than a "decision-procedure" and can encompass "indirect" strategies, this notion does give the book a practical, "how is one to live" or "what is to be done" orientation, despite Sidgwick's aversion to practical edification.

The "methods" that come to the fore in this treatment are, of course, egoism (that one ought to pursue one's own greatest good), "dogmatic" intuitionism (of the Whewellian variety, enjoining obedience to such common moral precepts or duties or virtues as veracity, promise keeping, justice, etc.), and utilitarianism (that one ought to seek the greatest good of the whole, of all sentient creatures) – the primary topics, respectively, of Books II, III, and IV. These books are bracketed by Book I, which gives an initial survey of the entire line of argument to come, and a "Concluding Chapter" on the "mutual relations of the three methods."

This basic structure was manifest in the first edition and preserved in every edition up to and through the last, seventh one (although Sidgwick's final revisions, for the sixth edition, went only through page 276 of the fifth). Some of the significant changes in later editions involved putting the treatment of "Kant's Conception of Free Will" in a separate appendix (the only such appendix) and toning down the pessimism of the concluding chapter (which is also retitled and set apart). But in fact, as will be noted, there were many others as well, some especially important for understanding Sidgwick's shifting views on the nature of practical reason and on ultimate good and its relation to virtue. In the Preface to the second edition, for example, which was also included in the separately published *A Supplement to the First Edition of the Methods of Ethics*,[21] he stated that he had, among other things, thought it desirable to explain "further my general view of the 'Practical Reason,' and of the fundamental notion signified by the terms 'right,' 'ought,' etc." and that this had led him to rework Book III, Chapter 13 on "Philosophical Intuitionism." This chapter "has been suggestively criticised by more than one writer," and Sidgwick "thought it expedient to give a more direct statement of my own opinions; instead of confining myself (as I did in the first edition) to comments on those of other moralists." Some commentators, notably Earnest Albee and Schneewind, have remarked that after the first edition Sidgwick eliminated some rather helpful references to, for example, Kant and Clarke, though all admit that that edition was extremely minimalistic in its treatment of such fundamental issues.[22]

It has often been said, and with justice, that the treatment of utilitarianism in the *Methods* is second in importance only to Bentham's *Introduction to the Principles of Morals and Legislation* and J. S. Mill's *Utilitarianism*, and that in terms of philosophical sophistication, it outstrips both together. Yet, as previously remarked, and as the opening passage from Schneewind so strongly urges, Sidgwick's work often clashes with the earlier utilitarian tradition. As Schneewind has encapsulated it, "the central thought of the *Methods of Ethics* is that morality is the embodiment of the demands reason makes on practice under the conditions of human life, and that the problems of philosophical ethics are the problems of showing how practical reason is articulated into these demands."[23] Put more fully:

> The starting-point of Sidgwick's argument is the demonstration, through reasoning and appeal to introspection, that we have a unique, irreducible concept of "being a reason for" as it applies to action and to desire. From this concept we learn that our own ability to reason involves a unique kind of demand on both the active and the sentient aspects of our nature, the demand that our acts and desires be reasonable. Since, therefore, it must be possible to give reasons for our desires and actions, a complex argument involving the elimination of various principles which might serve as the ultimate determinant of such reasons leads to the conclusion that a maximizing consequentialist principle must be the most basic principle of rationality in practice. Further eliminative argument shows that the end set for us by this principle must be interpreted hedonistically. These arguments bring out what the essence of rationality in practice is, given the facts of human existence. Further argument shows that it is possible to embody this rationality in daily life through a code like that exemplified in ordinary moral belief. At least it is possible up to a point.[24]

The sticking point is, of course, the dualism of practical reason, which forces Sidgwick "to the unhappy conclusion that the best that reason can do in coping with the actuality of human nature in the world as it exists, is to impose demands which in the end are incompatible" and to show "that the problem his historical analysis leads him to take as central to modern ethics cannot be fully resolved."

The dualism of practical reason aside, this orientation, which does appear to resonate happily with recent formulations of "the normative problem" that dogs anyone who reflects and acts, did not strike many of Sidgwick's contemporaries as obviously utilitarian. It was a very exasperated F. H. Hayward who complained that Sidgwick's disciple E. E. Constance Jones took all of Sidgwick's departures from utilitarianism as just so much common sense:

Sidgwick's identification of "Right" with "Reasonable" and "Objective"; his view of Rightness as an "ultimate and unanalysable notion" (however connected subsequently with Hedonism); and his admission that Reason is, in a sense, a motive to the will, are due to the more or less "unconscious" influence of Kant. Miss Jones appears to think that these are the common-places of every ethical system, and that real divergences only arise when we make the next step in advance. I should rather regard this Rationalistic terminology as somewhat foreign to Hedonism. I do not think that Miss Jones will find, in Sidgwick's Hedonistic predecessors, any such emphasis on Reason (however interpreted).[25]

For Hayward, the point was "not that Sidgwick should be classified as this or that, but that it is extremely difficult to classify him at all."

Plainly, Sidgwick does reject the empiricism, psychological egoism, and reductionism of much of the earlier tradition, qualities especially evident in the works of Bentham and James Mill, at least as commonly understood.[26] This comes through quite powerfully very early on – indeed, in the first book, where, for example, he explains that

Experience can at most tell us that all men always do seek pleasure as their ultimate end. . . . it cannot tell us that any ought so to seek it. If this latter proposition is legitimately affirmed in respect either of private or of general happiness, it must either be immediately known to be true, – and therefore, we may say, a moral intuition – or be inferred ultimately from premises which include at least one such moral intuition. (ME 98)

However, as we shall see, Sidgwick does not prejudge the ultimate validity of a proposition when he labels it an "intuition" – this is part of a complex, multicriterial epistemological strategy.

Sidgwick maintains that the basic concept of morality – something so fundamental that it is common to the terms "ought" and "right" – is unique and irreducible.[27] Morality, in short, is sui generis; in this Sidgwick is as insistent as any twentieth-century critic of the so-called naturalistic fallacy – most famously, his own student G. E. Moore, who at least did not include Sidgwick in the company of those who would reduce "ought" to "is."[28] He is, to resort to a recent idiom, profoundly convinced of the basic normativity of ethical judgments, how they concern what one *should* do or seek, rather than simply some set of facts about the world or about our feelings. Moral reasons are, after all, moral, not something that can be translated away into, say, wholly naturalistic factors. But they are also reasons – that is, prescribed or dictated by reason – and thus the kind of thing that can be contradicted, or supported by argument. Indeed, moral approbation is "inseparably bound up with the conviction, implicit or explicit, that the conduct approved is 'really' right – that is, that it cannot, without error, be disapproved by any other mind." Furthermore, the dictates of moral reason are "accompanied by a certain impulse to do the acts recognized as right," though Sidgwick recognizes that other impulses may conflict with this one. (ME 27)

Given such remarks as this last, most have read Sidgwick as at least a type of "internalist," such that, in David Brink's words, it "is not possible to think that a method of ethics is true and still ask whether there is reason to be moral, for the true method of ethics just states what it is ultimately reasonable to do." An externalist would deny any such internal or conceptual connection between morality and rationality. Brink has suggested some reasons for thinking of Sidgwick as sometimes vacillating between internalism and externalism, though his interpretation is admittedly more of a philosophical reconstruction and might also require a too-narrow construction of Sidgwick's epistemology, as will be explained.[29] At the least, it would be hard to blink Sidgwick's regular assertions that to have a moral reason is to have at least some degree of motivation to behave accordingly.

Sidgwick does deny, however, that the question of free will has the importance that some, notably Kant, have attributed to it in connection with this question of acting morally. It is, he holds, usually impossible in practical deliberation to regard the mere absence of adequate motive as "a reason for not doing what I otherwise judge to be reasonable," and this suggests the general irrelevance of the topic of free will to much that passes under the rubric of ethics, with the possible exception of questions of responsibility and punishment. Determinism might well be true, but that would make little difference to the way most people set about determining what they ought to do, especially since the truth of determinism would not, according to Sidgwick, help the case for psychological hedonism or other such controversial doctrines. At best, or worst, it might undermine purely retributive views of punishment, but no utilitarian, at least, should be much upset about that, since purely retributive views are better undermined, given their celebration of useless suffering, suffering with no deterrence value.

This rough handling of such long-standing topics as the nature of the moral faculty and the reality of free will is characteristic of Sidgwick's treatment of a number of other matters as well. Much of the controversy provoked by the *Methods* actually stems from the way in which Sidgwick's policy is to just steer clear of the metaphysical and psychological entanglements that such venerable topics carry with them. Oddly, in this respect, the argument of the *Methods* is conducted at arm's length from some of both Mill's and Sidgwick's basic intellectual commitments; for just as Mill took psychological investigation to be central to any work on the foundations of ethics, so too Sidgwick took his investigations into parapsychology and intuitive theism – investigations that were admittedly often of a highly personal nature, a kind of self-analysis – to be part and parcel of his research into ethics. What he apparently sought to do in the *Methods* was to see just what ethics might bring to this research from its own resources, independently of other disciplines and other areas of philosophy.[30]

Although one could read Sidgwick's general avoidance of metaphysical issues in the *Methods* as a form of proto-Rawlsian independent moral theory, such that ethics is treated as a discipline with its own distinctive problems and methods rather than as derived from or grounded upon more fundamental areas of philosophy, the danger of anachronism in any such reading is very great. Sidgwick did practice a certain limited form of the so-called method of avoidance, but as Schneewind has argued at length, in his *Sidgwick's Ethics and Victorian Moral Philosophy*, his purpose is most plausibly reconstructed in terms of the religious concerns of such figures as Whewell, Grote, and Maurice – that is, as an effort to test their common claim that the moral realm provided independent grounds for religious belief of some sort. Of course, as already suggested, Sidgwick himself did not end up believing that he had vindicated any such vision of a morally well-ordered world, which points up the need to reconsider just what alternatives he had in mind, by way of metaphysical commitments, and just where he might have been a little hasty or question-begging in his treatment of the views he was testing. After all, belief in free will is a common feature of the religious philosophies he was addressing.

Whether he also moves rather too quickly on certain ethical theoretical issues – for example, in reducing the number of methods to three (confusingly linking perfectionism to dogmatic intuitionism) and in collapsing egoism and utilitarianism into variants of hedonism – is a matter that has worried even those sympathetic to his commitment to independent ethical theory (and of course, Sidgwick himself). The remainder of this section will analyze in more detail some of the ways in which Sidgwick's constructions of the "right" and the "good" shape his formulation of the various methods and thus complement the famous arguments about the relations between the methods, described in the following two sections. Here it is particularly important to bring out the themes of the final chapter of Book I and the final chapter of Book III, which in all editions served as Sidgwick's main engagements with the question of how to understand "ultimate good." Also important, however, is the recognition that to survey the *Methods* from this perspective is (quite often, anyway) to survey the claims that Sidgwick found most debatable, the arguments that he allowed were "indirect" and less than fully compelling – in the ever-increasing realm of the "incalculable."

The themes discussed here, which often seem to involve indirect arguments about indirect strategies for achieving happiness, will reemerge in later sections, after Sidgwick's more direct epistemological claims are considered. Hopefully, the recapitulation at that point will clear up some of the obscurities of this preliminary treatment.

Now, again, the delineation of the three methods and their relations to such things as happiness is a crucial and controversial bit of agenda setting on Sidgwick's part. Much of this work is done in conjunction with his highly convoluted analysis of the "attractive" notions of "good" and "ultimate good," as contrasted with the "imperative" notions of what it is "right" to do or what one "ought" to do. The general contrast between the (characteristically ancient) concern with the ultimate, highest good or summum bonum – that which is good finally and in itself rather than as a means to something else – and the (characteristically modern) concern with what is right – the imperatives of duty concerning what one ought or ought not to do – is of course a fixture of much historically aware moral theory, as Sidgwick very well realized.[31] In a wide range of writings, he made reference to the distinctive "quasi-jural" nature of modern moral thought, running from Grotius and Pufendorf down to the present, though with some distant antecedents in the Stoics.[32] This was obviously a general orientation that he shared, what with his focus on the fundamental moral notion at play in such terms as "ought" and "right."

On Sidgwick's analysis of the "Right and the Good," judgments of ultimate good differ from judgments of right mainly in that they do not involve definite precepts to act or the assumption that we are capable of acting accordingly; they leave it open "whether this particular kind of good is the greatest good that we can under the circumstances obtain," whereas a judgment that one "ought" to do such and such implies that one *can* do such and such. That is, in "the recognition of conduct as 'right' is involved an authoritative prescription to do it: but when we have judged conduct to be good, it is not yet clear that we ought to prefer this kind of good to all other good things: some standard for estimating the relative values of different 'goods' has still to be sought" (ME 106). Furthermore, "good or excellent actions are not implied to be in our power in the same strict sense as 'right' actions – any more than any other good things: and in fact there are many excellences of behaviour which we cannot attain by any effort of will, at least directly and at the moment" (ME 113).

It would appear that on Sidgwick's line of argument, with its determined effort to avoid the naturalistic confusions of Mill's seeming equation of "what is good" with "what is desired," the notion of "good" is tied not to the merely desired, but to that which is desirable – or better, to what one ought to desire or generally seek to promote.[33] There has been some controversy over this because some of his remarks on the subject could be construed as defending a naturalistic "full-information" view of the "good" to the effect that the good is simply what one would desire if one actually had all relevant information available to one and so on.[34] Thus, his discussion takes its point of departure from Hobbes's view that one calls good whatever is the object of one's desires, and by successive qualifications and refinements reaches the position that

Indeed, we commonly reckon it among the worst consequences of some kinds of conduct that they alter men's tendencies to desire, and make them desire their lesser good more than their greater: and we think it all the worse for a man – even in this world – if he is never roused out of such a condition and lives till death the life of a contented pig, when he might have been something better. To avoid this objection, it would have to be said that a man's future good on the whole is what he would now desire and seek on the whole if all the consequences of all the different lines of conduct open to him were accurately foreseen and adequately realised in the imagination at the present point of time.

This hypothetical composition of impulsive forces involves so elaborate and complex a conception, that it is somewhat paradoxical to say that this is what we commonly *mean* when we talk of a man's 'good on the whole.' Still, I cannot deny that this hypothetical object of a resultant desire supplies an intelligible and admissible interpretation of the terms 'good' (substantive) and 'desirable,' as giving philosophical precision to the vaguer meaning with which they are used in ordinary discourse: and it would seem that a calm comprehensive desire for 'good' conceived somewhat in this way, though more vaguely, is normally produced by intellectual comparison and experience in a reflective mind. The notion of 'Good' thus attained has an ideal element: it is something that *is* not always actually desired and aimed at by human beings: but the ideal element is entirely interpretable in terms of *fact*, actual or hypothetical, and does not introduce any judgment of value, fundamentally distinct from judgments relating to existence; – still less any 'dictate of Reason.' (ME 11–12)

This sounds naturalistic, so much so that Tom Baldwin could even suggest that it is "not so clear why Moore exempted Sidgwick from the charge of committing the Naturalistic Fallacy," at least with respect to "good."[35] However, Sidgwick immediately proceeds to admit that to him it is "more in accordance with common sense to recognise – as Butler does – that the calm desire for my 'good on the whole' is *authoritative*; and therefore carries with it implicitly a rational dictate to aim at this end, if in any case a conflicting desire urges the will in an opposite direction."[36] We may, he allows, keep the notion of such a dictate "merely implicit and latent" by interpreting, in line with common sense, "ultimate good on the whole for me" as meaning "what I should practically desire if my desires were in harmony with reason, assuming my own existence alone to be considered." Or, as he concludes in the fifth edition,

'*my* ultimate good' must be taken to mean in the sense that it is 'what is ultimately desirable *for me*,' or what I should desire if my desires were in harmony with reason, – assuming my own existence alone to be considered, – and is thus identical with the ultimate end or ends prescribed by reason as what ought to be sought or aimed at, so far as reason is not thought to inculcate sacrifice of my own ultimate good. (ME5 112)[37]

Thus, the calm desire for one's "ultimate good on the whole," so construed, would seem to involve a form of rational authority that rules out such things as irrational desires and weakness of will. Analogously, "[u]ltimate good on the whole," Sidgwick tries to show, "if unqualified by reference to a particular subject, must be taken to mean what as a rational being I should desire and seek to realize, assuming myself to have an equal concern for *all* existence" – which is, of course, in contrast with "ultimate good on the whole for me" (ME 112–13).

But again, "good or excellent actions are not implied to be in our power." In either case, there may well be a difference between the judgment that such and such is good and the judgment that one ought to do such and such. It is only when the call to action takes shape, in practical deliberation, that the concern with promoting the good melds into the imperative of the right.[38]

Schneewind's summary of this tangled topic is hard to match:

The concepts of goodness and rightness then represent differentiations of the demands of our own rationality as it applies to our sentient and our active powers. Seeing this helps give us a better understanding of what Sidgwick takes the basic indefinable notion of practical rationality to be. It is what is common to the notions of a reason to desire, a reason to seek or aim at, a reason to decide or choose, a reason to do; it does not involve an authoritative prescription to act where there is barely reason to desire something, or even where there is fairly strong reason, but only where there is stronger reason to desire one thing than to desire anything else, and that one thing is within our powers. At this point it becomes the through-and-through "ought" or "right" of definite dictates claiming to give authoritative guidance to our conduct. If any "metaethical" answer to the question of the nature of the object of moral judgements is implicit in Sidgwick's position, it is that moral judgements embody the fact that we are reasonable beings who feel and act. In judging what is right or good, we are following out the implications of our rationality for the practical aspects of our nature.[39]

This seems plausible. The notion of "good" speaks to our sentient, feeling nature, and that of "right" to our agency, and the two meet when the authoritative pronouncements of the former come to yield concrete practical direction in the authoritative pronouncements of the latter.[40] But as Sidgwick admits, the differences in intuitional method that arise from this "variation of view as to the precise quality immediately apprehended in the moral intuition" are "peculiarly subtle and difficult to fix in clear and precise language" (ME 103). It was just this space for argument that would eventually produce the "ideal" utilitarianism of Moore, who resisted Sidgwick's interpretation of "good" and his supposed prioritizing of "ought." However, as Thomas Hurka has argued, the distance between these figures is hard to determine. Noting how Sidgwick recognized that his account of "ought" could be deemed problematic because inability to control irrational desires would suggest a violation of the principle that "ought" implies "can," Hurka explains:

> Sidgwick acknowledged this in earlier editions of *The Methods of Ethics*. After defining the good as what we ought to desire, he added that 'since irrational desires cannot always be dismissed at once by voluntary effort,' the definition cannot use 'ought' in 'the strictly ethical sense,' but only in 'the wider sense in which it merely connotes an ideal or standard.' But this raises the question of what this 'wider sense' is, and in particular whether it is at all distinct from Moore's 'good.' If the claim that we 'ought' to have a desire is only the claim that the desire is 'an ideal,' how does it differ from the claim that the desire is good? When 'ought' is stripped of its connection with choice, its distinctive meaning seems to slip away.[41]

Hence, the stock contrast between Sidgwick and Moore – with the former defining "good" in terms of the unanalyzable "ought" and the latter defining "right" in terms of the unanalyzable "good" – may be a bit simplistic. Rashdall, who knew them both, even claimed that Moore rightly recognized Sidgwick as his predecessor in holding "the idea of an indefinable good," but that he was preposterous in suggesting that this was an original discovery of the latter:

> To say nothing of writers who (like Mr. Moore and myself) learned the doctrine largely from Sidgwick, I should contend that it was taught with sufficient distinctness by Plato (whatever may be thought of his further attempt to show that only the good has real existence), Aristotle, and a host of modern writers who have studied in their school – by no one more emphatically than by Cudworth. The only criticism which I should make upon Mr. Moore's exposition of it is that he ignores the other ways in which the same notion may be expressed, and in particular the correlative notion of 'right' or 'ought.' He is so possessed with this idea that 'good' is indefinable that he will not even trouble to expound and illustrate it in such ways as are possible in the case of ultimate ideas.[42]

It was perhaps just this obsession that rendered Moore's notion of the good vulnerable to the charge that it failed to be sufficiently normative, sufficiently "ought-implying."[43] Furthermore, Rashdall's remark is illuminating not least for the way in which it brings out the common Platonic inheritance of Sidgwick and Moore – a point that, in light of the previous chapters, seems particularly revealing. Evidently, however, as later sections will explain, Sidgwick's efforts to explicate the "good" as what one "ought to desire" and his reluctance to talk about the "property" of "goodness" did make for serious differences with Moore when it came to the subject of egoism. At any rate, the division between Sidgwick and Moore in many ways comes down to the question of whether it makes sense to talk of agent-relative goodness, of the "ultimate good" of a particular person, generating reasons for that person but not necessarily for others, as in the case of egoism.[44]

Now, although the general scholarly consensus, past and present, thus appears to be that Sidgwick did not hold a naturalistic "full-information" view of the "good," there is some difference of opinion over just why he took this route.[45] And there have been some important dissenting positions as well, from Rawls down to the present. Thus, a rather different reading is given by Roger Crisp, in his essay "Sidgwick and Self-Interest."[46] Crisp maintains that "Sidgwick believed that self-interest is constituted by awareness of the fulfilment of certain desires one would have if special knowledge were available to one. In contemporary terms, this account comprises an Informed-desire Theory, constrained by an Experience Requirement." Crisp argues to the effect that Sidgwick's definition of the good in terms of "[w]hat I should practically desire if my desires were in harmony with reason" was not meant to contrast with the earlier definition – "what he would desire and seek on the whole if all the consequences of all the different lines of conduct open to him were accurately foreseen and adequately realised in imagination at the present point of time." Agreeing that the former was a response to the problem of weakness of will, Crisp nonetheless holds that it was a collateral, not contrasting, alternative, and that if the earlier definition "spells out what it is that makes someone's life go best," the later one "implies that seeking this is what one has most reason to do."[47] Which is to say, Crisp in effect denies that the "proper reasoning" requirement was meant to qualify the naturalism of the "full-information" or "informed desire" account.

However, Crisp allows that the interpretations advanced by Parfit and Schneewind are "more charitable," in that they make Sidgwick appear less incapable of recognizing "that desires may be irrational even in the conditions of full information he envisaged."[48] And of course, Sidgwick may have deliberately toned down his non-naturalism in the late editions of the *Methods*.[49]

Matters get even stickier when Sidgwick tries to work out a substantive account of ultimate good. If, as he insists, "the practical determination of Right Conduct depends on the determination of Ultimate Good," the devil is in the details, and Sidgwick's hedonistic answer is perhaps the feature of his work that has distanced it most from recent neo–utilitarianism (and from every other moral theory).[50] L. W. Sumner urges that as "Sidgwick conceives it, the contest at this point is between happiness on the one hand and various (subjective) perfectionist goods, such as knowledge and freedom, on the other." And as Sumner also notes, Sidgwick's form of hedonism, ostensibly treating pleasures as "a class of feelings" having the common property of pleasantness, betrays subtle differences from earlier utilitarian accounts.[51] As Sidgwick explains:

Shall we then say that there is a measurable quality of feeling expressed by the word 'pleasure,' which is independent of its relation to volition, and strictly undefinable from its simplicity? – like the quality of feeling expressed by 'sweet,' of which also we are conscious in varying degrees of intensity. This seems to be the view of some writers: but, for my own part, when I reflect on the notion of pleasure, – using the term in the comprehensive sense I have adopted, to include the most refined and subtle intellectual and emotional gratifications, no less than the coarser and more definite sensual enjoyments, – the only common quality that I can find in the feelings so designated seems to be that relation to desire and volition expressed by the general term 'desirable'. . . . I propose therefore to define Pleasure . . . as a feeling which, when experienced by intelligent beings, is at least implicitly apprehended as desirable or – in cases of comparison – preferable. (ME 127)

As Sumner cogently observes, both Mill and Sidgwick, by contrast with Bentham,

seemed to recognize that the mental states we call pleasures are a mixed bag as far as their phenomenal properties are concerned. On their view what pleasures have in common is not something internal to them – their peculiar feeling tone, or whatever – but something about us – the fact that we like them, enjoy them, value them, find them satisfying, seek them, wish to prolong them, and so on.[52]

One could, Sumner urges, rightly think of Sidgwick as advancing an "externalist, attitude" model of hedonism, rather than as returning to a pure, Benthamite "internalist" hedonism, with its "sensation model" emphasizing common hedonic tone and so forth. In either case, of course, "pleasures and pains are purely mental states," experiences that can be identified through introspection. However, on the internalist view, what is introspected is a particular internal quality, whereas on the externalist view, it is the external relation of being liked or disliked.[53]

Sidgwick certainly did defend this candidate theory of ultimate good in a wide range of writings, and it formed a crucial part of his treatment of egoism and utilitarianism, which got translated into "Egoistic Hedonism" and "Universalistic Hedonism," respectively. Yet, as the next section will show, he was never as confident about this hedonistic interpretation of good as he was of his general account of good and how it ought to be maximized, and he was ever troubled by whether he had really done justice to the perfectionist alternative, in its more compelling forms. And it is in this region that, ironically enough, one also finds much material that has a contemporary ring, despite the poor reputation of hedonism. As Shaver suggests, "Sidgwick works out what it is reasonable to desire, and so attaches moral to natural properties, by the ordinary gamut of philosopher's strategies – appeals to logical coherence, plausibility, and judgement after reflection. (Contemporary discussions of the ultimate good, such as those by Parfit, Griffin, Hurka, and Sumner, follow the same procedures.)"[54] In some respects, the bottom line is simply this:

[S]o far as we judge virtuous activity to be a part of Ultimate Good, it is, I conceive, because the consciousness attending it is judged to be in itself desirable for the virtuous agent; though at the same time this consideration does not adequately represent the importance of Virtue to human wellbeing, since we have to consider its value as a means as well as its value as an end. We may make the distinction clearer by considering whether Virtuous life would remain on the whole good for the virtuous agent, if we suppose it combined with extreme pain. The affirmative answer to this question was strongly supported in Greek philosophical discussion: but it is a paradox from which a modern thinker would recoil: he would hardly venture to assert that the portion of life spent by a martyr in tortures was in itself desirable, – though it might be his duty to suffer the pain with a view to the good of others, and even his interest to suffer it with a view to his own ultimate happiness. (ME 397)

However, Sidgwick's treatment of perfectionism is troublingly elusive at points, provoking questions about nonhedonistic and nonegoistic and nonteleological alternatives. Schneewind notes that "he does in effect consider the possibility of a fourth method, one involving a non-hedonistic teleological principle; and he need not, therefore, have linked dogmatic intuitionism as a method to perfection as an end. Had he not done so, it would have been clearer than it is that the dogmatic intuitionism he examines is a deontological, not a covertly teleological, method."[55] Plausibly, however, this mixing of the two positions was another aspect of the Whewellian view that so troubled him; at least, Whewell, in his *The Elements of Morality*, had often been at pains to demonstrate that his theory captured much of what was attractive in the notion of human perfection as an end.[56]

In the first edition of the *Methods*, Sidgwick had, in the chapter on "Good" concluding Book I, given a clear indication of how important these various considerations were for addressing the "method" of intuitionism:

Thus we are [provisionally] led to the conclusion that the only Good that can claim to be so intrinsically, and at the same time capable of furnishing a standard of conduct, is Perfection or Excellence of conscious life. And so we seem brought round again to the method discussed in the first part of this chapter, the form or phase of Intuitionism which takes "good" instead of "right" conduct as its most general notion. Only there is this important difference, that Conscious Life includes besides actions the whole range of feeling. We saw in chap. 7 that we had to distinguish the recognition of Excellence in feelings from the recognition of their Pleasantness: and that this distinction seemed to be implied in the contrast drawn by recent Hedonists between the *quality* of pleasures and their *quantity*. In aiming, therefore, at the Perfection of conscious life, we shall endeavour to realize this excellence in all our feelings. Now though Feeling is to some extent a subject of our common intuitions of right and wrong (as we think that actions, to be perfectly right, must be done from right motives), yet it seems to be so only in a subordinate and restricted manner: and there is much excellence of feeling (elevation or refinement of taste, &c.) which is not thus included. It seems then that the method which takes Perfection or Excellence of conscious existence as ultimate end, if we restrict its scope to the Perfection of the individual agent, coincides *primâ facie* with the ordinary form of Intuitionism, since Virtues are always recognised as the chief of human perfections: but that in so far as the former notion comprehends more than virtue, there is likely to be a certain practical divergence between the two methods. And if we take the Perfection of mankind in general as the ultimate end, this divergence may be increased indefinitely: for we cannot assume *à priori* that the best way for each man to attain his own perfection is by aiming at the perfection of others. We cannot but hope that this is the case, just as we cannot but hope that when an individual sacrifices his own happiness to that of others, the sacrifice will be in some way repaid him: but perhaps the constitution of things does not admit of this. (ME1 103–4)

The allusions to Mill here involve not only his doctrine of higher pleasures, but also his division between the ethical and aesthetic realms, something that also figures in Sidgwick's conception of ethics.[57] When Sidgwick
concludes his later treatment of the matter in Book III, however, he admits
that he is "forced to leave the ethical method which takes Perfection, as
distinct from Happiness, to be the whole or chief part of ultimate Good, in
a rudimentary condition." Such modesty is less marked in later editions:

If we are not to systematise human activities by taking Universal Happiness as
their common end, on what other principles are we to systematise them? It should
be observed that these principles must not only enable us to compare among
themselves the values of the different non-hedonistic ends which we have been
considering, but must also provide a common standard for comparing these values
with that of Happiness; unless we are prepared to adopt the paradoxical position
of rejecting happiness as absolutely valueless. For we have a practical need of
determining not only whether we should pursue Truth rather than Beauty, or
Freedom or some ideal constitutions of society rather than either, or perhaps
desert all of these for the life of worship and religious contemplation; but also
how far we should follow any of these lines of endeavour, when we foresee among
its consequences the pains of human or other sentient beings, or even the loss of
pleasures that might otherwise have been enjoyed by them.

I have failed to find – and am unable to construct – any systematic answer to
this question that appears to me deserving of serious consideration: and hence I
am finally led to the conclusion . . . that the Intuitional method rigorously applied
yields as its final result the doctrine of pure Universalistic Hedonism – which it
is convenient to denote by the single word, Utilitarianism. (ME 406)

Thus, perfectionism can be assimilated to dogmatic intuitionism
(because they supposedly coincide on ethical matters), which can in turn
be assimilated to utilitarianism, as we shall see in more detail presently.
And thus, again, the best candidate for ultimate good is the hedonistic
one: experiences of pleasurable or desirable consciousness. Put more precisely, the candidate is a "compromise" form of quantitative hedonism,
with both a preference element and a mental-state one.[58] Sidgwick cannot
shake the thought that the virtuous life loses its luster if we imagine it as,
say, conjoined to extreme pain. And throughout his meditations on the
good, he is convinced that consciousness must figure in whatever good
there is in the universe. When Moore, in *Principia Ethica*, insisted that
it was absolutely obvious that if there were two universes devoid of all
consciousness, one perfectly beautiful and one perfectly foul, it would be

better that the perfectly beautiful one should exist, he was responding to Sidgwick's argument that no one "would consider it rational to aim at the production of beauty in external nature, apart from any possible contemplation of it by human beings."[59]

Naturally, for Sidgwick, as for Moore, it would be quite wrong to claim, as Bentham did, that "ultimate good" simply means "pleasurable," since this would make it a mere tautology to say that pleasure is ultimate good, and a mere tautology is scarcely what fundamental ethical argument requires. Whether ultimate good should be interpreted in this hedonistic fashion is a significant, possibly mistaken, proposition – an open question. One needs to show how empty or circular notions of, for example, virtue as ultimate good actually are. What such hedonism has going for it, beyond the considerable brute force of the Benthamite argument that no one in their right mind supposes that sheer, needless, avoidable pain is a good thing, is mainly that it allows for a way to sort out and settle competing claims about particular goods – how, for example, to balance the claims of health against the claims of love or creativity. No other account that he is aware of allows for bringing at least some degree of precision and determinateness to judgments of good.

Appended to the foregoing passage is a note suggesting that the controversy over vivisection happily illustrates the way in which happiness serves as the final court of appeal, since no one "in this controversy has ventured on the paradox that the pain of sentient beings is not *per se* to be avoided." On this urgent question, Sidgwick thus falls in with what has been a proud utilitarian tradition from Bentham and Mill down to Peter Singer – namely, the view that the pains and pleasures of all sentient creatures morally matter and must therefore be included in the utilitarian calculus.[60] Another note explains, in faintly Aristotelian fashion, that "so long as Time is a necessary form of human existence, it can hardly be surprising that human good should be subject to the condition of being realised in successive parts."

Many critics, past and present, have felt that Sidgwick's insistence on determinateness amounts to a far-too-ambitious construction of rationality, involving the complete ordering of all possible acts or states of affairs. Yet the appeal to such an ideal is, in Sidgwick's work, a complex matter. Certainly, as should be evident, he is always keenly aware of how far short of such an ideal practical reason usually ends up, and one can typically take him as making the case for those who stress the impossibility of any such rational ordering. He is admittedly willing to recognize the ever-increasing sphere of the incalculable element in human affairs, however lamentable or problematic it may be. At any rate, it is far from obvious that many of his arguments would not survive translation into more recent idioms concerning real-world codes and indirect, incomplete methods of calculation; indeed, one is tempted to say that his critical and skeptical claims measurably contributed to these more recent idioms.[61]

Similar considerations of system and determinateness apply to both universalistic and egoistic hedonism, of course, though Sidgwick denies that commonsense morality is as receptive to the latter – it is "rather the end of Egoistic than of Universalistic Hedonism, to which Common Sense feels an aversion" (ME 403). Like Mill, he thinks that much of the hostility to utilitarianism comes from the confusion of it with egoism (narrowly construed) and a failure to appreciate how elevated pleasant consciousness can be, though he also allows that egoism has an important role to play in commonsense morality, as will be shown.[62]

At any rate, in both cases, the pursuit of happiness must, if it is to be effective, take an indirect route. This is an extremely important qualification, one that, Sidgwick believes, also helps to deflate much of the commonsense resistance to hedonism. It is vital to see that

from the universal point of view no less than from that of the individual, it seems true that Happiness is likely to be better attained if the extent to which we set ourselves consciously to aim at it be carefully restricted. And this not only because action is likely to be more effective if our effort is temporarily concentrated on the realisation of more limited ends – though this is no doubt an important reason: – but also because the fullest development of happy life for each individual seems to require that he should have other external objects of interest besides the happiness of other conscious beings. And thus we may conclude that the pursuit of the ideal objects . . . Virtue, Truth, Freedom, Beauty, etc., *for their own sakes*, is indirectly and secondarily, though not primarily and absolutely, rational; on account not only of the happiness that will result from their attainment, but also of that which springs from their disinterested pursuit. While yet if we ask for a final criterion of the comparative value of the different objects of men's enthusiastic pursuit, and of the limits within which each may legitimately engross the attention of mankind, we shall none the less conceive it to depend upon the degree in which they respectively conduce to Happiness. (ME 406)

The indirect nature of both egoism and utilitarianism has been appealed to in order to deflect criticism arising from conflicts with common sense, though the utilitarian version of this – which is, in effect, doubly indirect, indirect at both the individual and social levels – is especially important, at least for Sidgwick. As the next section will explain more fully, most of the work done by conceptual distinctions between acts and rules or decision procedures and standards is, in his case, done through appeal to the necessity of indirect strategies for maximizing happiness.[63] In familiar fashion, utilitarians of this type argue that if the acceptance of a rule will make for a greater number of optimal acts, because the suboptimal acts cannot be identified and countered in advance, then the acceptance is justified (even on "act-utilitarian" grounds, though this is an anachronistic idiom). Similarly, certain motives reliably productive of optimal acts ought to be fostered. One of the reasons why utilitarianism and egoism have been so often confused stems from the way in which the early utilitarians promoted laissez-faire economics, often failing to make sufficiently plain that their appeal to economic self-interest was part of an indirect strategy for maximizing general happiness. But other motives also importantly figure in indirect strategies. Most utilitarians past and present have insisted that special obligations to, or greater concern for, those near and dear must be justifiable on utilitarian grounds, as the best means to maximizing overall happiness in any society organized in a halfway-decent fashion. After all, one is usually best positioned to help oneself and those close to one; the efficient deployment of this information for the sake of the greatest good is all that the utilitarian is demanding. Sidgwick went still further, aiming to capture such perfectionist values as truth seeking in this way. Indeed, he had a keen eye for pleasures that one could experience only by radically changing one's nature: "the sacrifice of sensual inclination to duty is disagreeable to the non-moral man when he at first attempts it, but affords to the truly virtuous man a deep and strong delight" (ME 150).

Of course, there is some question here of just how coherent it would be to pursue, for example, truth for its own sake while recognizing that this is only "indirectly and secondarily" rational. How could one value truth for its own sake while knowing that this is only an indirect means to achieving what is really intrinsically valuable? The issue of moral schizophrenia – as some critics term such indirection or self-effacingness – has been effectively brought out by Bernard Williams, here in connection with Sidgwick's two-level utilitarianism:

Certainly it is empirically possible, and on the lines of Sidgwick's argument it must be true, that the dispositions will do the job which the Utilitarian theory has assigned to them only if the agents who possess those dispositions do not see their own character purely instrumentally, but rather see the world from the point of view of that character. Moreover, those dispositions require them to see other things in a non-instrumental light. Though Utilitarianism usually neglects the fact, they are dispositions not simply of action, but of belief and judgement; and they are expressed precisely in ascribing intrinsic and not instrumental value to various activities and relations such as truth-telling, loyalty and so on. Indeed, if Sidgwick is right in saying that the Utilitarian theory explains and justifies larger areas of everyday morality than had been supposed by the intuitionists, and that he has succeeded in his project of reconciling Utilitarianism and intuitionism by explaining in Utilitarian terms some of the phenomena on which the intuitionists were most insistent – if that is so, then it *must* be that in the actual world the dispositions do present themselves to their possessors, and also present other features of the world, in this non-instrumental light. It was these possessors who, just because they had these dispositions, were so strongly disposed to reject Utilitarianism and insist on the intrinsic value of these actions and of ends other than universal good.

It follows that there is a deeply uneasy gap or dislocation in this type of theory between the spirit that is supposedly justified and the spirit of the theory that supposedly justifies it. The gap is not very clearly perceived, if at all, by Sidgwick, nor, in my view, is its significance fully or at all adequately understood by later theorists who have adopted very much Sidgwick's position.[64]

As Williams recognizes, Sidgwick does have certain strategies for dealing with this dislocation not available to later utilitarians, albeit these are of a fairly elitist variety, such that the utilitarian theorists might be conceived as an elite class guiding, in Government House fashion, a less enlightened populace. But there are other responses to his critique as well, as later sections will explain, and it is mentioned here precisely because it applies more broadly than this passage suggests.

In fact, something akin to Williams's line of objection runs through a wide swath of criticism directed at the *Methods*, figuring in the arguments of perfectionists, virtue ethicists, anti-theorists, pragmatists, and others concerned to claim that Sidgwick just misses the point of the nonhedonistic alternatives.[65] Indeed, it is a venerable line of argument, and something very like it was given in Rashdall's review of the third edition of the *Methods*:

We must believe in a future life, Prof. Sidgwick tells us, because we must believe that the constitution of things is rational. And yet, according to Prof. Sidgwick, the universe is so constituted that the man who most completely succeeds in concealing from himself the true end of his being – or haply in never finding it out – will ultimately realise that end most thoroughly. *A priori* no one can deny that the universe may be so constituted; but where is the rationality of such a state of things? If we are to make assumptions, let them be such as will satisfy the logical demand on which they are founded. If we are to assume a rational order in the universe, surely the end prescribed to a man by his Reason must be his highest end. Man is so far a rational being that he is capable of preferring the rational to the pleasant. Surely, then, the reasonableness of such a preference cannot be *dependent* on its ultimately turning out that he has after all preferred the very things which his love of the reasonable led him to reject.[66]

Such objections have of course been seized on by many different critics of utilitarianism, anxious to demonstrate that this view cannot capture the recognition we accord to nonhedonistic values, or lives rather than acts, or other aspects of commonsense morality.[67] Obviously, elegant and subtle as Sidgwick's approach to happiness may be, it has not converted the legions of perfectionists or those defenders of "virtue ethics" who hold that the good life is one characterized by the exercise of certain excellences – courage, generosity, justice, and so forth – that are valuable for their own sake and constitute the happy life as parts of a whole, without requiring any reference to pleasure or desirable consciousness for their vindication.

Now, again, Sidgwick was not unappreciative of the force of such views, or of the efforts of the ancients – "through a large part of the present work the influence of Plato and Aristotle on my treatment of this subject has been greater than that of any modern writer" (ME 284) – but he could not persuade himself that they offered a genuinely constructive solution to the problems of ethics: "it seems worthy of remark that throughout the ethical speculation of Greece, such universal affirmations as are presented to us concerning Virtue or Good conduct seems always to be propositions which can only be defended from the charge of tautology, if they are understood as definitions of the problem to be solved, and not attempts at its solution" (ME 375–76).

Indeed, the Greek worldview was limited not only by its failure to artic-ulate the notion of disinterested duty. The "whole ethical controversy of ancient Greece," on Sidgwick's reading, was based on the assumption that "a rational individual would make the pursuit of his own good his supreme aim," and in claiming that the good was best conceived not in terms of pleasure but in terms of virtue – a nonhedonist eudaimonism – figures such as Aristotle simply lapsed into vagueness and tautology, defining virtue in terms of good and good in terms of virtue in a vicious circle (ME 375–76). Clarity in this department required that it be possible to compare and contrast, to quantify at least in a rough way, the happiness generated by one activity rather than another, or by one life rather than another. Falling back on some diffuse notion of "judgment" was no determinate solution at all.

Somewhat analogous objections are directed at the religious ethicist James Martineau, about whom, as Schneewind observes, Sidgwick wrote more than about any other contemporary excepting Herbert Spencer. For Martineau, the objects of ethical judgment are not things or acts per se but persons, and what is judged is always the "inner spring of action," assessed according to a scale of motives. But this is scarcely a system at all, according to Sidgwick; it is either as vague as unrefined common sense or must collapse into a utilitarian calculation of the consequences flowing from the different motives in action.[68]

As negative as Sidgwick is on these matters, he obviously took the lower, "Goethean" ideal very seriously, even if he awkwardly tried to fold it into Whewellian intuitionism or at least to divide it into that and nonhedonistic egoism. His later engagements with the work of Green, Rashdall, and Moore[69] would again suggest that he was in fact quite willing to treat this as, in effect, a separate method on its own terms, as he had in his earlier discussions with the Grote Club. Indeed, he was very appreciative of the classical influence on writers such as Green, and how this informed the rejection of any dualism of practical reason because, in T. H. Irwin's words, "[t]he full realization of one person's capacities requires him to will the good of other people for their own sake. We can show that the dualism of practical reason is avoidable if we can set out a true conception of a rational agent's good."[70] This was, obviously, not a result to which Sidgwick was emotionally averse. However, as Irwin stresses,

Sidgwick acknowledges Butler as the source of his own formulation of the dualism of practical reason; and he believes that Aristotelian non-hedonist eudaimonism allows us to think we have escaped the dualism simply because we mistake vague and useless formulations of substantive principles with practical consequences. Once we try to say more precisely what a person's good consists in, we will see that we are either assuming some highly controversial claim about the relation of morality to self-love or opening the very gap that Sidgwick calls to our attention.

Sidgwick, therefore, cannot take seriously any attempt to derive practical conclusions from a general conception of happiness such as the one Aristotle accepts; and he cannot endorse Aristotle's attempt . . . to show that self-love, correctly understood, requires acceptance of morality.[71]

For Irwin, and for many others drawn to perfectionism or virtue ethics, Sidgwick's main reason for rejecting nonhedonistic eudaimonism "rests on a demand for clarity that plays a highly controversial role at crucial points in *The Methods of Ethics*," and that begs the question of whether this kind of clarity "is necessary or appropriate in this case."[72] Both Aristotle and Green could be given more generous readings, on this basis, though Irwin, like Schneewind, does agree with much of what Sidgwick says about the difference between ancient and modern ethics.[73]

Yet as Thomas Hurka has argued,[74] Irwin is actually forced to concede on one truly fundamental issue, given the paradox of altruism:

On no plausible perfectionist view can a person's good consist entirely in promoting the good of others, and the other states that are good are ones for which conflict, especially over scarce resources, is possible. But Irwin does not state Sidgwick's argument in its strongest form. As (accurately) characterized by Irwin, Green's account of the good involves a vacuous circularity: each person's good consists entirely in promoting the good of others, which consists entirely in *their* promoting the good of others, which consists entirely in *their* promoting, etc. Unless there is something else that is good, there is nothing for all this promoting to aim at. This is Sidgwick's argument against the view that virtue, understood as pursuit of the good, can be the only intrinsic good. . . . And his response to Green therefore takes the form of a dilemma: for the good to be entirely non-competitive it must consist entirely in virtue, but then the theory of the good is vacuous; for the theory of the good not to be vacuous it must contain goods other than virtue, for which conflict is possible.[75]

Hurka goes on to observe, rightly, that Sidgwick's hedonistic account does not simply follow from such criticism, since even "if virtue cannot be the only intrinsic good it can be one intrinsic good among others, and its being so can make the good less competitive than on views like Sidgwick's." Such options have been explored by Moore, Rashdall, Ross, and, more recently, by Hurka himself, who endorses part of Rashdall's claim, against Sidgwick, that what the partisans of virtue value is "the settled bent of the will towards that which is truly or essentially good, and not a mere capacity or potentiality of pleasure-production such as might be supposed to reside in a bottle of old port."[76]

According to Hurka, the more plausible versions of perfectionism – untouched by Sidgwick's criticisms – make it clear that there "are initial goods such as the pleasure and knowledge of everyone, and then higher-level moral goods that consist in caring about those goods appropriately. That is a perfectionist view that values virtue but is not egoistic and not at all circular," and in this it differs from ancient perfectionism and "the virtue ethics that is its contemporary descendant," at least as these are understood by Irwin and many others. But Hurka also allows that many of the virtue ethicists who have objected to indirect or self-effacing forms of consequentialism have been guilty of an even severer form of moral schizophrenia. For consequentialists, including utilitarians, "the source of self-effacingness is a contingent psychological fact," whereas "virtue-ethical theory must be non-contingently self-effacing," since to "avoid encouraging self-indulgence, it must say that being motivated by its claims about the source of one's reasons is in itself and necessarily objectionable."[77]

As Sidgwick so often insisted, and as Hurka appears to admit, the Greeks can be plausibly understood as being in the main egoists, for whom cultivating one's perfection or virtue was, after all, cultivating one's own perfection or virtue. They were the forerunners of Arnoldian sweetness and light. One need only read, say, Aristotle on magnanimity to grasp how self-indulgent this orientation could become.[78] Thus, it must be allowed that Sidgwick's critical arguments carried and carry a good deal of force against some tremendously important ethical positions and thinkers, even if they cannot be credited with answering all the questions raised by his students Rashdall and Moore – who, after all, were developing Sidgwick's project on many fronts.

One might therefore conclude that however dismissive the treatment of Sidgwick's hedonism has been, his arguments and those of his contemporaries are nonetheless enjoying that curious vitality, characteristic of utilitarianism and egoism in general, that seems to come with having been pronounced dead so often.[79] Just how vital this discussion is will become clearer in the sections to follow. This preliminary survey of the issues is meant simply to highlight various controversial elements of Sidgwick's approach that need to be kept in mind in order to understand just how carefully qualified his claims for utilitarianism actually were, and how fertile in philosophical insight they have proved to be.

Of course, Sidgwick's hedonistic interpretation of ultimate good, it should be stressed again, also falls afoul of the conception of utility at work in most orthodox neoclassical economics, where the notion of minimally consistent preference satisfaction, disallowing any interpersonal comparisons of utility, serves as the last word on practical rationality (or at least has done so until recent decades).[80] Yet, as Book II of the *Methods* handsomely demonstrates, Sidgwick was as painfully aware of the difficulties involved in adding up and comparing utilities as any twentieth-century economist – asking, for example, "who can tell that the philosopher's constitution is not such as to render the enjoyments of the senses, in his case, comparatively feeble?" (ME 148) He was, however, also cognizant of the unavoidability of making "comparisons between pleasures and pains with practical reliance on their results," for purposes both of ethics and of everyday life (ME 150). The by now vast literature on the inadequacies of Pareto optimality as a substitute for justice, although often working in the service of Kantian alternatives to utilitarianism, at least points up the intelligence of Sidgwick's fundamental conviction – informed by a great deal of economic sophistication – that interpersonal (and intrapersonal) comparisons of some sort can hardly be avoided when discussing any marginally realistic social scheme.[81] The stronger point to make in this connection concerns the curious denouement for Benthamism that came with Sidgwick's candid, frustrated confession that "in the development of human nature, the incalculable element increases at a more rapid ratio than the calculable." How overly ambitious could he have been, when he claimed that "I think that with great trouble one may come to calculate the sources of such happiness as may then be found to be nearly valueless to us"?

III. *The Methods of Ethics*: Common Sense, Intuition, and Certainty

The orthodox moralists such as Whewell (then in vogue) said that there was a whole intelligible system of intuitions: but how were they to be learnt? I could not accept Butler's view as to the sufficiency of a plain man's conscience: for it appeared to me that plain men agreed rather verbally than really.

In this state of mind I had to read Aristotle again; and a light seemed to dawn upon me as to the meaning and drift of his procedure – especially in Books ii., iii., iv. of the *Ethics.* . . . What he gave us there was the Common Sense Morality of Greece, reduced to consistency by careful comparison: given not as something external to him but as what "we" – he and others – think, ascertained by reflection. And was not this really the Socratic induction, elicited by interrogation?

Might I not imitate this: do the same for *our* morality here and now, in the same manner of impartial reflection on current opinion?

Indeed *ought* I not to do this before deciding on the question whether I had or had not a system of moral intuitions? At any rate the result would be useful, whatever conclusion I came to.

So this was the part of my book first written (Book iii., chaps. i.-xi.), and a certain imitation of Aristotle's manner was very marked in it at first, and though I have tried to remove it where it seemed to me affected or pedantic, it still remains to some extent.

Sidgwick, ME xxi

Aristotelian virtue may have been rejected, but Sidgwick was, as has been stressed, very much in the grip of Aristotelian inquiry, at least of this Socratic and Apostolic variety. And nowhere is this more evident than in his famous analysis of commonsense or dogmatic intuitional morality, from which the ascent is made to the abstract axioms supporting utilitarianism.

But here again, there are so many different influences at work in Sidgwick that one may easily find it difficult to locate him in line with philosophical predecessors. The ancients, but also Descartes, Clarke, Butler, Kant, Reid, and Whewell, in addition to Mill, all loom large in his work, and one might also note that in the early 1870s, when he was slaving away again with his German, he found himself struggling to make sense of Hegel and post-Kantian German philosophy: "Day after day I sit down to my books with a firm determination to master the German Heraclitus, and as regularly I depart to my Mittagsessen with a sense of hopeless defeat. No difficulty of any other writer can convey the least conception even of the sort of difficulty that I find in Hegel." Still, "If Hegelianism shows itself in England I feel equal to dealing with it. The *method* seems to me a mistake, and therefore the system a ruin" (M 230, 238).

The residue of this intense stretch of Germanism is clearly evident in the *Methods*, especially in the first edition, which, as Schneewind has noted, includes such transcendental lines as: "we may perhaps say that this notion of 'ought', when once it has been developed, is a necessary form of our moral apprehension, just as space is now a necessary form of our sense perception" (ME1 93). Yet Schneewind is surely right to insist that, although "Sidgwick himself points out the Kantian affinities of his position, he is by no means simply a Kantian. He is deliberately developing a traditional mode of approach to basic axioms. In doing so, he brings out distinctly new possibilities within it."[82] Indeed, so great are the new possibilities that one suspects that the old Mauricean gambit was at work in Sidgwick's methods of composition, such that his own originality often ended up being masked. Among other things, his intuitionism manages to avoid most of the metaphysical entanglements usually associated with that form of epistemology, and his framing of the dualism of practical reason brings out the potential conflict between morality and self-interest much more acutely than, say, the work of Butler does, despite his professed indebtedness to Butler's handling of the issue.

Now, Sidgwick recognizes that his way of approaching the subject of ethics could lead to confusion. There is "difficulty in the classification and comparison of ethical systems; since they often appear to have different affinities according as we consider Method or Ultimate Reason." Thus,

In my treatment of the subject, difference of Method is taken as the paramount consideration: and it is on this account that I have treated the view in which Perfection is taken to be the Ultimate End as a variety of the Intuitionism which determines right conduct by reference to axioms of duty intuitively known; while I have made as marked a separation as possible between Epicureanism or Egoistic Hedonism, and the Universalistic or Benthamite Hedonism to which I propose to restrict the term Utilitarianism.

I am aware that these two latter methods are commonly treated as closely connected: and it is not difficult to find reasons for this. In the first place, they agree in prescribing actions as means to an end distinct from, and lying outside the actions; so that they both lay down rules which are not absolute but relative, and only valid if they conduce to the end. Again, the ultimate end is according to both methods the same in quality, i.e. pleasure; or, more strictly, the maximum of pleasure attainable, pains being subtracted. Besides, it is of course to a great extent true that the conduct recommended by the one principle coincides with that inculcated by the other. Though it would seem to be only in an ideal polity that 'self-interest well understood' leads to the perfect discharge of all social duties, still, in a tolerably well-ordered community it prompts to the fulfilment of most of them, unless under very exceptional circumstances. And, on the other hand, a Universalistic Hedonist may reasonably hold that his own happiness is that portion of the universal happiness which it is most in his power to promote, and which therefore is most especially entrusted to his charge. And the practical blending of the two systems is sure to go beyond their theoretical coincidence. It is much easier for a man to move in a sort of diagonal between Egoistic and Universalistic Hedonism, than to be practically a consistent adherent of either. Few men are so completely selfish, whatever their theory of morals may be, as not occasionally to promote the happiness of others from natural sympathetic impulse unsupported by Epicurean calculation. And probably still fewer are so resolutely unselfish as never to find "all men's good" in their own with rather too ready conviction. . . .

Nevertheless, it seems to me undeniable that the practical affinity between Utilitarianism and Intuitionism is really much greater than that between the two forms of Hedonism. . . . many moralists who have maintained as practically valid the judgements of right and wrong which the Common Sense of mankind seems intuitively to enunciate, have yet regarded General Happiness as an end to which the rules of morality are the best means, and have held that a knowledge of these rules was implanted by Nature or revealed by God for the attainment of this end. Such a belief implies that, though I am bound to take, as *my* ultimate standard in acting, conformity to a rule which is for me absolute, still the natural or Divine reason for the rule laid down is Utilitarian. On this view, the *method* of Utilitarianism is certainly rejected: the connexion between right action and happiness is not ascertained by a process of reasoning. But we can hardly say that the Utilitarian principle is altogether rejected: rather the limitations of the human reason are supposed to prevent it from apprehending adequately the real connexion between the true principle and the right rules of conduct. This connexion, however, has always been to a large extent recognised by all reflective persons. Indeed, so clear is it that in most cases the observance of the commonly received moral rules tends to render human life tranquil and happy, that even moralists (as Whewell) who are most strongly opposed to Utilitarianism have, in attempting to exhibit the "necessity" of moral rules, been led to dwell on utilitarian considerations. (ME 85–86)

There is a great deal of Sidgwick packed into the above passage. The view that "practical conflict, in ordinary human minds, is mainly between Self-interest and Social Duty however determined" is virtually a defining theme of the *Methods*, as is the view that the intuitionist method of someone like Whewell tacitly appeals to utilitarian considerations, which may, indeed, be more or less unconscious. Also evident here is the controversial way in which Sidgwick subsumes the moral content of ancient perfectionism – insofar as it is at all determinate – under intuitionism, and the way in which he is really concerned, in the final analysis, with both methods and principles. For it is one of the most prominent theses of the book that intuitionism of the Whewellian variety does not deliver on its claims for the validity of commonsense moral rules. In fact, running in parallel with the three methods we find several different understandings of the term "intuitionism," and the shifting between the use of the term to designate the Whewellian method of ethics and the use of it to designate the form of epistemology that Sidgwick endorses and applies to ultimate principles is one of the least felicitous features of Sidgwick's organization of his subject matter. But because he did organize his material in this way, it is easier to get a handle on the drift of his argument by tracking the varietes of intuitionism to which he makes reference. In this connection one confronts what Sidgwick, at least, regarded as the more definite results of his inquiry.

Indeed, Sidgwick allows that the three methods might be called "natural methods rationalised," since plain persons "commonly seem to guide themselves by a mixture of different methods, more or less disguised under ambiguities of language" (ME 12). In part, therefore, his task is to sort out the jumble of different and incompatible methods that often get mixed together in ordinary moral reasoning, and to make it clear how these are alternatives between which we are "necessarily forced to choose" when we attempt "to frame a complete synthesis of practical maxims and to act in a perfectly consistent manner" (ME 12). Although many seem to think that conscience delivers immediate judgments on the rightness of particular acts ("perceptional" or "ultra" or even "aesthetic" intuitionism), Sidgwick himself has "no doubt that reflective persons, in proportion to their reflectiveness, come to rely rather on abstract universal intuitions relating to classes of cases conceived under general notions." That is, the particular judgment, or truth, depends upon the more general truth, in a familiar form of abstract ascent from cases to rules. There is no one system of this type, but rather a range of views of different degrees of sophistication, from the commonsense morality of the Ten Commandments to the philosophically more developed "dogmatic intuitionism" of Whewell, which shares much with the better-known Kantian system.

The basic idea of this form of intuitional morality, which is not unlike the commonsensical view of the deliverances of conscience prevalent today, is that "the practically ultimate end of moral actions" is "their conformity to certain rules or dictates of Duty unconditionally prescribed," which rules are discerned with a "really clear and finally valid intuition" (ME 96, 101). One ought to do one's duty because one can just see that duty is something that ought to be done, that it is fitting to one's nature as a rational being. Every rational being can apprehend this, though the moral theorist can still play a special role in refining and developing the system of basic moral duties, rendering it a progressively better approximation to the truth. Whewell, for instance, holds that the general moral rules – such rules as telling the truth (veracity), promise keeping (good faith), and justice – are

implicit in the moral reasoning of ordinary men, who apprehend them adequately for most practical purposes, and are able to enunciate them roughly; but that to state them with proper precision requires a special habit of contemplating clearly and steadily abstract moral notions. It is held that the moralist's function then is to perform this process of abstract contemplation, to arrange the results as systematically as possible, and by proper definitions and explanations to remove vagueness and prevent conflict. (ME 101)

Of course, for Sidgwick, this is precisely what the dogmatic intuitional moralists do not succeed in doing; the process of the philosophical refinement of common sense needs to go much further. As he explains in a response to a review of the *Methods* by Henry Calderwood, another dogmatic intuitional moralist:

If I ask myself whether I see clearly and distinctly the self-evidence of any particular maxims of duty, as I see that of the formal principles "that what is right for me must be right for all persons in precisely similar circumstances" and "that I ought to prefer the greater good of another to my own lesser good": I have no doubt whatever that I do not. I am conscious of a strong impression, an opinion on which I habitually act without hesitation, that I ought to speak truth, to perform promises, to requite benefits, &c., and also of powerful moral sentiments prompting me to the observance of these rules; but on reflection I can now clearly distinguish such opinions and sentiments from the apparently immediate and certain cognition that I have of the formal principles above mentioned. But I could not always have made this distinction; and I believe that the majority of moral persons do not make it: most "plain men" would probably say, at any rate on the first consideration of the matter, that they saw the obligations of Veracity and Good Faith as clearly and immediately as they saw those of Equity and Rational Benevolence. How then am I to argue with such persons? It will not settle the matter to tell them that they have observed their own mental processes wrongly, and that more careful introspection will show them the non-intuitive character of what they took for intuitions; especially as in many cases I do not believe that the error is one of misobservation. Still less am I inclined to dispute the "primitiveness" or "spontaneousness" or "originality" of these apparent intuitions. On the contrary, I hold that here, as in other departments of thought, the primitive

spontaneous processes of the mind are mixed with error, which is only to be removed gradually by comprehensive reflection upon the results of these processes.
Through such a course of reflection I have endeavored to lead my readers in chaps.
2–10 of Book III of my treatise: in the hope that after they have gone through it
they may find their original apprehension of the self-evidence of moral maxims
importantly modified.[83]

Such remarks might well suggest how, for all his critical commentary on
ancient perfectionism, Sidgwick's procedure does indeed, as he insisted,
have distinct affinities with Aristotle's. Indeed, Sidgwick was ever ready
to insist that we must accept

Aristotle's distinction between logical or natural priority in cognition and priority
in the knowledge of any particular mind. We are thus enabled to see that a proposition may be self-evident, i.e. may be properly cognisable without being viewed
in connexion with any other propositions; though in order that its truth may be
apparent to some particular mind, there is still required some rational process
connecting it with propositions previously accepted by that mind.[84]

And there are two ways in which this might be done: by demonstrating
how "some limited and qualified statement" that is taken as self-evident
is actually only part of a "simpler and wider proposition," on which the
limitations turn out to be arbitrary, or by establishing some general criteria
"for distinguishing true first principles . . . from false ones," which are
then used to "construct a strictly logical deduction by which, applying
their general criteria to the special case of ethics, we establish the true
first principles of this latter subject."[85] Both ways are deployed in the
Methods, which develops but in no way retreats from the vision of Apostolic
inquiry.

Just how Aristotelian Sidgwick really was will be further considered
later on, when we will also further consider the viability of any such
strategy.[86] At present it need only be stressed that he obviously did distinguish between any final and authoritative system of intuitive truths and
the way in which an untutored or insufficiently reflective mind would at
length come to grasp such a system, by fighting its way free of the snares
and vague generalities of common sense. But so far, at least, Sidgwick's
approach would seem to have much in common with, for example, Jeff
McMahan's attempt to recast the method of reflective equilibrium in foundationalist form:

[D]eeper principles are explanatorily prior, we have to work our way to them via our intuitions in much the way that scientists work towards general principles via our perceptual data. The process of discovering and formulating the more general principles is evidently difficult and intellectually demanding.... as we grope our way towards the principles, we are discovering what we antecedently believe, albeit below the level of conscious awareness. The principles that we hope to uncover express deep dispositions of thought and feeling that operate below the level of consciousness to regulate our intuitive responses to particular cases.

Thus, "the order of discovery is the reverse of the order of justification."[87] McMahan resists calling the deeper principles intuitively "self-evident" rather than foundational, and he suggests that Sidgwick would differ in this respect. But the difference is not great, given that Sidgwick would not take the designation "self-evident" to mean finally valid, at least when applied by the philosophical intuitionist.[88]

As emphatically as Sidgwick insists that the morality of common sense is his "as much as any other man's," and that he is not engaged in "mere hostile criticism from the outside," one cannot come away from the famous Book III without the distinct feeling that the aversion to Whewell – and to the Whewell within himself – that he developed as an undergraduate must have been singularly intense, such is the remorselessness of the criticism flowing through these chapters. In summing up, Sidgwick urges that the

... Utilitarian must, in the first place, endeavor to show to the Intuitionist that the principles of Truth, Justice, etc. have only a dependent and subordinate validity: arguing either that the principle is really only affirmed by Common-Sense as a general rule admitting of exceptions and qualifications, as in the case of Truth, and that we require some further principle for systematising these exceptions and qualifications; or that the fundamental notion is vague and needs further determination, as in the case of Justice; and further, that the different rules are liable to conflict with each other, and that we require some higher principle to decide the issue thus raised; and again, that the rules are differently formulated by different persons, and that these differences admit of no Intuitional solution, while they show the vagueness and ambiguity of the common moral notions to which the Intuitionist appeals. (ME 421)

If this sounds rather familiar, as the kind of thing that Mill urged Sidgwick to do with his work on conformity and subscription, that is of course no accident. "Pious fraud" is addressed in Book III, Chapter 7, where Sidgwick cites Whewell's fishy endorsement of the methods of *suppressio veri* and *suggestio falsi* – turning a question aside and producing a false scent – as legitimate ways of avoiding a direct lie, noting that some would say that such methods still produce false beliefs in the inquirer and "that if deception is to be practised at all, it is mere formalism to object to any one mode of effecting it more than another" (ME 317). Sidgwick concludes that

> reflection seems to show that the rule of Veracity, as commonly accepted, cannot be elevated into a definite moral axiom: for there is no real agreement as to how far we are bound to impart true beliefs to others: and while it is contrary to Common Sense to exact absolute candour under all circumstances, we yet find no self-evident secondary principle, clearly defining when it is not to be exacted. (ME 317)

Thus, commonsense morality, or even the refined version of it represented by Whewell's dogmatic intuitional system, cannot stand on its own, cannot actually yield decisive practical answers.

However, the answer that Sidgwick, for all his impartiality, rather clearly favors is ready to hand. He strives to show how

> Utilitarianism sustains the general validity of the current moral judgements, and thus supplements the defects which reflection finds in the intuitive recognition of their stringency; and at the same time affords a principle of synthesis, and a method for binding the unconnected and occasionally conflicting principles of common moral reasoning into a complete and harmonious system. If systematic reflection on the morality of Common Sense thus exhibits the Utilitarian principle as that to which Common Sense naturally appeals for that further development of its system which this same reflection shows to be necessary, the proof of Utilitarianism seems as complete as it can be made. (ME 422)

In another passage more fully summing up the case, Sidgwick allies himself with Hume, whose account of the connection between commonsense morality and utility, although somewhat casual and fragmentary, was plainly on the right track. It can be shown, Sidgwick holds, that

> the Utilitarian estimate of consequences not only supports broadly the current moral rules, but also sustains their generally received limitations and qualifications: that, again, it explains anomalies in the Morality of Common Sense, which from any other point of view must seem unsatisfactory to the reflective intellect; and moreover, where the current formula is not sufficiently precise for the guidance of conduct, while at the same time difficulties and perplexities arise in the attempt

to give it additional precision, the Utilitarian method solves these difficulties and perplexities in general accordance with the vague instincts of Common Sense, and is naturally appealed to for such solution in ordinary moral discussions. It may be shown further, that it not only supports the generally received view of the relative importance of different duties, but is also naturally called in as arbiter, where rules commonly regarded as co-ordinate come into conflict: that, again, when the same rule is interpreted somewhat differently by different persons, each naturally supports his view by urging its Utility, however strongly he may maintain the rule to be self-evident and known *a priori*: that where we meet with marked diversity of moral opinion on any point, in the same age and country, we commonly find manifest and impressive utilitarian reasons on both sides: and that finally the remarkable discrepancies found in comparing the moral codes of different ages and countries are for the most part strikingly correlated to differences in effects of actions on happiness, or in men's foresight of, or concern for, such effects. (ME 425–26)[89]

This is, for Sidgwick, one aspect of the genuinely philosophical intu-itionism to which dogmatic intuitionism leads: that is, a third phase of intuitionism that "while accepting the morality of common sense as in the main sound, still attempts to find for it a philosophic basis which it does not itself offer: to get one or more principles more absolutely and unde-niably true and evident, from which the current rules might be deduced, either just as they are commonly received or with slight modifications and rectifications" (ME 102). This form of intuitionism allows the general rightness of commonsense morality, but also affords a "deeper explana-tion" of why it is largely right. And it is not "intuitional" in "the narrower sense that excludes consequences; but only in the wider sense as being self-evident principles relating to 'what ought to be'" (ME 102 n1). These are the sought-after axioms, about which there is a surprising degree of controversy.

In its general form, apart from the specifically intuitionist claims in-volved, Sidgwick's handling of commonsense morality plainly has as much in common with Mill as with Aristotle. However, one of the great virtues of Schneewind's classic, *Sidgwick's Ethics and Victorian Moral Philosophy*, is the way it details the far more complex and comprehensive structure of Sidgwick's inquiry, bringing out the difference between the "dependence" and "systematization" arguments.

As Schneewind has it, there is a dual purpose to Sidgwick's exam-ination of commonsense morality. First, there is the search for "really self-evident principles," and second, as the previously quoted passages illustrate, "there is the search for a principle superior in validity to other moral principles" – that is, a principle with superior moral rather than epistemological authority, which is what any complex moral code requires in order to determine the limits and exceptions of its component principles and be thoroughly rationalized. The latter process has two stages: a negative stage, which appeals to the "dependence" argument (that the principles of commonsense morality have only a dependent and subordinate validity), and a positive stage, which appeals to the "systematization" argument (that the utilitarian principle sustains commonsense moral judgments and affords a principle of synthesis). On the one side, Schneewind argues that, for Sidgwick, it is not "inevitable that a code of the kind which he takes to be a practical necessity in human life must have the characteristics of commonsense morality on which the dependence argument focuses attention."[90] On the other side, the examination of commonsense morality forms at least part of the case for utilitarianism. "For it shows, among other things, that the factual characteristics which are treated by common-sense moral rules as indicating rightness cannot be ultimate right-making characteristics." Thus, Schneewind argues in a crucial passage:

The dependence argument shows that certain features of received opinion which it would share with any equally complex code in an equally complex society, require us to go beyond its dictates to a different kind of principle. The appeal to self-evidence next yields rational principles of the kind required by the dependence argument. We then turn to see if these principles can systematize common sense. Since the first principles are obtained by a procedure not involving consideration of their systematizing power, the degree of their serviceability for this task provides an independent test of their acceptability. From the explanatory side of the systematization argument we learn that in so far as common-sense morality is already rational, the best explanation or model of its rationality is the utilitarian one. The rectificatory side of the systematization argument shows that in so far as received opinion still needs to be made rational, the best method of making it so is the utilitarian one. Thus the systematization argument is not meant to show that all our pre-theoretical moral opinions can be derived from the axioms. It is meant to show that the axioms provide an ideal or model of practical rationality which enable us to see that the kind of code we need for daily decision-making can be rational. The fact that one and the same ideal of rationality enables us to see that our actual code is to some extent rational and shows how it can have its rationality increased, provides stronger support for the ideal than any abstract argument can provide.[91]

This is one of the few commentaries on Sidgwick that truly captures the intricacy of his argument. Still, it is possible to exaggerate the differences from Mill resulting from Sidgwick's intuitionism, and a few reminders about the continuities between the two should prove helpful.

Recall that Mill, in *Utilitarianism*, lamented the chaos and indeterminateness of ordinary morality, but in contemplating "to what extent the moral beliefs of mankind have been vitiated or made uncertain by the absence of any distinct recognition of an ultimate standard," he thought it would "be easy to show that whatever steadiness or consistency these moral beliefs have attained, has been mainly due to the tacit influence of a standard not recognised." In other words, although

the non-existence of an acknowledged first principle has made ethics not so much a guide as a consecration of men's actual sentiments, still, as men's sentiments, both of favour and aversion, are greatly influenced by what they suppose to be the effects of things upon their happiness, the principle of utility . . . has had a large share in forming the moral doctrines even of those who most scornfully reject its authority.

Not to put too fine a point on it, Mill continues with a swipe at Whewell to the effect that "to all those à priori moralists who deem it necessary to argue at all, utilitarian arguments are indispensable," since no one refuses to admit the significance of happiness in some way, and the utilitarian method is often called in to settle conflicts or clarify duties within the system of common sense.[92]

Moreover, for all his criticisms of commonsense morality, especially in its dogmatic religious aspects, Mill sounded a very Sidgwickian note when he remarked that "mankind must by this time have acquired positive beliefs as to the effects of some actions on their happiness; and the beliefs which have thus come down are the rules of morality for the multitude, and for the philosopher until he has succeeded in finding better."[93] This was the cautious note that Sidgwick's far more extensive treatment of the subject sounded time and again. However much he was inclined to agree with Mill that commonsense morality as it stood was not good enough to yield the "middle axioms" of a genuinely scientific utilitarianism, he was clear that if the utilitarian theorist "keeps within the limits that separate scientific prevision from fanciful Utopian conjecture, the form of society to which his practical conclusions relate will be one varying but little from the actual, with its actually established code of moral rules and customary judgments concerning virtue and vice" (ME 474). Furthermore, both took some pains to present utilitarianism in a form that preserved certain commonsense notions – the difference between subjective and objective rightness, acting with the proper intention, and so forth. The *Methods* may even be said to outstrip Mill's exposition of these topics. Consider, for example, this summation, added in the second edition:

For no one, in considering what he ought himself to do in any particular case, can distinguish what he believes to be right from what really is so: the necessity for a practical choice between 'subjective' and 'objective' rightness can only present itself in respect of the conduct of another person whom it is in our power to influence. If another is about to do what we think wrong while he thinks it right, and we cannot alter his belief but can bring other motives to bear on him that may overbalance his sense of duty, it becomes necessary to decide whether we ought thus to tempt him to realise what we believe to be objectively right against his own convictions. I think that the moral sense of mankind would pronounce against such temptation, – thus regarding the Subjective rightness of an action as more important than the Objective, – unless the evil of the act prompted by a mistaken sense of duty appeared to be very grave. But however essential it may be that a moral agent should do what he believes to be right, this condition of right conduct is too simple to admit of systematic development: it is, therefore, clear that the details of our investigation must relate mainly to 'objective' rightness. (ME 207–8)

Thus, insofar as one is called upon to act directly with the intention of maximizing expected utility, one's action can rightly be assessed by considerations of objective rightness, the utility actually achieved by one's action, and by how well one sought to bring the two into accord. In this connection, mention might also be made of how Sidgwick construes the notion of an "intention" as extending to cover all the foreseeable consequences one's action (a point that, while it does not trouble utilitarians, has much provoked Catholic defenders of the so-called doctrine of the "double-effect").[94]

But the larger point here is that Sidgwick and Mill were quite at one in thinking that commonsense morality had evolved in a utilitarian direction and was undergirded by the utilitarian principle – or at least, by principles yielding utilitarian conclusions – even though the utilitarian must in turn make some resort to something like the rules of commonsense morality while continuing to work for its reform. As Mill eloquently argued,

to consider the rules of morality as improvable, is one thing; to pass over the intermediate generalizations entirely, and endeavour to test each individual action directly be the first principle, is another. It is a strange notion that the acknowledgement of a first principle is inconsistent with the admission of secondary ones. To inform a traveller respecting the place of his ultimate destination, is not to forbid the use of landmarks and direction-posts on the way.

And besides, "the multiplication of happiness is, according to the utilitarian ethics, the object of virtue: the occasions on which any person (except one in a thousand) has it in his power to do this on an extended scale, in other words, to be a public benefactor, are but exceptional."[95]

Furthermore, in the revealing little essay on "Utilitarianism" that Sidgwick delivered to the Metaphysical Society in December of 1873, just at the time he was completing the *Methods*, he explained that "Utilitarianism, as introduced by Cumberland, is too purely conservative; it dwells entirely on the general conduciveness of moral rules to the general good, and ignores the imperfections of these rules as commonly conceived. On the other side, the Utilitarianism of Bentham is too purely destructive, and treats the morality of Common Sense with needless acrimony and contempt."[96] The Millian space between these poles was precisely what Sidgwick sought to occupy, and if this seems to be at least a partial retreat to the "contemplative utilitarianism" of Hume and Smith, after the Benthamite juggernaut, that is not a filiation to which he would have objected, despite his very real differences from the cool, practical atheism of those figures from the previous century.[97]

Thus, if Sidgwick was carrying out a neo-Aristotelian research program, he was nonetheless doing it under very Millian guidelines. And as noted earlier, Christine Korsgaard has observed that Mill quite strikingly anticipates even Sidgwick's intuitionistic predelictions:

If there be anything innate in the matter, I see no reason why the feeling which is innate should not be regard to the pleasures and pains of others. If there is any principle of morality which is intuitively obligatory, I should say it must be that. If so, the intuitive ethics would coincide with the utilitarian, and there would be no further quarrel between them. Even as it is, the intuitive moralists, though they believe that there are other intuitive moral obligations, do already believe this to be one.[98]

Naturally, Mill puts this forward merely as a pregnant suggestion, since his own belief is that the moral feelings are acquired rather than innate.

Yet the distance between Mill and Sidgwick might be further reduced by stressing again that Sidgwick's version of intuitionism was not committed to claims about the "innateness" of moral principles; this he thought a confusion foisted on intuitionism by its critics. As Schneewind has put it, Sidgwick "takes 'intuitive' to be opposed, not, as the empiricists think, to 'innate,' but to 'discursive' or to 'demonstrative.'" Besides, the

empiricists themselves accept particular judgments as in this sense intuitively evident: Why do they reject universal intuitions? The reason they give is that the latter are sometimes mistaken. Sidgwick does not deny this. . . . But errors may be found even in apparent particular intuitions, if by this phrase we refer to more than the barest experiencing of feelings, for any cognitive claim about experience implies comparison and contrast and may go wrong. Moreover, it is impossible to see how 'he can establish upon his foundation the conclusions of science. . . . individual premises, however manipulated, cannot establish a universal conclusion,' and yet we all agree that such conclusions can be established.[99]

Thus, intuition "is simply a requirement for any sort of knowledge or reasoning at all – not a special mark of our moral insight or divine nature. It is needed for matter-of-fact knowledge, for mathematics, for logic, and for science as well as for morality."

But what did Sidgwick's "philosophical intuitionism" then amount to? How distant was he, really, from the fallibilism of Mill's empiricism and naturalism? And correspondingly, how free was he from the temptation to commit the "naturalistic fallacy"? If, as Schneewind, Shaver, and Crisp have all urged, Sidgwick's "antinaturalism" is of the most minimal kind, then perhaps he really is more properly situated in the line of descent from Mill to Dewey than in that from Mill to Moore, given the Platonic overtones of the latter's view of good as an independently existing property.[100] Did Moore's metaethics represent something of a metaphysical or ontological turn, when compared to Sidgwick's? As Schneewind remarks, although Sidgwick does "occasionally speak, especially in the earlier editions, of 'qualities' of rightness or goodness," which might suggest "a theory of the sort later put forth by Moore or Ross about the ontological status of what is known when we know that an act is right or good," any theory he might have "on this matter remains implicit."[101]

Although satisfactory answers to these questions would require a full-fledged account of "naturalism" and of how far Sidgwick's account really differed from Moore's, a few remarks might provide some helpful guidance. Obviously, Sidgwick was working with certain critical epistemological standards for assessing the success of the claims of systems such as Whewell's. He appreciates the difference, one of considerable historical importance, of "ethical writers . . . who have confined themselves mainly to the definition and arrangement of the Morality of Common Sense, from those who have aimed at a more philosophical treatment of the content of moral intuition" (ME 103n). Samuel Clarke, for instance, was one of the latter, but, useful as his early efforts were, "by degrees the attempt to exhibit morality as a body of scientific truth fell into discredit, and the disposition to dwell on the emotional side of the moral consciousness became prevalent." Until, that is, the noncognitivism of Hutcheson yielded the skepticism of Hume, at which point the defenders of morality grew alarmed and sought to show (with Reid and Hamilton, for example) that Hume was employing a mistaken view of the nature of empirical experience and morality. Even so, this school, with which Sidgwick has no little sympathy, "was led rather to expound and reaffirm the morality of Common Sense, than to offer any profounder principles which could not be so easily supported by an appeal to common experience" (ME 104).

Sidgwick clearly thinks that we must take a lesson from both Clarke and Reid, but with an admixture of Descartes and Kant. "Is there," he asks, "no possibility of attaining, by a more profound and discriminating examination of our common moral thought, to real ethical axioms – intuitive propositions of real clearness and certainty?" (ME 373) This is to ask, in other words, whether the philosopher might not aspire to rather more than the work of Reid and Whewell and seek "to do somewhat more than define and formulate the common moral opinions of mankind." Perhaps, indeed, the function of the philosopher is "to tell men what they ought to think, rather than what they do think," and thus to "transcend Common Sense in his premises" (ME 373). Perhaps "we should expect that the history of Moral Philosophy – so far at least as those whom we may call orthodox thinkers are concerned – would be a history of attempts to enunciate, in full breadth and clearness, those primary intuitions of Reason, by the scientific application of which the common moral thought of mankind may be at once systematised and corrected" (ME 373–74).

In this, Sidgwick seems to be sounding a call to philosophize meant to round up figures as far from each other as Clarke and Bentham, or Descartes and Bacon, who for all their differences were nonetheless at one in thinking it possible to improve on the mass of vague generality and superstition by which most people sought to guide their lives. Although he shows none of Bentham's nastiness and vituperation in attacking the received morality and politics, and goes beyond even Mill in casting utilitarianism as something both reasonable and respectable, a creed for decent people who are not mentally inert, he is at great pains not to confuse the true philosopher with the plain person, who mixes up different methods without even realizing it. This is, to be sure, a difficult (and highly Mauricean) balancing act, though a crucial one. Sidgwick's point, after all, is to present utilitarianism "as the final form into which Intuitionism tends to pass, when the demand for really self-evident first principles is rigorously pressed" – which is something that even Mill did not do,[102] thus leaving the famous supposed gap in his argument between the factual claim that people desire happiness and the normative one that the general happiness is what they ought to pursue (ME 388). Again, Sidgwick demands that his reader ask, when considering common sense, "(1) whether he can state a clear, precise, self-evident first principle, according to which he is prepared to judge conduct under each head: and (2) if so, whether this principle is really that commonly applied in practice, by those whom he takes to represent Common Sense" (ME 343).

What would it take to meet the first condition? According to Sidgwick, there "seem to be four conditions, the complete fulfilment of which would establish a significant proposition, apparently self-evident, in the highest degree of certainty attainable: and which must be approximately realised by the premises of our reasoning in any inquiry, if that reasoning is to lead us cogently to trustworthy conclusions" (ME 338). The careful phrasing here is, as we shall see, an essential part of Sidgwick's fallibilism, for he generally stops short of claiming, in the *Methods* and in his other writings, that humanity has at last got beyond "apparently self-evident" propositions and achieved absolute and final certainty.[103] On balance, Sidgwick is clear enough that principles or axioms of the "highest certainty" are still being sought in ethics.[104] At times, he does sound less doubtful – for example, in "Utilitarianism," which opens with the proclamation that it has been his object "to avoid all but incontrovertible propositions" and that he has been "careful not to dogmatize upon any point where scientific certainty did not appear to be attainable." But as he immediately explains, "in most discussions on Utilitarianism I find one or more of these propositions, at important points of the argument, implicitly ignored; and . . . a wide experience shows that an ethical or metaphysical proposition is not the less likely to provoke controversy because it is put forward as incontrovertible."[105]

The four conditions are as follows. The first, which he often refers to as the "Cartesian Criterion," is that the "terms of the proposition must be clear and precise. The rival originators of modern Methodology, Descartes and Bacon, vie with each other in the stress that they lay on this point: and the latter's warning against the 'notiones male terminatae' of ordinary thought is peculiarly needed in ethical discussion." Second, the

> self-evidence of the proposition must be ascertained by careful reflection. . . . A rigorous demand for self-evidence in our premises is a valuable protection against the misleading influence of our own irrational impulses on our judgements: while at the same time it not only distinguishes as inadequate the mere external support of authority and tradition, but also excludes the more subtle and latent effect of these in fashioning our minds to a facile and unquestioning admission of common but unwarranted assumptions. (ME 339)

This too is a test especially needed in ethics, since "it cannot be denied that any strong sentiment, however purely subjective, is apt to transform itself into the semblance of an intuition; and it requires careful contemplation to detect the illusion" (ME 339). Third, the "propositions accepted as self-evident must be mutually consistent," since it "is obvious that any collision between two intuitions is a proof that there is error in one or the other, or in both." This condition must not be treated lightly, as though the difficulty "may be ignored or put aside for future solution, without any slur being thrown on the scientific character of the conflicting formulae" (ME 341). Fourth and finally, since "it is implied in the very notion of Truth that it is essentially the same for all minds, the denial by another of a proposition that I have affirmed has a tendency to impair my confidence in its validity." Indeed, "the absence of such disagreement must remain an indispensable negative condition of the certainty of our beliefs," for "if I find any of my judgments, intuitive or inferential, in direct conflict with a judgment of some other mind, there must be error somewhere: and if I have no more reason to suspect error in the other mind than in my own, reflective comparison between the two judgments necessarily reduces me temporarily to a state of neutrality" (ME 341–42).

In other writings, Sidgwick tended to collapse the first two conditions into one, so that his philosophical intuitionism involved the three-pronged demand for clarity and ability to withstand critical reflection, consistency or coherence, and consensus of experts – all this conceived not as a guarantee of indubitable truth, but as the best way to reduce the risk of error.[106] All three methods are important; none can stand alone, though philosophy is especially concerned with the second, since its "ideal aim" is "systematisation – the exhibition of system and coherence in a mass of beliefs which, as presented by Common Sense, are wanting therein" (LPK 467). However, Sidgwick was always inclined to add that "the special characteristic of *my* philosophy is to keep the importance of the others in view." This deceptively simple statement will turn out to be of the first importance. In it there is a crucial link between Sidgwick's formal philosophical work and his general practice of inquiry: how, that is, science "sets before us an ideal of a consensus of experts and continuity of development which we may hope to attain in our larger and more difficult work" (PSR 231). The fellowship of Apostolic inquiry and the discussion society thus found formal expression in Sidgwick's epistemology, which is consequently far less vulnerable to the charge of celebrating the solipsistic individual knower.

Of course, much would ride on just how one determined the "sources" of likely error and, correlatively, the trustworthiness of fellow inquirers, and on this count, Sidgwick, as later chapters will show, ended up betraying some serious Eurocentric failings. Perhaps surprisingly, given the way in which system and coherence seem to be exactly what the dualism of practical reason undermines, Sidgwick explains in the *Methods* that his "chief business" in his analysis of commonsense morality has been with the first, Cartesian condition, "to free the common terms of Ethics, as far as possible, from objection on this score" (ME 339). As he frames it, his business has been to show how the purported "self-evidence" of commonsense or dogmatic intuitional morality scarcely even begins to meet the conditions of a genuine science. Thus, "what at first seemed like an intuition turns out to be either the mere expression of a vague impulse, needing regulation and limitation which it cannot itself supply, but which must be drawn from some other source: or a current opinion, the reasonableness of which has still to be shown by a reference to some other principle" (ME 342–43). For as soon as we attempt to give these glittering generalities the definiteness which science requires, we find that we cannot do this without abandoning the universality of acceptance. We find, in some cases, that alternatives present themselves, between which it is necessary that we should decide; but between which we cannot pretend that Common Sense does decide, and which often seem equally or nearly equally plausible. In other cases the moral notion seems to resist all efforts to obtain from it a definite rule: in others it is found to comprehend elements which we have no means of reducing to a common standard, except by the application of the Utilitarian – or some similar – method. Even where we seem able to educe from Common Sense a more or less clear reply to the questions raised in the process of definition, the principle that results is qualified in so complicated a way that its self-evidence becomes dubious or vanishes altogether. (ME 342–43)

Of course, as noted earlier, Sidgwick does not mean to frustrate altogether the "strong instinct of Common Sense that points to the existence of such principles," though he is also very sensitive to the fact that "the more we extend our knowledge of man and his environment, the more we realise the vast variety of human natures and circumstances that have existed in different ages and countries, the less disposed we are to believe that there is any definite code of absolute rules, applicable to all human beings without exception." Rather, what we find is that there

are certain absolute practical principles, the truth of which, when they are explicitly stated, is manifest; but they are of too abstract a nature, and too universal in their scope, to enable us to ascertain by immediate application of them what we ought to do in any particular case; particular duties have still to be determined by some other method." (ME 379)

In this way, the process of reflection actually leads Sidgwick to accept a number of intuitively justifiable principles of this formal and abstract nature, though there has been a remarkable disagreement among commentators as to just how many he sets out.[107] Even the derivation of utilitarianism is rather more complex than so far indicated, and involves considering "the relation of the integrant parts to the whole and to each other" in order to obtain

the self-evident principle that the good of any one individual is of no more importance, from the point of view (if I may say so) of the Universe, than the good of any other; unless, that is, there are special grounds for believing that more good is likely to be realised in the one case than in the other. And it is evident to me that as a rational being I am bound to aim at good generally, – so far as it is attainable by my efforts, – not merely at a particular part of it.

From these two rational intuitions we may deduce, as a necessary inference, the maxim of Benevolence in an abstract form: viz. that each one is morally bound to regard the good of any other individual as much as his own, except in so far as he judges it to be less, when impartially viewed, or less certainly knowable or attainable by him. I before observed that the duty of Benevolence as recognised by common sense seems to fall somewhat short of this. But I think it may be fairly urged in explanation of this that *practically* each man, even with a view to universal Good, ought chiefly to concern himself with promoting the good of a limited number of human beings, and that generally in proportion to the closeness of their connexion with him. I think that a 'plain man,' in a modern civilised society, if his conscience were fairly brought to consider the hypothetical question, whether it would be morally right for him to seek his own happiness on any occasion if it involved a certain sacrifice of the greater happiness of some other human being, – without any counterbalancing gain to any one else, – would answer unhesitatingly in the negative. (ME 382)

But it could take some doing to bring the plain person – not to mention the "sensual herd" – to this conclusion. And even the moral theorist has some ways to go. As Sidgwick had noted in the first edition, the

hedonistic interpretation which Mill and his school give to the principle of Universal Benevolence, seems inadmissible when the principle is enunciated as a self-evident axiom. In thus enunciating it, we must use, as Clarke does, the wider terms 'Welfare' or 'Good,' and say that each individual man, as a rational being, is bound to aim at the Good of all other men.

And this, Sidgwick continues, brings us back to the basic question of what is "Good," to which a return is made in the final chapter of Book III:

And here, perhaps, I may seem to have laboriously executed one of those circles in reasoning before noticed. For this question . . . is the fundamental problem of Ethics stated in its vaguest and widest form: in the form in which we find it raised at the very outset of the history of moral philosophy, when the speculative force of the Greek mind first concentrated itself on Practice. And here when, at the end of a long and careful examination of the apparent intuitions with which Common Sense furnishes us, we collect the residuum of clear and definite moral knowledge which the operation has left, we find the same problem facing us. We seem to have done nothing: and in fact we have only evolved the suppression of Egoism, the necessary universality of view, which is implied in the mere form of the objective judgement 'that an end is good,' just as it is in the judgement 'that an action is right.'

Whatever I judge to be Good, I cannot reasonably think that it is abstractly and primarily right that I should have it more than another. (ME1 366)

Again, the tone in later editions is more confident, though Sidgwick forever insists that the "identification of Ultimate Good with Happiness is properly to be reached ... by a more indirect mode of reasoning" (ME 389). And the expression the "suppression of Egoism" would, as will presently be shown, cause no end of bafflement, given his claims about the dualism of practical reason.[108] Moore's denial of agent-relative goodness would seem to be a development of just this line.

Still, Sidgwick seems to take some comfort in the fact that the principles that he finds in accordance with philosophical intuitionism have also been prominently featured in the works of such figures as Clarke, Butler, and Kant, as well as by the utilitarian theorists. And there is more to be had by way of axioms formulated by philosophical intuitionism. In fact, much in the fashion of such recent utilitarians as R. M. Hare, Sidgwick tries to appropriate nearly all of Kant's ethics for his own purposes. Thus, he is only too happy to accept "his fundamental principle of duty," namely, the "'formal' rule of 'acting on a maxim that one can will to be law universal,'" which is an "immediate practical corollary" of the self-evident principle that "whatever action any of us judges to be right for himself, he implicitly judges to be right for all similar persons in similar circumstances" (ME 386, 379). This, Sidgwick urges, is the core notion of the idea of justice. What is more, we find that when Kant

comes to consider the ends at which virtuous action is aimed, the only really ultimate end which he lays down is the object of Rational Benevolence as commonly conceived – the happiness of other men. He regards it as evident *a priori* that each man as a rational agent is bound to aim at the happiness of other men: indeed, in his view, it can only be stated as a *duty* for me to seek my own happiness so far as I consider it as a part of the happiness of mankind in general. (ME 386)

On this last, however, Sidgwick demurs, since he holds "with Butler that 'one's own happiness is a manifest obligation' independently of one's relation to other men." Even so, "regarded on its positive side, Kant's conclusion appears to agree to a great extent with the view of the duty of Rational Benevolence," though Sidgwick is "not altogether able to assent to the arguments by which Kant arrives at his conclusion." (ME 386) Among other things, he thinks that egoism could be universalizable, and that it is extremely unclear what a Kantian "self-subsistent" end could be ("ends" being things to be sought) and why respect for one's rational nature would entail respect for one's animal nature as well.[109]

As the remark on Butler perhaps suggests, Sidgwick's list of self-evident principles also includes, in addition to those of Rational Benevolence and Justice or Impartiality, a principle of Rational Prudence, enjoining "impartial concern for all parts of our conscious life" – or, in effect, "that Hereafter *as such* is to be regarded neither less nor more than Now" (ME 381). One common application of this is, of course, the familiar notion that "present *pleasure* or *happiness* is reasonably to be foregone with the view of obtaining greater pleasure or happiness hereafter" (ME 381), but, as in the case of the principle of Rational Benevolence, Sidgwick's strict formulation of it leaves open the question of whether the good should in fact be interpreted in this way (that is, hedonistically). He argues, as we have seen, that it should, but that is a separate argument, and perhaps less final than the basic principles of Benevolence, Prudence, and Justice. Furthermore, there is a great deal of confusion over how Rational Prudence gets translated into Rational Egoism in Sidgwick's view, a confusion aggravated by the fact that in the first edition, the discussion of the axioms in Book III, Chapter 13 is quite different, and, as Schneewind notes, "no axiom of prudence is presented as self-evident." The closest he gets to asserting the apparent self-evidence of egoism is in some brief remarks elsewhere about impartial concern for all parts of one's life and the need to accept Butler's view that it is reasonable to seek one's own happiness.[110]

This is singularly ironic because the first edition is the one with the strongest, most dramatic statement of the dualism of practical reason, in the concluding chapter. But before addressing this dualism, in the next section, a few summary cautions about the interpretation of Sidgwick's epistemology are in order.

Sidgwick's intuitionism has been the focus of much heated debate in recent decades. Some have sought to assimilate his approach to that of Rawlsian wide reflective equilibrium, interpreted as the search for system and coherence for our considered convictions at all levels; others have appealed to it precisely in order to oppose the (supposed) Rawlsian reliance on common sense, which is seen as relativistic and as failing to do justice to Sidgwick's cognitivist intuitionism. Rawls himself increasingly came to stress the contrasts between his own Kantian constructivism and any form of rational intuitionism, though he held that the method of reflective equilibrium can figure in both.[111] And these debates profoundly affect the interpretation of the dualism of practical reason, since the question of what to make, epistemologically speaking, of the conflict between utilitarianism and egoism depends in part on how one construes the intuitional support for the axioms undergirding these views. Unfortunately, much of this previous debate seems rather ungenerous and anachronistic in its depiction of Sidgwick, failing to grasp his fallibilistic, multicriterial approach in anything like its true complexity. Despite his evident commitment to fallibilism, there has been a remarkably persistent tendency to interpret his intuitionism on the "searchlight" (or "radar") and "hotline" model, taking it as a form of perceptual intuitionism involving the mental inspection of ontologically suspect esoteric qualities yielding indefeasible convictions.[112] Yet it is plain that his notion of intuitive truth works quite differently. And as Schneewind has shown, the first edition of the *Methods* contained a uniquely helpful statement suggestive of just how Sidgwick typically argued. Commenting on Clarke, he explains, in connection with benevolence and the similarity of its justification to the justification of equity, that

we must start with some ethical judgment, in order that the rule may be proved: and, in fact, the process of reasoning is precisely similar in the two cases. There, an individual was supposed to judge that a certain kind of conduct was right and fit to be pursued towards him: and it was then shewn that he must necessarily conceive the same conduct to be right for all other persons in precisely similar circumstances: and therefore judge it right for himself, in like case, to adopt it towards any other person. Similarly here we are supposed to judge that there is something intrinsically desirable – some result which it would be reasonable for each individual to seek for himself, if he considered himself alone. Let us call this the individual's Good or Welfare: then what Clarke urges is, that the Good of any one individual cannot be *more* intrinsically desirable, *because it is his*, than the equal good of any other individual. So that our notion of Ultimate Good, at the realization of which it is evidently reasonable to aim, must include the Good of *every* one on the same ground that it includes that of *any* one. (ME1 360)

Thus, as Schneewind glosses the passage,

all four axioms may be viewed as obtained by the procedure of eliminating arbitrary limitations on ethical propositions one is prepared to assert. If someone says that some consideration is a reason for him to do a specific act, he may be brought to see that the limitation to himself is arbitrary and unfounded: it cannot be a reason for him to act unless it would equally be a reason for anyone similar to act in the same way in relevantly similarly circumstances.[113]

The inferences typically demanded are therefore, as hinted earlier, generalizing ones, which at least suggests a certain affinity with the Kantian orientation; for all of the differences that Sidgwick insisted on and all of the changes to later editions, this remained part of his argument, giving it a different flavor from "demonstrations" of intuitive truth less sensitive to the dialectical demands of any defense of practical reason.

Schneewind also notes another singularly helpful passage that figured in the first edition – a brief but quite explicit statement concerning the nature of rationality, in which Sidgwick discusses how a reasonable person could deem a desire unreasonable if it conflicts with, or cannot be subsumed under, a general rule of conduct:

> But again, general rules and maxims may in their turn be found mutually inconsistent, in either sense: and here too conduct appears to us irrational or at least imperfectly rational, not only if the maxims upon which it is professedly based conflict with and contradict one another, but also if they cannot be bound together and firmly concatenated by means of some one fundamental principle. For practical reason does not seem to be thoroughly realised until a perfect order, harmony, and unity of system is introduced into all our actions. (ME1 25–26)

Bearing these various points in mind, one must conclude that Sidgwick was hardly a naive Victorian – or Cartesian – who simply took it for granted that ethics could be rationally justified because one "just saw" ethical truths courtesy of the natural light. His account of reason is far more complex. As Roger Crisp puts it, "Intuition for Sidgwick is a doxastic faculty, nothing more, or less, than a capacity for forming beliefs of a certain kind, with the possibility thereby of acquiring knowledge." And Sidgwick, "unlike Whewell perhaps, need not be seen as committed to any form of 'Platonist' metaphysics, but merely to the idea that there are reasons for action."[114] If one wishes to be anachronistic, one could read his commitments as no more objectionable than those of Rawls or McMahan, Parfit or Scanlon, when they urge that it makes sense to talk about reasons for action that are not purely instrumental, even if Sidgwick seems to have a keener sense of the need for unity and for a Socratic faith in common sense in general. This is important. Sidgwick was unmoved by worries that he was at odds with the more reductive and/or materialistic forms of naturalism, but he kept his metaethics so minimal – in the *Methods*, at least – that Deweyan pragmatists as well as Moorean Platonists could find his attitude congenial. In metaethics as in theology, he simply left the door open for any number of possible developments.

Continuing developments, of course. So much so that Crisp can argue that because of Sidgwick's "insight, impartiality, and exactingness, he was able to produce a version of intuitionism which, its boundaries duly drawn, and cleared of a misconception, should find more agreement among contemporary thinkers than the views of any of his predecessors, and is at least a serious contender for the strongest version of intuitionism yet developed." Put more exactly, on Crisp's rehabilitation of Sidgwick's approach:

Moral intuition is the capacity to form non-inferential, self-evident beliefs that certain actions, rules, or whatever are right or reasonable, and moral intuitions are such beliefs. The claim that we possess such a capacity should be kept apart from any other thesis, such as the radar view, the hotline view, or non-naturalism. So understood, the view that we have moral intuition is likely to be widely accepted.[115]

Still, some have argued that Sidgwick cannot have it all, that the complexity of his system ultimately renders it inconsistent, and that the appeal to Aristotle's distinction between logical priority and priority for any given individual is not apt in his case. In an important essay, Brink gives what is perhaps the reflective upshot of the earlier debates about Sidgwick and reflective equilibrium:

[I]t is hard to make sense of the idea that moral claims could be *self*-evident; asymmetrical epistemic dependence seems very troublesome. What is puzzling about philosophical intuitionism is that it reasonably insists that we can and should seek an inferential justification of moral beliefs about action tokens and types, even when they are indubitable or nearly so, but claims that the more abstract and more dubitable principles we produce as justifications do not admit of justification in terms of anything else. But how can a more abstract and more dubitable proposition be self-evident if a less dubitable one is not? Given that we permit the demand for explanation and justification in the first place, as Sidgwick allows we must if ethics is to contain debate and dialogue at all, philosophical intuitionism seems to limit the demand in an arbitrary and perverse way. In fact, moral philosophy, past and present, does assume that first principles are discursively justified; we challenge and defend moral theories by comparing their implications about particular cases with our independent moral beliefs about those cases. And this . . . is Sidgwick's other view about the justification of first principles; they are to be justified by showing that they are in dialectical equilibrium with beliefs that take common-sense morality as input.

Thus, whereas I do think that this interpretation of Aristotle's distinction allows us to reconcile asymmetrical metaphysical dependence with symmetrical epistemic dependence, it does not help Sidgwick resolve his dilemma, because it does not allow us to reconcile asymmetrical and symmetrical aspects of epistemic dependence. Sidgwick's epistemological views are not fully consistent; he must choose between his intuitionist and dialectical accounts of the justification of first principles.[116]

In effect, Brink is urging that there is a vicious circularity in the intuitionistic side of Sidgwick's argument, and that his appeal to Aristotle confutes the metaphysical and the epistemological. That is, on this account, Sidgwick is convicted of inconsistency, of deploying two fundamentally contrasting epistemological approaches: a dialectical or discursive one (systematizing common sense in the manner of Rawlsian wide reflective equilibrium) and a rational intuitionist form of foundationalism that disallows any "probative value or evidential role to common-sense morality." On the first, the "epistemic dependence between first principles and particular moral beliefs can be bi-directional," with the principle subsuming and explaining the particular judgment, and the particular judgment providing evidence of the principle. But on the second, "these first principles cannot be justified by their relation to anything less general, and, *ex hypothesi*, there is nothing more general than first principles in terms of which they might be justified."[117] The appeal to natural priority and priority for us is hard to make out in the epistemic way that Sidgwick uses it: "knowledge or justification seems precisely something that cognizers have (or lack); a cognizer's beliefs are justified or count as knowledge if they meet certain conditions. It is hard to understand what is being asserted if it is claimed that certain propositions are known (or justified) but by (or for) no one."[118] It is fine to talk about the metaphysical priority of first principles, since this "does not show that our evidence for what first principle is true cannot include our (defeasible) beliefs about what acts are right." But one cannot sensibly ask, of a first principle taken to be true, what further property makes it true.

Yet Brink does seem to be attributing to Sidgwick a view about intuitionism that he simply did not hold. Indeed, Brink seems not to appreciate either the force of Sidgwick's conception of self-evidence as a matter of degree or the point of his distinction between the (more limited) criterion of self-evidence and the larger justificatory process, including other tests for achieving a higher degree of certainty through the elimination of sources of error.

In part, the proper Sidgwickian response would seem to be that the process of reflection itself persuades the moral theorist that the "more dubitable" proposition is "less dubitable" – in other words, that it is possible to progress toward an ideal limit of self-evidence by grasping how one had not properly cognized the genuinely self-evident component of one's beliefs, which is to say, apprehended what real clarity involves. Hence, the special work of the moral theorist (or the Apostolic seeker). This is the intuitionist's equivalent of finding one's true faith, the core truth contained within a larger set of beliefs, some of which turn out to be adventitious or the result of one's being imperfectly receptive. And if the work of different theorists is such as to inspire confidence that they are approximating some common truth, as yet imperfectly formulated, then intuitionism can be taken as a promising research program. Brink's account would simply rule out from the start any claims to fundamental intellectual progress within an intuitionist – or for that matter, rationalist – epistemological framework.[119] Admittedly, such projects have often been accused of incoherence, circularity, and much else besides, but one would never guess from Brink's critique how vigorous and impressive their defense has been.

Brink admits that it is puzzling that Sidgwick himself seemed to anticipate so many of these concerns, and he seems somewhat troubled that his argument would disallow any effort to enhance the certainty had by intuition through discursive justification or the consensus of experts. In effect, he is charging Sidgwick with grotesque inconsistency, despite what would seem to be Sidgwick's perfectly clear apprehension of the issues. Notice, for a start, how in "Utilitarianism" Sidgwick concisely explains:

It may be said that it is impossible to 'prove' a first principle; and this is of course true, if by proof we mean a process which exhibits the principle in question as an inference from premisses upon which it remains dependent for its certainty: for these premisses, and not the inference drawn from them, would then be the real first principles. Nay, if Utilitarianism is to be *proved* to a man who already holds some other moral principles, say to an Intuitional or Common-Sense moralist . . . or an Egoist . . . the process must be one which establishes a conclusion actually *superior* in validity to the premisses from which it starts. For the Utilitarian prescriptions of duty are *primâ facie* in conflict, at certain points and under certain circumstances, both with Intuitional rule, and with the dictates of Rational

Egoism: so that Utilitarianism, if accepted at all, must be accepted as overruling Intuitionism and Egoism. At the same time, if the other principles are not throughout taken as valid, the so-called proof does not seem to be addressed to the Intuitionist or Egoist at all. How shall we deal with this dilemma? and how is such a process (certainly very different from ordinary proof) possible or conceivable? It seems that what is needed is a line of argument which, on the one hand, allows the validity, to a certain extent, of the principles already accepted, and on the other hand, shows them to be imperfect – not absolutely and independently valid, but needing qualification and completion.[120]

Now, what Sidgwick says here about taking the other principles "as valid" is quite significant. As Rob Shaver has urged, a short but nonetheless compelling counter to Brink's criticism is simply to interpret Sidgwick, as seems plausible, as allowing that such contending beliefs have an initial credibility without claiming that they are self-evident. Common sense does play more than a heuristic role in Sidgwick's arguments, but between heuristic value and self-evidence there are forms of initial credibility that are evidential but not final – for example, the "imperfect" certitude that common sense enjoys because it represents the experience of many generations, experience suggesting some presumptive evolutionary success. As Shaver has neatly put it, in defending the consistency of Sidgwick's approach, the basic point is simply:

I believe some self-evident proposition p on the basis of seeing its self-evidence and seeing that it agrees with common-sense morality. If I have no reason to trust common-sense morality other than noting p, seeing the agreement with common-sense morality should not increase my confidence in p. But where there is independent reason for believing in common-sense morality, agreement with it increases my confidence in p.[121]

To deny that there is any form of intuitionism that can countenance progress and such means for enhancing our confidence in apparently self-evident propositions would seem to be both arbitrary and ahistorical.

In fact, there is a larger point to be made here. Brink and Shaver are agreed that Sidgwick deploys both an intuitionist and a dialectical line of argument, and in this they part company with some earlier interpreters who would claim that Sidgwick was really just relying on one or the other. They differ over whether these arguments are compatible.

Now, Sidgwick himself sometimes allowed that there are two different epistemological strategies operating in his work. In a late essay, "Public

Morality," included in *Practical Ethics*, he argues that there are "two distinct ways of treating ethical questions," the first of which involves "establishing fundamental principles of abstract or ideal morality" and working "out deductively the particular rules of duty or practical conceptions of human good or well-being," and the second of which involves contemplating "morality as a social fact" and endeavoring "by reflective analysis, removing vagueness and ambiguity, solving apparent contradictions, correcting lapses and supplying omissions, to reduce this body of current opinions, so far as possible, to a rational and coherent system." Sidgwick observes, revealingly, that these methods are "in no way antagonistic" and that it is reasonable to think that "they must lead to the same goal – a perfectly satisfactory and practical ideal of conduct." He also allows that, unfortunately, given the current state of our knowledge, the results of the two methods may diverge and a rough compromise may be called for. (PE 53) Given the practical prominence of social verification, there is that much more reason to accept elements of common sense as a "working philosophy."

Sidgwick's description of these two methods here does not quite correspond to the distinction between the two methods described by Brink and Shaver; still, there is a rough overlap, and many other commentators have assumed that his intuitionism entailed something like the first method. But what is especially important to note is his eclectic attitude, his sense that truth is one and that our confidence in our beliefs can only be strengthened when different people committed to different views about truth and inquiry end up with the same conclusions. There is a certain unity in his determined effort to assault the deepest problems with every plausible method available. Perhaps this is a rather Rawlsian attitude – after all, even Rawls allows that we may end up wanting to call the convictions that survive the process of wide reflective equilibrium "intuitive" truths, and, as noted earlier, some have taken up the suggestion at least to the extent of casting reflective equilibrium in foundationalist form.[122] But whether or not this ecumenicalism is in keeping with Rawls's (shifting) arguments, it represents a very sober recognition that even those with fairly hardened and insulated foundationalist epistemological stances are susceptible to the sense of intellectual progress that comes from discovering a larger consistency and consensus in the web of belief. The Cartesian criterion is important, but it is not enough on its own. In an important passage to which Shaver has drawn attention, Sidgwick responds to the worry that self-evident principles cannot admit of "further substantiation":

[T]his view does not sufficiently allow for the complexity of our intellectual processes. If we have once learnt . . . that we are liable to be mistaken in the affirmation
of apparently self-evident propositions, we may surely retain this general conviction of our fallibility along with the special impression of the self-evidence of any
proposition we may be contemplating; and thus however strong this latter impression may be, we shall still admit our need of some further protection against
the possible failure of our faculty of intuition.[123]

In sum, the larger point to make in defense of the coherence of
Sidgwick's approach is that Brink's objections make it impossible to understand not only how Sidgwick could have attributed probative force to
certain elements of commonsense morality, but also how he could have
attributed justificatory force to the tests of coherence and consensus, and
how he could possibly have made sense of a progressive development in
the account of the self-evident axioms. An interpretive rupture of such
massive dimensions ought to suggest that something has gone awry in
the characterization of the position in question. And there is every reason
to think that this is so, in the case of the Apostolic inquirer who was so
convinced that he could and should learn from other sincere inquirers.
Sidgwick was obviously no Gramscian out to discredit the ideological
mystifications of common sense. But he was the Socratic inquirer who
could not see where else to begin and who had a certain faith in "things
in general" coupled with a terrific capacity for criticizing the particular
beliefs that came his way. His metaphysical reticence, combined with his
fertile skeptical probing, proved to be vastly inspiring for future generations of philosophers, however reluctant many of them were to recognize
his influence.

Part II. Chaos

I find that more than one critic has overlooked or disregarded the account of
the plan of my treatise, given in the original preface and in [section] 5 of the
introductory chapter: and has consequently supposed me to be writing as an
assailant of two of the methods which I chiefly examine, and a defender of the third.
Thus one of my reviewers seems to regard Book iii. (on Intuitionism) as containing
mere hostile criticism from the outside: another has constructed an article on the
supposition that my principal object is the 'suppression of Egoism'; a third has

gone to the length of a pamphlet under the impression (apparently) that the 'main argument' of my treatise is a demonstration of Universalistic Hedonism. . . . And as regards the two hedonistic principles, I do not hold the reasonableness of aiming at happiness generally with any stronger conviction than I do that of aiming at one's own. It was no part of my plan to call special attention to this "Dualism of the Practical Reason" as I have elsewhere called it: but I am surprised at the extent to which my view has perplexed even those of my critics who have understood it. I had imagined that they would readily trace it to the source from which I learnt it, Butler's well-known Sermons. I hold with Butler that "Reasonable Self-love and Conscience are the two chief or superior principles in the nature of man," each of which we are under a "manifest obligation" to obey: and I do not (I believe) differ materially from Butler in my view either of reasonable self-love, or – theology apart – of its relation to conscience.

Sidgwick, Preface to the second edition of *The Methods of Ethics*, 1877

At any rate, somehow or other, morality will get on; I do not feel particularly anxious about that. But my special business is not to maintain morality *somehow*, but to establish it logically as a reasoned system; and I have declared and published that this cannot be done, if we are limited to merely mundane sanctions, owing to the inevitable divergence, in this imperfect world, between the individual's Duty and Happiness.

Sidgwick's Journal to John Addington Symonds, March 16, 1887 (CWC)

IV. The Dualism of Practical Reason

Sidgwick's response to his critics, in the Preface to the second edition of the *Methods*, is rather puzzling, unless one recognizes that he genuinely felt that he was struggling, in this book, to impartially negotiate three methods, all of which he found within himself to some degree, albeit in evolving form. Nothing made the "Point of View of the Universe" bristle like the suggestion that he had somehow failed to sympathetically enter into the views he criticized. Immanent argument was second nature to him, despite his frustration with Hegel. Or rather, it was not Sidgwick the man taking sides – it was simply the spirit of impartial criticism inexorably working its way ahead. After all, although he disliked Hegel's dialectical method, he was drawn to his views about the rationality of the universe.

Yet the detachment was not quite sustainable. As we have noted, for all his success in synthesizing utilitarianism, intuitional morality, and intuitionism, Sidgwick allowed that something had gone terribly wrong. The chief failure with the *Methods*, in his eyes, came when he tried to press the critical examination of the axioms or principles still further, testing their consistency. The "dualism of practical reason" results when the principle of prudence is given a somewhat fuller (rather intricate) development, as the basic principle of the method of rational egoism, which is then cast as being in conflict with the fundamental principles yielding utilitarianism. But typically, Sidgwick rather simplifies his presentation of the conflict. His explication of this dualism in a later commentary on the *Methods*, "Some Fundamental Ethical Controversies," is clear and characteristic. As he explains, his philosophical intuitionism is such that, along with

(a) a fundamental moral conviction that I ought to sacrifice my own happiness, if by so doing I can increase the happiness of others to a greater extent than I diminish my own, I find also (b) a conviction – which it would be paradoxical to call 'moral', but which is none the less fundamental – that it would be irrational to sacrifice any portion of my own happiness unless the sacrifice is to be somehow at some time compensated by an equivalent addition to my own happiness.[124]

Each of these convictions has as much clarity and certainty "as the process of introspective reflection can give," not to mention a preponderant, if implicit, assent "in the common sense of mankind," and Sidgwick consequently regards this as a "fundamental contradiction in our apparent intuitions of what is Reasonable in conduct." Egoism, far from being suppressed, could rival utilitarianism as an independent principle of practical reason. A substantially similar account can be found in the little essay on "Utilitarianism," which could be taken as a summary of his thinking at the very point when he was completing the first edition of the *Methods*. He observes that the relation between utilitarianism and egoism is simpler than that between utilitarianism and intuitionism, though

it seems hard to state it with perfect exactness, and in fact, it is formulated very differently by different writers who appear to be substantially agreed, as Clarke, Kant, and Mill. If the Egoist strictly confines himself to stating his conviction that he ought to take his own happiness or pleasure as his ultimate end, there seems no opening for an argument to lead him to Utilitarianism (as a first principle). But if he offers either as a reason for this conviction, or as another form of stating it, the proposition that his happiness or pleasure is objectively 'desirable' or 'a good', he gives the requisite opening. For the Utilitarian can then point out that *his* happiness cannot be more objectively desirable or more a good than the happiness of any one else; the mere fact (if I may so put it) that *he is he* can have nothing to do with its objective desirability or goodness. Hence starting with his own principles, he must accept the wider notion of universal happiness or pleasure as representing the real end of Reason, the absolutely Good or Desirable: as the end, therefore, to which the action of a reasonable agent ought to be directed.

It is to be observed that the *proof* of Utilitarianism, thus addressed to the Egoist, is quite different from an exposition of the *sanctions* of Utilitarian rules; i.e., the pleasures and pains that will follow respectively on their observance and violation. Obviously such an exposition cannot lead us to accept Utilitarianism as a first principle, but only as a conclusion deduced from or a special application of Egoism. At the same time, the two, proof and sanction, the reason for accepting the greatest happiness of the greatest number as (in Bentham's language) the 'right and proper' end of action, and the individual's motives for making it his end, are very frequently confused in discussion.[125]

Interestingly, the concluding chapter of the first edition was titled "The Sanctions of Utilitarianism." This chapter, which in all editions has been the main statement of the dualism, was changed in the second edition to "The Mutual Relations of the Three Methods," the title in all later editions. In the preface to the second edition, he remarks that "I have yielded as far as I could to the objections that have been strongly urged against the concluding chapter of the treatise. The main discussion therein contained still seems to me indispensable to the completeness of the work; but I have endeavoured to give the chapter a new aspect by altering its commencement, and omitting most of the concluding paragraph."

From this and the other statements just cited, one might conclude that, to Sidgwick's mind, the critics had objected to his statement of the dualism as a problem but had done nothing to solve it. Such frustration may well have been appropriate, at least in many cases. Consider the conclusion of Leslie Stephen's review, from 1875:

The contradiction, in short, which Mr. Sidgwick discovers between different courses of conduct, both of which are equally reasonable, comes to this: First, he regards that conduct to be reasonable which would be approved by a perfectly impartial spectator, that is, by a being whose views would not be coloured by his own passions. This leads, as he says, to intuitional utilitarianism, or, as I should say, to pure Godwinism. Then he says that that conduct is reasonable which would be pursued by a man of private affections, but elevated above considerations of time. Any equal period of existence would be equally valuable to him. And thence, as it seems to be obvious that at each moment a man does what pleases him best, we arrive by a kind of integration at the conclusion that that course will please him best which gives him the greatest net result of pleasure. Between two such people there is of course an inevitable contradiction. As Mr. Sidgwick cannot find any mode of deciding which of these conceptions represents reason in the abstract, he is in a hopeless dilemma. Such a dilemma awaits anybody who thinks that reason can explain its own primary data, instead of reconciling the inferences from them. Meanwhile I am content to say that neither case represents any actual human being. Reason, on my view, necessarily produces different results when we start with different motives, just as reason brings out different conclusions if we start from different evidence. The fact that people ultimately agree in mathematical conclusions proves that their primary intuitions are the same, or at least analogous. The fact that they disagree in moral conclusions proves that their primary instincts are different. The resulting discord proves only that the universe is in this sense an embodiment of unreason, that it is full of conflicting impulses. That is a fact which will be explained when we know the origin of evil. To me the difficulty seems to be only a reflection upon the mirror of metaphysics of the indisputable truth that mankind is engaged in a perpetual struggle for existence, with the consequent crushing out – as we must try to hope – of the weakest and the worst.[126]

Such reactions were not uncommon in the era of evolution, but for Sidgwick they were merely suave evasions, a complete begging of the question of, say, whether the weakest were actually the worst. His student and colleague F. W. Maitland, in a review of the *Memoir*, rightly stressed Sidgwick's

watchful honesty which will not suffer any hope, however ardent, or any desire, however noble, to give itself the airs of proof. 'Well,' wrote Sidgwick in 1891, 'I myself have taken service with Reason, and I have no intention of deserting. At the same time I do not think that loyalty to my standard requires me to feign a satisfaction in the service which I do not really feel.' These words give us the core of the matter.[127]

It was not quite in Sidgwick to be cheerful about the irrationality of humanity in ethical affairs, and he did not want to concede it without a fight. Still, the changes between the different editions do suggest that he was willing to give the work a "new aspect." The infamous concluding lines of the first edition had read:

[T]he fundamental opposition between the principle of Rational Egoism and that on which such a system of duty [from the reconciliation of intuitional and utilitarian methods] is constructed, only comes out more sharp and clear after the reconciliation between the other methods. The old immoral paradox, "that my performance of Social Duty is good not for me but for others," cannot be completely refuted by empirical arguments: nay, the more we study these arguments the more we are forced to admit, that if we have these alone to rely on, there must be some cases in which the paradox is true. And yet we cannot but admit with Butler, that it is ultimately reasonable to seek one's own happiness. Hence the whole system of our beliefs as to the intrinsic reasonableness of conduct must fall, without a hypothesis unverifiable by experience reconciling the Individual with the Universal Reason, without a belief, in some form or other, that the moral order which we see imperfectly realized in this actual world is yet actually perfect. If we reject this belief, we may perhaps still find in the non-moral universe an adequate object for the Speculative Reason, capable of being in some sense ultimately understood. But the Cosmos of Duty is thus really reduced to a Chaos: and the prolonged effort of the human intellect to frame a perfect ideal of rational conduct is seen to have been foredoomed to inevitable failure. (ME1 473)

Sidgwick will allow nothing to diminish the drama of this tragedy. The supposition that there is a moral order to the universe reconciling egoism and utilitarianism is nothing less than "an hypothesis logically necessary to avoid a fundamental contradiction in a vast system of Beliefs: a contradiction so fundamental that if it cannot be overcome the whole system must fall to the ground and scepticism be triumphant over one chief department of our thought." Although Butler may have been the last name evoked by Sidgwick in this context, another precedes him by only a short space, one more profoundly expressive of Sidgwick's angst:

Still it seems plain that in proportion as man has lived in the exercise of the Practical Reason – as he believed – and feels as an actual force the desire to do what is right and reasonable as such, his demand for this premiss will be intense and imperious. Thus we are not surprised to find Socrates – the type for all ages of the man in whom this desire is predominant – declaring with simple conviction that 'if the Rulers of the Universe do not prefer the just man to the unjust, it is better to die than to live.' And we must observe that in the feeling that prompts to such declaration the desire to rationalize one's own conduct is not the sole, nor perhaps always the most prominent, element. For however difficult it may practically be to do one's duty when it comes into conflict with one's happiness, it often does not seem very difficult, when we are considering the question in the abstract, to decide in favour of duty. When a man passionately refuses to believe that the "Wages of Virtue" can "be dust," it is often less from any private reckoning about his own wages than from a disinterested aversion to a universe so fundamentally irrational

that "Good for the Individual" is *not* ultimately identified with "Universal Good."
(ME1 471–72)

This formulation, stressing the "disinterested aversion" to a perverse universe pitting duty against interest, is of the first importance, suggesting the complexity of Sidgwick's dualism. There is more to his worry than that what is good from one's own point of view may not square with what is good universally. As important as one's concern for one's own good may be, in driving home this conflict, one may also think it tragic or preposterous that others are called by duty to self-sacrifice. Hence, the infamous pessimism of the first edition of the *Methods*. There is no Nietzschean glee in Sidgwick's estimate of the significance of the death of God (ME1 473). He would later write to Alexander Bain that he had written his conclusion "at the very last minute, in a fit of candour."[128]

In later editions he would, as he put it in the Preface to the third, expand his treatment on certain points for the sake of completeness and for the book's "better adaptation to the present state of ethical thought in England." This apparently required a marked softening of his case, and a playing up of the constructive possibilities afforded by a rethinking of epistemology, rather than of religion. With the second edition, the conclusion becomes:

If we find that in other departments of our supposed knowledge propositions are commonly taken to be true, which yet seem to rest on no other grounds than that we have a strong disposition to accept them, and that they are indispensable to the systematic coherence of our beliefs; it will be difficult to reject a similarly supported assumption in ethics, without opening the door to universal scepticism. If on the other hand it appears that the edifice of physical science is really constructed of conclusions logically inferred from premises intuitively known; it will be reasonable to demand that our practical judgments should either be based on an equally firm foundation or should abandon all claim to philosophic certainty. (ME2 469)

Something very like this wording endured through all later editions, ultimately becoming, in the last:

If then the reconciliation of duty and self-interest is to be regarded as a hypothesis logically necessary to avoid a fundamental contradiction in one chief department of our thought, it remains to ask how far this necessity constitutes a sufficient reason for accepting this hypothesis. This, however, is a profoundly difficult and controverted question, the discussion of which belongs rather to a treatise on

General Philosophy than to a work on the Methods of Ethics: as it could not
be satisfactorily answered, without a general examination of the criteria of true
and false beliefs. Those who hold that the edifice of physical science is really
constructed of conclusions logically inferred from self-evident premises, may
reasonably demand that any practical judgments claiming philosophic certainty
should be based on an equally firm foundation. If on the other hand we find that
in our supposed knowledge of the world of nature propositions are commonly
taken to be universally true, which yet seem to rest on no other grounds than
that we have a strong disposition to accept them, and that they are indispensable
to the systematic coherence of our beliefs, – it will be more difficult to reject a
similarly supported assumption in ethics, without opening the door to universal
scepticism. (ME 509)

No doubt Sidgwick thought that if "failure" were not to be the last
word, then "scepticism," rather than "certainty," would be appropriate.

Some have suggested that the changes to the conclusion of the
Methods illustrate the changes in Sidgwick's epistemological stance.
Thus, Seth Pringle-Pattison, reviewing the memoirs of both Sidgwick
and Green, argued that there was "a change in Sidgwick's attitude in
the later years of his life" on the "question of the nature of proof."
That is, the younger Sidgwick had held to the "old ideal" of "conclusions logically inferred from self-evident principles," whereas the older
Sidgwick, "unconsciously influenced perhaps by the central Kantian idea
of 'transcendental deduction' . . . and by the debates which arose round
Mr. Balfour's *Foundations of Belief*," refers "to the analogy of physical
science and suggests (without absolutely committing himself to) the new
criterion of the truth of any proposition" – namely, the "systematic coherence of our beliefs."[129]

But this overstates the case. As argued in the previous section,
Sidgwick's epistemology was complex and multicriterial from the start. It
is true that in the first edition, he is more concerned to argue, for example:

I find that I undoubtedly seem to perceive, as clearly and certainly as I see any
axiom in Arithmetic or Geometry, that it is 'right' and 'reasonable,' and the 'dictate
of reason' and 'my duty' to treat every man as I should think that I myself ought
to be treated in precisely similar circumstances, and to do what I believe to be
ultimately conducive to universal Good or Happiness. But I cannot find inseparably connected with this conviction, and similarly attainable by mere reflective
intuition, any cognition that there actually is a Supreme Being who will adequately
reward me for obeying this rule of duty, or punish me for violating it.

Put more generally, "I do not find in my moral consciousness any intuition, claiming to be clear and certain, that the performance of duty will be adequately rewarded and its violation punished" (ME1 470). And in thus discussing whether it may be necessary to "borrow a fundamental and indispensable premiss from Theology" – either theistic or Buddhist, he allows – there is no parallel highlighting of the coherentist alternative. However, by the second edition, the wording of the final paragraph includes the lines,

> We have rather to regard it as an hypothesis logically necessary to avoid a fundamental contradiction in one chief department of our thought. Whether this necessity constitutes a sufficient reason for accepting the hypothesis, is a question which I cannot here attempt adequately to discuss; as it could not be satisfactorily answered, without a general examination of the criteria of truth and error.

And part of this had appeared, in more subordinated form, earlier on in the first edition.

Thus, Sidgwick clearly allows the possibility that something is wrong with a too-austere philosophical intuitionism if it leads to this result, so that more weight should be put on the coherence criterion and so on. And even in the first edition, as we have seen, he sets out the Cartesian criterion in connection with the others, allowing simply that it may "be of real use; if applied with the rigour which Descartes certainly intended, and not with the laxity which impairs the value of the important work of Reid" (ME1 318). Furthermore, as he would explain in retrospect,

> When I was writing my book on Ethics, I was inclined to hold with Kant that we must *postulate* the continued existence of the soul, in order to effect that harmony of Duty with Happiness which seemed to me indispensable to rational moral life. At any rate I thought I might *provisionally* postulate it, while setting out on the serious search for empirical evidence. (M 467)

That is, while setting out on his parapsychological investigations.

This retrospective account may seem slightly puzzling, given Sidgwick's emphatic statement in the first edition that he could not possibly

> fall back on the Kantian resource of thinking myself under a moral necessity to regard all my duties *as if they were* commandments of God, although not entitled to hold speculatively that any such Supreme Being exists "as Real." I am so far from feeling bound to believe for purposes of practice what I see no ground for holding as a speculative truth, that I cannot even conceive the state of mind which

these words seem to describe, except as a momentary half-wilful irrationality, committed in a violent access of philosophic despair. (ME1 471)

But as Sidgwick admitted, provisionally making such a postulation, on the grounds that the evidence is not all in, is a different matter. Hence the importance of recognizing that his work was an ongoing inquiry, extending to areas outside of ethical theory, even if the process was not the simple evolution described by Pringle-Pattison. As with theology, the emphasis was on the search that might achieve unity through Apostolic inquiry.

C. D. Broad famously objected that this effort to escape the dualism of practical reason was incoherent, since it did not meet the problem at the level of fundamental intuition but merely sought a contingent practical way of avoiding conflict. Whether or not God might exist, the principle of Rational Egoism and the principle of Rational Benevolence are still in flat opposition to one another.[130] But Broad was misguided in this, as William Frankena and many others have demonstrated. As C. A. J. Coady has neatly put it, Sidgwick seems to be envisioning a God that has so effectively harmonized the world of practical reason that both the principles are "true, and possibly self-evident, and it is the appearance of a contradiction between them that is wrong."[131] This seems exactly right, and it is of the first importance.

What is rather more puzzling, as noted in the previous section, is how Sidgwick could have been so dramatic in his early statement of the dualism, while in fact giving a rather weak account of the egoistic alternative. Shaver, for example, in a careful analysis, allows that Sidgwick's axioms do at least serve to locate the debate between the rational egoist and the utilitarian: "The issue turns on the rationality of taking up the point of view of the universe." But he claims that "Sidgwick's considered view is that rational egoism is neither self-evident nor of the highest certainty" but is "as credible as utilitarianism."[132] And this considered view is problematic because the credibility of egoism is scarcely made out.

The qualified wording here is important, since, on an ungenerous reading, Sidgwick's dualism would appear to involve a flagrant contradiction between the claim that both egoism and utilitarianism are self-evident, on the one side, and the use of the consistency criterion as a test of self-evidence, on the other. After all, how could two inconsistent propositions both be self-evident? Such supposed incoherence has been taken by some, such as Brink, as a reason for reading Sidgwick's account, in externalist fashion, as yielding a self-evident theory of rationality, in the shape of rational egoism, and a self-evident theory of morality, in the shape of utilitarianism – thus avoiding the incoherence by departmentalizing what it is rational to do separately from what it is moral to do.[133] Brink admits that this is a philosophical reconstruction, however, and that it does not seem to fit most of what Sidgwick actually says about rationality and morality, which he treats as a unity. Still, Sidgwick was not entirely consistent, especially in his earlier work.

Shaver's reading makes better overall sense. On this account, one possibility would be that the "consistency test is a test for the highest certainty, not for self-evidence," since self-evidence is the concern of the first criterion and the ultimate concern is the highest certainty (from eliminating sources of error) to be had by meeting all the criteria. Thus, it could be the case that egoism and utilitarianism are both self-evident and inconsistent and therefore not of the highest certainty. But there is a still better interpretation. Sidgwick's "considered view," according to Shaver, has him agreeing that

rational egoism and utilitarianism do not possess the highest certainty. But when he distinguishes between rational egoism and utilitarianism, on the one hand, and the "self-evident element" expressed by the axioms on the other, he suggests that neither rational egoism nor utilitarianism is self-evident. This is also the result one would expect from the "careful reflection" that yields self-evidence: Reflection on the inconsistency of rational egoism with other beliefs of the same certainty should (though need not) lead one to doubt its self-evidence. Sidgwick suggests exactly this when he writes that from the inconsistency "it would seem to follow that the apparently intuitive operation of the Practical Reason, manifested in these contradictory judgements, is after all illusory." (ME 508). In this way the puzzle raised by the critics is doubly dissolved. Sidgwick is left saying, plausibly, that rational egoism and utilitarianism really are inconsistent.[134]

This would seem to be the most sensible way to interpret Sidgwick's tendency to speak of "apparently self-evident" intuitions, and to be in keeping with Sidgwick's broadly fallibilistic attitude, though it must be allowed that Sidgwick often did put his case in simplified form, and that he at times seems to fit Shaver's other interpretive strategy. Often enough, he simply seems to be expressing his consternation that these two views, epistemologically forceful when considered on their own terms, can yield conflicting prescriptions when taken together and practically applied.

At any rate, these points are important not only in their own right, but also as preliminaries to addressing the question put earlier – namely, why is Sidgwick so persuaded of the rationality of egoism? This, it seems fair to say, is one of the most important and puzzling problems arising out of over a century of commentary on the *Methods*. All the more so given that it is manifest, as previous chapters have shown, that the problem of self-sacrifice dominated Sidgwick's life and in fact led him to produce the *Methods*. Was the life of self-sacrifice, be it Christian or Comtean, really the happiest one?

A key passage in the *Methods* points to the fundamental significance of the differences between persons. Explaining that the egoist may avoid the "proof" of utilitarianism offered in Chapter 2 of Book IV by declining to affirm that "his own greatest happiness is not merely the rational ultimate end for himself, but a part of Universal Good," Sidgwick continues:

It would be contrary to Common Sense to deny that the distinction between any one individual and any other is real and fundamental, and that consequently "I" am concerned with the quality of my existence as an individual in a sense, fundamentally important, in which I am not concerned with the quality of the existence of other individuals: and this being so, I do not see how it can be proved that this distinction is not to be taken as fundamental in determining the ultimate end of rational action for an individual. And it may be observed that most Utilitarians, however anxious they have been to convince men of the reasonableness of aiming at happiness generally, have not commonly sought to attain this result by any logical transition from the Egoistic to the Universalistic principle. They have relied almost entirely on the Sanctions of Utilitarian rules; that is, on the pleasures gained or pains avoided by the individual conforming to them. Indeed, if an Egoist remains impervious to what we have called Proof, the only way of rationally inducing him to aim at the happiness of all, is to show him that his own greatest happiness can be best attained by so doing. And further, even if a man admits the self-evidence of the principle of Rational Benevolence, he may still hold that his own happiness is an end which it is irrational for him to sacrifice to any other; and that therefore a harmony between the maxim of Prudence and the maxim of Rational Benevolence must be somehow demonstrated, if morality is to be made completely rational. This latter view, indeed . . . appears to me, on the whole, the view of Common Sense: and it is that which I myself hold. It thus becomes needful to examine how far and in what way the required demonstration can be effected. (ME 498)

Again, Sidgwick's own view is that both individual and universal happiness must be served, must be treated as that unity of which Mill spoke so eloquently, "to bid self-love and social be the same." His purpose is not the "suppression of egoism," but rather the assimilation of it to form a unified view free of irresolvable practical dilemmas – something akin to the harmony that had been claimed by earlier, theological utilitarianism. And again, egoism bears two aspects: interested and disinterested.

But as Shaver shows, following Schneewind, this passage "was added to the fourth edition of the *Methods*," having first appeared in "Some Fundamental Ethical Controversies" (*Mind* 14, 1889), and before this, Sidgwick admitted that he "had made no attempt to show the irrationality of the sacrifice of self-interest to duty." The point had been forcefully put by Georg von Gizycki, who, in a series of reviews, tried to get Sidgwick to provide some defense of rational egoism. His defense is weakest in the first edition, and after that he tends to link the axiom of temporal neutrality to rational egoism, as emerging out of it in a way suggesting that such egoism has a certain priority.[135] Still, according to Shaver, he did not appear to think that rational egoism was established by the axiom of temporal irrelevance, or that there were other absolutely compelling grounds for it arising from, say, general agreement. Thus, much rests on the so-called distinction passage, as the ultimate revelation, in the *Methods*, of how Sidgwick conceived the conflict on the egoistic side, beyond the bare assertion of self-evidence.

Yet for Shaver, the argument presented in the distinction passage scarcely seems able to support the weight Sidgwick puts on it. If it is supposed to involve a non-normative argument about personal identity, to the effect that challenges to self-interest stemming from a "reduction-ist" view of the self as a fiction falter because they rely on a false view of personal identity, then it would seem rather rudimentary and at any rate trained on only one line of objection. Parfit, in *Reasons and Persons*, has famously maintained just this line, defending the reductionist view of personal identity and suggesting that it remains a mystery just why Sidgwick clung to the "further fact" view of identity.[136] Parfit also argues that rational egoism is an "unstable hybrid" view. After all, how can one go along with Sidgwick in thinking that one should rationally be more concerned about one's own future than the future states of others, simply because it is one's own future, if there is need of a further argument to show why one should not be more concerned about one's present rather than future aims, as the so-called Present-Aim theory of rationality would urge?[137] Sidgwick himself had suggested how such arguments might be made:

I do not see why the Egoistic principle should pass unchallenged any more than the Universalistic. I do not see why the axiom of Prudence should not be questioned, when it conflicts with present inclination, on a ground similar to that on which the Egoists refuse to admit the axiom of Rational Benevolence. If the Utilitarian has to answer the question, 'Why should I sacrifice my own happiness for the greater happiness of another?' it must surely be admissible to ask the Egoist, 'Why should I sacrifice a present pleasure for a greater one in the future? Why should I concern myself about my own future feelings any more than about the feelings of other persons? It undoubtedly seems to Common Sense paradoxical to ask for a reason why one should seek one's own happiness on the whole; but I do not see how the demand can be repudiated as absurd by those who adopt the views of the extreme empirical school of psychologists, although those views are commonly supposed to have a close affinity with Egoistic Hedonism. Grant that the Ego is merely a system of coherent phenomena, that the permanent identical 'I' is not a fact but a fiction, as Hume and his followers maintain; why, then, should one part of the series of feelings into which the Ego is resolved be concerned with another part of the same series, any more than with any other series? (ME 418–19)[138]

Of course, Sidgwick did have reasons for rejecting such a view, reasons stemming from his metaphysics and his work in psychical research, which will be the subject of the following chapters. This side of his research is, to my mind, absolutely crucial for understanding his conviction that egoism is credible.[139] But even if Sidgwick's nonreductionism is viable, there are other objections to rational egoism, objections that bear heavily on more purely normative readings of the distinction passage.

Thus, as Shaver maintains, if that passage is meant to suggest that there are two and only two normative "points of view," that of the universe (the whole) and that of the individual (the part), then it is also too rudimentary for the purpose. Broad's well-known objection was that as far as common sense is concerned, self-referential altruism – the point of view of family, friends, perhaps country – seems to be the favored view, or at any rate is no more or less arbitrary than the point of view of the individual or of the universe.[140] Perhaps, then, there is a continuum of positions here, so that it needs to be shown why, whichever end one starts with, the same arguments would not lead one all the way to the other end or just as well stop at any point in between. Thus, the assertion "I am a Dane" seems no more arbitrary than the assertion "I am a separate individual," as an ontologically grounded counter to the demand that one take the point of view of the universe. And as previous sections have amply demonstrated, Sidgwick himself often points up the arbitrariness of the individual point of view; indeed, Shaver draws attention to some of the important passages in which Sidgwick seems to press the case in just this impartialist or neutralist way. In "The Establishment of Ethical First Principles," Sidgwick explains that if I hold that "it is reasonable for me to take my own greatest happiness as the ultimate end of my conduct," I need to show why the fact that it is mine makes a difference, and why I should not concede that "the happiness of any other individual, equally capable and deserving of happiness, must be no less worth aiming at than my own." He applies a similar argument to support concern for the happiness of animals – as Shaver notes, explicitly correcting "on utilitarian grounds, what some take to be common sense."[141]

Finally, if, following Parfit, the distinction passage is read as an early version of Rawls's "separateness of persons" objection to utilitarianism, bringing out the disanalogy between the rationality of (i) making a sacrifice for the sake of a greater benefit to oneself later on and (ii) making a sacrifice for the sake of greater benefits to others, then it is, according to Shaver, simply a bad reading. Sidgwick obviously admits the rationality of both forms of sacrifice, but he does not support the second on the basis of the first. When he discusses the part/whole analogy, Sidgwick, according to Shaver, "is simply noting a similarity. He is not claiming that the argument for (ii) stands on the truth of (i) and the similarity of the cases. (Indeed, in the first edition, he argues for (ii) without mentioning (i).)"[142] And besides,

Sidgwick endorses no alternative moral theory, other than rational egoism, by which utilitarianism stands condemned. He has argued that common-sense morality, which might condemn utilitarianism, collapses *into* utilitarianism. In rational egoism, Sidgwick does have a rival normative theory that condemns utilitarianism. And the distinction passage could be taken to express condemnation from the point of view of this theory. But then the distinction passage has not yielded any defence of rational egoism. It simply tells us what rational egoism says about utilitarianism. Just as the separateness of persons charge depends on, rather than establishes, the superiority of a non-utilitarian theory of justice, so the distinction passage would depend on, rather than establish, rational egoism.[143]

Thus, Shaver's conclusion is that "however it is read, the distinction passage does not give Sidgwick a convincing argument for rational egoism.

At best, on the personal identity interpretation, it defeats one argument against rational egoism." Add to this the arguments from Schneewind and Sverdlik to the effect that, on balance, Sidgwick demonstrates that common sense is better systematized by utilitarianism than by egoism, and it is, Shaver claims, that much more puzzling why Sidgwick finds egoism so troubling. True, Sidgwick admits that "Utilitarianism is more rigid than Common Sense in exacting the sacrifice of the agent's private interests where they are incompatible with the greatest happiness of the greatest number," and this renders the coincidence of egoism and utilitarianism even less probable than the coincidence of egoism and common sense. (ME 499) Nonetheless,

Sidgwick's point is that a rational egoist would face more difficulty capturing utilitarian demands than capturing the demands of common-sense morality. He does not, then, think his indirect considerations show that utilitarianism is no more demanding than common-sense morality. But it does not follow that common-sense morality supports rational egoism more than it supports utilitarianism, even when sacrifices alone are considered. For rational egoism is much *less* demanding than common-sense morality. Sidgwick can both make the quoted claim and say that common-sense morality supports utilitarianism over rational egoism. He can do so by holding that the departures rational egoism makes from common-sense morality, in the direction of being less demanding, are greater than the departures utilitarianism makes from common-sense morality, in the direction of being more demanding.[144]

Still, for Shaver, Sidgwick's most plausible (if not very plausible) reason for taking rational egoism seriously comes, not from Cartesian considerations, but from its "wide acceptance," amounting to social verification – the "preponderant assent" it has enjoyed in "the common sense of mankind" and "the history of ethical thought in England."[145] In the first edition of the *Methods*, Sidgwick states that "there seems to be more general agreement among reflective persons as to the reasonableness of its fundamental principle, than exists in the case either of Intuitionism or of . . . Utilitarianism." Citing everyone from Hobbes to Hume, from Butler to Kant, Sidgwick could naturally assume that "it is hardly going too far to say that common sense assumes that 'interested' actions, tending to promote the agent's happiness, are *prima facie* reasonable: and that the *onus probandi* lies with those who maintain that disinterested conduct, as such, is reasonable" (ME1 107).[146]

Perhaps, as seems likely, this is part of the explanation of why Sidgwick could be so passionate about the dualism of practical reason and yet so apparently casual about the defense of rational egoism. As we have seen, he was simply steeped in the problem of self-sacrifice, defined in part by the contrast not only with Bentham's (supposed) psychological egoism, but also with the eudaimonism of the ancients (or Goethe) and the Christian conception, found in Butler, of personal redemption. Egoism, one might say, was too close to see clearly, so prevalent was it in the Western tradition as understood by Sidgwick. This point will be reinforced in the chapters to follow, but it is worth recalling here his famous confession, to Symonds, that "I feel by the limitations of my nature incapable of really comprehending the state of mind of one who does not *desire* the continuance of his personal being. All the activities in which I truly live seem to carry with them the same demand for the 'wages of going on'." (M 471) How, without appeal to some form of egoism (interested or disinterested) could one possibly understand the force of the pervasive concern for personal survival of physical death?

But there remains the puzzle of why, in this case, the greater systematizing power of utilitarianism did not, in Sidgwick's eyes, render it more credible than egoism, at least on that level. Valuable as Shaver's analysis surely is, it does, in the end, cut two ways: he makes Sidgwick's epistemology sound much more sensible than Brink allows, thereby reinforcing the significance of the dualism as Sidgwick presents it, but he then leaves Sidgwick looking strangely dogmatic and vacuous on the core defense of egoism, thereby undercutting the force of the dualism as Sidgwick presents it. Indeed, Shaver in various respects simply fails to appreciate what really pained Sidgwick about the dualism – among other things, the perversity of an unjust universe, in which death is the end. And he also fails to capture just how Sidgwick worried about the direction of commonsense morality, and about the destructive potential of narrower forms of egoism, matters that are not altogether perspicuous in the *Methods*.

However, these points will be developed in the following section, after some additional stage setting. To reply to the charges made by Gizycki, Shaver, and so many other critics, a rather fuller account of Sidgwick on egoism is necessary. The remainder of this section will provide some background material useful for keeping the dualism of practical reason in proper perspective, and will try to tie together some of the themes raised earlier concerning Sidgwick's indirect arguments about indirect strategies, themes deeply suggestive of how, in practical terms, he dealt with this dualism. Understanding the gap between mundane experience with a theistic postulate and mundane experience without a theistic postulate would seem to be important for grasping Sidgwick's core concern about the chaos of practical reason – after all, why would not a nontheistic harmonization do as well as a theistic one, if it could be made out? Just how Millian was he willing to be about this vital matter?

In truth, many have worried about Sidgwick's understanding of the Western tradition and the place of the dualism of practical reason within it. Indeed, his claim that in formulating this dualism, he was simply proving himself to be a student of Butler would appear to be questionable. Thus, according to Stephen Darwall, Sidgwick's dualism "is actually closer to Hutcheson's notion that universal benevolence and calm self-love are the two independent 'grand determinations' than to anything in Butler"[147] and may even derive ultimately "from a contemporary of Locke's, Richard Cumberland."[148] But William Frankena has argued powerfully that "ethical dualism, at least in the form in which Sidgwick accepts it, did not work itself entirely clear in Butler and did not do so until Sidgwick himself worked on it, if even then."[149] That is,

In just what way, then, is Butler a dualist? He certainly is one in the sense of holding that there are (at least) two faculties or principles in human nature, one egoistic and the other not, each of which has some regulative power and authority as such and independently of the other. As far as I can see, however, he is not one in the further sense of thinking that they are fully coordinate in authority, obligation, and reasonableness, though Sidgwick seems to think he is. Their dictates are not *in principle* equally authoritative, obligatory, or reasonable for Butler; in principle, for him reasonable self-love is supreme. Sidgwick seems to think that a dualist will hold that his two faculties are coordinate in theory, in practice, or in both; but Butler does not hold them to be coordinate in either sense. Thus, by Sidgwick's own account, which I take to be correct, Butler is not as much of a dualist as he appears to think. Butler is an ethical dualist, but only in a rather qualified way. Sidgwick's early modern dualists are not as much on the same beam he is as he judges them to be.[150]

For Frankena, Sidgwick must have been on a "rhetorical high" when he suggested that the modern view, once worked clear, recognized two governing faculties in reason. For as Sidgwick himself notes in other contexts, there is no such thing as *the* modern or even British view about the number of governing faculties found, not even on his own account; he himself describes Hobbes and Spinoza as egoists, that is, as finding, as the Greeks did, that egoistic reason is the sole governing faculty in us. Nor, according to Sidgwick, do all of the British put all of the faculties they regard as operative in us under *reason*, as he implies . . . ; he expressly cites Shaftesbury as the first to transfer "the centre of ethical interest from the Reason . . . to the emotional impulses that prompt to social duty," specifically to our moral *sense* and our disinterested and altruistic *feelings*, and portrays Hutcheson, Hume, and Adam Smith as following Shaftesbury's suit, as many other have.[151]

Plausibly, then, Sidgwick himself was more original on this score than he let on. More to the point, it is quite possible that he outstripped his predecessors in compellingly and explicitly bringing out the force of the dualism as a potential moral dilemma for a post-Christian age. For there was something quite ingenious, or insidious, about his frequent invocations of Butler, as though the tacit question was: what becomes of Butler's system, or of any Christian ethical view, once the theological postulate is removed? In this way, Sidgwick positively invited consideration of how far the Butlerian view would collapse into chaos once there was no God to coordinate interest and duty, and duty was no longer certain. And the chaos might bear the color of reason.

But to come to terms with Sidgwick's subversive and unadmitted originality – characteristically Mauricean and Apostolic, to be sure – it is necessary to consider further just what kind of chaos he envisioned for practical reason, in practical terms. One leading concern, as we have seen, is just how constructive the method of egoism might be, how able to narrow or soften the conflicts of "mundane experience." Clearly, much depends on the interpretation of common sense and the reach of indirect strategies, egoistic and utilitarian, both for purposes of justification and for purposes of motivation. Again, how essential was the God of theism?

Even admitting Shaver's reservations, Sidgwick's treatment of the egoistic side of the dualism of practical reason was impressive on a great many counts, simply as an extensive, systematic formulation (if not justification) of the method, one also profoundly relevant for any discussion of the external and internal sanctions so often invoked by utilitarianism. Shaver perhaps does not go quite far enough in bringing out how Sidgwick struggled to determine the ways in which egoism had lent itself to constructive ethical theorizing. Having done so much to explain how Sidgwick could, consistently with his intuitionism, place some stock in common sense, Shaver should more readily allow the good sense of his worrying about just how egoistic common sense might really be, particularly given the Christian hope of a "happy immortality."[152] This is not to confuse proof with sanctions, but it is to try to measure the distance between God's moral order and mundane experience. And after all, Sidgwick was scarcely one to pronounce a priori that mundane experience was clearly contradictory, rather than only apparently so.

Thus, Sidgwick notes that Hobbes's system,

> though based on Materialism and Egoism, was yet intended as ethically construc-tive. Accepting in the main the commonly received rules of social morality, it explained them as the conditions of peaceful existence which enlightened self-interest directed each individual to obey; provided only the social order to which they belonged was not merely ideal, but made actual by a strong government. Now no doubt this view renders the theoretical basis of duty seriously unstable; still, assuming a decently good government, Hobbism may claim to at once ex-plain and establish, instead of undermining, the morality of Common Sense. (ME 103n)

Even the rather narrow egoism of the Hobbesian view might go some way toward underwriting commonsense morality, though Sidgwick reg-isters serious qualms about how far the artificial harmonizing of interests by institutional means could really go, in either Hobbes or Bentham. As he remarked in his 1877 essay on "Bentham and Benthamism,"

> [U]nless a little more sociality is allowed to an average human being, the problem of combining these egoists into an organisation for promoting their common happiness is like the old task of making ropes of sand. The difficulty that Hobbes vainly tried to settle summarily by absolute despotism is hardly to be overcome by the democratic artifices of his more inventive successor. (MEA 163)

This passage nicely captures Sidgwick's views about the limits of exter-nal (e.g., legal, institutional) sanctions for producing a utilitarian artificial harmony of interests, and it also points to his abiding concern with ex-ploring the potential of internal – especially dispositional – ones, which is where some of the most difficult and intriguing indirect strategies come into the picture. On this he was most explicit, and happy to ally him-self with the utilitarian tradition. Consider his early review of Grote's posthumous *An Examination of the Utilitarian Philosophy*:

> [I]n his remarks on Mill's 'Neo-utilitarianism' as he calls it, he is too apt to re-
> gard any deviations from Benthamism as alien elements, introduced from other
> sources and not really reconcilable with the fundamental principles of the system.
> Thus he points out very well the great difference between the innovating utili-
> tarianism of Bentham, which professed to reconstruct morality from (utilitarian)
> first principles: and the conservative utilitarianism of Mill, which takes *en bloc* the
> current rules of morality, as 'beliefs obtained from experience as to the effect of
> actions on happiness, to be accepted provisionally even by the philosopher'. But
> he does not see that the difference, important as it is, is yet one that may fairly
> exist *within* the school: both sides would agree that the question of accepting pro-
> visionally or throwing aside traditional rules of morality must be settled entirely
> on utilitarian grounds; and that, so far as innovation is necessary, the principle of
> utility must be the *principium innovandi et reformandi*. Again Mill is charged with
> 'importing' from Stoicism the consideration of man's social feelings as a sanction
> of utilitarian rules; and no doubt we have here another divergence from Bentham.
> But there again the difference is not ethical, but psychological: if men actually
> have social sympathies, with their attendant pains and pleasures, Bentham cannot
> without inconsistency refuse to recognise these latter as 'sanctions'; and indeed he
> does recognise them, in a later correction of his system (sent privately to Dumont
> in 1821).[153]

These latter strategies are, of course, also plainly suggestive of how, in practical terms, the world might be structured to soften the problem of the dualism of practical reason, even without benefit of deity. And Sidgwick analyzes them in terms of the type of character formation that utilitarianism should seek. His treatment of egoism works in parallel, also elaborating the most effective forms of socialization and going far beyond even a strategic, indirect version of Hobbesian egoism.[154]

For as we have seen, Sidgwick goes much further in making the case for egoism, urging also that egoism is more plausibly construed more high-mindedly, as the "Goethean" ideal. Even if he cannot quite see the point of aiming at virtue without producing some gain in desirable consciousness to someone, he does think that desirable consciousness is largely attached to the things praised as virtues. Again, much of this argument involves a complex account of the pursuit of happiness by indirect means:

> [B]esides admitting the actual importance of sympathetic pleasures to the majority
> of mankind, I should go further and maintain that, on empirical grounds alone,
> enlightened self-interest would direct most men to foster and develop their sym-
> pathetic susceptibilities to a greater extent than is now commonly attained. The

effectiveness of Butler's famous argument against the vulgar antithesis between Self-love and Benevolence is undeniable: and it seems scarcely extravagant to say that, amid all the profuse waste of the means of happiness which men commit, there is no imprudence more flagrant than that of Selfishness in the ordinary sense of the term, – that excessive concentration of attention on the individual's own happiness which renders it impossible for him to feel any strong interest in the pleasures and pains of others. The perpetual prominence of self that hence results tends to deprive all enjoyments of their keenness and zest, and produce rapid satiety and *ennui*: the selfish man misses the sense of elevation and enlargement given by wide interests; he misses the more secure and serene satisfaction that attends continually on activities directed towards ends more stable in prospect than an individual's happiness can be; he misses the peculiar rich sweetness, depending upon a sort of complex reverberation of sympathy, which is always found in services rendered to those whom we love and who are grateful. He is made to feel in a thousand various ways, according to the degree of refinement which his nature has attained, the discord between the rhythms of his own life and of that larger life of which his own is but an insignificant fraction. (ME 501)

Direct assault on one's happiness, or on one's good conceived in other terms, is likely, as with the direct assault on insomnia, only to chase it further and further from one's grasp. Again, both the egoist and the utilitarian can recognize this peculiar feature of happiness, and argue in a two-level fashion that the ultimate end to be sought can effectively be sought only by such indirect means as, say, cultivating sympathetic dispositions, abiding for the most part by rough commonsense moral rules, and so forth. In other words, though

the 'dictates of Reason' are always to be obeyed, it does not follow that 'the dictation of Reason' – the predominance of consciously moral over non-moral motives – is to be promoted without limits; and indeed Common Sense appears to hold that some things are likely to be better done, if they are done from other motives than conscious obedience to practical Reason or Conscience. (ME 395)[155]

And insofar as the utilitarian can go rather further in the assimilation of commonsense morality, this is not simply because egoism often takes the form of a self-defeating selfishness – Arnoldian complacency was not quite that. Recall Sidgwick's plea for fire and strength over sweetness and light, as well as his (partial) assimilation of perfectionism to dogmatic intuitional morality.

Thus, a significant part of Sidgwick's tactic in coping (or trying to cope) with the implications of the dualism of practical reason involved addressing how high-minded indirect strategies – as effective social policies – might or might not narrow the distance between egoism and utilitarianism. Yet in this region, where all the practical details of duty were to be worked out, some of the most important calculations only grew hazier. Indeed, an additional, quite insidious aspect of this conflict within practical reason is suggested by the way in which it could figure, in practical terms, even in a more highly evolved utilitarian society, since utilitarianism itself might on balance require the very dispositions that would create an analogous conflict:

> But allowing all this, it yet seems to me as certain as any conclusion arrived at by hedonistic comparison can be, that the utmost development of sympathy, intensive and extensive, which is now possible to any but a very few exceptional persons, would not cause a perfect coincidence between Utilitarian duty and self-interest. . . . Suppose a man finds that a regard for the general good – Utilitarian Duty – demands from him a sacrifice, or extreme risk, of life. There are perhaps one or two human beings so dear to him that the remainder of a life saved by sacrificing their happiness to his own would be worthless to him from an egoistic point of view. But it is doubtful whether many men, 'sitting down in a cool hour' to make the estimate, would affirm even this: and of course that particular portion of the general happiness, for which one is called upon to sacrifice one's own, may easily be the happiness of persons not especially dear to one. But again, from this normal limitation of our keenest and strongest sympathy to a very small circle of human beings, it results that the very development of sympathy may operate to increase the weight thrown into the scale against Utilitarian duty. There are very few persons, however strongly and widely sympathetic, who are so constituted as to feel for the pleasures and pains of mankind generally a degree of sympathy at all commensurate with their concern for wife or children, or lover, or intimate friend: and if any training of the affections is at present possible which would materially alter this proportion in the general distribution of our sympathy, it scarcely seems that such training is to be recommended as on the whole felicific. And thus when Utilitarian Duty calls on us to sacrifice not only our own pleasures but the happiness of those we love to the general good, the very sanction on which Utilitarianism most relies must act powerfully in opposition to its precepts. (ME 501–2)

This account suggests the possibility that even the best of mundane experience might be fairly rife with paradox and practical compromise. For Sidgwick, the unsatisfactoriness of the world without some form of religious enchantment is hard to blink. There may be irreducible trade-offs in trying to expand the circle of one's sympathetic concern, such that the attempt to render it more effective in the large may actually render it less effective in the small. It would, of course, be nice if there were more precise methods for comparing the various optimizing strategies, but these, on Sidgwick's account, are for the much further future. Ultimately, he rejects the attempts to find a deductive or "scientific short-cut to the ascertainment of the right means to the individual's happiness," a "high priori road," as it were, whether in the form of an account of the psychophysical sources of pleasure and pain or in the form of a Spencerian account of the preservation of life, and he does so because such efforts are still immature and at best yield only "a vague and general rule, based on considerations which it is important not to overlook, but the relative value of which we can only estimate by careful observation and comparison of individual experiences" (ME 195).[156] Thus, there can be no appeal beyond reflective experience, and reflective experience is deeply problematic and opaque. Why, after all, might not the evolution of common sense be replete with productive forms of delusion, perhaps ethical as well as religious?[157]

Still, Sidgwick's treatment of both the external and internal sanctions that utilitarianism might deploy is remarkably wide-ranging and not altogether unpractical. The strictures of utilitarianism may require that one painfully reign in even one's philanthropic impulses, if such charity in the small turns out to be the less effective means to the greatest happiness.

Or again, a man may find that he can best promote the general happiness by working in comparative solitude for ends that he never hopes to see realised, or by working chiefly among and for persons for whom he cannot feel much affection, or by doing what must alienate or grieve those whom he loves best, or must make it necessary for him to dispense with the most intimate of human ties. In short, there seem to be numberless ways in which the dictates of that Rational Benevolence, which as a Utilitarian he is bound absolutely to obey, may conflict with that indulgence of kind affections which Shaftesbury and his followers so persuasively exhibit as its own reward. (ME 503)[158]

Utilitarian sympathy was not to be confused with sentimentalism.

It is hard, in reading such passages, not to think back to the dilemmas of Sidgwick's resignation crisis, or to the issue of subscription generally, and all the ways in which the most painful of these conflicts had, in his mind, to do with those who acted hypocritically out of the best motives – "pious fraud" or "sweetness and light." Which is, of course, not to deny that he also worried about the "sensual herd," those who needed both reassurance about the motives of people in high places and orthodox religion as their "real elevator." Self-sacrifice was a problem across the board. But worrying about the force of the better argument and worrying about the force of the working class or "lower races" were not exactly the same thing. The *Methods*, for all its candor, does tend resolutely to stress the former and ignore the latter, veiling the social and political realities that made the dualism of practical reason a pervasive source of such practical anxiety for Sidgwick. And it hardly conveys the quite singular way in which this dualism was an abstract reflection of Sidgwick's personal struggle to unify duty and friendship, suggestive as the above passages may be. What if high-minded utilitarian soaring derived from such concrete particular relationships as Apostolic friendships?

As later sections and chapters will spell out, the *Methods* does take on a very different aspect when read in the light of Sidgwick's various life crises and other writings. His preoccupations did shape its construction, did influence what was said and what was left unsaid. Would Sidgwick have included himself among the "very few exceptional persons" capable of fully assimilating and acting upon the utilitarian orientation out of a superior sympathy? Could he thus be exempted from the dislocation between theory and practice (or justification and motivation) of which Williams complained? Just how many levels of moral thinking did he allow himself or other "moral saints"? How utopian was the "ideal" utilitarian society? How many trade-offs or compromises would it represent? What was the message of the *Methods*, on balance, when it came to that cultural evolution toward a more comprehensive sympathy and greater willingness for self-sacrifice that Sidgwick had apparently worked toward so assiduously in so many ways? For all his reluctance to enter into the details of psychology, he does suggest a tentative theory of moral psychological maturation:

Perhaps, indeed, we may trace a general law of variation in the relative proportion of these two elements as exhibited in the development of the moral consciousness both in the race and in individuals; for it seems that at a certain stage of this development the mind is more susceptible to emotions connected with abstract moral ideas and rules presented as absolute; while after emerging from this stage and before entering it the feelings that belong to personal relations are stronger. Certainly in a Utilitarian's mind sympathy tends to become a prominent element of all instinctive moral feelings that refer to social conduct; as in his view the rational basis of the moral impulse must ultimately lie in some pleasure won or pain saved for himself or for others; so that he never has to sacrifice himself to an Impersonal Law, but always for some being or beings with whom he has at least some degree of fellow-feeling. (ME 500–1)

Sidgwick's objections to sentimentalism notwithstanding, there is nothing far-fetched in finding in such passages anticipations of a distinctively utilitarian critique of neo-Kantian, Kohlbergian accounts of the stages of moral development.[159] Although it may not be terribly surprising that Sidgwick would interpret this process of maturation, both individual and social, as a growth through obedience to abstract rules to a capacity for empathy focused on real relations to other sentient beings, very little attention has been directed to his contributions in this area.[160] Obviously, his own Apostolic development took something like this form, what with his emphasis on friendship.

Still, where did all this sophisticated theorizing lead, when it came to the brute force of the dualism of practical reason as a potential reality of mundane moral experience? Where, in the end, did Sidgwick actually come down on how far the circle of sympathy might expand? How self-effacingly utilitarian might the egoist become? Sidgwick's view of utilitarianism often outdid Mill's in its high-minded soaring: "Universal Happiness, desirable consciousness or feeling for the innumerable multitude of living beings, present and to come" – this was "an end that satisfies our imagination by its vastness, and sustains our resolution by its comparative security." But just whose imagination did he have in mind? Was this clerisy a Eurocentric one? And was this a matter of reason, or of emotion? Of justification, or of motivation? And either way, why, with this vision of societal and individual maturation before him, was he always so terribly anxious about the future, his own and that of civilization?

V. Practical Chaos

Yet Prof. Sidgwick holds that Egoism is rational; and it will be useful briefly to consider the reasons which he gives for this absurd conclusion. 'The Egoist,' he says . . . 'may avoid the proof of Utilitarianism by declining to affirm,' either 'implicitly or explicitly, that his own greatest happiness is not merely the ultimate rational end for himself, but a part of Universal Good.' And in the passage to which he here refers us, as having there 'seen' this, he says: 'It cannot be proved that the difference between his own happiness and another's happiness is not *for him* all-important'. . . . What does Prof. Sidgwick mean by these phrases 'the

ultimate rational end for himself,' and '*for him* all-important'? He does not attempt
to define them; and it is largely the use of such undefined phrases which causes
absurdities to be committed in philosophy.

G. E. Moore, *Principia Ethica*

The logical contradiction involved in Egoism has been powerfully argued by
von Hartmann in his criticism of Nietzsche and Max Stirner. . . . More recently
Mr. Moore has incisively expressed the difficulty as follows: 'What Egoism holds,
therefore, is that *each* man's happiness is the sole good – that a number of different
things are *each* of them the only good thing there is – an absolute contradiction!
No more complete and thorough refutation of any theory could be desired. Yet
Professor Sidgwick holds that Egoism is rational,' a conclusion which he proceeds to characterize as 'absurd' (*Principia Ethica*, 1903, p. 99). I should agree
with him that the position is self-contradictory in a sense in which universalistic Hedonism is not, and that with all his subtlety Sidgwick failed altogether to
escape what was really an inconsistency in thought, even if he escaped an actual
or formal contradiction. But to point out this logical contradiction does not seem
to me quite so easy and final a way of refuting Sidgwick's position as it does
to Mr. Moore for these reasons: (1) The Egoist with whom Professor Sidgwick
is arguing would probably not accept Mr. Moore's (and my own) conception of
an absolute objective good, though I should admit and have contended . . . that
if he fully thought out what is implied in his own contention that his conduct
is 'reasonable' he would be led to that conception. (2) Sidgwick only admitted
that the Egoist was reasonable from one point of view – reasonable as far as he
goes, i.e. when he refuses to ask whether his judgements are consistent with what
he cannot help recognizing as the rational judgements of other men, and limits
himself to asking whether he can make his own judgements consistent with themselves from his own point of view. No doubt Sidgwick ought to have gone on
to admit that this imperfectly reasonable point of view was not really reasonable
at all, and to some extent he has done this in his last Edition. And (3) after all,
even if we admit that the Egoist is unreasonable, there remains the question 'Why
should he care to be reasonable?' It was largely the difficulty of answering this
question on universalistic Hedonist principles which drove Professor Sidgwick
to admit a 'dualism of the Practical Reason,' and I am not sure that the question
has been very satisfactorily answered by Mr. Moore who, though he is no Hedonist, appears to be unwilling to give the good will the highest place in his scale
of goods.

Hastings Rashdall, *The Theory of Good and Evil*

Although many may hope that Shaver is right in claiming that "neither
Hobbes nor Sidgwick provides good arguments for rational egoism" and

that "Sidgwick suggests good arguments against it," his suggestion that most philosophers after Sidgwick have been inclined to reject egoism, and that this view has been only weakly articulated for much of the last century, may well seem puzzling.[161] True, Moore, Rashdall, Ross, and Prichard were quite hostile to any such view, and many of the most prominent movements of the so-called great expansion in substantive moral theory – Rawlsianism chief among them – have shared various neo-Kantian assumptions about practical reason. But there is a fairly impressive consensus (including Shaver) that Moore and the rest responded to the dualism with arguments that were as unsatisfactory as they were curt – thus, for J. L. Mackie, "egoism can coherently resist any such proof by adhering to the use of such two-place predicates as 'right,' 'ought,' and 'good for': Objectivity and universalization with respect to these are powerless against it."[162] Moore, according to Mackie, was guilty of the worst sort of effrontery when he chastised Sidgwick for failing to define such expressions as "the ultimate rational end for himself," given how Moore himself had so insisted on the indefinable nature of "good." And Moore's claim that "good" must be a one-place predicate, absolute, was nothing but sheer assertion, or an unargued assumption that "an undefined one-place-predicate 'good' can be straightforwardly meaningful, but a two-place-predicate 'good for' or 'all-important for' cannot."[163] And as Skorupski has put it,

What is clear to him [Sidgwick] is that the egoistic principle can be stated in a rational and universal form. Of course an egoist who thinks his own good is the *only* good thing, the only thing that everyone has reason to promote, can be convicted of attaching irrational significance to his good as against that of others. Such an egoist thinks his own good the only thing that is 'agent-neutrally' good, the one thing that provides everyone with reasons for action. (The term is not used by Sidgwick; it comes from more recent moral theory.) But egoism need not appeal to the idea of the *agent-neutrally* good. The egoist may instead hold simply that his own good is the only good relative to him – this is not a tautological doctrine. And he can put this in universal terms by saying that everyone ought to pursue what is good relative to them, namely their own good.

It now becomes clear that hedonism is a doctrine about what a person's good is. To advance from it to utilitarianism we need at least to add that every person's good is *agent-neutrally* good. The rational egoist can block our considerations at this point, unless we can make it plausible that reasons as such are agent-neutral.[164]

Even if one claims, as Skorupski does, that pure practical reason as such does rest with agent-neutral reasons, the vanquishing or subordination of agent-relative reasons, including those deployed by rational egoists, is not generally regarded as simply the correction of an obvious mistake. Indeed, many defenders of agent-neutral reasons – including both Skorupski and Thomas Nagel – end up in partial retreat, allowing that agent-relative reasons cannot be altogether discounted. Crisp goes even further down the Sidgwickian path, defending a dual-source view of practical reason that admittedly incorporates "a version of what Henry Sidgwick called 'the dualism of practical reason.'"[165] And this allows the rational egoist considerable room for maneuver, as Samuel Scheffler, long associated with a similar dualistic account, has also observed.[166] Thus, Hurka, in a recent defense of perfectionism, framed his argument by explaining that in "the absence of a compelling argument that goodness must be understood in the . . . Moorean way, I will assume with Sidgwick that claims about agent-relative goodness are coherent, and ask how they may affect the recursive account of self-interest and altruism."[167]

To be sure, to cast Sidgwick's dualism in this way is to invite again the question of why he narrowed the contenders down to utilitarianism and egoism.[168] That is, Moore's claim was that the expressions "my own good" and "good for me" are misguided because such talk can only mean that "something which will be exclusively mine, as my own pleasure is mine" is also "good absolutely," but if "it is *good absolutely* that I should have it, then everyone else has as much reason for aiming at *my* having it as I have myself." If the Sidgwickian counter to this is simply that there is such a thing as agent-relative goodness – such that, as Hurka puts it, "the question is only whether there are different ultimate ends for different people" – then egoism is only one variety of the challenge to agent-neutral reasons, Broad's "self-referential altruism" being one of many other options.[169]

This is not to deny that, on Sidgwick's rendering, as we have just seen, egoism houses many different alternatives, from Aristotle to Hobbes to Goethe. Still, for all its richness in representing "the personal point of view," egoism plainly does not encompass all agent-relative reasons, and when Sidgwick broaches the matter of nonegoistic agent-relative reasons, he is often less than perspicuous. Interestingly, however, he also on occasion gestures toward further indeterminacies in practical reason, conflicts between agent-neutral reasons, as when he invokes the Socratic complaint about the *injustice* of a universe in which virtue goes unrewarded. And it may be in part for this reason that some commentators have suggested that what really bothered Sidgwick was not merely the specific challenge of egoism, but the general indeterminacy of practical reason.[170]

In this connection, it should be added that the contrast between Sidgwick and Moore is not quite as simplistic as the just-quoted passages make it sound. As Hurka spells it out,

[T]he concept of Sidgwick's that Moore rejected was not well-being but agent-relative goodness. And his main reason for rejecting it was his belief that goodness is an unanalysable property. If goodness is this kind of property, it is hard to see how an object can have it "from one point of view" but not "from another"; surely it must either have the property or not. Compare squareness. An object cannot be square from one point of view but not from another; it is either square or not. (The object can look square from one point of view but not from another, but looking square is not the same as being square.) So it must be with goodness if that is a simply property. But Sidgwick held that goodness can be analyzed, in particular as what a person ought to desire, and it is perfectly possible to say that what each person ought to desire is different, say, just his own pleasure.[171]

Plausibly, this is the conflict, though as remarked in the last section, it is hardly obvious why Sidgwick's "ought" did not share various features of the Moorean "good" in its idealizing. Still, his greater metaethical caution made a difference, allowing the cogency of agent-relative reasons generally.

For all that, it is difficult to deny that Sidgwick was fairly obsessed with the varieties of egoism, and this concern has struck many as apt, given the power of egoism as a source for agent-relative reasons, the "personal point of view." Thus, it is not surprising that Kurt Baier, for example, in his recent account of the subject, should suggest that rational egoism is "the most deeply entrenched normative theory of egoism" and that "the jury on this case is still in disarray." Sidgwick, he allows, was engaged with just this form of the theory, in a weak version admitting that even if it is always rational to act out of self-interest, acting against one's interest may also be rational.[172]

In fact, in his major work, *The Rational and the Moral Order*, Baier addresses Sidgwick's views at length, particularly the dualism of practical reason:

How serious is Sidgwick's problem? In my view . . . it is quite serious, especially if one starts, as many do, from Sidgwick's unfortunate formulation of it. Thus, his bifurcation of practical reason need not give rise to a contradiction, even on those occasions when, as surely sometimes happens, the two principles do conflict. A contradiction would arise only if both the reasons they supported were what I called requiring rather than merely permissive, and even then only if they were indefeasible. If even only one of them is merely permissive, if it is simply perfectly rational or reasonable, say, to act for one's own good, but not necessarily always irrational or unreasonable not to act for one's own good, then one could act for the general good and contrary to one's own without its necessarily being the case that when the two principles offer reasons for incompatible actions, one both ought to act for the universal good and not for one's own, *and* that one ought to act for one's own and not for the universal good.

However, as Sidgwick seems to have sensed, there is still a problem even if this is granted. For if my argument . . . is sound, then Sidgwick's position would allow that it may always be in accordance with reason to promote the universal good and always in accordance with reason to promote one's own good and that, when one cannot do both, it is in accordance with reason to do *either*. Nevertheless, Sidgwick also appears to have thought, and it would seem to agree with common sense, that moral reasons, which he took to be those based on the universal good, defeat, if not all other kinds, surely at least prudential ones. . . . Sidgwick seems to have grasped this much, even if perhaps only obscurely. For in various places in which he produces arguments designed to persuade the Egoist to see the rationality of Universal Hedonism, their thrust is always to show not merely that the Universal Hedonist is *also* or *equally* rational, but that the Egoist ought to give up his position and become a Universal Hedonist. The thrust of his argument "from the Point of View of the Universe," for example, appears to be that everyone should look at things from that point of view, and that anyone who does must adopt the principles of Universal Hedonism as defeating that of Egoistic Hedonism when the two conflict. Thus Sidgwick seems to have sensed the need for a demonstration that moral reasons have a greater defeating force than prudential ones, hence his argument from the point of view of the universe. In any case, whether or not he sensed it, he is surely wrong in his claim . . . that a completely rational morality requires a demonstration of a "harmony" (i.e., coextensionality) between the maxims of prudence . . . and of benevolence.[173]

These remarks both situate Sidgwick's dualism as a live issue and indicate some different ways of tackling it. What is perhaps especially instructive is that, like Moore and Rashdall, Skorupski and Shaver, Baier is basically drawn to Sidgwick's universalizing challenge to the egoist: why is *your* good so special? How, then, does one stop on the slippery slope before reaching the point of view of the universe? Thus, for Baier, the better alternative to any attempted proof of the harmony or moral order of the universe is the demonstration that when morality and prudence conflict, "the requirements of morality defeat those of prudence."

But again, a more thoroughly Sidgwickian view is possible. Crisp argues that "Sidgwick is sometimes described as a utilitarian. But it is more precise to ascribe to him a version of the dual-source view, held on the basis of the neutral argument for the existence of options." Quoting the distinction passage, he explains that (contra Shaver) it makes "a clear appeal to the separateness of persons as grounding a counterbalance to the reason to promote the good." And for Crisp,

Sidgwick was rightly pessimistic about the reconciliation of Rational Egoism and Utilitarianism. His version of the dual-source view contains at its heart an irreconcilable tension between two ultimate and comprehensive principles of rationality. But this is not to say that any dual-source view must fail to provide any practical guidance. To take two extreme cases: when I can promote a very great good at a very small cost to myself, other things being equal my strongest reason overall is to make the sacrifice; likewise, if I can add to the overall good only a little at very great cost to myself, other things being equal my strongest reason is not to make the sacrifice. In other words, the strength of the reasons grounded in the simple thought or the separateness of persons varies according to the good or bad at stake. The dilemma of practical reason is not quite what Sidgwick took it to be. It arises most starkly in those cases where I can produce a great increase in overall good at a great cost to myself. Here the simple thought and the separateness of persons pull hard against one another. The problem here is essentially a Hegelian (or Freudian) one. The intuitions about rationality and reasonableness we consult in such cases will have been shaped by an upbringing in a culture itself imbued with a particular understanding of the relative strengths of the reason to promote the good and the reason to promote one's own good.[174]

Arguably, Sidgwick would have appreciated the reference to Hegel and felt himself equal to dealing with it, providing his own account of moral maturation. At any rate, on Crisp's intricately developed line, the question of "whether morality permits one to pursue one's own good at the expense of the overall good" invites the following response:

[T]his gets things the wrong way round. If we are asked what morality consists in, we can identify it if we wish with the reason to promote the overall good. But there is no need for any notion of morality, prior to the reason to promote the good and the competing reason based on the separateness of persons, that will rule on whether one is permitted or required to act on certain reasons on certain occasions."[175]

In addressing Shelley Kagan's penetrating attempt to defeat all such reasons arising from the personal point of view, Crisp develops some strikingly Sidgwickian themes:

> But what about the practical implications of the dual-source view? Am I seriously arguing that we should see killing and letting die as on a par, and be prepared to kill in pursuit of our own good? Am I suggesting that this is how we should bring up our children? These consequences may be *so* counterintuitive that the arguments for the dual-source view will have to be rejected.
>
> The dual-source view does not have these practical implications. First, since we have been brought up to accept common sense morality, and since we live in a culture based on common sense morality, killing is likely to be far more psychologically and socially costly than letting die. Secondly, these facts militate against educating any individual child to use the dual-source view in practice. Further, it would probably be a mistake for *all* of us to begin educating children to be practical dual-source theorists. Human beings are not creatures of pure reason. We have an evolutionary background and an emotional make-up which cannot be ignored in moral theory. In particular, we show a particular concern for those visibly near us, and for what we *do* to them. It may well be that these concerns, though they might not withstand close intellectual scrutiny, are somehow central to our becoming and continuing to be rational agents. The risk that this is so would be sufficient to justify not radically changing the moral education of our children. What is needed is common sense morality with a far greater emphasis on the importance of distributive justice and personal generosity.[176]

As Crisp notes, these arguments "parallel those for a 'split-level' version of utilitarianism." Clearly, they resonate powerfully with Sidgwick's views about the potential limitations of even a more highly evolved utilitarian society, absent any cosmic ordering, and the nature of moral maturation and cautious utilitarian reform. Crisp is, in effect, picking up the Sidgwickian project without the parapsychological and theistic or Buddhist options.

Doubtless there is much to be said for all these interpretations and reconstructions of Sidgwick's dualism, which collectively ought to convey something of the continuing relevance of the issues raised by the *Methods*. Beyond a certain point, however, it is just very difficult to say, for example, whether Sidgwick shifted his views on the question of "permissive" reasons, given that he did not use such terminology.

But at least on the question of whether Sidgwick's axiomatic grounding of egoism is really as elliptical as Shaver claims, it must be owned that a great many commentators have followed Sidgwick in moving too quickly to identify "prudence" with egoism, when giving a summary exposition of the dualism. Even Crisp, for example, flatly states that Sidgwick "took it as self-evident that one ought to aim at one's own good on the whole, accepting that this good was merely a particular part of the general good."[177] And Marcus Singer, in a recent work, simply states that the "fundamental principles of Philosophical Intuitionism are the intuitively self-evident axioms of prudence or egoism, justice, and rational benevolence."[178]

However, in a footnote, Singer does call attention to the interpretation anticipating Shaver's advanced by Sidgwick's student W. R. Sorley, in his *A History of English Philosophy*:

It would appear . . . that this dualism was not adequately tested by [Sidgwick] and that it really arises from the ambiguity of the term prudence. Prudence may mean either "regard for one's own good on the whole" or (what is not the same thing) the principle that "hereafter as such is neither less nor more valuable than now." Both forms of statement are used by Sidgwick; but only the latter has a claim to express an absolute ethical principle; and it is not inconsistent with the axiom of benevolence.[179]

This would certainly suggest some powerful support for treating the move from axioms to egoism with much greater caution.

Furthermore, Schneewind's account, which remains the most extensive, ends up reformulating Sidgwick's axiom of prudence to read "Maximizing the agent's own good is an ultimate right-making characteristic" and his axiom of benevolence to read "Maximizing the universal good is an ultimate right-making characteristic." His claim is that "these formulations seem to express Sidgwick's understanding of the two principles involved in the dualism of the practical reason, and they reveal its structure more plainly than his own statements do."[180] If the world does not have the requisite moral order, then it is "logically impossible" for both of these to be true, for "it cannot be true that it is actually right to do an act maximizing own-good and not actually right to do it."

Thus we have found the contradiction, removable by a factual proposition, which lies at the heart of Sidgwick's problem. The urgency of the difficulty it creates can perhaps be brought out by recalling that Sidgwick has tried throughout the *Methods* to discover what reason demands of action when applied under the most fundamental conditions of human life. What he finds at the end is that because of one such basic and undeniable fact about human life, practical reason inevitably makes contradictory demands on action. If this is not a formal contradiction within reason itself, its bearing on Sidgwick's real hope for philosophical ethics is sufficiently devastating to make it clear why he thinks his endeavour ends in failure.[181]

And Phillips would also seem to have a point insofar as he suggests that Sidgwick was also exercised – justifiably or not – about the simple indeterminacy of permissive reasons on both sides, because this still, to his mind, amounted to a failure to provide an ultimate unification of practical reason. Consider Sidgwick's pointed and quite characteristic criticism of John Grote's position:

> The non-critical part of Mr. Grote's book I can scarcely call constructive. It is not even a sketch of a system; it is a collection of sketches. He considers that utilitarians are right in the general assertion (carefully explained to be meaningless) that all action is aimed at happiness. But he would distinguish the study of the general effects of Conduct on happiness, from the enquiry into the principles of Duty, or right distribution of happiness, and from the investigation of the Virtues, or generous dispositions, which must be left freely to follow their special altruistic aims, and not made to depend on a utilitarian first principle. What the last two methods are to be, and how the three enquiries are to be harmonized, Mr. Grote does not clearly explain. In his desire to comprehend the diversity of human impulses, he has unfortunately neglected the one impulse (as human as any) which it is the special function of the philosopher to direct and satisfy: the effort after a complete and reasoned synthesis of practical principles.[182]

Here again one feels the force of the (frustrated) ambition that was behind the *Methods*, and the refusal to "compress the world into a system." What Irwin complained of as an ungrounded demand for clarity at key points in the *Methods* was also in large measure a demand for determinateness, for the type of clear guidance that Sidgwick lamented losing along with his faith.

But in any event, the illuminating point here is that even Schneewind requires a reconstruction of Sidgwick's axioms in order to make sense of the dualism. This, too, supports Shaver's general account, though on Schneewind's reading, Sidgwick's pursuit of harmonization is clearly much more of a necessity. Shaver, in fact, admittedly takes his point of departure from Schneewind's analysis, agreeing with him that it explains – in a way that Broad's account does not – much of what Sidgwick says about how the axioms are merely "consistent with and needed to prove utilitarianism, and that the issue between rational egoist and utilitarian turns on the rationality of taking up the universe's point of view." Certainly, as we have seen, Sidgwick was extremely insistent that the axioms were too abstract to provide much practical guidance about anything – everything needed still to be filled in.

It would be rash, then, to deny what Shaver, Schneewind, and apparently Sidgwick himself – in his more considered statements – all expressly claim in this connection: namely, that the axiomatic basis of egoism is insufficient in itself to render egoism truly rather than apparently self-evident, much less of the highest certainty. And yet it is also possible to think that Shaver has gone too far in discounting the force of the argument for rational egoism in Sidgwick's work, and in painting a picture of what Sidgwick "was really getting at" that comports too easily with the impartialist attempt to defeat egoism. Schneewind's work supports just such a critique.

To be sure, Shaver's view has great advantages. It makes admirable sense of Sidgwick's tendency to describe his own views as "utilitarian," without much qualification. And it suggests how, taking moral theory as a going project, Sidgwick could have continued to develop his account of the self-evident grounding of utilitarianism, getting beyond the treatment of it as only "apparently" self-evident, without then running into the problem of a similar development of the egoistic principle producing a conflict – an impossible conflict – of genuinely self-evident propositions of the highest certainty. After all, Sidgwick manifestly aspired to greater certainty in this department, even if he did not find it. Furthermore, it helps to explain how so many of those inspired by the *Methods* and/or by Sidgwick himself – from Rashdall, Moore, and Russell down to Baier, Kagan, Singer, and Shaver – could take this as the *obvious* direction for the progress that Sidgwick sought but failed to find.

On the other side, however, Sidgwick clearly did lean toward a nonreductionist view of personal identity that undercut a number of potential challenges to rational egoism, as the following chapter will show. His articulation of moral theory was, for better or worse, steeped in the religious orientation of his youth, which had in effect involved a form of reconciliation. And he did tend, as Crisp suggests, to wield the distinction passage as an independent argument for at least the personal point of view, and not simply as an objection to utilitarianism. Consider his response, in the very paper presenting the distinction passage – the relatively late "Some Fundamental Ethical Controversies" – to Rashdall's objection that he fails to reconcile duty and self-interest because he assigns a "different end to the individual and to the race." On Sidgwick's rendering, Rashdall, trying to avoid the paradox of altruism apparent in Green's account of the common good, held that if

"it is pronounced right and reasonable for A to make sacrifices of his own happiness to the good of B," as this must be equally right and reasonable for B, C and D, "the admission that altruism is rational" compels us to conceive "the happiness which we ought to seek for society," not as mere happiness but as "moral happiness." The ultimate end, for the race as well as for the individual, thus becomes composite: it consists of a higher good, Virtue, along with a lower good, Happiness, the two being so related that in case of conflict the higher is always to be preferred to the lower.[183]

Sidgwick grants "to the full" Rashdall's starting point, the basic charge that he "assigns a different end to the individual and to the race." But he is "unable to see why it constitutes a difficulty, since the individual is essentially and fundamentally different from the larger whole – the universe of sentient beings – of which he is conscious of being a part: just because he is conscious of his relation to similar parts of the same whole, while the whole itself has no such relation." Thus,

[W]hile it *would* be reasonable for the aggregate of sentient beings, if it could act collectively, to aim at its own happiness only as ultimate end – and *would* be reasonable for an individual to do the same if he were the only sentient being in the universe – it is yet *actually* reasonable for an individual to make an ultimate sacrifice of his happiness for the sake of the greater happiness of others, as well as reasonable for him to take his own happiness as ultimate end; owing . . . to the double view which he necessarily takes of himself as at once an individual essentially separate from other individuals, and at the same time essentially a part among similar parts of a larger whole."[184]

However odd it may seem, Sidgwick does here imply that the dualism would also be overcome by the destruction of all sentient beings save one, though this is obviously not the type of harmonization he favors. But at any rate, Sidgwick's use of the argument against Rashdall shows that he, at least, viewed it as more than an objection to utilitarianism. Besides, and contra Shaver, the charge that one is "an individual essentially separate from other individuals" is not even a serious objection to utilitarianism unless it carries the normative upshot that the unity of the personal point of view ought somehow to be recognized. What would be the purpose of asserting it, in either Sidgwick's work or Rawls's, if it merely meant "here is a normatively tinged, metaphysically grounded view of the person different from the utilitarian one"? As Samuel Scheffler has observed, when Rawls makes the charge that classical utilitarianism "does not take seriously the distinction between persons," this is regarded as a "decisive objection" provided that "we assume that the correct regulative principle for anything depends on the nature of that thing, and that the plurality of distinct persons with separate systems of ends is an essential feature of human societies."[185] Moreover, Schneewind concludes his account of the introduction of the distinction passage by stating "the conviction that the egoist is not irrational in adopting a basic principle resting on the reality and significance of the distinction between his own consciousness and the consciousness belonging to others is one reason for Sidgwick's concern with the dualism of practical reason."[186]

In fact, Schneewind also provides a wealth of argument indicative of just how Sidgwick regarded the separateness of persons as a very deep truth – the "dualism comes from the same kind of consideration as the axioms themselves. It represents the requirements action must satisfy if it is to be reasonable, given the most basic facts of human life. Each of us is a self-conscious possessor of a private consciousness."[187] The crucial point, however, is that if "own-good is logically prior to universal-good, and P3 to B1, the inescapability of the egoistic aspect of practical rationality is evident." "P3" refers to the axiom of temporal neutrality, and what it "essentially involves is that there exists a plurality of times during which a sentient or conscious being is aware of good or evil. It is thus the axiom about what reason demands over time in one life, as B1 [that the good of one is no more important than the good of another] is the axiom about what reason demands over many lives." Thus,

Logical priority, as Sidgwick understands it . . . is not a matter of more or less certainty. It is a matter of the order in which concepts must be explicated and propositions proven if clarity and cogency are to be attained. If we look at the axioms with this in mind, we shall find it helpful to suppose that Sidgwick thinks P3 and its associated concept of own-good are logically prior to B1 and its concept of univeral-good. This order of priority helps explain several points. For instance, it helps explain the way in which the definition of the concept of universal good is developed. Sidgwick sees the concepts of right and good as representing the demands of reason, the one on the active aspect, the other on the sentient aspect, of our nature. He begins his account of good by considering the goods of an individual, as determined by what the individual thinks desirable. The next step is to develop the notion of what is 'good on the whole' for one individual, and only after this notion is defined does he move to the concept 'good on the whole' *simpliciter*, without the limitation to ownership by one consciousness. (ME 7, pp. 111–13) The same order, from the momentary goods of one individual to the universal good, is followed when the axioms are obtained. After P3 is given Sidgwick comments that in obtaining it we have been constructing a concept 'by comparison and integration of the different "goods" that succeed one another in the series of our conscious states', that is, in the time-series of a single life. In the same way, he says, we construct 'the notion of Universal Good by comparison and integration of the goods of all individual human – or sentient – existences'. (ME 7, p. 382) In both cases, own-good is plainly treated as the logically prior concept, the concept which must be explained before and in order that the others may be clearly explicated.

The hypothesis of the logical priority of own-good also helps explain why Sidgwick treats the egoist as building his theory with the concept of own-good and refusing to move to the concept of universal-good, but never suggests that by parity of reasoning we can see the utilitarian as starting with the concept of universal-good and refusing to move to the concept of own-good. The concept of own-good on the whole carries the concept of integration over time with it. It is only because it does that the concept of universal-good, constructed by integrating own-goods, includes the temporal condition under which reason must be applied to practice. But without the temporal condition it is impossible to make sense of the ideas of action and of rational demands on action. Thus own-good is logically simpler than universal-good, and P3 must be presupposed if B1 is to generate a requirement of practical rationality.[188]

Oddly, Shaver does not attempt any serious discussion of this all-important passage, nor do other recent efforts to undercut Sidgwick's presentation of egoism.[189] Admittedly, the notion of "logical priority" would seem to make for additional complications to an already very complicated analysis of Sidgwick's methodology. But the points that Schneewind makes about Sidgwick's way of proceeding are well taken and go far toward explaining how Sidgwick could have attached such importance to rational egoism, even if they do not afford a full-fledged Sidgwickian justification of egoism along the lines that Shaver demands. Perhaps, as some have claimed, his hedonism reinforced such views, but that is surely not obvious from the passages Schneewind cites. The force of this "logical priority" will be further illustrated in later chapters.

Interestingly, and in line with Hurka's views on the incompleteness of the critique of perfectionism to be found in the *Methods* and its close approximation to Moore's account of good, Sidgwick concludes his critique of Rashdall with the confession "I am not prepared to deny that a consistent system might be worked out on the basis of such a composite End as Mr. Rashdall suggests, and I shall not attempt to prove, before seeing it in a fully developed form, that it would be more open to attack on the score of paradox than my own." But he, Sidgwick, is still reluctant to "aim at making my fellow-creatures more moral, if... as a consequence of this they would become less happy," and he would "make a similar choice as regards my own future happiness," which is why he finds it misleading "to say that Virtue is an ultimate good to the individual as well as Happiness." Again, although the dictates of reason are always to be obeyed, it must be "determined by empirical and utilitarian considerations" whether the "dictation of Reason is always to be promoted."[190]

Thus, even as late as 1889, Sidgwick is still calling the (nonegoistic) perfectionist alternative a promising research program, in the very paper presenting the explicit "defense" of egoism.[191] It would, therefore, be ill-advised to be dogmatic about just what he was really after in seeking philosophical progress. Still, when he discusses "the inevitable twofold conception of a human individual as a whole in himself, and a part of a larger whole," and urges that there "is something that it is reasonable for him to desire, when he considers himself as an independent unit," it is very hard to think that he was terribly hopeful about the defeat of the egoistic alternative.[192]

Thus, Schneewind's account would seem to remain, on key points, the better reading of Sidgwick on the force of rational egoism. And this account helps to explain not only the *Methods*, but much else in Sidgwick's life and work. Yet perhaps the chief flaw running through all these interpretations is that they approach the issue of the dualism from a too narrowly analytical perspective. In a word, they cannot render comprehensible the urgency of Sidgwick's struggles with the dualism, or his insistence on the theistic alternative, harmonization, and the unsatisfactoriness of mundane experience. For him the dualism was as fraught, culturally speaking, as Nietzsche's death of God.

Recall Sidgwick's own worries about the consequences of failing to overcome the dualism:

I do not mean that if we gave up the hope of attaining a practical solution of this fundamental contradiction, through any legitimately obtained conclusion or postulate as to the moral order of the world, it would become reasonable for us to abandon morality altogether: but it would seem necessary to abandon the idea of rationalising it completely. We should doubtless still, not only from self-interest, but also through sympathy and sentiments protective of social wellbeing, imparted by education and sustained by communication with other men, feel a desire for the general observance of rules conducive to general happiness; and practical reason would still impel us decisively to the performance of duty in the more ordinary cases in which what is recognised as duty is in harmony with self-interest properly understood. But in the rarer cases of a recognised conflict between self-interest and duty, practical reason, being divided against itself, would cease to be a motive on either side; the conflict would have to be decided by the comparative preponderance of one or other of two groups of non-rational impulses. (ME 508)

This scenario is described purely in terms of the failure of the effort at harmonization – through, for example, the theistic postulate, or a Buddhist metaphysic – and the concern is that should practical reason be unable in itself to direct action one way or the other, nonrational impulses will step in to do the job. No doubt this helps to explain why Sidgwick was so passionately interested in moral development and education, the shaping of nonrational impulses.[193] Obviously, he was not unconcerned with the problem of just which nonrational impulses would be performing this function in the future. The texture of emotional life would, on his prognosis, likely prove decisive for the fate of future generations. In due course, perhaps the psychologist and the sociologist would be doing the work of the church.

And besides, if natural theology, in the form of psychical research, might eventually be able to demonstrate that the dualism did not involve even the indeterminacy of conflicting permissive reasons, why should not other (partly naturalistic, empirical) arguments – for example, about indirection – turn up similarly hopeful prospects, however unlikely that might seem? Perhaps the further developments of philosophical argument might also help in rendering mundane experience at least somewhat less unsatisfactory. The failure of perfectionist and Idealist attempts in this direction did not permanently settle the matter. Poor as such a substitute may be, for lost faith in a cosmic guarantee, it could provide some consolation. At least, mundane experience could help, and could not be ruled out a priori as involving some form of category mistake about what a solution must entail.

Clearly, however, Sidgwick was not sanguine about the alternative of simply asserting the force of agent-neutral reasons. Even if he doubted that egoism and utilitarianism were either ultimately self-evident or certain, and gave egoism only cryptic support, he nonetheless took his task – as Baier observed – to be demonstrating their harmonization (along with the cultivation of nonrational utilitarian impulses), at least in very large measure. The degree to which he did so indicates the degree to which he refused to admit the weakness of the case for egoism, and not simply the degree to which he recognized the mundane force – rational or not – of egoistic tendencies. Sidgwick wanted it all: a rational, orderly universe that unfailingly maximized both collective and individual happiness. He wanted the philosopher to be armed with a cognitivist defense of the moral order of the universe that could substitute for the theologian's and convert both the clerisy and the "sensual herd."

This is crucial. It is perishingly difficult to make sense of Sidgwick's many remarks to both friends and critics about the challenge of egoism – how he came to feel so strongly "this opposition" between own and other happiness, and the paradox of its denial – without the supposition that he at least took it to be an extremely plausible "apparent intuition." In one of his most explicit statements on the subject, a response (in 1877) to an essay on the *Methods* by Alfred Barratt, Sidgwick charges Barratt with holding "a fundamental misapprehension of the drift of my treatise." Allowing that he had avoided "stating explicitly" his own "ethical view," Sidgwick insists that it should have been "pretty clear to the reader that it is not what Mr. Barratt controverts as the 'Suppression of Egoism', but rather what, in No. V. of *Mind*, I attributed to Butler, describing it as 'the Dualism of Practical Reason.'" After quoting Butler's "Third Sermon on Human Nature," Sidgwick continues:

My difference begins when we come to consider what among the precepts of conscience we really do see to be reasonable. Here my view may be briefly given by saying, that I identify a modification of Kantism with the missing rational basis of the ethical utilitarianism of Bentham, as expounded by J. S. Mill. I consider the fundamental formula of conscience to be that one ought not to prefer one's own good to the greater good of another: this (like Kant's Categorical Imperative) is a purely formal principle, and is evolved immediately out of the notion of 'good' or 'desirable', if this notion is used absolutely; as it then must mean 'desirable from a universal point of view', or 'what all rational beings, as such, ought to aim at realising'. The substantial difference between me and Mr. Barratt is that he rejects this notion, at least as applied to concrete results. On this point I confidently appeal to the common moral consciousness of mankind: (e.g.) it is certainly the common belief that the design of the Creator of the world is to realise Good: and in this belief the notion 'good' must be used absolutely. But I should admit Mr. Barratt's objection to the reasoning by which (see p. 360), I endeavour to exhibit the self-evidence of this formula, if that reasoning were intended – as Mr. Barratt has taken it – as a confutation of the principle of Rational Egoism. Since, however, it is manifest, at the close of the treatise, that I do not consider the principle of Rational Egoism to have been confuted, but only contradicted; and since I carefully explain, on p. 392, how in my view this confutation is avoided, I confess that I can hardly understand my critic's misunderstanding.[194]

Here Sidgwick is actually appealing to common sense to support the axiomatic grounding of utilitarianism, but doing so by linking it to the "common belief that the design of the Creator of the world is to realise Good." And he is insistently denying that egoism has been confuted by any of the arguments presented in the first two editions (by "contradicted" he could mean "shown to be inconclusive by the equal rationality of utilitarianism," but this is not obvious), even going so far as to concede the weakness of the case for utilitarianism. He uses the expression the "dualism of practical reason" as a label for his own "ethical view," and his indignation is reminiscent of that expressed in the *Methods* over the possibility that the wages of virtue could be "dust." Puzzlingly, Shaver does not consider this exchange in any detail. But it both affirms Sidgwick's dualism in uncompromising terms and vividly expresses his worry about how the moral content of common sense might be dependent on religious belief.

True, in "Some Fundamental Ethical Controversies," Sidgwick did admit that he had earlier set out rational egoism "without a sufficient rational justification," as Gizycki had claimed. And he allowed the tenability of Gizycki's view that "the preference of Virtue or general happiness to private happiness is a dictate of reason, which remains no less clear and cogent, however ultimate and uncompensated may be the sacrifice of private happiness that it imposes," because "even if the reality and essentiality of the distinction between one individual and another be granted, I do not see how to prove its fundamental practical importance to anyone who refuses to admit it." Yet, revealingly, Sidgwick concludes this passage by flatly stating "but I find such a refusal impossible to myself, and I think it paradoxical."[195]

Impossible? Paradoxical? Why "impossible," of all things, unless something along the lines of Schneewind's interpretation is correct?

Sidgwick does also appeal to common sense, but in a curious way that admits that the explicit articulation of egoism has not been all that common:

> I admit that it is only a minority of moralists who explicitly accept this dualism of rational or governing principles; but I think myself justified in inferring a wider implicit acceptance of the dualism from the importance attached by dogmatic moralists generally to the conception of a moral government of the world, and from the efforts of empirical utilitarians to prove – as in Bentham's posthumous treatise – that action conducive to greatest happiness is always also conducive to the agent's greatest happiness.

If his own statement of the dualism has proved controversial, and thus somewhat confidence-shaking, nonetheless his confidence is partly restored by the fact that "while to some critics the sacrifice of self to others seems solely rational, others avow uncompromising egoism; and no one has seriously attemped to deny that the choice between one or other alternative – according to any forecast of happiness based on mere mundane experience – is occasionally forced on us."[196] If Gizycki and Rashdall fell on one side, Barratt fell on the other.

Thus, the upshot would seem to be that common sense in fact contains, in implicit form, a potentially explosive contradiction, waiting to emerge once the religious worldview fades. Put differently, Sidgwick questions, in a way that other secular utilitarians did not, the degree to which the utilitarian evolution of morality may in fact, perhaps paradoxically, have depended on the evolution of Christianity. Lurking behind the minimal metaphysics of the *Methods* is the hope that secular morality will be able to go it alone, but also the profound worry that this may prove impossible.

One is strongly tempted to interpret this in the light of Sidgwick's personal struggles and his reluctance to openly attack religion. That is, as the material presented in Chapter 3 strongly suggests, Sidgwick was profoundly uncertain about the degree to which commonsense morality would lean toward utilitarian justifications of self-sacrifice, should religious skepticism grow more pervasive, and a fuller discussion of egoism's grounding would necessitate the very thing he had determined not to give: an open, explicit critical discussion of the failings of theology. It was one thing to claim that practical reason required a theistic postulate for its unity; it was something else again to demonstrate why theology could not provide this and how that might undermine the moral force of self-sacrifice, as embedded in common sense. Sidgwick was so obviously exercised by what would happen when the religious worldview finally came apart in the popular consciousness, and so drawn to the view (despite his criticisms of Seeley) that utilitarianism captured in a refined way the virtue of Christian benevolence, that the possibility that utilitarianism was actually drawing on intellectual capital supplied by the Christian inheritance was for him a rather natural worry. Yes, common sense on balance supported utilitarianism, and carried some justificatory force. But common sense was evolving, hard to pin down, and at least somewhat divided. Could the aversion to frank egoism be sustained without a broadly religious consciousness? How else to explain the characteristic confession:

[T]he reason why I keep strict silence now for many years with regard to theology is that while I cannot myself discover adequate rational basis for the Christian hope of happy immortality, it seems to me that the general loss of such a hope, from the minds of average human beings as now constituted, would be an evil of which I cannot pretend to measure the extent. I am not prepared to say that the dissolution of the existing social order would follow, but I think the danger of such dissolution would be seriously increased, and that the evil would certainly be very great. (M 357)

Presumably, Sidgwick was not being silently horrified at the prospect of further progress toward a society of ideal utilitarians of an enlightened secular bent, or even a society of perfectionists. Yet Shaver's account supplies no explanation whatsoever of this fundamental Sidgwickian concern. At most, Shaver explains that Sidgwick

thinks utilitarianism provides a good explanation of differences in common-sense morality over time, place, and occupation. For example, theft is venial where labour is unnecessary. . . . He also thinks utilitarianism can be seen as what common-sense morality is coming increasingly to approximate. . . . This supports the conclusion that utilitarianism underlies common-sense morality. Sidgwick does not claim that rational egoism provides a poorer explanation or destination, and he has some reason not to do so: since rational egoists and utilitarians will usually make the same recommendations, the appeal to differences over time, place, and occupation may be insufficiently fine grained to reveal a winner. However, Sidgwick does record one change that favours utilitarianism. Rational egoism has difficulty explaining duties to those who cannot reciprocate. But such duties have become increasingly popular: Sidgwick notes the condemnation of exposing infants and the extension of aid for the sick and poor. (ME 455n) He might now add the concern with animal welfare. If so, utilitarianism better explains not just our verdicts and reasoning, but also changes in common sense.[197]

To emphasize, during the era of Herbert Spencer, the utilitarian support for protecting the vulnerable was surely admirable, and Shaver is correct to call attention to this part of Sidgwick's argument. But clearly, none of this goes very far toward explaining how Sidgwick could at the same time be so worried about the direction of commonsense morality and the undermining of the social order. Shaver himself goes on to observe:

It is quite plausible to think Sidgwick overestimates the force of his indirect utilitarian considerations. Utilitarianism is probably more demanding than he supposes. It is less plausible, but still possible, that he underestimates the force of the indirect rational egoist considerations. If so, common-sense morality may be friendlier to rational egoism, and more hostile to utilitarianism, than has been argued. This, I think, shows the importance of Sidgwick's appeal to common-sense moral reasoning and to historical change. Provided these favour utilitarianism over rational egoism, Sidgwick might concede that, when attention is confined to the dictates of each regarding sacrifices, the case for choosing utilitarianism over rational egoism on the basis of common sense is inconclusive.[198]

But of course, if Sidgwick were worried about precisely such potential errors in his assessment, and not very confident in his – or anyone else's – ability to predict the direction of historical change, then he would be much more anxious about the viability of egoism, in this respect, than Shaver suggests, and rightly so.

There can be little doubt that Sidgwick was more agnostic in just this way, and that this in part explains his deep gloom over the "failure" of the *Methods*. In June of 1872, he had written to Myers:

As for my philosophy, it gets on slowly. I think I have made out a point or two about Justice: but the relation of the sexes still puzzles me. It is a problem with ever new x's and y's emerging. Is the *permanent* movement of civilized man towards the Socialism of force, or the Socialism of persuasion (Comte), or individualism (H. Spencer)? I do not know, and yet everything seems to turn on it.[199]

This is not an idiosyncratic expression of ignorance. Quite the contrary. As Sidgwick wryly argued in his essay on "Political Prophecy and Sociology":

[I]nnovators whose social and political ideals are really in their inception quite unhistorical, are naturally led to adopt the historical method as an instrument of persuasion. In order to induce the world to accept any change that they desire, they endeavour to show that the whole course of history has been preparing the way for it – whether 'it' is the reconciliation of Science and Religion, or the complete realisation of Democracy, or the fuller perfection of Individualism, or the final triumph of Collectivism. The vast aggregate of past events – many of them half-known and more half-understood – which makes up what we call history, afford a malleable material for the application of this procedure: by judicious selection and well-arranged emphasis, by ignoring inconvenient facts and filling gaps of knowledge with convenient conjectures – it is astonishing how easy it is plausibly to represent any desired result as the last inevitable outcome of the operation of the laws of social development; the last term of a series of which the formula is known to the properly instructed historian. (MEA 218–19)

Or the properly instructed theologian, moral theorist, and so on, and on.

Naturally, this also suggests the importance of the complications arising from the various indirect forms of utilitarianism and egoism, when it came to making out the direction of common sense and its epistemic worth. What could be more obvious than Sidgwick's overwhelming sense that he had succeeded only in bringing out the incalculable nature of so much that was of importance in human affairs, rendering the particular demands of duty highly uncertain and contestable? This was a most ironic fate for someone with utilitarian sympathies, who had prized the objective, conflict-resolving features of this position, but it is hard to deny that it was Sidgwick's, especially given the tentativeness of his major treatises on economics and political theory. The point will be spelled out in later chapters.

And this penumbra of uncertainty about the nature of good – how to interpret it, how to calculate it, and consequently how to estimate the value of indirect strategies – goes far toward providing a reasonable explanation of the depth of Sidgwick's anxiety about the death of God as it bore on ethics. This is not only concern about the disenchantment coming with the popular realization that the life of virtue might be dust (though it is certainly that as well), but also concern that narrower, materialistic forms of egoism could be that much harder to dismiss. Consider, by way of example, the spectre of James Fitzjames Stephen, an illustrious old Apostle whose infamous attack on Mill, *Liberty, Equality, Fraternity*, was reviewed by Sidgwick in 1873, just as he was completing the *Methods*:

The third part of the treatise is so far original that it attacks the one element in Christian teaching which the most virulent antagonists of Christianity have hitherto left unassailed – the sentiment of human brotherhood. In discussing 'Fraternity' Mr. Stephen seems to confound two very distinct issues, how far men actually do love each other, and how far it would be for their mutual benefit that they should. Sometimes, indeed, the discussion seems to be almost narrowed to the question whether Mr. Fitzjames Stephen loves his fellow-men: which, he assures us, is only the case to a very limited extent. Life, to Mr. Stephen, would be intolerable without fighting: a millennium where the lion is to lie down with the lamb, presents to him a very flat and tedious prospect: he has no patience with the sentimentalists who insist on pestering him with their nauseous affection. These facts are not without interest for the psychological student: and we may admit that they exhibit forcibly the difficulty of realising the evangelical ideal.[200]

Sidgwick claims that these are not "serious arguments against the practical doctrine that any possible increase of mutual goodwill among the members of the human family is likely to be attended with an increase of their common happiness." But he allows that Stephen "generally assumes that every one must necessarily wish to impose his own idea of happiness upon every one else: indeed in one place he goes so far as to say that if two persons' views of what constitutes happiness are conflicting, they cannot have a mutual wish for each other's happiness."[201]

Worth recalling in this context is Sidgwick's statement, in the first edition of the *Methods*, that

we cannot even concede to Hobbes that *under existing circumstances* it is a clear universal precept of Rational Self-love that a man should "seek peace and ensue it:" since some men gain, by the disturbance of society, wealth, fame, and power, to an extent to which in peaceful times they could not hope to approximate: and though there is always some risk involved in this mode of pursuing these goods, it may be reduced to a small amount by a cool and skilful person who has the art of fishing in troubled waters. It may be admitted that this road to success is over-hazardous for prudent persons in tolerably good circumstances. But even these, though they will not assist in producing social disorder, are not likely to make any great sacrifices to avert it: it will often be sufficient for them to defer it, and even when it is imminent prudence may counsel evasion rather than resistance. In short, though a society composed entirely of *rational* egoists would, when once organized, be in a condition of stable internal equilibrium: it seems very doubtful whether this would be the case with a community of pure egoists, among whom the average degree of enlightenment and self-control was no greater than it is among ourselves. (ME1 150–51)

Needless to say, Fitzjames Stephen was an admirer of Hobbes, and a closer threat, in Sidgwick's eyes. This Stephen was even more abhorrent to Sidgwick than his younger brother Leslie, on the subject of the wicked and the weak. No doubt part of Sidgwick's worry about this harsh view was its potential for molding the "irrational" impulses determining human action, particularly in the event that the suspect foundations of religion and ethics became more widely known. What can be said, in support of Brink's emphasis on an externalist interpretation, is that Sidgwick certainly was concerned about molding character and motivation, and that he did, as the passage just quoted indicates, seem to think that enlightened egoism might all too easily collapse into unenlightened egoism – the sensualness of the "sensual herd" – given the limitations of the age. Perhaps the spectre of ancient Greece did have a hold on him after all. At any rate, Rashdall was on to something when he observed that with Sidgwick, concern about the dualism of practical reason was also a concern about reason period, as a force for defending ethics.

It is, however, a delicate question to just what degree Sidgwick was also persuaded that disagreeable forms of egoism could genuinely bear the color of reason. By his own admission, his indirect arguments about the good, the dictation of reason, and so on were less than conclusive, and nothing in the axiomatic account of egoism could claim, on the basis of self-evidence, to rule out such interpretations. He was even inclined to admit that egoistic calculations were easier to make than utilitarian ones, giving egoism the advantage of clarity.

Much of this case will need to be spelled out in connection with Sidgwick's politics and practical ethics, the subjects of later chapters. And as noted, the following chapter on Sidgwick's psychical research is also crucial for filling in his views on personal identity and the viability of the theistic postulate, and for tracing the supposed evolution of these views. My own view goes even further than Schneewind's in stressing both how seriously Sidgwick took egoism and how little his views on overcoming the dualism of practical reason actually changed.[202] Why else would his chief intellectual investment have been in psychical research? Indeed, as

remarked earlier, his Christian orientation and correlative longing for personal survival of physical death powerfully reinforced his conviction that
egoism was as rational as the alternative principles of practical reason.

For all that, he wanted reason to lead him somewhere. His faith in
"Things in General" was, as he painfully recognized, just another faith.

VI. Integrity at Government House

The truth is that the *"Weltschmerz"* really weighs on me for the first time in my
life: mingled with egoistic humiliation. I am a curious mixture of μεγαλάψυχος
and μικρόψυχος: I cannot really care for anything little: and yet I do not feel
myself worthy of – or ever hope to attain – anything worthy of attainment.

Ethics is losing its interest for me rather, as the insolubility of its fundamental
problem is impressed on me. I think the contribution to the *formal* clearness &
coherence of our ethical thought which I have to offer is just worth giving: for a
few speculatively-minded persons – very few. And as for all practical questions of
interest, I feel as if I had now to begin at the beginning and learn the A B C.

Why this letter has been so long in writing I do not know. Perhaps it is owing to
a peculiar hallucination under which I labour that I shall suddenly find my ideas
cleared up – say the day after tomorrow – on the subjects over which I brood
heavily.

Sidgwick to H. G. Dakyns, February 1873 (M 277)[203]

My book drags on: but I think it will be done in a way by Easter, thrown aside for
the May Term and then revised in June and published in the Autumn. At least I
hope for this. It bores me very much, and I want to get it off my hands before it
makes me quite ill. . . . As for my inner life, it is hollowness, chaos and gloom.

Sidgwick to H. G. Dakyns, February 1874 (CWC)[204]

That was what was so remarkable in Henry Sidgwick – the perpetual hopefulness
of his inquiry. He always seemed to expect that some new turn of argument, some
new phase of thought, might arise and put a new aspect upon the intellectual
scenery, or give a new weight in the balance of argument. There was in him
an extraordinary belief in *following* reason – a belief and a hopefulness which
continued up to the last.

Bishop Charles Gore (M 557)

Although the previous sections give only the barest sketch of the rich
argumentation of Sidgwick's *Methods*, perhaps this is sufficient to indicate
how Sidgwick's magnum opus, for all its vast reservoirs of close reasoning,

failed to make the hoped-for contribution to the solution of "the deepest problems of human life." As far as it surely went in advancing independent, secular moral theory, and in articulating the utilitarian program while redirecting its energies, the *Methods* did not vindicate practical reason in the way that Sidgwick thought best, both for philosophy and for purposes of cultural advance. Indeed, he worried that it had not vindicated practical reason at all.

Still, it has undeniably contributed much to more recent moral theory. Since the revival of substantive ethical theory in the post-positivist Anglo–American philosophical world, it has been impossible even for critics – be they Aristotelian, Kantian, Nietzschean, or whatever – to ignore Sidgwick's monumental volume. When Rawls, in *A Theory of Justice*, famously drew out the supposedly counterintuitive implications of Sidgwick's utilitarianism with respect to questions of distributive justice and population growth, the better to advance his own theory of justice as fairness, he effectively put the *Methods* at the very heart of the great expansion of substantive ethical theory that marked the last third of the twentieth century. Rawls's objection that "classical utilitarianism fails to take seriously the distinction between persons" because the "principle of rational choice for one man is taken as the principle of social choice as well" was, above all, a challenge to Sidgwick, albeit one aimed at only half of the dualism, that promoting the "impartial sympathetic spectator" who represents "the conflation of all desires into one system of desire."[205]

In responding to such objections, contemporary utilitarians have, ironically, been able to take considerable comfort in Sidgwick's steadfast, honest confrontation with the shortcomings of utilitarianism – and of every other method of ethics. Certainly, as we have seen, with Sidgwick, utilitarianism was presented in connection with nearly the whole extraordinary menu of practical and theoretical difficulties that have dogged it ever since: the problem of its rational grounding, especially as against egoism; the problem of formulating "indirect" or "two-level" theories in order to accommodate traditional or commonsense moral rules and/or dispositions; the problem of accounting for friendship and integrity, and, relatedly, the "demandingness" of utilitarianism, especially versus the personal point of view; the problem of supererogation; the problem of universalizability and the special demands of justice, which seem to pose alternative conceptions of impartiality and equitable social arrangements (as opposed to utilitarian aggregation and maximization); the differences between total and average utility calculations, as brought out by the question of optimal population size; the complexities involved in drawing inter- and intrapersonal comparisons of utility; and, not least, the importance for utilitarianism of the nature of personal identity over time. When one looks at the most serious recent attempts to defend utilitarian ethical theory – works such as R. M. Hare's *Moral Thinking*, R. B. Brandt's *A Theory of the Good and the Right*, Derek Parfit's *Reasons and Persons*, John Skorupski's *Ethical Explorations*, Brad Hooker's *Ideal Code, Real World*, and Peter Singer's *How Are We to Live?* – one finds that they make constant reference to Sidgwick and the agenda that he set.

However, although recent utilitarian theorizing has often reached a very high level of sophistication, the appeal to Sidgwick in such work often seems rather opportunistic. Even Rawls's characterization of the *Methods* scarcely does justice to, say, Sidgwick's search for a harmonization of egoism and utilitarianism, such that the practical overcoming of the dualism would hardly have left individuals in the position of necessarily regretting the "sacrifices" demanded of them. Schneewind was profoundly right to stress, in *Sidgwick's Ethics*, how crucial it is to read Sidgwick in the context of the religious debates of the mid-Victorian era. Of course, better historical readings of Sidgwick can make him look both more interesting and less interesting, more probing and less probing. Marcus Singer has rightly noted the strangeness of Sidgwick's famous treatment of the population question, his argument that "strictly conceived, the point up to which, on Utilitarian principles, population ought to be encouraged to increase, is not that at which average happiness is the greatest possible . . . but that at which the product formed by multiplying the number of persons living into the amount of average happiness reaches it maximum" (ME 415–16). As Singer observes,

Sidgwick is aware of what he calls the 'grotesque . . . show of exactness' exhibited by such reasoning. That is not the main problem. The main problem is that Sidgwick rejects out of hand, without argument, the average happiness criterion in favor of the total happiness criterion, and never even questions the appropriateness of either criterion. And Sidgwick is not simply reporting on what the utilitarian view is, he is actually supporting this view, and never asks whether the point made is a point in its favor or against it. But this implication of the 'strictly conceived' utilitarian principle is surely paradoxical, even on Sidgwick's own conception of paradox.[206]

Singer goes on to remark insightfully on how the apparent corollary of this view – Sidgwick's claim that "a universal refusal to propagate the human species would be the greatest of conceivable crimes from a Utilitarian point of view" – would also appear to be related to his beliefs about colonization and the duty of "civilized nations" to "civilize the world."

These are crucially important issues, to be discussed at length in later chapters. The troubling point, however, is that they have scarcely been discussed at all in the vast analytical philosophical literature devoted to utilitarianism and the population question.[207]

Now, given the influence of Rawls and Rawlsian debates over Sidgwickian utilitarianism, it is strange that the single most important work on the *Methods* – Schneewind's *Sidgwick's Ethics* – is also the one most determined to downplay its utilitarianism. As we have seen, Schneewind is fairly consistently puzzled over the gap between the axioms and the substantive views of egoism and utilitarianism, and one aspect of his puzzlement concerns the central matter of maximization. In discussing the filling out of the principle of benevolence, he asks: "Why, then, are we to *maximize* goodness?" This, he observes, "seems to follow simply from the definitions of rightness and goodness," which might seem problematically question-begging in itself. Moreover, the "definitional point that rightness is conceptually *tied* to creating maximal goodness does not yield the utilitarian principle just by itself. An ultimate principle must present a characteristic that *makes* right acts right, and the definition does not establish that maximizing goodness has this status."[208]

Of course, Schneewind recognizes that, by Sidgwick's lights, what "shows that maximizing goodness is what makes right acts right is . . . the negative result of the examination of common-sense morality, that none of the purely factual properties can serve as an ultimate right-making characteristic." Thus, it must be that "bringing about the most good is what makes right acts right." But as Schneewind argues at length, this is to treat commonsense morality as covertly teleological, rather than deontological.[209]

Still, Schneewind does for the most part take Sidgwick at his word in terms of his claims about setting aside the need to edify in the interests of impartial inquiry, and his arguments are deeply supportive of the Rawlsian reading of Sidgwick as a seminal figure in the growth of substantive, academic moral theory, out to judiciously compare and contrast the leading contenders in a very modern way. On this count, the assessment of the

Methods is highly positive and somewhat surprising: "If in its attention to detail as well as in its range of concern the *Methods of Ethics* challenges comparison, as no other work in moral philosophy does, with Aristotle's *Ethics*, in the depth of its understanding of practical rationality and in its architectonic coherence it rivals the work of Kant himself."[210] In his concluding paragraph, Schneewind muses on how Sidgwick would have reacted to future developments:

> Most of all [Sidgwick] would have welcomed attempts to work out an alternative to utilitarianism as systematic, as comprehensive, and as powerful as he himself showed that utilitarianism could be. If one of the foundations of his own moral position was a belief about the demands of rationality, the other was the conviction that there is no alternative principle satisfying those demands as well as the utilitarian principle. To this second claim no one in his lifetime offered a cogent and compelling reply. Yet such a reply would have seemed to Sidgwick to present the most desirable kind of challenge a philosopher could want. Whether it has yet been provided or not is a matter still under discussion.[211]

Presumably, Schneewind had the neo-Kantian, autonomist trend in moral theory in mind when he penned this passage, coming as it did in the wake of Rawls's *Theory*. And he had good reason for thinking that Sidgwick would have welcomed such efforts; indeed, much of the analysis in *Sidgwick's Ethics* is devoted to bringing out the Kantian proclivities of the *Methods*. For Schneewind, more than anyone, has stressed the ways in which Sidgwick was indebted to moral theorists who were outside of and hostile to the utilitarian tradition. Clarke, Butler, and Kant – Sidgwick readily admitted that these figures were also his masters. But those critics of utilitarianism closer to home – such as Maurice, Whewell, and John Grote – also constantly pressed upon him the need to reconcile utilitarianism with the perspective of agency and the requirements of rational intuition. And of course, the view that ethics might somehow vindicate, or at least warmly support, Christian faith was hardly part of the legacy of Bentham and Mill, though it was a vital component of the ethics of Kant and the "Cambridge Moralists."[212] Schneewind in fact insists (contra Frankena, Darwall, and Shaver) that to "no major historical figure does Sidgwick have closer affinities than to Bishop Butler," though he "moves well beyond Butler in the thoroughness with which he works out the view that our moral beliefs are or can be rational. Where Butler refused to elaborate a theory, Sidgwick, like Whewell, holds that the development of a systematic understanding of our moral experience is the central task of ethics." Which brings us not only to Whewell, but also to Kant:

It is tempting to describe the dominant philosophical strategy which Sidgwick uses to carry out this task as a Kantian attempt to work out the sole conditions under which reason can be practical. Certainly his basic aim is similar to Kant's, but, as his many points of disagreement with Kant suggest, the Kantian aspect of his thinking needs to be defined with some care. He detaches the issue of how reason can be practical from the most distinctive aspects of Kantianism. He rejects the methodological apparatus of the 'critical philosophy', the Kantian distinction of noumenal and phenomenal standpoints, and the association of the issue with the problem of free will. He treats the question of the possibility of rationally motivated action as answerable largely in terms of common place facts; he does not attribute any special synthesizing powers to reason beyond those assumed in ordinary logic; and he does not take morality to provide us with support for religious beliefs. In refusing to base morality on pure reason alone, moreover, he moves decisively away from Kant, as is shown by his very un-Kantian hedonistic and teleological conclusions. These points make it clear that the Kantian strain in Sidgwick's thought is most marked in his central idea about rationality of first principles. Substantive first principles of morality are not the most basic embodiment of practical rationality. The rationality of these principles is a consequence of requirements set by more formal principles which themselves delineate the general activity of reasoning, when the formal principles are applied in the circumstances of human life. Intuition is then explicable as the understanding a reasonable being has of the nature of his own activity as reasonable. If this is Kantianism, then it is not inaccurate to think of Sidgwick as a Kantian.[213]

In fact, in a variety of later works, Schneewind has developed this theme somewhat, maintaining that Sidgwick's emphasis on the "methods" of ethics also reflected a very Kantian view of the ordinary person's capacity for moral knowledge and direction – like Mill, but unlike Bentham, Sidgwick tried to show "how normal adults can see for themselves what morality requires in daily life [and] how each person could be moved to act morally, regardless of legislatively engineered sanctions."[214] The link he finds involves the moral democracy of this form of self-direction.

That there is much that is profoundly right about Schneewind's interpretation is undeniable, for reasons that by this point ought to be quite obvious. Schneewind is perfectly well aware of the novel features of Sidgwick's approach, but after all, Sidgwick himself was most anxious to identify his work with that of Butler and Kant, despite his differences on the subjects of determinism, intention, and the ultimate nature of moral knowledge. His interpretations of his "masters" may not have been the most perspicuous, but his sense of indebtedness is plain. A brief recapitulation of Sidgwick's own account of his Kantian filiations may help to put Schneewind's reading in perspective and to throw into sharper relief a number of the points made in earlier sections.

As Sidgwick explained the evolution of the *Methods*, he had been led back to Kantism after the inadequacy of Mill's treatment of egoism – and of Mill's reading of Kant – had been borne in on him, and he "was impressed with the truth and importance of its fundamental principle. . . . That whatever is right for me must be right for all persons in similar circumstances – which was the form in which I accepted the Kantian maxim – seemed to me certainly fundamental, certainly true, and not without practical importance." (ME xix)

Of course, as we have seen, it is also important to appreciate just what kind of use Sidgwick made of the autonomist tradition:

Kant's resting of morality on Freedom did not indeed commend itself to me, though I did not at first see, what I now seem to see clearly, that it involves the fundamental confusion of using 'freedom' in two distinct senses – "freedom" that is realised only when we do right, when reason triumphs over inclination, and "freedom" that is realised equally when we choose to do wrong, and which is apparently implied in the notion of ill-desert. What commended itself to me, in short, was Kant's ethical principle rather than its metaphysical basis. (ME xix)

Moreover, Sidgwick deemed Kant's fundamental principle "inadequate for the construction of a system of duties," unable to really help with the problem of the dualism of practical reason, the "subordination of Self-Interest to Duty."

For the Rational Egoist – a man who had learnt from Hobbes that Self-preservation is the first law of Nature and Self-interest the only rational basis of social morality – and in fact, its actual basis, so far as it is effective – such a thinker might accept the Kantian principle and remain an Egoist.

He might say, "I quite admit that when the painful necessity comes for another man to choose between his own happiness and the general happiness, he must as a reasonable being prefer his own, i.e. it is right for him to do this on my principle. No doubt, as I probably do not sympathise with him in particular any more than with other persons, I as a disengaged spectator should like him to sacrifice himself to the general good: but I do not expect him to do it, any more than I should do it myself in his place."

It did not seem to me that this reasoning could be effectively confuted. No doubt it was, from the point of view of the universe, reasonable to prefer the greater good to the lesser, even though the lesser good was the private happiness of the agent. Still, it seemed to me also undeniably reasonable for the individual to prefer his own. The rationality of self-regard seemed to me as undeniable as the rationality of self-sacrifice. I could not give up this conviction, though neither of my masters, neither Kant nor Mill, seemed willing to admit it: in different ways, each in his own way, they refused to admit it. (ME xix–xx)

Kant and most neo-Kantians have always emphatically denied that egoism could be consistently willed as a universal law or defended as an independent principle of practical reason, but Sidgwick, as we have seen, is not impressed with such denials. This was the realization that left Sidgwick "a disciple on the loose, in search of a master," and in turn led him back to Butler, in whom he claimed to find an anticipation of his own thinking about the dualism of practical reason, as well as much effective criticism of psychological hedonism. Thus, it was Butler who finally persuaded him of the "existence of 'disinterested' or 'extra-regarding' impulses to action, [impulses] not directed towards the agent's pleasure," and consequently, Sidgwick found himself "much more in agreement with Butler than Mill" concerning the "Psychological basis of Ethics," not to mention further confirmed in his intuitionistic tendencies:

And this led me to reconsider my relation to Intuitional Ethics. The strength and vehemence of Butler's condemnation of pure Utilitarianism, in so cautious a writer, naturally impressed me much. And I had myself become, as I had to admit to myself, an Intuitionist to a certain extent. For the supreme rule of aiming at the general happiness, as I had come to see, must rest on a fundamental moral intuition, if I was to recognise it as binding at all. And in reading the writings of the earlier English Intuitionists, More and Clarke, I found the axiom I required for my Utilitarianism . . . in one form or another, holding a prominent place. (ME xxi)

What is singularly interesting in this story of Sidgwick's intellectual wanderings, however, is the way in which he travels from Mill to Kant to Butler to Clarke and then back to Aristotle, as though the pull of his classicist background always proved irresistible. Thus, he had "theoretically as

well as practically" accepted the "fundamental moral intuition" of rational
benevolence, along with the Kantian one, and "was then an 'intuitional'
moralist to this extent: and if so, why not further?" That is to say, why not
go all the way with something like Whewell's system, which after all found
a place for rational benevolence, or charity, as one principle alongside the
others? At this, though, Sidgwick balks: "The orthodox moralists such as
Whewell (then in vogue) said that there was a whole intelligible system
of intuitions: but how were they to be learnt? I could not accept Butler's
view as to the sufficiency of a plain man's conscience: for it appeared to me
that plain men agreed rather verbally than really." (ME xxi) And it was in
this state of mind that he looked to "Aristotle again; and a light seemed to
dawn upon me as to the meaning and drift of his procedure – especially
in Books ii., iii., iv. of the *Ethics*."

Indeed, as we have seen, the light of Aristotle proved to be brilliantly
illuminating, and crucial to the assembling of the *Methods*, with Sidgwick
seeking, like Aristotle and Socrates, to reduce "to consistency by careful
comparison" commonsense morality, what "we" think, "ascertained by
reflection." (ME xxii–xxiii)

Obviously, the result of this Aristotelian examination of common sense
only succeeded in bringing out "with fresh force and vividness" the differences between the "maxims of Common Sense Morality" and the intuitions associated with utilitarianism and the Kantian principle, though
it had "continually brought home" how commonsense morality is a system of rules "tending to the promotion of general happiness" (ME xxii).
Indeed, there was "no real opposition between Intuitionism and Utilitarianism," because the "Utilitarianism of Mill and Bentham seemed to me to
want a basis: that basis could only be supplied by a fundamental intuition;
on the other hand the best examination I could make of the Morality of
Common Sense showed me no clear and self-evident principles except
such as were perfectly consistent with Utilitarianism." To be sure, given
how the "merely empirical examination of the consequences of actions is
unsatisfactory" and how practically imperfect is the "guidance of the Utilitarian calculus," it was crucial to "treat with respect, and make use of, the
guidance afforded by Common Sense in these cases, on the ground of the
general presumption which evolution afforded that moral sentiments and
opinions would point to conduct conducive to general happiness." Still,
this could be overruled by "a strong probability of the opposite, derived
from utilitarian calculations." (ME xxii–xxiii)

Given the account in earlier chapters of Sidgwick's Apostolic truth seeking, this invocation of Aristotle on common sense, as the figure carrying on the true work of the Socratic *elenchus*, should seem remarkably apt, as should the suggestion that the project was carried on by Mill. The *Methods* effectively provided the formal philosophical underpinnings for Sidgwick's Apostolic love of philosophical conversation that was intense and personal, a matter of individual self-revelation, fellowship, growth, and experimentation as much as abstract truth. Recall his Mauricean insistence that all three methods gave expression to some enduring features of his own being. Here are the social dimensions of his epistemology.[215]

Now, this recapitulation of the genesis of the *Methods* is meant to suggest just how much care must be taken when applying to such a book broad labels like "Millian" or "Kantian" or "Aristotelian" (etc.). Even Schneewind's extremely sensitive Kantian interpretation may underestimate other influences, such as the Aristotelian one. Yes, Sidgwick accepted the universalizability principle and, in a general way, agreed with Kant – and with Whewell, for that matter – that morality is a matter of practical reason and that the moral theorist must determine the preconditions for applying reason to practice in human life. But he did not, as Schneewind would admit, quite capture the essence of the Kantian orientation, whether expressed by Kant or by Green.[216]

Thus, as Darwall has observed, intuitionists and autonomists from Butler to Kant to the present do share a certain normative idea of the will, of "an agent who can step back from her various desires – for example, from her desires for her own good or the goods of others, or of all conceived impartially – and ask which she should act on." However, whereas "the intuitionists take practical reasoning and action to have an implicit *material* aim, namely, to track independent normative facts, autonomist internalists take the implicit aim of practical reasoning to be entirely *formal* – guidance by considerations that we can reflectively endorse, thereby realizing autonomy."[217] Arguably, Sidgwick's complex philosophical intuitionism actually falls midway between these poles, since it places such weight on being guided by a certain kind of authority, achieved via free, critical inquiry, etc. It is neither a pure practical reason theory nor a pure intuitionist one (on the older models), and that is just what makes it hard to classify.

To be sure, one might feel that the popular contrasts between the pure Kantian view and rational intuitionism are somewhat stylized and overdrawn; Sidgwick's intuitionism insists on the procedural and reflective aspects of practical deliberation, making one's views one's own through the application of reason, being self-directed, and so forth.[218] And this is the strong point of Schneewind's interpretation. Cast in terms of the account of Sidgwick's Apostolic commitments, one could say that with Sidgwick, the intuitionist conception of the self as seeker, friend, and discussant was not all that thin. The dialectical side of his approach was absolutely crucial.

Unfortunately, however, the different shadings of emphasis here do translate into some very important substantive differences in ethical principle. An important corollary to all such Kantian and neo-Kantian views involves the so-called "publicity" criterion. As Kant himself put it, in an appendix to *Perpetual Peace*: "All actions affecting the rights of other human beings are wrong if their maxim is not compatible with being made public."[219] This feature of the Kantian orientation is clearly at work in Rawls's arguments.

The basic idea, simply built into the Rawlsian position, is that it is crucial to the notion of a "public conception of justice" that all citizens would at least have some grasp of the basic principles of justice and of their justifying reasons, their derivation from a point of view representing the conditions for reaching a fair agreement on such principles. After all, how can one freely, of one's own will, obey the law one gives oneself if one does not know what it is? Here, the kinds of legitimating conditions that Rousseau found in direct democracy are translated into the abstract conditions for reasoning to moral conclusions – or, in Rawls's case, to principles of political justice. As Rawls frames it:

It is fitting, then, that the fair terms of social cooperation between citizens as free and equal should meet the requirements of full publicity. For if the basic structure relies on coercive sanctions, however rarely and scrupulously applied, the grounds of its institutions should stand up to public scrutiny. When a political conception of justice satisfies this condition, and basic social arrangements and individual actions are fully justifiable, citizens can give reasons for their beliefs and conduct before one another confident that this avowed reckoning itself will strengthen and not weaken public understanding. The political order does not, it seems, depend on historically accidental or established delusions, or other mistaken beliefs resting on the deceptive appearances of institutions that mislead us as to how they work. Of course, there can be no certainty about this. But publicity ensures, so far as practical measures allow, that citizens are in a position to know and to accept the pervasive influences of the basic structure that shape their conception of themselves, their character and ends. As we shall see, that citizens should be in this position is a condition of their realizing their freedom as fully autonomous, politically speaking. It means that in their public political life nothing is hidden.[220]

   Although Rawls is here adapting the Kantian idea to the construction of a distinctly political view, the larger analogies should be evident enough. When Kantian and neo-Kantian reconstructions of "conscience" – that is, each rational agent's capacity for acting freely and responsibly – focus on the capacity for moral self-direction, on the ordinary person's ability to grasp what morality requires and to act on it, the publicity condition is in play. When one is called upon to extend to others the respect that one accords oneself, as a creature able to rise above inclination and to act freely and responsibly, the demands of reasonableness are inseparable from the demands of publicity.

   And it is perhaps at this juncture that one can best appreciate how Sidgwick parted from the Kantian project. For one of the most notorious features of his utilitarian orientation concerns exactly this issue of publicity. The charge that Sidgwick's view amounts to "Government House" utilitarianism amounts to the charge that he rejects any such principle of publicity as a sine qua non for moral principles. As we have seen, the point has been sharply put by Bernard Williams – a perceptive critic of both utilitarianism and Kantianism – who urges that Sidgwick's utilitarianism is "the morality of an élite" such that "the distinction between theory and practice determines a class of theorists distinct from other persons, theorists in whose hands the truth of the Utilitarian justification of non-Utilitarian dispositions will be responsibly deployed. This outlook accords well enough with the important colonial origins of Utilitarianism."[221]

   Williams points up some of the most notorious passages in the *Methods*, namely, those having to do with the possibility of an "esoteric morality." Thus, in discussing when exceptions to the ordinary rules of morality should be permitted, Sidgwick allows that there may be cause for further doubt, beyond the clearer instance where exceptional ethical treatment would involve a class of cases and would be acceptable to a community of enlightened utilitarians. This is the "doubt whether the more refined and complicated rule which recognises such exceptions is adapted for the community in which he is actually living; and whether the attempt to introduce it is not likely to do more harm by weakening current morality than good by improving its quality." That is,

Supposing such a doubt to arise . . . it becomes necessary that the Utilitarian should consider carefully the extent to which his advice or example are likely to influence persons to whom they would be dangerous: and it is evident that the result of this consideration may depend largely on the degree of publicity which he gives to either advice or example. Thus, on Utilitarian principles, it may be right to do and privately recommend, under certain circumstances, what it would not be right to advocate openly; it may be right to teach openly to one set of persons what it would be wrong to teach to others; it may be conceivably right to do, if it can be done with comparative secrecy, what it would be wrong to do in the face of the world; and even, if perfect secrecy can be reasonably expected, what it would be wrong to recommend by private advice or example. These conclusions are all of a paradoxical character: there is no doubt that the moral consciousness of a plain man broadly repudiates the general notion of an esoteric morality, differing from the one popularly taught; and it would be commonly agreed that an action which would be bad if done openly is not rendered good by secrecy. We may observe, however, that there are strong utilitarian reasons for maintaining generally this latter common opinion; for it is obviously advantageous, generally speaking, that acts which it is expedient to repress by social disapprobation should become known, as otherwise the disapprobation cannot operate; so that it seems inexpedient to support by any moral encouragement the natural disposition of men in general to conceal their wrong doings; besides that the concealment would in most cases have importantly injurious effects on the agent's habits of veracity. Thus the Utilitarian conclusion, carefully stated, would seem to be this; that the opinion that secrecy may render an action right which would not otherwise be so should itself be kept comparatively secret; and similarly it seems expedient that the doctrine that esoteric morality is expedient should itself be kept esoteric. Or if this concealment be difficult to maintain, it may be desirable that Common Sense should repudiate the doctrines which it is expedient to confine to an enlightened few. And thus a Utilitarian may reasonably desire, on Utilitarian principles, that some of his conclusions should be rejected by mankind generally; or even that the vulgar should keep aloof from his system as a whole, in so far as the inevitable indefiniteness and complexity of its calculations render it likely to lead to bad results in their hands. (ME 489–90)

Of course, it hardly seems that this would be a case of the vulgar keeping aloof, and Sidgwick also allows that in an "ideal community of enlightened Utilitarians this swarm of perplexities and paradoxes would vanish," since in such a society all would share the same principles and abilities. Hence, as a form of indirect utilitarianism – a version of the claim that the utilitarian end is best achieved by having people reason according to largely nonutilitarian standards or decision procedures – Sidgwick's position may seem somewhat compromised, since it would not extend to the ideally enlightened community.[222] As Williams notes, however, "it is not generally true, and it was not indeed true of Sidgwick, that Utilitarians of this type, even though they are pure theorists, are prepared themselves to do without the useful dispositions altogether," which is why they still might have the problem of "reconciling the two consciousnesses in their own persons – even though the vulgar are relieved of that problem, since they are not burdened with the full consciousness of the Utilitarian justification."[223] This would seem to be in line with Sidgwick's reservations about the limits of even a more highly evolved utilitarian society, absent the theistic postulate.

As suggested earlier on, Williams himself finds such views flatly incredible, a virtual abdication of the task of moral reflection. The dispositions to truth telling and the rest that Sidgwick describes as having utilitarian value

turn out to be a very valuable element in the world of practice. But that means that divergences of sentiment and various kinds of conflict that flow from those dispositions are themselves part of the world of practice, and the answers that they demand have to come from impulses that are part of the situation as it is actually experienced in the world of practice. It follows that a theory which stands to practice as Sidgwick's theory does cannot actually serve to eliminate and resolve all conflicts and unclarities in the world of practice, though *they* are the conflicts that were complained of when the method of intuitionism was unfavourably reviewed.[224]

The problem, once again, is "that the moral dispositions, and indeed other loyalties and commitments, have a certain depth or thickness: they cannot simply be regarded, least of all by their possessor, just as devices for generating actions or states of affairs." On the contrary, they

will characteristically be what gives one's life some meaning, and gives one some reason for living it; they can be said, to varying degrees and variously over time, to contribute to one's practical or moral identity. There is simply no conceivable exercise that consists in stepping completely outside myself and from that point of view evaluating *in toto* the dispositions, projects, and affections that constitute the substance of my own life.[225]

Hence the worries of perfectionists, virtue ethicists, and Sidgwick himself concerning the limits of indirection and the alternative to moral schizophrenia being moral elitism of a rarefied variety.

Not surprisingly, Williams also finds Parfitian-style accounts of esoteric morality, cast as self-effacing moral theories, altogether peculiar: "Parfit's emphasis is on the question whether the fact that an ethical theory has one or another of these properties [being self-effacing or self-defeating] shows that it is untrue. I am less clear than he is about what this means. The discussion . . . concerns what kind of life, social or personal, would be needed to embody such a theory."[226]

Curiously, Schneewind's discussion of these passages from the *Methods* defining Sidgwick's esotericism seems not to recognize the provocation that such a view represents to Kantian publicity. As he glosses it:

[T]he utilitarian will be led, more generally, to the conclusion that it is undesirable to have everyone calculating everything on a utilitarian basis, since the unavoidable indefiniteness of such calculations leaves scope for the wicked and the weak to construct specious excuses for their misbehaviour. . . . The point raises in turn the more general question of the significance of divergent moral beliefs in a society. If common-sense moral rules are generally taken to be valid, what is the utilitarian to do when there are conflicting opinions each claiming that status? Sidgwick thinks that while contradictory moral beliefs cannot both be correct it may be advantageous at times to have conflicting opinions held by different social groups — one is reminded here of John Stuart Mill's passionate defence of diversity of opinion – and so it may be best that one person should commit an act, for which he is condemned by a segment of society. Sidgwick illustrates this with the case of rebellion.[227]

This, however, does not really engage the concern. Although Schneewind obviously does see that Sidgwick went much further than any of his utilitarian predecessors in invoking indirect strategies to counter the charge that utilitarianism flies in the face of received opinion, it is quite evasive to treat this potential for moral elitism in such a sanitized fashion, as a ringing endorsement of diversity.[228] Sidgwick may have, in Mauricean fashion, downplayed the provocation, but that was his way.

Now, this notion of a sophisticated or two-level utilitarianism that might even go so far as to countenance a completely esoteric morality points up just how difficult it is to find in Sidgwick's idea of a method of ethics an effectively Kantian endorsement of the plain person's capacity for moral self-direction. The method of the plain person may, under certain conditions, be completely but justifiably bricked off from any reflective grasp of the justifying grounds of ultimate principle. (Again, this also points up the way in which both Sidgwick and Mill would have largely circumvented worries as to whether they were at bottom "act" utilitarians, since how one should calculate is something that is itself subject to the utilitarian principle: it is a contingent, empirical question what the best strategy or decision procedure would be for advancing the general happiness.) Insofar as people would in the main do best by calculating according to rules, such as the rules of commonsense morality, that is the policy recommended; insofar as they approximate the community of enlightened utilitarians, more sophisticated calculations might be allowed.[229] One need not suppose that the plain person should or could have a full philosophical grasp of the justification of morality to think that Sidgwickian esotericism violates Kantian publicity. And this only underscores Sidgwick's uncertainty about the direction of "civilised" opinion.

Against the naive objection that if Sidgwick had believed anything of this sort he would not have gone about proclaiming it in his great work, it should be observed that he did add a carefully crafted footnote to the relevant section, in which he explains that "Common Sense to a certain extent" does accept the idea of such indirection, in that "it would be commonly thought wrong to express in public speeches disturbing religious or political opinions which may be legitimately published in books" (ME 489n). And of course, he did rather bury his claims in a very long tome, one replete with various Mauricean subterfuges.

Clearly, this last thought was very much from the heart, and suggestive of his general Apostolic tendencies towards esotericism, given the way in which he had sought to negotiate the aftermath of his resignation crisis. At a time when the literate public, though growing, was still very small, and universal public education was only just on the horizon as a genuine reality, Sidgwick's attitude was perfectly plausible. In his historical context, the clerisy, or intellectual aristocracy, could take much for granted about the smallness and clubbiness of their world. One need only ask how many readers the *Methods* is likely to attract even today to understand how he could be so complacent about his message failing to reach the "sensual herd." Again, his position was nicely expressed in a letter to his old Rugby friend Major-General Carey:

[M]y creed, such as it is, is sufficient to enable me to live happily from day to day, hoping for more light from some quarter or other. But experience has convinced me that what contents me would not content others; and therefore for the last ten years – since in 1870 I gave up, to avoid hypocrisy, my Fellowship at Trinity – I have 'kept silence even from good words,' and never voluntarily disclosed my views on religion to any one. (M 346)

It was in this context too that he had explained to J. R. Mozley, in a letter quoted earlier:

[T]he reason why I keep strict silence now for many years with regard to theology is that while I cannot myself discover adequate rational basis for the Christian hope of happy immortality, it seems to me that the general loss of such a hope, from the minds of average human beings as now constituted, would be an evil of which I cannot pretend to measure the extent. (M 357)

However, what Sidgwick goes on to say in the next lines marks the crucial qualification to his own qualified, practical endorsement of esoteric morality:

But I am not prepared to say that this will be equally true some centuries hence; in fact, I see strong ground for believing that it will *not* be equally true, since the tendency of development has certainly been to make human beings more sympathetic; and the more sympathetic they become, the more likely it seems to me that the results of their actions on other human beings (including remote posterity) will supply adequate motives to goodness of conduct, and render the expectation of personal immortality, and of God's moral order more realised, less important from this point of view. At the same time a considerable improvement in average human beings in this respect of sympathy is likely to increase the mundane happiness for men generally, and to render the hope of future happiness less needed to sustain them in the trials of life. (M 357–58)

Such passages also indicate some important qualifications to Williams's analysis, which is cast strictly in terms of the arguments for utilitarianism in Book IV and fails to catch the significance of the dualism of practical reason for Sidgwick's larger position. Thus, the concern here – once again apparently covering both justification and motivation – would seem to be cast in terms of the harmonization project, such that moral maturation will yield an increase in general and individual happiness, rendering the problem of self-sacrifice less compelling. The complications on the egoistic side of this effort, given the failure of deductive approaches and the limits of indirection, would need to be addressed as well, and Williams does not do this. But how this argument would run is evident from Sidgwick's conclusion to his chapter on "Happiness and Duty" in Book II:

> To sum up: although the performance of duties towards others and the exercise of social virtue seem to be *generally* the best means to the attainment of the individual's happiness, and it is easy to exhibit this coincidence between Virtue and Happiness rhetorically and popularly; still, when we carefully analyse and estimate the consequences of Virtue to the virtuous agent, it appears improbable that this coincidence is complete and universal. We may conceive the coincidence becoming perfect in a Utopia where men were as much in accord on moral as they are now on mathematical questions, where Law was in perfect harmony with Moral Opinion, and all offences were discovered and duly punished: or we may conceive the same result attained by intensifying the moral sentiments of all members of the community, without any external changes (which indeed would then be unnecessary). But just in proportion as existing societies and existing men fall short of this ideal, rules of conduct based on the principles of Egoistic Hedonism seem liable to diverge from those which most men are accustomed to recognise as prescribed by Duty and Virtue. (ME 175)

This and the previous passage might suggest how, in certain humors, Sidgwick did express some less guarded thoughts about the potential of an ideal enlightened community – future community, anyway – of utilitarians. Plainly, his own sense of duty compelled him to work assiduously to at least try to push the sympathetic development of humanity forward, if mainly in that Millian fashion described earlier, so that the normal person might come to sincerely wish to pursue his or her own interests only in ways compatible with the general happiness. But as we have seen, he was, on reflection, quite guarded and tentative in his hopes for future society and social prognoses, much more alert to how little could confidently be said about the laws of historical development and the shortcomings of any future society, in a godless universe. Comte, Spencer, Marx, and even Mill were to his mind wildly optimistic in this department. And his own psychological work, with the experiments in intuitive theism, was less than conclusive when it came to the matter of the basic fabric of human nature. Hence, the persistent anxiety running through his expressions of uncertainty. Precisely what was it in human nature that was responsible for this maturation of the sympathetic tendencies? How crucial, and how natural, was the religious impulse or some form of reverence? How responsible was it for his own faith in "Things in General," or for the more self-sacrificing tendencies of the public? The theistic postulate offered so much more by way of hope for reconcilation, but it had yet to be vindicated.

Thus, there can be little doubt that the sections of the *Methods* devoted to esoteric morality were among the most personal and revelatory of any in the entire book, and not merely theoretical speculations of purely hypothetical interest. Here was the philosophical expression of Mauricean paternalism; here was the philosophical payoff of pursuing Mill's advice about looking into the touchy matter of the utility of truth. Obviously, Sidgwick was walking a very carefully constructed path, taking solace not only in the possibility of future progress, but also in the way that the germ of such progress appears to be one of the elements of commonsense morality. Thus, the man who

earnestly and successfully endeavours to realise the Utilitarian Ideal, however he may deviate from the commonly-received type of a perfect character, is likely to win sufficient recognition and praise from Common Sense. For, whether it be true or not that the whole of morality has sprung from the root of sympathy, it is certain that self-love and sympathy combined are sufficiently strong in average men to dispose them to grateful admiration of any exceptional efforts to promote the common good, even though these efforts may take a somewhat novel form. To any exhibition of more extended sympathy or more fervent public spirit than is ordinarily shown, and any attempt to develop these qualities in others, Common Sense is rarely unresponsive; provided, of course, that these impulses are accompanied with adequate knowledge of actual circumstances and insight into the relation of means to ends, and that they do not run counter to any recognised rules of duty. And it seems to be principally in this direction that the recent spread of Utilitarianism has positively modified the ideal of our society, and is likely to modify it further in the future. Hence the stress which Utilitarians are apt to lay on social and political activity of all kinds, and the tendency which Utilitarian ethics have always shown to pass over into politics. For one who values conduct in proportion to its felicific consequences, will naturally set a higher estimate on effective beneficence in public affairs than on the purest manifestation of virtue in the details of private life: while on the other hand an Intuitionist . . . still commonly holds that virtue may be as fully and as admirably exhibited on a small as on a large scale. A sincere Utilitarian, therefore, is likely to be an eager politician. (ME 495)

Sidgwick concludes, however, that it is not within the scope of his treatise to show "on what principles" this kind of "political action ought to be determined." Rather, that issue would be at the core of his next two major treatises, *The Principles of Political Economy* and *The Elements of Politics*, which would extend his utilitarian method into a truly comprehensive practical philosophy.

Given this denouement, Williams is correct to suggest that it is profoundly ironic that a treatise that had started out by carefully defining ethics in terms of the problem of what one ought to do here and now should by the end have left practical ethics in such a state of doubt and uncertainty on "all questions of practical interest." This much Sidgwick roundly admitted, but without concluding that the reflective excursion was without interest or value, at least for the philosophical few. What is truly ironic, however, is the way in which Sidgwick, the high-minded utilitarian saint who had a reputation for scrupulous honesty and a detestation of hypocrisy, was here theorizing in detail the justification for an esoteric morality.[230]

Indeed, the passages quoted here should suggest how the question of esoteric morality must be pursued through a consideration of Sidgwick's larger psychological, social, and political theory, as an extension of his utilitarianism or dualism and, of course, of his personal struggles with "the deepest problems." Surely, he meant himself to be one of those exemplary utilitarians winning the praise of plain persons and contributing to the development of the utilitarian elements in common sense. Williams's presentation of Sidgwick's position makes it sound too much like that of a Victorian-era Plato, thoroughly persuaded of the permanent limitations of nonphilosophers. Sidgwick, one wants to say, was more truly Socratic, albeit with less Socratic irony and more Millian sympathy. Furthermore, his stress on harmonization and positive infatuation with matters of hypocrisy and integrity point to the curious ways in which Williams's critique of the demandingness of utilitarianism is in fact highly Sidgwickian, and does not respond to Sidgwick's own efforts at reconciliation.[231]

Perhaps this provides at least some oblique support for the picture of a less elitist Sidgwick painted by Schneewind's Kantian interpretation, though it would nonetheless seem to be true that Sidgwick's notion of a method of ethics, by encompassing such indirect strategies, differed in fundamental respects from any Kantian decision procedure. He took his esotericism very seriously, and it must be allowed that Williams gets closer to the heart of the matter. In fact, Williams's take on Sidgwick has been given a very important feminist turn by Margaret Urban Walker in her book *Moral Understandings: A Feminist Study in Ethics*. Like Williams,

Walker pays Sidgwick a backhanded compliment, declaring that he was at least clearer about how to negotiate the different levels of moral thinking than recent indirect utilitarians.[232] Her claim is that Sidgwick advanced a perversely elitist and patriarchal epistemological project.

Walker, as we shall see, misses crucial aspects of Sidgwick's epistemology and of his practical politics, including his feminism and the way in which his life and work brought the problem of esotericism into connection with that of the "epistemology of the closet" – the distinctive ethical and political dilemmas about publicity associated with same-sex erotic love. However, she does, like Williams, raise many of the crucial questions about the ultimate meaning of the *Methods*. After all, to the degree that the book did embody Sidgwick's Apostolic quest, might it not also reflect the highly elitist and highly gendered perspectives – not to mention Eurocentric perspectives – of so many of the actually existing Apostles?[233] As sophisticated and defensible, in narrowly analytical terms, as many of Sidgwick's arguments may be, they clearly need to be fleshed out in more concrete terms – in terms, that is, that really capture the notions of experts and expertise that went into his much-sought-after "consensus of experts." What if the Mauricean and Millian efforts on behalf of the higher education of women were of a piece with their views about civilizing the so-called "lower races"? And what were their views, and Sidgwick's, about the larger mission of "civilization"?

A last reiteration. What is missing even from quite sympathetic treatments of the *Methods* is an adequate appreciation of the importance, in Sidgwick's overall project, of the notion of inquiry, of the ways in which his philosophical intuitionism was cast in a fallibilist epistemology that also underscored the social dimensions of knowledge and relied upon Apostolic notions of friendship and integrity. On Rawls's reading, Sidgwick's epistemology is as individualistic as that of Descartes or Kant – that is, there is insufficient appreciation of Sidgwick's conviction that his method can only reduce the risk of error and can do this only by also working to establish coherence and consensus. What the Rawlsian description of "rational intuitionism" misses is the Millian and Mauricean vitality of ethical inquiry, as a matter of the larger culture. Manifestly, Sidgwick's conception of free, critical inquiry was not that of the pure and attentive mind absorbed in its own individual study. Nor was it that of the solipsistic self of the empiricist, reducing all knowledge claims to its own sense-data. No, to build the educating society and the new culture would take much more than egoistic ropes of sand, be they ethical or epistemic. It is here, in his construction of notions of consensus and authority, that one must search for Sidgwick's deeper views about publicity as they bear on matters of sex, class, and race.

How, then, to reconcile the demands of inquiry with the esotericism of the utilitarian method? Of the pursuit of truth and the pursuit of the greatest happiness? And both of these with one's own happiness? What kind of culture hero did Sidgwick think the times demanded, and what kind did he conceive himself to be? How could he even talk about an ideal community of enlightened utilitarians while avoiding the "illimitable cloudland" of utopian conjecture? What could even an eager politician do when confronted with such complexity? How many selves needed to be sacrificed?

With such problems before him, what was an Apostle to do? For Sidgwick, the answer was clear: hunt ghosts. Harmony and esotericism of a rather literal sort had not yet failed.

5

Spirits

I. Preliminaries and Cautionaries

The battle is to be fought in the region of thought, and the issue is belief or disbelief in the unseen world, and in its Guardian, the Creator-Lord and Deliverer of Man.

W. E. Gladstone[1]

Occultism is the metaphysic of dunces.

Theodor W. Adorno[2]

Whatever one may think of parapsychology, it is impossible to appreciate Sidgwick's worldview without recognizing his commitment to such investigations.[3] Like Gladstone and so many others who feared that dogmatic materialism was on the rise and orthodox religion in serious peril – which in the 1860s and 1870s, especially, it seemed hard to deny – Sidgwick regarded these studies as the vital avenue by which to meet the challenges thrown down by the likes of T. H. Huxley, "Darwin's Bulldog." Just as the Idealism of Green and Bradley was a reaction to the growing climate of unbelief, so too Sidgwick's parapsychology was a bit of philosophizing with strategic intent, a return to the concerns of Swedenborg to parallel the return to the concerns of Kant (though of course, one could also view it as carrying forward certain forms of Romanticism). It certainly proved to be a happy vehicle for the poetic imagination, as both subject and object.

As noted in Chapters 1 and 2, Sidgwick appears to have been fascinated by ghosts for practically his entire life, quite possibly as a result of being exposed to so many deaths in his early years. He would sometimes refer, in his letters, to his "ghost-seeing" tendencies. Even his mentor, Benson, had shared this fascination, helping to found the Cambridge "Ghost Society" during his time there, an institution that Sidgwick then participated in when he was a Cambridge undergraduate.[4] By the time of his graduation, he was already a fund of tales about supposed paranormal happenings, though these were more or less held in check by his orthodox religious views and skeptical doubts about the quality of the evidence. Anglican orthodoxy for the most part disapproved of any untoward interest in ghosts.

Again, as recounted in Chapter 3, it was the battering dealt his Anglican beliefs during his years of "storm and stress," when he came to struggle so with the entire issue of the evidence for miraculous happenings, that pushed him to accord a truly cosmic significance to these interests, theological and ethical, and to surround himself with a circle of (mostly younger) friends of similar disposition willing to seek firmer support for such claims. Quickly becoming known as the Sidgwick Group, after their researches took systematic form in the 1870s, they became the respectable core of the official Society for Psychical Research, which was born in 1882, with Sidgwick as its first president, the others serving on its Council, and a membership list of some one hundred names, many of them highly respectable. By the mid-eighties it had 600 members and associates – everyone from Gladstone to Tennyson to Lewis Carroll – and Sidgwick was confident that it could "run without further nursing." When it crested, in about 1920, it had 1,303 members and associates as well as a respectable endowment fund, the result of various bequests. Its *Proceedings of the Society for Psychical Research* were very widely read; it had an in-house *Journal*; and it was busy assembling a fine library to support its researchers. After 1885, there was also an American version, which, though not as flourishing as the original, attracted such leading intellectual figures as William James and worked in close collaboration with the British organization, of which it was officially a branch from 1887 until 1905.

As a piece of cultural and social history, therefore, psychical research is clearly a fascinating development, affording a wealth of insights into the assumptions and practices governing knowledge, expertise, and inquiry during this period. In Sidgwick's case, this endeavor to reenchant the universe was of course bound up with his worries about the chaos of the dualism of practical reason and the grounding of egoism; as indicated in the previous chapters, such concerns were absolutely crucial to him, and he regarded the empirical investigation of the paranormal as a form of theological study that could help to vindicate belief in the moral order of the universe, the harmony of duty and interest. Also noteworthy, however, is the way in which this line of inquiry took the same form as so many of his other Apostolic quests, becoming in large part an intimate fellowship of seekers revealing to each other their deepest concerns. Thus, Sidgwick's parapsychology happily illuminates the larger social dimensions of his epistemology as well as his metaphysical views, extending even to his political concerns. The "failure" of *The Methods of Ethics* had only strengthened his interest in "psychological experiments in ethics and intuitive Theism," and in the "miraculous" as perhaps a permanent element in human history – the defining interests of his years of storm and stress. How curious that it fell to ghosts to prove that the wages of virtue were not dust.

Of course, given the subsequent record of inconclusive and fraudulent research in parapsychology, which in recent times has been so mercilessly exposed by such critics as Martin Gardner and a professional magician, "The Amazing Randi," it is difficult to recapture anything like the rectitude and intellectual aspirations of the early psychical researchers. And to be sure, even at the start, the Society had its divisions, with the "scientific" contingent on one side and the séance-loving "Spiritualists," led by Stainton Moses, on the other. One could safely say, however, that it was largely because of the comparative sobriety that Sidgwick early on brought to the Society that their work enjoyed the long period of respectability that it did. And still more importantly, the work of the psychical researchers proved to be a very fertile breeding ground for many different forms of psychological research; their work on such topics as hypnosis and the various forms of unconscious thought was entangled with the developments that would later be absorbed into various regions of clinical and experimental psychology. Although these investigations remain controversial, they are not usually placed in the same category as attempts to communicate with the dead. It is also important to stress that psychical research, perhaps because of its novelty, provided an important vehicle for the work of independent, intellectually motivated women – for example, Eleanor Mildred Balfour, whose marriage to Sidgwick in 1876 only reinforced her commitment to a life of research and educational activity. Ironically, however, the SPR has also been described as a highly gendered (and orientalist) effort, reinscribing male authority and at odds with some of the very movements that were, albeit in strange ways, empowering women – notably, the Theosophical movement.[5]

Yet Sidgwick and his group apparently regarded all such work as an open and fair field. Again, he embarked on it in the same spirit of Apostolic truth seeking that characterized his work on religion and ethics, insisting that however potentially important the results might be, the method had to be one of impartial, disinterested inquiry rather than advocacy. And on the whole, his views of the results were rather measured: he did think that there was sound evidence for telepathy and unconscious thought processes (as demonstrated by hypnotism), but he did not think that the results of his other parapsychological inquiries had been very successful. Such modest, mostly negative results would in due course mean that all of his anxieties about the corrosive impact that his skepticism might have would return with renewed force. Indeed, the people involved in psychical research were often uniquely subject to the force of Sidgwick's skepticism, and they did not always react very appreciatively: another eminent member of the SPR would comment, after Sidgwick's death, that "[t]here are some people so constituted that nothing psychic will take place in their presence. Prof. Sidgwick was one."[6] Mediums were apt to complain that he was too "fidgety."

Still, unpopularity with the spirits may have served Sidgwick well, and it was in this region that he did the most to spell out his philosophy of mind and the moral psychology that informed his other efforts. And his more philosophical criticisms of empiricism, materialism, and idealism make much more sense when read with the example of his psychical research in mind. Here, surely, he had found the "deepest problems," for which a solution had to be sought.

II. The Fellowship

After Death

I have been buried for seven long days;
Here in the cold deep grave I lie:
Dark, all is dark! tho' the sun's warm rays
Slumber above on the earth close by.

For seven more days shall I wait fast bound
In coffin and shroud, tho' I seem but dead;
While the spirits of those whom I wronged flit round,
And fill me with torture and horrible dread.

What men call wicked was I on the earth,
What men call lost am I here below:
For twice seven days ere I have new birth
Shall the souls that I wronged flit to and fro.

I am theirs for a while: they may do what they will
With my poor body and pitiful soul,
While I lie in the vault where all life is still,
Where dank air sickens and far sound roll.

Where the stones seem heavy and like to sink
With the weight of the woe that I wrought in my life,
And crush me, or hurry me over the brink,
Down, down, to a pit of unending strife.

But I know that ere long I shall find release;
When twice seven days and nights are sped
I shall change. Shall I soar to the realms of peace?
Or down shall I fall to the place of the dead?

> Poem, signed "Σ," published in *The Cliftonian*,
> November 1877 (believed to be by either Arthur
> or Henry Sidgwick)[7]

As we have seen, Sidgwick's skepticism was only heightened by his work on the *Methods*, which failed to vindicate an independent, justifiable ethical system and consequently aggravated, if anything, his anxieties about the future of religious belief and, correlatively, the future of civilization. Again, his early inclination to "provisionally postulate" the "continued existence of the soul in order to effect that harmony of Duty with Happiness which seemed to me indispensable to rational moral life" had involved, as he later explained, "setting out on the serious search for empirical evidence" (M 466–67).[8] This retrospective suggests just how his concerns became so focused on psychical research, during the period from 1865 to 1875, and what his priorities were. Eleanor Mildred Sidgwick, née Balfour, whom Sidgwick first met and began working with during this period, was also quite clear about the formative interests of the Sidgwick Group and the SPR:

The question whether good scientific evidence of survival – as distinct of course from philosophical or theological reasons for believing it – could be obtained, is probably one which from the foundation of the Society in 1882 has interested the majority of the members more than any other branch of our enquiries, because of the far-reaching consequences its solution would carry with it. One consequence would be a decisive argument against materialism, and it is this that leads some of those who hold dogmatically a materialistic view of the universe to oppose, not only any conclusion that survival can be proved, but any enquiry into the subject, with a virulence resembling that of medieval theologians.[9]

This was to be a common theme of the Sidgwick Group – namely, the dogmatism of so many of those who professed to be representing science. Much of their initial energies went into simply trying to persuade people that the evidence was not all in yet, one way or the other, and that empirical inquiries were a promising alternative to the inconclusive, question-begging answers coming from theology and philosophy, or from those spiritualists who regarded all such experimental investigations of the paranormal as wrong "because they must be the work either of the devil or of familiar spirits, with whom the Bible forbid us to have dealings."[10] Still, the fiercest opposition was from the scientists, not from the religiously inclined. As Sidgwick retrospectively put it, in his SPR presidential address of 1888:

We believed unreservedly in the methods of modern science, and were prepared to accept submissively her reasoned conclusions, when sustained by the agreement of experts; but we were not prepared to bow with equal docility to the mere prejudices of scientific men. And it appeared to us that there was an important body of evidence – tending *primâ facie* to establish the independence of soul or spirit – which modern science had simply left on one side with ignorant contempt; and that in so leaving it she had been untrue to her professed method, and had arrived prematurely at her negative conclusions. (CWC)[11]

This attitude was shared by most of the important founding members of the Sidgwick Group. Myers, for example, many of whose insights into Sidgwick's early Cambridge years have been appealed to in early chapters, was of special importance in connection with psychical research, as well as with psychology in general. Sidgwick would in later life write that "[f]or many years Frederic Myers has been as dear to me as the dearest of brothers – there is no one so qualified to enrich and make brighter and nobler the lives of those he loves."[12] No other member of the Sidgwick Group, with the possible exceptions of Eleanor Sidgwick and Edmund Gurney, had a closer perspective on the evolution of Sidgwick's thinking in this area, and Myers's own work – including his posthumously published magnum opus, *Human Personality and the Survival of Bodily Death* (1903), which was dedicated to Sidgwick and Gurney – is a rich mine of material for understanding at least the kinds of beliefs to which Sidgwick was drawn and with which he was forced to engage. Not surprisingly, Sidgwick, here as elsewhere, was always the more skeptical friend.

In his obituary of Sidgwick, part of which was quoted in Chapter 3, Myers recalled his own parallel development and the events leading to their collaboration:

My own entry into his inquiry, at any rate, was in an hour of deep inward need. "Faith at her zenith, or all but lost in the gloom of doubts that darken the schools": – I had passed through all these stages, and visiting Cambridge again in 1869 to examine for the Moral Sciences Tripos, I felt drawn in my perplexities to Henry Sidgwick as somehow my only hope. In a star-light walk which I shall not forget (December 3rd, 1869), I asked him, almost with trembling, whether he thought that when Tradition, Intuition, Metaphysic, had failed to solve the riddle of the Universe, there was still a chance that from any actual observable phenomena, – ghosts, spirits, whatsoever there might be, – some valid knowledge might be drawn as to a World Unseen. Already, it seemed, he had thought that this was possible; steadily, though in no sanguine fashion, he indicated some last grounds of hope; and from that night onwards I resolved to pursue this quest, if it might be, at his side. Even thus a wanderer in the desert, abandoning in despair the fair mirages which he has followed far in vain, might turn and help an older explorer in the poor search for scanty roots and muddy water-holes.[13]

Myers goes on to admit that his was "a slow and late conversion to the sense, which so many men had already reached, of Sidgwick's penetrating wisdom." Still, in the end, only Arthur Balfour and Edmund Gurney rivalled him in admiration – the "attitude as of 'companions of Socrates': – as it were, say, a Kritias of happier omen, a Theages, a Simmias, – feeling an essential stimulus to self-development in his intellectual search, his analysing *elenchus*; – and feeling also in the steadfastness of his inward aspiration a prophylactic, as each man might need it, against dilettantism, or self-indulgence, or despair." On Myers's account of it, he and Sidgwick "had caught together the distant hope that Science might in our age make sufficient progress to open the spiritual gateway which she had been thought to close; – to penetrate by her own slow patience into the vestibule of an Unseen World."[14] And they even occasionally remarked with pride that it was the stereotypical English mind and method, with its fact-gathering ploddingness, that might at last crack the secret of the universe – "where the German had been satisfied with embracing the cloud – where the Frenchman's logic had lightly accepted negation – the dogged Anglo-Saxon might yet wrest some secret from silent Fate." For Myers, no one was more English in this respect than Sidgwick, that "veritable incarnation of beneficent wisdom":

And Sidgwick possessed, in an almost unique degree, that motive for dogged persistence which lay in a deep sense of the incurable incoherence of the intelligible world, as thus far grasped by men. More thoroughly than any other man known to me he had exhausted one after another the traditional creeds, and accredited speculations; – had followed out even to their effacement in the jungle the advertised pathways to truth. Long years of pondering had begotten in him a mood of mind alike rare and precious; – a scepticism profound and far-reaching, which yet had never curdled into indifference nor frozen into despair.[15]

In fact, however, Myers would also insist that "Sidgwick was not only cautious, systematic, self-controlled, he was also unresting, undeviating, inwardly ardent to the end; – possessed, as Plato has it, with that 'iron sense of truth and right' which makes the least indication of intellectual as well as of moral duty fall on the heart as an intimate and urgent command." This somewhat less English-sounding Sidgwick had his "true core" in "ardour" rather "than in circumspection, in force of will rather than in pondering hesitancy."[16]

One suspects that such praise reveals more about Myers than about Sidgwick, however. In an 1869 letter to Anne Clough, Sidgwick would remark, by way of explaining how Myers's appreciation of it proved the ever-increasing relevance of Arthur Hugh Clough's poetry, that "Myers is a man whose turn of mind is so antagonistic to subtle scepticism that he *could* not have appreciated these poems except that he is, as every susceptible youth must be, *de son siècle*" (M 215).

In many ways, Myers, born in 1843, may have seemed an unlikely intimate of Sidgwick's. Although he had a similar background – a clergyman father; well-to-do relatives (including his self-made uncle William Whewell); an early sensitivity to and preoccupation with religious matters; and a Trinity College, Cambridge education, marked by study of classics gradually giving way to an interest in the moral sciences – he was certainly far more expressive and hopeful by temperament, and apparently far more capable of alienating people. Alan Gauld has nicely pointed up the contrast: "Sidgwick was ascetic and cool-headed, a political and academic liberal and a practical reformer. Myers, by contrast, was not merely a man pulled this way and that by turbulent emotions and irrepressible sensuality; he was at this period of his life a snob, a name-dropper, an arch-tory."[17]

As Gauld further describes him:

To Myers' undergraduate contemporaries he appeared an eccentric and a *poseur*. His extreme sensibility led him to express his feelings in an unrestrained way and to dramatise scenes and incidents which others were likely to find merely trivial or silly. It led also to an arrogance and a vanity which made him widely unpopular, for his emotions had to him at times a momentous, cosmic import, and he could hardly help regarding himself as singled out by Fate, for some high destiny. His pride was augmented by his early successes; and he was perhaps not unaware of possessing personal advantages – a tallish (though somewhat plump) figure, a handsome face and silky beard, a delicately flexible voice – denied to many others. Few liked him, and some detested him. His closest friend during his early years at Cambridge was Arthur Sidgwick, a clever young classic in the year above him. Their relationship was of an emotional and aesthetic kind, and its intenseness may well have caused unfavourable comment, so adding to Myers' unpopularity.[18]

That Myers and Arthur Sidgwick were linked to the John Addington Symonds circle at this earlier point (from about 1863), and widely recognised as intimate, is clear from Symonds's own letters.[19] And all of them shared a similar "Arcadian" development, grounded in the classics. As Myers explained:

That early burst of admiration for Virgil of which I have already spoken was followed by a growing passion for one after another of the Greek and Latin poets. From ten to sixteen I lived much in the inward recital of Homer, Aeschylus, Lucretius, Horace, and Ovid. The reading of Plato's *Gorgias* at fourteen was a great event; but the study of the Phaedo at sixteen effected upon me a kind of conversion. At that time, too, I returned to my worship of Virgil, whom Homer had for some years thrust into the background. I gradually wrote out Bucolics, Georgics, Aeneid from memory; and felt, as I have felt ever since, that of all minds known to me it is Virgil's of which I am the most intimate and adoring disciple.

Plato, Virgil, Marcus Antoninus; – these, to speak summarily, are the three great religious teachers of Graeco-Roman antiquity; and the teaching of Plato and that of Virgil are in the main identical. Other pathways have now led me to something like the creed which they foresaw; but it is still, and more than ever, the support of my life.

The discovery at seventeen, in an old school-book, of the poems of Sappho, whom till then I had only known by name, brought an access of intoxicating joy. Later on, the solitary decipherment of Pindar made another epoch of the same kind. From the age of sixteen to twenty-three there was no influence in my life comparable to *Hellenism* in the fullest sense of that word. That tone of thought came to me naturally; the classics were but intensifications of my own being. They drew from me and fostered evil as well as good; they might aid imaginative impulse and detachment from sordid interests, but they had no check for lust or pride.

When pushed thus far, the "Passion of the Past" must needs wear away sooner or later into an unsatisfied pain. In 1864 I travelled in Greece. I was mainly alone; nor were the traveller's facts and feelings mapped out for him then as now. Ignorant as I was, according to modern standards, yet my emotions were all my own; and few men can have drunk that departed loveliness into a more passionate heart.[20]

Thus it would appear that something astonishingly close to the Oxford Hellenism of Symonds was very much alive at Cambridge. Myers was quite clear that his Hellenism "was an intellectual stimulus, but in no way a moral control. Entirely congenial to my temperament, it urged me onwards . . . into intellectual freedom and emotional vividness, but exercised no check upon either sensuality or pride. Hellenism is the affirmation of the will to live; – but with no projection of the desired life into any juster or sterner world." For Myers, Plato was right about love being "an inlet into the spiritual world."[21]

These "Uranian" connections of the early psychical researchers were quite significant, as we shall see again in the next chapter. Arthur, however, was also an Apostle, and although he and Henry worked hard to get Myers elected, they were unsuccessful in this. Myers would often talk about how many of Henry's "contemporaries and juniors in his early student days" regarded him with a certain "coldness" – he was 'High, self-contain'd, and passionless,' like the mystic Arthur."[22] But it would seem that Myers was the more roundly disliked of the two.

As noted in Chapter 3, Myers's bad reputation was considerably aggravated by the plagiarism controversy that surrounded his prize poem for the Camden Medal competition of 1863, for which he appropriated without proper acknowledgment (though apparently in good faith) a number of lines from a book of earlier Oxford prize poems. The result was that he had to return the prize and endure a new crop of enemies, who would keep the memory of this event alive for many years to come. Myers himself, in his "Fragments of Inner Life," is brutally clear that the "swaggering folly" of his earlier self made this incident more characteristic than not.

At any rate, whatever the degree of Sidgwick's earlier aloofness, Myers was clearly the more controversial and disliked figure, in the Cambridge of the 1860s, and it is consequently not very surprising that he also ended up resigning his lectureship in 1869, though this was apparently in order to devote himself more fully to women's higher education. Eventually, he became a school inspector, and after 1875 was assigned to the Cambridge district, a turn that proved to be most convenient. Perhaps Sidgwick was able to accept him because, as the more senior and philosophically adept member of the partnership, he was less exposed to Myers's overbearingness than others, and because he had often heard Arthur – who really was his "dearest brother" – speak favorably of him. And Myers's more expressive side must have been a complement to Sidgwick's greater reserve and intellectuality. At least, according to Gauld, Myers "was endowed in the highest degree with that capacity for *delight* which, in the wake of the Romantic Revival, seemed to many the most essential mark of a poet," and the "emotional and poetic side of him felt that everyday events and scenes are somehow reflections of a deeper order of things from which they take their meaning and by which they are in some obscure way harmonised and guided to good ends."[23] Doubtless this struck a chord in Sidgwick's ultra-poetic soul.

Gauld's reading certainly seems right – Myers was always obsessed with the "subliminal uprush" of genius, and in his psychological research, at least, there was a pronounced, even Nietzschean, sense of the dangers of normalization:

Thus 'mad-doctors' tend to supplant theologians, and the lives of lunatics are found to have more lessons for us than the lives of saints. For these thinkers know well that man can fall *below* himself; but that he can rise *above* himself they can believe no more. A corresponding ideal is gradually created; an ideal of mere sanity and normality, which gets to look on any excessive emotion or fixed idea, any departure from a balanced practicality, with distrust or disfavour, and sometimes rising to a kind of fervour of Philistinism, classes genius itself as a *neurosis*.[24]

That Myers so evidently supposed himself to have been subject to such assaults on passionate, individual genius may suggest why his popularity was less than maximal. Yet Myers had real poetic gifts, which Sidgwick admired. One his poems, "An Epithalamium," expresses his admiration for the Sidgwicks, though it is perhaps not numbered among his better-known works. Poetically and of course philosophically, his outlook was always deeply colored by his Hellenism, especially by his love of Plato and Virgil.[25] Again, this was a common bond linking him to the Sidgwicks, Symonds, and the Platonic revival of the nineteenth century – "the affirmation of the will to live," in contrast to the "deadness and bitterness" of his more agnostic periods.[26] But with Myers, especially, Platonism became a vision of cosmic evolution:

I seem to foresee that the centre of interest must shift from the visible to the invisible world. I believe, – paradoxical as it now sounds, – that the day will come when the small problems of this earth – population, subsistence, political power – will be settled and gone by; when Science will be the absolutely dominant interest, and Science will be directed mainly towards the unravelling of the secrets of the Unseen.[27]

The closed, materialistic world of the nineteenth century, he prophesied, would be hard to imagine in future ages.

Thus, the longing for immortality that his literary interests suggested, coupled with what by all accounts was an overly eager willingness to believe, eventually, along with other sources, led Myers to this "Final Faith," an eclectic mix of elements tending to cosmic optimism. The "drawback" of Christianity was

the growing sense of unreality, of insufficiency; the need of an inward make-believe. The Christian scheme is not cosmical; and this defect is felt so soon as one learns to look upon the universe with broad impersonal questioning, to gaze onward beyond the problem of one's own salvation to the mighty structural laws on which the goodness or badness of the Cosmos must in the last resort depend.

Thus, although he has no wish to contrast his views with Christianity, Myers regards them as a "scientific development of the attitude and teaching of Christ," who was "a Revealer of immortality absolutely unique," but whose work "grows more and more remote," so that it is harder "to follow along that legendary way." Religion in "its most permanent sense" is rather "the adjustment of our emotions to the structure of the Universe," and what is needed for moderns "is to discover what that cosmic structure is."[28]

Myers's various early efforts to hang on to or revive his belief in higher realms, after his first painful bouts with agnosticism, took some forms that

Sidgwick found hard to swallow, such as an infatuation with the piety of Josephine Butler. Apparently, his early interest in spiritualism was also given a boost by his relationship with the future Lord and Lady Mount-Temple, who "lived as Lord Palmerston's heirs at Broadlands, one of the stateliest of English homes."[29] But for all their differences, both early and late, Myers and Sidgwick shared, at some crucial junctures, a certain similar pattern of disillusionment with orthodoxy – "from increased knowledge of history and of science, from a wider outlook on the world."[30] During the sixties and early seventies, Myers's bleak outlook and "cynical preference of the pleasures of the passing hour" led Sidgwick to write to him that "it would delight me much to know that you were prosperously betrothed . . . in order that Cupid may 'Get his sop and hold his noise' and leave room for other enthusiasms and impulses of self-development." Myers, it seems, needed stability, and Sidgwick was none too sure that in this case egoism would prove enlightened and self-limiting. Eventually Myers would fall utterly in love with Annie Marshall, the wife of a cousin, and the effort to contact her after her premature death would animate much of his later research, even when he was married to Eveleen Tennant.

And in the end, it was Myers who, with disarming simplicity, put the question that, above all, animated the efforts of the Sidgwick Group: is the universe friendly? Ultimately, this was the basic concern behind the manifold activities of the Sidgwick Group, their investigations into everything from table turning and spirit rapping to hypnotism and the source of the creative imagination. By "friendly" they meant in effect well-ordered ethically, and in a theistic way. This is important to bear in mind, when thinking about how Sidgwick's psychical research was addressed to the dualism of practical reason as presented in the *Methods*. Sidgwick rather clearly hoped that Myers would turn out to be right in some fundamental way, and this put him at some distance from those agnostics, such as George Eliot, who sought a substitute for religious reverence in reverence for ethical duty in and of itself. Myers recalled how Eliot had once asked him if he realized that "the triumph of what you believe would mean the worthlessness of all that my life has been spent in teaching?"[31]

If there was any member of the group who was less than preoccupied with the question of his own personal survival, it was Edmund Gurney. Myers observed that "Gurney had *not* a strong personal craving for a future life – had not even that kind of confidence in Providence, or in evolution, which leads most of us to take for granted that if that life exists, then for us and for the universe all must in the end be well."[32] Even so, as Myers allowed, Gurney reasoned "not that if there were a future life the universe *must* be good, but that if there were a future life the universe *might* be good; and that without such a life the universe could *not* be good in any sense in which a man moved with the sorrows of humanity ought to be called upon to use that word." Thus, his approach was begotten "neither by cravings nor by fears" but rather was the "deliberate outcome of a penetrating survey of the possibilities of weal for men."[33] Indeed, Myers was always eager to praise Gurney for his "disinterestedness," his "readiness, in Plato's words, 'to follow the argument whithersoever it leadeth' – a genuine, instinctive delight in the mere process of getting at truth, apart from any consideration of the way in which that truth might affect his own argument."[34] But it was Sidgwick who gave the shrewder summation, when in 1886 he commented on how the SPR had benefitted from "the peculiar combination of reckless impulsive independence of thought & action with laboriousness which characterises Gurney, & the passion for immortality which rules Myers."[35]

Gurney was certainly a fascinating personality. Born in 1847, he too had a father in the church and, after receiving a somewhat spotty private education, went up to Trinity College, Cambridge, and an extremely successful study of classics. His great passion in life, however, was not classics but music. As Myers remarked,

Called upon to choose between classical and mathematical studies, he chose classics almost at hazard, and worked at them, one may say, in the intervals of his practice on the piano. In spite of this divided interest... his singular acuteness in the analysis of language, his singular thoroughness in leaving no difficulty unsolved, secured him high honours and a Trinity Fellowship. Few men have attained that position by dint of studies which formed so mere an episode in their intellectual life.[36]

Although he had a modest independent income, Gurney sought, especially after his marriage in 1877, to cultivate a career. Rather tragically, he was denied the one object in life that he most desired: he proved to be insufficiently talented as a composer or performer to pursue a musical career. As this became clear, he turned to medicine as a possible alternative, but his successful studies in this department were not matched by an aptitude for the clinical side – he could not bear the messy part of the clinical setting and practice. He followed with a spurt of legal studies, though this also faded. His gifts were apparently consistently of a scholarly and analytical nature. Eventually, he would turn these to his first love, producing a pathbreaking piece of aesthetics entitled *The Power of Sound* (1880) and many essays of a philosophical, literary, and aesthetic bent, some collected in *Tertium Quid* (1887). The preface to the second of these works contains some illuminating remarks on his cast of mind:

The subjects treated being too various for any brief comprehensive description, the uniting idea had to be found, if at all, in the method of treatment. Now it happens that most of the papers deal with matters of contemporary controversy, as to which two antagonistic opinions have been strongly entertained and enforced, each with distinct and direct reference to the other. Thus, the Positivist view of life has had to reckon almost exclusively with the view of more or less orthodox Christianity; the aim of 'Natural Religion' has been simply to refute and supplant Supernaturalism; those who doubt whether life is 'worth living' have directed all their weapons against the fallacious confidence of the Materialistic school; Vivisectionist and Anti-vivisectionist have thrust and parried each as if his only possible critic or accuser were the other; 'evidence in matters extraordinary,' devoured or rejected *en bloc*, has been used as the gauge alike of popular credulity and of scientific arrogance.

Or to turn to aesthetic subjects. The most conspicuous artistic creator of our time [Richard Wagner] has been either worshipped as a prophet or decried as a charlatan; in Music, the issues between classical form and free romanticism have been contested with none the less earnestness and conviction for being totally unreal; and the same may be said of a good deal of the chronic disputes as to the relative greatness of poets, and the relative value of form and content, sound and sense, in Poetry.

In most of these questions I am conscious of 'a great deal to be said on both sides,' and also of a strong aversion to saying it in the ways which have chiefly attracted the public ear. In most of them the truer view seems to me to depend on taking a standpoint, or in recognising facts and principles, other than those which partisans have usually recognised or taken. And this truer view, if such it be, is not one that would extenuate differences, or induce lions to lie down with lambs, or generally tend towards compromise in the ordinary sense; its immediate tendency, on the contrary, is rather to make each of the duels triangular. In short, it is a *tertium quid*.[37]

Yet even these works do not do justice to Gurney's wide-ranging mind. One of his primary fascinations, which made him receptive to the call of Myers and Sidgwick, was hypnotism – or mesmerism, as it was then often called – and his contributions to that field put him in the same league as Charcot, Janet, and Richet.[38] Much of this work was done in collaboration with Myers, on whom he, like Sidgwick, acted as something of an intellectual brake, though it is astonishing how fertile and philosophically suggestive their collaboration turned out to be. For instance, in anticipation of recent discussions of the nature of personal identity, Gurney would suggest that hypnotism might illustrate "the spontaneous alternations in cases of '*double consciousness*,' where a single individual lives in turn two (or more) separate existences."[39] Hypnotism was thus early on linked to questions of identity, the unconscious, and split or multiple personalities.

Gurney's writings, which in due course won him the friendship and admiration of William James, thus reflect what Gauld has called his "general love of speculation and enquiry" and "complete disrespect for conventional lines of thought."[40] Moreover, he was noted for another "leading feature" of his personality – "his extreme sensitivity to pain; not just to physical pain, but to grief and suffering of all kinds," which made him "excruciatingly aware of the predicaments of his fellow-men."[41] His deep aversion to "hopeless suffering" played a key role in his philosophical outlook. Small wonder that he could not pursue medicine beyond the textbook, or that for all his triangulation, he ended up being considered an early advocate of animal rights. He was perhaps the most lovable of all the members of the Sidgwick Group, and served George Eliot as a model for the title character in *Daniel Deronda*. But he also suffered from cycles of depression (was, indeed, quite possibly manic-depressive), and his premature death in 1888, from an overdose of chloroform prescribed for insomnia and neuralgia, has been interpreted by some as a suicide. Sidgwick himself confessed to "painful doubts."[42] His depressions had been seriously worsened by a tragic boating accident on the Nile that had killed three of his beloved sisters in 1875.

However, it was just before this terrible blow to his family that Gurney took up with Myers in an especially fateful development. As Gauld describes it:

On 9th May 1874 there occurred an event which decisively influenced the whole course of Myers' life. Accompanied by his friend Edmund Gurney, another of the younger Trinity Fellows, he went to the home of his aunt, Lady Mount-Temple, to meet Stainton Moses. Moses, a man of university education, gave them a first-hand account of the strange phenomena of which he was the focus; and they could not but feel impressed by his 'manifest sanity and probity'. 'He spoke frankly and fully; he showed his notebooks; he referred us to his friends; he inspired a belief which was at once sufficient, and which is still sufficient, to prompt to action.' On his return Myers persuaded Sidgwick to join him in organising a 'sort of informal association' for the investigation of the phenomena; into this association were sooner or later drawn Edmund Gurney, Walter Leaf and Lord Rayleigh (all Fellows of Trinity); Arthur Balfour and his sisters Eleanor and Evelyn (Lady Rayleigh); the John Hollands; and various others. Up till this time Sidgwick's investigations of Spiritualism and related phenomena had been fitful, waxing and waning as his opinions vacillated; but for much of the rest of his life he was to be constantly prodded into action by the eager and relentless Myers.[43]

One could say, then, that the two camps that would later produce so much divisiveness within the SPR began in a more symbiotic, cooperative relationship. Spiritualism was the issue, communicating with the spirits of the dead, and the Sidgwick Group was truly born at this point. Myers was the ringleader, and Gurney was at first reluctant – as Sidgwick wrote to Myers, Gurney "will give us – his warmest *sympathies* (but no more), in spiritualistic investigation." Eleanor Sidgwick would comment on this: "It is interesting to find that Edmund Gurney, who soon after became, and remained to the end of his life, one of the most important collaborators in the movement, hesitated at first about joining it" (M 288–89). But it appears that Gurney was simply for this stretch still struggling with his problematic career opportunities.

Clearly, the Balfours and Rayleighs were also there at the creation. Indeed, as a set, they formed an extraordinarily important part of the group, what with Arthur Balfour, Gerald Balfour, Eleanor Balfour, and John Strutt (later Lord Rayleigh, husband of Evelyn Balfour and, as noted, a winner of the Nobel Prize for chemistry) all taking an active part in the research from the very start, and all in due course taking their turns as president of the SPR. The members of this set would weave through Sidgwick's life in manifold ways, beyond his marriage to Eleanor. Most shared his speculative interests and membership in such organizations as the Metaphysical Society and the Synthetic Society, and much of Sidgwick's life outside of Cambridge was divided between the Balfour estate in Whittingehame, Scotland, the Rayleigh's Terling Place, and the various London homes of the family members.

Sidgwick's first contact with them had come through Arthur Balfour, who became his student in the late sixties. In fact, Balfour was one of Sidgwick's favorite pupils, and one of the very first students to be examined

under the newly remodeled Moral Sciences Tripos, in 1869. He was thus
one of Sidgwick's first proper students in philosophy. Balfour's admiration
for Sidgwick was unstinting:

I came up from Eton to Cambridge in 1866 with no Academic ambitions, but with
the highest expectations as to the gratifications which Academic life had to offer,
both in the way of ideas and in the way of amusements. That these expectations,
so far as the first head is concerned, were in no wise disappointed was largely due
to Sidgwick. My philosophic equipment when I first became his pupil was but
slender – being, indeed, little more than what I had acquired at Eton for my own
entertainment. Nor did I find it easy to increase this modest stock of learning
by attendance at ordinary lectures, which others besides myself have found a
somewhat irksome and ineffectual means of increasing knowledge. Few teachers
would, in these circumstances, have taken either much trouble or the right kind of
trouble with so unsatisfactory a pupil, and certainly any teacher would have been
justified in leaving me to my own devices. Fortunately for me Henry Sidgwick took
a more tolerant view. In addition to his other lectures he had at that time a small
class for those specially interested in the metaphysical side of the 'moral sciences'
Tripos, a class so small indeed that it consisted, if I remember right, only of one
other student besides myself. We met in Sidgwick's own rooms. The teaching was
largely in the nature of conversational discussion; and though I cannot, at this
distance of time, recall it in detail, I retain a vivid recollection of the zest with
which these hours were enjoyed. (M 309–10)

As Balfour goes on to explain, this was in part owing to Sidgwick's
method, which allowed them "to forget that we were preparing for an
examination, an oblivion which may or may not be desirable in other
branches of study, but is almost essential if the pleasures of speculation
are to be enjoyed without alloy." Moreover, Sidgwick "did not unduly
force upon us the historic method of studying philosophy," and "never
drove us into those arid regions of speculation where, to the modern
mind, the arguments seem without cogency and the conclusions without
interest." (M 310) But most important, Balfour allows, was his teacher's
disinterestedness:

What most people want in order to do their best is recognition; and the kind of
recognition from a distinguished man of eight-and-twenty which is most valued
by a boy of eighteen is the admission that his difficulties are worth solving, his
objections worth answering, his arguments worth weighing. This form of conveying encouragement came naturally to Sidgwick. Of all the men I have known he

was the readiest to consider every controversy and every controversialist on their merits. He never claimed authority. . . . (M 311)

It is worth noting that this frequently cited assessment must have, at least in part, reflected Balfour's experiences with Sidgwick in psychical research.

Now, for all of his admiration for Sidgwick as a friend, teacher, and brother-in-law, Balfour was always at a far remove from him on theological matters. Such works as his *A Defence of Philosophic Doubt* (1879) and *The Foundations of Belief* (1895) were, as Janet Oppenheim has rightly stressed, largely devoted to demonstrating "the validity of doubting that scientific methodology provided the only legitimate way to make inquiries about man and the universe," and he "consistently refused to acknowledge that science and religion could be at cross-purposes, that the former could fatally undermine the latter."[44] If such attitudes were not always entirely at odds with Sidgwick's distaste for dogmatic materialism, his more expressly Christian views surely were. For throughout his life, Balfour never really doubted immortality or the existence of a personal God, "a God whom men can love, a God to whom men can pray, who takes sides, who has purposes and preferences, whose attributes, howsoever conceived, leave unimpaired the possibility of a personal relation between Himself and those whom He has created."[45] This was not Sidgwick's thin, theistic faith.

Thus, as Oppenheim observes, Balfour "did not need the SPR to prop up a sagging faith, nor to afford the evidence without which he could enjoy no peace of mind." His theology "was grounded, not on sublime certainty, but rather on the conviction of man's spiritual needs. Again and again, his arguments reduced themselves to this: Human life was meaningless and valueless without religious faith. Religion was worth fighting for because it was an indubitable 'benefit' to mankind."[46] For Sidgwick, both of these points might well be true, but it was nonetheless important not to confuse hope with justified belief.

Yet for all that, Balfour was obviously deeply persuaded that the work of the Sidgwick Group and the SPR was of profound importance, since at the least they would demonstrate "that there are things in heaven and earth not hitherto dreamed of in our scientific philosophy." If his faith never sagged or demanded support, he was nonetheless delighted to add this form of buttressing, which clearly appealed to his speculative cast of mind.

The Balfour children came by their religion honestly. Their father had died prematurely in 1856, of tuberculosis, and afterwards they were very much in the keep of their evangelical mother, Lady Blanche Gascoigne Cecil. In a remarkable article, "A Mother's Role, a Daughter's Duty: Lady Blanche Balfour, Eleanor Sidgwick, and Feminist Perspectives,"[47] Oppenheim has brought out the significance of this family context, in connection not only with Eleanor but also with the ways in which Eleanor became a kind of surrogate mother for her younger brother Arthur – "Prince Arthur," as it was sometimes joked. Drawing on two unpublished memoirs that Eleanor – the eldest surviving child, born in 1843 – wrote about her mother, Oppenheim gives a vivid description of the family backdrop:

The dominant image of Lady Blanche that emerges from her eldest daughter's memoirs is, somewhat paradoxically, that of a domestic angel with an iron will. Incidents illustrating her capacity for self-sacrifice abound, most of them associated with the zealous nursing of her family through repeated health crises. Although exhausted from a decade of childbearing, she devotedly, and almost single-handedly, ministered to her young husband, James Maitland Balfour, as he slowly died of tuberculosis between 1854 and 1856. In the years that followed, Sidgwick recorded, she successfully nursed her offspring through bouts with diptheria, typhoid fever, and whooping cough, at serious personal cost. The impression conveyed is of a mother literally killing herself for her children. Sidgwick was also deeply impressed that Lady Blanche, a 'naturally sociable' woman, relinquished the pleasures of society after her husband's death, when she was only thirty-one, in order 'to use the little strength she had' for her eight children, all under the age of eleven.

Lady Blanche's seemingly endless capacity for self-denial was coupled in her daughter's memory with masterful self-discipline. Both Eleanor Sidgwick and Evelyn Rayleigh recollected her vigorous attempts to crush all manifestations of personal vanity, particularly in matters of fashion and adornment.... Lady Blanche was also quick to extirpate evidence of pride in Eleanor's conduct, as Mrs. Sidgwick appeared to relish telling her brothers' and sister's children. Once when the family grocer in Edinburgh gave her a little box of sweets, Eleanor wanted to refuse the gift until her mother persuaded her to accept. 'She convinced me afterwards,' Sidgwick explained, 'of the ungraciousness of such an action and how the impulse was in my case rooted in pride. She did that sort of thing without giving any impression of scolding or preaching.' At an unspecified date, perhaps in the wake of this incident, Lady Blanche gave Eleanor a set of uncompromising directions 'for prayer and self-examination,' which began: 'Have I given way to pride, conceit, vanity, temper, waste of time or dawdling, exaggeration or inexactness of speech, unkindness or selfishness?' After queries about Eleanor's Bible reading and relationship to God, the instructions ended with a final question no less relentless than the first: 'Have I omitted any opportunity of doing good or of making others happy?' Although Sidgwick claimed that the strong evangelicalism of Lady Blanche's youth had mellowed into a much broader religious outlook as she matured, enough of it evidently remained to leave her children little room for moral lapses.[48]

It should be tolerably evident that this type of intense, delicate soul searching, so characteristic of the widespread evangelicalism of the Victorian era, was the type of thing that could very easily dispose one to more sophisticated philosophical or psychological pursuits, as with the Apostles. The habit of intense scrutiny of one's own motives was, at any rate, something that Eleanor and Henry shared from the start (recall his instructions to the "Initial Society"). This was his form of prayer.

As Oppenheim notes, in later life the other Balfour children would also deny that, in Arthur's words, their mother was a "goody" and fondly recall her amusing and brilliant talk. In her last years, before her death in 1872, Lady Balfour spent more time traveling, and sought comfort in spas to help restore her strength. Thus, "as she grew older, Eleanor filled her mother's role with greater success. During Lady Blanche's absences from Whittingehame, she seems to have functioned as the stable center of the household, the person to whom the brothers at school or university turned for family news."[49] But this assumption of "maternal services for her brothers," was not, as Oppenheim stresses, mere matriarchy. Lady Blanche had been the very able administrator of a very large estate – Whittingehame covered over 10,000 acres, and the family resided in an eighty-room mansion – which she carefully trained Eleanor to manage, ensuring that she knew not only how to keep the books, but also how to do the housework, cook, and perform other tasks that would help her to "run a household from positions of knowledgeable authority, never at the mercy of the servants." Moreover,

Eleanor was pressed into service as her mother's philanthropic agent as soon as she reached sufficient age. On Lady Blanche's behalf, she helped a needy, but deserving, family in Edinburgh and did 'some visiting of poor families in London too at one time.' With other siblings, she made up the Christmas parcels of old clothes and delivered them, while Lady Blanche 'strongly encouraged' all her children to allocate a fixed portion of their allowance 'for giving.'[50]

Also notable, given Eleanor's later career, is the fact that Lady Blanche helped to establish an elementary school at Strathconan, where the family had another estate, and that at Whittingehame she began a parish lending library.

To be sure, much of this was a schooling in noblesse oblige, meant to ensure – as in fact it did – that Eleanor would "associate the special position and comforts she enjoyed with an abiding sense of duty not privilege." Eleanor certainly regarded her mother's ends as "unfailingly beneficent," and as something that "far more than wealth or rank, betokened membership in the ruling class." Still, as Oppenheim goes on to argue, if Eleanor's lessons "about the responsibilities of class were straightforward and unambiguous . . . her lessons on the responsibilities and rewards of womanhood were anything but." Although the daughters were not sent away to school, Lady Blanche herself apparently provided them with a stimulating education, imparting to Eleanor considerable love of and skill in mathematics – something for which she would be noted in later life, especially when she collaborated on scientific papers with her brother-in-law Rayleigh. If, after the death of her husband, she ended up placing a lesser value on the education of her daughters than on that of her sons, she nonetheless "carefully arranged that the girls would be financially independent of their brothers, free to lead their own lives, without any pressure to marry if they chose to remain single."[51] Eleanor's position and family would in some significant ways allow her to escape the "subjection of women" that Mill and Taylor so accurately depicted.

Thus it was that, shortly after the death of her mother, Eleanor Mildred Balfour – "Nora" to her friends – felt sufficiently independent to collaborate with Lord Rayleigh, during a trip up the Nile, and, in the autumn of 1875, to move to Cambridge to live in the newly completed Newnham Hall while studying mathematics with Norman Macleod Ferrers, later the master of Caius College. Henry Sidgwick had, as noted, been busy at work in building Newnham, the "positive" work that served as counterpoint to the "negative" work of relinquishing his Fellowship. Inspired by Mill's writings and Maurice's actual collegial collaboration, he had rented and furnished the original house, at 74 Regent Street, when Anne Clough and the first five students began residence there in 1871, and he was a moving force in all the developments that led to the building of Newnham Hall, which in October of 1875 had Eleanor Balfour and twenty-nine other students in residence. Women's higher education and the investigation of spiritualism had brought them together, and the Sidgwick Group was born.

III. Love and Ghosts

I would have written to you before, but I have unfortunately nothing to communicate on the interesting subject of Spiritualism – in fact, I find that I must give up the subject for the present, as I am behindhand with my work. I hope, however, to take it up again at some future time. It is certainly a most perplexing subject. There is so much crass imposture and foolish credulity mixed up with it, that I am not at all surprised at men of science declining to have anything to do with it. On the other hand, no one who has not read Crookes's articles in the *Quarterly Journal of Science*, or some similar statement, has any idea of the weight of the evidence in favour of the phenomena. As a friend of mine (who is a *dis*believer) says: 'There are only three alternatives – Crookes is either affirming a tissue of purposeless lies, or a monomaniac, or the phenomena are true,' and we seem to me to be driven to one of these conclusions. And then there is the startling fact that while all this is going on Crookes is exhibiting before the Royal Society experiments of novel and great interest on the motive force of heat. Altogether I am surprised that the thing is not attracting more attention. We have had tremendous heat in London, which has made me almost unable to work; I am now going back to Cambridge for a few days to finish my book, which I shall put into the printer's hands (I hope) before very long. It is a book too technical to give me any general reputation; indeed it can scarcely be said to belong to Literature, but I hope it will at least show that I am not altogether idle – as most of us academic residents are supposed to be. I shall be very glad to have it done, as then I shall be able to have a little real rest. . . . If you say anything to the Bishop about Spiritualism, please say that *no one* should pronounce on the *primâ facie case for serious investigation* – this is really all that I maintain on behalf of Spiritualism – who has not read Crookes's *Researches*.

Sidgwick to his mother, July 1874[52]

In writing thus to his mother, in the summer of 1874, Sidgwick nicely brought together the way in which the completion of the *Methods* was entwined with his growing concern to investigate the claims of spiritualism, which Myers had done so much to stimulate. Of course, as early as 1863 he had written to Dakyns that although he had "not yet investigated

Spiritualism," he was "bent on doing so" as soon as he got the opportunity. After all, the spiritualists were the ones who seemed to speak most directly to the concern for a reformed religious outlook, making sense of the "miraculous" as a universal and continuing phenomenon. If they were too eager to believe, at least they often pointed to the kinds of beliefs that Sidgwick thought were needed, after the havoc that had been sown by biblical criticism, biology, and geology. Although officially he was simply advocating the case for investigation, he was certainly hopeful in what he dreamed the investigations would succeed in revealing.

Sidgwick was much impressed by the work of Sir William Crookes, who, in Oppenheim's sharp words, "followed no prescribed paths to success, and blazed his own highly individual trail to knighthood in 1897, the Order of Merit in 1910, and the presidency of the Royal Society from 1913 to 1915."[53] In the early 1870s, Crookes, already well on his way to becoming an eminent chemist, published a number of accounts of his experimental research on spiritualism, claiming that he had witnessed genuine spirit materializations with the help of the medium Florence Cook. Crookes's scientific reputation for close and accurate observation apparently lent great credibility to his accounts of the evidence he claimed to derive from his séances with Cook and a long list of other famous mediums, including Daniel Douglas Home, Kate Fox, and Stainton Moses.

In retrospect, the only real mystery in his work was how it could have so impressed Sidgwick, since the "experiments" were completely unrigorous. In any event, the shocks and disappointments came quickly for the Sidgwick Group. Their initial investigations concerned two professional mediums, a C. Williams and a Mrs. Annie Eva Fay, from the United States. There followed investigations of various mediums celebrated by the burgeoning Spiritualist Association in Newcastle, including Miss C. E. Wood, Miss Annie Fairlamb, and the Petty family. Most of these made claims to be able to materialize various spirits. While sitting with their hands and feet tied, or bound up in some sort of cabinet, in a darkened setting, they would purportedly summon up the spirits, who would move about the room in a ghostly way, play musical instruments, or perform other acts to demonstrate their presence. As Gauld has remarked, the next quarter of a century saw a rather tiresome repetition of the same pattern: "Myers would become enthusiatic about such-and-such a medium; the Sidgwicks would acquiesce far enough to support or participate in an investigation; and everyone would in the end be more or less disappointed. . . . Myers sat, often several times, with practically every famous medium, public or private, of that time; and the Sidgwicks sat with many of them."[54]

But the initial burst of enthusiasm was always followed by the exposure of imposture or at least the serious suspicion of such. The only positive result in these early efforts, a number of which took place at Arthur Balfour's London home at 4 Carlton Gardens, was that Henry apparently got to do a lot of scientific hand holding with Eleanor, while they were serenaded by the spirits in the darkened séance settings. "She is not exactly perfect," the ever judicious philosopher wrote to his mother, "any more than other people, but it *is* true that whatever defects she has are purely negative: all that is positive in her is quite quite good. I cannot even imagine her doing anything wrong." (CWC) He married his vision of integrity on April 4, 1876.

Few harbored any doubts about the uniquely appropriate nature of this pairing of minds. William James would later describe them, in a critical tone, as "the incarnation of pure intellect – a very odd appearing couple."[55] Clearly, Eleanor was as rarefied a being as Henry, if not more so. As her biography records, she once confessed to her friend Alice Johnson that "mathematics especially appealed to her in early youth because she thought a future life would be much more worth living if it included intellectual pursuits." Johnson speculated that mathematical abstraction probably struck her as "adapted to a disembodied existence."[56] The tacit suggestion is that she began her preparations for this at a very early age.

Theirs was a union with a mission. In June of 1876, not long after their marriage and honeymoon trip to France, Sidgwick writes to Dakyns, "On July 5th I go back to London for another bout of ghosts. When your letter came I was just going in for three weeks of experiments, all of which failed, or nearly so; the 'phenomena' would not occur under the conditions we wished to impose. I do not know what to say now about the thing." (M 289) The next month, he writes to Dakyns that it is probably not worth his while to come to Newcastle to learn about spiritualism:

We are applying . . . a test which seems to us as conclusive as any that can be devised; we had *seven* seances, nearly altogether unsuccessful, and on Friday and Saturday last we had two which were even more suspicious in their partial success than the previously unsuccessful ones, so much so that two members of our circle have announced their intention of withdrawing, as from a proved imposture. (M 299)

In 1876, the Sidgwicks also began their investigations of the celebrated Dr. Slade, an American medium who supposedly could invoke the spirits to answer questions from the audience by writing that appeared inside a locked double slate, and of the still more successful slate-writing medium William Eglinton. Of the former, he wrote "I went to Slade several times, and, as far as my own experience goes, should unhesitatingly pronounce against [him], but there is a good deal of testimony for him, quite untouched by any explanation yet offered" (M 324–25). Another remark was inspired by the fear that he would be subpoenaed to appear in a court case charging Slade with fraud: "I want to keep out of it, being anxious not to appear before the public in connection with Spiritualism until I have a definite conclusion to announce" (M 324). Yet such investigations of the so-called physical phenomena of spiritualism would carry on for a long time, and by Eleanor Sidgwick's later account would remain the least successful of the SPR's endeavors. In fact, the exposure of Eglinton by the amateur conjurer S. J. Davey, in the mid-eighties, provides an excellent example of how the SPR, under Sidgwick's leadership, actually set the stage for the debunking work of such recent conjurers as "The Amazing Randi." This exposure utterly alienated the spiritualists in the SPR.

In any event, it seems fairly plain that the spirits of the Sidgwick Group, at least, were kept up during these tedious and disappointing investigations mainly by Myers's enthusiasm, and that, after the summer of 1876, things took a rather more desperate turn. As already remarked, Myers had fallen deeply in love with Annie Marshall, the wife of a troubled first cousin of his. His autobiographical accounts always discreetly refer to her as "Phyllis," when they are not celebrating the "sea-like sapphire of her eyes" or how she was a "fountain of vivifying joy." She "wrought upon" him an effect "which neither Mrs. Butler's heroic Christianity nor Henry Sidgwick's rightness and reasonableness had ever produced. . . . I knew in the deep of the heart that Virtue alone was safe, and only Virtue lasting, and only Virtue blest; and Phyllis became to me as the very promise and earnest of triumphant Virtue."[57] But in the spring of 1876, Annie's husband, Walter, was certified insane, and the strains that the family situation caused her over the course of the summer led to her suicide in September. Myers later responded in verse: "Then came the news that, on me hurled, / At once my youth within me slew, / Made dim with woe the reeling world, / And hid the heaven that shone therethrough."

From this point on, Myers could no longer abide even a whiff of his earlier agnosticism, and he began the pattern of responding to grief with belief that would eventually characterize so many members of the SPR.

He first began receiving supposed messages from Annie in July of 1877, in sittings with a Mme. Rohart; in due course, especially during the 1890s, he was absolutely convinced that she had communicated with him and that therefore survival was a reality. The reputation of the Society, in the twentieth century, would suffer greatly from the general impression that it was basically a vehicle for collective, sublimated mourning for both lost religion and lost loved ones, since virtually all of the original members who survived until 1920 became similarly converted, including Arthur Balfour and Eleanor Sidgwick.[58]

In the late 1870s, however, and despite Myers's hopes, things looked very different. In June of 1878, Sidgwick could write to Roden Noel that "I have not quite given up Spiritualism, but my investigation of it is a very dreary and disappointing chapter in my life." Had their research continued in this vein, Sidgwick would quite probably have ended up devoting much more of his life to philosophy. But at this crucial juncture, fresh enthusiasm was brought to the Sidgwick Group by William Barrett, who must be counted the actual proximate cause of the SPR. As Gauld reports:

The foundation of the Society for Psychical Research was not primarily the work of those who afterwards became its leaders. Those chiefly responsible were Professor W. F. Barrett and certain prominent Spiritualists. Barrett had for many years been interested in the question of thought-transference, and in 1876 he had offered the British Association a paper on his experiments. The paper was accepted by the Anthropological sub-section, by the casting vote of its Chairman, Alfred Russell Wallace, but it was not published. It was none the less reported in detail in the Press and caused much talk. Barrett was also interested in the phenomena of Spiritualism, and during the eighteen-seventies had become acquainted with Myers and Gurney, who assisted him in some of his later experiments on thought-transference. He conceived the idea that if a group of Spiritualists, who would join forces in dispassionate investigation with a group of scientists and scholars, who would possess the funds and the training to conduct proper experiments, the phenomena might perhaps be elucidated. Accordingly he convened a conference of persons likely to be interested. The conference met in London at 38 Great Russell Street on 5th and 6th January 1882. The foundation of the Society was proposed, and a committee (of which Myers, Gurney and Sidgwick were members) was set up to consider the question. The committee met at Hensleigh Wedgwood's house on 7th and again on 9th January. Myers and Gurney were not hopeful about the prospects of such a Society, and made their support conditional upon Sidgwick's accepting the Presidency. Sidgwick, remembering the many dreary hours which he had already passed to no avail in psychical investigations, was likewise pessimistic; but he felt that recent experiments in thought-transference gave fresh grounds for hope, and he agreed to become President. The conference met again on 20th February, and the Society for Psychical Research was formally constituted. Its stated aim was 'to investigate that large body of debateable phenomena designated by such terms as mesmeric, psychical and spiritualistic,' and to do so without prejudice or prepossession of any kind, and in the same spirit of exact and unimpassioned enquiry which has enabled Science to solve so many problems, once not less obscure nor less hotly debated.'[59]

The Council of the SPR began further sorting out the subjects to be investigated. Thought reading – or, in Myers's terminology, "telepathy" – was certainly a high priority, but so too was hypnotism, which had long been one of Gurney's chief interests, and of course such things as the physical phenomena of spiritualism, apparitions, and haunted houses. Curiously, Eleanor Sidgwick's name is not listed with the Society until January 1884, and she would later state: "I do not distinctly remember the cause of this delay, but I think it was due to my holding in 1882 a responsible position in another youthful institution – Newnham College (for Women) at Cambridge. It was probably not thought desirable to risk associating the College in the public mind with what was likely to be regarded as a cranky Society." Still, she also admits that though "not technically a Member I was entirely cognizant of the doings of the Society and its Council from the beginning," which is hardly surprising, since many of them took place at the Sidgwicks' new home, Hillside, on Chesterton Road in Cambridge.[60]

Apparently, there were few fears for the reputation of Sidgwick, the author of *The Methods of Ethics* and the soon-to-be-published *Principles of Political Economy* and *Outlines of the History of Ethics*, who during the eighties would reach the height of his prestige, becoming Knightbridge Professor, a Fellow of Trinity College, and president of the economic section of the British Association. Chastened by his experiences with fraudulent mediums and spiritualists, he threw himself into the work of the Society with an uncompromising demand for rigor and with zero tolerance for fraud. In his first presidential address to the Society, delivered on July 17, 1882, he urged

the point which is chiefly characteristic of the method of investigation which our Society will, I hope, in the main use. Though it would be a mistake to lay down a hard and fast rule that we may not avail ourselves of the services of paid performers or paid mediums, still we shall, as much as possible, direct our investigation to phenomena where no ordinary motives to fraud, – at any rate I may say no pecuniary motives, – can come in. There has, of course, always been a mass of evidence of this kind. In fact, I think every one who has become convinced of the reality of the phenomena, or has become strongly and persistently convinced that there is a *primâ facie* case for investigation, has had his attention first attracted by narratives of what has gone on in private families or private circles, where none but relatives or intimate friends have been concerned.

Now, the great gain that I hope may accrue from the formation of this Society is that the occurrence of phenomena – *primâ facie* inexplicable by any ordinary natural laws – may be more rapidly and more extensively communicated to us who desire to give our time to the investigation, so that in the first instance we may carefully sift the evidence, and guard against the danger of illusion or deception which even here may, of course, come in; and then, when the evidence has been sifted by accumulation of personal experiments, make it more available for the purpose of producing general conviction. (CWC)

To be sure, Sidgwick did strike a positive note in this address, speaking far too highly about the prima facie evidence, the work of Crookes and Wallace, among others. He allowed, too graciously, that he did not presume to be able to offer evidence of better quality than that offered by such colleagues, but only recognized on behalf of the Society that "however good some of its evidence may be in quality, we require a great deal more of it." He did not voice his own more pessimistic views, which he had expressed so often in correspondence, but instead urged that

the important point to bear in mind is that every additional witness who, as De Morgan said, has a fair stock of credit to draw upon, is an important gain. Though his credit alone is not likely to suffice for the demand that is made on it, his draft will help. For we must not expect any decisive effect in the direction at which we primarily aim, on the common sense of mankind, from any single piece of evidence, however complete it has been made. Scientific incredulity has been so long in growing, and has so many and so strong roots, that we shall only kill it, if we are able to kill it at all as regards any of those questions, by burying it alive under a heap of facts. We must keep 'pegging away,' as Lincoln said; we must accumulate fact upon fact, and add experiment upon experiment, and, I should say, not wrangle too much with incredulous outsiders about the conclusiveness of any one, but trust to the mass of evidence for conviction. The highest degree of demonstrative force that we can obtain out of any single record of investigation is, of course, limited by the trustworthiness of the investigator. We have done all that we can when the critic has nothing left to allege except that the investigator is in the trick. But when he has nothing else left to allege he will allege that. . . . We must drive the objector into the position of being forced either to admit the phenomena as inexplicable, at least by him, or to accuse the investigators either of lying or cheating or of a blindness or forgetfulness incompatible with any intellectual condition except absolute idiocy. (CWC)

What such statements so nicely illustrate is simply another facet of Sidgwick's obsession with hypocrisy. Throughout his work as a psychical researcher, he was engaged in an investigation that ran parallel to his worried writings about conformity and subscription, as well as his other ethical concerns. So much depended on defining what counted as expert opinion and trustworthy testimony, on formulating a better definition of the "consensus of experts" than he had ever had to do, and on finding a place for the contributions of nonexperts. Just as he would still be struggling with the question of religious hypocrisy in the last decade of his life, so too, in such late pieces as "Disinterested Deception," he would continue to try to come to terms with the general nature of deceit and credibility. As we shall see, many of his claims about the human condition and potential – claims directly related to his concern about practical reason as a chaos – would directly or indirectly reflect his experiences as a psychical researcher. Furthermore, as in the religious case, he would find himself caught in the dilemma of how to deal with the potentially unfortunate social effects of the negative results of his investigations, which, he feared, could very well be used by the more aggressive enemies of religion.

For the present, it is sufficient to simply note one of the more obvious commonalities. Sidgwick went further than any of the other psychical researchers in insisting that once a medium or subject was seriously suspected of fraud, no further use could be made of that person or any evidence gathered therefrom. This was very far from the attitude of most of the psychical researchers, though some of those who came on board in the late seventies, especially Frank Podmore, did develop in due course something of Sidgwick's acute skepticism. It is instructive to compare William James's attitude, when he wrote:

Falsus in uno, falsus in omnibus, once a cheat, always a cheat, such has been the motto of the English psychical researchers in dealing with mediums. I am disposed to think that, as a matter of policy, it has been wise. Tactically it is far better to believe much too little than a little too much; and the exceptional credit attaching to the row of volumes of the SPR's Proceedings, is due to the fixed intention of the editors to proceed very slowly. Better a little belief tied fast, better a small investment *salted down*, than a mass of comparative insecurity.

But, however wise as a policy the SPR's maxim may have been, as a test of truth I believe it to be almost irrelevant. In most things human the accusation of deliberate fraud and falsehood is grossly superficial. Man's character is too sophistically mixed for the alternative of 'honest or dishonest' to be a sharp one. Scientific men themselves will cheat – at public lectures – rather than let experiments obey their well-known tendency towards failure. I have heard of a lecturer on physics, who had taken over the apparatus of the previous incumbent, consulting him about a certain machine intended to show that, however the peripheral parts of it might be agitated, its center of gravity remained immovable. 'It *will* wobble,' he complained. 'Well,' said the predecessor, apologetically, 'to tell the truth, whenever *I* used that machine I found it advisable to *drive a nail* through the center of gravity.[61]

James was also speaking from experience, and went on to relate how he had cheated in such demonstrations.

No doubt James made about as strong a case as anyone could for believing that fraud in one instance does not mean a person is always defrauding, and that mediums might resort to trickery in order to serve what they honestly held to be the truth about psychic phenomena. But he allowed that he looked on nature with "more charitable eyes" than the scientist. For James, there "is a hazy penumbra in us all where lying and delusion meet, where passion rules beliefs as well as conduct, and where the term 'scoundrel' does not clear up everything to the depths as it did for our forefathers." The psychical researchers were, for their part, perhaps not much better than their subjects, though against the charge that "dabbling in such phenomena reduces us to a sort of jelly, disintegrates the critical faculties, liquefies the character, and makes of one a *gobe-mouche* generally," he would respond by

thinking of my friends Frederic Myers and Richard Hodgson. These men lived exclusively for psychical research, and it converted both to spiritism. Hodgson would have been a man among men anywhere; but I doubt whether under any other baptism he would have been that happy, sober and righteous form of energy which his face proclaimed him in his later years, when heart and head alike were wholly satisfied by his occupation. Myers's character also grew stronger in every particular for his devotion to the same inquiries. Brought up on literature and sentiment, something of a courtier, passionate, disdainful, and impatient naturally, he was made over again from the day when he took up psychical research seriously. He became learned in science, circumspect, democratic in sympathy, endlessly patient, and above all, happy.[62]

It is noteworthy that Sidgwick got classed rather differently, given how the "liberal heart which he possessed had to work with an intellect which acted destructively on almost every particular object of belief that was offered to its acceptance."[63] And it was Sidgwick who was at the helm of the British SPR from 1882 to 1885, and again from 1888 to 1992, and he made it clear that he had, if anything, less tolerance for fraud in this department than in religious matters, even if the fraud might be construed as a kind of pious hypocrisy in the service of a good cause. This was not because he was altogether insensitive to human foible and peculiarity. In fact, in some of his earliest examinations of spiritualism, in 1867, he had heard Mazzini tell a story of how in Italy he had once encountered a group of people who were all mysteriously staring up at the sky. When asked what they were doing, one replied "The cross – do you not see it?" Mazzini plainly saw nothing at all, and when he took one of the gazers by the arm and gave him a slight shake, saying "There is no cross at all," the man awoke as if from a dream and admitted that there was nothing there. This story made a lasting impression on Sidgwick, as illustrating the power of group suggestion and the problem of determining the credibility of witnesses.[64] He was forced, against his instincts, to accept the idea that people might deceive on a grand scale for trivial or weird reasons, and that they might, even when testifying in the best of faith, be subject to mistakes and delusions of which they had no inkling and that were largely invisible to an investigator.

What was it, then, about the research on telepathy that so impressed Sidgwick, encouraging him to take on the burdens of leading the SPR? According to Eleanor Sidgwick, this early concentration on telepathy was not

the result of any deliberate plan on the part of the Council. Telepathy forced itself on the Society rather than was sought by it. In far the greater part of the spontaneous cases sent to us which seemed to afford evidence of some supernormal process, the process was apparently telepathic, or at least a telepathic explanation was consistent with the facts as reported; and opportunities of experimenting in telepathy presented themselves more than they have done in later years.[65]

Interestingly, she recalled that the "idea of thought-transference was, as it were, in the air, in this country at least, in the early eighties, because of an amusement called the 'willing game' which was in vogue both in private drawing-rooms and on public platforms."[66] Some action, perhaps fairly complicated, was decided upon, to be performed by a participant who was out of the room. When the person returned, the "willer" would place his or her hands on the "percipient," perhaps on the forehead, and, while avoiding any overt indication of what was being willed, would concentrate on getting the percipient to perform the action – often, it was claimed, with great success, the nature of which stimulated much debate.

But as Eleanor Sidgwick's recollections make clear, it was not the popular parlor games that impressed the SPR, but the work done by Barrett and various others, including the highly regarded Professor Charles Richet in France. At the time that the Society was founded, Barratt had already done work with the Creery family, work that would quickly be further pursued by the SPR's "thought-transference" committee. Many of these investigations are presented in excellent thumbnail descriptions in Appendix A of Gauld's *The Founders of Psychical Research*, which also make it clear just how much the "experiments" had in common with the popular game. As Gauld summarizes it:

The first subjects with whom members of the SPR conducted extended and seemingly successful experiments on thought-transference were the family of the Rev. A. M. Creery, Buxton. The percipients were various of Mr. Creery's five daughters, acting singly. The agents generally acted in a group, and at various times included Mr. Creery himself, members of his family, Barrett, Professor Balfour Stewart (the SPR's second President), Professor Alfred Hopkinson, Gurney, Myers, and other members of the thought-transference committee. The usual procedure was as follows. The daughter who was to act as percipient would leave the room, whilst the group of agents selected a target. This would be written down rather than spoken. The girl would be called in, and the company would concentrate on the target. Targets might be a name chosen at random, an object from the house, a two-figure number, or a playing card out of a full pack.

The girls achieved some startling successes, even when members of their family were not among the agents. They succeeded not merely in their father's home (where the first experiments were carried out in 1881–82), but at Cambridge (July to August 1882) and Dublin (November 1882). For instance at Cambridge they between them guessed correctly 17 out of 216 playing cards; and at Dublin 32 out of 108.[67]

As Gauld observes, however, their "ability began to wane in 1882; and in some further experiments . . . two of them were detected in the use of a rather weak code. Though of course it could have been effective only when one of the sisters was amongst the agents."

Many other experiments also took place during this period, including the "Smith–Blackburn" ones that brought G. A. Smith into contact with Myers and Gurney, but the general format was always quite similar. The main advances concerned an ever-increasing ability to detect subtle codes devised by the participants, guarding against such things as voluntary or involuntary whispering, perhaps observed in the throat and neck rather than the lips. But when Sidgwick himself examined Smith for such maneuvers, he came away quite satisfied that this was not the explanation of Smith's performances.[68] At any rate, the basic parameter of these studies was very largely what it would continue to be, with greater technical and statistical sophistication, throughout the twentieth century: significantly above-chance performances by "sensitives" on guessing the answers to questions generated by some controlled, randomized process.

To be sure, Sidgwick would have his periods of doubt about telepathy, just as he did about everything else. But even at his darkest and most skeptical – for example, during the period 1887–88 – he would allow that he was "not yet hopeless of establishing telepathy." Furthermore, it should be kept in mind that establishing telepathy was something of a mixed blessing, given Sidgwick's main priorities. On the one side, as Eleanor Sidgwick later explained: "Telepathy, if a purely psychical process – and the reasons for thinking it so increase – indicates that the mind can work independently of the body, and thus adds to the probability that it can survive it."[69] Relatedly, as the work on hypnotism revealed, increased "knowledge about the subliminal self, by giving glimpses of extension of human faculty and showing that there is more of us than we are normally aware of, similarly suggests that the limitations imposed by our bodies and our material surroundings are temporary limitations." But, on the other side, telepathy often afforded an alternative explanation for purported communications from beyond the grave – suggesting, for example, that a supposed medium could be getting the communicated information from the minds of living friends and relatives, rather than from the departed. Thus, the research of the Society was complicated by the discounting of "all communications purporting to come from the dead where the matter communicated is known to any living person directly or indirectly in touch with the medium." Unfortunately, as Eleanor Sidgwick went on to note, "matters unknown to any living person can seldom be verified."[70]

Add to this concerns about unconscious thought processes, and things get very tricky indeed:

[T]he mere claim to come from the dead is invalidated, because the subliminal consciousness concerned in automatic writing and trance speaking has been found liable to claim more knowledge and power than it possesses, to say things which are not true, and to offer false excuses when the untruth is discovered. This subliminal trickiness may be found in the case of persons who in their normal life are upright and honourable; – just as in dreams we may behave in a way that would shock us in our waking life. Another embarrassing circumstance from the evidential point of view is that the subliminal memory does not coincide with the supraliminal, and can draw upon a store not accessible to the normal consciousness. And further, things may be subliminally taken note of, which do not enter, or scarcely enter the normal consciousness at all.[71]

Thus, telepathy often yielded the most parsimonious account of paranormal happenings. Why, for example, assume the reality of ghosts, when in so many cases supposed apparitions could be accounted for as telepathic communications from the dying person? This approach was seemingly supported by the comparative infrequency, according to the SPR, of well-evidenced postmortem apparitions. And who could tell what the unconscious self, partly unveiled in hypnosis, might be capable of, by way of sending and receiving such communications?

One might well suggest, therefore, that with their work in the Society, the Sidgwicks ended up engaged in their most tormented soul searching of all, with the old worries about selfishness and sinfulness transmuted into anxieties about the tricky and dangerous subliminal self and the vagaries of its telepathic doings. Much of the work that would follow – "Phantasms of the Dead," *Phantasms of the Living*, and the *Census of Hallucinations*, for example – would be aimed at sorting out these difficulties, differentiating thought transferences from apparitions and coming to terms with the question of whether claims concerning these really were inexplicable statistically.

But before surveying these monumental productions of the Sidgwick Group, there is another tribute to be paid to their negative and critical accomplishments. For early on in the SPR's existence, a powerful alternative to spiritualism presented itself to them as the chief aspirant to becoming the religion of the New Age. Madame Blavatsky came to Cambridge.

IV. Koot Hoomi on *The Methods of Ethics*

We all went to a Theosophic lunch with Myers. Madame de Novikoff was there; certainly she has social gifts, but she does not interest me. Our favourable impression of Mme. B[lavatsky] was sustained; if personal sensibilities can be trusted, she is a genuine being, with a vigorous nature intellectual as well as emotional, and a real desire for the good of mankind. This impression is all the more noteworthy as she is externally unattractive – with her flounces full of cigarette ashes – and not prepossessing in manner. Certainly we like her, both Nora and I. If she is a humbug, she is a consummate one: as her remarks have the air not only of spontaneity and randomness but sometimes of an amusing indiscretion. Thus in the midst of an account of the Mahatmas in Tibet, intended to give us an elevated view of these personages, she blurted out her candid impression that the chief Mahatma of all was the most utter dried-up old mummy that she ever saw. She also let us behind the scenes of all the Transcendental Council. It appears that the desire to enlighten us Westerns is only felt by a small minority of the Mahatmas, who are Hindoo: the rest, Tibetans, are averse to it: and it would not be permitted, only Koot Hoomi, the youngest and most energetic of the Hindoo minority, is a favourite of the old mummy, who is disposed to let him do what he likes. When the mummy withdraws entirely from earth, as he will do shortly, he wants Koot to succeed him: but Mme B. thinks he won't manage this, and that a Thibetan will succeed who will inexorably close the door of enlightenment.

Sidgwick, journal entry for August 10, 1884 (CWC)

The Theosophical Society was founded in New York in 1875 by Madame Helena Petrovna Blavatsky and Colonel Henry Steel Olcott (the former a Russian, the latter an American), but it quickly became an international force, with offices in England, India, France, and other countries. In so many ways, it was the natural product of the period that, in America and England especially, spawned spiritualism and a fascination with things occult and mystical. The Rosicrucians, the Hermeticists, the reincarnationists, followers of Aleister Crowley and Samuel Liddell – all helped to provide a context in which Theosophy might find an eager audience. The esoteric wisdom of the mysterious East had a very big and very credulous market. Materialism and scientism had produced a mystical and occultist reaction – a reaction that often went far beyond the séancing of the spiritualists, many of whom were apt to decry the exclusivity and cultlike practices of occultists.[72]

Theosophists, of course, did seek to capture much of the same audience as the spiritualists, even if they did come to alienate many of them in the process. Their creed was an eclectic soup of esotericism. As Oppenheim describes it:

Blavatsky herself stressed the roots of her teaching in the venerable texts of the Far East, but the very term 'theosophy' conjured up a rich variety of associations with the cabalist, neo-Platonic, and Hermetic strands in western philosophic and religious thought. Meaning 'divine wisdom,' or 'wisdom of the gods,' theosophy was a familiar term in the vocabulary of the occult long before Madame Blavatsky stamped it with the mark of her own impressive personality. Belief in the existence of specially initiated adepts, or of secret documents that held, in coded signs and symbols, the key to understanding nature's deepest enigmas, had haunted the fringes of European thought for centuries, tantalizing susceptible minds with the possibility of attaining truly godlike power over the natural world. C. C. Massey dubbed the Jewish cabala 'a system of theosophy,' while Hargrave Jennings used the label 'theosophists' to describe the Paracelsists of the sixteenth and seventeenth centuries. The links between the new, Blavatsky brand of Theosophy and the older tradition related to Hermetic teaching were nicely encapsulated in Annie Besant's claim to have been none other than Giordano Bruno himself in a previous incarnation.[73]

Different planes of existence, astral and ethereal bodies, the miraculous time-and-space-defying feats of yogis and more "highly evolved" beings – all were displayed with a flourish in Blavatsky's first major esoteric text, *Isis Unveiled* (1877). She was, she claimed, receiving instruction in ancient wisdom from the mahatmas of Tibet and India, though more critical eyes had trouble discerning in her work anything more than a cheap pilfering of various Hindu and Buddhist sources.[74] Although it would be nice to be able to read such cultural developments as a meaningful reaction against Western rationalism and orientalism, the Theosophists in the end did more to demean multicultural understanding than to advance it, though the investigation of them by the SPR did do much to shape the way the Sidgwick Group thought about anthropology and history. As Joy Dixon has observed, Theosophy was "a kind of middle-brow orientalism (in Edward Said's sense), which reinscribed divisions between eastern mysticism and western science."[75]

What made Theosophy so provocative to all sides involved in the SPR was the way in which it objected to so much of the spiritualist endeavor. That is, spiritualism was

> predicated on the proposition that, after death, a person's spirit could remain in close touch with the living and could relay messages to them with the help of a medium. Theosophical denial of this principle, and denunciation of séance practices, seemed to many an angered spiritualist an attempt to cut the very heart out of their faith. But Theosophists had learned from Madame Blavatsky the dangers that followed all attempts to commune with spirits around the séance table.[76]

After all, after death one was supposed to evolve and reincarnate; the astral plane was populated by all sorts of unsavory spooks and elementals, primitive and sometimes malicious forces that might pretend to be the dear departed, but were not. Bringing such things into contact with the living was risky and, at any rate, beside the point, as far as one's spiritual progress was concerned. One's aim should rather be to advance one's spiritual evolution, to cultivate the higher elements in one's being over the lower, animal elements. Resort to mediums – or to priests, for that matter – was a diversion from communing with one's higher self, which was immortal and evolving according to karmic laws. And of course, according to the Theosophical hard sell, this was all the more urgent because the mahatmas might soon decide to stop wasting their efforts on Westerners. This was, to mix a metaphor, a window of opportunity on the doors of perception.

Thus, the Theosophists and spiritualists really were at odds over how to deal with the spirit world, much as they agreed that there was such a world and that the material universe was only a form of delusion imprisoning lower beings. The Theosophists offered up a much more ambitious rendering of the perennial philosophy, claiming that the basic tenets of their wisdom formed the root of all the great world religions; this belief, in good Idealist fashion, allowed them to exercise much charity in interpretation, allowing that all worldviews had some piece of the truth. This rather Mauricean theme, coupled with the elite and esoteric mode of inquiry that the Theosophists represented, would have been a natural draw for old Apostles like Sidgwick. But it was scarcely apt to appeal to orthodox believers, since it granted no special place to any one religion, though Buddha did tend to be the first among equals. And the Theosophical belief in reincarnation was quite alien to most spiritualist and Judeo-Christian audiences, who tended to regard this as a puzzling complication of the already much-too-tricky problem of personal identity.

In England, the Theosophists had quickly established friendly relations with many members of the SPR, including Myers, and their representatives had been invited to attend the initial meetings of the Society. When Madame Blavatsky came to England for an extended stay, in 1884, the Society sent a delegation to interview her in London, and followed this up with an invitation to come to Cambridge for more extensive exchanges. The SPR was especially interested in her and her followers because, despite the Theosophical disclaimers about séances, etc., Blavatsky claimed to have been a successful medium, in some sense, and much of the attractive force of her new religion came from claims that she could perform paranormal feats. Thus, it was widely reported that mysterious letters from her mahatmas would materialize out of thin air, dropping from the ceiling. Such reports ensured that when Madame, the colonel, and their collaborator Mohini held a public reception in Oscar Browning's rooms, the crowd was overflowing.

The Sidgwicks were undeniably impressed – at one point in his journal, Sidgwick refers to Blavatsky as a "Great Woman." As was so often the case, their initially favorable impression had a great deal to do with what they took to be the personal credibility of the people involved and the absence of any obvious motive to deceive. Thus, Sidgwick would write to James Bryce, in May of 1884:

I did not answer your question about Olcott as I was really in doubt what to say. He has been here and I am favourably impressed with him as regards honesty and sincerity: but he has no experiences to relate which are conclusive on the mere supposition that he is honest: it is possible to suppose that he has been taken in – only to take him would require an elaborate plot in which persons would be involved who appear to have no more motive for trickery than the twelve apostles in Paley's evidences: one at least – as we are credibly informed – has sacrificed wealth and position to follow after the Masters of Theosophy. (CWC)[77]

But by this time, suspicions were gathering about Madame Blavatsky, and Sidgwick reports that "what I hear is rather too mixed: in at least one case there is well-grounded suspicion of her trickery – though she again has no obvious motive as she is giving money to the cause." Indeed, Sidgwick's confidence in his estimate of people and their motives was to be very quickly and very badly shaken. In November of 1884, he records in his journal how

Psychical Research is growing dark & difficult: I am shaken in my view of telepathic evidence by the breakdown of Sir E. Hornby's narrative in the XIXth Century. Here is a man tells an elaborate story of what happened to him less than ten years ago, and his wife (who was an actor in the drama) confirms it, and her mother bears witness that the wife told her next morning: and yet the story is altogether inaccurate in fundamental points – it is indeed difficult to understand how any of it can be true. And yet Gurney who has been to see them says that he and his wife are thoroughly good witnesses, and clearly believe every word they say! This is much worse for us than if they were bad witnesses, as tending more to lower one's general confidence in human testimony. This one case seems to me to make a great hole in our evidence. (CWC)

Worse was to come. The SPR appointed a young Australian member, Richard Hodgson, to travel to the Theosophical headquarters in Madras, India, in order to do a thorough investigation of the purported Theosophical marvels, and when he returned to England, in April of 1885, his report was utterly damning.

It would have been difficult for Sidgwick to ignore Hodgson's work even if he had wanted to, since Hodgson had in 1881 taken an honors degree in the moral sciences from Cambridge, and Sidgwick himself had encouraged (and paid for) him to abandon his post as university extension lecturer in order to go off to investigate Theosophy. Eventually Hodgson would become a leader of the American SPR and a full-time psychical researcher, for which his work on Theosophy proved to be sobering training. While in India, he had managed to recruit a couple, the Coulombs, who were disgruntled former assistants to Madame Blavatsky and who had in their possession various letters from the founder detailing just how to perform the "marvels" under investigation. Thus, the letters-out-of-thin-air stunt was revealed as requiring no more explanation than a porous ceiling and a long piece of thread with a confederate on the other end of it, safely out of view. The mahatmas were revealed as Blavatsky's own fictions, whose communications had been lifted out of various obvious sources. And Hodgson even suspected that Blavatsky was in the pay of the Russians, who wanted her to foment discontent in India.

As Oppenheim shows, the report did not move the true believers:

They accused Hodgson of undertaking his Indian inquiries, not in a mood of impartial research, but as prosecutor, judge, and jury all at once. The integrity of the Coulombs was, with justice, assailed, and Blavatsky complained that she had never even been shown the incriminating letters which, she insisted were largely fabrication. Sinnett accused the SPR of pandering to public opinion in its denigration of Theosophy and triumphantly concluded that Hodgson's logic served no purpose, because Blavatsky's complex character was not explicable 'by any commonplace process of reasoning.'[78]

But the Sidgwick Group took this sobering lesson to heart. Some time later, Myers, in the Introduction to *Phantasms of the Living*, would note the importance of this lesson in cultural anthropology:

Acting through Mr. Hodgson . . . a committee of the Society for Psychical Research has investigated the claim of the so-called 'Theosophy,' of which Madame Blavatsky was the prophetess, to be an incipient world-religion, corroborated by miraculous, or at least supernormal, phenomena, – and has arrived at the conclusion that it is merely a *réchauffé* of ancient philosophies, decked in novel language, and supported by ingenious fraud. Had this fraud not been detected and exposed, and had the system of belief supported thereon thriven and spread, we should have witnessed what the sceptic might have cited as a typical case of the origin of religions.[79]

Sidgwick himself would later contribute a prefatory note to another exposé of Theosophy, Solovyoff's *A Modern Priestess of Isis* (1895), in which he would strike a similar note:

[S]uch English readers as were likely to be interested in learning anything more about Madame Blavatsky would not so much desire additional proof that she was a charlatan – a question already judged and decided – but rather some explanation of the remarkable success of her imposture; and Mr. Solovyoff's vivid description of the mingled qualities of the woman's nature – her supple craft and reckless audacity, her intellectual vigour and elastic vitality, her genuine *bonhomie*, affectionateness and (on occasion) persuasive pathos – afforded an important element of the required explanation, such as probably no one but a compatriot could have supplied. Whether the Theosophical Society is likely to last much longer, I am not in a position to say; but even if it were to expire next year, its twenty years' existence would be a phenomenon of some interest for the historian of European society in the nineteenth century.[80]

Especially illuminating, on this score, is the way in which the experience with the Theosophists led the Sidgwick Group to think about the nature of evidence and credibility. In a draft of a letter to Lord Acton that Myers apparently wrote in 1892, he explained the nature of the criteria used by the Society to determine untrustworthy evidence. In addition to evidence that was "other than first-hand," or that involved "persons apparently hoping to receive therefrom money, fame, or reverence," or that was not written down for more than ten years after the fact, or that came from informants about which nothing more could be determined, there was: "All evidence depending wholly on the testimony of (1) uneducated persons, (2) persons with a strong bias in favour of the supernatural, (3) Asiatics, (4) the lower races, (5) children." Of this, he explains that the "exclusion of *Asiatics*, & the addition of the expectation of *reverence* to the causes of suspicion, were forced upon us by Mr. Hodgson's exposure of Mme. Blavatsky' frauds, & of the gross credulity of some even able & educated Hindoos. Mme. Blavatsky (one may say) was within an ace of founding a world-religion merely to amuse herself & to be admired."[81]

Now, lamentably, Myers is presumably speaking for the Sidgwick Group, at the very least. Certainly Sidgwick, in a variety of writings, had consistently urged the "Society to accumulate testimony, to overcome opposition by the gradual accession of witnesses of good intelligence and character." In his exchange with C. C. Massey, Sidgwick had explained that he wanted "evidence obtained in private circles of relatives or friends, where no professional medium was employed," and that he certainly wanted to exclude consideration of mediums "whose trickery was proved and admitted."[82] As always, he was uniquely impressed with the testimony that emerged in small societies of close friends. The sweeping bigotry of Myers's statement, with its wholesale discounting of the experiences of the "uneducated," the "lower races" and "Asiatics," does not quite seem to capture Sidgwick's views, at least insofar as there is any extensive record of them. But, as later chapters will show, Sidgwick did harbor such prejudices, at least in a weaker form, which may explain why he did not actively protest Myers's policy. And surely, if this was the policy of the Sidgwick Group, it would suggest that his notions of credibility and expertise could be appropriately described as part of a "Government House" utilitarianism, in which the "lower" classes and "lower" races are put on a level with children. After all, Sir E. Hornby apparently did not fit the above categories, yet there was no move to exclude the testimony of knights. Was this the type of thinking that lay behind, for example, his views on the value of colonization?

This is a matter of vital importance. But a further discussion of it must await a fuller treatment of the other dimensions of psychical research and politics, and of the further shocks that Sidgwick's notions of "good intelligence and character" were to be dealt. As the following chapters will show, Sidgwick's notions of race and class ended up being rather worse, and certainly no better, than J. S. Mill's. The best one can say is that he did a great deal to defend some of the accomplishments of other historical civilizations, that he thought nurture far more important than nature in determining human differences, and that he was mainly impressed by European achievements in science and constitutional government, while always remaining ready to remind the reader of the evils of religious bigotry and slavery that Western civilization had also produced. On the whole, his writings reveal someone who, like Mill, had a decided Eurocentric bias in his understanding of "civilized" education, but who was also potentially receptive to the claims of the other world historical civilizations.[83] In these ways, at least, his skepticism served him well, though not well enough.

For he was not immune to the pervasive and offensive – often offensively casual – racism of his environment, the prejudice that far too few of his Cambridge colleagues even thought to question. He entertained, as serious hypotheses, the views of such figures as Charles Henry Pearson about the "yellow peril," and he occasionally used the (generic) derogatory term "nigger" in his correspondence. One cannot confront this side of Sidgwick without worrying deeply about just how limited his notions of "educated common sense" and social verification might have been, and about whether Theosophy – which he certainly hoped would turn out to be true – might have resonated with him in part precisely because of its elitism and orientalism. And as Dixon has noted, Theosophy was engaged in a very paradoxical effort: "to proclaim publicly occult or esoteric truths, truths that by definition are secret, hidden, and known only to the initiated."[84] This was a paradox after his own Apostolic heart.

V. Their Finest Hour

When I was young and "erotion" (cf. Clough) I used to repeat to myself
the end of Iphigenia's prayer (Goethe, favourite play of mine) for wholesome
warning –

> Ye Gods, . . .
> in calm repose,
> Ye listen to our prayer, that childishly
> Beseeches you to hasten, but your hand
> Ne'er breaks unripe the golden fruits of heaven.
> And woe to him who with impatient grasp
> Profanely plucks and eats unto his death
> A bitter food.
>> Sidgwick to Myers, May or June 1871[85]

So far, one might think that the Sidgwick Group, for all its hopefulness
about personal survival of death and gullibility about prima facie evidence
calling for investigation, partly redeemed itself through its critical debunking of spiritualists and Theosophists, and by its fashioning of such
tactics as the deployment of conjurers to expose conjuring as just that
and nothing more. Their fascination with hypnotism turned out to be
productive and indeed the most enduring of their positive contributions,
and no doubt there are some who would make a similar claim on behalf
of their work on telepathy. If their research reflected various forms of
prejudice and bigotry, that, given their time and place, is unfortunately
to be expected. They were part of the culture of imperialism, and their
images of truth, expertise, evidence, progress, and so on could not help
but reflect and project this to varying degrees. It was, they really felt, the
solid English who were going to discover the "secret of the Universe."
This would, of course, be altogether fitting in their eyes, given that it was
the solid English who largely ruled the Universe. The opacity of the other
world was related to the opacity of other regions of this world; both called
for penetration through sympathetic unity. How else could consensus and
reconciliation come to pass?

One thing that can be safely said is that the SPR followed Sidgwick's
command to pile testimony on top of testimony, and it is worth considering
in greater detail just what the nature of that testimony ended up being,
since it does not seem to comport with Myers's strictures.

For most of the 1880s, the Sidgwick Group was engaged in compiling the material that would go into Eleanor Sidgwick's "Phantasms of the Dead" and the remarkable joint production of Myers, Gurney, and Podmore, *Phantasms of the Living*. In helping with the former, Henry had gone out to interview some 300 persons who had contributed ghost stories, but he had concluded that not more than twenty or thirty were any good, and that "[i]t looks as if there was *some* cause for persons experiencing independently in certain houses similar hallucinations. But we are not at present inclined to back ghosts against the field as *the* cause."[86]

Phantasms of the Living was in another category, with its massive array of case studies selected to prove the reality of telepathy, and to demonstrate that "phantasms (impressions, voices, or figures) of persons undergoing some crisis, – especially death, – are perceived by their friends and relatives with a frequency which mere chance cannot explain."[87] C. D. Broad insisted that this "is undoubtedly an epoch-making work, in the strict sense that it laid the foundations of a new subject and still remains a classic indispensable to all students in its own field."[88] Despite the official authorship, the Sidgwicks were very much involved in the production, and Eleanor would later produce an updated (and abridged) version of the study.

As Myers explained the title:

[U]nder our heading of 'Phantasms of the Living,' we propose, in fact, to deal with all classes of cases where there is reason to suppose that the mind of one human being has affected the mind of another, without speech uttered, or word written, or sign made; – has affected it, that is to say, by other means than through the recognised channels of sense.

To such transmissions of thoughts or feelings we have elsewhere given the name of *telepathy*; and the records of an experimental proof of the reality of telepathy will form a part of the present work. But, for reasons which will be made manifest as we proceed, we have included among telepathic phenomena a vast class of cases which seem at first sight to involve something widely different from a mere transference of thought.

I refer to *apparitions*; excluding, indeed, the alleged apparitions of the *dead*, but including the apparitions of all persons who are still living, as we know life, though they may be on the very brink and border of physical dissolution. And these apparitions, as will be seen, are themselves extremely various in character; including not visual phenomena alone, but auditory, tactile, or even purely ideational and emotional impressions. All these we have included under the term *phantasm*; a word which, though etymologically a mere variant of *phantom*, has been less often used, and has not become so closely identified with *visual* impressions alone.[89]

After reviewing various suggestions about how such investigations relate to anthropology and history (which include the remarks on Theosophy), Myers goes on to pose "a still larger and graver question": "What (it is naturally asked) is the relation of our study – not to eccentric or outlying forms of relgious creed – but to central and vital conceptions; and especially to that main system of belief to which in English-speaking countries the name of *religion* is by popular usage almost confined?"[90] He notes that the members of the SPR have heretofore "studiously refrained from entering on this important question," and this because they "wished to avoid even the semblance of attracting the public to our researches by any allurement which lay outside the scientific field," since they "could not take for granted" that their inquiries would "make for the spiritual view of things, that they would tend to establish even the independent existence, still less the immortality, of the soul." They held it to be essential to "maintain a neutral and expectant attitude," conducting their "inquiries in the 'dry light' of a dispassionate search for truth."[91]

This is still their position, Myers explains, and their book does not try to deal with all "the most exciting and popular topics which are included in our Society's general scheme." Still, even if the "master-problem of human life" may require more deliberate approaches, psychical research is now no longer a matter of mere anticipation, but can claim "a certain amount of actual achievement." Thus,

We hold that we have proved by direct experiment, and corroborated by the narratives contained in this book, the possibility of communications between two minds, inexplicable by any recognised physical laws, but capable (under certain rare spontaneous conditions) of taking place when the persons concerned are at an indefinite distance from each other. And we claim further that by investigations of the higher phenomena of mesmerism, and of the automatic action of the mind, we have confirmed and expanded this view in various directions, and attained a standing-point from which certain even stranger alleged phenomena begin to assume an intelligible aspect, and to suggest further discoveries to come.

Thus far the authors of this book, and also the main group of their fellow-workers, are substantially agreed.[92]

Beyond this, Myers allows, more caution must be exercised in claiming any sort of consensus. But for all that, he does carry on, at length, in a quite positive way, about

how much support the preliminary theses of religion may acquire from an assured conviction that the human mind is at least *capable* of receiving supernormal influences, – is not closed, by its very structure, as the Materialists would tell us, to any 'inbreathings of the spirit' which do not appeal to outward eye or ear. And somewhat similar is the added reality which the discovery of telepathy gives to the higher flights, the subtler shades, of mere earthly emotion.[93]

In brief, the psychical "element in man" must, Myers claims, "henceforth almost inevitably be conceived as having relations which cannot be expressed in terms of matter."[94] But the other side of this argument is, obviously, that the case for religion and the case for psychical research were being brought into intimate connection in public.

This was the theme to which Myers would continue to warm, as he grew ever more convinced that

Science is now succeeding in penetrating certain cosmical facts which she has not reached till now. The first, of course, is the fact of man's survival of death. The second is the registration in the Universe of every past scene and thought. This I hold to be indicated by the observed facts of clairvoyance and retro-cognition; and to be in itself probable as a mere extension of telepathy, which, when acting unrestrictedly, may render it impossible for us to appear as other than we are. And upon this the rule of like to like seems to follow; our true affinities must determine our companionships in a spiritual world.[95]

For Myers was personally persuaded that there was no longer any reason to deny that the investigations into telepathy had led on to a vindication of his cosmic faith in the "other world" – or rather, the "friendly universe." And the "subliminal uprushes" of genius and mutual recognitions of sensitive seekers carried for him a cosmic importance, as though the Apostolic brotherhood had been written into the structure of the universe.

This evidently worried Sidgwick a good deal. In a singularly revealing journal entry, he explains:

The Book – *Phantasms of the Living* – is getting on. Yesterday we heard Myers read the first half of his introduction. I am rather troubled about the part of it which relates to religion. M. says roundly to the Theologian, 'If the results of our investigation are rejected, they must inevitably carry your miracles along with them.' This is, I doubt not, true, but is it wise to say it? Also it is only true as regards the *ultimate* effect. I do not doubt that if we ultimately reach a negative conclusion, this inquiry of ours will *in time* be regarded by sceptics as supplying the last element of proof necessary to complete the case against Christianity and other historic religions; but for many generations – perhaps many centuries – the only difference will be that Christianity, Mohammedanism, etc., will have to *support* their miracles instead of being supported by them; and the historic roots of these great institutions are surely quite strong enough to enable them to do this for an indefinite period – in fact until sociology has been really constructed, and the scientist steps into the place of the priest. (M 415)[96]

But he would not remain even this sanguine for long, and the *Phantasms* volume would actually trouble him a great deal. He had, in fact, been working rather hard at getting Myers to tone down his enthusiasms. In a journal passage from January 4, 1885 – one excised from the *Memoir* – he recorded for Symonds's benefit how he

Had rather an agitating discussion at Massey's about the book on 'Phantasms of the Living'. Hitherto we have agreed that Myers & Gurney are to write it jointly: but I have come to the conclusion that all our appearances in print ought to be conducted on the principle of individualising responsibility. In this obscure and treacherous region, girt about with foes watching eagerly for some bad blunder, it is needlessly increasing our risks to run the danger of *two* reputations being exploded by one blunder: it is two heads on one neck: "hoc Ithacus velit." Let us have the freest and fullest mutual criticism – so that if possible each of us may feel himself *morally* responsible for our friends' blunders – but let the responsibility *before the world* be always to *one*, that we may sell our reputations as dearly as possible.

I urged this view, but I did not prevail: it was a delicate matter as I was palpably aiming at ousting F. M. and leaving E. G. as sole author: estimating the superior trustworthiness of the latter in scientific reasoning as more important than his literary inferiority. I could see M. was annoyed; but he bore it admirably. Ultimately we compromised thus: M. to write a long introduction and G. the body of the book. (CWC)

Thus, as this exceptionally candid and accurate assessment reveals, Sidgwick was indirectly responsible for Myers's Introduction, though he apparently would rather have kept Myers out of the volume altogether. Myers was altogether too ready to believe, and in highlighting the religious significance of psychical research in the way that he did, he gambled too much, too precipitously. For what if the critics could make a strong counterattack? Gurney's handling of the volume was, as Sidgwick predicted, much more restrained, and often struck a note quite different from Myers's. Interestingly, Gurney concluded that

though 'psychical research' is certain in time to surmount ridicule and prejudice, and to clear for itself a firm path between easy credulity on the one side and easy incredulity on the other, the rate of its advance must depend on the amount of sympathy and support that it can command from the general mass of educated men and women. In no department should the democratic spirit of modern science find so free a scope: it is for the public here to be, not – as in anthropological researches – the passive material of investigation, but the active participators in it. We acknowledge with warm gratitude the amount of patient assistance that we have received – how patient and forbearing in many instances, none can judge who have not tried, as private individuals, to conduct a system of strict cross-examination on a wide scale. But unless this assistance is largely supplemented, our undertaking can scarcely hold its ground. . . . And here is the practically interesting point; for, till the general fact is universally admitted, the several items of proof must ever tend to lose their effect as they recede further into the past. This peculiarity of the subject cannot be gainsaid, and must be boldly faced. For aught I can tell, the hundreds of instances may have to be made thousands.[97]

This conclusion, coming at the end of two fat volumes carefully and analytically reporting some 702 instances of supposed telepathic happenings of every conceivable stripe, no doubt reflected the kind of cautious enjoining of "more research" that Sidgwick, at least, thought most appropriate. Surely, as Gauld observes, Gurney had "found his *métier*" – he had written up most of the cases, included a wealth of additional material on the canons of evidence, and, during this same period, had also been beavering away at hypnosis and carrying out his duties as the SPR's honorary secretary and editor.

As Gauld nicely summarizes it, the "central thesis" of *Phantasms* is this:

[C]risis apparitions [those occurring within twelve hours, either way, of the death of the supposed agent] . . . are best interpreted as *hallucinations* generated in the percipient by the receipt of a *telepathic* 'message' from the dying agent. That ghosts are *hallucinatory* is suggested by their complete or almost complete failure to leave any physical traces behind them, and by the fact that they occasionally behave in ways impossible to physical objects. . . . That crisis apparitions are caused by the receipt of a telepathic 'message' from the dying person is strongly suggested by the fact that they can be placed at the end of an unbroken series of cases, a series of which cases of experimental and spontaneous telepathy form the early and middle terms. First of all come the instances of experimental telepathy in which, let us say, a percipient in one place is able to reproduce a drawing held before the eyes of an agent in another place. Then come cases of spontaneous telepathy, which most commonly occur when the agent is undergoing some shock or strong emotion; thus a lady lying in bed early one morning felt a pain in her mouth at the moment when her husband was struck painfully in the mouth by the tiller of his yacht. Next we have more complex cases of spontaneous telepathy, where the percipient's experience is not, so to speak, a reproduction of that of the agent, but is rather *founded* upon it, the details coming from the percipient's mind. An example would perhaps be that of 'arrival' cases, in which a person about to arrive at a given spot is actually seen there in advance of his arrival by someone not expecting him; here what the percipient sees – the agent as he appears to people other than himself – is most unlikely to correspond closely with what is in the agent's mind, so that the *details* of the picture must presumably be in some way supplied by the percipient. Finally come crisis apparitions themselves, in which the details of the phantom, which often behaves normally and is normally clad, would seem necessarily to have come from the percipient's mind; for the agent may be at the bottom of the sea, or lying in night clothes upon his death-bed.[98]

The care and thoroughness of the detailing of these cases has certainly impressed most everyone subsequently involved in psychical research. As Gauld suggests, to pass "from even the ablest of previous works to *Phantasms of the Living* is like passing from a mediaeval bestiary or herbal to Linnaeus' *Systema Natura*."[99] But the book did have some formidable early critics, including C. S. Peirce, who argued that it did not make a strong enough case that these incidents were not simply chance occurrences. The Sidgwick Group had certainly recognized that they needed to make some sort of case against the alternative theory of chance coincidence, and that they needed "to try to estimate the proportion of the population which has the experience of seeing a recognised apparition and the proportion of these cases in which the apparition was veridical." Gurney himself had attempted something of a census, receiving answers from approximately 5,700 persons about their experiences with apparitions, but this was not deemed sufficient, even by the psychical researchers. Hence, his concluding plea for greater public involvement in this form of research must be read as an altogether serious effort at improving his sampling techniques and establishing some more reliable baseline for determining the frequency of such apparitions.

Gurney had made various approaches to this in *Phantasms*, and it was manifestly the type of work that he wanted to carry on. His untimely death, on June 25, 1888, was of course a terrible blow to these efforts. Sidgwick wrote to his widow on behalf of the SPR that

nothing that can be said in public will really express our sense of loss. . . . We are determined that the work shall be carried through to whatever result the laws of the Universe destine for it; we feel it to be now not only a duty owed to humanity, but also to the memory of our friend and colleague, that the results of our previous labour should not fail from any faint-heartedness. (M 493)

As recorded earlier, he was "not yet hopeless of establishing telepathy" and was now "specially anxious, for Edmund Gurney's sake, that his six years' labour should not be lost" (M 494–95).

It was thus partly as a tribute to Gurney that the Sidgwick Group decided on their next big project: the *Census of Hallucinations*. This ambitious project was directly aimed at supplying the evidence that Gurney had so wanted concerning the statistical occurrence of apparitions. The work began in April of 1889 and carried on, through a series of publications and partly under the auspices of the International Congress of Experimental Psychology, until the final massive report appeared in 1894, as Volume X of the *Proceedings*, written mostly by Eleanor Sidgwick and Alice Johnson. Although the investigators had set out to collect some 50,000 answers, this turned out to be a bit impractical, and they had in the end to content themselves with some 17,000 answers. As Broad summarizes the conclusion:

About one visual hallucination in *sixty-three* occurs within a period of twenty-four hours round about the death of the person whose apparition has been 'seen'. If such death-coincidences were purely fortuitous concurrences of causally independent events the proportion would be about one in *nineteen thousand*. There is a most elaborate and careful discussion of the fallacies to which such statistics are liable, and a very clear and detailed statement of the precautions which the committee took to avoid them. . . . [This is] a uniquely and meticulously careful contribution to an important branch of their subject.[100]

According to Eleanor Sidgwick, the work "fully confirmed" the claim of *Phantasms*: "that between deaths and apparitions of the dying person a connection exits which is not due to chance alone."[101] Indeed, this was the conclusion endorsed by the entire Sidgwick Group.

It should be stressed, however, that this piling on of case after case does not fully do justice to the sense that the Sidgwick Group had that there was clearly something to telepathy. In a letter to William James, Gurney had explained:

I cannot describe to you the effect on my own mind which my hundreds of personal interviews have had. It has only been in a very small number of cases ... that a case which seemed genuine and sound on paper has not been *strengthened* by the impression (& often by the details) which conversation and careful cross-questioning added. ... The viva voce account has consistently struck me as just what you or I might give of a singular experience, which *did happen*, but which was wholly isolated & inexplicable.[102]

Such sentiments were often echoed by Sidgwick – for example, when he confessed to the SPR that "part of my grounds for believing in telepathy, depending, as it does, on personal knowledge, cannot be communicated except in a weakened form to the ordinary reader of the printed statements which represent the evidence that has convinced me."[103] Hence, his abiding conviction that he had to put his character on the line in this form of research, just as he had had to do on all those Apostolic Saturday evenings.[104] Such conclusions about the nature of personal knowledge ought to be kept in mind when considering Sidgwick's epistemology and his criticisms of empiricism, idealism, etc. – recall the very personal nature of his rejoinder to Gizycki, his flat confession that he found the rejection of egoism "impossible." Moreover, his sense of the possibilities of sympathetic unity, a true mingling of minds, must be understood as in part involving this quite literal way of achieving it, which was of course the work of special, sensitive minds.

Still, whatever sense of the uncanny was shared by Gurney and Sidgwick, their more straightforward similarities had to do with the critical faculties that they brought to bear on their work. Sidgwick's disparagement of his own abilities, in comparison to Eleanor's quite pronounced scientific abilities, has become rather famous:

[I]n Psychical Research the only faculty that I seem able to exercise is the judicial; I feel equal to classifiying and to some extent weighing the evidence – so far as it depends on general considerations – but I do not feel the least gift for making a legitimate hypothesis as to the causes of the phenomena, and I am too unobservant and unimaginative about physical events generally to be at all good at evaluating particular bits of evidence. For to tell whether a 'psychical' experiment or narrative is good or not evidentially requires one to imagine with adequate accuracy and exhaustiveness the various possibilities of 'natural' causation of the phenomenon, and judge the degree of improbability of each. Nora is much better at all this than I am: and I mean to give her the work to do, on this ground, so far as she will take it. (M 388)

As for Sidgwick, had he not felt duty-bound to be pursuing psychical research, he would, circa the mid-eighties, have preferred to give himself over to the luxury of working on "the evolution of political ideas," since his mind was

adapted for seeing things – relations – for myself in the history of Thought: when I read what other people say, I seem to see that they have not got it quite right; and then, after an effort, what seems to be the truth comes to me. This is as near the sense of original production as I ever get, and only intellectual work that gives me this experience really takes hold on me. (M 387)

This is an intriguing gendering, given how often the Victorians are presented as linking scientific rationality to manliness and character, and how often the various forms of spiritualism are interpreted as historical constructions of the private and feminine. But spiritualism was in fact an arena for the contestation of gender roles, as the career of the redoubtable Madame Blavatsky might suggest.[105]

At any rate, Sidgwick did devote an enormous amount of time to exercising his judicial faculties on the case for psychical phenomena, and *Phantasms* and the *Census* were very obviously deeply indebted to him for their more sensible aspects. After all, the work was being subjected to different interpretations. Myers was clearly not as circumspect in interpreting the telepathy explanation as Gurney or Sidgwick, favoring instead the possibility that clairvoyance might be invoked to explain various cases, and that there was somehow an actual externalization or materialization of the dying person's conception of himself. Against this, Gurney wrote to James that Myers's argument was "a hopeless attempt to present a frankly material view of ghosts with elimination of the material element," against which he had made decisive objections.[106]

Later chapters will further consider just how Myers continued to argue for ghosts, communications from the other world, and so on, and for their religious significance. In the 1890s, psychical research took another turn, and work on the so-called cross-correspondence cases provided Myers with the kind of material on which he believed he could build a case. At this point, however, what calls for emphasis is the way in which the Sidgwick Group turned out to be rather divided internally, what with the more orthodox Balfour element and the more spiritualist Myers. Much as Sidgwick may have loved Myers, one suspects that his refrain about how he was as dear to him as the "dearest of brothers" is some sort of dry comment on his relationship with Arthur, and perhaps on the emotional nature of their attachment, more brotherly than intellectual. Intellectually, at least, Sidgwick and Gurney were somewhat more alike, and with the latter's passing in 1888, the Sidgwick Group would never be the same. When in that year Sidgwick again took over the presidency of the SPR, it was with a heavy sense of responsibility for maintaining the respectability of their endeavors.

Here it is important to accent just how destructive the Sidgwick Group's research had been during the eighties – disposing of mediums, spiritualists, Theosophists, and so many others. The entire intellectual context was now harsher; as Sidgwick would explain when discussing the shifts in the significance of Tennyson's *In Memoriam* – that Bible of the Apostles – from the sixties to the eighties:

Hence the most important influence of *In Memoriam* on my thought, apart from its poetic charm as an expression of personal emotion, opened in a region, if I may so say, deeper down than the difference between Theism and Christianity: it lay in the unparalleled combination of intensity of feeling with comprehensiveness of view and balance of judgment, shown in presenting the *deepest* needs and perplexities of humanity. And this influence, I find, has increased rather than diminished as years have gone on, and as the great issues between Agnostic Science and Faith have become continually more prominent. In the sixties I should say that these deeper issues were somewhat obscured by the discussions on Christian dogma, and Inspiration of Scripture, etc. . . . During these years we were absorbed in struggling for freedom of thought in the trammels of a historical religion: and perhaps what we sympathised with most in *In Memoriam* at this time, apart from the personal feeling, was the defence of 'honest doubt,' . . . Well, the years pass, the struggle with what Carlyle used to call 'Hebrew old clothes' is over, Freedom is won, and what does Freedom bring us to? It brings us face to face with atheistic science: the faith in God and Immortality, which we had been struggling to clear from superstition, suddenly seems to be *in the air*: and in seeking for a firm basis for this faith we find ourselves in the midst of the 'fight with death' which *In Memoriam* so powerfully describes. (M 539)[107]

Tennyson, for Sidgwick, had not only captured the intensity of the feelings provoked by atheism, the refusal to "acquiesce in a godless world," but also expressed them in conjunction with "a reverent docility to the lessons of science which also belongs to the essence of the thought of our age." But Sidgwick's experiences in such venues as the Metaphysical Society, an illustrious intellectual setting during the eighties, had not left him much doubt about the spirit of the age, or about the direction of the various inquiries on which he had pinned his hopes back when he was concluding the first edition of the *Methods*.

Most importantly, Sidgwick himself regarded the massive investigations of telepathy as mainly a *negative* result, a matter of winning a battle and losing the war. This is evident from some of Myers's own writings, bits that he had composed for his autobiography but that were excluded from the published version. Speaking of the evidence for survival, he wrote:

Gurney, up to the time of his death, was quite uncertain on this capital point. He still held that all proved phenomena were possibly explicable by new modes of action between living men alone. Sidgwick often thought this too; and his wife, though more steadily inclining to a belief in survival, was averse to pronouncing herself on the matter. I had therefore often a sense of great solitude, and of an effort beyond my strength; – 'striving,' – as Homer says of Odysseus in a line which I should wish graven on some tablet in my memory, – 'striving to save my own soul, and my comrades' homeward way.'

It was as late as November, 1887, that these doubts reached their worst intensity. The group who had consulted over *Phantasms of the Living*, – the group whom some regarded as facile in belief, – were certainly then in no credulous mood. Sidgwick's natural scepticism and self-criticism asserted themselves more strongly than ever before. The collapse of Madame Blavatsky's so-called Theosophy, – a mere fabric of fraud, – had rendered all of us severer in our judgment of the human evidence on which our own conclusions depended. Sidgwick urged that all that we had actually proved was consistent with eternal death. He thought it not improbable that this last effort to look beyond the grave would fail; that men would have to content themselves with an agnosticism growing yearly more hopeless, – and had best turn to daily duties and forget the blackness of the end.

His words touched many a latent doubt in my own bosom. As I have implied, the question was for me too vital to admit of my endeavouring for a moment to cheat myself into a false security. My mind had been ever eagerly on the watch for indications telling either way; and for a few days I was now overshadowed by Sidgwick's loss of hope.[108]

It is at this point, one might say, that one finds Sidgwick himself really and truly coming to terms with his work as "the negative result of a theological investigation," as Schneewind described the *Methods*. Psychical research fifteen years on was beginning to take the familiar, patiently self-undermining shape of most other Sidgwickian inquiries – the "deepest problems of human life" were turning out to be quite deep and not at all congenial to the English mind. On March 7, 1886, he writes in his journal: "I feel, however, that the natural drift of my mind is now towards total incredulity in respect of extra-human intelligences; I have to remind myself forcibly of the arguments on the other side, just as a year ago I had to dwell deliberately on the sceptical argument to keep myself properly balanced" (M 441).

What was the value of all these forms of thought transference, if all they amounted to were the desperate communications of all-too-mortal human beings, fragments of psychic e-mail that carried little real meaning or larger significance? Supplemental modes of communication between meaningless lives was not the answer he had sought. Nor was it a comfort to be handed so many Jamesian lessons in the stranger warps of human nature, blurring the lines between hypocrisy and good faith, error and evidence, irresponsibility and responsibility. The "true self" was disintegrating under scrutiny.

The pain of this experience, for Sidgwick, can scarcely be overestimated. The filiations between his psychical research and his religious and ethical concerns – including, indeed, his deep commitment to Apostolic inquiry – were so strong and extensive that this later crisis of faith was about as stormy and stressful as his earlier one. The mode of inquiry, the very language of truth, had all the same confessional aspects. Consider how, in an undated letter to Myers, Sidgwick put the question of whether to include their friend Henry Graham Dakyns in their efforts: "Dakyns, with whom I am staying, would like to come to about half a dozen seances – the first four and one or two afterwards. Should he be let in? He is a sympathetic person, and would I should think be good – but possibly there is no room."[109]

Curiously, psychical research, like Mauricean Apostolic inquiry and utilitarian moral maturation, demanded the same extension of the sympathetic tendencies, the same receptiveness to and willingness to learn from others, albeit in a rather extreme form. In this sense, the evolution of sympathy was a matter not simply of changing sentiment, but of crucial epistemological significance – an evolution of sympathetic understanding.[110] And the intimate inquiring of the Sidgwick Group functioned within the larger, more formal, and less effective institutional environment of the SPR in much the same fashion as the Apostles did within the framework of the university. In both cases, the real action was taking place in the elite, vanguard element, the "leaven in the loaf."

Frank Podmore, one of Sidgwick's younger and congenially critical comrades in psychical research, gave a vivid impression of the force of Sidgwick's Apostolic tendencies in the conclusion to his review of the *Memoir*:

Mr. Haldane, in his recent address to the University of Edinburgh, has described what should be the function of a University in the national life: that the best minds should there receive their training for the highest service to the state. I do not know where there could be found a finer example than that exhibited by Henry Sidgwick of the "dedicated life" which Mr. Haldane describes – a life dedicated, however, not to the state, but to humanity – a life wholly given to the strenuous search for Truth, and finding in that search its sole and sufficient reward. Nearly all lives – our own or others – as we look back on them must seem desultory and incomplete. But Henry Sidgwick's had a unity and completeness beyond that of most men. I do not mean that it was complete if measured by the results, for of the results we are scarcely yet able to judge. But if we consider not the achievement but the purpose, we shall find that Sidgwick's life presented more than others a symmetrical whole. Its symmetry was marred by no infirmity of endeavour, by no self-seeking, by no petty personal aims. His years were continuously spent from youth upwards in the one high impersonal quest. In looking back on such a life we can see "age approve of youth, and death complete the same."[111]

What so struck Podmore was how "to Sidgwick nothing was common or unclean. And just as no fact was to him too insignificant to be worthy of study, so no person was so foolish but that something might be learned from him." Henry advised Eleanor to "get yourself into the state of mind of taking a large amount of misunderstanding and misrepresentation as inevitable, and merely endeavour to extract the grains of useful suggestion" (M 395).

Doubtless this attitude sustained Sidgwick in his psychical research, but of course, not just anyone was allowed a place at the séance. Yes, psychical research made some curiously democratic demands, as Gurney had noted, and yes, the experience of the researcher with those struggling to explain their paranormal experiences was virtually an intimate form of depth psychotherapy. But the Apostolic searcher was still "exceptional," the one who solicited and interpreted the rough truth, dimly perceived, of ordinary (or not-so-ordinary) experience. Even if he was fidgety.

For all that, what if all this sympathetic openness and self-revelation did not produce the unifying thread? And what was the responsibility of the Socratic intellectual to the larger, unphilosophical, and potentially dangerous public? Clearly, Podmore's account notwithstanding, Sidgwick ardently did hope to crack the "secret of the Universe." The world of mundane experience might be improved somewhat, but it was bound to end up a sorry compromise compared to what a new theistic religion could offer, especially by way of harmonizing duty and interest.

Was this later crisis, then, the disintegration of Sidgwick's strong belief in personal identity – effectively, belief in some type of soul surviving bodily death – and with it, of the value of seeking the harmony of reason and duty in the moral order of the universe? That, of course, was precisely what was at issue, though Sidgwick did not quite take the turn. As he summed matters up in 1891:

My attitude towards Christianity is briefly this. (1) I think Optimism in some form is an indispensable creed – not for every one, but for progressive humanity as a whole. (2) I think Optimism in a Theistic form – I mean the belief that there is a sympathetic soul of the Universe that intends the welfare of each particular human being and is guiding all the events of his life for his good – is, for the great majority of human beings, not only the most attractive form of optimism, but the most easily acceptable, being no more unproven than any other form of optimism, and certainly more satisfying to the deepest human needs. (3) I think that no form of Optimism has an adequate rational basis; therefore, if Theism is to be maintained – and I am inclined to predict the needs of the human heart will maintain it – it must be, for Europeans, by virtue of the support that it still obtains from the traditional belief in historical Christianity. (M 508)

It is in this connection that Sidgwick laments the pains that come with having "taken service with Reason." The "blackness of the end" threatened to crush the most viable form of optimism he knew. While his experiments in "intuitive Theism" had continued to impress upon him the needs of the human heart, his experiments in psychical research, like those in philosophical ethics, had left him feeling that the theistic postulate, the thing that might harmonize duty and interest, was in deep trouble.

In some ways, Sidgwick's felt relationship to humanity at large had found expression in the small in his relationship to Myers, in a way that also goes far to explain his attitude toward teaching. In 1873, while working on the *Methods*, he had written to him:

You know that in spite of my love of truth, I am too fond of you not to be keenly pleased by your overestimate of me: I only feel bound from time to time to warn you that you will find me out. My only merit (if it be a merit) is that I have never swerved from following the ideal

> Evermore unseen
> and fixt upon the far sea-line

but I have a double sorrow first that I cannot come to know the relation of the ideal to the actual, and secondly that I myself show so mean and uncomely to my own vision. Further as to you, I have another sadness in feeling that during the years in which we have exchanged thoughts I have unwillingly done you more harm than good by the cold corrosive scepticism which somehow in my own mind is powerless to affect my 'idealism', but which I see in more than one case acting otherwise upon others.

Still your friendship is one of the best delights of my life and no difference of ethical opinion between us can affect this, though it may increase my despondency as to things in general.[112]

By the late eighties, Sidgwick's idealism had been dampened, and he felt ever more the "Great Either-Or" – pessimism or faith. The friends of this Socrates rightly worried about his despair over "Things in General," the loss of confidence in that cosmic invisible hand that he had always deemed an essential supplement to any mundane harmonizing of interests.

It is singularly odd that philosophical commentary on Sidgwick has failed to look for the sources of his belief in the "deep truth" about personal identity in this rather obvious place. Although his profound aversion to materialism and guarded optimism about the possibility of personal survival do not quite in themselves yield a metaphysical defense of a nonreductionist view of personal identity, the larger dimensions of his project – the emergent depth psychology, including the sense of the uncanny that came from his experiences in interviewing the people reporting "phenomena" – point to the ground of his unshakeable sense of the logical priority of egoism, of egoism as a reflection of the true self that somehow endured.[113] After all, he was genuinely excited about the prospects for Theosophy.

To grasp the import of this singular Sidgwickian crisis, however, it is essential to introduce at greater length another crucial character, one whose pioneering explorations of human psychology, in self and other, were of vital interest to Sidgwick and perhaps of more lasting value than those of the Sidgwick Group. This, of course, is Sidgwick's intimate friend John Addington Symonds. Exploring their friendship, which brought forth Sidgwick's candid thoughts and feelings like no other, will bring out other dimensions of Sidgwick's psychological views and their bearing on his philosophical work, and also set the stage for consideration of the larger political and social vision that informed his worries about the practical implications of the dualism of practical reason. Once again, Sidgwick's inquiry should not be construed simply in narrow philosophical terms: along with his larger metaphysical concerns, there was a very highly developed sense of the political context of the morality of common sense, and of the task of the enlightened dualist. After all, this account of his work in psychical research has only raised again, rather than answered, all of the difficult questions about just how elitist, patriarchal and orientalist the Sidgwickian "consensus of experts" might have been.

6

Friends versus Friends

Part I

Henry Sidgwick told me something about his spirits, but nothing new. He spoke on a more important subject, [letter incomplete]
John Addington Symonds to Henry Graham Dakyns, May 3, 1864[1]

I. Idealisms

Sidgwick's life project, as should by this point be clear, involved an effort to find some evidence for the thin theistic postulate capable of resolving the dualism of practical reason and, of course, undergirding his casuistry. If his psychical research was a logical development of his theological and ethical interests – his chosen path for restoring the moral order of the universe in a way that recognized the force of egoism as part of the religious hope for a happy immortality – it was also yet another manifestation of his Apostolic love of intimate fellowship in the service of inquiry into the "deepest problems." Such inquiry, as it transpired, positively demanded new forms of intimacy and sensitivity, new horizons for the Millian and Mauricean attempt to achieve sympathetic unity. The confessional had become the depth psychological, the romantic the experimental, the empathetic the telepathic. In an age of transition, the notion of a clerisy had itself been transformed, but there was still a good deal of the poetic and romantic inspiring Sidgwick's transfigured utilitarianism. His educational ideal of culture may have underscored the importance of science, but his conception of science was being reconfigured by something akin to the depth psychological recognition that intimate confession and drawing out were what it took to get at the deeper truth about human nature. Even the *Methods* represented an extended testimonial to his efforts to penetrate his "true self." Sidgwick's school of sympathy was to be a very Millian one and a very Apostolic one, but still, in the end, it can only be described as a special Sidgwickian one, his own synthesis.

Was it, for all that, a men's school, or club? Worse, an elite and very Eurocentric men's school that, in its own skeptical and reticent way, was also a rival to Green's Idealistic training school for statesmen to run the empire? After all, the Society for Psychical Research, despite Eleanor Sidgwick's involvement in it, has been charged with being a force against many developing modes of feminism, and with reinscribing patriarchal notions of "rational" male authority. Furthermore, as already noted, it certainly betrayed some extremely Eurocentric prejudices, an orientalism that was at times overtly racist. Did Newnham College do so as well? Given the Apostolic roots of Sidgwick's educational ideal, it can scarcely be above suspicion. After all, just who were his friends and fellow seekers?

These are very serious questions, questions that point up the larger epistemological and political significance of Sidgwick's views on sex, gender, and race. To truly grasp what he had in mind when he sought the "consensus of experts" – a refashioned notion of aristocracy that cast it basically as a clerisy with more professional opportunities – it is simply imperative that one have some sense of how he delimited the social dimensions of authority, and of whatever gendering and orientalism were at work in his construction of expertise and understanding. What, at the limit, so to speak, did sympathetic unity really require, in terms of sameness and difference, familiarity and otherness?

This chapter will, in due course, begin to address the matter of elitism in Sidgwick's feminism and in his work with such reformist institutions as Newnham College, but this will be via a further examination of his Apostolic notion of friendship, with its powerful homosocial/homosexual undercurrents. It is here, with this latter, that one finds his deeper meditations on hypocrisy, publicity, sex, friendship, and the inconclusiveness of ethics and experiments in intuitive theism. Appropriately enough, however, it is best to approach this matter with some indirection, albeit indirection of a metaphysical stripe that will help to tie together some of the themes of the last two chapters. For just as Sidgwick had a closet full of theological concerns, so too he had a closet full of metaphysical ones, which, in so many ways, were the very stuff of his intimate soaring. His closest friends – Frederic Myers, John Jermyn Cowell, Henry Graham Dakyns, Roden Noel, John Addington Symonds – were all irredemiably metaphysical in their cast of mind, albeit in a rather Shelleyan fashion, and Sidgwick's minimal metaethics was in truth a tenuous middle way between the extremes of sense and speculation. And just how passionate and metaphysical he could be has not yet been demonstrated. At times, it could well seem that a precondition for his personal affection and philosophical admiration was to have some serious thoughts about immortality and the grounds for Cosmic Enthusiasm, with all the erotic charge that the Victorian Platonic revival could muster. His best friends typically stimulated him with their visions of immortality or of alternative cosmic faith that could do without personal survival. Only such souls were attuned to the "deepest problems." Awakened by poetry, alive to philosophy, and always, always voyaging, the friends of Socrates knew what soaring was all about.

As Symonds explained, when recounting some of Tennyson's views on how "moral good is the crown of man," though it would be nothing "without immortality" – views that were expressed at a dinner party also including Symonds, his father, and Gladstone:

In all this metaphysical vagueness about matter, morals, the existence of evil, and the evidences of God there was something almost childish. Such points pass with most men for settled as insoluble after a time. But Tennyson has a perfect simplicity about him which recognises the real greatness of such questions, and regards them as always worthy of consideration. He treats them with profound moral earnestness. His "In Memoriam" and "Two Voices" illustrate this habit. There is nothing original or startling – on the contrary, a general common-placeness, about his metaphysics; yet, so far as they go, they express real agitating questions – express, in a poet's language, what most men feel and think about.[2]

Ironically, then, Sidgwick's "club" was a very metaphysically engaged one. Given this, and his philosophical erudition, the obvious question that presents itself is why he was not more receptive to the Kantian–Hegelian answers to the problems that he had so labored over. Kant and Kantism also spoke to the issue of the dualism of practical reason, and they also offered up a solution couched in the language of immortality. How could a mind as philosophically penetrating as Sidgwick's have pronounced parapsychology the more promising prospect?

Thus, a more extensive comparison between Sidgwick's project and the Idealist one might prove singularly helpful. After all, many of the questions to be addressed concern the degree to which Sidgwick was, in his own peculiar fashion, in fact engaged in a project akin to Green's, or for that matter Jowett's, both of whom he knew and admired as fellow academic liberals. Next to evolutionism, it was Idealism – whether in the older, more Platonic form represented by Jowett, or in the newer Kantian–Hegelian synthesis represented by Green and Bradley – that exercised Sidgwick as a philosophical and political rival, a more serious rendering of the perfectionist alternative than Arnold's. And it did so in part because the entire Oxford philosophical context reflected in its own way the Apostolic ethic of personal growth through intimate (if tutorial) friendships between teachers and students. Indeed, later Victorian Oxford carried this to a pitch rather beyond tranquil Cambridge, though the differences between the two institutions are often overstated. Symonds was an Oxford product, a student of Jowett, Green, Conington, and the other lights of liberalism. Green, as it happened, would end up marrying Symonds's sister, Charlotte.

To be sure, there was much straightforward philosophical debate over Sidgwick's work, particularly over the *Methods*, emanating from Oxford. The later objections of Moore and Rashdall, mainly directed at Sidgwick's defenses of egoism and hedonism, were all anticipated earlier on, particularly by Green and Bradley (but also by others who resist easy classification, notably such Cambridge figures as Goldsworthy Lowes Dickenson and James Ward – two more of Sidgwick's spiritual offspring).[3] But Green, more than these others, was Sidgwick's immediate rival, the friend and contemporary who also represented the academic liberal agenda and whose influence, like Jowett's, extended far beyond the academic setting. He represented much more, to Sidgwick, than a mere alternative academic philosophy.

In so many respects, Green is the bridge to Sidgwick's deeper concerns – speculative, social, and sexual. An earnest academic liberal with deep religious convictions worked into an Idealist philosophy bordering on spiritualism, and an inspiring teacher who, among other things, coached Symonds in Plato, Green was the one who invariably appeared whenever Sidgwick looked over his shoulder. They virtually began philosophizing together; Sidgwick would recall how Green was stimulated to philosophize by his classics, such that when "he was out walking one day with Green, they came upon a bridge which his companion attempted to prove was a different bridge for each of them."[4] Green too was pained that the

most intelligent critics had rather, it would seem, that the ideas which poetry applies to life, together with those which form the basis of practical religion, should be left to take their chance alongside of seemingly incompatible scientific beliefs, than that anything calling itself philosophy should seek to systematise them and to ascertain the regions to which they on the one side, and the truths of science on the other, are respectively applicable.[5]

Green, as noted in previous chapters, had no use for psychical research and found in Idealist metaphysics the revivifying intellectual and cultural force that would fill the void left by disintegrating Christian orthodoxy. Or rather, he took his philosophical mission to be one of supporting Christian orthodoxy, albeit of the Mauricean, Broad Church variety, mixed with his own Evangelical Puritanism, an aspect of his familial background for which he always evinced some sympathy. As he put it to a former pupil in 1872, he could find no greater satisfaction "than to think that I at all helped to lay the intellectual platform for your religious life." If he were "only a breeder of heretics," he would suspect his philosophy, which, if it is "sound," ought "to supply intellectual formulae for the religious life whether lived by an 'orthodox' clergyman or (let us say) a follower of Mazzini." Green, that is, "never dreamt of philosophy doing instead of religion," and his own interest in it "is wholly religious" in "the sense that it is to me . . . the reasoned intellectual expression of the effort to get to God."[6]

Thus, Green's attitude may well seem quite different from Sidgwick's. As Schneewind has it, for Sidgwick, "philosophy is the rational search for truth, and if Christianity turns out to possess it, so much the better for Christianity. For Green, it seems, philosophy has the task of showing that Christianity does possess the truth, and if the philosopher fails to come to that result, then it follows that he has more work to do."[7] But this is not quite right. Plainly, Sidgwick worried considerably about his philosophical results being so hard on the human heart, and kept searching.

It is scarcely odd that Sidgwick and Green should have shared much by way of the religious attitude. Green was also a Rugby product – indeed, one of Sidgwick's old Rugby friends. During the sixties, both were hammering out their distinctive philosophical worldviews and often doing so by direct exchange – for instance, while on a walking tour of the continent in 1862. Sidgwick would later confess, in his "Reminiscences of T. H. Green," that he was at this point "in a crude and confident stage of utilitarianism" and consequently "quite unappreciative" of Green's line. And plainly, he did not appreciate his "sniffing" at psychical research. Green was a strange figure, the model for a character named Professor Grey in Mary (Mrs. Humphrey) Ward's *Robert Elsmere*, a novel about an earnest young man who loses his orthodox faith but finds a new one in working for the underprivileged, inspired in part by professor Grey. By all accounts, Green was, if not as austere as some claimed, exceedingly earnest and lost in his own soul searching. As Melvin Richter has judiciously described him:

> There was general agreement about the quality of Green's mind. 'You never talked to him without carrying away something to remember and ponder over.' Yet it seemed highly unlikely that he would accommodate himself to university life any better than he had done to Rugby. The classical philology that bulked so large in the Greats curriculum bored him. In his first trial by examination, he failed to distinguish himself. Absorbed in his efforts to articulate views unusually personal and deeply felt, he was notorious for puzzling on Monday over essays that had been due the previous Friday. None of this augured well for a successful university career. And yet the class of degree achieved by a poor clergyman's son might fix the course of his future life. With First Class Honours doors would be opened to him, beyond which he otherwise could not hope to penetrate. Left to himself, Green's character might have manifested itself in a mediocre record which would have condemned him to eking out an existence as a schoolmaster, or to burying himself in an obscure government post. But Green fortunately profited from the ministrations of his tutor, that Pascal of the undergraduate heart.
>
> Jowett saw something worth stimulating in this gauche freshman.[8]

Just what Jowett saw in his earnest young Anglican Evangelical is, as Richter explains, most illuminating: "As he said many years later, the only person in his experience who at all resembled this singular young man was another Rugbeian who had entered Balliol twenty years before, Arthur Hugh Clough." If Clough was the "more indolently dreamy" of the two, and Green the more abstract, Jowett was nonetheless a shrewd judge of his students. As Richter puts it, referring to Clough and Green: "Reserved and self-contained, they moved in a detached sphere of almost inhuman high principle. Society and politics were to them intimate realities, the great problems of which it had fallen to them personally to resolve."[9] Had Sidgwick taken up the Balliol option, following Rugby, there might have been another young Cloughian in Jowett's care and keeping.

But as he would shortly discover with yet another dreamy student – namely, Symonds – Jowett found that Green needed more than a little prodding.

Jowett decided that it was only through his Puritan sense of duty that Green could be made to work. And so, particularly after Green disappointed his friends and family by taking a Second in Moderations, his tutor began to prod. Green's essays, he remarked, were much too dry and dull, a fault which might be repaired by reading poetry. But Jowett's major stroke was yet to come. One day he said casually: 'If you do not get your First, Green, *I* shall have a good deal to answer for.' This remark Green later recalled as the turning point of his life. Knowing how much the prestige of the college meant to his tutor, Green's sense of duty was called into play: the gospel of work taught by Carlyle, Dr. Arnold, and Jowett had now to be applied to himself and his conditions. And so he plunged into the task ahead.[10]

With the support and stimulus of Jowett, and the help of C. S. Parker and John Conington – the University Professor of Latin and another old (though strikingly radical) Rugbeian – Green was stirred up, transformed, and in due course, after many walks and many talks and many reading parties, became a successful First, the first lay Fellow of Balliol, and in due course Professor. He became a fixture of the "Old Mortality Society," the somewhat less secretive Oxford equivalent of the Apostles that included such notable figures as Symonds, Bryce, Dicey, Walter Pater, and Algernon Swinburne. All in all, he represented the virtues of that very personal and intimate form of education that had come to mark Oxford, an outgrowth, in part, of the Tractarian movement's transformation of the tutorial into a transfiguring personal experience, a spiritual awakening. It was common Oxbridge ground that, in the words of Noel Annan, "all fellows, certainly all directors of studies and tutors, should try, as far as they were able, to become the guide, philosopher and friend of those they taught."[11] Education was a very important and a very personal business – indeed, not a business at all, but a special form of intimacy. The Platonic revival came to fruition in Jowett's Oxford.

But Green imbibed this in a fashion that mixed Platonic elitism with a good deal of Puritan moral democracy. W. L. Newman gave a famous, and by all accounts accurate, description of him:

His habitual dress of black and grey suited him well and was true to his character. He was drawn to plain people, to people of the middle and lower class rather than to the upper, to the puritans of the past and the nonconformists of the present, to Germans, to all that is sober-suited and steady-going. One judged from his feeling for homely, unadorned and solid worth what he must feel for things showy, brilliant and hollow.[12]

Of course, Sidgwick was also in love with things German, and in the sixties he vied with Green for superior knowledge of German biblical criticism and philosophy. In 1864, he had explained to Dakyns: "I should like to get at this Oxford *Hegelianism* and see what it means. I used to talk with Green, but I did not draw much." (M 102) Again, Sidgwick was always perfectly ready to admit the importance of Kant and Kantism. Indeed, he began his lectures on the metaphysics of Kant by observing that "it is partly at least to Kant that we trace the origin of the systems of metaphysical thought which have most vogue at the present day – the Agnosticism of Spencer (though here the influence is indirect, through Hamilton and Mansel), and more directly the Idealism or Spiritualism of which I take Green as a representative" (LPK 1).[13] Thus, he found the root of *both* Spencer's evolutionism and Green's Idealism in the works of Kant, which suggests how he attached much more importance to the latter than the arguments of the *Methods* reveal.

Now, as many have observed, when Green translated his general predispositions into philosophical Idealism, it was in a somewhat more democratic and reforming fashion than that of many later Idealists, such as his student F. H. Bradley. Little wonder that, whereas Sidgwick's exchanges with Bradley were marked by an unusual asperity on both sides, his exchanges with Green were far more congenial.

Green, of course, in good Hegelian fashion, did not fear the growth of the state in quite the way that most of the old Benthamites or Millians did, but rather regarded it as potentially a positive force for spiritual development, for positive freedom, especially when it came to education.[14] The disciples of Jowett may have been concerned with the practical business of running the empire on Platonic grounds, but the disciples of Green – notably Arnold Toynbee – also went on to produce the settlement movement and nurse the work of Mary Ward and Jane Addams, who went far toward implementing the Mauricean social gospel of bringing the classes together and opening up educational and cultural opportunities to all. The library fireplace at Mary Ward House (formerly the Passmore Edwards Settlement, an early settlement that complemented Toynbee Hall) bore the initials T. H. G., in honor of its philosophical inspirer, after whom the library was named.[15] Ironically, in the late 1890s it would also house the London School of Ethics and Social Philosophy, of which Sidgwick was a vice president and another of Green's disciples, Bernard Bosanquet, president, and at which the young G. E. Moore gave the lectures on the "Elements of Ethics" that would serve as a dry run for *Principia Ethica*.[16]

It is important to bear in mind that Ward and Addams were also the result of that academic liberalism and Mauricean Christian socialism, with more than a dash of Ruskin and Arts and Crafts, that shaped both Green and Sidgwick, since concerns about paternalism (or maternalism) and patriarchy (or matriarchy) appear rather different when viewed in light of their work.[17] Again, the disciples of Green were mostly not like Bradley in harboring a Whewellian reverence for the status quo, which, they felt, left a lot to be desired as a realization of the Divine Spirit. As Richard Symonds has urged, what "Ruskin, Jowett (who taught what he called 'the new economics'), Green and Toynbee had in common was a detestation for the consequences of the economic policies of *laissez-faire*, and their pupils carried this out into the Empire."[18] Needless to say, in this they were the harbingers of the New Liberalism, the liberalism attuned to the positive functions of the state and the inevitable growth of larger organizations that would, in the twentieth century, make the Millian vision seem like a distant libertarian romance.[19] And this brought in its train a wealth of complaints about paternalism, authoritarianism, and creeping socialism from those who identified with what they took to be the classical liberalism of the older utilitarian tradition – not to mention concerns about imperialism, or "spiritual expansion." The infamous Alfred Milner, architect of British imperialism in South Africa, was another student of Green's, also a friend of Toynbee's and a champion of "social service."

Not surprisingly, Sidgwick turns out to be difficult to classify, though as later chapters will show, he was in many respects more with the new forces than against them. However, during this formative age when Jowett's Oxford began ruling the world, the Millian strains were a complex and considerable element even in the work of Green. Even the early Millian strains, those of the early editions of his *Political Economy*. For Green was still a believer in private property and self-help, and he never had anything like a full-blooded Prussian adoration of the state, even if he was willing to encourage it to use liquor licensing and zoning to cultivate temperance among the working class in ways that the Millians regarded as paternalistic. Nowhere is his ambivalence more evident than in the work his students Charles Loch and Bernard Bosanquet did – apparently with his blessing – as leaders of the Charity Organisation Society, an organization widely regarded as devoted to effectively implementing the New Poor

Law, and one that would unite Marx and Dickens in their scorn for the cruelty of capitalism. The COS was essentially founded on the belief that pauperism was the result of weak character, a lack of industry and foresight, and that poor relief must not dampen incentives to self-help. Much of its effort went into screening applicants for relief, so that the "deserving poor" would be aided, while the undeserving went off to the workhouses. As the following chapter will show, Sidgwick was also very much entangled in this distinctively Victorian institution, and his involvement was similar to Green's in sitting uneasily with other elements of his political philosophy.[20]

Green's tragic premature death in March of 1882 robbed the philosophical world of what would surely have turned out to be one of the most famous and fruitful intellectual rivalries in the history of philosophy. Still, even to the degree that it was played out, their mutual stimulus was important. When Green's *Prolegomena to Ethics* appeared (posthumously, in 1883), it marked, among other things, a serious extended engagement with Sidgwick's *Methods*. Indeed, it is striking how far Green went in positively trying to claim Sidgwick for his side. Like Hayward at a later date, Green finds it baffling how Sidgwick could identify with the older utilitarian tradition – the tradition that he, Green, had steadily tried to demonstrate the incoherence of:

Now in this theory [Sidgwick's] it is clear that an office is ascribed to Reason which in ordinary Utilitarian doctrine, as in the philosophy of Locke and Hume on which that doctrine is founded, is explicitly denied to it. To say that as *rational* beings we are bound to aim at anything whatever *in the nature of an ultimate end*, would have seemed absurd to Hume and to the original Utilitarians. To them reason was a faculty not of ends but of means. As a matter of fact, they held, we all do aim at pleasure as our ultimate end; all that could properly be said to be reasonable or unreasonable was our selection of means to that end. They would no more have thought of asking why pleasure ought to be pursued than of asking why any fact ought to be a fact. Mr. Sidgwick, however, does ask the question, and answers that pleasure ought to be pursued because reason pronounces it desirable; but that, since reason pronounces pleasure, if equal in amount, to be equally desirable by whatever being enjoyed, it is universal pleasure – the pleasure of all sentient beings – that ought to be pursued. It is not indeed an object that every one ought at all times to have consciously before him, but it is the ultimate good by reference to which, 'when we sit down in a calm hour,' the desirability of every other good is to be tested.

In this procedure Mr. Sidgwick is quite consistent with himself. His rejection of 'Egoistic' in favour of 'Universalistic' Hedonism rests upon a ground which in Mr. Mill's doctrine it is impossible to discover. His appeal to reason may be made to justify the recognition of an obligation to regard the happiness of all men or all animals equally, which, upon the doctrine that pleasure is the one thing desirable because the one thing desired, can only be logically justified by the untenable assumption that the only way to obtain a maximum of pleasure for oneself is to have an equal regard for the pleasure of everyone else. But Mr. Sidgwick's way of justifying his Altruism constrains us to ask him some further questions. What does he understand by the 'reason' to which he ascribes the office of deciding what the one 'ultimately and intrinsically desirable end' is; not the means to it, but on the nature of the end itself? In saying that it is reasonable to pursue desirable consciousness, is he not open to the same charge of moving in a circle which he brings against those who say it is reasonable to live according to nature, or virtuous to seek perfection, while after all they have no other account to give of the life according to nature but that it is reasonable, or of perfection but that it is the highest virtue? What does he mean by desirable consciousness but the sort of consciousness which it is reasonable to seek?[21]

Green goes on to maintain that although Sidgwick tries to avoid such a circle by "describing the desirable consciousness as pleasure," it would nonetheless seem, given his impartialism, and the equivocating way in which he describes pleasure, that "his doctrine comes to this, that it is reasonable to seek as ultimate good that form of conscious life which is reasonably to be desired" – a singularly revealing upshot. For according to Green, by criticizing Sidgwick's view in this manner, he sought "not to depreciate it, but to show how much more truth there is in it, from our point of view, than in the common statement of utilitarianism." The circle, that is, is virtuous rather than vicious:

We have previously explained how it comes about that any true theory of the good will present an appearance of moving in a circle. The rational or self-conscious soul, we have seen, constitutes its own end; is an end at once to and in itself. Its end is the perfection of itself, the fulfilment of the law of its being. The consciousness of there being such an end expresses itself in the judgement that something absolutely should be, that there is something intrinsically and ultimately desirable. This judgement is, in this sense, the expression of reason; and all those who, like Mr. Sidgwick, recognise the distinction between the absolutely desirable and the *de facto* desired, have in effect admitted that reason gives – is the source of there being – a supreme practical good. If we ask for a reason why we should pursue this end, there is none to be given but that it is rational to do so, that reason bids it, that the pursuit is the effort of the self-conscious or rational soul after its own perfection. It is reasonable to desire it because it is reasonably to be desired. Those who like to do so may make merry over the tautology. Those who understand how it arises – from the fact, namely, that reason gives its own end, that the self-conscious spirit of man presents its own perfection to itself as the intrinsically desirable – will not be moved by the mirth.[22]

Not moved by their mirth, and not at all tempted to try to "escape the charge of tautology by taking the desirableness of ultimate good to consist in anything else than in the thought of it as that which would satisfy reason – satisfy the demand of the self-conscious soul for its own perfection." Pleasure is no help, since "this notion cannot be determined by reference to anything but what reason has itself done; by anything but reflection on the excellences of character and conduct to which the rational effort after perfection of life has given rise." Thus, Green's self-conscious spirits will

appeal to the virtues to tell them what is virtuous, to goodness to tell them what is truly good, to the work of reason in human life to tell them what is reasonably to be desired; and that is the only appropriate procedure, because only in the full attainment of its end could reason learn fully what that end is, and only in what it has so far attained of the end can it learn what its further attainment would be.

In this, they could take some inspiration from Sidgwick, while asking him for some reason why "having accepted principles, as it would seem, so antagonistic to those of the philosophic Utilitarians," he should "end by accepting their conclusion."[23]

Manifestly, there is in such a view a good deal of the old Maurican Platonic soaring toward the form of the Good, apprehended in this world only through a glass darkly. But the nature of Green's position may be rather hard to make out without a fuller sense of his metaphysical system. This is not easily summarized. In fact, Sidgwick came about as close to giving an accurate thumbnail account of it as anyone: "Briefly, then, a spirit's thinking activity is the source of a system of notions, by which the world is constituted, but it cannot itself be thought under any of these. It is the former proposition that leads me to call Green's view Idealistic: it is the latter which leads me to call it Spiritualistic. . . ." That is, for Green, as for the Germans, a "mentalistic" metaphysics is crucial. "Nature, or the world of space and time, is conceived as a single, unalterable, all-inclusive system of relations: and these relations are thought-relations; they result from the activity of thought." Hence, Green's Idealism.

However, Green does not follow Hegel in viewing Thought as having completed itself in Spirit, "so that the Universe of Reality would have been truly thought as Thought itself." Rather, Green rejects such a view, holding instead that the all-inclusive system of thought relations "implies something other than itself, as a condition of its being what it is." It "presupposes the activity of a thinking being, a 'self-distinguishing, self-objectifying, unifying, combining consciousness' whose synthetic activity is the source of the relations by which the knowable world is unified: and we are entitled to say of this entity, that the relations which result from its synthetic action are not predicable of it." This is the Divine Spirit, outside of space and time, the great unifying consciousness that cannot be another object to itself, on a par with the phenomena it unifies. This is what constitutes the world, while remaining itself unconditioned. And it is a macrocosmic analogue of the Kantian transcendental "I" that finds itself reproduced microcosmically in the individual person. As "knower," "each man's consciouness is nothing but the eternal consciousness itself, reproducing or realising itself in a limited form in connexion with the man's animal organism which it makes its vehicle, and whose sentient life it uses as its organ. It is as such a reproduction or realisation of the one Divine Mind that a man is also a 'self-distinguishing, self-objectifying consciousness,' a 'self-conscious personality' or briefly a 'spirit.'" (LPK 257–58)[24] As an irreverent contemporary Balliol rhyme so famously had it:

> I am the self-distinguishing
> consciousness in everything;
> the synthetic unity
> one in multiplicity,
> the unseen nexus of the seen
> sometimes known as TOMMY GREEN

Evidently, even Sidgwick's powers of luminously clear exposition were taxed to the limit in his account of Green's metaphysics. Still, it should be tolerably plain that Green held that there was a Mind that constituted the world but remained separate from it. He was, in effect, rehabilitating the notion of God by developing – out of a critical account of the incoherence of empiricism in accounting for itself, free will, the knowing subject, or the kind of uniformity of experience required even by scientific explanation – an account of the world that portrays it as the unified thought processes of one big consciousness, with some of the thoughts, namely persons, more closely reflecting the nature of the Divine Thinker than others, as the consciousness of free will indicates. As Skorupski puts it, for Green,

> Self-consciousness, or Thought as such, is not to be identified with this or that empirical thought, since all such particular thoughts are within experience. Self-consciousness is rather a single, actively self-distinguishing spiritual principle: which expresses itself in temporal human intelligence, in something like the way that the whole meaning of a text is potentially present throughout the temporal act of reading.[25]

This is phenomenalism made honest, brought into holistic coherence after the devastation of Hume. There is, manifest in persons as knowers and free moral agents, a principle of originality and creativity that will ever defy naturalistic science, will ever frustrate science because science presupposes it and science, even if it can catch its own tail, can never swallow itself whole.

This is recognizably a critical philosophical friend of the familiar Christian conception of human beings as the children of God – souls endowed with free will and somewhere in between the beasts and the angels, striving or being drawn to ever fuller awareness of the Divine spark within, the very ground of one's being. Persons are special; the experience of freedom that each has is revelatory of how much more there is than the natural world. Sidgwick would always admit the force of the key analogy: "If the aggregate of thoughts and feelings into which the world as empirically known to me is analysable has every element of it connected by reference to a self-conscious subject, we may argue from analogy that there must be such a subject similarly related to the Universe" (LPK 227). Consciousness, as so many philosophers of mind continue to urge, just does manifest a special unity and integration.[26] With Green, there is a further Hegelian admixture in this, since the striving for perfection involves a world-historical form of spiritual progress, but his is decidedly a Hegel moderated by Kant and by a warmer feeling for the achievements of English civilization.

The Hegelian twist in Green's remarks, to the effect that a deeper logic can account for the necessary appearance of circularity in ordinary reasoning – which was just bound to be incoherent when it bumped up against its limits – would appear time and again in Idealist criticisms of Sidgwick. In fact, the first Idealist salvo against Sidgwick's *Methods*, in print at least, came not from Green but from Bradley, whose *Ethical Studies* appeared in 1876. This work, often regarded as the breakthrough statement of British Idealism, makes some reference to Sidgwick, who in turn reviewed it in *Mind* – rather unfavorably:

At any rate, whatever the author may have intended, I venture to think that uncritical dogmatism constitutes the largest and most interesting element of Mr. Bradley's work. It is true that his polemical writing, especially his attack on ethical and psychological hedonism . . . is always vigorous, and frequently acute and suggestive: but often again, just at the *nodes* of his argument, he lapses provok-ingly into mere debating-club rhetoric; and his apprehension of the views which he assails is always rather superficial and sometimes even unintelligent. This last defect seems partly due to his limited acquaintance with the whole process of English ethical thought, partly to the contemptuous asperity with which he treats opposing doctrines: for really penetrating criticism, especially in ethics, requires a patient effort of intellectual sympathy which Mr. Bradley has never learned to make, and a tranquillity of temper which he seems incapable of maintaining. Nor again, does he appear to have effectively criticised his own fundamental po-sitions, before putting them before the public. His main ethical principle is that Self-Realisation is the ultimate end of practice: but in Essay II . . . the reader is startled by the communication that Mr. Bradley "does not properly speaking know what he means when he says 'self' and 'real' and 'realise'." The frankness of this confession disarms satire. . . .[27]

Manifestly, Sidgwick was out to teach his obnoxious, irritable junior from Oxford a few Apostolic lessons about how to pursue truth. This review was followed up, in *Mind*, by an unrepentant reply from Bradley and a further rejoinder from Sidgwick – if anything even more damning, though also quite revealing:

Mr. Bradley seems to be under a strange impression that, while professing to write a critical notice of his views on ethics, I have been or ought to have been – defending my own. I entertain quite a different notion of a reviewer's 'station and duties.' In criticising his book (or any other) I put out of sight my own doctrines, in so far as I am conscious of them as peculiar to myself: and pass my judgments from a point of view which I expect my readers generally to share with me. Hence the references in his reply to my opinions would be quite irrelevant, even if he understood those opinions somewhat better than he does. I passed lightly over his attack on Hedonism in Essay III for the simple reason – which I gave – that I thought it less interesting and important than other parts of his work. Much of it, as he must be perfectly aware, either has no bearing on Hedonism as I conceive it, or emphasises defects which I have myself pointed out: the rest consists chiefly of familiar anti-hedonistic commonplaces: the freshest argument I could find was one with which I had made acquaintance some years ago in Mr. Green's Introduction to Hume. This, as stated by Mr. Green, I have taken occasion to answer in the course of an article in the present number of this journal. The attack on my book appended to Essay III, though not uninstructive to myself, is far too full of misunderstandings to be profitable for discussion. It is criticism of the kind that invites explanation rather than defense: such explanation I proposed to give in its proper place – which was certainly not my notice of Mr. Bradley.[28]

In short, Sidgwick has "nothing to retract or qualify on any of the points raised by Mr. Bradley – except a pair of inverted commas which were accidentally attached to a phrase of my own." Apparently, he held to this (plausible) judgment that whatever was interesting in Bradley was due to Green and that he was better off addressing the latter; at least, he would continue to write and lecture about Green's philosophy, while flatly ignoring Bradley's further productions, including the long pamphlet on "Mr. Sidgwick's Hedonism" that appeared in 1877.

As Schneewind has suggested, Sidgwick was largely right to be unimpressed by Bradley's early statement of the Idealist case. The best one can say of Bradley's charges – for example, that the very notion of a sum of pleasures is incoherent, like all the rest of phenomenal appearances – is that they "depend on certain doctrines, concerning either the internality of relations, which makes certain types of abstraction illegitimate, or the concrete universal as the necessary structure of the moral end, which makes it impossible that the end should be a 'mere aggregate'," and these doctrines are scarcely developed in either Bradley or Green when they criticize Sidgwick.[29] Indeed, Bradley's larger view in *Ethical Studies* rests "on the unstated Hegelian idea that the world spirit, operating through us, moves ever onward to new stages in its development. The task of the philosophical owl that flies at twilight is to articulate the developments the world spirit has already undergone. Philosophy can no more anticipate its evolution in morality than it can in science." Thus, as Schneewind notes, this position is fundamentally at odds "with Sidgwick's belief that the same principle which provides an adequate explication of the 'morality current in the world' must also provide the basis for a method of rectifying that morality."[30] Bradley's plain man, who has identified with the moral spirit of his community and acts out of decent unreflective habit, has no need of the philosopher, who, if it is Bradley, will insist that the philosopher is indeed perfectly useless and has absolutely nothing to contribute to ordinary practice, to making the world a better place.

Given the general fate of Idealist metaphysics and logic, it would be easy to conclude that what was lurking behind the Idealists' criticisms of Sidgwick was not such as to seriously threaten the viability of his views, however powerful the academic standing of Idealism was during its heyday.[31] And in fact, when Sidgwick does address Green, it is for the most part in a remarkably effective manner. For Green rather obviously misunderstood utilitarianism from beginning to end, more or less constantly confusing it with hedonistic psychological egoism and rendering it as a mishmash of the least compelling parts of Bentham and Mill. Sidgwick, in addressing the bits from the *Prolegomena* quoted earlier, has a fairly easy time of it, given the gulf of implausibility lying between his minimal metaethical account of reason and the full-blooded Idealist account, with all its perfectionist elements:

If such objects, then, as Truth, Freedom, and Beauty, or strictly speaking, the objective relations of conscious minds which we call cognition of Truth, contemplation of Beauty and Independence of Action, are good, independently of the pleasures that we derive from them, it must be reasonable to aim at these for mankind generally, and not at happiness only: and this view seems, though not the prevailing one, to be widely accepted among cultivated persons.

When I compare the cognition of Truth, contemplation of Beauty, volition to realise Freedom or Virtue, with Pleasure, in respect of their relation to Ultimate Good, I would justify my own view that it is Pleasure alone, desirable Feeling, that is ultimately and intrinsically good, by the only kind of argument of which the case seems to me to admit. I would point out that we may be led to regard as mistaken our preferences for the conditions, concomitants or consequences of consciousness, as distinguished from the consciousness itself, and in order to show this, I would ask the reader to use the same twofold procedure that I have regarded as applicable in considering the absolute and independent validity of common moral precepts. I would appeal, firstly, to his intuitive judgment after due consideration of the question fairly placed before it: and, secondly, to a comprehensive comparison of the ordinary judgments of mankind. As regards the first argument, to me at least it seems clear that these objective relations of the conscious subject, when distinguished in reflective analysis from the consciousness accompanying and resulting from them, are not ultimately and intrinsically desirable, any more than material or other objects are, when considered out of relation to conscious existence altogether.

Now, how does Green answer this argument? So far as I can see, he ignores it. He answers . . . an argument, involving Psychological Hedonism, which I do not use; and which he admits that I do not use. (GSM 126–27)

Here again, as described in Chapter 4, Sidgwick, the man so heavily laden with a finely tuned cognitive apparatus, thinks his way to a celebration of Feeling, the "other" of his psyche, as the source of intrinsic value.[32] He does not, in his sensitive discrimination of the various pleasures, altogether relinquish the appeal to their feeling tone. Indeed, as for the charge of "tautology," Sidgwick deems it "quite unwarrantable." Even considering only the presentation of the argument in the *Methods*, Book III, Chapter 14, Green's case fails:

For the object of a great part of this argument is carefully to distinguish pleasure or happiness – desirable *Feeling* – from other elements of conscious life, which I do not, in a reflective attitude, regard as ultimately desirable. To say that the 'only thing that reason declares to be ultimately desirable is some kind of feeling,' whatever it is, is not a tautology, nor the same thing as saying that it is some kind of conscious life. But again, Green's statement of my view leaves out the further determination of the kind of feeling which is given in the definition of Pleasure, and which I fondly supposed that the reader would carry with him from Book II. I there define Pleasure as 'the kind of feeling which, when we experience it, we apprehend as desirable or preferable' – as 'feeling that is preferable or desirable, considered merely as feeling, and therefore from a point of view from which the judgment of the sentient individual is final.' The statement that Ultimate Good is feeling of a certain quality, the quality being estimated by the judgement of value implicitly passed on it by the sentient being at the time of feeling it, – this proposition is certainly not a tautology.

A similar want of understanding of my distinction between 'desired' and 'desirable' appears in Green's subsequent arguments. . . . I do not argue that the reason why 'no one denies pleasure to be a good' is merely 'because he is conscious of desiring it,' for I maintain that we all have experiences of desires directed to wrong objects, and also to objects clearly not ultimately desirable – e.g. in resentful impulse I desire another's pain, but on reflection I do not judge this pain to be desirable because I desire it, but because it is necessary for the determent or reformation of the offender.

Again, I cannot conceive why 'desirable' should exclude the 'actually desired,' as is argued by Green. . . . Of course we should not apply the idea of 'desirable' as distinct from 'desired,' unless we had empirical evidence that we desire pleasures to some extent out of proportion to their value as pleasures; but it does not follow that feeling actually desired is not normally, in the main, feeling judged desirable when fruition comes: as overwhelming experience shows to be in fact the case. (GSM 129–31)

Thus, although Sidgwick was wary of identifying, in Benthamite fashion, one particular mental quality of pleasure or pain, he did invoke the family of feelings that counted as desirable consciousness.[33] And this was important, pointing to how he in effect used an "experience requirement" (as noted in Chapter 4) to show that his account of Good did not bump up against the limits of thought as the Idealists claimed.

In fact, the upshot of this engagement with Green is to turn the tables, to seek to recruit Green for the Sidgwickian camp:

With part of Green's controversy against Mill – that which is directed against Psychological Hedonism – I am almost entirely in accord – that is to say, I agree with his conclusion that the object of conscious desire and voluntary aim is not pleasure only. And I agree in the main with the explanation he gives of the prevalence of the opposite error – that is, that pleasure normally accompanies the attainment of the desired object, and that hence it is easy to conceive this pleasure as the real object aimed at. But the same analysis which shows me that I do not always aim at my own pleasure, shows me equally that I do not always aim at my own satisfaction. I reject, in the one case as in the other, the conscious egoism of the form in which human choice is conceived – except in the insignificant sense that I am conscious that what I desire and aim at is desired and aimed at by me – a tautological proposition. In fact, I find a considerable difficulty in distinguishing what Green calls self-satisfaction from pleasure. And so far as I can distinguish them, – so far as I can conceive the consciousness of attainment of a desired object separated from pleasure, – it is something I do not desire. (GSM 103)[34]

As in the case of Bradley, Sidgwick cannot make out what Green really means by "Self-satisfaction," or whether he has any coherent notion of it. And this is crucial, since Green seems to be offering up his Idealism as a philosophical form of the reconciliation project, achieving through the notions of "good" and "perfection" what Sidgwick had called in the theistic postulate to deal with. But Sidgwick wonders whether, despite Green's claims, he does not fall prey to some form of dualism:

[I]f we take Green's wider notion of Perfection, namely, *complete realisation of capabilities*, and understand this to include (as he expressly affirms it to include) the development of Science and Art, of the faculties of knowledge and artistic production and appreciation, we cannot say that our own perfection or approximation to perfection and others' perfection are not liable to be presented as alternatives, unless we ignore the facts of experience and the actual conditions of human life. And Green's own language, in speaking of Justice, Self-denial, Self-sacrifice, etc., involves a similar conception of 'Good to one' incompatible with 'Good to another' – notwithstanding his assertion that True Good does not consist in objects that admit of being competed for.

So again as regards . . . the uncertainty of hedonistic calculation – I have aimed in *The Methods of Ethics* at bringing out clearly the uncertainties of hedonistic calculation, and all that I will now observe is, that the uncertainties on Green's view seem to me indefinitely greater, – both more complex and more fundamental, – if a wider conception of the end as the complete realisation of capabilities is taken. All the alternatives presented for practical choice involve different realisations of different capabilities. What criterion does Green offer for preferring one sort of realisation to another? I find none whatever; and if the comparison of quantities of pleasure is difficult and doubtful, the comparison of different realisations of capabilities seems to me indefinitely more difficult and more doubtful. (GSM 107)[35]

Sidgwick would end up forever lamenting the mysterious logical chasms separating the Idealist metaphysics from the Idealist ethics and both from the Idealist practice. His last philosophical lecture, delivered to the Oxford Philosophical Society in May 1900, was on "The Philosophy of T. H. Green," and it drew all the chief representatives of Oxford Idealism. According to F. C. S. Schiller, who attended, the disciples of Green mostly admitted the fairness of the criticism that Green's view was incoherent, though when a prominent Hegelian suggested that the incoherence pointed to the dialectical limits of thought in the world of appearance, Sidgwick confessed that "he had never been able to make out from the school to which he [the critic] evidently belonged how they managed to distinguish the contradictions which they took to be evidence of error from those which they regarded as intimations of higher truth" (M 586).[36]

This was more than a Sidgwicked witticism. The talk distilled decades of critical Sidgwickian engagement with Green's views, and it posed with special force the challenge to Green's Spiritualism: "Let us first take Green's positive account of Spirit, and ask, point by point whether we can definitely think the qualities or functions he attributes to it, without, in so thinking, predicating of it some of the relations which, according to Green, result from its combining and unifying activity, and are therefore not properly predicable of it." Point by point, Sidgwick answers no:

And this view, I think, will be confirmed by a rigorous examination of Green's main argument for establishing the existence of a spiritual principle in nature. It is the source of the relations that constitute experience a connected whole: but where lies the logical necessity of assuming such a source? Green answers that the existence of the relations involves 'the unity of the manifold, the existence of the many in one. . . . But,' he adds, 'a plurality of things cannot of themselves unite in one relation, nor can a single thing of itself bring itself into a multitude of relations . . . there must' – therefore – 'be something other than the manifold things themselves which combines them.' The argument seems to me unthinkable, because, as Green has emphatically declared, I cannot even conceive the manifold things out of the relations: and therefore I cannot even raise the question whether, if I could so conceive them, I should see them to require something other than themselves to bring them into the relations. (LPK 260, 264)

This was an important point, one that Sidgwick had often stressed in his class lectures. As he alternatively put it, for Green, nature is "conceived as essentially a single unalterable all-inclusive system of relations, by which all phenomena are combined into a systematic whole: and the source of connexion, the combiner and unifier, must be a non-natural or Spiritual Principle." But then,

How, as no element of nature is conceivable out of relation, can we conceive it as requiring a non-natural principle to bring it into relation? It seems that in order to exhibit the evidence for a non-natural principle Green has first to conceive Nature as analysed into elements; yet this in the same breath he declares to be irrational and inconceivable! (LPK 240)

Should Green appeal to self-consciousness as yielding a "positive conception of the action of the Divine Mind in the universe," Sidgwick counters that, as for himself, "I seem to *find*, not to *originate*, truth"; but even granting the consciousness of "action absolutely from itself" – human freedom – how "can we infer from this the action of the Universal Mind, consistently with Green's theory of the human spirit?" After all, "if my self-consciousness is to be the *causa cognoscendi* of the causality of the *unifying* principle in the world, that self-consciousness must surely include an indubitable cognition of the essential unity of the self: but in trying to think Green's conception of the human spirit, I find that notion of its essential unity vanishes." Green, that is, has not reconciled the mental and the physical, despite his appeal to the analogy of a two-sided shield: "For I see clearly that a shield not only *may* but *must* have two opposite sides, united into a continuous surface by the rim: whereas I cannot see how one indivisible self can possibly have as its two sides an animal organism and a self-limiting eternal consciousness" (LPK 264–65). In the fuller formulation of the point in Sidgwick's lectures:

> One of the things I am most certain of is the unity of myself. Green says that (1) I am really two things, so disparate as an eternal consciousness out of time, and a function of an animal organism changing in time; and yet at the same time that (2) I am one indivisible reality contemplated from two different points of view. I submit that Green is bound to reconcile this contradiction, which he does not do by simply stating that both contradictory propositions are true. As it is, his doctrine is rather like the theological doctrine of the Athanasian Creed, only the Athanasian Creed does not profess to give an intelligible account of the mysteries it formulates. (LPK 247)

For his part, Green would probably have thought this a prime example of the cheap mirth one ought to expect from utilitarians. But for Sidgwick, from the self-contradictions of empirical experience Green has only produced a self-contradictory metaphysics, unable to present its own basic tenets in a consistent and coherent fashion. What can't be said can't be said, and it can't be whistled either, as later Wittgensteinians were fond of singing.

It is not stretching it to find in these and many other passages of Sidgwick's critique the springboard for the (not much) later arguments of Moore and Russell, particularly during their early, realist period of rebellion against Idealism.[37] Sidgwick had urged in his lectures that "when Green draws the inference that this knowing consciousness is not a 'phenomenon,' not an 'event in the individual's history,' he seems to be confounding the knowing consciousness with the object known" (LPK 234).[38]

And of course, Russell attacked head on the central Idealist doctrine that, as he put it, "Every apparently separate piece of reality has, as it were, hooks which grapple it to the next piece; the next piece, in turn has fresh hooks, and so on until the whole universe is reconstructed." Russell, like Sidgwick, found this question-begging, a view that presupposed that existing incomplete things demanded the existence of other things, and that the nature of a thing was constituted by all the truths about it. Russell argued that the relations that a thing has do not necessarily constitute its nature, and that one can know things by direct acquaintance while remaining quite ignorant of many other relations:

I may be acquainted, for example, with my toothache, and this knowledge may be as complete as knowledge by acquaintance ever can be, without knowing all that the dentist (who is not acquainted with it) can tell me about its cause, and without therefore knowing its 'nature' in the above sense. Thus the fact that a thing has relations does not prove that its relations are logically necessary.[39]

Sidgwick had struggled hard with analogous claims in Green, concerning internal relations. He confessed himself unable to make out how Green could claim that "the single things are nothing except as determined by relations which are the negations of their singleness, but they do not therefore cease to be single things. . . . On the contrary, if they did not survive in their singleness, there could be no relation between them – nothing but a blank, featureless identity." Among other things, Sidgwick wondered why the "fact that they survive in their singleness" – whatever that singleness is – should show "that they need something other than themselves to make them so survive" (LPK 220). Furthermore, as John Gibbins has plausibly suggested, Russell's appeal to knowledge by acquaintance versus knowledge by description can be traced back through Sidgwick to John Grote.[40] In any event, Sidgwick plainly recognized the crucial point of the distinction, and the problematic that would animate much of Russell's epistemological work, at least during its phenomenalistic and reductionistic phases:

Let us suppose that both Materialists and Mentalists agree to affirm (1) that we immediately know the external world, so far as it is necessary to know it for the purpose of constructing physical science; (2) that we immediately know nothing but our own consciousness; and (3) that these two statements are perfectly consistent. It still remains to ask who are the 'we' who have this knowledge. Each one of us can only have experience of a very small portion of this world; and if we abstract what is known through memory, and therefore mediately, the portion becomes small indeed. In order to get to what 'we' conceive 'ourselves' to know as 'matter of fact' respecting the world, as extended in space and time – to such merely historical knowledge as we commonly regard not as 'resting' on experience, but as constituting the experience on which science rests – we must assume the general trustworthiness of memory, and the general trustworthiness of testimony under proper limitations and conditions. I do not for a moment say that we have no right to make these assumptions; I only do not see how we can prove that we have such a right, from what we immediately know. (LPK 389–90)[41]

However, it must be allowed that on various points, Sidgwick, while clearly pointing to the possibility of a program resembling Russell's logical atomism, would have resisted any overly ambitious formulation of it out of a fairly robust sense of the theory-ladenness of obervation, a sense of just how conceptualized perception, in any useful sense, always already is:

> The truth seems to be that the indubitable certainty of the judgment 'I am conscious' has been rather hastily extended by Empiricists to judgments affirming that my present consciousness is such and such. But these latter judgments necessarily involve an *implicit* comparison and classification of the present consciousness with elements of past conscious experience recalled in memory; and the implied classification may obviously be erroneous either through inaccuracy of memory or a mistake in the comparative judgment. And the risk of error cannot well be avoided by eliminating along with inference this implicit classification: for the psychical fact observed cannot be distinctly thought at all without it: if we rigorously purge it away, there will be nothing left save the cognition of self and of we cannot say what psychical fact. Nay, it is doubtful whether even this much will be left for the Empiricist's observation: since he may share Hume's inability to find a self in the stream of psychical experience, or to maintain a clear distinction between psychical and material fact. Thus the Empiricist criterion, if extended to purge away comparison as well as inference, may leave us nothing free from error but the bare affirmation of Fact not further definable. (LPK 453–54)[42]

Sidgwick takes pains to explain that he does not want to deny "the value of the Empirical criterion" and that he has no doubt of "the importance of distinguishing the inferential element in our apparently immediate judgments as far as we can, with a view to the elimination of error." The point is simply that "the assertion that we can by this procedure obtain a residuum of certainly true cognition seems to me neither self-evident nor confirmed by experience." Often enough, in Sidgwick's eyes, the "given" turned out to be a myth.[43]

Thus, although Sidgwick was well aware of the type of neo-Humean direction that empiricism might take – and later would take, in the work of the mature Russell – his own conception of experience held on to some of the more holistic and nonreductive elements of Idealism, in at least proto-pragmatist fashion. The empiricists and the rationalists offered up "useful" criteria for "guarding against error," but neither their schools nor any other had found the key to infallibility.[44] This comports well with the account of his epistemology set out in Chapter 4 in connection with the *Methods*.

Beyond all this, Sidgwick always found the whole Idealist business just terribly overimpressed by thought, at the expense of feeling.[45] In his final talk, as in so many other places, he explained of Green:

He is equally willing to admit that there is 'no such thing as mere thought'; and in fact only to contend that feeling and thought are inseparable and mutually dependent. And he expressly affirms this mutual dependence of thought and feeling, not only in the case of our empirical consciousness, but in the case also of 'the world-consciousness of which ours is a limited mode.' But if this be so, I do not see how Green is justified – or thinks himself justified – in making the thought element so prominent, and the feeling element so subordinate in his account of Nature; or in speaking of Nature as a system of relations, instead of related feelings; or in resolving – as we saw – the particularity of a feeling entirely into relations. And finally, if 'mutual independence of thought and feeling has no place in the world-consciousness,' difficult questions arise to which Green suggests no answer. For instance, if any feeling is attributed to the world-consciousness, must not all feeling in the world be so attributed? or how are we to distinguish? does God then feel the pleasure and the pain of the whole animal kingdom? And if so, is not the ground cut from under the anti-hedonistic position of Green's Ethics? (LPK 265–66)

Thus, Sidgwick concluded his last public philosophical talk by saying "But I perceive that this topic will introduce so great a wave of discourse – as Plato says – that I must reluctantly abandon it, and apologise for the extent to which I have already tried your patience."[46]

A neat twist: it is intriguing that in this final encounter, Sidgwick would end up charging the Idealists with harboring the image of one great calculating utilitarian consciousness, and thus tacitly admitting the coherence of a sum of pleasures, etc.[47] But in any event, he had again made plain his distaste for an unfeeling universe, whether championed by Huxley or by Green, and from this, it was only a few short steps to an aestheticism revolving around the fine discrimination of the pleasures of friendship, love, art, and the other Bloomsbury passions, as we shall see. And it was not even a short step to the critique of Idealism framed by William James, who would in due course lampoon Bradley's "sort of religious principle against admitting 'untransformed' feeling into philosophy," which he tracked back to "the old and obstinate intellectualist prejudice in favor of universals," revered as "loftier, nobler more rational objects than the particulars of sense":

The motive is pathetically simple, and any one can take it in. On the thin watershed between life and philosophy, Mr. Bradley tumbles to philosophy's call. Down he slides, to the dry valley of 'absolute' mare's nests and abstractions, the habitation of the fictitious suprarelational being which his will prefers. Never was there such a case of will-to-believe; for Mr. Bradley, unlike other anti-empiricists, deludes himself neither as to feeling nor as to thought: the one reveals for him the inner *nature* of reality perfectly, the other falsifies it utterly as soon as you carry it beyond the first few steps. Yet once committed to the conceptual direction, Mr. Bradley thinks we can't reverse, we can save ourselves only by hoping that the absolute will re-realize unintelligibly and 'somehow,' the unity, wholeness, certainty, etc., which feeling so immediately and transparently made us acquainted with at first.[48]

To opt with Bradley for the road leading inevitably to "the whole bog of unintelligibilities through which the critical part of 'Appearance and Reality' wades" is for James virtually to choose death over life:

When the alternative lies between knowing life in its full thickness and activity, as one acquainted with its *me's* and *thee's* and *now's* and *here's*, on the one hand, and knowing a transconceptual evaporation like the absolute, on the other, it seems to me that to choose the latter knowledge merely because it has been named 'philosophy' is to be superstitiously loyal to a name. But if names are to be used eulogistically, rather let us give that of philosophy to the fuller kind of knowledge, the kind in which perception and conception mix their lights.[49]

James's vital, nonreductive "radical empiricism" was rather plainly resonant with Sidgwick's eclectic and only qualifiedly empiricist epistemology. Indeed, James not only shared the Sidgwickian concern over the way Idealism inexplicably voided the universe of its feeling side, but also, as James Kloppenberg has urged, followed Sidgwick on the dualism of practical reason, resisting both Idealist and naturalist efforts to show how something other than theism might resolve the conflict.[50] Of all the pragmatists, James was the one who was most truly a kindred Sidgwickian spirit, and what with their shared subversions of the traditional epistemological and ethical projects, and their shared enthusiasm for the fresh facts of psychical research, it was a remarkably close kinship. Although Dewey may have been the one to coin the expression the "quest for certainty" as a summary assessment of what was wrong with the Great Tradition,

Sidgwick and James – both so sensitive to the attractions of soaring – were ahead of him in discovering that infallibility was nowhere to be found, and that Idealism, in particular, afforded no fresh hope. After all, Sidgwick too, however grudgingly, had ended up with a keen appreciation of the distance between abstract, universal ethical truth and the demands of practical action. The gap between axioms and actions called for pragmatic measures.

What is astonishing about Sidgwick's critique is not only its cogency, but also how consistent it was over the decades. Such leading concerns about Idealism's unsatisfactoriness were to some extent evident even in his review essay on the *Prolegomena*, which appeared in *Mind* in 1884 and in which he complained that, although Green

recognizes that it is the function of philosophy to supply men with a '*rationale* of the various duties' prescribed to them, I cannot perceive that the enthusiasm for human well-being which the whole treatise breathes has actually impelled him to furnish such a *rationale*, or even to provide his readers with an outline of a coherent method by which a system of duties could be philosophically worked out.[51]

The slipperiness of Green's practical ethics had fairly appalled Sidgwick for quite some time, particularly when he considered how Green, with all his Idealist theological unorthodoxy, could seriously entertain the idea of becoming a deacon of the Anglican Church. As he wrote to Dakyns, in 1864: "I talked to Green in Oxford; I was horrified by his idea of diaconising; it is only in such a *milieu* as Oxford that a high-minded man could think of it" (M 105).[52] Even if the great Mill had urged liberal-minded young clergymen to stay in the church and reform it, Sidgwick, as we have seen, thought the cost of this form of hypocrisy too high. Fortunately, Green was spared the necessity of having to affiliate himself with any particular institutional orthodoxy.

Ironically, then, for all his earnest reformism, Green was in the end left in much the same position as Bradley, theoretically speaking.[53] And against both Green and Bradley, Sidgwick often appeared as the defender of pleasure and progress, the brighter light of academic liberalism. But as we have seen, outside the realm of philosophical polemics, and some-times even within it, he was plagued by uncertainty. His project was not as positive or confident as Green's; it did not breathe moral uplift in the fashion of the Idealists. Consider Sidgwick's famous 1884 bout of introspective self-scrutiny, provoked by an attack on him by Alfred Marshall, fresh from stints at Bristol and Oxford, who among other things blasted him for his mania for "over-regulation" and invidiously compared Sidgwick's "lecture-room, in which a handful of men are taking down what they regard as useful for examination, with that of Green, in which a hundred men – half of them B.A.'s – ignoring examinations, were wont to hang on the lips of the man who was sincerely anxious to teach them the truth about the universe and human life." Sidgwick pondered his "failure to attract men on a large scale" and, in assessing his "Character and Opinions," borrowed some lines from Bagehot's description of Clough:

Though without much fame, he had no envy. But he had a strong realism. He saw what it is considered cynical to see – the absurdities of many persons, the pomposities of many creeds, the splendid zeal with which missionaries rush on to teach what they do not know, the wonderful earnestness with which most incomplete solutions of the universe are thrust upon us as complete and satisfying.

As he noted, this "represents my relation to T. H. G. and his work." Destiny had been good to him, had bestowed upon him

richly all external sources of happiness – friends, a wife, congenial occupation, freedom from material cares – but, feeling that the deepest truth I have to tell is by no means 'good tidings,' I naturally shrink from exercising on others the personal influence which would make men [resemble] me, as much as men more optimistic and prophetic naturally aim at exercising such influence. Hence as a teacher I naturally desire to limit my teaching to those whose bent or deliberate choice it is to search after ultimate truth; if such come to me, I try to tell them all I know; if others come with vaguer aims, I wish if possible to train their faculties without guiding their judgements. I would not if I could, and I could not if I would, say anything which would make philosophy – my philosophy – popular. (M 394–96)

Missionary "zeal" and "wonderful earnestness" – all in the service of very incomplete solutions to the deepest problems – seem a pretty shrewd assessment of Green. Where would Green's Idealism lead, without the concrete experience of the church? The Idealist temperance movement was as baseless as the Millian antitemperance movement. Green's philosophy merely reproduced in new terms an unfeeling Universe, the dualism of practical reason, egoism, complacency with (some types of) orthodox religion, and all the rest of Sidgwick's worries. In fact, all the old theological conundrums arise again in connection with Idealism. Consider the problem of evil, the suffering of innocents. Sidgwick, sounding a note more often associated with Russell's atheism, wondered "Why does the eternal spirit, reproducing itself so many million times in connexion with so many organisms, produce so much error and so much vice? I find no serious attempt to answer this in Green." (LPK 254) Worse still, no one, not even Green's fondest admirers, could make out just where he stood on the question of personality – that is, whether God has a personal nature (that one might pray to) and whether there is such a thing as personal immortality.

Perhaps the cogency of Sidgwick's critique of Green was in part a result of his own intense ambivalence over the allures of German philosophy. He had, like Green, found himself uniquely attracted to German erudition and civilization. But, as we have seen, in some crucial respects he had already thought and fought his way free of the great source of Green's project – the Kantian conception of the self. In a vital, deeply revealing section of his lectures on "The Metaphysics of Kant," Sidgwick argued, concerning Kant's conception of the "Transcendental I" as barren of content:

Now perhaps this language is justifiable if the 'I' of the thought 'I think' is treated as strictly transcendental and examined in rigorous abstraction from experience. But in saying that 'in inner perception there is nothing permanent, for the "I" is simply the consciousness of my thinking,' Kant has abandoned the transcendental ground; and here I think he is guilty of a transition as illegitimate as that which he rightly attributes to his opponents, although in an opposite direction. That is, he tries to reduce the notion of Self as object of inner experience to the meagreness of the 'I' of transcendental thought. Now of the self which introspection presents to us as a thinking thing, introspection doubtless tells us little enough: all the particularity of the mind, all that interests us in our thought of ourselves and other minds as relatively permanent objects of thought in contrast with the more transient states of consciousness, we only know by inference from the transient and ever-varying element of inner experience. But still it is going too far to say that the self presented in inner experience is merely thought as a logical subject *without* predicates. However little 'I' know of 'myself' in introspection, I still know myself as *one* and *identical*, perduring through the empirical stream of thoughts, feelings, and volitions.

This cognition may be liable to error – I find infallibility nowhere in human thought – or again it may seem unimportant: but it is presented as immediate and is as certain as any empirical cognition, and in it I certainly find 'given' – if anything is ever 'given' – the empirical permanence which Kant – in the *Kritik* – denies. (LPK 150–51)[54]

The actually experienced self was richer than the Kantians or the Idealists owned, and here was an opening for psychical research, made all the more imperative by the total failure, to Sidgwick's mind, of the Kantian and neo-Kantian efforts to wrest from the critical philosophy a resolution of the dualism of practical reason. In one of his most explicit pronouncements on this all-important subject, as handled by Kant, he stated:

> In the case of Immortality, speculative reason – the non-empirical study of the soul, when duly critical – appears to do nothing but guard against materialistic explanations of mental phenomena. Rational psychology, with its idea of an absolute subject, 'is merely a discipline which prevents us . . . from throwing ourselves into the arms of a soulless materialism,' and serves as a regulative principle totally to destroy all materialistic explanations of the internal phenomena of the soul – for these can never account for self-consciousness, – but it gives no ground for inferring the permanence of the soul beyond the period of mundane life. I may observe that as regards the practical postulate of Immortality, Kant's ideas appear to have undergone a development between the *Critique of Pure Reason* (1781) and the *Critique of Practical Reason* (1788). In the former, he does not distinguish between the belief in immortality and the belief in 'a future life' or 'future world' in which the connexion which reason demands between morality and happiness may be realised. But by the time he came to compose the *Critique of Practical Reason*, it seems to have occurred to him that the postulate of a future life, adequate to the rewarding of desert with happiness, does not necessarily involve endlessness of life. Here, accordingly, he rests the argument for immortality on the necessity for the realisation of the highest good by man, of 'perfect harmony' between this disposition and the moral law. 'Such a harmony,' he says, 'must be possible, as it is implied in the command to promote the highest good' – a form in which the command to do duty may be conceived; on the other hand, 'a finite rational being' cannot *attain* moral perfection, it is only 'capable of infinite progress towards it.' Hence, as we must postulate that our 'existence should continue long enough to permit of the complete realisation of the moral law,' we must postulate that it will continue for ever. I shall have occasion to refer to this argument later. It always seems to me to illustrate well both the ingenuity of Kant and what I may perhaps be allowed to call his *naïveté*. (LPK 18–19)

Understandably, Sidgwick was specially attuned to those bits of Kant, often ignored in more recent commentary, that flesh out the Kantian view that without a God, "and without a world not visible to us now but hoped for, the glorious ideas of morality are indeed objects of applause and admiration, but not *springs of purpose and action*." For Kant was clear that the "Highest Aim" of the transcendental reason was directed toward comprehending the "freedom of the will, the immortality of the soul, and the existence of God." When it comes to Rational Theology, Sidgwick explained, "for Kant the sole important question is, Can the theorising reason of man prove, what a rational man, who has to act in the world no less than to know it as completely as possible, must believe?" (LPK 179–80, 183) These were the questions that had made Kant one of his masters when he was composing the *Methods*.

Much as he agreed with Green in rejecting the Kantian appeal to the noumenal realm of "things in themselves" and other points of the original critical philosophy, Sidgwick nonetheless held that Kant was near the heart of the "deepest problems." Unfortunately, he cannot discern a successful Kantian answer, only an ultimate resort to the demands of a coherent morality that speculative reason is powerless to defend. And inner experience and the world of feeling were richer resources than the Kantians and Idealists allowed. Although many have shared John Skorupski's view that there "is more to be learnt from the idealist notion of a person's good than Sidgwick allows; there is also more to be learnt from the idealist notion of freedom than he allows," Sidgwick found the Idealist moral psychology too thin to capture the richness of inner experience and the importance of feeling.[55] And this was an approximation to James's views – Sidgwick was a whole-hearted admirer of James's *Principles of Psychology*, a complementary copy of which had been sent him by his SPR colleague.[56]

Indeed, this is a point of the first importance. For as urged in the previous chapter, Sidgwick was very much in the vanguard that was producing complex forms of depth psychology, leaving behind the older schools of associationism and introspectionism. Freudianism, with its prioritizing of the therapeutic perspective, was only one offshoot of this; another was Jamesian pragmatism, which also stressed the role of the unconscious, and which was in fact deeply indebted to the work of Myers on the "Subliminal Self." Both Myers and Symonds figure prominently in James's *Varieties of Religious Experience*:

The *subconscious self* is nowadays a well-accredited psychological entity; and I believe that in it we have exactly the mediating term required. Apart from all religious considerations, there is actually and literally more life in our total soul than we are at any time aware of. The exploration of the transmarginal field has hardly yet been seriously undertaken, but what Mr. Myers said in 1892 in his essay on the Subliminal Consciousness is as true as when it was first written: 'Each of us is in reality an abiding psychical entity far more extensive than he knows – an individuality which can never express itself completely through any corporeal manifestation. The Self manifests through the organism; but there is always some part of the Self unmanifested; and always, as it seems, some power of organic expression in abeyance or reserve.' Much of the content of this larger background against which our conscious being stands out in relief is insignificant. Imperfect memories, silly jingles, inhibitive timidities, 'dissolutive' phenomena of various sorts, as Myers calls them, enter into it for a large part. But in it many of the performances of genius seem also to have their origin; and in our study of conversion, of mystical experiences, and of prayer, we have seen how striking a part invasions from this region play in the religious life.[57]

Fascinatingly, what James draws from this speaks directly to the religious concerns of the Sidgwick Group:

Let me propose, as an hypothesis, that whatever it may be on its *farther* side, the 'more' with which in religious experience we feel ourselves connected is on its *hither* side the subconscious continuation of our conscious life. Starting thus with a recognized psychological fact as our basis, we seem to preserve a contact with 'science' which the ordinary theologican lacks. At the same time the theologians's contention that the religious man is moved by an external power is vindicated, for it is one of the peculiarities of invasions from the subconscious region to take on objective appearances, and to suggest to the Subject an external control. In the religious life the control is felt as 'higher'; but since on our hypothesis it is primarily the higher faculties of our own hidden mind which are controlling, the sense of union with the power beyond us is a sense of something, not merely apparently, but literally true.[58]

The question is, of course, what sense to make of the "farther" side; but in any event, to cast matters in this way is, James holds, at least a doorway into the scientific study of the subject, one mediating a variety of conflicting views.

As we have seen, this was very much the problematic that had emerged in the Sidgwick Group, and it is well to bear in mind that when Sidgwick discussed the fallible sense of the perduring self, through the flux of experience, he had James's "stream of consciousness" and Myers's "Subliminal Self" before his mind. This was the work that rather obviously had his sympathy. In James's immortal rendering of the sense of personal identity:

[T]he thoughts which we actually know to exist do not fly about loose, but seem each to belong to some one thinker and not to another. Each thought, out of the multitude of other thoughts of which it may think, is able to distinguish those which belong to it from those which do not. The former have a warmth and intimacy about them of which the latter are completely devoid, and the result is a Me of yesterday, judged to be in some peculiarly subtle sense the *same* with the I who now make the judgment.[59]

Like Sidgwick, James was sensitive to the appeal of Idealism, particularly against reductive forms of empiricism and materialism, while in the end finding it unsatisfactory – too ambitious, too antiscientific, and ultimately, too inhuman.

Some have suggested that this entire phase of British philosophy – featuring first Sidgwick versus Bradley and Green, and then James, Russell, and Moore versus Bradley and McTaggert – was something of a backwater in the larger currents of history. Richard Rorty, in a witty comparison of twentieth-century textualism with nineteenth-century Idealism, wrote of the latter:

[B]y the time of Marx and Kierkegaard, everybody was saying that the emperor had no clothes – that whatever idealism might be it was not a demonstrable, quasi-scientific thesis. By the end of the century (the time of Green and Royce) idealism had been trimmed back to its Fichtean form – an assemblage of dusty Kantian arguments about the relations between sensation and judgment, combined with intense moral earnestness. But what Fichte had been certain was both demonstrable truth and the beginning of a new era in human history, Green and Royce disconsolately knew to be merely the opinion of a group of professors.[60]

Yet clearly, the principal players did not see it that way. Here was a group of professors who were out to rule the world, and who profoundly shaped the men who actually did. The importance of being earnest was never so palpable, philosophy never more relevant, even if it was becoming professionalized. The world needed revitalizing, and philosophy was never more charged. Neither Sidgwick nor Green had any clear sense that their efforts to professionalize philosophy might at some future time drain it of the passion and personal investment that had so marked their own formative soaring.

And Green's world had much more in it than any reduction of it to the professionalization of philosophy and canon formation would indicate, even if Green was responsible for imposing Hume versus Kant as the testing ground for students. Indeed, however unsatisfactory his philosophical efforts may have been to Sidgwick, the larger Cosmic Optimism they represented was to emerge as a profound challenge to some of Sidgwick's deepest beliefs when it found expression in the life and work of Symonds. Symonds was not a professional philosopher. But to Sidgwick's mind, he knew where the deepest problems were to be found, and his psychological explorations brought home to Sidgwick the problems of inner experience and the unity of the self in ways that the Idealists never could. For whatever else he was, Symonds was a voyager in the inner world and a shaper of the future of psychology. James singled him out as beautifully articulating mystic and Whitmanian notions of cosmic consciousness, and for his part, Symonds was utterly persuaded of the importance of Myers's work on the unconscious, the subliminal "uprush" of genius being especially appealing. And Symonds was, with Walter Pater, a formidable proponent of the lower, Goethean alternative, recast as a revitalizing "New Chivalry" or, more accurately, "New Paganism."

Patently, the Oxford of Jowett and Green was destined to shape Sidgwick's consciousness in myriad ways. His connections to the famous rival institution were manifold and intense – his brothers Arthur and William would both end up as Oxford dons, and Henry was in constant contact with Oxford life through such vehicles as the Ad Eundem Society, a dining club founded by William in 1864 precisely in order to foster such fellowship. For all his Cambridge ways, Sidgwick, too, owed much to Jowett, and he would owe even more to Symonds – another of Jowett's discoveries, for whom education was a very personal affair that might save the world.

II. Liberty of the Heart

Seen in the context of such other politically liberal undergraduate essay societies as the Cambridge Apostles of Tennyson and A. H. Hallam or the Decade of Matthew Arnold and A. H. Clough, the Old Mortality society of Pater and Symonds, T. H. Green and James Bryce thus stands forth as a two-handed engine of cultural transformation by which liberal influences are to be introjected into the larger society . . . as well as into Tory Oxford itself. The language of this transforming influence would always be that of the Oxford intellectual elite: the discursive vocabulary of the Greats course with its intermixture of Plato, Hegel, and J. S.

Mill, that procreant combination Pater's essay adopts when it joins the 'forgotten culture' of philosophic love to the cultural anxieties of *On Liberty*. Pater thus allows his 'hearer' to understand that precisely the answer to Millian fears about the 'regeneration of the world' or about 'our collective life' sinking 'to the level of a colourless uninteresting existence' ('Diaphaneitè' 252) may indeed mean returning to the Platonic eros, as to 'a relic from the classical age, laid open by accident to our alien modern atmosphere' (251) – Pater's central image for cultural renaissance to which he would constantly recur.

Sharing in Pater's sense of a dawning moment of extraordinary cultural expansion and possibility, Symonds, writing in an 1863 prize essay, had already read enough Michelet and Burckhardt to be able to declare that the Renaissance itself began when the Aristotle of the medieval schoolmen yielded his place to Plato, whose 'sublime guesses and far-reaching speculations suited the spirit of the awakening age' (*Renaissance* 47). On the most obvious level, one readily apprehensible to themselves, Pater and Symonds are both participating in the moment when the full mission of the reformed Greats curriculum was being carried out in the spirit of Mill's ringing dictum in *On Liberty* – that one's first duty as a thinker is 'to follow his intellect to whatever conclusions it may lead' (242). Pater and Symonds are quietly determined to do nothing less than follow Mill's notion of a culturally reinvigorating liberty of opinion and experience to its boldest conclusion: a 'liberty of the heart,' as Pater was to call it in *The Renaissance* (3), so free as to encompass even male love.

> Linda Dowling, *Hellenism and Homosexuality in Victorian Oxford*

Peculiar as it may seem to affiliate Sidgwick with the growth of depth psychology and Jamesian pragmatism, that is a context of singular importance for understanding his work. If Sidgwick did not go all the way with the cheerful, insouciant Jamesian "will to believe" or think of himself as naturalistic in the same way as the pragmatists, nonetheless, as we have seen, he was at one with James on a great many counts. Besides, whatever "naturalism" marked James's view of the universe, it was one capacious enough to include psychical research and the normative structure of practical reason. Sidgwick's minimal metaethics was just on the other side of the line demarcating any such naturalism from non-naturalism. His reticence about postulating any Moorean "objective property" of goodness, much less any special faculty of intuition, and his sticking instead to the less ontologically ambitious claim that, simply put, in any given situation there is something that ought to be done, made it difficult for pragmatists to find anything in his metaphysics that they did not in some way share.

To be sure, if the Jamesian enthusiasm for the rich particularity of life was for James a healthy restorative from the soaring of Idealism, whether Platonic or Hegelian, Sidgwick tended to find himself more regretful, with a sense of the loss involved in such a retreat from the great ambitions of capital-P Philosophy. Even so, the arc of their thought was similar. After all, Sidgwick's skeptical results, and his sense that infallibility was nowhere to be found, were in their way every bit as heretical as the pragmatists' rather breezier acceptance of fallibilism, particularly from the standpoint of orthodox Christianity. However reverential he was about the great philosophical quest, to deny that universal moral truth was known was the type of thing that, under certain circumstances, could get one into a great deal of trouble. Especially if one was given to pursuing pleasurable consciousness with the wrong people.

Yet there was something utterly characteristic about this graceful Victorian decanting from airy Platonism to earthy life. Sidgwick's restless tossing between the high of sympathetic unity and the low of Goethean harmonious development was almost written into the times, with the journalistic world invoking the contrasts of "sympathy" and "egotism" at every turn. James may have been somewhat readier to endorse this tossing on its own terms, but even he would pale beside Sidgwick's intimate friend Symonds, when it came to Cosmic Optimism sustaining a vacillation between the other-worldly and the this-worldly. Symonds's arc carried him from a youthful infatuation with Plato to a mature worship of Walt Whitman, whose healthy naturalness made him "more truly Greek" than any other modern. Of course, the figure of Goethe was always there smiling in the background, as another towering genius breathing life into ancient perfectionism.

Indeed, the Platonic revival that Mill and the seminal Apostles had advanced, and that Jowett had brought into effective academic realization, would reach a new level of knowing self-awareness with the figures of Pater and Symonds, both of whom made it unmistakably clear that Plato meant what he said about eros. Swinburne had also, in his earlier years, been a fine flower of the eroticized Oxford Hellenism, but he was in due course to suffer a serious attack of homosocial panic and repudiate his earlier attachments, even coining the expression "Whitmania" to describe all that was wrong with his old friends from the Old Mortality. But in the bloom of the 1860s and 1870s, Oxford was the Arcadia that would inspire such breakthrough works as Pater's *Studies in the History of the Renaissance* (1873)[61] and Symonds's *Studies of the Greek Poets* (first series 1873) and *The Renaissance in Italy* (first volume 1875). What Pater and Symonds found in the Italian Renaissance was, of course, the rebirth of paganism and a renewed appreciation for Plato, just the things that they found in Goethe and in Goethe's inspirer, the seminal art historian Johann Joachim Winckelmann, in whom Goethe found the ideal of "wholeness, unity with one's self, intellectual integrity."

Of course, the Goethean ideal could forgive Winckelmann much hypocrisy for the sake of his aesthetic growth. What matter if, as Richard Dellamora puts it, "a diplomatic conversion to Catholicism enabled him to move to Rome, where alone his life's work could be done"?[62] And what matter if this paganism were true to its source, and celebratory of male love? As Dellamora notes, quoting G. S. Rousseau, the "villa of Winckelmann's Roman patron, Cardinal Albani, 'was an unrivaled nervecenter for combined antiquarian and homosocial activity.' "[63] For Goethe, as for Pater, this was also part of the dream, the realization of their passion for male love, albeit in a double life. Hypocrisy wore a double face, religious and sexual, but this was simply the price of admission to a truly liberating spiritual growth.

Like Goethe and Winckelmann, Pater and Symonds would find that the route to ancient perfectionism went through Renaissance Italy, and the route to Renaissance Italy went through modern Italy. Such a curious paradox, that while Sidgwick and Green were adoring the Germany shaped by Goethe and Winckelmann, Symonds and Pater were following the example of Goethe and Winckelmann and fleeing south, to the source of art and love. As Goethe confessed: "Only in Rome have I found myself, only here have I become happy and wise in the intimate harmony of my being."[64] Such predilections also carried a certain risk in terms of one's academic career, particularly when the battle lines were being drawn with such erudite clarity. As David DeLaura has argued, Pater's "Winckelmann" was

so centrally a response to Arnold's 'Pagan and Medieval Religious Sentiment' that ... the very structure of his argument parallels Arnold's. By rejecting the uniqueness and value of the medieval religion of sorrow, by qualifying Arnold's views on the alleged superficiality of Greek popular religion, and finally by proposing a version of Arnold's Hellenic solution in a larger historical perspective, Pater consciously sets out to re-adjust the relations among the major factors in Arnold's own complex equation.[65]

Pater was fairly emphatic on how the Greek "immersion in the sensuous was, religiously, at least, indifferent." Unlike Christian asceticism, "Greek sensuousness, therefore, does not fever the conscience: it is shameless and childlike." Winckelmann is free of that "intoxication" that comes from artistic interests resulting from a "conscious disavowal of a spiritual world," and "he fingers those pagan marbles with unsinged hands, with no sense of shame or loss. That is to deal with the sensuous side of art in the pagan manner."[66] The lesson, for moderns, is that it is not "the fruit of experience, but experience itself" that is the end. What is demanded of us is that we "be for ever curiously testing new opinions and courting new impressions, never acquiescing in a facile orthodoxy, of Comte, or of Hegel, or of our own." Philosophy must be subordinated to this: "The theory or idea or system which requires of us the sacrifice of any part of this experience, in consideration of some interest into which we cannot enter, or some abstract theory we have not identified with ourselves, or of what is only conventional, has no real claim upon us."[67] Of this wisdom, "the poetic passion, the desire of beauty, the love of art for its own sake, has most. For art comes to you proposing frankly to give nothing but the highest quality to your moments as they pass, and simply for those moments' sake."[68]

Pater suffered for his forthright defense of the lower Goethean vision. Although he was a Fellow of Brasenose College, Jowett consistently passed him over in his bid for the post of proctor, which position ultimately went to one John Wordsworth – a grandnephew of the great poet – who had candidly told Pater of his concern about *Studies in the History of the Renaissance*:

After a perusal of the book I cannot disguise from myself that the concluding pages adequately sum up the philosophy of the whole; and that that philosophy is an assertion, that no fixed principles either of religion or morality can be regarded as certain, that the only thing worth living for is momentary enjoyment and that probably or certainly the soul dissolves at death into elements which are destined never to reunite.[69]

Such views, Wordsworth avowed, had to be opposed openly. Furthermore, when Pater stood for the professorship of poetry, in 1877, Jowett ended up opposing him, and the victorious candidate turned out to be J. C. Shairp, who was elected with the support of Arnold, who had held the professorship from 1857 to 1867.

This episode in academic politics was a significant turning point in the history of Oxford Hellenism. It was not merely the defeat of Pater's paganism at the hands of old Arnoldian Hellenism, cleansed of sensuality. For Jowett had also been forced into opposing another of his old students, one he tended to favor over Pater – namely, Symonds. And Symonds had been urged to stand by, among others, Henry Sidgwick, who, along with Green, openly supported his candidacy. As Symonds wrote to Clough's widow, in January of 1876: "I think the chief new thing to be told about myself is that I am thinking of standing for the Poetry Professorship at Oxford. A great many people have urged me to do this, & Henry Sidgwick says he thinks it is very important for my literary reputation." By contrast, Jowett "sententiously pronounces that to get it would confer no honour."[70] Given the seriousness with which these figures regarded education and the business of professorships, it is intriguing in the extreme to contemplate the meaning of Sidgwick's and Green's support for the academic legitimation of Symonds's brand of paganism, which in so many respects – not all – overlapped with Pater's. All the more so given the visibility of the issues that the year 1877 witnessed. As Linda Dowling has observed, by this point Pater's orientation was an open secret – he was "Mr. Rose"

I rather look upon life as a chamber,' says Mr. Rose in W. H. Mallock's *New Republic* (1877), his voice like a lonely flute, 'which we decorate as we would decorate the chamber of the woman or the youth that we love' (21). Mr. Rose's utterance marks the moment when the sexual ambivalence within Oxford Hellenism, so plausibly depicted by Pater as the very engine of past and future cultural regeneration, is thrust into a scandalous visibility upon the national stage.[71]

Beyond this, however, there was the infamous attack on the new paganism issuing from Richard St. John Tyrwhitt, who, as Dowling notes, would also go on to "assault the pretensions of Balliol Hellenism by glorifying forthright, fox-hunting, aristocratic passmen in *Hugh Heron, Christ Church*." Tyrwhitt, the rector of St. Mary Magdalen, Oxford, had been fairly scandalized by Symonds's *Studies in the Greek Poets*, in which Symonds had been openly lyrical about classical Greek life, including male love. This was another pathbreaking work in aestheticism and Oxford

Hellenism, with Symonds urging, among other things, that

When we speak of the Greeks as an aesthetic nation, this is what we mean. Guided by no supernatural revelation, with no Mosaic law for conduct, they trusted their αἴσθησις, delicately trained and preserved in a condition of the utmost purity. This tact is the ultimate criterion in all matters of art – a truth which we recognize in our use of the word aesthetic, though we too often attempt to import the alien elements of metaphysical dogmatism and moral prejudice into the sphere of beauty. This tact was also for the Greeks the ultimate criterion of ethics. . . . A man in perfect health of mind and body, enjoying the balance of mental, moral, and physical qualities which health implies, carried within himself the norm and measure of propriety. Those were the days when 'love was an unerring light, and joy its own security.'[72]

This was too much for Tyrwhitt, who, in "The Greek Spirit in Modern Literature," set out to quash Symonds's run for the professorship. It was a brilliant polemic, firmly reminding readers of how different Arnold's Hellenism was when it came to commonsense morality, and bringing in some of Jowett's more emphatically homophobic remarks about how "there is a great gulf fixed between us and them [the ancient Greeks], which no willingness to make allowance for the difference of ages and countries would enable us to pass." Indeed, however customary it may be to deride Tyrwhitt's views, there was a good deal of wit and intelligence in his case:

[T]hese essays are full of descriptive beauty, good scholarship, high poetic feeling, and artistic culture, as distinguished from artistic knowledge. But their drift is polemical Agnosticism. Mr. Symonds really means, in every page, to set up the higher side of Athenian life – its rejoicing in beauty, its bodily training, its content with nature and itself, its balanced *sophrosyne*, by which each man knew what every part of him was fit for, and what he himself was fit for – against the Christian faith, its self-distrust and restraint, its unrest in this world, its sense of sin, and hopes of heaven. And he sees that the faith, theism, and morality are irrevocably bound together, and determines that they shall go together.

These pages are a rebellion against nature as she is here, in the name of nature as described in Athens. And the word nature now brings us unavoidably on awkward ground. Mr. Symonds is probably the most innocent of men; we certainly cannot look upon him in any other light. He might not return the compliment, for everybody who objects to suggestive passages of a certain character is now called prurient by their authors, and this reproach we propose to incur. The emotions of Socrates at sight of the beauty of young Charmides are described for him by Plato, in the dialogue which bears the name of the latter. Socrates' purity, and indeed his asceticism of life are freely and fully vindicated elsewhere by Plato, and will never be disputed here. The expressions put in his mouth are, no doubt, typically Hellenic. But they are not natural: and it is well known that Greek love of nature and beauty went frequently against nature. The word is used equivocally in this book – for the outward shows of creation, and for the inward impulses of man; and it is assumed that because the former are generally beautiful, the latter are invariably to be followed. Neither are good, for what is good? They are both here, and must be taken for what they are.

Other assertions seem to be made rather, it must be said, in the spirit of the persecutor; that is to say, in order to inflict moral outrage instead of physical. Such are the passage about a phallic ecstasy perfectly free from pruriency ... the talk about the frank sensuality of Priapus as a right object of Greek sculpture, and the concluding exhortation to follow Walt Whitman as far as our Hebraistic training and imperfect nature will enable us. The critic glides over the whole subject of Greek slavery and its utterly demoralizing consequences in a short note; and well he may, for it destroys his whole argument. He affirms with bland confidence that Retribution, the Eumenides, the θεῖον φθονερὸν, and the Corinthian worship of Aphrodite were Asiatic introductions and foreign intrusions, in fact not Greek. And we must say again, that he cannot know his historians as well as he does his poets; or he would have remembered that unnatural practices between men were foreign intrusions from Greece into Asia.

In this sense, then, Hellenism means, at the present day and when you come to work it, the total denial of any moral restraint on any human impulses. And let us now set forth our own duller notions of a quasi-Greek training, based on the old distinction, between an original, true, or better nature of man, and an actual or fallen nature which lusts against the other. Perhaps such an education is as yet, and for a time, inaccessible to the poorer, or lower-artisan classes of our own days. But so was ancient culture to Athenian slaves, who did all the hard work of the State, and who seem to have been as un-Hellenic as colliers.[73]

In sum, Symonds was "against nature," understood in anything like the Christian sense. And as for evil, Tyrwhitt can only lament the passing of the "rougher time" of his own earlier undergraduate world at Oxford, when vice "was less recondite, and the devil was more of a roaring lion, and did not glide about with the polite hiss of modern days." At least then, before being "cultured into Hellenism," the men "accepted Nature for what she is; but, on the other hand, decency was considered decent and not 'prurient.'"

Although Symonds naturally complained of Tyrwhitt's attack, which he thought was "meant to be nasty," it would be hard to deny that Tyrwhitt

had, from an orthodox Anglican orientation, provided a pretty fair statement of the real issues. Especially in the section on "The Genius of Greek
Art," Symonds had been most eloquent on how the Greek notion of "living according to nature" had great advantages, and even in later editions
of the *Studies*, such as that of 1879, he was not actually very conciliatory
toward such critics as Tyrwhitt.[74] Indeed, his celebration of the Greeks
was remarkably consistent over his mature career; their ethics

do not place between us and the world in which we have to live and die the will
of a hypothetical ruler, to whom we may ascribe our passions and our fancies,
enslaving ourselves to the delusions of our own soul. Nor, again, do they involve
the monstrous paradox of all ascetic systems, which assert that human nature
is radically evil, and that only that is good in us which contradicts our natural
appetites and instincts.

For Symonds, "the truest instinct of the Greeks" involved eliminating "the
mysterious and the terrible, to accentuate the joyous and the profitable for
humane uses."[75] After a brief review of Marcus Aurelius and Goethe,
whose Stoic–Epicurean search for well-ordered conduct without either
asceticism or licence he would emulate, the moral and the mission come
out:

Thus the Greek conception of life was posed; the Christian conception was
counterposed; the synthesis, crudely attempted in the age of the Renaissance,
awaits mature accomplishment in the immediate future. The very ground-thought
of Science is to treat man as part of the natural order – not, assuredly, on that
account excluding from its calculation the most eminent portion of man, his reason and his moral being – and to return from the study of nature with profit
to the study of man. It does not annihilate or neutralise what man has gained
from Christianity; on the contrary, the new points of morality developed by the
Christian discipline are of necessity accepted as data by the scientific mind. Our
object is to combine both the Hellenic and the Christian conceptions in a third,
which shall be more solid and more rational than any previous manifestation of
either, superior to the Hellenic as it is no longer a mere intuition, superior to
the ecclesiastical inasmuch as it relies on no mythology, but seeks to ascertain the
law.[76]

But there is all the difference in the world between the Greek and
the Christian: "the whole bearing of a man who feels that his highest
duty consists in conforming himself to laws he may gradually but surely
ascertain, is certainly different from that of one who obeys the formulae

invented by dead or living priests and prophets to describe the nature of a God whom no man had either seen or heard."[77] Fortified by the example of science, in a Whitmanesque sense, Symonds asks if it is really impossible to "dream that morality will be one branch of the study of the world as a whole, a department of τὰ φνσικά, when φύσις regarded as a total unity, that suffers no crude radical distinction of Mind and Body, has absorbed our scientific attention?"[78] What is needed is chiefly suspension of judgment, and the recognition that "we have no reason to apprehend that personal licence should result from a system of purely positive ethics based upon that conception of our relation to the universe which Science is revealing."[79] The Greek Pantheon might be viewed as "an exhaustive psychological analysis. Nothing in human nature is omitted: but each function and each quality of man is deified." And just as "the unity of the Greek religion was not the unity of the One but of the Many blent and harmonised in the variety that we observe in Nature, so the ideal of Greek life imposed no commonplace conformity to one fixed standard on individuals, but each man was encouraged to complete and realise the type of himself to the utmost."[80] This was an ancient Greece that had a good deal of J. S. Mill in it.

Needless to say, the difficulty of the task ahead is also brought out, and much of this difficulty does seem to involve shaking off "the Hebraistic culture we receive in childhood." This is evident even in the first edition of the two *Studies*. The Greeks, in contrast to moderns in a world grown old, "had no Past." To find anything resembling the vital Greek spirit, some "living echo of this melody of curving lines," modern Englanders "must visit the fields where boys bathe in early morning, or the playgrounds of our public schools in summer, or the banks of the Isis when the eights are on the water, or the riding-schools of young soldiers."[81] After all, the Genius of the Greeks was mostly stimulated by male beauty, was indeed personified in the

young man newly come from the wrestling-ground, anointed, chapleted, and very calm.... Upon his soul there is no burden of the world's pain; the whole creation that groaneth and travaileth together, has touched him with no sense of anguish; nor has he yet felt sin. The pride and the strength of adolescence are his – audacity and endurance, swift passions and exquisite sensibilites, the alternations of sublime repose and boyish noise, grace, pliancy, and stubbornness and power, love of all things and splendours of the world, the frank enjoyment of the open air, free merriment, and melancholy well beloved.

Of this "clear and stainless personality, this conscience whole and pure and reconciled to nature, what survives among us now?" After all, the "blear-eyed mechanic, stifled in a hovel of our sombre northern towns" was hardly even in a position "to envy the pure clear life of Art made perfect in Humanity, which was the pride of Hellas." How can such a one "comprehend a mode of existence in which the world itself was adequate to all the wants of the soul, and when to yearn for more than life affords was reckoned a disease"?[82]

When it came to the celebration of Greek boy love – or more accurately, young man love – Symonds made Pater seem like a model of circumspection and understatement. Indeed, Pater would grow more conciliatory toward Christianity, albeit a Christianity that valorized the body and demoted St. Paul. Symonds's higher synthesis was hardly such as to fool anyone with even a trace of religious orthodoxy in his or her soul.

But of course, this was the danger. The conservative critics of Jowett's religious heresies and Platonist pedagogy were all too ready to urge that these had spawned the sexual heresies of Pater and Symonds. Recall that Jowett had been one of the contributors to the 1860 *Essays and Reviews*, and early on had been known for his unorthodox views, shaped in part by the German critics. Among other things, he found conventional explanations of the Atonement to have an offensively "commercial" tone. If he became a giant figure in the Balliol of Symonds's day, this was after years of nasty academic battling and public controversy. He was pressured to sign the Thirty-nine Articles again when he was appointed Regius Professor, and was no doubt another prime example of what Sidgwick deemed high-minded laxness, though Leslie Stephen observed that Jowett was, after all, following Mill's advice about reforming the church from within. At least, many of the academic liberals took him to be on their side, and he joined with Sidgwick in contributing a piece to *Essays on Liberal Education*. For Jowett, the emphasis on Plato was pretty clearly an alternative to an emphasis on religion.

To be sure, Jowett was a very strange man – at once shy and sarcastic, apparently opposed to academic research in favor of "usefulness in life," he hated to see his students become antipractical, even while he was in subtle ways bringing them to a lifelong interest in the Plato that he was busy translating. He was not exactly the ideal of the aggressive reformer, though in some respects he was a model for Sidgwick. As Annan notes, after Pusey had (unsuccessfully) launched proceedings against Jowett for publishing heretical doctrines (in the *Essays and Reviews*), "never again was Jowett to express his theological opinions in public." And if he was not quite what one would call a "friend" to the undergraduates, nonetheless:

Jowett was not the first don to institute reading parties in the vacation, but he was the first head of house to know something about all his men, and a great deal about some of them. The list of Balliol graduates in 1873–8 included Asquith, Curzon, Gell, Milner, Baden-Powell, Leveson-Gower and W. P. Kerr. As undergraduates they would have been invited to meet the Master's guests – among them Turgenev, George Eliot and G. H. Lewes, Bishop Colenso, Archbishop Tait, Lord Sherbrooke and Tyndall. He made a point of mixing the different types of undergraduates at his parties – 'Jowett's Jumbles', they were called – yet Balliol was judged to be the most cliquey of all colleges.[83]

And certainly when it came to Green and Symonds, it was Jowett's personal touch that had turned them into educated men – indeed, into educators themselves, who appreciated the sheer labor involved in cultural understanding. But this was just the point. As Dowling has argued:

[T]he darker, subversive dimension to Jowett's and, more generally, to all tutorial Socraticism would always be the fatal character of Socrates as a 'corrupter of youth.' In the aftermath of the conservative clerical challenge to Jowett's religious orthodoxy which made him such a hero to undergraduates during 1860–63, this darker Socratic character was never to be far from the foreboding imaginations of many at Oxford. Even Brodrick himself, a political ally of Jowett's, did not absolutely reject the notion that Jowett may have deliberately instilled theological doubt into his pupils, while the judgement of Richard St. John Tyrwhitt, as voiced by a character in his novelistic memoir *Hugh Heron, Christ Church* (1880), would express a deep mistrust of all such tutors who 'take pleasure in unsettling lads' minds, and think they were like Socrates whenever they succeeded in that' (166).[84]

Amazingly, however, given Jowett's distance from utilitarianism, his Plato was in many respects the fearless and sexless Socratic doubter of Mill. Indeed, Jowett might well seem a textbook case of homosocial panic, trying to deny that education was a sexually charged business and that Plato's language concerning this had been anything but figurative. Swinburne, after his homophobic turn, would remark on "such renascent blossoms of the Italian Renaissance as the Platonic amorist of blue-breeched gondoliers who is now in Aretino's bosom," assuring his readers that the "cult of the calamus, as expounded by Mr Addington Symonds to his fellow

calamites, would have found no acceptance or tolerance with the translator of Plato." And in truth, as Annan records, the "translator of Plato
did indeed on one occasion take action. A Balliol undergraduate, William
Hardinge, sent Pater sonnets praising homosexual love. Pater responded
by signing himself 'Yours lovingly'. Jowett was told: confronted both,
expelled Hardinge from Balliol and never spoke to Pater again."[85] It was
apparently this event, in 1874, that brought the proctorship to Wordsworth
rather than Pater.

In due course, Symonds was the one who would try to drive home to
Jowett how impossibly conflicted the Balliol Platonic Revival was. In a
touching letter of February 1, 1889, he wrote about how glad he was that
Jowett had abandoned the "idea of an essay on Greek love."

It surprises me to find you, with your knowledge of Greek history, speaking of
this in Plato as 'mainly a figure of speech.' – It surprised me as much as I seem to
surprise you when I repeat that the study of Plato is injurious to a certain number
of predisposed young men.–

Many forms of passion between males are matters of fact in English schools,
colleges, cities, rural districts. Such passion is innate in some persons no less than
the ordinary sexual appetite is innate in the majority. With the nobler of such pre-
determined temperaments the passion seeks a spiritual or ideal transfiguration.
When, therefore, individuals of the indicated species come into contact with the
reveries of Plato, (clothed in graceful diction, immersed in the peculiar emotion,
presented with considerable dramatic force, gilt with a mystical philosophy, throb-
bing with the realism of actual Greek life), the effect upon them has the force of a
revelation. They discover that what they had been blindly groping after was once
an admitted possibility – not in a mean hole or corner – but that the race whose
literature forms the basis of their higher culture, lived in that way, aspired in that
way. For such students of Plato there is no question of 'figures of speech,' but of
concrete facts, facts in the social experience of Athens, from which men derived
courage, drew intellectual illumination, took their first step in the path which led
to great achievements and the arduous pursuit of truth.

Greek history confirms, by a multitude of legends and of actual episodes, what
Plato puts forth as a splendid vision, and subordinates to the higher philosophic
life.

It is futile by any evasion of the central difficulty, by any dexterity in the use of
words, to escape from the stubborn fact that natures so exceptionally predisposed
find in Plato the encouragement of their furtively cherished dreams. The Lysis, the
Charmides, the Phaedrus, the Symposium – how many varied and unimaginative
pictures these dialogues contain of what is only a sweet poison to such minds!

Meanwhile the temptations of the actual world surround them: friends of like temper, boys who respond to kindness, reckless creatures abroad upon the common ways of life. Eros Pandemos is everywhere. Plato lends the light, the gleam, that never was on sea or shore.

Symonds continues this remarkable letter by growing even more emphatic and more personal. He urges Jowett to

Put yourself in the place of someone to whom the aspect of Greek life which you ignore is personally and intensely interesting, who reads his Plato as you would wish him to read his Bible – i.e. with a vivid conviction that what he reads is the life-record of a masterful creative man-determining race, and the monument of a world-important epoch.

Can you pretend that a sympathetically constituted nature of the sort in question will desire nothing from the panegyric of paederastic love in the Phaedrus, from the personal grace of Charmides, from the mingled realism and rapture of the Symposium? What you call a figure of speech, is heaven in hell to him – maddening, because it is stimulating to the imagination; wholly out of accord with the world he has to live in; too deeply in accord with his own impossible desires.

Greek love was for Plato no 'figure of speech,' but a present poignant reality. Greek love is for modern students of Plato no 'figure of speech' and no anachronism, but a present poignant reality. The facts of Greek history and the facts of contemporary life demonstrate these propositions only too conclusively.[86]

By the time that he penned this letter, Symonds had long been persuaded that he himself had been "born that way," and moreover that there was nothing morbid about his tendencies. But he was harking back sympathetically to the tortured time of his youth, when he was much more conflicted. Symonds may have been rather more in the grip of a repression-versus-release view of sexual passion than Pater, who had a delicate (almost Foucauldian) appreciation for the paradoxical stimulus to desire that repression can bring. And he may have been more masculinist than Pater in his readings of the Greeks, Whitman, and everything else. But for all that, his life and explorations defy the stock Foucauldian and constructivist categories for characterizing Victorian sexual discourse. Dellamora has suggested how "a proliferation of sexual-cultural discourses after 1850 provides rich resources for meditation on what, in the second volume of *The History of Sexuality*, Foucault refers to as an 'aesthetics of existence' intimately related with a variety of male-male sexual practices, relationships, and fantasies."[87] Indeed, Symonds and his circle are a wonderful case in point, and the vital and life-sustaining friendships among them have scarcely even been noted, much less extensively researched.[88] As important as Symonds's paganistic partnership with Pater surely was, it was quite secondary and less personal than his alliances with Graham Dakyns, Arthur and Henry Sidgwick, and Horatio Forbes Brown.

There is a pleasant irony in the fact that 1877 witnessed Symonds coming forward as a candidate for the professorship of poetry – in effect, a public plea for the legitimation of his version of the Platonic Revival. For in February of the very same year, just when he was in the thick of his campaign for the professorship and soliciting the support of as many influential friends and acquaintances as he could muster, he had also come forward in an effort to rid himself of some of his old conflicts about his tendencies. He had, for the first time, visited a male brothel, and become truly fully sexually active with men. As his candid *Memoirs* explain:

In February 1877, I think, I gave three lectures on 'Florence and the Medici' at the Royal Institution. This took me of course to London; and, as it happened, an acquaintance of old standing asked me one day to go with him to a male brothel near the Regent's Park Barracks. I consented out of curiosity. Moved by something stronger than curiosity, I made an assignation with a brawny young soldier for an afternoon to be passed in a private room at the same house. Naturally, I chose a day on which I was not wanted at the Royal Institution. We came together at the time appointed; the strapping young soldier with his frank eyes and pleasant smile, and I, the victim of sophisticated passions. For the first time in my experience I shared a bed with one so different from myself, so ardently desired by me, so supremely beautiful in my eyes, so attractive to my senses. He was a very nice fellow, as it turned out: comradely and natural, regarding the affair which had brought us together in that place from a business-like and reasonable point of view. For him at all events it involved nothing unusual, nothing shameful; and his simple attitude, the not displeasing vanity with which he viewed his own physical attractions, and the genial sympathy with which he met the passion they aroused, taught me something I had never before conceived about illicit sexual relations. Instead of yielding to any brutal impulse, I thoroughly enjoyed the close vicinity of that splendid naked piece of manhood; then I made him clothe himself, sat and smoked and talked with him, and felt, at the end of the whole transaction, that some at least of the deepest moral problems might be solved by fraternity.[89]

"Soldier Love" was destined to become Symonds's special passion. But it was much more than a personal affair. In a touching letter to Sidgwick from September of 1871, some years earlier, he had made clear how busy he was theorizing in advance of practice. Referring to their difficult, critical perspective on the work of another of their close, poetically inclined friends, Roden Noel – who was in all probability the "acquaintance of old standing" – Symonds wrote:

As for Noel and his controversy with you – some echoes of it I have heard. My opinion about his actual achievement is not greatly altered, except that I think he has improved in style and not lost in energy. But my admiration for him as a being has vastly increased. I am sure I have said nothing to justify him in supposing that I think him superior to Swinburne, or myself on a level with Morris. On the contrary I vexed him much last June by telling him that I thought both he and I had no chance in the long run against poets our superiors in delicacy of expression and energy of imagination. Afterwards, alone among the hills, my Prophecy of Love of Comrades as a future institution of Democracy came upon me; and I began to believe more in my own poetic vocation.[90]

Symonds also noted that he had read Sidgwick's "'Verification of Belief' at Mürren and was much impressed with its force, compression, and overwhelming destructive accuracy of analysis. It is the most wholly sceptical thing I have ever read. If you write a whole book in that way, it will be about as hard as Aristotle. Oh for the precision of your well-thewed and well-trained mind!"[91] Sidgwick, as we shall see, had been challenged by Symonds to prove that he was truly capable of skepticism.

Thus, the future candidate for the Oxford professorship had been planning his platform for some years; his vision of the new Renaissance was akin to Pater's, but more Whitmanesque, more openly celebratory of the love of comrades.[92] Strange as it may seem, Symonds's assignation really was in his eyes politically freighted – a stimulation of comradeship across the classes that represented the Whitmanian vision of the democratic future. The new pagans thus aspired, like the old clerisy, to stimulate social change through a new, revitalizing literature, a new poetic language, that would transform human sensibilities. This was recognizably a version of the old Apostolic tradition, even if brought into a demand for academic reform. Certainly, it resonated deeply with Sidgwick's aspirations. One of Symonds's dearest comrades, Sidgwick counselled him at every turn. To him, Symonds confessed, after he withdrew from the running in favor of Shairp:

I believe it is really better for me in some ways not to have the Chair; though for my mental health I should have liked it. The Renaissance is an odd atmosphere to live in and a bad milieu to live into. I seriously feel as if I were losing my sense of what is fitting & decorous in conduct & were adopting the moral indifferentism of those people. To all this the P. P. [Poetry Professorship] would have been a good corrective.[93]

"Moral indifferentism" could be a rather dangerous thing, especially in the years leading to the Labouchère Amendment Act of 1885, the law that would be used to ruin Oscar Wilde a decade later. Even if Symonds was guilty less of a "common-sense" moral indifferentism and more of a highly ethical differentism, he often had a curiously weak grasp of how dangerous public reaction to his work might be. On the very eve of the Wilde trials, Henry James, who had ungenerously portrayed Symonds in "The Author of 'Beltraffio'," wrote a shrewd assessment of him to their mutual friend Edmund Gosse. In contrast to Pater, who had been "negative & faintly grey," a "mask without a face" for the purposes of public consumption, Symonds had been "almost insane" in his "need of taking the public into his *intimissima* confidence."[94] Fortunately for Symonds, his friend Sidgwick was an expert on the limits of commonsense morality and the casuistry of hypocrisy.

III. Arcadia and the Augenblick

This terrible and lonely communing of his spirit face to face with the widest abstractions which his intellect could compass, seems to me to contain the essence of Symonds' psychological quality. He had carried speculation in the abstract, and the audacious interrogation of the Universe, to their utmost limits. It was inevitable that, if he survived the strain, he would ultimately abandon the vacuum of abstractions in which he was stifling, for the concrete world of men and things about him.

Having boldly plunged into the 'abyss,' having learned that when sounded by the plummet of the human intellect, it is actually void and bottomless, the instinct of self-preservation, the shrinking from the *'seuil de la folie'* – caused him to cling to the antithesis of the void, the concrete manifestations of life, actual, visible, sensible, as the one salvation in the *mare magnum* of speculation. This is, probably what he meant when he said that 'the crisis at Cannes gave him a religion.' He did not attempt to fill the void with some definite concept of a Deity – that is what many have done – but Symonds's twofold psychical structure debarred him from such a salvation. Emotionally, he desired the warmth of a personal Deity; intellectually, he rejected as *ipso facto* inadequate any concept of Deity which the human intellect could construct and therefore enclose. He abandoned the effort to grasp the *Idée*, and accepted the *erscheinungen*, by the study and interrogation of which he might

still reach all that was humanly knowable of God. But the analytical, inquiring, sceptical spirit, and the passion for the absolute still retained the regency of his mind; therefore, for him all *erscheinungen*, all phenomena, are to be studied, none neglected, humanity is to be sounded to its depths, life to be 'drunk to the lees.'
Horatio Forbes Brown, *John Addington Symonds, A Biography*[95]

. . . the Alps are my religion . . .
John Addington Symonds to Henry Sidgwick, June 23, 1867[96]

The year 1877 marked a turning point for Symonds, and the turn was toward a healthier and happier existence – a coming out of sorts, and a coming to terms. His failure to join the Oxford faculty, and his success with his soldier, made it that much easier for him to distance himself from the English environment that was, both psychologically and physically, proving increasingly hazardous to his health. Indeed, it was later in the very same year that chance would carry him to Davos, Switzerland, where the bracing Alpine climate was considered particularly salubrious for those who, like Symonds, suffered from tuberculosis. Ever afterward, he would live much of his life in Davos, punctuated by long visits to Venice, where his friend, former student, and literary executor Horatio Brown lived a life of liberal scholarship and sexual liberty that would have been impossible in liberal England. If Symonds was often dangerously out of touch with the prejudices of the English, that was no doubt because he had gone far to remove himself from them. Sidgwick would be a frequent visitor to Davos, as would Dakyns.

As the passage from Brown's biography suggests, the roots of Symonds's mature philosophy, the Whitmania he would have carried with him into academia, are to be traced to an earlier psychological crisis – the "crisis in Cannes," which took place in late 1867. It was then that the Platonism of his youth imploded into something close to a Jamesian love of worldly particulars, into his own idiosyncratic mix of paganism and proto-pragmatism, in which the Greek and Goethean ideal got transformed into a Cosmic Enthusiasm fired by real-world male love and a Darwinian sense that the world was enough. As always, Sidgwick was there. Their friendship, an intense intermingling of the philosophical, the theological, and the personal, was for both an inquiry into the "deepest problems" like no other. This was what "soaring" meant, even when it involved subjecting the Platonic to some very serious reversals. For the "true self" that Symonds was obsessed with trying to understand and come to terms with was the sexual self beneath the veneer of consciousness.

Symonds was an experiment in ethics and intuitive theism who challenged Sidgwick's hopes to the very core, in a way so powerful that he would make it into James's *Varieties of Religious Experience* as well as Havelock Ellis's *Studies in Sexual Inversion* (originally as a coauthor). To understand Sidgwick, with all his yearning for immortality and concern over the rationality of egoism and the fate of his own hypocritical civilization, one must understand Symonds, who debated these matters with him in journals and letters unmatched in their intense candor and intimacy. With Symonds, one finds, in the shape of an intimate friend, the challenge that had troubled Sidgwick ever since his undergraduate Apostolic days, when he wrote about the "symmetrical people," such as the ancient Athenians, who could be happy with the world as it is, needing no comforting religious thoughts about immortality. And with Symonds, one finds the new paganism inexorably moving toward both the new pragmatism and the new depth psychology, the depth psychology that would, paradoxically, in short order produce a medicalized discourse about sexuality that would classify the "homosexual" as "pathological," a sickness rather than a sin, albeit a rare criminal disease. As it transpired, the new psychological science would embody the clinical attitudes of Symonds's father – an eminent physician for whom the disease model came easily – rather than the liberationist dreams of his son. The inaugural discourse of heterosexual/homosexual binarism, worked into medical classifications of character types and pathologies, was virtually a Symonds family affair.[97]

Earlier on, however, everything was in the air, and Symonds could legitimately hope, in a way parallel to Sidgwick's hope for parapsychology, that "fresh facts" and scientific authority could befriend the poetics of the new religion and the yearnings of the "true self." Just as Sidgwick would seek to redeem his deeper religious self with parapsychology, so Symonds would seek to redeem his deeper sexual self with depth psychology (and cultural history). Like Myers, whose work on the subliminal self he so admired, Symonds knew well the trouble with normal. But to appreciate just how the "crisis in Cannes" came about, and what it meant for the Symonds–Sidgwick friendship, a good deal of fleshing out of the Symonds biography is necessary.

Dr. Symonds was a very accomplished, prominent, and successful Bristol physician and a man of cultivated tastes, a mix of science and poetry, medicine and art, combined with a steadfast political liberalism. He had had to be both father and mother to his children, since John Addington's mother had died of scarlet fever in 1844, only four years after his birth.

Although Symonds senior had grown into a fairly enlightened, latitudinarian form of faith, away from his familial Puritanical and Evangelical rigorism and open to "the influence of the age in which he lived," his son developed a "morbid sense of sin and screamed at night about imaginary acts of disobedience."[98] Symonds was to suffer from forms of visionary and/or hallucinatory experience for much of his life, and his unique ontological insecurity was part of what made him so attractive to Sidgwick and to James.

Certainly, he had a rough childhood, being plagued by everything from bed-wetting to "night terrors" to sleepwalking. His education was painful even in its more conventional aspects, especially when he got to Harrow, which he thought of as "the camp, where I had to brace myself to discipline," compared to the Capua of Clifton Hill House, the family home in Bristol. Particularly disturbing, however, was the "low moral tone" – like the other public schools, Harrow was a remarkably licentious environment:

Every boy of good looks had a female name, and was recognized either as a public prostitute or as some bigger fellow's 'bitch'. Bitch was the word in common usage to indicate a boy who yielded his person to a lover. The talk in the dormitories and the studies was incredibly obscene. Here and there one could not avoid seeing acts of onanism, mutual masturbation, the sports of naked boys in bed together. There was no refinement, no sentiment, no passion; nothing but animal lust in these occurrences. They filled me with disgust and loathing. My school-fellows realized what I had read in Swift about the Yahoos.[99]

Symonds managed to remain "free in fact and act from this contamination." Although the "beasts" tried to seduce him, they apparently ultimately decided that he was "not game." He acquired his own set of friends – Gustavus Bosanquet, Randall Vickers, and Alfred Pretor among them – and survived mainly by managing to separate his "inner and real self" from the "outer and artificial self." In fact, so "separate were the two selves, so deep was my dipsychia, that my most intimate friends there . . . have each and all emphatically told me that they thought I had passed through school without being affected by, almost without being aware of, its peculiar vices. And yet those vices furnished a perpetual subject for contemplation and casuistical reflection to my inner self."[100]

Symonds had long been aware of his own tendencies towards male love. Although he was often enough – not always – disgusted with such actual sexual encounters as he had in his youth, his "earliest recollections" included "certain visions, half-dream, half-reverie, which were certainly erotic in their nature." Thus, often before falling asleep, he would fancy himself "crouched upon the floor amid a company of naked adult men: sailors, such as I had seen about the streets of Bristol. The contact of their bodies afforded me a vivid and mysterious pleasure."[101] This fantasy is explained more graphically in his "case history": "he imagined himself the servant of several adult naked sailors; he crouched between their thighs and called himself their dirty pig, and by their orders he performed services for their genitals and buttocks which he contemplated and handled with relish."[102] Upon exposure to Shakespeare's "Venus and Adonis," before he was ten, the "shaggy and brawny sailors, without entirely disappearing, began to be superseded in my fancy by an adolescent Adonis."[103] He also loved the Hermes of Homer and "was very curious to know why the Emperors kept boys as well as girls in their seraglios, and what the male gods did with the youths they loved."[104]

Dr. Symonds was apparently rather clueless about his son's inclinations, which were indeed kept from him. He later told him that "he sent me with undoubting confidence to Harrow, because he had no conception that I was either emotional or passionate."[105]

If Harrow would teach him to detest what he had so fantasized, he held himself to have "transcended crude sensuality through the aesthetic idealization of erotic instincts." His imagination steeped in the "filth" of his schoolmates, Symonds was "only saved from cynicism" by the "gradual unfolding" of "an ideal passion which corresponded to Platonic love. This idea was not derived from Greek literature; for I had not yet read the works of Plato and Theocritus. It sprang up spontaneously, proving that my thought was lodged in ancient Hellas." Thus, while his fellows deemed him passionless, he was busily "theorizing, testing and sublimating the appetites which they unthinkingly indulged."[106] He would later come to regard this as a big part of his problem, but this was not until the "crisis in Cannes."

Of course, Plato was soon to make a grand appearance. Symonds, age seventeen and in the sixth form, was supposed to be studying the *Apology*, and for the purpose had bought "Cary's crib." During a visit to London, he went to bed with his crib and, stumbling on the *Phaedrus*, read it straight through, following it up with the *Symposium*, which made for a sleepless night but "one of the most important nights of my life." For

Here in the *Phaedrus* and the *Symposium* – in the myth of the Soul and the speeches of Pausanias, Agathon and Diotima – I discovered the true *liber amoris* at last, the revelation I had been waiting for, the consecration of a long-cherished idealism. It was just as though the voice of my own soul spoke to me through Plato, as though in some antenatal experience I had lived the life of philosophical Greek lover.

Harrow vanished into unreality. I had touched solid ground. I had obtained the sanction of the love which had been ruling me from childhood. Here was the poetry, the philosophy of my own enthusiasm for male beauty, expressed with all the magic of unrivalled style. And, what was more, I now became aware that the Greek race – the actual historical Greeks of antiquity – treated this love seriously, invested it with moral charm, endowed it with sublimity.

For the first time I saw the possibility of resolving in a practical harmony the discords of my instincts. I perceived that masculine love had its virtue as well as its vice, and stood in this respect upon the same ground as normal sexual appetite. I understood, or thought I understood, the relation which those dreams of childhood and the brutalities of vulgar lust at Harrow bore to my higher aspiration after noble passion.[107]

This was, as Symonds allowed, a most timely revelation, one proving "decisive" for his future. It confirmed "my congenital inclination toward persons of the male sex, and filled my head with an impossible dream, which controlled my thoughts for many years." After all, Symonds had his youthful self in mind when he penned that 1889 letter to Jowett about the effects of Plato. Remarkably, however, he could not really, with justice, blame Jowett for having exposed him to Platonic love, given the way he had come upon it quite on his own initiative. In a sense, it was Symonds himself who brought the Hellenic eros to Oxford.

Shocked by his friend Pretor's revelation that he was having a love affair with none other than their headmaster, C. J. Vaughan, Symonds was thrown into a good deal of casuistical turmoil and cynical reflection about hypocrisy in high places. Plato helped, as did Aristophanes, the erotic dialogues of Lucian and Plutarch, Theognis, Theocritus, and the *Greek Anthology*. He threw himself ever more passionately into things Greek. Now, the "lord" of his life "was love," and his "mental and moral evolution proceeded now upon a path which had no contact with the prescribed

systems of education."[108] A visit home to Clifton for the Easter holi-
days, with his "soul lodged in Hellas" while his body was in the Bristol
Cathedral, led to his infatuation with the chorister Willie Dyer, "the
only beautiful, the only flawless being I had ever seen." He arranged
a meeting, "on the morning of 10 April 1858," and it was from "that
morning I date the birth of my real self. Thirty-two years have elapsed
since then; and still I can hardly hold the pen when I attempt to write
about it."[109]

Of course, not much had happened between them, by Harrow standards. Symonds had taken "Willie's slender hand into my own and gazed
into his large brown eyes fringed with heavy lashes." Many meaningful
walks together in Leigh Woods would follow, culminating in a couple of
kisses. Symonds plucked a white anemone on the spot of the first kiss,
a treasure that he would still possess decades later, keeping it pressed in
his Theocritus beside the phrase "Men *were* of the Golden Age long ago,
when the beloved boy returned one's love."[110] It was all so ethereal, so
high-minded, so Platonic in the idealization of beauty.

Still, Symonds knew well enough "that if I avowed my emotion to
my father or his friends, I should meet – not merely with no sympathy
or understanding or credence – but that I should arouse horror, pain,
aversion."[111] And the casuistical intricacies of his situation were soon to
grow even more complex. Happily transported to Oxford, he was taking
up with a new and infinitely more agreeable set of people, one of the
more important being John Conington. Although Symonds had presented
himself to Jowett, armed with a letter of introduction from his father,
Jowett had unexpectedly rebuffed him, and would only warm to him
during his later undergraduate years. His Apostolic-style awakening was
mainly courtesy of Conington:

The association with Conington was almost wholly good. It is true that I sat up
till midnight with him nearly every evening, drinking cup after cup of strong tea
in his private lodgings above Cooper's shop near University. This excited and
fatigued my nerves. But the conversation was in itself a liberal education for a
youth of pronounced literary tastes. Now and again it turned on matters of the
affections. Conington was scrupulously moral and cautious. Yet he sympathized
with romantic attachments for boys. In this winter he gave me *Jonica*; and I learned
the love story of its author William Johnson (now Cory) the Eton master, and the
pretty faced Charlie Wood (now Lord Halifax) of Ch.Ch. who had been his pupil.
That volume of verse, trifling as it may appear to casual readers, went straight to

my heart and inflamed my imagination. It joined on in a singular manner to my recent experiences at Harrow, and helped to form a dream world of unhealthy fancies about love. I went so far as to write a letter to William Johnson, exposing the state of my own feelings and asking his advice. The answer, addressed to O.D.Y. at the Union, duly came. It was a long epistle on paiderastia in modern times, defending it and laying down the principle that affection between people of the same sex is no less natural and rational than the ordinary passionate relations. Underneath Johnson's frank exposition of this unconventional morality there lay a wistful yearning sadness – a note of disappointment for forced abstention. I have never found this note absent in lovers of my sort and Johnson's, unless the men have cast prudence to the winds and staked their all on cynicism.[112]

Avoiding such cynicism, while rediscovering something of the joy of the ancients in male love, would become his guiding task.

Although his normal studies were suffering (Symonds was "ploughed in Smalls for Greek Grammar"), he was educating himself after his fashion. He kept before his mind, as a sort of maxim, an oracle from Herodotus: "You ask me for Arkadia; a great request you make of me. I will not grant it." Be that as it may, he avidly discussed the subject of Arcadian love with Conington, and in the course of some of these discussions, during a reading party at Whitby that also included Green, Albert Rutson, and Cholmeley Puller, he informed his tutor about Vaughan's affair with Pretor. Conington insisted that Symonds should go to Clifton to inform his father about these goings-on.

This Symonds did, with the result that his father now became rather more aware of his son's inner workings. But Symonds was terribly conflicted about the intricacies of this "new casuistry":

I had become the accuser of my old headmaster, a man for whom I felt no love, and who had shown me no special kindness, but who was after all the awe-inspiring ruler of the petty state of Harrow. My accusation rested solely upon the private testimony of an intimate friend, whose confidence I violated by the communication of his letter to a third party. To complicate matters, I felt a deeply rooted sympathy with Vaughan. If he had sinned, it had been by yielding to passions which already mastered me. But this fact instead of making me indulgent, determined me to tell the bitter truth. At that period I was not cynical. I desired to overcome the malady of my own nature. My blood boiled and my nerves stiffened when I thought what mischief life at Harrow was doing daily to young lads under the autocracy of a hypocrite.[113]

Dr. Symonds was not so conflicted, and with the guidance of Conington successfully pressured Vaughan to resign from Harrow. But the young Symonds was troubled by the "sense that I appeared disloyal to my friends." Pretor and some other old schoolmates let him know that they did not agree that this was the action of Conscience. Symonds's "brain and moral consciousness – the one worn with worrying thought, the other racked by casuistical doubts – never quite recovered from the weariness of those unprofitable weeks."[114] Loyalty to friends would remain for him a burning issue, calling for the best of one's soul searching. Among his manuscript remains is a little piece entitled simply "Loyalty to Friends," which reads:

The truly loyal friend, is not merely staunch in his adherence – for this he might be from a sense of duty – nor devoted in his love – for this he might be through passion: he is both staunch & devoted; but he is also true in every corner of his soul to his friend, honouring & respecting him, incapable of believing evil in him, betraying his secrets to none, criticizing him to none, never complaining of him, waiting if wronged by him in the hope of explanation; & if such a friend has to break from his friend at last he still honours the past & is silent preferring to suffer before the world rather than to throw blame on one whom he once greatly loved.[115]

Quite possibly this was penned with Pretor in mind. In any case, such meditations were classic Symonds: he would develop a "genius" for male friendship.

The curious casuistical web spun round this affair – the betrayal of a friend's confidence, the partial ruin of a friend's uncle (Green was Vaughan's nephew), the hypocritical condemnation of hypocritical boy love by appeal to a father (whom he had consistently deceived) at the behest of a decidedly Arcadian tutor – surely did help to determine Symonds's ethical course in profound ways. He would forever be engaged in struggling to work out the new casuistry that so troubled him, enlisting the aid of such philosophical friends as Sidgwick, who, needless to say, shared his absorbing interest in the issue of hypocrisy.

But the more immediate effect of the Vaughan matter was to bring his father into his confidence in an altogether new way. Dr. Symonds had not changed his stripes. This new parental intimacy led to more filial pain, and more betrayal, what with Symonds being pressured to give up his precious Willie Dyer: "The back of my life was broken when I yielded to convention, and became untrue in soul to Willie." The cathartic poetry flowed.

This was only the beginning. Another chorister, Alfred Brooke, would follow in Willie's place, with similar results. Worse still, Symonds himself was very nearly brought into scandal by one of his Oxford friends. His academic career had been turned around, thanks to the stimulus of Conington and Jowett, the latter having entered the scene during Symonds's last two years at Balliol. He had also been spurred by a conversation between Conington and Green that he had accidentally overheard, in which his seniors had worried that "Barnes" (their nickname for him) would not "get his First." The "sting" of this assessment "remained in me; and though I cared little enough for first-classes, in comparison with lads' love, I then and there resolved that I would win the best first of my year."[116] He did – "a first-class in Litterae Humaniores – the best first of my year" – along with a Magdalen Fellowship. And it was while at Magdalen that he was nearly ruined by C. G. H. Shorting, whom he had befriended in 1859. Shorting's "conduct with regard to boys, especially the choristers at Magdalen, brought him into serious trouble," and Symonds in retrospect found "that my whole nature was harassed by the quarrels, reconcilements, jealousies, suspicions, which diversified our singular sort of comradeship."[117] Shorting "the troublous friend, who had chosen the broad way of self-indulgence, plagued me by his influence – by the sympathy I felt for him, my horror of his course, the love I nourished in my bosom for a man I could not respect."[118]

Annoyed by Symonds's efforts to restrain him, Shorting, in November of 1862, "had sent a document defamatory of myself, and containing extracts from my private correspondence and my poems, to six of the Magdalen fellows. His object was to prove that I had supported him in his pursuit of the chorister Goolden, that I shared his habits and was bent on the same path."[119]

Symonds's conscience may have been "clear," but the nastiness of the whole matter was considerable. Magdalen was largely hostile to the Balliol liberalism that Symonds practically embodied, and to the system of open fellowships that had brought him in, which factors made him suspect that his trial would be something of a show. In the event, he did go down in November to prepare his defense and "received letters of support from some of the most distinguished men in Oxford and in England – numbers of them – which were placed in the President of Magdalen's hands, together with my own statement. . . . After some time, on 18 December, a general meeting of the College of Magdalen acquitted me of the charges brought by Shorting."[120]

Symonds was acquitted, and Shorting left Oxford in disgrace, but once again the vague sense of betraying a friend and denying his true self insured that the psychic cost would be considerable. Besides, the whole atmosphere of Oxford was now poisoned. Suspicion clung to him, and although he continued in residence at Magdalen for the rest of the year, it was a painful time. He was determined, however, to do some good work as a partial redemption of himself in his father's eyes. Despite collapsing health, in part brought on by his continuing psychic agonies and pining for Brooke, he completed his pathbreaking study of the Renaissance, which won the Chancellor's Essay Prize. This was to be the capstone of his official Oxford career – a celebration of Platonism in the Renaissance.

To be sure, the Shorting affair had also strengthened his father's hand in counselling about the dangers to health and reputation that could be found in Arcadia. The crushing, undeniable power of paternal guidance, combined with the ineradicable quality of his own feelings and tendencies, ensured that the 1860s would be years of "storm and stress" for Symonds as well as for Sidgwick. Shorting's malicious gambit had brought home to him how vulnerable he really was. More infatuations and more unstable friends only worked to keep the influence of Dr. Symonds in the ascendant. Whitney Davis has suggested that during this crucial period, Dr. Symonds was applying the ideas of James Cowles Prichard, whose delineation of "'moral insanity' extended Philippe Pinel's identification, in 1791, of a mania 'confined to the moral feelings and the emotions, just as in other cases the perceptive and reasoning powers are the sole subjects of disorder.'" Thus, for both Prichard and Dr. Symonds, "the 'perversions' of 'moral insanity' included inexplicable marital jealousy, uncontrolled temper, financial recklessness, and excessive fascination with sexual matters. They recommended that the affected person separate himself totally – or be forcibly separated – from the objects towards which the disordered feelings were directed." Even if the elder Symonds would not have pronounced either his son or Vaughan altogether "morally insane," he did prescribe, in both cases, something very much like this form of treatment. This "liberalized approach," Davis observes, "stood midway between the long-established canonical and juridical condemnation of sodomy and other heteroclite affections, and the later medical-psychiatric therapy of 'homosexuality' and other supposed sexual anomalies." [121]

Here it is well worth bearing in mind that, despite the cogency of various broadly Foucauldian claims about the webs of power and domination built into psychiatric discourse, Dr. Symonds's tactics compared somewhat favorably to the use of the gallows and the pillory, the corrective measures that a rabidly homophobic England had employed for most of the nineteenth century. Louis Crompton, in his classic study, *Byron and Greek Love: Homophobia in 19th-Century England*, has extensively documented the singularly brutal way in which England dealt with male love, which stands in marked contrast to the liberalizing tendencies of the Continent:

It was totally out of keeping that England, under the circumstances, should have invoked its parliamentary statute to hang sixty men in the first three decades of the ninetenth century and have hanged another score under its naval regulations.

When we consider that England's gay male minority at this time must have numbered several hundred thousand (if we use modern statistics as a guide), it is obvious that only a tiny proportion were touched by the law in its severest form. Yet the threat of the gallows was always present to darken these men's perception of themselves as outcasts and to justify a multitude of lesser, but still onerous, forms of persecution. As one of Byron's closest friends at Cambridge put it in a letter to the poet about their shared inclinations: 'We risque our necks.' At the time this letter was written, Byron was on his way back from his first journey to Greece. Charles Skinner Matthews's remark was inspired by a visit he had made with their common friend Scrope Davies to see two convicted men, an army lieutenant and a sixteen-year-old drummer, in Newgate. The man and boy were hanged shortly after before a huge crowd, which included a royal duke, who had himself recently figured in a scandal that had encouraged alarming rumors. [122]

As Crompton insightfully observes, Georgian England was simply in love with the death penalty, and thus Bentham's remarkable work on pederasty stands out as all the more remarkable – as an utterly pathbreaking analysis that would not find its emancipatory equal until the work of Symonds. For Bentham, the pointless, obfuscatory, pleasure-hating nature of the law on this subject was an illustrative, extreme example of all that needed reforming. But most of those who would have agreed with him in the following decades – Byron and his Cambridge set, Shelley in some humors, Clough, Tennyson, and so many of the Apostles, including Lord Houghton, the "greatest living Angel" in Sidgwick's day – had nothing like his courage, not to mention his legal expertise. And of course, even

Bentham had kept this side of his legal reformism underground. Both old Benthamite and young Apostle knew why Plato had been pushed out of English education to begin with, and needed reviving. The Byronic hero – all "the gloom, alienation, wounded pride, and guilt embodied in the literary archetype that in many ways reflected Byron's own personality" – was to be replayed in William Johnson's sadness, Sidgwick's gloom, and Symonds's "self-loathing."[123]

At any rate, the younger Symonds had come to appreciate just how dangerous a business his sexuality was, how class and connection had their protective limits, and how much his father wanted him to marry. A trip to Europe with Green in late spring of 1863 – a trip at the behest of Dr. Symonds, who thought it would prove restorative – led to Symonds's two most important relationships with women, and to much else as well. It was on this trip that he first met Catherine North. She was a "dreamer and thinker," in love with sketching, and Symonds felt he "could soon have fallen in love with her" had she not had to depart with her family after a week at Mürren, where they met. And after Catherine departed, Symonds developed a rather wild crush on the fifteen-year-old Rosa Engel, the niece of the innkeeper. She had come from Thun to help out her uncle over the summer, little knowing that she was going to inspire thoughts of Faust's Margaret in the strange English gentleman. Unfortunately, Symonds had to go off to meet Green in Zurich, as they had planned. Green, who was busy thinking great German thoughts, was none too pleased about Symonds's insisting that they return – through a blizzard – to Mürren to meet his potentially normalizing love. All for nought, as it turned out, since Rosa had wisely decided that little good was likely to come of his attentions.

Green at length insisted that Symonds continue with their planned journey together, and although the latter insisted on a side trip to Thun so that he could search (unsuccessfully) for a picture of Rosa, in due course they made it to Dresden, where they shared a pension with none other than Henry and Arthur Sidgwick, along with J. R. Mozley and Oscar Browning. As for the Cambridge men, he had a supremely disengaged perspective:

The Pension we are in is comfortable. . . . There are numbers of young Cambridge men in the house, who, one & all, play the piano & spend their time in nothing but learning German & talking about music. This is somewhat of an infliction.

Arthur Sidgwick is among them. Altogether, I feel as if I should be well off here; very well, if my eyes wd let me read; but there is something sad in coming back to old ways of going on, old gossip, old College talk, old associations of foregone life, much of wh I wd be glad to spurn for good, after the fresh divine existence wh I led among the mountains. There I did nothing common or mean, but everything was new & had a definite import. Here there are the thousand indifferences & little interests that vulgar life brings with it.[124]

This must have been an inauspicious meeting with Henry, who was always decidedly unmusical, but Symonds did find himself traveling part of the way home with Arthur, whom he found a most attractive companion. In October, he would apparently try to induce Arthur to travel to Italy with him, explaining, "I have to-day a desire to embrace at once all that is beautiful and deeply thought in Art, Philosophy, and Nature." In December, he would instruct Dakyns, "If you see Arthur please tell him of me & make him feel me the never forgetting never to be forgotten but of speech and sight much thirsting wh things for reasons are not easily obtained."[125] Dakyns was another friend from this period. Over the course of a pretty miserable fall back in Clifton, the only bright spot had been Dakyns, a new master at Clifton College:

He was a Rugby-Cambridge man, the friend of Arthur Sidgwick whom I knew, and of Henry Sidgwick, whom I was destined to know. All these names will recur frequently in my memoirs. Of Graham, I need only say here that his perfervid temper of emotion, his unselfishness, his capacity for idealizing things and people, the shrewdness of his intellectual sense, and the humour of his utterance (style almost of Jean-Paul Richter), made their immediate impression on me. In philosophy he inclined to Comtism, chiefly because of its altruistic theories. He was physically robust, athletic at football, courageous and spirited, but withal very nervously excitable and irritable. Gentle exceedingly and sweet in converse – ποθεινὸς τοῖς φίλοις. Masculine to the back-bone.[126]

Dr. Symonds was apparently less enthusiastic, and vetoed his son's plan to invite Dakyns along on an Italian trip.

Thus, at the precise time when Symonds was placing himself so thoroughly in his father's care and keeping, and even feeling affectionate toward certain select women, his most intimate circle of male friends had started to take shape. The preceding lines in the letter to Dakyns were:

I cannot tell you exactly as I wish how deeply I feel the more than kindness of your words, & yet how much I fear them. I know I am not worthy of them. I dread lest they should make me selfish, & lest a time should come when I might have to cry in vain for them & be alone. – Still they are gifts wh I take as I sh take any great gift of God wh came to me & made me live.[127]

He sends his new friend a book as a gift, in all likelihood his old copy of Shelley.

Needless to say, there was much felt conflict in all this – more guilt, more health problems, more drift. And there was much else going on with his life beyond his new – and hardly unsuspicious – friends. Symonds was, after all, casting about for a career. This took him to London, later in the spring of 1864, where he went "to eat dinners at Lincoln's Inn, and to make a pretence of studying law."[128]

In London, Symonds socialized, he poeticized, he philosophized. He did not in any serious way study law, instead preferring to read and think "at random in the club." Meditations on Goethe's Proemium to "Gott und Welt," a favorite of his, took up more of his time than studying Blackstone. And of course, "I rode in the park, rowed on the Serpentine, and went sculling up the river with a waterman of Surbiton. Characteristically enough, I began to fall in love with this young fellow."[129] His father again intervened, and with the additional support of the eminent surgeon Sir Spencer Wells, encouraged his son to get married. "Then, by inspiration, the memory of Catherine North returned to me. She was connected with the best and happiest period of my past confused existence." Symonds set out in pursuit of her, receiving, later in the summer, after some initial overtures, her parents' permission to follow the family to Pontresina, which proved a fateful turn. Thus, hanging about the entrance at the Hotel Krone, he "met Catherine; and our life together began."[130]

As the *Memoirs* continue, the "best would have been to have died there on the top of the Pitz Languard," where they had had "a day of days" and exchanged rings. Symonds was plagued by doubts straight off: "I loved her ardently. . . . But was it not too pure, too spiritual, too etherialized, this exquisite emotion?" He "missed something in the music – the coarse and hard vibrations of sex" and wondered whether his love was really "perfect for her, such a holocaust of self as she had a right to expect?" But he managed to compare this love to that of "Dante and his Beatrice," and told his "heart it did not signify," this want of passion.

The marriage duly took place, at Hastings on November 10, 1864, and the honeymoon almost immediately confirmed Symonds's fears. He "felt no repugnance at first, but no magnetic thrill of attraction," no magic, no cure. It was all so awkward:

The organ of sex was vigorous enough and ready to perform its work. My own ineptitude prevented me for several nights from completing the marital function; and at last I found the way by accident – after having teased and hurt both my wife and myself, besides suffering dismally from the humiliating absurdity of the situation. She afterwards told me that such manifest proofs of my virginity were agreeable to her. But all the romance and rapture of sexual intercourse, on which I had so fondly counted, were destroyed by this sordid experience.[131]

Symonds would come to admit that this marriage was a colossal mistake. Catherine was a very sophisticated and intelligent women, who preferred the socializing of Clifton to the beauties of remote Davos, and her pain and isolation were often palpable during their years together.

Symonds did try, in at least some limited ways, to protect Catherine. It is curious that even the quite candid case history was slightly censored in the first English edition, which reads: "He found that he was potent, and he begot several children, but he also found, to his disappointment, that the tyranny of the male genital organs on his fancy increased." The German text reads a touch differently: "He found that he was potent, and he begot several children. But he also found, to his disappointment, that he only slept with his wife faute de mieux. The dependence on picturing male genitals was so great that visions of men pursued him even in the very act of marital copulation."[132]

Just how well Catherine understood her husband's inner life is not easy to determine. Naturally, he supposed that they would be in a deep sense friends, a school of sympathy for their children. Symonds was, after all, a liberal who had read his Mill and his Maurice and was determined to do his bit for women's higher education. And in fact, his children – ironically, all girls – profited from his ambitions for them. But of course, his sexual interests were so thoroughly intwined with an aesthetic celebrating the superiority of male beauty that there was a pervasive, often unconscious, masculinism that hung about his life and work. Like the Greeks, he held male beauty to be paramount.

Needless to say, Symonds's "health gave way." If he did at this time do much to hone the literary style that would figure in his future works, it was always in a haze of pain and discomfort. Troubled by the failure of the "marriage cure," he would recognize in retrospect that "[w]hat was really happening was that I was pining away through the forcible repression of my natural inclination for the male sex. I could not keep my thoughts from running on this subject; I could not prevent myself from dreaming at night about it; I could not refrain from poetizing the passion in a hundred forms."[133] When introduced to Whitman's *Leaves of Grass* in 1865, by Myers, he had been immediately struck by the moving celebration of male comradeship. But explicit graffiti and a proposition from a soldier in Leicester Square only served to drive home how fragile his equilibrium really was. Still, things were coming to a head, and the year 1867 would prove as fateful for Symonds as it had been for Sidgwick.

Just what a state he was in became evident during the hot summer of that year, after their return to London. Symonds was in "a perpetual fever" and would later describe his own writings from that period as "hysterical." As the *Memoirs* recount, he would rise early in the morning "from a sleepless bed, walk across the park, and feed my eyes upon the naked men and boys bathing in the Serpentine." It was a cosmic experience:

I was Hypnos gazing on Endymion in the cave of Latmos. Golden hair, and white neck, and breasts brighter than twin stars, and belly softer than the down of doves, and dewy thighs, and awful beauty of love's minister beneath the tuft of crispy curls, and slender swelling legs, and rosy feet, and long lithe languid arms. I had them all pressed to my body there, flank to flank – kissed every part and member of the lad – with wandering hand tasted them one by one, and felt the fervous of smooth buttocks glowing and divine. In a day dream: O Jupiter!

Four young men are bathing in the pond by the embankment. I pass; the engine screams and hurries me away. But the engine has no power to take my soul. That stays, and is the pond in which the bathers swim, the air in which they shout, the grass on which they run and dress themselves, the hand that touches them unfelt, the lips that kiss them and they know it not.[134]

Not surprisingly, Symonds "began writing poetry again during the hot summer weather," and all of his poems "were composed upon the subject of masculine love. The second half of 'John Mordan', 'Diego', 'Love and Music', 'The Headmaster', together with a great number of dithyrambic pieces in the style of Walt Whitman, belong to those months." However uncertain he was of his own talents, he simply could not stop.

And of course, it was at precisely this moment that the ascetic, tormented, and poeticizing Henry Sidgwick was to enter his life in an intimate and permanent way. As the *Memoirs* explain:

Henry Sidgwick, whose acquaintance I had recently made, was also staying in London – philosophizing, going to spiritualistic seances, and trying to support himself (for an experiment) on the minimum of daily outlay. Our acquaintance ripened rapidly into a deep and close friendship, which has been of inestimable value during the last twenty-two years. It would be difficult to say how much I owe to the rarely noble character, the wisdom, the extraordinary mental originality, the inexhaustible sympathy and kindness of this most remarkable man.[135]

For its part, the dryly evasive *Henry Sidgwick, A Memoir*, actually quotes Symonds on the "inestimable value" of this friendship, noting that for "Sidgwick, too, this friendship was one of the things he most valued in life" (M 166).

Apparently, each found the confessions of the other profoundly interesting right from the start. A long letter to Sidgwick, dated June 23, 1867, spells out how much talk was being devoted to the "deepest problems":

I wonder what I have done to deserve being classed among the infidels, who imagine human delusion to be the origin of all religions. I am far too sceptical for that. The explanation of Comte seems to me more puerile and less consonant with the laws of our nature than Theism. But yet I am not a Theist. I should like to know very much what made you one, or whether you never ceased to be one. I would give a great deal to regain the Christian point of view, or rather, since all modern people are ethically Christian, to regain the sentiment of belief in the Deity – the personal, creative, conscious Deity. But I nowhere find Him. I see that this age has no definition of Him. I cannot construct one. Theists, each and all in different ways, continue the old anthropomorphism and self-worship. They derive the Deity from man, refining their conceptions proportionately to the advancing refinement of the world. It is possible that this may be good evidence of the Deity: an innate impulse to worship God in our own image may have been implanted in us by Him. But scepticism requires evidence from the other side. In a word, nothing appears to me satisfactory by way of proof but revelation; and I do not feel myself forced at present to credit any revelation. All the revelations, like the Theistic ideals, seem products of the human soil; good, bad, or indifferent, according as clay, sand, peat, and the like are mixed. I wonder whether you think you may lay your finger in spiritualism on some point affecting revelation. If you do, you have the secret. I could believe anything if somebody first knocked me flat with a club – if all the conceit were taken out of me by the proof of agencies beyond our experience revealing God, I could prepare myself for mysticism. Here says the teleologist, are not thought, conception of seed, the growth of plants, miracles enough for you? Undoubtedly they are miracles. But, in order to make me a Theist, connect them with God, prove their inevitable emanation from Paternal Intelligence – I am not Atheistic, or scoffing; I am merely helpless, painfully surrounded by miracles. My pen upon this paper, these letters, and what they mean, assuredly these things are miracles; it is this very thing that distracts me; miracles are so plentiful. I turn aside and think of the past myriads of centuries; I look across the stars and see billions flying into sight suddenly down the tubes of the telescopes; are there not more miracles than blackberries? But not one teaches me God. Or if I talk of God, worn out with these inexplicable wonders, I feel this to be cowardice; God, so spoken of, is a merely otiose *summum genus*, a general term to include everything, the O which ends an infinite series. In other words, again, if God is everywhere He is as good as nowhere. I have forgotten His definition. The world cannot supply me with one. I sprawl simply. Then what makes you a Theist? Is it the moral world? Is it your intellect? In the moral and intellectual miracles I do not find more than in those of the material world, except that, because my whole being depends on them essentially, they seem to me more marvellous and more inexplicable. Yet when I try to abstract them, and when I throw myself into a state of trance, proceeding in my ascent from *infimae species* to the *summum genus*, I eventually eliminate everything but naked consciousness, which tells absolutely no tale. It is an appalling solitude. My head reels, my heart seems ceasing, I catch myself upon the verge of madness, and roll down the mountain of meditation again, only too glad to be among the *infimae species* at the bottom. Long ago, even as a child, I had the morbid faculty of such self-abstraction, and when doubt first insinuated itself into my mind this spiritual nakedness made itself horribly remembered. I thought, will death be like that, and when our eyes are closed for ever, will even that last sense of existence, naked, solitary, formless, unimpressed, which I so much hate, be also lost? I can imagine annihilation thus. What I call my soul is simply the embroidery of sense upon this blankness. I can reduce it to its primal blankness by abstracting sense; and when sense is finally abstracted from me, what, to call 'Myself,' will be left? With the conception of the soul disappears that of God. Then both irresistibly rush back and assert themselves. Then comes the problem of human history. The philosophy of religion says its say. Physical science perplexes more than it illuminates. Its new horizons are merely great in bewilderment. The struggle of the soul begins to wax faint. It ceases and atomic scepticism gets in. Therewith there is nothing left to live for. Every faculty droops; the whole man becomes etiolated; death intervenes, and at last – the great secret.

But such a helpless condition is awful – ἀθεὸς ἐν τῷ κόσμῳ. Four words rarely meant more than these. Objectively they contradict themselves, for "quis Deus incertum est, habitat Deus"; subjectively, in relation to the aching brain and unsatisfied heart, and incomplete intelligence and weak moral nature, they contain a volume of sad significance. "Malgré moi l'infini me tourmente." The whole question revolves on the quis, quis Deus. If there be no other God, what Is is a God – not Jah, but ὄν – yet who, having heard of Moses and of Christ, can be satisfied with Parmenides? Even Spinoza will not do for me. I would sooner have Comte than the worshippers of *Ens*. My human weakness clamours for a personal God, and – let not Congreve hear me – for some assurance of either immortality or annihilation. It is the indefinite which is so cruel, the perpetual "perhaps," which will not be dismissed.

The only thing I know which will restore my physical tone and give me health is living in the Alps. The only prospect of obtaining spiritual tone and health seems to be the discovery of some immaterial altitudes, some mountains and temples of God. As I am prostrated and rendered vacant by scepticism, the Alps are my religion. I can rest there and feel, if not God, at least greatness – greatness prior, and posterior to man in time, beyond his thoughts, not of his creation, independent, palpable, immovable, proved. The sense of the Alps was a long time coming to me. Perhaps even now that grander sentiment is on its way. [incomplete][136]

The significance of this letter cannot be overestimated. Brown's biography of Symonds, effectively coauthored by Sidgwick and Dakyns, was a thematization of the line about being knocked flat as a prerequisite for mysticism. Clearly, this seminal letter struck right at the very heart of Sidgwick's deepest concerns, and he would use it when thinking about how to construct his departed friend's biographical treatment. There was something extremely judicious about this, a subtle recognition of a moment in their lives that had been a defining one, however painful. Indeed, the letter brings out the curious religious interest of Symonds's various dissociative states, how his dipsychia often took quite literal forms. He had often, when growing up, been strangely affected by light in certain natural settings and had "passed from the sense of a tangible presence into a dream," a "very definite phase of experience, approaching hypnotism in its character." Moreover, he was also subject to "a kind of trance."

Suddenly, at church, or in company, or when I was reading, and always when my muscles were at rest, I felt the approach of the mood. Irresistibly it took possession of my mind and will, lasted what seemed like an eternity and disappeared in a series of rapid sensations which resembled the awakening from anaesthetic influence.

One reason why I disliked this kind of trance was that I could not describe it to myself. I cannot even now find words to render it intelligible, though it is probable that many readers of these pages will recognize the state in question. It consisted in a gradual but swiftly progressive obliteration of space, time, sensation and the multitudinous factors of experience which seemed to qualify what we are pleased to call ourself. In proportion as these conditions of ordinary consciousness were subtracted, the sense of an underlying or essential consciousness acquired intensity. At last nothing remained but a pure, absolute, abstract self. The universe became without form and void of content. But self persisted, formidable in its vivid keenness, asking or rather feeling the most poignant doubt about reality, ready as it seemed to find existence break as breaks a bubble round about it. And what then? The apprehension of a coming dissolution, the grim conviction that this state was the last state of the conscious self, the sense that I had followed the last thread of being to the verge of the abyss and had arrived at demonstration of eternal *maya* or illusion, stirred or seemed to stir me up again. The return of ordinary conditions of sentient existence began by my first recovering the power of touch, and then by the gradual though rapid influx of familiar impressions and diurnal interests. At last I felt myself once more a human being; and though the riddle of what is meant by life remained unsolved, I was thankful for this return from the abyss – this deliverance from so awful an initiation into the mysteries of scepticism.[137]

As if Symonds's grasp on reality were not shaky enough, he had these mystical, dissociative states to contend with, accentuating his sense of ontological insecurity. This was an all-too-literal Platonic sense of "the phenomenal unreality of all the circumstances which contribute to a merely phenomenal consciousness." Often, upon awakening from "that formless state of denuded keenly sentient being," he asked himself "which is the unreality: the trance of fiery vacant apprehensive sceptical self from which I issue, or these surrounding phenomena and habits which veil that inner self and build a self of flesh-and-blood conventionality?" What would happen if "the final stage of the trance were reached. . . . Could another garment of sensitive experience clothe again that germ of self, which recognized the unsubstantiality of all that seem to make it human?"[138] Such states would return "with diminishing frequency" until Symonds was twenty-eight – curiously, until 1868, after the "crisis in Cannes."

Symonds worried that he might have been a bit too intense, too over-whelming for Sidgwick, after they had been so much together over the long, hot summer. They planned to meet up again "in the dim distance of the Riviera." But Symonds wrote to explain "that much which I have told you about myself must seem painful. My past life has been painful in many ways, and I bear in my body the marks of what I have suffered." Thus, he allows that

when my nervous light burns low in solitude, then the shadows of the past gather round, and I feel that life itself is darkened. . . . I dread that art and poetry and nature are unable to do more for what Dante, with terrible truth, called 'Li mal protesi nervi' [badly strained nerves]. These darknesses, which Arthur calls my depression fits, assail me in splendid scenery, among pictures and statues, wherever, in fact, I ought to enjoy most and be *most alive*. It is only the intercourse of friends which does me really any good.[139]

This was a revealing reversal from his attitude in 1864, when he had written to his sister concerning Arthur Sidgwick, "it seems necessary to blunt all my sensibilites at present, & therefore the more I like a companion the less he is esteemed a healthy one."[140] And it would prove prophetic.

Needless to say, in all this Symonds had touched Sidgwick's Apostolic soul in just the right way, eliciting perhaps the most passionate letter that Sidgwick ever penned:

My dearest friend I cannot tell you all I feel: I have drunk deep of happiness: I have said to the Augenblick, 'du bist so schön' – I am so glad you say I have done you good: I must have given you my best: my best never comes out except when I am played upon & stirred by affection and subtle sympathy combined: when I do not get this, I become lethargic. Among the 'dim' common populations I seem to change and become common. I am so glad you let me stay with you so long; I might have felt that what of strange, new, delicious, rich had come into my life might pass out of it like a dream. I feel now that you are 'not something to be retracted in a certain contingency.'[141]

And Symonds knew his power: he wrote to Dakyns that "Henry Sidgwick has been with me a week. He is numbered among mine."

Symonds had put the great questions to Sidgwick with unrivalled force. What was the great secret? the true, enduring self? the proof of theism? the human cost of skepticism? the significance of altered psychological states? And he had tied them together with a warm appreciation of how friendship, duly aestheticized, was the sustaining and enabling element in a life absorbed in such inquiries. Here was the friend that Sidgwick had so long sought, with whom the soul could flow in soaring talk. No one, in the years to come, would do so much to bring out his best. Goethean hypocrisy had its Apostolic virtues.

Part II

IV. The Point of View of the Universe

At about the age of 30, unable to endure his position any longer, he at last yielded to his sexual inclinations. As he began to do this, he also began to regain calm and comparative health. He formed a close alliance with a youth of 19. This *liaison* was largely sentimental, and marked by a kind of etherialised sensuality. It involved no sexual acts beyond kissing, naked contact, and rare involuntary emissions. About the age of 36 he began freely to follow homosexual inclinations.

At the same time, when he had begun to indulge his inborn homosexual instincts, he rapidly recovered his health. The neurotic disturbances subsided.

He has always loved men younger than himself. At about the age of 27 he began to admire young soldiers. Since he yielded freely to his inclinations the men he has sought are invariably persons of a lower social rank than his own. He carried on one *liaison* continuously for 12 years; it began without passion on the friend's side, but gradually grew to nearly equal strength on both sides. He is not attracted by uniforms but seeks some uncontaminated child of Nature. The methods of satisfaction have varied with the phases of his passion. At first they were romantic and Platonic, when a hand-touch, a rare kiss, mere presence, sufficed. In the second period sleeping side by side, inspection of the naked body of the loved man, embracements, occasional emissions after prolonged contact. In the third period the gratification became more frankly sensual. It took every shape: mutual masturbation, intercrural coitus, *fellatio*, *irrumatio*, occasionally *paedicatio*, always according to the inclination or concession of the beloved male. He himself plays the active masculine part. He never yields himself to the other, and he asserts that he never has the joy of finding himself desired with ardour equal to his own. He does not shrink from passive *paedicatio*; but it is never demanded of him. Coitus with males, as above described, always seems to him healthy and natural; it leaves a deep sense of well-being, and has cemented durable friendships. He has always sought to form permanent ties with the men whom he has adored so excessively.

He is of medium height; not robust, but with great nervous energy, with strong power of will and self-control, able to resist fatigue and changes of external circumstance. In boyhood he had no liking for female occupations, or for the society of girls, preferring study and solitude. He avoided games and the noisy occupations of boys, but was only non-masculine in his indifference to sport, was never feminine in dress or habit. He never succeeded in his attempts to whistle. Is a great smoker, and has at times drunk much. He likes riding, skating and climbing, but is a poor horseman, and is clumsy with his hands. He has no capacity for the fine arts and music, though much interested in them, and is a prolific author.

He has suffered extremely throughout life owing to his sense of the difference between himself and normal human beings. No pleasure he has enjoyed, he declares, can equal a thousandth part of the pain caused by the internal consciousness of Pariahdom. The utmost he can plead in his own defence, he admits, is irresponsibility, for he acknowledges that his impulse may be morbid. But he feels absolutely certain that in early life his health was ruined, and his moral repose destroyed, owing to the perpetual conflict with his own inborn nature, and that relief and strength came with indulgence. Although he always has before him the terror of discovery, he is convinced that his sexual dealings with men have been thoroughly wholesome to himself, largely increasing his physical, moral, and intellectual energy, and not injurious to others. As a man of letters he regrets that he has been shut out from that form of artistic expression which would express his own emotions. He has no sense whatever of moral wrong in his actions, and he regards the attitude of society towards those in his position as utterly unjust and founded on false principles.

Case History of John Addington Symonds[142]

As Symonds explained in the case history, there was a certain periodization in his sexual maturation, such that he moved from a more sublimated, Platonized form of sexuality with Willie Dyer, through a somewhat more direct middle period, when he took up with the nineteen-year-old Clifton student Norman Moor, and on to an amazingly libidinous middle age, when he would become intimate comrades with the Swiss peasant Christian Buol and the Venetian gondolier Angelo Fusato.[143] If 1877 marked the transition from the second to the third stage, the transition from the first to the second came in 1867, with the "crisis in Cannes." Once Henry Sidgwick came on the scene, Symonds was to become a less divided self. Strange as it surely must seem to readers of *The Methods of Ethics*, Sidgwick's vision of education and culture was worked out in his intense interplay with Symonds, who in turn was a vivid, forceful presence at nearly every major crisis point in Sidgwick's life.

Now, this account of the concrete sexual practices underlying Symonds's sometimes more lyrical or etherealized public presentations of them is of considerable value for interpreting his relationship with Sidgwick, who, needless to say, was never quite as forthcoming about the particulars of his sexual existence. Or rather, insofar as he was, the record has in large part been either destroyed or protected from public exposure. This, naturally enough, has made the so-called "friendship problem" more of an issue in his case. As Louis Crompton has eloquently framed it: "the central issue confronting gay studies may be called 'the friendship problem.' If a novel, poem, or essay describes or expresses ardent feelings for a member of the same sex, when are we to regard them merely as reflections of what is usually called romantic friendship?"[144]

If this is no longer quite the problem that it was when Crompton wrote, it is thanks in part to work on Symonds, who provided a very accurate means for decoding just how sexualized his more elusive pronouncements really were. Admittedly, much has been written to show how a proper contextual, historical understanding of Victorian friendship precludes any ready translation of it into the sexual and gender categories of more recent times. Thus, it has variously been claimed, passionate, emotional expressions of brotherly love were not necessarily sexual, and effeminate behavior was not necessarily sexual, and many forms of same-sex behavior were not necessarily construed as any indication of a deeper underlying identity or character. And no doubt considerable caution is needed in trying to understand the complex web of acts and identities of the Victorian period.

Still, the case of Symonds does rather put the lie to any attempt to interpret in a desexualized manner the notions of comradeship at play in the English Whitmanians and others of a Hellenistic bent. The record of his inclinations and activities leaves no doubt whatsoever about precisely what was figurative and what literal. What seems clear, from his case, is that even his more etherealized periods often involved a good deal of body contact, foreplay, and physical arousal, even if he did swear that he was being "chaste." Thus, he could spend a long evening with the young Norman Moor during which, as his diary of January 28, 1870, so zealously explains: ·

I stripped him naked, and fed sight, touch and mouth on these things. Will my lips ever forget their place upon his breast, or on the tender satin of his flank, or on the snowy whiteness of his belly? Will they lose the nectar of his mouth – those opened lips like flower petals, expanding neath their touch and fluttering? Will my arms forget the strain of his small fragile waist, my thighs the pressure of his yielding thighs, my ears the murmur of his drowsy voice, my brain the scent of his sweet flesh and breathing mouth? Shall I ever cease to hear the metallic throb of his mysterious heart – calm and true – ringing little bells beneath my ear?

I do not know whether, after all, the mere touch of his fingers as they met and clasped and put aside my hand, was not of all the best. For there is the soul in the fingers. They speak. The body is but silent, a dumb eloquent animated work of art made by the divine artificer.

Beneath his armpits he has no hair. The flesh of his throat and breast is white as ivory. The nipples of his breats are hardly to be seen, they are so lost in whiteness and so soft. Between them, on the breastbone, is a spot of dazzling brightness, like snow or marble that has felt the kisses of the sun. His hips are narrow, hardened where the muscles brace the bone, but soft as down and sleek as satin in the hollows of the groin. Shy and modest, tender in the beauty-bloom of ladhood, is his part of sex χύπριν ποθοῦσαι ἤδη – fragrant to the searching touch, yet shrinking: for when the wandering hand rests there, the lad turns pleadingly into my arms as though he sought to be relieved of some delicious pang. . . . Ah, but the fragrance of his body! Who hath spoken of that scent undefinable, which only love can seize, and which makes love wild mad and suicidal.[145]

Symonds could actually go on to say that "neither then, nor afterwards, nor before, did any one of those things take place between us which people think inseparable from love of this sort," seemingly implying, in some oblique way, that what he was doing was somehow not really licentious because ejaculation was not the set aim.

Admittedly, this affair was after the "crisis in Cannes," and by contrast, in 1866, Symonds could write disapprovingly to Dakyns about the reckless behavior of Arthur Sidgwick with a boy:

I do not intend to discuss his conduct much more. I shall long to hear of him, every new thing; & I believe in his goodness. But that he is in a dangerous position cannot be denied; when I think of him I range the matter somehow in question & answers like the following–
Is this ἔρως Greek? No.
If it were Greek, is it what Plato wd allow? No.
Is it what the world at large wd call romantic, sentimental, effeminate, on the verge of vice? Yes.
Supposing the world wrong in a special instance, may not its general verdict be right? I think so.
What is the source of Arthur's love? Is it intellectual sympathy? No.
Is it moral good? No.
Is it consentaneity of tastes? No.
Is it chiefly aesthetical enjoyment & pleasure of highly refined sensuousness? Yes.
Are these likely to produce moral & intellectual strengths? No.
Are they capable of producing moral or intellectual debility? Yes, *capable*.
What has yr experience been of this ἔρως? That if uncontrolled it is evil.
In all cases of possible harm, what does Duty say? Avoid all appearance of evil.

In case moral injury were to accrue, where wd the evil fall most heavily? On the
boy, & if on him then through him on his fellow boys.
Does Arthur expose himself to external danger? Yes, to a very gt extent.
These questions by no means settle or exhaust the matter. It is a case of absolutely
new casuistry. There is no rule by wh to measure it as yet.[146]

Here in fine is the Platonic conscience of Symonds (and his friends)
in his first phase. Still, as the line about believing in Arthur's goodness
suggests, the Platonic conscience could be pleasantly lenient about sensual
lapses. And it was certainly fascinated by them.

In fact, Symonds had been introduced to Norman in December of
1868 by Dakyns, who long had had a similar infatuation with the young
Cecil Boyle. In another long letter from 1866, Symonds bemoans at length
the fact that he could not accompany Dakyns and Boyle on a trip to the
Riviera: "it is exceedingly bitter that you should be there & not I, you &
your Myrtilus, & that Theocritus should be once more alive."[147] Their
correspondence from this time is largely devoted to boy love. Dakyns
even helped bring Symonds to Clifton as a lecturer – the better to pursue Norman at close quarters – and their correspondence simply exudes
exuberant hyperbole about their boys.

Hence, it is in this context that one has to read Sidgwick's involvement with Symonds, particularly during its formative moment, in the
decade of storm and stress. Nearly all of Sidgwick's closest, most enduring
male friends were homosexual or bisexual: Symonds, Dakyns, his brother
Arthur, Myers, Browning, Noel.[148] And these men were not simply prone
to the standard passing phase of schoolboyish same-sex behavior. Quite
the contrary, they were – with the exception of Myers – devoted to a life
of Uranian activity and philosophizing. That is, they were all more or less
like Symonds in finding a larger political – even cosmic – meaning in their
"inversion," one that shaped their understandings of culture and education. And this could take a remarkably flamboyant form. Oscar Browning,
for example, has grown into an extraordinary (if dubious) Cambridge legend, and his story shares many of the telltale marks. Annan describes
Browning's personal touch when it came to being an educational inspirer
for boys who were not part of the smart set:

He opened their minds by making them mix with the elegant sprigs. He educated the sprigs, too, by puncturing their ideas of good form. Class differences
evaporated in his rooms, where at his parties one would find foreign professors,

diplomats, apprentice teachers, merchant seamen and soldiers in full regimentals. He would strum Wagner on the piano and Desmond MacCarthy remembered how after he had sung 'Voi che sapete' a Tommy in scarlet uniform picked him up and spanked him for singing false notes. He was senior treasurer to dozens of undergraduate societies, including the Union. It was he rather than Seeley who got the history school in the university afloat and it was he who first set up a teacher training college and became its principal. . . . Browning left behind him 10,000 letters, of which 2,000 were from soldiers or sailors and some from a few shady characters. He never concealed his interest in young men and wrote an ode in alcaics to the penis ('Partner of our days, King potent over men, Troublesome author of anxieties you are . . . '). Some Victorians were privately less shocked by demonstrations of homosexual affection than their successors and were even indulgent towards spooning and swooning over choristers. As a boy Browning had been revolted by the scenes of animal lust in college at Eton and there was never any evidence that he stole even a kiss from the undergraduates he befriended.[149]

Doubtless Browning was the one manning the piano at that Dresden pension in the summer of 1863. At Eton, he had been a student of none other than William Johnson Cory, and as noted, when he went up to Cambridge he was one of Sidgwick's Apostolic brethren – indeed, the one who eventually donated the cedarwood chest, known as the "Ark," in which the Society stored its papers. And he was laughably far from being above suspicion. Although he returned to Eton after Cambridge and became a popular teacher, he was driven out in 1875 because of the close relationships he established with the boys, particularly the future Lord Curzon. Symonds and Sidgwick worked behind the scenes on his behalf, unsuccessfully attempting to undercut Browning's nemesis, the headmaster Hornby.[150] Sidgwick deemed Browning rather than Hornby the more advanced educator, and Browning's transition to Cambridge was aided by his Apostolic friends. Sidgwick, like nearly everyone else, had reservations about Browning's scholarship. This, however, in no way impeded their friendship or collaboration in the cause of educational reform. Much the same assessment could be given of Sidgwick's relationship with Dakyns, who was also by all accounts a most inspiring schoolmaster.[151] Stimulating the intellect was their mission, not promoting sports.

Consider also Noel, the aristocratic Apostle who identified himself as a radical and poet, and who was, if anything, even more flagrantly sexually active and politicized than Symonds (and was, in all probability, the one who persuaded Symonds to take up with his soldier). As Symonds summed him up:

Noel was married, deeply attached to his wife, a poet of high soaring fancies, a philosopher of burning nebulous ideas. He justified passion to his own eyes and preached it to others in an esoteric quasi-Manichean mysticism. He was vain of his physical beauty, which was splendid at that epoch; and his tastes tended to voluptuousness. The attraction of the male governed him through this vanity and this voluptuousness. He loved to be admired. He enjoyed in indolent sultana fashion the contact of masculine desire, the *attouchements* of excited organisms, the luxurious embracements of nakedness. Strange to say, the indulgence of these tastes did not disturb his mental equilibrium. Both as poet and thinker, he remained vigorous and grew in comprehension. Finally, I think, he overlived, absorbed, and clarified by religious mysticism the grossness of his passions. But for me the conversation of this remarkable man was nothing less than poisonous – a pleasant poison, it is true.[152]

Symonds would also appreciatively suggest that the "exaltation of enthusiasm which distinguishes Goethe, Wordsworth, Shelley, appears rarely in their contemporaries and successors. Only perhaps in Roden Noel does the cult of Nature rise to the fervour point of philosophical and religious inspiration."[153]

As remarked earlier, Noel, who would die the year after Symonds, in 1894, also sought a literary career (following a disastrous attempt at business), soliciting the patronage of Lord Houghton (Richard Monckton Milnes). This made sense, given that, as noted, Lord Houghton was the greatest living Angel and a decided "invert." During the sixties, Sidgwick was extremely close to Noel, perhaps closer to him than to anyone else, with the possible exceptions of Dakyns, Cowell, and later on, Symonds. The *Memoir* includes a letter from Sidgwick to Noel's widow, which reads:

I must write a few lines – though I feel how useless words are – to tell you how much shocked and grieved I was by the news of Roden's death. I have been thinking ever since of him and of your trouble; and also of the early years of our friendship, when we talked and wrote to each other, in the eagerness of youth, on all things in heaven and earth. I have always felt that, though he was keenly disappointed by the world's inadequate recognition of his genius, he did his work in life none the less resolutely, and brought out his great gifts, and remained nobly true to his ideal. I never knew any one more free from what Goethe calls – "was uns alle bändigt, das Gemeine." After conversing with him I always felt that the great realities of

Life and Thought and Art, the true concerns of the human spirit, became more real and fresh and vivid to me.

I am afraid that in later years I often vexed him somewhat by unsympathetic criticism of his poetic work: but I am glad to think that this never made any division between us, – he knew that I recognised in him the "deep poetic heart" and the rare constructive force and vividness of poetic imagination in which he was second to none among his contemporaries. (M 531)

Noel, as Desmond Heath has observed, called himself "an Advanced Liberal with Democratic Leanings," though he was one who also worried, like Mill, about socialism's possible antagonism to individuality and eccentricity. Unlike "Blake, Roden was a nature worshipper, but unlike Wordsworth, he faced her 'disinterest' quite squarely, declaring that 'Truth must embrace both horns of the dilemma'."[154] All this perforce made him exceptionally congenial to Sidgwick and Symonds, however critical they both were of many (not all) of his poetic productions. Sidgwick judged his friend a "poetical man," if not exactly a poet, and he criticized Noel's willingness "to take a poet as a philosopher" as opposed to an artist providing the matter for philosophy, "special" by virtue of emotional fine tuning. Still, he admitted that *A Modern Faust*, Noel's most autobiographical poem, was a very special appreciation of the difficulties confronting "the most sympathetic, thoughtful and sensitive amongst ourselves." The tenor of their Apostolic friendship is suggested by some lines from the letter, cited in Chapter 3, that Sidgwick wrote to Noel when the latter was traveling in Syria, in 1860:

If you throw any light on Platonic mysticism, bring out any esoteric doctrines that our uninitiated eyes are now blind to, why, we shall be proud of you as a man and a brother. Our [Apostolic] discussions have of late taken a slightly political and social turn – for instance, I am now engaged on an essay on the "Over-population" theory – but every now and then we have a good speculation, than which nothing has a more rousing and quickening effect. I wish you could have discussed with us last term "Whether Life Culminated," viz. Whether the noblest view of man's course *inter utramque facem* was not that of continued progress instead of first ascent and then descent. (M 48)

It was also in a letter to Noel that Sidgwick wrote about taking the lines from Shelley's "Hymn to Apollo" as the motto of a true metaphysic. Shelley was another special bond between Sidgwick, Noel, and Symonds, and it is illuminating that, as Crompton shows, "Shelley was unique in challenging accepted sex mores in his prose as well as in his verse. Both his Godwinism and his deep immersion in Greek literature gave him a point of view remote from his countrymen."[155] Shelley would virtually rank with Goethe as a sort of poetic encoding of the great questions, the deepest problems.

Noel was also dear friends with Cowell and a member of the Alpine Club, and thus his links to Sidgwick were singularly close. Symonds met Noel through Sidgwick. And happily, Noel also contributed an anonymous case history to Symonds, for inclusion in *Sexual Inversion*:

He dreams indifferently about men and women, and has strong sexual feeling for women. Can copulate, but does not insist on this act; there is a tendency to refined, voluptuous pleasure. He has been married for many years, and there are several children of the marriage.

He is not particular about the class or age of the men he loves. He feels with regard to older men as a woman does, and likes to be caressed by them. He is immensely vain of his physical beauty; he shuns *paedicatio* and does not much care for the sexual act, but likes long hours of voluptuous communion during which his lover admires him. He feels the beauty of boyhood. At the same time he is much attracted by young girls. He is decidedly feminine in his dress, manner of walking, love of scents, ornaments and fine things. His body is excessively smooth and white, the hips and buttocks rounded. Genital organs normal. His temperament is feminine, especially in vanity, irritability and petty preoccupations. He is much preoccupied with his personal appearance and fond of admiration; on one occasion he was photographed naked as Bacchus. He is physically and morally courageous. He has a genius for poetry and speculation, with a tendency to mysticism.

He feels the discord between his love for men and society, also between it and his love for his wife. He regards it as in part, at least, hereditary and inborn in him.[156]

Noel's case falls under the classification "Psychosexual Herma-phroditism," which is probably where Sidgwick's case history would have been placed had he only contributed one – though of course, Sidgwick was by all accounts impotent with women.[157] Noel apparently believed his bisexuality inborn in part because his great uncle was none other than Percy Jocelyn, the bishop of Clogher, who in 1822 "was apprehended with a guardsman of the First Regiment in the White Lion Tavern near the Haymarket, a well-known place of assignation."[158] His gender bending and decadence complicate any straightforward identification of him with the Whitmanians, though he too professed to worship at that shrine.

Lamentably or not, there is no such frank record of the particulars of Sidgwick's sexual tendencies, though there is such a mountain of evidence about his filiations that such a record is scarcely needed. There is little ambiguity about his longing wondering, in his diary, if Oscar Browning might be "the friend I seek."[159] Perhaps E. E. Constance Jones realized, when she described Sidgwick's "Horatian" wit, that "Horatian" was a well-known code word for bisexual. As one of Sidgwick's literary executors, she may well have known what Eleanor and Arthur so clearly knew about Henry's deeper self.[160] No doubt Myers, at any rate, knew exactly what he was suggesting when he recalled Sidgwick's habit of nervously munching on his beard while sitting in chapel staring at the choristers.[161] And among the various fragmented jottings contained in the Sidgwick Papers, one finds such Symondsish thoughts as the following, entitled "My Friends":

1. These are my friends – beautiful, plain-featured, tender-hearted, hard headed.
2. Pure, spiritual, sympathetic, debauched, worldly, violent in conflict.
3. Their virtue and vice are mine and not mine: they were made my friends before they were made virtuous and vicious.
4. Because I know them, the Universe knows them and you shall know them: they exist and will exist, because I love them.
5. This one is great and forgets me: I weep, but I care not, because I love him.
6. This one is afar off, and his life lies a ruin: I weep but I care not because I love him.
7. We meet, and their eyes sparkle and then are calm.
8. Their eyes are calm and they smile: their hands are quick and their fingers tremble.
9. The light of heaven enwraps them: their faces and their forms become harmonious to me with the harmony of the Universe.
10. The air of heaven is spread around them; their houses and books, their pictures and carpets make music to me as all things make music to God.
    * * *
13. Some are women to me, and to some I am a woman.
14. Each day anew we are born, we meet and love, we embrace and are united for ever: with passion that wakes no longing, with fruition that brings no satiety T.O.
15. We pour the Cana-wine of converse: the first poured is good, and the last poured is better, and what is not poured is best.[162]

This is marked "(May 1867 to JAS)," suggesting that Sidgwick and Symonds were growing close even before their summer visit.

Admittedly, Sidgwick was conflicted, perhaps more conflicted than Symonds and certainly more consistently repressed. He was less passionate by far, and for Symonds, comparable to rhubarb in his sobriety. In an exchange concerning a sex scandel, in 1861, Noel wrote to him: "nor by the way did I accuse you of 'sympathy with Immorality!' (I know you a little better, au contraire *you* are the Ascetic and I the Libertine!)" Sidgwick, as noted, had a reputation for health-imparing asceticism, being at war with his "clay." But what Noel goes on to say is suggestive. He admits that "There is also some truth in what you say, I fear, about the low tone of morals prevailing in society, and the hypocritical cant that conceals its own vileness, and perchance even lays a salve to its own conscience (a poor crippled thing easily gagged) by raising a virtuous howl when somebody is found out." But what, Noel asks, is the inference? "Not 'Yelverton is to be let off with a shrug of the shoulders,' but that of W. M. Thackeray, 'We are surrounded by infernal scoundrels more than we think for.' And then, probably you will say, after all this, let us look *within*! Well, if you say that, you will be right. But are we hypocrites? I hope not."[163]

At any rate, the upshot here is that, whatever his ascetic tendencies – so odd for a professed Benthamite – it is simply incredible to suppose that all of Sidgwick's profoundly intimate friendships were somehow sexually veiled or repulsive to him. The Apostolic worship of "In Memoriam," the adoration of Clough and Shelley, the orientalist studies (emerging at the very time of Noel's travels), a taste for de Musset, Swinburne, Whitman, and Pater, not to mention an astounding knowledge of Plato – all these things, and much else besides, put him in a very precisely delimited circle of comrades. And of course, beyond the (for Sidgwick) passionate exchanges with Symonds, there are the passionate exchanges with Dakyns, with the language of Greek love plastered all over them. For example, Dakyns wrote to him, in January of 1869:

This is perhaps the only news I have to give you: except, (unless you have divined it) that I am grown & growing cynical. It is not a pretty ending I am going to have I believe. It is also a little curious; to be so much begotten of your own age that when you are most exalted, & believe yourself on the "verge of something real" old ante philistering period slang you remember – "heaven's gate opening, to have tasted the uranian food" then you find yourself anatomically becoming one of Balzac's heroes; and struggle & writhe under the reproach as you may, seek to cloak yourself with a vesture of original sanctity as you will, for don't we all live from the beginning the first-born of the Father? is not original righteousness imputed to us who believed? struggle writhe seek – but find not unless it be more spiders web and serpent coil, and hollow-heaven which is bottomless hell I think it wd. make a capital nightmare for an archangel with an attack of indigestion to fall asleep one with christ by doubleconsciousness a dream a godly dream awake find himself a witless apollyon: hearing also some ape repeating "we told you so." I hope my dear you have σύνεσις, as I have not φωνή. (CWC)[164]

Difficult as it may be to decipher Dakyns's manic outpourings, the line about "heaven's gate opening, to have tasted uranian food," coupled with the complaint about "anatomically becoming one of Balzac's heroes" – corpulent, presumably – make it plain enough that this is a complaint about growing old after a fitter Uranian youth. Dakyns was hardly writing to an unsympathetic party. Indeed, there is a long "love poem" from Sidgwick, seemingly dated September 22, 1866, that reads in part:

> My dearest,
> So it's over then, at last,
> The envious days that could not let us stay
> Among the fairest places of the earth,
> The envious days, that as the time went on,
> Grew shorter ever and shorter, and the sun
> That could not hide himself and could not hide
> The glory of the mountains of the Lord,
> Yet quicker, quicker thro' the heavens fled.–
> At length their envy is accomplished
> And the short hour of loveliness is past.
> Yet, howsoever it be past, I know
> It is but buried in the fruitful earth
> Even as a root; and in the aftertime
> Such evergreen of fragrant memories
> Shall spring and spread luxuriant around
> That these brief days, tho' dead, yet live for ever.

Another stanza – following some lines about how he had simply set out with his brother for a "healthy life & happy, in the hills," which if it rained would have them "smoke cigars / Or play picquet, écarté, or bezique– / Or read some Positive Philosophy" – reads:

> A healthy life and happy, I repeat–
> Tho' just perhaps a little *superficial.*
> You know the truth – how different it was.

The life I lived – the joy & happiness
That God permitted me to taste & see–
It was not on the surface, nor external–
Nay, for it entered deep into my soul.
They two, whose nerves and red 'arterial blood'
Most closely thrill & beat in unison
With mine, These two did God vouchsafe to me.
And when the time was ripe for him to go–
That great pure tender heart & sensitive
The gift that only in the latter years
So suddenly was given to my life–
Then straightway came the other – in his eyes
And in the welcome flavour of his word
The mutual love and deep-struck sympathy
That thro' the thirteen years of sweet & sad
Of boyhood and of manhood ever more
Has bloomed and blossomed to the perfect flower –
He came – and as it were one day had set
And one had risen, with no night between. (CWC)

This poetic effort, which few would associate with the author of the *Methods*, suggests that there was no gulf of understanding between the members of the Symonds circle. It might refer to any number of trips, perhaps even to the voyage of the summer of 1863. But some trip in 1866 seems the most likely – his old Rugby friend Dakyns had known Sidgwick "the thirteen years of sweet & sad."

To be sure, Sidgwick did on occasion express some ardour for young women.[165] His years of storm and stress held even more romantic turbulence than has been indicated, albeit of a curious Sidgwickian variety. Thus, there was the frustrating experience with Meta Benfey, the daughter of Professor Benfey, with whose family Sidgwick stayed for a time while studying in Germany in 1864. After a painful misunderstanding with her, apparently involving some type of crush on Sidgwick's part, he wrote to Dakyns:

Friendship between the sexes is you know after all a devilish difficult thing. How are you to prevent mistakes on the one side or the other. It is not as if the human heart was only capable of the one or other definite emotion blue or red: then it would be comparatively easy to distinguish which was proffered: but on the contrary there are all sorts of purples which run into one another. (M 118)[166]

By December of 1864, he can write of her: "Dear little girl: I know now I should be glad to hear she was engaged to be married. which is a safe test." (CWC)

In fact, Sidgwick's singularly revealing ideas about love and marriage at this time emerge in sharp relief in Noel's letters. In May of 1862, Noel had written to Sidgwick about his own good news:

As one of my best friends I must first announce to you my *engagement to be married*! I think you know the lady. She is (without any humbug!) the best, purest and most loving of her sex. To enable me to marry consistently with the duties one owes to a wife and family I am obliged to look out for some occupation more remunerative than Literature and though I believe in the right of every man to follow his own line and believe in a purely intellectual life (if study of men and experience of life be made the basis of it) which I myself always meant to follow till I found my ideal woman, yet I do believe that to live is above writing about it and that, at least for most natures, to rough it in the world, to marry the woman of one's choice, is the primary duty, even as a question of self-culture. I agree with a remark I saw the other day that the greatest thinkers and writers have been practical active men like others, not dreamers. The mind needs such food, needs to be strengthened for its work by the Heart and Will, disciplined and fully exercised in active life. But this is not to be laid down as a rule for *all*, as no rule is.[167]

Such thoughts were evidently right up Sidgwick's critical line, for a hot correspondence ensues, and it is in this connection that Noel is pushed to explain defensively to Sidgwick that we must "let the eye of Conscience be well open," seeing that it sometimes may be our duty to take "our largest cut" of pleasure. This letter ranks as a singularly fine flowing of soul, much of it swirling around the lower Goethean ideal. Apparently, whatever congratulations he may have offered, Sidgwick also managed to convey that Noel was falling off the Apostolic pedestal, opting for the lower rather than the higher, the partial over the universal. With this, Noel took issue:

Then again there are men, fully men, (but these are a select few indeed, and perhaps can be developed only at certain great crises) who *are* penetrated with the feeling and passion of the universal heart without yielding more particularly to any special individual affection – there may be crises in which such men, who will give up all special binding ties of affection, are needed. But in them there is no lack of Humanity. Yet again, there may be circumstances which preclude a man from forming marriage ties with real advantage to himself and others. This may be the case with anyone of us, either always, or at a given time of our lives.

Or suppose, still more simply, that he had not fallen in love: well then your ideal is doubtless the right one for him, if he is intellectual. Only should circumstances change, and his feelings change, you see I would not lay this down as the grand and binding ideal for myself for ever, unless I know and feel sure I am not a man but a student, or that I am one of the great prophets, or at least specially called to a great special work whose due performance involves giving up near social ties. I would be pretty sure of this latter before I did so. I am far from saying that the life of a professional man is a better thing than the life of an intellectual man, far from that. I like your life at Cambridge for instance. But as much as you can be in contact with the younger men, so as to draw them out and be yourself refreshed body and soul by them the better. Then you don't *want* to marry just now, but if you ever do, then I mean that I don't know that it would be the grand thing to resist and refuse to adopt some mode of life which would enable you to do so, seeing that you would be brought into contact with another phase of social national life; certainly would double your individual life, your being – and acquire a much deeper wider sympathy with the universal heart. Here I come to my favourite theme. You send a shudder through me with your blasphemy (excuse the word) about "marriage consecrating selfishness." Hear a beautiful sentence from Maurice's kind letter to me when I told him of my marriage– "you will be always encouraged to be your very best without any temptation to be proud of it, for it is Love that prompts you." I am sure that common men like me most fully acquire the universal sympathy you speak of in marriage. There is apt to be something vague, sentimental, unreal, fitful in it. The more we come in contact with life and reality the better. Else we may get simply dreamy, at last selfish. Marriage does not necessarily involve giving up one's intellectual life. My ideal would be – Love – the throng and busy life of men – and contemplation – combined. And then "give me neither poverty nor riches" – Yet we cannot always have all we like – and no doubt, our business is to carve the best ideal we can see out of the materials we have got and not be craving too much for others. This was my idea in the latter part of the poem you allude to. I am glad and I may say proud to know that anything I have felt and striven to express has gone home to you. Again, how much danger is there lest "the native hue of resolution be sicklied o'er with the pale cast of thought." What a fine poem is Browning's "Statue and Bust." It strikes me that that man is *the* great poet of the age. We must not strive too much after more perfection of theory than is attainable, we shall have constantly to modify it. Only let us act up to our light. The value of will and action are intense, and in so far as thought paralyses them it must be usurping a place not its own. Every situation has its use, and though we ought to consider what we are most fit for, yet we can adapt ourselves pretty easily to nearly any in which circumstances may for the time place us, if we do not "consider it too curiously." One thing, however, is certain, that the most valuable truths, as you say, are those which grow dim in the closet. Only there are of course various ways of connecting oneself with social and national life. I hesitated long before I gave up my full leisure for thinking and writing, but I have gained in every way, though I am far from thinking everyone should follow my example. You are, however, quite mistaken in thinking that I condemn a life of "pure thought." What I condemn is precisely the life you describe as your ideal, at least condemn it abstractedly *as* an *ideal*, not to be departed from at any time. Let the mere student be content to be a mere student, all well. But let him not hope to acquire a fuller sympathy with the "universal heart of humanity" than the practical man, by the process of placing himself above or outside of humanity and contemplating it, (or rather contemplating his idea of it formed a priori and from books.) A curious sympathy surely will result. He despises common humanity as vulgar, and will not condescend even to experience the most sacred of its emotions, because every ignorant poor man seems capable of these – too gross for the illuminati, and so, delicately sniffing at common humanity and passing by holding his nose, he expects to sympathize with the "universal heart" of man, that heart with its unsounded depths and infinite variety, its good and evil, storms and calms, all in a manner sacred as belonging to it. Can he fitly expound history who enters not into the commonest yet profoundest Life experience before him? And to work well at the truly pressing problems of the time implies no shrinking from common experience, if it comes in our way at least. He will be doing good work may be in expounding differences of text, varieties of reading, certainly in expounding physical truths, perhaps metaphysical, but *History* scarcely seems to be the domain for him. Your ideal seems to be an etherialized Goethe, but he will have infinitely less power, for he contemns experience. Intellect is the Deity of Goethe. But to furnish food for intellect he sees the fullest experience to be necessary. Yet both the practical and the etherial Goethe is in [sic] radically wrong, Intellect is not the most Divine element. In my creed, it is Love. . . . It is plain that if Goetheism is right, we should have a series of isolated, well-cultivated human units, only working for Society when it is clearly seen to be their interest, but self being the end of all. If Christ's spirit is right, Love and universal sympathy with all good would actuate each and unite each to all by an indissoluble bond, binding not by the intellect only, but by the very root fibres of the whole being, the whole man. Is not the harmony of wills our desire for men? And is not this the spirit by which it can be most certainly attained? But I remember your saying that in advocating a many-sided experience I was inconsistent, as *this* is self-culture, Goetheism, as opposed to sacrificing oneself and one's culture for others. I think not. The spirit and object is the point of difference. Does a man apply himself to the study of Truth for the love of Truth – to intercourse with mankind from sympathy with mankind – to particular social affections for the sake of the Love and the beloved objects? Or is it all done half-heartedly with one eye upon himself and all in order only to cultivate himself? This makes the difference. A man must have some general bias, or some plan more or less defined according to which he regulates his life. Is this self-interest, or is it the good of others – the attainment of Truth? That one may be fitted to be an instrument of good, one must cultivate oneself – and one must have that genuine sympathy which prompts us to put ourselves in the position of others, to share their infirmities, put up with their imperfections, and oppose only this want of love. I myself look upon marriage – a true wise deliberate union – (as a general rule I mean) as the holy school for those best affections which are to radiate from them, as from a centre, upon mankind, or as much of mankind as lies within our reach, warmer and more substantial if not so highflown and etherial as those of the philosophic philanthropist; affections which can blossom into perfection only under a serener sky. Then you philosophers are so particular – you must find it seems an actual intangible angel. This would not do for men of common clay – ought not a *man*'s ideal to be "a spirit, yet a woman too"?[168]

Apparently, Sidgwick really did envision "a philosophical bachelor life" guided by the "universal heart of humanity," with, Noel thought, the "danger of the general public to whose benefit a man resolves to devote himself melting – from the largeness and vagueness of his object – into the image of himself only, and of his undertaking *no* definite work in their favour after all." The hope, Noel suggested, was that his "teaching and coming in contact with the young" would serve as a corrective, though in the decades to come Symonds would join Noel in lamenting Sidgwick's curious bookish abstraction when it came to human relations. Obviously, Sidgwick's etherializing tendencies made even his Goethean side look a lot less attainable for the normal man. And this is not to mention the side devoted to altruism and self-sacrifice, as befits a superior man above inferior attachments. If he and Noel shared much when it came to valuing love over thought, they evidently had some sharp differences about just how one entered into the heart of humanity, cultivated sympathy, and so on. And Noel's challenges had a serious impact on the practical-minded Rugbyean and future author of the *Methods*, who was forever complaining about the abstraction and practical uselessness of his results and about the irresolvable tensions between egoism and utilitarianism that might be embedded even in high-minded utilitarian society.[169] Should not a good Millian challenge academic celibacy as well as idleness?

That Noel had some real insight into Sidgwick's other-worldly mentality is also suggested by one of Sidgwick's early poems, "Goethe and Frederika," which he published anonymously in *Macmillan's Magazine* in

1860, the first stanza of which runs:

> Wander, O wander, maiden sweet,
> In the fairy bower, while yet you may.
> See, in rapture he lies at your feet;
> Rest on the truth of the glorious youth,
> Rest – for a summer day.
> That great clear spirit of flickering fire
> You have lulled awhile in magic sleep,
> But you cannot fill his wide desire.
> His heart is tender, his eyes are deep,
> His words divinely flow;
> But his voice and his glance are not for you;
> He never can be to a maiden true;
> Soon will he wake and go. (M 51)

Upon reading Lewes's biography of Goethe, however, Noel had some further, rather alarming thoughts about that ideal:

[T]he impression I derive from it is very distinct, that Goethe conceived a manifold Life experience to be essential to his self-culture, and the Love of many different women to be an important element of it, that he conceived his soul to be a very great soul and the culture of such a soul to be of paramount importance compared to which the happiness or unhappiness of meaner souls was of little moment. They might be indeed and ought to be happy in their connexion with him whatever that might be. Looking round with his broad dispassionate gaze, he saw that this seemed to be the Law of all Nature, the weak absorbed in the strong, and all forming the grand Pantheistic order of the Universe. Other men, with natures not so elevated as that of Goethe, have expressed such a theory more coarsely and acted on it more coarsely than he, and do so still and will do so.[170]

Noel cannot go along with this and wants rather to be the poet of wedded love. "But is there a sacred mystery whose deeps Love may explore, is there a capacity for varied development Love may quicken and feed on, in one truly chosen object? Is wedded Love the best and happiest school for self-denial, for steady devotion to the good of others, strengthening and widening character?" Nor does it ever occur to him that he might be somehow unfitted for this mission. By his lights, Sidgwick is the strange one, with his esoteric, Apostolic pride and taste for Swinburne's wildly aestheticized poetry, coupled with the enforced bachelorhood of an academic Fellowship.

A weird letter written to Dakyns, also from 1862, sheds further light on Sidgwick's feelings:

If a man only could make up his mind not to marry! But the longer I live the more I believe in that institution for all men but those of very sympathetic disposition: though I retain my old theory about the perfection of the human race coinciding with its removal *en masse* from this planet. I believe also, that by a perverse law of human nature marriage is more necessary to a man not engaged in practical work. (M 87)

This would seem to reflect the impact of his arguments with Noel.

Whether Sidgwick regarded Meta Benfey as having lulled him awhile in magic sleep cannot be determined with any exactitude, but it is plain that she somehow managed to shake his self-image. In November of 1864, he confesses to Dakyns, in a somewhat facetious tone, that he is "an inferior man – a sort of χαλκεὺς φαλακρὸς καὶ σμικρός," who must "cultivate principally the art of οἰκονομική."[171] The "inferior man" need not study "abstruse ancient history," which is irrelevant to religion, and may be "a *bona fide* member of the Church of England if he hold his tongue, though speculatively a pure Theist." However, "marriage is necessary to the inferior man therefore £600 per annum is necessary to him." Since it "will be precious hard to become at once humble, industrious, practical & silent," he considers himself "lucky" that he is only twenty-six and a half years old. Still, he admits that "I have one or two friends, who will always think it is my own fault I am not a superior man: also I shall always have a bitter doubt whether it is not really so." He prays "for enough epicureanism" to endure such thoughts. (CWC)

Interestingly, Sidgwick's views often do seem rather more Goethean – or at least the usual vacillating alternation between and synthesis of Goethe and Comte – than Pauline, than the Pauline sentiment as regards marriage, that it is better than burning in hell. As he writes in a letter from December 1864, "Plato is better than St. Paul. . . . 'Earth outgrows the mythic fancies / Sung beside her in her youth / And those debonair romances / Sound but dull beside the truth'." Indeed, another letter from this time carries a remarkable parable, entitled "A Memorable Fancy," involving a Devil conversing with an Angel:

The Devil answered; 'bray a fool in a mortar with wheat yet shall not his folly be driven out of him: if Jesus Christ is the greatest man, you ought to love him in the greatest degree; now hear how he has given his sanction to the law of ten commandments: Did he not mock at the Sabbath & so mock the Sabbath's God? murder those who were murdered because of him? turn away the law from the woman taken in adultery? steal the labour of others to support him? bear false witness when he omitted making a defence before Pilate? covet when he pray'd for his disciples, and when he bid them shake off the dust of their feet against such as refused to lodge them? I tell you no virtue can exist without breaking these ten commandments; Jesus was all virtue, and acted from impulse, not from rules.'

When he had so spoken, I beheld the Angel who stretched out his arms embracing the flame of fire and he was consumed and arose as Elijah.

Note. This Angel, who is now become a Devil is my particular friend: we often read the Bible together in its infernal or diabolical sense, which the world shall have if they behave well. (CWC)

Such pure Apostolic insouciance was not presented in full force in *Henry Sidgwick, A Memoir*, which quite downplayed any overt suggestion that the "superior man" might be above the rules of commonsense morality.[172] And this is not to mention the near-total excision of Sidgwick's more literary and poetic productions, which appeared with some frequency in his letters. There is a much more Bloomsbury-style elitism at work in Sidgwick than is apparent from the abridged versions of his letters – apparently the only versions actually read by the Bloomsberries. After all, the superior man might have a fairly esoteric morality, and certainly one with an eye for aesthetics, even if he did worry about "men using their higher culture to add an extra zest to their material enjoyments."

Circa 1864, there had of course been much worrying about marriage on the part of Sidgwick's other friends as well, not only by Symonds but also by Dakyns. Dakyns, in fact, had taken an interest in Symonds's sister Charlotte at this time, before she married Green. In April of that year, Sidgwick had written to him: "You seem to be rapidly changing roles with me. You under the influence of adorable Symondses, (male and female) are growing so clear, self confident epigrammatic; so passionate and poetical – while I unbraced by work, absorbed in the futile struggle to comprehend the Universe am growing timid, amiable, profound inexpressible – in fact a Great Inarticulate Soul." (CWC) But Dakyns was apparently not the kind of match that Dr. Symonds had in mind for his daughter, and his displeasure with the prospect was communicated through his son. The delicate state of things was summed up in a letter from Sidgwick, feeling very Goethean, trying to console Dakyns:

I think I understand everything now I suppose you have had no communication since with S. I have burnt his letters. I am desponding but not hopeless. I of course guess in the dark not knowing the people. The one important sentence in S's letter is where he says that 'he is quite certain his sister has no idea' etc. Now with 99 brothers out of a 100 I should consider this inconclusive. But S may be the 100th: you know better than I do. I may also misunderstand his meaning, but it seems to me he wishes to leave it open to you to withdraw after hearing the paternal sentence. He does it most delicately but does it not mean this? I should not do it myself, (1) because I am an egotist & (2) because I believe that love often first starts into conscious life in a woman when she knows she is loved. I suppose you have not seen them since. You only heard the father's decision through the son. (CWC)

Revealingly, it is in just this way – pressing one's claims in love – that Sidgwick keeps invoking the image of the egoist: "But you being in love do you believe in it or not? If you do you must push on to the crisis now just as a rational Egoist does." The dualism of practical reason is implicated, as Noel so cogently observed, in cultivating in the particular the very thing that is demanded from the moral point of view – namely, love – at least if the moral point of view is to be rendered effectual.[173]

Thus, in his years of storm and stress, Sidgwick simply could not make up his mind about the nature and general consequences of marriage – he went from chiding Noel for "consecrating selfishness" by getting married to encouraging Dakyns to be an egoist and pursue his love in good conscience.[174] Still, if he was at this time rather far from the Millian perspective on friendship in marriage as a school of sympathy, his views were obviously in flux, and he treated the institution of marriage to a critical consequentialist scrutiny that hardly suggests any undue reverence for it. Intriguingly, he never seemed to doubt that his male friends would serve as a school of sympathy, albeit of the Hellenizing type.

In a sense, Dakyns was revenged, since his effervescent happiness with Cecil Boyle was one of the things that, earlier in 1867, drove home to Symonds how hollow his own marriage was, how much he relished his male companions. When Dakyns did ultimately marry, in 1872, this did not dim his enthusiasm for homogenic love, any more than it did with Symonds or Noel.

Elaborating on these matters, concerning how Sidgwick and his friends hashed out the issues of sex and marriage, ought to suggest just how stormy and stressful the sixties were, as well as fixing the context for discussing Sidgwick, Symonds, and the "crisis in Cannes." There has been much misunderstanding surrounding this affair, and about Sidgwick's sympathies in general. Indeed, he has been cast as reprising the role of Dr. Symonds, when it came to urging "Johnnie" to stifle his impulses and any poetic expression of them. Or worse, as a prime example of "homosocial panic," someone who reacted badly to the sexual suggestiveness of the dangerously close bondings with his male friends. Any such portrait, however, simply fails to do justice to the facts, encoded as they may have been. If Sidgwick's vision of sympathetic unity seemed strange in its absorption in parapsychology, how much stranger that it was also linked to Symonds's vision of the special sensitivity of Uranian love, of being attuned to the aura of sympathetic fellows, alert to the clues that bespoke a comrade. This was the sympathetic unity that required no words, that was somehow conveyed, that simply vibrated the special sensitivity of the evolved soul. Esotericism and dipsychia, joined to Apostolic-style inquiry into the deepest problems, were never so perfectly realized as in Symonds's alternative to the Idealistic and Theosophical visions of the New Age.

V. Crisis Redux

Since your visit nothing very remarkable has happened except a visit from Jowett and one from Norman – both memorable. Were there a school of sculptors in bronze, he (Norman) might make a fortune as a model; or were I a painter, I might even in that inferior art of colour give the world a new, true, original transcript of Hellenic life. . . .

Jowett has much to say, chiefly about my work on Elizabethan literature which he wishes me to undertake in a severely historical spirit – also about more grave matters, especially the future of religious feeling and opinion in England. He complains bitterly of the 'flabbiness' of our present religious consciousness and rejects my facile belief that the civilized world must, in its present highly intellectualized scientific condition, advance after a needful period of putrid softening, towards a new synthesis. His firm conviction of the possibility of continuing for centuries in a slough of lightly worn and morally obstructive dogmas, prejudices, permanent attitudes of traditional acceptance, startled and appalled me. I have grown to believe myself in the centre of a transformation scene, and to expect that ere long (I do not much care if I reckon by decades or by centuries) the scenary and figures will be fixed for a new action. . . . It provokes me to think of your enormous fertility of ideas and power of elaborating thought.

John Addington Symonds to Henry Sidgwick, January 29, 1870[175]

The "crisis in Cannes" took place in January of 1868. Symonds had been in London until late August, and had continued to write Sidgwick passionate letters. In one from the fourteenth, he allows that he has been "reading Noel's poems all this morning" and found "in them a singular earnestness and purity of feeling. There are passages of real pathos, and a few of liquid beauty," even if the form is much too "rough hewn," an ore in need of much "smelting." As always, he worries about his own capacities as well as Noel's. "But no sooner is this written than I remember the things I have to say, the poem of life which I should not like to die without expressing somehow, the excellences in another line which I can claim."[176] On the twenty-second, he writes, apparently in answer to a letter from Sidgwick discussing the trials of being in advance of his age, that to "be a Moses upon Pisgah is not a 'feeble failure,' " but is rather "the best thing which one who believes in progress can at this moment hope for." This was a decidedly Sidgwickian sentiment, as was the following Goethean aspiration: "At all events, I feel, let us not acquiesce in anything but Wholes; let us feebly grasp, or powerfully bear, displaying strength in our weakness; until the Whole is made clear to us." The next line was the slightly glum Sidgwickian: if "it is never in this life revealed, *n'importe*. There are plenty of men to come, and nature is prodigal of her dear ones."[177] For his part, Sidgwick was also busily pondering the utility of truth, having written to Mill on the subject in late July, just after his stay with Symonds.

After a quick trip to Clifton, the Symonds family is off on the planned European trip, eventually to take them to the Riviera. But all the while Symonds is boiling and brooding. On September 20, he writes to Sidgwick that "[y]our squirrel moods gratify me immensely, for then, like Jacque [in *As You Like It*] you are full of matter. My obliteration is proceeding quickly. There are four οἰκεῖα κακα from which I habitually suffer in the flesh – overworn nerves, weak eyes, delicate lungs, and a peculiar derangement of the digestive organs, which affects more subtle parts of the economy."[178] Unfortunately, all of these "are in a bunch upon me now, so that rest and beauty have but little meaning, and like the happy man in Aristotle, my chance of noble action consists in maintaining serenity amid a crowd of evils." Still, he a confesses that he feels his "own to be one definite human situation, and am satisfied." But in a prophetic afterthought, he admits, "I have seen so little into the nature of anything here – I am so utterly blind to everything hereafter – love and life have so many flowers for me that

I have not yet mortified myself into recognising a possible early death as part of this human situation, which I would not exchange. I hate diffusing the scent of the charnel." It is amazing, he adds, "what calm there is in suffering."[179]

But he is terribly vexed. Conington has criticized his "shady fluency" and touched a nerve. He needs "guidance," feeling that he "might work, if well counselled, to better purpose," and asks Sidgwick for criticism. Catherine is depressed and sick, and, having reached Cannes, he writes to Dakyns that he wishes he "could go to sleep at night without chloral" and that "I could say what is in me like a cloud, & I wish I had got something to say." By Christmas, things are apparently a little better. He writes to Charlotte:

It is sad. I think over & over again of my literary impuissance, & have a fellow feeling for Sir Egerton Brydges who, when he was past 60, still eagerly thirsted for the assurance of poetical genius, trying to prove to himself he had it by writing 200 lines a night, yet confessing that the assurance never came. Sidgwick is magnanimous on similar occasions of self bewailment: he satisfies himself with remembering that Nature works on a large scale. For one being that she succeeds with, she produces many apparent failures; yet these very failures are of value – they go, as it were, to make up the perfect being, or at least to prove his sovereignty & completeness. 20 men e.g. with only the embryos of eyes or nose or arms & the desire to having these useful members complete, should be glad to testify by their abortiveness to the law that has been thwarted in them. Positivism is a serene philosophy if it so annihilates self. – I am getting better in health & spirits though I have not quite lost the pain in my chest.[180]

But events then take a nasty turn. Out walking with his new friend Edward Lear, the celebrated writer of nonsense verse, he sprains his ankle and has to walk nearly two miles in pain in order to return home. Thus, just before Sidgwick is set to arrive for a visit, Symonds is completely bedridden. The visit is a disaster, as he explains to Mrs. Clough in a letter of January 22:

Three weeks ago I sprained my ankle very badly & I have been on the sofa ever since – partly owing, I think, to the awkwardness of the doctor who attended to it. . . . Unfortunately the confinement, together with other reasons, brought on a violent attack of brain weakness, wh is still oppressing me. I cannot read or write or think or speak, but I lie for hours together in mere nervous prostration & misery. I do not know how it is to end. Work will be impossible for many weeks if not months. Unluckily, Henry Sidgwick arrived just at the beginning of my troubles. He had come out on purpose to see & cheer me; & when he came I cd do nothing. I had not time to stop him by telegram before he left England; & I had not heart to send him back as soon as he came, wh I ought to have done. So his visit of nearly 3 weeks proved a great source of disappointment to both of us & tended to prolong & aggravate my weakness.[181]

This was putting it mildly. The *Memoirs* provide a rather vivider description of his state:

All the evil humours which were fermenting in my petty state of man – poignant and depressing memories of past troubles, physical maladies of nerve substance and of lung tissue, decompositions of habitual creeds, sentimental vapours, the disappointment of the sexual sense in matrimony, doubts about the existence of a moral basis to human life, thwarted intellectual activity, ambitions rudely checked by impotence – all the miserable factors of a wretched inner life, masked by appearances, the worse for me for being treated by the outside world as mere accidents of illness in a well-to-do and idle citizen, boiled up in a kind of devil's cauldron during those last weeks at Cannes, and made existence hell. The crisis I passed through then was decisive for my future career. But I did not foresee the point to which it was about to lead me. I only knew for certain that I must change my course, and that I would never repeat, come what might, that infernal experience of the Riviera.[182]

Among his papers from that time, he found an "incoherent document" testifying to just how bad things had been. He contemplated suicide, but "death is not acceptable; it offers no solution. I loathe myself, and turn in every direction to find strength. What I want is life; the source of life fails me."

In my present state of entire negation I cannot get the faith without the strength, or the strength without the faith. . . . The last night I spent in Cannes was the worst of my whole life. I lay awake motionless, my soul stagnant, feeling what is meant by spiritual blackness and darkness. If it should last for ever! As I lay, a tightening approached my heart. It came nearer, the grasp grew firmer, I was cold and lifeless in the clutch of a great agony. If this were death? Catherine who kept hold of me, seemed far away. I was alone, so utterly desolate that I drank the very cup of the terror of the grave. The Valley of the Shadow was opened, and the shadow lies still upon my soul.[183]

As Symonds explained, he was undergoing what in "another nature" might have been a "conversion experience." But with him it "was different.

I emerged at last into Stoical acceptance of my place in the world, combined with Epicurean indulgence of my ruling passion for the male. Together, these two motives restored me to comparative health, gave me religion, and enabled me, in spite of broken nerves and diseased lungs, to do what I have done in literature." It was, in this sense, a conversion experience of a certain sort. He found "indifference very shortly in the study of Marcus Aurelius, the *Imitatio Christi*, and Walt Whitman. Later on, I found the affirmation of religion and contentment in love – not the human kindly friendly *love* which I had given liberally to my beloved wife and children, my father and my sister and my companions, but in the passionate *sexual love* of comrades." Now he was beyond the sense that his view of love was a sin; "when, in the stage of indifference, I became careless about sinning, then, and not until then, I discovered love, the keystone of all the rest of my less tortured life."[184]

As noted, it is from this period that his renewed enthusiasm for homo-erotic versifying dates. Clearly, this form of cathartic expression was part of his cure. And there was still more such literary expression. Despite his claims about literary impotence, it is evident that during the autumn and early winter of 1867 he completed a draft of one of his most enduring works, "A Problem in Greek Ethics." As the *Memoirs* explain:

I have been busy, and have greatly tired myself by writing an essay on Platonic love. To do so has been often in my mind, and some time ago I collected the materials for it, but had to lay the work aside. My object is to explain the feelings of the Greeks about passion, to show how paiderastia was connected with their sense of beauty, and how it affected their institutions. It is not by any means finished. I am once again compelled to lay my pen down breathless. The subject appeals too deeply to my sympathies, while its more repulsive aspects are painful. I stumbled on till I came to grief in my brain.[185]

Part of the work went into *Studies of the Greek Poets*, though the original was rewritten "at Clifton in 1874, and privately printed under the title of 'A Problem in Greek Ethics.'" This would be revised again for inclusion in *Sexual Inversion*, and would in general serve as a crucial source of many other of his works. It was, as much as the *Memoirs*, Symonds's signature work, the fruition of his exposure to Whitman's *Leaves of Grass*:

I was sitting with F. M. Myers in his rooms at Trinity, Cambridge, when he stood up, seized a book and shouted out in his nasal intonation with those brazen lungs of his, 'Long I thought that knowledge alone would content me.' This fine poem, omitted from later editions of *Leaves of Grass*, formed part of 'Calamus'. The book became for me a sort of Bible. Inspired by 'Calamus' I adopted another method of palliative treatment, and tried to invigorate the emotion I could not shake off by absorbing Whitman's conception of comradeship. The process of assimilation was not without its bracing benefit. My desires grew manlier, more defined, more direct, more daring by contact with Calamus. I imbibed a strong democratic enthusiasm, a sense of the dignity and beauty and glory of simple healthy men. This has been of great service to me during the eleven years I have passed at Davos. I can now declare with sincerity that my abnormal inclinations, modified by Whitman's idealism and penetrated with his democratic enthusiasm, have brought me into close and profitable sympathy with human beings even while I sinned against law and conventional morality.

The immediate result of this study of Walt Whitman was the determination to write the history of paiderastia in Greece and to attempt a theoretical demonstration of the chivalrous enthusiasm which seemed to me implicit in comradeship. Both these literary tasks I accomplished.[186]

Thus, it would appear that work on this remarkable piece – the world would not see its like until Sir Kenneth Dover's *Greek Homosexuality* appeared in 1978 – was part of what precipitated Symonds's crisis.[187] It was, as much as his poetry, a frank endorsement of the healthiness of Greek love – popular more than Platonic – albeit one cast in a remarkably erudite and anthropologically astute manner. Interestingly, in the very same letter to Mrs. Clough in which Symonds complained of how difficult the visit with Sidgwick had been, he also explained:

Since this illness began I have read & of course have written nothing. Yet I have so much both to read & write. One little piece of satisfaction I got from Sidgwick who read an essay of mine written this winter on 'Platonic Love' among the Greeks, & who told me it ought to create a change in the opinion of scholars respecting some social questions of Gk history. I cannot publish it, & I do not wish any one to know that I have written it except my most intimate friends. But it is gratifying, when so helpless & lamed in the race, to find that I can still contribute my share to the thoughts of stronger men & more assiduous students. Sidgwick works 10 hours a day. I at my best work 2 or 3. With respect to Zeller I am in great difficulty. Sidgwick read some of the translation & pointed out a few linguistic errors wh make me feel my grasp of German to be too feeble & uncertain. I cannot give the whole thing up. . . . I do not know what I wd not give for a little more horse power of work. As soon as I feel the collar, crack I go & all study is impossible. Problems wh I want to work out in verse fare just in the same way.[188]

He goes on to say that there is one "book I have tried to see through the haze of my vapours," and it is none other than *Essays on a Liberal Education*, which holds much "to interest anyone who cares for education, for the intellectual prospects of the English upper classes, & for the kind of thought prevalent in our great schools – especially if such an one has a boy to be taught." Sidgwick's contribution is singled out as one of the best.

What is singularly instructive about all this is how it indicates both the respect that Symonds had for Sidgwick as a scholar and educator, and the way in which he counted him as one of his "most intimate friends," one who could be trusted with "A Problem in Greek Ethics." And Sidgwick in turn was obviously impressed.

It is also noteworthy that Catherine, as her daughter Margaret would later recall,

had the greatest affection and trust for Mr Henry Sidgwick. There is a note in one of her letters about all he was prepared to do for her husband at that period: 'Henry Sidgwick is wonderfully nice and gentle and good, but he is so strong bodily and intellectually, that it is almost impossible for him to bring himself down to the level of an invalid, and I think the contrast makes J. feel his own weakness more painfully. Think of Henry's gravely proposing, after finding a few small faults in the translation of J.'s German, to go through the whole, line by line, with the original, in the Easter Vacation, and correct it. Few friends would undertake such a work, I think.'[189]

This admiration and trust on Catherine's part would prove enduring.

What also seems so striking, however, is the way in which Symonds's thoughts of death and suicide hit Sidgwick hard. As he wrote to Dakyns, shortly after his return to Cambridge:

I left the Garden on Monday week. When I say the garden, I speak chiefly objectively and only partly subjectively. I thought as I was on my way that it would be odd if something did not happen – something to make this mixed like the rest of life. When I got to Cannes I found it had happened. Johnnie had sprained his ankle a day or two before. The confinement to the house brought on a return of a cerebral complaint from which he suffers. It became doubtful whether I ought to stay, and indeed, on looking back, I am afraid I feel sure I ought not: but I sophisticated myself into staying, and made a permanent effort (with what doubtful and varying success you know me well enough to imagine) to avoid fatiguing topics. It was sad and painful, though I myself was so happy as to feel unsympathetic.

But some life has the Divine in it as a felt element, and everything else seems to vanish in comparison – just as it does from the point of view of mysticism. Why cannot we all have it always?

For should I prize thee, could'st thou last,
At half thy real worth

I wonder. It is only my belief in Providence, my optimism, that makes me even disposed to entertain a doubt.

But this is about myself. I am – now that I am gone – unhappy and anxious about them. Catherine looks worn and jaded rather: has a cold that she is unable to throw off, which is a sign of lowered vitality. She refuses to believe that there is any reason to take care of herself – a state of mind which is good on one side and bad on the other. Johnnie is often very depressed. I felt terribly that I had

. . . Neither faith nor light,
Nor certitude, nor any help in pain, . . .

as Matthew Arnold says. My religion, which I believe is sincere, seemed such a weak and feeble thing when I endeavoured to communicate it in need. What can I do? I cannot, as Clough says, 'be profane with yes and no' – subjectively it would be profanity. Oh, how I sympathise with Kant! with his passionate yearning for synthesis and condemned by his reason to criticism.

Forgive me, dearest, I am going to say something which may annoy you and which offends my own taste – but I wish you would write to Johnnie. He keeps thinking that there must be a barrier of his raising. I endeavoured to make him understand my understanding of you: but when one is ill subtle calculations have to be simplified both to the brain and to the heart.

I had written so far when a letter came from Johnnie. I copy out part. It is partly discrepant with what I have just written – but that is all the more reason (The 'letter' is your last to me). Do not tell him I showed it you. You feel that I would not have written these words but for my strong feeling that he needs shewn sympathy just now. I would send you the whole letter but it is too painful. (CWC)[190]

And Sidgwick was probably not feeling as robust as he seemed. He had in fact arrived in Cannes straight from the funeral, in December, of his dear friend Cowell, whose death had been a source of intense pain to him. Evidently, he was looking forward to this visit with Symonds as an opportunity for intimate soul-knitting thoughts at a time when he, too, was in need. Cowell, it should be recalled, was the intimate with whom Sidgwick had engaged in experiments in automatic writing.

Thus, having watched one intimate friend die a wretched, tubercular death, Sidgwick was now struggling with a "great invalid" who could mount a penetrating challenge to many of his cherished notions. In fact, as the months wear on, Symonds starts gaining in horsepower, agreeing with Sidgwick that "when people talk of 'Hell' they often mean a state of their nerves" and allowing how he has learned "that for Life a square is needed: Health, Home, Occupation, Faith or Philosophy," though it is health that is the "matter" of happiness.[191] And he is meditating away, on Clough, Goethe, Whitman and the rest, despite Sidgwick's apparent suggestion that what he needs "is healthily animalizing." As in the golden moments of their earlier conversations, he is pondering Goethe's maxim "Resolve to live in the Whole, the Good, the Beautiful." But Sidgwick appears to be growing gloomier over the spring, even eliciting Symonds's sympathy, mixed with remonstrance:

You do not write in the best spirits, and you say you have never felt scepticism really till now. I do not believe that any man who is healthy and active can know the pinch of scepticism – what there is wretched and weak and morbid in it. Life is so good a thing to the strong, that no despair about the essence underlying its pleasing shows can make them valueless. It is only when the phantasmagoria of the world becomes sickly or menacing that the intolerable burden of not knowing whence, where, whither, how, etc., makes itself oppressive. . . . As for the garbage of the world, and the really good things in it, I cannot weigh them against each other. In the infinity of the universe they seem to merge and become as one. At all events for me, who am a grain of clay upon this tiniest of little worlds, and who live for less than a moment in the short minute of its terraqueous aeons, when I think of the chaos of greater universes and the irrevocable circles of eternity, and when I remember it was but yesterday that the like of me imagined sun, moon, and stars made to give them light – I fold the wings of aspiration and of discontent, and wait in patience till the chemistry of the years resolves me into my elements. I do not wish for death, since life has many beautiful things in it. But I am incapable of living for any purpose, or of raising my soul to the altitude of a delusion. Let us eat and drink, for tomorrow we die. Let us weep and pray, for tomorrow we die. Let us laugh and sing, let us paint pictures and write poems, let us love and kill, let us improve our species and disseminate disease, let us parade the destinies of man and draw our lineage from the ape, for tomorrow we die. 'One is prone,' you say, 'in scepticism to make semi-practical the idea that nothing matters.' Yes; and then you proceed: 'it is so easy to show the absurdity of this semi-practicality.' If it is so easy, show it me; tell me what is practical, if anything is practical, or if any sect except the *peisithanatoi* were final and irrefutable.[192]

Evidently, Symonds is feeling strong enough to set Sidgwick all the old challenges to his faith and then some. And Sidgwick feels the pinch in the worst way. As Symonds carries on, in a letter from June 21:

Perhaps by this time you are out of scepticism and in McCosh. So I will not discuss that part of your letter – except to say that I think you hit the most intolerable part of the world's riddle in the eternity *a parte ante*. But it oppresses me just as much if I try to imagine no God as if I try to state the absurdity of a God emerging from somnolence into world-creative activity. I wish I could, like you, embrace Positivism as ἐμοὶ βέλτον, it is just what I could not do. I feel that the instant I endeavour to take the ἐμοὶ and not the ἁπλῶς point of view I resent the attempt to impose upon myself. No healthy reaction takes place, but I am thrown back upon a moral helplessness inclining to materialism, and to the feeble hope (yearly more vain) of perhaps living so as to enjoy myself without doing any positive harm.

Then again, as to wickedness; your inclined plane is a just statement; but what is to arrest one on this plane, and (from another point of view) why should I seek to be arrested? . . . I am here in the same see-saw as about Scepticism, and end in the same temporizing, modified by an agonizing sense of there being somewhere a clear truth – a something ἁπλῶς and not ἐμοὶ or even πόλει, but plain and unmistakable when once perceived.[193]

Clearly, as all these intimations of Moore intimate, Symonds is not being "knocked flat" by any of Sidgwick's arguments or evidence. Still, Symonds wants to see Sidgwick as soon as he returns to England, "if only to remove the nightmare recollection of those Cannes days when I could not talk to you." There is much exchange about poetry, with both Sidgwick and Dakyns, that finds Symonds urging, for example, that much as he would have liked to have written Clough's "Dipsychus," "even this poem is now behind the age. Its handling of religious and sexual matters is quite timid." Revealingly, he is at work studying the life of Byron, being persuaded that the "time is come for a return to Byronism in literature," the better to "free ourselves of the nightmare of Tennyson." The latter plays "into the hands of conceited Academical pedantic priggish verbal supersubtilizing critics of the Cambridge-Coningtonian sort."[194] But he is genuinely torn about his dipsychical self and about the creative, sublimative potential of it, writing to Dakyns:

I am afraid of forming a permanent double consciousness in my own mind, of being related to this world of phantoms, & moving meanwhile in the world of fact. But the phantoms are so beautiful to me & so real. Last night we had a dinner party, & over our wine I was listening to a certain Dr Marshall droning in a saccharine medical medicinal voice about local politics, when suddenly Myronides appeared before me, as he fell on Theron's neck & the dawn overspread the hills of Attica.

It was too good. I enjoyed my double consciousness; for I talked to Dr Marshall about Lewis Fry & John Miles, & all the while I heard Athenian night breezes shuddering in the myrtle groves of Harmodius.[195]

He continues by explaining "what are the chief things written for this 'Doric Muse' & what, if it were not for the trouble & the ostracism, I wd write into the big fair book you gave me yesterday for a monument of Love Heroic." This concerns a sketch of how he would assemble his homoerotic verse, including his tribute to "John Morden" and "Lelio, the Florentine Platonist, a subject suggested by Henry." But as he explains, all these and the essay on "A Problem in Greek Ethics" "will be consigned to Coutts erelong; & you & Henry & Catherine are to have them to do what you think fit with if you survive me – that is, unless I make some other disposition regarding them."

This last refers to the way Symonds was going to lock up his homoerotic verse in storage with his banker, Coutts. In fact, what transpired made for a famous story about Sidgwick's attitude toward Symonds's poetry. As Grosskurth describes it:

Late in December [of 1868] Symonds wrote a poem entitled 'Eudiades' on the theme of a Greek boy and his older lover. When Henry Sidgwick arrived for a fortnight's visit in the middle of January, Symonds showed him 'Eudiades' and a number of other poems of the same nature. Sidgwick read them with horror and warned him of the dangers he invited by pursuing his erotic interests. He persuaded him to lock up all his poetry in a black tin box (except the MS. of 'Eudiades' which Symonds had given to Dakyns and which Dakyns loyally refused to surrender) and on 23 January, Sidgwick stood on the bank of the Avon and dramatically flung the key into the water.

On the 27th, Norman came to dine alone with Symonds for the first time. Despite Sidgwick's warnings, Symonds deliberately set about winning Norman's affection and from the outset he did not deceive himself about the possible consequences of such a course. All his previous warnings to Arthur Sidgwick, all his exhortations to Graham Dakyns and his fear of his father's reaction were completely disregarded as he eagerly succumbed to the excitement of this new attraction.[196]

As should by now be obvious, any such description hardly captures the tenor of Symonds's relationships with Sidgwick and Dakyns, both of whom shared his poetic enthusiasms at some level. Grosskurth was so keen on making Sidgwick out to be an echo of Symonds's father that she

even mistakenly claimed that he was the one who alarmed Symonds about
the danger of "John Morden," his paean to a London newsboy.[197] It was
of course not Henry but Arthur Sidgwick who moved Symonds to write
to Dakyns, in November of 1866: "A letter from Arthur has stung me to
this recoil upon myself. It is all really well with him, but wild fire is abroad
in the world & who am I that I should offend against God's elect?"[198]

Symonds's description of Henry's reaction strikes a different chord:

Early in January 1869 Jowett paid us a visit; and on 15 January my daughter
Margaret was born. Next day Henry Sidgwick came to stay, and we thoroughly
investigated the subject of my poems on Erôs. His conclusion was that I ought to
abandon them, as unhealthy and disturbing to my moral equilibrium. I assented.
We locked them all up in a black tin box, with the exception of 'Eudiades'. . . .
Having done this, Henry threw the key into the river Avon on the 23rd.

There was something absurd in all this, because I felt myself half-consciously
upon the point of translating my dreams and fancies about love into fact. And on
27 January occurs the entry, 'Norman dined with me alone: χάλλιστος, ἄδρητος,
εἰρωνιχός. I was launched upon a new career, with the overpowering sweetness
of the vision of Eudiades pervading my soul.[199]

And in fact, once again it is Arthur rather than Henry who sounds "horrified" about Symonds's verse. When Dakyns showed it to him, he pronounced it "degrading to whoever wrote and whoever reads," and his "high
and mighty ways" nettled Symonds to no end, making him write in turn:

What matters it if ephemerals like 'Eudiades' perish? This brain holds a dozen
Eudiadeses. And you were quite at liberty, so far as I am concerned, to burn it.

But about 'Eudiades' I have still something to say. This poem was written with
an attempt to realize a historical situation. You asked me what I meant by the
temptation of the lovers. I chose to depict one of those young men of Plato's
Phaedrus, who recoil from acts which were permissible in Hellas. But I admit
there is an element of pathos in the poem, which makes it what you called 'orectic'
and therefore inartistic.[200]

Symonds was of course lecturing at Clifton during this period, which
inspired Arthur to lecture him on how he should enter into his teaching in
a "philanthropic" spirit, rather than as a hunt for "emotional excitement."
Still, there "was no rift in the lute" of their friendship.[201]

When Symonds visited him later in April, Henry's reaction, was slightly
different:

I showed my diary to Henry, who said, 'It fills me with terror and pain. I admire your spiritual gifts so much, the versatility of your intellectual interests,

your power of poetizing life. But this thread of etherealized sensuality.' In spite of the uneasiness which I too felt, and which these remarks accentuated, I was pledged to meet Norman in London. My foot was in, and could not be drawn out.[202]

But this too is easily misinterpreted. Of Sidgwick's January visit, so different from the one the year before, Symonds wrote to Mrs. Clough: "Sidgwick has been here nearly a fortnight – is just gone. I have enjoyed his visit much, but I am overdone."[203] Of their encounter in April, Symonds wrote to Dakyns: "Henry read my μῶρον βίβλον & lectured me as severely as *he* can. It did clearly not agree with him or please him. I confess that what he said pricked my conscience & I was made very sick & sorrowful." Consequently, when he gets together with Norman, he has "been able to readjust my view of the life wh I had designed for us two. Henry has modified it permanently & in the right direction. But Norman's presence has restored its transcendentalism. And Catherine understands."[204] Sidgwick was, after all, addressing Symonds in his own idiom, and with an effort to sympathize.

Thus, during this interval from December 1868 through spring of 1869, Symonds is busily composing the lectures that would go into *Studies of the Greek Poets*, and he is pursuing Norman with some ardor, clear in his mind that "the fruition of my moderate desires brought peace and sanity and gladness." Sidgwick, who had deeply sympathized with him ever since the summer of 1867, and who had been counted as an intimate friend to share his sexual writings with, has been gently challenged in his cautiousness and not so gently challenged in his philosophizing, and decides that, as with religion, silence may be his best course, explaining to Dakyns: "I have stayed with Symonds. What shall I say of Symonds? I will keep silence even from good words. Some day I will tell you, if you care." (CWC) Symonds also writes to Dakyns to say that he and Sidgwick "are to have now 'a long silence' about his concerns."[205]

Only two weeks would pass before Symonds would write to Dakyns to discuss Sidgwick's letter to him (Dakyns) about the resignation of his fellowship:

Here is Henry's letter wh I hardly like to return, it is so good. Your own is a proper pendant to it. But he has the clear advantage of a crisis. I have always said that the real tragedy of a life is when its crisis is no crisis – a prolonged struggle & protracted anéantissement. Coleridge says somewhere it is a duty to hope. Then let us do our duty. But I know not if the voice of that stern mother is ever more maddening than when she bids us be of a hopeful spirit & of a cheerful heart in the midst of the Valley of the Shadow – the Valley is so long, about as long as the Rhone Valley.[206]

No doubt Symonds had helped Sidgwick avoid the tragedy of a life with a crisis that is no crisis. But so had Dakyns, who in May had written Sidgwick a strange letter complaining about the silence of his friends:

Their names are (besides J.A.S.) H.S: A.S: J.R.M: and many others H.W.E: W.C.S: and many more. But they have come now to regard him as dead, who long played the part of corpse. The only resource left is to read over old letters, & think what each of them wd. be likely to say if the channel of communication cd. suddenly again burst open. Yours are full of very plain prophecy – & strong tender expostulation & it is marvellous that the adder in me was so deaf. Verily I say unto you I have my reward. But will you not do violence to natural psychological laws – & forgetting the hideous hiatus – speak? I believe I shall understand. There are moreover on a lower level far a thousand things I want to hear you say which may be said – without galvanising forfeited friendship: *amicus olim amico loquitur*.

v. My opinion is that the 13th public are about ripe for his poems – at any rate an excerpt. It amuses me to see the gigantic gudgeon swallowing certain passages in "sketches" most complacently – On the other hand I ask myself more now, whether it would not have been better long ago like Shelley or even like Swinburne to have put the poems forth at once in toto regardless of consequences. But I can't explain my point of view except *viva voce*. I dare say *festina lente* was Shakespeare's motto. The sonnets weren't allowed to damage him. But what nonsense was there any need for caution or thought of it in those days? (CWC)

However demented, this letter nonetheless makes the case for Symonds's coming out in print, the consistent Dakynsean line. After all, in January, before the celebrated tossing of the key into the Avon, Dakyns had written to Sidgwick in a pitch of enthusiasm: "I have not solved the mystery of the universe. I have the finest poem of all in my portmanteau. It is called Eudiades." This was the very same letter that had gone on about having tasted "uranian food." Again, Sidgwick had been counted as an insider, one who knew everything there was to know about the veiled homoerotic meanings of Symonds's work, not to mention the work of Swinburne, Shelley, and Shakespeare. The problem was the public, that "gigantic gudgeon."[207]

Soon the friendships are all back on course. Symonds produces his collection of Clough's works, which inspires Sidgwick to write his essay on Clough, which in turn inspires Symonds to write that Sidgwick's essay "is really the best thing I have ever seen of yours and a celestial luminary among Reviews.... You have, I think, said the *dernier mot* about Clough on a great many points."[208]

Feeling the pinch of skepticism, of hypocrisy, and something more, Sidgwick had finally managed a real crisis. And he was becoming rather famous for his studied silences.

What, precisely, was the faith that had seemed so inadequate in the face of Symonds's crisis and Sidgwick's casuistry? A letter to Noel from January of 1870, a letter that beautifully captures the quality of the metaphysical thinking refracted in the *Methods* (and this with reference to a discussion society), is illuminating on a number of counts:

Are you going to the Metaphysical on the 12th? If so will you take me in at Kew that night, and then we can discuss Palingenesis & the Immortality of the Soul. I should have written but have been busy in various ways finishing up odds & ends of work here. I send back your papers. As to Green I do not know whether I advise sending it to him. He is in the state of mind in which he does not care about other people's opinions, & rather shuns them – a state of mind not unnatural in an original, rather lethargic intellect, conscious of thoughts unworked out. At least he does not care a bit about *my* opinions: he might care more about yours. Only my vanity you see, will not allow me exactly to *promise* you that he will.

If you like I will ask him. I think he would quite allow that he had made Aristotle Hegelianize and would maintain that A. can only so be made profitable.

Your arguments on the [Imm.?] seem to me very able and closely put. In fact I have rather delayed to answer from a wish to answer them more satisfactorily: I can only make one or two remarks (1) as to the Unity of consciousness I see you revive what is ordinarily regarded as Locke's paradox on Personal Identity. I admit that personal identity as a doctrine of *consciousness*, ascertained by Empirical Psychology, is only coextensive with memory, or if not with actual memory at any rate with possible memory. But one may fairly ask, how can you limit possible memory? How can you be sure that *all* our past consciousnesses are not potentially reversible, as we know some to have been actually recovered when they were to all appearances irretrievably lost.

At any rate as a *Belief of Common Sense*, personal identity is held to extend through the whole of a stream of consciousness where there has been no break of continuity, (as in the life of a normal man).

However this [is] all beside the mark to my mind: as I have never based my belief in immortality on our consciousness of the oneness of Self. I have always considered Kant's 'Paralogisms' conclusive as against that.

What I really base it on (apart from the evidence supplied by Spiritualism, and apart from religious grounds) is on *Ethics*, as Kant, supported by Common Sense. But I do not state the argument quite as you answer it: but thus.

In face of the conflict between Virtue & Happiness, my own voluntary life, and that of every other man constituted like me, i.e. I believe, of every normal man is reduced to hopeless anarchy.

Two authorities roughly speaking Butler's 'self-love' and 'Conscience' claim to rule, and neither will yield to the other.

The only way of avoiding this intolerable anarchy is by the Postulate of Immortality. But you may say – 'you cannot believe it because you want to'.

I reply; I find

1) in me an inherited predisposition to this faith.

2) In human history the belief is that of the best part of mankind: it has nearly, though not quite, the authority of a belief of Common Sense.[209]

Not only is the dualism of practical reason presented here in unvarnished form, but also the various possible resolutions of it – theistic (or spiritualistic), epistemological, and ethical. But perhaps most noteworthy is Sidgwick's simple confession that he has "an inherited predisposition to this faith," in the Postulate of Immortality, a faith that he thinks so widespread as to nearly have the authority of common sense. This is nearly to say that his belief in the harmony of the Universe was on a par with Symonds's sexual inversion – he was simply born that way. Hence, their inner voyaging after the "true self" was a remarkable case of elective affinities, twinning the religious and the sexual. And doubtless this deep conviction of his own immortality goes far to explain how he could have been so persuaded of the rationality and logical priority of egoism, just as much as it was a reflection of the grip egoism had on him. For on Sidgwick's rendering, is not the appeal to one's immortal soul typically egoistic? Whether in Plato or in Christianity, is it not the final strategy for marrying self-interest and justice? What point would there be in depicting an eternity of self-sacrifice? Would one wish that on one's loved ones?

But what was at the bottom of this? Thought? Feeling? Knowledge? Hope? Evolutionarily useful dispositions? Small wonder that Symonds found this philosophy unsatisfactory. So did Sidgwick, and the decades to come would only play out their struggles with their "abnormality."

VI. Sunspots

Your letter gave me the keenest pleasure I have felt for a long time. I had not exactly expected to hear from you. Yet I felt that if you liked my poem you would write. So I was beginning to dread that I had struck some quite wrong chord – that perhaps I had seemed to you to have arrogantly confounded your own fine thought & pure feeling with the baser metal of my own nature. What you say has reassured me and has solaced me nearly as much as if I had seen the face and touched the hand of you – my Master! For many years I have been attempting to express in verse some of the forms of what in a note to Democratic Vistas (as also in a blade of Calamus) you call "adhesiveness." I have traced passionate friendship through Greece, Rome, the medieval & the modern world, & I have now a large body of poems written but not published. In these I trust the spirit of the Past is faithfully set forth as far as my abilities allow.

It was while engaged upon this work (years ago now) that I first read Leaves of Grass. The man who spoke to me from that Book impressed me in every way most profoundly and unalterably; but especially did I then learn confidently to believe that the Comradeship, which I conceived as on a par with the Sexual feeling for depth & strength & purity & capability of all good, was real – not a delusion of distorted passions, a dream of the Past, a scholar's fancy – but a strong & vital bond of man to man.

John Addington Symonds to Walt Whitman, February 7, 1872[210]

Here, then, was the creation of Sidgwick's favored candidate for the Oxford Professorship of Poetry. Symonds sought a Platonic revival that was, of all things, somehow eroticized and blended into the emergence of a new democratic culture. Such later published essays as "Democratic Art, with Special Reference to Walt Whitman" and "The Dantesque and Platonic Ideals of Love" would play and replay the themes of *Studies of the Greek Poets,* pointing to how the new democratic culture should try to achieve some higher synthesis of the Greek and Christian – or better, Dantesque – ideals of love:

What subsists of really vital and precious in both ideals is the emotional root from which they severally sprang: in Greece the love of comrades, binding friends together, spurring them on to heroic action, and to intellectual pursuits in common; in mediaeval Europe the devotion to the female sex, through manly courtesy, which raised the crudest of male appetites to a higher value.

Even if it may be "a delusion to imagine that the human spirit is led to discover divine truths by amorous enthusiasm for a fellow creature," nevertheless, "there are delusions, wandering fires of the imaginative reason, which, for a brief period of time, under special conditions, and in peculiarly constituted natures, have become fruitful of real and excellent results."[211]

But in the first half of the 1870s, Symonds would continue to forge his distinctive style of homoerotic verse, his "peccant pamphlets," of which "Eudiades" had marked a new beginning.[212] Although his reputation as a poet has always been weak, he did write some decidedly memorable verse, including "A Vista," a poem that was later set to music by John Ireland as the famous "These Things Shall Be," an anthem of the socialist movement.[213] Whitman himself had pronounced "Love and Death" a success: "a beautiful poem – just barely lacks real greatness – is in places virile: a bit too decorative, here and there, maybe – on the whole triumphantly worth while." In the same pronouncement, to his friend Horace Traubel, Whitman went on: "Symonds has got into our crowd in spite of his culture: I tell you we don't give away places in our crowd easy – a man has to sweat to get in."[214]

"Love and Death" was in fact written for Whitman, was "suggested by his teaching of Comradeship as the binding emotion of the nations; & in particular by some poems out of Calamus." Thus, the Master had received and praised the tribute, and an exultant Symonds writes to Sidgwick: "Did I tell you I had had a very kind letter from Walt Whitman to whom I sent a copy of my poem 'Love and Death' – that only. He says he thinks it 'of the loftiest, strongest and tenderest,' and wants to know more of me. Consequently I have begun a correspondence."[215] Although Whitman would ultimately deny – hypocritically deny – his Uranian orientation when Symonds pressed him too explicitly, for most of the years to come their correspondence was remarkably warm and mutually supportive.[216]

The genesis of "Love and Death" was explained in the letter to Sidgwick from September 24, 1871:

It was very jolly being with Graham in Switzerland. He became better and stronger in soul and body than I have ever known him. I, too, shook off there for the time my physical disabilities – could walk, endure cold and heat, sleep, eat, etc., like an ordinary healthy man. I also wrote – Poems in Terza Rima, notably one called 'Love and Death,' another called 'With Caligula in Rome,' a third 'The Eiger and the Monk,' together with less aspiring works. I used to write them in my head when walking over the glaciers or along the slopes and valleys of Mürren and the

Scheinige Platte (a very fine place for poet or painter or for nature worshipper). I will send you these in print.[217]

It is in this letter that Symonds talks about believing in his own poetic vocation, how he stands "utterly aloof from all discussions of who is first and who is last and who is above whom. To believe in one's Poesy or Prophecy, to believe in oneself is the great point. Then to sing and preach. The rest the world must do and the man must leave unnoticed." Still, he does want Sidgwick's criticism; Sidgwick, he holds, is "the almost absolute *lumen siccum*" and he is "most grateful" to him for everything he says: "When you praise, I feel it is such praise as the strong will give; when you blame, I know I am inadequate." As for Sidgwick's book:

I hope to be one of the readers of your book – for this reason; my meditations of late, carried on mostly between sea and skies after reading bits of Helmholtz' lectures, which I have with me, make me believe that on the method of Ethics will depend the future of the human race. One such discovery as Newton's law of gravitation in the field of morals would advance us aeons forward in all that concerns spiritual life. We beat about the bush so long because we have not found the scientific starting-point of ethics. This is what I meant when I said in my Greek book that science was to be our Deliverer.[218]

Both Symonds and Sidgwick were at this point especially taken up with critically assessing Noel's poetry, with all its nature worship – a task that Noel did not always appreciate[219] – and for all of Sidgwick's sophistication about the irreducibility of the normative, he too was out to discover psychological laws bearing on moral development.

In November of 1870, Symonds had written to assure him, "You will find my black box and all my poems gone, evanished quite, not merely keyless but buried. I want to be the historian of Italian Literature and so I trundled away my stumbling-blocks." And he had prematurely exclaimed that the "incurable itch" to poeticize was nearly dead in him.[220] Far from it. Symonds was about to enter some of the most literarily productive years of his life, of course, and in the next cycle of production, he would be working ever more closely with Sidgwick to ensure the viability of his scholarly reputation. Dr. Symonds had died early in 1871, on February 25. Symonds writes to Sidgwick that he "had hardly expected to feel the blow of his loss so crushing," but it has come and "it cannot be surpassed in heaviness." Shortly before his death, Dr. Symonds had explained to his son that all his thoughts upon "the great questions" had been "resolved into the one thought of God as good, and of trust in Him."[221] Interestingly, Symonds undertakes the assemblage of *Miscellanies* for both his father and Conington, who had died shortly before.

Back in Clifton Hill House as its master, however, Symonds is clearer in his mind than ever about taking on a literary career, and his work positively flourishes – including his poetry. And some remarkable letters from early summer of 1874 suggest just how much interest Sidgwick took in this work, giving much shrewd, cautious advice to someone who harbored ambitions to public literary fame:

Your last letter has perplexed me a little: you put so lucidly the different points of view that you leave a judicial but indecisive mind little to do. It *is* vexatious that what are certainly your best things cannot be published: but it seems to me clear that they cannot, at present certainly, so that it is useless to contemplate this source of vexation. My view of what is possible – my choice between admissible alternatives is somewhat as follows:

1. I think you ought to publish for the reasons you give yourself, and because I think that any poems of yours are sure to have at least a *success d'estime*, and certainly to do no harm to your growing literary reputation.

2. I do not think you can include *any* poems of which Hellenic sentiment is the subject without a certain risk of disagreeable things being said. If you wish to be *quite* on the safe side, I advise you only to print the David and Jonathan, which is under the aegis of the Bible. But I think that the risk of printing 'Love and Death' and 'Callicrates' might be run without real imprudence, if you carefully exclude every phrase that passes the line which separates passionate friendship from ἔρως.

3. I think that, as far as the poems themselves are concerned you might also include 'In the Stone Quarries' and one or two more. But here comes in another consideration. I do not think you ought to have enough of these poems in the book to give it a distinct character: and that is why I proposed to limit you to the above-mentioned, which seem to me on the whole the most striking.

I feel that a reviewer *may* be nasty about these: but then I feel that we shall have a strong case against him. We shall say that he introduced the nastiness himself: we shall say that as long as the attention of mankind is so much directed to the life of Greece in its prime, it is absurd to ignore this sentiment altogether: and that as long as Plato is put into the hands of youth etc. etc. Now I do not feel that these arguments apply equally well to the loves of Imperial Rome: and that is why I should exclude Antinous. I feel that I could not defend it myself if it were attacked. (Of course you will understand that I say this not as passing a decision on the propriety of your work, but as trying to ascertain from my own feelings what the average more-or-less cultivated man would feel.)[222]

Symonds responds, "I owe you a great debt of gratitude for the trouble you have taken about these poems."[223] But Sidgwick takes even more trouble; he continues the correspondence, changing his mind about the poetic value of "Callicrates" and recommending instead that Symonds go with "In the Stonequarries" and "Before the Hêrôon &c."

Although the Rev. Tyrwhitt had not mentioned Sidgwick when discussing the "polite hiss" of the devil in more recent days, he would no doubt have found in these letters an utter vindication of his claims about pagans cynically using the charge of "prurient" to deflect criticism from the perspective of orthodox religion. This was the undeniably cynical strategy that Sidgwick was proposing. He was obviously in deep sympathy with Symonds's project – which would appear in due course as the volume *Many Moods* – and completely understood his Whitmanian ambitions. The book was to be an "experiment," a test of what commonsense morality – that "great gudgeon," the public – could handle.

As suggested in previous sections, commonsense morality badly failed the test in the mid-1870s, what with the abortive campaign for the professorship and Tyrwhitt's smoking out of Symonds. All the more remarkable, then, that during this period Sidgwick was working in an exceedingly collaborative humor with his more sensual friend. Indeed, in a letter from October of 1873, when he was hard at work on the *Methods*, he had even written to Dakyns that he should tell "Johnnie I am meditating a study of the Greek Mind with the guidance of his book. If only Time was longer!" (CWC)

When *Many Moods* appeared, in 1878, well after Tyrwhitt's attack, it contained not only an altered version of "The Lotus Garden of Antinous," but also a touching dedication to Roden Noel that suggestively explained, "It has always seemed to me that there are some thoughts which a writer, who dares not claim the sacred name of poet, may express better in rhyme and metre than in prose, and that the verses so produced have a certain value." The apologia for weak poetry – then as in recent decades – was that it allowed for the special expression of special sentiments, particularly homoerotic ones. But Symonds continued:

Condemned by ill health to long exile, and deprived of the resource of serious study, I wish to gather up the fragments that remain from stronger and it may be happier periods of life, in order that some moods of thought and feeling, not elsewhere expressed by me in print, may live within the memory of men like you, as part of me.

The "unity of tone" of the volume is achieved by focusing mainly on "the themes of Love, Friendship, Death, and Sleep," and the work is offered to Noel "in token of a friendship founded upon sympathies of no common strength or quality."[224] As Symonds remarked to Gosse, who was to receive a complimentary copy, "You may see from the dedication that I am not unprepared for plain speech in my own critical mood."[225] However, to Noel he wrote:

I am glad, very glad, that you like my Dedication. How could I but always feel what I have said there, & for {?} for you – for a man to whom I have so unreservedly given myself once, & to such a man as you – not to be forgotten & to be loved for the very contradictions in him? No one alive has seen into me in the same way as you; on no one have I felt that I could to the same extent depend for sympathy & understanding of dark troublous things; no one perhaps has more influenced me; & of no one do I so much respect & admire the warfare & ascendant aspiration; the fuliginous volcanic glow half hail with rapture & half tremble at!

I do not think I have inserted in my selection a single poem you could object to – except "The Lotus Garland of Antinous"; and *that* has been so radically castrated of all that was allusive to Roman foulness that I believe nothing but a pageant & a tragic mystery is left.[226]

This letter suggests that Noel tended to agree with Sidgwick in urging caution.

For their part, the reviewers heartily agreed with Symonds that he was not a poet. His friends were more receptive, of course. Sidgwick wrote to Noel: "Symonds's *Many Moods*. I should like to talk to you about them. Some of the newer things gave me unexpected delight – some of the sonnets of death; and especially some Dream-pieces." (M 336) And Symonds wrote to Dakyns: "I was born Dipsychic. I dont get my poems much reviewed, & I like to hear what friends have to say about them. They differ very much. Noel e.g. likes all the celebrations of young men & the tales: Henry cares for "Dream Pictures" most: and here are Mozley & Brown pitching on the little Lyrics."[227]

Symonds was in fact now also spending more time with Horatio Brown, whose "Aesthetical Sybaritism" – learned from the very decadent William Frederick Howlett – he had noted long before, when teaching him at Clifton.[228] But he was also seeing a good deal of Sidgwick, now married, who in fact visited him at Davos in the summer of 1878, when *Many Moods* first appeared. The visit went well, with Symonds informing Dakyns that

Sidgwick is "as always: herrlich wie am ersten Tag, shall we say? – He counts his future by years, by decades – giving so many to this title page & so many to that." But Symonds worries that his friend has "too many irons in the fire" and that he "has become too analytical of Kleinigkeiten in his own sensations: he makes one hear too much of them." Still, "why find spots on the sun?"[229]

Noel is very much on the scene at this time, and in a singularly illuminating letter, from September, Sidgwick writes to him, in connection with some new verse:

As for the great question of Immortality, there was one line of thought I wanted to suggest, in which, from time to time, I find a kind of repose – which, curiously enough, I find is that in which Browning's poem on the subject ("La Saisiaz") concludes. It is that on moral ground, *hope* rather [than] *certainty* is fit for us in this earthly existence. For if we had certainty there would be no room for the sublimest effort of our mental life – self-sacrifice and the moral choice of Good as Good, though not perhaps good for us here and now. From this point of view I feel that on the one hand I could not endure an unjust universe, in which Good Absolute was not also good for each; and on the other hand that the *certain knowledge* that Justice ruled the universe would preclude the unselfish choice of Good as Good. What weakens and obscures this argument is that from time to time I feel so very doubtful about "Good Absolute," what it is and how it is to be attained. (M 338–39)

The book in question was one of Noel's most popular – and least homoerotic – productions, *A Little Child's Monument*, inspired by the tragic death of his five-year-old son Eric. This particular letter drew from Noel another remarkable Apostolic flow of soul, one almost supernaturally designed to speak to the author of the *Methods*. Dated September 9, 1878, it reads:

I used to think that argument good, as to hope being better for us than certainty as making for disinterestedness in virtue. But I own I feel now that if the whole thing is likely to be a sell, there is no sense at all in being good for the sake of being good – you may if you like, but it is a matter of fancy – there is no obligation – there *is* no good – it must in such a case be all illusion together – virtue and summum bonum no less than existence, life. There cannot *be* good at all unless there be life, existence, identical with, or wrapped up in it as its condition. I often used (when I did not believe in a future for the individual) to try and realize self-sacrifice that should look on alien good alone as its end, realizing at the same time its own utter and absolute annihilation, and I could never really conceive that, the ground felt shaky, it seemed the acme of lofty and sublime virtue, and yet it seemed, – well nonsense, too – absurdly unreasonable and vain, and this especially so when I further saw that, if the individual is absolutely impermanent, a kind of illusion, a flash in the pan, (what are a few years measured absolutely more than a few seconds? we are not at all if we are not now and for ever; we are ourselves mere illusions!) so is the race, so is the world, and finally (as some of our scientific men expressly teach us) so is the universe, for after all individuals make up the whole. I am to sacrifice myself – for what – a vast illusion, an impermanent flash in the pan, a mere congeries of phenomena, transitory, vain, non-substantial, unreal, like myself!!! Is it not absurd to talk of absolute good and evil on this supposition? Can there be any such thing? Nay, but if *I* am not real, permanent, eternal, true and absolute, and if *you* are not, how can there be any such thing at all? I conceive it, I look out of myself to it, I worship and try to live up to it, seek it and find it, and would conform to it more and more; yet I have no part nor lot in it, neither has any individual spirit that conceives seeks and talks of it. Where and what then is it? The Absolute must be in all that is, yet nothing that we know, not even we ourselves, *are* – are real, permanent, abiding, but transitory phenomena only! Yet how can a chain be stronger than its weakest link? And in this case all the links are alike weak! But an absolute which we can think and aspire after and yet in which we have no part is absurd. Sum. I am. And in that certain assurance alone to my mind is the pledge and proof ever and certainly of our immortality. Then to seek the Higher life, the Summum Bonum, then to seek the good of others, as real, as permanent as ourselves, we in them and they in us, all in God, in the Divine Humanity, not an abstraction, but the Spirit of spirits – then such a life seems reasonable. Virtue, as Tennyson has expressed it, seeks its own continuance, its own permanence. And Kant justly points to the desire of happiness as co-existing with the categorical imperative. There is nothing in the world but spirit – spirits, and the thoughts of spirits – all in God, and yet with their own distinction and identity; but not necessarily narrow and limited as now and here, but with a sense of the Divine universality and communion, intuitive, rather than ratiocination. As to "matter," I am sure that is spirits in communion with us: that was Hinton's thought, a modification of Berkeley's. Hegel is right, all is ideal, but the ultimate and only substance is Spirit, personal, without the present illusive limitations of personality, and we in Him. I believe all is ideal – but our understanding is not ultimate. There is higher consciousness than ours, and this supports, involves, explains ours. Christianity in its highest teaching seems to me therefore on the whole the least one-sided and the most human spiritual teaching we have had.[230]

Apart from the last, more Idealistic lines, the bulk of this letter surely captures much of Sidgwick's own conviction about the "wages of carrying on," the moralized mix of egoism and universal benevolence that defined the reconciliation project in response to the dualism of practical reason. The sheer, desperate angst at an unjust universe in which death is the end provides, in effect, the missing pages from the *Methods*. And it represents precisely the perspective that Sidgwick would be increasingly pressed to defend against Symonds, of all people.

Sidgwick's thoughts were very much on the "great question" at this time, since his mother's condition was steadily worsening (she would die the following January). And this was a fairly characteristic way he had of consoling himself when the reconciliation project seemed hopeless; echoes of it would reverberate through Moore and Bloomsbury. With Sidgwick, the issue was also cast as a matter of being able to free oneself from any lingering doubt about the altruism of one's actions. The problem, as always, was one of being able to penetrate one's innermost self, to smoke out the trickster egoist within.

It is somewhat perverse that Symonds found in Sidgwick such a glorious Apollonian robustness, even if the latter was at this point addicted to lawn tennis, walking, and even jogging (this last representing his more econom-ical alternative to the horseback riding recommended by his physician). Symonds seems to have found it very difficult to understand or sympathize with Sidgwick's more depressive moments – what did Sidgwick know of real suffering? In a revealing letter to Noel, from May of 1874, he wrote:

I wished much to be at Cambridge when you were there & Sidgwick wrote to urge me to come. But it is no use trying to do what one cannot; & as long as the Eastwinds lasted I was an invalid.

There is something very gloomy about Sidgwick's letters of late – more than usual, it seems to me. Does he feel his vie manquée do you think? And yet how is it more manquée than that of most people? I think there is a sort of duty to oneself to be sanguine & careless & young in spite of all things & to live in Eternity's sunrise if even by some desperate effort at self-delusion.[231]

Clearly, Sidgwick's friends did not always recognize just how much they affected him or how much he needed them. Sidgwick was of course feeling all the strains of the unsatisfactory conclusion of the *Methods* during this period, but Symonds was not inclined to indulge any of his self-pity, especially given the appreciative critical reception of Sidgwick's work:

My first impression after running through the *Saturday* on you was: well here is another instance of an author who wants *all*, and who is not satisfied with language of respect and the patient homage paid to his work by an able man who does not wholly take his point of view. I would give much for such testimony to my acknowledged ability. It is in fact what I wanted and have never got.

How are you to expect your seniors (if this is Mark) to stoop lower to crown you? How can you seek that they should exactly apprehend the originality they discern and conscientiously point out. It will remain for younger minds to fill the void up by learning from you, getting you by heart, and taking, like new wax, the mould of your thought. I have so much more passion in me than you, and am so habitually moved by passionate impulses, that I dare say I do not really comprehend your attitude about writing and study. I cannot quite picture to myself a man who has done this, and will not, for the love of the thing, *con amore*, do more – moved by Erôs, only son of Penia and Poros. Perhaps you are right in thinking yourself a successful imposter; and perhaps this is the first sign of your being found out. *Je n'en sais rien.*

I think it is dangerous to attach importance to the opinion of people in print or otherwise (except in matters of personal prudence, good taste and so forth). The real thing is to discover if you enjoy literary work. You will not cumber the world with books more than you do already with your body, and oblivion covers both quickly as far as both are perishable. For a man to do what he likes best is the right course, since his liking is the surest sign of his capacity – far surer than the estimate of critics or of friends. Love is the only law. This is the one Great Gospel that is true.[232]

This advice, apparently referring to Sidgwick's complaining about the review of the *Methods* in the *Saturday Review*, was clearly heartfelt. As Symonds put it to him in November of 1877:

Who, dearest Henry, is to be happy about the Universe, if you are not? It is a bad business for everybody if you feel as you say you do. I, for my part, try to live without asking many questions. I do not want to be indifferent to the great problems of morals, immortality and the soul; but I want to learn to be as happy as my health and passions will allow me, without raising questions I am convinced no one will ever answer from our human standpoint. You, however, have made it your business to inquire, and it is aggravating to arrive at bewilderment; only I feel you will do the world good service if you stoutly proclaim this bewilderment, and attack the false idols of knowledge. If we cannot build, we can dissipate illusions.[233]

Difficult as it may be to emerge from these exchanges without thinking that Symonds did Sidgwick a world of good by being less than impressed by his Cosmic Pessimism, surely Symonds was being slightly disingenuous, given the way he so often profoundly engaged with the themes of "Love, Friendship, Death, and Sleep." Sidgwick plainly found him absolutely entrancing as a life with the Divine as a felt element – a raiser of the dead. However distanced Symonds may have been from enthusiasm for ghosts, he was a walking case history for the SPR, given its larger interests in abnormal states of consciousness. As remarked, his sexual dipsychia was part of a larger constellation of trance states and dissociative psychological experiences.

When William James addressed the question of mysticism, including Symonds's experiences, he was utterly persuaded that

> our normal waking consciousness, rational consciousness as we call it, is but one special type of consciousness, whilst all about it, parted from it by the filmiest of screens, there lie potential forms of consciousness entirely different. We may go through life without suspecting their existence; but apply the requisite stimulus, and at a touch they are there in all their completeness, definite types of mentality which probably somewhere have their field of application and adaptation.[234]

To illustrate the point, James quotes the section of Brown's biography that recounts Symonds's experiences during a visit to the dentist. In fact, the bit James quotes is taken from a letter to Sidgwick dated February 20, 1873, which prefaces the account thusly:

> I have a strange, deep, inexplicable power of suffering that belongs not to natures more finely strung than the average, I think, but to those which require for their mere existence some frequent tasting of the *âpres jouissances* of mere nature – savage and bitter to the taste. All the sweet refined fruits, the grapes and the peaches, of poetry and art, are mine: and I care not for them one jot, if I may not press from time to time against my lips the sharp, rough husk of the wild drupe. As I must not pluck and taste these wilding berries, I pine with a distempered appetite, and am cloyed with over suavity.
>
> I am going to write out for you the account of a curious psychological experience I had the other day. On Tuesday I was put under the influence of chloroform and laughing gas together. I felt no pain; but my consciousness seemed complete, and I was occupied with the strange thoughts which you shall read. Tell me what you think about it. If this had happened to a man in an uncritical age, would it not have carried conviction, like that of Saul of Tarsus, to his soul? A violent deepening of despair – a sense of being mocked and cheated – remains with me.

After this, the following account is given:

> After the choking and stifling of the chloroform had passed away, I seemed at first in a state of utter blankness: then came flashes of intense light, alternating with blackness, and with a keen vision of what was going on in the room round me, but

no sensation of touch. I thought that I was near death; when, suddenly, my soul became aware of God, who was manifestly dealing with me, handling me, so to speak, in an intense personal present reality. I felt Him streaming in like light upon me, and heard Him saying in no language, but as hands touch hands and communicate sensation, 'I led you, I guided you; you will never sin, and weep, and wail in madness any more; for, now, you have seen Me.' My whole consciousness seemed brought into one point of absolute conviction; the independence of my mind from my body was proved by the phenomena of this acute sensibility to spiritual facts, this utter deadness of the senses; Life and Death seemed mere names, for what was there then but my soul and God, two indestructible existences in close relation. I could reason a little, to this extent that I said; 'Some have said they were convinced by miracles and spirit-rapping, but my conviction is a real new sense.' I also felt God saying, 'I have suffered you to feel sin and madness, to ache and be abandoned, in order that now you might know and gladly greet Me. Did you think the anguish of the last few days and this experience you are undergoing were fortuitous coincidences?' Then as I gradually awoke from the influence of the anaesthetics, the old sense of my relation to the world began to return, the new sense of my relation to God began to fade. I suddenly leapt to my feet on the chair where I was sitting, and shrieked out, 'It is too horrible, it is too horrible, it is too horrible,' meaning that I could not bear this disillusionment. Then I flung myself on the ground, and at last awoke covered with blood, calling to the two surgeons (who were frightened), 'Why did you not kill me? Why would you not let me die?' Only think of it. To have felt for that long dateless ecstasy of vision the very God, in all purity and tenderness and truth and absolute love, and then to find that I had after all had no revelation, but that I had been tricked by the abnormal excitement of my brain.

Yet, this question remains, Is it possible that the inner sense of reality which succeeded, when my flesh was dead to impressions from without, to the ordinary sense of physical relations, was not a delusion but an actual experience? Is it possible that I, in that moment, felt what some of the saints have said they always felt, the undemonstrable but irrefragable certainty of God?[235]

Symonds appeared to be "knocked flat," at least for a time. He wrote to Dakyns a little later that the

vision I had in London of God still haunts me. It was not all a dream. 'Behind the veil' has an odd meaning for me now; & yet I stick to your idea of writing out a series of memories. What remains to us upon this shore of oblivion but to place some waifs & strays of our dying selves – some portion of that which made us be – upon ledges above the surf & spray? Because such a work is introspective it has not therefore no value, nay rather it has therefore its value. Up then! Woo beauty, while yet you may. Love – for Art is Love – while you still can.

But this was indeed a *felt* experience. As he later explained to Green, in June of 1878:

I always feel that theological philosophy starts with a *petitio principii* about God, and that the subjective proof to which you so eloquently appeal is unsatisfactory to the very people who require to be convinced – those who have it not. . . . Why Nature should not be without a thinking subject . . . I could never comprehend. I am so obtuse that I cannot get over the reflection of what Nature must have been before man appeared, and is where man is not. That the spirit of man is no part of what we call nature may be conceded *arg.gr.* without the corollary that God is to be sought in it, or that it is the creative principle of the Universe. It is just this latter position: viz. that humanity is Deity in the sense of effectuating Nature by its thought, which seems to me to divide you, and those who think with you, from those who, however they feel the Divine in the Universe, do not venture to assert its cognisability.[236]

Thus, Symonds's vision of God was the type of unphilosophized, raw, paranormal psychological experience that James and Sidgwick, at least, found so suggestive and promising. Symonds the nonphilosopher, rather than Green the philosopher, was the one raising the right question – and this at the very time that Sidgwick was completing the *Methods*. And this sensibility, of tenuous dying selves falling before a greater reality, was stamped all over *Many Moods*, particularly the parts that Sidgwick admired. As ever, Sidgwick was positively addicted to "psychological experiments." However, there is no evidence that he shared Symonds's habit of using sleep-inducing drugs, and even such recreational items as hashish, to stretch his own consciousness in such ways.[237]

Yet with the retreat to Davos and the Alps, Symonds's consciousness was to take a new turn. Already, with his academic hopes smashed and his happy experience with soldier love, he was mentally very much beyond *Many Moods* and the forms of dipsychia that England had fostered in him. The last of his peccant pamphlets, *Rhaetica*, was perhaps the boldest of all. About this, Sidgwick was feeling none too cooperative. As Symonds related to Dakyns, in June of 1879:

I found here yesterday an awful letter from H. Sidg about Rhaetica. If I were not so ill & hopeless & impervious, it would have crushed me. But as it is, I am bored & less sanguine than before.

The gist is that I am on the brink of a precipice, on the verge of losing my reputation & bringing disgrace on Henry & you & all who call me friend. Rhaetica, if smelt out by a Critic, would precipitate me altogether.

I think I ought to ask you, under these conditions, to destroy the peccant pamphlet, together perhaps with all my confounded verse in print or out of it. I am sure they are not as well worth keeping as they seem to be perilous, & to you they must only now be very ancient bores – pathetic perhaps & a little humorous, if we think about them in the past. If you don't wish to burn them, make a packet of the things addressed to me, to be consigned by your executors or burned unseen if I am dead first.

I think this is due to Henry, who is really in a state.[238]

Among other things, *Rhaetica* included a poem "To H. F. B." and another called "What Might Have Been," with the lines "The love we might have known, if we / Had turned this way instead of that; / The lips we might have kissed, which he / For whom they parted, pouted at!" It is uncertain just when this poem was penned, but it carries a peculiar resonance with a certain turn of phrase common to Symonds, Dakyns, and Sidgwick. In a letter of uncertain date, but surely from sometime in 1872, just around the time of his wedding, Dakyns had in his singular way challenged Sidgwick:

I saw one letter (the last?) from you to Johnnie about the various scepticisms, & your right to comprehend them. It was a ray of light – (to continue the ancient simile of me regarding you by a disciple of K'ung fou tsze regards the earth or sun without need of speech resting under or upon the general embrace – but now if the sun be dark, or earth thorny, then the disciple no more believes in the existence of benign unseen powers). So I liked one ray. But you don't comprehend vermicular scepticism I think & rejoice to think. It perhaps isn't worth even classification *e fango é mondo*. (CWC)

Dakyns apparently shared Symonds's shrewd assessment of the limits of Sidgwick's sympathy and skepticism, as suggested by the brilliant phrasing "vermicular scepticism."

In a letter just prior to this, carrying the salutation "Dear Friend" and written to accept the role of trustee for Dakyns's marriage settlement, Sidgwick had written, in a passage carefully abridged in the *Memoir*:

As for our past – you do not think that I have any such thoughts as you suggest. I feel often as unrelated and unadapted to my universe as man can feel: except on the one side of friendship: and there, in my deepest gloom all seems strangely good: and you among the best. And if you might have been more – I know nothing of Might-have-been, and suspect too that if I did enquire, the fault would turn out to be my own.

But 'golden news' expect none unless I light perchance on the Secret of the Universe, in which case I will let you know. (CWC)[239]

Coincidence? What "Might-have-been" but for Henry's fault?

At any rate, it is not at all surprising that by the time of *Rhaetica*, Sidgwick should worry about any potential scandal that might erupt over Symonds and his poetry. Sidgwick is married, building an academic career (in part as an ethicist), and sheparding Newnham College into existence, along with his psychical research. And he is of course generally known as one of Symonds's friends and supporters, who sought to place him in a professorship at Oxford. In short, he has a great deal to lose, should Symonds, safely off in Davos, provide Tyrwhitt and his ilk the ammunition to mount another attack on the pagans and their circle. The whole cause of university reform, of reducing the influence of religion in academics, could suffer immeasurable damage if the academic liberals could be linked to the Platonic revival and then to a paganism in sharp conflict with commonsense morality. Sidgwick knew full well precisely how stupid conservative religious opinion could be in general, and particularly when it came to anything having to do with sex. His "new casuistry," in connection with Symonds's coming out, is perfectly consistent with his old casuistry, in connection with his resignation, despite the different resultant actions – if uncertain, remain silent, and everything depends on just what the public is ripe for. Moral rigorism was subject to consequentialist reckoning. And now, Sidgwick was Praelector of Moral and Political Philosophy, and an aspirant to the Knightbridge Professorship.

What happens after his "awful letter"? Once again, there is no "rift in the lute." To the contrary, Symonds repairs to Davos permanently; Sidgwick is his frequent visitor; and to compensate for the lack of personal contact, they decide on an exchange of their private confidential journals, kept intermittently from 1884 to 1892. *Rhaetica* never sees the light of day – in its original, naked, pamphlet version – and Symonds is increasingly steered, by Sidgwick and others, to channel his candor into a course bearing the stamp of scientific legitimacy – as in his work with Havelock Ellis. It was all just too shrewd. Plainly, if anyone deserves the credit – or blame – for keeping Symonds from something like the scandal that engulfed Oscar Wilde, it was his very well-connected friend Sidgwick, who, however deficient in vermicular skepticism, had a much better feel for the deficiences of commonsense morality.

Sidgwick received a great deal in return. His invalid, sexually active, God-feeling friend would shepard him into and out of another very real crisis.

VII. Vermicular Skepticism

Weaving throughout all these encounters between Sidgwick and Symonds, Noel and Dakyns, one finds, in slightly altered, more immediate, personalized form, so many of the very same conflicts informing Sidgwick's better known philosophical work: the haziness of practical ethics, the claims of egoism, the problem of self-sacrifice, the mystery of the true self, the importance of immortality, the worries about hypocrisy, and so on and on. Indeed, the very language of Sidgwick's religious and philosophical struggles was rife with allusions to and appropriations of the pregnant poetry of Symonds.[240] And nowhere, outside of this nexus, is it more striking just how esoteric much of Sidgwick's moral thinking was. Sidgwick wanted Symonds's Whitmania relegated to the enlightened future rather than the bigoted present.

But ultimately, what was so remarkable to Sidgwick about the Symonds "psychological experiment" was the paradoxical way in which Symonds's ongoing invalidism effectively rendered him a case study in attitudes toward death – the great test for any working philosophy. For all of Symonds's envy of Sidgwick's robustness and strength, he was very perceptive in challenging Sidgwick's estimate of his own sympathetic powers, and, ironically enough, of the normality of the human longing for personal immortality. Here, after all, was someone who at many points counted his life by days or months rather than by years – particularly after 1877, when the graveness of his consumptive condition was impressed upon him by various eminent physicians, leading to his sojourn to Davos. How was Sidgwick supposed to lecture him about attitudes toward death?

Recall how, in his early Apostolic days, some such issues had figured in that paper for the "Wise and the Good" in which Sidgwick considered whether prayer would "be a universal function of the ideal humanity" and challenged his religious sentiments with an appreciation of "a rather rare and very admirable class of men: men that are in mind what the models of the Greek Statues were in body, healthy, finely moulded, well nerved, symmetrical." His defense of prayer invoked the "one trial that may befall the most symmetrical – old age which is rarely borne as well as youth by the non-religious." Impending death was the final test of unbelief. To be sure, religion was "not yet quite fitted to become the crown of glory of a symmetrical nature." But he looks "forward to a type of man combining the highest pagan with highest medieval excellences" – that is, with a much greater capacity for sympathy and benevolence." (CWC) Like Symonds, Sidgwick was working on a new religion, a new synthesis. And his interest in the "symmetrical people" was evidently lifelong: he addressed the very same issue at a meeting of the Synthetic Society held on May 25, 1900 – the last such philosophical meeting (this one private) that he would attend.

But Symonds increasingly put the lie to the claim that ill health or an unfavorable constitution or the confrontation with death could not be borne without the comfort of belief in personal immortality, theistic if not orthodox. Paradoxically enough, despite (or because of) his invalidism, Symonds lived and breathed the ideal of symmetry – in the Greeks, in Goethe, in Whitman. By contrast, Sidgwick's reconciliation project appears asymmetrical and weak, more modern and less Hellenistic, more distrusting of the deeper self.

The in-built tensions in their friendship come to a head in the 1880s, when Sidgwick finds himself in another crisis, a crisis that in a great many respects was the old one over subscription revived. In 1887 and 1888, Sidgwick finds all his familiar bothers coming back to haunt him. Although he has won many honors,[241] he has also, like Symonds, suffered woe upon woe – the death of various old friends; being passed over for the mastership of Trinity; frustration with the economy, academic politics, and his work for women's higher education – and appears to be headed toward a midlife crisis along with his fiftieth birthday. But worst of all, of course, is the news from psychical research. As shown in the previous chapter, it is at just this juncture that he seems utterly despairing of being able to find evidence for survival of death, and the "blackness of the end" is making him feel acutely asymmetrical.

All is confessed in his journals to Symonds, naturally. And it is in January of 1887 that he pens the famous passage about how fifteen years before, when finishing the *Methods*, he "was inclined to hold with Kant that we must *postulate* the continued existence of the soul, in order to effect that harmony of Duty with Happiness which seemed to me indispensable to rational moral life." He had, as shown, "provisionally" postulated it, while setting out on his hunt for evidence. Now, the question is:

If I decide that this search is a failure, shall I finally and decisively make this postulate? Can I consistently with my whole view of truth and the method of its attainment? And if I answer 'no' to each of these questions, have I any ethical system at all? And if not, can I continue to be Professor and absorb myself in the mere erudition of the subject.

As always, he has "mixed up the personal and general questions, because every speculation of this kind ends, with me, in a practical problem, 'What is to be done here and now.'" That, he feels, is the question that he simply must answer, "whereas as to the riddle of the Universe – I never had the presumption to hope that its solution was reserved for *me*, though I had to try." (M 466–67) Of course, he did have more than his share of presumption, as Symonds was fond of pointing out.

Sidgwick describes his state as a "mental crisis." He finds himself mostly "fingering idly" the old "Gordian knot." Symonds is not so sure. He answers:

I am alluding to the passage of your Diary, in which you announce your expectation of having to abandon in this life the hope of obtaining proof of the individual soul's existence as a consciousness beyond death. What this implies for yourself, in its bearing I mean, upon Moral Philosophy, and its bearing upon the sustained quest of twenty years, I am able to appreciate.

And I may add that it was for myself also a solemn moment, when I read that paragraph in the Diary, through the measured sentences of which a certain subdued glow of passion seemed to burn. I do not pretend that I had ever fixed my views of human conduct clearly or hopefully upon the proof of immortality to our ordinary experience. I do not deny that I never had any confidence in the method you were taking to obtain the proof. I will further confess that, had you gained the proof, this result would have enormously aggravated the troubles of my life, by cutting off the possibility of resumption into the personal-unconscious which our present incertitude leaves open to my sanguine hope.

Ethics, I feel, can take care of themselves – that is to say, human beings in social relations will always be able to form codes of conduct, profitable to the organism and coercive of the individual to the service of its uses. In humanity, as in nature, 'est Deus, quis Deus incertum.'

I have no apprehension for civil law and social and domestic institutions, even though the permanence of personal consciousness after this life remain undemonstrated. Those things are necessary for our race, of whose position in the universe we are at present mainly ignorant; and a sanction of some sort, appealing to imagination, emotion, unformulated onward impulses, will always be forthcoming. Man has only had about 6,000 years of memory upon this planet; and the most grudging of physicists accord him between ten and twenty millions to come. Dislocations of ethical systems, attended by much human misery, possibly also by retrograde epochs of civilisation, are likely to ensue. History, if it teaches anything in its little span of past time, prepares us to expect such phases in the incalculably longer future. But our faith lies in this: that God, in the world, and in humanity as a portion of the world, effectuates Himself, and cannot fail to do so. I do not see, therefore, why we should be downcast if we cannot base morality upon a conscious immortality of the individual.

But I do see that, until that immortality of the individual is irrefragably demonstrated, the sweet, the immeasurably precious hope of ending with this life the ache and languor of existence, remains open to burdened human personalities.

A sublime system of ethics seems to me capable of being based, in its turn, upon that hope of extinction. Demonstration, *ex argumento ipso*, will not here be attained. But I am of opinion that the persuasion, if it comes to be reasonably entertained, of man's surcease from consciousness when this life closes, will afford quite as good a basis for submission to duty as any expectation of continuance in its double aspect of hope and fear has lately been.[242]

This hit Sidgwick about as hard as any psychological experiment possibly could. In February he is rereading Tennyson's *In Memoriam*, amazed at the "intensity of sympathy" with which he does so. The explanation is of course the obvious one, though now Sidgwick owns up to his own presumption: "This is due, I think, to my final despair of obtaining – I mean *my* obtaining, for I do not yet despair as regards the human race – any adequate rational ground for believing in the immortality of the soul." Tennyson is "the representative poet of an age whose most characteristic merit is to see both sides of a question." (M 468–69)

Sidgwick remains in a meditative funk over these matters for the rest of the winter, in March responding:

I have been thinking much, sadly and solemnly, of J.A.S.'s answer to my January journal. In spite of sympathy of friendship, I feel by the limitations of my nature incapable of really comprehending the state of mind of one who does not *desire* the continuance of his personal being. All the activities in which I truly live seem to carry with them the same demand for the 'wages of going on.' They also carry with them concomitant pleasure: not perhaps now – aetat 49 – in a degree that excites enthusiasm, but quite sufficient to satisfy the instinctive claims of a man who has never been conscious of having a creditor account with the universe. Whether if this pleasure failed I could rely on myself to live from a pure sense of duty I do not really know; I hope so, but I cannot affirm.

But at present the recognised failure of my efforts to obtain evidence of immortality affects me not as a Man but as a Moralist. 'Ethics,' says J.A.S., 'can take care of themselves.' I think I agree with what is meant, but should word it differently. I should say 'morality can take [care] of itself,' or rather the principle of life in human society can take care of morality. But how? Perhaps always by producing an illusory belief in immortality in the average man, who must live content with Common Sense. Perhaps he will always
Fix perfect homes in the unsubstantial sky,
And say what is not will be by and by.

At any rate, somehow or other, morality will get on; I do not feel particularly anxious about that. But my special business is not to maintain morality *somehow*, but to establish it logically as a reasoned system; and I have declared and published that this cannot be done, if we are limited to merely mundane sanctions, owing to the inevitable divergence, in this imperfect world, between the individual's Duty and his Happiness. I said in 1874 that without some datum beyond experience 'the Cosmos of Duty is reduced to a Chaos.' Am I to recant this conviction – which no one of my numerous antagonists has yet even tried to answer? Or am I to use my position – and draw my salary – for teaching that Morality *is* a chaos, from the point of view of Practical Reason; adding cheerfully that, as man is not after all a rational being, there is no real fear that morality won't be kept up somehow. I do not at present see my way to acquiesce in either alternative. But I shall do nothing hastily, *non ego hoc ferrem calidus inventa*, but the 'consulship of Plancus' is long past.[243]

This would appear to be about as plain an affirmation of the rationality of egoism as one could want from Sidgwick – he is not sure that he himself is up to living "from a pure sense of duty."[244] As in the case of pursuing love, so in the case of fearing death, is it not paradoxical to deny that one is pressing the claims of a separate self, the personal point of view? And if even Sidgwick could doubt his ability to follow self-sacrificing duty without this reassurance, what of the "sensual herd"? Even if ethics could take care of themselves in the long run, a reduction to this worldly forms of egoism would, to Sidgwick's mind, prove pretty rough on the social order. How very odd that the Goethean Symonds should turn out to be so much more able than Sidgwick to overcome self with a vision of Cosmic Enthusiasm. This baffled Sidgwick; if he had long felt that the "alternatives of the Great Either-Or seem to be Pessimism or Faith," he could not see his way to this form of faith. (M 340)

Symonds gave another such account to Roden Noel, making note of Sidgwick's attitude:

I should call my attitude a highly spiritualized Stoicism rather than Calvinism. The latter assumed *inequality* in the Divine dealings with man. All my notions about Law & and homogeneity of the Universe lead me to expect absolute equality.

Only I feel that I have no power & no right to speculate on what may be; but, like a private soldier in a campaign, to accept orders & discipline. I do not understand or criticize. . . . Practically I believe that our opinions differ (I do not mean merely yours & mine, but those of all people) very much according to their want to go on living – the attraction that immortality has for them. I have always been singularly apathetic about that. Sidgwick tells me I am quit abnormal in my indifference – an indifference which, if I indulged one part of it, would make me as desirous of annihilation as other people are averse to it.

I am therefore in the peculiar position of an optimist who is prepared to accept extinction. This enables me to feel a really passionate interest in the spectacle of the Universe, & a firm conviction that its apparent injustice & inequalities must have a meaning, imply *a good in process*. At the back of my thought lie two perceptions 1) our incapacity of formulating the future & what we want in the future 2) our right to assume that manly & cheerful acquiescence in this state of ignorance, combined with continued effort to get the utmost out of our lives by work in our own way, one man's way being action, another's art, another's service of his fellows in philanthropy, & so forth, is the best preparation for any grace that may be granted to us, & the best energizing for the totality of human nature.

It is extremely difficult to state what sort of *hope* I have and I can readily believe that my idiosyncratic indifference regarding immortality makes my attitude of faith unintelligible. It may also make it seem frigidly unsympathetic toward those who have had far less of good in this life than I have.

How very imperfect and unsympathetic historical Christianity has been in this respect – especially toward the unnumbered millions who built our race up before Christ's Gospel was preached. I counterpose my Stoicism to *this*, not to any philosophical construction* which provides a sphere for *all* souls – including beasts & trees etc.[245]

The asterisked note reads "Bruno attracts me so much because he speculated so evidently in this direction."

Sidgwick had used the very same image of his taking his intellectual position "as a soldier takes a post of difficulty" (M 354). This was the practical upshot of the Symonds–Sidgwick experiments in living, but there was a big difference. When Sidgwick had used the expression, it was in the course of explaining to his sister how he did not want to bring her around to his position. His worldview was "an inevitable point in the process of thought," but he could take neither the "responsibility of drawing any one else to it" nor "the responsibility of placing obstacles in their way" (M 354).

At any rate, Symonds, Sidgwick reflects, has not quite caught his approach on one point – namely, how he has "tried *all* methods in turn," only to find that "all in turn have failed – revelational, rational, empirical methods – there is no proof in any of them." Now it is Sidgwick pushing the skeptical challenge. Symonds's inner voyaging may have revealed much about the deeper layers of his sexual self, but Sidgwick is not being knocked flat by the Cosmic Optimism that resulted. The mystic "phenomena" continue to elude him; the felt Divine remains beyond him. It is not merely the poverty of philosophy that has crushed his hopes.

Still, the tide of vermicular skepticism recedes and the Socratic faith remains: it is "premature to despair," and he is "quite content to go on seeking while life lasts; that is not the perplexing problem; the question is whether to profess Ethics without a basis" (M 472–73).

Of course, he did do so, and the very next edition of the *Methods* was none other than the famous fourth edition, with the more direct statement concerning the rationality of egoism. Like Symonds, perhaps, Sidgwick in the late 1880s was getting rather bolder with – if also more anxious about – his expressions of his deeper doubts, suggesting that the famous first edition of the *Methods* may have been the less overtly skeptical one. In his last decade, he would spend more time teaching politics and metaphysics, and working with the "ethical culture" movement to foster greater ethical behavior without dwelling on the ultimate questions of ethical justification. Of course, in the 1890s, psychical research began to offer new rays of hope.

In any case, whether he had an inherited predisposition toward it or a painful series of buried childhood memories concerning it, Sidgwick never could shake his conviction that immortality was the great question, or fully enter into Symonds's "abnormal" way of dealing with the matter. He was – at this point, as in 1867 – rather tactless in his philosophical self-importance. For this exchange about the afterlife and its human importance was going on at precisely the time that Symonds's eldest daughter, Janet, was succumbing to tuberculosis. She died on April 7, at the age of twenty-one, and yet Sidgwick's journal finds him still in his

introspective turmoil, even after having received notification of the death
from Symonds:

[W]hile I find it easy enough to *live* with more or less satisfaction, I cannot at
present get any satisfaction from *thinking* about life, for thinking means – as I am
a philosopher – endeavouring to frame an ethical theory which will hold together,
and to this I do not see my way. And the consideration that the morality of the
world may be trusted to get on without philosophers does not altogether console.
(M 475)

Apparently, Sidgwick did write Symonds a separate letter of consolation, as can be judged from Symonds's painful response:

The pain of losing Janet was very great, and the *desiderium* will remain permanent.
There seems to be something pitiful in this extinction of a nature formed for really
noble life. It is extraordinary from how many unexpected quarters the echo of her
personality, the impression she made on those who knew a little of her, comes to
us. You tell me that you have "no consolation to offer." But really I do not want
any. I know that I cannot get any. The loss is there, and may not be made up to
me. I have long since bent and schooled myself to expect no consolation of the
ordinary sort. And I do not think I feel less brightly and less resignedly than those
who are basing their hopes upon unimaginable re-uniting with their loved ones,
in heaven only knows what planet. You go on to say that "despair in our ignorance
is the prompting of blind passion, not of reason." I have no comprehension what
"despair" is. I have ceased to wish for immortality, and therefore ceased to hope
for it. If I am to have it, I have it at the hand of the same Power which gave me
mortal life. If I am not to have it, is a matter of contentment to me; for I have
found that all life is a struggle, and neither for myself nor my fellow-creatures do
I desire the prolongation of the struggle. Being what we are, it is obvious that the
continuation of consciousness in us must entail a toilsome *Entwickelung*.

So I am content to leave these things until the very end, until the very new
beginning if that comes, upon the knees of It, of Him, who is for me responsible.

Such a word as "despair," the counterpart of hope in personal immortality, does
not exist in my vocabulary. This fact I have tested while sitting by my daughter's
corpse, while consigning it to the earth. And I want to utter this now, because, as
you observe, "the perplexities of theory have strangely entwined themselves with
the inexorabilities of life in our correspondence."

The net result of my present experience is to corroborate my previous opinions.
It has roused in me no new longing, no new regrets, laid its finger on no lurking hope
and no concealed despair. Only it has confirmed my conviction that the main point
in the whole position is that of Euripides, τοὺς ξῶντας εὖδρᾶν. Upon this point
I have only the purest satisfaction with regard to Janet. She attained to spiritual

perfection in her life. What troubles me about myself is the sense of shortcomings, rendering the part I play in life less worthy of man's station in the world.

I have proved in my own person that St. Paul was wrong when he exclaimed, "If Christ be not risen, then are we of men most wretched." We may be happy and calm and submissive to the supreme order, to Zeus and ἡπεπρωμένη, without a resurrection. I perceive that his *argumenta ad hominem* in I Cor. xv., "Else what shall they do that are baptised for the dead," &c., "If after the manner of men I have fought with beasts at Ephesus," &c., are blots upon the splendid inspiration of his rhetoric, appeals to human love of profit. Love and good, and the desire of righteousness, do not need the bribe of immortality, and have to be reasoned now upon quite different principles.

I would not willingly bore you with these observations, but it is incumbent upon me to tell you how the last week of severance from my first-born has acted like a test upon the convictions I began to express some weeks ago.[246]

To an unknown correspondent, Symonds would explain that Janet had told him "that she could cheerfully & contentedly give back her life to Him who bestowed it on her, without repining even though it should be renewed upon the same inadequate terms of happiness as she enjoyed in this world." This, he said, was "the perfectly *religious* spirit" and the one in which he tried "to take her loss."[247]

Sidgwick was apparently aware of the imperfect nature of his sympathy, writing in his journal:

While at Miss Ewart's I received J.A.S.'s answer to my letter of sympathy: – from which it seems clear that I must have sympathized not with him but with myself imagined in his circumstances. I suppose it is difficult to avoid this: yet I of all people ought to be able to avoid it: – for no one can feel more strongly that J.A.S.'s state of thought about the Universe is likely – for most people – to be more conducive both to happiness and to virtue than mine: no one is more inclined than I to give thanks that everybody does not think as he does. Still the only way to truth is to follow out one's own intellectual process: one cannot change it *per saltum* by jumping resolutely into another line of thought: at least I do not think I could. (CWC)[248]

Symonds's Whitmania, it would seem, had the same utilitarian merits as Green's Idealism, to Sidgwick's mind – though the further irony is that Symonds was, in effect, pursuing Mill's line about the religion of the future dispensing with the doctrine of personal immortality.

By early 1888, Sidgwick is becoming rather jaded about his state: "For my inner life, I have nothing new to say. I think over 'Gordian knots' but come to no further solution. Silence is best." But by April, the clouds are lifting, apparently. He has again been intensely, if internally, debating "the tenability of my position here as a teacher of Ethics." The problem, as he sees it, is that ethics falls between science and theology, the former demanding doubt, the latter a creed. Which analogy is right for philosophical ethics? But for all his doubt, he has had it: "Enough! this is longer than I intended. What I intended to say is that I have emerged from my tunnel by an act of will, and do not mean to let my mind turn on this hook any more for the present." Slightly earlier in the month, he had explained his changing attitude in terms sounding distinctly Symondsish:

The change is great in my own mind since I left off the journal: – and, though the loss is great, I am obliged to confess to myself that the change is not altogether for the worse. I take life more as it comes, and with more concern for small things. I aim at cheerfulness and I generally attain it. I have a stronger *instinctive* repugnance to cause pain or annoyance to any human being – in old times, when the old idea of a judgment at which all would be known still hung about me, I was more concerned about being *in the right* in my human relations – about having as Bp. Andrews says, "defensionem bonam" ante tremendum tribunal. But now I have let this drop into the background, and though I still feel what Carlyle calls the "Infinity of Duty," it is only in great matters I feel it: as regards the petty worries of life, I feel that both the Universe and Duty *de minimis non curat*: – or rather the one Infinite duty is to be serene. And serene I am – so far! (M 485–86)

He and Nora are now "too much bored with the SPR: we only acquiesce in the time and trouble required to keep it up because we feel the need of an advertisement for scientific purposes – to hear of subjects." In fact, he is enjoying reading Symonds on aesthetics, an article in "Fortnightly which I agreed with and liked very much – terse and pregnant, interesting & suggestive." (He differs on some points: "what Goethe creates appeals to Thought not Fantasy.") And he is in fact looking at the bright side of leaving Cambridge, which "everything points to." That is, "I do not think I was made to be a teacher of age and dignity: I like talking to young men, but I like talking to them as an equal – and this becomes harder as the years go on." If they leave, "Cambridge will miss my wife more than me," and this gives him pause, though Arthur has "stirred my desire to go to Greece." (M 488–89)

By his birthday:

My fiftieth birthday! I find that now my whole nature is beginning to sway in the direction of leaving Cambridge. Two old impulses raise their heads and sing in tune within me – (1) the desire to travel to know the world of West-European civilisation thoroughly and as a whole, and (2) the desire of literary independence to be able to speak when I like as a man to men, and not three times a week as a salaried teacher to pupils. I understand the teacher who said that his classes were his "wings": but in my deep doubt whether what now appears to me true leads to edification I find them rather chains than wings. (M 489)

All of this simply screams the example of Symonds, of course. And Sidgwick is spending a great deal of time in Davos, eventually helping with the book that Symonds would publish as *Essays Speculative and Suggestive*, a work as representative of Sidgwick's aesthetics as of Symonds's. In July of 1890, Symonds writes Dakyns:

> Henry Sidgwick is here, & is dissecting my essays under my eyes. He is doing me the compliment of reading them & trying to get something useful out of them.
>
> Good Lord! in what different orbits human souls can move.
>
> He talks of sex, out of legal codes, & blue books. I talk of it, from human documents, myself, the people I have known, the adulterers & prostitutes of both Sexes I have dealt with over bottles of wine & confidences.
>
> Nothing comes of discussions between a born doctrinaire & a born Bohemian. We want you to moderate between us. And you are not enough. We want a cloud of witnesses.
>
> Shall we ever be able to see human nature from a really central point of view? I doubt this now. Though we redouble our spectacles, put scores of our neighbours' glasses on our own, in order to obtain the typical impression, shall we reach the central standpoints?
>
> Books are trifles in the current of life. What we write, is the smallest part of what we are. And what we are, is an insignificant globule in the vast sea of nature.
>
> So we must be content to remain with pores & tentacles wh. find no sympathetic response in our deepest brethren – nay in the wife of our bosom, the comrade who sleeps beside us & the children who grow up separately from ourselves; all of whom, soul & body, in their several ways we passionately love.[249]

To be sure, Sidgwick actually liked the book. Only ten days later, Symonds would write to Dakyns again, this time explaining that "Henry Sidgwick here has helped me in the same way, or a similar. These Essays have suggested for twelve days constantly recurring conversations, and have set speculation on the wind. They would not have done so with him, had they not had stuff. And do you know, I was beginning to fear I had no stuff left in me?"[250]

The reviewers did not think that *Essays Speculative and Suggestive* had the right stuff, making Symonds wonder why he supposed he "could do things of that sort well."[251] But that he had a great deal of stuff left in him was plain. It was at this time that he began so much of the work that would mark the final, "scientific" period of his sexual writings, including "A Problem in Modern Ethics" and his memoirs. Among other things, he presses Whitman on the sexual meaning of "Calamus," visits the great sex researcher Karl Ulrichs in Italy, sets to work on his massive biography of Michelangelo ("if he had any sexual energy at all . . . he was a U"), starts his collaboration with Ellis (in the course of which he begins collecting stories and "case histories" from Urnings all over the globe), becomes friendly with the very out and politically active Whitmanian Edward Carpenter, and appears to be circulating photographs and reproductions of beautiful (and naked) young men among his intimate friends. Oscar Wilde is counted as one of his admirers, but Symonds has reservations:

Oscar Wilde sent me his story. I have read it with interest. But I do not like this touch upon moral psychological problems, wh have for myself great actuality, & ought I think to be treated more directly. I am afraid that Wilde's work in this way will only solidify the prejudices of the vulgar – to wit, that aesthetics are inseparable from unhealthiness or inhumanity, & that interest in art implies some corruption in its votaries. My Essays are meant in a large measure to remove this error.

Wilde's manner is "morbid & perfumed." But if the British public will stand *The Picture of Dorian Gray*, "they can stand anything."[252]

Through it all, Sidgwick the disenchanted is visiting Davos at every turn, and in "excellent form." That he was critical of Symonds's work signifies little, since he was critical of everyone's work, including his own. Indeed, Symonds had written to their friend Noel – the "Centaur" – in 1892 that "if you had shown as much contempt for my verses as F. Myers & H. Sidgwick do, it would not have made any difference in my feeling for you."[253] Which is to say, everyone, with the possible exception of Dakyns, criticized Symonds's verses. Symonds even worried about Brown's reaction:

I do not want to send you any more of my verses. I can always tell you what I think. But verse is form. I hope this will not prevent you from sending me what you write. About twenty years ago I used to show my verse productions to Henry Sidgwick and F. Myers. I discovered that they were curious about them on account of what I said, but did not like the form. So I stopped doing so, and there has been no interruption of the freest closest exchange of thought and feeling. Henry is only a little plaintive when "Vagabunduli Libellus" appears, and I do not send it him, and will not discuss it with him. But he has made the situation. It is easy enough to do without a man's sympathy, but difficult to go on seeking it and not getting it. . . . if I must sing, I will sing to myself and God, not to you and Henry and F. M.[254]

If Symonds was worried that Brown and Noel would criticize his verse after the manner of Sidgwick, the criticism at issue could not have had much to do with male love in and of itself. Henry is only a "little plaintive" about one of Symonds's most graphic verse productions, and in fact wants to bring Symonds to Cambridge to meet Arthur Balfour.

But, even if Symonds was a psychological experiment in living of the first importance, one whose serene attitude was seeping ever more steadily across Sidgwick's mental landscape, he was not in the end the example that Sidgwick chose to follow. Sidgwick remained in Cambridge, and, as noted in the previous chapter, would be working ever more religiously for the SPR and women's higher education. To appreciate why he took the road that he did, it is vital to consider how Symonds's concerns figured in his vision of educational reform and the relations between the sexes, which, on the face of it, does not appear very Whitmanian.

VIII. Women

I duly received the gift of your book "Towards Democracy" in its third edition, & have been reading it with sustained interest ever since it came into my hands. It is certainly the most important contribution which has as yet been made to the diffusion of Whitman's philosophy of life, & what I think we may now call the new religion. . . .

What you have done has been to give a thoroughly personal, a specifically English, & if I may so put it, a feminine (as implying other strains of sensitiveness, humour, ways of regarding particular modes of (social life), interpretation upon the leading ideas).

Insofar, then, as "Towards Democracy" is read & appreciated, it will do more than any amount of analysis or criticism to diffuse the teaching wh inspires you.

You know how deeply I sympathize with all that is involved in the new religion. The circumstances of my own existence & having been early married, & then reduced to a state of comparative physical inefficiency, have rendered it not only a necessity, but a duty also, & what is more, the best practical form left for me of service – to carry on my own work as a scholar, a writer, a student of history, an analyst. I have been unable to do what I should have preferred, had I been vigorous

& unentangled, namely to join the people in their lives. Still I have endeavoured more & more to approach them, & learned more & more from them. A large portion of my happiness in later years has come to me from frank companionship, wholesome comradeship, & mutual fellow-service with these Swiss mountaineers among whom my lot has been cast.

John Addington Symonds to Edward Carpenter, March 20, 1892[255]

Given the controversial, radical nature of the manner in which Symonds had found relief from the hypocrisy of his own English milieu and of England generally, it is very curious that Sidgwick would say of him the same thing he had said of Green – namely, that people would be better off believing something like that, rather than accepting the views of the author of the *Methods*. Ironic, too, since in the end what Symonds mostly had to offer was also a simple felt faith in "Things in General." Of course, it was Whitman, not Socrates, who kept Symonds from becoming "a mere English gentleman" and made him instead an aspirant to symmetry, or rather, made him someone who could defy Sidgwick's claims about even the symmetrical people needing the comforts of belief in personal immortality when confronting old age and death.[256] In this, Symonds was also the better Millian, consistently resisting the bribes of orthodox or even theistic belief in framing the "new religion."

Yet however serene these two – Symonds and Sidgwick – were trying to become in middle age, neither was really inclined to let ethics look after themselves. Work for the new religion took many forms, of course, but one of the most important involved appeal to the authority of science in the cause of legal reform. This was a most interesting denouement for Sidgwick's early positivistic phases, and for his cultural and educational ideal, with its consistent incorporation of the scientific attitude along with that of culture and many-sidedness. As another battle line in the academic liberal war against the influence of orthodox religion, it made tremendous good sense.

Certainly, legal reform was needed. As Symonds summarized the state of things, following the Labouchère Amendment of 1885: "Any act of 'gross indecency' between males, in private or public, is a Misdemeanour punishable with two years imprisonment and hard labour. Connection per anum, with or without consent, is a penal servitude for life." This, of course, was the law used against Wilde, the law that was supposed to be something of an advance over the previous use of capital punishment.

But as Symonds wrote a friend: "Whatever view the psychologist may take of homosexual passions, every citizen of a free country must feel that Labouchere's Clause is a disgrace to legislation, because of its vague terminology & plain incitement to false accusations." His course was clear, as he wrote to Ellis:

I am glad to hear that Arthur Symons told you what I wrote to him about a book on "Sexual Inversion," and that you are disposed to consider it.

This, I feel, is one of the psychological and physiological questions which demand an open treatment at last. The legal and social persecution of abnormal natures requires revision. And enquiry may lead to some light being thrown upon that *terra incognita*, the causes of sexual differentiation.

I have written and privately printed two treatises on this subject. One deals with the phenomenon as recognised and utilized in Ancient Greece; the other with the same phenomenon, under adverse conditions, in the modern world.

It is absolutely necessary to connect those two investigations in any philosophical handling of the problem. The so-called scientific "psychiatrists" are ludicrously in error, by diagnosing as necessarily morbid what was the leading emotion of the best and noblest men in Hellas. The ignorance of men like Casper-Liman, Tardieu, Carlier, Taxil, Moreau, Tarnowsky, Kraft-Ebing, Richard Burton is incalculable, and is only equalled to their presumption. They not only do not know Ancient Greece, but they do not know their own cousins and club-mates. The theory of morbidity is more humane, but it is not less false, than that of sin or vice.

If it were possible for us to collaborate in the production of an impartial and really scientific survey of the matter, I should be glad. I believe it might come from two men better than from one, in the present state of public opinion. I would contribute the historical analysis (ancient Greece), which I am sure must form a basis for the study. You are more competent than I am to criticize the crudest modern medical and forensico-medical theories. But I might be of use here by placing at your disposition what I have already done in "getting up" the material, and in collecting data of fresh cases. We should have to agree together about the *legal* aspects of the subject. I should not like to promulgate any book, which did not show the absurdity and injustice of the English law. The French and Italian Penal Codes are practically right, though their application is sometimes unfair. (Do not imagine that I want to be aggressive or polemical.)

I am almost certain that this matter will very soon attract a great deal of attention; and that it is a field in which pioneers may not only do excellent service to humanity, but also win the laurels of investigators and truth-seekers.

If you do not feel able to collaborate with me, I shall probably proceed to some form of solitary publication, and I should certainly give my name to anything I produced.[257]

Even if the great Whitman himself was reluctant to go this far, Symonds, as he put it to Whitman's disciple Traubel, is confident that "in Europe" there are "signs of an awakening of enthusiastic relations between men, which tend to assume a passionate character."[258]

Symonds brought to this task both his personal commitment and the larger perspectives of the cultural historian and proto-anthropologist, and his sense of the grotesque naïveté of the "medical men" was acute and perfectly justified. He seemed to be working almost in tandem with Sidgwick and the psychical researchers, in the effort to pay science its due while recognizing that many of the scientists were actually promoting their own religious or nonreligious agendas. For his part, Sidgwick was continuing to feel a very similar frustration. Elected to preside over a large London meeting of professional psychologists, he exclaimed in his journal: "Behold me then President elect of a Congress of Experimental Psychologists – most of them stubborn materialists, interested solely in psychophysical experiments on the senses; whereas *I* have never experimented except in telepathy. Water and fire, oil and vinegar, are feeble to express our antagonism!" (M 515–16)[259]

Thus, the sense that psychological science *might* be emancipatory, but mostly was not, formed a common bond between Sidgwick and Symonds. Their often overlapping visions of education recognized the limitations of both classicist notions of culture and scientistic notions of science, and sought to use each to correct the other. Both – Symonds with sex research, and Sidgwick with psychical – would begin exploring a larger, more participatory, and more depth psychological conception of scientific research. Just as the psychical researchers had been increasingly driven to regard their investigations as a cooperative venture between subject and object, the investigators and the investigated, that demanded a certain intimacy, so too would Symonds recognize that his investigations were premised on being able to give voice to those being investigated, a politicized business from beginning to end. As Jonathan Kemp has put it:

Unlike the *Memoirs*, however, Symonds's privately printed essay, *A Problem in Modern Ethics* (1891), which both Grosskurth and Weeks see as a counterpart to the *Memoirs*, circulated within the homosexual underground of the early 1890s, and it was undoubtedly a signal text in the emergence of a coherent sense of the 'homosexual' as a particular type of person/personality. Only 50 copies of the book were printed and, despite the appearance on the title page of the disclaimer

'Addressed especially to medical psychologists and jurists', it appears to have been sent out mainly to fellow-inverts.

Grosskurth testifies that Symonds received hundreds of letters from men who identified with *A Problem in Modern Ethics*, who saw within its pages a mirror-image of their own feelings; men whose lives were characterized by constant conflict and furtiveness. For the first time, men whose sexual interest was predominantly – if not exclusively – in other men could read about themselves in a way that did not classify their desires as the product of sin or sickness. The margins of *Modern Ethics* were wide open in order that recipients could return their copies with written comments, thus reversing the discourse and giving homosexuals a vehicle to speak out via this pseudo-scientific text, or, as Koestenbaum argues, making the readers collaborators. In this way, Symonds hoped to open up the debate to include inverts.[260]

But this pragmatizing of sex research was, like Sidgwick's psychical research, as much a challenge to medical discourse in the name of cultural history as a ratification of its terms. The "vulgar," it seems, were to be found across all classes and professions. And the "better vulgar" of science needed more poetry and personal experience, as well as greater historical understanding. The sympathy of Apostolic-style friendship was indeed crucial to inquiry after all. Intimacy and growth, education in the larger transfigurative mode – this was the common currency of Symonds's Oxford and Sidgwick's Cambridge, at least in their visions.

Still, as always, Sidgwick was given to fits of depression over just what his own personal touch might produce. As we have seen, time and again he found himself concluding that he left a great deal to be desired as an inspirer – he would speak candidly if doubting students came to him, but otherwise he would train their faculties and leave their faith alone. He was no Green, nor did he have Symonds's talents for raising the dead or Cowell's for communicating with them. He was, quite simply, too conscientious, too careful, and too skeptical, more Cloughian than Whitmanian. John Scott Lidgett, one of Maurice's most distinguished disciples, noted how Sidgwick's intellect acted as cold water on reforming zeal:

Dr. Paton, Dr. Percival – then Bishop of Hereford – and others were seeking to constrain the Government to revise the restrictive conditions which at that time made the establishment of Evening Continuation Schools difficult, if not altogether impossible. I was requested to approach Professor Sidgwick on their behalf, in order to secure his signature to the Memorial they had prepared for submission to the Minister of Education. Unfortunately, however, for this purpose, the Memorial spoke of this object as "the most important educational reform" then urgent. But Professor Sidgwick wrote to tell me that he was unable to sign because, though in full sympathy with the Memorialists, he could not conscientiously say that the proposed reform, though very important, was "the *most* important" education improvement that was then called for! It is to be feared that such meticulous exactitude and sense of proportion, while no doubt desirable, would, as things go, chill and check the endeavours of many enthusiastic reformers, who can only secure the necessary momentum for their efforts by seeing them as, for the time being, the one and only end of social improvement.[261]

Just as he worried about his effect on Myers, so he worried about his effect on so many others, including Symonds. Surely this made for some painful dilemmas, especially when following out his own "intellectual process" seemed to drive away the "phenomena" he was seeking to explore, whether spirits or Symonds's homoerotic feelings. Too often, he seemed to himself to be the monster in the closet. And he was, after all, an educator and a reformer. He did not leave Cambridge. He remained in his post, and it is interesting that in the section of the *Memoir* following the bit to Symonds about the "Infinite duty" to be serene, Eleanor and Arthur comment:

Sidgwick was liable to periods of depression all his life after his illness as an undergraduate, generally accompanied – perhaps caused – by a tendency to lie awake at night. During the latter part of his life he used, as indicated in the passage just quoted, to make a great effort to conceal depression from those he was with. To a great extent he succeeded, and he found the effort beneficial to himself. He never took drugs to relieve sleeplessness. He had been warned against this by a doctor early in life, and never wavered from the principle he had adopted. Nor did he read in bed; he generally found it best to lie still, and get rest if he could not get sleep. He used to find making plans for the future a soothing occupation under these circumstances. (M 486)

Who was the crisis–driven dipsychic now? Perhaps, like Plato, Sidgwick feared the lower self that came out in dreams. Intriguing it is that he was fantasizing an independent literary life with plenty of European travel – Symonds's life, to be sure. Intriguing as well that he may have been masking his depression from his friend, sensing a want of sympathy there or perhaps, once again, a potentially deleterious impact on his part – or both. Symonds may have cast doubt on his convictions about normality and sought to dethrone Philosophy, but to Sidgwick's mind, his friend had not grasped the horror of an unfriendly universe in which death is the end and reason is powerless, much less the pain of the age of transition.

Clearly, Sidgwick had a lot to be depressed about. The work of reform went on, but he was not as serene about how the future was shaping up as Symonds or his other friends were. Why did he stay in Cambridge? There was no one reason; duty beckoned from many different sides. With psychical research, there were, as noted in the previous chapter, some big developments in 1888, just when all seemed to be lost. Partly, this resulted from the tragic death of Gurney; as the journal records:

Edmund Gurney died in a hotel at Brighton on Friday night (22? June). Arthur Myers was telegraphed for on Saturday morning: on Saturday evening and Sunday the calamity was communicated by him to one or two relatives and friends. Nora and I and Fred Myers learnt it (from Arthur M) on Sunday. The inquest took place on the Monday: but the news was not generally known in London till the Tuesday. On Sunday in London Miss F. a friend of Fred Myers, known to him (and to me) through psychical research, – who has already had more than one apparently telepathic impression – wrote the following lines in her diary (which Myers has seen)

"Sun. Is Mr Myers in trouble? Involuntary, and I hope meaningless note of sympathy floating by my mind since yesterday morning. Wrote it down but still present. 'one offers an expression of sympathy chiefly perhaps for one's own sake, – for all else silence is best. Your friend is out of sight, your fellow-worker still with you. Believe this I speak as one who knows.'

What *can* this mean?"

Miss F says that the 'note of sympathy' was written down by her on a separate scrap of paper on Saturday evening, after floating in her mind since the morning: and then copied into her diary on Sunday. She had no idea what it could mean: she only felt a vague dread of some calamity having happened to Myers; which led her to call on another friend of his on the Monday, on the chance of hearing what (if anything) had happened. She is quite sure she knew nothing of E.G.'s death till the Tuesday. We think her a perfectly trustworthy witness.

Can this be pure coincidence? If not, what can be the explanation? This we anxiously ask ourselves. (CWC)

Again, Gurney's death galvanized the psychical researchers, and the positive turn this work took through the 1890s was undoubtedly one reason why Sidgwick felt that his academic prestige was still needed by the society, which he again headed. When he blazed forth, if he ever did, it was to be with maximal efficacy.

But there was much else going on as well, though on many fronts the story was less encouraging. The 1880s were for Sidgwick a decade of extremely active academic politicking, politicking which had taken its toll. And there was a certain Whitmanian flavor, paradoxical as that may sound, to his work for the "general academic reorganisation." The *Memoir* explains how important the new statutes proposed by the university commission were, when they came into effect in 1882. The new "General Board of Studies" was to carry out this major program of reorganization, and Sidgwick would be much involved with it: "Sidgwick joined the General Board, when it was first constituted in November 1882, as the representative of the Special Board for Moral Science, and, with the brief interruption caused by his absence in Italy in the Lent term of 1883, served on it continuously till the end of 1899," by which time he had partly lost interest in administration because Cambridge "had seemed to him to show want of adequately progressive action in several instances" (M 371).

But work with the General Board was to be an exceedingly difficult and painful task:

Among the most important duties of the new Board was that of administering to the best advantage a common fund for University purposes composed of contributions exacted from the Colleges by the new statutes – contributions which were to increase at intervals of three years to a stated maximum. By means of this additional income the University was to establish Professorships, Readerships, and University Lectureships, to increase the emoluments attached to some of the existing Professorships, to provide necessary buildings, and otherwise to enlarge its work and render it more efficient; and it was the business of the General Board to co-ordinate the demands of different departments so as to present to the University a workable scheme which should give the utmost efficiency possible under the circumstances. When, however, the demands of the Special Boards were formulated it became "immediately obvious," as the General Board said in a report in May 1883, "that the funds at the disposal of the University would be for the present wholly inadequate to supply the wants which the several Boards considered to be urgent," and it will be seen that the work of adjusting these claims was necessarily a very delicate and difficult one. The difficulty was, moreover, greatly increased by the unforeseen effect of agricultural depression, which by impoverishing the Colleges, whose property was and is largely agricultural, rendered it impossible to exact from them the full tax counted on by the Commissioners in framing the statutes. (M 371–72)

Naturally, however, this project of academic reform was "an object which Sidgwick had long had in view and had long been working for." It was, he hoped, to be turned in the direction of the academic liberals:

He desired on the one hand to extend the influence of the University, and to open its doors as widely as possible to different classes of serious students, and on the other so to organise the teaching offered as not only to provide as far as possible for all subjects required, and (for industrious students) do away with the need of private tuition, but also to avoid the overlapping, and consequent waste of funds and energy, apt to arise from the separate organisation of the Colleges.

This he took very, very seriously:

Of his desire to open the doors of the University to different classes of students his work for women is an example, but by no means the only one. The maintenance and development of teaching for Indian Civil Servants was an object to which he devoted both time and money, and in May 1883, when there had been some question, on pecuniary grounds, of discontinuing the attempt to provide adequately for them, he said, in a discussion in the Arts Schools, that his own "opinion was well known that research should be much more considered and encouraged in the University than now; still, the discredit of abandoning the connection with these students [Indian Civil Servants] would be so grave that he would rather postpone important research than incur the loss." The view here expressed is typical; he sympathised with every effort to enlarge the field of University influence both on the literary and scientific sides, and the development of departments of study which by some were viewed with distrust as too narrowly professional, such as – besides the Indian Civil Service studies – engineering, agriculture, and the training of teachers, was always encouraged by him. His desire to extend the sphere of influence of the University in the interest of sound learning was one of the reasons which made him wish that the imposition of Greek on all its members would be done away with, since he believed that this would make it possible for the University to put itself at the head, as it were, of the modern sides of schools as well as of the classical sides, and also at the head of those "modern" schools, already numerous and certain to increase, of whose curriculum Greek was not a regular part. (M 372–73)

The aim here was less that of Mr. Gradgrind than that of Green and Symonds, who agreed about the Greek. It is not in the least to be wondered at that he "had on the Board a few strong opponents, and many half-convinced supporters who might turn at any time into opponents," or that he won a reputation as "a very dangerous person." "Himself a professor, and a *very* conscientious one, he took a large and generous view of the work which a professor should be expected to do. The professors, however, resented the proposed regulations." (M 377, 378, 375)[262] It was at this time that he received the severe dressing-down from Alfred Marshall.

Now, it is certainly appropriate to wonder just how elitist such educational work was. This talk of opening the university to all classes did not, it would seem, translate into any actual reverence for political democracy in and of itself, much less for revolutionary economic reform. Indeed, the new Whitmanian rhetoric often had a lot in common with the old Mauricean Christian socialism or Millian agnostic socialism, allowing for the celebration both of fellowship and of a guiding intellectual aristocracy, a clerisy.

The attitude was happily captured in a piece by Roden Noel explaining the significance of Whitman and how his views demanded qualification:

[I]s equality a truth in the manner in which he asserts it? I believe not; and if not, it must be so far mischievous to assert it. That common manhood is a greater, more cardinal fact than any distinctions among men which raise one above another I most firmly believe. Still these distinctions do exist, and so palpable a fact cannot be ignored without very serious injury. If great men could not have been without average men, and owe most to the grand aggregate soul of the ideal unit, humanity – which is a pregnant truth – yet, on the other hand, this grand aggregate soul could never have been what it is, could never have been enriched with the treasures it now enjoys, without those most personal of all personalities – prophets, heroes, men of genius. . . . I do not believe that the mere proclamation of friendly love as between comrades (any more than of sexual love and equal union between man and woman) is at all sufficient. Veneration, reverence, also must be proclaimed, as likewise necessary; and the great point we ought to aim at, in helping to solve the momentous question of the social future, seems in that respect to be this – that mankind be taught, and gradually accustomed, to place their reverence where reverence is indeed due, and not upon mere idols of popular superstition.[263]

This passage explains what to many has seemed either absolutely ludicrous or utterly hypocritical about the English Whitmanians – that is, the way in which so many of them could celebrate Whitman without abandoning or compromising their vanguardist belief in some sort of clerisy or intellectual aristocracy that would play a vital role in cultural and political leadership and reform. Whitman is valuable in that "he corrects the prevalent tending of advanced thought to rely on more or less questionable social Utopias, leaving the nature of individuals unchanged; teaching that each is honourable in his own position and calling." However, he "is defective in not granting more unreservedly the need of spiritual regeneration, and of that heavenlier Civil Constitition, or City of God, which the noblest have ever anticipated and aspired to as slow and sure consummation of such regeneration, social and individual."[264] Perhaps Whitman himself "may be so morally well-knit, and sweet-natured that he may not need that repentance and renewal, which the Tannhäusers amongst us, and the average men, do so sadly, and unquestionably require." Still, he "does now and then distinctly acknowledge the claims of greatness to lead mankind, insisting on the supreme worth of ideal manhood, strong mastering personality."[265]

Noel's *Essays on Poetry and Poets* was dedicated to none other than Symonds, who had enthusiastically encouraged him to publish it. And it won Sidgwick's approval as well: "For relaxation from 'Value' and 'Capital' I have been reading and meditating on Roden Noel's book. On the whole I find it solidly satisfactory: and it removes a lurking fear in my mind that in spite of his originality, vigour, and flow of ideas he would be found not exactly to 'come off' as an essayist – would, in fact be rather eccentric than original." Of course, "the fundamental difference between him and me is that he thinks the Poet has Insight into Truth, instead of merely emotions and an Art of expressing them." (CWC)

Even so, the poets, like the subjects of psychical research, are for Sidgwick all-important as vehicles for getting at the emotions, for understanding the true self and reforming the current one. Feeling, not Thought, is the source of ultimate value, but it needs cultivating, and Sidgwick wanted the modern curriculum to include modern literature for just that reason. It had to be studied with all the care an Apostle could muster. As a later, Bloomsbury Apostle, E. M. Forster, put it: "The poet wrote the poem, no doubt, but he forgot himself while he wrote it, and we forget him while we read. What is so wonderful about great literature is that it transforms the man who reads it towards the condition of the man who wrote, and brings to birth in us also the creative impulse."[266]

Needless to say, Sidgwick himself was constitutionally incapable of being the whole-hearted Whitmanian worshipper of the people, much as he was touched by the efforts of Symonds and Noel. If he shared much with them by way of the search for a new synthesis and new casuistry, and a sense of the incoherence of commonsense morality and the importance of the investigation of the deepest problems via intimate conversation, the appreciation of art, and so forth, he was for all that inclined to worry about "powerful uneducated persons," not to celebrate or seduce them. He did, under the influence of his friends, descend somewhat from the Apostolic pedestal, allowing that "constructing a Theory of Right" cannot "be thoroughly well done by philosophers alone," because they must learn from people "in the thick and heat of the struggle of active life, in all stations and ranks, in the churches and outside the churches" (PE 20, 22). Entering into the Universal Heart of Humanity did, he now realized, involve experiencing the messy realities of actual people. But in the end, he remained the more critical, Millian philosopher who tended to view his friends' lives as challenging experiments for testing the horizons of happiness, for demonstrating the potential of new cultural alternatives capable of fostering happiness and avoiding social strife in a post-Christian era. His Millianism was eclectic enough to appropriate elements of these visions for the effort to advance culture and education. After all, Mill and Maurice agreed about the importance of poeticizing life, and how could Sidgwick resist any plea to foster sympathetic friendship for the sake of reform? Still, Whitmania, like Idealism, was always set against his Apostolic conscience and his skeptical doubts.

Quite possibly Symonds and Noel were not all that radical either. Eve Sedgwick has dismissed Symonds as a "glib rationalizer," by comparison with the genuine Whitmanian socialist Carpenter, even on matters of sex: "the difference between Symonds' political ideal and the bourgeois English actuality of sexual exploitation, for cash, of proletarian men and women is narrow and arbitrary. It seems to lie mostly in the sanguine Whitmanian coloration of Symonds' rhetoric and erotic investment."[267] This is too harsh, but it is true that Symonds's rejection of "civilization" was not as radical as Carpenter's activism; it was a very selective affair that managed to think well of most of Sidgwick's academic reformist efforts.

Indeed, the practical task, whether for Mill and Maurice or for Sidgwick and Symonds, was how to make their visions of culture and cultural advance flourish, fostering some new balance of friendship and individuality, comradeship and greatness. And curiously, given the masculinist overtones of talk of Dorian comradeship and individual greatness – especially pronounced in Symonds and Noel – all of these figures held that a crucial part of the program involved supporting higher education for women. Indeed, Sidgwick's most famous reformist efforts, the arena in which he could claim to rival Green as an inspirer, concerned women's higher education. It was work in this connection that specially illustrates

Sidgwick's dilemmas during the 1880s. If his frustration with the General Board and the SPR had contributed to his depression in 1887 and 1888, so had his work for Newnham College.

This is not to deny that he found this "positive" side of his reformism quite rewarding. He certainly did, and his collaboration with Eleanor in this endeavour – with Newnham College, Cambridge as their enduring monument – well illustrates just how far he was willing to go in translating the Apostolic ideal of friendship into the Millian ideal of friendship between the sexes. If in the process he clung to his tactic of reserving his deepest teaching for the elect who were already on his rocky path – the kind of Apostolic personal education that flourished in the closets of the universities – he nonetheless devoted a remarkable amount of energy to less esoteric modes of improving his students, fostering the Millian vision of culture that had always defined his larger educational ideal.

Of course, the longer the Sidgwicks worked for the cause, the less they were given to the more nervous, cautionary aspects of Millian agnosticism (not the aspects that Mill and Taylor had emphasized, to be sure). Their experience, or "experiments," with the women of Newnham suggested that women would be able to meet any test that men might throw down. In contrast to those of their parapsychological research, their "results" in this domain were altogether positive, except when it came to the conservative reaction against them from a very threatened male establishment.

The story of the Sidgwicks and Newnham has been well told by Rita McWilliams Tullberg, in her *Women at Cambridge*.[268] As she shows in detail, the Sidgwicks' work for Newnham was almost from the start caught up in an unfortunate rivalry with Emily Davies's work for Girton, which had actually begun at neighboring Hitchin:

As early as 1870, Emily Davies and her committee were considering plans for building a college, the location of which was again a point of controversy. Sidgwick pointed out the advantages of joining forces; a college built in Cambridge meant a ready supply of lecturers and the chance for women to attend the public lectures of University professors. The Hitchin scheme had proved very expensive and this had been a deterrent to many students. But Emily Davies could not agree with Sidgwick; she objected strongly to the use made of the examinations for women and had very definite views on the dangers of siting her college in the University town. For his part, Sidgwick objected to the use of the Previous, and the official connection which the Hitchin college had with the Established Church.

Co-operation was impossible; Emily Davies and Henry Sidgwick went their own ways.[269]

Perhaps McWilliams Tullberg should have said that they went forward into a relationship of intense and heated rivalry. Davies once described Sidgwick's work as "the serpent gnawing at our vitals."

Still, it is far from clear that Sidgwick and his group were wrong to be unimpressed with the notion of exactly identical treatment for women and men. Sidgwick wanted women's education to be better than that of men – after all, men's education was precisely what he had been trying to improve. As Hunt and Barker have summarized the points at issue, Davies

and her supporters saw the creation of any special rules and exceptions for women as fundamentally unhelpful to their cause. In particular, they believed that anything that made women's education easier would devalue women's accomplishments. By contrast, Sidgwick's goal was to improve women's higher education, and he was willing to make separate arrangments for women (such as the Higher Locals) if these were likely to improve women's participation in higher education. At the same time, Sidgwick was a vocal campaigner for university reform in other areas, and combined other efforts with his campaign for women's status.[270]

Sidgwick was perfectly frank about the worthlessness of the Previous Examination (the fourth-term university exams requiring Greek and Latin) and the Pass Degree – more so than he was about the worthlessness of Christian theology – and he could not see the point of subjecting women to the same bad schemes that had been inflicted on men. This would turn out to be a lifelong cause; as he put it to the Royal Commission on Secondary Education in 1894:

I think that no reform in our academic system is at present so urgently needed as a change in the previous examination which would bring it into correlation with the modern system of education, now so widely established in secondary schools; and I trust that the influence of the Commission will be directed to the attainment of that end. I think that the change would tend ultimately to improve the quality of classical as well as of modern education; since it would render it easier to raise the standard of knowledge of Latin and Greek required from boys trained in the classical system.

I may observe that in this respect the relation of both Cambridge and Oxford to the school education of girls is in a far more satisfactory condition, since both universities have refrained, in the case of women, from requiring a knowledge of

Latin and Greek as a condition of entering the examinations that test academic work. (CWC)[271]

Newnham did in fact thrive with a crowd of independent spirits, highly motivated and scarcely open to any charge of seeking laxer standards. And this without benefit of so much as a chapel.

In any event, there can be no doubt about Sidgwick's devotion to the cause. He was first drawn into the business in the 1860s, when he was concerned with the problems confronting governesses and school mistresses, who often complained of inadequate training. From 1871, when he leased premises on Regent Street to provide a residence for the handful of women students coming to Cambridge to take advantage of the lectures being offered, to 1875, when the first permanent building of Newnham opened, to the triumph of 1881, when women gained the right to take the Tripos examinations, to the bitter and unsuccessful campaigns of the late 1880s and 1890s for full university membership for women, Sidgwick devoted as much time and money to this work as he possibly could. With the help of the Balfour fortune, the Sidgwicks effectively built out of their own pockets much of the Newnham that stands today, though it took until 1947 for the university to finally grant the demands they were making in the 1880s and 1890s.

The Sidgwicks oversaw this creation with considerable shrewdness and academic skill. Nowhere was this more evident than in their recruit for the first principal position:

Miss Clough was already 51 when she came to Cambridge; she was the sister of Arthur Hugh Clough, poet and principal of University hall, London, who had set up lectures and classes for girls in Liverpool, her home city, Manchester, Leeds and Sheffield. By 1867 she had created the North of England Council for the Promotion of the Higher Education of Women, and this was one of the inspirations which led Owens College, Manchester, to consider admitting women in 1869 – and so to the admission of women to the Victoria University comprising Manchester, Liverpool and Leeds when it was formed in 1878. Sidgwick (himself a Yorkshireman) and several of his colleagues had met her through these lectures, and been impressed by her ability and dedication. She represented a very distinct national element in the formation of Newnham.[272]

Doubtless Sidgwick did sometimes fall into an overly cautious approach to reform, as in his 1887 opposition to a move for full membership for women because of his conviction that this would only be defeated and prove counterproductive – might in fact end by undoing the gains made, of their sitting the Tripos and being awarded a certificate if they passed. This was an ugly dispute, with Sidgwick inadvertently creating much tension between Newnham and Girton. As McWilliams Tullberg explains:

The dispute caused confusion amongst the women at Newnham. Sidgwick's influence was very strong there; his wife . . . was Vice-Principal of the College and shouldered an increasing amount of responsibility as Anne Clough grew old. If the University was going to receive Memorials from groups supporting and opposing women in Cambridge, Newnham could hardly stay silent. But their dilemma was, as Helen Gladstone (at that time Eleanor Sidgwick's secretary) put it, 'to compose a memorial so as not to ask for degrees, but not to appear to reject them if they are offered.' Sidgwick made this delicate situation even more difficult by bringing the dispute into the open. In a letter to the *Daily News* on 1 July 1887, he explained his opposition to the London Committee's plans. He was not opposed in principle to the identity of conditions for the two sexes in University examinations and he supported in principle the idea of a mixed university. But he believed that the demand for degrees was inopportune and impolitic, since it was too soon to judge the effect of Newnham and Girton on the life of the University. Further, if women gained admission at the expense of having to take the Previous examination, they would have struck an extremely bad bargain. He suggested that the matter be dropped for four or five years, by which time the Greek of the Little-Go might have disappeared and there could be less talk of 'inexperience' of the effects of women on the University environment. The issues were now becoming clearer. Sidgwick wanted the women to have their degrees; his real worry was that imposing the Previous on women candidates would lengthen the life of the examination that he was so committed to change. Emily Davies' brother, Llewelyn Davies, who replied to Sidgwick in the columns of the same paper four days later, quickly pointed out the opposite interpretation to him. He too was opposed to compulsory Greek, but in his opinion the prescription would be abolished all the sooner if women were involved in it, since it would then be very clearly unreasonable. Who might have been right is a matter for conjecture, though Llewelyn Davies was quite mistaken if he thought reason would be the guiding star in Cambridge disputes about Greek.[273]

That is putting it mildly. Indeed, the stunning unreason of which Cambridge was capable became clear less in the debate over Greek than in that over admitting women to degrees. Sidgwick was ever the cautious reformer, fearing backlash. Unfortunately, he was mostly right. All that came of the pleas that Cambridge should get with the times and, like the newer universities, recognize women was an inflammation of reactionary feelings in favor of traditional, "special" Cambridge. College life was, for so many Cambridge men, essentially a period of male bonding to set the stage for mature life; to have women in the middle of it, as opposed to having them as a few second-class citizens off in their own colleges and available for dating, would be an intolerable intrusion. In February of 1888, the Council of the Senate met to consider the case for granting women full membership, and the result was precisely what Sidgwick had feared: the university would make no more concessions.

As we have seen, circa 1887–88, about everything that could possibly go wrong for Sidgwick was going wrong. This crisis with his cherished cause of women's higher education was surely another weighty factor in his depression, rivaling the crisis of the SPR. And what followed was certainly cause for further gloom. Throughout most of the 1890s, work for women's higher education at Cambridge was cause for discouragement after discouragement, coming as it did from the university upon which he had pinned so many of his reformist hopes. Virtually no progress was made in the 1890s; in fact, when the issue of full membership was pressed again, in 1897, the defeat was even nastier, with jeering undergraduates hanging an effigy of a gowned women in bloomers outside the Senate House and terrorizing the town with bonfires and firecrackers. After the voting, the dons lined up in the Senate House yard to await the result. But "Someone threw a cracker over the palings and this was the signal for the commencement of a general bombardment. Cooped up like sheep in a pen, the devoted dons, some thousands in number, were pelted with fireworks of every description, while smoke rose in clouds over their heads."[274]

Sidgwick, who missed the battle because he had returned to Newnham immediately after voting, really did not by this point require any further confirmation of his opinion that the University was caught up in a "hidebound and stupid conservatism." Indeed, he had again feared a bad reaction, but was reluctantly pressed into coming forth, arguing passionately:

The University of Cambridge in 1881 gave the substance; it is now considering whether or not it should give the symbol. You have evidence laid before you, showing that the symbol is required to produce a due popular valuation of what our students trained here have done and the examinations they have successfully passed. The symbol is required, but it would be a great mistake to suppose that the country taken as a whole is so unintelligent as to value the symbol more than the substance. That is not the case. The view throughout the circles in which the truth with regard to educational matters is known, is that the Universities have already taken the most important step. That in my view is the reason why it is not only the interest of women, but I should say, quite as much the interest of the University to take the further step that is to-day proposed. From the point of view of the provinces the question of membership falls into a subordinate place. What they mean by a degree is a recognised stamp of the fact that the student has successfully passed through a course of education at Oxford or Cambridge. They cannot understand your action in refusing it. At first they do not believe it; they do not believe when they are told that the students of Newnham and Girton have passed through the same course as the undergraduate students pass through. When they do believe it, they think the University is either absurd or unjust. You will remove that impression throughout the country, I believe, by adopting the recommendations of the Syndicate. (M 550–51)

Perhaps it was good that Sidgwick did not live to see the further defeats of the cause in the early twentieth century. As Richard Symonds has observed, a year after Oxford admitted women (in 1920), when the question again came before the Cambridge University Senate:

[O]nce more the dinosaurs staggered in from their rural dens to vote. The proposal to give women full membership of the University was defeated by 904 to 712. Many of the clergy, who often had daughters at Cambridge or other universities, had been converted. Much of the opposition now came from the medical profession and the scientists who stressed the physiological and psychological differences between men and women. Once more male students rioted and even damaged the memorial gates of Newnham. Menaced by the possibility of interference by a Royal Commission and by Parliament, the Senate now conceded that women might write BA after their names. It was not until 1948 however that they became full members of the University with the same standing as men in its governance.[275]

Thus, Sidgwick's feminist reformist work was to suffer a fate similar to that of his reformist work with Symonds, with the medical and psychiatric establishments proving to be as bad as the Christian Church when it came to the disciplinary "normalizing" of sex and gender roles. No doubt he would have recalled his experience with the scientific opposition to the SPR, or how slow Cambridge had been to allow Fellows to marry.

If Sidgwick's pessimism about what the university was ripe for turned out to be all too apt, he could at various times have gone on record with a more emphatic Millian statement. A planned article on "Women," like a planned article on Mill, apparently never got written, and consequently one must piece together his feminist views from various bits and pieces of evidence. Like Mill and Taylor, he was much more than a "first-wave" feminist calling for thin legal equality. The Sidgwicks came to appreciate just how much was riding on changing the nature of the family, work, love, and so on.

To be sure, as indicated, the Sidgwicks did evolve in their feminist understandings over the course of their careers. Olive Banks, in *The Biographical Dictionary of British Feminists*, argues that:

Like that of her husband, Nora's feminism developed slowly and when she was first involved with Newnham she had doubted whether women were either intellectually or physically fit for a full university education. These doubts were eventually resolved, and by 1896 she was fully committed to equality in the higher education of men and women. Nevertheless, she continued to believe that marriage and motherhood was the natural career for a woman, and that most women would choose marriage rather than a career if the opportunity came. By the 1880s, however, she was an enthusiastic supporter of women's suffrage and always presided at pro-suffrage lectures given at the college. She was, however, never drawn into sympathy for the militant movement, believing that it damaged women's reputation for good sense.[276]

As previously remarked, Henry, back in the days of the Initial Society, had also had a somewhat limited view of the matter. Elaborating on the theme of the inferior man, he had argued:

How can we assume that happiness is 'intended' to be the lot of all on earth – The question arises here as so often, are we speaking of the few or the many. The Few (for whom I have an unfeigned admiration) can find their happiness in self-culture or some absorbing enthusiasm. But the many *need* domestic life. Otherwise they become either selfish (the greatest misery) or they find, in spite of the most conscientious efforts, a want of solid interest in the world. Is it practically any use telling the mass of women that when they can't get married they must take an interest in politics, speculation, poetry, music etc.? No doubt the best thing for them is to get some active work of benevolence: but even this won't fill the void. (Holme Lee describes this well in one of her novels, Kathie Brande, I think). As to 'old maids' I do not think that if they make themselves worthy of respect they fail to obtain it: but we cannot blink the fact that for very many women the only chance of proper development as well as happiness is matrimony: this alone can give them depth: otherwise they remain frivolous and trivial to the end of their days. I except of course the *few* whom society does not prevent embracing a profession. I confess that the more I think of it the less I can blame such women for their much-satirized efforts to obtain a husband.[277]

As he went on to explain, he did not think

celibacy a unique evil, considered in its effect on general happiness. . . . This being the case it always seems to me rather a noble thing for a person of great natural elevation not to marry, except under peculiar circumstances. If other human relations develop in us an equal flow of love and energy (the primary and paramount branch of self culture) there is no doubt that the greater freedom of celibacy, the higher self denial of its work, the time it leaves for useful but unlucrative pursuits, the material means it places at our disposal for the advantage of our fellow-creatures ought to have great weight in the balance.

Sidgwick concludes that he entirely agrees with Elisabeth Rhodes "as to the immense educational influence in the hands of single women, if they are but trained to see and use it." They could be the "leaven in the loaf" – as Mary Ward and Jane Addams, among others, would ultimately demonstrate.

Sidgwick had also informed the Society:

Always argue with a man, if at all, in private: with a woman, if at all, in public. A man wants not to convince so much as to conquer: he does not care so much about the opinion you hold in your heart, but he wishes to prove the opinion you express to be inferior to his own. By arguing in public you stimulate his vanity too much. A woman does not argue for conquest but for harmony: she does not care about proving your statements absurd, she wishes you to surrender your inner convictions to hers: her anxiety to do this may grow undesirably intense if you argue with her in private; while in public this danger is lessened, as she will most likely have one of the company on her side: finding the agreement she wants somewhere, she will care not more than enough about finding it in you.[278]

Yet it is not quite obvious just when Sidgwick took himself to be describing gender roles and when endorsing them. Certainly, his entire conception of Apostolic inquiry weighed in against the masculinist view of argument as "conquest," as opposed to listening and sympathetically drawing out. There was at least a Millian particle in his outlook even in the early 1860s, when it came to thinking of the potential of marriage as a school of sympathy for the inferior person but also as something to which there ought to be other options. And by the time Mill died, Sidgwick was quite willing to express just how much admiration he had for the more "radical" of Mill's writings:

> On the other hand his essays on *Liberty* and *The Subjection of Women*, though somewhat less close and careful in argument than his larger works, have great literary excellence, and were perhaps the most effective of his writings – perhaps because the intense enthusiasm for human progress which the studied composure of his philosophical style partly conceals was allowed freer expression in these popular essays. This is not the place to speak of Mill's public career; but our notice would be incomplete if we did not dwell for a moment on the simple and noble passion for the universal realization of a high ideal of human well-being which burns like a hidden flame at the core of his social philosophy.[279]

Shortly before he died, Mill had "come forward like a woman" to donate money to Newnham for creating scholarships.

Early on in his reform efforts, Sidgwick discovers, as he wrote to his supporter Oscar Browning, that "I am growing fond of women. I like working with them. I begin to sympathise with the pleasures of the mild parson." (M 247) By this point, in fact, Sidgwick could be very far from mild – even fairly scorching – in his response to hypocritical opposition to Millian feminism. In his review of James Fitzjames Stephen's harsh attack on Mill and all that Mill stood for, Sidgwick sarcastically countered that Stephen

> is unexpectedly checked by the consideration that any minute examination of the differences between men and women is – not exactly indecent, but – 'unpleasant in the direction of indecorum.' We should be sorry to encourage any remarks calculated to raise a blush in the cheek of a Queen's Counsel: but as the only conceivable ground for subjecting women, as a class, to special disabilities, must lie in the differences between them and men, it is obviously impossible to decide on the justice – or if Mr. Stephen prefers it, the 'expediency' – of those disabilities, without a careful examination of these differences. And in fact Mr Stephen's sudden delicacy does not suffice to hinder him from deciding the question with his usual rough dogmatism: it only renders his discussion of it more than usually narrow and commonplace.[280]

Arguably, when Symonds took his "scientific" turn, it was partly under the influence of such arguments used on behalf of feminism (and Ellis was insisting that they needed to address female as well as male inversion). At least, Sidgwick was consistent across the board when it came to thinking these subjects fit for impartial inquiry. He would have none of the stupid jokes that constituted most of the conservative opposition. As he wrote of Courthope's long poem "Ludibria Lunae," an "'allegorical burlesque' intended to satirise the efforts of women to get rid of their Subjection," Courthope was "hampered by the nature of his subject," since, although no "topic offers more facilities to a satirist than the Emancipation of Women," the "fertility of the field has attracted reapers, and most of the quips, gibes, and taunts that the subject affords have been already harvested by the comic and semi-comic Conservative journals."[281] He was hopeful about the prospects for women's higher education, he wrote to his mother, because "all of the jokes have been made."

If Henry and Eleanor were not quite destined to go down in history as on a level with John and Harriet, there was nonetheless a remarkable degree of Millian friendship in their relationship. And it must be said that there was a good deal of gender bending in the Sidgwick marriage. As Ethel Sidgwick, her niece, described Eleanor:

Calculation, comparison, neat adjustment of means to ends, were her lifelong habit. She liked fundamentals, the bones of things, and would, if she could, have touched and handled materials. Miss Edith Sharpley described once how she came on her in early days with Miss Clough, walking about planks and over builder's litter in the foundations of what would one day be North hall – only the air, at present, overhead. Such surrounding would have suited her.

Mrs. Sidgwick was called over-critical, like her husband. She was 'cold.' In a Victorian world of overflowing feelings, and 'charming' letter-writers, she thought statistically, and wrote sparingly, with a kind of dainty precision – locking each statement behind her as she went. But she loved the exercise of her art, whatever it might be called: it was satisfaction and relief. After one of the most cruel sorrows of her life, she confessed in private that to work out, in solitude, a problem in mathematics relieved her heart more than any condolences. She gently pressed her favourite study on others, teachers or learners whom she was asked to address; and the only passage in her writing that might be called purple is in its praise.[282]

Small wonder that Symonds could write to Mrs. Clough:

I saw Miss Balfour in London. She is very quiet, but impressive. A fine mixture of intellect & birth & breeding & feminine bonté and self-composed personality. Of course I do not know her, & only record a first impression. But there seems to be a general consent that she is the right woman for H. S. He meanwhile is perfectly happy & declares that now he comprehends emotion for the first time. Yet he has written a book on Ethics![283]

Symonds would remain impressed, going on record as admitting that Mrs. Sidgwick was up to any challenge put to her.

Interestingly, Eleanor apparently regarded her marriage to Henry as in some respects a liberation from the domestic bondage of looking after her brothers, to whom she had become a substitute mother. When Henry began courting her in the 1870s, she slyly deployed one of the notes he sent to her at Carlton Gardens. It "began: 'My dear Miss Balfour', and finished, after some business, 'I want sympathy, yours best of all, if you will give it to me. . . .' Miss Balfour had laid this sheet open on the chimney piece, for the brothers to see, 'Hullo, what's Sidgwick writing 'my dear' to Nora for?' they asked in turn as they took it up."[284]

Again, to his credit, Sidgwick was always warmly supportive of Eleanor's intellectual, academic, and political interests. He was delighted when Eleanor became principal of Newnham, ungrudgingly giving up their privacy and their unhappy haunted house at Hillside to move back into a college: "the more I think of it the more I feel that the position of appendage to the Principal is one I was born to fit. . . . You will have all the responsibility for the entertainment and I shall have only the function of free critic."[285]

Such modesty was somewhat false – Sidgwick was a very busy person when it came to this work. As McWilliams Tullberg puts it: in "this era of educational reform, young dons like Sidgwick undertook college lectures, inter-college lectures, extension lectures, lectures to women outside Cambridge, advanced classes and coaching to resident women, and in some cases acted as correspondence tutors, as well as serving on various University Syndicates and College Committees."[286] And Sidgwick did more than most, beavering away at everything from correspondence courses to workingmen's colleges to plans to set up an entirely new university.[287] At his best, he was nudging the reformism of Maurice and Mill toward the reformism of Addams and Dewey, even establishing a Teacher's Training College.

The move to Newnham, it should be explained, was in some ways an antidote to Sidgwick's later depression, though it did involve a severe pruning of the Sidgwick library:

The trial, in the first year of her Principalship, must have been severe, the more for its agitating effect on her husband. In April, sorrow came on him, – John Addington Symonds died in Rome: a calamity "long expected but irreparable."

Henry had forthwith to bring his best gifts to help the biographers: as he had done in his living services to that sick friend. He was barely well at the time, dogged by sleeplessness, feeling the consequent drain on his daytime energy. Here and there in his letters, and the last pages of the journal written for "Johnnie's" eye, there comes to the surface a deep conviction that the time allotted him, to complete his own task, would not be long.

However, the move into Newnham, and the utterly insoluble problem of reducing his over-grown library to fit their destined rooms, on the first floor of the new buildings, were a useful diversion. Mrs. Sidgwick's own description of their establishment there in New Year 1894 bears marks of relief at planting him in fresh and pretty surroundings and what was then modern comfort. . . . Students' rooms were on the floor above them; and from the windows they had a wide view of cheerful red and white buildings, trees and grass, with groups of girls moving about; a space where Mr. Sidgwick could walk and air his thoughts, "absently stroking his beard on the under side and holding it up against his mouth – a gesture very habitual to him while meditating." They had their own dining-room, for purposes of entertainment. As for the books, they soon over-flowed again the shelves in the long passage and his study, "somewhat small" as at Hillside. . . . Now and again a crisis would occur, and there was nothing for it but a drastic tidying up. "After an hour or two of this had resulted in the destruction of much rubbish, and the reduction of the rest of the accumulated masses to comparative order, he would triumphantly invite a sympathetic inspection of the transformation effected."[288]

At any rate, even prior to the move, this work also provided forceful reasons to remain at Cambridge. However dejected he was over the reactionary backlash, the accomplishments of his students were an intense source of pride. Philippa Fawcett, the daughter of his old friends Henry and Millicent Fawcett, surpassed all expectations when she headed the list in the Mathematical Tripos of 1890.

Indeed, the increasing success of his students and of his collaboration with Eleanor convinced him that the setbacks the women's movement suffered were purely the result of the obtuse opposition of men – often religiously conservative ones. Especially illuminating, however, was a conflict with Alfred Marshall in the 1890s. Marshall, an early supporter of the cause, turned against the Sidgwicks in the 1880s, when he was also hostile to Sidgwick as a "tyrant" of the Moral Sciences Board. and delivered his infamous invidious comparison of Sidgwick to Green. He was a case in point of the type of reaction Sidgwick feared would result from pushing the case for full admission. This was revealed in another contretemps, in 1896, that according to McWilliams Tullberg came from Marshall's bigotry on such subjects as mixed lectures and including women in informal at-home instruction. As Marshall confessed:

As regards the informal instruction and advice given 'at home', I do not admit women to my ordinary 'at home' . . . but make occasional special appointments for them. I adopt this course partly because of the difficulty of getting men and women to open their minds freely in one another's presence, and partly because I find the questions asked by women generally relate to lectures or book work and/or else to practical problems such as poor relief. Whilst men who have attended fewer lectures and read fewer books and are perhaps likely to obtain less [sic] marks in examinations, are more apt to ask questions showing mental initiative and giving promise of original work in the future.[289]

Marshall apparently did not entertain the possibility that these differences were the result of societal sexism in shaping gender roles that called for opposition rather than endorsement. Clearly, he had a low opinion of women's potential, and at about this time he produced a pamphlet claiming that young women had special responsibilities to their families and that it would be immoral (even unhealthy) for them to meet the residence requirements of men, since at least half their time should be devoted to the domestic sphere. This was of course a vital issue, given that continuous residence at Cambridge – studying with one's peers or in a "room of one's own" – was regarded as a crucial part of the educational experience, especially for women who needed to escape the crushing demands of domesticity,[290] But Marshall even quashed the academic career of his wife, Mary Paley.

Such challenges emanating from a former ally led Eleanor Sidgwick, now principal of Newnham, to issue one of her most forceful statements:

I may perhaps remind Professor Marshall that the whole course of the movement for the academic education of women is strewn with the wrecks of hasty generalisations as to the limits of women's intellectual powers. When the work here began, many smiled at the notion that women, except one or two here and there, could be capable of taking University honours at all. When they had achieved distinction in some of the newer Triposes, it was still confidently affirmed that the highest places in the time-honoured Mathematical and Classical examinations were beyond their reach. When at length a woman obtained the position of Senior Wrangler, it was prophesied that, at any rate, the second part of the Mathematical Tripos would reveal the inexorable limitations of the feminine intellect. Then, when this last prophecy has shared the fate of its predecessors, it is discovered that the domestic qualities of women specially fit them for Tripos examinations of all kinds, but not for vigorous mental work afterwards. With this experience, while admiring the pertinacity and versatility of our opponents, we may be pardoned for distrusting their insight and foresight; and in any case we hope that the University will not hesitate to allow women who satisfy its intellectual tests unrestricted opportunities for cultivating whatever faculties they possess for receiving, transmitting, and advancing knowledge.[291]

This was a powerful Millian counter, one not hedged about with worries that the case for women was still in the experimental stage. Eleanor simply flattened the father of modern economics, on count after count. As McWilliams Tullberg summarizes the full scope of her counter:

Eleanor Sidgwick made an able reply to Marshall's pamphlet, providing him with hard facts about unmarried women, the health of students who try to combine home commitments and study, and stressing the professional disadvantages of having a qualification, a Tripos Certificate, the value of which was not universally understood. She accepted that facilities for non-residential degrees were needed by men and women alike and reminded Marshall of what was already available. But college residence was a most valuable part of Cambridge education, mentally, morally and physically, and those women who could take advantage of it should not be denied it. As far as intellectual potential was concerned, Eleanor Sidgwick challenged Marshall's claim that women were not capable of constructive work. What opportunities had women had for higher work? There were no fellowships, prizes or academic posts available to them.[292]

Eleanor may have referred to herself as "Mrs. Henry Sidgwick," but she was not exactly the champion of a "feminine feminist" ethic. As Janet Oppenheim has argued, if

she thought that most women would find their greatest joy in marriage, she denounced the notion that marriage was the only career worth having and warmly sympathized with the need felt by many women for 'the kind of happiness which can only come from work' and from 'the habit of reasonable self-dependence in thought and study'. . . . The most rewarding life for a woman, she believed, necessarily combined 'intellectual autonomy with emotional bonds to friends and family.'[293]

As Eleanor herself put it,

There will always be gaps in domestic life which can best be filled by unmarried girls and women of the family; help wanted in the care of old people and children and invalids, or in making the work of other members of the family go smoothly, to which a woman may well devote herself at some sacrifice of her own future – a sacrifice she will not regret. This kind of work can best be done by women, not only because they are generally better adapted to it, but because the sacrifice is not so clear nor so great in their case as it would generally be in that of a man. Only let the cost be counted and compared with the gain, and do not let us ask women to give up their chance of filling a more useful place in the world for the sake of employing them in trivial social duties from which they might be spared with little loss to anyone.[294]

Thus, if Eleanor "never discounted the legitimacy of family claims on a woman's time, she always balanced her gospel of self-renunciation for others with a paean to the joys of nurturing one's own mental garden." In truth, Eleanor plainly had no doubt that women could enter into the true spirit of the university, "the love of knowledge for its own sake and apart from its examination and professional value." Among such women

will be found a few who will add to our literary stores, and a few who will help in advancing knowledge by reflection, observation, experiment, or research, or – more humbly – by rendering accessible the work of others. Those who advance knowledge will not probably be many – there are not many among men – but the others if they have been really interested will not have wasted their time; and will have received a training which will directly or indirectly help them in any work they may undertake, and they will form part of the audience – the cultivated, interested and intelligent public – without which scientific progress and literary production is well nigh impossible.

The true university was, for both the Sidgwicks, in this way a model of Millian friendship, affording "the sense of membership of a worthy community, with a high and noble function in which every member can take part," along with "the habit of reasonable self-dependence in thought and study." Eleanor went on record often and emphatically with her hope that the institutions of higher education "will never cease to aim at producing that intellectual grasp and width of view which Mill regarded as their chief object," even if this must increasingly be done by teaching individuals "in connection with their prospective careers."[295]

Clearly, Eleanor, like her husband, wanted it all – wanted the university to open itself wider and extend itself further, to provide career training for a more diverse and mixed student body but without relinquishing the liberal, Millian ideal of imparting the culture that could form the basis for a high-minded, sympathetic life and high-minded, sympathetic friendships, including marital ones. Women, too, might achieve greatness.

Although she denied that a university education would "disincline a woman for marriage" and was prepared to agree that "for most women marriage, provided it is marriage to the right man, offers the best prospect of carrying out our ideal in the most satisfactory manner," she nonetheless insisted that "a cultivated mind and developed intelligence is likely to make her a better companion for a man similarly endowed, and a better guide and helper for her children." Indeed, "any development of her faculties is likely to give a woman a higher standard and therefore to some extent to make her less likely to find the man she can care for among the men she happens to be thrown with. But this of course is one of the ways in which the chance of ill-assorted marriages is diminished."[296]

Thus, the Millian universities to be – Mill had of course despised the actually existing ones, though he grew more hopeful when the academic liberals came along – were to play a powerful part in reforming the family along Millian lines. Again, Newnham had no religious trappings and was educationally innovative – was, as Sidgwick allowed, a piece of practical Millian and Mauricean reformism. And there is no evidence to suggest that Henry was anything but supportive of the more radical points that Eleanor advanced.

In truth, Eleanor, despite her class background, had a real feel for the Millian ideal. A Cecil and a Balfour, she had been raised so that her independence, both financial and intellectual, was guaranteed. As Oppenheim urges:

When we hear [Eleanor] Sidgwick telling Helen Gladstone to consider her own opportunities to perform meaningful work before sacrificing herself to the care of elderly parents; when we read about her confidently arguing with Bertrand Russell over college finances; when we see her, as a married lady, spending hours away from home and husband for the sheer delight of working in the Cavendish laboratory – then we begin to feel confident that Lady Blanche did not destroy Eleanor's sense of self or capacity for self-assertion. It seems clear that Eleanor learned as much from her mother about exercising authority as submitting to it.[297]

Eleanor had, as noted, a love of, and gift for, mathematics and scientific research, and she is listed as a coauthor, with her brother-in-law Rayleigh, of a number of papers published in the Royal Society's *Philosophical Transactions*. Henry was only too happy to recognize and support his wife's intellectual interests, freely admitting that, as in psychical research, she had much the better scientific mind. This judgment would appear to be vindicated in their work for the SPR.

However, once again, it must be allowed that Sidgwick's attitude toward women had undergone a good deal of evolution. In his youthful debates with the "Initial Society," he had actually come out as far less advanced in his views than Dakyns on the matter of women's political equality:

Granting for the moment, a radical difference between masculine and feminine minds, it surely does not follow that this difference should be increased rather than diminished by bringing it into prominence as early as possible. Just as it is thought best for boys, of the most different natures and destined for the most different pursuits, to receive up to a certain age an exactly similar education: so it might improve both boys and girls if the point, at which their respective trainings branch off from one another, were deferred as long as possible. Miss Martineau has well urged the great importance of an improved physical training for girls; in respect of exercise and gymnastics this would approach more nearly to boyish education. On the other hand the roughness that is expected from, and encouraged in boys, makes some of them little brutes, and the lives of others miserable. E.R. seems to despair of a change in this respect, because mothers will always bring up their daughters like themselves: but surely on this principle the world would not have progresseed at all. It is only because parents have generally a desire to raise their children, if possible, *above* themselves, that we are not now savages running wild in the woods.

As to the further question I agree with H.G.D. that it is not necessary to say beforehand whether women could ever become like men. I would rather ask "could their education and position in society be assimilated to that of men with advantage." For example (1) E.R. confesses that their mental training is miserably deficient: it ought therefore to be altered: the only conceivable ways of altering it would render it more like that of men. (2) I agree with H.G.D. that we ought to give women certain rights which they may fairly claim, and which we at present withhold from them. I am amused however with my friend professing a desire to proceed with the greatest moderation: and then coming out with a measure so violently radical as that of giving women votes in election . . . but I think that simple justice would make us give them a right to hold property, and throw open to them such professions as they can be qualified for. When these are done (the latter is being done), and when further by an insensible elevation of public opinion, the social stigma attaching to "old maids" is entirely removed (so that the *disproportionate* cultivation of the arts of attraction which must be degrading, ceases): then it will be time to reconsider the evidence for the "natural inferiority" of women to men. E.R. asks "Why have they let themselves sink" etc. She forgets that the progress of civilization is only a *gradual emerging* from the savage state, in which the relations of the sexes is determined *solely* by physical force. The conditions of women has always improved as a nation has become more civilized: but it has taken a long time for them to shake off a yoke that ages of barbarism have hardened. It is not too much to say that in no time or country have women had a fair opportunity of measuring their natural mental powers with those of men.[298]

Following the selection from these remarks reproduced in *Henry Sidgwick, A Memoir*, there is a footnote explaining that "Some twenty years later Sidgwick's view on the franchise question had changed." Thus, in a letter on the subject addressed to the *Spectator* for May 31, 1884, he insists that

in refusing to treat sex alone as a ground of disfranchisement, the Legislature would simply recognise in our political constitution what the best reflection shows to be an established fact of our social and industrial organisation. . . . So long as the responsibility is thrown on women, unmarried or widows, of earning their own livelihood in any way that industrial competition allows, their claims to have the ordinary constitutional protection against any encroachments on the part of other sections of the community is *primâ facie* undeniable. (M 73)

This position would be elaborated in *The Elements of Politics*, where Sidgwick declares the "most important consideration on the other side is the inferiority of women in physical force and their unfitness for warfare," an argument he regards with appropriate scorn.

Hence, despite their greater political conservatism, one can still find in Sidgwick's early statements at least the roots of a fairly Millian view about the progress of civilization being gauged by the progress of women, with the savage and slow history of human progress being sufficient to explain women's supposed inferiority. Education, in both the broad cultural sense and the narrow institutional one, is the key to further such progress, which will involve not only political equality but also the larger cultural reform, the growth of sympathetic capacities resulting from better marriages, independence, and so forth. The school of sympathy was, for the Sidgwicks, rather literal.

But of course, there was the matter of the "superior man." Did this work somehow betray a patriarchal mentality that filtered through everything from epistemology to sex? It would be much easier to answer this question if Sidgwick had been good enough to submit a case history to Symonds for his work on *Sexual Inversion*, or had at least composed a major treatise on women and women's higher education. That he did not is also revealing in its way, indicative of Sidgwick's conflicts. Plausibly, he really did, like Mill, wish to maintain an agnosticism about just where gender traits and relations would end up, once reform had really got under way. Gender traits seemed to puzzle him, more than provoke him. Certainly, though, like Mill, the Sidgwicks did tend to prioritize intellectual inquiry and autonomy in a curiously disembodied way – as both Symonds and James recognized.

Consider Henry's assessment of Millicent Garrett Fawcett:

On Saturday was the Newnham Council, and Mrs Fawcett came to stay with us. We had pleasant and instructive talk and yet I felt that she did not quite satisfy me as a "political woman": – and, again, that I was wrong in being dissatisfied. She discussed things in an attitude that was neither feminine nor unfeminine, but simply that of a thoroughly reasonable and sensible unsexual being – who happened to have taken up the enfranchisement of women as her business. But somehow one demands that a woman going into politics should exhibit all feminine excellences and no feminine defects! – which is asking too much. (CWC)

This critical self-interrogation, sparked by failing to appreciate as such "a thoroughly reasonable and sensible unsexual being," would seem to be quintessential Sidgwick and suggestive of a certain presumption about who defines reason and how. One should remember, however, that his conception of "feminine excellences" undoubtedly owed much to George Eliot,[299] a warm admirer of the Sidgwicks, who held that "there lies just that kernel of truth in the vulgar alarm of men lest women shuld be 'unsexed'. We can no more afford to part with that exquisite type of gentleness, tenderness, possible maternity suffusing a woman's being with affectionateness, which makes what we mean by the feminine character." If Eliot was no Virginia Woolf, at least she was equally far from Eliza Lynn Linton and, like more recent "feminine feminists," cautiously persuaded that the special relationships of care and dependence had produced some admirable character traits worth preserving.[300] Needless to say, however, Eliot also had a "strong conviction" that

women ought to have the same fund of truth placed within their reach as men have; that their lives (i.e. the lives of men and women) ought to be passed together under the hallowing influence of a common faith as to their duty and its basis. And this unity in their faith can only be produced by their having each the same store of fundamental knowledge. It is not likely that any perfect plan for educating women can soon be found, for we are very far from having a perfect plan for educating men. But it will not do to wait for perfection.[301]

Eliot's great novel *Middlemarch*, a favorite of Sidgwick's, had had the following line excised from it:

... it was never said in the neighbourhood of Middlemarch that such mistakes [Dorothea's] could not have happened if the society into which she was born had not smiled on propositions of marriage from a sickly man to a girl less than half his own age – on modes of education which made a woman's knowledge another name for motley ignorance – on rules of conduct which are in flat contradiction with its own loudly-asserted beliefs.[302]

Plainly, moreover, Eleanor herself cannot easily be pigeonholed according to recent stereotypes of Victorian feminism: Lady Bountiful, Florence Nightingale, Eliot, and so on. True, she had Tory sympathies and gravitated toward the Jane Addamsish, and she was not happy with the "New Woman" given to "disorderly conduct." When Virginia Woolf questioned whether there might not be some connection between good thought and good food, and carried on at witty length – in the wonderfully titled *A Room of One's Own* – about the prunes served to the fictional guest lecturer at "Fernham College" Cambridge, she canonized the difference that Bloomsbury sought to place between itself and Sidgwickian feminism.

For all that, Bloomsbury was simply another offshoot of the "New Chivalry," and Woolf would for the most part find her enemies in just the same institutions that the Sidgwicks did – the church, the traditional university, the medical men, and the aesthetically uninclined. Yopie Prins, in a cogent discussion of Newnham and such Newnham successes as Jane Ellen Harrison, has argued that

In their imaginative identification with Greek maenads, these Victorian spinsters redefined spinsterhood not only in their different styles of writing but also in the lifestyles they chose for themselves. As various critics have argued, the generation of unmarried middle-class women that came of age in the 1870s and 1880s played an important role in the transition from mid-Victorian Old Maid to fin-de-siècle New Woman; during the last three decades of the century, single women were beginning to redefine familial relations and conventional female domesticity. Thus Bradley and Cooper turned the relationship between aunt and niece into an alternative marriage, while Harrison, resolutely refusing to become "Aunt," chose the communal life of a women's college where she cultivated passionate friendships with colleagues and students.[303]

Education, with the personal touch and a sexual undercurrent, producing at least the work of transition to the New Woman – this was surely something that Sidgwick would have happily recognized.

It would appear, then, that the Sidgwicks' feminism came to something like this: themselves a near-perfect embodiment of the Millian notion of high-minded, highly intellectualized marital friendship – indeed, a more-than-Millian model of a mutually active, professional academic couple – they nonetheless remained cautiously open and flexible about just what assortment of feminine/masculine gender traits would emerge as women progressed toward greater intellectual autonomy and social independence. Neither cared for the "frivolous and doll-like women," any more than they cared for the Hugh Herons. Although earlier on, they both had harbored various doubts about what women might ultimately prove themselves capable of, and about what degree of political equality they might be given, these doubts had rapidly diminished once they began actively working for women's higher education, and they ultimately allowed that women had demonstrated their capacity for even the most "masculine" intellectual and political endeavors (e.g., physics and mathematics, political reformism). Consequently, they favored women's suffrage and greater opportunity for women across the board in higher education and career opportunities. Treating the universities as the chief vehicles for reform and societal guidance generally, they hoped that the ancient and most influential ones would become "mixed," just as the newer ones were. Correlatively, while recognizing that many women would naturally prefer to continue along the paths to which they had been socialized, they favored reducing the pressure to marry as opposed to considering other options, hoping that higher education would also make for better (more Millian) marriages. The pressures of a suffocating domesticity were, of course, linked to precisely the religious orthodoxy that both thought a relic of an earlier era.

Newnham even stressed that women were capable of physical education and sports. Indeed, it could afford a quite wonderful existence for its fortunate students. As a student from the nineties would (much) later recall:

Our lives were so excitingly novel. We worked, some of us, ten hours a day, and there were so many College societies and preoccupations that there was little time or energy for anything else. There were the Political, Debating, Sharp Practice societies, the Historical, Classical, Scientific societies, The Browning, Shakespeare and other Literary societies, the Sunday Society, the Musical Society and many others. Those were recognised by authority, and there were many not recognised and indeed concealed from authority. (I remember my special contribution was a secret society called the L.S.D. And the letters hadn't the significance they have now; they didn't even mean pounds, shillings and pence. They merely meant 'Leaving Sunday Dinner'. A small group of us signed off for Sunday dinners and we hired a room in Grantchester Street, I think for 8s 6d a term. Each of us had in turn to provide a meal for the group. And there I may add we used to make our own cigarettes after a fashion.) For athletics there were tennis, hockey, cricket, fives, boating and the fire brigade. Life was never dull.[304]

Interestingly, smoking was prohibited only "because it was pointed out that parents wouldn't send their daughters to Newnham if they thought that they might get contaminated by the pernicious habit."

Naturally, there was a good deal of social control, curfews, chaperones, and the like. And again, the Sidgwicks were plainly not interested in the female equivalents of Hugh Heron. For them, education was a sacred and serious business; one year, when the women won only five Firsts, Eleanor warned them about devoting too much time to the societies. Still, the women themselves found it liberating.

Also interestingly, despite the rampant talk of eugenics during this era, nothing came of a proposed scheme by Frances Galton to create a "dower fund": "to be used in rewarding candidates who had been selected by a board of women for their good physique and morale, 'especially such as appeared to have been hereditarily derived and therefore to be the more probably transmissible', with £50 on marriage, if before the age of twenty-six and £25 on the birth of each and every living child.'"[305]

Thus, Newnham was to be different – different from the men's education at Cambridge generally, and different from Girton's imitation of the masculine domain. Different right down to the architecture:

When Philip Webb, Norman Shaw and Bodley began to design houses, not in ponderous stucco or bewildering gothic, but in the potpourri of styles which came to be known as Queen Anne, some members of the intellectual aristocracy responded. Henry Sidgwick at Cambridge and the philosopher T. H. Green at Oxford both commissioned houses designed in the new style of sweetness and light, with bay windows, verandas, inglenooks and crannies crammed with a clutter of objects intended to delight the eye and interest the mind. Girton College was built as a spartan, spare building in the Tudor-gothic style of Waterhouse, everything geared to proving that women could compete on equal terms with men. But Sidgwick got his friend Champneys to design Newnham in the Queen Anne style: the students' rooms were papered with Morris wallpaper, and his wife . . . insisted that the corridors should have windows on both sides for cheerfulness.[306]

Sidgwick was even responsible for the road called Sidgwick Avenue, which was built to accommodate the expanding college, though the battle to get it built put him at odds with his old Apostolic friend Jebb, whose property was appropriated for the purpose. (M 503–4)

None of this is to deny, of course, that both the Sidgwicks were cautious reformers in the extreme, worrying at every turn that Cambridge was not ripe for change. If Newnham was effectively a Millian experiment in living, involving various experiments in fostering individuality, autonomy, and marital friendship, it was therefore just the kind of thing that could be threatened by excessive public recognition of its radicalness. And if Mill could have witnessed their sad experience in the 1890s, he would have reverted to his low opinion of the ancient universities. Moreover, it was in this painful context that Sidgwick took up the business of the Symonds biography. He lost Symonds, Noel, and Benson in quick succession, but the death of the first was in many ways the hardest. And beyond his disenchantment with Cambridge politics, there was the public spectacle of Oscar Wilde's ruin, at the very point when he was working on assembling the biography. His justified sense that matters of sex reform were being threatened by a conservative backlash surely helps to explain why he so insistently guided Horatio Brown to ensure that Symonds's sexual concerns would be carefully masked to appear as good old religious agonizing.

Still, it bears repeating that the Sidgwicks were more than "first-wave" feminists focused on changing such legal impediments to women as disenfranchisement. They clearly did recognize the insidious elements of domination in marriage, the family, and domesticity that kept women back, kept them from even thinking of taking up the new educational and career opportunities for which they were fighting. If they were predictably restrained and decorous when it came to the politics of the body and of sex, they were at least engaged in a determined effort to reduce the pressures to marry and to improve the sympathetic quality of future marriages. (And given Henry's ambivalent and limited libido, he cannot be accused of dominating or brutalizing via sex in his own marriage.) Nor is it at all far-fetched to think that Henry's views on marriage had been shaped by his friendship with Symonds. As he well knew, there were many reasons why marriage was not for everyone, why people capable of other forms of sympathetic development ought to be allowed to follow out their own processes. On many fronts, Sidgwickian feminism was a complementary force to Symonds's Whitmanian challenge to sex law and custom. As the following chapter will show, this is evident even in the *Methods*. Sidgwick was plainly persuaded, with Symonds, that the whole vast region of sex, male and female, was another in which free and open inquiry had been quashed by religious orthodoxy and dogmatism posing as science. How, given his work with Newnham, could he have been anything but an interested supporter of Symonds and Ellis in their investigations?

And in the end, his work did have the personal touch. Ironically, Reba Soffer has even compared Eleanor Sidgwick and Newnham to Jowett and Balliol: "shy, diminutive Eleanor Sidgwick consistently thought of herself as Henry Sidgwick's wife rather than as a public figure"; nonetheless, "warning her graduates that marriage was no substitute for an engaged life, she forcefully pushed them into public activity. Newnham's graduates, like Balliol's, were meant to succeed not for their own sakes, but for college and country."[307] In fact, the Sidgwicks did make a point of getting to know their students, and Eleanor was apparently rather happy to allow her appendage to range about as a free critic – a role to which he was much looking forward as a compromise escape from his station and its duties.[308] He had been practicing for many years. As one of the very first Newnham students, Mary Paley (later Marshall) recalled:

Mr Sidgwick was the most delightful conversationalist on any subject. I have known only one to equal him, Henry Smith of Oxford. Every subject Mr Sidgwick touched upon was never the same again. As someone said of him: 'If you so much as mentioned a duster in his presence he would glorify it on the spot.' His conversation made him sometimes inattentive to ordinary affairs and one day when he was helping us at dinner after using a tablespoon for the soup he pulled out the entire contents of the apple pie with the soup ladle, to our great delight. Though we were only five he found us rather troublesome. In another letter he writes: 'There is such a strong impulse towards liberty among the young women attracted by the movement that they will not submit to maternal government.'[309]

Eleanor was of course among the early women students attending Cambridge lectures. And as her best friends were wont to say, she was not really shy – she was silent "only because she was thinking hard."[310]

And she could and did advise her students in a way bespeaking the old Balliol mode of personal guidance. One of her students gave an account:

I asked her when I might come, and went rather in fear and trembling on Wednesday night. I had nearly 1 1/2 hours alone with her, and she was angelic, talking *so* much herself. . . . She told me of a good many things I could do in a *political* way, organising and speaking, etc., but she advised me if I did that, only to do *one* question – perhaps Education – study it theoretically *and* practically – try to get on a County Council Committee. . . . But what she really advised me to do was to go on with my work for some time, and perhaps try to write some little thing, because she said with a view to my doing college work ultimately . . . it would rather stand me in place of a degree. . . . The marvellous thing is that though she hardly ever talks to a student, she seems to know by instinct exactly what stages of thought they are all in. I don't know what people may call her, but to me she seems to be one of the most deeply religious women I've ever met, and one feels able to talk to her about religion in a perfectly free and natural way, which one couldn't do if she was the least out of sympathy.[311]

Such encounters suggest that the comparison to Jowett is judicious, except that Jowett used to explain that people were wrong to suppose that he was thinking when he remained silent. The Sidgwicks as a team, an early example of the academic couple, achieved a similar but more benign effect than Jowett:

He [Henry] liked the presence of youth all about him again. There can be no doubt that having him at hand, through a thin partition, to sweeten her intercourse with the students, as well as to counsel in private, altered the aspect of her daily task to Mrs. Sidgwick – how much, she was realising when those passages in the *Life* were written. She and he dined once a week in hall with the staff and students, and third - and fourth-year girls were invited, four at a time, to breakfast: those fearful occasions to which old students have referred. Mrs. Sidgwick was "at home" to the girls once a week, when the master would extract himself from the mazes of his books to wander about the drawing-room with a teacup and talk to them, or read aloud from the newest poet. Students could now come to and fro under cover on the stormiest evening; there was the pleasant sense of being "all under one roof." The doors between the halls were open, day and night, and the new rooms over the Principal's lodging took in the last wanderers from without – at present. The spirit of growth was not extinct.[312]

Given the "stupid conservatism" of so many of the male Cambridge undergraduates – including Sidgwick's nephew A. C. Benson – it is perhaps not surprising that his increased dealing with independent young women

students did help stave off his depressive tendencies. When he was not
"boring" Russell and Moore with his one-joke lectures – the lectures that
he hated giving, since he thought the whole practice another worthless
educational encumbrance – he was lecturing to the women of Newnham.
But better still, from his angle, was this opportunity to deploy his sympathetic conversational talents in helping young women feel at home in
the academic men's club that was Cambridge. Sidgwick the talker still
believed in the value of talk. And he no longer had to worry very much
about making his students too much resemble him – they were not likely
to go too far in submitting to his maternal government. Indeed, in his last
decade he was beginning to think that the students, whether religious or
agnostic, needed rather more skepticism.

Perforce, Newnham was a remarkably well-connected place, largely
thanks to "Nora." In June of 1888, no less than three of the honorary
degrees awarded to Cambridge were to her relatives: "Nora's brother and
brother-in-law and uncle" – that is, "A. J. Balfour, Lord Rayleigh, and
Lord Salisbury." The occasion made for a memorable "Garden Party" at
Newnham:

[I]t was an exciting time, especially as we achieved for Newnham the triumph of
getting all the Swells (including the Prince and Princess of Wales) to come to its
Garden Party. This was partly due to the cordiality of the Vice-Chancellor, who
was, I think, anxious to show that though Cambridge will not give women degrees,
it does not in any way draw back the hand it has held out to them.

We had the Premier, Lady Salisbury, and Gwendolen Cecil, as well as Arthur
and Alice Balfour [staying with us]. It strained the resources of our humble
establishment, but I like having the Salisburys. I think Lord S. is particularly
attractive in private life – one recognizes the style of his speeches in his hu-
mourous observations; otherwise I should describe his manner as simple, gentle,
and unassuming. (M 490–91)

Given the nature of Newnham, its leadership and political connections,
it might well seem as elitist as Jowett's Balliol, committed to training young
women, if not to go out and rule the world, at least to go out and work
as intellectual equals with the men who were. Was this, then, the form
that Sidgwick's supposed "Government House" utilitarianism actually
took? Was the Millian and Mauricean ideal meant strictly for domestic
consumption, for the vanguard of English civilization? And even then
only for the fortunate few? Precisely when was the promotion of that

Millian vision of saving sympathetic friendship and expanded culture an egalitarian matter, and when not?

The larger political context of the Sidgwicks' reform efforts is of course troubling and calls for further investigation. But before moving on, it is worth adding here that the epistemological side of Sidgwick's educational and cultural vision was neither as crude nor as masculinist as some feminist critics have charged. The notions of knowledge and authority that Henry and Eleanor shared were, admittedly, shaped by what they deemed the successes of scientific method. But they were also seeking a different understanding of the forms of inquiry that might be necessary in parapsychology or depth psychology, covering research on sex and gender.[313] Indeed, the eclectic, social epistemological form of intuitionism described in earlier chapters allowed for precisely this type of interpretation and implementation: much sensitive soul searching was required in the effort to penetrate to one's deepest convictions, and much sympathetic listening was required in order to find common ground, the free consensus of impartial inquirers. This was especially true in the realm of the "deepest problems," the problems that Henry and Eleanor, like Henry and Johnnie, were so thoroughly devoted to exploring.

7

Colors

Both the last talkers deal much in points of conduct and religion studied in the 'dry light' of prose. Indirectly and as if against his will the same elements from time to time appear in the troubled and poetic talk of Opalstein. His various and exotic knowledge, complete although unready sympathies, and fine, full, discriminative flow of language, fit him out to be the best of talkers; so perhaps he is with some, not *quite* with me – *proxime accessit*, I should say. He sings the praises of the earth and arts, flowers and jewels, wine and music, in a moonlight, serenading manner, as to the light guitar; even wisdom comes from his tongue like singing; no one is, indeed, more tuneful in the upper notes. But even while he sings the song of the Sirens, he still hearkens to the barking of the Sphinx. Jarring Byronic notes interrupt the flow of his Horatian humours. His mirth has somethng of the tragedy of the world for its perpetual background; and he feasts like Don Giovanni to a double orchestra, one lightly sounding for the dance, one pealing Beethoven in the distance. He is not truly reconciled either with life or with himself; and this instant war in his members sometimes divides the man's attention. He does not always, perhaps not often, frankly surrender himself in conversation. He brings into the talk other thoughts than those which he expresses; you are conscious that he keeps an eye on something else, that he does not shake off the world, nor quite forget himself. Hence arise occasional disappointments; even an occasional unfairness for his companions, who find themselves one day giving too much, and the next, when they are wary out of season, giving perhaps too little.

Robert Louis Stevenson, "Talk and Talkers"[1]

I. Purity and Suicide

Symonds did not much care for his friend Stevenson's characterization of him as "Opalstein." It mistook the species for the genus, he suggested. Yet Stevenson had a fine ear for this world of talk and talkers, in which so much rested with the conversational virtues; the author of *The Strange Case of*

Dr. Jekyll and Mr. Hyde knew a dipsychical self when he saw one, and these were times when he often saw little else. A complex and many-faceted affair, the frank surrender of Apostolic soaring was not easily achieved in the larger and often unsympathetic world, even though, as we have seen, this aspect of the Platonic revival figured in nearly everything Symonds and his friend Sidgwick had to say about culture and education, inquiry and change. The serious business of pursuit of truth always devolved into one or another web of intimate friendships, with the companions of Socrates looking a lot like new groups of Apostles probing the recesses of the "true self." But the drift of politics, in the late Victorian world, was not making things easier. Hypocrisy remained, even as religion declined.

The nexus with Symonds illuminates the various core concerns defining Sidgwick's effort to shed light on the "deepest problems of human life," yielding nothing less than the primary source material for Sidgwick's experimentalizing struggles with the meaning of death, particularly for morals. In their exchanges, one discerns the concrete ways in which Sidgwick worried out the possibilities of the lower Goethean ideal, the symmetrical people, and the serious limits of the "sensual herd" when it came to achieving even that limited ideal. The urgency that he felt about his work – from psychical research to women's higher education – manifestly had a great deal to do with his fear about the impotence of practical reason and his conviction that a powerful reshaping of human sentiment – a new religion – was needed to move civilization in the right direction. In many ways, such fears and convictions fell in with Symonds's diagnosis of the state of things, even if Sidgwick could not regard the peril to philosophical reason with anything like his friend's insouciance (or James's insouciance).

Obviously, Sidgwick's worst anxieties were not always evident on the surface of either his life or his writings. Clearly, as shown, he was much obsessed with sexual hypocrisy, as well as with religious hypocrisy, and he was not at all averse to esoteric moral reasoning when it came to his religious, parapsychological, and sexual doubts. If he was in some ways suited for his skeptical results, the larger public, he was confident, was not. Silence was often best, outside of the knowing elite.

Yet, if many of the Apostolic and Millian dimensions of Sidgwick's practical reformist efforts – above all, of his educational efforts – are by now tolerably clear, the full force of his thinking on all of these matters can only be appreciated by engaging with his economic and political writings, writings that often develop the positions set out in the *Methods*. These help to flesh out both his views on the social implications of the dualism of practical reason and the broader nature of his evolving academic liberalism – the ways in which, for good or ill, he did share many of the presuppositions of Jowett and Green, as well as of Symonds, and this despite his greater skeptical reticence and his worries about making people come to resemble him. Of course, Sidgwick was still Sidgwick, and his thinking about economic and political matters has the clarity and toughmindedness that one would expect from the author of the *Methods*. If he shared the Idealist's sense of the Philistinism of capitalism, he was also capable of dissecting the debates over the economic system with all the rigor of a professional economist. The new discipline of political science could also regard him as one their own. Often dry and abstract, his *Principles of Political Economy* and *Elements of Politics* were not designed to whip up enthusiasm.

Still, strange as it may seem, in his major works – the *Methods*, the *Principles*, and the *Elements* – Sidgwick appears to have applied the lessons that he had set out so many years before, for his friends in the Initial Society. That is, he became quite expert at masking the originality and subversiveness of his claims by the Mauricean tactic of presenting them as mere developments of received belief, cloaking his real insights with massive tomes of respectable opinion so that few could apprehend how destructive his criticism was. Each of his three major treatises follows the same pattern, burying the reader in a great mass of the relevant received wisdom – commonsense morality or political common sense – such that the critical working free of "respectable" opinion seems comparatively modest and respectful. Perhaps, as with the *Methods*, Sidgwick always felt that the respectable views he criticized were enduring elements of his own being, and that his criticism really was a form of self-scrutiny, an inner Socratic dialectic rather than "hostile criticism from the outside." Certainly, this was the attitude of spectatorship toward his own inner reactions that he offered up to his friends when criticizing their poetry, and that led Symonds to describe him as a perfect "scientific thermometer." At any rate, the result was invariably a single-minded attempt to articulate through extended sympathy some consensus that could then be worked over in a way that made it difficult to feel that the criticism involved a failure to see the other side. In this way, his books were reflections of his conversational ideal, albeit lacking the zest. Common sense helped with the opening moves; the end game was another matter.

Consequently, if one digs into these tomes a bit more deeply, one finds that they often do address, in abstract, oblique fashion, the burning questions that were so evident in his personal crises and more candid writings. Again, one must read the works in light of the life, as well as the life in light of the works. Indeed, before addressing Sidgwick's political economy, political theory, and political practice, it might prove helpful to further illustrate how the *Methods* reflects various of the preoccupations that emerged in his exchanges with Symonds and work with Newnham. Reading the *Methods* in light of these matters should help to indicate how his other major works might be similarly interrogated in order to bring out how they reflect his deeper concerns about politics and civilization.

Clearly, some of the discussions in the *Methods* directly relate to Sidgwick's dealings with Symonds. The most obvious case in point is the material in Book III, Chapter 11, section 7, which in an almost eerie way reflects their exchanges. This is the section of his "Review of the Morality of Common Sense" that concerns duties to self and covers such matters as suicide and the regulation of sex. Earlier in the book, in his summation of commonsense morality, Sidgwick had rightly noted that this morality actually insisted that any too-close inquiry into the issue of sex was itself morbid, and thus not to be indulged. But when he gets to his review of this morality, he in effect pleads the case of Symonds and Ellis, not to mention Bentham:

In the case, however, of the sexual appetite, a special regulation seems to be prescibed on some independent principle under the notion of Purity or Chastity. In chap. ix. of this Book, where we examined this notion, it appeared that Common Sense is not only not explicit, but actually averse to explicitness, on this subject. As my aim in the preceding chapters was to give, above all things, a faithful exposition of the morality of Common Sense, I allowed my inquiry to be checked by this (as it seemed) clearly recognisable sentiment. But when it becomes our primary object to test the intuitive evidence of the moral principles commonly accepted, it seems necessary to override this aversion: for we can hardly ascertain whether rational conviction is attainable as to the acts allowed and forbidden under this notion and its opposite, without subjecting it to the same close scrutiny that we have endeavoured to give to the other leading notions of Ethics. Here the briefest account of such a scrutiny will be sufficient. I am aware that in giving even this

I cannot but cause a certain offence to minds trained in good moral habits: but I trust I may claim the same indulgence as is commonly granted to the physiologist, who also has to direct the student's attention to objects which a healthy mind is naturally disinclined to contemplate. (ME 356–57)

The discussion that follows is a model of Sidgwick's subversive chipping away at orthodox belief. After observing that since "the normal and obvious end of sexual intercourse is the propagation of the species, some have thought that all indulgence of appetite, except as a means to this end, should be prohibited," he goes on to note, ever so briefly, that "this doctrine would lead to a restriction of conjugal intercourse far too severe for Common Sense" (ME 357). And against the idea that purity would forbid any such sensuous activities except as prescribed by law, he sensibly holds that as in the case of justice, the law is very imperfect in any such regulation of conduct, and that it is essential to ask "what kind of sexual relations we are to call essentially impure, whether countenanced or not by Law and Custom?" But here, "there appear to be no distinct principles having any claim to self-evidence, upon which the question can be answered so as to command general assent." Indeed:

It would be difficult even to state such a principle for determining the degree of consanguinity between husband and wife which constitutes a union incestuous; although the aversion with which such unions are commonly regarded is a pe-culiarly intense moral sentiment; and the difficulty becomes indefinitely greater when we consider the *rationale* of prohibited degrees of affinity. . . . if legal polyg-yny is not impure, is Polyandry, when legal and customary – as is not unfrequently the case among the lower races of man – to be so characterised? and if not, on what rational principle can the notion be applied to institutions and conduct? Again, where divorce by mutual consent, with subsequent marriage, is legalised, we do not call this an offence against Purity: and yet if the principle of free change be once admitted, it seems paradoxical to distinguish purity from impurity merely by less rapidity of transition; and to condemn as impure even 'Free Love,' in so far as it is earnestly advocated as a means to a completer harmony of sentiment between men and women, and not to mere sensual license.

Shall we, then, fall back upon the presence of mutual affection (as distinguished from mere appetite) as constituting the essence of pure sexual relations? But this, again, while too lax from one point of view, seems from another too severe for Common Sense. . . . Again, how shall we judge of such institutions as those of Plato's Commonwealth, establishing community of women and children, but at the same time regulating sexual indulgence with the strictest reference to social ends? Our habitual standards seem inapplicable to such novel circumstances. (ME 358–59)

Hence Sidgwick's destructive analysis of the coherence of commonsense morality: he would like to believe in purity, but what could it possibly mean? Common sense leads only to yet another dualism, and to indecision:

The truth seems to be, that reflection on the current sexual morality discovers to us two distinct grounds for it: first and chiefly, the maintenance of a certain social order, believed to be most conducive to the prosperous continuance of the human race: and, secondly, the protection of habits of feeling in individuals believed to be generally most important to their perfection or their happiness. We commonly conceive that both these ends are to be attained by the same regulations: and in an ideal state of society this would perhaps be the case: but in actual life there is frequently a partial separation and incompatibility between them. But further, if the repression of sexual license is prescribed merely as a means to these ends, it does not seem that we can affirm as self-evident that it is always a necessary means in either case: on the contrary, it seems clear that such an affirmation would be unreliable apart from empirical confirmation. We cannot reasonably be sure, without induction from sociological observations, that a certain amount of sexual license will be incompatible with the maintenance of population in sufficient numbers and good condition. And if we consider the matter in its relation to the individual's perfection, it is certainly clear that he misses the highest and best development of his emotional nature, if his sexual relations are of a merely sensual kind: but we can hardly know *a priori* that this lower kind of relation interferes with the development of the higher (nor indeed does experience seem to show that this is universally the case). And this latter line of argument has a further difficulty. For the common opinion that we have to justify does not merely condemn the lower kind of development in comparison with the higher, but in comparison with none at all. Since we do not positively blame a man for remaining celibate (though we perhaps despise him somewhat unless the celibacy is adopted as a means to a noble end): it is difficult to show why we should condemn – in its bearing on the individual's emotional perfection solely – the imperfect development afforded by merely sensual relations. (ME 359)

Characteristically, Sidgwick goes on to explain that he has said nothing to "show that we have not distinct moral impulses, claiming authority over all others, and prescribing or forbidding kinds of conduct as to which there is a rough general agreement, at least among educated persons of the same age and country." The notions of justice, purity, and so forth are not necessarily "emptied of significance," since the "main part of the conduct prescribed under each notion is sufficiently clear: and the general rule prescribing it does not necessarily lose its force because there is in each case a margin of conduct involved in obscurity and perplexity, or because the rule does not on examination appear to be absolute and independent." The morality of common sense "may still be perfectly adequate to give practical guidance to common people in common circumstances." (ME 360–61)

But what about common people in extraordinary circumstances? Or, more to the point, extraordinary people – sensitives such as Symonds and Noel – under any circumstances? The superior man or woman might on this account find his or her best development outside of marriage, and even remain undiminished by a certain degree of license. Sidgwick himself, in his younger days, had aspired to be a chaste "superior" man, a virtual Platonic guardian, albeit one without breeding duties.

When he returns to the subject, in Book IV, Chapter 3, section 6, he is in the midst of a utilitarian attack on the double standard of sexual morality. Although he allows that the double standard, by which unchastity in men is accepted more readily than unchastity in women, could be said to reflect the unconscious utilitarianism of common sense, he thinks that this standard still threatens the security of family life and encourages women to ruin their reputations, and that even socially countenanced prostitution would risk the "contagion of unchastity" and thus override the arguments on the other side. His defense has a Millian ring: "the Virtue of Purity may be regarded as providing a necessary shelter under which that intense and elevated affection between the sexes, which is most conducive both to the happiness of the individual and to the wellbeing of the family, may grow and flourish." Still, he admits that the particulars are problematic, even for the utilitarian. Thus,

[I]t is not necessary that the line between right and wrong in such matters should be drawn with theoretical precision: it is sufficient for practical purposes if the main central portion of the region of duty be strongly illuminated, while the margin is left somewhat obscure. And, in fact, the detailed regulations which it is important to society to maintain depend so much upon habit and association of ideas, that they must vary to a great extent from age to age and from country to country. (ME 452–53)

In this region, the connections between ethics, law, and custom get particularly complicated.

Read in the light of his relationship to Symonds, these passages take on a peculiar significance. For what Sidgwick is so plainly allowing is that commonsense morality is a somewhat crude instrument on this matter, that it may allow for practical guidance for common people but is inadequate for special cases, and that any prescriptions on this count must remain flexible and somewhat vague. Beyond procreation, the morality of sexual relations involves fostering friendship and sympathy – a point that neatly admits both Millian and Uranian interpretation. After all, procreation is not always the aim even in heterosexual relations, and what if friendship could be fostered in other relationships and contexts? Besides, Symonds, Noel, Dakyns, Arthur Sidgwick – all had done their duty by way of procreation. The Greeks did their duty by way of procreation. Sidgwick's reference to Plato in this context, while guarded enough, is surely not coincidental. Nor, given Symonds's empirical and historical investigations, should this call for sociological evidence seem at all strange. And it is noteworthy that any discussion of how rational egoism might tackle these questions is carefully avoided.

Interestingly, on this point, Sidgwick and Moore were rather similar in being disposed to think that commonsense moral rules, mostly negative and of limited range, left a great deal of room for maneuver for the reformer trying to bring about as much goodness as possible. And despite Sidgwick's hedonism, in practice he would have approved of the pursuit of Moore's "unmixed goods" – "the love of beautiful things or of good persons." Here, of course, was the Bloomsbury religion, and a good deal of Symonds's. Curiously, however, one could urge that *Principia Ethica* was actually rather more puritanical than the *Methods*, what with Moore's pronouncements on lust:

With regard to the pleasures of lust, the nature of the cognition, by the presence of which they are to be defined, is somewhat difficult to analyse. But it appears to include both cognitions of organic sensations and perceptions of states of the body, of which the enjoyment is certainly an evil in itself. So far as these are concerned, lasciviousness would, then, include in its essence an admiring contemplation of what is ugly. But certainly one of its commonest ingredients, in its worst forms, is an enjoyment of the same state of mind in other people: and in this case it would therefore also include a love of what is evil.[2]

Sidgwick was not so dogmatic. How curious that no one thought to apply to the "inconclusive" *Methods* what Beatrice Webb said of Moore's *Principia*, in condemnation of Bloomsbury – namely, that it was "a metaphysical justification for doing what you like."[3]

At any rate, Sidgwick's arguments on the topic of purity are present in all editions of the *Methods*, from the first to the last, though in the first edition the two arguments are distinguished as "external" and "internal." But there is another argument in this section that seems to have materialized at a time especially suggestive of the influence of Symonds. Section 7 of Chapter 11 of Book III deals with how "even the prohibition of Suicide, so far as rational, seems to rest ultimately on utilitarian grounds." As in the case of purity, the emotion surrounding the issue is no indication of the clarity of the moral principles involved:

[I]t is true that among what are commonly called 'duties to self' we find the duty of self-preservation prescribed with apparent absoluteness, – at least so far as the sacrifice of one's life is not imperatively required for the preservation of the lives of others, or for the attainment of some result conceived to be very important to society. I think, however, that when confronted with the question of preserving a life which we can foresee will be both miserable and burdensome to others – e.g. the life of a man stricken with a fatal disease which precludes the possibility of work of any kind, during the weeks or months of agony that remain to him, – though Common Sense would still deny the legitimacy of suicide, even under these conditions, it would also admit the necessity of finding reasons for the denial. This admission would imply that the universal wrongness of suicide is at any rate not self-evident. And the reasons that would be found – so far as they did not ultimately depend upon premises drawn from Revelational Theology – would, I think, turn out to be utilitarian, in a broad sense of the term: it would be urged that if any exceptions to the rule prohibiting suicide were allowed, dangerous encouragement would be given to the suicidal impulse in other cases in which suicide would really be a weak and cowardly dereliction of social duty: it would also probably be urged that the toleration of suicide would facilitate secret murders. In short, the independent axiom of which we are in search seems to disappear on close examination in this case no less than in others. (ME 356)

Suicide had of course long been one of the most provocative issues in moral theory. David Hume had shocked the religious world when he defended, on a utilitarian basis, the possibility of permissible suicide, and it is perhaps not surprising that Sidgwick steered clear of this issue in earlier editions of the *Methods*. He had, as early as 1862–63, given the issue some (rather glib) thought; in connection with the candid exchanges fostered by the Initial Society, he observed that "the real reason why a virtuous suicide seems a paradox is that we can conceive no circumstances under which a man so unselfish as to kill himself for the sake of humanity would not benefit humanity more by living." For public purposes, however, the issue begins to appear only in the third edition of 1884, in the form of a note appended to Chapter 2 of Book II that reads:

> It is sometimes thought to be a necessary assumption of Hedonists that a surplus of pleasure over pain is actually attainable by human beings: a proposition which an extreme pessimist would deny. But the conclusion that life is always on the whole painful would not prove it to be unreasonable for a man to aim ultimately at minimizing pain, if this is still admitted to be possible; though it would, no doubt, drive a rational egoist to immediate suicide. (ME3 127)

The fuller discussion materializes in the fourth edition, of 1890, without any attention being called to it in the new Preface, although Sidgwick regularly indicated any important changes in that place. But the point is that he seems to have first felt compelled to address the topic in print at the very time when he was again discussing it with Symonds. In the summer of 1883, Symonds had had another collapse, was growing pessimistic about Davos, and had been getting bad news about Janet's condition. Sidgwick visited him during that period, and in a letter written to him afterwards explained:

> I do not like to answer the question you put to me about prolongation of life except in an absolutely sincere way; and, speaking quite unreservedly I must say that there are cases in which it does not seem to me that any one is morally bound to prolong his life, – supposing he can avoid causing to those dear to him the pain which anything recognised as suicide would cause, and the moral shock and painful stigma which anything publicly known to be such involves. For instance if I could foresee with approximate certainty that the last two years of my life would be what my poor mother's were, a long gradually intensified lethargy both of faculties and of emotional susceptibilities, I should think it right to cut these two years of my life in any *latent* manner that I could. I mention this because I believe my physical constitution to be very like my mother's, and so habitually contemplate this termination as a possibility – though of course not yet near enough for any practical considerations as to how to avoid it. But I cannot apply this general view to your case: for I cannot doubt that any three years you may be able to add to your life by wise management will be years of thoroughly effective human existence, – even if your power of literary work should become less vigorous and sustained. (CWC)[4]

The letter is incomplete, and breaks off with Sidgwick explaining how he is at work on "the third edition of his . . ." – but this could only be a reference to the third edition of the *Methods*.

Evidently, sex and suicide, coupled with Symondsish pessimism, provided Sidgwick with some additional cases where the egoist and the utilitarian might differ, and where the dualism of practical reason would carry serious force. Despite the guarded statement in the *Methods*, it is plain from his correspondence what Sidgwick really thinks: as in the case of hypocrisy and veracity, he allows the possibility of a more or less esoteric approach, allowing suicide but not the publicizing of it. And he also urges that he would resort to "latent" means – negative inaction rather than positive action, as in the case of the expression of his religious views. But the exact meaning of "thoroughly effective human existence" is left unclear – the phrase does not, on the face of it, settle the difference between the egoist and the utilitarian. Here Sidgwick's esotericism seems to be of the utilitarian sort, but as in the case of sex, he avoids an extended confrontation with the rational egoist, even while admitting in passing that here would be a more provocative challenge that he could not meet. After all, the challenge of the egoist on suicide is simply the flip side of the egoist on immortality: absent belief in the latter, what becomes of the prohibition of the former?

Given the suicide craze that hit England in the 1890s, and the fate of various Bloomsberries, it is ironic that Sidgwick's discussion of suicide was more forthright than anything in Moore. The "Yen," as Strachey had dubbed Moore, apparently lacked a certain penetration when it came to this problem. But for Sidgwick the issues of egoism, immortality, and suicide were intertwined, were in fact the recurrent matter of his relationship with Symonds, clearly lending additional force to the urgency he felt about the reconciliation project. His depressive periods, like Symonds's, invariably brought thoughts of suicide, kept in check largely by that all-too-thin theistic hope. Living out of a sense of duty alone could be very hard.

At any rate, these two issues, like the issue of veracity, illuminate the artful evasions at work in the *Methods* – the dry way in which Sidgwick leads the reader only so far down the road of honest questioning on matters that he is personally struggling with day in and day out, and that he clearly regards as of supreme ethical significance. And it is only an interpretive effort of this form that can effectively bring out the various ways in which

Sidgwick's project, for all his skeptical reticence, did betray many of the same elitist and Eurocentric prejudices evident in the work of Jowett and Green. Like his Oxford comrades, Sidgwick was a reformer concerned about the increasing "Philistinism" of democratic market society; if he was "the last of the Benthamites," he nonetheless went far toward burying the "Benthamite" defense of laissez-faire, and he was certainly not as complacent or conservative as the term "Government House" utilitarian suggests.[5] Still, his esotericism was quite real, and, again like his Oxford comrades, he had a vision of a revitalized civilization that could take some very disturbing turns. The Balliol of Jowett and Green had, after all, inspired Lord Curzon and Alfred Milner, as well as Mary Ward and Jane Addams. The tensions at work in such groups as the Apostles and Old Mortality did not always have a satisfactory resolution.

II. Socialisms

In the opening chapters of the *Methods*, Sidgwick carefully delineates how his study relates to politics and speculation about ideal societies. He notes how some thinkers, such as Spencer, hold that theoretical ethics ought to take the form of "Absolute Ethics,"

> ... an investigation not of what ought to be done here and now, but of what ought to be the rules of behaviour in a society of ideally perfect human beings. Thus the subject-matter of our study would be doubly ideal: as it would not only prescribe what ought to be done as distinct from what is, but what ought to be done in a society that itself *is* not, but only *ought* to be. (ME 18)

For Sidgwick, however, "it is too paradoxical to say that the whole duty of man is summed up in the effort to attain an ideal state of social relations; and unless we say this, we must determine our duties to existing men in view of existing circumstances: and this is what the student of Ethics seeks to do in a systematic manner" (ME 20).

To be sure, Sidgwick allows that ethics and politics are both departments of practical philosophy, and that both are to be distinguished from the sphere of the positive sciences by their concern with "the determination of ends to be sought, or rules to be unconditionally obeyed." And of course, insofar as politics is concerned with ideal rather than positive law, the links with ethics will be important. A view that the law of property is unjust, for example, will affect one's deliberations concerning moral duty.

Still, for Sidgwick, "the extent of this influence is vague and uncertain."

Suppose I am a slave-owner in a society in which slavery is established, and become convinced that private property in human beings should be abolished by law: it does not therefore follow that I shall regard it as my moral duty to set free my slaves at once. I may think immediate general abolition of slavery not only hopeless, but even inexpedient for the slaves themselves, who require a gradual education for freedom: so that it is better for the present to aim at legal changes that would cut off the worst evils of slavery, and meanwhile to set an example of humane and considerate treatment of bondsmen. Similar reasonings might be applied to the abolition of private property in the instruments of production, or in appointments to offices, civil or ecclesiastical. Speaking generally, the extent to which political ideals ought to influence moral duty would seem to depend partly on the apparent remoteness or nearness of the prospect of realising the ideal, partly on its imperativeness, or the expediency of immediate realisation: and the force attached to both these considerations is likely to vary with the political method adopted; so that it belongs to Politics rather than Ethics to determine them more precisely. (ME 17)

Somehow, after all political debate has been aired, there remains the question of what the individual ought to do here and now, the sphere of ethics proper.

Yet for all that, as we have seen, Sidgwick also admits that with utilitarianism, as opposed to alternative ethical conceptions, the links between ethics and politics are especially intimate, and the demands of duty more problematic. He frames this claim with considerable caution, in a lengthy passage (part of which was quoted earlier) that sheds a flood of light on his own personal strategies:

Perhaps we may say generally that an enlightened Utilitarian is likely to lay less stress on the cultivation of those negative virtues, tendencies to restrict and refrain, which are prominent in the Common-Sense ideal of character; and to set more value in comparison on those qualities of mind which are the direct source of positive pleasure to the agent or to others – some of which Common Sense scarcely recognises as excellencies. . . . Nay, we may even venture to say that, under most circumstances, a man who earnestly and successfully endeavours to realise the Utilitarian Ideal, however he may deviate from the commonly-received type of a perfect character, is likely to win sufficient recognition and praise from Common Sense. For, whether it be true or not the whole of morality has sprung from the root of sympathy, it is certain that self-love and sympathy combined are sufficiently strong in average men to dispose them to grateful admiration of any exceptional efforts to promote the common good, even though these efforts may take a somewhat novel form.... And it seems to be principally in this direction that the recent spread of Utilitarianism has positively modified the ideal of our society, and is likely to modify it further in the future. Hence the stress which Utilitarians are apt to lay on social and political activity of all kinds, and the tendency which Utilitarian ethics have always shown to pass over into politics. For one who values conduct in proportion to its felicific consequences, will naturally set a higher estimate on effective beneficence in public affairs than on the purest manifestation of virtue in the details of private life: while on the other hand an Intuitionist (though no doubt vaguely recognising that a man ought to do all the good he can in public affairs) still commonly holds that virtue may be as fully and as admirably exhibited on a small as on a large scale. A sincere Utilitarian, therefore, is likely to be an eager politician: but on what principles his political action ought to be determined, it scarcely lies within the scope of this treatise to investigate. (ME 494–95)

Thus, while admitting that the dualism of the *Methods* on balance demonstrates the greater role for calculation – and hence uncertainty – in ethics, as compared to Whewellian intuitionism, Sidgwick is nonetheless at pains to urge the utilitarian reformer that it would not be very utilitarian to incur "general condemnation," a reactionary backlash. Still, there is no question that common sense needs reforming, and that the negative, side-constraint conception of morals and virtue needs to evolve in such a way as to make for a more positive, utilitarian character type. Given the going mix of self-love and sympathy, common sense at least contains the seeds of an appreciation for the high-minded utilitarian reformer.

Of course, what the *Methods* does repeatedly say, in this connection, is that such efforts at reform must be exercised with the greatest care, given the fledgling state of sociology and most of the social sciences that would be instrumental in designing societal improvement. Much as he admires the sweep of Spencer's system, and the powerful emphasis on personal altruism in Comte, Sidgwick is forever trying to rein their efforts in, to avoid the "illimitable cloudland" of utopian speculation. Thus,

I hold that the utilitarian, in the existing state of our knowledge, cannot possibly construct a morality *de novo* either for man as he is (abstracting his morality), or for man as he ought to be and will be. He must start, speaking broadly, with the existing social order, and the existing morality as a part of that order: and in deciding the question whether any divergence from this code is to be recommended, must consider chiefly the immediate consequences of such divergence, upon a society in which such a code is conceived generally to subsist. No doubt a thoughtful and well-instructed Utilitarian may see dimly a certain way ahead. . . . he may see a prospect of social changes which will render a relaxation of other parts of the moral code expedient or inevitable. But if he keeps within the limits that separate scientific prevision from fanciful Utopian conjecture, the form of society to which his practical conclusions relate will be one varying but little from the actual, with its actually established code of moral rules and customary judgments concerning virtue and vice. (ME 473–74)

Sidgwick clearly regarded himself as a "thoughtful and well-instructed" utilitarian, one who would win the praise and not the censure of common sense through his efforts to promote a more comprehensive sympathy, while paying due court to the "Thou shalt nots" of traditional morality. Certainly, as we have seen, the negative virtues played a considerable role in his personal efforts to avoid hypocrisy, though viewed from this angle, his reticence could be regarded as a utilitarian compromise with the common regard for a decorous silence with respect to painful topics. That is, it suggests that his somewhat puzzling acceptance of the difference between acts and omissions – puzzling for a utilitarian – made sense in utilitarian terms as a necessary compromise with the established code. And a pretty convenient one, from his perspective, one that could certainly afford him a defense against any charge of "corrupting youth."

The note in these warnings against an excess of reforming or revolutionary zeal seems to be steadfastly Millian – a resolute agnosticism about what we can claim to know about the potential of individuals and societies, and a correlative call for piecemeal experimentation rather than a vague faith that a "Cosmos" might arise out of a "Chaos." And this is, of course, no coincidence, given how all the while Sidgwick was struggling with religious and ethical issues, he was also struggling with the study of political economy and politics, balancing the one interest against the other.

But the *Methods* scarcely indicates the complex content of Sidgwick's politics. Its few references to the "socialistic ideal" are not particularly enthusiastic. Thus, in Chapter 5 of Book III, he recognizes that various political thinkers "hold that Justice requires a mode of distributing payment for services, entirely different from that at present effected by free competition: and that all labourers ought to be paid according to the intrinsic value of their labour as estimated by enlightened and competent judges." If this socialist ideal could be effected "without counterbalancing evils," he allows, "it would certainly seem to give a nearer approximation to what we conceive as Divine Justice than the present state of society affords." But of course, he sets up this ideal only to demolish it by showing how impracticable it would really be, exposed to all the difficulties of the hedonistic method and then some. Thus, common sense "regards as Utopian any general attempt to realise this ideal in the social distribution of the means of happiness," and in the

> actual state of society it is only within a very limited range that any endeavour is made to reward Good Desert.... the only kind of Justice which we try to realise is that whi.h consists in the fulfilment of contracts and definite expectations; leaving the general fairness of Distribution by Bargaining to take care of itself. (ME 289–90)

Similarly, in a somewhat heated letter in response to Sir Louis Mallot, Sidgwick denies that he is a radical favoring big government: "Nor do I anywhere propose to 'throw on government the task of dispensing distributive justice.' Nor do I 'propose' that the community should take possession of private capital employed in production: I expressly say that such a proposal is not even ripe for practical discussion." Allowing that there is "a 'growing inequality' in distribution, if the difference between the highest and the lowest class was increasing," he nonetheless explains that the "loose phrase that the 'rich are getting richer and the poor poorer' is one that I should never use." (CWC)[6]

Yet these sharp cautionary disclaimers do not capture the more progressive aspects of Sidgwick's view. Mallot, like Friedrich Hayek in more recent times, was not really off base in suspecting Sidgwick of working with great subtlety to undermine the foundations of laissez-faire, one of the basic components of the old Benthamite platform. In an interesting piece of appropriation, Albert Venn Dicey, in *Law and Public Opinion*, would approvingly quote his friend Sidgwick's confession that "we were as much surprised as the 'general reader' to learn from Mill's *Autobiography* that our master, the author of the much-admired treatise, 'On Liberty,' had been all the while looking forward to a time when the division of the produce of labour should be 'made by concert.'" But Dicey excises the next line in Sidgwick's confession, which reads:

> But though Mill had concealed from us the extent of his Socialism, we were all, I think, conscious of having received from him a certain impulse in the Socialistic direction: he had at any rate ceased to regard the science of Political Economy as opposing a hard and fast barrier against the Socialistic conception of the ideal goal of economic progress.[7]

The quotation misleadingly employed by Dicey is from Sidgwick's late essay "The Economic Lessons of Socialism" (1895) – a piece that, along with the other relevant essays in *Miscellaneous Essays and Addresses*, does an admirable job of presenting in short compass some of Sidgwick's serious meditations on the question of socialism in their more or less final form. In these essays, what Mill and Taylor had only suspected by way of the coming relevance of socialism is taken for granted: "The present unmistakable drift towards Socialism in Western Europe is a fact of great interest, and a reasonable source of alarm to some, and perhaps of hope to others, from the political and economic changes to which it tends" (MEA 235). A somewhat earlier essay, "Economic Socialism" (1886), flatly states that "Socialism is flowing in upon us with a full tide" (MEA 200). Although Sidgwick does not follow Mill in the full blush of his enthusiasm, he does allow that the controversies generated by an increasingly open-minded political economy on the one side, and an increasingly implacable Marxism on the other, have had a valuable result, though he concludes that "the next lesson of importance will come through experiment rather than reasoning." This is not an experiment in socialist communes or cooperatives of the sort Mill had admired and encouraged, New Harmony or Rochdale. Sidgwick recognizes that the experiment must be tried at a more ambitious level, and he dryly suggests that "the post of honour" in this branch of knowledge go to Germany.

Just how destructive of Benthamite orthodoxy Sidgwick's arguments could be is well brought out by "Economic Socialism," which in fact follows in brief the lines of his *Principles of Political Economy*. The case for laissez-faire, or economic individualism, is described thusly:

[A]ssuming that the conduct of individuals is generally characterised by a fairly intelligent and alert pursuit of their private interests – regard for self interest on the part of consumers will lead to the effectual demand for the commodities that are most useful to society, and regard for self-interest on the part of producers will lead to the production of such commodities at the least cost. If any material part of the ordinary supply of any commodity A were generally estimated as less adapted for the satisfaction of social needs than the quantity of another commodity B that could be produced at the same cost, the demand of consumers would be diverted from A to B, so that A would fall in market value and B rise; and this change in values would cause a diversion of the efforts of producers from A to B to the extent required. On the other hand, the self-interest of producers will tend to the production of everything at the least possible cost; because the self-interest of employers will lead them to purchase services most cheaply, taking account of quality, and the self-interest of labourers will make them endeavour to supply the best paid – and therefore most useful – services for which they are adapted. Thus the only thing required of Government is to secure that every one shall be really free to buy the utility he most wants, and to sell what he can best furnish. (MEA 201)

Having thus set out the case with his customary impartiality, Sidgwick goes on just as carefully to tick off the exceptions that he suggests are "due to the manifest limitations under which abstract economic theory is necessarily applied to the art of government." Thus, it obviously assumes that individuals are sensibly self-interested, and "even the extremest advocate of *laisser-faire* does not extend this assumption to children," which means that the condition of children must be discussed on entirely different principles. Moreover, the political economists are concerned with wealth, which is only one element of the statesman's concerns. Wealth may rightly be subordinated to considerations of physical or moral well-being:

If we regard a man merely as a means of producing wealth, it might pay to allow a needle-grinder to work himself to death in a dozen years, as it was said to pay some American sugar-planters to work their slaves to death in six or eight; but a civilised community cannot take this view of its members; and the fact that a man will deliberately choose to work himself to death in a dozen years for an extra dozen shillings a week is not a decisive reason for allowing him to make the sacrifice unchecked. In this and similar cases we interfere on other than economic grounds: and it is by such extra-economic considerations that we justify the whole mass of sanitary regulations; restrictions on the sale of opium, brandy, and other intoxicants; prohibitions of lotteries, regulation of places of amusement; and similar measures. (MEA 203)

The political economist might investigate the effects of such regulations, but strictly speaking, the principles on which the interference is based fall outside the competence of the discipline.[8] Indeed, when it comes to classical political economy, the distinction between giving an account of how the free market might enhance the production of a nation and assessing the justice of the resulting distribution of wealth is all-important. Unlike various French political economists (e.g., Bastiat), the English school has never been persuaded that enhancing the production of wealth has much to do with reward in accordance with desert:

[G]enerally speaking, English political economists, however 'orthodox,' have never thought of denying that the remuneration of workers tends to be very largely determined by causes independent of their deserts – e.g. by fluctuations in supply and demand, from the effects of which they are quite unable to protect themselves. If our economists have opposed – as they doubtless have always opposed – any suggestion that Government should interfere directly to redress such inequalities in distribution, their argument has not been that the inequalities were merited; they have rather urged that any good such interference might do in the way of more equitable distribution would be more than outweighed by the harm it would do to production, through impairing the motives to energetic self-help. . . . If, however, we can find a mode of intervention which will reduce inequalities of distribution without materially diminishing motives to self-help, this kind of intervention is not, I conceive, essentially opposed to the teaching even of orthodox political economy – according to the English standard of orthodoxy; for orthodox economy is quite ready to admit that the poverty and depression of any industrial class is liable to render its members less productive from want of physical vigour and restricted industrial opportunities. Now, an important part of the recent, and the proposed, enlargement of governmental functions, which is vaguely attacked as socialistic, certainly aims at benefiting the poor in such a way as to make them more self-helpful instead of less so, and thus seeks to mitigate inequalities in distribution without giving offence to the orthodox economist. This is the case, e.g., with the main part of governmental provision for education, and the provision of instruments of knowledge by libraries etc. for adults. (MEA 204–5)

Furthermore, against the objection that such public goods can be supplied only by taxation, and that it is immoral to tax one class for the benefit of another, Sidgwick replies that if the thing in question serves the good of the community as a whole, it is right to tax the community as a whole. Beyond that, he is keenly aware of the logic of public goods, of cases where the market will necessarily fail to provide the good in question because of such problems as nonexclusion. Thus, he describes the case where "a particular employment of labour or capital may be most useful to the community, and yet the conditions of its employment may be such that the labourer or capitalist cannot remunerate himself in the ordinary way, by free exchange of his commodity, because he cannot appropriate his beneficial results sufficiently to sell them profitably" (MEA 209). Here he gives the stock example of the lighthouse, whose beacon will shine even for shipowners who do not help pay for it. Moreover, he appreciates the problem of collective action generally:

Take, for instance, the case of certain fisheries, where it is clearly for the general interest that the fish should not be caught at certain times, or in certain places, or with certain instruments; because the increase of actual supply obtained by such captures is much overbalanced by the detriment it causes to prospective supply. We may fairly assume that the great majority of possible fishermen would enter into a voluntary agreement to observe the required rules of abstinence; but it is obvious that the larger the number that thus voluntarily abstain, the stronger inducement is offered to the remaining few to pursue their fishing in the objectionable times, places, and ways, so long as they are under no legal coercion to abstain. (MEA 208)

And of course, Sidgwick also lists the familiar examples of market failure due to monopoly – noting that the advance of civilization seems to favor combination as much as competition – and what are nowadays referred to as "negative externalities," such as pollution, destroying valuable resources such as rare plants and animals, and so on.

Now, the combined effect of all these counterexamples to the logic of the market was undoubtedly to dampen the fervor of those dogmatically attached to the doctrine of laissez-faire. Sidgwick admits that he has not shown that in all such cases government interference would be best, since it may be, in any given case, impossible to effect a correction in a worthwhile fashion. But what he has done, of course, is to show how much rides on empirical evidence that could go one way or another. His only real concern about socialism is the quite modern one that it might, barring a change in human motivation, mean splendidly equal destitution.

Naturally, as a "mere empirical utilitarian," Sidgwick has very little patience for doctrines of "natural rights," in this department as in others. Any such creed leads to impossible muddles, or to very different conclusions from those suggested by the more doctrinaire advocates. As he shows at length in the case of Spencer:

For what, according to Mr. Spencer, is the foundation of the right of property? It rests on the natural right of a man to the free exercise of his faculties, and therefore to the results of his labour; but this can clearly give no right to exclude others from the use of the bounties of Nature: hence the obvious inference is that the price which – as Ricardo and his disciples teach – is increasingly paid, as society progresses, for the use of the 'natural and original powers of the soil,' must belong, by natural right, to the human community as a whole; it can only be through usurpation that it has fallen into the hands of private individuals. Mr. Spencer himself... has drawn this conclusion in the most emphatic terms. That 'equity does not admit property in land'; that 'the right of mankind at large to the earth's surface is still valid, all deeds, customs, and laws notwithstanding'; that 'the right of private possession of the soil is no right at all'; that 'no amount of labour bestowed by an individual upon a part of the earth's surface can nullify the title of society to that part'; that, finally, 'to deprive others of their rights to the use of the earth is a crime inferior only in wickedness to the crime of taking away their lives or personal liberties'; – these conclusions are enforced by Mr. Spencer with an emphasis that makes Mr. Henry George appear a plagiarist. (MEA 211–12)

But what is more, such conclusions cannot be contained to the case of land. Clearly, "the original and indefeasible right of all men to the free exercise of their faculties on their material environment must – if valid at all – extend to the whole of the environment; property in raw material of movables must be as much a usurpation as property in land." By such arguments, Sidgwick drives the principles of the great social Darwinian defender of individualism ever further away from the notion of a market society:

The only way that is left of reconciling the Spencerian doctrine of natural right with the teachings of orthodox political economy, seems to be just that 'doctrine of ransom' which the semi-socialists have more or less explicitly put forward. Let the rich, landowners and capitalists alike, keep their property, but let them ransom the flaw in their titles by compensating the other human beings residing in their country for that free use of their material environment which has been withdrawn from them; only let this compensation be given in such a way as not to impair the mainsprings of energetic and self-helpful industry. We cannot restore to the poor their original share in the spontaneous bounties of Nature; but we can give them instead a fuller share than they could acquire unaided of the more communicable advantages of social progress, and a fairer start in the inevitable race for the less communicable advantages; and 'reparative justice' demands that we should give them this much. (MEA 213)

Sidgwick is of course aware that the apostle of social Darwinism would hardly go all the way with this generous reconstruction, even though his remarks really were departing from Spencer's views on land, and he also admits that the semisocialist argument needs a good deal of working out in legislative details and has often incurred just criticism. In fact, this line of argument, which Sidgwick repeated in a number of places, drew an irate response from Spencer himself, whose (limited) correspondence with Sidgwick is largely concerned with asking him to alter such misrepresentations in future editions (something Sidgwick apparently chose not to do).[9] Interestingly, however, Sidgwick also makes it plain enough that his version of mere empirical utilitarianism has a good deal of sympathy for such semisocialism, and that his chief objections to governmental interference are not objections to socialism per se.

Thus, it is the remarkable, careful accumulation of the arguments compromising or rendering indeterminate the case for the market that makes Sidgwick appear as much on the side of the socialists as on that of orthodox political economy. What is so often missing in his critical remarks on ideal socialism or utopianism is this keenly balanced account of the failings on the other side, the impossibility of believing anything like the old Benthamite case for laissez-faire. To appreciate his considered opinions, it is essential to grasp just what he thought of gradual change in a socialist direction. To be sure, the socialism with which he was most in accord, owing so much to Mill and Maurice, was in many respects a conservative, counterrevolutionary alternative. But with the retrospect afforded by the history of socialism in the twentieth century, his views on the matter often seem singularly sane.[10]

Much the same line of argument is advanced in one of Sidgwick's best-known essays, "The Scope and Method of Economic Science," which was his presidential address to the economic and statistics section of the British Association in 1885. There, too, he makes it quite clear that "the absolute right of the individual to unlimited industrial freedom is now only maintained by a scanty and dwindling handful of doctrinaires, whom the progress of economic science has left stranded on the crude generalisations of an earlier period." Under the "more philosophic guidance of J. S. Mill, English political economy shook off all connection with these antiquated metaphysics, and during the last generation has been generally united with a view of political principles more balanced, qualified, and empirical, and therefore more in harmony with the general tendencies of modern scientific thought." (MEA 175, 174) Indeed, Sidgwick is rarely more emphatic than in his disparagement of that "kind of political economy which flourishes in proud independence of facts; and undertakes to settle all practical problems of Governmental interference or private philanthropy by simple deduction from one or two general assumptions – of which the chief is the assumption of the universally beneficent and

harmonious operation of self-interest well let alone." The "more completely this survival of the *a priori* politics of the eighteenth century can
be banished to the remotest available planet, the better it will be . . . for the
progress of economic science." (MEA 171)

Moreover, the "assumption that egoism ought to be universal – that the
prevalence of self-interest leads necessarily to the best possible economic
order – has never been made by leading English writers," their only concern being "the actual prevalence of self-interest in ordinary exchanges of
products and services." However, he admits that the political economists
ought to adopt a different tone in their work, one less blandly accepting of
the role of self-interest, and that they ought to stress more clearly the ways
in which their account of self-interested action is circumscribed. Thus,

it should be noted that the ordinary economic man is always understood to be
busily providing for a wife and children; so that his dominant motive to industry
is rather domestic interest than self-interest, strictly so-called. And it has never
been supposed that outside his private business – or even in connection with it if
occasion arises – a man will not spend labour and money for public objects, and
give freely gratuitous services to friends, benefactors, and persons in special need
or distress. (MEA 184)

These considerations certainly point up, once again, the need for sup-
plementing economic analysis with historical and sociological study. The
problem, for Sidgwick, is that the other forms of knowledge needed to
supplement political economy are in a far more rudimentary state, and
the claims of many of the great founding figures of disciplines such as
sociology border on the ridiculous. Thus, with reference to an issue as
dear to him as any:

Take, for example, the question of the future of religion. No thoughtful person
can overlook the importance of religion as an element of man's social existence;
nor do the sociologists to whom I have referred fail to recognise it. But if we
inquire after the characteristics of the religion of which their science leads them
to foresee the coming prevalence, they give with nearly equal confidence answers
as divergent as can be conceived. Schäffle cannot comprehend that the place
of the great Christian Churches can be taken by anything but a purified form
of Christianity; Spencer contemplates complacently the reduction of religious
thought and sentiment to a perfectly indefinite consciousness of an Unknowable
and the emotion that accompanies this peculiar intellectual exercise; while Comte
has no doubt that the whole history of religion – which, as he says, 'should

resume the entire history of human development' – has been leading up to the worship of the Great Being, Humanity, personified domestically for each normal male individual by his nearest female relatives. It would certainly seem that the science which allows these discrepancies in its chief expositors must be still in its infancy. . . . when we look closely into their work it becomes only too evident that each philosopher has constructed on the basis of personal feeling and experience his ideal future in which our present social deficiencies are to be remedied; and that the process by which history is arranged in steps pointing towards his Utopia bears not the faintest resemblance to a scientific demonstration. (MEA 193–94)

Thus, when the "statesman" turns to Sidgwick for guidance, he would seem to get only a compromised political economy and a dismissive account of how laughably speculative sociology was – small wonder that Sidgwick was regarded as a hostile critic by the early sociologists eager to establish their disciplinary credentials.

Yet for all of his worries about the "illimitable cloudland" of utopian speculation, Sidgwick was nonetheless warmly sympathetic to semisocialistic views derived from a more nuanced and historical approach to political economy. About the only point in Bentham's political economy that he adopts without qualification is the principle of declining marginal utility, such that there is a prima facie case for equality, given how much more utility a poor person gets out of a dollar than a rich one. What is more, in the *Elements of Politics* he would argue that "most of us would readily accept, as a moral ideal, what I may call *ethical* as contrasted with *political* socialism; that is, the doctrine that the services which men have to render to others should be rendered, as far as possible, with a genuine regard to the interests of others" (EP 42). Here again he expresses his admiration for Mill, for the view that "every person who lives by any useful work should be habituated to regard himself, not as an individual working for his private benefit, but as a public functionary" – that is, as someone working for the benefit of society.

What this sketch might suggest is that Sidgwick's destructive, critical analysis also worked to open up various possibilities, possibilities for the future that, while not underwritten by any laws of historical progress, were at least not constrained by the narrowness of Benthamite political economy. Reformers could actively create a better future by cultural improvement; the responsibility for doing so fell on them, not on "history" or "human nature." This is, of course, not exactly Whitmania, or even that society of "ideal" utilitarians with perfect information and motivation, and no one has ever charged Sidgwick's *Principles of Political Economy* and *Elements of Politics* with being utopian. But then, their critical potential has never been fully appreciated either.

III. Methods and Principles

In a great many ways, Sidgwick's treatises on the *Principles of Political Economy* and the *Elements of Politics*, as well as his posthumous *The Development of European Polity*, were companion works. He had been laboring on these topics ever since his Apostolic days and his first exposure to Mill's *Logic*, *Principles of Political Economy*, and *Considerations on Representative Government*. "Mill's influence," it should be recalled, led him "as a matter of duty" to "study political economy throughly, and give no little thought to practical questions, social and political" (M 36). In 1861, he wrote to Dakyns, "I live a lotus-eating life, unmingled with introspection (just at present), but not free from many anxieties as to the future; and tempered with political economy, which I am studying just as a ballast to my necessarily busy selfishness, which would otherwise be intolerable to my real self" (M 66).

And this study was more or less constantly taking place alongside various relevant practical activities in politics and university reform. In an exuberant letter of 1875, he explains to C. H. Pearson how "we had separated History from Law and ballasted it with Political Philosophy and Economy and Intenational Law in order to make the course a better training for the reasoning Faculties – in fact, to some extent carried out Seeley's idea of identifying History and Politics." His colleague Seeley's idea of "inductive" political science was based on the twofold conviction that "the right method of studying political science is an essentially historical method, and . . . the right method of studying political history is to study it as material for political science." Sidgwick observed that this training for statesmen was objected to by some historical "fanatics." (M 295)

But the Millian optimism of the mid-Victorian era was to undergo increasing strain during the seventies and eighties, thanks in no small part to the economic reversals and agricultural depression that would make it evident to figures such as Sidgwick that free trade was not the cure-all that had been advertised. As E. J. Feuchtwanger describes it, in a chapter entitled "The 1880s: Victorian Confidence Falters," the year "1873 marked the end of one of the most frantic booms of the nineteenth century both in the international and the British economy." There was no spectacular crash, but only a

slackening of business activity and profits accompanied by a prolonged drop in prices, and unemployment – although the word itself was hardly yet established in the vocabulary and there were no reliable statistics for it. All this was not a new phenomenon, but it seemed more prolonged than in previous slumps, for by the end of the 1870s there were only slight signs of recovery. A renewed down-turn in the middle 1880s reinforced the feeling that the Golden Age was a thing of the past.[11]

Agriculture, now threatened by cheap grain imports from North America, was no longer protected in the event of bad harvests and low prices, and it led the slump. After the long interlude, the eighties would mark the resurgence of labor unrest and demands for democracy. Thus, Sidgwick's personal depression was a microcosm of the larger national depression as well.

At any rate, at this earlier point, during the latter half of the 1870s, Sidgwick is understandably increasingly concerned with political econ-omy, writing and lecturing on it. And in a still more practical vein, he finds himself "drawn more and more into some local quasi-philanthropic work at Cambridge.... it is the business of reconstructing the old 'Mendicity' Society on the principles of the London Charity Organisation Society."

Sidgwick finds this practical philanthropy singularly instructive:

Though we have not yet much to do, the work is very interesting, not less that the *positive* part of it is very perplexing. The negative part, the elimination of impostors, is in the main very easy; the profesional mendicants either do not come to our office to be inquired into or their case soon breaks down for the most part. But the positive work, the helping of people who ought to be helped, presents great difficulties; for the people we have to deal with are so often just trembling morally on the verge of helpless pauperism, and it is very hard to say in any case whether the help we give will cheer and stimulate a man to help himself, or whether it will not just push him gently into the passive condition of letting society take him in hand and do what it will with him. (M 342)

Apparently, this work also kept Sidgwick tossing and turning at night, wrestling with his conscience about his casuistry.

Sidgwick had in fact been involved with the old Mendicity Society since 1871, and he would continue to be very actively involved with the new version, the Cambridge Charity Organisation Society, which he did as much as anyone to found. He chaired its executive committee in 1880, 1881, and 1882, and from 1886 to 1890, during the years when he was also active in the Political Economy Club and served as president of section F of the British Association. Thus, in this case, as with the *Methods*, his academic work was developed in conjunction with various personal practical involvements that were masked by his abstract, neutral style. The topic of charity, in particular, would serve him as a conduit for many of his ethical and political investigations, posing difficult problems for the effort to render people more sympathetic. And this is not to mention how much he influenced such figures as his troublesome colleague Alfred Marshall, H. S. Foxwell, and F. Y. Edgeworth, whose pathbreaking *Old and New Methods of Ethics* and *Mathematical Physics* were friendly gestures toward Sidgwick's work.

In short, Sidgwick was, like Mill, an ethicist completely versed in the economic science of his day, and a theorist with a practical bent as well. There was, it would seem, nothing he relished more than putting together some minutely detailed scheme for finance or taxation, as is evident from his correspondence with Arthur Balfour and from such works as his "Memorandum to the Royal Commission on Local Taxation."[12] He appears even to have been involved with the Cabinet Makers Cooperative in Cambridge, and to have done a considerable amount of economic counseling for the university during its times of financial trouble.[13] But Mill had died just before England had entered its long downturn and the imperialistic reaction that was to follow it. Sidgwick would be forced to reconsider political economy in this more trying historical context.

Sidgwick's *Principles* was widely regarded as important mainly for the care with which it set out conceptual clarifications of such notions as wealth and value, and for its lengthy systematizing of the exceptions to the individualistic principle. Indeed, the book is organized in much the same way as the various essays discussed earlier, an organization that would also feature in the *Elements*, with which it is very closely linked. It was part of Sidgwick's characteristic approach to political economy to insist on being absolutely clear about the difference between economic science, with its empirical claims about how people do behave in certain contexts, and the art of public economic policy, with its judgments about how people, or society, ought to behave and the best public policies for government. He insists that the divisions of the study be respected:

Political Economy, as commonly studied, has included a theoretical and a practical branch, which it is important to distinguish clearly, since there is a popular disposition to confound their respective premises and conclusions. For brevity, it seems convenient to refer to them as the Science and the Art of Political Economy; the latter being historically the subject to which the term was mainly applied in its earlier use, whereas among English political economists from the beginning of the nineteenth century there has been a tendency to restrict it to the former. The science of Political Economy deals with a certain class of social activities having an economic aspect, as well as more or less influence on the activities with which Political Economy is more specially concerned. . . . the Art of Political Economy, which deals with a special department of governmental interference, designed to improve either the social production of wealth or its distribution, may be partially, but only partially, separated from the general art of legislation or government. . . . (PPE 33)

And the volume is thus divided into three books, the first on production, the second on distribution and exchange, and the third on the art of political economy. There are also several rather famous introductory chapters dealing with the "present state of economic controversies," the scope of political economy, and its method – chapters that also served as the material for Sidgwick's contributions to Palgrave's *Dictionary of Political Economy* – but these were added only for the third and final edition, which appeared posthumously.

In all editions, however, the work is presented as affording a reconciliation between the conflicting doctrines of recent days, which have done so much to set back the hopeful progress of the discipline as it had existed in Mill's day. Thus, he explains:

My primary aim, then, has been to eliminate unnecessary controversy, by stating these results in a more guarded manner, and with due attention to the criticisms and suggestions of recent writers. Several valuable contributions to abstract economic theory have been made by Cairnes, Jevons, and others, who have written since Mill; but in my opinion they generally admit of being stated in a form less hostile to the older doctrines than their authors suppose. In the same way the opposition between the Inductive and Deductive Methods appears to have been urged by writers on both sides in needlessly sharp and uncompromising terms. An endeavour will be made to shew that there is an important part of the subject to which economists are generally agreed in applying a mainly inductive or 'realistic' treatment. On the other hand, there are probably few who would deny the utility and even indispensability of deductive reasoning in the Theory of Distribution and Exchange; provided only the assumptions on which such reasoning proceeds are duly stated, and their partially hypothetical character continually borne in mind. I fully admit the importance of this latter proviso; accordingly in those parts of this work in which I have used chiefly deductive reasoning, I have made it my special aim to state explicitly and keep clearly in view the limited and conditioned applicability of the conclusions attained by it. (PPE 7)

The tone is not unlike that of the *Methods*, with its sustained attempt to get beyond present controversies in the search for common ground. And as in the *Methods*, this involves a great deal of reworking of the old Benthamite position. Clearly, given how receptive he is to the inductive, or historical, form of analysis, Sidgwick is not about to reprise the role of Bentham or James Mill in the controversy with Macaulay, extending the a priori or deductive form of rational–actor analysis to economics, politics, and everything else. Indeed, he would seem to be especially concerned to insinuate a good deal more historical analysis into the very heart of economic theory. His approach to the social sciences generally would seem especially indebted to Macaulay and the various neo-Romantic forces that Mill had partially assimilated. Custom and habit, very much matters of historical variation, are for Sidgwick, as for Mill, prominent features of human action that no student of human society can afford to ignore. Sidgwick even goes quite beyond Mill in highlighting at least the potential importance of "national character" in connection with such things as "habitual energy," and this in some very questionable, possibly racialist ways.

At any rate, Sidgwick explains,

[I]n declaring that the method of Political Economy, regarded as a concrete science, is necessarily to a great extent inductive, we also declare that it is necessarily historical, in a wide sense of the term; for the facts of which it seeks to ascertain the empirical laws, in order to penetrate their causal connexions, are facts that belong to the history of human societies. The question can only be how far the history to be studied is recent or remote.

And on this question, he has a very characteristic point to make against the historical approach:

[I]t may be worth while to point out to the more aggressive 'historicists' that the more the historian establishes the independence of his own study, by bringing into clear view the great differences between the economic conditions with which we are familiar and those of earlier ages, the more, *primê facie*, he tends to establish the corresponding independence of the economic science which, pursued with a view to practice, is primarily concerned to understand the present. (PPE 48)

Thus, the more effectively the historian demonstrates the inapplicability of economic analysis to medieval conditions, the more medieval conditions may appear inapplicable to ours. Progressive history poses such dilemmas for economics, just as it does for religious doctrine.

Just how successful Sidgwick was in this attempt to fashion a more eclectic, diversified approach to economic analysis is hard to say. Although he is sometimes designated one of the two founders of the Cambridge school of economics – the other of course being Marshall – he is often treated only glancingly, if at all, in histories of economic theory. Phyllis Deane, in *The New Palgrave*, expresses the view of many: "The fact is that the *Principles* owed more to the classical tradition of J. S. Mill than to what contemporaries were then calling the 'new political economy' of Jevons and Marshall."[14] Similarly, Mark Blaug states that "Cairnes' *Leading Principles* (1874) and Sidgwick's *Principles* (1883) were entirely cast in the old mold," though he goes on to say that the "dominant view among English economists in the 1870s and 1880s was that of the Historical School," that such historicism "was an indigenous growth, whose roots go back to Carlyle's and Ruskin's protests against the narrow scope of classical political economy," and that this "English *Methodenstreit*" was finally "put to rest by John Neville Keynes's *Scope and Methods of Political Economy* (1890) and by Marshall's conciliatory attitude in the *Principles* (1890), by which time the new movement had successfully vanquished all vestiges of classical economics."[15] Howey, in the *Rise of the Marginal Utility School*, also insists that economists "must add something to and take something away from hedonism, as ordinarily construed, before it becomes marginal utility economics. Jevons and Gossen could make the transformation; Sidgwick never could."[16]

Scott Gordon, in at least partial contrast, has argued that the "orientation of Marshall's work to what is today called 'welfare economics' was due in part to Sidgwick's contribution to economic theory and his connection of it to the philosophy of utilitarianism," and he also notes how Edgeworth's efforts at a science of "hedonometry" were consciously indebted to Sidgwick.[17] And Blaug actually cites sources that argue that Sidgwick was the link between Marshall and Pigou's welfare economics, as well as noting that the *Principles* "seems to have been the first to question the traditional idea that technical change is necessarily capital-using."[18]

Sorting out Sidgwick's various connections to Marshall, Keynes, Edgeworth, H. S. Foxwell, P. Wicksteed, and all the other eminent figures in the history of economics with whom he had close intellectual dealings would be a very difficult task. This is in part because, as close as this group may have been in its Oxbridge connections, there was a good deal of division and conflict among them when it came to the nature and direction of political economy. In fact, as previously noted, once Marshall became professor of political economy at Cambridge, in 1884, he lost no time in seeking a hostile confrontation with Sidgwick over his views on the teaching of economics as part of the Moral Sciences, and much else besides. Sidgwick's response, in addition to comparing himself to Clough, allowed that "not knowing what road is best for humanity to walk in, I want all roads that claim to be roads to be well made and hedged in" (M 396). Little wonder that Sidgwick thought of his teaching as an effort at "concentrating fog," or that the Moral Sciences Board would often feature Sidgwick v. Marshall.

As far as the direction of teaching economics was concerned, Marshall was clearly the one in the ascendant. It was Marshall, as much as anyone, who fought to establish the new discipline of economics, rather than rehabilitating the old one of political economy. The emphasis on marginal utility theory, and on formal analysis generally, the increasing mathematicization of the profession, would play no small role in making Sidgwick's *Principles* look antiquated. Thus, a reviewer in *The Athenaeum* charged that notwithstanding his expression of gratitude to Jevons, "it is doubtful whether Mr. Sidgwick has caught the full bearings of the former's fructifying idea of 'final utility.' He rejects with Cairnes the application of mathematical conceptions to economics, ignoring the possibility of a treatment akin to that of the calculus of variations and dealing with indeterminate quantity."[19]

And yet for all that, one can make a strong case that Sidgwick's careful distinctions between the science and art of political economy, and his measured introduction of the inductive, historical side of the methodology, did end up shaping the course taken by Marshall and Keynes, both of whom clearly owed him a great deal. If Marshall would go on to favor what Sidgwick (like many since) regarded as ill-defined biological analogies, as tools for thinking about the evolution of social systems, he would also insist on the historical side of his work. For all his differences with Sidgwick, Marshall's work, as Ronald Coase has observed, "always emphasizes induction, collection and assembly of facts, and plays down what we would term 'theory,' a word which . . . he did not much like when applied to economics."[20] Furthermore, J. S. Nicholson, another prominent economist of this era, would in a survey article in 1913 give a notably generous assessment of Sidgwick's contribution that linked him directly to Marshall's hand-picked Cambridge successor:

Sidgwick showed very clearly that the principle of utility needed serious qualifications, and in the end, in spite of his thorough-going support of utilitarianism, he considers 'only very mild and gentle steps towards the realisation of the socialistic ideal as at all acceptable in the present state of our knowledge.' Prof. Pigou's economy of reference to Sidgwick is even more strange than his reticence regarding Adam Smith. For not only does the younger writer apply the same general principle of utility, but the main trend of the argument is the same. Yet Sidgwick's name is only mentioned in connexion with one or two points of minor detail. If Prof. Pigou had really appreciated the work of Sidgwick, he would have been saved from some unfortunate inconsistencies, and from some appalling lacunae in his argument.[21]

In the end, Marshall too expressed considerable admiration for Sidgwick's work, calling the section in the *Principles* on the art of political economy the best thing of its kind in any language.

Now, whatever its failings in formal analysis, Sidgwick's treatment of the issues of wealth and value and the "Art" of political economy is extremely carefully thought out, and he took some pride in the "elaborateness" of his discussion. He analyzes at great length the difficulties involved in giving any very precise general content to the basic terms of political economy. As he conceives it, the basic questions for the theory of production are: "What are the causes that make the average annual produce per head of a given community at a given time greater than that of another whose primary wants are not materially different, or greater than its own produce at a previous state of history?" and "What are the laws of their operation?" (PPE 99) As for exchange and distribution, the main question is:

'According to what laws is the new increment of commodities, continually produced by the combination of the labour and unequally distributed capital (including land) of different members of the community, shared among the different classes of persons who have co-operated in producing it, either by their personal exertion – bodily or mental – or by allowing others to use their wealth, knowledge, or other resources?' . . . Our object is to study the causes of the different extents of command over 'necessaries and conveniences,' obtained respectively by different members of the community, through the complicated system of co-operation by means of exchange on which the life of modern society depends; and since some portion of each one's money income is spent in purchasing not material wealth but education, professional advice, &c., we must regard these utilities, no less than the material products of industry, as practically 'distributed' through the medium of the money payments that determine the nominal incomes of individuals: and the laws that govern the exchange values of these immaterial commodities concern us as much as those regulating the values of material products.

These topic questions are very carefully put, reflecting the numerous qualifications that Sidgwick introduces in his discussions of the basic elements of value and wealth, and in his assessments of the various notions of use value, real value, and exchange value. As he summed up the lengthy account of just what it would mean to enhance the wealth of a nation:

[I]n studying the Wealth of Nations what we are concerned to know is, Under what conditions different communities of men, or the same communities at different times, come to be 'better or worse supplied with all the necessaries and conveniences for which they have occasion.' Hence our attention should be concentrated upon those directly useful commodities which I have called consumers' wealth to distinguish them from the instruments and materials which are only useful and valuable as means of producing other wealth. Again in comparing – with any aim at precision – the supply of such commodities enjoyed by different communities, or the same community at different times, we must limit ourselves to cases in which the primary needs of the persons concerned are not materially different. Further the durability of a portion of consumers' wealth must not be left out of sight in estimating the community's command over the 'conveniences' – and even the 'necessaries' – of life. A man's house does not the less shelter him from the elements because it was built in the reign of Elizabeth; and if we ask why England now is richer than England 300 years ago, a part of the answer must be that each generation has added somewhat to the stock of such durable wealth as is not, except accidentally, destroyed in the using.

At the same time . . . this stock of wealth requires continual expenditure of labour upon it in various ways; and it is often convenient to neglect the small element of inherited consumable commodities and consider society as continually supplying what it continually consumes, in respect of the comparatively durable part of its consumers' wealth no less than of that which is rapidly destroyed and reproduced. But we must not forget the amount of error involved in this limitation of view; and we must also bear in mind that carelessness in preserving what has been produced, and the instability of taste and fashion which impairs the satisfaction derived from it, tend practically to reduce the available supply of commodities.

Further; I argued that, in a complete view of the conveniences of life, we ought to consider along with consumers' wealth what I have called, for analogy's sake, 'consumable service': and I accordingly propose to extend the terms 'produce' and 'commodities,' so as to include such services as well as material products. I also pointed out that, since a portion of wealth consists of books, pictures, microscopes, and other material means of literary, artistic, and scientific culture, and since the utilities embodied in these objects cannot be realised except by persons who have been more or less elaborately trained, it would be a mistake for us to leave out of sight the culture that results from this training, and the skill that is acquired and used as a source of immediate enjoyment, as a private person's skill in painting or piano-playing. Though we do not call permanent skill and culture, any more than transient services, by the name of wealth; still, since they resemble wealth in the two important characteristics of being results of labour and sources of satisfaction, the economist no less than the statesman or the philanthropist must keep them in view, in contemplating the growth of the resources of refinement and elevation of life which the progress of civilisation tends to furnish in continually increasing abundance. (PPE 98)

These last points are essential for appreciating just how qualified Sidgwick's account of the importance of political economy really is. For he admits that it would be hard to extend the usual forms of economic analysis to cultural life; the "most important changes that have taken place as regards the possession and enjoyment of culture" are quite different in their nature and cause from those involved in increasing material wealth. Trying to squeeze into political economy an explanation of "the varying quality and abundance of the services of painters, poets, educators, even priests, would . . . take us into regions very remote from that of political economy as ordinarily understood." (PPE 98) On the other hand, confining the discipline to a focus on material commodities seems arbitrary in any number of ways, and it is important to bear in mind that lots of commodities – such as railways and telegraphs – do not comport with the image of durable goods being exchanged from producer to consumer, but instead create a different infrastructure in which economic life more narrowly construed takes place. Indeed, Sidgwick is fairly emphatic that questions of wealth are completely entangled with more basic questions of value.

Thus, Sidgwick is certainly not going to jump to any hasty conclusions about just when a society is really better off, given all the difficulties involved in measuring intangible advances in such areas as culture and science, art and professional services, not to mention all of the difficulties involved in trying to compare the wealth of a country such as England with that of countries in very different historical and cultural settings – say, ancient Greece – in which people had different needs and wants. In political economy, as in politics, he would often deploy the historical method in order to demonstrate precisely how difficult it is to make – much less to draw any lessons from – global comparisons of past and present.

Nor does he think that the notions of value – even Ricardo's notion of real value in terms of labor expended – are going to eliminate the vagaries of political economy. Certainly, he at least appreciated the logic of Jevons's contribution in qualitative terms: "as Jevons had admirably explained, the variations in the relative market values of different articles express and correspond to variations in the comparative estimates formed by people in general, not of the *total* utilities of the amounts purchased of such articles, but of their *final* utilities; the utilities, that is, of the last portions purchased." (PPE 82) Sidgwick described himself as a disciple of Jevons on this point, though he does go on to observe that

It is not, I think, quite convenient to say with Professor Jevons that 'useful' is that which gives pleasure; and to measure 'utility,' in the Benthamite way, by the balance of pleasurable over painful consequences. For *primâ facie* there are many valued things – alcohol, opium, &c. – which not only have an actual tendency to produce a balance of painful consequences to their consumers, but are even known to have this tendency by many of the persons who nevertheless value and consume them. And in dealing with the determination of value we are not concerned – except in a very indirect way – with these painful consequences: what we are concerned with is the intensity of the desire or demand for the articles in question, as measured by the amount of other things, or of labour, that their consumers are prepared to give for them. (PPE 63)

Sidgwick the economist was evidently content to work with a definition of utility that was warmer to the notion of revealed preference – that is, the idea of grounding economic analysis simply on the actual choices that people make – than Jevons's account, though again, one carefully framed so as not to apply to "persons or communities living respectively at different times or in distant places." Otherwise, a host of difficulties arise –

[W]hen we have to compare aggregates of wealth made up of heterogeneous elements, it becomes necessary to reduce the units of quantity of these different elements to some common standard of measurement; and if we adhere to our original standard of exchange value, we have to deal with the problem of keeping this measure identical, in spite of the variations in relative value among the elements measured. (PPE 79)

Sidgwick was also exceptionally clear in his criticisms of the contributions of Ricardo and his disciple McCulloch – "all economists – except those Socialists who have perverted Ricardo's inconsistency into an argument against the remuneration of capitalists – would now agree that in McCulloch's estimate of cost 'labour and delay' (or some corresponding term) must be substituted for 'labour' simply." Although with such emendations, Ricardo's notion of "real value" might be tenable as an interpretation of the common notion, there are serious drawbacks to all such talk:

[W]e see how the exchange value of a permanent instrument of production, such as land, may be different from what we may fairly call its 'real' value in exchange: for – owing, let us say, to a 'scare' as to the prospects of agriculture – the future exchange value of its produce may be underestimated, and the present exchange value of the land may be proportionally depressed. In this case what we mean by 'real' value, is the hypothetical exchange value which would result from the substitution of truth for error in the minds of actual and possible purchasers. This use of the term 'real value' is convenient in ordinary discourse. I think, however, that it should as a rule be avoided in any discussion that aims at scientific precision; and, when the term is used, a careful explanation should be given of the particular kind of error or ignorance which we seek to eliminate. For in many cases, we should find various kinds and degrees of error in the minds of the persons whose judgments determine the price of a commodity; and it would generally be quite arbitrary to select one of these and regard its elimination as the one thing needful to make the current opinion of value correspond to the reality. And if, in order to determine the real value of any thing, we were to suppose knowledge of all facts materially affecting its value, in the estimate of intelligent persons, to be substituted for ignorance and error in the minds of all the persons concerned, we should often get a hypothesis so remote from reality that it would be at once impossible to calculate the hypothetical value, and absurd, if we could calculate it, to call it 'real.' For the limitations of knowledge actually existing in the minds of producers, dealers, and consumers are among the most important of the facts on which any particular intelligent dealer bases his estimate of value: the removal of such limitations would be a fundamental alteration of the facts. (PPE 76)

At any rate, when Sidgwick turns his attention to the "Art" of political economy, as opposed to the science, all of these historicist considerations and more figure prominently. Here again, true to form, he finds all of the going definitions wanting in clarity, such that it is not really enough to talk about this subject as involving the practical policies by which governments might maximize production and rightly distribute the produce among members of the community. Thus, "for completeness," this "Art" would also consider "the actions of private persons for the same end, so far as it is not prompted by the ordinary motives of pecuniary self-interest or regulated on commercial principles." This is especially important concerning distribution, "where gratuitous labour and expenditure have, especially in modern times, largely supplemented the efforts of governments to mitigate the distressing inequalities in the distribution of produce." (PPE 398) Hence, the importance of charity or philanthropy.

Now, in his usual fashion, Sidgwick again gives a fair-minded account of the case for laissez-faire, which he allows "has much force," only to follow up with an altogether damning list of "important qualifications and exceptions." In fact, the theoretical logic of economic individualism is belied even in the simple case of bequest:

The free play of self-interest can only be supposed to lead to a socially advantageous employment of wealth in old age, if we assume that the old are keenly interested in the utilities that their wealth may furnish to those who succeed them: but if they have this keen interest, they will probably wish to regulate the employment of their wealth; while again in proportion as they attempt this regulation by will, they will diminish the freedom of their successors in dealing with the wealth that they bequeath; and, therefore, according to the fundamental assumption of the system of natural liberty, will diminish the utility of this wealth to those successors. Of this difficulty there is, I think, no theoretical solution; it can only be settled by a rough practical compromise. (PPE 405)

A similar paradox holds in the case of contract, where absolute freedom of contract would allow people to sell themselves into slavery.

In a more empirical vein, Sidgwick reviews at length all the familiar cases of market failure – monopoly, public goods and collective action problems generally, negative externalities. He is particularly sensitive to issues involving time and future generations – especially, as in the *Methods*, as concerns questions of optimal population growth. Also covered in detail are the cases where government intervention promotes production (everything from railways to education are dealt with here) and the advantages of temporary protective measures (for example, to foster a new industry or promote a nation's development). There is perhaps the most extended discussion in any of Sidgwick's writings of the nature of distributive justice, a discussion that, as usual, culminates in a treatment of communism and socialism. Here again he has no doubt at all that laissez-faire does not reward workers according to desert, which is an unattainable ideal for both free marketers and their opponents. But, on the other side, he is equally insistent that

> The proposal to organise society on a communistic plan, so as to distribute the annual produce of the labour and capital of the community either in equal shares, or in shares varying not according to the deserts but according to the needs of the recipient, is one of which the serious interest has now passed away; though a generation ago it had not a few adherents, and was supported with earnestness and ability by more than one competent writer. And, notwithstanding what has been urged in the preceding section, the proposition that a communistic distribution would produce more happiness than the present system, if it could be realised without materially affecting production, or removing needful checks to population, is at any rate a very plausible one. But even if it were completely true, I cannot doubt that the removal of the normal stimulus to labour (bodily and intellectual) and to care, which the present individualistic system supplies, would so much reduce the whole produce to be divided, that any advantage derived from greater economy of distribution would be decidedly outweighed – even supposing that no material change took place in population. Probably few of my readers will dispute this; but I may suggest to any one who is inclined to doubt it, to compare the average energy and perseverance in labour displayed by even respectable and conscientious rich persons, even when they select their own work, with the average energy and perseverance of professional men. (PPE 525–26)

Furthermore, Sidgwick thinks that the problem of population growth, under communism, would be serious; although he does not regard it as insoluble, he cannot see "how the difficulties in which it is involved are to be overcome without such a revolution in the traditional habits and sentiments regulating the relations of the sexes as no thoughtful person could contemplate without alarm and disquiet" (PPE 526). And he also appreciates the "serious danger that a thoroughgoing equalisation of wealth among the members of a modern civilised community would have a tendency to check the growth of culture in the community." This, of course, is an especially contentious matter, and he recognizes that many of the champions of cultural advance would not think it any compensation if a loss in culture were counterbalanced by a gain in general happiness. The perfectionists of this type

have a conviction, for which they could not give an empirical justification, that a diffusion of culture may be expected in the future which has no parallel in the past: and that any social changes which cripple its development, however beneficent they may be in other respects, may involve a loss to humanity in the aggregate which, if we look sufficiently far forward, seems quite immeasurable in extent. (PPE 523–24)

There are, Sidgwick recognizes, several issues at stake here – the happiness of the few, cultivated rich as against "the additional happiness that might be enjoyed by the poor if wealth were more equally distributed," the extent to which "whatever happiness is derived from culture by the many poor depends at any given time on the maintenance of a higher kind of culture among the few rich," and "the prospective addition to happiness when culture shall have become more diffused," which might be endangered by hampering the existing cultured elite. Any estimate of these developments would be, he admits, "necessarily vague," but he does urge that one point seems clear: "they apply far more strongly against any sudden sweeping equalisation than they do against a more slow and gradual movement towards this result, – accompanied (as it naturally would be) by an improvement in the average intellectual condition of the classes who would benefit pecuniarily by the equalisation." (PPE 524) Here, in a nutshell, is his educational program.

The wider or more comprehensive terms "Socialism" and "Socialistic" are harder to define than "Communism," but also suggestive of these more acceptable possibilities, and it is in connection with them that Sidgwick actually dares to advance a bit of imaginative speculation on one possible course for the future:

Suppose that, in civilised countries generally, governmental administration of all kinds of business were shewn to be economically superior, in a marked degree, to the present competitive management: it is obvious that the State might gradually buy up the land and fixed capital of different industries, paying for them out of the increased proceeds of its superior management; and the process, when once commenced, would go forward with continually increasing rapidity. The field of investment thus becoming gradually more and more limited, the return to private capital – supposing saving to continue as at present – would probably begin to fall. 'Spending' would then increase at the expense of saving, and private capital would gradually diminish from being eaten up. It would be important that the State should purchase the land of the community, and other permanent instruments of production tending to rise in value – if there be any – at any early stage of this process: not merely to gain the unearned increment, but because, as interest sinks towards zero, the selling value of land at a given rent tends to rise proportionally. The process might conceivably go on until the payment for the use of capital, as distinct from insurance against risk, became nearly evanescent; so that only such an amount of private capital would be kept up as men would be willing to keep for security of future use and enjoyment, without any view to profit. And finally when the instruments and materials of all industries had become the property of the government, the aggregate of private savings – leaving out of account the non-usurious lending and borrowing among private persons that might still go on – could only be in the form of "consumers' capital," i.e., houses, gardens, furniture, jewels, pictures, &c. Suppose further that, at the same time, by a comprehensive system of free education, elementary, technical, and professional, the present scarcity values of the higher grades of labour had been reduced, so that all such skill as average persons can acquire by training was remunerated by merely a fair return for the additonal outlay on sustenance during the period of education. We should thus have arrived at something very like the ideal of economic distribution which German socialists have put forward, without any sudden shock to the expectations formed by the present system of private property. Society would voluntarily have converted its private capital into consumers' wealth; and, through the agency of its government, would have produced for itself the public capital used in its place. The income of all individual members of the community would be entirely derived from labour of some kind, – or, in the current phrase of the socialists, labour would obtain its 'full product' of consumable commodities (subtracting only whatever additional public capital had to be provided for the increase of its future produce). (PPE 527–28)

 As one would suspect, Sidgwick has some trouble sustaining such an imaginative exercise, and immediately goes on to caution that he need hardly say "that any such increase in social production through governmental administration as we have above imagined is beyond the limits of any rational forecast of the future development of society," and perhaps even beyond the dreams of "the most sanguine socialist." His point is simply to suggest how government might take steps toward the socialist aim, and to insist that "it is only such mild and gentle steps towards the realisation of the socialistic ideal that I can regard as at all acceptable, in the present condition of our knowledge of man and society." This is his updating of the Millian call for more socialistic experimentation, albeit in a very carefully phrased way, so that improving distribution is typically tied to means that will also improve production. And, cautious as his statement may be, he makes it absolutely clear that he can "see no reason to regard unqualified *laisser faire* as tending to realise the most economical production any more than the best possible distribution of wealth: and it seems . . . quite possible that a considerable extension of the industrial functions of government might be on the whole advantageous, without any Utopian degree of moral or political improvement in human society." Such improvements must be gradual, should begin in the areas where the market conspicuously fails (as in monopoly conditions), and should strive "to maintain as far as possible in the governmental organisation of industry an effective stimulus to individual exertion, and to allow scope for invention and improvement of methods." (PPE 529)

He also suggests that "if we condemn 'sweaters,' slop-shop dealers, and other small traders who 'grind the faces' of the poor by taking full advantage of competition, it should be rather for want of benevolence than for want of justice; and the condemnation should be extended to other persons of wealth and leisure who are aware of this disease of the social organism and are making no efforts to remove it." He admits that such efforts do need to be made, though "the exact form that they will take if most wisely directed must depend upon the particular conditions of the labourers in question." (PPE 587)

Having said this, Sidgwick is nonetheless about as close as he would ever come to proposing a substantive theory of distributive justice, as opposed to his usual puzzling over the indeterminacy involved in notions of impartiality, the impossibility of giving each person his or her due, and so forth. On his view, the "only hope" of effecting anything resembling a distribution according to desert would involve "getting rid of all removable differences in remuneration that are due to causes other than the voluntary exertions of the labourers." And this his scheme might do to a considerable extent, as long as "the means of training for the higher kinds of work were effectually brought within the reach of all classes, by a well organised system of free education, liberally supported by exhibitions for the children of the poor." After all, the inequalities resulting from

the payment of interest to private capitalists as such, or of profit to employing capitalists, would, speaking broadly, have ceased to exist; and though it would be impossible, without intolerable constraint on the freedom of action of individuals, to prevent the children of persons earning larger incomes or owning accumulated wealth from having a somewhat better start in life than the rest, still this advantage might be reduced to a minimum by such an educational system. (PPE 530)

And Sidgwick even thinks that his creeping socialistic civilization will help with population growth and with such matters as sloth and fraud in public assistance:

If we suppose a community in which the aggregate remuneration of labour is increased by most of the share that now forms interest on individuals' capital, while the emoluments and dignities attached to the higher kinds of labour are brought within the hopes of all classes by a system of education which at the same time makes general such a degree of foresight and intelligence as is now possessed by the higher grade of artisans, – it seems quite possible that in such a community a minimum of wages might be guaranteed to all who were unable to find employment for themselves, without drawing an ever increasing crowd of applicants to claim the guaranteed minimum, and without a serious deficit arising from the inefficient work of such as did apply. (PPE 531)

This was a subject very dear to Sidgwick's heart, of course, and it is interesting not only that he found the question of population (and relatedly, sexuality) to be so closely allied to the problems of poor relief, but also that he had such faith in the possibilities of education for fostering intelligence and foresight throughout the population. These issues were also bound up with that of colonization, which provided another possible form of "poor relief," though one also requiring considerable educational development.

Evidently, then, and as unlikely as it may seem, Sidgwick's *Principles* ends up admittedly straining the bounds of political economy in its effort to come to terms with culture and education, the sources of gradual semisocialism. Here was a vision of the educating society, one involving concrete suggestions for both educational institutions narrowly conceived and the broader advance of culture. As in the *Methods*, Sidgwick had buried a subversive account of moral (or social) development within an extensive and seemingly respectful treatment of the received wisdom that had no utopian intentions.

Ironically, it may well be that these more lyrical moments in Sidgwick's work were composed in Rome, during the Italian tour when he was busily studying art with the help of Symonds's *Renaissance* volume on the subject. He had meant to finish the work before departing England, but, as he wrote to Symonds, "fate ordained" that he would have to continue working on it while visiting the Eternal City and its monuments (CWC). However, the Eternal City also made him quite ill, and his digestive disorders made it impossible for him to continue on to Greece as he had hoped to do.

To be sure, Sidgwick's claims reflect the socialist legacy of Mill and Maurice rather than of Marx and Morris, and they do not even approximate the "ideal" utilitarian society sometimes invoked in the *Methods*. Experimental and gradualist, anti- and perhaps even counterrevolutionary, and ever celebratory of individual and elite efforts at high-minded social improving, this was the type of movement that Marx himself had attacked as hopelessly bourgeois. Indeed, on this score, Marx had famously attacked not only Mill but also Mill's chief Cambridge disciple, Henry Fawcett, the blind political economist who had done much to tutor Sidgwick in Mill, but who had had the temerity to criticize the principles of the First International.[22] In this respect, Sidgwick remained altogether Millian.

Indeed, as Sidgwick heads toward the conclusion of his volume, he returns again to the question of the relation of economics to morality, posing the question of whether "the whole individualistic organisation of industry, whatever its material advantages may be, is not open to condemnation as radically demoralising." Although there is nothing in Sidgwick's writings that quite reaches the lyricism of Mill's laments about the possible stagnation and loss of solitude in the future, he is nonetheless also keenly sensitive to the attractions of an alternative ethos, one in which life in society promises fellowship. He recognizes that the divergences between private and common interest, and the antisocial temper of individualism, have led many "thoughtful persons" to sympathize with socialism, and that even many who are not socialists "yet feel the moral need of some means of developing in the members of a modern industrial community a fuller consciousness of their industrial work as a social function, only rightly performed when done with a cordial regard to the welfare of the whole society, – or at least of that part of it to which the work is immediately useful." It is of course from this point of view that so much importance attaches to attempts at increasing the role of cooperatives in economic activity. But what is more, since "it is always open to any individual who dislikes the selfish habits of feeling and action naturally engendered by the individualistic organisation of society, to counteract them in his private sphere by practising and commending a voluntary redistribution of wealth for the benefit of others," the subject of poor relief again comes to the fore. (PPE 590–91)

Now, it is important not to overestimate the subversiveness of Sidgwick's gradualist arguments, particularly on matters such as immediate aid to the poor. Again, the subject of poor relief was a particularly fraught one for him, given how much time and energy he had invested in it, and how it was bound up with the other matters of justice and the potential for socialism. Despite his keen awareness of the long Christian tradition of almsgiving, Sidgwick finds it impossible to think well of it when the activity proceeds in ignorance of political economy, and he often expresses his disgust with "sentimental" politics. Political economy has, on the one side, tended "to impress powerfully on the mind the great waste of the material means of happiness that is involved in the customary expenditure even of the most respectable rich persons." But it has also, on the other,

tended to make the common view of these dangers [of almsgiving] more clear, definite, and systematic. It has impressed forcibly on instructed minds the general rule that if a man's wants are supplied by gift when he might have supplied them himself by harder work and greater thrift, his motives to industry and thrift tend to be so far diminished; and not only his motives, but the motives of all persons in like circumstances who are thereby led to expect like gifts themselves.

In sum, "there is reason to hope that, in minds of nobler stamp, the full perception of the difficulties and risks attending the voluntary redistribution of wealth will only act as a spur to the sustained intellectual activity required for the successful accomplishment of this duty." (PPE 592)

The point is that private almsgiving was often seen as a necessary supplement to the work of the English Poor Law – with its infamous workhouses – but it was "largely impulsive, unenlightened, and unorganised," so that it gave serious encouragement to "unthrift, and even to imposture." Conceivably then, the "government might with advantage undertake the *organisation* of eleemosynary relief, in order to make its distribution as economical, effective, and judicious as possible," although the *provision* of the funds for such relief "might be left mainly to voluntary gifts and bequests, with a certain amount of assistance from government, if experience shews it to be necessary, but without any legal right to relief." (PPE 535) This would be the model of the French system, which Sidgwick thinks does work in certain respects, though on the whole he actually favors the English system, the very object of so much Dickensian satire.

Thus, like Mill, Sidgwick took a fairly sour view of what the existing poorer members of society were capable of, by way of advancing the semisocialistic future. Still, again like Mill, that future also held out the possibility of a general improvement in education and culture that would pervade all levels of society – indeed, would help to reduce if not eliminate the gap between the better-off and the worse-off. And this was, as Maurice had also urged, quite possibly essential to social harmony.

Fuller discussion of this sensitive topic – on which many would say Sidgwick sounds more like Mr. Gradgrind than Whitman – must await the treatment of his magnum opus in politics (which subject, it should be plain, was constantly on his mind as he was working through his more purely economic views). But before proceeding to that, it should perhaps be underscored yet again just how different Sidgwick's political economy was from that of the orthodox Benthamites or even the Millians.[23] For Sidgwick strikes at the very heart of economic analysis. He does not merely invoke the familiar forms of irrationality due to custom and habit. Rather, he wonders about the condition even of "a community where the members generally were as enlightened and alert in the pursuit of their interests as we can ever expect human beings to become," in which it still might be the case that "the defects of private enterprise" needed to be overcome by "the action of the community in its collective capacity" (PPE 414). In a more abstract consideration of the conditions under which "even where we do not regard the intervention of government as at present desirable, we may yet look forward to it, and perhaps prepare the way for it," he finds it possible to doubt that social progress "is carrying us towards a condition in which the assumption, that the consumer is a better judge than government of the commodities that he requires and of the source from which they may be best obtained, will be sufficiently true for all practical purposes." Indeed,

[I]n some important respects the tendencies of social development seem to be rather in an opposite direction. As the appliances of life become more elaborate and complicated through the progress of invention, it is only according to the general law of division of labour to suppose that an average man's ability to judge of the adaptation of means to ends, even as regards the satisfaction of his everyday needs, is likely to become continually less. No doubt an ideally intelligent person would under these circumstances be always duly aware of his own ignorance, and would take the advice of experts. But it seems not unlikely that the need of such advice, and the difficulty of finding the right advisers, may increase more markedly than the average consciousness of such need and difficulty, at any rate where the benefits to be obtained or the evils to be warded off are somewhat remote and uncertain; especially when we consider that the self-interest of producers will in many cases lead them to offer commodities that *seem* rather than *are* useful, if the difference between seeming and reality is likely to escape notice. (PPE 416–17)

Skepticism about these fundamental comforts of orthodox political economy would seem, potentially, to throw a rather heavy burden of responsibility on the "expert" or enlightened guidance that Sidgwick looks to as the way out, though he admits that how "far government can usefully attempt to remedy these shortcomings of self-help is a question that does not admit of a confident general answer." The "nature and extent of such collective action" as would correct for such failings is hard to capture in any system of practical rules, "owing to the extent to which the construction of such a system ought reasonably to be influenced by the particular social and political conditions of the country and time for which it is framed." (PPE 418)

Given this nearly Hegelian sensitivity to the particulars of historical community, what could *The Elements of Politics* possibly have to say that would count as Benthamite? Indeed, for all Sidgwick's insistence on the importance of political economy, his *Principles* ends up being nearly as subversively inconclusive as his *Methods*, given his accounts of the heavily qualified claims for maximizing wealth, the limited role of the art of political economy in the wider range of politics, and the importance of advancing culture and other goods that the political economist has very little understanding of and that are intrinsically resistant to calculation. Once again, private duty (e.g., charity) has disappeared in a haze of empirical uncertainty.

When Mill had objected to Jevons's marginalism as yielding only a false precision, and serving only to render technical and obscure a subject that needed to be made as accessible as possible for the sake of educating and pacifying the working class, he had sounded the note of the public intellectual, of the public educator opposed to obfuscating details.[24] Many of Sidgwick's writings, particularly his essays, might be thought to heed this Millian injunction, and of course his wide-ranging efforts to extend educational resources – for example, the time he devoted to lecturing at the Cambridge Working Men's College in the early sixties, and his aid to Oscar Browning's University Day Training College for teachers in the nineties – also suggest that he was struggling to follow the example of both Mill and Maurice concerning the pacification of the working class through education. Somehow, though, Sidgwick's work, even when most accessible, betrays a kind of ambivalence and equivocation, not to mention an unfailing regard for the complexities of the subject, that would seem capable only of stirring doubt – a doubt that, as he well knew, could cut many different ways.

Thus, for example, another one of the stronger policy stances issuing from his art of political economy involved an insistence on the virtues of "bimetallism" – that is, the use of both silver and gold as monetary standards. In Sidgwick's mouth, of course, this could never turn into a polemic about the economy being crucified on a cross of gold, or the depression being aggravated by a dogmatic adherence to the gold standard.[25] As ever, he calls only for a "careful and impartial" forecast of the comparative disadvantages of bimetallism versus the alternatives, reaching the guarded conclusion that

It thus appears that the adoption of a double standard will, up to a certain point, prevent variations in supply from affecting the relative market-value of the two metals, as it will tend to produce changes in demand sufficient to absorb their effect. But variations of a certain magnitude cannot be thus counteracted; on the contrary, such variations will nullify the formal adoption of a double standard, and render the currency practically monometallic. (PPE 257)

Still, the patient reader has carried away arguments against all sides.

Notoriously, Sidgwick found that he had a hard time recommending his political economy to students or friends. He sent Symonds a copy, for the record, but also wrote to tell him that he should not even think of reading it.[26]

IV. Principles and Elements

What candidate wanted to tell his voters that he considered them too stupid and ignorant to know what was best in politics, and that their demands were as absurd as they were dangerous to the future of the country? What statesman, surrounded by reporters carrying his words to the remotest corner tavern, would actually say what he meant? Increasingly politicians were obliged to appeal to a mass electorate: even to speak directly to the masses or indirectly through the megaphone of the popular press (including their opponents papers). Bismarck had probably never addressed other than an elite audience. Gladstone introduced mass electioneering to Britain (and perhaps to Europe) in the campaign of 1879. No longer would the expected implications of democracy be discussed, except by political outsiders, with the frankness and realism of the debates which had surrounded the British Reform Act of 1867. But as the men who governed wrapped themselves in rhetoric, the serious discussion of politics retreated to the world of the intellectuals and the educated minority public who read them. The era of democratization was also the golden age of a new political sociology: of Durkheim and Sorel, Ostrogorski and the Webbs, Mosca, Pareto, Robert Michels and Max Weber.... When the men who governed really wanted to say what they meant, they had henceforth to do so in the obscurity of the corridors of power, the clubs, the private social evenings, the shooting parties or country-house weekends where the members of the elite met each other in a very different atmosphere from that of the gladiatorial comedies of parliamentary debates or public meetings. The age of democratization thus turned into the era of public political hypocrisy, or rather duplicity, and hence also into that of political satire.... For what intelligent observer could overlook the yawning gap between public discourse and political reality?

> Eric Hobsbawm, *The Age of Empire, 1875–1914*[27]

These days at Whittingehame, with Political Economy, Howarth, and other Tories were instructive but depressing. Their criticism of the present phase of Radicalism seems to be unanswerable. Am I then becoming a Tory? Perhaps, but a strange one.

> Sidgwick in January 1885, after meeting with members of Arthur Balfour's Manchester Conservative Association (M 398)

In an important passage in the posthumous *Philosophy, Its Scope and Relations*, Sidgwick explained:

The distinction between Ethics or Politics and Philosophy is not so clear: still I think that some distinction is vaguely made in ordinary thought, and might with advantage be made somewhat more explicit. It is vaguely recognised that it is the business of *Ethics* to supply an answer to questions as to details of duty or right conduct – so far as they are questions which it is held legitimate, and not idle, to ask – but that this is not the business of Moral or Ethical *Philosophy*, which is primarily concerned with the general principles and methods of moral reasoning, and only with details of conduct so far as the discussion of them affords instructive examples of general principles and method. It is commonly felt that an attempt to work out a complete system of duties would inevitably lead us out of Philosophy into Casuistry: and that whether Casuistry is a good thing or a bad thing, it certainly is not Philosophy. . . . A similar distinction may, I think, be applied to Politics: – accordingly when I had to select a title for a bulky volume in which I attempted to treat systematically the chief questions for which the statesman has to find answers, I called the book 'Elements of Politics,' not 'Political Philosophy' or 'Political Science.' I did not call it Political Philosophy, since it aims at determining the rules for governmental action, and for the construction of governmental organs with more fulness of detail than it belongs to Philosophy to do: nor, again, did I call it Political Science, since it is primarily concerned with polity as it ought to be, and not with politics as they are, have been, and – so far as we can foresee – will be. (PSR 25–26)

This statement does appear to be in harmony with the professed aims of the *Elements*, which offers the statesman a more comprehensive form of practical guidance than the *Principles*, and a more politically oriented form of argument than the *Methods*. He was impressed, he allowed, with the need for a book "which would expound, within a convenient compass, and in as systematic a form as the subject-matter might admit, the chief general considerations that enter into the rational discussion of political questions in modern states" (EP v).

In fact, Sidgwick moves quickly to establish the difference between politics and ethics. The very first paragraph of the *Elements* suggests that the citizens of the modern state, in deciding political questions, will typically arrive at answers "as the result of conscious reasoning from certain general principles or assumptions," whereas on moral questions most are "accustomed from comparatively early years to pronounce confident decisions; sometimes arrived at intuitively, or at least without conscious processes of reasoning, sometimes the result of rational processes of more or less length." Thus, as in economics, the move from principle to policy, or from virtue to the common good, has nothing like the immediacy of intuitions of rightness. The fourth book of the *Methods* finds its natural continuation here. And like the *Methods*, the *Elements* disclaims any great originality – the aim is "not to supply any entirely new method of obtaining reasoned answers to political questions; but rather, by careful reflection, to introduce greater clearness and consistency into the kind of thought and reasoning with which we are all more or less familiar." (EP 1)

Sidgwick is also at some pains to distinguish this kind of work, which "treats of political societies regarded in their political aspect: – i.e. as under government," from the larger and to some degree different pre-occupations of sociology. Here, however, his qualms about sociology are directed at Mill as well as the familiar targets, and he wants to deny that he is developing the Millian study of ethology, according to which "Theo-retical Politics can only be scientifically studied as one part or application of the Science or Philosophy of History." In a vital passage, he explains: "I think that, for the purpose of general political reasoning that has a practical aim, induction from the political experiences which history records can only be employed in a secondary way." "But if this is so," he continues, "by what other rational method can we deal with the questions of Practical Politics?" Thus,

The method commonly adopted in political reasoning that appeals to general principles is the following: we assume certain general characteristics of social man – characteristics belonging not to mankind universally, but of civilised man in the most advanced stage of his development; and we consider what laws and institutions are likely to conduce most to the welfare of an aggregate of such beings living in social relations. The present work is an attempt to render this method more systematic and precise: the practical principles defined and applied in it are accordingly based on certain general assumptions as to human motives and tendencies, which are derived primarily from the ordinary experience of civilised life, though they find adequate confirmation in the facts of the current and recent history of our own and other civilised countries. (EP 11)

A note to this statement observes that despite Mill's claims for ethology, the method he employs in such works as *Considerations on Representative Government* was closer to this deductive approach, which is in part the method inherited from the Benthamites.

Now, this insistence on the primary importance of the analytical or deductive method inherited from the Benthamites may seem to fly in the face of all the cautious historicizing tendencies of such works as the *Principles*, and to make the problem of "difference" loom very large indeed. How, for example, could it be reconciled with the frank confession, in "Bentham and Benthamism," that Macaulay's rejoinder to James Mill had been very powerful, and that this "spirited criticism of the deductive politics of James Mill, though it was treated with contempt by its object, had a powerful effect on the more impartial and impressible mind of the younger Mill"? (MEA 169)

In truth, however, Sidgwick's methodological struggles in the *Elements* were largely continuous with those of the *Principles*, with only a slight shifting of emphasis to stress the limitations of the historical method. Although he did admit that the question "how far knowledge of the past is important for a scientific grasp of the present, is one that will *primâ facie* receive a different answer in relation to different inquiries," he did not seek to drive a historicist wedge between politics and the art of political economy. The essence of the deductive method in economics is that in

all abstract economic reasoning which aims at quantitative precision, there is necessarily a hypothetical element; the facts to which the reasonings relate are not contemplated in their actual complexity, but in an artifically simplified form; if, therefore, the reasoning is not accompanied and checked by a careful study of facts, the required simplification may easily go too far or be inappropriate in kind, so that the hypothetical element of the reasoning is increased to an extent which prevents the result from having any practical value. (PPE 37–38)

It is just this type of limited priority that the analytical or deductive approach should have in politics as well.

In other words, Sidgwick's way of deploying the deductive approach still has very little in common with the universalistic or ahistoricist Benthamism that Macaulay had so effectively demolished.[28] His "homo economicus" and "homo politicus" are the products of the social conditions of modern European civilization, and the political policies appropriate to them will be, like the economic policies, carefully tailored to the specifics of their culture and political system. If anything, Sidgwick's insistence on the priority of the analytical method reflects his acute sense of historical change, of just how little of political relevance is to be found in the study of other times and places. Again, he was happy to admit that the arch-historicists had demonstrated how different the modern world was from, say, the medieval one: the lesson then to be learned was how little guidance moderns could take from the medieval situation.

Thus, the *Elements* resembles the *Principles* in taking its point of departure from the effort to assimilate the historicizing tendencies of the nineteenth century. And despite Sidgwick's gestures toward Bentham, this very different methodological mentality was quite evident to contemporary reviewers. Although some rehearsed the old charge of Benthamism – the *Edinburgh Review* predictably charged him with having "discarded almost throughout his work the teachings of experience," founding "his theory of politics on reasoning which is mainly or purely deductive" – most found his professions of allegiance to Bentham less than persuasive. W. A. Dunning, writing in *The Political Quarterly*, shrewdly argued that

> As a matter of fact we find everywhere in Professor Sidgwick's work, along with a most rigorous adherence to the forms of *a priori* reasoning, evidence that the substance of his thought is inductive. While he tries to derive existing institutions from his fundamental principles, he really is conforming the principles to the institutions. It is hard to believe, for example, that his chapter on 'Federal and Other Composite States,' represents a laborious deduction from the dogmas of utilitarian ethics rather than an intelligent generalization from the constitution of the United States and one or two similar documents.[29]

And none other than Woodrow Wilson, the future U.S. president, then a professor of political science at Princeton, insisted that Sidgwick's "procedure is deductive . . . but his treatment is of course more or less saturated with experience." Wilson's review was generally favorable, but he did sharply observe that "[t]here may be Elements of English Politics, or of American, or of French or Prussian; but the elements of general politics, if cast into general considerations, must either be quite colorless or quite misleading. The considerations urged by Professor Sidgwick are for the most part quite colorless."[30] But perhaps the most infamous review, marshalled on behalf of the notion of natural rights, came from D. G. Ritchie, a pugnacious defender of Green's Idealism:

> Perhaps one might safely characterize the 'Elements of Politics' as a discussion of most political problems of present-day politics, with some hints towards their partial solution. The discussion is distinctly of today, not of yesterday, and with just a slight regard for tomorrow morning early. Although we are told that 'the primary aim of the theory of politics as here expounded is to determine what the constitution and action of government *ought* to be,' we must not expect to find a sketch of an ideal state. Professor Sidgwick argues deductively from 'psychological propositions not universally and absolutely true, but approximately true of civilized men,' and yet, somehow, the conclusion again and again turns out to be

just what we have in the present British constitution. Thus our unpaid members of parliament, and our parliaments of five, six, or even seven years' duration, are exactly the results at which Professor Sidgwick arrives by deductive arguments about what ought to be. He nowhere arrives at any conclusion which would differ very widely from that of the average man of the professional and commercial middle-class at the present day. The method is Bentham's; but there is none of Bentham's strong critical antagonism to the institutions of his time, and the mode of thought is much more what we might expect from an end-of-the-nineteenth-century Blackstone, or from an English Hegel, showing the rationality of the existing order of things, with only a few modest proposals of reform. If this is Benthamism, it is Benthamism grown tame and sleek.[31]

Ritchie does go on to say some nice things about the "immense value of his calm discussion, carried on in the undogmatic spirit of a sane and sober, if rather old-fashioned, utilitarianism," but his criticisms have endured longer than his compliments.

Between Wilson and Ritchie, Sidgwick felt the pinch. He often expressed some doubt himself as to the nature of his work, whether it was not either colorless or a longish summary of the principles of British politics. During the extremely long gestation period of this 632-page tome, he was prone to all the usual disparagements of his work – "Labor Improbus," he called it, and one can almost hear the groan. In February of 1889, he would respond to Bryce's comments on his proofs:

I quite agree with your general criticism that the whole thing is too English. I will try to remedy that a little, so far as my knowledge allows. Something about America is to come in a later chapter on 'Local and Federal Government': something more in a chapter on 'Parties and Party Government.' But I will try and put some more references to American Conditions and expedients in the chapters that you have seen. (CWC)[32]

Although he had long rumbled about doing a book on politics, Sidgwick apparently first began to think seriously about writing the *Elements* in the mid-1870s, when he began lecturing on political economy and related subjects. Thus, the *Memoir* has him writing to Browning in June of 1876: "I should like to talk to you about Political Philosophy. I am preparing myself to write 'Elements of Politics,' and am thinking of printing some 'outlines of Politics' to use for my lectures, and also to get criticised as regards arrangement, etc., before I write my book." (M 322)[33] The next explicit reference is in a journal entry from February 1886, when he is particularly distressed about Gladstone's campaign for Irish Home Rule:

For the first time for weeks I am moved to write about Politics, chiefly to mark, with some alarm, the extent of my alienation from current Liberalism. We are drifting on to what must be a national disaster, and the forces impelling are Party organisation and Liberal principles. The stability of the dual organisation of parties makes it difficult for the average politician to see any way out of the trouble without satisfying the Irish; and Liberal principles make it seem right to let them have what they want. So the good man closes his eyes and hopes that what they want will not turn out, after all, so ruinous to England as some people think.

My personal trouble is that I do not quite see what to do about my book on Politics. My political ideal is nearly written out – and lo! I begin to feel uncomfortable about it; I begin to find something wooden and fatuous in the sublime smile of Freedom. (M 439)

The last part of the eighties, following Sidgwick's crisis period, appears also to have marked the most intense period of work on the *Elements*. His journal for April 1888 explains: "During the last fortnight I have settled all my literary hesitations; determined to bring out two books (1) *Elements of Politics*, and (2) *Development of European Polity*; have made out the plan of (1) – twenty-three chapters, of which sixteen are more or less written – have sent off the first three to the printer, and got three more ready for sending." (M 487) In January 1889, he explains, "We are both of us very busy: I have two books on Politics – one deductive and analytical going through press, one (smaller), inductive and historical, getting ready for press – on my hands" (M 500). By December he is announcing "Well, term is over, and eighteen chapters of my book on *Politics* are ready for printing off, and of the thirteen that remain about eleven are wholly or partially in type, and the other two half-written" (M 503). It was at this point that he was busily sending proofs to various friends in the field – Bryce, Dicey, and F. W. Maitland – soliciting their critical feedback. He had earlier in the decade given Bryce extensive commentary on the proofs of his *The American Commonwealth*, and their friendship and collaboration was a particularly close one, of special significance for interpreting Sidgwick's views, as we shall see. By the end of 1890, he is complaining to Noel that he has lost interest in his book, "which makes it harder to finish," and it is only the next July that he can write to Bryce, "I have just sent off my last sheet!" (CWC)

It is interesting that during the period leading up to his crisis about psychical research and its bearing on his professional position, Sidgwick should also have been so wholly absorbed in politics as well. His journal to Symonds records how he has

a certain alarm in respect of the movement of modern society towards Socialism, i.e. the more and more extensive intervention of Government with a view to palliate the inequalities in the distribution of wealth. At the same time I regard this movement as *on the whole* desirable and beneficent – the expectation of it belongs to the cheerful side of my forecast of the future; if duly moderated it *might*, I conceive, be purely beneficent, and bring improvement at every stage. But – judging from past experience – one must expect that so vast a change will not be realised without violent shocks and oscillations, great blunders followed by great disasters and consequent reactions; that the march of progress, perturbed by the selfish ambitions of leaders and the blind appetites of followers, will suffer many spasmodic deviations into paths which it will have painfully to retrace. Perhaps – as in the movement of the last century towards Liberty – one country will have to suffer the pains of experiments for the benefit of the whole system of States; and if so, it is on various grounds likely that this country may be England. . . . My recent fear and depression has been rather of a different kind: has related rather to the structure of Government than the degree of its interference with property and contract. I have hitherto held unquestioningly the Liberal doctrine that in the modern industrial community government by elected and responsible representatives was and would remain the normal type. But no one has yet found out how to make this kind of government work, except on the system of alternating parties; and it is the force of resistance which this machine of party government presents to the influence of enlightened and rational opinion, at crises like this, which alarms. I find myself asking myself whether perhaps, after all, it is Caesarism which will win in the competition for existence, and guide modern industrial society successfully towards its socialistic goal. However, I do not yet think this; but it is a terrible problem what to do with party government. (M 441–42)

Caesarism? Perhaps the model of Bismarck's Germany ushering in the welfare state? Such doubts suggest just how uncertain Sidgwick was about the direction of civilization, and how exasperated with the crude self-interest of party politics. A Godless universe above and vulgar party politics below were the two poles of Sidgwick's midlife crisis.

These last few passages sum up quite a bit of Sidgwick's political orientation, especially the anxiety about the "selfish ambitions of leaders and the blind appetites of followers." An academic Liberal favorably disposed to Gladstone, he had broken with him over Home Rule for Ireland. Optimistic about socialist drift, he nonetheless wanted it to be gradual and high-minded; the raucous corruption of democratic party politics – studied so diligently by his friend Bryce, with his famous account of Boss Tweed – worried him greatly. In 1885, he is even invited – by "Hall of Six Mile Bottom" – to stand as a Liberal candidate for Parliament for the county, an offer to which he gives serious consideration:

> I was tempted; but I communed with my political conscience and discovered that I could not come forward as a Liberal at this juncture without hypocrisy. I am a Utilitarian, and would be a hypocrite if I were convinced that the country required this sacrifice; but I cannot rate my political value so high. In fact the temptation was really this: I want to write a great book on Politics during the next ten years, and am afraid it will be too academic if I do not somehow go into the actual struggle. (M 407)

In a further note on this, which Trevelyan advised Eleanor Sidgwick to leave out of the *Memoir*, he recalls that "Hall ventured the prediction that about one-third of the agricultural labourers in these parts would give their votes by *chance*, owing to inability to read the name of their candidate."[34]

Revealingly, he is also at this time "studying Plato again, in spite of my despair as to the possibility of making out what he means." Perhaps Symonds was having some effect, however, since he confesses that he is

> coming to the conclusion that his myths are *not* as I once thought the drapery of a half-philosophised creed to which he clings while conscious that it is not philosophy. I now think he was not half poet, half philosopher, but philosopher to the core, as determined as Descartes to believe nothing but the clearest and most certain truth, who only used his imagination in myths to dress up δόξαι for the vulgar, as near the truth as their minds could stand, but that a long way off. (M 407)[35]

All of these would be auspicious happenings for his work on the *Elements*. If much of Sidgwick's hands-on dealing with politics came from his academic reformism, he was also deeply involved in some larger causes (and certainly loved the political gossip that came his way from Bryce and Arthur Balfour). True, he was ever the academic in politics. Collini has insightfully argued that Sidgwick does not quite fit the mold of the earnest, politically active "public moralist" of the mid-Victorian era, but instead foreshadows a rather different type:

In European terms, Sidgwick perhaps corresponded more to the older figure of the 'notable', a personage who was of consequence in the community partly through social connection, partly through institutional role, and partly by virtue of personal gifts or capacities. In English terms, he may have been an early example of a type which became more familiar by the mid-twentieth century: the socially well-connected don, one who made a career by attaining eminence in a branch of scholarship, but one whose social experience gave him both the confidence and means of access to contribute directly and indirectly to the policy-making process, largely by-passing general public debate.[36]

This is a helpful description, as long as one remembers that in Sidgwick's day, prior to the politicized rift between liberal and professional or vocational education, it was possible to think that one could somehow have it all, that one's politics could envision both culture and professionalization flourishing.

Before turning to the text, it should be underscored just how entangled in certain real-world political events Sidgwick was. The very long controversy over Home Rule for Ireland, from 1886 through 1921, was a political event that captured the political and intellectual energies of Sidgwick and such friends as Seeley, Bryce, and Dicey like no other. In the early phases of the dispute, though not later, it clearly had what Dicey termed a "civil Gladstonian" quality, with influential friends and brothers lined up in decorous opposition: Dicey against, Bryce for; Morley against, Stephen for; Henry Sidgwick against, Arthur Sidgwick for; and George Trevelyan changing sides. Harvie observes that it "was all rather like Walter Raleigh's description of the contest between Faith and Doubt, as refereed by Henry Sidgwick: the combatants spent more time shaking hands, exchanging compliments and costumes, than in actually fighting. Each had more trouble establishing his own identity than hitting his opponent."[37]

Sidgwick's position on the matter was in essence this:

In the most important parts of the discussion that is now being carried on, I agree with the opposition: that is, I think, as I have always thought, that if there were no attack on property combined with the political movement for semi-independence of the Irish nationality, I should think it on the whole best to yield to this movement. I am optimistic as regards the connexion of Ireland with England; I think this connexion will subsist – for purposes of common defence and offence and unrestricted internal trade – whether we give Home Rule or refuse it; but I think we shall have somewhat less political trouble with Ireland if we give it than if we refuse it. But to abandon the landowners of Ireland to the tender mercies of the people who have for eleven years carried on an unscrupulous private war against their rights of property – rights which those of us who supported the Land Bill of 1881 morally pledged ourselves to secure to them – this is a national crime and deep moral disgrace in which I can have no part. The fact that even Tory speakers lay no stress on this danger only makes me feel it more strongly; they know that the landlords are not a popular class, and that the spoliation of them will arouse very feeble indignation in the breast of the average household suffrager. (M 524)

And of course, for Sidgwick, this issue was very much a family affair. In 1887, when Hicks-Beach resigned as chief secretary for Ireland, the Tory political forces settled on Balfour as his successor, a move that worried the Sidgwicks, who were, as the journal records, "much depressed, from a conviction that he will not be able to stand it physically, and will break down" (CWC). To the contrary, Sidgwick's pupil proved his grit by putting the lie to what had been one of Bryce's main arguments in favor of Home Rule – namely, that "the Democracy will not coerce, and therefore we must come to this in the end; so we had better take it at once quietly." Sidgwick allowed, as early as 1886, that "the only tolerable alternative for Home Rule *now* is Coercion, and vigorous coercion; any intermediate scheme has become irrelevant, even to the point of stupidity" (M 445). Balfour agreed and acted quickly to pass his infamous Crimes Act, which would allow him to impose a serious crackdown on the opposition in Ireland –

Courts of summary jurisdiction were to be used for the prosecution of certain offences, among them boycotting, conspiracy to withhold rent, illegal gatherings and intimidation. Cases involving trial by jury could now be moved from one district to another to avoid prejudiced verdicts; the Lord Lieutenant was given the power to 'proclaim' those parts of the country which were to be governed under the terms of the act, and certain assemblies were declared unlawful.[38]

As Sidgwick's journal from 1887 reveals, Balfour discussed his measures with Sidgwick in detail.

The Crimes Act led to the infamous riot in Mitchelstown. The National League had called a meeting there to protest a trial that was under way, that of the Irish nationalist M. P. William O'Brien. As Egremont describes it:

O'Brien was charged with inciting resistance to the proposed evictions on Lady Kingston's estate at Mitchelstown; Dillon and Henry Labouchère, the English radical, came, together with several other members of parliament, to protest against this. A riot erupted in which the vastly outnumbered police opened fire on the crowd, killing three men and wounding more. Liberals and Nationalists united to condemn the killings.

In Parliament there was an outcry. Balfour would not give an inch. Labouchère, supported by the Liberal front bench, launched an impassioned attack on the Chief Secretary although the opposition moved no vote of censure against the government. Balfour instituted an inquiry into the debacle but quashed the verdict of wilful murder passed against the police by the local coroner's jury. He knew the affair had been badly mishandled by the authorities and that the police had panicked, yet officially he admitted no error.[39]

Supposedly, ever afterward, Gladstone would murmur "remember Mitchelstown" when the subject of Balfour came up. The Irish dubbed him "Bloody Balfour."

Again, Sidgwick was quite in the thick of all this, however depressed he was about his spirits. He and Nora would visit Arthur in Ireland and come away impressed by his "coolness and courage." His journal is packed with references to Balfour and the Irish issue, and his other correspondence also testifies to his not-insignificant advisory role in this case and with regard to Balfour's career in general (though his letters float wildly from detailed assessments of various plans for taxation and land purchase schemes to resolve the Irish tensions, to minute questions of copyright law, to Hegelian metaphysics, to plans for the Albert University in London). Despite his vast admiration for Gladstone, he simply could not go along with the shift in the Liberal Party, which he deemed "a pusillanimous surrender of those whom we are bound to protect, and of posterity" (M 434). The Home Rule controversy, along with escalating labor unrest at home, did much to render him jaded with party politics, and these trials weighed heavily on him at precisely the time of his great crisis over immortality, a time when he was also "trying to absorb myself in my Opus Magnum on *Politics*." As he put it to Symonds:

My position is that I seem to myself now to have grasped and analyzed adequately the only possible method of dealing systematically with political problems; but my deep conviction is that it can yield as yet little fruit of practical utility – so doubt whether it is worth while to work it out in a book. Still a man must work – and a Professor must write books. I look forward with much interest to your new departure in literary criticism; you certainly have the gift of perennial youthfulness of spirit. I do not think I have, except in my general attitude towards life, which is very like that of a somewhat pessimistic undergraduate. (M 481)

When Sidgwick's book finally appeared, it was somewhat puzzling even to his friends and colleagues. In fact, there was little agreement on just what was the most Sidgwickian part of it. Hastings Rashdall suggested, for the benefit of the reader who wanted to skim some, that "if he wants to get at Professor Sidgwick's best and most characteristic work, he should read the last few chapters of it."[40] But Bryce felt that it was rather the first part of the book, on the functions of government, that succeeded best. And Maitland, one of Sidgwick's protégés, whose position at Cambridge Sidgwick himself had funded, deemed the part on international law and morality "the best thing that I have read about the subject," though he also expressed delight in the critique of Austin, "for the formal jurisprudent sits heavy upon us and you will deprive him of his terrors.[41]" (For all the praise of Bentham, the *Elements* contains a damning indictment of the theory of sovereignty advanced by his famous disciple.)

As should be clear from Sidgwick's planning of the work, he himself regarded the *Elements* as only a partial fulfillment of his project. Eleanor Sidgwick, in her Preface to *The Development of European Polity*, would give a concise statement of the overall plan:

It had of later years been more and more decidedly the author's view – as he has left on record – that a threefold treatment of politics is desirable for completeness: – first, an exposition analytical and deductive, such as he attempted in his work on the *Elements of Politics*; secondly, an evolutionary study of the development of polity within the historic period in Europe, beginning with the earliest known Graeco-Roman and Teutonic polity, and carried down to the modern state of Europe and its colonies as the last result of political evolution; thirdly, a comparative study of the constitutions of Europe and its colonies in connexion with the history of what may be called the constitution-making century which has just ended. The present book is an attempt at a treatment of political science from the second point of view. . . . In reading the book it should be borne in mind that it does not deal with theoretical politics as such. The theory of politics is treated in *Elements of Politics*, where the work and structure of the modern state are examined, and though the present book is complete in itself, it is intended that, for a full view of the subject, both books should be read. As a matter of fact, Mr. Sidgwick often gave a course of lectures on Political Theory along with the lectures contained in this book – some of his pupils attending both courses. (DEP v)

She also notes that Sidgwick had the keen (if impractical) wish to spend much more time in Europe, engaged in the direct study of comparative politics.

It is curious, and suggestive of how misleading the *Elements* was in some respects, that when *The Development of European Polity* finally appeared, pieced together from materials that Sidgwick had left at the time of his death, both Dicey and Bryce observed, in the latter's words, that "Few among Sidgwick's friends knew till this second book appeared how wide was the range of his historical knowledge, and how complete his mastery of historical method."[42] Thus, perhaps one reason why the *Elements* has struck some as a retreat from the more historically minded critique of Benthamism in the *Principles* is simply that one part of Sidgwick's political studies has been mistaken for the whole.

In any event, these are crucial points to bear in mind when considering the claims that the *Elements* makes on behalf of the analytical or deductive method. The analytical side of his project must still, after all, work with a self-consciously historicized account of human nature and the common sense of humanity, of the political and economic context, and it is still only one part of the larger task that involves inductive and comparative investigations as well. Sidgwick did not share Dicey's view that the historical bent was responsible for everything from nationalist bigotry to sickly emotionalism, though he did think that nationalist sentiment was something of an unfortunate halter on cosmopolitan utilitarian internationalism. In all of his major treatises, he insists that any concrete applications of the utilitarian principle must involve detailed analysis of the actual social conditions in question. As he described this aspect of his work in *Philosophy, Its Scope and Relations*: "the historical method could hardly be distinguished from the inductive method; and its alleged 'invasion' would not mean more than a spread of a tendency in all departments of thought to pay more attention to facts and less to deductive reasoning from general premises, assumed or supposed to be self-evident" (PSR 126).

Again, one of Sidgwick's primary concerns in emphasizing the primacy of the deductive method is simply that this is rendered all the more appropriate by the success of historical consciousness in general. If the world has changed – presumably for the better – if society has evolved as well as nature, then perforce the lessons of earlier times will be of limited applicability to the present, except perhaps in relation to other countries at different stages of historical progress. The historical method cannot be dispensed with, of course, and has practical value as well as being appropriate to its own sphere. Historical examples can always undermine sweeping generalizations – as in the part of Symonds's argument stressing that the example of classical Greece demonstrated that same-sex behavior need not be abnormal, pathological, or decadent. But of course, even Symonds allowed that there was no going back, and like Sidgwick, instead thought that a new synthesis was necessary.

As usual, however, Sidgwick's chief point is the familiar one that the more ambitious historical and sociological forecasts "can only be vague and general, if they are kept within the limits of caution and sobriety; and any guidance that may be derived from such forecasts for the problems of practical politics must be mainly negative and limitative, and can hardly amount to positive direction" (EP 8). But as he put it in *Philosophy*,

> Especially in the departments of Ethics and Politics, with which I have been specially concerned, do I recognise the importance of studying in historical order the variations in political ideas and beliefs in their double relation partly as cause and partly as effect of change in political facts; and similarly in studying the changes in ethical ideals in connexion with changes in other elements of social structure and in the relations between societies. And of course in both these studies, since they are departments of history, we must use a historical method. (PSR 162)

Recall again his worries, highlighted in Chapter 4, about the direction of commonsense morality.

Of course, another point that Sidgwick is eager to emphasize is that

> History cannot determine for us the ultimate end and standard of good and bad, right and wrong, in political institutions; – whether we take this to be general happiness, or social wellbeing defined somehow so as to distinguish it from happiness. This ultimate end we cannot get from history; we bring it with us to the study of history when we judge of the goodness or badness of the laws and political institutions which history shows us. (EP 7)

But history does show us just what kind of material we must work with.

Now, after all of this methodological preliminary, what did Sidgwick's analytical method actually yield?

The *Elements* proceeds in the fashion of so many of his works on the art of political economy, though in even more encyclopedic detail. Thus, he begins with a careful elaboration of the individualistic principle, the basic principle at work in the argument for laissez-faire. Taken as the main guide for legislation and governmental interference, it means that

what one sane adult is legally compelled to render to others should be merely the negative service of non-interference, except so far as he has voluntarily undertaken to render positive services; provided that we include in the notion of non-interference the obligation of remedying or compensating for mischief intentionally or carelessly caused by his acts – or preventing mischief that would otherwise result from previous acts. This principle for determining the nature and limits of governmental interference is currently know as 'Individualism'.... the requirement that one sane adult, apart from contract or claim to reparation, shall contribute positively by money or services to the support of others I shall call 'socialistic.' (EP 42)

As usual, Sidgwick explains how this principle reflects various psychological and sociological presuppositions – for example, that sane adults are the best judges of their own interests – and that these are only approximate generalizations and subject to important limitations. In the *Elements*, especially, he is very careful to disentangle these presuppositions, noting how the argument for laissez-faire requires "besides the psychological proposition that every one can best take care of his own interest" the "sociological proposition that the common welfare is best attained by each pursuing exclusively his own welfare and that of his family in a thoroughly alert and intelligent manner" (EP 145). And he stresses how no actual nation

is composed of individuals having only the few simple and general characteristics which are all we can include in our conception of the civilised man to whom our abstract political reasoning relates. An actual nation consists of persons of whom the predominant number have, besides the general characteristics . . . a certain vaguely defined complex of particular characteristics which we call the 'national character' of Englishmen, Frenchmen, etc.; among which sentiments and habits of thought and action, formed by the previous history of the nation, must always occupy a prominent place: and a consideration of these particular characteristics may properly modify to an important extent the conclusions arrived at by our general reasoning. (EP 13–14)

This fixation on "national character" was, as previously noted, pervasive during this period, a legacy of Romanticism that had passed into the post-Darwinian ethos, and one that can be found throughout the work of Sidgwick and his various social scientific friends. It is quite central to Sidgwick's thought, complementing his account of commonsense morality.

Clearly, Sidgwick is once again setting up the individualistic (or nonpaternalistic) principle for an extended beating, decorously disguised by his admission that it is in the main sound and the best point of departure for considering admissible deviations. He wastes no time in explaining that it will not do either as a basic or ultimate principle or as the means of advancing human happiness. In fact, the *Elements* goes a bit further, claiming

general – if not universal – assent for the principle that the true standard and criterion by which right legislation is to be distinguished from wrong is conduciveness to the general 'good' or 'welfare.' And probably the great majority of persons would agree to interpret the 'good' or 'welfare' of the community to mean, in the last analysis, the happiness of the individual human beings who compose the community; provided that we take into account not only the human beings who are actually living but those who are to live hereafter.

At any rate, he continues, this is his view, and thoughout this treatise he will "take the happiness of the persons affected as the ultimate end and standard of right and wrong in determining the functions and constitution of government" (EP 38). Of course, in Millian fashion, he owns that "when we have agreed to take general happiness as the ultimate end, the most important part of our work still remains to be done: we have to establish or assume some subordinate principle or principles, capable of more precise application, relating to the best means for attaining by legislation the end of Maximum Happiness" (EP 40). Obviously, this is where the individualistic principle comes in.

This is, to be sure, a fairly generous assessment of the general political consciousness, one that cannot help but make many of Sidgwick's concerns about the dualism of practical reason fade into the background, at least somewhat, though this is consistent with his statements about common sense being only implicitly or potentially as receptive to egoism as it is to utilitarianism, with the decline of religion. The actual rational egoistic arguments of Hobbes or Bentham (or of orthodox political economists, for that matter) find little resonance in the *Elements*, and the generous reconstruction of political common sense would seem to be at odds with

Sidgwick's worries about the rank selfishness evident in party politics. Not surprisingly, it was of the *Elements* that Hayek complained that although it was "in many respects an admirable work," it scarcely "represents what must be regarded as the British liberal tradition and is already strongly tainted with that rationalist utilitarianism which led to socialism."[43] Hayek was not one to be put off the scent by Mauricean subterfuges.

Indeed, the list of deviations from individualism that Sidgwick assembles is quite daunting, covering again a vast range of items such as education, defense, child care, poor relief, public works, collective bargaining, and so forth. He delicately teases apart the different degrees of intervention, according to whether the government "merely regulates, and perhaps subvents," or "itself undertakes a department of business," or actually "establishes a legal monopoly of the business in its own favour – as in the case of the post office in England" (EP 153). He stresses two cases that he thinks point up in a quite obvious way the limitations of the individualistic principle: "the humane treatment of lunatics, and the prevention of cruelty to the inferior animals." Such restrictions do not aim at securing the freedom of the lunatics or the animals, but are "a one-sided restraint of the freedom of action of men with a view to the greatest happiness of the aggregate of sentient beings." An unfortunate note explains that the "protection of inferior races of men will be considered in a subsequent chapter." (EP 141–42)

In typical manner, such considerations lead Sidgwick back to the discussion of socialism. Many of the cases discussed shade imperceptibly from individualism to socialism – thus, "when it is evident that children are, through their parents' poverty, growing up in such a way as to render them likely to be burdensome or dangerous to society, it seems *prima facie* a prudent insurance against this result for the community to assist in their support and education." Here, Sidgwick recognizes, there is indeed a slippery slope, though not one that can realistically be avoided. For "similar arguments may be used to justify a governmental provision of sustenance for adults, in order that they may not be driven into criminal courses: and if either kind of governmental assistance is once admitted as justifiable in principle, it is not very easy to limit the burden that may be thrown on industrious and provident individuals by the improvidence of others." This question lands us in "the debatable territory between Individualism and Socialism." (EP 141) But Sidgwick is starting to sound much more like Green on temperance than Mill on liberty.

In the *Elements*, the extremist form of socialism is labelled "collectivism" rather than "communism." Against collectivism or communism
Sidgwick, as usual, urges that it would under the present circumstances
"arrest industrial progress," in such a way that "the comparative equality
in incomes which it would bring about would be an equality in poverty"
(EP 158). But in this book, much more a product of the turbulent eighties
that witnessed the rebirth of working-class activism, he seems far less confident that the extreme form of socialism has had its day, and admits in less
qualified fashion that such a scheme "has much attraction for thoughtful
and sympathetic persons; not only from its tendency to equalise wealth,
but also from the possibilities it holds out of saving the waste and avoiding
the unmerited hardships incident to the present competitive organisation
of business; and of substituting industrial peace, mutual service, and a
general diffusion of public spirit, for the present conflict of classes and
selfish struggles of individuals" (EP 158). The general case of socialistic
interference is presented in, if anything, an even more favorable, politically relevant light than it was in the *Principles*, and the evolution toward collectivism is cast as "quite conceivable," through "improvements
in the organisation and working of governmental departments, aided by
watchful and intelligent public criticism – together with a rise in the
general level of public spirit throughout society" (EP 158–59). The collectivist idea is only impracticable "at the present time or in the proximate
future."

Allowing that much of the relevant discussion is a matter for political
economy, Sidgwick is nonetheless anxious to "point out certain general
considerations which must to some extent govern our estimate of the expediency" of socialistic schemes especially concerned with "the mitigation
of the harshest inequalities in the present distribution of incomes" (EP
160). He thinks it "indubitable that the attainment of greater equality in
the distribution of the means and opportunities of enjoyment is in itself
a desirable thing, if only it can be attained without any material sacrifice
of the advantages of freedom," and he accepts, as he did in the *Methods*
and the *Principles*, "Bentham's view, that any given quantum of wealth
is generally likely to be less useful to its owner, the greater the total of
private wealth of which it forms a part . . . that the utility of a given quantum of any particular commodity to its possessor tends to be diminished,
in proportion as the total amount of the commodity in his possession
is increased" (EP 160). While admitting the force of the arguments for

maintaining incentives to productivity, and for the "effective maintenance and progress of intellectual culture" through "the existence of a numerous group of persons enjoying complete leisure and the means of ample expenditure," Sidgwick still insists that "at least the removal of the extreme inequalities, found in the present distribution of wealth and leisure, would be desirable, if it could be brought about without any material repression of the free development of individual energy and enterprise" (EP 161).

The discussion that follows is hardly what one would call utopian, with its account of the English Poor Law as guilty of diminishing "the inducements to industry and thrift, without any counterbalancing tendency to stimulate labour by enlarging its opportunities" – such systems "simply and nakedly take the produce of those who have laboured successfully to supply the needs of those who have laboured unsuccessfully or not at all." Again, he tends to favor measures that avoid such controversy, because their "primary aim is not to redistribute compulsorily the produce of labour, but to equalise the opportunities of obtaining wealth by productive labour, without any restriction on the freedom of adults." (EP 162) Interestingly, against the objection that even such schemes as these cost money, and will have to be funded by taxation that is effectively redistributive, he argues that such arguments ignore the fact

that the institution of private property as actually existing goes beyond what the individualistic theory justifies. Its general aim is to appropriate the results of labour to the labourer, but in realising this aim it has inevitably appropriated natural resources to an extent which, in any fully peopled country, has entirely discarded Locke's condition of 'leaving enough and as good for others.' In any such country, therefore, the propertied classes are in the position of encroaching on the opportunities of the unpropertied in a manner which – however defensible as the only practicable method of securing the results of labour – yet renders a demand for compensation justifiable from the most strictly individualistic point of view. It would seem that such compensation may fitly be given by well-directed outlay, tending either to increase the efficiency and mobility of labour, or to bring within the reach of all members of a civilised society some share of the culture which we agree in regarding as the most valuable result of civilisation: and in so far as this is done without such heavy taxation as materially diminishes the stimulus to industry and thrift of the persons taxed, this expenditure of public money, however justly it may be called Socialistic, appears to be none the less defensible as the best method of approximating to the ideal of Individualistic justice. (EP 163)

This passage, reflecting the familiar line of argument dealing with Spencer's inconsistent individualism, marks again Sidgwick's penetrating assessment of how the champions of laissez-faire have tended to "tacitly assume" conditions of equality of opportunity – or at least, "the loss to the community arising from the restricted opportunities of large masses has been tacitly overlooked." Given that, when he wrote this, it was still the case that some 80 percent of the land in England was owned by the aristocracy, the whiff of Ricardian radicalism about the conflictual components of the English economy is undeniable.[44] And the conclusion Sidgwick derives is, as we have seen, more general than the Ricardian one, given the difficulty of drawing the line between property in land and property in manufacturing or financial assets.

The ensuing discussion, concerning poor relief, draws together a number of Sidgwick's arguments on the topic, from his various unpublished lectures on the "Theory of Almsgiving" and the "Poor Law," to his introduction to the English translation of Aschrott's book on *The English Poor Law System*, a work that he much admired. After reviewing the French system, with its dependence on private charity, he sums up the English system and introduces a comparison to the German one. The English system

secures adequate sustenance from public funds to all persons who are in complete destitution, while it aims at minimising the encouragement thus offered to idleness and unthrift by attaching unattractive – though not physically painful – conditions to the public relief given to ordinary adult paupers. Practically, it succeeds better as regards industry than thrift. So far as able-bodied men are concerned, experience has shown that the required combination of unattractiveness with sufficiency of provision for physical needs is attainable by insisting that the recipient of relief shall submit to the constraints of a 'workhouse.' But the system has hitherto failed to bring about the general provision against old age, which – for the most part – might be made without difficulty even by unskilled labourers in the period of early manhood, if they were content to defer marriage for a moderate term of years. Further, it would be unpractically severe to insist on the condition of entering the workhouse in the temporary disablement of breadwinners through sickness or accident; while to dispense with it even in these cases involves a serious discouragement to providence. These evils are avoided by the German method – so far as can be applied – of compulsory insurance against sickness, accidental disablement, chronic infirmity, and old age. This method, it may be observed, involves governmental interference, which is in one aspect greater than that entailed by the English method, since the provision compulsorily made extends to labourers generally, whereas the English system only provides for the destitute: on the other hand, the method of compulsory insurance is, from another point of view, less anti-individualistic, so far as the burden of the provision is thrown on the persons who receive the benefit of it. (EP 165–66)

Sidgwick goes on to suggest that a "careful combination" of all three systems – regulated private almsgiving, public relief, and compulsory insurance – would probably yield the "practically best plan" for dealing with poverty, but at the same time he admits that just how to combine them, and in what degree, are problems to which there is no general theoretical solution. Consequently, he is only willing to conclude that "the proper nature and limits of governmental action for the relief of indigence must largely depend upon (1) the actual extent of effectiveness of voluntary association among the citizens, and (2) on the amount of philanthropic effort and sacrifice habitually devoted by private persons to the supply of social needs, and the wisdom with which these efforts and sacrifices are directed." These lessons are similar to those drawn in other departments – thus, "we actually find that the promotion of education and culture, and the cure of diseases, have been largely provided for in modern civilised communities . . . by the donations and bequests of individuals. So far as these needs can be adequately met in this way, there is an advantage in avoiding the necessity for additional taxation." (EP 166) Should the state start intervening in an area where private beneficence had been effective, "there is a serious danger of the latter withdrawing from it, unless the spheres of action appropriate to the two agencies respectively are well and clearly defined."

These general remarks do not actually convey Sidgwick's more detailed convictions, the result of his work with the Cambridge Charity Organization Society. For example, in an unpublished lecture on the "Poor Law," delivered to the London COS, he explained that he did not think that the English system, workhouses and all, was fundamentally misguided, despite the attacks on it as "hard-hearted" by sentimental socialists, trades union congresses, and so on. Moreover, he opposed transferring to the government the tasks of discriminating desert and dealing with specially deserving cases – which was the "the semi-official work of experts" such as the COS. At most, he favored an intermediate course of reform: "keeping the work-house system as at present, we might supplement it – so far as out-door relief is concerned – by something like the French system – some cooperation with local governments which should yet keep the financial and administrative basis of the work mainly voluntary." Presumably, this is where he hoped for the involvement of minds of "nobler stamp," as he had put it in the *Principles*. His fear was that

an astute socialistic leader, taking advantage of popular sentiment, might easily construct a series of apparently moderate steps by which our existing system of poor-relief might be transformed into a system securing a fairly comfortable provision for old-age and industrial emergencies, for the manual labour classes; so that it might serve as a valuable military basis enabling them to conduct their industrial wars with more staying-power than at present. (CWC)[45]

Now, such sentiments and affiliations were hardly likely to win Sidgwick a reputation for radicalism. Again, the Charity Organisation Societies were generally regarded as bastions of the laissez-faire thinking that went into the Poor Law reforms of 1834, the first result of the reformed Parliament, which did away with the Speenhamland system that had sheltered rural England against the first ravages of capitalism. As Polanyi put it in his classic work, *The Great Transformation*,

To the bewilderment of thinking minds, unheard-of wealth turned out to be inseparable from unheard-of poverty. Scholars proclaimed in unison that a science had been discovered which put the laws governing man's world beyond any doubt. It was at the behest of these laws that compassion was removed from the hearts, and a stoic determination to renounce human solidarity in the name of the greatest happiness of the greatest number gained the dignity of secular religion.[46]

Altruistic rightness of heart was being subordinated to utilitarian hardness of heart, a focus on consequences as calculated by experts.

What is missing from such an imputation of want of human feeling and solidarity is, at least in the case of Sidgwick, any recognition of how he simply sought to combine altruistic feeling with effective giving, and how he held out the hope that human nature would change and that a far more socialistic system would prove possible. Moreover, he did think the English system too purely deterrent. After all, he himself had effectively undermined most of the orthodox attempts to legitimate the economic system, and his brief was against industrial war, not creeping socialism.

It was this curious combination of countenancing too many of the complacencies of orthodox political economy with respect to the present, while recognizing the empirical, debatable nature of the issues and keeping an open and hopeful mind about the future obsolescence of libertarian theory and practice, that made Sidgwick such an elusive, easily misunderstood figure. A revealing case in point involved the famous socialist playwright George Bernard Shaw, who used to enjoy recounting how Sidgwick had stormed out of one of his socialist speeches, while loudly objecting that he would have no truck with anyone advocating the theft of property. Sidgwick's journal, however, leaves a different impression:

The Committee had invited a live Socialist, redhot 'from the Streets,' as he told us, who sketched in a really brilliant address the rapid series of steps by which modern society is to pass peacefully into social democracy. The *node* of the transition was supplied by urban ground-rents (it is interesting to observe that the old picture of the agricultural landlord-drone, battening on social prosperity to which he contributes nothing, is withdrawn for the present as too ludicrously out of accordance with the facts). It is now *urban* ground-rent that the municipal governments will have to seize, to meet the ever-growing necessity of providing work and wages for the unemployed. How exactly this seizure of urban rents was to develop into a complete nationalisation of industry I could not remember afterwards, but it seemed to go very naturally at the time. There was a peroration rhetorically effective as well as daring, in which he explained that the bliss of perfected socialism would only come by slow degrees, with lingering steps and long delays, and claimed our sympathy for the noble-hearted men whose ardent philanthropy had led them to desire to cut these delays short by immediate revolution and spoliation. It was, indeed, a mistake on their part; the laws of social development did not admit of it; but if we were not quite lost in complacent selfishness we should join him in regretting that this shorter way with property was impossible.

Altogether a noteworthy performance: – the man's name is *Bernard Shaw*: Myers says he has written books worth reading. (M 498)

This encounter at the British Association was in September of 1888, well after the publication of Sidgwick's *Principles* and his own quasi-Millian sketch of the possible transition to socialism through the increasing success of public industries. According to legend, when Shaw was finally confronted with this passage from the *Memoir*, he was rendered quite speechless.[47]

One of the primary reasons why Sidgwick's views on gradual socialism and the growth of government interference were so cautious in the case of such matters as poor relief has to do with his more general fears about the corruption of the political process. Thus, he concludes his chapter on "Socialistic Interference," with its discussion of poor relief, with an expression of concern about the disadvantages of governmental action. These disadavantages involve:

(1) the danger of overburdening the governmental machinery with work, (2) the danger of increasing the power capable of being used by governing persons oppressively or corruptly, (3) the danger that the delicate economic functions of government will be hampered by the desire to gratify certain specially influential sections of the community: – for instance, when legislation is in the hands of a representative assembly, the more the functions of Government are extended in a socialistic direction, the greater becomes the risk that contested elections will exhibit an immoral competition between candidates promising to procure public money for the benefit of particular classes and districts. (EP 167)

Along with these dangers, he warns that the work of government is apt to be done by persons lacking some of the drive of persons in the private sector, and that it is therefore a mistake to conclude "that governmental interference is always expedient, even where *laisser faire* leads to a manifestly unsatisfactory result; its expediency has to be decided in any particular case by a careful estimate of advantages and drawbacks, requiring data obtained from special experience."

Clearly, Sidgwick feared that government, too, was under the going conditions insufficiently high-minded, and that the evolution of public spirit had some ways to go. Indeed, with the increasing democratization coming with the reforms of 1867 and 1883, he was inclined to think that short-sighted party strife was becoming even more of a danger. When, in Part II of the book, he finally comes around to an extended discussion of democracy, he makes it abundantly plain that his conception of democracy – quite like Mill's – would not harbor any excessively generous view of the capabilities of the plain man. Thus,

There seem to be two competing principles, one or other of which is more or less definitely assumed in current arguments for democratic institutions. One of these, – which I myself accept, with important qualifications, – is 'that government should rest on the active consent of the governed'; the other is 'that any one honest and self-supporting citizen is, on the average, as well qualified as another for the work of government.' This latter proposition I in the main reject; but I admit that, in one view of the proof of the first proposition, the second is to some extent implied, and that where democracy – as defined by the first proposition – is fully developed, there is likely to be a tendency to accept and act upon the second to some extent. (EP 610)

The qualifications have to do especially with the legislative side of government (Sidgwick accepts the familiar threefold division of executive, judicial, and legislative), and on many counts they follow Mill's *Considerations on Representative Government*. Yet he is, if anything, even pickier about expertise than Mill, and often sounds very like a precursor to Walter Lippmann, with his scathing assault on the myth of the "omnicompetent citizen" in *Public Opinion*.[48] Thus, the

> ideal legislator ought to know law as well as the lawyer, but he ought to know much more than law. He must have an insight . . . into the actual relation of the laws to the social life of the community regulated; the manner in which they modify the conduct of the individuals whom they affect; the consequences, proximate and remote, that are likely to result from any change in them.

But getting a body of legislators who, in addition to general knowledge, "combine special experience in different departments of social life" is only one part of the problem. Harder still is to secure "in legislators a keen *concern* for the interests of the various elements of the community for which they legislate." This requires the familiar solution of a "system of popular election for a limited time," which even when it yields bad laws, at least makes the legislation more acceptable to the governed. (EP 370–71)

Needless to say, Sidgwick has little patience for the claims of direct democracy, or for a natural right to self-governance. The latter he treats as akin to the individualistic principle, as something that may be justified on utilitarian grounds, but only with important exceptions and qualifications. On the former, he insists that legislation is "a difficult art, the mastery of which requires such an expenditure of time and energy as the citizens at large – even if otherwise qualified – cannot ordinarily afford." Although he allows that under certain conditions, it could be justifiable to rely more rather than less heavily on such direct democratic means as the referendum, this does not translate into any sympathy for the idea of doing away with representation. Against the claim that the incompetence of the electorate for directly producing legislation will simply translate into an incompetent choice of legislators, he thinks it sufficient

> to reply that, in the division of labour which civilisation has brought, ordinary members of a community organised on an individualistic basis have continually

to choose experts for skilled work of which the chooser does not understand the methods: and the result is commonly accepted as tolerably satisfactory. Thus ... most men value highly the control that they acquire, by the free choice of their physician, over the operation of applying drugs to the cure of their diseases; though they know themselves to be wholly unable to prescribe medicines for themselves.

If this cannot be exactly imitated in the case of government's coercive power, nonetheless "we imitate it as far as we can by giving the individuals coerced a share in the appointment of the supreme organ of legislation." (EP 374–75)

Yet it must be said that Sidgwick was awfully sensitive to the inadequacies of the people. All of Mill's fears – or Tocqueville's – about the potential tyranny of the majority loom large for him, in the context of the 1880s, though in somewhat altered form. He is not one to suffer any confusion about the multiple meanings of "freedom":

When a writer speaks of 'Free' institutions he sometimes means to imply that the government leaves the individual alone to look after his own affairs; sometimes that the private members of the community collectively exercise an effective control over the government: sometimes he seems to imply both together, apparently assuming a necessary connection between the two facts, which we may conveniently distinguish as 'civil' and 'constitution' freedom respectively.

But there is no such necessary connection; alluding to a favorite example of Mill's, he notes "that Government does nothing to prevent a man from getting as drunk as he likes in Russia: whereas the vigorous democracy of North America has established in several States severely restrictive liquor-laws." (EP 375–76)

Sidgwick is of course well aware of how the demand for voter confidence might undercut the point of democracy, since a legislature representing only certain class interests could be even harsher toward those excluded than a despot with fewer prejudices. But for all that, he is quite liberal in excluding people from the franchise:

On the whole it would seem that the permanent exclusion of any class of sane self-supporting adults, on account of poverty alone, from the share of the control over legislation which the representative system aims at giving to the citizens at large, is not easily defensible in face of a strong and steady demand for their admission. It is less difficult to maintain such an exclusion in the case of avoidable ignorance of an extreme kind: i.e. to refuse the suffrage to persons who have not attained a certain educational standard, provided that facilities for education are within the reach of all classes. Various other exclusions are permanently defensible on different grounds. Thus it seems reasonable to withhold the suffrage – partly as a deterrent, partly as a security against its perversion – from persons who have committed grave offences of any kind; also from all who have been convicted of buying or selling votes, or intimidating electors. In some cases, disgraceful conduct not amounting to crime seems a sufficient ground for exclusion – e.g. the keeping of a brothel, where this is tolerated. It also seems reasonable to disfranchise temporarily persons who without crime have so far failed to maintain their economic independence as to receive support as paupers from public funds; on the ground that their use of the vote as a protection of their political interests is specially unlikely to be advantageous to the public. Other temporary exclusions appear to be desirable for reasons that involve no sort of discredit. Thus, as we have seen, the ordinary objections to electoral restrictions do not apply in the case of exclusion on the ground of youth and inexperience; and it seems reasonable to impose, as a condition of the suffrage, an inferior limit of age somewhat higher than that of ordinary legal maturity; so that a man may not have a share in the control of public affairs until after some years of the experience gained by the independent management of his own affairs. Again, when we examine the possibilities of bringing the motive of private interest into illicit operation in political elections, we are led to distinguish a special class of persons in whose case this operation cannot effectually be excluded, except by a partial withdrawal of the right of voting. I mean persons employed by candidates or their friends for the work of an election. A similar danger exists in some measure in the case of permanent employment, private or governmental: but not such as to justify a sweeping disfranchisement of employees, provided that the independence of the latter is tolerably secured by the protection of the ballot or otherwise. There is, however, a special ground for excluding from the exercise of the suffrage such employees of government as are charged with the function of physical coercion – policemen or soldiers on service – on the score of the peculiar importance of keeping them impartial in political conflicts. (EP 383–84)

As one might expect, there is a fairly nuanced discussion of the enfranchisement of women, though Sidgwick admits that, sad to say, "if we seek for a definition of democracy applicable to modern facts, it seems necessary to limit the 'governed' whose consent is required to 'sane lawabiding adult *men*'" (EP 611). But he can see "no adequate reason for refusing the franchise to any sane self-supporting adult otherwise eligible, on the score of her sex alone." Indeed, "there is a danger of material injustice resulting from such refusal, so long as the State leaves unmarried women and widows to struggle for a livelihood in the general industrial competition, without any special privileges or protection." (EP 385)[49] Sidgwick makes short, rather sarcastic work of the claims that the franchise belongs to those who can defend the country when attacked, or who represent a preponderance of physical force: the "manifest superiority of trained soldiers in physical conflict" would, on this argument, require that they receive "electoral power out of proportion to their numbers" (EP 385).

The matter of race as a possible ground for exclusion from the franchise is one that Sidgwick treats in a much more gingerly fashion. He appears to have maintained a certain agnosticism on the subject that allowed him to remain at least somewhat loyal to Mill's emphasis on racial equality. Thus,

Exclusion on the ground of race alone may be expedient if the general intellectual or moral inferiority of the race excluded is sufficiently clear. But a political society in which such exclusion is an important question, will be necessarily different from that which has been generally contemplated in the discussions of the present treatise, and will be likely to require different laws in other matters besides the franchise. (EP 387)

The "present treatise" had of course considered such countries as the United States and Australia. Furthermore, in a note to his discussion on colonization, he remarks,

Of course if it should become clear that the social amalgamation of two races would be debasing to the superior race, or otherwise demonstrably opposed to the interests of humanity at large, every effort ought to be made to carry into effect some drastic and permanent measures of separation. But I do not think that any proof has yet been brought adequate to support such a conclusion. (EP 326)

This is Sidgwick's characteristic way of commenting on the issue. In correspondence, he repeatedly states that there is no evidence worthy of the designation "scientific" for inherent racial differences when it comes to such things as intelligence and moral capacity. But his views on race and prejudice are perhaps not so innocent, and will be treated more fully later, when discussing the issues of colonialism and imperialism.

In addressing Sidgwick's conception of democracy, with its severe limitations on the franchise, it is vital to bear in mind that his main worry was how to ensure justice in legislation: "I did not mean to imply that good legislation is a kind of bargain struck between conflicting class-interests; it is the interest of the whole, which includes justice to all the parts, at which the statesman should aim: and justice, as Mill says, consists in giving a man not the half of what he asks, but the whole of what he ought to have" (EP 388–89). Restriction of the suffrage admittedly runs the risk that the interests of the unenfranchised class will be unfairly sacrificed, but on the other side, "a widely extended suffrage involves a danger . . . that the ultimate interests of the whole community may be sacrificed to the real or apparent class-interests of the numerical majority of the electors, either through ignorance or through selfishness and limitation of sympathy" (EP 389). Sidgwick thinks that the latter danger "may be more or less effectively met by giving the wealthier and more educated classes a representation in the legislature out of proportion to their numbers," which is in effect the aim of most bicameral legislative structures.

But the general means and principles by which this might be done are very problematic. Given Mill's views on the matter, Sidgwick is naturally appreciative of the importance of weighted or plural voting schemes, according to which either certain classes or certain individuals are given proportionately more voting power. He allows that there are some arguments for so weighting the votes of the rich, since "man for man, the rich have more important interests to defend than the poor." But he is more impressed by the idea that "superior political knowledge and insight" come

to be possessed on the average by the classes with larger incomes; partly from their more advanced education, and the habits of reading and thought thus acquired, partly from the exercise of intellect involved in the management of property, in the direction of industrial and commercial undertakings, and in the work of the 'learned' professions and other higher forms of skilled labour.

Still, superiority of this form "does not universally, or at all uniformly, accompany wealth," and any system of weighted voting would have to allow the poor to demonstrate that they had the requisite intellectual superiority. (EP 390–91)

In fact, on balance, Sidgwick finds these schemes to be faced by very grave difficulties. Any plan for implementing the recognition of the superiority of wealth or intelligence would have to be "to a great extent arbitrary: we have no means of determining, with any pretence to exactness, how much additional electoral power is due to wealth on account of the implication of social with private interests, or how much properly corresponds to any available evidence of probable superiority in political judgment." Any scheme would have to be left open to change, and would more or less perpetually encourage political agitation in some direction. Furthermore, as for any balance of interests, "it is impossible to divide society into classes which remain identical and equally distinct for all legislative purposes: as we pass from one proposed law to another, we find that the important lines of division are continually changing." Thus, sometimes the conflicts are between agricultural interests and manufacturing ones, sometimes between manual laborers and artisans, and so on, so that any weighting of the vote in favor of wealth might aggravate "the natural inequalities of a modern industrial society by adding artificial political inequalities to correspond" and "cause a real injustice corresponding to the appearance." (EP 391–92) Finally, weighting in terms of superior political knowledge and judgment is also bound to be arbitrary:

For, in the present state of the political art, such superiority is largely derived from personal experience, and reflection on such experience: and in any case requires a steady direction of thought to political questions, of which, in most cases, a satisfactory guarantee is not afforded either by prolonged education, or certificates of scholastic attainments, or the exercise of professinal functions. A thoughtful artisan who has only had an elementary education may easily have more political insight – and even knowledge – than e.g. a schoolmaster, physician, or engineer whose intellectual energies are absorbed in his special pursuit. (EP 392)

As Sidgwick goes on pointedly to observe, even without formal advantages in voting power, the rich "are likely always to count practically for more than one vote each." Bribery cannot be altogether prevented, nor intimidation, and more importantly, "gratitude for services, private or public – and hopes of similar services in the future – will always be motives operating on the side of wealthy candidates, or candidates with wealthy backers." Something of the same applies to superior intelligence, since when directed to "political exposition and persuasion" it will also wield great indirect electoral power.

Such considerations as these "somewhat reduce the danger that a widely extended suffrage *prima facie* involves, of legislation in which the interests of the rich minority are sacrificed to those of the poor majority in a manner disadvantageous to the community as a whole." They do not, however, demonstrate that such dangers are "immaterial," and Sidgwick allows that they are "likely to become more formidable in the future history of Western Europe and America." After all, "we have not yet seen the working of a thoroughly organised democracy, with a strong urban element, in a crowded country with very marked contrasts of wealth and poverty." Still, Sidgwick thinks it preferable, if at all possible, "to meet this danger by developing the natural and legitimate influence of wealth, when used as a means of performing social services, and of intelligence, when directed to political instruction and persuasion." Should these prove inadequate, then artificial weighting measures might be called for, and the plural vote would be more workable than unequally represented classes. In any event, if the weighted-vote scheme is to work, "the standard either of wealth or intellectual attainment should be low, so that the increased electoral power allotted to them may be widely shared, and the invidiousness of heaping votes on a privileged few may be avoided." (EP 393–94)

In the course of these discussions, Sidgwick makes some singularly illuminating remarks, delicately tucked away in notes. Thus, he wants to make it clear, however discreetly, that the unequal share of wealth of any given rich individual does not call for special protection on utilitarian grounds, given that inequality is *prima facie* not in accord with the general happiness. But with an eye toward Mill, he goes on to explain that we "cannot indeed say that every man's happiness is of equal importance as an element of the general happiness; because development of intellect and refinement of taste generally imply a capacity for superior pleasures. But it is just because this higher kind of happiness is at present enjoyed by few that a distribution of wealth much less unequal than the present would be undoubtedly desirable if it could be effected without any material diminution in the total amount to be distributed." (EP 390) Moreover, he has high hopes for the future progress of economic and political science. He doubts that "the value of political insight is underrated by thoughtful persons generally in any class." If the less educated "have now a difficulty in determining where it lies, and are liable to take a charlatan for a statesman, it is largely because educated opinion is so divided; – because the 'royal art' of government, as judged by the criterion of 'consensus of experts,' is still in so rudimentary a condition." In the future, as knowledge progresses, "disinterested students of politics should come to greater agreement," and consequently it is "reasonable to hope that the less educated will in preponderant numbers follow their lead." (EP 393–94) Clearly, the advancement of the educating society is a matter of some urgency.

Interestingly, when Sidgwick comes to the matter of legislative districts and the issue of proportional representation, he strongly dissents from the plan of Thomas Hare, which had been so enthusiastically endorsed by Mill in *Considerations*.[50] The idea of obtaining a truer representation by "the formation of constituencies by free combination, independent of locality," suffers from any number of problems. First, there "is a danger of losing a valuable protection against demagogy, if we remove the natural inducements which local divisions give for the more instructed part of the community to exercise their powers of persuasion on the less instructed." In local divisions, "the wiser few" can exploit their position, and "the natural sociability springing from neighbourhood tends to become a channel of political education." (EP 395) Also, if "the citizens are left to aggregate themselves into constituencies by free combination they are likely to form electoral bodies of a more uniform character, whether the combination is based upon identity of interests or similarity of opinions," losing the breadth of view and variety of ideas that locality fosters. Sidgwick worries that the simplicity of Hare's and similar schemes "is artificial, and involves the disadvantage of breaking up for electoral purposes portions of the community, – such as towns generally are, – which tend to have an intimate internal coherence in their economic and social life, and consequently important common interests." (EP 397) Any national political figure ought to be able to find some local basis of support.

And there are more specific problems with Hare's notion of preferential voting, according to which "each elector only gives one vote, but he is allowed to deliver a voting-paper on which the names of candidates may be written in any number not exceeding the number of places to be filled up." The names are to be in order of preference, so that "if a vote for the name first on the list turns out to be superfluous, because the candidate's quota of votes is already made up, the vote is counted for the name second on the list; and similarly, if need be, for the third, and so on." The "weak point of this scheme is that no thoroughly satisfactory method has been devised for selecting the particular votes that are to count for any candidate who has votes in excess of the required quota" – consequently, the results could be juggled, depending on which "winning votes" were counted, and so on. (EP 398)

At any rate, Sidgwick bestows no great favor on any concrete plan for legislative districting, and contents himself with the general conclusion that "it is important to provide for a rectification of the division from time to time, to meet changes in population." This rectification, however, should not be regarded as a constitutional change, but "should be performed regularly, as a natural consequence of a periodical census; and where party government prevails, it will be better that it should not be performed by the legislature but by a permanent commission – in order to avoid or reduce the danger of 'gerrymandering.'" (EP 399)

When it comes not to the right to elect but to the eligibility to be elected, Sidgwick, not surprisingly, reveals many of the same concerns, so that "crime, infamous trade, loss of economic independence, extreme poverty and ignorance, should disqualify equally in both cases: and if a minimum of age higher than that of ordinary legal maturity be adopted for electors, it will be reasonable to put the same restriction on candidates" (EP 400). Naturally, the same problems of arbitrariness would plague direct attempts to make riches or intelligence the criterion of holding office. Thus, "in order to obtain the varied empirical knowledge and the sympathetic insight into the needs of all sections of society, which we say to be the characteristic merit of this form of government, it is necessary that every class of electors should be free to choose its own members." Limitations "must have a tendency to diminish the interest taken by the poorer classes in the election of legislators, and to weaken their confidence in the legislators elected." (EP 401) However,

These arguments seem to me very strong against any formal limitation of eligibility by the requirement of definite pecuniary or educational qualifications: but they do not apply with anything like equal force to an arrangement which without excluding any class would yet operate very decidedly in favour of candidates possessing such qualifications. And this result, I conceive, may be simply attained by attaching no salary to the post of legislator. In this case, it will still be possible for any class in the community to select representatives from its own ranks: only if they have no independent means they will require to be supported by voluntary contributions: and the electors are hardly likely to tax themselves for this purpose unless they have a very decided preference for such candidates. (EP 401)

Sidgwick admits that "it may be necessary to provide public remuneration for the work of legislation in poor communities." Still, he thinks that "in societies as wealthy as modern states generally are, it cannot be difficult to find an adequate number of persons, qualified by nature and training and enjoying pecuniary independence, to devote themselves to this important and interesting work: which, if public opinion is in a healthy state, they will regard as at once a duty and an honour." This principle would establish a high standard of "pecuniary incorruptibility." Moreover,

If it be said that an assembly in which comparatively rich men preponderate will tend, in framing legislative measures, to have special regard to the class-interests of the rich, I should reply that this tendency, in a country where the suffrage is widely extended, may reasonably be regarded not as a drawback, but as a valuable security for just legislation; in view of the grave danger already noticed that the apparent interests of the poor, who form the numerical majority, will be preferred to the real ultimate interests of the whole community. (EP 402)

This is not to mention the arguments to be made on behalf of some form of upper chamber, exercising a further check on the democratic tendencies of the lower. With an eye to the comparison of the U.S. Senate and the British House of Lords, Sidgwick argues at length that

assuming that a Senate is desirable, I should reject as generally inexpedient modes of appointing senators – under the social and political conditions of a modern state – co-optation, inheritance, and those modes of election which manifestly render the elected chamber representative of a *section* of the whole body of citizens. Among the acceptable modes of appointment I should distinguish (1) those that aim at securing *personal* weight in the senators; and (2) those that aim at securing *representative* weight. I should place in the former class nomination on the ground of eminence by the executive, and appointment as a consequence of holding or having held for a certain time certain high offices. In the latter class I should include all modes of election which would render the persons elected representative in some way of the whole body of citizens. The methods included in the first class appear to me well adapted for the purpose of providing a chamber that is only designed to have the power of delaying, and not that of permanently resisting, the legislative measures approved by the primary representative assembly: but if a chamber with really co-ordinate powers is wanted, I think that the weight required for the conflicts it must be prepared to face is most likely to be secured by some method that will render it undeniably representative, though perhaps in an indirect way, of the nation at large. (EP 477)

The former is the method "adapted to Parliamentary government," while the latter requires "some such careful separation of legislature from executive as is realised in the 'presidential' system of the United States of America."

Now, the foregoing remarks should make it tolerably plain how and why Sidgwick favors the account of democracy as resting on the active consent of the governed rather than on the idea of the omnicompetent citizen. The latter notion perhaps really did find an application in ancient Athens, but Sidgwick has a host of reservations about its modern applicability and favors instead an adaptation of Aristotle, when it comes to the forms of government. Thus, he notes that there has been an unfortunate obliteration in recent times of the distinction between oligarchy and aristocracy. The former connotes rule by the wealthy few in their own interests, but the latter involves rule by the "best" and still carries at least a more neutral sense. Thus,

[T]he 'aristocratic' element of a modern community is vaguely understood to be not merely rich, but to have acquired, on the average, through hereditary wealth, leisure, and social position, a cultivation of mind above that of the 'masses' and also certain valuable traditions of political experience: so that its claim to a share in government disproportionate to its numbers is based on a belief in its superior intellectual qualifications. It therefore seems to me possible, without doing too much violence to current usage, to give the term a signification akin to the Aristotelian; accordingly I shall mean by 'aristocracy' the government of persons specially qualified by abilities, training, and experience for the work of government. (EP 608)

With this understanding, which simply criss-crosses notions of liberal culture and professional expertise, Sidgwick is perfectly happy to have his political theoretical efforts understood as an attempt to marry the virtues of democracy with those of aristocracy. As he sums it up:

[I]t is generally admitted by theoretical advocates of democracy in modern times that the part of governmental work which is entrusted to particular individuals or elected assemblies should be entrusted to persons specially qualified. And so far as this is admitted, the principle of aristocracy . . . that the work of government is a form of skilled labour which should be in the hands of those who possess the requisite skill – is implicitly accepted. Hence, I do not consider representative government – even when the suffrage is universal – as merely a mode of organising democracy, but rather as a combination or fusion of democracy and aristocracy.

This fusion or combination may become less or more aristocratic in character through various minor modifications. Thus, it may be made less aristocratic by increasing the intervention of the people at large in legislation – through measures like the 'referendum' and 'initiative' . . . – by shortening the time for which the legislature or the executive is appointed, by the habit of demanding elaborate pledges at elections, or even imposing 'mandates' at other times to which the representative submit, and by the practice of appointing executive officials on grounds other than their qualifications for office. Correspondingly it tends to be made more aristocratic by lengthening the duration of parliaments, by the habit of choosing representatives for proved ability, and abstaining from the exaction of pledges and the imposition of mandates, and by the practice of giving executive appointments to the persons best qualified to fill them. But these latter modifications can hardly be said to make it less democratic, in the sense in which I first defined – and in which alone I accept – the democratic principles: at least so long as the consciousness of active consent remains vigorous in the citizens generally. (EP 616–17)

Even with all of these safeguards, however, precipitous pressure on legislators to promote sectional interests, or the equalization of happiness at the expense of the truly utilitarian end, remains a worry. Sidgwick simply concludes that he is "inclined to hope" that the danger

may be materially reduced if the legislators receive no salary; since they will then be more independent, and being drawn in the main from the minority of persons of wealth and leisure, will be generally disposed, from training and habit, and also from regard to the sentiment of their class, to do justice to the reasonable claims of the rich in any disputed question on which rich and poor are opposed.

This policy measure is, Sidgwick enthusiastically proposes, easier to maintain "against a strong drift towards democracy than other oligarchical expedients – limited suffrage, plural vote, etc. – because it has the advantage, which the poor are likely to appreciate, of saving money." And again, the measure can in some degree be neutralized by "combinations of the poor to elect members of their own class and pay them a salary." (EP 618)

On other points, Sidgwick is generally open to the constitutional and parliamentary solutions that he sees around him. As for the monarchy, he simply takes it that

the monarch in the most monarchical modern State must normally govern along with a legislature independently elected, and judges whom he cannot of his own sole will dismiss. . . . it seems to me not inconsistent with the principle of democracy ... that a power of this latter kind should be held for life, and even transmitted by inheritance, instead of being obtained for a short period by election. (EP 622)

Such mixed systems of the Western European type will conduce to stability, avoiding the swings between democracy and despotism that marked ancient Greece.

Much of the charming innocence of Sidgwick's vision no doubt stems from his truly heroic effort to come to terms with the forms and functions of the modern state, while holding onto the dream of avoiding party politics, the strife of "faction." He writes most movingly of the principles of the *Federalist Papers*, and of Justice Story's *Constitution of the United States*, in which there is scant recognition of the emerging two-party system as a permanent fixture of the political world. "And even J. S. Mill," he exclaims, "hardly seems to contemplate a dual organisation of parties as a normal feature of representative institutions" (EP 590). Like Mill's, Sidgwick's sympathies for socialism were in inverse ratio to his enthusiasm for radical democratization, given the state of popular morality.[51]

The evils of party are vast: corruption, bribery, and the general intellectual perversion of being pressured to go with a platform and a slate rather than make up one's mind independently on each issue and each candidate. Despite what might seem to be the obvious permanent party division – that between rich and poor, over such issues as taxation – there are, Sidgwick urges, any number of issues, from protectionism to war, on which there may be considerable internal class division. Thus, party formations ought, in any natural form, to be "of a complicated and shifting kind" and "almost certainly have a multiple and not a dual character" (EP 593). Which leads, obviously, to the question of just why they do tend toward a dual character.

Here Sidgwick's analysis is unsparing. In electoral systems where inadequate provision is made for the representation of minorities,

if the vacancies are filled up by the candidates of one party, the candidates of any other party can only be elected accidentally, unless the parties have formed an alliance, and agreed upon a common list of candidates. Hence arises an important influence, tending to reduce the number of competing electoral combinations to two. It seems not unlikely, however, that such combinations would be very transient, and would vary from place to place, if the sole concern of the electors were to choose representatives for the purpose of legislation: the decisive impulse towards a permanently dual organisation of parties appears to be given by entrusting to the constituencies, along with the election of members of a central legislative assembly, the practical choice of the chief or leading members of the central executive. This choice . . . takes place in strikingly different forms in the English and American systems respectively; still, its effect both at the quadrennial presidential elections in the United Sates, and at ordinary general elections in England, is to concentrate the interest of the whole country on an electoral struggle, in which, if any political combination does not form part of the victorious majority, it has failed so far as this contest is concerned. This gives a powerful and continually operating inducement to the absorption of minor parties in one or other of two great combinations; the force of which is further increased in the United States by the 'Spoils system' – the practice of making extensive changes in the minor posts of the executive to reward members of the winning party – and by the control over legislation which the veto gives to the President; while in England, again, it is importantly increased by the practical control over legislation which the Cabinet has come to possess. (EP 594–95)

Thus it is that two permanently opposed and competing parties tend to gain control over the political process. Relatedly, "the hostile criticism of governmental measures, carried on in the press and public meetings, is mainly directed and largely supplied by the systematic effort of a defeated party to discredit and supplant its dominant rival." Although this system may make for a certain stability in the political world, foster party feeling in the average citizen, and help to ensure that "the leaders of the opposition tend to criticise keenly, from desire to oust the holders of power, and yet circumspectly, being aware of the responsibilities and difficulties which success, bringing power, must entail," it is on balance a serious handicap to high-minded leadership. Rendering party spirit "more comprehensive and absorbing," it means that "the sentiment of 'loyalty to party' becomes almost as tenacious and exacting as patriotism, and sometimes almost equally independent of intellectual convictions; so that a man remains attached to his party from old habit and sentiment, or from fear of being called a renegade, when he can no longer even imagine that he holds its 'fundamental principles.'" (EP 596–97) But once "sentiment and habit are thus semi-unconsciously substituted in many cases for intellectual agreement as the bond of party-union, the fundamental principles of either party become obscure" and attacks on the opposition become more "factious and disingenuous."

Thus, even beneficial legislation has to be avoided by the party in power, if and when "it can be successfully discredited by partisan ingenuity." (EP 598)

Indeed, an oily insincerity and hypocrisy poison the whole political process:

[T]he dual system seems to have a dangerous tendency to degrade the profession of politics: partly from the inevitable insincerity of the relation of a party leader to the members of his own party, partly from the insincerity of his relation to the party opposed to him. To keep up the vigour and zeal of his own side, he has to maintain the fiction that under the heterogeneous medley of opinions and sectional interests represented by either the 'ins' or the 'outs' at any particular time there is a fundamental underlying agreement in sound political principles; and he has to attribute to the other side a similar agreement in unsound doctrines. Thus the best political talent and energy of the country acquires a fatal bias in the direction of insincere advocacy; indeed the old objection against forensic advocacy as a means of obtaining right judicial conclusions – that one section of the experts employed are professionally required to make the worse seem the better reason – applies with much more real force here than in the case of the law-courts. For in the case of the forensic advocate this attitude is frankly avowed and recognised by all concerned: every plain man knows that a lawyer in court is exempt from the ordinary rule that binds an honest man only to use arguments which he believes to be sound; and that it is the duty of every member of a jury to consider only the value of an advocate's arguments, and disregard, as far as possible, the air of conviction with which they are uttered. The political advocate or party leader tends to acquire a similar professional habit of using bad arguments with an air of conviction where he cannot get good ones, or when bad ones are more likely to be popularly effective; but, unlike the forensic advocate, he is understood, in so doing, to imply his personal belief in the validity of his argument and the truth of the conclusions to which he desires to lead up. And the case is made worse by the fact that political advocacy is not controlled by expert and responsible judges, whose business it is to sift out and scatter to the winds whatever chaff the pleader may mingle with such grains of sound argument as his belief affords; the position of the political advocate is like what that of a forensic advocate would be, if it was his business to address a jury not presided over by a judge, and largely composed of persons who only heard the pleadings on the other side in an imperfect and partial way. (EP 598–99)

This "demoralising effect of politics under the party system" is really behind a great many of Sidgwick's political concerns, including his conviction that the "business of statesmanship" should be as far as possible unremunerated. The business of keeping a party together and victorious, if it becomes a trade, becomes "a vile trade." The party politician would seem to compare very unfavorably even to Sidgwick's earlier nemesis, the hypocritical priest.

As we shall have occasion to see, this attitude was one that Sidgwick developed in collaboration with his friend Bryce, whose *American Commonwealth*, which influenced him profoundly, was filled with indictments of the corruptions of American party politics and explanations of why the "best men" did not go into politics to begin with.[52] American culture, the culture of democracy, was, Bryce argued, vital and strong, but this had little to do with the character of politicians. Still, Bryce, even more than Sidgwick, admired the marriage of aristocracy and democracy to be found in the American Constitution. It was the cultural and institutional moderating of democratic passions – and inexpertise – that these old academic Liberals admired so. And whatever their differences with the antidemocratic conservatism of figures like Henry Sumner Maine, who regarded the British democratic reforms of the eighties as the beginning of the end of civilization, they certainly agreed that the merits of these newer forms of aristocracy needed to be driven home to a public that was showing too much reckless enthusiasm for social change.[53]

Sidgwick admits that it is difficult to gauge the dangers of party very exactly, since they largely depend on "the condition of political morality," but he does not doubt that they are grave. The potential solutions are "partly political, partly moral." Thus, making "the Supreme Executive elected by the legislature, with subordinate officials holding office independently of party ties" would help, as would withdrawing substantial portions of legislative and administrative work "from the control of the party system, under the influence of public opinion, aided by minor changes in parliamentary rules and in the customary tenure of executive offices." (EP 601) Establishing a custom such that, barring a vote of no confidence, ministers need not resign because their legislation was defeated – "unless the need of these measures was regarded by them as so urgent that they could not conscientiously carry on the administration of public affairs without them" – might also help to "allow free play to the natural working of political convictions without increasing the instability of government" (EP 601–2). And some increased reliance on the referendum might also work in this direction.

But in the end, Sidgwick thinks the most important question is the moral one:

Finally, the operation of the party-system might be checked and controlled – more effectually than it now is in England and the United States – by a change in current morality, which does not seem to be beyond the limits of possibility. It might be regarded as the duty of educated persons generally to aim at a judicial frame of mind on questions of current politics, whether they are inside parties or outside. If it is the business of the professional politician to prove his own side always in the right, it should be the point of honour of the 'arm-chair' politician, if he belongs to a party, to make plain when and why he thinks his party in the wrong. And probably the country would gain from an increase in the number of persons taking a serious interest in politics who keep out of party ties altogether. (EP 602–3)

From this last injunction, one can appreciate just how much there was behind Sidgwick's celebration of the sympathetic but trained minds of a nobler stamp who would be leaders in philanthropic work and the educators of public opinion generally, bringing to it the refined arguments hammered out in endless discussion societies and meetings of minds. Here was the growth of sympathetic understanding – of a Socratic/Apostolic sort – that would characterize the eager utilitarian politician in the effort to be genuinely practical, to avoid party and international strife. Here was the sense of justice, in Sidgwick's view, and the lesson would also inform his essays on *Practical Ethics*, reflecting his work with the Ethical Culture Society in the 1890s. What is more, it is impossible to contemplate the core of Sidgwick's political thinking in this respect without recalling his passionate concern with hypocrisy and religious conformity, the questions of subscription and professional duty. True, one can certainly feel the effects of his proximaty to the Balfour clan, and appreciate why in his later years he tended to vote more independently, going with the Tories in a way he would never have considered when younger. But his object, manifestly, was to avoid the demoralizing effects of "insincere advocacy" and party politics, to engage in the kind of moral leadership that was a descendant of the Millian clerisy, though one adapted to a new, rougher, and more Darwinian era. And it was one that carried at least some odor of the qualified version of Whitmania advanced by Noel and Symonds, with the effort to befriend all ranks.

This is a heavy burden to place on the aristocratic element in his political vision. But there is no mistaking the parallel between Sidgwick's politics and his views of the clergy and ethics. Indeed, on this sensitive topic, the *Elements* expounds at some length on points of direct relevance to the discussion of the dualism of practical reason. Thus, when the question is posed of whether the state should teach morality, and posed in its most relevant form, in relation to "a civilised community in which there is either no religion having general acceptance or important influence, or else only religions that have no important connection with morality," the answer would bring to the fore "one of the most fundamental questions of moral philosophy: viz. whether the performance of social duty can be proved scientifically – with as strong a 'consensus of experts' as we find in established sciences generally – to be certainly or most probably the means best adapted to the attainment of the private happiness of the agent." Now, even if the answer were affirmative, it would not follow that morality "ought to be based on self-interest alone." Sidgwick's point, which lucidly captures all his nervousness about the destructive potential of the dualism of practical reason, is only that "it would clearly be an important gain to social wellbeing to correct the erroneous and short-sighted views of self-interest, representing it as divergent from duty, which certainly appear to be widely prevalent in the most advanced societies, at least among irreligious persons."[54] For the government to supply teachers of this view might even be "indirectly individualistic in its aim, since to diffuse the conviction that it is every one's interest to do what is right would obviously be a valuable protection against mutual wrong," though it would probably detract from the credibility of such teachers if they were salaried servants of the state. (EP 213–14)

Were this the case, the political economists and psychical researchers would presumably have their work cut out for them as cultural functionaries. But this last objection is even stronger "if we regard it as impossible to prove by ordinary mundane considerations that it is always the individual's interest in the present condition of human society to do his duty; or if, granting the evident coincidence of self-interest and duty, it is still held that self-regard should not be the normal motive to moral action." In these cases,

the only teaching likely to be effective is such as will powerfully affect the emotions of the taught, no less than their intellects; we should, therefore, generally speaking, need teachers who themselves felt, and were believed to feel, sincerely and intensely, the moral and social emotions that it was their business to stimulate; and governmental appointment and payment would hardly seem to be an appropriate method of securing instructors of this type. If a spirit of devotion to a particular society or to humanity at large, and readiness to sacrifice self-interest to duty, are to be persuasively inculcated on adults, the task should, generally speaking, be undertaken by persons who set an example of self-devotion and self-sacrifice; and therefore by volunteers, rather than by paid officers. (EP 214–15)

Under these circumstances, as Sidgwick's own life attested, the dualism of practical reason made the promotion of social harmony a much more difficult enterprise: recall again how he did not wish his own philosophy to affect the larger populace in the way that it had affected Myers. Tommy Green and Johnnie Symonds (and Jane Addams) were better volunteers than the self-doubting philosopher. Still, in his own energetic way, he clearly did his bit for the cause of culture, even if he himself was fitted to be neither politician nor prophet and had to remain more esoteric than enthusiastic.

In descending from principle and considering how governments might be justified in intervening to promote morality in actual modern European communities, Sidgwick returns to the intimate connection between the church and the dualism, arguing that:

For ordinary members of such communities, the connection of any individual's interest with his duty is established by the traditional Christian teaching as to the moral government of the world, and the survival of the individual after his corporeal death. Accordingly, this traditional teaching – though it by no means relies solely on appeals to self-interest – still always includes in its store of arguments appeals of this kind, having irresistible cogency for all hearers who believe the fundamental Christian doctrines. So far as the rules of duty thus taught are those commonly accepted by thoughtful persons, the value of the aid given to the work of government by this supply of extra-mundane motives to the performance of social duty can hardly be doubted. But the expediency of governmental action to secure this aid is importantly affected by the fact that the teachers who give it are actually organised in independent associations called churches, whose lines of division differ from – and to an important extent cut across – the lines of division of political societies; and which for the most part would resist strongly any attempt to bring them directly and completely under the control of the secular government. The practical question therefore is, whether government should leave these churches unfettered – treating them like any other voluntary associations based on free contract – or should endeavour to obtain a partial control over them in return for endowments or other advantages. (EP 215–16)

But this, Sidgwick explains, is bound to be a very difficult question, since "so far as the priest or religious teacher seeks not merely to provide a harmonious and satisfying expression for religious emotion, but also to regulate the behaviour of man to his fellows in domestic and civil relations, – using as motives the hope of reward and fear of punishment from an invisible source, – his function obviously tends to become *quasi-governmental*." And when Sidgwick returns to the topic, in his chapter on "The State and Voluntary Associations," he considers it from the perspective of "how the State should proceed in order that the advantages derivable from them [voluntary religious associations] may be the greatest possible, and the dangers that they involve may be avoided or reduced." Insisting that the Christian churches "meet a social need of fundamental importance," and that given their "systematic teaching of morality," the state gains from their being vigorous and effective, he nonetheless concludes that they "are likely to fulfil their function better if kept independent of the State. For, if the clergy acquire the character of officials appointed and paid by the State, they become exposed in some degree to the objections . . . against a governmental organisation for teaching morality: and are therefore likely to be less effective in rendering the service for which the State appoints and pays them." (EP 584)

Naturally, Sidgwick takes a firm stand for religious freedom.

Direct prohibition of any religious teaching not clearly inciting to illegal conduct, or otherwise immoral in its tendency, is invidious and objectionable, as interfering with the free communication of beliefs on which the development of human thought depends; and it is likely to be ineffective or worse in the most dangerous cases, from the ease with which opinions and sentiments hostile to government may be secretly propagated among persons united by a community of religious feeling, and the increased violence that they are likely to assume from the resentment caused by repression.

Better than any actual repression of religious beliefs or practices seriously inimical to the government is the effort "to secure a certain control over religious teaching, by the grant of privileges the withdrawal of which would only reduce the Church to the level of other voluntary associations." Such favoritism, "without anything like establishment or endowment," could avoid conflict, though there might also be various minor degrees of endowment, such as tax breaks and the provision of religious facilities, and it is important for the state to avoid "the awkward dilemma of either endeavouring to make one set of religious opinions prevail over others held by equally educated persons, or of endeavouring to moralise the community by imparting a number of mutually inconsistent beliefs." (EP 586) And there are further measures, such that, for example, "Government may refuse to admit any religious society to the position of a corporation capable of holding and administering property, unless its organisation fulfils certain conditions, framed with the view of preventing its 'quasi-government' from being oppressive to individual members of the association or dangerous to the State" (EP 587).

Thus, one sees how Sidgwick's concern about hypocrisy in high places shifts effortlessly between state and church, political leadership and religious leadership. What one does not see, however, is anything like a frank confrontation with the possibility that the impossibility of achieving a scientific morality and the consensus of experts might lead to the impossibility of finding teachers with the requisite sincerity and enthusiasm – a bunch of Sidgwicks, arguably the thing that most worried him. Nor, obviously, does one find in Sidgwick's political work that "science of society" that could actually explain how the more optimistic future that he envisions, with high-minded, far-seeing leadership gradually opening the way for ethical socialism and semisocialism in economics, might come to pass. The normative analysis – the enjoining of civilized, utilitarian minds to resist through self-sacrifice the demoralizing effects of the modern world – is always primary.[55]

Manifestly, for all the usual dry evasion, a very big part of Sidgwick's answer is: education, understood in the broad sense of fostering an educating society, fostering Millian culture if not esoteric doubt. Education is what is supposed to produce an aristocracy worthy of the name, and an electorate willing to recognize the superior judgment of representatives and grant them the power to govern, rather than serve as mere delegates following the popular mandate. In an early and singularly revealing letter to Oscar Browning, in part quoted earlier, Sidgwick had made his ultimate commitment pretty evident:

[O]f course people who make the lucky hits are uneducated generally, but that is just the point; if you could get all classes properly educated in the highest sense of the term, a man who came into a fortune by 'striking ile' would not waste it: and if he did not become a patron of Art, he might bring up his children to be so. . . . What I want to do is to put an end to the existing and threatening strife between Labour and Capital by any possible means. (M 132–33)

Again, the concern is to get "all classes properly educated" – not simply the "lower" orders, but also the "upper" ones – and this in the "highest sense of the term," while also gradually reducing the economic distance between the two. That any such effort would include the kind of mingling of minds effected in some of the various discussion societies and other educational efforts in which Sidgwick had participated was, alas, perhaps too much taken for granted by him, so that he did not adequately theorize all of the educational resources that he deployed or admired.[56] Emphatic enough on the kinds of corruption involved in the growth of the party system and the forms of political debate it fostered, he did not, in the *Elements*, succeed in completely articulating the very thing that he had himself done so much to advance in practice, as a vehicle for elevating the quality of public debate and spreading culture – the very thing that set his reformism apart from ideological indoctrination. Even freedom of the press receives a fairly perfunctory treatment:

We have seen that the control over government given to the governed by periodical elections is likely to be comparatively ineffective and ill-directed, unless the danger of blindness or apathy on the part of the governed be met by full and free criticism of current legislation and administration. At the same time, such criticism is likely to be often very distasteful to the governmental organs criticised, even when it is highly useful: hence there is a *prima facie* reason for including in any rigid constitution rules protecting the citizen's right 'to speak the thing he will' from undue governmental interference. But with a view to the maintenance of order, it seems important that this protection should only be given to criticism that (1) is *bona fide* intended to recommend only legal methods for obtaining the reform of what is criticised, and (2) would not be understood as an incitement to illegality by a person of ordinary intelligence. . . . Hence any constitutional rule restraining the legislature from 'abridging freedom of speech or of the press' will require to be qualified by a tolerably comprehensive permission to prohibit seditious utterances. (EP 570)

Writing in the aftermath of the French Commune and the social-ist agitation in England that had resulted in Bloody Sunday – the po-lice attack on a peaceful procession of radicals, members of the Irish

National League, and socialists in Trafalgar Square on November 13, 1887 – Sidgwick's balancing of stability against liberty might sound rather worse than "utilitarianism grown tame and sleek."[57] And yet of H. M. Hyndman, the forceful socialist leader and collaborator with William Morris, Sidgwick could write to Foxwell: "I am interested in what you say of Hyndman. He is a man I am disposed to like – though he does call me an eclectic bourgeois." (CWC) Moreover, he continued to be on friendly terms with William Morris, whose socialist poems he found "touching."

Thus, the puzzles about Sidgwick's politics run deep. Previous narratives have tried to fit him into both the conservative reaction to Gladstone and the growth at century's end of a progressivist "via media" determined to get beyond the dead ends of earlier religious, philosophical, and political disputes.[58] For some, he was merely an old Millian elitist, an "aristocratic liberal" and "public moralist" unwittingly bolstering the application of Enlightenment thinking to the mission of British imperialism. For others, he was a force for changing times, on the road to pragmatism.

What is missing from most such accounts is a willingness to take Sidgwick on his own (philosophically sophisticated) terms, an appreciation of his efforts to synthesize or reconcile the wide range of views that moved him. Even Symonds's Whitmania is at least somewhat evident in Sidgwick's celebration of America and the need for a culture of harmonization, beyond party and class strife. He was impressed enough with the intelligence of the artisans, and he certainly recognized the need for a new cultural formation, with an enthusiasm for devotion and self-sacrifice, for true comradeship and the growth of sympathetic understanding, stimulated by all the resources of literature and culture in the larger sense. The vision of a cosmic unity, of the overcoming of strife and the achievement of a harmony of duty and interest – this always gripped him, whether coming from Maurice, or Myers, or Symonds. Under the circumstances, he was not prepared to reject an enthusiastic teacher with poetic talent. And after all, Whitman himself had some distaste for the realities of political institutions. What Noel, Myers, and Symonds found in him was not Rousseauian democracy but something much more Platonic:

I hail with joy the oceanic, variegated, intense practical energy, the demand for facts, even the business materialism of the current age, our States. But woe to the age or land in which these things, movements, stopping at themselves, do not tend to ideas. As fuel to flame, and flame to the heavens, so must wealth, science, materialism – even this democracy of which we make so much – unerringly feed the highest mind, the soul.[59]

To hate hypocrisy and endless strife was the common currency; to create a new, enthusiastic cultural vision of the unity of humanity – what precisely was Sidgwick to find objectionable in this? Even Greek love, if duly refined and conducing to intellectual growth, was a force in this direction, not that it was always to be openly proclaimed. Internal sanctions rather than revolution, personal growth rather than industrial war, comradeship rather than class conflict – all of this spoke to Sidgwick. For him,

the deepest problems presented by war, and the deepest principles to be applied in dealing with them, are applicable also to the milder conflicts and collisions that arise within the limits of an orderly and peaceful community, and especially to those struggles for wealth and power carried on by classes and parties within a state. Indeed, these latter – though conducted by the milder methods of debate and vote – often resemble wars very strongly in the states of thought and feeling that they arouse, and also in some of the difficulties that they suggest. (PE 49)

"External" methods for resolving such conflicts – for example, arbitration – can go only so far, and cannot be relied upon "for a complete and final removal of the evils of strife." For this, "spiritual" methods are needed, and, recognizing the risk of ineffective rhetoric on behalf of justice,

we may none the less endeavour to develop the elements from which the moral habit of justice springs – on the one hand, sympathy, and the readiness to imagine oneself in another's place and look at things from his point of view; and on the other hand, the intelligent apprehension of common interests. In this way we may hope to produce a disposition to compromise, adequate for practical needs, even when the adjustment thus attained can only be rough, and far removed from what either party regards as ideally equitable. (PE 61)

This is not political deal-making, but a practical extension of the sympathetic understanding and harmonization that Sidgwick so prized. But was it really possible to avoid hypocrisy, after 1887?

V. Spiritual Expansion

There may be Elements of English Politics, or of American, or of French or Prussian; but the elements of general politics, if cast into general considerations, must either be quite colorless or quite misleading.

Woodrow Wilson, review of the *Elements of Politics*

Mohammedanism is such a very inferior article to Judaism that I do not think much is to be gained from comparing the two. And then I do not believe that the earlier prophets admitted even the qualified hypocrisy one finds in Mohammed. However, when one gets to the heresies, one may get hold of some laws of religious progress.

Sidgwick to Dakyns, October 22, 1862 (M 87)

As regards the Chinese nightmare – what troubles me is that in the year 1900 when so many have gone to and fro and the knowledge of the world in which we live is increased so much, we are still so very ignorant of what is really going on and has been going on in this great state embodying the one civilization that it remains to Europe to overcome. I have always thought that the collision and interpenetration of European science and Chinese institutions – which it seemed to me must come – will be an interesting phenomenon of the 20th century, but the present shock of the two civilizations in battle is something quite different and what will come of it I know not.

Sidgwick to George Young, August 13, 1900 (M 597)

For all his fear of inappropriate historical analogy, Sidgwick's politics did tend to reflect his early convictions about the fate of Socrates – it was the hypocritical, incoherent public that represented the true sophist, not the philosophers or the promoters of the "new learning." And the danger was largely of a potential, rather than actual, nature, something ready to emerge in the vacuum left by traditional religion. Philosophy was, or ought to be, the answer, the helpmate to a (genuine) aristocracy.

Clearly, Sidgwick came close to personally realizing his vision of the high-minded reformer, despite (or because of) his deeper doubts. His contributions to the educational enterprise were even more extensive than those sketched in earlier chapters. Money, time, and expertise were given unstintingly to academic service and institutional growth – it was Sidgwick who funded positions for Maitland (in law), Ward (in psychology), and Michael Foster (in physiology), and the overflow of his library was always distributed to various colleges. His devotion to higher education in general, and to Newnham College in particular, are in so many ways difficult to fault. Much of his esotericism, or "Government House" utilitarianism, was in the name of such things as educational reform and challenging dogmatic religious (and sexual) orthodoxy. Cautious vanguardism, not reactionary conservatism, for the end of universal happiness.

True, Sidgwick's socialism was cautious, gradualist, and conservative in many of the same ways as that of Mill and Maurice. Cast in a certain light, however, his reformist educational politics can appear quite noble, despite his persistent tendencies toward Apostolic elitism. The ethical culture movement was in many ways complementary to the settlement movement, when it came, in Addams's words, to the aim of bringing "into the circle of knowledge and fuller life, men and women who might otherwise be left outside."[60] The universal heart of humanity at least throbbed over opening up new worlds for those with few prospects; no one was to be left out.

But this vision, whether in Sidgwick or in Green, plays out rather differently when applied beyond the domestic context, to other countries and cultures, where the self-sacrificing moral educator tends to take on the trappings of the missionary. What, then, is the content and function of the instruction? The spread of culture becomes the spread of civilization, with the "experts" involved all coming from the small club of European nations. Many of Sidgwick's Cambridge colleagues were notorious representatives of the imperialist mentality that so shaped the later Victorian era – Seeley, Maine, Trevelyan, Pearson, and others were some of the most illustrious architects of the ideology of British imperialism in its most flourishing state. If the Balliol of Jowett and Green produced a great raft of philosophical statesmen, Sidgwick's Cambridge also did its part. Indeed, the step from old academic liberal to new imperialist was short and effortless.

Hence, the importance of the questions broached time and again in earlier chapters: how elitist was Sidgwick's reformism, especially when considered in relation to the empire? Correlatively, was Sidgwick's work infected with those forms of racism that were becoming ever more virulent in this imperialistic and post-Darwinian context, cutting across socialism, imperialism, liberal unionism, progressivism, and every other political movement? What did he mean by those references to the "lower races" and the possibility of "race degradation"? Was he also a "Government House" utilitarian in the way charged by Williams and Walker? Or a Cambridge orientalist?

Given the long history of utilitarian involvement in and philosophizing about India, an imperialist enterprise that provided both James and John Stuart Mill with much of their livelihood, it is striking how comparatively little Sidgwick had to say about these issues.[61] Unlike so many of his contemporaries and colleagues in the post-Darwinian period, he scarcely dwelt on the subject of race at all. In his writings, he resolutely focused on the world that he knew best. This in itself was unusual, and makes it that much more difficult to decipher just where he stood on so many of the political controversies swirling around him. But he wrote and did enough to put together a rough picture.

Some sense of the imperial mission of Sidgwick's Cambridge can be gained by considering his connections with the work of Seeley and Maine, two of the "competent authorities" to whom he would make frequent reference. They profoundly shaped his conception of the historical method and his views of India, China, Egypt, and even Ireland.

Seeley was, of course, slightly senior to Sidgwick, having been born in 1834. As we have seen, he was the anonymous evangelical author of *Ecce Homo*, which Sidgwick had so admired, however critically, during his years of storm and stress. He went up to Christ's College, Cambridge, in 1852, graduating in 1857 at the top of the Classical Tripos, but, like Sidgwick, with a strong performance in mathematics as well. He was appointed a Fellow and lecturer in classics, wrote poetry, and left Cambridge, becoming in 1863 professor of Latin at University College, London. In 1869, while on his honeymoon, he received a letter from Gladstone offering him the professorship of modern history at Cambridge, which Charles Kingsley had resigned. At Cambridge, he was, unlike Sidgwick, an enormously popular lecturer, with very large classes filled with students from many different departments. If he was not generally known outside Cambridge, his influence was nonetheless great. As Sheldon Rothblatt has observed: "As a don and professor his achievements were no less important than those of other, more celebrated reformers, his contemporaries (and Oxford heroes) Jowett and Pattison, for examples, with whom his efforts compare."[62]

As Rothblatt also observes, Seeley's general method of argument "was sociological. His concern was with the institutions responsible for social stability, and he therefore laid primary emphasis on the family, regarding

it as an early form of political organization." One of his successors, George
Prothero, summed up Seeley's approach this way:

Though he did not coin the phrase 'History is past politics, and politics present
history,' it is perhaps more strictly applicable to his view of history than to that
of its author. 'The indispensable thing,' he said, 'for a politician is a knowledge of
political economy and of history.' And again, 'our University must be a great sem-
inary of politicians.' . . . The statesman was to be taught his business by studying
political history, not with a view to extracting arguments in favour of particular
political theories, but in order to understand, by the comparative and historical method, political science, the science of the State. . . . Modern history being
specially applicable to existing political problems, he lectured by preference on
modern times.[63]

For Seeley, historical facts "pure and simple" had no allure. The facts
called for interpretation, "deducing from them the main lines of historical
and political evolution." As Prothero goes on to note:

In the year 1883, Professor Seeley's lectures on the foreign policy of Great Britain
in the 18th century were published under the title 'The Expansion of England.'
This book aroused as wide-spread an interest as 'Ecce Homo,' and its reception
was more uniform. The applause which it met with was almost universal. So
vigorous and thoughtful an apology for the British Empire, and for the way by
which it had been founded, had never before appeared. It brought together in one
concise survey and regarded from one point of view a number of occurences which
historians had previously treated in a disconnected manner. Its conclusions were
easily grasped: they appealed to a large audience: they were immediately applicable
to one of the greatest questions of the day. In its clear-cut, animated style, its
deliberate omission of all superfluous detail, its concentration of illustrative facts
on the main thesis, and the confidence with which that thesis is maintained, the
book is a model of what an historical essay, with a practical end in view, should
be.[64]

Of Seeley's knighthood, bestowed in 1894 when the Liberal Rosebery
became prime minister, Prothero remarks that he "had the satisfaction of
receiving public acknowledgement of the services which by his writings
and addresses he had rendered to the empire." Seeley, Prothero urges,
"was a good citizen, with a high sense of political responsibility." He was
a "Liberal so far as domestic progress was concerned, anxious for the
wider spread of education, for the open career," but he was "ardently

conservative of what he conceived to be the foundation of the state." For Seeley, a

little England, an England shorn of Empire, was . . . synonymous not only with national degradation but national ruin. To foster an enthusiasm for the British State, to convince the people that it is worth preserving, to eradicate the Turgot view of colonies, and to set men thinking how the existing union may be preserved – such were the aims of many lectures and addresses delivered during his final years.

The same convictions led him to become, with Sidgwick and Dicey, a "vigorous opponent of Irish Home Rule, regarding it as a first step towards a dissolution of the empire."[65]

Sidgwick had of course known Seeley ever since his undergraduate days, when he was disappointed that he could not get his older friend into the Apostles. They shared a great deal by way of efforts at academic reform, with Seeley being, if anything, even more radical than Sidgwick about introducing modern subjects and downplaying classics. Thus, they would both be writing in support of the reform of the Classical Tripos in the mid-sixties, though Seeley wrote from his perch at University College. Seeley was also a supporter of higher education for women and, like Sidgwick, found the Girton program problematic in part because it was aimed at replicating the same curriculum that he found objectionable in the case of men. At any rate, he would lecture and examine for both Girton and Newnham, and also be much involved in efforts to spread education generally, lecturing at the Working Men's College in London, Toynbee Hall, and at the various locations that marked the beginning of the university extension movement. Thus, Seeley was undeniably part of that group of Cambridge reformers – Sidgwick, Browning, Myers, Jackson, and all the rest – trying both to extend education and to professionalize it, to adapt it to the needs of the children of the rising middle class.

In fact, Sidgwick thought so highly of Seeley's contribution to Cambridge life that in the late seventies he anonymously supplemented Seeley's (rather modest) professorial income by about £200 per year, in order to help him leave off extracurricular activities designed mainly to bring in revenue. And it should be recalled again how he had in 1875 enthusiastically written to Pearson that "we had separated History from Law and ballasted it with Political Philosophy and Economy and International Law in order to make the course a better training for the reasoning Faculties – in fact, to some extent carried out Seeley's idea of identifying History and

Politics" (M 295). Although they would naturally enough have various differences, especially about Sidgwick's work on the General Board (when most of his friends abandoned him), nevertheless when Seeley died in 1894, Sidgwick lamented, "it makes Cambridge feel diminished and poor to have lost within a year two men so remarkable as him and Robertson Smith. We have no young men coming on of the same mark – at any rate, outside mathematics and physical science." (M 535)

After Seeley's death, Sidgwick read and advised the publication of the material that became *Introduction to Political Science*, a work that profoundly influenced his own *Development of European Polity*. His Editor's Preface to this work contains various fond recollections of Seeley, including this rather Sidgwickian-sounding appreciation of his teaching method by J. R. Tanner. Seeley, too, had the personal touch in education:

His old pupils carry with them grateful recollections of his 'Conversation Class.' The subject was political science studied by way of discussion, and discussion under the reverential conditions that prevailed resolved itself into question and answer – Socrates exposing the folly of the Athenians. It was mainly an exercise in the definition and scientific use of terms. What is liberty? Various definitions of the term would be elicited from the class and subjected to analysis. The authors of them would be lured by a subtle cross-examination into themselves exposing their inconsistencies. Then the professor would take up his parable. He would first discuss the different senses in which the term had already been used in literature. . . . From an examination of inconsistent accounts the professor would proceed to the business of building up by a gradual process, and with the help of the class itself, a definition of his own. . . . It was not told us on authority as something to remember, but we assisted ourselves at the creation of it.[66]

And Sidgwick himself gives a generous summation of Seeley's work and historical method:

As regards the general view that these lectures enforce and illustrate – the two-sided doctrine (1) that the right method of studying political science is an essentially historical method, and (2) that the right method of studying political history is to study it as material for political science – I think it may be said that this was one of his deepest and most permanent convictions. . . . it grew stronger and clearer as years went on, and assiduous study enlarged his knowledge and deepened his insight into the development of historic polity. Indeed, he once said to me that he valued the wide popularity of his *Expansion of England*, not only for the effects that might be hoped from it in furthering practical aims that he had at heart, but also not less because the book seemed to have proved itself a persuasive example of his method: because it had brought home to Englishmen throughout the Empire, that, in order to know what England ought to be and do now, they must study what she has been and done in the past.[67]

Seeley obviously had no sympathy for a priori method in historical study; his methodological lineage had altogether different heroes – Aristotle, Burke, Macaulay, Maine.[68] For him, the family and the state are the pervasive facts of history, and to examine them even in the case of "primitive" societies is crucial. Still, for all his comparative methodological dogmatism, one hears echoes of Sidgwick's voice in the closing lecture of the *Introduction*, when Seeley addresses "how the name 'aristocracy,' originally one of the most respectable of all political names, has come in recent times to have disagreeable, almost disreputable associations." Recalling its meaning as "government by the best," he goes on to explain how enduringly important this bit of taxonomy is to political science:

In every community there is a part which has ordinarily no share in those movements which constitute political vitality. In many communities this part is infinitely larger than the part which is disturbed by them. Imagine the condition of the Russian populations for many centuries. . . . In such a state aristocracy is not only real, but is, as it were, the chief reality. It arises not by contrivance, not out of a theory that some qualifications are necessary, not out of any design on the part of the rich to exclude the poor in order that they may have more freedom to oppress them; it arises inevitably and naturally. The population falls of itself into two parts. On the one side are seen those who have thoughts and feelings about the public welfare; on the other are those who have no such thoughts and feelings. In one sense all are included in the state, for the state protects all and imposes duties upon all. But one of these two classes is normally passive; nothing, therefore, can prevent the other from monopolising public affairs. For purposes of action, or in the eyes of foreign statesmen, these active citizens are the state, and the passive class, often the great mass of the population, do not count.[69]

Seeley goes on to explain that although he has appealed to the extreme case of Russia, the England of the previous century might provide "another case in order to show that aristocracy of this natural, necessary kind is by no means uncommon." With truly Burkean relish, and no little nostalgia, he patiently explains how

not only the whole lower class, but a very large proportion of the middle class, were excluded from the franchise, and therefore had no share whatever in the government of the country or in making the government. Now, there was at that time nothing artificial in this exclusion; it caused no discontent; no cry was then raised for an extension of the franchise. It would seem that the vast excluded class acquiesced contentedly in its exclusion, and that it was conscious of having no serious political opinions.

The "genius of aristocracy," he triumphantly proclaims, is that "political consciousness or the idea of the state comes to some minds before it comes to others. Those monopolise all the powers of the state who alone enter into its nature and understand it. These are the good people." Of course, these "good people are by no means saints," and there is always the temptation of corruption, of possible degeneration into oligarchy.[70]

The "advance spirits" will likely be of one class – "those to whom wealth has given leisure, freedom of mind, and the habit of dealing with large affairs." And in case the moral is slow in hitting home, Seeley indulges in a little futuristic speculation, imagining that "some test better than birth and wealth has been invented, by adopting which the danger should be avoided of introducing oligarchy under the name of aristocracy; and that this test is also safe against the objections which are urged against competitive examination." The result, a "pure and true aristocracy," would be such that "every one would hail it with delight," and it "would appear at once that all the invective against aristocracy to which we have grown accustomed in recent times is like a letter which has been misdirected; it ought to have been addressed to oligarchy."[71]

Now, such remarks, besides recalling Sidgwick's worries over the fate of the word "aristocracy" and the ways in which he followed Bryce in deploring party politics and the failure of the "best men" to lead, also call to mind the work of another Cambridge historian, Maine. Maine, born in 1822, was of course one of the Cambridge giants – a brilliantly successful undergraduate at Pembroke College, Cambridge – and an Apostle – after which he became a tutor of Trinity Hall and in 1847, Regius Professor of Civil Law. He resigned the Regius Professorship in 1852, devoting much more time to writing and producing his classic work on *Ancient Law*, which appeared in 1861. The enthusiastic reception of this book led to his becoming very deeply involved with British rule in India, serving on the Council of the Governor-General from 1863 to 1869 and being named "Knight Commander of the Star of India" and given a permanent appointment to the Council of the Secretary of State for India. He would also become Corpus Professor of Jurisprudence at Oxford, eventually returning to Cambridge as the Whewell Professor of International Law in 1887. And he must have regarded Sidgwick as a sympathetic fellow Apostle, since when, in 1886, he started feeling out the possibilities for a return to Cambridge as the Whewell Professor, one of the first things that he did was to solicit Sidgwick's support, authorizing him to declare his candidacy.[72]

Maine and Seeley made natural colleagues, though the latter was less shaped by the passion for utilitarian institutions that marked Maine's policy views, despite his historical approach. It was Maine who gave currency to the view that the basis of legal and social institutions of the Aryan family had evolved historically from "Status to Contract," in the famous phrase, and his studies of the evolution of legal and political institutions, especially in India, would provide much of the basis for Seeley's – and Sidgwick's – claims about that country, and about England's governance of it.[73] All of the luminaries of the Victorian era, including Spencer and Mill, cited Maine's work on historical and comparative methods (especially as applied to India), which were perceived as systematizing and rendering scholarly the antideductivist work of the Macaulay school. Moreover, as Thomas Thornely, a later Cambridge political scientist, once remarked, for Maine "democracy" was "almost a term of contempt." He completely shared – for that matter anticipated, from a less liberal perspective – Seeley's warm arguments about aristocracy, believing that change and progress were always the work of the energetic few. When, in the aftermath of the democratic reforms of the eighties, Maine revised his antidemocratic essays for publication in book form, he added a remark that would seem to capture very well the Cambridge of Seeley and Sidgwick:

Whether – and this is the last objection – the age of aristocracies be over, I cannot take upon myself to say. I have sometimes thought it one of the chief drawbacks of modern democracy that, while it gives birth to despotism with the greatest facility, it does not seem to be capable of producing aristocracy, though from that form of political and social ascendancy all improvement has hitherto sprung.[74]

It is extremely intriguing that Sidgwick could have thought so highly of Maine's work, suggesting how he was coming to feel the strains in the Liberal Party. As Shannon explains, at this point there

was grave disquiet at the pattern of Liberal appeasement of challenges to ruling authority: 'Socialism' at home; Afrikaners in the Transvaal; Parnellism in Ireland;

the 'Ilbert Bill' giving way to nationalist agitation in India. The revealing symptom of this anxiety in 1885 was Henry Maine's *Popular Government*, in which he argued that the assumption of progress integral to democratic idealism was 'not in harmony with the normal forces ruling human nature, and is apt therefore to lead to cruel disappointment and serious disaster.'[75]

Even Tennyson weighed in, with his tale of Liberal disillusionment, "Locksley Hall Sixty Years After."

Here, then, was the common problem, another face of the worry running throughout Sidgwick's *Principles* and *Elements*, to the effect that so little is known about what makes for a vital culture, for scientific and artistic progress and religious development – all the things that slip past the work of political economy. And plainly, Seeley and Maine provided a great deal by way of in-the-flesh example of the historical method to which Sidgwick was so concerned to do justice.

But before further pointing up just what Sidgwick shared with this gallery of "competent authorities," it would be helpful to rehearse in slightly more detail their visions of India and of spiritual expansion in general. In a striking account of the "benefits" of British civilization, Seeley explained:

India then is of all countries that which is least capable of evolving out of itself a stable Government. And it is to be feared that our rule may have diminished what little power of this sort it may have originally possessed. For our supremacy has necessarily depressed those classes which had anything of the talent or habit of government. The old royal races, the noble classes, and in particular the Mussulmans who formed the bulk of the official class under the Great Moguls, have suffered most and benefited least from our rule. This decay is the staple topic of lamentation among those who take a dark view of our Empire; but is it not an additional reason why the Empire should continue? Then think of the immense magnitude of the country; think too that we have undermined all fixed moral and religious ideas in the intellectual classes by introducing the science of the West into the midst of Brahminical traditions. When you have made all these reflexions, you will see that to withdraw our Government from a country which is dependent on it and which we have made incapable of depending upon anything else, would be the most inexcusable of all conceivable crimes and might possibly cause the most stupendous of all conceivable calamities.[76]

This smacks of the "white man's burden," while admitting that the white man did quite a bit to create the burden in the first place.[77] Seeley does, however, also offer this consoling background report on how, strictly speaking, the British did not conquer India at all:

If we begin by remarking that authority in India had fallen on the ground through the decay of the Mogul Empire, that it lay there waiting to be picked up by somebody, and that all over India in that period adventurers of one kind or another were founding Empires, it is really not surprising that a mercantile corporation which had money to pay a mercenary force, should be able to compete with other adventurers, nor yet that it should outstrip all its competitors by bringing into the field English military science and generalship, especially when it was backed over and over again by the whole power and credit of England and directed by English statesmen.[78]

Thus, the "conquest of India" was not really the "act of a state," and besides, India was not really a state properly so called:

[I]n India the fundamental postulate cannot be granted, upon which the whole political ethics of the West depend. The homogeneous community does not exist there, out of which the State properly so called arises. . . . The majority of the Governments of India were Mussulman long before the arrival of the Mogul in the sixteenth century. From this time therefore in most of the Indian States the tie of nationality was broken.[79]

Thus, although Seeley is far from any jingoism, there is the weariness of the weight of moral responsibility running through his claims about India. The poor English founded the empire "partly it may be out of an empty ambition of conquest and partly out of a philanthropic desire to put an end to enormous evils. But, whatever our motives might be, we incurred vast responsibilities, which were compensated by no advantages." Unlike the colonial empire, which has "grown up naturally, out of the operation of the plainest causes," British India "seems to have sprung from a romantic adventure; it is highly interesting, striking and curious, but difficult to understand or to form an opinion about." And when it comes to whether the British have actually done the Indians any good, Seeley is all humility:

I have asserted confidently only thus much, that no greater experiment has ever been tried on the globe, and that the effects of it will be comparable to the effect of the Roman Empire upon the nations of Europe, nay probably they will be much greater. This means no doubt that vast benefits will be done to India, but it does not necessarily mean that great mischiefs may not also be done. Nay, if you ask on which side the balance will incline, and whether, if we succeed in bringing India into the full current of European civilisation, we shall not evidently be rendering her the greatest possible service, I should only answer, 'I hope so; I trust so.' In the academic study of these vast questions we should take care to avoid the optimistic commonplaces of the newspaper. Our Western civilisation is perhaps not absolutely the glorious thing we like to imagine it. Those who watch India most impartially see that a vast transformation goes on there, but sometimes it produces a painful impression upon them; they see much destroyed, bad things and good things together; sometimes they doubt whether they see many good things called into existence. But they see an enormous improvement, under which we may fairly hope that all other improvements are potentially included, they see anarchy and plunder brought to an end and something like the *immensa majesta Romanae pacis* established among two hundred and fifty millions of human beings.

Another thing almost all observers see, and that is that the experiment must go forward, and that we cannot leave it unfinished if we would. For here too the great uniting forces of the age are at work, England and India are drawn every year for good or for evil more closely together. Not indeed that disuniting forces might not easily spring up, not that our rule itself may not possibly be calling out forces which may ultimately tend to disruption, nor yet that the Empire is altogether free from the danger of a sudden catastrophe. But for the present we are driven both by necessity and duty to a closer union. Already we should ourselves suffer greatly from disruption, and the longer the union lasts the more important it will become to us. Meanwhile the same is true in an infinitely greater degree of India itself. The transformation we are making there may cause us some misgivings, but though we may be led conceivably to wish that it had never been begun, nothing could ever convince us that it ought to be broken off in the middle.[80]

Thus, Seeley hopes that his meditations on the expansion of England will impress upon the reader "that there is something fantastic in all those notions of abandoning the colonies or abandoning India, which are so freely broached among us." After all, he inquires,

Have we really so much power over the march of events as we suppose? Can we cancel the growth of centuries for a whim, or because, when we throw a hasty glance at it, it does not suit our fancies? The lapse of time and the force of life, 'which working strongly bind,' limit our freedom more than we know, and even when we are not conscious of it at all.[81]

Indeed – and most importantly, by Seeley's reckoning – the English do not for the most part really have an empire at all, on the good old Roman model: "our Empire is not an Empire at all in the ordinary sense of the word. It does not consist of a congeries of nations held together by force, but in the main of one nation, as much as if it were no Empire but an ordinary state." That is, the union of "Greater Britain" – the true essence of which is the white Dominions – is "of the more vital kind. It is united by blood and religion and though circumstances may be imagined in which these ties might snap, yet they are strong ties, and will only give way before some violent dissolving force."[82] India might be a moral responsibility, but when "we inquire then into the Greater Britain of the future we ought to think much more of our Colonial than of our Indian Empire."[83] And behind all of this pleading, there is a simple conviction: "We in Europe . . . are pretty well agreed that the treasure of truth which forms the nucleus of the civilization of the West is incomparably more sterling not only than the Brahmanic mysticism with which it has to contend, but even than the Roman enlightenment which the old Empire transmitted to the nations of Europe."

India, and Egypt, a convenient route to India that the British under Gladstone had blunderingly continued to maintain after the breakup of the Ottoman Empire and Disraeli's purchase of the Suez Canal, might well have appeared at this time to be quite resistant to any vital unity with England. And with the British busily deploying their military to crush the leaders of the Sepoy Mutiny, the insurrections of the Arabi Pasha and the Mahdi, and Zulus whenever and wherever, the impartial observor ought to have quickly realized that talk of spreading civilization scarcely did justice to the flavor of imperial rule.[84] The stirrings of colonial liberation were already perfectly evident, and hardly incoherent, even if Queen Victoria was the very proud Empress of India. Hence, Seeley's fond outpourings about the importance, for the future of the empire, of racial and religious unity. He was, after all, the author of *Ecce Homo*.

And though he was no Rudyard Kipling, Seeley's pleas for maintaining the empire, cast in the tones of the academic, carried a great deal of weight with those who were ever ready to feel the pangs of conscience and moral responsibility. As George Woodcock has observed, Seeley, with his stress on the white Dominions, really did introduce "a new element into imperial thinking," something not present in "open imperialists like Disraeli and the crypto-imperialists like Gladstone."[85] Ensor has it that after Disraeli's death, "the single influence which did most to develop the imperialist idea was the very powerful and popular book *The Expansion of*

England. . . . Seeley, who was a specialist on the rise of Prussia and the career of Napoleon, was a believer in the beneficence of rule by the strong."[86] Indeed, as Shannon puts it, he was seeking "an English equivalent of the great reconstructor of the Prussian state, Stein, to fulfill the prophecies of *The Expansion of England.*"[87]

Maine's arguments about the fate of India were somewhat different but no more sympathetic to claims for Indian independence than Seeley's. Stocking has remarked that although some have seen Maine as "a progenitor of Cromer and Lugard and the later imperialism of 'indirect rule,'" he was actually "a strong advocate of active central government and legislative reform," and went far to break down in India "existing barriers to individual personality and property rights." In Maine's view, it was only the English who held back the "pent-up flood of barbarism" in this country, where the inheritance of the past was of "nearly unmixed evil."[88] The English, he urged, needed to rebuild India on English principles.

As Gauri Viswanathan has argued, in *Masks of Conquest*, Maine played the harsh Dickensian utilitarian when it came to Indian education, particularly the study of literature. For this study "assumed a mind that was capable of being driven by reason, an assumption that Maine felt was entirely inappropriate in the Indian context." Thus, Maine urged that liberal, classical education only "gave Indians the illusion that they could be better than they actually were and that they were being empowered to change their personal destiny and affect the course of things." He was blunt: "We may teach our students to cultivate language, and we only add strength to sophistry; we teach them to cultivate their imagination, and it only gives grace and colour to delusion; we teach them to cultivate their reasoning powers, and they find a thousand resources in allegory, in analogy, and in mysticism, for evading and discrediting truth."[89]

Thus, the revitalized "aristocrat" was beginning to look quite white and quite manly, less Millian and more Dorian. Did the work of Seeley and Maine (and Balfour's example) provide the case for the "Caesarism" that Sidgwick so wondered and worried about?

Certainly it inspired, among other things, the formation of the Imperial Federation League, in 1884, which was eagerly supported by such liberal imperialists as Lord Rosebery – not to mention Bryce and other academic liberals – despite the lingering anti-imperialist sentiments of Gladstonian liberalism.[90] Enhanced federation, at least, was something to which Sidgwick looked forward, as a possible evolution of empire from the colonial formation, and this was often very much an extension of the imperial idea, with the "Concert of Europe" – the "civilized" states – creating a more extensive framework of international law. He especially looked forward "to the kind of federal union of civilized states that will prevent war," even if progress will be "slow." As the *Memoir* records, he put a great deal of faith in the potential of federation: the "federation of the Australian Colonies interested Sidgwick greatly. He believed that in federation there and elsewhere lay the best hopes of the peace and progress of the world." (M 576) Indeed, his posthumous *Development of European Polity*, the historical side of his political inquiries, would labor through 439 pages to the carefully hedged (albeit prescient) conclusion that

The future of constitutional monarchy I was unwilling to prophesy: but I feel more disposed to predict a development of federality, partly from the operation of the democratic tendency just noticed, partly from the tendency shown through-out the history of civilisation to form continually larger political societies – as Spencer would say, 'integration' – which seems to accompany the growth of civilisation. . . . We have seen the same tendency in recent times in the formation of Germany and Italy: and we have in North America an impressive example of a political society maintaining internal peace over a region larger than Western Europe. I therefore think it not beyond the limits of sober forecast to conjecture that some further integration may take place in the West European states: and if it should take place, it seems probable that the example of America will be followed, and that the new political aggregate will be formed on the basis of a federal polity.

When we turn our gaze from the past to the future, an extension of federalism seems to me the most probable of the political prophecies relative to the form of government. (DEP 439)

The "democratic tendency just noticed" concerned the "establishment of secured local liberties, mainly under the influence of the sentiment of nationality, in states that were previously of the unitary type."

Mention might also be made, in this regard, of one of the more ambitious forcasts of the *Elements*:

[I]f the boundaries of existing civilised states undergo no material change, the rela-tive strength of the United States, as compared with any one of the West-European States, will before the end of the next century so decidedly preponderate, that the most powerful of the latter will keenly feel its inferiority in any conflict with the former. And even apart from this motive to union, it seems not impossible that the economic burdens entailed by war, the preponderantly industrial character of modern political societies, the increasing facilities and habits of communication among Europeans and the consequently intensified consciousness of their common civilisation, may, before many generations have passed, bring about an extensive federation of civilised states strong enough to put down wars among its members.

He admits, however, that "this ideal is at present beyond the range of practical politics." (EP 219)

Now, the figures dealt with here are especially revealing of the most powerful academic and political forces at work on Sidgwick, and of the changing context in which he found himself, with the transition from Millian academic Liberalism, half realized in Gladstone, to the ideology of empire, influentially purveyed by colleagues he had personally praised and supported. Apparently, his feelings for a new (genuine) aristocracy infused with fire and strength shaded into some admiration for the twist given such ideas in the new imperialism. This is much more than guilt by association. Recall, too, how Sidgwick himself was instrumental in the "maintenance and development of teaching for Indian Civil Servants" and "served on the Board for Indian Civil Service Studies from May 1883 to December 1896, and from 1884 to 1888 himself provided £200 a year towards the expense of the teaching required" (M 373). In 1889, he wrote to Dakyns that he has "been engaged in constructing a scheme for the Competitive Examination by which a fair chance is to be given to University Graduates; and a job it has been, as we had to adjust and balance the relative claims of Classics, Mathematics, and Natural Science, not to speak of other subjects, and at the same time balance the claims of Oxford and the claims of Cambridge so that neither may feel postponed to the other" (M 503). But presumably Sidgwick thought it worth the effort; he in all probability shared the view of his friend Trevelyan, whose family was also much caught up in India, that "the Indian Civil Service was a fine career, which held out splendid prospects to honourable ambition. But better far than this, there was no career which so surely inspired men with the desire to do something useful in their generation; to leave their mark upon the world for good, and not for evil."[91]

Moreover, Sidgwick apparently had a warm regard for none other than Edward Robert Bulwer Lytton (1831–1891), the first Earl Lytton, who became viceroy of India in 1876. Lytton was a statesman, poet, and literary figure who sometimes published under the pen name Owen Meredith. His works included *Clytemnestra*, *The Earl's Return and Other Poems*, *The Wanderer*, *Chronicles and Characters*, *After Paradise*, and *King Poppy*, among many others, and under his rule the controversial and problematic role of the British in India was growing ever more evident. Under Lytton and the Beaconsfield government, the British were led to a series of entanglements with Afghanistan, with such results as the massacre of their delegation at Kabul; his exploits provided Gladstone with much of the material needed for his anti-imperialist speech making during the Midlothian campaign against Disraeli. Intolerant of the Indian press and Eurocentric in the extreme, Lytton left India in 1880, and in 1887 took up the more congenial position of ambassador to France. His mother was Lady Rosina Bulwer-Lytton, the novelist who caused a scandal with her public (and quite sane) attacks on her husband and was eventually forcibly committed to an asylum, with her care in later life largely falling to her son. Lytton's daughter married Eleanor's brother Gerald, and Lytton himself lived long enough to be recruited into the Society for Psychical Research.

Sidgwick found in Lytton the ideal reader for his *Elements*, and, as with Bryce and Dicey, solicited his comments while preparing the book:

My dear Lord Lytton

I am exceedingly obliged to you for your very full and interesting letter; and much gratified to find that you do not take more objections to my formulation of international duty, and that your disagreements are only on minor points. I was probably led to exaggerate our difference from the fact that, as you say, we approached the matter from opposite [sic] – your object being to show that the ordinary moralist had got considerably out of his proper place and function in his dealings with international questions, and *my* object being rather to put him if possible in his proper place and keep him there!

I thought all you said in your address about the feminine personalities of nations and the [sic] misleading effects opportune as well as entertaining. I quite feel that popular talk on this subject is rife with absurdities which are liable to become worse than ridiculous in their practical effect. I have sometimes thought that the uncertainty whether national identity depends on physical continuity of *race* or identity of *land* inhabited was perhaps the most striking cause of muddled sentiment on the subject. Do you remember how in Tennyson's 'Boädicea' the queen is consoled by loosely robed prophetesses depicting power and glory awaiting the "isle" in the future? – when it would be inhabited by Angles who had managed to extirpate Boädicea's kinsfolk, except from "Little Wales"! All the same I suppose you would agree that as the notion of national identity is indispensable if we are to have any international morality, all this muddled sentiment does more good than harm *on the whole*, – though it is an excellent thing that it should be from time to time sharply criticized.

I am much interested in what you say of the perplexities of Federal States in international relations. I suppose however that they would only come in so far as matters of "*international comity*" are concerned, as distinct from matters of *strict duty* according to the received law of nations. I mean, at least, that U.S.A. took this view of the treatment of British niggers by South Carolina in 1849–51, for the Federal Government is constitutionally bound to punish "offences against the law of nations."

I should myself be inclined to say that this distinction between Offices of "Comity" and duties of strict obligation was required in applying my principle that "internal Constitution" cannot be an excuse for neglecting international duty. I am particularly pleased with your approval of what I have said about this; as it seems to me one of the points – they are perhaps few! – in which a theoretical, systematic treatment of international duty may really do practical good. For I can hardly conceive any one approaching the subject from a theoretical point of view, and considering the question in relation to the received principle that no nation's internal Constitution is to be interfered with by other nations – I can hardly conceive him not coming to my conclusion. And yet the opposite view has often been loudly maintained by Englishmen, at the time of the Conspiracy Bill to which you refer and at other times. I think it partly belongs to a conviction that the moral superiority of a free country, quâ free, justifies it in taking liberties that cannot be allowed to despots!

Still on this point, as I said, I should distinguish between points of strict duty and points of mere friendliness or courtesy. It seems to me that as regards the latter "internal Constitution" may fairly be considered. To adapt your metaphor, a man with a wife whom he cannot control must not be therefore excused from paying his just debts, but he may be excused for not asking his friends to stay with him.

Now a word or two as regards minor points of disagreement. I am afraid I have no effective answer to what you say about my discussion of the moral validity of compacts imposed by "unjust victors." I am afraid it must seem all rather "in the air," to practical statesmen. All I would urge is that the international moralist is bound to have some view on the morality of breaking treaties, and he cannot quite bring himself to say that a defeated State *may* legitimately tear up an irksome treaty whenever it has a favourable opportunity or feels strong enough. And though the moralist may have but little influence on the decision of such a question, do you not think that he may have *some* – always supposing that a tolerably complete *consensus* of moralists could be attained? At least if the Statesmen of such a State were balanced between the *pros* and *cons* on the question of tearing up a treaty, would not the probable verdict of impartial moral opinion have some weight? And might I not even quote the case of Russia and the Black Sea on my side? Do you think Russia would have dared to do what she did (say) ten years earlier, and with no excuse of breaches on the other side?

As to arbitration, – I am impressed with what you say of the objections to it as a means of solving the minor disputes to which alone we agree in thinking it possible to apply it effectively. Do you think that your objection would be at all removed or diminished by adopting Maine's suggestion (in his last posthumous book) of a permanent Court of Arbitration appointed by the Concert of Europe to deal with all questions that might be referred to them by any state? This seems to me partly to get over the danger of *conscious* and *interested* partisanship of the arbitrator.

I am really most grateful to you for giving so much attention to my proofs. I fear very few will read my chapters carefully *even once*, when published – except unhappy wights preparing for examination – but one must at least imagine readers, so in writing the rest I shall imagine you.[92]

In this remarkable letter, addressed to the former Viceroy, the "consensus" of moral experts appears as possible support for Maine's proposals for overcoming international strife by resort to the "Concert of Europe," and all this as part of a finely argued plea for the practical relevance of the moralist for the business of the statesman, in passages replete with offensive remarks on race and gender. Does the satiric reference to Boädicea suggest, with Seeley, the superiority of race to land as a criterion of national identity? Perhaps Sidgwick hoped that Lytton would learn something from the *Elements*, but this letter does not suggest any contempt for this renowned Government House poet. Lytton is duly thanked in the acknowledgments, along with Bryce, Dicey, Maitland, and others.

That Sidgwick's gallery of competent authorities for his political writing should include so many eminent figures committed to imperial rule, in both theory and practice, is singularly revealing, as is his jarring use of the term "nigger." Was he then, like his friends and colleagues, a whole-hearted champion of "spiritual expansion," whose views of imperial rule reflected fundamentally racist constructions of the populations ruled? What, in his mind, did the growth of federation entail for the larger world, at the hands of the "Concert of Europe"? Or were Seeley and the rest simply more enthusiastic teachers, whose support was utilitarian in the shorter run? This last possibility would suggest an extreme paradox: that Sidgwick's esoteric morality might have been beyond the rulers as well as the ruled.

As one would expect, Sidgwick's deeper views do seem to be decidedly more complex and ambivalent than those of his colleagues. Much, though not all, of what Sidgwick published on such issues is contained in the chapters in the *Elements* on "Principles of International Duty," "The Regulation of War," "International Law and Morality," and "Principles of External Policy," chapters covering other concerns as well. The emphasis is very much on colonialism – the word "imperialism" scarcely figures – and there is a great deal of detailed comparison of the different possible colonial situations. These issues are effectively framed in a characteristically Sidgwickian way, with the stress being on how to apply ethical criteria to larger transnational contexts, and Sidgwick is often singularly original in his development of utilitarian thinking in connection with cosmopolitianism, immigration, colonization, population control, and the development of legal and moral measures for global application. Indeed, his case for utilitarian impartialism in international affairs, shorn of its more offensive aspects, continues to attract defenders.[93]

As in the letter just quoted, Sidgwick draws a crucial distinction between international law and international morality – that is, between "rules of strict international duty, to the performance of which a State may rightly be compelled by force, and rules of international courtesy or comity, the breach of which justifies – generally speaking – moral disapprobation and complaint, but does not justify the use of violence." This roughly corresponds to the distinction between "legal and merely moral obligations in the sphere of civil conduct," though Sidgwick recognizes an inevitable looseness in applying such terms as "law" to the international context. In the domestic case, on his complex account, however "much I may think that a man ought to be punished for mischief he has caused, and however decidedly public opinion may be on my side, still if he has not committed any act that has already been determined to be a crime either by precedent or by statute, the judge if really an expert will not condemn him to punishment." The moral claim and the claim of positive law are thus distinct. Since

it has come to be recognised that the proper source of new law is a special legislative organ distinct from the judicature, it is clearly seen that there are two distinct species or grades of 'what ought to be,' in respect of legal coercion: – there are rules which the judge actually ought to enforce by punishing the violation, and there are other rules which (in a sense) it ought to be his duty to enforce, but is not. (EP 291)

With international law, however, as with positive versus reflective morality, it is harder to make out the distinction between the generally accepted and that which ought to be accepted. That is, for many "international jurists the distinction between what is and what ought to be an established rule seems to be obscure and imperfect," and there appears to be "a strong indisposition to recognise that a rule which seems to the disputant right is not an accepted duty." But still, there are also reasons for thinking that international law occupies "an intermediate position between ordinary law and ordinary morality":

[I]n the case of international law, though there is no regular organ of legislative innovation, the concerted action of States, in the way of treaties and conventions, plays an important part in the introduction of changes, to which there is no counterpart in the development of positive morality. This is due chiefly to the limited number of the States among whom the system of rules and usages that constitute modern international law is actually established: they are so few in all that the agreement of even a small group of them to adopt a new rule may be an important – in many cases even a decisive – step towards the general acceptance of this rule. . . . Further, the concerted action . . . is not the only method by which the rules of international law have been modified; it is undeniable that international law, like civil law, has been gradually made more definite and coherent by a series of arguments of the ordinary legal kind, terminated in some cases by judicial or quasi-judicial decisions; and it is conceivable that this process might be continued until international law should reach something like the systematic precision which parts of our own common law have attained through judicial interpretation alone. (EP 293–94)

For Sidgwick, this is a consummation devoutly to be wished, even if on many crucial matters he doubts that "the currently accepted principles for judging of international rights and wrongs have as yet been brought to legal precision and systematic coherence." Consequently, he thinks that it will be very difficult to regulate satisfactorily, in this quasi-legal way, such vital matters as "expansion into territory not yet occupied by civilised nations," which must "for a long time to come at any rate" be "left to international morality, in the sense in which it is distinguished from law: and this may be given as a final reason for not sharing the hopes of certain optimists who look forward to getting rid of wars between States by increasing the use of arbitration." (EP 296) He is all in favor of arbitration, to be sure, for both international and domestic strife, but confidence in that method will be better advanced if the distinction between international law, as a system of rules that experts can adjudicate on the model of law courts, and international morality, the vaguer and more contestable set of principles, is maintained.

Maitland had written to him:

I admire the chapter on International Law and Morality; it is the best thing that I have read about the subject. In my view the great difficulty in obtaining a body of international rules deserving the name of law lies in the extreme fewness of the 'persons' subject to that law and the infrequency and restricted range of the arguable questions which arise between them. The 'code' of actually observed rules is thus all shreds and patches.[94]

Still, it was clear enough that, beyond concrete particulars about the treatment of ambassadors, noncombatants, and so forth, the general principles of international duty are "abstinence from aggression and observance of compact," which work rather in parallel with the individualistic principle domestically. Sidgwick allows that, for all the differences that may arise over particular rules meant to interpret or apply these principles, still "the general principles on which these rules are avowedly based, are of much wider application," and there "seems to be no class of societies – civilised, semi-civilised, or savage – in dealing with which a civilised State can be exempted from the obligation to observe these principles, unless it has adequate grounds for expecting that they will be violated on the other side." But he does hold that in dealing "with uncivilised or semi-civilised communities difficult questions arise as to the interpretation of the duty of abstinence from aggression, and the manner in which it is to be reconciled with the legitimate claim of civilised communities to expand into unoccupied territory, and their alleged right – or even duty – of spreading their higher type of social existence." (EP 244). He recognizes that, alas, "in discussions among civilised States as to the occupation of new territory, the claims of the uncivilised tribes to the lands in some sort occupied by them nave been usually ignored."

Note here the assertion about the "alleged right – or even duty" of spreading civilized social existence. This was a fixture – a puzzling fixture – of Sidgwick's political thinking:

> With each successive generation the demand for expansion on the part of civilized nations is likely to grow stronger; and the more serious the interests involved, the more difficult it will be to obtain acquiescence in the rules determining the legitimate occupation of new territory, which must inevitably be to some extent arbitrary. And the question is complicated by the differences in grade of civilization . . . for the nations most advanced in civilization have a tendency – the legitimacy of which cannot be broadly and entirely disputed – to absorb semicivilized states in their neighbourhood, as in the expansion of England and Russia in Asia, and of France in Africa. As, I say, the tendency cannot be altogether condemned, since it often seems clearly a gain to the world on the whole that the absorption should take place; still it is obviously difficult to define the conditions under which this is legitimate, and the civilized nation engaged in this process of absorption cannot be surprised that other civilized nations think that they have a right to interfere and prevent the aggression. (PE 57)

And in *Lectures on the Ethics of T. H. Green, H. Spencer and J. Martineau*, he had also urged that the utilitarian mission is to "civilize the world," which may well involve "acts which cannot but be regarded as aggressive by the savage nations whom it is their business to educate and absorb" (GSM 236).

But the upshot of this conviction is less than transparent, since Sidgwick was of course as stringent a moralist in the international sphere as in the national one, utilitarianism knowing no such bounds. He is emphatic in maintaining that any claim to the effect that states are not properly subject to any restraints on the pursuit of their interests is "essentially immoral." Thus, for a state, "as for an individual, the ultimate end and standard of right conduct is the happiness of all who are affected by its actions," though of course, "for an individual no less than for a State – as the leading utilitarian moralists have repeatedly and emphatically affirmed . . . the general happiness is usually best promoted by a concentration of effort on more limited ends." National interest, like self-interest, thus has a certain limited role to play as an indirect means to the greatest happiness. But in the "exceptional cases in which the interest of the part conflicts with the interest of the whole, the interest of the part – be it individual or State – must necessarily give way. On this point of principle no compromise is possible, no hesitation admissible, no appeal to experience relevant."

(EP 299)[95] Again, Sidgwick was as horrified by neo-Machiavellian global politics as he was by narrowly egoistic party politics, and he favored federation in part because he recognized and feared other tendencies, those making for strife. As usual, on his view of the reconciliation project, egoism was supposed to get lifted up to high utilitarian duty.

Indeed, some nineteen years after Sidgwick's death, in the immediate aftermath of the first World War, Bryce and Eleanor edited a small volume entitled *National and International Right and Wrong*, consisting of two of Sidgwick's essays from *Practical Ethics* – "Public Morality" and "The Morality of Strife." It was a touching tribute to Sidgwick's continuing relevance:

> Sidgwick had already perceived more than twenty years ago that the current of German thought, beginning to run in an anti-moral direction, was returning to the doctrines promulgated by Machiavelli but provided with a new basis by the Hegelian doctrine of the omnipotent state. Some of us had latterly observed that not in Germany only was there a decline from the moral standards of eighty years ago, but no one (so far as I know) has explained with so much ingenuity the causes that have contributed to this change.[96]

Sidgwick pointed out "in words that ought to be pondered to-day what may be hoped for from the sedulous cultivation of what he calls the spiritual methods of avoiding both international and industrial strife."

Bryce's reading was certainly shared by Eleanor. In "The Morality of Strife in Relation to the War," she quoted her late husband's observation that the affirmation of national egoism almost always had the practical aim of emancipating "the public action of statesmen from the restraints of private morality."[97] This was followed by the observation that when "it is deliberately maintained by a powerful State that Might makes Right, that a nation is a law to itself, and not only has no duties to other nations but is bound to aim solely at what it conceives to be its own interests irrespective of all considerations of justice, veracity, and good faith – when a State holds this it is obvious that trouble is bound to come." Individual egoism and national egoism, both apt to be much less than rational or Goethean, were parallel problems. Small wonder that Sidgwick felt the urgent need to write a book on "Kant and Kantism in England."

Here it might also be recalled how the *Methods* had stressed the necessity of coming to terms with narrower circles of sympathy and attachment, and had even made reference to race, as well as nationality, as a commonsense criterion for partiality:

We should all agree that each of us is bound to show kindness to his parents and spouse and children, and to other kinsmen in a less degree: and to those who have rendered services to him, and any others whom he may have admitted to his intimacy and called friends: and to neighbors and to fellow-countrymen more than others and perhaps we may say to those of our own race more than to black or yellow men, and generally to human beings in proportion to their affinity to ourselves. (ME 246).[98]

Now, predictably, as an intermediate principle, the national one – or the racial one, for that matter – must be as qualified as the individual one. Certainly, no such thing could serve as an absolute, as opposed to a qualified indirect means to achieve the greatest happiness. For Sidgwick,

According to the national ideal, the right and duty of each government is to promote the interests of a determinate group of human beings, bound together by the tie of a common nationality – with due regard to the rules restraining it from attacking or encroaching on other States – and to consider the expediency of admitting foreigners and their products solely from this point of view.

On the "cosmopolitan ideal, its business is to maintain order over the particular territory that historical causes have appropriated to it, but not in any way to determine who is to inhabit this territory, or to restrict the enjoyment of its natural advantages to any particular portion of the human race." But the latter, Sidgwick owns, "is perhaps the ideal of the future," since it "allows too little for the national and patriotic sentiments which have in any case to be reckoned with as an actually powerful political force, and which appear to be at present indispensable to social wellbeing." Indeed, these sentiments cannot at present find a substitute "in sufficient diffusion and intensity" in the "wider sentiment connected with the conception of our common humanity." (EP 308–9)

Thus, for example, the "governmental function of promoting moral and intellectual culture might be rendered hopelessly difficult by the continual inflowing streams of alien immigrants, with diverse moral habits and religious traditions." And of course, the "efficient working of the political institutions of different States presupposes certain characteristics in the human beings to whom they are applied; and a large intermixture of immigrants brought up under different institutions might inevitably

introduce corruption and disorder into a previously well-ordered State."
(EP 309)

Still, the conclusion is that even if it might not at present be "in the
interest of humanity at large" to "impose upon civilised States generally,
as an absolute international duty, the free admission of immigrants," this
path is to be encouraged, since such free admission "will generally be
advantageous to the country admitting them." The admitting state would
be "thus enabled to share the advantage of the special faculties and empirical arts in which other countries excel," which is partly a matter of
"the diffusion of mutual knowledge and sympathy among nations." Once
again, Sidgwick suggests a brighter future: "Over a large part of the earth's
surface the union of diverse races under a common government seems to
be an almost indispensable condition of economic progress and the spread
of civilisation; in spite of the political and social difficulties and drawbacks
that this combination entails." (EP 310) At one level, at least, this was
indeed a shrewd recognition of how nationalism had evolved far beyond
the earlier, often Romantic proto-nationalistic identity politics that had
inspired so many mythical accounts of the spiritual bonds uniting Celts,
or Gauls, or Teutons (etc.) – or Boädicea's kinsfolk.[99]

But the cosmopolitan ideal would appear to welcome emigration as well
as immigration, and on this it sounds rather less enlightened. In discussing
the matter of "increase of population as a subordinate end at which a statesman should aim, with a view to the promotion of the general happiness,"
Sidgwick rehearses the shifting attitudes from the pre-Malthusian period
down to the present one, noting that it would be "generally agreed" that
"emigration apart," a "government that took measures for the direct purpose of adding to the population of a country as fully peopled as England
or France, would be assuming too great and dangerous a responsibility;
owing to the danger that the increase of numbers would be accompanied
by a lowering of the average quality of life in the increased population."
He continues:

Indeed, since Malthus, an important group of thinkers have urged that measures
should be taken tending to restrict the growth of the population: and it seems not
improbable that at some future time the governments of civilised countries will
have to face this problem, unless measures of this kind are spontaneously adopted
by the governed. But in the present condition of the world any such measures
would seem to be objectionable so far as they tend to check the expansion of

civilised humanity; – assuming that the increase of the amount of human life in the world, under its present conditions of existence in civilised countries, is a good and not an evil; except so far as increase of numbers tends to be accompanied by increase of disease, or even of physical discomfort not involving disease. If this assumption be granted, we may clearly regard as a benefit to humanity the stimulus to population which organised emigration and colonisation would tend to give – accompanied as it would be with a tendency to improve the average condition of the human beings in the colony and mother country taken together. (EP 317–18)

Puzzlingly, in a rare inconsistency, in these passages Sidgwick keeps referring to the "average quality of life," rather than to the total utility criterion that he had defended in the *Methods*.

At any rate, the claim that colonization was a vehicle for utilitarian policy in this respect was also something of a fixture of Sidgwick's thought. As early as 1861, he had written to Dakyns:

I forget whether you agree with Mill's population theory. I think the way he blinks the practical morality of the question is the coolest thing I know. And I know many cool things on the part of your thorough-going theorists. I believe in 'Be fruitful and multiply.' I think the most crying need now is a better organised colonisation. To think of the latent world-civilisation in our swarms of fertile Anglo-Saxon pauperism.

A follow-up letter flatly puts it: "colonisation is unanswerable, I think; if not, please answer it." (M 66–67)

Sidgwick was the first to admit that England was the great colonizer, and he appreciated the complex forms it had taken. In a broadly sympathetic review of Cairnes's *Essays*, he especially complimented the one on "Colonisation," which

presents very effectively in sharp outline and impressive contrast the three stages of English colonisation: the first period, closed by the war of American Independence, when the aims of colonisation were commercial, while in other matters the habits and genius of our race produced an unwatched and half-unwarranted freedom of self-government; the second period, of Colonial-Office control and convict settlement; the third period, 'initiated by an event as obscure as the War of Independence was famous,' the formation of the Colonisation Society in 1830. Mr. Cairnes . . . dwells with justifiable pride on the success of this latter movement, certainly one of the "most remarkable triumphs of constructive theorising that English history has to show." He does allow, however, that the "bursting of the

Wakefield bubble" with the early bankruptcy of South Australia and Wakefield's failures in New Zealand were serious setbacks. Still, he concludes "we may fairly attribute the present prosperity of Australia and New Zealand to the Colonisation Society of 1830. (CWC)[100]

But ultimately, Sidgwick's bottom line on colonization is not quite so simple:

Experience, however, seems to show that, generally speaking, taking into account the risk of conflict with aborigines and of collisions with other civilised states, the cost of founding a colony will outweigh any returns obtainable to the public treasury of the mother country; and that the extra cost cannot be thrown on the colonists, since, so long as the colony is weak, it is too poor to bear it, while, when it has grown richer, it will also have grown stronger, and will refuse to pay. Still . . . even where colonisation is a bad investment from the point of view of public finance, it may still be remunerative in one way or another to the community as a whole. (EP 319)

On the economic side, then, Sidgwick would seem to align himself more closely with the skeptical approach to colonies taken by Smith, Turgot, and Bentham and by eighteenth-century political economy generally, according to which the economic gains from colonies are doubtful. He allows, however, the possibility that "substantial gains are likely to accrue to the conquering community regarded as an aggregate of individuals; through the enlarged opportunities for the private employment of capital, the salaries earned in governmental service, and especially, in the case of a commercial community, through the extended markets opened to trade." Moreover, he thinks they may be of doubtful help in terms of war and national defense, noting that the British possession of India was, if anything, a handicap in this respect.

So it is with this mass of qualifications and warnings that Sidgwick at last broaches more directly the relations between "civilized" and other states or peoples:

As between old fully-peopled States like those of Western Europe and civilised States like the American, with a large amount of unoccupied land, the transfer of population tends to be more extensive and one-sided; the old States – even when they are growing in numbers and wealth – send to the newer countries a considerable excess of both over what they receive. When, however, emigration takes place from civilised States into regions uninhabited except by savage tribes – whose political organisation would hardly be held to justify the name of

'States' – it is in modern times normally combined with extension of the territory of the State from which it takes place, and may be regarded as a process of Expansion of the community as a whole. (EP 310)

The term "colonisation," he explains, often refers to "the occupation by a civilised community of regions thinly inhabited by uncivilised tribes; in which, accordingly, even supposing the 'aborigines' to be treated with equity and consideration, there is room for a new population of immigrants far exceeding the old in numbers" (EP 314). But this does not apply to all cases, and some colonization has involved conquest of not-so-thinly populated areas. And he allows that

The case is different when the conquered, though not uncivilised, are markedly inferior in civilisation to the conquerors. Here, if the war that led to the conquest can be justified by obstinate violation of international duty on the part of the conquered, the result would generally be regarded with toleration by impartial persons; and even, perhaps, with approval, if the government of the conquerors was shown by experience to be not designedly oppressive or unjust; since the benefits of completer internal peace and order, improved industry, enlarged opportunities of learning a better religion and a truer science, would be taken – and, on the whole, I think, rightly taken – to compensate for the probable sacrifice of the interests of the conquered to those of the conquerors, whenever the two came into collision. (EP 311)

Indeed, it is in this context that Sidgwick warmly recounts some of the genuinely "remunerative" factors involved in colonization:

[T]here are sentimental satisfactions, derived from justifiable conquests, which must be taken into account, though they are very difficult to weigh against the material sacrifices and risks. Such are the justifiable pride which the cultivated members of a civilised community feel in the beneficent exercise of dominion, and in the performance by their nation of the noble task of spreading the highest kind of civilisation; and a more intense though less elevated satisfaction – inseparable from patriotic sentiment – in the spread of the special type of civilisation distinctive of their nation, communicated through its language and literature, and through the tendency to imitate its manners and customs which its prolonged rule, especially if on the whole beneficent, is likely to cause in a continually increasing degree. (EP 313)

This is "spiritual expansion," such as occurred, he suggests, with the French in Algeria. The contrast is supposedly with the "physical expansion which takes place when the conquered region is so thinly populated as to afford room for a considerable immigration of the conquerors." Unfortunately, Sidgwick rather glosses over the ways in which this might be associated with unjustifiable as well as justifiable conquests, and instead turns his attention back to the more common denotation of the term "colonisation," given earlier, observing that the "rational motives to colonisation, in this narrower sense, are partly the same as those that prompt to the conquest of semi-civilised countries." (EP 314).

In a revealing note, he admits that it is often difficult "to estimate the force of the desire for national expansion, – including the desire of cultivated minds to spread the special type of civilisation which they enjoy – as distinguished from the more primitive impulse to the amelioration of the emigrants' condition." He goes on to discuss the peculiar relationship between Great Britain and the United States, observing that despite their economic and political rivalry, "if we derive any satisfaction from the expansion of the English race, and of the English type of civilisation as communicated through its language, literature, and law, the prosperous growth of the community inhabiting the United States must be regarded as the most important means to this end – and perhaps more important than if the colony had remained in political connexion with England." In one of his better forecasts, he explains that "if any existing language should ever become the one common language of civilised man it will probably be English: and the chief cause of this result, if it should be brought about, will probably be the growth and commercial pre-eminence of the United States." (EP 315)

Thus, spiritual expansion may actually be at odds with the expansion or maintenance of the colonial empire and at any rate needs to be distinguished from more narrowly self-interested aims. And it is at this juncture that Sidgwick finally addresses in a more direct fashion some of the explosive racial questions arising out of colonial expansion:

It remains to speak of the management of the relations between civilised settlers and the uncivilised tribes inhabiting the district into which immigration takes place – commonly called the 'aborigines.' It is not without hesitation that I venture to touch this question, as I can only treat it in a very brief and general way; while any student of the history of European colonisation must be profoundly impressed with its difficulty. What a well-informed writer [Merivale], by no means unduly sentimental, called the 'wretched details of the ferocity and treachery which have marked the conduct of civilised men in their relations with savages,' forms one of the most painful chapters in modern history; all the more painful from the frequent evidence it gives of benevolent intentions, and even beneficent efforts, on the part of the rulers of the superior race. At present in England there is a general agreement that the wellbeing of the uncivilised first-comers, found in regions colonised by civilised men, should be earnestly and systematically kept in view by the governors of these latter; and that the 'aborigines' should be adequately compensated for any loss that they may suffer from the absorption of their territory – and ultimately of themselves – by the expanding civilised societies. It is therefore permissible to hope that in the future some closer approach may be made to the realisation of this ideal than has been made in the past. (EP 322–33)

At least Sidgwick fretted over this subject a good deal. In a letter to Bryce, complaining about his slow progress, he explained that "there is a horrid new chapter on 'Principles of External Policy' which has been giving me trouble for weeks: I am trying to find something judicious to say on the treatment of 'aborigines' but have not yet succeeded." Bryce responded: "The greatest difficulty about the aborigines question seems to be the question of their lands – as to which there are many American [duties?] but none that clear up the practical perplexities of reconciling justice with the 'progress of civilization.'" (CWC)

As Sidgwick sees it, one central issue concerns the difference between colonies "where the manual labour can be and will be supplied by the civilised race" and those where "it can only supply capital and superior kinds of labour."

In the first case the main difficulties of the problem are likely to be transient; the incoming tide of civilised immigration will gradually modify or submerge the barbarism of the aborigines; so that ultimately the question, how to deal with such of them as may survive without becoming really fit for civilised work, will sink into a part of the general question of dealing with the incapable and recalcitrant elements found in all civilised communities. But in its early stages the collision of races is likely to be more intense in colonies of this class; since the process of settlement inevitably involves more disturbance of the economic conditions of the life of the aborigines.

On the other hand, in colonies where the superior race does not supply the manual labour, the difficulties of governing a community composed of elements very diverse in intellectual and moral characteristics must be expected to last indefinitely longer; but there is no stage at which the conflict of interests need be quite so acute as in the former. (EP 323)

Sidgwick believes that the former case has been more important historically, but that "its importance is rapidly diminishing, and in most of the territories open to the future expansion of civilised European States, manual labour is likely to be mainly performed by non-European races." But he also tries to downplay the significance of his remarks, explaining that he will not discuss either case in detail, but only "indicate briefly the nature of the problems that arise and the principles *prima facie* applicable to them, in accordance with the general view of politics taken in the present treatise." Astonishingly, he actually goes on to say that he will "not attempt to distinguish between the international duty and the interest of the civilised nation aiming at expansion," because "here, as elsewhere, duty and interest are mostly coincident." Still, he would have it understood that he has in view "as ultimate end, the aggregate happiness of all the human beings concerned, civilised and uncivilised – native or imported." If it "does not seem possible – even if it were desirable – to check the expansion of civilised Europe," then "the problem of regulating and governing composite social aggregates, with a civilised minority superimposed on a semi-civilised majority, must be regarded as one of the most important proposed for European statesmanship in the proximate future." (EP 323–24) With this statement, the growth of federation starts to look more worrisome, as a way of regulating the behavior of the "civilised minority superimposed."

And now, having thus done his best to cast a soft light on the hard realities of European expansion, stress the importance of the issue, and confess the inadequacies of his treatment of it, Sidgwick finally brings himself to some broader statements of principle. On the topic of the "civilised" State claiming supreme control over the territory in question:

It would be going too far to say that no exercise of power over these latter is justifiable, unless the general consent of the persons subjected to it may be presumed from agreements formally made by their chiefs or on some other adequate ground. But we may say that no serious interference of the civilised government with the aborigines should take place without such evidence of consent, except under circumstances which afford a special justification for it; – as (e.g.) when the civilised State has been victorious in a war provoked by the aggression of the inferior race, or when the interference is necessary for the security of its own subjects in the exercise of rights that they may fairly claim, or to protect the natives from the evils of intercourse with the most lawless and degraded elements of civilised society. Further, the claim of sovereignty should not be understood to carry with it any obligation to interfere with the laws and customs of the aborigines, even when opposed to civilised morality. Such interference should be regulated by an unprejudiced regard of the social wellbeing of the tribes subjected to it; which might be seriously impaired by the sudden abolition even of pernicious customs. (EP 325)

Government may also have to control the sale and purchase of lands, in order to prevent the aborigines from being taken advantage of. Even when the aborigines may not have conceptualized their "property rights," compensation should be made "for the loss of the utilities in the way of hunting, fishing, etc., which they have been accustomed to derive from such lands."

As for further restrictions on the free interaction between settlers and aborigines, these need to be worked out on a case-by-case basis. The familiar examples of the "prohibition of the sale of intoxicating liquors, and the prohibition of the sale of firearms" being in principle defensible, Sidgwick goes further, suggesting that "in some cases a more complete separation of races, and a more thorough tutelage of the inferior race, would seem to be temporarily desirable." But he hastens to add that it is "hardly likely that this kind of artificial isolation can ever be more than partially successful," and that "such measures should generally be regarded as essentially transitional, and only adopted – if at all – in order better to prepare the aborigines for complete social amalgamation with the colonising race." It is in this connection that he allows, in the footnote quoted earlier, that there has been no proof adequate to support the conclusion that "the social amalgamation of two races would be debasing to the superior race," though if this were clearly demonstrable, permanent forms of separation would be justifiable. (EP 326)

Furthermore, the government must ensure that the punishment of crimes against the settlers proceed "within the limits of strict justice," though the crucial object is less to achieve "pedantic adhesion to the forms of civilised judicial procedure" and more to "impress the intellect of the aborigines with the relation between offence and punishment." On the matter of education, however, Sidgwick is insistent that the aborigines are owed much more than mere "industrial education." The educational task

should include all kinds of instruction required to fit the inferior race to share the life of civilised mankind. In particular, though the religion of the settlers should not be compulsorily imposed on the natives, every encouragement should be given to the effort of missionaries to teach it. Experience seems to show that the potency of such teaching as an instrument of civilisation varies very much in different cases, but few will doubt the desirability of allowing full scope to its application. (EP 327)

Finally:

One of the most indisputable services that – as we may hope – the expansion of civilised States is destined to confer on uncivilised humanity is the abolition of the evils of enslavement, and of the wars and raids that have enslavement for their object; and, ultimately, of the condition of slavery. But it may often be expedient that this latter result should be only gradually attained: while, on the other hand, even where the status of slavery is formally excluded by law, special restrictions on freedom of contract between natives and settlers are likely to be required in the case of contracts of service; since, if such contracts are left unrestricted, there is some risk that the inferior race may be brought too completely into the power of private employers. This point is of course peculiarly important in the case of colonies in which the superior race cannot or will not undertake the main part of the manual work required: in this case the demand of the capitalist employer for a steady supply of reliable labour led modern civilisation in its earlier stage back to the institution of slavery in an extreme form: and prompts even now to longing aspirations after some system of compulsory labour, which shall have the economic advantages of slavery without its evils. But I know no ground for thinking that such a system can be devised: and should accordingly deprecate any attempt to approximate to it. I do not therefore infer – as some have inferred – that contracts of long duration ought to be prohibited altogether; but only that they ought to be carefully supervised and closely watched. The need for this vigilance arises equally – it may be even greater – when the labourers in question are not natives, but aliens belonging to a lower grade of civilisation; at the same time there are strong economic reasons for introducing labour from abroad in colonies of this class, where the natives are either not sufficiently numerous or wanting in industrial capacity. (EP 327–28)

Indeed, Sidgwick insists that in

regulating the relations between aborigines and settlers, the care of Government will be specially needed to prevent the interests of the former from being damaged through the occupation of land by the latter. We may lay down that the aborigines should never be deprived of any definite rights of property without full compensation; and that, so far as possible, such rights should be only ceded voluntarily. I cannot, indeed, hold that compulsory transfer is in principle inadmissable; since I cannot regard savages as having an absolute right to keep their hunting-grounds from agricultural use, any more than an agricultural occupant in a civilised State has a right to prevent a railway from being made through his grounds. Still, compulsory deprivation should be avoided as far as possible, even where it may seem abstractly justifiable, on account of the violent resentment that it is likely to cause. (EP 325)

And with that, Part I of the *Elements* comes to an inconclusive close. Sidgwick returns to the topic only one more time, briefly, in the chapter on "Federal and Other Composite States." There he reiterates his conviction that the mother country must take a hand in regulating relations between colonists and aborigines, since the "greater impartiality that may be reasonably attributed to the home government seems to render it generally desirable that the management of the aborigines should not be regarded as an 'internal affair' of the colony, so long as there is any serious danger of a conflict of races or persecution of the inferior race" (EP 550). More alarmingly, however, he also adds some further discussion of the case "where the manual labour can never be in the main supplied by the superior race: since here the composite character of the population must be regarded as permanent unless the races blend."

To a society so constituted the governmental structure sketched in the preceding chapters is *prima facie* unsuited: but the extent and nature of the modifications that should be introduced into it must vary very much with the degree of civilisation actually reached by the inferior race, and its apparent capacity for further improvement. It will be difficult to prevent a simple oligarchy of the superior race from being tyrannical: on the other hand, it seems a desperate resource to give equality of electoral privileges to members of the inferior race while admittedly unfit to control the operations of government, in the mere hope that experience may in time educate them up to a tolerable degree of fitness. So long as the composite society presents this dilemma, it will probably conduce to its wellbeing as a whole that the colony should remain a dependency; so that, even where the business of government is mainly left in the hands of the colonists, the control of the central government may prevent or mitigate any palpable oppression of the inferior race. (EP 550)

What can be said on behalf of Sidgwick's treatment of these questions, with all its dismal, disturbing talk of "lower" races and "higher" grades of civilization? Against the overwhelming tide of neo-Darwinian racism, he holds out somewhat, with an agnostic claim that no seriously "debasing" inherent racial differences have been demonstrated scientifically, and thinks assimilation possible. Against the overwhelming realities of British imperial expansion, he urges that actual spiritual expansion may not necessarily take the form of extended or enduring empire, and that although colonization is often a good thing, the rights of semicivilised and aboriginal peoples must be protected – especially from the less-than-impartial colonists themselves. Despite his warm feelings about the spread of his "higher" civilization, he favors the cosmopolitan ideal and clearly hopes for more extensive and effective international law and custom to regulate all such relations and to help avoid war. His anti-Machiavellianism and belief in external and internal sanctions and suasion for enhancing world peace would thus appear to circumscribe – subject to utilitarian calculation – any imperialistic ventures that the energetic "good people" might take on. Indeed, Sidgwick recognizes how abysmally cruel the treatment of native populations has been, by the "civilised" states, even when statesmen were well-intentioned, and he thinks of denying independence as in part a measure to ensure that the exploitation by the colonists is not perpetuated. And against any educational program that would merely underwrite the inferior social and economic position of the "lower races," he demands full educational opportunity to share in the benefits of "civilisation" – the "better religion" and "truer science," as he elliptically puts it. Again, colonial rule, in Sidgwick's eyes, might advance the general happiness of humanity, gradually undermining the prescientific superstitions and institutions – such as slavery – that have contributed only to human misery (not to mention the subjection of women).

On the other side, of course, is the breathtaking fatuity with which Sidgwick designates unfamiliar peoples "lower" or "semi-civilised" or "savage," with perfect insouciance consigning their ways of life to extinction. How, given his own skeptical cast of mind and distance from spiritual or political orthodoxy, could he have been so unreflectively Eurocentric, so easily forgiving of what in other contexts he immediately recognised as the phenomenon of missionaries rushing out to preach things they did not know? And what did it mean, in practice, to be so warmly appreciative of the greater impartiality of the home governments, so that their benevolence was linked to maintaining British dependencies? "Spiritual expansion" sounds deeply suspicious, even when Sidgwick fails, in his all-too-evasive way, to give it much concrete content. Moreover, just how lenient was he willing to be about lapses in international duty or comity, when it came to "the duty" of spiritual expansion? Was this like Greek love? And what, concretely, did he have in mind when referring to such things as the different capacities for manual labor and the possibility of "race degradation"? How did he construct racial difference?

The frustrating feature of Sidgwick's writings on this score is his abstract way of describing the issues, the way in which he intentionally tries to steer clear of too much concrete political reference, the better to foster agreement on principle. Just which peoples did he suppose to be "savage" and which "semi-civilised"? What was his list of the future cases where the colonists were unlikely to engage in manual labor? What did he mean by "race," and which races did he think would be conquered or fused, and which endure? Precisely why was Europe bound to "overcome" Chinese civilization?

Clearly, a great deal of what Sidgwick said about aborigines – like a great deal of what he said about the lower classes – derived from his impressions of the United States, Australia, South Africa, India, and New Zealand, and his impressions of these countries were based entirely on indirect sources, chiefly novels and a few select academic works, mostly those of his friends and colleagues. As mentioned earlier, Bryce's *American Commonwealth* was another such work. It is worth dwelling on Bryce's book at length, given Sidgwick's intimate acquaintance with and high regard for it. Bryce was, of course, one of the old cohort, part of the group of academic liberals and friends – including Sidgwick, Green, and Symonds – who had toured Europe together back in the early sixties, arguing religion, philosophy, and politics at every turn. He had accompanied Sidgwick on his fateful trip to Italy, was a frequent houseguest, and a most welcome source of political gossip. He became not only an influential academic, holding the Regius Professorship of Civil Law at Oxford from 1870 until 1893, but also a dedicated and conscientious public servant – the 1895 Bryce Commission on Secondary Education, which urged "a comprehensive central authority to formulate policy and the constitution of local authorities to administer secondary education," was of the first importance for pushing ahead the improved secondary education that would undergird the improvement of higher education.[101] A longtime Liberal MP, he was invited to serve on the India Council (but declined), though he did serve as chief secretary to Ireland under Campbell-Bannerman, and as ambassador to the United States, not to mention as president of the American Political Science Association. An absolutely inveterate traveler, Bryce had experienced firsthand not only the United States, which he knew quite well, but also Canada, Australia, Egypt, South Africa, India, and any number of other lands, in addition to the Eurocentric circuit to which Sidgwick had limited himself. He wrote about most of the places he visited, and it would not be stretching matters to say that he served as Sidgwick's "competent authority" in chief when it came to factual information on the past and present possessions of the British Empire. Both Sidgwick and Bryce, in the nineties, would be viewed as remnants of the academic liberals of the sixties. Both in due course had become members of the Synthetic Society, with Sidgwick regarding his friend as in effect a fellow Apostolic inquirer, one with whom he could share his excitement over developments in para-psychology. And again, Sidgwick had followed Bryce in insisting on the importance of the historical and comparative methods; he thought the *American Commonwealth* a "great work."

Sadly, Bryce was also a veritable fund of the offensive racial stereotypes characteristic of the late Victorian era, and often these come through with special clarity in his discussions of African Americans. Thus, a number of key passages in his chapter on the "Present and Future of the Negro," in the *American Commonwealth*, yield a series of perfectly idiotic claims concerning both African and Native American civilizations. Summing up the "character and gifts of the Negro," he writes:

He is by nature affectionate, docile, pliable, submissive, and in these respects most unlike the Red Indian, whose conspicuous traits are pride and a certain dogged inflexibility. He is seldom cruel or vindictive – which the Indian often is – nor is he prone to violence, except when spurred by lust or drink. His intelligence is rather quick than solid; and though not wanting in a sort of shrewdness, he shows the childishness as well as the lack of self-control which belongs to the primitive peoples. A nature highly impressionable, emotional, and unstable is in him appropriately accompanied by a love of music, while for art he has – unlike the Red Indian – no taste or turn whatever. Such talent as he has runs to words; he learns languages easily and speaks fluently, but shows no capacity for abstract thinking, for scientific inquiry, or for any kind of invention. It is, however, not so conspicuously on the intellectual side that his weakness lies, as in the sphere of will and action. Having neither foresight nor 'roundsight,' he is heedless and unthrifty, easily elated and depressed, with little tenacity of purpose, and but a feeble wish to better his condition. Sloth, like that into which the Negroes of the Antilles have sunk, cannot be generally charged upon the American coloured man, partly perhaps because the climate is less enervating and nature less bountiful. Although not so steady a workman as is the white, he is less troublesome to his employers, because less disposed to strike. It is by his toil that a large part of the cotton, rice, and sugar crop of the South is now raised. But anyone who knows the laborious ryot or coolies of the East Indies is struck by the difference between a race on which ages of patient industry have left their stamp and the volatile children of Africa.[102]

It was, he argues emphatically, a mistake, an excess of the American fanaticism about identifying citizenship and voting, to have precipitously granted Negros the vote in 1870, when generations of slavery had rendered them totally unfit to exercise it effectively.

Bryce goes on to consider the ways in which schools, churches, literature, industry, and business are "moulding the Negro," and his conclusions are less than optimistic. He thinks that there "is something pathetic in the eagerness of the Negroes, parents, young people, and children, to obtain instruction. They seem to think that the want of it is what keeps them below the whites." And as for religion, "Among the Negroes, it took a highly emotional and sensational form, in which there was little apprehension of doctrine and still less of virtue, while physical excitement constantly passed into ecstasy, hysterics, and the other phenomena which accompany what are called in America camp meetings." Furthermore, in some of "the pure Negro districts further south," there have "been relapses into the Obeah rites and serpent worship of African heathendom. How far this has gone no one can say. There are parts of the lower Mississippi valley as little explored, so far as the mental and moral condition of the masses is concerned, as are the banks of the Congo and the Benué."[103] Bryce also suggests that the former slaves have witnessed an "increase of insanity, marked since emancipation, and probably attributable to the increased facilities which freedom has given for obtaining liquor, and to the stress which independence and education have imposed on the undeveloped brain of a backward race." And he also buys into white fears of black criminality and sexuality, noting "the large amount of crime. Most of it is petty crime, chiefly thefts of hogs and poultry, but there are also a good many crimes against women."[104]

Furthermore, because the "most potent agency in the progress of the humbler and more ignorant sections of a community has always been their intercourse with those who are more advanced," and as this presupposes the absence of "race repulsion" and the possibility of intermarriage, the American Negro faces special problems: "The day of his liberation was also the day when the whites began to shun intercourse with him, and when opinion began to condemn, not merely regular marriage with a person of colour, for that had been always forbidden, but even an illict union." The problem of lynching has become serious, rendering the whites cruel and lawless and the "docile Negroes" increasingly distrustful of their former masters.

Bryce recognizes that the problem of the color line in America is in many ways unique, "a new one in history." The "relations of the ruling and subject races of Europe and Asia supply no parallel to it." Thus,

In all such cases . . . though one race or religion may be for the moment dominant, there is no necessary or permanent distinction between them; and there is, if the religious difficulty can be overcome, a possibility of intermarriage. Other cases may be suggested where a fusion is improbable, as between the British and the natives in India, or the colonists and the natives in South Africa. But the European rulers of India are a mere handful in comparison with the natives, nor do they settle in India so as to form a part of its permanent population. In New Zealand, the Maoris, hitherto a diminishing body, though now just maintaining their numbers, live apart on their own lands, but seem likely to be ultimately absorbed by the whites. In western South America the Spanish settlers have, in some regions, very largely mingled their blood with that of the native Indians, and may ultimately become as much blent with the latter as has befallen in Mexico. The peculiar feature of the race problem as it presents itself in the United States is, that the Negroes are in many districts one-third or even one-half of the population, are forced to live in the closest local contiguity with the whites, and are for the purposes of industry indispensable to the latter, yet are so sharply cut off from the whites by colour and all that colour means, that not merely a mingling of blood, but any social approximation, is regarded with horror, and perpetual severance is deemed a law of nature.[105]

There are fatal objections to any plans for a "Back to Africa" solution, the chief of them being that the Negroes would not go and that the whites could not afford to let them go because it would mean that much of the country would then "remain untilled and useless." But intermarriage seems equally impossible:

Even at the North, where the aversion to Negro blood is now less strong, 'miscegenation,' as they call it, is deemed such a disgrace to the white who contracts it that one seldom hears of its occurrence. Enlightened Southern men, who have themselves no dislike to the black race, justify this horror of intermarriage by arguing that no benefit which might thereby accrue to the Negroes could balance the evil which would befall the rest of the community. The interests of the nation and of humanity itself would, in their view, suffer by such a permanent debasement of the Anglo-American race as would follow. Our English blood is suffering enough already, they say, from the intrusion of inferior stock from continental Europe; and we should be brought down to the level of San Domingo were we to have an infusion from Africa added. This is the argument to which reason appeals. That enormous majority which does not reason is swayed by a feeling so strong and universal that there seems no chance of its abating within an assignable time. Revolutions in sentiment are, no doubt conceivable, but they are more rare than revolutions in politics.[106]

But for all the ghastly prejudice that he both describes and exhibits himself, Bryce does in the end hope for a revolution in sentiment. The evils of this situation are to be measured not just in terms of political stability, but

also by the diminution of happiness which they cause, by the passions hurtful to moral progress they perpetuate, by the spirit of lawlessness they evoke, by the contempt for the rights of man as man which they engender. In a world already so full of strife and sorrow it is grievous to see added to the other fountains of bitterness a scorn of the strong for the weak, and a dread by the weak of the strong, grounded on no antagonism of interests, for each needs the other, but solely on a difference in race and colour.

Political progress is possible, and such things as lynching must be sternly repressed. But for the

social difficulty, rooted deep in the characters of the two races, none but moral remedies have any promise of potency, and the working of moral remedies, sure as we believe it to be, is always slow. . . . one must place one's hopes on what physicians call the healing power of Nature, and trust that the forces which make not only for equality, but also for peace and goodwill among men, will in due time reduce these evils, as they have reduced many others.[107]

In some ways, Bryce recognized the harsher realities of British imperialism and his own compromised position: "the Englishman, who knows how not a few of his own countrymen behave to the ancient and cultivated races of the East whom they have conquered, feels that he is not entitled to sit in judgment.[108] That Bryce himself is sitting in judgment is perfectly clear, however, and he would appear to have made a powerful, if unwitting, advance case for Said's thesis that British imperialism involved the construction of "the lower races" as the chief ideological prop for domination.[109]

Moreover, his construction of race often incorporated notions of Millian vitality transformed into Seelyan strength:

> In most men the want of individual Will – that is to say, the proneness to comply with or follow the will of another – is the specially conspicuous phenomenon. It is for this reason that a single strenuous and unwearying will sometimes becomes so tremendous a power. There are in the world comparatively few such wills, and when one appears, united to high intellectual gifts, it prevails whichever way it turns, because the weaker bow to it and gather round it for shelter, and, in rallying to it, increase its propulsive or destructive power. It becomes almost a hypnotizing force. One perceives this most strikingly among the weaker races of the world. They are not necessarily the less intelligent races. In India, for instance, an average European finds many Hindus fully his equals in intelligence, in subtlety, and in power of speech; but he feels his own volitions and his whole personality to be so much stronger than that of the great bulk of the native population (excluding a very few races) that men seem to him no more than stalks of corn whom he can break through and tread down in his onward march. This is how India was conquered and is now held by the English. Superior arms, superior discipline, stronger physique, are all secondary causes. There are other races far less cultivated, far less subtle and ingenious, than the Hindus, with whom Europeans have found it harder to deal, because the tenacity of purpose and the pride of the individual were greater. This is the case with the North-American Indians, who fought so fiercely for their lands that it has been estimated that in the long conflict they maintained they have probably killed more white men than they have lost at the hands of the whites. Yet they were far inferior in weapons and in military skill; and they had no religious motives to stimulate their valour.[110]

Is this "fire and strength" or the "triumph of the will"?

Bryce's work could helpfully be taken as providing something of a key for interpreting Sidgwick's more abstract account. Nor is this at all surprising, given how closely they collaborated in their political work. It is here that one finds the issues of national character, manual labor, and "debasement of the race" versus fusion raised, and the problem of the color line in the United States used as a unique way of categorizing the various forms of interaction between different populations. The "coolie" and the "ryot" were industrious compared to the "Negro," and the "ancient and cultivated races" of India and China did not pose quite the same problems as the "savage" aboriginal populations of the Congo, the Australian wilderness, and the American West. These were the concrete examples behind Sidgwick's colorless arguments about race and colonization. He had supplied Bryce with extensive commentary on his proofs, and the points that he did not query are as important as the ones he did.

Quite possibly, Sidgwick actually played a role in stimulating Bryce's extended meditations on the subject of race. The extensive correspondence that they maintained during the eighties has Sidgwick complaining, of Bryce's claims about the future of the United States, that "Only people of European origin appear to be contemplated in this forecast. Is the nigger no longer a problem, and is the Mongolian played out?" And a letter from October of 1888 explains, "I enclose an extract from the Times of today about the nigger: it represents a view I have heard more than once expressed with much confidence: but I am glad to hear that the best authorities do not share it." This continues with the suggestion: "For 'antecedent theory' I should be inclined to suggest 'prevalent views of heredity': as I do not think that there [has] ever been any theory deserving the name of scientific which has professed to determine the relative influences of physical heredity and social environment." (CWC)[111]

The peculiar dissonance that comes from Sidgwick's casually lapsing into offensive slang – slang that he, like Bryce, scrupulously avoids in all his published works, and that even Maine found offensive – while at the same time denying the very ground of the racism that Bryce had described, is hard to absorb. One can convict Sidgwick of many failings – Eurocentrism, certainly, and also falling in with any number of ridiculous stereotypes that were legitimated under the rubric of "national character" – but it should have seemed – on the face of it, at least – difficult to convict him of harboring racist convictions appealing to hereditary inferiority, and for much the same reason that it is difficult to convict Mill of harboring any such convictions.[112] And yet the jarring usage and easy acceptance of it are still apt to leave doubts about just where to locate him and his colleagues. After all, as noted, his friend Cowell had softened him to the Southern cause during the American Civil War, which he tended to treat in legalistic terms as a matter of the right of secession and noninterference.[113]

It is possible that Sidgwick increasingly adopted this (long-familiar) usage during the eighties, as a result of his readings in American literature.[114] The year 1885 finds him reading *Adventures of Huckleberry Finn*, the title character of which he describes as "a kind of boyish, semi-savage Gil Blas, of the low – the lowest – Transatlantic life, living by his wits on the Mississippi. The novelty of the scene heightens the romantic *imprévue* of his adventures: and the comic *imprévu* of his reflections on them is – about once every three times – irresistibly laughable." (M 406) But the "n word" was a fixture of many of his literary sources, most of whom were more racist than Twain.[115] Tennyson, for example. When in 1865, the young Symonds got to accompany his father to a dinner party featuring Tennyson and Gladstone, among others, and the talk of the evening turned to race and Governor Eyre of Jamaica: "Tennyson did not argue. He kept asserting various prejudices and convictions. 'We are too tender to savages; we are more tender to a black than to ourselves.' 'Niggers are tigers; niggers are tigers,' in *obligato, sotto voce*, to Gladstone's declamation."[116]

In any event, the potential affinities between Sidgwick and Bryce, on this as on other issues, are certainly worrisome. Even if they were not completely at one on all matters, it is very hard to say just where (if at all) they would have parted company. It is also worth emphasizing in this connection that, of the two, Sidgwick was in some ways more sympathetic to, albeit worried about, the socialist future. It was Sidgwick who had taxed Bryce, in correspondence, for insisting too strongly that there was "[n]o sign of class hatred" in the forces shaping America's future: "But the formidable class hatred of the present and future is that between labour and capital: and is not the development of boycotting in U.S. and the action of the Knights of Labour, something of a sign of this?" Sidgwick explains that he would

lay more stress on the general movement towards Socialism in the modern civilised community, and which is marked in the recent economics of America – the 'Katheder Sozialisten' . . . seem to predominate. Are they likely to lead the move-ment when the time of pressure comes? And to what will they lead it? Perhaps however you are prudent in leaving out here any specific reference to the movement of ideas. (CWC)

Bryce's "prudence" extended a good deal further than this last remark suggests, since his account of the labor struggles in the United States, including even the Pullman case, was uniformly hostile to labor.

But still, having socialist or collectivist sympathies and a background in academic liberalism was no guarantee at all, during the late Victorian era, that one would be immune to racist beliefs and eugenic policy prescriptions (or to imperialistic tendencies).[117] A very wide range of figures – Balfour, the Fabian socialists, Havelock Ellis, even Bertrand

Russell and Edward Carpenter – would soon make it patently obvious that no party was unreceptive to the views of Frances Galton, and worse. Indeed, Sidgwick's connections to such figures as Seeley and Bryce are not even the most alarming ones in this respect. Another noteworthy concern is how over the course of some decades, he would warmly support the career and work of Charles Henry Pearson. Born in 1830, Pearson, who had studied at King's College, London, under F. D. Maurice, and at Oriel College, Oxford, where he became friends with John Conington and eventually a Fellow, would go on to become education minister in Victoria, Australia, and a stalwart of the Liberal Party in general. He was brought to Cambridge by Sidgwick just at the time of the latter's resignation, when the changes in the curriculum meant that Sidgwick would no longer have to teach history as part of the Moral Sciences. They would work together closely for two years and correspond for many years afterward, and Sidgwick even came to think and hope that in the mid-1870s Pearson would receive a professorship in history. At any rate, Sidgwick thought very highly of Pearson, and in a telling review, which appeared in the *National Review* in 1894, he warmly praised Pearson's book *National Life and Character*:

I will begin by remarking that prophecies are not always put forward, even by the most highly educated prophets, as based on a scientific grasp of the laws of social evolution. Indeed, in the most impressive book of a prophetic nature which has appeared in England for many years – I mean Pearson's *National Life and Character* – the prophecies are not announced with any such pretensions; they always rest on a simply empirical basis, and only distinguish themselves from the common run of such forecasts by the remarkably wide and full knowledge of relevant historical facts which the writer shows, and the masterly skill with which the facts are selected and grouped. His predictions are almost always interesting and sometimes, I think, reach a degree of probability sufficient to give them a real practical value. (MEA 219)

The distressing thing about this encomium is that Pearson's book was concerned to make such arguments as the following, in which Mill's worries about the loss of cultural vitality get transmuted into a Nietzschean mode, not that one would ever guess it from Sidgwick's review:

Summing up, then, we seem to find that we are slowly but demonstrably approaching what we may regard as the age of reason or of a sublimated humanity; and that this will give us a great deal that we are expecting from it – well-ordered

polities, security to labour, education, freedom from gross superstitions, improved
health and longer life, the destruction of privilege in society and of caprice in family life, better guarantees for the peace of the world, and enforced regard for
life and property when war unfortunately breaks out. It is possible to conceive
the administration of the most advanced states so equitable and efficient that
no-one will even desire seriously to disturb it. On the other hand, it seems reasonable to assume that religion will gradually pass into a recognition of ethical
precepts and a graceful habit of morality; that the mind will occupy itself less and
less with works of genius, and more and more with trivial results and ephemeral
discussions; that husband and wife, parents and children, will come to mean less
to one another; that romantic feeling will die out in consequence; that the old
will increase on the young; that two great incentives to effort, the desire to use
power for noble ends, and the desire to be highly esteemed, will come to promise
less to capable men as the field of human energy is crowded; and generally that
the world will be left without deep convictions or enthusiasm, without the re-
generating influence of the ardour for political reform and the fervour of pious
faith which have quickened men for centuries past as nothing else has quickened
them, with a passion purifying the soul. It would clearly be unreasonable to murmur at changes that express the realisation by the world of its highest thought,
whether the issue be good or bad. The etiolated religion which it seems likely we
shall subside upon; the complicated but on the whole satisfactory State mech-
anism, that will prescribe education, limit industry, and direct enjoyment, will
become, when they are once arrived at, natural and satisfactory. The decline of
the higher classes as an influence in society, the organisation of the inferior race
throughout the Tropical Zone, are the natural result of principles that we cannot
disown if we would. It would be impossible for a conservatively-minded monarch
to reconstruct the nobility of the eighteenth century in the twentieth; and even
now no practical statesman could dream of arresting Chinese power or Hindoo
or negro expansion by wholesale massacres. The world is becoming too fibre-
less, too weak, too good to contemplate or to carry out great changes which imply
lamentable suffering. It trusts more and more to experience, less and less to insight
and will.

An admirer of Nietzsche and Ibsen, Pearson frets endlessly about the
fate of a society of weak men, a society that "has no purpose beyond
supplying the day's needs, and amusing the day's vacuity." What has such
a society "to do with the terrible burden of personality?" But there "seems
no reason why men of this kind should not perpetuate the race, increasing
and multiplying till every rod of earth maintains its man, and the savour
of vacant lives will go up to God from every home."[118]

The precise nature of the human predicament, according to Pearson, has everything to do with race:

Even during historical times, so-called, the world has mostly been peopled by races, either like the negro very little raised above the level of brutes, or at best, like the lower-caste Hindoo and the Chinaman, of such secondary intelligence as to have added nothing permanent to our stock of ideas. At this moment, though the civilised and progressive races have till quite recently been increasing upon the inferior types, and though the lowest forms of all are being exterminated, there seems, as we have seen, good warrant for assuming that the advantage has already passed to the lower forms of humanity, and indeed it appears to be a well-ascertained law that the races which care little for comfort and decency are bound to tide over bad times better than their superiors, and that the classes which reach the highest standard are proportionally short-lived. Nay, so profusely is life given in excess of what we can account the efficient use made of it, so many purposeless generations seem to pass away before humanity is in travail of a prophet or a thinker, that some inquirers have actually defined the method of creation as a law of waste.[119]

Pearson is willing to console the reader with invocations of the Norse "twilight of the gods" as the possible future, when, although there may be a "temporary eclipse of the higher powers," even the losing struggle is a kind of vindication. This Nietzschean thought continues:

We are so accustomed to the fierce rapture of struggle and victory, to that rough training of necessity by which the weak are destroyed, to revolutions of the political order, transferences of power and wealth, and discoveries in science, that we can hardly conceive a quiet old age of humanity, in which it may care only for sunshine and food and quiet, and expect nothing great from the toil of hand or thought.... It is now more than probable that our science, our civilisation, our great and real advance in the practice of government are only bringing us nearer to the day when the lower races will predominate in the world, when the higher races will lose their noblest elements, when we shall ask nothing from the day but to live, nor from the future but that we may not deteriorate. Even so, there will still remain to us ourselves. Simply to do our work in life, and to abide the issue, if we stand erect before the eternal calm as cheerfully as our fathers faced the eternal unrest, may be nobler training for our souls than the faith in progress.[120]

Pearson's passionate racism makes Sidgwick's concern with colonization and manual labor look singularly suspicious, as though his doubts about progress and faith in federation and the "Concert of Europe" might have reflected an all-too-conservative faith in a saving remnant of civilization holding out against the peril of the "lower races." After all, his views on the difficulty of determining what made for scientific and cultural change and development certainly left a very wide field for alternative explanations, such as Pearson's. And it is all too clear what Pearson has in mind, given his account of the attitudes that he deems overly complacent:

No one, of course, assumes that the Aryan race – to use a convenient term – can stamp out or starve out all their rivals on the face of the earth. It is self-evident that the Chinese, the Japanese, the Hindoos, if we may apply this general term to the various natives of India, and the African negro, are too numerous and sturdy to be extirpated. It is against the fashion of modern humanity to wish that they should suffer decrease or oppression. What is assumed is that the first three of these races will remain stationary within their present limits, while the negro will contribute an industrial population to the states which England and Germany will build up along the Congo or the Zambesi. The white man in these parts of the world is to be the planter, the mine-owner, the manufacturer, the merchant, and the leading employee under all these, contributing energy and capital to the new countries, while the negro is to be the field-hand, the common miner, and the factory operative. Here and there, in exceptional districts, the white man will predominate in numbers, but everywhere he will govern and direct in virtue of a higher intelligence and more resolute will.[121]

Pearson is insistent that the "character of a race determines its vitality more than climate," and he strikes a pessimistic note, arguing that the day will come when the globe is "girdled with a continuous zone of the black and yellow races, no longer too weak for aggression or under tutelage, but independent, or practically so. . . . The citizens of these countries will then be taken up into the social relations of the white races, will throng the English turf, or the salons of Paris, and will be admitted to intermarriage. It is idle to say, that if all this should come to pass our pride of place will not be humiliated." As Pearson elaborates on this vision, those who had been struggling "for supremacy in a world which we thought of as destined to belong to the Aryan races and to the Christian faith" will wake up to find themselves "elbowed and hustled, and perhaps even thrust aside by peoples whom we looked down upon as servile, and thought of as bound always to minister to our needs." Against the "solitary consolation" that the changes were "inevitable," he confesses that "in some of us the feeling of caste is so strong that we are not sorry to think we shall have passed away before that day arrives."[122]

And Pearson's worries about an evolution toward socialism that amounts to a triumph of base security and mediocrity – the contented herd – are connected with his interpretation of the global drift. The "lower races" are multiplying more rapidly than the higher, and the greater humanity of war favors them. This forecloses certain outlets for domestic unrest:

More and more as we approach the stationary state – as there are no countries to receive immigrants; as war is more and more dreaded for its chances, or recoiled from for its barbarity; as commerce and invention are restricted because there are no new regions to open up – will the old outlets for discontent or unsatisfied ambition be closed. What are now the governing classes will have to arrange reasonable compromises, by which the condition of the poor is made endurable. It may be that there will be less enthusiasm in those days, because there will be less hope; but it may be assumed that there will be less misery, more resignation, and it may even be more content.[123]

There is of course a great deal of romanticism in Pearson's lament for greatness, which on many points sounds very like Myers's views on the decline of genius, or at least on the declining appreciation of it (a point Freud would later adopt wholesale). But in this case, as Harvie rightly observes, the "persistent re-statement of the inferiority of the coloured races did much to stimulate 'yellow peril' agitation and 'white Australia' policies. As a convinced and hard-working radical, his assessment of the tendencies making for collectivism was shrewd and not unsympathetic; but the book was penetrated by searing, pessimistic judgements about the consequences for human personality of such development."[124] Could this really be the book that Sidgwick deemed "the most impressive book of a prophetic nature which has appeared in England for many years"?

Lest there be any underestimating just what was behind Harvie's still much-too-delicately-put charge, consider how in Pearson's very Introduction he defensively explains:

The fear of Chinese immigration which the Australian democracy cherishes, and which Englishmen at home find it hard to understand, is, in fact, the instinct of self-preservation, quickened by experience. We know that coloured and white labour cannot exist side by side; we are well aware that China can swamp us with a single year's surplus of population; and we know that if national existence is sacrificed to the working of a few mines and sugar plantations, it is not the Englishman in Australia alone, but the whole civilised world, that will be the losers. Transform the Northern half of our continent into a Natal with thirteen out of fourteen belonging to an inferior race, and the Southern half will speedily approximate to the condition of a Cape Colony, where the whites are indeed a masterful minority, but still only as one in four. We are guarding the last part of the world, in which the higher races can live and increase freely, for the higher civilisation. We are denying the yellow race nothing but what it will find in the home of its birth, or in countries like the Indian Archipelago, where the white man can never live except as an exotic.

If, however, the white race is precluded by natural laws from colonising on a large scale anywhere except in the Temperate Zone, it seems certain that the condition of old countries will be powerfully modified. The eager and impetuous element that has hitherto found an outlet in new communities, will be pent up in the overpeopled countries of Europe.[125]

The book had actually opened with a half-lament that the contemporary statesman confines his attention too much to the immediate future, even though his forecasts of this are often more misguided than his longer-term visions – thus, "the transportation of an inferior race, like the negroes of the United States, to a country where they would be harmless, is too vast, and of too uncertain benefit, to be readily attempted."

Pearson makes little mention of Bryce or Sidgwick; he smugly cites the former on how the United States has increasingly limited the influx of Chinese immigrants, and the latter on the obscurity of the notion of patriotism, the duties of which would bear on the morality of "voluntary expatriation," a subject obviously close to his heart after his move to Australia.

But in his contribution to *Charles Henry Pearson: Memorials by Himself, His Wife, and His Friends*, Sidgwick makes it perfectly evident not only that he knew Pearson very well and thought highly of him, but also that the general drift of Pearson's thinking was evident even back in his somewhat more optimistic Cambridge period.

It may be noticed that I have said little that is definite of Pearson's opinions, political, sociological, or theological. The fact is that, though I had much interesting
talk with him on these subjects, the impression derived therefrom has become, in
the main, blended with or obliterated by the impression derived, more than twenty
years later, from his remarkable book on 'National Life and Character'; so that I
could not now hope to reproduce it with any accuracy. I can only say generally
that many of the startling conclusions of that book were certainly held by him at
the earlier date, though his tendency to pessimistic forecast seemed to me to have
grown stronger in the interval. One point I seem to remember clearly: he used to

talk forebodingly of the probable results of the removal of the barriers that now separate European and Chinese civilisations; but I do not think he then conceived the danger as at all political, but as solely economical. Centuries of keen struggle for existence, he argued, had made the Chinaman a more economical machine for most kinds of work than the European. Thrifty, industrious, and tolerant of privations, he would successfully underbid the European in industrial competition; so that, if the then Liberal ideal of open competition were maintained, the human world would gradually become mainly yellow, with a black band round the tropics, and perhaps an aristocratic film of white on the surface![126]

Thus, when Sidgwick was doing his best to keep his "catch," Pearson, in Cambridge, teaching history in the new curriculum, he was not under any misconceptions about his views. Indeed, he thought that Pearson was a most impressive intellect and a warmly sympathetic friend, though he did observe that he "was certainly one of the small class of persons whose practical adhesion to their convictions is only made more resolute by its colliding with popular sentiment or with self-interest; the position of 'Athanasius contra mundum' would certainly always have had an attraction for him." He was, Sidgwick noted, deploying "an Anglo–Indian phrase then current," a man "to go tiger-hunting with." He

had little respect for prevalent prejudices, he had a great respect for facts; he was always self-critical as well as critical of others, and alert and disengaged in the collection and valuation of evidence on all sides of any question in which he was interested speculatively or practically. He was even circumspect in the sense of being anxious to avoid contests on badly chosen grounds; and the enthusiasm for human progress, which was strong in him, was kept in check by his intellectual habit of steadily and clearly distinguishing his ideals and aspirations from his expectations.[127]

Sidgwick was especially impressed by the patient, minutely detailed arguments that Pearson marshalled to demonstrate why France was bound to win in the Franco–Prussian War, a belief that only final crushing defeat managed to shake.

Bryce, too, was counted amongst Pearson's friends, and his contribution to the memorials recalls how Pearson had been regarded as "one of the most brilliant men of an unusually brilliant generation" at Oxford, and how he was "a strong Liberal, advocating University Reform and the abolition of university tests, as well as most of the political measures, as, for instance, for the extension of the suffrage, which the Liberal Party had taken up." It was to Bryce that Pearson sent the syllabus of *National Life and Character*, in order to help him find a publisher. "The firm to which I showed it accepted it at once, struck, no doubt, as I had been, by the breadth and power with which the subject had been conceived."[128]

After the book appeared, Pearson sent Sidgwick a complimentary copy, to which gesture the latter replied:

> I am much obliged to you for sending me your book which I am reading with much interest. When I find myself too depressed by it, I console myself by thinking that sociology is not yet an exact science, so that the powers of prediction possessed by the wisest intellect are limited.
>
> I am glad to see that the reviews are giving you justice – so far as I see them.[129]

Set in this context, Sidgwick's tergiversating abstraction starts to look much less like cool agnosticism or impartiality. It is impossible to imagine Mill, say, reading Pearson or even Bryce with so much admiration and so little indignation. To the degree that he thought Pearson indicated the likely direction of scientific progress on racial matters, and posed the right research agenda, his skeptical resistance would appear to have had little practical consequence. How could Sidgwick and Bryce have been so warmly respectful of Pearson's claims? Bryce himself had warned that just as

> there are historians and politicians who, when they come across a trait of national character for which no obvious explanation presents itself, set it down to 'race,' so there are writers and speakers who, too indolent to examine the whole facts of the case, or too ill-trained to feel the need of such examination, pounce upon the political institutions of a country as the easiest way to account for its social and intellectual, perhaps even for its moral and religious peculiarities.[130]

But Pearson's views were apparently thought to be well within the orbit of competent authority. In fact, at many points, they may well have over-lapped with those of Balfour (who, incidentally, was the one who could be credited with injecting the new imperialist ideas into the Tory Party). When in 1908, the former prime minister undertook to deliver the Henry Sidgwick Memorial Lecture at Newnham College, he used the occasion to speak to the theme of "Decadence." The type of decadence he considered was that which infected the Roman Empire – "the decadence which attacks, or is alleged to attack, great communities and historic civilisations: which is to societies of men what senility is to man, and is often like senility,

the precursor and the cause of final dissolution." This is the type of decadence, or degeneration, that occurs when "through an ancient and still
powerful state, there spreads a mood of deep discouragement, when the
reaction to recurring ills grows feebler, and the ship rises less buoyantly
to each succeeding wave, when learning languishes, enterprise slackens,
and vigour ebbs away."[131]

Balfour worried that Western European civilization might not be quite
as lucky as the Roman Empire. If cultural advance in these states "is some
day exhausted, who can believe that there remains any external source
from which it can be renewed? Where are the untried races competent to
construct out of the ruined fragments of our civilisation a new and better
habitation for the spirit of man?" The inexorable conclusion, of course, is:
"They do not exist; and if the world is again to be buried under a barbaric
flood, it will not be like that which fertilised, though it first destroyed, the
western provinces of Rome, but like that which in Asia submerged forever
the last races of Hellenic culture." Thus, he would emphatically not infer
that "when some wave of civilisation has apparently spent its force, we
have a right to regard its withdrawing sweep as but the prelude to a new
advance."

True, in conclusion Balfour strikes the requisite hopeful note:

[W]e cannot regard decadence and arrested development as less normal in human
communities than progress; though the point at which the energy of advance is exhausted (if, and when, it is reached) varies in different races and civilisations. . . . as
regards those nations which still advance in virtue of their own inherent energies,
though time has brought perhaps new causes of disquiet, it has brought also new
grounds of hope. . . . there are so far, no symptoms either of pause or of regres-
sion in the onward movement which for more than a thousand years has been
characteristic of western civilisation.[132]

And Balfour makes a strong Sidgwickian case for science, as a new
force on the horizon the advance of which is not easily explained, though
he of course is not one to suppose that science could prove ultimately
satisfying to the religious consciousness of ordinary people. Democracy
too is addressed, and finds its due place as a regulative force in at least
some modern societies. But though the forward movement of humanity
"may be controlled or checked by the many; it is initiated and made
effective by the few," which was why it is a good thing that even in the
advanced societies there is, in terms of mental capacity, "a majority slightly

below the average and a minority much above it." He denies that "any attempt to provide widely different races with an identical environment, political, religious, education, what you will, can ever make them alike. They have been different and unequal since history began; different and unequal they are destined to remain through future periods of considerable duration."

Balfour's Sidgwick Lecture found a fascinated and receptive audience in the person of the president of the United States, the Bull Moose Progressive Teddy Roosevelt. Roosevelt, who had fond memories of Balfour as the man who kept England from interfering in the Spanish American War, agreed heartily with much of what his British friend had to say. He had "ugly doubts as to what may befall our modern civilisation" and thought it an "irritating delusion" that there would necessarily be forward progress, about which there was nothing inevitable or necessary. In writing to Balfour, Roosevelt explained that "[i]t is equally to the interest of the British empire and of the United States that there should be no immigration in mass from Asia to Australia or North America. It can be prevented, and an entirely friendly feeling between Japan and the English speaking people preserved, if we act with sufficient courtesy and at the same time with sufficient resolution."[133]

As Kenneth Young observes, it was quite possibly this letter from Roosevelt that "decided Balfour early in 1909 to put some of his most cherished and far-seeing ideas on the future before the President. Among the Royal papers there is a very remarkable document headed 'The Possibility of an Anglo–Saxon Confederation,' " which was apparently sent to Roosevelt. In it, Balfour outlined the necessity for England and America to confront the twentieth century as firm allies, insisting that disarmament was a dream, that a few nations were bound to control the world, and that peace would come "only when these powers have divided the world between them." He worried about the expansion of Russia and Germany, but as for most of Africa, it will never be the "home of whites," being already possessed by "many millions of an inferior black race with whom white men cannot live and work on equal terms," and besides, "the climate is not suitable for hard manual labour." Thus, the "progressive races" might develop some commerce or military installations, but in the main, "It will be given over to the negro and, in the North East, to the Mohammedans."[134] Still, such underpopulated areas as Australia and South Africa were desirable: "Not until these countries are more thickly populated than they are today can their future as Anglo–Saxon states be assured, unless they are protected by a power invincible at sea."

As Young suggests, here we find Balfour's real thoughts about the empire. He held that the "future for a rapidly overpopulating Britain, equally rapidly becoming completely unself-supporting, lay in closer integration with the Empire," but the problem was that – support the navy though he did – there could scarcely be an "invincible" sea power.[135] Balfour's point was that the United States and Britain should federate in order to "be a more than equal counterpoise to the other great nations of the future and also partly in order to secure to them the undisputed possession and development of the still thinly populated areas of the world." Otherwise, they will end in conflict, and to what end? "If England and America do not federate, the history of the world will continue to be one of warfare, for a number of world powers will be competing for the supremacy," but if they unite, they will "be beyond attack."[136]

Whatever Balfour's prescience by way of anticipating the political configurations of the twentieth century (his scheme barely got beyond the theorizing stage), the crucial point is that he sounds very much like an advocate of "spiritual expansion" who had read his Seeley and Pearson and been tutored in the dangers of philosophical doubt. That so much of his vision was contained in his memorial lecture for Sidgwick is surely revealing, if alarming. The deep-seated prejudice that it reveals – a smug bigotry that must have been a fixture of Sidgwick's home life, when off at 4 Carlton Gardens, or Whittingehame, or Terling Place – cannot help but make one wonder whether Sidgwick himself was ever really as agnostic as his publications would make him sound. Was this more "prudence," as with Bryce's evasion of the issue of labor strife?

Just how evasive Sidgwick's prophesying could be is evident from that review essay on Pearson. It is a singular Mauricean performance. For after praising the book as the "most impressive book," and so on, Sidgwick goes on to make it clear that this is not a field governed by high standards of impressiveness. Thus, although Pearson's views are not like the sweeping claims of positivists and Marxists concerning the laws of social evolution, and "rest on a simple empirical basis" made impressive by a "remarkably wide and full knowledge of relevant historical facts," and although his "predictions are almost always interesting, and sometimes . . . reach a degree of probability sufficient to give them real practical value," still, Sidgwick continues, there is "no book which brings

home to one more forcibly the imperfection of all such empirical forecasts."
(MEA 219–20). As Sidgwick explains, predictions of the direction of social change "may be classed under two heads, in respect of the general
procedure employed in them: they either proceed on the assumption that
what is will continue to be, or that what has happened will happen again."
Each procedure may have its place, under proper conditions, but each
also has its own imperfections. Sidgwick of course recognizes that these
familiar assumptions would be hard to do without, and that for a good
many purposes – say, predicting how many children will be born a year
hence – they serve well enough, especially given the increasing sophistication of statistical forecasting. Still, the "best knowledge of history, even
if confined to current history, prevents us from accepting the proposition that what has been will be, in its crudest form, in which it excludes
change," and it is in the subtler shape of expecting a process of change
to "continue in the same direction" that it is liable to be abused. Indeed,
Pearson relied on it "somewhat too much," and in doing so, got tripped up
on the other assumption that what has happened before will happen again.
Thus,

> Mr. Pearson found that in the last twenty years – I do not think that the ex-
> perience on which he based his forecast goes farther back – the functions of
> Government have shown a tendency to expand (especially in the colony of
> Victoria): he also found that the influence of religion has shown a tendency
> to diminish, especially the belief in a future life, which our age tends to re-
> gard as 'nothing more than a fanciful and unimportant probability': and, as-
> suming these tendencies to continue, he predicted certain depressing effects on
> national life and character. Now, the tendency to Socialism is undeniable; and
> I am not prepared to deny that a drift to secularism is traceable in what may
> be in a wide sense called the educated classes; and I should quite agree with
> Mr. Pearson, that if both tendencies together continue operating long enough
> they are likely to affect our national character very seriously. But I hesitate to infer
> confidently that this effect will be produced, when I reflect how short a time it is
> since a more fully developed Individualism seemed to thoughtful minds 'in the
> van of progress,' and how impossible it would practically have been to prophesy
> on empirical grounds any of the revivals of religious sentiment that have taken
> place during the history of Christianity. (MEA 221–22)

Sidgwick proceeds by hauling out his favorite target, Herbert Spencer,
observing that Spencer "formed, before 1850, the opinion that a completed Individualism was the ultimate goal of human progress; and to this

opinion he remains true in 1894, regarding the Socialistic drift of the last twenty years as a lamentable temporary divergence from the true and main movement of political thought and fact." Moreover, against any too-ready acceptance concerning the drift toward secularism, Sidgwick rhetorically asks whether it is "not a historical commonplace that the tendency towards a practically secular view of human life has rarely been more marked than it was in the educated class – including the clergy of the most civilised country in Europe – in the age that preceded Luther?" (MEA 222)

The point, Sidgwick explains, is that "prophecies, based on analogous historic cases" are always "very imperfect," and though the history of civilization is a history of change that is usually gradual, the change is "still sufficiently rapid to establish profound differences between any two stages separated by a considerable interval of time." These doubts and cautionaries – quintessential Sidgwick – lead him back to the question of whether we have any real knowledge of the "fundamental laws of social evolution as a whole," since "only a positive answer to this question can justify us in confidently forecasting the future of society for any considerable way ahead." And of course, Pearson's claims had rested on precisely this argument, to the effect that it was often easier to forecast the big developments of social evolution than the nearer and more specific future. "Fortunately," Sidgwick argues, concerning whether there really is any science of social dynamics worthy of the name, "there is a simple criterion of the effective establishment of a science – laid down by the original and powerful thinker who must certainly be regarded as the founder of the science of society, if there is such a science – the test of Consensus of experts and Continuity of scientific work." This criterion, derived from Comte, shows "that the social science is not yet effectively constructed – at least so far as the department of 'social dynamics' is concerned – since it is certain that every writer on the subject starts *de novo* and builds on his own foundation." (MEA 224)

Curiously, amazingly, Sidgwick does not directly address Pearson's racialist claims.[137] One could read his review without appreciating what Pearson's fundamental worry actually was. Yet, with what were apparently Pearson's most firmly grounded claims now skilfully undercut, the reader is left to imagine the havoc that Sidgwick's considerations could make with them. And what Sidgwick does do is to delicately divert attention to a work on *Social Evolution* by Benjamin Kidd, which serves as the object of a thoroughly effective, highly sarcastic assault on the mingling of biology and sociology. In fact, Kidd comes off as the kind of singularly moronic camp follower of social Darwinism that the Spencers and Comtes had left in their wake. Kidd is like a youthful student of history who gets carried away by – infatuated with – vast generalizations, generalizations that more mature study would end up loading "with qualifications and reserves." When it comes to the

> general moral superiority of the Anglo–Saxon in his dealings with inferior races –
> I think that any Anglo–Saxon who will study with strict impartiality the 'wretched
> details of ferocity and treachery which have marked the conduct of civilised men
> in their relations with savages,' is not likely to rise from the study thanking heaven
> that he is not a Frenchman or a Spaniard; but rather with a humble hope that the
> page of history recording these details is now turned for West-European nations
> generally, and that the future historian of the Europeanisation of Africa will have
> a different tale to tell. (MEA 231–32)

And the inevitable conclusion is, of course: "Scientific prevision of this kind will perhaps be ultimately attained, as the slow fruit of long years of labour yet to come; – but even that is one of the things which it would be rash confidently to predict."

Yet it is very difficult to know just what to make of this piece. Why did Sidgwick avoid all mention of race? More Brycean prudence? Another Mauricean dodge? After all, if Sidgwick casts aspersions on the supposed moral superiority of Anglo–Saxons, he nonetheless still assumes that they are dealing with "inferior races." If he hopes that the Europeanization of Africa will not be a repeat of the Europeanization of, say, America, he nonetheless accepts the legitimacy of the Europeanization of Africa. Against Pearson, or other segregationists, Sidgwick would quite clearly insist on affording the "inferior races" every opportunity to "prove" themselves, particularly via education. But they would still be proving themselves, and the education would still be that designed by Sidgwick and his colleagues. This is at the least highly Eurocentric, and quite possibly racist. And if Bryce could contemplate the possibility of permanent segregation in the United States, and Pearson do likewise with respect to Australia, both of them duly impressing Sidgwick with their work, how candid could the *Elements* have been, in stating that exclusion from the franchise on grounds of race was a question for political societies "necessarily different from that which has been generally contemplated in the discussions of the present treatise"?

For despite his doubts, how could Sidgwick have said what he said, without being all-too-impressed by Pearson's quasi-Nietszchean perfectionist remnant and Balfour's racial progressivism and brutal attitudes? Is this not simply another facet – or possible facet – of the much-sought-after, reinvigorating new religion?

A fundamental question remains, however. It is very far from plain that these different figures actually held anything even faintly resembling a coherent biological notion of race,[138] or even the same one, however confused. Balfour's notion of race, for instance, was an odd mix of Lamarckian speculation and ethnic bigotry, linked to a virtually mystical notion of national character. And Bryce, in his 1902 Romanes Lecture on "The Relations of the Advanced and Backward Races of Mankind," at least admitted that "[a]ll the great peoples of the world are the result of a mixing of races" and allowed that some "of the races now deemed backward may show a capacity for intellectual and moral progress greater than they have been credited with. The differences between them and the advanced races lie not so much in intelligence as in force of will and tenacity of purpose."[139] True, he again seemed to envision the possible advisability of permanent segregation in some cases, and to view race repulsion as virtually ineradicable. Upon revisiting the United States in later years, however, he was led to produce an additional chapter, "Further Reflections on the Negro Problem," in which his old views were further moderated. Now, he held that the progress of blacks was indisputable, and if there was something to the claim that they were inefficient workers, the cause was probably environmental. He was much moved by DuBois's *The Souls of Black Folk*, and he concluded by wondering, when "the sentiment of a common humanity has so grown and improved within a century as to destroy slavery everywhere, may it not be that a like sentiment will soften the bitterness of race friction also?"[140]

Consider in this context a most illuminating letter from Dicey to Bryce, dated Christmas 1901, which conveys in short compass a keen sense of the shifting utilitarian perspective on race:

Your subject for the Romanes Lectures which I am delighted to hear you are going to deliver is an excellent one. "The Contest Between Civilized and Uncivilized Races" is perhaps the most important of the time and will become more and more important as the century goes on and happily as yet it has not become a party question. Accidental circumstances have recently called my attention to it.

There is a terrible danger that, as we cannot talk of human equality with the same confidence with which the best men of the 18th and the earlier 19th century spoke of it, and as we are compelled to attach more importance than they did to race, we may come to give up faith in the truth, of which I think they had a firm hold, that the qualities which races have in common are at least as important as (I should say more important than) the characteristics in which they differ. Then the whole matter is complicated to my mind by the growth of an idea, which I think may be true that the races with different ideals and different moralities had best live apart. I cannot myself feel at all sure that the cry for a "White Australia" is not at bottom a sound one. But all I want at present to urge is the great advantage of your taking up this topic and dealing with it in your lecture.[141]

Dicey, the old Benthamite, here regretfully insists on the increasing importance of race as a political issue, expressing some doubts as to whether Pearson might not be right about keeping Australia white. But this comes as part of a congratulatory message to Bryce for his willingness to tackle head-on a baffling subject that needs thinking through, made the more poignant by the manifest confusion of race with something closer to ethnic identity.

Perhaps something akin to these Diceyan and Brycean notes are important for considering Sidgwick, marking as they do the slightly more moderate, slightly more agnostic attitude amid a veritable sea of grotesque prejudice. Indeed, Sidgwick goes well beyond all these figures in keeping matters of race far in the background, and this may well have been, not only the retreat to the private sphere described by Hobsbawm, but also, at least in part, that characteristic Sidgwickian silence when doubtful. If his doubts did not end up effectively neutralizing his racist presuppositions, they at least moderated them somewhat.

The most straightforward comments that Sidgwick makes on the subject would seem to support this reading. Thus, crucially, *The Development of European Polity* does not contain any specific projections about race to speak of, though surely this is where Sidgwick would have put them, out of all his major works. He does discuss the future of federation, with an eye to Home Rule, explaining how in Croatia

there has been since 1872 a separate Parliament which legislates on a part of those matters that are *not* regarded as common to the whole of the territories of the Hungarian Crown, the rest of such matters being legislated on in the Hungarian Parliament at Buda Pest, to which Croatia sends deputies; the Croatian deputies voting in the Hungarian Parliament not on all matters, but only on such matters as are not legislated on separately in the Croatian Parliament. (DEP 428)

There is much disputing with Maine over the evolution of patriarchy, custom, and law in ancient Greece and Rome, but China, India, Africa, and even Australia are nearly absent even as counterpoints. There is the stock point – "competent judges hold that it might have prevented serious mistakes in our government of India, if the governing statesmen had had before their minds the historical development of land-tenure, as we now conceive it to have taken place in European countries" – which Sidgwick repeated in a half-dozen different works to illustrate how the past might afford "instructive analogies." But there is little effort to demonstrate any serious familiarity with non-European states or any serious reliance on the concept of race, after the manner of Pearson. The reason for this is embedded in the very structure of the book. As Sidgwick explains in his opening chapter, he is going to confine his attention "mainly to the political institutions of the ancient Greeks and Romans, and of Western Europe and its colonies in post-Roman times." Thus,

Though there are societies – groups of gregarious men – in which the 'differenti-ation' into governors and governed is barely perceptible, such societies constitute a very insignificant portion of humanity: it is almost universally true that a man is a 'political animal' in the sense of being either ruler or ruled, either obeying or constituting a government of some kind. But there is a sense in which *higher* polit-ical development has originated almost exclusively in, and is still mainly confined to certain portions of the white, or – as some still call it – Causcasian race. They alone have developed, along with the development of their civilisation, governing organs of which the members are accustomed 'to rule and obey alternately' – whether (1) the supreme ruler is merely elected by the citizens for a limited time, and then gives up power and may be formally called to account for his exercise of it, or (2) the supreme rule is in whole or in part exercised collectively by a body of citizens meeting from time to time.

In the history of political institutions these forms interest us most, not only as citizens of a modern West-European State, but as students of Political Science: just as the highest forms of life have a special interest for the biologist. I shall accordingly confine my attention mainly to the nations who have shown a power of developing them. And among them the most important and conspicuous of those whose history is known to us are certainly the Greeks, Romans, and West-Europeans. They stand pre-eminent among the civilised portions of humanity as having developed, up to the highest point that their civilisation has yet reached, not only political *ins*titutions, but *constitutions* and constitutional ideas and theories. (DEP 9)

Obviously Sidgwick is here simply taking for granted the prejudices of his time, since he plainly knew nothing whatsoever of, say, the Iroquois nation or the Arapesh. Yet what is noteworthy, in addition, is that he is working with a fairly etiolated biology of race, comparatively speaking, such that few features of "national character" appear to be attributable to it. *Development* in fact gives one of Sidgwick's clearest and most extensive statements on the subject:

Some explanation is required of these notions of 'race' and 'family of nations.' Firstly, in speaking of the 'white race,' I do not mean to imply that there are four or five original stocks of human beings, distinguishable by colour and other marks, as 'white,' 'brown,' 'yellow,' and 'black' races. In the present state of anthropology there is no ground for assuming any such original differences of stocks; and the physical differences actually existing are more numerous and complicated, and shade off into each other more gradually, than the popular nomenclature suggests. And since all varieties of human beings are zoologically of one species – inter-marriage between any two generally producing fertile offspring – the physical differences of race historically presented may be to an indefinite extent referable to crossing of breeds. A special instance of this is perhaps presented by the marked differences we find between the fair whites, prevalent in Northern Europe, and the dark whites prevalent in Southern Europe and parts of Asia; – as the latter are considered by leading anthropologists to be probably due to a crossing of the fair whites with a darker race. It is to be observed that this distinction cuts across that which Comparative Philology would lead us to draw between Aryan or Indo-Germanic and Semitic nations; and this illustrates another uncertainty in which the application of the notion of 'race' is involved, from the difficulty of separating, among the mental characteristics that distinguish average members of different societies, what comes from physical heredity and what from social influence. In consequence of this affinities of language are a very imperfect guide to affinities of race. Hence, in speaking of the 'Indo-Germanic family of nations,' I must not be understood to imply that the nations thus grouped together are all physically derived from one stock; but only that they are connected with one ancient social group by a continuous social life, evidenced by continuity of language and at least partly due to continuity of race.

At the same time there are certain broad distinctions of physical race which have remained nearly permanent during the range of history. As Mr. Tylor says, on the wall-paintings at Thebes we can distinguish red-brown Egyptians, Ethiopians like those of the present day, captives from Palestine with the well-known Semitic profile, thick-lipped negroes, and fair-skinned Libyans. And these examples may remind us that civilisation is not a monopoly of the white race, in the widest sense of that term. 'At the dawn of history, the leaders of culture were the brown Egyptians, and the Babylonians,' whose language is not connected with any known language of white nations; while the yellow Mongoloid Chinese have been 'for four thousand years or more a civilised and literary nation.' The civilisation that spread round the Mediterranean was not originated by the dark whites – Phoenicians, Greeks, Romans – but only carried on by them. Still we may perhaps say that higher *political* civilisation, the capacity for developing constitutional government in a *civilised state*, belongs primarily to the white race; and mainly to branches of the white race which speak an Indo-Germanic language, and therefore show a partial continuity of descent from one single original group. (DEP 12–13)

Sidgwick goes on to address the importance of climate and geography in shaping peoples, roughly following the line shared with Bryce. The primary source of any racial pride that he is willing to record, in this highly tentative and ambivalent way, thus concerns the European development of liberal constitutionalism.

These distinctions between race, civilization, and political civilization would seem to be of some importance for appreciating the particulars of Sidgwick's position. He had long been sharply critical of those who pronounced in too-dogmatic fashion on just where civilization was to be found. Of special note is an 1872 review of Lord Ormathwaite's *Astronomy and Geology Compared* – one of the tartest things Sidgwick ever wrote – in which he complains of the "lucid and well-bred tediousness" of the "store of platitudes" by which the author attempts to challenge Darwin. But the "climax of complacent commonplace" is only reached when Ormathwaite tries to show "how entirely progress and civilization have been confined to the European branch of the human race." According to him, Asiatic nations "never seem to have been inspired by any of the loftier motives which animate Europeans" – they cannot "recognize among them patriotism, or honour, or moral principle" and seem never to have "possessed any body of works worthy to be termed a literature." For such ignorance Sidgwick can scarcely conceal his scorn: the problem with the book arises "entirely from the matter."

If only he had continued the thought.

As noted earlier, both Bryce and Dicey thought that many of Sidgwick's friends were slightly surprised by *Development*. Eleanor Sidgwick had consulted both of them, and Leslie Stephen, on the publication of it, and they were enthusiastic in recommending it. In fact, Bryce went so far as to write that in "the main principles or statements of fact there was nothing to differ from," and that he was especially impressed by Sidgwick's treatment of Rome – a subject on which, of course, Bryce had written extensively.[142]

Perhaps enough has now been said to indicate the more worrisome peculiarities of Sidgwick's description of himself as a political "independent, with Tory sympathies." As the nineteenth century wore on, he was more and more out of sync with political developments and more and more worried about the direction of civilization, even as he was ever more entangled with such matters. The great mystery is how he could have been so alienated and so skeptical and yet remain so supremely confident in the moral mission of English civilization, which in the end he prized mainly for its political institutions and greater emphasis on science. Clearly, at the least, he warmly entertained far too many possibilites when it came to the future of race and rule, relations between "higher" and "lower" civilizations, and a vigorous new aristocracy. His agnosticism did not lean far enough in the right direction – did not, that is to say, push him far enough toward a truly critical engagement with the concept of "Race." Vermicular skepticism might have served him and his students very well.

8

Last Words?

Never, surely, was the English mind so confused, so wanting in fixed moral principles, as at present.

> Sir John Seeley, "Ethics and Religion," paper delivered to the
> Cambridge Ethical Society in 1888[1]

I share to the full the general disillusionment of political idealists, perhaps all the
more fully that I am spending my time in trying to finish a book on the Theory
of Politics, with a growing conviction that the political results of the coming
generation will be determined by considerations very unlike those that come to
the pen of a theoretical person writing in his study.

> Sidgwick to A. J. Patterson, December 27, 1889 (M 504)

The brutalism that was reviving in Europe was displayed most grimly in the
'Congo Free State' sanctioned by the Berlin Conference on Africa in 1885, and
from then until 1908 a private empire of King Leopold of the Belgians. Here
could be seen private enterprise at its worst, free from all public inquiry or
check, and the new plutocracy at its glossiest, with a royal manager. Its devi-
ous origins show how missionary zeal, like all Europe's better impulses, could be
exploited by money-grubbers. A titular Archbishop of Carthage launched with
papal approval a campaign for stronger action against slave-trading; he invited
Christian soldiers to volunteer, and dreamed of a new order of knights-errant.
Leopold encouraged the idea, and when his 'Free State' was set up humanitarians
rejoiced.

His agent for the preliminary spadework or collection of 'treaties' was H. M.
Stanley, the Anglo-American explorer whose chief performance in Africa was
his expedition to find Livingstone in 1871–2. . . . In the Congo it was as easy as
elsewhere to employ Africans of one tribe against another. Leopold assembled
a mercenary army with, by 1905, 360 officers from up and down Europe, and
16,000 natives. Its business was to ensure quick profits in rubber, ivory, or palm-
oil collected as tribute or by forced labour. The consequences were of a sort and

on a scale not seen again in the world until the Nazi epoch, when they were seen in Europe itself.

V. Kiernan, *The Lords of Human Kind*[2]

I. The Universal Heart of Darkness

Sidgwick's abiding faith in the supreme value of Western civilization and its expansion makes for very depressing reading. No doubt he was in many ways innocent and ignorant of the brutal realities of the growth of empire; certainly, he detested the militarism and barbarism of which he was aware. But he was nonetheless horribly smug about his "grade" of civilization. Someone so keenly aware that he was living in a Millian age of transition, and possessing such an acute skeptical intellect, might have done better, even if so many others certainly did worse. But then, notions of "spiritual expansion" just did permeate the Oxbridge air, and Sidgwick was in the business of educating the sentiments in the hope of overcoming "strife," at home and abroad, the strife that threatened to increase as opportunities for colonization waned. Sidgwick's major depressive crisis in 1887 occurred in the very year of the birth of the Labour Party.

In politics, in ethics, in philosophy, and in parapsychology – not to mention in educational reform and sexual censorship – Sidgwick in the 1890s was very much continuous with his earlier self, even if he had grown more politically depressed and eclectic. At the very end of his life, in fact, he was again much animated by a political cause, opposition to the Boer War. He felt keenly that Britain's efforts in this case were ill conceived, acidly remarking that it would be very convenient for future schoolchildren if the British Empire were to fall in the easily remembered year of 1900. As his nephew Rayleigh recalled:

During the Boer War his attitude certainly verged on the anti-patriotic. He considered the action of this country indefensible, I think on the general ground that the Boers had retreated to the Transvaal in order to get away from British rule, and that if British subjects had followed them there they did so at their own risk, and must put up with such legal and political status as the Boer government chose to accord. I do not remember how he dealt with the rather technical questions about British suzerainty which were involved. Mrs Sidgwick did not see eye to eye with him on this subject, and when he discussed it she was sometimes perceptibly irritated – a rare event indeed with her.[3]

Rayleigh also observed that

One of Sidgwick's traits was a pronounced anti-militarist tendency. When after the Omdurman campaign, Lord Kitchener came to Cambridge to receive an honorary degree, some enthusiastic young woman said that he was her hero. When Mrs Sidgwick mentioned this, Sidgwick remarked that he did not think it heroic to mow down savages with machine guns – it might be necessary, but that was the best that could be said of it. He was not tempted to think of himself as a man of action.[4]

The "Storm Along John" jingoism singing forth from every dance hall in the late nineties only disgusted Sidgwick, who never showed any great love of soldiers. But of course, this was characteristic of many of his friends, notably Dakyns and Bryce, and was in no way inconsistent with warm feelings about spreading civilization. To Bryce, in fact, he confided:

As for the war, I do not mind telling you privately that no political event in my lifetime has ever been so odious to me. It seems to me the worst business England has been in since the war with the American Colonies, – and I cannot help foreboding that it will end similarly, in an independent Dutch republic. But I console myself by perceiving that I stand almost alone in this forecast. (CWC)

On Sidgwick's analysis, if the war was due to any one person, it was Milner. Revealingly, however, he held that the "war has manifested the force and genuineness of the Imperial sentiment in the Colonies; that is the brightest aspect of the whole matter."

For all that, he could not bring himself to sign a petition, sent to him by James Sully, calling for a halt to the war:

I should rather like to explain why, after thinking over your paper . . . I could not sign it. Perhaps it is partly my personal connection with the Government which makes me think, in considering a question of this kind, 'What should I do if I were the Government?' Now there is no doubt that if I were constituted the Government *now*, and took up the matter at this state, I should not think it right to bring the war to an end except under conditions that gave adequate security against its recurrence, provided for the equality of Dutch and English throughout South Africa, and also for the payment of some part of the cost by the gold-bearing districts. I should think this my duty, taking up the matter at this stage, in spite of my strong condemnation of the diplomacy that brought the war about. This being so, I have tried hard to think of any conditions that we could offer the Boers such that a 'brave people, jealous of their independence' could be 'expected' to acquiesce in, which will also realise the ends above mentioned, especially security against the recurrence.

I think that the only terms England can offer, consistently with the attainment of practically necessary ends, are such as the Boers *cannot* be expected to accept at present. . . . (M 582)

Indeed, Sidgwick would constantly lament the way in which, with jingoistic political rhetoric everywhere about him, "the old idea of national independence as a priceless good for which a brave man may willingly die had vanished into a dim and remote past." He was, in a sense, right about the meaning of the war. There is some consensus that the "Boer War marked the end of a period of territorial expansion of the empire, and led to a time of imperial rethinking and reorganization. The setbacks and defeats of the first stage of the war, and the unexpectedly long drawn-out closing stage poured cold water over imperial enthusiasm, but they did not lead to any suggestion of imperial withdrawal."[5]

Yet this final phase of Sidgwick's political and spiritual disillusionment is again oddly revealing, for scarcely anywhere in his recorded opinions is there any serious consideration of the issues posed by the war in connection with the black populations of the contested territories. Ironically, most of the blacks apparently favored the English over the Boers, who were notoriously more racist. What, then, is to be made of this example of Sidgwickian silence?

Once again, Bryce was the man with the details needed to fill in Sidgwick's colorless abstractions. When Bryce wrote about South Africa, he well knew that there were more racial questions at issue than the relations of the Dutch and the English. Indeed, he envisioned South Africa's becoming like the southern United States, with "two races, separated by the repulsion of physical differences," having "no social relations, no mixture of blood" and effectively forming two different nations – though with "the nexus of industrial interest, for the white employer will need the labor of the black." Still, if "the whites realize, before the colored people have begun to feel aggrieved, that they have got to live with the natives, and that the true interests of both races are in the long run the same," then the difficulties faced will be less "formidable." In fact,

the whites will in South Africa hold the position of an aristocracy, and may draw from that position some of the advantages which belong to those who are occupied only on the higher kinds of work and have fuller opportunities for intellectual cultivation than the mass of manual laborers enjoy. A large part of the whites will lead a country life, directing the field work or the ranching of their servants.[6]

Here one finds again the abysmal stereotypes attached to notions of national character, linked to vague, Pearsonian notions about fitness for certain types of labor, and making Sidgwick's warm feelings for rehabilitating the notion of aristocracy look quite sinister. Bryce was effectively providing a brief for overcoming strife by means of apartheid.[7] He had yet to read DuBois.

"Race repulsion" and "race debasement" were notions that Sidgwick ought to have treated with all the destructive force of his skeptical intelligence. But he did not, and what Bryce spelled out as a likely future scenario, Sidgwick countenanced in abstract terms, maintaining that "greater impartiality of tone" that could mask so much. It is instructive how he could criticize Spencer for failing on this count, for giving in to "cheap sneers at bishops for their warlike sentiments," which sounded too much like "the one-sided rhetoric of a professional advocate of the Peace Society." Yes, there was surely "plenty of barbaric feeling surviving in the so-called civilised world," but such sneers are "not what we expect from a philosopher." Insists Sidgwick, in a passage quoted earlier:

Theoretically it is one-sided, and practically it gives no guidance. Civilised nations, so long as they are independent, have to fight; and, in performance of their legitimate business – for it is their legitimate business on utilitarian principles – of civilising the world, they have to commit acts which cannot but be regarded as aggressive by the savage nations whom it is their business to educate and absorb. From both points of view the problems presented by International Morality are very difficult. (GSM 236–37)

Sidgwick may have been antimilitaristic and genuinely committed to impartial justice, but his efforts on behalf of moralizing war and advancing international law were grounded on Eurocentric prejudice. When his dear old friend Dakyns wrote to him in January of 1899, it was with a question that would well define what were seen as the political alternatives:

I have just been reading John Morley's speech. If the spirit moves you – I wish you would write me your views on his attitude. With his spirit and his 'Uranian' *versus* 'Pandême Imperialism' and his anti jingoism I have the utmost sympathy. But I fancy that neither Lord Salisbury nor your Brother in Law are pandême imperialists. I think Joe Chamberlain is – and I half suspect Roseberry to be – and so is more than half the population of the British Isles – is it not?

I want to know whether it strikes you that John Morley's attitude is in any respect illogical – and his counsel except as a counsel of perfection impractical, unstatesmanlike? I don't want to be swept along by the Destiny-of-the-British-Race-daemon – at the cost of abandoning all my noble principles (Xtian, positivistic, dakynsian). Neither do I want to go to sea in a sieve with Labouchère – to float round & round a duckpond & my own axis. Whom are they going to send as Peace Commissioner to the Czar's Congress? I hope it may be perhaps yourself or if not Arthur Balfour. But I don't see how the latter can be spared from his Parliamentary Duties. *Ergo* it is you who have got to go. (CWC)

Unfortunately, the spirits did not move Sidgwick to reply, though he would no doubt have expressed a good deal of sympathy for Morley and Uranian imperialism. Morley was another long-standing friend of Sidgwick's, one who had opposed him over Home Rule for Ireland, but who was otherwise a prudent reformer of the type that Sidgwick always admired – indeed was very much a representative of the old Millian party, which insured some memorable confrontations with Balfour. He would in due course become secretary of state and, ironically, would work hard to undo the damage done to India by Lord Curzon, who was of course a product of the educational methods of Browning himself.[8] The "Czar's Congress," interestingly, was the first Hague Conference, which produced a revision of the "laws of war" (if they could be called that) and the establishment of the very thing Sidgwick so desired – a court of arbitration. Unfortunately, Germany effectively killed the Russian proposals aimed at a steady reduction of "excessive armaments." Sidgwick would no doubt have made an excellent representative.

Nor is it far-fetched to think he might have been one. He was very busy in public life during the nineties, what with his connections to Balfour, and despite being steadily crushed in his efforts for women's higher education. His correspondence with his brother-in-law often had a decidedly practical bent; it involved much eager planning of such institutions as the School of Social Ethics, a "teaching University for London," and what would become the British Academy. And Sidgwick was an active participant in various royal commissions, producing such works as "Note on the Memorandum of Sir R. Giffen to the Royal Commission on the Financial Relations of Great Britain and Ireland," "Memorandum in Answer to Questions from the Royal Commission on Secondary Education," and "Memorandum to the Royal Commission on Local Taxation." (CWC)

He had some pangs of conscience about declining such duties, writing to Balfour, "When you asked me . . . whether I should like to be on the new Commission, I answered the question simply, I should not like it. But if you asked me to undertake the work as a public duty, I should not think it right to refuse. To have a right to refuse I should require a much stronger conviction than I actually have of the value to mankind of my philosophic studies."[9]

But these were very strange days. From the Home Rule controversy, to the Wilde trial, to the Boer War, Sidgwick found himself decidedly alienated from the tempo of the times; materialism and militarism did not enhance his belief in common sense. In the nineties, the anticipations of war were everywhere – marked, as Hobsbawm observes, by crazy Nietzschean prophesies of a militarized Europe and a war that would "say yes to the barbarian, even to the wild animal within us."[10] D. H. Lawrence and T. E. Lawrence were looming on the horizon, and as Kiernan has put it, in a vivid redescription of the colonial mentality:

What was really about to erupt was the first of Europe's two great internecine wars, its own relapse into savagery. When white men in the most desolate parts of Africa recoiled from scenes of massacre and ravage, they were in a way recoiling from something lurking in their own souls. Caliban, the African, was the baser self that Christendom with its dualistic philosophy of soul and flesh had always been conscious of; he was the insecurely chained Adam of the Puritan preachers, the Hyde of Stevenson's novel, the *id* of the Freudians. When he was let loose the same devastation that Africans or invaders had inflicted on Africa would fall on Europe.[11]

The "beast" that had so racked Sidgwick's soul did seem, to the Sidgwicks of the world, very much on the loose, and after all, the dualism of practical reason had always carried with it a whiff of the older Christian dualism. Symmetry and sympathy remained only possibilities, the human potential rather than the reality of the "normal" person. All the old problems were still alive with Sidgwick, and then some.

Of course, there was a sense in which Sidgwick went into his last decade with a resolve to throw off depressing speculations and keep himself trained on the practical. Again, the bleak end of the eighties had found him busily working with the Ethical Societies of Cambridge and London – warning them, in effect, to watch out for too much soaring.

When he addressed the Cambridge Ethical Society, in May of 1888, it was in bittersweet tones:

In order to set an example of frankness, I will begin by saying that I am not myself at all sanguine as to the permanent success of such a society in realizing what I understand to be the design of its founders, i.e., to promote through discussion the interests of practical morality. I think that failure in such an undertaking is more probable than success: but, lest this prognostication should be too depressing, I hasten to add that while permanent success in realizing what we aim at would be a result as valuable as it would be remarkable, failure would be a very small evil; indeed, it would not necessarily be an evil at all. Even supposing that we become convinced in the course of two or three years that we are not going to attain the end that we have in view by the method which we now propose to use, we might still feel – I have good hope that we shall feel – that our discussions, so far as they will have gone, will have been interesting and, in their way, profitable; though recognizing that the time has come for the Ethical Society to cease, we may still feel glad that it has existed, and that we have belonged to it.

This cheerfully pessimistic view – if I may so describe it – is partly founded on an experience which I will briefly narrate.

Many years ago I became a member of a Metaphysical Society in London; that was its name, although it dealt with ethical questions no less than those called metaphysical in a narrow sense. It included many recognized representatives of different schools of thought, who met animated, I am sure, by a sincere desire to pursue truth by the method of discussion; and sought by frank explanation of their diverse positions and frank statement of mutual objections, to come, if possible, to some residuum of agreement on the great questions that concern man as a rational being – the meaning of human life, the relation of the individual to the universe, of the finite to the infinite, the ultimate ground of duty and essence of virtue. Well, for a little while the Society seemed to flourish amazingly; it was joined by men eminent in various departments of practical life – statesmen, lawyers, journalists, bishops and archbishops of the Anglican and of the roman persuasion: and the discussions went on, monthly or thereabouts, among the members of this heterogeneous group, without any friction or awkwardness, in the most frank and amicable way. The social result was all that could be desired; but in a few years' time it became, I think, clear to all of us that the intellectual end which the Society had proposed to itself was not likely to be attained; that, speaking broadly, we all remained exactly where we were, "Affirming each his own philosophy," and no one being in the least convinced by any one else's arguments. And some of us felt that if the discussions went on, the reiterated statement of divergent opinions, the reiterated ineffective appeals to a common reason which we all assumed to exist, but which nowhere seemed to emerge into actuality, might become wearisome and wasteful of time. Thus the Metaphysical Society came to an end; but we were glad – at least, I certainly was glad – that we had belonged to it. We had not been convinced by each other, but we had learnt to understand each other better, and to sympathize, in a certain sense, with opposing lines of thought, even though we were unable to follow them with assent. (PE 3–5)

With these remarks in mind, Sidgwick goes on to urge the Ethical Society not to emulate the Metaphysical Society, but instead to "give up altogether the idea of getting to the bottom of things, arriving at agreement on the first principles of duty or the Summum Bonum." By contrast with his statement of purpose in the *Methods*, "the aim of such an Ethical Society, in the Aristotelian phrase, is not knowledge but action: and with this practical object it is not equally necessary that we should get to the bottom of things." Rather than seeking agreement on first principles, the aim is simply "to reach some results of value for practical guidance and life."

This was something of a reversal of the priorities of the *Methods*, and bespoke the hard lessons life had taught the old Apostle, whose pragmatic tendencies always stemmed from his sense of duty and his despair of the higher soaring that he so loved. Suggestively, one of the finest philosophical pieces in *Practical Ethics* is an incisive number on "Unreasonable Action," on "voluntary action contrary to a man's deliberate judgement as to what is right or best for him to do." Although Sidgwick thought it more common for people to sophisticate or rationalize, to shy away from uncomfortable truths, he admitted the reality of the rarer case, where "a man with his eyes open simply refuses to act in accordance with his practical judgment, although the latter is clearly present in his consciousness, and his attention is fully directed towards it." With "habitually reflective persons," he dryly explained, this usually involves "negative action, non-performance of known duty," since it is "far easier for a desire clearly recognized as conflicting with reason to inhibit action than to cause it." (PE 138, 141–42)[12]

As Rashdall had observed, Sidgwick was as exercised by unreason as by divided reason. The aim of the Ethical Societies was to edify and elevate, much as the settlement movement sought to edify and elevate.

All very well, but Sidgwick had imbibed too much of the Platonic Revival to rest content for long with any Jamesian embrace of real, unreasonable people. Ultimately, he could not put such a low estimate on his philosophical work or its urgency, whether his work on "Kant and Kantism in England" or with the SPR. He took over financial responsibility for the philosophical journal *Mind* in 1892 and in due course helped found the "Mind Association." The old Apostolic lure was always irresistible, and as the *Memoir* records,

In 1896 a discussion society called the Synthetic Society, somewhat like the old Metaphysical Society, had been formed through the action of a group of persons differing from each other in theological opinions, and yet equally desirous of union in the effort to find a philosophical basis for religious belief. It met in London five or six times in the season, and among its members it counted A. J. Balfour, James Bryce, F. W. Cornish, Albert Dicey, Canon Gore, R. B. Haldane, Baron Frederic v. Hugel, R. H. Hutton, Sir Oliver Lodge, Sir Alfred Lyall, Dr. James Martineau, F. W. H. Myers, the Bishop of Rochester (Dr. Talbot), Father Tyrrell, Mr. Wilfrid Ward, who was one of its most energetic founders and with Mr. George Wyndham acted as secretary, and later Professor James Ward. Sidgwick had early in its progress been asked to join the Society, but the tendency of an exciting evening to produce a wakeful night made him hesitate. However, his interest in the questions discussed, and his old love of good discussion, were irresistible, and he was elected a member, first joining in the discussion in 1898. (M 556)

Wilfrid Ward (1856–1916) is often described as a "biographer and Catholic apologist," in part because of his massive, loving biography of his father, William George Ward, known as "Ideal" Ward, who had been a leader of the Oxford Movement. Ward and Sidgwick knew each other as members of their London club, the famous Athenaeum, and grew friendly during the nineties. Sidgwick much admired the two-volume biography, *William George Ward and the Oxford Movement* (1889) and *William George Ward and the Catholic Revival* (1893), and contributed some reminiscences to the latter volume, based on his participation with Ward senior in the old Metaphysical Club.

Clearly, the Synthetic Society featured many of the old comrades. It was in connection with his contributions to the Society, of which he became the "heart and soul" (as well as vice president), that Gore had praised Sidgwick's "perpetual hopefulness."[13] The designation was certainly apt, at least in this context, for here was Sidgwick again engaging the "deepest problems," rather than trying to forget the "blackness of the end."

There was much highly philosophical back-and-forth with Ward, and with Balfour. Thus, he wrote to the latter, on April 9, 1897:

I agree broadly with your attack on Haldane: except that I do not, I fear, grasp his position sufficiently to judge precisely how far your attack hits. I thought it was a *fundamental* doctrine of Hegelian Logic that what is logically prior is – being more abstract – *less* real than what is logically posterior. Yet H's argument seems based on the opposite assumption. The Neo-Hegelian epistemology is a Proteus that eludes my grasp: it is always appearing in new form! . . . I also agree with much of Rashdall, whose turn of mind suits mine – only I am more realistic & common sensical as regards the physical world than he, or perhaps than you – I mean than you would be if forced to dogmatize.[14]

Whatever "realism" Sidgwick may have contemplated was of course only of the mildest and most nonreductive form. In some very interesting (slightly earlier) notes on Balfour's theological/ethical views, he stated:

But is Reverence incompatible with Naturalism? It did not seem so to me 20 years ago when I wrote M. of E. p. 473.
  It still seems to me that the feeling with which we contemplate the essential condition of the wellbeing of that larger whole of which the individual feels himself a member will be not without an element of what we call reverence.[15]

Reverence, a prayerful attitude, these were things Sidgwick would not give up, elements of what he took to be the religiously oriented psychology of human beings. A materialistic science dismissive of such things was simply another form of dogmatism. In a letter to Ward from the same year, Sidgwick elaborated:

As regards the two points mentioned in your letter, I think I agree mainly with Balfour on the first, and with you, to a great extent on the second.
  That is (1) I am not able to separate my conception of the external world into "physical" and "metaphysical," in the manner which you seem to regard as simple and accepted. I do not say that a distinction *may* not be drawn between the two ways of regarding and investigating matter; but that it is much more difficult to draw than is commonly supposed by students of physical science who have a turn for philosophizing, and who find it a convenient way of gliding over the contradictions into which their philosophizing tends to involve them, to put their view into two compartments. This kind of dualism always reminds me of the more

simpleminded people who are content to regard a proposition as "true in theory but not in practice."

I do not of course say this with regard to *your* view, but only to indicate "where I am" in the matter.

On the other hand, as regards Reason and Authority, I am on the whole decidedly with you: I am thinking of printing something on the subject. If I do, I will send it you; if not, I will send you the rough notes suggested by your article.[16]

The work referred to in this last paragraph is surely what became "Authority, Scientific and Theological," a paper read to the Synthetic Society on February 24, 1899, and included, along with another paper for the Society, "On the Nature of the Evidence for Theism," in the *Memoir*. Both papers testify to the continuity of Sidgwick's thinking on the "deepest problems." By "authority," he maintains, is usually meant "a ground or source of human belief," the "implied antithesis" of which is not "Reason simply" but "the independent reason of one or more individuals." Thus, in theological debates, the contrast between propositions that one believes because, for example, they are "self-evident" and those that one believes "because of the decisions of other persons that they ought to be believed" ends up getting muddled because of confusion over the meaning of the second view. The authority involved in the latter view can be understood "in two essentially distinct ways: either (a) because I believe them to be held by others with better knowledge than myself of the matters in question, or (b) because other persons command me to hold them, and I am afraid that they will do me some harm if I do not obey." (M 608) Naturally, as ever, Sidgwick links the latter to a supposed theological "consensus." And he even goes on to appropriate some of the wording from his earlier writings:

Taking Authority in this sense [as opposed only to "the independent exercise of private reason"], I think that its place in determining the actual beliefs, speculative and practical, of ordinary educated persons, is not only very large, but tends to grow with the growth of science and civilisation, on account of the increasing specialisation in the pursuit of knowledge which is an inevitable accompaniment of this growth. Probably there never was a time when the amount of beliefs held by an average educated person, undemonstrated and unverified by himself, was greater than it is now. But it is no less true – and it much concerns us here to note – that men are more and more disposed only to accept authority of a particular kind: the authority, namely, that is formed and maintained by the unconstrained agreement of individual experts, each of whom is believed to be seeking truth with unfettered independence, and declaring what he has found with perfect openness and the greatest attainable precision. This authority, therefore, is conceived as the authority of the living mind of humanity, and as containing within itself, by the very nature of its composition, adequate guarantees for the elimination of error by continual self-questioning and self-criticism; it is not an authority – such as that of our Supreme Court of Appeal was once held to be – that refuses to question its own past decisions; on the contrary, it encourages to the utmost any well-reasoned criticism of the most fundamental among them. It is for this kind of authority that the wonderful and steady progress of physical knowledge leads educated persons to entertain a continually increasing respect – accompanied, I think, by a corresponding distrust of any other kind of authority in matters intellectual. (M 609–10)

As he put it in another letter to Ward, the

struggle between Freedom and Authority, in this department, must certainly go on, and I do not pretend to forecast its ultimate issue, though quite willing to discuss sympathetically any suggestion of a *modus vivendi* between the two principles: but my special point is that it will be carried on under better conditions, intellectual and moral, if we uphold and enforce the simple ethical demand for sincerity in solemn utterances of theological beliefs. (CWC)[17]

Deference to genuine Apostolic inquirers who say what they mean was what Sidgwick had in mind, for a culture cultivating both literature and science, and the social epistemological point is underscored by the more formal treatment given in other late essays, notably "The Criteria of Truth and Error," with appendix, reprinted in the posthumous *Lectures on the Philosophy of Kant and Other Philosophical Lectures and Essays*. These works – some of Sidgwick's clearest on formal epistemology – reiterate many of the explications of his *Methods* that he had supplied in earlier years. Thus, there are extensive discussions of Descartes and the failings of the Cartesian criterion: "perhaps the most important case of the kind is a conflict between a universal judgment accepted as self-evident, and the particular judgments of perception, or inference from these." Consider, he urges, the "fate of the belief that 'a thing cannot act where it is not'." This apparently self-evident belief "was found to con-flict apparently with the hypothesis of universal gravitation, which rested on a multitude of particular observations of the position of the heav-enly bodies; and this has, I think, destroyed any appearance of intuitive certainty in it for most of us." (LPK 462) By way of further illustration, he recalls

> the method by which in my work on Ethics Common Sense is led to Utilitarianism. This was, indeed, suggested by the method of Socrates, whose ethical discussion brought to light latent conflicts of this kind. It was evident (e.g.) to Polemarchus that 'it was just to give every man his own'; but being convinced that it is not just to restore to a mad friend his own sword, his faith in his universal maxim was shaken.
>
> Now it is possible that what I have called the Intuitive Verification might exclude error in some of these cases, one of the conflicting intuitions being due to inadvertence. If we had examined more carefully the supposed universal truth, or the supposed particular fact of observation, we might have detected the inadvertence, or at any rate have seen that we had mistaken for an intuition what was merely inference or belief accepted on authority. But the history of thought shows that I cannot completely rely upon the Intuitive Verification alone. (LPK 462)

What is crucial, of course, is to supplement "the Intuitive or Cartesian Verification" with "a second, which I will call the Discursive Verification, the object of which is to exclude the danger of the kind of conflict I have indicated." And this in turn calls for the third epistemological criterion. The Cartesian criterion "lays stress on the need of clearness, distinctness, precision, in our thought," and the discursive criterion "brings into prominence the value of *system*" – of special interest to philosophers, since this "is the kind of service which Philosophy may be expected to render to the sciences." What to do, however, when the conflict is not simply between two apparently self-evident beliefs held by one person, but rather involves the beliefs of different persons? Then the philosophic mind demands that "the conflicting intuitor has an inferior faculty of envisaging truth in general or this kind of truth," and if this cannot be shown, then one "must reasonably submit to a loss of confidence in any intuition of his own that thus is found to conflict with another's."

> We are thus led to see the need of a third Verification, to supplement the two former; we might call it the Social or Oecumenical Verification. It completes the process of philosophical criteria of error which I have been briefly expounding. This last, as we are all aware, with many persons, probably the majority of mankind, is the Criterion or Verification practically most prominent; if they have such verification in the case of any belief, neither lack of self-evidence in the belief itself, nor lack of consistency when it is compared with other beliefs, is sufficient to disturb their

confidence in it. And its practical importance, even for more reflective and more logical minds, grows with the growth of knowledge, and the division of intellectual labour which attends it; for as this grows, the proportion of the truths that enter into our systematisation, which for any individual have to depend on the *consensus of experts*, continually increases. In fact, in provisionally taking Common Sense as the point of departure for philosophical construction, it was this criterion that we implicitly applied. The Philosopher, I conceive, at the present day, starts with the particular sciences; they give the matter which it is his business – I do not say his whole business, but a part of his business – to systematise. But how is he to know what matter to take? He cannot, in this age, be an expert in all sciences; he must, then, *provisionally* accept the judgment of Common Sense. Provisionally, I say, not finally; in working out his Epistemological principles in application to the sciences, he may correct or define more precisely some fundamental conception, point out a want of cogency in certain methods, limit the scope of certain premises and certain conclusions. Especially will he be moved to do this when he finds confusion and conflict in comparing and trying to reduce to system the fundamental conceptions, premises, and methods of different sciences. (LPK 464)

But this is to say that the growth of modern science and academic specialization reinforces the old Socratic lesson, absorbed by the Apostles, that one can and must seek to learn from others, in a fellowship of high-minded inquiry. Philosophy specializes in employing the discursive criterion, aiming at system, but the "special characteristic" of Sidgwick's philosophy "is to keep the importance of the others in view." Given the nature of the controversies surrounding the *Methods*, addressed in Chapter 4, it would be very difficult to deny that this was a special characteristic of his work throughout.

Hence, the more or less constant – and, alas, sometimes all-too-sinister – invocation of the "consensus of experts" in his political work concerned with spiritual expansion. Coupled with this, however, is the slight but increasing endorsement of a kind of practical pluralism, a faint proto-political liberal sense of the enduring nature of difference. In March of 1898, he would write to Ward that he was glad to hear that the discussion of Oliver Lodge's paper seemed to Lodge to "make for approximation to agreement," since "the phrase exactly expresses what I think we ought to aim at: it would be idle to expect more" (CWC).[18] And coupled with this is some growing sense, still faint, of the limits of the philosopher in his study. Thus, he has not forgotten his message in "The Aims of an Ethical Society," which enjoined the moral philosopher to "study with reverent and patient care the Morality of Common Sense. I referred to the moral judgements – and especially the spontaneous unreflected judgments on particular cases, which are sometimes called moral intuitions – of those persons, to be found in all walks and stations of life, whose earnest and predominant aim is to do their duty." These are the persons of whom the verse rang that "though they slip and fall, / They do not blind their souls with clay," and they are such that "after each lapse and failure recover and renew their rectitude of purpose and their sense of the supreme value of goodness." Sidgwick has in mind here not the denizens of "hermitages and retreats," but persons

in the thick and heat of the struggle of active life, in all stations and ranks, in the churches and outside the churches. It is to them we have appealed for aid and sympathy in the great task that we have undertaken; and it is to their judgments on the duties of their station, in whatever station they may be found, that the moral philosopher should, as I have said, give reverent attention, in order that he may be aided and controlled by them in his theoretical construction of the Science of Right. (PE 22–23)

But again, the study of common sense, the normal man of the Benthamites now become a medical classification, was in Sidgwick's hands a very worried affair, the piercing of the veil to get at the true self that was rapidly becoming the study of abnormal psychology. Knowing what made people tick ethically remained for him an inquiry of the utmost urgency, and consequently theism was, as always, very much on the agenda during this gathering up of the "fragments that remain."

II. Reasonable Persons

For Sidgwick's part, as his letters to Ward and Balfour demonstrate, he was still under no illusions about the difference between hoping that theism was true and actually showing that it was. As he unmistakably put it in *Philosophy, Its Scope and Relations* – by his own account one of the most finished of his unpublished works and one that he thought might suitably be published[19] – although many thoughtful persons have been persuaded of the truth of theism,

I myself regard Theism as a belief which, though borne in upon the living mind through life, and essential to normal life, is not self-evident or capable of being cogently demonstrated. It belongs, therefore, to a class of beliefs which I do not dispute the general reasonableness of accepting, but which I think have to be considered carefully and apart in estimating the grounds of their acceptance – assumptions for which we cannot but *demand* further proof, though we may see no means of obtaining it. (PSR 242)[20]

All his old views about the spirit of the age being theistic, but with Christianity still playing a valuable social role, emerge again in this context. He has some sympathetic feeling for those who turn to external authority in search of faith, but he cannot follow them. What he still feels so acutely is the emotional unsatisfactoriness of his views:

[I]n opposing your argument [Ward's on the role of saints], I intended to limit myself to the sociological point of view: from which morality does not seem to me to lead us to Theism. But I did not mean to say that I could be *satisfied* to regard morality exclusively from this point of view: quite the reverse: I hold strongly that sociological inquiry cannot answer the deepest questions which the individual, reflecting on his moral judgments and impulses, is inevitably led to ask. And where Sociology fails, the need of Theism – or at least some doctrine establishing the moral order of the world – seems to me clear.

As to the definition of Theism – I should think a provisional definition would not be difficult to agree on, if any one wants it. But I should have thought we might wait till any serious divergence in our conceptions disclosed itself. (CWC)[21]

Of course, various deep differences did appear. One crisis came when early on Myers wanted to give a paper "to discuss what he conceives to be the limitations of Christianity from the point of view of a wider religious outlook," which Sidgwick did not think a bad subject, though "it had better come later." When it came, the "wider religious outlook" clearly had a lot of Whitmanian Cosmic Enthusiasm in it, and caused Father Tyrrell no little pain. Myers had apparently been "quite unaware of 'thunder in the air' " and claimed to have expressed himself "in simple confidence in the general good humour that he thought prevailed." And Sidgwick urged that "I feel *very strongly* that anything like 'crowing' over 'adhesion' as Tyrrell calls it is a great mistake: it must tend to repress the perfect frankness on which both the pleasure and the profit of such debates depends." (CWC)[22]

"Adhesiveness" was of course Whitman's term of art for spiritualized but sensual male comradeship, and Myers may well have sounded a good deal like Symonds, though it may also be that Father Tyrrell was thinking of adhesion in the narrower sense of religious conformity.

To be sure, Sidgwick had not given up exploring the various possibilities for harmonizing duty and interest. "On the Nature of the Evidence for Theism" in fact reads like a continuation of the conclusion of the *Methods*, especially after the third edition. The entire problematic is set out in just the same fashion:

Theism is a philosophical doctrine: it is the primary aim of philosophy to unify completely, bring into clear coherence, all departments of rational thought; and this aim cannot be realised by any philosophy that leaves out of its view the important body of judgments and reasoning which form the subject matter of Ethics. And it seems especially impossible, in attempting the construction of a Theistic Philosophy, to leave Ethics on one side. No view of Theism – as X [presumably Ward] says – "is of much importance to mankind which does not include the conception of a Sovereign Will that orders all things"; and if – as he goes on to say – "the only form of dogmatic religion worth arguing about is Christianity," I think we may agree to add one word to the statement previously quoted, and say "A Sovereign Will that orders all things *rightly*." For this reason I cannot agree to discard from our discussions – even provisionally – "arguments drawn from the indications of ethical experience."

But here again I should like to go as far as I can to meet X's views. I quite admit that when we contemplate human morality from the point of view from which the historian or sociologist naturally contemplates it – regarding it as a body of rules of conduct supported by social sentiments of approval and disapproval, which a normal member of society shares, and through sympathy with others applies reflectively to his own conduct as well as to the conduct of others – it certainly does not seem "easy to prove that the Theistic hypothesis is necessary to account for its existence." Especially when we direct our attention to the variations in prevalent moral opinion and sentiment, which are observable as we pass in our contemplative survey from age to age, and from one contemporary society to another; the fluid and changing results that impartial observation thus seems to yield hardly even suggest the hypothesis of "super human institution"; they are more naturally viewed as a part of the complex adaptation of social man to the varying conditions of gregarious existence, civilised and uncivilised. Nor would the fact that saints generally have found themselves irresistibly led to regard moral rules as the dictates of a Divine Ruler weigh with me much on the other side; unless I were assured that the saints in question had made a systematic attempt to contemplate the variations in positive morality from a sociological point of view – which is not, so far as I know the case. But all such sociological observation of morality ignores the question which, from the point of view of the reflective individual, is the fundamental question of ethics, 'Why should I, always and in all circumstances, do what is most conducive to the well-being of my society, or of humanity at large?' To answer this question satisfactorily, we have to find a solution of the *primâ facie* conflict between an individual's interest and his social duty, which the actual conditions of human life from time to time present. Optimistic moralists of the last century attempted to obtain the required solution by establishing a perfect coincidence of interest and duty on a strictly empirical basis; but such attempts are now, I think, abandoned by serious thinkers; and yet some solution must be found, if the normal judgments of our practical reason are to be reduced to a coherent system. It is this consideration which led Kant to affirm with so much emphasis the indispensability of Theism in the construction of an ethical system: "Without a God and without a world, not visible to us now but hoped for, the glorious ideas of morality are indeed objects of applause and admiration, but not springs of purpose and action, because they fail to fulfil all the aims which are natural to every rational being." This language is too sweeping to express my own convictions: still, the importance of the conception of the moral government of the world, in giving the required systematic coherence to Ethics, seems to me so great that I cannot consent to discard this consideration – even provisonally – in seeking a 'working philosophy' of Theism. (M 604–5)

This is a nice appropriation of Jamesian language and, as usual, a shrewd assessment of Kant's deeper concerns,[23] but as Sidgwick realizes, the natural objection is that this establishes only the convenience of believing in theism, not the evidence of its truth. Again, he sounds much the same note as that struck in the *Methods*: "To this I should reply by asking whether any philosophical theory can ever be established, if we are not to accept as evidence of its truth the fact that it introduces unity, harmony, systematic coherence into our thought, and removes the conflict and contradiction which would otherwise exist in the whole or some department of it?" (M 605)

The main difference is that Sidgwick goes on to explore this possibility at greater length, addressing in more detail the matter of "the analogy between hypotheses that are verifiable and those that are not verifiable by human experience." He readily admits that "those sciences which can point to exact particular predictions, made before the event and realised by the event, acquire thereby a claim to our confidence, which must be wanting to any philosophy of Theism, based on the data which we at present possess." Theism ought to predict "the complete realisation of Divine Justice in the ordering of the world of humanity and the individual lives of men: and it admittedly cannot show the realisation of this prediction in past experience." Still, Sidgwick confesses that he is not willing to

admit "that verification by particular experiences and cogent demonstration from incontrovertible premises are the only modes of attaining the
kind and degree of certitude which we require for a 'working philosophy.'"
And here Sidgwick adds some very interesting (and personal) insights and
examples, arguing against a too-narrow construction of "verification by
experience."

The criterion that we find really decisive, in case after case, is not any particular
new sense-perception, or group of new sense-perceptions, but consistency with
an elaborate and complex system of beliefs, in which the results of an indefinite
number of perceptions and inferences are combined. Let me take a case of some
current interest. Many of the vulgar and a few educated persons still believe
that there are such things as 'ghosts' moving about in space. The vulgar naively
consider that this general statement is 'verified' by the numerous experiences
of 'seeing ghosts,' which undoubtedly do occur to some persons from time to
time. But no educated person thinks that the mere fact of A's 'seeing' a ghost
is any evidence at all for the above generalisation: he unhesitatingly concludes
that the apparent vision of an external object is in this case merely apparent, an
'hallucination.' And why? Surely because the existence of something so material as
to produce through the organ of vision the apparent perception of a human figure,
and yet so immaterial as to pass through the wall of a room, is incompatible with
his general conception of the physical world. Suppose this general conception
different, and the "verification" might be accepted by a mind far from credulous.
Indeed, the history of thought shows this. Epicurus was not in his age regarded
as prone to superstition, but rather as the great deliverer from the terrors of
superstition; yet Epicurus held it to be an important argument for the existence
of Gods that phantasms of them appear to men in dreams and visions.
    It seems to me, then, that if we are led to accept Theism as being, more than
any other view of the Universe, consistent with, and calculated to impart a clear
consistency to, the whole body of what we commonly agree to take for knowledge –
including knowledge of right and wrong – we accept it on grounds analogous to
those on which important scientific conclusions have been accepted; and that,
even though we are unable to add the increase of certitude derivable from verified
predictions, we may still attain a sufficient strength of reasoned conviction to
justify us in calling our conclusions a "working philosophy." (M 607–8)

But this is a very big "if." Although this may appear to be a rather
more holistic, coherentist sentiment than that expressed in the *Methods*,
the notion of a "working philosophy" may not be all that different from
the "provisional" postulate that had kept Sidgwick going until his crisis
in the eighties. He was, after the fashion of Mill on theism, in that region of

legitimate hope that had not been foreclosed by the evidence. It was still, as he argued in *Philosophy, Its Scope and Relations*, not possible to give theism a completely "cogent" demonstration, however reasonable it might seem. Interestingly, when Ward reviewed *Henry Sidgwick, A Memoir*, Eleanor Sidgwick would write in response: "I am glad you dwell on the optimism. Some have said that the life gives them a sad impression. Of course there was an element of disappointment that he had not been able to find the truth he sought, but his life was certainly a happy and a hopeful one in spite of occasional depression."[24] This should be read as an affirmation that Sidgwick remained less than fully convinced by and content with the coherentist argument. As Maitland observed, if Sidgwick had not been Sidgwick, "he might, as others often do, have forgotten the exact point where proof ended and only hope remained." But he never did.

Plausibly, Sidgwick's final position did lend some support to the nascent pragmatist movement. Had he been able to embrace mere reasonableness as what the human world offers and to shake off the feeling that he was provisionally settling for a second-best, functional view, he might deserve such a designation as pragmatist. But the quest for certainty, the old Apostolic soaring, had too strong a grip on him; if this was a shadow of the Christian aspiration, then it is all the less surprising that he could never fully reconcile himself to the loss of the grander project. It was in his cycles of soaring and sinking that the shapes of things to come were discernible.

Furthermore, despite his work with the ethical societies, Sidgwick had still, to his mind, left a great deal to the mundane realm of contestable calculation. As he explained to Bishop Creighton, in a letter of August 30, 1898:

But I should like to say that the omission you note in my essay on Public Morality is one of which I am quite conscious: and I entirely agreed with what you said about it. The difficulty of weighing material gain against moral loss is one which I was conscious of not being able to deal with in a manner that would satisfy or edify the 'plain man,' for whom my little volume was supposed to be written. I have no moral scales in which I can balance these disparate values: that is, when anything like a delicate balance is required. Practically, I find that when my mind comes to a clear decision on a particular problem of this class, it is not because I can establish any sort of 'ratio of exchange' – so much material gain = so much moral loss – but because one or other of the values compared, either the gain or the loss, seems to me much more certain than the other in the particular case. (M 569)

In fact, the problem is even more pervasive. His admiration for Symonds's aesthetics points to many further dilemmas, poignantly expressed in "The Pursuit of Culture":

Both art and morality have an ideal, and the aim in both cases is to apprehend and exhibit the ideal in a reality that does not conform to or express it adequately; but the ideals are not the same, and it is just where they most nearly coincide – in dealing with human life and character – that some conflict is apt to arise. Morality aims at eradicating and abolishing evil, especially moral evil; whereas the aesthetic contemplation of life recognizes it as an element necessary to vivid and full interest. The opposition attains its sharpest edge in modern realistic art and literature; but it is by no means confined to the work of this school. Take, for example, the *Paradise Lost* of Milton – a writer as unlike a modern realist as possible. The old remark, that Satan is the real hero of *Paradise Lost*, is an epigrammatic exaggeration; but he is certainly quite indispensable to the interest of the poem; and the magnificent inconsistency with which Milton has half humanized his devil shows that he felt this. (PE 127)

Consequently, the more that we admire the poem aesthetically, "the more satisfaction we must find in the existence of the devil, as an indispensable element of the whole artistic construction; and this satisfaction is liable to clash somewhat with our moral attitude towards evil."

Needless to say, by "art" Sidgwick does not mean "the mere misuse of technical gifts for the gratification of base appetites." But even with art "worthy of the name," this form of conflict cannot be "altogether overcome," since its "root lies deep in the nature of things as we are compelled to conceive it." Thus, we have "an unsolved problem of philosophy, which continually forces itself to the front in the development of the religious consciousness." For the "general man is convinced that the war with moral evil is essential to that highest human life which is the highest thing we know in the world of experience; and yet he is no less convinced that the world with all its evil is somehow good, as the outcome and manifestation of ideal goodness." If the realm of art involves the latter, then it has a place "along with our moral effort," with the result that

we must endeavour to make the moods of aesthetic and ethical sentiment alternate, if we cannot quite harmonize them; the delighted contemplation of our mingled and varied world as beautiful in its mixtures and contrasts, though it cannot be allowed to interfere with the moral struggle with evil, may be allowed to relieve it, and give a transient repose from the conflict.

And on the whole we must be content that science and art and morality are for the most part working on the same side, in that struggle with our lowest nature through which we "move upward, working out the beast." Perhaps they will aid each other best if we abstain from trying to drill them into perfect conformity of movement, and allow them to fight independently in loose array. (PE 127–28)

This might seem like just the type of "generous resolution" that Sidgwick had found so objectionable in Mill's work, but despite his yearning for some more exact determination of duty, much the same tolerance can be found in the *Methods*, as shown in Chapter 4. At any rate, Sidgwick's ethics thus leaves considerable space for the lower Goethean personal point of view, whether material or aesthetic, even suggesting that it might give one a refreshing break from the weight of duty. The agenda was set for Bloomsbury.

Of course, as already shown, in the practical realization of Sidgwick's vision everything seemed to ride on the sincerity of the inquirer and the degree of civilization that he or she represented. And of course, as his involvement with the Synthetic Society might suggest, Sidgwick had not actually forsaken his hope of so long ago, expressed in his diary:

1. Why should not God be willing to give us a few glimpses of the unseen world which we all believe exists; 2. as to law of Nature, it may be that God governs Spirits not according to rules similar to physical rules & that we can no more expect to find out the law of these appearances than the law of the action of grace in our own hearts. 3. as to cause, the appearance may be (besides 1,) to work effects on the spirits of the seers which we cannot expect to know. (CWC)

The nineties had produced fresh evidence of "phenomena." His toying with the coherentist justification for theism must be read in light of his continuing efforts at harmonizing duty and interest with the aid of the "other world" – his "working philosophy" was, as always, entangled in parapsychology, though Sidgwick was not quite ready to come out.

III. Dreams and Visions

We shall contemplate the relation of virtue to the happiness of the virtuous agent, as we believe it actually to be in the present world, and not refer to any future world in which we may hope for compensation for the apparent injustices of the present. And in thus limiting ourselves to mundane motives we shall, I hope, keep a middle path between optimism and pessimism. That is, we shall not profess to

prove that the apparent sacrifices of self-interest which duty imposes are never in the long run real sacrifices; nor, on the other hand, shall we ignore or underrate the noble and refined satisfaction which experience shows to attend the resolute choice of virtue in spite of all such sacrifices –
"The stubborn thistles bursting
Into glossy purples, which outredden
All voluptuous garden-roses."

It may, however, be said that it is not merely the function of Churches to supply motives for the performance of duty, but also to teach what duty is, and that here their work must inevitably coincide – and perhaps clash – with that undertaken by an Ethical Society. My answer would be that there is at least a large region of secular duty in which thoughtful Christians commonly recognize that an ideal of conduct can be, and ought to be, worked out by the light of reason independently of revelation; and I should recommend our Society to confine its attention to this secular region. Here no doubt some of us may pursue that quest of moral truth by study or discussion in a non-religious spirit, others in a religious spirit; but I conceive that we have room for both.

Sidgwick, "The Scope and Limits of the Work of an Ethical Society" (PE 9)

Sidgwick's "middle way," defining his work with the ethical societies, reflected his state of mind in 1888, when his disillusionment with psychical research inclined him to focus on daily duty and forget the "blackness of the end." But as his work with the Synthetic Society so amply testifies, his interest in the deepest problems would persist. George Eliot's stance was something he could admire, but not quite emulate. He would still finger the "old Gordian knot," even while gathering up the "fragments that remain." There was only so much serenity to be found, in his true self.

Surely a big part of what determined Sidgwick's direction during his last decade had to do with the reinvigoration of his hopes for psychical research. Notoriously, there was Eusapia Palladino, the Neapolitan medium who was the object of McTaggart's nasty remarks to the Apostles about Myers's erotic interests. She was by all accounts an earthy, illiterate woman who did indeed add a highly sensuous element to the séance. According to Oppenheim:

The SPR connection with Palladino began in 1894, when Myers, Lodge, and the Sidgwicks held séances with her in southern France, as guests of Charles Richet, professor of physiology in the Paris Faculty of Medicine. Myers and Lodge were certain that they were witnessing the real thing, at least some of the time. The

Sidgwicks were, as ever, guarded and noncommittal, but not unwilling to have another round with Palladino. She was, accordingly, invited to Cambridge for a long visit in the summer of 1895.[25]

But Oppenheim has not caught the genuine excitement over Palladino that Sidgwick showed. Consider the following letter to Bryce, from August of 1894, marked *"Private"*:

My wife hoped to have had an opportunity yesterday of explaining to you the sudden change in our plan of foreign travel: but fate did not permit. The truth is, the call of duty has descended on us in connexion with the S.P.R. – in whose affairs a crisis is impending. Three chief members of our group of investigators: F. Myers, O. J. Lodge, and Richet (Professor of Physiology in Paris) have convinced themselves of the truth of the physical phenomena of Spiritualism! They have been experimenting with an Italian "medium" Eusapia Palladino, on a small island in the Mediterranean, close to Hyéres, which is Richet's private property: they have had her alone there, no one being on the island but Richet's servants and the experimenters: we have read the notes taken from day to day of the experiments, and it is certainly difficult to see how the results recorded can have been produced by ordinary physical means.

At the same time as the S.P.R. has now for some years acquired a reputation for *comparative* sanity and intelligence by detecting and exposing the frauds of mediums; and as Eusapia's "phenomena" are similar in kind to the frauds we have exposed, it will be rather a sharp turn in our public career if our most representative men come forward as believers. Consequently we both feel bound to accept Richets' invitation and go for ten days or a fortnight to the "Ile Roubaud", and if possible, obtain personal experience. (CWC)[26]

Sidgwick goes on to say that this "will be rather a bore," but his excitement is palpable. In fact, in a follow-up letter from August 30, 1894, he is on the brink of conversion:

I promised to write and tell you the results of our experiments here: if I have delayed it has been partly from the uncertainty of our plans, but still more from a desire not to *fix* my ideas prematurely. But we are now near the end of our series of sittings, and it is improbable that any of the experiences which remain will materially alter my view.

In brief, then, we have no doubt that our experiences confirm those of Lodge, Myers and Richet: that is, if I can rely on myself and my wife to know whether or not we have hold of a medium's hand in the dark, then it is certain that effects are somehow produced, similar to those which human hands would produce, when actually there are no hands so employed. The effects are of a very elementary kind – touches, grasps &c or movements of objects such as billiard balls, melons &c – and they occur in the dark, or in a very dim light: so that everything depends on the reliance to be placed on any investigator's statement that he *is* holding a hand, foot, or head, at the time that a 'phenomenon occurs.' Now I shall not be surprised if I find that statements of this kind are regarded as unreliable: and I do not think I should be disposed to rely on them, except when made by experienced persons – aware of the tricks by which one hand may be made to appear two &c. But then my wife and I have had a good deal of experience: and so have our friends Richet and Lodge (who is here). Accordingly our present state of mind is that we *do* rely on ourselves and each other, for the purpose of such holdings: meanwhile, we continue the experiments at intervals of two or three days, varying and if possible improving the conditions. (CWC)

In a letter from September, there are some doubts as to whether the views of Myers and Lodge had been completely confirmed, but even so,

we do not see any way – even so far as our own experiences go – of avoiding the conclusion that effects are produced such as human hands would produce, when no such hands are there to produce. Thus we are able to confirm a *part* of the experiences which have led Myers, Lodge & Richet to the conclusion that we have at last got hold of a genuine case of the 'physical phenomena' which the Spiritualists attribute to Spirits. Nothing, however, that we have seen at all supports the Spiritistic hypothesis, so far as we can judge. (CWC)

Perhaps the gullibility that Sidgwick brought to such investigations suggests how he could have been so gullible on other counts – say, the activities of the empire. What could he have supposed was being proved by the mysterious moving of a melon? The Theosophists had at least had some familiar mystical philosophizing attached to their phantom letters and so forth, of the sort that would again become popular with Aldous Huxley's *Perennial Philosophy*, a sacred text of the 1960s.

But at any rate, the thrill of discovery could not survive the more sober scrutiny that Palladino met with when she visited Cambridge, a scrutiny that came from none other than the old debunker of Theosophy Richard Hodgson.[27] As Oppenheim explains:

In this quandry, during the 1895 Cambridge sittings, they sent for Richard Hodgson, who was in Boston serving as executive secretary of the American Society for Psychical Research, affiliated with the British SPR at the time. With Myers and Sidgwick paying for his transportation, Hodgson crossed the ocean in August, in time to render judgment on Palladino. Her talents, he ruled, included

nothing more noteworthy than the ability, through a variety of deceptive movements, to wriggle hands and feet free from the control of sitters. That agility,
Hodgson was convinced, explained all her so-called spiritualist phenomena, and
as far as the Sidgwicks and Podmore were concerned, Hodgson's was the last
word on Eusapia Palladino. Their worst suspeicions had been confirmed; there
was nothing further to add.[28]

It was this uncompromising rejection of all the evidence for a medium
upon any demonstration of fraud in a particular instance that struck fellow
researchers like William James as unduly ungenerous. But in this case,
Sidgwick was clearly right to be more suspicious of the will to believe.

The case of Eusapia Palladino was only part of the excitement attending
psychical research in the nineties, and her reception may in fact have been
colored by the excitement over other cases. Most importantly, there was
also the trance mediumship of one Leonora Piper, whose automatic writing supposedly reflected communications, via an other-worldly control,
from various deceased persons. The evidence from such sources utterly
convinced (the always credulous) Myers of the reality of personal survival, and appears even to have brought Sidgwick nearer the conclusion
that there was evidence for survival after all, sufficient to merit further
investigation. In fact, this form of inquiry would continue well into the
twentieth century, to such a degree that C. D. Broad could write, in the
1950s, that

Controls and ostensible communicators often display a knowledge of facts about
the past lives of dead persons and about the present actions and thoughts and
emotions of living ones, which is too extensive and detailed to be reasonably
ascribed to chance-coincidence, and it is quite inexplicable by reference to any
normal sources of information open to the medium. I do not think that this would
be seriously questioned by anyone, with a reasonably open mind, who had made a
careful study of the recorded facts and had had a certain amount of experience of
his own in these matters: though it is often dogmatically denied by persons who
lack those qualifications.[29]

Ironically, the case of Piper, an American, had come to the SPR as a kind
of godsend at the moment of Sidgwick's despair. She had been investigated
by William James as early as 1885 and later by none other than the skeptical
Hodgson, who found that this was a case he could not crack. The intensive
investigations of her that began in 1889 and extended over the next decade,
according to Morton Prince, "wrecked Dick Hodgson who had one of

the most beautiful minds I ever knew."[30] At any rate, it was Piper, with Hodgson as her champion, who converted the eminent physicist Lodge, who after this point came to be a believer in human survival of physical death.

What was the nature of the evidence? It was much along the lines described by Broad. As Oppenheim records:

Piper's first visit to England in 1889–90 added Lodge, recently elected a Fellow of the Royal Society, to the list of her admirers. Together with Myers and Leaf, he formed a committee to study her mediumship, an inquiry that they pursued in Cambridge, London, and Liverpool. Usually they invited other guests to meet Piper and these, introduced under assumed names, frequently marveled at her ability to recount personal information about themselves and their families that, they were convinced, she could not have acquired through normal means. Sometimes it seemed that her knowledge could only have come to her from the deceased. Trickery or purposeful deception on her part appeared out of the question. In Boston, Hodgson had hired detectives to follow her and ascertain whether she had confederates who supplied her with information, or whether she herself did research on potential sitters. Piper successfully passed that test and while in England was most cooperative in allowing SPR investigators to search her luggage and to scrutinize her mail. There was nothing to suggest that she turned to outside sources, human or literary, for the contents of her trance conversations.[31]

As usual, the psychical researchers sought to explain Piper's performance as involving "nothing more" than telepathic communication between living persons, rather than communications from the "other world." But this could not, it seemed, fully account for her occasional ability to produce material that had been unknown to any living person. Myers visited Piper in Cambridge, Massachusetts, in 1893, and came away absolutely persuaded, as he told Lodge, "that spirits are talking & writing to us thro her."[32] Similar evidence was obtained from a medium named Rosina Thompson. In both cases, the psychical researchers argued, a "spirit presence" was controlling the automatist productions in the trance state. Indeed, Myers was certain that he had been in touch with his beloved Annie Marshall.

The more skeptical psychical researchers struggled hard with the strangeness of the Piper case. She claimed that she was under the guidance of the spirit of a deceased French physician, the "Phinuit control," but when William James addressed the control in French, it seemed not to comprehend. James speculated that this "spirit" was some form of unconscious construction, quite fictitious. But he grew more receptive to other interpretations when Piper was supposedly taken over by a new control, during the period from 1892 to 1905. As Robert Almeder has summed up the evidence that baffled James and converted Hodgson:

George Pellew had been a young man of philosophical and literary talent who had been killed in New York two weeks before he became Mrs. Piper's control. Five years earlier, Pellew had – under a pseudonym – attended one and only one sitting with Mrs. Piper. According to A. Gauld, out of 150 sitters who were introduced to G.P. during the sittings, G.P. recognized 29 of the 30 who had been known to the living Pellew. (The thirtieth, whom G.P. recognized after an initial failure, was a young person who had "grown up" in the interval.) G.P. conversed with each of them in an appropriate manner and showed an intimate knowledge of their careers and of his own supposed past relationships with them. According to Gauld, rarely did G.P. slip up badly in these matters, as he sometimes did when discussing certain philosophical questions that had interested him during life.

It was during this time that Hodgson came to believe that Mrs. Piper's controls were sometimes what they claimed to be – namely, surviving disembodied persons. Presumably, the reason was that G. P. – in identifying the thirty people known to him when alive, and in describing his own personal (and sometimes intimate) relationships with them – manifested a very systematic, coherent, and personal set of memories that one would have expected of Pellew. Also, it seemed unlikely that Mrs. Piper was successfully dramatizing the personality of Pellew, because she had met him only once, briefly, five years earlier, when he sat with her anonymously.[33]

James still resisted, believing that Hodgson had too quickly discounted forms of telepathy as the basic explanation. But on the whole, he was softened:

If we suppose Mrs. Piper's dream-life once and for all to have had the notion suggested to it that it must personate spirits to sitters, the fair degree of virtuosity need not, I think, surprise us. Nor need the exceptional memory shown surprise us, for memory seems extraordinarily strong in the subconscious life. *But I find that when I ascend from the details of the Piper Case to the whole meaning of the phenomenon, and especially when I connect the Piper case with all the other cases I know of automatic writing and mediumship, and with the whole record of spirit-possession in human history, the notion that such an immense current of human experience, complex in so many ways, should spell out absolutely nothing but the word "humbug" acquires a character of unlikeness.* The notion that so many men and women, in all other respects honest enough, should have this preposterous monkeying self annexed to their personality seems to me so weird that the spirit theory immediately takes on a more probable appearance. The spirits, if spirits there be, must indeed work under incredible complications and falsifications, but at least if they are present, some honesty is left in the whole department of the universe which otherwise is run by pure deception.[34]

James, it would appear, was capable of mustering a Sidgwickian abhorrence for the perversity of a universe in which all spiritual experience turned out to be the diddlings of the "monkeying self."

The Sidgwicks, naturally, were more resistent still, but they too were deeply impressed, and one suspects that it was precisely this bit of Jamesian coherentism that was informing Sidgwick's thoughts on theism. As the *Memoir* notes, in addition to Sidgwick's further – and seemingly successful – experiments in telepathy and hypnosis, there came in 1889 "Mrs. Piper – a medium who in a trance state seemed to have a power of getting information telepathically from the minds of those who sat with her, and sometimes something beyond this." Furthermore, "Sidgwick took an active part in the investigation, and though he did not himself have any success with her, the experiences of his friends impressed him very strongly." As Sidgwick would write to Roden Noel, with respect to Lodge's SPR report on Piper, "I think we are on the verge of something important." (M 502, 507) Eleanor Sidgwick would later sum up matters as follows: after Hodgson's second report on Piper, when she was under the G. P. control, "though all did not agree that the evidence for survival was yet conclusive, all who studied the subject felt, I think, that at any rate there was evidence that had to be taken account of."[35]

Set in this context, Sidgwick's enthusiasm for Eusapia Palladino makes more sense; his most skeptical and stalwart companions in psychical research (Hodgson, Lodge, Podmore, Eleanor) were all going over to optimism – some more slowly than others, but the drift was clear. It was a prime triumph for Myers when Sidgwick in 1898 would respond to Hodgson's report on Piper that, as for the spirit interpretation, "he could not say more than that a *prima facie* case had been established for further investigation, keeping this hypothesis in view." The time was indeed ripe for the Synthetic Society.

Of course, the theorizing that came of such developments was itself wild beyond belief. Myers, as one would expect, was the wildest of all. Here was a companion of Socrates who took it that Socrates was psychic.

The flights of psychological fancy that would become *Human Personality* had been released from Sidgwickian skepticism, though the results were proving paradoxical. Between the subliminal and the supraliminal, and the emphasis on the former not as a sink of base instinct, but as a source of artistic inspiration and creativity, the psychology of the individual was not looking very individualistic. As Oppenheim has rightly observed:

> Aiming above all else to prove that the human personality survived bodily death, he had virtually destroyed the human personality. In Myers's theory of the subliminal self, man emerged as a not particularly well integrated bundle of many parts; strata and streams of consciousness did not form one seamless web, but remained distinct entities. Myers vastly confused the question of what distinguished one single personality from another. Was personality composed of all the layers of subliminal consciousness taken together, or of one in particular? Was it, perhaps, the sum total of subliminal and supraliminal selves combined? Whatever its constitution, it was liable to abandon its own home, leaving that vulnerable to invasion and possession by an alien personality. Leaf was expressing an understandable opinion when he remarked that Myers's work weakened his own sense of personality. Myers had definitely not, Leaf explained, proved "the survival of what we call the living spirit, the personality – a unit of consciousness, limited and self-contained, a centre of will and vital force, carrying on into another world the aspirations and the affections of this."[36]

Myers knew how this deconstruction of the unitary agent was beginning to frighten people – Father Tyrrell probably found it strange – but he had to content himself with a faith "that there *is* an incandescent solid," albeit one that "is beneath our line of sight." Symonds in fact loved this development, though he would give it a less personalist twist. As he wrote to Sidgwick, in a letter strongly suggestive of the limits of his scientific attitude:

> I am fascinated by Myers' treatise on the Subliminal Consciousness. I doubt whether he himself suspects how far the hypothesis involved in his argument carries. Rightly, he confines himself to proof or plausible inference from more or less accredited phenomena.
>
> I could talk more than it seems convenient to write, upon the deductions and corollaries which must ensue from this doctrine, if it is established. It will prove a great prop to Pantheism, the religion of the Cosmic mind.[37]

The reference is presumably to Myers's seminal articles on "The Subliminal Self" that appeared in the SPR's *Proceedings* in 1892. And in fact, Myers was leading the way, setting the terms of the debate. Complex competing accounts of the phenomena – was it telapathic or direct control by departed spirits, or perhaps telapathic communication from departed spirits? – were all speaking Myers's depth psychological language. As Gauld demonstrates, the differences between the various members of the Sidgwick Group "seem on the surface to be quite considerable; and no doubt from a practical point of view they *are* considerable. But they did not involve the members of the Sidgwick Group in quite the theoretical differences one might expect, for believers and non-believers alike came in greater or in less measure to accept much the same sort of theoretical framework or at any rate theoretical terminology." And "this framework was principally developed by Myers."[38] Thus,

That Myers believed in survival whilst Sidgwick doubted it was not to any great extent due to the former accepting phenomena which the latter dismissed as fraudulent. The evidence had reached such a state . . . that rejecting the survivalist point of view involved about as much credulity (in the way of supposing sensitives and mediums to possess fantastic powers of telepathy and clairvoyance) as upholding it did, so that the side one took might well be decided by one's constitutional optimism or pessimism, or by one's suspicions as to one's prospects in another existence.[39]

Admittedly, it may seem quite fantastic to think of the ever-skeptical Sidgwick taking this type of psychological speculation so seriously. But he manifestly did, and it is worth reiterating that from an early age he had an abiding belief in quirky unconscious thought processes. Myers's *Human Personality* actually contains a report that Sidgwick belatedly wrote in 1885, recounting his experiments with his friend Cowell in the 1860s:

The experiences which I mentioned to you as similar to those described in your paper – so far as the mere effects of unconscious cerebration are concerned – occurred about twenty years ago. An intimate friend of mine who had interested himself somewhat in Spiritualism, and had read Kardec's book, discovered almost by accident that his hand could write, without any conscious volition on his part, words conveying an intelligible meaning – in fact, what purported to be communications of departed spirits. He asked me to come and stay with him, in order to investigate the phenomenon; he had been rather struck by some things in Kardec's book, and was quite disposed to entertain the hypothesis that the writing might be due to something more than unconscious cerebration, if it should turn out that it could give accurate information on facts unknown to him. The experiments, however, that we made in order to test this always failed to show anything in the statements written down that might not have been due to the working of his own brain; and at the end of my visit we were both agreed that there was no ground for attributing the phenomenon to any other cause but unconscious cerebration. At the same time we were continually surprised by evidences of the extent to which his unconscious self was able to puzzle his conscious mind. As a rule, he knew what he was writing, though he wrote involuntarily; but from time to time he used to form words or conjunctions of letters which we were unable to make out at first, though they had a meaning which we ultimately discovered.[40]

The report continues with several examples of the peculiar nature of Cowell's automatic writing – for example, they once puzzled over an apparently meaningless word before realizing that it was a transliteration of Greek for "farewell," the spirit apparently signing off in impressive fashion. Sidgwick found the experiments intriguing, and – though inconclusive on the question of spirit controls – certainly pointing to strong evidence for unconscious thought processess. Indeed, Sidgwick "had absolute reliance" on his friend's "*bona fides*," and did not suspect him of trying to mystify or defraud him.

Thus, it is important to bear in mind that all the close introspection of mental processes and appeal to unconscious belief pervading Sidgwick's philosophical ethics was increasingly informed by what he took to be genuine experimental evidence calling for a sophisticated depth psychological theory of the unconscious. He believed in telepathy, hypnosis, split personality, and a host of other depth psychological phenomena, and he had no scruples about their being legitimate objects of inquiry – in this he certainly paved the way for such pragmatists as James, and for Freudianism. Myers, like Symonds, was a fellow explorer of the human potential, an investigator of more or less Whitmanian forms of Cosmic Optimism who was working the right field. And Sidgwick allowed that with mediums like Piper, the *prima facie* case was made. Here was a working philosophy, reasonable, if not conclusive, evidence. The "blackness of the end" was turning to gray.

Eleanor Sidgwick in fact went on to publish a good deal on Piper, including "A Contribution to the Study of the Psychology of Mrs. Piper's Trance." Interest in the Piper case could not help but continue, given the further shock that came in 1905. Hodgson suddenly died, and according to Mrs. Piper, his spirit was now directing her trance states. And this was only one piece of the new and ever more complex evidence that the psychical researchers were proclaiming. New mediums, such as Mrs. Willett, were supposedly in communication with the spirits of none other than Sidgwick and Myers, who died within a half-year of each other, as well as with those of Hodgson and Gurney. According to C. D. Broad, Piper's

> mediumship has been of the utmost importance because it gave results which are quite certainly supernormal and which seem, *prima facie*, to be very difficult to explain without going beyond telepathy from the living. It is roughly true to say that Sidgwick's death happened at a transition point in the history of the subject. In the past were the comparatively straightforward problems of the experimental and statistical establishment of the transference of simple concrete ideas and emotions. In the future lay the subtle and complex problems of cross-correspondences, book-tests, and so on, in which we are still immersed. Mrs. Piper's mediumship is the connecting link between the two stages, and Sidgwick lived only long enough to participate in the very early phases of the investigation. . . . Mrs. Sidgwick survived her husband for many years and maintained up to the end her active interest in the Society and her invaluable work on the subject. We have her own authority for stating that, in her opinion, the evidence as a whole provides an adequate ground for believing that human beings survive bodily death. One would give a great deal to know whether the facts which became available after 1900 would have caused Sidgwick himself to accept so positive a conclusion.[41]

But before considering Sidgwick's death and possible posthumous writings, a little more needs to be said about the esotericism of his inquiries and his morality. For the nineties witnessed a great many Sidgwickian communications marked "Private."

IV. Pious Fraud

But again, I admit cases in which deception may legitimately be practised for the good of the person deceived. Under a physician's orders I should not hesitate to speak falsely to save an invalid from a dangerous shock. And I can imagine a high-minded thinker persuading himself that the mass of mankind are normally in a position somewhat analogous to that of such an invalid; that they require for their individual and social well-being to be comforted by hopes, and spurred and cured by terrors, that have no rational foundation. Well, in a community like that of Paraguay under the Jesuits, with an enlightened few monopolizing intellectual culture and a docile multitude giving implicit credence to their instruction, it might be possible – and for a man with such convictions it might conceivably be right – to support a fictitious theology for the good of the community by systematic falsehood. But in a society like our own, where every one reads and no one can be prevented from printing, where doubts and denials of the most sacred and time-honoured beliefs are proclaimed daily from house-tops and from hill-tops, the method of pious fraud is surely inapplicable. The secret must leak out; the net of philanthropic unveracity must be spread in the sight of the bird: the benevolent deceiver will find that he has demoralized his fellow-men, and contributed to shake the invaluable habits of truth-speaking and mutual confidence among them, without gaining the end for which he has made this great sacrifice. The better the man who sought to benefit his fellow men in this strange way the worse, on the whole, would be the result; indeed, one can hardly imagine a severer blow to the moral well-being of a community than that that element of it which was most earnestly seeking to promote morality should be chargeable with systematic unveracity and habitual violation of solemn pledges, and be unable to repell the charge.

Sidgwick, "The Ethics of Religious Conformity" (PE 74)

P.S. I really think that the power of combining sympathy and *lumen siccum* does belong to me – and the unpleasant is as human (um) as the pleasant.

Sidgwick to H. G. Dakyns, summer of 1864 (CWC)

Sidgwick's work with his various discussion societies and the SPR was very much a part of his own experimentation, a psychological exploration of his own possibilities as well as those of the general human condition. The old Apostolic ideal was ever-evident: frank, unfettered bearing witness, an encounter group for the parts of the soul. Sidgwick's worries about Father Tyrrell suggest just how much he continued to prize creating an intimate environment for the free expression of thought and feeling. The sympathy needed to get the spirits to speak applied to this world as well as to the other world, and it consequently makes perfect sense that Sidgwick should have moved effortlessly between the séance, religious counseling, educational counseling, and sexual counseling. The sincere expression of sexual doubt was on a par with the sincere expression of religious doubt – or for that matter, with the sincere expression of paranormal mental happenings in one's hidden depths. Certainly, there was a form of esoteric morality at work here, but with a strange aura of therapeutic confidentiality about it, intermingled with fear both of the "dim, common masses" and of what might materialize from within. Candor always seemed, for Sidgwick, to carry explosive consequences. Irresistible, but dangerous.

No doubt this did, in its way, comport very well with the spirit of the age insofar as it reflected the social construction, as it were, of intimacy and domesticity, the birth of the novel and the discovery of the unconscious, all mixed with notions of national and individual character building. The end of the Victorian era was the age of identity, as well as of empire. The two went together, becoming pressing issues in fine Hegelian fashion, just when they had become deeply problematic. The Boer War spelt the beginning of the end of empire. The spirits were speaking, but where was the soul? As always, Sidgwick was worried.

In a way, it scarcely does justice to Sidgwick to label him a "Government House" utilitarian or advocate of esoteric morality. Somehow, as we have seen in so many different ways, esotericism was virtually second (or perhaps first) nature to him. Even his vision of science, carrying all his plans for professionalization, involved the sincere testimonial, and therapeutic witnessing, of high-minded seekers. If he did not believe in "idle fellowships" and mere donnish erudition, he did somehow manage to transmute many of the gentlemanly ideals of seventeenth-century science into the idioms of the late nineteenth century. It was one thing to train people's faculties, to overcome the rift of the two cultures – humanistic and scientific – and to strengthen the societal role of forward-looking educational institutions. All this was well enough, but there was still the need of a clerisy, of leading thinkers on the cutting edge, and these might need protection from the public gaze.

And of course, when it came to the "deepest problems," paths of inquiry of a yet more intimate and esoteric nature were required.[42] One simply did not get at the "true self," its buried roots, without Apostolic inquiry, hypnosis, the analysis of dreams and hallucinations, and all the techniques that would shortly become clinical psychology. Sidgwick's own explorations were meant to be mind-altering, as transformative as any therapeutic experience could be. To mingle one's thoughts with others' was to be at risk, open to discovery and change of the most fundamental sort. As he had confessed in his diary, he was eager to "plunge into the tide of self-formation" (CWC). Moreover, literature, including classical literature, had a very important role to play, even if "the intuitions of literary genius will not avail to reduce to scientific order the complicated facts of psychical experience" (EP 123); his was the old Apostolic vision reworked in light of Mill and then again in light of parapsychology, Myers, and Symonds. In the age of scientific specialization, literature might help to give "the kind of wide interest in, the versatile sympathy with, the whole complex manifestation of the human spirit in human history," and might help to produce a "harmony of feeling in our contemplation of the world and life," even if it falls to philosophy to try to deliver a "reasoned harmony" (PE 125). Either way, such soul craft required the right form of discussion.

Was it secrecy or confidentiality that mattered so to Sidgwick? As noted in previous chapters, Sidgwick and Cowell were caught up in an early controversy about the very issue of Apostolic secrecy, and they had been advised by Lord Houghton, who thought that "little good would come from talking about the Society 'to the general world who are more likely to mistake its objects & misunderstand its principles', and urged a policy of secrecy."[43] Cowell's letter to Houghton read:

I was anxious to know whether in your time in Cambridge the Society was kept a secret, or whether the brothers openly talked of it. According to all traditions in my time, it was considered that the Society ought not to be talked about by its members and that much of its utility depended upon its being kept to a great extent secret. This seemed to me so obvious that I had always supposed it was the rule from the earliest times of the Society; until about two years ago some brothers started a new practice and told all about the Society to their friends and acquaintances at Cambridge. . . . The innovators maintain that they are only reverting to the primitive system which prevailed till twelve years ago. Would you tell me whether:
1st. publicity or secrecy was the rule?
2nd. the rule varied, and, if so
3rd. when? and with what results?
4th. whether publicity or secrecy was the rule during the years preceding 1847 and 1848 when the Society was nearly coming to an end.[44]

John Burwell Payne, elected in 1863, had complained that "Past indiscretions by members of the Society have caused some members to wish to keep our thoughts underground. May they be defeated." Sidgwick had some real sympathy and regard for Payne, with his hatred of hypocrisy. But on this issue he appears to have gone with the Angel's advice. As Deacon argues, the "sudden passion for secrecy in this period" was surely a result of the mission of the Apostles at that time: "Some members wanted to use the Society as a spearhead group to undermine the Church of England's domination of University life, and especially to remove the statutory obligations of the Thirty-Nine Articles." Thus, an excellent reason for secrecy was "to prevent victimisation by the Church."[45] This appeared to be the only road to free and frank inquiry.

Again, the connection with Lord Houghton, Richard Monckton Milnes, is telling. An Urning, a "defender of Keats, lately the patron of young Swinburne,"[46] and apparently a sometime collector of pornography, Houghton was one of the chief protectors and resources for the Apostles, facilitating their social position and efficacy. According to Allen, he "became a father figure to the younger Apostles[,] . . . and he used his very considerable social influence to benefit the Society and its members in whatever way he could."[47] He and Sidgwick were close in many respects, and back in the heady days of storm and stress, each had contributed an essay to the pathbreaking *Essays on a Liberal Education*. Though something of a dilettante, Houghton, too, wanted reform, a "larger and wiser instruction of our governing classes, if they are to remain our governors." Sidgwick of course also wanted to free liberal studies from "the clergy and persons of a literary bias," and to advance a notion of culture that would incorporate a truer Platonic Revival, being bound up with modern languages and modern science. The schools and the schoolmasters, like Dakyns and Browning and Eleanor Sidgwick, were to become the leaven in the loaf, loosening the hold of the church. This was manifestly not the form of Platonic Revival known in more recent times, though it certainly shared the aspiration of civilizing the rulers. Lord Houghton also practised mesmerism, which he had learned from Harriet Martineau.

The one club that Sidgwick apparently did not join was Cowell's Alpine Club, though it did represent for him a kind of premonition of Symonds at Davos. Many Apostles were members, and as Lubenow notes, the club was meant to foster comradeship: "it mingled life's mental, emotional and social properties. The life of physical exertion complemented mental exertion. Alpining allowed them to experience feelings of courage, vigour, physical pain, and being at one with nature in an immediate way. The struggle with and against nature gave a powerful sense of personal identity." Cowell, according to Trevelyan, "carried *camaraderie* to the highest point in our set and generation."[48] And even if he did not take to mountaineering with the same gusto, Sidgwick regarded Cowell as an intimate friend and was distraught over his premature death in 1867 – the year he wrote to Mill and took up with Symonds.

But there were so many other clubs, and they all took such similar form, sounding more or less Masonic in their organization. Consider Lubenow's description of the Savile club:

The Apostles also became members of less distinguished clubs which were as notable for their fellowship as for their learning. The Savile Club had a number of pronounced apostolic characteristics. One was the taking of common meals at a common table as a means of fostering friendly as well as social relations. Another was the club's conscious policy of electing members who differed from each other in their occupations, tastes, accomplishments, and interests. Henry and Arthur Sidgwick, J. B. Payne, Lord Houghton, and Henry Lee Warner were founding members of the Savile Club, and many other Apostles joined it in later years.[49]

Or his account of the Ad Eundem:

The Ad Eundem Club, founded to encourage university reform, was another enterprise of the Apostles as well as another of Henry Sidgwick's particular projects. Henry Jackson called it 'one of Henry's good works.' Composed of twenty members, ten from Cambridge and ten from Oxford, five resident and five non-resident, it met once a term to dine and discuss university affairs. It was strewn with Apostles on the Cambridge side: Henry and Arthur Sidgwick (though Arthur was in residence at Oxford after he left Rugby to take up his lectureship at Corpus Christi College), Jermyn Cowell, W. H. Thompson, G. O. Trevelyan, Richard Jebb, Henry Jackson, James Duff Duff, and G. M. Trevelyan. Cowell welcomed membership, but feared for the rules by which members would pay for their dinners.... The Ad Eundem Club represented a half century's commitment to university reform and liberal values which the Apostles shared with like-minded colleagues at Oxford.[50]

Or A. W. Brown's account of the formative influences on the Metaphysical Society:

The Apostles continued to influence the intellectual life of England throughout the century. When the Metaphysical Society was founded in 1869, Tennyson, Alford, Lushington, Thirlwall, and soon Maurice, Fitzjames Stephen, W. K. Clifford, and other Apostles were asked to join the new society. James Martineau, who although not a Cambridge man had sometimes attended meetings of the Apostles, and J. R. Seeley, who, Sidgwick said, should have been a member, were both among the founders of the Metaphysical Society. The Essay Club, the Apostles' lesser light at Oxford, contributed Gladstone and Henry Acland. Thus more than a sixth of the members of the Metaphysical Society were men who, at one time or another, had been under the influence of the Apostles. The success of the Metaphysical Society, whose aims and procedure were in some ways so similar to those of the older society, was perhaps in no small measure owing to the demanding discipline of mind and manner obtained in the weekly meetings of the Apostles.[51]

The Synthetic Society in its turn would be devoted to such questions as: "The evidence for the operation, in the process of the world and especially in human history, of a power that 'makes for righteousness,' in a manner or degree not to be accounted for by naturalistic explanations of the origin and development of morality, or, briefly the Moral Order or Moral Government of the World." The Society's "concessions" included recognition of the "general value" of religion and the "failure of attempts to find a socially effective substitute for Christian Theism."[52] But the approach, what with Sidgwick, Myers, Bryce, and Balfour attending, was very much on the old lines.

To be sure, these other discussion societies were not wrapped in quite the same aura of secrecy as the legendary Apostles. Still, for all practical purposes, their exclusiveness rendered them safe from any larger, unwanted public scrutiny. Preventing victimization by the church – or the dim masses – turned out to be a lifelong task for Sidgwick. How deeply ironic that his worst failings came from an excess of missionary zeal displaced, with civilization taking over for Christianity.

And as we have seen, he was, if the occasion called for it, perfectly willing to shade privacy into secrecy into more or less overt deception. At any rate, Apostolic inquiry required throwing a good many people off the scent in rather aggressive ways.

How else to interpret his advice about how to handle the more negative results of the SPR? Or about Balfour's political machinations? Or, most troubling, his evasions on the issue of race?

How else to regard his handling of Symonds's public persona, both during the latter's lifetime and posthumously? Recall the careful criticism of Symonds's poetry, the construction of biblical cover for homoerotic verse that he knew to be precisely that (indeed, that he admired as such). And as we noted, Horatio Brown's *John Addington Symonds, A Biography* was very much a joint effort of Brown, Dakyns, and Sidgwick. Sidgwick was the one who realized the degree to which public reaction to Symonds's erotic activities and Whitmania – particularly during the

years of the Wilde trial – could ruin everyone involved, completely discrediting him in his position at Cambridge and undermining all his efforts at reform. In fact, Balfour appears to have involved himself in the
Wilde case, being somewhat sympathetic to Bosie Douglas; according
to George Ives, Balfour cautioned Rosebery against intervening to help
Wilde, Rosebery already being widely suspected of homosexuality. And
George Ives, incidentally, was the founder of the Order of Chaeronea, a society based on the Masons but devoted to the reform of the laws concerning
homosexuality.[53]

Like Symonds, Sidgwick in fact recognized the importance of treating
these issues with all the resources of scientific respectability. The constant
worry that Symonds's writings on the subject were "too literary," and that
physicians such as Ellis were the ones who had to lead the way, is revealing.
Sidgwick brought to sexual issues the same keen sense of how to reassure
the public that he brought to the SPR. And when in the 1890s, Brown and
Dakyns were caught up both in assembling the Symonds biography and
in admiration for Edward Carpenter's work, it was quite in the tone set by
Sidgwick. In a letter to Carpenter from February of 1895, Brown set out
at some length the point of view:

I have just finished reading your pamphlet on Homogenic Love which Mr.
Havelock Ellis was kind enough to send me.

I should like to tell you with what admiration, sympathy & enthusiasm I have
read it. It is in this cool, quiet, convincing, scientific way that I think this difficult
&, at present, obscure problem should be brought to the notice of an ignorant and
hostile society.

At present I am rather afraid of the effect upon the world if the polemic is
confined to the region of *belles lettres*. I ought to say it more simply; I mean that I
think we want a cool, unimpassioned statement of the situation, & that Doctors &
Lawyers must be induced to take off their spectacles and look. If Lord H [?] had
been alive I should certainly have sent him your admirable Essay.[54]

"Lord H" was presumably Lord Houghton, who had died in 1885.

In a follow-up letter, Brown adopts a very Sidgwickian tactic:

You ask my opinion about publishing: as I said in my last letter to you, I feel
that the main object just now is to get doctors & lawyers to give intelligent attention to the subject; if publication will reach & touch them I should say publish by all means. It is the uninformed & prejudiced majority who require to be
instructed.

If you publish I should venture to suggest the omission of the word "delights" in the first line. I may be wrong, but I have an idea that the sympathetic colour of the word might prejudice the already prejudiced against the argument; the whole tone of which strikes me as cool, grave, admirable except for "delights.". . . Did it ever strike you how young both spiritually & physically the homosexuals remain![55]

The lines in question read: "Of all the many forms that Love delights to take, perhaps none is more interesting (for the very reason that it has been so inadequately considered) than that special attachment which is sometimes denoted by the word Comradeship." Brown, by his own account, was altogether a literary person, but the matter of comradeship was something that he, like Symonds and Sidgwick, wanted to see treated with all the authority of the scientific establishment, even if he thought it clear enough what science would prove.

In due course, when he assembled his sole volume of (somewhat) homo-erotic poetry, *Drift*, in the spring of 1900, Brown too sought and followed Sidgwick's "wisdom." Sidgwick, even on his deathbed, urged caution; according to Brown, Sidgwick was afraid that "the enemy" might use *Drift* for purposes of an "attack" on both Brown and Symonds.[56] Brown came to feel very close to Sidgwick, toward the end of the latter's life, finding him a uniquely sympathetic friend. Sidgwick, like Symonds and like Dakyns, was on his side, against "the enemy."

It is scarcely surprising that "Henry's wisdom" in these matters should have been so insightful and so effective, given how he had so long honed his skills at leading a double life in order to pursue the "deepest problems" in sympathetic fellowship while avoiding "victimisation by the Church." In this, at least, his efforts were a success. And he clearly did keep Symonds from becoming a public scandal. He was intensely engaged with Brown and Dakyns in the assembly of the Symonds biography, candidly describing their "care" to "keep things secret." The flavor of their lengthy and detailed exchanges – puzzling, for example, over whether they dare mention the name of the sex researcher Ulrichs – may be gleaned from one of Brown's letters to Sidgwick, from November of 1894:

I have to thank you very much for two long letters of most valuable criticism; one I ought to have answered sooner, the other has just arrived. Of course they both raise a most important point in the construction of the book. The variance between us is, as it always has been, upon the question of how much. There are two reasons why I should hesitate to hold by my own selection, as against your excisions;

(1) I have excised so much already that, to me, what I have left in seems harmless; but it is possible that I have 'poisoned my eye' as painters say.

(2) You are so much more experienced than I am; & you are in England; in touch with the best of it.

On the other hand I sometimes fancy that there must be another public – not a vicious one necesarily, but perhaps less influenced by traditions of cultivated society, to whom these things would not appear shocking.

I also feel that this book, if it is going to live at all, will probably be appealing to people long after all who are immediately concerned with it are gone, and it is a pity that its readers should not get some idea of the emotional side of the life that is portrayed.

I notice that you take it for granted that wherever passion, emotion, affection, for other is mentioned the public will take it for that kind of passion, emotion, affection which we are not to introduce. I do not think there is anything in the pages of the book itself to warrant that conclusion.

But then, as you say, there is that wretched *Key of Blue*, (I think there is nothing I regret so much as the existence of that book). Personally I feel that where emotion, passion, affection, play a large part in a man's life, it does not matter much what the precise complexion of that passion etc. was; and the student of a man's life need not enquire too closely. . . . But I suppose we should not agree here; and I am very far from asserting that I am right.

I do not think I am incautious, & I feel the weight of your wisdom; and yet I think if I came to this book as an outsider I should only gather from the Davos pages indications of a man who made warm friendships with many people not of his own class. However there are one or two considerations in myself, which make me doubtful whether I am a competent judge; and I daresay I shall excise again as I have done before almost all that you query.[57]

The letter would go on to explain that "in the end I shall be governed by the consensus of yourself & H.G.D." and to ask Sidgwick to indicate the degree of his alarm at various passages. In fact, as all concerned recognized, Sidgwick was also working at the request of the Symonds family – Catherine had written to Dakyns, in November of 1894, about how glad she was "to have Henry's wisdom for *final* reference."

Although some have suggested that Sidgwick effectively spoiled Brown's work, it should be stressed that they were actually very much in accord and for the most part happily collaborative. The book cast all of Symonds's agonizing purely in the religious terms of those intense exchanges with Sidgwick, back in in the long hot summer of 1867, when Symonds was longing to be "knocked flat" and was unimpressed with his friend's theistic faith. This was the stance that Brown would maintain throughout, even in defending the work to the much admired (though puzzled) Carpenter:

About the Biography, though well aware how large a part of Symonds' later life was occupied by this question [Inversion], I have always felt & still feel convinced that it was not the main thread in his psychology. I have by no means omitted the topic altogether; there are passages on the theory of fellow service, on the theory of class distinctions, etc. which contain some of the most important of Symonds' views on this subject – and which will be understood by those who can understand the matter at all; but of course I was bound to consider the whole life and to observe proportion.[58]

Fine, Mauricean Apostolic evasion and myth making is about the most generous construction that one can put on this, with truth being left between the lines for the knowing eye. Sidgwick's hand, so practiced from his exercises in literary criticism and censorship, was obviously the one guiding the entire effort. In another letter to Carpenter, Brown somewhat heatedly explained:

You probably do not know that the very last words he wrote, when he was past speech, and within a few hours of death, were a strong injunction to me to regard his family in all matters of publication. An appeal from one of his family; the strongly expressed opinion of his oldest and most intimate friends when I got to London; the best legal & medical opinion I could obtain; all combined to make me take the steps I did: although I may not have done quite what he would have liked (but did not do), I think I have done what he would have done in the circumstances.[59]

Of course, the biography, supposedly grounded on Symonds's very frank memoirs, was only one part of the effort to "keep things secret." There was, after all, Symonds's work with Ellis on *Sexual Inversion*, which was in a fairly advanced state. This was apt to blow everything. Grosskurth describes how Brown handled Ellis:

At first Symonds's literary executor, Horatio Brown, from Venice gave every encouragement possible. On August 8th, 1895, he wrote, after reading the manuscript: 'I think that it is admirable in its calmness, its judicial unbiased tone. And if anything can persuade people to look the question in the face this should.' But Mrs. Symonds – who apparently never saw the manuscript – felt nervous and wanted her husband's old friend, the philosopher Henry Sidgwick, to look it over carefully. Sidgwick insisted on some omissions, and Brown, now in London, was obviously beginning to waver and told Ellis that he fully agreed with Sidgwick. Suddenly, in July 1897, Ellis received word from Brown that he had consulated both Herbert Asquith and a Professor George Poore (an authority on sanitation), who advised that the publication 'will do more harm to Symonds's name than good to the cause'. The matter, be believed, should be left entirely to medical men. As for Asquith, he believed the treatment was far too 'literary'. Pressure was being put on Brown from all sides, and while he personally might have liked to have seen the publication of the book as it was (as well as the publication of Symonds's autobiography), he felt obliged to ask Ellis to remove Symonds's name from the title page as well as all material attributed to Symonds. He would not allow further distribution of the book and, after buying up the entire edition from de Villiers, had it destroyed.[60]

That Sidgwick orchestrated all this is highly likely – "Henry's wisdom" was the "final" reference in all such matters. And thus it was that "Soldier Love" and much else that Symonds had written went underground until late in the twentieth century. Sidgwick may have had a reputation, during his lifetime and since, for saintly honesty and candor. But he did not deserve it. This massive falsification was not merely one of his golden silences: it was an extended campaign to create and control Symonds's posthumous public reputation. The new casuistry apparently had room for pious fraud after all.

But if this was a very big lie, it was at least not a betrayal. Sidgwick, Dakyns, and Brown were too much in accord about matters, and their efforts quite possibly did reflect Symonds's final thoughts about how wise it would be to take the public into one's intimate confidence. Wilde was a martyr and Carpenter a hero, in the eyes of the later gay liberation movement. Sidgwick must go down as someone who was politically astute, loyal to friends, and very, very good at keeping a secret. He never did come out, with sexual or psychical research, but had he done so, the reaction would probably have been even more depressing than it was in the case of women's higher education. From Sidgwick's perspective, the "yellow nineties" must have been rather blue, personally and politically, with the problem of hypocrisy weighing on him more heavily than ever. One can well imagine what spectres kept him awake at night – visions of blazing forth on psychical research or women's higher education only to be attacked by his old religious antagonists, newly armed with a sex scandal and coverup, courtesy of his old friend Symonds.

V. The Voyage

My religion *if I were dying* is this verse of Whitman's. It is not poetry, few hymns (but Clough's) are
"Unchanged through our changes of spirit and frame
Past, now and henceforward the Lord is the same
Though we sink in the darkness, his arms break our fall,
and in death as in life he is Father of all."
Simple words for a dying man. I do not wish to die but I think of it – the "word proceeding out of the mouth of God" is often bitter food.

Sidgwick to H. G. Dakyns, spring 1866 (CWC)

Early in the month of May 1900 Sidgwick, by his Cambridge physician's advice, consulted an eminent surgeon in London, and learnt the serious nature of the illness which had recently affected him. He was suffering from an internal cancer, which must ultimately prove fatal, and which within a very short time would necessitate an operation of a grave character. For nearly a fortnight he told no one but his wife. It was easier to carry on life in a normal manner when no one knew. But he began to set his affairs in order. He felt full of vigour and vitality, and minded very much leaving this life and all the work he was doing and was interested in; and he was especially troubled because he was leaving so much literary work unfinished. There was the book on the *Development of European Polity*, already in an advanced state, but which he had had to lay aside, feeling that he could not give to it the time and labour required to make it as scholarly a work as he desired while giving courses of lectures on metaphysics; there was an Introduction to Philosophy which he was gradually evolving into a book. And in a more fragmentary state there were other metaphysical lectures which in his own mind were books in embryo. He did what he could to arrange these and his other papers, fearing, what proved to be the case, that after the operation he might not be able to do any more work; but he had promised to give an address on the Philosophy of T. H. Green to the Oxford Philosophical Society on May 20, the preparation of which required time, and prevented his spending as much time in putting his papers into order as he would have liked.

Henry Sidgwick, A Memoir[61]

It was characteristic of Sidgwick to carry out his commitments in this way. He and Eleanor went to Oxford on May 19, staying with the Diceys.

He had a last Ad Eundem dinner that evening, and gave his final philosophical lecture the next night, also working in a meeting "to establish
the *Mind* Association, which was to take over from him and carry on the
philosophical journal *Mind*." No one at the meetings knew what had befallen him, and he did not tell, though he did take the occasion of being in
Oxford to explain to his brother Arthur how matters stood. Arthur later
recalled Henry's visit in a letter to his half-brother-in-law, James Maurice
Wilson, who had written him a letter of condolence:

On the Sunday in May – the most sorrowful day I have known, for my mother
died in ripe old age after we had been long prepared for it, and my father I do
not remember – that Sunday when he came over to tell us what was impending –
there will always abide with me the memory how he calmly told me, that when the
blow fell and he heard that he was doomed, he reviewed his whole life, considering
whether under the new solemn certainty (as he then thought) of imminent death
his thoughts and beliefs stood fast, and whether, or how far, he could feel he had
done his work and lived his life as he had meant;

    and how he did not see, after fullest reflection, that the coming death
brought any new light on his intellectual beliefs or shifted or modified in any way
the grounds on which the truths (as he had long held them) had commanded his
assent:

    how as to his work, he felt that [he] had in the main and to the best of his
power carried out what he had meant to do, – whatever the worth of it;

    but in regard to the daily life and conduct he saw many points of shortcom-
ing in spite of effort, and faults of character too indulgently treated, and practices
which would have been salutary not adopted, from insufficient consideration –
here he gave examples, some of which he thought might be useful to others, and
to me.

    The whole left a *deep impression* of mixed sincerity, and humility, and high moral
aims, and genuine devotion to truth, and anxious effort to avoid all forms of self
deception, and complete detachment from any personal motive – a deep sense of
responsibility and the truest and rarest disinterestedness.[62]

Sidgwick was precisely the type to review his life in this way, and although there do seem to be conflicting impressions of just how content he
was with the state of his work, there is greater consensus on the matter of
his refusal to let death alter his philosophical convictions. This was plainly
something that he, more than anyone, regarded as a vital test of one's true
self, a crucial part of the experiment to determine the religious leanings
of individual psychology, the universality of some form of theistic belief.

It would of course have been most helpful if Arthur had elaborated on just which practices "would have been salutary not adopted," but that was not something he was likely to do at that point, when he was in fact being highly protective of his reputation.[63] But Sidgwick must not have been too censorious with his younger brother, though he still wanted him to take on an ambitious piece of work, and willed him some money for that purpose. Arthur had always felt his "function to be to *distribute*, not *produce*, knowledge."[64] At any rate, the younger brother was deeply moved; he wrote to George Trevelyan, on August 20, that Henry's "quiet review of his own life" was "what we can none of us forget. It was the last and best example of what he was and is – as I have known since I knew anything, and you have known for over forty years." (M 598)

What was uppermost in Sidgwick's mind may in fact have been better expressed to Dakyns. He had written to Dakyns on May 29 – just two days before the operation, which took place on his sixty-second birthday – telling him of the "incurable complaint of the bowels" and how he would "try to bear it as a man should":

I think much of old times and old friends and especially of your unfailing love and sympathy. It is through human love that I try to touch the Divine and "faintly trust the larger hope."
If I have given a hint, I shall be happy. (M 589)

After the operation and a brief convalescence at the Cliftonville Hotel in Margate, when there were still hopeful signs, Sidgwick was taken to Terling Place, the Rayleigh estate in Essex. Dakyns was a frequent visitor, extremely concerned about his old friend. Like Arthur, he was also privileged to hear Sidgwick's review of his life, though he also heard much about beauty and love; about the continuing need humanity had for prayer, or at least self-examination; and about the much-too-ready acceptance of agnosticism, as simply a foregone conclusion, on the part of the younger Cambridge men (this last matter being aimed at Graham's son, who was at Cambridge and a friend of Bertrand Russell's).[65]

Thus, Sidgwick at the end was very far from worrying about his overly introspective self, and was very well aware of and unimpressed by the insouciance of the younger Apostles on religious issues. They had, to his mind, a tendency to miss the deeper side of human existence, the emotional unsatisfactoriness of the universe being constructed by modernity. Crude atheism, crude materialism, crude conversation – he had always rejected these for the finer ambivalences of human existence. It is singularly interesting that when Arthur and Eleanor assembled *Henry Sidgwick, A Memoir*, they provided so much detail about the Apostles – something that caused the younger Brethren much consternation, and of course discussion.[66] It was a curious exposure, coming from the "Pope's" widow and an old Apostle and brother of the "Pope."

At any rate, when it came to possessing a sense of the gravity of the issue, he was closer to Nietzsche's grasp of the world-shattering importance of the death of God, or at least to James on the variety of religious experience and Dewey on a common faith, than to Keynes and Russell.[67]

Prayer was a prominent theme throughout Sidgwick's last months. Father Tyrrell had written to him a "very kind and sympathetic letter," and Sidgwick felt it necessary to respond that he valued "sincerely the prayers of all whose kindness prompts them to pray for me, and especially of those who devote themselves to the betterment of man's spiritual life." But this value, he emphasized, was "entirely independent of agreement in theological beliefs," and he was quite well aware "of the different attitudes towards the endurance of pain and sorrow in which our respective intellectual conclusions place us." Sidgwick had recognized "that truth long ago in days of health and happiness," and it is a subject on which he may, if he has any future capacity for work, try to put his thoughts "into an orderly form for the help of others." (M 595)

Moreover, there was the farewell to Myers, in some ways the most revealing of all. Sidgwick had written to Myers on May 24:

I went to Leckhampton this afternoon to tell you face to face our trouble. But you were away and I must write.

I have an organic disorder (bowels) which – the expert said more than a fortnight ago – must soon render an operation necessary. I am, by my Cambridge physician's advice, going to see him again tomorrow. He may say 'at once.' I believe that the chances of the operation are on the whole favourable: I mean that the probabilities are that I shall not die under it, but *how long* I shall live after it is uncertain. At any rate it will be only an invalid halflife.

I have hoped till today to defer telling this till after your brother's visit. I have shrunk from grieving those who love me. But today I am telling brothers and sisters and *one* or *two* intimate friends. *Only* them: please tell no one.

We may of course have to put our visitors off. If so, we shall telegraph to you tomorrow afternoon. If not, all will go on as arranged, and in that case I shall probably come to the Synthetic though not to the dinner.

Life is very strange now: very terrible: but I try to meet it like a man, my beloved wife aiding me. I hold on – or try to hold on – to duty and love; and through love to touch the larger hope.

I wish now I had told you before: as this may be farewell. Your friendship has had a *great place* in my life, and as I walk through the Valley of the Shadow of Death, I feel your affection. Pray for me.[68]

Sidgwick had supposed that the operation was to take place very shortly after this letter, but a second expert, thinking that his pulse was too weak, ordered him to "eat, drink, and be merry for a few days first." Sidgwick did attend the Synthetic, and as Myers would recall:

I learnt his sentence from his own lips just before he presided at a meeting of the Synthetic Society, at which Mr. Arthur Balfour read a paper upon Prayer. And thus it came about that my friend's last utterance, – not public, indeed, but spoken intimately to a small company of like-minded men, – was an appeal for pure spirituality in all human supplication; a gentle summons to desire only such things as cannot pass away. I will not say how his countenance showed then to my eyes; – eyes dimmed, perhaps, with secret knowledge of what so soon must be.[69]

The intimate company of "like-minded men," the companions of Socrates – this was just the image that Myers would seek to capture. How fitting, too, that the topic of the evening should be prayer. This had obviously been a preoccupation of Sidgwick's for his entire life – recall his youthful essay for the Apostles entitled "Is Prayer a Permanent Function of Humanity?" And his attitude at the end appears to have been much the same as his attitude at the beginning:

Men pray not merely as a means to an end, but to indulge a profound abiding and imperious instinct, and the function does not merely generate emotions, which produce moral results, but is closely bound up with a whole group of thoughts and feelings which we may call religious (in a narrow sense of the term). It is not impossible to imagine a genuine Theism as existing and producing the best effects on the character, without prayer: but it is not possible to conceive an emotional relation existing between man and unknown powers, without states of consciousness that are in substance prayer.[70]

He was not willing to let go of some sense of reverence for the larger whole, despite his sense that he was living on reasonableness rather than reason. He was never one of the symmetrical people.

At a luncheon party at Myers's Leckhampton on May 27, Sidgwick would be in good form, discussing Swinburne's poetry. A friend who attended recalled: "He taught me there how calmly and manfully death and suffering could be faced, as he recited without a break in his voice the lines which I could hardly bear to hear, from 'Super Flumina Babylonis,' ending 'Where the light of the life of him is on all past things, / Death only dies.' " (M 588)

Myers said his goodbye to Sidgwick shortly before his death in late August. It had been a difficult summer, with some glimmers of hope, but mostly a steady wasting away of life and energy. Sidgwick had not been in pain, but the discomfort, caused chiefly by his dyspepsia, was acute, and by mid-August even his closest friends and relatives were simply wishing for a serene end. Dakyns had been sending him their old correspondence to go over, which stimulated his thoughts about his past life. And with the cumulative effect of so much reflection in his mind, his message to Myers was a particularly significant one:

"As I look back on my life," – almost his last words to me were these, – "I seem to see little but wasted hours. Yet I cannot be sorry that you should idealise me, if that shows that I have made my ideals in some degree felt. We must idealise, or we should cease to struggle."[71]

Perhaps Sidgwick had in mind the many hours wasted in psychical research. But if so, it would appear that Myers did not quite agree. Sidgwick "did not indeed bequeath to us his wisdom in the shape of crisp metaphysical bank-notes, which the Universe would ultimately decline to cash. Nor did he, like the old man in the fable, tell us to dig everywhere for a treasure which in reality was only to consist in the strengthening of our own minds." No, there was more to Sidgwick than the disciplining of the faculties and the concentrating of fog: "he pointed to a definite spot; he vigorously drove in the spade; he upturned a shining handful, and he left us as his testament, *Dig here*."[72]

Sidgwick died at about 3 P.M. on August 28, and the funeral was held on the thirty-first, at Terling. Dakyns went down, but otherwise only members of the family were there, in the beautiful, peaceful corner of the old country churchyard. The Church of England funeral service was used, it being a village churchyard, even though Eleanor knew that "not to use it was what seemed to him most in harmony with his views and actions in life." He had not left specific instructions, but he had in fact composed an alternative: "Let us commend to the love of God with silent prayer the soul of a sinful man who partly tried to do his duty. It is by his wish that I say over his grave these words and no more." (M 599) These words were used to conclude the *Memoir*.

There is a report that Sidgwick insisted on being buried in a wickerware coffin, though his rationale for this remains unclear. At any rate, a beautiful monument of red Whittingehame sandstone was placed on the grave, carrying a simple inscription: "In Thy Light Shall He See Light."[73]

There were many obituaries, tributes, letters of condolence. Bryce, Maitland, Balfour, Myers, and so many others saw to that. Yet as Alan Gauld has noted, one of the most touching testimonials came in the shape of a letter that Frank Podmore had written to Sidgwick on August 27, which he probably never saw:

You have counted for so much in my life: and I have valued so highly your friendship. Apart from all that you have done for our common work, I feel that I personally owe so much of my intellectual development to you: that you have helped me to see more clearly and to weigh more soberly and justly.

And in other ways, that I can hardly find words for, your life and character have meant a great deal to me. I am not sure now that I very much care whether or not there is a personal, individual immortality. But I have at bottom some kind of inarticulate assurance that there is a unity and a purpose in the Cosmos: that our lives, our own conscious force, have some permanent value – and persist in some form after death. And – if you will let me say it – you and some others, just by being what you are, constantly revive and strengthen that assurance for me. I feel that there is a meaning in things.[74]

This is the kind of tribute that Sidgwick would have singled out – he had done something for someone to restore faith in "things in general."[75] As he wrote to Baron von Hugel: "it is a deep satisfaction to any one who has to look back on his life's work as something nearly finished to think that the incompleteness of his work and the imperfection of his manner of performing it have not altogether obscured his ideal from the recognition of his fellow-men" (M 592). Indeed, Eleanor seems not to have been terribly impressed with the more florid tributes. As her biography notes:

Many good and consolatory things were said of her husband, as at the Memorial Meeting in Cambridge of November 1900; but from the more emotional expressions her nature shrank. ("I don't think Henry was like that," she said once, long afterwards, of one of these more florid tributes. She once or twice asserted that she and he were "grey," – "grey people"). Her old students' letter, from the Newnham College Club, – of which Miss Clough was the Cambridge representative – she answered at once. "We wanted you to know," they wrote, "that we realise that we owe to him opportunities which have altered our whole lives, that we feel it to have been an honour and a privilege to be even indirectly under his influence, and that we understand at least something of the value of what we have lost."[76]

The Sidgwick Memorial Lecture at Newnham was instituted as a fitting remembrance – the first being given by Bryce, in 1902 – though one might well think that the winning of Newnham's freehold and their burgeoning Fellowship Fund were the better memorials, especially given Balfour's contribution to the lecture series. Eleanor would remain at the helm of Newnham for another ten years, as well as being a mainstay of the SPR. She also kept up her work for women's education and suffrage, and for such causes as the Charity Organization Society.

But in the immediate aftermath of Henry's death, she was tired. Friends and family convinced her, curiously enough, to journey to Egypt, where her niece, an Oxford student named Maggie Benson, was heading to excavate tombs. Thus it was that, ironically, Eleanor packed up various of Henry's literary remains and correspondence in order to sort through them at Karnak, in a house "with a lovely view of Luxor and the eastern hills beyond." The trip apparently restored her. She divided her time between arranging *The Development of European Polity* and joining in the work in the tombs, tracing the wall paintings.

Apparently, the plan for the *Memoir* emerged fairly early on, when Eleanor realized how much material was available for the purpose. At any rate, she almost immediately set about rounding up as much of Henry's correspondence as possible. Doubtless it was with thoughts of the Symonds biography in mind that she wrote to Horatio Brown in September, who responded on October 3:

I am sure you will not have attributed to want of sympathy the fact that I have not written to say how deeply I feel for you in this great loss. For Henry, who only longed to go, to rest at the close of a noble life, & for him there can be no sorrow, no fears. But for you, for us, who have to go on without him, how bitter is the loss. I do not think a day has passed without my recalling him, his sympathy, his understanding, his support so generously given; and if I feel it so what must it be for you? He said to me in a letter "I think you will not forget me." That I never shall.

The great packet of Henry's letter-journals to Mr. Symonds was returned to him long ago & must either be among his papers or have been destroyed by him. But I will look out whatever other letters I have from him to Mr. Symonds; not many; as the journal formed the real correspondence.[77]

Brown's sympathy was clearly sincere. And surely Eleanor's concern was not unlike that of Symonds's widow. After all, if one counts the students of Newnham, Henry had left far more than three surviving daughters whose reputations might suffer, should the founding father be disgraced. And of course, there were the Balfour political careers, and so on and on.

Is it in the least bit shocking that the *Memoir*, like *John Addington Symonds, A Biography*, decorously leaves out all reference to sexual matters? The Symonds poetry, Arthur's doings, the Brown biography – all these the *Memoir* enfolds in silence. It was a silence that continued for a very long time indeed. Quite possibly the Valley of the King's witnessed some fresh burials, during Eleanor's time there.

But there was a yet stranger aftermath to Sidgwick's death. One would expect the leading psychical researchers to seek to devise new, more inventive tests for communicating with the other world, and this they did. Both Sidgwick and Myers, who died on January 17, 1901,[78] left sealed envelopes with messages inside, the hope being that some medium would be able to divine the contents. The researchers gave the test over eight years, and Eleanor reported the results to James in a letter dated February 26, 1909:

We opened the Myers envelope which you sent over and the envelope my husband left, on Tuesday last, in the presence of Sir Archibald Geikie (President of the Royal Society), my brother Gerald Balfour, Mr Walter Leaf, Mr Piddington, Mr Fielding, Miss Johnson and myself. The result was a blank. So far as we can at the moment remember the scripts of the different automatists, there is no evidence of any attempt to communicate the contents of either envelope.

Mr Myers', dated July 25 1890, contained two lines from Wordsworth's Laodama:
The invisible world with thee hath
 sympathised;
Be thy affections raised and
 illuminised
My husband's, dated May 16, 1900, contained two texts
 I keep under my body and
 bring it into subjection.
 Shall we receive good at the

hands of the Lord and shall
we not receive evil.
These were headed "To be remembered" and below them was written
"For remembrance H Sidgwick"[79]

But the failure of the experiment did not much move Eleanor: "I have
always doubted whether posthumous envelopes were likely to give us good
results, because I am so certain I should forget anything I put in one
myself."

It was of course just like Sidgwick to leave a couple of biblical texts, particularly one about bringing his body into subjection. Noteworthy, in this
connection, is the date of the Sidgwick letter, suggesting that it was penned
shortly after the tragic diagnosis by Dr. Allingham. But Eleanor was to
come to a more optimistic conclusion as a result of other developments –
the cross-correspondence cases mentioned earlier. As Broad has described
the fresh evidence:

Certain parts of what follows [a discussion of Mrs. Willett's mediumship] would
not be intelligible unless it were prefaced by a few words about the so-called
'cross-correspondences', which were in 1908 and for many years afterwards being
reported, analysed, and commented upon in the S.P.R. *Proceedings*. These scripts
came through the hands of a number of non-professional automatists, several
of whom were personally strangers to each other and living in various parts of
the world. They purported to come from the surviving spirits of F.W.H. Myers,
Edmund Gurney, Henry Sidgwick, and certain of their friends. It was claimed
in the scripts themselves, that these persons, after their deaths, had devised and
were using a method of communication which would rule out telepathy from the
living as a possible explanation of the out-of-the-way and characteristic bits of
information displayed in the automatic writings.

In essence the method was this. In the script of each automatist there would
be fragmentary and allusive items, without special significance for the person in
whose script they occurred. But these were highly significant for any investigator, acquainted with the personalities, interests, and acquirements of the alleged
communicators, who might compare and put together the contemporary scripts
of the various automatists in the group.[80]

The extraordinary complexity and arcane nature of the scripts from
Mrs. Willett, Mrs. Verrall, and the other mediums certainly brought out
the most gymnastic hermeneutical talents of the psychical researchers,
who struggled to decipher weird references to the "Ear of Dionysius" and
so forth.

The timing of these developments is curious. It is shortly before the failure of the envelope tests, in her presidential address to the SPR in May of 1908, that Eleanor explains how those

who follow the work of the Society carefully will, I think, perceive that in these scripts we have at least material for extending our knowledge of telepathy. They will probably be disposed further to admit that the form and matter of the cross-correspondences that occur between the different scripts (produced at a distance from one another) afford considerable ground for supposing the intervention behind the automatists of another mind independent of them. If this be so the question what mind this is becomes of extreme interest and importance. Can it be a mind still in the body? or have we got into relation with minds which have survived bodily death and are endeavouring by means of the cross-correspondences to produce evidence of their operation? If this last hypothesis be the true one it would mean that intelligent cooperation between other than embodied human minds and our own, in experiments of a new kind intended to prove continued existence, has become possible, and we should be justified in feeling that we are entering on a new and very important stage of the Society's work.[81]

The cross-correspondence cases were thus taken as an ingenious bit of posthumous experimentalizing by the senior members of the Sidgwick Group, and were treated with all the seriousness and diligence that the SPR could muster. Needless to say, few since their time, or at least since Broad's, have been quite so impressed by this body of evidence. Indeed, the reputation of the SPR suffered a good deal from what looked like a prolonged obsession with mourning the lost founders, carried on by a group of insiders irretrievably lost to a truly bizarre interpretive method. Some flavor of this can be had from an unpublished lecture on telepathy that Eleanor Sidgwick gave at Cambridge on January 25, 1912:

Three years ago, on January 6th [1909], Mrs. Verrall's script produced sixteen lines of verse which might be intended for a description of St. Paul's experience on the road to Damascus at the time of his conversion – and following these verses came the words, "That is partly what I had to say, but I think you have confused it somewhere. There should be an allusion to the Chemin de *Damas*. Remember what Renan wrote about it. – F.W.H.M." (F.W.H.M. were the initials of Mr. Frederic Myers.) On January 8th, in another part of the country, Mrs. Willett obtained in her automatic script the sentence "I want you to do something for me, to write to Mrs. Verrall and say these words: Eikon Renam. Eikon Renam (twice repeated). No, don't send yet. – Myers."

The word *eikon*, Greek for image, was known to Mrs. Willett (who is not a Greek scholar) in connection with the sacred pictures used in the Greek Church, but Renam – RENAM – conveyed nothing to her, and it would probably have conveyed nothing to any of us if it had not been for the mention in Mrs. Verrall's script two days before of the French writer on the early Christian narratives, M. Renan – RENAN. But when we find Renan mentioned in a script of Mrs. Verrall's on January 6th, which is signed with Mr. Myers' initials, and Renan emphasised in Mrs. Willett's script on January 8th in a message to Mrs. Verrall also signed by Myers, the conclusion is irresistible that the substitution of M for N in Mrs. Willett's script was a slip of the automatist's.

We have these three coincidences – the scripts were both connected with Mrs. Verrall, were both signed by Myers and both referred to Renan or Renam.

They led Mrs. Verrall to look up in Renan's book on the Apostles (which neither she nor Mrs. Willett had ever read) his account of the journey to Damascus to which her script referred her; and she then discovered that Renan describes St. Paul as having seen the figure of Jesus – *eikon* in Greek – for which there is no warrant in the original account in the Book of Acts. It struck her – and very plausibly, I think when we remember that her script called special attention to what Renan said – that the introduction of the word *eikon* in connection with Renam may have been intended to indicate this discrepancy.[82]

Perhaps this is evidence of something, though it is difficult to say just what. At any rate, the continuation of such exercises is what ultimately brought Eleanor to belief. When as honorary president she gave her address to the SPR on the occasion of its fiftieth anniversary, she again struck the positive note, albeit guardedly: "The general effect produced by the study of these scripts is that some intelligence behind the communications is acting by design." Arthur Balfour, with her permission, followed up with the announcement:

That concludes the Address of your President of Honour. May I be allowed, before we separate, to add one or two sentences of my own? Some of you may have felt that the note of caution and reserve has possibly been over-emphsised in Mrs Sidgwick's paper. If so, they may be glad to hear what I am about to say. Conclusive proof of survival is notoriously difficult to obtain. But the evidence may be such as to produce *belief*, even though it fall short of conclusive *proof*. I have Mrs Sidgwick's assurance – an assurance which I am permitted to convey to the meeting – that, upon the evidence before her, she herself is a firm believer both in survival and in the reality of communication between the living and the dead.[83]

Belief short of conclusive proof – whether the message came from the departed Henry Sidgwick or not, it was certainly in the spirit of his final views on the theistic postulate. As Barrett observed, in *Psychical Research*, the Sidgwick persona of the scripts "retains his propensity for awaiting results with scrupulous patience, though he has now, as well he may, added to patience a confident hope."[84]

Strangely enough, however, the scripts would make it appear that Sidgwick had finally reached the point where he was not talking:

We no more solve the riddle of death by dying than we solve the problem of life by being born. Take my own case – I was always a seeker, until it seemed to me at times as if the quest was more to me than the prize. Only the attainments of my search were generally like rainbow gold, always beyond and afar. It is not all clear; I seek still, only with a confirmed optimism more perfect and beautiful than any we imagined before. *I am not oppressed with the desire that animates some of us to share our knowledge or optimism with you all before the time. You know who feels like that; but I am content that you should wait.* The solution of the Great Problem I could not give you – I am still very far away from it. And the abiding knowledge of the inherent truth and beauty into which all the inevitable uglinesses of existence finally resolve themselves will be yours in due time.

Maybe his faith was working after all. But as another script has it:

[B]ut Sidgwick will *speak* of this later. He feels the burden of unuttered words Do they think of him as standing dry and secure above the seas roar careless of the turmoil in which he himself was once a buffeted swimmer He pondered deeply on many things pondered all his life with a sort of serene patience which yet was not dull or drugged but was partly the result of a belief in the possibility of obtaining any answer underline the word *any* and partly the realision [sic] that the time had not yet come when the time honoured answers had proved to be completely unsatisfying to the sons of men the thought that he was by his own labour and by loyalty to his Spirits Vision – hastening that hour made him often uneasy for he had no solution to offer in the place of those which he destroyed – destroyed quite as much by his silence as by the spoken word.[85]

Clearly, we have here a very deep problem indeed: how much of the Apostolic Sidgwick's success came, not from his sympathy, but from his silence?

Notes

Chapter 1. Overture

1. Sidgwick Papers, Wren Library, Add.Ms.c.105.47. There is a second, tidied up, version of this crucial statement at Add.Ms.c.96.20, and it is also reproduced in *Henry Sidgwick, A Memoir*, pp. 33–34.
2. Sidgwick's casuistry has received scant attention in the century following his death, a recent exception being Sissela Bok's new edition of Sidgwick's *Practical Ethics* (New York: Oxford University Press, 1998). But see also my review of this in *Ethics* 109, no. 3 (April 1999), pp. 678–84.
3. As Walter Houghton has so aptly described it; see his *The Victorian Frame of Mind, 1830–1870* (New Haven, CT: Yale University Press, 1985).
4. See, e.g., Russell's *Portraits from Memory* (New York: Simon and Schuster, 1956), p. 63.
5. C. D. Broad, *Five Types of Ethical Theory* (London: Routledge and Kegan Paul, 1930), p. 143. To be sure, Broad's admiration for Sidgwick was to some degree shared by such figures as Hastings Rashdall.
6. This is perhaps the most famous, or infamous, pronouncement ever made on Sidgwick; it originally appeared in Keynes's letter to his friend Bernard Swithinbank, dated March 27, 1906 (Keynes Papers, King's College, Cambridge). Keynes's *Essays in Biography* (New York: Horizon, 1951) was kinder.
7. See also Keynes, "My Early Beliefs," in *The Bloomsbury Group: A Collection of Memoirs and Commentary*, ed. S. P. Rosenbaum, rev. ed. (Toronto: University of Toronto Press, 1995), p. 85.
8. Quoted in Michael Holroyd, *Lytton Strachey: The New Biography* (New York: Farrar, Straus, and Giroux, 1994), pp. 140–41. Strachey was of course the leading apostle of the "higher sodomy."
9. Ibid., p. 140.
10. Quoted in Paul Levy, *Moore: G. E. Moore and the Cambridge Apostles* (New York: Oxford University Press, 1981), p. 234.
11. In *Moral Discourse and Practice: Some Philosophical Approaches* (New York: Oxford University Press, 1997), p. 3.
12. Just how continuous Moore's views were with Sidgwick's is happily brought out in the following works: Tom Regan's edition of Moore's *Elements of Ethics*

(Philadelphia: Temple University Press, 1992), the early set of lectures from which the *Principia* was largely derived; Jennifer Welchman's "G. E. Moore and the Revolution in Ethics: A Reappraisal," *History of Philosophy Quarterly* 6 (1989), pp. 317–329; and Thomas Hurka's "Moore in the Middle," *Ethics* 113 (2003), pp. 599–628.

13. I am indebted to Thomas Hurka for cogently pressing me about the significance of this lineage.

14. See my "Bertrand Russell in Ethics and Politics," *Ethics* 102 (April 1992), pp. 594–634, for some suggestions along these lines; among other things, Russell certainly represented a very Sidgwickian ability to work enthusiastically for social reform while maintaining a highly skeptical attitude toward the cognitive claims of ethics.

15. Leonard Woolf, "Cambridge Friends and Influences," p. 137, and "Old Bloomsbury," p. 144, both in Rosenbaum, ed., *The Bloomsbury Group*.

16. Alan Donagan, "A New Sidgwick?" *Ethics* 90 (1980), p. 283.

17. John Rawls, *A Theory of Justice* (Cambridge, MA: Harvard University Press, 1971); John Rawls, *Political Liberalism* (New York: Columbia University Press, 1996).

18. Rawls's reading of John Stuart Mill as inconsistent in his efforts to qualify Benthamite hedonism is seriously problematic. For an important defense of Mill's consistency, see Elizabeth Anderson, "John Stuart Mill and Experiments in Living," *Ethics* 102 (October 1991), pp. 4–26. I am especially indebted to Anderson's work.

19. For a good summary of Rawls's take on Sidgwick, see his Foreword to Sidgwick's *Methods*, 7th ed. (Indianapolis: Hackett, 1981), and various of the essays in his *Collected Papers* (Cambridge, MA: Harvard University Press, 1999), especially "The Independence of Moral Theory," pp. 286–302.

20. J. B. Schneewind, *Sidgwick's Ethics and Victorian Moral Philosophy* (Oxford: Clarendon Press, 1977). I am profoundly indebted to Schneewind's seminal work.

21. Derek Parfit, *Reasons and Persons* (Oxford: Oxford University Press, 1984).

22. Peter Singer raised the issue in a pointed way in his contribution to a centennial symposium on the *Methods*; see his "Sidgwick and Reflective Equilibrium," *Monist* 58 (1974), pp. 490–517. And the theme has been forcefully developed by David Brink – for example, in "Common Sense and First Principles in Sidgwick's Methods," *Social Philosophy and Policy* 11 (1994), pp. 179–201. Rob Shaver's *Rational Egoism* (New York: Cambridge University Press, 1999) provides a reading of these issues from a perspective somewhat congenial to mine.

23. On this latter point, see especially Rob Shaver's insightful essay "Sidgwick's Minimal Metaethics," in "Sidgwick 2000," *Utilitas* 12, no. 3 (November 2000), pp. 261–77. Intuitionism of the minimal Sidgwickian type is now finally receiving its due, as will be made evident in Chapter 4.

24. James Kloppenberg, *Uncertain Victory: Social Democracy and Progressivism in European and American Thought, 1870–1920* (New York: Oxford University Press, 1986). Indeed, Kloppenberg hardly seems to recognize how intuitionism differs from pragmatism.

25. Keynes, in "My Early Beliefs," famously praised Bloomsbury for having tossed off both Christianity and Benthamism, construed as a narrow obsession with efficiency.

26. *An Introduction to the Principles of Morals and Legislation*, ed. J. H. Burns and H. L. A. Hart, with a new Introduction by F. Rosen, in *The Collected Works of Jeremy Bentham* (Oxford: Clarendon Press, 1996), pp. 13–14.

27. This essay, part of a much larger set of manuscripts, has been edited and published by Louis Crompton in *The Journal of Homosexuality*, vol. 3, no. 4 (Summer 1978) and vol. 4, no. 1 (Fall 1978); all references are to that edition.

28. Louis Crompton, *Byron and Greek Love: Homophobia in 19th-Century England* (Swaffham: The Gay Men's Press, 1998; first published in 1985), pp. 20–21. I am much indebted to Crompton's classic work and to Richard Dellamora's *Masculine Desire: The Sexual Politics of Victorian Aestheticism* (Chapel Hill: University of North Carolina Press, 1990).

29. Mary Lyndon Shanley, "The Subjection of Women," in *The Cambridge Companion to Mill*, ed. J. Skorupski (Cambridge: Cambridge University Press, 1998), p. 419.

30. "The Subjection of Women," in *Sexual Equality: Writings of John Stuart Mill, Harriet Taylor Mill, and Helen Taylor*, ed. A. Robson and J. Robson (London: University of Toronto Press, 1994), p. 393.

31. "John Stuart Mill's Liberal Feminism," *Philosophical Studies* 69 (1993), pp. 156–57.

32. When Russell, during the First World War, was composing his *Principles of Social Reconstruction*, he began by explaining how the traditional liberalism of Bentham and Mill too readily assumed that people generally knew what motivated them, whereas in truth they generally did not. See Ray Monk, *Bertrand Russell: The Spirit of Solitude* (London: Jonathan Cape, 1996), p. 446.

33. Much as I disagree with Margaret Urban Walker's remarks on Sidgwick, in her *Moral Understandings: A Feminist Study of Ethics* (New York: Routledge, 1998), I am inclined to think that she raises many of the right questions. See my "Sidgwick's Feminism," in "Sidgwick 2000," *Utilitas* 12, no. 3 (November 2000), pp. 379–401.

34. Bryce, "Henry Sidgwick," in his *Studies in Contemporary Biography* (New York: Books for Libraries Press, 1971; first published 1903), p. 335. Bryce, as Chapter 7 will show, was a particularly important friend of Sidgwick's, and his work often affords more concrete understandings of issues that Sidgwick left dryly abstract.

35. See, for example, the contributions by Schultz, Frankena, Mackie, Deigh, and Brink in *Essays on Henry Sidgwick*, ed. Bart Schultz (New York: Cambridge University Press, 1992). It was my work on this volume that suggested to me most of the interpretive questions addressed in the present work.

36. See Crisp's helpful recent defense of Sidgwick's insights on this count, "The Dualism of Practical Reason," *Proceedings of the Aristotelian Society* 46, new series (1995/96), pp. 53–73. For a lucid short statement of Sidgwick's dilemma, see J. L. Mackie, *The Miracle of Theism* (Oxford: Oxford University Press, 1982), pp. 111–14.

37. These lines are from the chapter on "The Morality of Strife," which was originally an 1890 address to the London Ethical Society. Ironically, Rawls's account of Sidgwick's views appears not to recognize these elements of a theory of justice.

38. The roots of the Jamesian view, evident in both his own *Principles of Psychology* (1890) and the work of his student W. E. B. DuBois, have not often been traced back to these works.

39. See M. Foucault, *The History of Sexuality* (New York: Vintage, 1990), p. 43. Unfortunately, Foucault's understanding of utilitarianism was slight, and he appears not even to have known about Bentham's work on pederasty.

40. Symonds's most revealing pronouncements are to be found in *In the Key of Blue* (New York: Macmillan, 1893), *Essays Speculative and Suggestive* (London: Chapman and Hall, 1893), *Studies in Sexual Inversion* (New York: AMS, 1975, a reprint of a privately printed edition of 1928, bringing together "A Problem in Greek Ethics" and "A Problem in Modern Ethics"), and, most importantly, his memoirs, published as *The Memoirs of John Addington Symonds: The Secret Homosexual Life of a Leading Nineteenth-Century Man of Letters*, edited and introduced by Phyllis Grosskurth (New York: Random House, 1984).

41. Linda Dowling's excellent *Hellenism and Homosexuality in Victorian Oxford* (Ithaca, NY: Cornell University Press, 1994) goes far to situate Symonds in the political context of Jowett's Oxford.

42. The allusion here is to Eve Kosofsky Sedgwick's *Epistemology of the Closet* (Berkeley: University of California Press, 1990); her earlier work *Between Men: English Literature and Male Homosocial Desire* (New York: Columbia University Press, 1985) included a very dismissive account of Symonds that, like scholarly work on Sidgwick, quite neglected his actual political practices and circle of friends.

43. For a "textbook" treatment, see *Utilitarianism and Its Critics*, ed. J. Glover (New York: Macmillan, 1990). However, in considering the broader significance of this issue, it is also important to locate Sidgwick within Habermas's classic narrative concerning the growth and decay of the liberal public sphere, as bringing into sharper relief many of the tensions that Habermas finds in Mill between the quantity and quality of public democratic discourse. See J. Habermas, *The Structural Transformation of the Public Sphere: An Inquiry into a Category of Bourgeois Society*, trans. T. Burger and F. Lawrence (Cambridge, MA: MIT Press, 1989).

44. Williams, "The Point of View of the Universe: Sidgwick and the Ambitions of Ethics," reprinted in his *Making Sense of Humanity, and Other Philosophical Essays* (New York: Cambridge University Press, 1995), affords the prime example of such criticism, cast in a purely theoretical mode.

45. Some help can be gained from Christopher Harvie's *The Lights of Liberalism* (London: Lane, 1976); Stefan Collini, Donald Winch, and John Burrow, *That Noble Science of Politics: A Study in Nineteenth-Century Intellectual History* (Cambridge: Cambridge University Press, 1983); Stefan Collini, *Public Moralists: Political Thought and Intellectual Life in Britain, 1850–1930* (Oxford: Clarendon Press, 1991); and H. S. Jones, *Victorian Political Thought* (London: Macmillan, 2000).

46. On this count, it must be stressed that the works cited in the previous note are wholly inadequate to the task. Even such recent pieces as Collini's "My Roles and Their Duties: Sidgwick as Philosopher, Professor and Public Moralist," and the response to it by Jonathan Rée (in *Henry Sidgwick*, ed. R. Harrison [Oxford: Oxford University Press, 2001]) succeed only in gracefully dodging all questions of race and imperialism in connection with Sidgwick.

47. See L. Zastoupil, *John Stuart Mill and India* (Stanford, CA: Stanford University Press, 1994), and G. Varouxakis, *Mill and Nationality* (London: Routledge, 2002).

48. See Chapter 7; for some brief remarks, see my "Snapshot: Henry Sidgwick," *The Philosopher's Magazine* (Winter 1999), p. 58.

49. The subtleties of the different strands of imperialist philosophizing are quite extraordinary, as later chapters will show. I am much indebted to such classic works as Richard Symonds, *Oxford and Empire: The Last Lost Cause?* (New York: St. Martin's Press, 1986).

50. In this way, the later utilitarians compare unfavorably with the earlier ones. For an insightful account of Bentham on these matters, see Jennifer Pitts, "Legislator of the World? A Rereading of Bentham on Empire," in *Classical Utilitarianism and the Question of Race*, ed. B. Schultz and G. Varouxakis (Lanham, MD: Lexington Books, 2004).

51. My approach to the interpretation of philosophers is not unlike Said's approach to novelists, in *Culture and Imperialism* (New York: Knopf, 1993), and I share his sense that however disturbing it may be to discover imperialist and racist subtexts in canonical works, there can be no avoiding such interpretive efforts.

Chapter 2. First Words

1. In *John Stuart Mill and Jeremy Bentham: Utilitarianism and Other Essays*, ed. A. Ryan (New York: Penguin Books, 1987), p. 229.

2. For Balfour's statement, see *The Letters of Arthur Balfour and Lady Elcho, 1885–1917*, ed. J. Ridley and C. Percy (London: Hamish Hamilton, 1992), p. 173; for Mill's, see Michael St. John Packe, *The Life of John Stuart Mill* (London: Secker and Warburg, 1954), p. 507.

3. Frank Podmore, "Review: *Henry Sidgwick, A Memoir*," Sidgwick Papers, Wren Library, Cambridge University, Add.Ms.c.102.1, pp. 446–47.

4. See his "A Lecture against Lecturing," reprinted in MEA.

5. Here I borrow from Alan Ryan's *Liberal Anxieties and Liberal Education* (New York: Hill and Wang, 1998), p. 40. Ryan is right to claim that the notion of a vigorously self-educating society, in which social intelligence is fostered by the fabric of the culture and not simply by certain educational institutions, is common ground for Mill and Dewey. Unfortunately, he does not remark at all on how Sidgwick also belongs in this camp, possibly as the most significant figure between Mill and Dewey.

6. See Brand Blanshard's engaging study of Sidgwick in his *Four Reasonable Men* (Middletown, CT: Wesleyan University Press, 1984), pp. 181–243, a shorter version of which appeared in the symposium on Sidgwick in the *Monist* 58 (1974).

7. F. W. Maitland, "Henry Sidgwick," *Independent Review* (June 1906), pp. 534–35. It should be noted that, despite his earlier abstemiousness and lifelong aversion to luxurious expenditure, the mature Sidgwick was not averse to oiling the conversational wheels: "He used to tell how, at one time, he had . . . severely simplified the entertainment at his dinner parties, cutting off the champagne or other expensive wine, and generally reducing it below the prevailing standard. But an unforeseen difficulty arose. He felt the need under these circumstances of making it up to his guests by added conversational brilliance; and the strain of this weighed so heavily upon him that he abandoned the effort and went back to the champagne!" Lord Rayleigh, "Some Recollections of Henry Sidgwick," *Proceedings of the Society for Psychical Research* 45 (1938), p. 170.

8. Sorley, "Henry Sidgwick," *International Journal of Ethics* 11 (1900–1), p. 171.

9. A good survey of Russell's jibes can be found in his *Portraits from Memory*.

10. James Bryce, "Henry Sidgwick," in his *Studies in Contemporary Biography* (London: Macmillan, 1903), pp. 338–39.

11. Myers Papers, Wren Library, Cambridge University, 13.22.

12. E. E. C. Jones, "Review: *Henry Sidgwick, A Memoir*," *The Journal of Education* (April 1906), p. 264.

13. F. W. H. Myers, *Fragments of Poetry and Prose*, ed. E. Myers (London: Longmans, Green, 1904), pp. 97–98.

14. Ryan, *Liberal Anxieties*, p. 54.

15. Ibid., p. 71.

16. It is worth remarking on just how enduring most of Sidgwick's major intellectual interests were; he would continue his enthusiastic reading in all of these areas for the rest of his life, and of course in such areas as parapsychology.

17. During Sidgwick's early period of active membership, the Society included James Clerk Maxwell, Henry Montagu Butler, Henry Brandreth, Roden Noel, E. E. Bowen, C. H. Tawney, Oscar Browning, J. J. Cowell, George Trevelyan, and Richard Jebb. His younger brother Arthur was elected in 1861. Among the most valuable studies of the Apostles are Paul Levy, *Moore: G. E. Moore and the Cambridge Apostles* (Oxford: Oxford University Press, 1981); Peter Allen, *The Cambridge Apostles: The Early Years* (Cambridge: Cambridge University Press, 1978); and William Lubenow, *The Cambridge Apostles, 1820–1914: Liberalism, Imagination, and Friendship in British Intellectual and Professional Life* (Cambridge: Cambridge University Press, 1998).

18. Remarks made during a 1908 dinner toast by Donald MacAlister, an Apostle from the 1870s. Quoted in Allen, *Apostles*, p. 218.

19. Sheldon Rothblatt, *The Revolution of the Dons* (Cambridge: Cambridge University Press, 1968), p. 134.

20. See Chapter 6 and my essay "Sidgwick's Feminism," in "Sidgwick 2000," *Utilitas* 12, no. 3 (November 2000), pp. 379–401.

21. Actually, as important as the *Memoir* is, what follows draws on a variety of other sources as well, including A. C. Benson's *The Life of Edward White Benson* (London: Macmillan, 1899); Ethel Sidgwick, *Mrs. Henry Sidgwick, A Memoir*

(London: Sidgwick and Jackson, 1938); and the many obituaries of Sidgwick and reviews of the *Memoir*, for which see Bart Schultz and J. B. Schneewind, "Henry Sidgwick, A Bibliography," in *The Cambridge Bibliography of English Literature*, 3rd ed. (Cambridge: Cambridge University Press, 1999).

22. Some of the notes from this genealogical inquiry are preserved in the miscellaneous Sidgwick materials held by University Library, Cambridge University. F. Galton regarded the Sidgwicks as an impressive case of family genius.

23. William Everett, "Henry Sidgwick," *The Atlantic* 108 (1906), p. 93.

24. "The Ural Mountains: A New Parlour Game," *Macmillan's Magazine* (March 1862), p. 409. I am indebted to Dr. C. A. Stray, of Swansea University, for reminding me of Sidgwick's reference to this piece in his correspondence with Dakyns; he deserves the credit for correcting the Wellesley Index in its attribution of the essay solely to Bowen.

25. Sidgwick's two best-known poems are "The Despot's Heir" and "Goethe and Frederika," both published in the *Memoir*; see Chapters 5 and 6 for more examples of his work. A poetic sensibility was also a defining Apostolic trait, and in this respect Sidgwick certainly continued the Millian reaction against Bentham's supposed distaste for the genre.

26. Though there should be little doubt that the "low moral tone" that concerned Sidgwick senior had to do with sexuality, and that Rugby, (like Harrow, Eton, Clifton, etc.) continued to house the homoerotic activities described in Chapter 6.

27. Bowen to Arthur Sidgwick, Sidgwick Papers, Wren Library, Cambridge University, Add.Ms.b.71.3.3-4.

28. Benson, *Life of Benson*, p. 148.

29. Sidgwick to Minnie Sidgwick, 1859, Sidgwick Papers, Wren Library, Cambridge University, Add.Ms.c.100.

30. See E. F. Benson, *Mother* (London: Hodder and Stoughton, 1925), especially pp. 12–13. The entire dreary account makes it evident that Mary, like her brother Henry, suffered from periods of serious depression. There are other sources of evidence concerning the Sidgwicks' early family life that I am researching for a future essay on "Young Sidgwick," including Mary Benson's diaries, Arthur Sidgwick's diaries, and other recollections by friends and family members.

The Benson family has, in fact, been the object of considerable research. Two especially helpful works for understanding the unhappy fate of "Minnie" Sidgwick are Betty Askwith, *Two Victorian Families* (London: Chatto and Windus, 1971) and Brian Masters, *The Life of E. F. Benson* (London: Chatto and Windus, 1991). My construction of Sidgwick's life and work owes much to these and other works dealing with the Bensons versus the Sidgwicks. Indeed, it has often struck me that Henry's various (mature) concerns – from religion, to ghosts, to women's higher education, to sympathetic understanding, to same-sex relationships – uncannily reflected his evolving sympathy for his sister's side of things against the tyrannical force of Benson. As Askwith has judiciously observed, Archbishop Benson "had the Mid-Victorian virtues: intellectual and physical energy, devotion to duty,

unswerving rectitude and sincere religious feeling. The qualities he lacked included imagination and the power of putting himself into another's place. He was
unceasingly strenuous, vital, dogmatic and domineering and from early on he had
armed himself with the triple authority of paterfamilias, schoolmaster and priest."
(Askwith, *Two Victorian Families*, p. 109) Askwith also notes that, unlike Benson,
Minnie "approached god through the love of human beings" and sought a "harmonious" life, which was deemed by Benson "a kind of longing for *comfortableness*
and not specially worthy" (p. 145). Minnie was sympathetic, somewhat volatile,
and given to trance states as well as very deep attachments; after Benson's death,
she shared her bed with her close friend Lucy Tait. It is also noteworthy that
after Mary's mother's death, the Benson family retained the services of the redoubtable Elizabeth (Beth) Cooper, the same adored nurse who had raised Minnie
and her brothers, and who thus ultimately devoted some eighty years of service to
the family.

31. Benson, *Life of Benson*, pp. 250–51.
32. Rothblatt, *Revolution*, p. 134.
33. Benson, *Life of Benson*, p. 251.
34. In fact, when Sidgwick was dying, in August of 1900, his old friend Dakyns would
    try to sound a hopeful note by recalling how he had bounced back from this earlier
    and very alarming illness, when he had seemed to his friends to be at death's door.
    See the various letters from August 1900 included in *Strange Audacious Life*.
35. Maitland, "Henry Sidgwick," p. 326.
36. See Alison Winter, *Mesmerized: Powers of Mind in Victorian Britain* (Chicago:
    University of Chicago Press, 1998), especially Chapter 12.
37. Sidgwick Papers, Wren Library, Add.Ms.d.68.
38. Thus, having learned the trick of indirection, he applied it to such things as his
    insomnia; he discovered that the best approach was simply to lie in bed for a
    set time come what may, content to rest at least physically, instead of fruitlessly
    struggling to sleep. The intriguing question of how he dealt with his impotence
    will be considered in a later chapter.
39. Sidgwick to Dakyns, August 1864 (CWC).
40. See Browning, *Memories of Sixty Years at Eton, Cambridge, and Elsewhere* (London:
    John Lane, 1910), p. 40.
41. Sidgwick Papers, Wren Library, Cambridge University, Add.Ms.d.70.
42. Benson, *Life of Benson*, p. 151, pp. 249–50.
43. F. D. Maurice, *Moral and Metaphysical Philosophy*, vol. 1 (London: Macmillan,
    1873), p. 126.
44. Quoted in Allen, *Apostles*, p. 56.
45. The significance of Grote and the Grote Club will be noted again in later chap-
    ters. For some helpful background, see John Gibbins, "John Grote and Modern
    Cambridge Philosophy," *Philosophy* 73 (July 1998), pp. 453–77, and the entry on
    Grote by Gibbins and Schultz in the *Routledge Encyclopedia of Philosophy*, ed.
    E. Craig (London: Routledge, 1998). Grote was constitutionally averse to the
    polemics between Whewell and Mill and, like Maurice, sought to be a unifying

force. The discussants included Alfred Marshall, John Venn, J. R. Mozley, and W. K. Clifford.

46. This is from an account by Alfred Marshall; see also Keynes, *Essays*, pp. 131–34.

47. Melvin Richter, *The Politics of Conscience: T. H. Green and His Age* (Cambridge, MA: Harvard University Press, 1964), pp. 48–49.

48. This passage is from an 1868 letter to T. Erskine, reproduced in *Toward the Recovery of Unity: The Thought of Frederick Denison Maurice*, ed. J. Porter and W. Wolf (New York: Seabury Press, 1964), p. 232.

49. Most Marxists have dismissed Christian socialism as a sham, but it had a very considerable following in its day, and both Mill and Sidgwick regarded it as on the whole a force for the good. In essence, the message was that capitalism was indeed cruel and unfair to the working man, and degrading to the capitalists themselves, but that community, religious fellowship, and self-improvement were the answer, not revolution. Both Mill and Sidgwick looked to new, post-Christian forms of religion to do the job, but they shared the inclusive, reformist outlook.

50. Maurice, *Toward Unity*, p. 234.

51. Ibid., pp. 35–36.

52. F. D. Maurice, *The Life of Frederick Denison Maurice, Chiefly Told in His Own Letters* (New York: C. Scribner's Sons, 1884).

53. J. S. Mill, *Autobiography* (London: Longmans, Green, Reader, and Dyer, 1873), pp. 152–54.

54. Maurice, *Toward Unity*, p. 20.

55. Owen Chadwick, *The Victorian Church*, Part One (London: SCM Press, 1987), p. 349–50.

56. Schneewind, *Sidgwick's Ethics*, pp. 99–100.

57. Mill, "Coleridge," in Ryan, ed., *Utilitarianism and Other Writings*, p. 177.

58. Allen, *Apostles*, p. 78.

59. Allen, *Apostles*, p. 71, p. 80.

60. See Dowling, *Hellenism*, on this development.

61. Allen, *Apostles*, p. 86.

62. Especially in its insistence on personal testimony, putting one's life on the line, and being transfigured by philosophy. This larger vision of the philosophical life continues to attract defenders – e.g., Pierre Hadot, *What Is Ancient Philosophy?* (Cambridge, MA: Harvard University Press, 2002).

63. Rothblatt, *Revolution*, p. 144, p. 150.

64. Maurice, *Life*, vol. 1, p. 54.

65. Nussbaum, *Cultivating Humanity* (Cambridge, MA: Harvard University Press, 1997), p. 26.

66. See G. Vlastos, *Socrates, Ironist and Moral Philosopher* (Ithaca, NY: Cornell University Press, 1991), and his *Socratic Studies* (Cambridge: Cambridge Univeristy Press, 1994), especially the chapter entitled "Socrates and Vietnam."

67. Maurice, *Life*, p. 56.

68. Quoted in Frank Turner, *The Greek Heritage in Victorian Britain* (New Haven, CT: Yale University Press, 1981), p. 370. I am much indebted to Turner's

fascinating work, though it pays insufficient attention to such later developments as J. A. Symonds's use of Plato.

69. Maurice, *Life*, vol. 2, p. 608.

70. Richard Deacon, *The Cambridge Apostles* (New York: Farrar, Straus and Giroux, 1985), p. 44.

71. Though Bentham himself often had very harsh words for Socrates and Plato, referring to the latter as the "master manufacturer of nonsense." See, for example, Jeremy Bentham, *Deontology*, ed. A. Goldworth (Oxford: Oxford University Press, 1983), pp. 135–37. It would appear that James Mill played a crucial role in strategizing the utilitarian co-optation of Socrates and Plato that Grote and the younger Mill would play out. See the insightful essay by Kyriacos Demetriou, "The Development of Platonic Studies in Britain and the Role of the Utilitarians," *Utilitas* 8 (March 1996), pp. 15–37, which shows just how the early utilitarians "approached Plato as the exponent of critical epistemology, who replaced the authority of the commonplace with the sovereignty of undisguised intellect. The effective method of the Platonic *elenchus* in discussing moral issues was an antidote to the traditional prejudices which have been always detrimental to social and political progress" (p. 36). As Demetriou also shows, Grote's polemic was more complex and brought out more of Plato's constructive side, albeit in a way congenial to utilitarianism: "First, it prevented Plato from being seen as a religious idealist, an interpretation favoured by the British university scholars of his times; and secondly, contrary to narrow German perfectionism, it exposed Plato's philosophical complexity" (p. 37).

72. See Irwin, "Mill and the Classical World," in *The Cambridge Companion to Mill*, ed. J. Skorupski (Cambridge: Cambridge University Press, 1998), p. 424.

73. Turner, *Greek Heritage*, pp. 251–52.

74. See his "Henry Sidgwick, Cambridge Classics, and the Study of Ancient Philosophy: The Decisive Years (1866–69)," forthcoming. I discuss Todd's claims further in the next chapter.

75. Henry Sidgwick, "Review: *Essays on the Platonic Ethics*," *The Academy* (September 15, 1871), pp. 440–41.

76. These essays were originally published in *The Journal of Philology* in 1872 and 1873.

77. Sidgwick shows remarkable insight in these claims, which are in line with, e.g., Irwin's account in *Classical Thought* (Oxford: Oxford University Press, 1989), which notes that the Greek *sophistês* simply means "expert," not necessarily with unfavorable connotations (see p. 231, n. 37). The sophists were, however, contrasted with the rhetoricians.

78. One should bear in mind here the sexual side of popular morality in ancient Greece, as so marvelously described by Kenneth Dover in *Greek Popular Morality in the Time of Plato and Aristotle* (Indianapolis: Hackett, 1994) and *Greek Homosexuality* (Cambridge, MA: Harvard University Press, 1978, 1989). The treatment of Sidgwick and Symonds in later chapters will return to this question of how the hypocrisy of Greek popular morality served as a source for them in considering the hypocrisy of their own day.

79. These passages are drawn from Sidgwick's posthumous *Development of European Polity*, which was based on lecture notes that he had assembled over many years of teaching the subject. See, especially, p. 114 and pp. 112–13.

80. Vlastos, *Socratic Studies*, p. 9, p. 10. For further discussion of Sidgwick and the Grotes on Plato, see Chapter 7.

Chapter 3. Unity

1. "Initial Society Papers," in the Sidgwick Papers, Wren Library, Cambridge University, Add.Ms.c.96.4.29f.

2. "On the Classical Tripos Exam," p. 5. This pamphlet was circulated in 1866.

3. It was included in *Essays on a Liberal Education*, ed. F. W. Farrar (London: Macmillan, 1867).

4. Christopher Brooke, *A History of the University of Cambridge*, vol. 4 (Cambridge: Cambridge University Press, 1993), pp. 16–17. This valuable work gives a quite appreciative account of Sidgwick's importance to the creation of modern Cambridge.

5. I am indebted to Robert Todd for sending me his extremely interesting work on Sidgwick and the creation of the Moral Sciences Tripos – "Henry Sidgwick, Cambridge Classics, and the Study of Ancient Philosophy: The Decisive Years (1866–69)."

6. Todd, "Henry Sidgwick, Cambridge Classics, and the Study of Ancient Philosophy," pp. 8–9.

7. Ibid.

8. *Macmillan's Magazine* (April 1867), p. 468.

9. The Sidgwick brothers in fact devoted a great deal of time and effort to bridging the gap between Cambridge and Oxford, via such dinner/discussion societies as the Ad Eundem, which was initiated in the 1860s for this express purpose.

10. Henry Sidgwick, "Liberal Education," *Macmillan's Magazine* (April 1867), p. 465.

11. See especially his essays "Philosophy at Cambridge" and "Liberal Education," though as his correspondence with Dakyns at this time makes clear, he may for polemical purposes have slightly exaggerated his antipathy toward the standard method of teaching Latin and Greek.

12. The original is in the Sidgwick Papers, Wren Library, Trinity College, Cambridge University, Add.Ms.c.96.2.

13. He was, of course, not so uniformly upbeat. His more pessimistic side was evident in an undergraduate letter to Mary: "I am in very low spirits – continually preaching myself profitless sermons on the following texts: 1. There's nothing true & nothing new & it do'nt matter. 2. This world is'nt much. 3. Science is laborious frivolity, philosophy wordy emptiness, knowledge a wearisom dream, love 1/20th honey concealing 19/20th gall, fame a shadow, & even that only obtained by desperate bigotry or deliberate hypocrisy & – but let's stop this bosh." Sidgwick Papers, Wren Library, Trinity College, Cambridge University, Add.Ms.c.100.4.

14. Sidgwick's linguistic studies of Arabic, German, and Hebrew were quite intensive, and he made some four trips to Germany during this period expressly for this

purpose. As Chapter 6 will show, on one of these he developed a certain romantic interest that stimulated his exchanges with Noel on the value of marriage for the philosopher.

15. Strauss's *The Life of Jesus* had been translated into English in 1846 by none other than George Eliot, with whom Sidgwick formed something of a mutual admiration society. See her *Selected Essays, Poems and Other Writings* (London: Penguin, 1990) for material on Strauss.

16. My thanks to J. B. Schneewind for reminding me of just how complex the history of philological and historical criticism of the Bible had been in the seventeenth and eighteenth centuries as well. Renan and Strauss were not the first of their breed, though on the history of philology, Edward Said's observation that Renan regarded philology as "a comparative discipline possessed only by moderns and a symbol of modern (and European) superiority" should serve as a reminder of the agenda for philology that one finds in his work – see Edward Said, *Orientalism* (New York: Vintage, 1979), p. 132.

17. Quoted in Blanshard, *Four Reasonable Men*, pp. 114–15.

18. Ibid., p. 116.

19. Said, *Orientalism*, pp. 133–34.

20. Desmond Heath, *Roden Noel: A Wide Angle* (London: DB Books, 1998), p. 33. This valuable and delightful work tells the story of how Noel's papers ultimately came into the possession of his great granddaughter, Silvia Putterill, who married Heath.

21. This letter is dated January 1865 and can be found in the Noel Papers, Archives and Special Collections, Brynmoor Jones Library, University of Hull, DNO/1/3. Unfortunately, Noel's letters to Sidgwick exist only in partial, typescript form, though they are a most important resource even in that abridged condition. More unfortunately still, only a handful of Sidgwick's letters to Noel have been located to date. As in so many other cases, however, it is to be hoped that future research will turn up more material.

22. Noel to Sidgwick, October 15, 1863, Noel Papers, Archives and Special Collections, Brynmoor Jones Library, University of Hull, DNO/1/2, p. 93. This remarkable letter, which is singularly helpful for understanding Sidgwick's dualism of practical reason, will be analyzed in great detail in Chapter 6. The (presumably) Greek expression is missing in the typescript letter.

23. Sidgwick tried, unsuccessfully, to get Seeley into the Apostles and would remain supportive of him throughout his life. Said has also noted Seeley's contribution to orientalism – see especially his *Culture and Imperialism*.

24. Maurice, *Towards Unity*, pp. 218–19.

25. Owen Chadwick, *Secularization of the European Mind in the Nineteenth Century* (Cambridge: Cambridge University Press, 1975), p. 263.

26. The section of this letter marked by ellipses is torn in the original, with a piece missing; see CWC.

27. The Greek line is from 1 Corinthians, 7:21: "Art thou called being a servant? Care not for it: but if thou mayest be made free, use it rather."

28. Although it may seem a rather commonplace psychological observation, one cannot help but think that Sidgwick was, at some level, understandably obsessed with father figures, and perhaps more shaped (and depressed) by the early loss of his actual father than has commonly been recognized. Such losses are determining factors in increasing the likelihood of clinical depression.

29. The Greek expression means "theological and moral truths."

30. See Charles Gore, *Belief in Christ* (New York: Charles Scribners Sons, 1923), p. 137, note).

31. Sidgwick to Dakyns, December 1862 (CWC); this letter is inaccurately transcribed in the *Memoir* (M 89).

32. Henry Sidgwick, "Review: *Letters, Lectures, and Reviews*," *The Academy* (July 15, 1873), p. 267.

33. Henry Sidgwick, "Review: *Essays Theological and Literary*," *The Academy* (July 1, 1871), p. 325.

34. Ibid., p. 326.

35. Noel to Sidgwick, July 3, 1871, Noel Papers, Archives and Special Collections, Brynmoor Jones Library, University of Hull, DNO/1/2, p. 191.

36. In "Is Philosophy *the Germ* or the Crown of Science?" he had stated that "psychology is as it were the vestibule and entrance chamber of philosophy," which made somewhat more forgivable the tendency of some schools of philosophy to reduce it to the study of the human mind (CWC).

37. Sidgwick to Dakyns, June 9, 1862 (CWC, M 81–82); the Greek term means "enthusiasm."

38. See Chapter 10.

39. The original is in the Sidgwick Papers, Wren Library, Trinity College, Cambridge University, Add.Ms.c.96.5.

40. One might well think that some of Sidgwick's most cheerful letters come when he seems ready to fall back into some form of egoistic perfectionism. See, for example, his letter to Dakyns from December 1862: "I have worked away vigorously at the selfish morality, but I cannot persuade myself, except by trusting intuition, that Christian self-sacrifice is really a happier life than classical insouciance." And "The effort to attain the Christian ideal may be a life-long painful struggle; and therefore, though I may believe this ideal when realised productive of greater happiness, yet individually (if it is not a question of life or death) my laziness would induce me to prefer a lower, more attainable Goethean ideal. Intuitions turn the scale" (M 89–90). Such lines contain the seeds of much of Sidgwick's later struggle with the dualism of practical reason, which for him was often cast as a struggle with the lower "Goethean" ideal, against the self-sacrifice demanded by utilitarian universal benevolence, which was for the future. See Chapters 4 and 6, especially.

41. Though not entirely; he was certainly intimately familiar with the emphasis on associationist psychology in the utilitarian tradition, and with the developments in physiological psychology – indeed, he contributed financially as well as intellectually to the growth of physiological studies at Cambridge. But on his psychology,

see Chapters 5 and 6, which show how far he went in opening up the newer regions of depth psychology.

42. Sidgwick to Mary Sidgwick, circa 1858, Dep. Benson 3/10, Bodleian Library, Oxford University.

43. J. Oppenheim, *The Other World* (New York: Cambridge University Press, 1985), p. 127.

44. Sidgwick Papers, Wren Library, Trinity College, Cambridge University, Add.Ms.c.100.159.

45. See the sketch of Sidgwick in Myers, *Fragments of Prose and Poetry*, ed. E. Myers (London: Longmans, Green, 1904).

46. Deacon, *The Cambridge Apostles*, pp. 47–48. Deacon notes, interestingly, that "Lowes Dickinson, another Apostle, attended meetings of the SPR for a time and studied esoteric Buddhism," though he apparently "soon lost interest" (p. 49). Dickinson would be a crucial figure in the transformation of the Apostles into a more openly and aggressively "gay" organization, and he was in many ways deeply influenced by Sidgwick, who was in spirit green (versus black) tie.

47. Sidgwick Papers, Wren Library, Trinity College, Cambridge University, Add.Ms.d.68; Sidgwick's (locked) diary is reproduced in CWC.

48. See the many letters to Dakyns from the late spring and summer of 1900, reproduced in CWC.

49. The next lines read "Mill is an exception. He will have to be destroyed, as he is becoming as intolerable as Aristeides, but when he is destroyed, we shall build him a mausoleum as big as his present temple of fame – of that I am convinced."

50. Gibbins,"John Grote and Modern Cambridge Philosophy," p. 458. Gibbins, I think, rather overstates the case for Grote's importance as a formative philosophical force, but he provides a useful corrective to the rather extraordinary neglect that this "Cambridge Moralist" has suffered. Of course, one of the great merits of Schneewind's *Sidgwick's Ethics* is the way in which it calls attention to the importance of Grote and Maurice. John was George's younger brother, but philosophically quite different.

51. Lubenow, *Cambridge Apostles*, p. 35. The letter, as Lubenow notes, is to be found in the Sidgwick Papers, which suggests that it was indeed circulated, though Cowell and Sidgwick were such singularly close friends that they would surely have discussed the matter in any event.

52. Rothblatt, *Revolution*, p. 133.

53. Hobsbawm, *The Age of Empire, 1875–1914* (New York: Pantheon Books, 1987), p. 85.

54. Quoted in W. A. Speck, *A Concise History of Britain, 1707–1975* (New York: Cambridge University Press, 1993), p. 87.

55. In 1861, Sidgwick wrote to Dakyns: "I read through Mill's *Representative Government* in one morning. It is extremely good, I think, though I cannot get over my scepticism as to the elaborate Hare-ian scheme." He goes on to write, however, "As to population . . . colonisation is unanswerable, I think; if not, please answer it." In a slightly earlier letter, he had said, about Mill's population theory, that "the way he blinks the practical morality of the question is the coolest thing I

know. And I know many cool things on the part of your thorough-going theorists. I believe in 'Be fruitful and multiply.' I think the most crying need now is a better organised colonisation. To think of the latent world-civilisation in our swarms of fertile Anglo-Saxon pauperism" (M 66–67). This issue, all too suggestive of Sidgwick's debt to Renan, is discussed at length in Chapters 8 and 9.

56. The Greek expression means "families of ancient wealth." See also the extensive correspondence with Browning reproduced in CWC.

57. Sidgwick to Dakyns, May 1861 (CWC).

58. Ryan, *Liberal Anxieties*, pp. 90–91.

59. Dickens's *Hard Times* has perhaps done more damage to the reputation of utilitarianism than Marx and Foucault combined.

60. Ryan, *Liberal Anxieties*, pp. 91–92.

61. Ibid., p. 89.

62. Plainly, Mill as much as Maurice found his religion in sympathetic unity – these passages are from the conclusion of the brilliant third chapter of "Utilitarianism." See Roger Crisp, ed., *Utilitarianism* (Oxford: Oxford University Press, 1998) and his *Routledge Guide* to this essay (London: Routledge, 1997).

63. Matthew Arnold, *Culture and Anarchy*, ed. S. Collini (New York: Cambridge University Press, 1993), p. 141.

64. J. S. Mill, *Three Essays on Religion* (Amherst, NY: Prometheus Books, 1998), pp. 249–50.

65. It should be noted that, for all Sidgwick's misgivings about spreading views that would be appropriate only for an educated public, he certainly fell in with the burst of enthusiasm for the semipopular periodical press, at least during the sixties and seventies. His work for *Macmillan's Magazine*, the *Spectator*, the *Contemporary Review*, and the *Academy* reached a very wide public. As Alan Brown has observed: "No development since the invention of printing itself has had a more important influence on public opinion and cultural history than the astonishing growth of periodical journalism in the nineteenth century. Between 1800 and 1900 more than one thousand new magazines of various kinds were started in London alone, catering to every kind of person, every kind of mind, and every pocketbook. This development was of course made possible by the application of steam power to the printing press – an event which bore its first fruit in the rapid expansion of daily newspaper journalism. The cheap and rapid production of schoolbooks which also resulted, in its turn encouraged an increase of literacy and an extension of the habit of reading which provided an audience for all kinds of periodical literature. . . . These reviews soon became even more influential than the anonymous roar of the mighty *Edinburgh* and *Quarterly*." Alan Brown, *The Metaphysical Society* (New York: Octagon Books, 1973), pp. 167–68.

66. Henry Sidgwick, "The Pursuit of Culture," *University College of Wales Magazine* (October 1897), p. 5, pp. 6–7, pp. 8–9. This essay was chopped into two pieces, with one part, that on Arnold, appearing in *Practical Ethics* and the other in *Miscellaneous Essays and Addresses*. This was an unfortunate division, however, since the longer piece forms a wonderfully coherent whole that provides perhaps Sidgwick's best, most considered thoughts on Arnold and the meaning of "culture." My own

conception of Sidgwick's educational reformism refects the arguments of this piece at every turn.

67. Ibid., p. 12.

68. Ibid., p. 13.

69. Ibid., pp. 13–14.

70. Ibid., pp. 14–15.

71. Ibid., pp. 16–17. Interestingly, Mill's very similar attitude owed something to Plato. See Geraint Williams, "The Greek Origins of J. S. Mill's Happiness," *Utilitas* 8, no. 1 (March 1996), p. 9.

72. Ibid., p. 19.

73. Sidgwick to Symonds, June 1867; the letter is reproduced in full in Chapter 6.

74. Noel to Sidgwick, May 6, 1861, Noel Papers, Archives and Special Collections, Brynmoor Jones Library, University of Hull, DNO/1/2, pp. 81–82.

75. Noel to Sidgwick, October 15, 1863, ibid., p. 92.

76. See Lynn Zastoupil, *John Stuart Mill and India* (Stanford, CA: Stanford University Press, 1994) for an excellent discussion, especially on p. 13, p. 39, and p. 41. Neither the Mills nor Macaulay nor Sidgwick entertained much doubt as to just who was to play the role of educator when it came to teaching other "races," as later chapters will detail.

77. To this list one might add "the worth of honest investigations into human gender and sexuality," as we shall see in later chapters.

78. Consider, too, the often rather Millian sympathies of Christopher Lasch's *The Revolt of the Elites and the Betrayal of Democracy* (New York: Norton, 1995), which is suggestive of how, in some respects, actual elite rule is even more morally disgraceful today than it was during the Victorian era.

79. Michael Maurice, quoted in Maurice, *Life*, vol. 1, p. 72.

80. Maurice, *Life*, vol. 2, pp. 504–5.

81. Quoted in Owen Chadwick, *The Victorian Church, Part II: 1860–1901* (London: SCM Press, 1972), p. 132; I am deeply indebted to Chadwick's exceedingly erudite and comprehensive work.

82. Sidgwick to Dakyns, June 20, 1862; the letter is reproduced in part in M 83.

83. As Jim McCue put it, in his fine introduction to *Arthur Hugh Clough: Selected Poems* (London: Penguin, 1991).

84. Maurice was also a warm admirer of Clough's poetry and, along with others, tried to draw the poet into the Christian socialist movement, though without success. See David Young's fine study, *F. D. Maurice and Unitarianism* (Oxford: Clarendon Press, 1992).

85. Quoted in Noel Annan, *Leslie Stephen: The Godless Victorian* (Chicago: University of Chicago Press, 1994), p. 43. There is also much useful background material in Annan's *The Dons: Mentors, Eccentrics and Geniuses* (London: HarperCollins, 1999), and in Keynes, *Essays*.

86. The original is in the Hutzler Collection, Eisenhower Library, Johns Hopkins University. I am grateful to J. B. Schneewind for confirming the discovery of this letter and for help with the transcription.

87. See the discussion in Schneewind, *Sidgwick's Ethics*, pp. 37–38.

88. Noel to Sidgwick, July 8, 1869, Noel Papers, Archives and Special Collections, Brynmoor Jones Library, University of Hull, DNO/1/2.

89. Chapter 6 will show how Sidgwick and John Addington Symonds were both in effect struggling with the problem of how to take the public into their confidence in some fashion, however much they may have differed over just what the English public was "ripe" for.

90. It is perhaps worth noting that Sidgwick's views here again illustrate how the actual utilitarians were not happily representative of supposedly "utilitarian" accounts of science as thinly instrumental, a stock piece of early Frankfurt School mythology. For a better critical theoretical perspective, one should read Sidgwick generally as part of the Millian struggle with the communicative ethics of the public sphere – a continuation of, or another moment in, the tensions between the growth of democracy and the quality of public debate. See the classic work by J. Habermas, *The Structural Transformation of the Public Sphere: An Inquiry into a Category of Bourgeois Society*, trans. T. Burger and F. Lawrence (Cambridge, MA: MIT Press, 1989), and his more recent *Between Facts and Norms: Contributions to a Discourse Theory of Law and Democracy*, trans. W. Rehg (Cambridge, MA: MIT Press, 1996). As the latter notes, "After Kant it was above all John Stuart Mill and John Dewey who analyzed the principle of publicity and the role an informed public opinion should have in feeding and monitoring parliament" (p. 171). Sidgwick, one might say, forms a missing but very important link.

91. John Dewey, *Democracy and Education* (Carbondale: Southern Illinois University Press, 1980), p. 187.

92. As the final chapter will show, Sidgwick's attitude toward authority was another remarkably consistent element in his overall vision; it emerges again at the end of his life, especially in his work with the Synthetic Society and his correspondence with Wilfrid Ward (reproduced in CWC).

93. In Schultz, ed., *Essays*, p. 140.

94. A point noted by Brad Hooker in "Sidgwick and Common-Sense Morality," in "Sidgwick 2000," *Utilitas* 12, no. 3 (November 2000), p. 351 note 5.

95. Schneewind, *Sidgwick's Ethics*, p. 51.

96. Mill to Sidgwick, Nov. 26, 1867. The two letters that Mill wrote to Sidgwick were first published in the *Mill Newsletter*, 9, no. 2 (Summer 1974) and have since appeared in the collected late correspondence in *Additional Letters of John Stuart Mill*, vol. 32 of *The Collected Works of John Stuart Mill*, ed. M. Filipirk, M. Laine, and J. M. Robson (Toronto: University of Toronto Press, 1991). The originals are in the Sidgwick Papers, Wren Library, Cambridge University, Add.Ms.c.94.133.

97. See D. E. Winstanley, *Later Victorian Cambridge* (Cambridge: Cambridge University Press, 1947).

98. See the relevant volumes of *The Gladstone Diaries*, 14 volumes, ed. M. R. D. Foot and H. C. G. Matthew (Oxford: Clarendon Press, 1968–94).

99. Chapter 6, especially, will bring out the affinities between Sidgwick's thinking on conformity and subscription and his counsel to Symonds on sexual matters. However, it should also be noted that another (unintended) consequence of Sidgwick's resignation, and of his 1875 appointment as Praelector in Moral and Political

Sciences, was that he was allowed to marry; he became an Honorary Fellow in 1881 and regained his full Fellowship only in 1885, when opposition to the marriage ban on fellowships was finally triumphing.

100. In *The Letters of John Addington Symonds, 1844–1868*, ed. H. M. Schueller and R. L. Peters (Detroit: Wayne State University Press, 1967), p. 742.

Chapter 4. Consensus versus Chaos

1. *Fraser's Magazine* 91 (March 1875), pp. 306–25.
2. For a helpful recent overview, see J. W. Burrow, *The Crisis of Reason: European Thought, 1848–1914* (New Haven, CT: Yale University Press, 2000). Such early works in Victorian studies as W. Houghton, *The Victorian Frame of Mind, 1830–1870* (New Haven, CT: Yale University Press, 1985), and Richter's *The Politics of Conscience* also remain quite useful.
3. Chadwick, *Victorian Church*, pt. two, p. 121.
4. The Greek means "useful either for the private or public good." Horace was one of Sidgwick's favorite classical authors; the significance of this is discussed in Chapter 6.
5. This is in a letter to Dakyns dated Oct. 12, 1873; only part of the letter is reproduced in the *Memoir* (M 284), and it does not contain the quotation from Descartes.
6. F. H. Hayward, *The Ethical Philosophy of Sidgwick* (Bristol: Thoemmes Press, 1993; originally published in 1901), p. xix note.
7. Sidgwick to Pearson, May 10, 1873, Bodleian MS. Eng. Letters d.190; 170.
8. Very short and surprisingly restrained, this piece appeared in the *Academy* (May 15, 1873).
9. Sidgwick to Pearson, May 10, 1873, Bodleian MS. Eng. Letters d.190; 170.
10. Quoted in Annan, *The Dons*, p. 68.
11. The Greek means "and things connected with it."
12. Sidgwick Papers, Wren Library, Trinity College, Cambridge University, Add.Ms.c.104.65.
13. Mill, "The Utility of Religion," in *Three Essays on Religion*, p. 122.
14. See the further discussion of this letter in Chapter 6.
15. Sidgwick was quite moving on his love for Cowell, whom he described as "one of the very very few men I love" (M 134). What Sidgwick found in him is perhaps not surprising: "But one had to know him well to appreciate – it was some time before I did myself – his unvarying graceful unselfishness carried out into the smallest details, and his profoundly sympathetic considerateness, that was never in the least superficial, but always so unreservedly given" (M 178). See Chapters 5, 6, and 10 for more about their special relationship.
16. Skorupski, "Desire and Will in Sidgwick and Green," in "*Sidgwick 2000*," *Utilitas* 12, no. 3 (November 2000), p. 314.
17. In Schultz, ed., *Essays*, p. 94.
18. John Rawls, *The Methods of Ethics* (Indianapolis: Hackett, 1981), p. v. See also Rawls's famous statement in "The Independence of Moral Theory."

19. The allusion is to Rob Shaver's excellent essay "Sidgwick's Minimal Metaethics," in "Sidgwick 2000," *Utilitas* 12, no. 3 (November 2000), pp. 261–77, but see Hurka, "Moore in the Middle," for some challenges to this reading of the differences between Sidgwick and Moore.

20. Some of Sidgwick's most important commentary on his own *Methods* addresses the matter of principles: see, for example, "The Establishment of Ethical First Principles," *Mind* 4 (1879), pp. 106–11. For further discussion, and criticism of C. D. Broad's account in *Five Types of Ethical Theory*, see Marcus Singer, "The Many Methods of Sidgwick's Ethics," *Monist* 58 (1974), pp. 420–48, and his introductory essay to his collection of Sidgwick's essays, *Essays on Ethics and Method* (Oxford: Clarendon Press, 2000). Singer has also endorsed Janice Daurio's claims in her essay "Sidgwick on Moral Theories and Common Sense Morality," *History of Philosophy Quarterly* 14 (1997), pp. 425–45.

21. Sidgwick published these, with Macmillan, for both the first and second editions, and he offered to do so again for the third edition, but Macmillan demurred (the relevant correspondence is in the Macmillan papers, British Library). Sidgwick's half-completed notes for his projected sixth edition are in the Sidgwick Papers, Wren Library, Cambridge University, Add.Ms.b.70.

22. See Schneewind, *Sidgwick's Ethics*, p. 291 and p. 300, to be discussed in the next section. Schneewind suggests, controversially, that after "the second edition no philosophically important changes occurred, despite a fair amount of condensing and rearranging of the text" (p. 291). Albee, in his workmanlike section on Sidgwick in *A History of English Utilitarianism* (New York: Macmillan, 1901), also has a keen eye for changes between the different editions, remarking that probably "it is not without significance that chapter iii. of Book I. . . . has successively borne the titles 'Moral Reason,' 'Reason and Feeling,' and 'Ethical Judgments,'" though he agrees that the "more important changes . . . seem to have been made in the second edition (1877)" (p. 362). Still, Albee prudently cautions that it is important to keep in mind that the work was carefully revised five times, "for the numerous references to current ethical literature in the later editions of the *Methods* might give the impression that the book in its present form had been more recently planned and written than is actually the case" (p. 359). My own treatment, in the text of this chapter, follows the example of Albee and Schneewind, appealing to the final edition but with cautionary references to changes from earlier ones.

23. Schneewind, *Sidgwick's Ethics*, pp. 303–4.

24. Ibid., pp. 417–18.

25. See Hayward, "A Reply," *International Journal of Ethics* 11 (1900–1), p. 361. This is a reply to E. E. Constance Jones's reply to Hayward's "The True Significance of Sidgwick's 'Ethics,'" all in the same issue. Constance Jones was one of Sidgwick's prize students in later life, and edited some of his posthumous work. Sadly, her views on Sidgwick have been almost entirely neglected in scholarly commentary on him.

26. Though such works as P. J. Kelly's *Utilitarianism and Distributive Justice: Jeremy Bentham and the Civil Law* (Oxford: Clarendon Press, 1990) powerfully suggest

that Bentham's moral psychological theory was not as simplistic as the common understanding has it.

27. Schneewind observes that he grew less tentative about this in the second edition of the *Methods*; see *Sidgwick's Ethics*, p. 233.

28. It has often been noted that the references to Sidgwick in Moore's *Principia Ethica* are by far the most numerous of all his references. For some excellent comparisons between the *Methods* and the *Principia*, see Bernard Williams's "The Point of View of the Universe," in his *Making Sense of Humanity* (Cambridge: Cambridge University Press, 1995), pp. 153–71; and Hurka, "Moore in the Middle." As I stressed in Chapter 1, Hurka's argument is largely the line that I have taken in this book, insofar as he maintains that "*Principia Ethica* is best seen, not as starting a new era, but as coming near the middle of a sequence of ethical writing that runs roughly from the first edition of Sidgwick's *Methods of Ethics* in 1874 to Ross's *Foundations of Ethics* in 1939" (p. 600).

29. See Brink, "Sidgwick and the Rationale for Rational Egoism," in Schultz, ed., *Essays*, p. 202; and "Sidgwick's Dualism of Practical Reason," *Australasian Journal of Philosophy* 66 (1988), pp. 291–307. As Brink notes, William Frankena, in such works as "Sidgwick and the Dualism of Practical Reason," *Monist* 58 (1974), pp. 449–67; and "Sidgwick and the History of Ethical Dualism," in Schultz, ed., *Essays*, has provided a more internalist reading. But see also Frankena's "*The Methods of Ethics*, Edition 7, Page 92, Note 1," in "Sidgwick 2000," *Utilitas* 12, no. 3 (November 2000), pp. 278–90. Brad Hooker has suggested classing Sidgwick along with Nagel and others as an "internalist cognitivist," which seems justifiable. See his "Is Moral Virtue a Benefit to the Agent?" in *How Should One Live?* ed., R. Crisp (Oxford: Oxford University Press, 1996), p. 147, note 15.

30. A point stressed by Schneewind throughout *Sidgwick's Ethics*, pursued by Schultz in *Essays on Henry Sidgwick*, and developed further by Shaver in "Sidgwick's Minimal Metaethics" and *Rational Egoism* (New York: Cambridge University Press, 1999), particularly with respect to twentieth-century metaethics.

31. The historical dimensions of Sidgwick's account of the Right and the Good will be considered more fully in connection with the dualism of practical reason. But it is important to stress throughout how emphatic he was about this: "Virtue or Right action is commonly regarded as only a species of the Good: and so, on this view of the moral intuition, the first question that offers itself, when we endeavour to systematise conduct, is how to determine the relation of this species of good to the rest of the genus. It was on this question that the Greek thinkers argued, from first to last. Their speculations can scarcely be understood by us unless with a certain effort we throw the quasi-jural notions of modern ethics aside, and ask (as they did) not 'What is Duty and what is its ground?' but 'Which of the objects that men think good is truly Good or the Highest Good?' or, in the more specialised form of the question which the moral intuition introduces, 'What is the relation of the kind of Good we call Virtue, the qualities of conduct and character which men commend and admire, to other good things?' " (ME 106).

32. Recently given brilliant coverage in J. B. Schneewind's *The Invention of Autonomy* (New York: Cambridge University Press, 1997). Schneewind has long urged that Sidgwick's basic historical account is right as far as it goes and only requires adding some depth and detail. See his "Modern Moral Philosophy: From Beginning to End?" in *Philosophical Imagination and Cultural Memory*, ed. P. Cook (Durham, NC: Duke University Press, 1993), pp. 83–103. Schneewind's sympathetic reading of Sidgwick's historical work has received weighty support from many quarters, perhaps most importantly from T. H. Irwin, in, e.g., his "Happiness, Virtue, and Morality," *Ethics* 105, no. 1 (1994), pp. 153–77.

33. In *Utilitarianism*, Mill infamously advanced an inappropriate analogy with vision in this connection, the visible being that which is seen. See the discussions in Crisp's *Mill on Utilitarianism*, Chapter 4, and Berger's *Happiness, Justice, and Freedom* (Berkeley: University of California Press, 1984), Chapter 2. Although Moore typically receives credit for spotting the confusions in this (not very characteristic) section of Mill's work, Sidgwick (and indeed, John Grote and James Ward) anticipated him on nearly every count. I am grateful to J. B. Schneewind for stressing to me that there is "nothing" new in Moore's criticism.

34. See Connie Rosati, "Persons, Perspectives, and Full Information Accounts of the Good," *Ethics* 105 (1995), pp. 296–325; and David Soble, "Full Information Accounts of Well-Being," *Ethics* 104 (1994), pp. 784–810. Schneewind, Shaver, Parfit, and Hurka are united in rejecting any such interpretation, and Hurka goes so far as to insist that Sidgwick's notion of "good" is distinct from contemporary interpretations of it in terms of "well-being."

35. See his Introduction to his edition of *Principia Ethica* (Cambridge: Cambridge University Press, 1993), p. xv, note 16.

36. See Rob Shaver, "Sidgwick's False Friends," *Ethics* 107 (1997), pp. 314–20.

37. See also, e.g., ME4, pp. 110–12, where Sidgwick's resistance to the full-information view is somewhat clearer.

38. Schneewind, *Sidgwick's Ethics*, is particularly good on the changes in Sidgwick's treatment of ultimate good through the various editions. It is not often noted, for example, that in the first edition neither "the distinctive arguments in support of the rationality of moral judgements nor the definition of 'good' as 'what is reasonably desired' are presented" (p. 233). See also Stephen Darwall, "Sidgwick, Concern, and the Good," in "Sidgwick 2000," *Utilitas* 12, no. 3 (November 2000), pp. 291–306. I am also grateful to Thomas Hurka for impressing upon me the significance of Sidgwick's revisions concerning "good" even in later editions.

39. Schneewind, *Sidgwick's Ethics*, p. 226; see also the discussion in Parfit, *Reasons and Persons*, pp. 493–502.

40. Sidgwick's concern to address the charge that utilitarianism neglected the importance of agency may well have stemmed, in significant measure, from his constant exposure to the views of John Grote, who, again, was George Grote's younger brother and the Grote behind the "Grote Club." See Grote's posthumously published *An Examination of the Utilitarian Philosophy*, ed. J. B. Mayor (Cambridge: Deighton Bell, 1870), for a remarkably prescient and penetrating

series of criticisms of utilitarianism, including the claim that it speaks only to half of our nature.

41. Hurka, "Moore in the Middle," pp. 603–4.

42. Hastings Rashdall, *The Theory of Good and Evil*, vol. 1 (London: Oxford University Press, 1924; 1st ed. 1907), pp. 135–36, note 1. I would like to thank Thomas Hurka for stressing the importance of this passage to me; see his "Moore in the Middle," p. 599, note 3.

43. This was the basis for the powerful criticisms of Moore's position advanced by William Frankena, who, not coincidentally, thought very highly of Sidgwick's *Methods*. See Stephen Darwall's "Learning from Frankena," *Ethics* 107 (July 1997), pp. 685–705, for a lucid overview of Frankena's work on both Moore and Sidgwick.

44. Though, as Hurka notes, Moore was perhaps more original on some counts, such as his claims about organic unities and intrinsic value. For Moore, intrinsic value precludes relational properties – hence his famous "isolation test" for a purported intrinsic value, asking whether a universe with nothing else in it would be good. Sidgwick apparently allowed the possibility of relational properties – e.g., when he allowed that "A man may prefer the mental state of apprehending truth to the state of half-reliance on generally accredited fictions, while recognising that the former state may be more painful than the latter, and independently of any effect which he expects either state to have upon his subsequent consciousness" (ME 399).

45. For Shaver, the implication is that "Sidgwick's complaint against a full information account, understood without a 'proper reasoning' addition, is that in cases of weakness of will, such an account declares rational or good what is surely not rational or good." Furthermore, although Sidgwick does not explicitly admit that adding the "proper reasoning" requirement compromises the naturalism of the full-information view, "this, presumably, is why he highlights the naturalism of the full information account he rejects." See his "Sidgwick's False Friends," p. 316, p. 317. Schneewind focuses on a slightly different point, stressing how Sidgwick's final account eliminates the possibility "that a particular decision about what is good might be influenced by the desires one merely happened to have at the present moment in a way that would not be reasonable if one took into account all one's future desires." See *Sidgwick's Ethics*, p. 225. Parfit, in *Reasons and Persons*, goes further than either in suggesting how Sidgwick might be approximating an "objective list" account of well-being, such that the best life is that containing the things that are good for us, whether we want them or not (see p. 500). For an excellent overview, see Robert Merrihew Adams, *Finite and Infinite Goods: A Framework for Ethics* (New York: Oxford University Press, 1999), pp. 84–93, though Adams seems not to recognize how, at a more general level, Sidgwick was so often engaging with precisely the Platonic perfectionist alternative he favors.

46. Roger Crisp, "Sidgwick and Self-Interest," *Utilitas* 2 (November 1990), pp. 267–80.

47. Ibid., p. 271, pp. 268–70.

48. Ibid., p. 278.

49. Allan Gibbard, in such works as "Normative and Recognitional Concepts," *Philosophy and Phenomenological Research* 64 (January 2002), pp. 151–67, very interestingly seeks a subtle rehabilitation of Moore, though the result sounds rather more like Sidgwick, in its metaphysical reticence.

50. Interestingly, however, something close to classical hedonism is making a comeback; see such works as Daniel Kahneman, "Objective Happiness," in *Well-Being: The Foundations of Hedonic Psychology*, ed. D. Kahneman, E. Diener, and N. Schwarz (New York: Russell Sage Foundation, 1999); and Allen Parducci, *Happiness, Pleasure, and Judgment: The Contextual Theory and Its Applications* (Mahwah, NJ: Erlbaum, 1995). This hedonism is informed by the most sophisticated tools of decision theory and experimental psychology, but in core respects it marks a return to the views of F. Y. Edgeworth, who was the first to try to throw Sidgwick's hedonism into a formal decision-theoretic mode. See his *New and Old Methods of Ethics* (Oxford: Parker & Co., 1877), which was one of the first extensive treatments of Sidgwick's *Methods*.

51. See Sumner, *Welfare, Happiness and Ethics* (Oxford: Clarendon Press, 1996), p. 86, p. 91.

52. See his "Something in Between," in *Well-Being and Morality*, ed. Roger Crisp and Brad Hooker (Oxford: Clarendon Press, 2000), p. 5; the point is made at greater length in Sumner, *Welfare, Happiness, and Ethics*, pp. 84–87, p. 91.

53. Sumner, *Welfare, Happiness, and Ethics*, p. 91.

54. Shaver, "Sidgwick's Minimal Metaethics," p. 270.

55. Schneewind, *Sidgwick's Ethics*, pp. 203–4.

56. Indeed, the earlier nineteenth-century intuitionists – Whewell, Grote, etc. – simply did not parse moral theory in the way that has become so common in the twentieth century, and were in fact closer to idealism than has been supposed. See, for example, John Gibbins, "John Grote and Modern Cambridge Philosophy."

57. See, for Mill, Alan Ryan's eloquent statement in "Mill in a Liberal Landscape," in Skorupski, ed., *Cambridge Companion to Mill*, pp. 536–37.

58. Again, see Sumner, e.g., *Welfare, Happiness and Ethics*, p. 91. See also Griffin, *Well-Being: Its Meaning, Measurement, and Moral Importance* (Oxford: Clarendon Press, 1986), for many of the classic arguments that Sumner takes as his point of departure. Other especially useful works on these issues include Shelly Kagan, *Normative Ethics* (Boulder, CO: Westview Press, 1998); R. B. Brandt (long a defender of quantitive hedonism), *A Theory of the Good and the Right* (Oxford: Oxford University Press, 1979); and T. L. S. Sprigge, *The Rational Foundations of Ethics* (London: Routledge and Kegan Paul, 1988). It is, of course, the "mental state" aspect of Sidgwick's view that has brought down upon it much of the stock criticism of hedonism, such as the reductio argument having to do with "experience machines" capable of simulating any and every experience and thus of maximizing pleasure by wholly delusional means. See, e.g., Robert Nozick, *The Examined Life: Philosophical Meditations* (New York: Touchstone, 1989), Chapter 10.

59. *Principia Ethica*, p. 135; as Thomas Hurka has stressed to me, this element of Moore's (early) views was not shared by such figures as Rashdall and McTaggart

and should not be taken as essential to perfectionism – see his *Virtue, Vice and Value* (Oxford: Oxford University Press, 2001), Chapter 8.

60. See Peter Singer, *Animal Liberation*, 2nd ed. (New York: New York Review/ Random House, 1990), and his very Sidgwickian *How Are We to Live?* Sidgwick's views on this point (to my mind a great strength of the utilitarian tradition) will be considered in a different context in Chapters 5 and 6.

61. See, for the type of argument that I have in mind, the contributions by Crisp and Hooker in Crisp and Hooker, eds., *Well-Being and Morality*, along with Griffin's replies. I am inclined to agree with Crisp that Griffin, even in such works as *Value Judgement: Improving Our Ethical Beliefs* (Oxford: Clarendon Press, 1996) with its call for modesty in ethical theory, is after all much more Sidgwickian than he allows. See also John Skorupski, *Ethical Explorations* (Oxford: Oxford University Press, 1999).

62. It is a delicate question just how independent the issues of what is good and whether good is to be sought indirectly ultimately are. Some, such as Thomas Hurka, treat them as altogether independent, but on the broad, holistic view of argument and justification described by Shaver it is not plain why this should be so.

63. Though some, notably Brad Hooker, argue powerfully that the distinction survives. See his contributions to Crisp and Hooker, eds., *Well-Being and Morality*, and to "Sidgwick 2000," *Utilitas* 12, no. 3 (November 2000), and his important book *Ideal Code, Real World: A Rule-Consequentialist Theory of Morality*, in all of which he urges that Sidgwick is not best regarded as an indirect consequentialist. Most of what I urge in this chapter is consistent with Hooker's description of Sidgwick as a "direct consequentialist," since he recognizes how this view finds a place for indirect optimizing strategies involving the internalization of various dispositions, decision procedures, etc.

64. Williams, "Point of View," pp. 164–65.

65. I hasten to add that I am not suggesting that all of these critics share a positive ethical perspective, only that they share certain reservations about Sidgwick.

66. Rashdall, "Prof. Sidgwick's Utilitarianism," *Mind*, old series 10 (1885), p. 221. Rashdall was one of Sidgwick's keenest critics on issues of conformity and subscription, the virtual model of the admirable defender of pious fraud. Their exchanges in the 1890s will be discussed in later chapters, but it is curious how they could share so much by way of ethical theory and so little when it came to casuistry.

67. For a good summary statement, see Roger Crisp's Introduction to his edited volume *How Should One Live?* Many of the contributions to this collection, such as those by Irwin, Hooker, and Driver, point to the dilemmas that arise from the confrontation between Sidgwick and most forms of virtue ethics.

68. See Schneewind, *Sidgwick's Ethics*, Chapter 8, for an excellent treatment (and a testament to scholarship, since Martineau was surely one of Sidgwick's most tedious controversialists).

69. The extent of his response is in descending order of magnitude, since he obviously had comparatively little opportunity to respond to Moore's work. However, he

had some; Tom Regan's edition of Moore's early work, the basis for *Principia Ethica*, reveals much about their interaction – see Moore, *The Elements of Ethics*, ed. T. Regan (Philadelphia: Temple University Press, 1991). Among other things, Regan notes that Moore delivered the *Elements* as a lecture series in 1898 at the London School of Ethics and Social Philosophy, an institution with Sidgwick as one of its vice presidents. See also Regan's *Bloomsbury's Prophet: G. E. Moore and the Development of His Moral Philosophy* (Philadephia: Temple University Press, 1986) for a full account of their interaction, including Sidgwick's views on Moore's fellowship dissertations.

70. T. H. Irwin, "Eminent Victorians and Greek Ethics: Sidgwick, Green and Aristotle," in Schultz, ed., *Essays*, pp. 281–82. Irwin nicely brings out the Sidgwickian obsession with clarity and determinateness.

71. Ibid., pp. 286–87; Irwin is at some pains to urge that Green gives the better reading of Aristotle.

72. Ibid., p. 287.

73. Ancient theories, he argues, held "that all our rationally justified concerns must be fitted into some harmonious and coherent set of values" and were thus monistic about practical reason. See Irwin, "Happiness, Virtue, and Morality."

74. Similar points have been forcefully presented by John Skorupski, e.g., in his review of Schultz, ed., *Essays* in the *Times Literary Supplement* (July 1993).

75. Thomas Hurka, "Review: *Essays on Henry Sidgwick*," *Canadian Philosophical Reviews* 12, no. 5 (October 1992), p. 358.

76. Hurka, *Virtue, Vice and Value*, p. 32.

77. Ibid., p. 247. Thus, Michael Stocker and Julia Annas, among others, would be open to such charges.

78. Brink's recent "Eudaimonism, Love and Friendship, and Political Community," *Social Philosophy and Policy* 16 (1999), pp. 252–89, nicely brings out many of the problems that arise from the unstable Greek combination of virtue and egoism, though Brink in fact provides a defense of indirect forms of, e.g., friendship that would apply in various respects to Sidgwick. At any rate, this essay conveys some sense of the richness and vastness of the debates over the issue of whether one can value friends for their own sake and as a crucial element of one's own good.

79. This is, of course, only a bare sketch of some central issues. See Crisp, *How Should One Live?* and Hurka, *Virtue, Vice and Value*, for trenchant discussions of the various strategies of (and differences between) perfectionists and virtue ethicists. Some very interesting philosophical rehabilitation of Green is currently under way: see, e.g., David Brink, "Perfectionism and the Common Good: Aristotelian Themes in T. H. Green"; and Avital Simhony, "The Reconciliation Project: T. H. Green and Henry Sidgwick," both unpublished papers delivered at the conference ISUS 2000, held at Wake Forest University, March 2000.

80. As previously noted, however, hedonism is in fact enjoying something of a revival. In addition to the works by Parducci and Kahneman cited earlier, see Torbjorn Tannsjo, *Hedonistic Utilitarianism* (Edinburgh: Edinburgh University Press, 1998); and Fred Feldman, *Utilitarianism, Hedonism, and Desert*

(New York: Cambridge University Press, 1997). Good critical overviews of the sorry development of rational choice and utility theory in general can be found in such works as D. P. Green and I. Shapiro, *Pathologies of Rational Choice Theory: A Critique of Applications in Political Science* (New Haven, CT: Yale University Press, 1994); Richard Thayer, *Quasi-Rational Economics* (New York: Russell Sage Foundation, 1994); and Sen, *On Ethics and Economics*, though there is of course a vast and highly technical literature in this area. Again, the various works by and on James Griffin cited in previous notes afford excellent insights into how such debates bear on Sidgwick's arguments.

81. One should also mention here the works of Russell Hardin, e.g., *Morality within the Limits of Reason* (Chicago: University of Chicago Press, 1988).

82. Schneewind, *Sidgwick's Ethics*, p. 286.

83. "Professor Calderwood on Intuitionism in Morals," *Mind*, no. 4 (1876), pp. 563–66 at, p. 564.

84. This explication is from "The Establishment of Ethical First Principles," pp. 106–7.

85. Sidgwick, "Establishment," pp. 106–7.

86. See T. H. Irwin, *Aristotle's First Principles* (Oxford: Oxford University Press, 1988), p. 533, note 9. Irwin, as we shall see, is highly critical of this form of intuitionism.

87. See Jeff McMahan, "Moral Intuition," in *The Blackwell Guide to Ethical Theory*, ed. H. LaFollette (Oxford: Blackwell Publishers, 2000), pp. 105–6. This is noteworthy in part because McMahan takes himself as presenting an alternative to Sidgwick's view.

88. Unfortunately, much of the recent Rawlsian-inspired discussion of Sidgwick's method has been warped by the extremely simplistic description of "rational intuitionism" given in Rawls's later work; see *The Cambridge Companion to Rawls*, ed. A. Freeman (New York: Cambridge University Press, 2002), p. 27, for a case in point.

89. These core claims were quite consistent across the different editions.

90. Schneewind, *Sidgwick's Ethics*, pp. 264–65, pp. 284–85.

91. Ibid., p. 350.

92. See Mill, *Utilitarianism*, p. 51.

93. Ibid., p. 70.

94. It certainly provoked G. E. M. Anscombe, anyway; her tirade on "Modern Moral Philosophy" took Sidgwick as the kind of "corrupt mind" emblematic of the failings of all modern moral theory. This tradition of abuse has been carried on by Alasdair MacIntyre in his *Three Rival Versions of Moral Inquiry* (Notre Dame, IN: Notre Dame University Press, 1990), though with little gain in plausibility.

95. Mill, *Utilitarianism*, p. 70, p. 66.

96. Henry Sidgwick, "Utilitarianism," reprinted in "Sidgwick 2000," *Utilitas* 12, no. 3 (November 2000), p. 259.

97. However, see Chapter 1 for some suggestions on how Mill was indebted to Bentham even on the matter of the unconscious utilitarianism of common sense, and on much else besides. The designation of Hume and Smith as "contemplative utilitarians"

is of course controversial, though I think highly plausible, particularly if utilitarianism is understood in a broader way, with less of a fixation on "maximizing" as opposed to "satisficing." See, especially, T. D. Campbell's excellent work *Adam Smith's Science of Morals* (London: Allen and Unwin, 1971); Ian Simpson Ross's *The Life of Adam Smith* (Oxford: Clarendon Press, 1995) gives a clear and concise statement of the view, and some helpful points of comparison with Hume – see, e.g., p. 167.

98. Mill, *Utilitarianism*, p. 76.

99. J. B. Scheewind, "Sidgwick and the Cambridge Moralists," in Schultz, ed., *Essays*, p. 111.

100. Interestingly, Skorupski has also noted how, from certain angles, Mill and Sidgwick seem closer than has been supposed: "the difference between Mill and Sidgwick is not great. Both think that fundamental principles of reasoning are located by reflective scrutiny, which identifies what our most fundamental commitments are. In both cases there is also an appeal to the systematic coherence a principle can provide, and to the general agreement it can secure. Nor does Mill deny that a fundamental principle, either of theoretical or of practical reasons, is a requirement of *reason*. . . . his standpoint on reason is naturalistic, not sceptical. And on the other hand Sidgwick does not put his self-evident rational intuitions into an explicitly anti-naturalistic Kantian or Platonic setting." See his *English-Language Philosophy, 1750–1945* (Oxford: Oxford University Press, 1993), p. 68. Hurka, in "Moore in the Middle," takes sharp issue with any such account of the differences between Sidgwick and Moore, questioning "whether there is a significant difference between non-naturalisms that do and do not posit non-natural properties" (p. 608). But he leaves it open how to draw the larger moral: "that Moore's metaethics were no more metaphysically suspect than Sidgwick's, or that Sidgwick's were as hopelessly extravagant as Moore's." Gibbard's "Normative and Recognitional Concepts" is suggestive of how to push the former line, though Gibbard's own expressivist position is rather similar to Russell's noncognitivist appropriation of Sidgwick's intuitionism in *Human Society in Ethics and Politics*. Sidgwick and Moore remained cognitivists, taking ethical claims as having truth value.

101. Schneewind, *Sidgwick's Ethics*, p. 205.

102. Sidgwick, it must be admitted, did much to contribute to the unfortunate tendency to seize on some of the less perspicuous passages of Mill's *Utilitarianism* in order to demonstrate his supposed failings as a logician. See Crisp's critical discussion of Mill in his edition of *Utilitarinism* and his *Mill on Utilitarianism*. That Mill did not suffer from many of the confusions critics have attributed to him is plain. To assess the worth of Sidgwick's argument, however, it is necessary to ask why he was so persuaded that only intuitionism could afford a rational justification of first principles.

103. An especially helpful discussion, produced while work was proceeding on the *Methods*, is to be found in Sidgwick's "Verification of Beliefs," *Contemporary Review* 17 (July 1871), pp. 582–90. The earlier and in some ways more revealing

version of this, delivered to the Metaphysical Society, is reproduced for the first time in CWC.

104. See the excellent discussion in Shaver, *Rational Egoism*, pp. 62–73.

105. Sidgwick, "Utilitarianism," p. 253.

106. See, e.g., PSR.

107. Thus, William Frankena, in "Henry Sidgwick," in *The Encyclopedia of Morals*, ed. V. Ferm (New York: Philosophical Library, 1956), finds eight; Schneewind, in *Sidgwick's Ethics*, ultimately settles on four. The latter seems the more helpful account.

108. It is this gap, between what the axioms actually accomplish by way of crediting the powers of pure practical reason, and the greater claims of utilitarianism on the matter of the nature of the good and its maximization, that suggests how close Skorupski's "generic" or "philosophical" utilitarianism actually is to Sidgwick's position–see his *Ethical Explorations* for an extended account. The parallels are even more striking if one holds, as Shaver does, that Sidgwick's account of the justification of egoism is not on the same level or as compelling as his defense of universal concern or impartiality; see the discussion in the following sections of this chapter.

109. Sidgwick in fact wrote extensively about the Kantian system as a whole, and at the time of his death was contemplating a book on "Kant and Kantism in England." The drift of his larger interpretation, which is more cogent than the *Methods* conveys, is given in the posthumous LPK. The best discussion of the complex Kantian elements in Sidgwick's ethics remains Schneewind, *Sidgwick's Ethics*, which is treated at greater length in the final section of this chapter. It is curious that the interest in Kantianism was another matter on which Moore was apparently more indebted to Sidgwick than he allowed; the lecture course on *The Elements of Ethics* that Moore gave in 1898 was to be followed by a series on Kant's moral philosophy, and the original title of the first series was A Course of Ten Lectures on *The Elements of Ethics, with a View to the Appreciation of Kant's Moral Philosophy*. See Moore, *The Elements of Ethics*.

110. See Schneewind, *Sidgwick's Ethics*, pp. 290–91.

111. Schneewind's early essay "First Principles and Common Sense Morality in Sidgwick's Ethics," *Archiv für Geschichte der Philosophie* 45, no. 2 (1963), pp. 137–56, might be seen as setting the stage for a Rawlsian interpretation, as it was by Peter Singer in "Sidgwick and Reflective Equilibrium," *Monist* 58 (1974), pp. 490–517, who defends Sidgwick as closer to Hare in the rejection of received opinion. A good summary is in Steven Sverdlik, "Sidgwick's Methodology," *Journal of the History of Philosophy* 23 (1985), pp. 537–53, and as will be shown, the debate has been revisited more recently by Brink, "Common Sense and First Principles in Sidgwick's Methods," and Shaver, *Rational Egoism*, especially pp. 99–108.

112. Again, on this see Shaver, "Sidgwick's Minimal Metaethics," and Darwall, "Learning from Frankena." It is noteworthy that intuitionism is also undergoing something of a revival. Robert Audi, though he scarcely recognizes the

significance of Sidgwick as his intellectual godfather, has importantly worked out a form of fallibilistic intuitionism that "is free of some often alleged defects of intuitionism: arbitrariness, dogmatism, and an implausible philosophy of mind." See his *Moral Knowledge and Ethical Character* (New York: Oxford University Press, 1997), p. 4. Also important in this connection is Roger Crisp's "Sidgwick and the Boundaries of Intuitionism," in *Ethical Intuitionism: Re-evaluations*, ed. Philip Stratton-Lake (Oxford: Clarendon Press, 2002), pp. 56–75. Crisp suggests that Sidgwick took a "step backwards" when he disparaged "aesthetic intuitionism," or judgment in particular cases, and that this was left to Ross to develop. Even so, "[F]reed of the mistaken emphasis on practical precision . . . Sidgwick's intuitionism provides a powerful method for the resolution of debates in normative ethics, though much remains to be done in working out the details and implications of his conditions for self-evidence" (p. 75). For a sharply contrary view about the "step backwards," see the works by Donagan cited in note 119.

113. *Sidgwick's Ethics*, pp. 300–301.
114. Crisp, "Sidgwick and the Boundaries of Intuitionism," p. 59.
115. Crisp, "Sidgwick and the Boundaries of Intuitionism," p. 57, p. 64. Crisp, like Skorupski, takes a profoundly Sidgwickian approach to ethics and metaethics, one far less anachronistic or opportunistic in its appropriation of the *Methods* than most such efforts. As remarked earlier, it remains an open question just how far Sidgwick can be cast in "naturalistic" terms. There is something mildly peculiar in the idea that he was deeply averse to postulating ghostly entities in metaethics, when he was, after all, so receptive to the existence of ghosts generally.
116. Brink, "Common Sense and First Principles," pp. 197–98. As Brink notes, the dialectical method is common to Aristotle and Mill.
117. Ibid., p. 201, p. 190.
118. Ibid., p. 196.
119. Schneewind's *Sidgwick's Ethics* demonstrates how progressivism was a distinctive feature of mid-nineteenth-century intuitionism; see also Alan Donagan, "Sidgwick and Whewellian Intuitionism," in Schultz, ed., *Essays*; "Whewell's *Elements of Morality*," *Journal of Philosophy* 71 (1974), pp. 724–36; and "Justice and Variable Social Institutions," in *Midwest Studies in Philosophy*, vol. 7, *Social and Political Philosophy*, ed. P. French et al. (Minneapolis: University of Minnesota Press, 1982). Donagan was a distinguished defender of the Whewellian project who argued, like Schneewind, that Sidgwick had treated it unfairly by failing to appreciate how alternative, deontological fundamental principles could succeed in systematizing commonsense morality. However, he did credit Sidgwick for having resisted the move to an Aristotelian defense of "prima facie" reasons, the course that Ross would later take.
120. Sidgwick, "Utilitarianism," p. 258.
121. Shaver, *Rational Egoism*, pp. 70–71. Shaver's work provides an excellent defense of Sidgwick's epistemology, avoiding many of the crudities of earlier interpretations, though it does admittedly develop points made by Schneewind and Schultz in defense of Sidgwick's consistency.

122. See Rawls's discussion in *Political Liberalism*, pp. 95–96, though his (brief) characterization of Sidgwick as sharing the rational intuitionism of Clarke and Price conceals more than it reveals. Again, see McMahan, "Moral Intuition"; Shaver, *Rational Egoism*; and Audi, *Moral Knowledge and Ethical Character*.
123. Sidgwick, "The Establishment of Ethical First Principles," pp. 108–9.
124. Sidgwick, "Some Fundamental Ethical Controversies," p. 483.
125. Sidgwick, "Utilitarianism," pp. 259–60.
126. Stephen, "Sidgwick's Methods of Ethics," p. 325.
127. "Henry Sidgwick," *The Independent Review* (June 1906), p. 330.
128. See the letter from Sidgwick in Alexander Bain, *Autobiography*, ed. W. L. Davidson (London: Longman, 1904).
129. Seth Pringle–Pattison, "Critical Notice: Henry Sidgwick and Thomas Hill Green," *Mind*, new series, 17 (1908), p. 95.
130. Broad, *Five Types*, p. 253.
131. See C. A. J. Coady's helpful piece, "Henry Sidgwick," in the *Routledge History of Philosophy, Vol. VII, The Nineteenth Century*, ed. C. L. Ten (London: Routledge, 1994), p. 140. William Frankena had long urged the plausibility of this form of response to Broad; see his "Sidgwick and the Dualism of Practical Reason," and other essays reprinted in *Perspectives on Morality*, ed. K. E. Goodpaster (Notre Dame, IN: University of Notre Dame Press, 1976); and "Sidgwick and the History of Ethical Dualism," in Schultz, *Essays*.
132. Shaver, *Rational Egoism*, p. 82.
133. See, e.g., David Brink, "Sidgwick's Dualism of Practical Reason," pp. 291–307, and "Sidgwick and the Rationale for Rational Egoism," in Schultz, ed., *Essays*, pp. 199–206.
134. Shaver, *Rational Egoism*, pp. 79–80.
135. Ibid., p. 77.
136. See *Reasons and Persons*, especially pp. 137–42, where Parfit discusses the distinction passage.
137. Parfit suggests that Sidgwick's hedonism may have misled him here, making him confuse the present-aim view with the (absurd) "hedonistic egoism of the present" view that one should maximize one's happiness now. See *Reasons and Persons*, pp. 137–44.
138. In the first edition, p. 389, there is a similar suggestion: "If the unity of the Ego is really illusory, if the permanent identical 'I' is not a fact but a fiction . . ."
139. Shaver, like most other philosophical commentators on Sidgwick, ignores it entirely.
140. See C. D. Broad, "Self and Others," in *Broad's Critical Essays in Moral Philosophy*, ed. D. Cheney (London: George Allen and Unwin, 1971), pp. 262–82. It should be noted that Broad concludes this essay with a sketch of an argument for the Sidgwickian "neutralist": "Even if Neutralism be true, and even if it be self-evident to a philosopher who contemplates it in a cool hour in his study, there are powerful historical causes which would tend to make certain forms of restricted Altruism or qualified Egoism *seem* to be true to most unreflective persons at

all times and even to many reflective ones at most times. Therefore the fact that common-sense rejects Neutralism, and tends to accept this other type of doctrine, is not a conclusive objection to the *truth*, or even to the *necessary* truth, of Neutralism" (p. 282). See also Allan Gibbard's "Inchoately Utilitarian Common Sense: The Bearing of a Thesis of Sidgwick's on Moral Theory," in *The Limits of Utilitarianism*, ed. H. B. Miller and W. H. Williams (Minneapolis: University of Minnesota Press, 1982), pp. 71–85; and Crisp, "Sidgwick and Self Interest."

141. Shaver, *Rational Egoism*, pp. 91–92.

142. Ibid., pp. 96–97.

143. Ibid., p. 97.

144. Ibid., pp. 103–4.

145. The passages are from "Some Fundamental Ethical Controversies," p. 483.

146. The passages are quoted by Shaver, *Rational Egoism*, p. 110.

147. Stephen Darwall, *The British Moralists and the Internal 'Ought' 1640–1740* (New York: Cambridge University Press, 1995), p. 244, note 1.

148. Stephen Darwall, "Reason, Norm, and Value," in *Reason, Ethics, and Society: Themes from Kurt Baier, with His Responses*, ed. J. B. Sehneewind (Chicago: Open Court, 1996), pp. 29–30.

149. William Frankena, "Sidgwick and the History of Ethical Dualism," in Schultz, ed., *Essays*, p. 177. Frankena's work on Sidgwick rightly stressed the importance of comparing ME to OHE, which grew out of Sidgwick's entry on "Ethics" for the ninth edition of the *Encyclopaedia Britannica*. There are some interesting student notes on Sidgwick's lectures on the history of ethics in the archives at King's College, Cambridge, mostly taken by John Neville Keynes.

150. Ibid., pp. 183–84.

151. Ibid., p. 177.

152. Of course, Shaver does address these matters to a degree. But he is fairly impatient with the religious orientation that Sidgwick took so seriously, regarding it more as a source of potential error that should have led Sidgwick to discount the importance of consensus among the theologically inclined (see *Rational Egoism*, p. 109). Sidgwick was at least slightly more receptive to the idea of enlightened, Apostolic theological inquiry.

153. Henry Sidgwick, "Review: J. Grote's *Examination of the Utilitarian Philosophy*," *Cambridge University Reporter* (February 8, 1871), pp. 182–83.

154. Popular in recent neo-Hobbesian theory – on this, see, e.g., David Brink, "Rational Egoism, Self, and Others," in *Identity, Character, and Morality*, ed. O. Flanagan and A. Rorty (Cambridge, MA: MIT Press, 1990).

155. See also p. 345, p. 404.

156. But on this, see the important paper by David Weinstein, "Deductive Hedonism and the Anxiety of Influence," in "Sidgwick 2000," *Utilitas* 12, no. 3 (November 2000), pp. 329–46.

157. Parfit's *Reasons and Persons* is of course famous for its extensive treatment of such self-effacing moral theories, often considered in connection with varieties of the Prisoner's Dilemma.

158. Julia Annas, in her important study *The Morality of Happiness* (Oxford: Oxford University Press, 1993), cites this passage in criticism of the Stoics: "A demand of reason, that one treat all alike, is not the conclusion of a process of extending personal affections: that can only result in weak partiality, not in impartiality" (p. 270). But her account does not catch the significance that Sidgwick attached to expanded sympathy; difficult and conflictual as it may be, it was still the best bet, when properly understood. Moreover, she underestimates just how far Sidgwick went in considering "virtue" as a candidate for ultimate good, stating that "[i]t is a great puzzle, why Sidgwick's analysis, which demotes the virtue aspects of commonsense morality to a sub-theoretical level, has been so successful." However, she admits, parenthetically, that "Sidgwick at least struggles with the problem of what to do with our concern with virtue, character and disposition, whereas his successors have dismissed these matters as though solved" (p. 455).

159. It is interesting that Rawls, who did so much in Part III of *Theory* to draw attention to Kohlberg's work on the stages of moral development, was also willing to grant that the utilitarian might present a plausible alternative account, and in this connection cited the above passage from the *Methods* (see *Theory*, p. 477).

160. However, Peter Singer's approach in *How Are We to Live?*, which also raises the issue of how a utilitarian moral psychology seems to comport well with a distinctly feminine voice, is thoroughly Sidgwickian in this respect.

161. Shaver, *Rational Egoism*, pp. 1–2, pp. 157–58. The conclusion of Shaver's book is rather too sketchy to be taken as a serious attempt to do justice to the vitality of rational egoism in twentieth-century philosophy, but what he does say seems highly questionable.

162. Mackie, "Sidgwick's Pessimism," in Schultz, ed., *Essays*, p. 174. One is almost inclined to suggest that, outside of ethical theory, across such stretches of academia as economics and political science, Mackie's claim would still be taken as stating the obvious.

163. Ibid.

164. Skorupski, *English-Language Philosophy*, p. 69.

165. Roger Crisp, "The Dualism of Practical Reason," *Proceedings of the Aristotelian Society*, new series 46 (1995/96), p. 53.

166. See Scheffler's *The Rejection of Consequentialism* (Oxford: Clarendon Press, 1982), especially pp. 69–70. Thus, Scheffler is concerned to argue that although one is always permitted to act for the best outcome according to consequentialist reckoning, one is not always required to do so, and there is an agent-centered prerogative that justifies according more weight to the personal point of view. And he admits that any nonegoistic rendering of this prerogative must "ultimately come to grips with the egoist challenge," that is, the egoist appropriation of this defense of the trumping value of the personal perspective (p. 70). My thanks to Michael Green for confirming that Scheffler's view was much influenced by the *Methods*.

167. Thomas Hurka, "Self-Interest, Altruism, and Virtue," in the symposium on "Self-Interest," *Social Philosophy and Policy* 14, no. 1 (Winter 1997), p. 300.

Rational egoism in various guises is certainly well represented in the contributions to this recent collection.

168. A point forcefully brought out by Skorupski in his "Three Methods and a Dualism," in Harrison, ed., *Henry Sidgwick*; see my review of this volume in *Utilitas* 14 (July 2002).

169. Hurka, "Moore in the Middle," pp. 611–12. One of the most powerful efforts to undercut egoism is of course Parfit's *Reasons and Persons*.

170. A line stressed by David Phillips, in "Sidgwick, Dualism and Indeterminacy in Practical Reason," *History of Philosophy Quarterly* 15 (January 1998), pp. 57–78.

171. Hurka, "Moore in the Middle," p. 612.

172. Kurt Baier, "Egoism," in *A Companion to Ethics*, ed. P. Singer (London: Blackwell, 1993), p. 204, p. 202.

173. Kurt Baier, *The Rational and the Moral Order: The Social Roots of Reason and Morality* (Chicago: Open Court, 1995), pp. 121–23.

174. Crisp, "The Dualism of Practical Reason," pp. 64–65.

175. Ibid., p. 71.

176. Ibid., pp. 67–68.

177. Ibid., p. 64.

178. Singer, ed., *Essays on Ethics and Method*, p. xxi.

179. Ibid., p. xxii, note 6.

180. Schneewind, *Sidgwick's Ethics*, pp. 373–74.

181. Ibid., p. 374.

182. Henry Sidgwick, "Review: J. Grote's *Examination of the Utilitarian Philosophy*," *The Academy* (April 1, 1871), p. 198. Sidgwick actually wrote two reviews of Grote's work (see CWC).

183. "Some Fundamental Ethical Controversies," p. 45.

184. Ibid., pp. 45–46.

185. Rawls, *Theory*, p. 29. Scheffler's discussion of the passage is in his "Rawls and Utilitarianism," in Freeman, ed., *The Cambridge Companion to Rawls*, pp. 426–53. Parfit's *Reasons and Persons* makes the forthright counter that "persons," so construed, do not exist.

186. Schneewind, *Sidgwick's Ethics*, pp. 365–66.

187. Ibid., pp. 369–70.

188. Ibid., pp. 367–68.

189. E.g., Darwall, in "Sidgwick, Concern, and the Good." Darwall, however, also appears to underestimate the importance of sympathy in Sidgwick ethical theory – see his discussion in his *Welfare and Rational Care* (Princeton, NJ: Princeton University Press, 2002), especially p. 26 and pp. 31–43. As previously noted, I think that Sidgwick's view could be developed in some very psychologically sophisticated ways, along the lines of A. Damasio's *The Feeling of What Happens* (New York: Harcourt Brace, 1999).

190. Sidgwick, "Some Fundamental Ethical Controversies," p. 46.

191. Rashdall would in due course fall in with Moore. Thus, in his little volume on *Ethics* (New York: Dodge Publishing, n.d.), a synopsis of sorts of his massive

Theory of Good and Evil, he argued against Sidgwick that "all Egoism . . . is absolutely and irredeemably irrational, since it involves a contradiction." Thus, "Good means 'ought to be pursued,' and Egoism makes it reasonable for me to assert that 'my good is the only thing that ought to be pursued,' while it pronounces that my neighbour is right in denying that proposition and in asserting that his pleasure is the only thing to be pursued. Therefore contradictory propositions are both true. But I must not further develop this point, which no one has pushed home so thoroughly as Mr. Moore in his brilliant *Principia Ethica*" (p. 63). Hurka, in *Virtue, Vice and Value*, defends what he takes to be a better Rashdallian claim: "He thinks virtue is a greater good and vice a greater evil because he thinks any virtuous or vicious attitude, though outweighed by some base-level values, has more positive or negative value than the specific base-level state that is its direct or indirect object." (p. 133).

192. As Schneewind notes, the passage occurs in the third edition, on p. 402.

193. Ross Harrison has insightfully suggested that this side of Sidgwick's argument could be seen as a stimulus for later emotivist developments. See his "Henry Sidgwick," *Philosophy* 71 (1996), pp. 423–38. Certainly, as previously noted, Russell could be viewed as a true disciple of Sidgwick on many counts; even Moore came to have some doubts about cognitivism.

194. Henry Sidgwick, "Mr. Barratt on 'The Suppression of Egoism'," *Mind* 2 (1877), pp. 411–12.

195. Sidgwick, "Some Fundamental Ethical Controversies," pp. 44–45.

196. Ibid., pp. 43–44.

197. Shaver, *Rational Egoism*, p. 102.

198. Ibid., p. 104.

199. Myers Papers, Wren Library, Cambridge University, Add.Ms.c.100.2.83.

200. Henry Sidgwick, "Fitzjames Stephen on Mill on Liberty," *Academy* (August 1, 1873), p. 294.

201. Ibid.

202. Schneewind appears to underestimate the extent to which Sidgwick considered the constructive potential of egoism – see *Sidgwick's Ethics*, pp. 360–61.

203. The Greek terms mean "magnanimous" and "mean-spirited," respectively.

204. M 287 gives part of this letter.

205. Rawls, *Theory*, pp. 187–88.

206. Singer, *Essays on Ethics and Method*, pp. xxxvi–xxxvii.

207. See Chapter 8.

208. Schneewind, *Sidgwick's Ethics*, pp. 307–8. As noted earlier, if one resists Sidgwick's treatment at just this point, something closer to Skorupski's "philosophical" or "generic" utilitarianism results. See his *Ethical Explorations*, especially Chapter 3. Philosophical utilitarianism "abstracts from classical utilitarianism by allowing (1) functions other than the aggregative function of classical utilitarianism from individual well-being to good – so long as they are positive and impartial functions and (2) different interpretations of well-being to the classical utilitarians' view of it as consisting exclusively of happiness" (p. 57). Skorupski's

sophisticated approach represents another deeply Sidgwickian project, albeit a version of the moralist or impartialist attempt to defeat egoistic reasons (which are nonetheless treated as reasons, reasons stemming from a different source than pure practical reason). See also his "Three Methods and a Dualism: A Reassessment of Sidgwick's Methods of Ethics," in *Henry Sidgwick*, ed. R. Harrison.

209. Schneewind, *Sidgwick's Ethics*, p. 308. See also the works by Donagan cited in previous notes.

210. Ibid., p. 422.

211. Ibid. Needless to say, although Schneewind had in mind Rawls's work, a number of other projects, such as Skorupski's, Crisp's, and Hurka's, could make powerful claims to be developing precisely the options that Sidgwick had deemed most promising.

212. Again, see Hayward, "A Reply," p. 361. Hayward was responding to Jones's piece, in the same issue, on the "True Significance of Sidgwick's 'Ethics.'" There is no little irony in the charge that Sidgwick, who accused dogmatic intuitionists of being unconscious utilitarians, was himself an unconscious Kantian.

213. Schneewind, *Sidgwick's Ethics*, pp. 419–20.

214. J. P. Schneewind, "Classical Republicanism and the History of Ethics," *Utilitas* 5, no. 2 (November 1993), p. 207.

215. Kloppenberg's *Uncertain Victory*, while recognizing that Sidgwick was not in the grip of a solipsistic epistemology, fails to bring out the specific connections between his theory and practice in this way. See also his "Rethinking Tradition: Sidgwick and the Philosophy of the Via Media," in Schultz, ed., *Essays*, for a shorter account of his claims; Kloppenberg does carefully bring out just how profoundly indebted James and Dewey were to Sidgwick's work.

216. On this, see Skorupski's important paper "Desire and Will in Sidgwick and Green." This is, of course, a point long harped on by Rawls and Rawlsians – see the various contributions to Freeman, ed., *The Cambridge Companion to Rawls* – e.g., p. 365, note 17.

217. Darwall, *Internal 'Ought'*, p. 329. For a helpful survey of "internalisms" in ethics, see his "Reasons, Motives, and the Demands of Morality," in Darwall, Gibbard, and Railton, eds., *Moral Discourse and Practice*, pp. 305–12. As Darwall elsewhere recognizes, Sidgwick is not happily cast as a "perceptual internalist" on the model of Clarke or Price; see also his "Learning from Frankena."

218. It is worth noting that both Alan Donagan and William Frankena would have urged, in different ways, that such classifications are unsatisfactory and simplistic. Donagan held that both Kant and Whewell were engaged in a common rationalist project that Sidgwick appreciated somewhat, though inconsistently (see his *The Theory of Morality*).

219. Included in *Kant's Political Writings*, ed. H. Reiss (New York: Cambridge University Press, 1991).

220. Rawls, *Political Liberalism*, p. 68.

221. Williams, "The Point of View of the Universe," p. 166.

222. A point stressed by John Gray in his illuminating essay "Indirect Utility and Fundamental Rights," in his *Liberalism: Essays in Political Philosophy* (London: Routledge, 1989). See also Jonathan Bennett, *The Act Itself* (Oxford: Clarendon Press, 1995); Peter Railton, "Alienation, Consequentialism, and the Demands of Morality," *Philosophy and Public Affairs* 13 (1984), pp. 134–71; Hare, *Moral Thinking*; and Parfit, *Reasons and Persons*.

223. Williams, "The Point of View of the Universe," p. 166.

224. Ibid., p. 168.

225. Ibid., pp. 169–70.

226. *Ethics and the Limits of Philosophy*, p. 215, note 12.

227. Schneewind, *Sidgwick's Ethics*, p. 347.

228. I am most grateful to Jerry Schneewind for his extremely generous and constructive feedback on this material, and for agreeing that he did not handle these issues in a perspicuous way. For his response to my criticisms, see his "Comment" on my "The *Methods* of J. B. Schneewind," both of which are forthcoming in *Utilitas* 16, no. 2 (July 2004); as this exchange demonstrates, Schneewind's interpretation of Sidgwick remains highly – and controversially – Kantian.

229. In a letter to Sidgwick's friend John Venn, Mill advanced another consideration, explaining that "I agree with you that the right way of testing actions by their consequences, is to test them by the natural consequences of the particular action, and not by those which would follow if every one did the same. But, for the most part, the consideration of what would happen if every one did the same, is the only means we have of discovering the tendency of the act in the particular case." Quoted in Mill, *Utilitarianism*, p. 17.

230. Compare the account in Blanshard, *Four Reasonable Men*, which more or less canonized the image of Sidgwick as a man of saintly honesty.

231. Furthermore, the charge of elitism rings a bit hollow when issuing from a self-described Nietzschean.

232. Walker, *Moral Understandings*, pp. 45–46.

233. And, to be sure, Millians.

Chapter 5. Spirits

1. Quoted in Janet Oppenheim, *The Other World: Spiritualism and Psychical Research in England, 1850–1914* (New York: Cambridge University Press, 1985), p. 63.

2. Theodor W. Adorno, *The Stars Down to Earth and Other Essays on the Irrational in Culture*, ed. S. Crook (London: Routledge, 1994), p. 130.

3. This chapter is deeply indebted to C. D. Broad, "Henry Sidgwick and Psychical Research," *Proceedings of the Society for Psychical Research* 45 (1938), pp. 131–61, and *Lectures on Psychical Research* (London: Routledge and Kegan Paul, 1962); Alan Gauld, *The Founders of Psychical Research* (New York: Schocken Books, 1968); Oppenheim, *Other World*; Alison Winter, *Mesmerized: Powers of the Mind in Victorian Britain* (Chicago: University of Chicago Press, 1998); and Joy Dixon, *Divine Feminine: Theosophy and Feminism in England* (Baltimore: The

Johns Hopkins University Press, 2001). Although my own interests are more congenial to the concerns of Winter and Dixon, who address the links between psychical research and the history of gender/sexuality and the culture of imperialism, the other works just listed are standard reference guides for anyone working on these topics and represent highly valuable research efforts. Roger Luckhurst's valuable study, *The Invention of Telepathy* (Oxford: Oxford University Press, 2002), appeared just as I was preparing the final version of this manuscript for the press, but it appears to comport well with the analysis of this chapter. Although Luckhurst's book contains surprisingly little on Sidgwick, it goes far to fill in the cultural context of the psychical researchers and is particularly valuable on such figures as Myers.

4. See also Oppenheim, *Other World*, pp. 123–24, for some discussion of Sidgwick's early efforts.

5. This is one theme of Dixon's insightful work, *Divine Feminine*.

6. Quoted in Oppenheim, *Other World*, p. 124. This statement was made by William Crookes, to be discussed.

7. I am grateful to R. L. Bland, a recent headmaster of Clifton, for calling this poem to my attention and explaining its possible authorship.

8. See the discussion of this passage in the previous chapter.

9. Eleanor Sidgwick, "On the Development of Different Types of Evidence for Survival in the Work of the Society," *Proceedings of the Society for Psychical Research* 29 (1917), p. 246.

10. In Sidgwick's December 9, 1882, address to the SPR (CWC); this first appeared in the *Proceedings of the Society for Psychical Research* 1 (1882).

11. This first appeared in the *Proceedings of the Society for Psychical Research* 5 (1888).

12. Myers quoted the relevant testimonial at length at the end of his own obituary to Sidgwick, included in his posthumously published *Fragments of Poetry and Prose*, ed. Eveleen Myers (London: Longmans, Green, 1904). This work contains a somewhat abridged version of Myers's autobiography, "Fragments of Inner Life," the excised portions of which are available in the Myers Papers, Wren Library, Trinity College, Cambridge. What follows draws heavily on the latter.

13. Myers, *Fragments*, pp. 98–99.

14. Ibid., p. 100.

15. Ibid., pp. 105–6.

16. Ibid., pp. 109–10. Sidgwick doubtless would have regarded Myers's passionate idealization of him as rather characteristic.

17. Gauld, *Founders*, p. 100.

18. Ibid., p. 90. Sidgwick rather clearly took a certain delight, however mixed with disapproval, in Myers's sensual side. One of his more intriguing letters to Myers has him moving directly from admiration of Kant to admiration of flirtation. On Nov. 20, 1871, he wrote to Myers: "Each day I have wished to write to you how delightful and salutary your visit has been to me. You always do me good, though you make me feel more deeply the perplexities of conduct. I wish I had more wisdom to impart to those whom I love: it is not for want of seeking it. Sometimes

I console myself for fundamental scepticism by the feeling that it is necessary, if we are to choose Good per se: if we were too sure of personal happiness, this unselfish choice would be impossible. I do not think with Kant that Noble Choice is the *only* good thing in man: but I do think it a great good. However at other times this seems to me a very over-drawn and metaphysical consolation. Now as I write it is real to me.

Your narrative is of thrilling interest: I have no doubt you were the right man for the situation – (see Testimonial). I confess I tremble a little at the thought of the amount of emotional Electricity generated by your passage through these feminine atmospheres: but I rely on you: if only you will not so systematically court danger. Please regard me henceforward as thoroughly convinced of your power. I will idealize you if you like into a sort of Genius of Flirtation: with 'loving eyes a little tyrannous,' leonine splendour of countenance. . . . " A marginal note beside "the situation" reads: "Something about a Schoolmistress who had got into a mess," and Sidgwick notes that the phrase in quotation marks is from an unpublished poem of his. Sidgwick Papers, Wren Library, Trinity College, Cambridge University, Add.Ms.c.1000, pp. 221–22.

19. Indeed, at this point, Symonds was far closer to Arthur Sidgwick, who along with Henry Graham Dakyns formed his most intimate early group. In a letter of 1863, Symonds wrote of Myers: "He is a scapegrace: but he will be a considerable man: and a turbulent, even a presumptuous & criminal, youth may be ignored in silence when there is hope of so great a manhood" (Symonds, *Letters*, vol. 1, p. 387). This was an improvement on his still earlier judgment; when he first met him in 1861 he was fairly aghast at Myers's conceit and anti-intellectualism. But it was Myers who would first and fatefully introduce Symonds to the poetry of Walt Whitman, and who would continue to stimulate his psychological – if not parapsychological – interests, as the discussion in the following chapter will demonstrate.

20. This passage is taken from the original proofs of Myers's memoir – Myers Papers, Wren Library, Trinity College, Cambridge University, 13.30(1). The published version is more carefully censored, delicately dropping the word "lust" from the line about "no check for lust or pride."

21. Myers Papers, Wren Library, Trinity College, Cambridge University, 13.50.15, p. 23.

22. Myers, *Fragments*, p. 97.

23. Gauld, *Founders*, pp. 90–91.

24. F. W. H. Myers, Introduction to *Phantasms of the Living* (New York: Arno Press, 1975), pp. xxiv–xxv.

25. Myers, *Fragments*, p. 17.

26. Ibid., p. 46.

27. Myers Papers, Wren Library, Trinity College, Cambridge University, 18.76.12, p. 3.

28. Myers, "Fragments of Inner Life," pp. 36–37.

29. Myers, *Fragments*, p. 39.

30. Myers, "Fragments of Inner Life," pp. 36–37.

31. Myers Papers, Wren Library, Trinity College, Cambridge University, 18.76.11, p. 2.
32. Myers, *Fragments*, p. 64.
33. Ibid.
34. Ibid., p. 76.
35. Sidgwick, journal entry for October 27, 1886 (CWC); the manuscript of Sidgwick's journal is in the Sidgwick Papers, Wren Library, Trinity College, Cambridge University, Add.Ms.c.97.25.
36. Myers, *Fragments*, pp. 56–57.
37. Gurney, *Tertium Quid* (London: Kegan Paul, Trench, 1887), p. 1.
38. Oddly, Gurney receives scant attention in Winter's important study, *Mesmerized*.
39. Gurney, "The Stages of Hypnotism," *Proceedings of the Society for Psychical Research* 2 (1884), pp. 69–70.
40. Gauld, *Founders*, p. 155.
41. Ibid., p. 157.
42. Though the evidence for any such conclusion is scarcely compelling, and gains force mainly from the fact that a number of Gurney's friends and colleagues feared as much. The psychical researchers, as we will see, thought there was some evidence for Gurney's personal survival of death and communication from the other side. A full account, and one appropriately skeptical of the suicide hypothesis, is in Gauld, *Founders*, pp. 178–82. Gordon Epperson, *The Mind of Edmund Gurney* (Cranbury, NJ: Associated University Presses, 1997), is an admiring overview of Gurney's work, and very dismissive of the suicide hypothesis, but does not really engage the thoughts of the psychical researchers on this score. Oppenheim's *The Other World* also suggests that the evidence for suicide is inconclusive and likely to remain so. The main argument for the suicide hypothesis is Trevor Hall's *The Strange Case of Edmund Gurney* (London: Duckworth, 1964, 2nd ed. 1980), which holds that Gurney committed suicide because he was depressed by various events, particularly the discovery that G. A. Smith, his secretary and one of the subjects from whom he had gained positive evidence for telepathy, had been engaged in fraud and thus that his evidence was discredited. Smith always denied this, but an early partner of his in the experiments later claimed that they had tricked Gurney and Myers. Even if this were so, however, the specific links to Gurney's death in the St. Albion's Hotel in Brighton are all purely speculative, since there is no sound evidence that Gurney had discovered any such thing.
43. Gauld, *Founders*, p. 104.
44. Oppenheim, *Other World*, p. 130.
45. Quoted in Oppenheim, *Other World*, p. 131.
46. Ibid.
47. Oppenheim, "A Mother's Role, a Daughter's Duty: Lady Blanche Balfour, Eleanor Sidgwick, and Feminist Perspectives," *Journal of British Studies* 34 (April 1995), pp. 196–232. I am much indebted to this essay, which suggests how valuable Oppenheim's planned biography of Eleanor Sidgwick would have been, had she lived to complete it.

48. Oppenheim, "A Mother's Role," pp. 204–5.
49. Ibid., p. 207.
50. Ibid., pp. 209–11.
51. Ibid., p. 212.
52. Sidgwick Papers, Wren Library, Trinity College, Cambridge University, Add.Ms.c.99.
53. Oppenheim, *Other World*, p. 338.
54. Gauld, *Founders*, p. 107.
55. Quoted in Linda Simon, *Genuine Reality: A Life of William James* (New York: Harcourt Brace, 1998), p. 225. The wedding was held at St. James Church, London.
56. In Ethel Sidgwick, *Mrs. Henry Sidgwick: A Memoir* (London: Sidgwick and Jackson, 1938), p. 66.
57. Myers, "Fragments of Inner Life," excised sections, Myers Papers, 13.50(16).
58. Ironically, given the role of the SPR and Myers in calling attention to Freud's work, one could do a very interesting Freudian interpretation of their form of mourning and melancholia. For suggestive arguments about how to apply this side of Freud to some such social analysis (though not with specific reference to the psychical researchers), see Peter Homans, *The Ability to Mourn: Disillusionment and the Social Origins of Psychoanalysis* (Chicago: University of Chicago Press, 1989).
59. Gauld, *Founders*, pp. 137–38.
60. The house still stands, and some of its older neighbors can recall hearing, when they were growing up, that it was haunted. But its recent residents, mainly Cambridge students, have not to my knowledge reported any difficulties with apparitions.
61. William James, "The Confidences of a 'Psychical Researcher,'" in *William James: Writings 1902–1910* (New York: Library of America, 1987), pp. 1252–53.
62. Ibid., pp. 1259–60.
63. Ibid., p. 1250.
64. He recounted it in *Phantasms of the Living*, though the same account is reproduced in the *Memoir*, pp. 165–66.
65. Henry Sidgwick, "The Society for Psychical Research: A Short Account of Its History and Work on the Occasion of the Society's Jubilee, 1932," *Proceedings of the Society for Psychical Research* 41 (1932–33), p. 126.
66. Ibid., p. 7.
67. Gauld, *Founders*, pp. 356–57.
68. See Sidgwick's essay on "Involuntary Whispering" (CWC); the original appeared in the *Proceedings of the Society for Psychical Research* 12 (1897).
69. Eleanor Sidgwick, "On the Development of Different Types of Evidence," p. 247.
70. Ibid., pp. 248–49.
71. Ibid., p. 248.
72. The best attempt to situate the Theosophists in their proper historical contexts is Dixon, *Divine Feminine*.
73. Oppenheim, *Other World*, p. 163.
74. It is worth noting here that another of the accomplishments of F. D. Maurice was to have given a comparatively sober account of Hinduism and Buddhism, in

Moral and Metaphysical Philosophy, and that Sidgwick would have been familiar with this.

75. Dixon, *Divine Feminine*, p. 11.
76. Oppenheim, *Other World*, p. 165.
77. Sidgwick's correspondence with Bryce is in Bryce MSS, Modern Political Papers, Bodleian Library, Oxford University.
78. Oppenheim, *Other World*, p. 178. Remarkably, the Theosophical Society would long continue to publish rebuttals of Hodgson's report.
79. Myers and Gurney, *Phantasms*, p. xviii.
80. "Prefatory Note" to V. Solovev's *A Modern Priestess of Isis*, abridged and translated by W. Leaf for the APR (London, 1895).
81. Quoted in Gauld, *Founders*, pp. 366–67.
82. Henry Sidgwick, "The Possibilities of Mal-Observation (discussion with C. C. Massey)," *Proceedings of the Society for Psychical Research* 4 (1886), pt. 10 Sidgwick's exchanges with Massey – another stalwart of the SPR – are extremely illuminating, and deeply suggestive of his Apostolic faith in the truth-promoting properties of discussion among intimate friends.
83. On Mill, see various works by Georgios Varouxakis, including "John Stuart Mill on Race." See also the essays in Schultz and Varouxakis, eds., *Classical Utilitarianism and the Question of Race*; and the cogent essay by Graham Finlay, "John Stuart Mill on the Uses of Diversity," *Utilitas* 14, no. 2 (July 2002), pp. 189–218.
84. Dixon, *Divine Feminine*, p. xii.
85. Sidgwick Papers, Wren Library, Trinity College, Cambridge University, Add.Ms.c.100.
86. Journal entry for August 11, 1884 (CWC).
87. Myers and Gurney, *Phantasms*, p. xxxii.
88. Broad, "Sidgwick and Psychical Research," p. 141.
89. Myers and Gurney, *Phantasms*, p. ix.
90. Ibid., p. xix.
91. Ibid.
92. Ibid., p. xx.
93. Ibid., p. xxv.
94. Ibid., pp. xx–xxi.
95. Myers, "Fragments of Inner Life," p. 37.
96. Compare the remarks at the conclusion of the previous chapter concerning the evolution of sympathy.
97. Myers and Gurney, *Phantasms*, p. 520.
98. Gauld, *Founders*, pp. 162–63.
99. Ibid., p. 164.
100. Broad, "Sidgwick and Psychical Research," pp. 144–45.
101. Sidgwick, "Society," p. 13.
102. Quoted in Gauld, *Founders*, p. 166.
103. "The Canons of Evidence in Psychical Research," May 10, 1889 (CWC); this paper originally appeared in *Proceedings of the Society for Psychical Research* 6

(1889). Interestingly, Sidgwick's studied silence about his paranormal experiences much perturbed Alfred Russel Wallace, who deemed it a betrayal of those who went public (Oppenheim, *Other World*, p. 300).

104. Indeed, a significant part of the personal knowledge to which Sidgwick alludes had to do with his psychical experiments with his intimate Apostolic friend Cowell, during the sixties. Sidgwick's description of these, which was included in Myers's later work *Human Personality and Its Survival of Bodily Death*, is given Chapter 8.

105. On this, I largely follow the line of Dixon, *Divine Feminine*, who also shows in detail how, despite the efforts of the SPR, the Theosophical movement went on to thrive, becoming a serious political force in the early twentieth century.

106. See Gauld, *Founders*, p. 171.

107. Interestingly, even during the sixties, when his adoration of Clough was so intense, Sidgwick could marvel at how Tennyson's "The Voyage" had "caught the spirit of the age" (M 119–20).

108. Myers Papers, 3.50(20).

109. Sidgwick to Myers, Sidgwick Papers, Wren Library, Trinity College, Cambridge University, Add.Ms.c.100.98. The extensive, matched correspondence between Sidgwick and Myers, now in the Sidgwick Papers, was held by Arthur Sidgwick, when working on the *Memoir*, to be nearly as fascinating as the correspondence with Dakyns, but it is overwhelmingly concerned with the details of their psychical research.

110. Again, this is a point of fundamental importance for understanding why Sidgwick's discussions of sympathy did not reduce to an exploration of internal sanctions. See also the following chapter.

111. Frank Podmore, "Review: *Henry Sidgwick, A Memoir*," Sidgwick Papers, Wren Library, Cambridge University, Add.Ms.c.102.1, p. 450.

112. Sidgwick Papers, Wren Library, Trinity College, Cambridge University, Add.Ms.c.100.2–99.

113. Naturally, the allusion in the foregoing remarks is to Parfit's work, particularly *Reasons and Persons*. My own misgivings about Parfit's reductionist alternative can be found in "Persons, Selves, and Utilitarianism," *Ethics* 96, no. 4 (July 1986), pp. 721–45, which includes a "Comment" by Parfit. Interestingly, and controversially, Parfit in some fundamental ways agrees with Sidgwick about the importance of empirical evidence for supporting or undermining a nonreductionist view of identity (see *Reasons and Persons*, pp. 227–28). What he fails to appreciate, however, is the force of Sidgwick's view that evidence from different forms of depth psychology, including neurophysiology, might as yet be unable to fix the nature and significance of psychological continuity and connectedness. For example, the importance of the body – indeed, of deeper forms of organic awareness – in the growth of the conscious sense of self-identity is emphasized by Damasio, in *The Feeling of What Happens*. Sidgwick would no doubt have rejected any such account as materialistic, but he nonetheless found the problem of the deeper sources of the conscious self to be of fundamental importance. One of the stranger

ironies in this history is that Freud, who so profoundly influenced the Bloomsbury group, made his published debut in England courtesy of Myers and the SPR. On this, see Luckhurst, *Telepathy*, pp. 270–75.

Chapter 6. Friends versus Friends

1. *The Letters of John Addington Symonds*, vol. 1, ed. H. M. Schueller and R. L. Peters (Detroit: Wayne State University Press, 1967), pp. 467–68. The incompleteness of this and other highly revealing letters may well reflect the censoring efforts of Eleanor Sidgwick and Arthur Sidgwick when they were at work on *Henry Sidgwick, A Memoir*.

2. In *Letters and Papers of John Addington Symonds*, ed. Horatio F. Brown (New York: Charles Scribner's Sons, 1923), pp. 6–7. At the same dinner party, Tennyson had openly avowed his conviction that "Niggers are tigers" and other expressly racist views, corollaries to his imperialist sentiments. See the discussion in Chapter 7.

3. As noted, Dickenson was an influential and much-loved figure who had a considerable impact on the Apostles, setting the stage for the more openly avowed "higher sodomy" of Strachey and Keynes. (Dickenson's father painted a posthumous portrait of Sidgwick that today hangs in Trinity College.) James Ward was in some respects another of Sidgwick's discoveries. Raised in a narrow Congregationalist environment, he steadily expanded his intellectual horizons by, among other things, studying in Germany and becoming versed in the philosophy of Lotze; eventually he made his way to Cambridge, where Sidgwick helped him to advance through the ranks from student to Fellow to professor (in 1897). Ward was very well-versed in science as well, and in some respects his attack on naturalism and defense of theism, in such works as *Essays in Philosophy* and *The Realm of Ends, or Pluralism and Theism*, was less important, even as a development of Sidgwick's concerns, than his pioneering efforts in psychology. Ward's arguments in such works as his article on "Psychology" in the ninth edition of the *Encyclopaedia Britannica* and his book *Psychological Principles* advanced a sophisticated "genetic" psychology and helped finish off the old associationism. Thus, Ward provides yet another example of the emergent (pragmatist and phenomenological) concerns that Sidgwick deemed promising, and a close, extended comparison of their work would be most valuable. Among other things, Ward was Bertrand Russell's chief tutor in philosophy, and he edited two of Sidgwick's posthumous works – *Lectures on the Philosophy of Kant* and *Philosophy, Its Scope and Relations*.

4. Sidgwick, "Reminiscences of T. H. Green," Balliol College Library, University of Oxford. Symonds also composed such "Reminiscences," which are included in *The Letters of John Addington Symonds*, vol. 2.

5. T. H. Green, *Prolegomena to Ethics*, ed. A. C. Bradley (Oxford: Clarendon Press, 1890; first edition 1883), p. 2. Much as Green loved Tennyson's "In Memoriam," he felt that the poet was overly impressed with science – the very thing that Sidgwick liked about Tennyson. Green would no doubt have urged, unfairly, that Sidgwick himself was too willing to let poetry take its chances, rather than really

taking up the call to bring in systematic philosophy to vindicate poetically expressed truth.

6. Green to Henry Scott Holland, quoted in Schneewind, *Sidgwick's Ethics*, pp. 401–2.

7. Ibid.

8. Richter, *The Politics of Conscience: T. H. Green and His Age*, pp. 73–74.

9. Ibid., p. 74.

10. Ibid., p. 75.

11. Annan, *The Dons*, p. 111.

12. Quoted in Richter, *Politics of Conscience*, p. 79.

13. These points are developed in a number of other places, such as the "Introductory: Kantian Influence in England" that heads the lectures on "The Philosophy of Mr. Herbert Spencer" in the same volume.

14. Green rather famously tackled the Millian arguments, in *On Liberty*, against the temperance movement; see his famous lecture on "Liberal Legislation and Freedom of Contract," in T. H. Green, *Lectures on the Principles of Political Obligation, and Other Writings*, ed. P. Harris and J. Morrow (Cambridge: Cambridge University Press, 1986). The best discussion of the political views of the Idealists is Peter Nicholson, *The Political Philosophy of the British Idealists: Selected Studies* (Cambridge: Cambridge University Press, 1990).

15. And Jane Addams, the remarkable founder of Chicago's Hull House – perhaps the most successful of the U.S. settlement houses – took her inspiration directly from a visit to Toynbee Hall in London, which began life when Arnold Toynbee moved there, to Whitechapel, "to experience firsthand the notoriously poor living conditions endured by Londoners of humble means." See the sympathetic account in Jean Bethke Elshtain, *Jane Addams and the Dream of American Democracy* (New York: Basic Books, 2002), p. 74; but see also my review of Elshtain's work in *Ethics* 113 (January 2003). As Elshtain remarks, "Toynbee Hall offered something new: In place of old-fashioned modes of relief to the poor, it provided mutual engagement across class lines and a broad education for working men and women. Run by the impressive Canon Barnett, Toynbee Hall emphasized the importance of art and culture to a 'people's university.' " (p. 74) This was but another of the educational experiments meant to ease the pain of capitalism and the democratic transition through a Mauricean mingling of the classes; see Chapter 7 for more details about Sidgwick's perspective on this very important development.

16. For these details about the school and the Passmore Edwards Settlement, see Tom Regan's Introduction to his edition of Moore's *The Elements of Ethics*, especially pp. xv–xix.

17. Which is of course not to deny that they remain concerns. The settlement movement has often been charged with reflecting the elitism and even racism that infected the Progressivist currents that would usher in the twentieth century. Besides, Alfred Milner, the architect of much of England's imperialist ventures in South Africa – who was tutored by Green and befriended by Toynbee – also represented the philosophy of "social service." And Ruskin, like Tennyson, was

a notorious champion of the spiritual "destiny of the British race" form of imperialist ideology. Milner and Toynbee, along with Oscar Wilde and others, were
recruited by Ruskin for the cause of the dignity of labor, which for him involved
doing road construction between North and South Hinksey. See, e.g., Symonds,
Oxford and Empire, p. 41 and pp. 25–26.

18. Ibid., p. 30.

19. Bertrand Russell, in so many ways an authentic voice of the Victorian era carried on
through the mid twentieth century, was always at his most eloquent in describing
the massive changes to the Millian world and worldview that came with the growth
of large-scale social organization; see, for instance, his valuable study *Freedom
versus Organization, 1814–1914* (New York: Norton, 1934). Just how easily Green's
Idealism could be naturalized and transformed into Dewey's pragmatism (which
in many respects precisely paralleled it in its political program, support for the
settlement movement, etc.) has been brought out by Robert Westbrook in *John
Dewey and American Democracy* (Ithaca, NY: Cornell University Press, 1991).

20. See Richter, *Politics of Conscience*, pp. 330–39, for a valuable discussion of how
Green and his disciples supported the COS, though this account does not provide
an accurate account of the larger organization and its history. On this, see the
following chapter.

21. Green, *Prolegomena to Ethics*, pp. 409–10.

22. Ibid., pp. 410–11.

23. Ibid., pp. 411–12.

24. This summary is from Sidgwick's late lecture "The Philosophy of T. H. Green,"
included as an appendix to "The Metaphysics of T. H. Green" (LPK).

25. Skorupski, *English-Language Philosophy, 1750–1945*, p. 87.

26. See, for an updated account, John Searle's *The Rediscovery of Mind* (Cambridge,
MA: MIT Press, 1992), pp. 128–41. Sidgwick might well have shared Searle's bafflement at the many and varied materialist and behaviorist efforts in the twentieth
century to evade rather than address the nature of consciousness. The deficiencies
of the Wundtian forms of introspection were one thing, but the rejection of the
philosophical concern with the subjective point of view was something else entirely.

27. Henry Sidgwick, "Bradley's *Ethical Studies*," *Mind* o.s. 1 (1876), p. 545.

28. *Mind* o.s. 2 (1877), p. 125–26.

29. Schneewind, *Sidgwick's Ethics*, p. 395.

30. Ibid., p. 399.

31. It is curious that Sidgwick is rarely recognized for having approximated many
of the objections to Idealist logic, especially the doctrine of internal relations,
that would later be championed by Russell and Moore. Peter Hylton's otherwise
excellent work *Russell, Idealism and the Emergence of Analytic Philosophy* (Oxford:
Clarendon Press, 1990) makes no mention of Sidgwick whatsoever, even in its
extended discussions of Green and Bradley.

32. As explained in Chapter 4, this would of course turn out to be one of the biggest
bones of contention in the critical reception of Sidgwick's work. In addition to
the better-known criticisms advanced by Moore and Rashdall, there were also

objections coming from James Ward, whose *The Realm of Ends, or Pluralism and Theism* addressed some of the (very) similar passages in the *Methods*:

> Now, first of all, is there not here a radical confusion ... between analytical distinction and actual separation? To say that 'we may take conscious life in a wide sense as including objective relations' implies that we may also take it in a narrow sense as excluding these. But the psychologist assuredly has no such choice: he must take what he always finds. No reflexion will enable him to take the consciousness *accompanying or resulting from* objective relations apart from these relations themselves; for there is no consciousness, or as we had better say, no experience, unless these form an integral part of it. It is clear, from the context, I allow, that what Sidgwick here meant by consciousness was pleasure (or pain). But it is equally clear that feeling alone, a purely subjective state, though always an element in consciousness or experience, is never the whole of it. We cannot talk of pleasure or happiness or, to speak generally, of pure feeling as in any measure an *alternative* to the cognitions or actions from which it is inseparable. And yet Sidgwick not only admits this inseparability, but even urges that 'if we finally decide that ultimate good includes many things distinct from Happiness,' hedonism becomes 'entangled in a vicious circle.' But if the inseparability be admitted, how is that decision to be avoided? (pp. 346–47).

But to this, Sidgwick would surely have replied that the moral philosopher must utilize methods of reflection, including thought experiments, that perforce go beyond the actual psychology of lived experience. Ward, interestingly, also clearly formulates the population problem as an objection: "Maximum pleasure being the end of the world, it would seemingly be indifferent whether the number of conscious individuals were increased and their capacity *pro tanto* diminished, or *vice versa*. ..." (p. 348).

33. Sumner, in *Welfare, Happiness and Ethics*, does not quite bring out this side of Sidgwick's argument.

34. Sidgwick's remarks here make it pretty evident that he did not agree with Green (or Mill) that, as Skorupski puts it, "whatever is desired is desired as part of one's own good," though doubtless he could have been rather more forthcoming on various points. See Skorupski, "Desire and Will in Sidgwick and Green," e.g., p. 328.

35. Intriguingly, some similar thoughts turn up in a very early essay, "On Foundations of Ethics," by Sidgwick's then-student Bertrand Russell, which puzzles over how Green could possibly think "that self–sacrifice is a good in itself." This essay is included in *The Collected Papers of Bertrand Russell*, vol. 1, ed. K. Blackwell et al. (London: George Allen and Unwin, 1983), pp. 209–10; this volume also includes the papers that Russell wrote for Sidgwick and records many of Sidgwick's professorial comments on his student's work. A particularly revealing one concerns a paper on "The Ethical Bearings of Psychogony" in which Russell had "pointed out the very serious advantages of Suttee," eliciting Sidgwick's comment, "Savages can overeat themselves without being the worse for it. Don't want to take responsibility for all your illustrations. Morality of civilized societies not wholly

due to natural selection." (p. 222) Sidgwick knew Russell personally not only from tutorials, but also from their membership in the Ethical Club and Sidgwick's continuing participation in the Apostles.

36. As the *Memoir* makes patent, Sidgwick really slaved to come to terms with Green's views, though he always found himself unable to see how they could hang together: "I have been busy lately reviewing Green's posthumous book – *Prolegomena to Ethics*. I read it twice over carefully: the first time much impressed with its ethical force and persuasiveness: the second time unable to resist the conviction that my intellect could not put it together into a coherent whole – in fact, that it would not do – and yet that probably it was better that young men should be believers in it than in anything I can teach them. This is a conviction adapted to make a Professor cynical." (M 380) That Sidgwick did have a touch of cynicism is perhaps suggested by the famous story of how, upon reading McTaggart's fellowship dissertation, he said to his fellow examiners: "I can see that this is nonsense, but is it the right kind of nonsense? (see Blanshard, *Four Reasonable Men*, p. 221). McTaggart, for his part, produced one of the best, most sensitive, short overviews of Sidgwick's life and work ever penned – "The Ethics of Henry Sidgwick," *Quarterly Review* ccv (October 1906), pp. 398–416 – in which he cogently observed that Sidgwick "was above all things a student."

37. Moore, in his famous "The Refutation of Idealism," had argued that "the most striking results both of Idealism and of Agnosticism are only obtained by identifying blue with the sensation of blue: that *esse* is held to be *percipi*, solely because *what is experienced* is held to be identical with the *experience of it*." In *G. E. Moore: Selected Writings*, ed. T. Baldwin (London: Routledge, 1993), p. 36.

38. Worth stressing in this connection is the way in which many of Noel's letters to Sidgwick from the 1860s make it clear that Sidgwick was arguing for the realist case, rather than for any phenomenalistic version of positivism.

39. Bertrand Russell, *The Problems of Philosophy* (Oxford: Oxford University Press, 1912), pp. 144–45.

40. See Gibbins, "John Grote and Modern Cambridge Philosophy."

41. From "The Incoherence of Empirical Philosophy" (LPK).

42. From "Criteria of Truth and Error" (LPK).

43. There are points in Sidgwick's discussion where he appears to come strikingly close to the upshot of more recent debates over the "Myth of the Given " – e.g., John McDowell's suggestions in *Mind and World* (Cambridge, MA: Harvard University Press, 1994), pp. 42–43. It is also worth noting that Sidgwick did have something of a nascent philosophy of language – he corresponded with Lady Victoria Welby on semiotics – and was far from oblivious to many of the concerns that would emerge with the "linguistic turn."

44. See the very illuminating Appendix to "Criteria of Truth and Error" (LPK 461–67) for an exceptionally clear statement of Sidgwick's fallibilism.

45. It is interesting that James Ward would go on to address this issue at length, ultimately trying to keep "feeling" in a subordinate place, cognitively speaking, and denying that either it or the self could be noninferentially known.

46. The allusion is of course to the famous passage in Book 5 of Plato's *Republic* that introduces the idea of the philosopher king.

47. It might be added that the theological (or in some cases contemplative) versions of indirect utilitarianism in general – not, of course, Green's Idealism – do afford much argument to rebut the criticisms of indirect utilitarianism advanced by Williams and others. When the utilitarian standard invokes an appeal to the direct utilitarian decision procedure of a benevolent and all-knowing God, there seems little reason why mortals should suffer from moral schizophrenia, as opposed to an acute inferiority complex.

48. William James, "Bradley or Bergson?," in *William James, Writings 1902–1910* (New York: Library of America, 1987), pp. 1269–70.

49. Ibid., p. 1270.

50. See Kloppenberg, *Uncertain Victory*, pp. 124–28.

51. Henry Sidgwick, "Green's Ethics," *Mind* o.s. 9 (April 1884), p. 184.

52. The situation arose because, as Richter explains, "to take his degree of MA, he would have to subscribe again to the Thirty–nine Articles of the Church of England; and if he decided that he could in good conscience do so, ought he then go on to take deacon's orders? The situation in relation to University Tests between 1854 and 1874 was that although a student could take his BA without any religious profession, he could not become an MA, the almost invariable condition of holding a fellowship, without signing the Articles." (*Politics of Conscience*, p. 86) Sidgwick found Green's breezy attitude toward subscription – "one kiss does not make a marriage" – perfectly revolting.

53. Interestingly, when the young G. E. Moore did start presenting his ethical views to the philosophical public – including the working–class philosophical public – at Passmore Edwards House, one of the things that persuaded the Idealists in attendance that here was a student of Sidgwick's was Moore's stress on practical ethics and casuistry. See Regan's Introduction to Moore, *The Elements of Ethics*, and Jennifer Welchman, "Moore's *Principia*."

54. Thus, Sidgwick's position would appear to be a variant of what Parfit, in *Reasons and Persons*, labels the non-Reducationist view of personal identity, albeit one that ends up being fairly elusive about the "Further Fact."

55. See Skorupski, "Desire and Will in Sidgwick and Green," p. 327. His concern is that the "Greenian (or German idealist) conception of a person's good importantly focuses on the way in which what comes to belong to an agent's good results in part from his or her self-identifying choices. My good is not *determined* by the identity I evolve, as the idealist conception can seem to claim. . . . My good is sufficiently independent of that identity to provide a criterion for criticizing it; but certainly it is shaped by my identity and my identity is something I help to make." (p. 327) Sidgwick has more to say about this than Skorupski realizes.

56. James also unsuccessfully tried to recruit Sidgwick for a visit to Harvard; it is quite possible that Sidgwick declined the offer, and limited his travels generally, because of his tendency to seasickness (which when crossing the English Channel he sought to overcome by getting absorbed in the recitation of poetry).

57. William James, *The Varieties of Religious Experience: A Study in Human Nature*, in *William James: Writings 1902–1910* (New York: Library of America, 1987), p. 457.

58. Ibid., pp. 457–58.

59. William James, *Psychology: Briefer Course*, in *William James: Writings 1878–1899* (New York: Library of America, 1992), p. 196.

60. Richard Rorty, "Nineteenth–Century Idealism and Twentieth–Century Textualism," in his *The Consequences of Pragmatism* (Minneapolis: University of Minnesota Press, 1982), p. 147.

61. See the recent edition, Walter Pater, *The Renaissance: Studies in Art and Poetry*, ed. D. L. Hill (Berkeley: University of California Press, 1980), p. 141.

62. Dellamora, *Masculine Desire*, p. 113.

63. Ibid., p. 115.

64. Quoted in Franco Paloscia's *Goethe Strolling in Rome* (Milano: E.S.T.E. Srl, 1997), p. 123. For Goethe's own erotic verse, see J. W. von Goethe, *Erotic Poems*, trans. D. Luke (Oxford: Oxford University Press, 1988), with a helpful introduction by Hans Rudolf Vaget that details how Rome "became the site of Goethe's sexual liberation" (p. xvii).

65. Quoted in Pater, *The Renaissance*, p. 412; cf. Dellamora, *Masculine Desire*, p. 113.

66. Pater, *The Renaissance*, p. 177.

67. Ibid., pp. 188–89.

68. Ibid., p. 190.

69. Quoted in Dellamora, *Masculine Desire*, p. 159.

70. *Letters of John Addington Symonds*, vol. 2, p. 402.

71. Dowling, *Hellenism and Homosexuality*, p. 104.

72. J. A. Symonds, *Studies of the Greek Poets*, second series (London: Smith, Elder & Co., 1876), p. 379. The Greek means "percipient reason." The first version of "The Genius of Greek Art," the most famous, provocative part of the *Studies*, is reproduced in John Addington Symonds, *Male Love: A Problem in Greek Ethics and Other Writings*, Foreword by R. Peters, ed. J. Lauritsen (New York: Pagan Press, 1983).

73. Richard St. John Tyrwhitt, "The Greek Spirit in Modern Literature," *The Contemporary Review* (March 1876), pp. 556–58.

74. In fact, contrary to a popular view, later editions were in some ways less conciliatory, dropping the inclusion of pederasty in the list of the "evils" of the ancient Greeks.

75. Symonds, *Studies*, second series, p. 398 and pp. 401–2.

76. Ibid., pp. 391–92.

77. Ibid., p. 402.

78. Ibid., p. 412. The Greek terms mean "natural science" and "nature," respectively.

79. Ibid., p. 401.

80. Ibid., p. 137.

81. Symonds, "Genius," in *Male Love*, p. 121 and p. 130.

82. Ibid., p. 121.

83. Annan, *The Dons*, p. 71.

84. Dowling, *Hellenism and Homosexuality*, pp. 76–77.
85. Annan, *The Dons*, pp. 74–75.
86. *The Letters of John Addington Symonds*, vol. 3, pp. 345–47.
87. Dellamora, *Masculine Desire*, p. 3.
88. It is striking how some of the most famous commentaries on Symonds emerging from gay studies have been almost completely uninformed about Symonds's intimate circle of friends – e.g., Dakyns, Brown, and the Sidgwicks. See, for example, Eve Sedgwick's *Between Men* (New York: Columbia University Press, 1985) and Paul Robinson's *Gay Lives: Homosexual Autobiography from John Addington Symonds to Paul Monette* (Chicago: University of Chicago Press, 1999). With very few exceptions, the recent scholarly research on Symonds has been as disappointing as it has been derivative.
89. Symonds, *Memoirs*, pp. 253–54. Grosskurth's edition of the *Memoirs* is in fact a much abridged version of the famous (unpublished) manuscript, which was kept under embargo at the London Library for fifty years following Symonds's death.
90. Symonds, *Letters and Papers*, p. 46.
91. Ibid., p. 47.
92. Though interestingly, in a letter written before he actively considered becoming a candidate, he had written to his sister (who was married to Green): "If I had stood for the Poetry Professorship & got it, I think I should have lectured on the AEsthetik of Hegel. It is an extremely interesting book & full of the most brilliant things: all the discussion of Classic Art & Sculpture seems to me luminous in the last degree. But just what a critic most wants, & what ought to form the ground question of Esthetics, Hegel hardly touches upon – the principle of beauty." (*Letters of John Addington Symonds*, vol. 2, p. 390)
93. Ibid., p. 478. Symonds withdrew his candidacy shortly after learning that Shairp was in the race; he had been assured, in January, that Shairp would not be a candidate.
94. Quoted in Eric Haralson, "Henry James's 'Queer Comrade'," in *Victorian Sexual Dissidence*, ed. R. Dellamora (Chicago: University of Chicago Press, 1999), p. 205. Interestingly, this James, who shared Symonds's orientation, was less sympathetic to him than his brother William, who did not.
95. Brown's biography, as explained in the final chapter, was effectively the joint work of Brown, Dakyns, and Sidgwick; although it is a carefully censored work, the treatment of Symonds's religious views is nonetheless illuminating and reflective of how his closest friends were apt to understand him.
96. *The Letters of John Addington Symonds*, vol. 1, p. 738.
97. The full significance of Symonds for the changing structure of sexual discourse has yet to be fully appreciated, though Jeffrey Weeks's classic works on the history of sexuality do, unlike Foucault's, highlight Symonds's pioneering efforts in what would eventually become gay studies and gay liberation – see, especially, *Coming Out: Homosexual Politics in Britain from the Nineteenth Century to the Present* and *Sex, Politics and Society: The Regulation of Sexuality since 1800* (London: Longman, 2nd ed. 1989).

98. Symonds, *Memoirs*, p. 39.

99. Ibid., p. 94.

100. Ibid., pp. 95–96.

101. Ibid., p. 62.

102. Included in Havelock Ellis and John Addington Symonds, *Sexual Inversion* (London: Wilson and Macmillan, 1897; reprint edition by Ayer Company Publishers, 1994), p. 58. Symonds composed his own case history, and collected similar accounts from many others, in the last years of his life, when he was actively collaborating with Ellis on *Sexual Inversion* (which would appear only after Symonds's death).

103. Symonds, *Memoirs*, p. 63.

104. Symonds, *Sexual Inversion*, p. 59.

105. Symonds, *Memoirs*, p. 82.

106. Ibid., p. 96.

107. Ibid., p. 99.

108. Ibid., p. 107.

109. Ibid., p. 104.

110. Ibid., p. 105.

111. Ibid., p. 106.

112. Ibid., pp. 109–10.

113. Ibid., p. 112.

114. Ibid., p. 114.

115. This fragment is in the Symonds Papers, Special Collections, University of Bristol Library.

116. Symonds, *Memoirs*, p. 119.

117. Ibid., p. 118.

118. Ibid., p. 130.

119. Ibid., p. 131.

120. Ibid., p. 132.

121. See Davis, "Symonds and Visual Impressionability," in *John Addington Symonds: Culture and the Demon Desire*, ed. Pemble, p. 64. This volume, based on the first academic conference ever devoted expressly to Symonds and his work, stands out as a serious scholarly effort to come to terms with his legacy.

122. Crompton. *Byron and Greek Love*, pp. 17–18.

123. Ibid., p. 8. Crompton's wonderful study does not make the particular connections to Sidgwick and Symonds that I have emphasized, though it does bring out the significance of the Benthamite background in an absolutely unparalleled way.

124. *The Letters of John Addington Symonds*, vol. 1, p. 421.

125. Ibid., p. 425 and p. 435.

126. Symonds, *Memoirs*, pp. 148–49. The Greek means "longed for by his friends."

127. *The Letters of John Addington Symonds*, vol. 1, p. 454.

128. Symonds, *Memoirs*, p. 150.

129. Ibid., p. 151.

130. Ibid., pp. 154–55.

131. Ibid., p. 157.
132. Symonds, *Sexual Inversion*, p. 61. Again, the variations between the different editions are pieced together for the first time in *Strange Audacious Life*.
133. Symonds, *Memoirs*, p. 166.
134. Ibid., pp. 166–67.
135. Ibid., p. 165.
136. *The Letters of John Addington Symonds*, vol. 1, pp. 736–38. The Greek expressions mean "godless in the world" and "being," respectively.
137. Symonds, *Memoirs*, pp. 57–58.
138. Ibid., p. 58.
139. *The Letters of John Addington Symonds*, vol. 1, p. 747.
140. Ibid., p. 486.
141. The original letter is in the Symonds Papers, Special Collections, Bristol University Library.
142. Ellis and Symonds, *Sexual Inversion*, pp. 62–63. Again, the German edition adds some significant details: "he seeks strong fellows between 18 and 25 years of age who have full members, are sexually potent and always below his social station," and every "part of the desired body appears to him to be equally worth caressing."
143. Though this is a little too tidy, and it is impossible to say just how many entanglements Symonds really had. He allowed that, especially with his friends Roden Noel and Ronald Gower, he occasionally gave in to some very decadent goings on. Roger Fry, who was profoundly influenced by Symonds, called him "the most pornographic person" he had ever met, though not at all "nasty."
144. Crompton, *Byron and Greek Love*, p. 6.
145. From his diary, reproduced in part in Symonds, *Memoirs*, pp. 209–10. The Greek means "now longing for passion." Norman Moor would go on to become a very successful master at Clifton College.
146. *The Letters of John Addington Symonds*, vol. 1, p. 614. The Greek is of course "eros."
147. Ibid., p. 682.
148. To be sure, Sidgwick had a remarkable number of close friends, and some of the others may or may not have been sexually unorthodox. Cowell was in all likelihood also Hellenic in his tastes, though the evidence about him is thin; the same might be said of G. O. Trevelyan (see Chapter 7). Other intriguing possibilities include Edmund Henry Fisher, a fellow Apostle who tenderly nursed Sidgwick during his undergraduate illness, and J. B. Payne, a younger Apostle who died prematurely, in 1869. Payne was an aspiring writer (and publisher of Swinburne) who told Sidgwick "If you want anybody assassinated morally in the P.M.G. [Pall Mall Gazette], no questions asked, I am your man." (Sidgwick Papers, Wren Library, Trinity College, Cambridge University, Add.Ms.a.95.30.) Another is A. J. Patterson, who eventually moved to Hungary and wrote about Hungarian politics, who figures in the 1860 diary, and with whom Sidgwick would have a lengthy correspondence (see Sidgwick Papers, Wren Library, Trinity College, Cambridge University, Add.Ms.c.98). However, Browning's *Memories of Sixty*

Years leaves little doubt about such figures as F. W. Cornish and Richard Jebb.

149. Annan, *The Dons*, pp. 102–3. Browning contributed the entry on "Education" to the ninth edition of the *Encyclopaedia Britannica*, and his views resembled Seeley's.

150. For the stock (though incomplete) treatment, see Ian Anstruther, *Oscar Browning, A Biography* (London: John Murray, 1983); but see also Jane Marcus, "Review of *Oscar Browning, A Biography*," *Victorian Studies* 28 (1985), pp. 556–58, and David Gilmour, *Curzon: Imperial Statesman* (New York: Farrar, Straus, and Giroux, 2003), pp. 13–17.

151. See the various remarks about him in Jeremy Potter's *Headmaster: The Life of John Percival, Radical Autocrat* (London: Constable, 1998), e.g. p. 33. This book gives a vivid picture of the Clifton of Dakyns and Symonds, of which Percival was the founding headmaster.

152. Symonds, *Memoirs*, pp. 191–92.

153. This is from a fragment found in the box of Noel's papers that formed the basis for Desmond Heath's *Roden Noel: A Wide Angle* (London: Edwin Mellen, 1997) and is quoted from Heath's "Roden Noel: A Legacy of Words" <http://www.hull.ac.uk/lib/archives/paragon/1998/noel.html>.

154. Heath, "Roden Noel: A Legacy of Words."

155. Crompton, *Byron and Greek Love*, pp. 284–85. Crompton notes that Shelley's "Discourse on the Manner of the Ancient Greeks Relative to the Subject of Love" was not half as bold as either Bentham's work or Symonds's. Intriguingly, Crompton also implies that John Stuart Mill must have known more about the topic than he let on. Mill had in 1834 bitterly complained that Plato's "boundless reputation" was not matched by actual knowledge of his works, and he "tried to compensate in some measure by providing partial translations of the *Protagoras* and the *Phaedrus*." Yet as Crompton noted, the taboo concerning Plato's "forbidden side" was firmly in place: "Though the theme of homosexuality is woven into the very warp and woof of the *Phaedrus*, Mill managed to excerpt the dialogue in such a way as to leave no hint of its presence. Nor did his introductory discussion make any reference to what had been left out" (pp. 286–87). Even George Grote had been more forthcoming.

156. Ellis and Symonds, *Sexual Inversion*, pp. 75–76.

157. This is a familiar charge, which was already taken as given in Strachey's day. It was formally suggested in E. M. Young's biography of Arthur Balfour, and it has been personally confirmed to me by the Right Honorable Guy Strutt, a descendant of Lord Rayleigh, who, with the current Lord Rayleigh, most generously allowed me to tour Terling Place and to visit Sidgwick's grave. See E. M. Young, *Arthur James Balfour: The Happy Life of the Politician, Prime Minister, Statesman, and Philosopher, 1848–1930* (London: G. Bell and Sons, 1963), p. 40: "Sidgwick was sexually impotent; no wonder that years later Nora remarked that she had had a 'grey life,' and that she liked winking because 'it is the least tiring expression of emotion.'" Young's work also contains some interesting remarks on the Apostolic

outlook: "there was another side to the 'apostolic' outlook: if it was agreeably undogmatic, it was also somewhat cool, with a suggestion of *surtour point de zèle*, even of superiority to the common mass (though the latter was carefully concealed)" (pp. 21–22).

158. Crompton, *Byron and Greek Love*, p. 300.

159. The diary, from the spring of 1860, reads: "Walked with Cornish – cannot mingle my mind with his to generate soul-knitting thoughts. Browning came up – He might be the friend I seek si non aliuno – Is Cornish worthy of him?" (CWC)

160. Again, there can be virtually no doubt that Eleanor and Arthur were responsible for destroying or suppressing a great deal of compromising material. At any rate, it is also instructive that when Symonds died, the only thing that Sidgwick requested from his widow was a single book: "it is a little *Horace*. In 1867 he gave me a *Virgil*, and the Horace is a fellow to it – a little Parisian edition with a few delicate engravings." Symonds Papers, Special Collections, Bristol University Library. The fate of Symonds's literary remains is discussed in Schultz et al., *Strange Audacious Life*.

161. See his "Account of My Friendship with Henry Sidgwick," Myers Papers, Wren Library, Trinity College, University of Cambridge, Myers 13.22(1).

162. Sidgwick Papers, Wren Library, Trinity College, University of Cambridge, Add.Ms.c.96.19.6+4. I discovered this piece quite by accident, when combing through the Sidgwick Papers, and to the best of my knowledge, it has never been so much as noted by scholars writing on Sidgwick.

163. Noel to Sidgwick, May 6, 1861, Noel Papers, Archives and Special Collections, Brynmoor Jones Library, University of Hull, DNO/1/2, pp. 81–82; this is the letter in which Noel chides Sidgwick for his "esoteric pride," characteristic of the Apostles.

164. The Greek expressions mean "understanding" and "faculty of speech," respectively.

165. This comes through most clearly in his correspondence with Myers, some of which was discussed in Chapter 5.

166. The original letter continues: "Where do these lines come? The heart bereaved of why and how/Unknowing, knows but that before/It had, what e'en to memory now/Returns no more, no more." In a letter from November, he says that he "has got over" his "little emotional difficulty."

167. Noel to Sidgwick, May 8, 1862, Noel Papers, Archives and Special Collections, Brynmoor Jones Library, University of Hull, DNO/1/2, pp. 83–84.

168. Noel to Sidgwick, October 15, 1863, Noel Papers, Archives and Special Collections, Brynmoor Jones Library, University of Hull, DNO/1/2, pp. 89–95.

169. Though in his *Diary*, at least, Sidgwick had even wondered "is my intellect much worth cultivating & even if it is why should I not narrow it to England & social science?" (CWC)

170. Noel to Sidgwick, April 10, 1864, Noel Papers, Archives and Special Collections, Brynmoor Jones Library, University of Hull, DNO/1/2, p. 100–1, p. 104.

171. The Greek phrases mean "blacksmith, bald–pated and small" and "domestic economy," respectively. Again, the allusion appears to be to Plato's *Republic*, Book VI, 495 e., referring to someone unfitted to be a guardian.

172. Just how far Sidgwick was from orthodoxy is also suggested by the way he refused to be "godfather" to one of his own nephews and to one of Dakyns's sons. He explained that he simply could not take the Apostle's Creed into his mouth. Intriguingly, however, Benson presided at his 1876 wedding service.

173. Recall the rather more abstract discussions of this in Chapter 4 – for example, in connection with Crisp's dualism.

174. Of course, Noel was an Apostle and Dakyns was not.

175. *The Letters of John Addington Symonds*, vol. 2, pp. 100–102.

176. *The Letters of John Addington Symonds*, vol. 1, p. 748.

177. Ibid., p. 750.

178. The Greek means "evil natures."

179. *The Letters of John Addington Symonds*, vol. 1, pp. 758–59.

180. Ibid., p. 781.

181. Ibid., p. 789.

182. Symonds, *Memoirs*, p. 173.

183. Ibid., p. 174.

184. Ibid., p. 176.

185. Ibid., p. 172.

186. Ibid., pp. 189–90.

187. It is noteworthy that Gregory Vlastos, who admired Dover's work, was also an admirer of Symonds's pathbreaking effort. See his insightful little piece "Sex in Platonic Love," in his *Platonic Studies* (Princeton, NJ: Princeton University Press, 1973, 1981), p. 40. There is a variorum edition of "Problem" in Schultz et al., *Strange Audacious Life*.

188. *The Letters of John Addington Symonds*, vol. 1, pp. 790–91.

189. Ibid., p. 792. The translation of Zeller – urged on Symonds by Jowett – was eventually taken over by Sarah Francis Alleyne, and after her by Evelyn Abbott; it appeared in the 1880s as *Outlines of the History of Greek Philosophy*.

190. This letter is reproduced in part in the *Memoir*, p. 177.

191. *The Letters of John Addington Symonds*, vol. 1, pp. 795–96.

192. Ibid., pp. 808–9.

193. Ibid., pp. 817–18. The Greek expressions respectively mean "best for me," "simply, absolutely" (repeated in reverse order in the last line), and "for country."

194. Ibid., p. 839. Perhaps a jab at Sidgwick? As Schueller and Peters note, "Symonds found an important precedent for the poetic treatment of exotic matter in Byron's narrative works." "Erotic" matter would be more to the point.

195. Ibid., p. 829.

196. Phyllis Grosskurth, *The Woeful Victorian: A Biography of John Addington Symonds* (New York: Holt, Rinehart and Winston, 1964), pp. 128–29.

197. Ibid., p. 116.

198. *The Letters of John Addington Symonds*, vol. 1, p. 678.

199. Symonds, *Memoirs*, pp. 195–96. The Greek means "most fair, untamed and deceitful."

200. Ibid., p. 201.

201. Ibid., p. 202. Grosskurth's edition of Symonds's *Memoirs* does get this interaction right, correcting the mistaken claim, by Schueller and Peters, that this letter was addressed to Henry.

202. Ibid., p. 202.

203. *The Letters of John Addington Symonds*, vol. 2, p. 40.

204. Ibid., p. 65. The Greek expression means "dull man's book."

205. Ibid., p. 74.

206. Ibid.

207. Which was apparently swallowing the periodical publication of the various essays that eventually went into such books as *Studies* and *Sketches in Italy and Greece* (1874). It is interesting that the list of initials includes reference to W.C.S. – surely William Carr Sidgwick, the oldest Sidgwick brother, who also had a reputation for "Sidgwickedness." Reference is also made to J. R. Mozley, another important old friend of Sidgwick's, from the Grote Club.

208. *The Letters of John Addington Symonds*, vol. 2, pp. 88–89.

209. I am most grateful to Desmond Heath for generously gifting this letter to me. To the best of my knowledge, it has never before been published or cited.

210. *The Letters of John Addington Symonds*, vol. 2, pp. 201–2.

211. Symonds, "Dantesque and Platonic," in his *In the Key of Blue* (London: Elkin Mathews and John Lane, 1893), pp. 85–86.

212. For a precise account of Symonds's homoerotic poetic productions, see Ian Venables, "Symonds's Peccant Poetry," in Pemble, ed., *John Addington Symonds: Culture and the Demon Desire*, Appendix.

213. See Schultz et al., *Strange Audacious Life*, which transcribes various poems from the original peccant pamphlets.

214. Quoted in *The Letters of John Addington Symonds*, vol. 2, p. 203.

215. Ibid., p. 206.

216. On the Symonds–Whitman relationship, see, in addition to the recent biographies of Whitman, Jonathan Ned Katz, *Love Stories: Sex Between Men before Homosexuality* (Chicago: University of Chicago Press, 2001), especially pp. 277–85. It should be noted in this connection that Symonds did not like the term "homosexual," with its bastardized etymology, much as his work with Ellis helped to popularize it. He preferred a richer language for male love – Uranian, Urningthum, comradeship, adhesion, homogenic love, Calamite, Arcadian, etc. etc. Moreover, as ought to be clear from the text, it is hardly fair to describe his work in stock Foucauldian terms of "reverse discourse," such that "homosexuality began to speak on its own behalf . . . often in the same vocabulary, using the same categories by which it was medically disqualified" (Bristow, *Effeminate England* [New York: Columbia University Press, 1995], pp. 136–37). Nor is it quite right to claim reductively that his "strategy was not subversion, but conversion – and this can look like complicity in the light of Foucauldian theories about homosexuality as a 'construction' that legitimizes the power of the medico-legal authority to 'cure',

to punish, and to silence" ("Preface" to Pemble, ed., *John Addington Symonds*, p. xi). Symonds's "science" was more Greek and more attuned to cultural history and anthropology.

217. *The Letters of John Addington Symonds*, vol. 2, p. 161.

218. Ibid., p. 322.

219. Indeed, Sidgwick's published review of Noel's volume *Poems*, which appeared in *The Spectator* (February 13, 1869), was fairly harsh: "being easily moved to strong feeling, he writes down whatever affects him strongly in the first language that occurs to him, and then takes it for poetry if it will only rhyme and scan. There are poets, no doubt, so instinctively melodious that their thoughts appear to run spontaneously into exquisite tunes; but Mr. Noel is hardly one of these." Noel's letters in the following years are heatedly defensive of his "poetic genius," and reveal, among other things, just how galled he was by Sidgwick's more favorable critical assessment of Swinburne as a poetic "Master": "I believe that the school of poetry (art pour art) you patronize will soon become as vapid and absurd (and that as a direct and necessary consequence of the teaching of your school of criticism) as Messrs. Moore Armitage etc. have already become in painting." Noel does, however, take some inspiration from Sidgwick's resignation, when it comes to giving up his "Court place": "But do you consider that I am by profession and necessity a writer, and that radical sentiments conflicting with a position of this kind, either shackle and make a writer dishonest or feeble – or seem inconsistent with such a position and unwarrantable? I take the pay and the old coat and that more or less muzzles my mouth. That is the chief difficulty, and it is one, even though I do not think that monarchy and court ceremonial . . . should be at once abolished. But I do think the public mind ought to be gradually prepared for the abolition of this and of hereditary aristocracy. So you see I am quite as radical as you. And what makes me feel the chains especially just now is that my essay on Whitman is of course redolent with democratic sentiment." Noel to Sidgwick, July 8, 1871, and October 2, 1869, Noel Papers, Archives and Special Collections, Brynmoor Jones Library, University of Hull, DNO/1/2.

220. *The Letters of John Addington Symonds*, vol. 2, p. 716.

221. Ibid., p. 135.

222. The Greek word is "eros." This letter is reproduced in my "Eye of the Universe: Henry Sidgwick and the Problem Public," *Utilitas* 14 (July 2002), pp. 174–75.

223. *The Letters of John Addington Symonds*, vol. 2, p. 352.

224. J. A. Symonds, *Many Moods* (London: Smith, Elder, 1878), pp. v–vi.

225. *The Letters of John Addington Symonds*, vol. 2, p. 551.

226. This correspondence between Symonds and Noel is in the Bodleian Library, Oxford University, MS.Eng.Litt.c308; it is not reproduced in *The Letters of John Addington Symonds*.

227. *The Letters of John Addington Symonds*, vol. 2, p. 561. Interestingly, the term dipsychic, which literally means "double–minded," comes not from classical Greek, but from the Epistle of St. James, which is where Clough discovered it. See McCue's notes in *Arthur Hugh Clough*, p. 245.

228. Ibid., p. 132.

229. Ibid., p. 558. The suggestion that Sidgwick was "[a]s splendid as on the first day of Creation," even if too analytical of "trifles," again points up just how far he was from Symonds's invalid condition.

230. Noel to Sidgwick, Noel Papers, Archives and Special Collections, Brynmoor Jones Library, University of Hull, DNO/1/2.

231. Symonds to Noel, Bodleian Library, Oxford University, MS.Eng.Litt.c308.

232. *The Letters of John Addington Symonds*, vol. 2, pp. 358–59.

233. Ibid., p. 497.

234. James, *Varieties of Religious Experience*, p. 349.

235. Brown, *Biography*, vol. 1, pp. 77–80.

236. Ibid., p. 555.

237. A fairly hilarious reminiscence by Symonds's friend Arthur Symons recalls a pleasant afternoon they had together smoking hashish and entertaining a troop of young female dancers. See his "John Addington Symonds," in *Studies in Two Literatures* (London: Leonard Smithers, 1897). But references to hashish occur much earlier in Symonds's correspondence, and one cannot help wondering if this was another thing that Noel introduced him to.

238. *The Letters of John Addington Symonds*, vol. 2, p. 396.

239. The *Memoir* excises the line about how Dakyns "might have been more."

240. The influence obviously went both ways. Consider, for example, *Animi Figura* (London: Smith, Elder, 1882), with the poem "Gordian Knot," p. 79. The title of this collection was suggested to Symonds by his friend (and critic) Robert Louis Stevenson. It is one of his better collections, unusual in winning the praise of both Stevenson and Catherine.

241. Including honorary degrees from the Universities of Glasgow, Edinburgh, St. Andrews, and Leipzig; in due course he would also recieve degrees from Oxford and Budapest, and be awarded memberships in the American Academy of Arts and Sciences and the Royal Danish Academy of Science (the Athenaeum had elected him in 1879). He had also at last won the Knightbridge Professorship, in 1883, and thus finally overcome the slight that he suffered during his first run for it, in 1872, when he lost out to the relatively undistinguished but more orthodox T. R. Birks (who had succeeded Maurice).

242. *The Letters of John Addington Symonds*, vol. 3, pp. 206–7.

243. Ibid., pp. 471–72. The allusion is to one of Sidgwick's favorite authors, Horace, and it is intriguing. The final stanza of the ode "Herculis ritu" reads: "Greying hair mellows the spirit / that once relished disputes and violent quarrels; / I wouldn't have stood for this in the heat of my youth / when Plancus was consul." As David West notes, "In 42 BC, when Plancus was consul and Horace fought against Octavian at Philippi, Horace's disputes and quarrels were not all amorous." See *Horace: The Complete Odes and Epodes*, trans. D. West (Oxford: Oxford University Press, 1997), p. 93 and p. 171.

244. And it is certainly suggestive of how Brink's "externalist" interpretation, addressed in Chapter 4, appears to fit some of what Sidgwick says, though as noted, Sidgwick's "internalism" allowed for motives conflicting with the moral one.

245. Symonds to Noel, Bodleian Library, Oxford University, MS.Eng.Litt.c308.

246. *The Letters of John Addington Symonds*, vol. 3, pp. 231–32. The Greek expressions mean "those who are alive are well off" and "destiny," respectively.

247. Ibid., p. 234.

248. These lines are not included in the *Memoir*.

249. *The Letters of John Addington Symonds*, vol. 3, p. 476.

250. Ibid., p. 481.

251. Ibid., p. 511.

252. Ibid., p. 479, p. 477.

253. Symonds to Noel, August 17, 1892, Bodleian Library, Ms.Eng.Lett.c.308.

254. *The Letters of John Addington Symonds*, vol. 3, pp. 705–6.

255. Ibid., vol. 3, pp. 674–76.

256. Ibid., p. 667.

257. Ibid., pp. 693–94.

258. Ibid., p. 553.

259. Experiments in ethics and intuitive theism were of course another matter.

260. See his "A Problem in Gay Heroics: Symonds and *l'Amour di 'impossible,'*" in *John Addington Symonds: Culture and the Demon Desire*, p. 57.

261. The story is told in Lidgett's *My Own Guided Life* (London: Methuen, 1936), pp. 108–9. My thanks to the Rev. Dr. David Young for calling this to my attention.

262. These are views expressed by Sidgwick's old friend Henry Jackson and G. F. Browne, the bishop of Bristol, who was the one told to watch out for the dangerous Sidgwick. Of course, Sidgwick had long been known as someone of suspect religious views, which means that, in a sense, the wariness of him was nothing new.

263. Roden Noel, *Essays on Poetry and Poets* (London: Kegan Paul, Trench, 1886), pp. 329–34.

264. Ibid., pp. 333–34.

265. Ibid.

266. E. M. Forster, "Anonymity: An Enquiry," in his *Two Cheers for Democracy* (New York: Harcourt Brace, 1967; first edition 1938), p. 84.

267. Sedgwick, *Between Men*, pp. 210–11. What Sedgwick's work mostly brings home is how little understanding there really is of Symonds's notions of sex and gender. For all his reservations about Pater and Wilde, his Dorian distrust of "effeminacy," he could still praise Carpenter for giving Whitman a more "feminine" twist.

268. Rita McWilliams Tullberg. *Women at Cambridge* (Cambridge: Cambridge University Press, 1998); I am profoundly indebted to this excellent work, a classic in the field.

269. Ibid., p. 53.

270. F. Hunt and C. Barker, *Women at Cambridge: A Brief History* (Cambridge: Cambridge University Press, 1998), p. 9.

271. "Memorandum in Answer to Questions from the Royal Commission on Secondary Education." This memorandum also nicely illustrates Sidgwick's abiding concern for improving the training of teachers, especially in secondary education. He notes that "though fifteen years ago, at the request of a committee of headmasters, the university of Cambridge established a system of lectures and examinations in the theory, history and practice of education, it has remained

almost inoperative up to the present time, so far as the schoolmasters for whose benefit it was primarily instituted are concerned; though it has been used to an important extent by women preparing for secondary teaching. I have no doubt that the theory of education should be taught at the universities, and that some systematic practical training should be given to all teachers in secondary schools; though whether the practical training should be carried on at the universities, in conjunction with theoretical study, or afterwards in the form of apprenticeship at the schools . . . is a question which I have no experience that would justify me in expressing a confident opinion. I should be disposed to allow free scope for both methods." (CWC) See also Browning, *Memories of Sixty Years*, pp. 262–3.

272. Brooke, *A History of the University of Cambridge, Vol. IV, 1870–1990*, pp. 303–4.

273. McWilliams Tullberg, *Women at Cambridge*, pp. 76–77.

274. Ibid., p. 116.

275. Symonds, *Inside the Citadel: Men and the Emancipation of Women, 1850–1920* (London: Macmillan, 1999), p. 97.

276. Olive Banks, "Sidgwick, Eleanor Mildred (Nora)," in *The Biographical Dictionary of British Feminists*, vol. 1 (New York: New York University Press, 1985), p. 184.

277. Sidgwick Papers, Wren Library, Trinity College, Cambridge University, Add.Ms.c.96.4.22–23.

278. Ibid.

279. Henry Sidgwick, "Obituary Notice of John Stuart Mill," *Academy* 15 (May 1873).

280. Henry Sidgwick, "Review of J. F. Stephen's *Liberty, Equality, Fraternity*," *Academy* 1 (August 1873).

281. Henry Sidgwick, "Review of Courthope's *Ludibria Lunae*," *Spectator* (August 7, 1869).

282. Ethel Sidgwick, *Mrs. Henry Sidgwick*, pp. 64–65.

283. *The Letters of John Addington Symonds*, vol. 2, p. 402.

284. Ethel Sidgwick, *Mrs. Henry Sidgwick*, p. 48.

285. Ibid., p. 119.

286. McWilliams Tullberg, *Women at Cambridge*, p. 54.

287. Sidgwick's educational work would make a book in itself, and a most valuable one. Here, as in so many other areas, one can only lament that so much research remains to be done.

288. Ethel Sidgwick, *Mrs. Henry Sidgwick*, pp. 131–32.

289. Quoted in McWilliams Tullberg, *Women at Cambridge*, p. 104.

290. And these could be thoroughly crushing. For a superb overview of the distinctive issues surrounding domesticity and the law at this point, see Mary Lyndon Shanley's *Feminism, Marriage, and the Law in Victorian England* (Princeton, NJ: Princeton University Press, 1989).

291. E. M. Sidgwick, Flysheet dated 12 February 1896, Newnham College Archives, reproduced in Ethel Sidgwick, *Mrs. Henry Sidgwick*.

292. McWilliams Tullberg, *Women at Cambridge*, p. 96.

293. Oppenheim, "A Mother's Role, a Daughter's Duty," p. 198.

294. Eleanor Sidgwick, "The Place of University Education in the Life of Women: An Address Delivered at the Women's Institute, London, on November 23rd, 1897," Newnham College Archives, Sidgwick Papers, Box 1.

295. E. M. Sidgwick, "University Education for Women" (Manchester, 1913), p. 16, p. 20, and p. 7.

296. Ibid., p. 18.

297. Oppenheim, "A Mother's Role, a Daughter's Duty," p. 226.

298. "Initial Society Papers," Sidgwick Papers, Wren Library, Cambridge University, Add.Ms.c.96.4.46–48.

299. See the correspondence in CWC. The Sidgwicks worked to see that Eliot was properly honored after her death, when religious conservatives pronounced her too unorthodox to be awarded a plaque in Westminster Cathedral.

300. George Eliot, quoted in F. R. Karl, *George Eliot, Voice of a Century* (New York: Norton, 1995), p. 428.

301. Quoted in Brooke, *A History of the University of Cambridge, Vol. IV, 1870–1990*.

302. Karl, *Eliot*, p. 512, note.

303. Yopie Prins, "Greek Maenads, Victorian Spinsters," in Dellamora, ed., *Victorian Sexual Dissidence* (Chicago: University of Chicago Press, 1999), p. 46.

304. For this and many other fascinating reminiscences, see the marvellous little work *A Newnham Anthology*, ed. Ann Phillips (Cambridge: Newnham College, 1979, 1988), p. 46. See also *Letters from Newnham College, 1889–1892* (Cambridge: Newnham College, 1987), by Catherine Durning Holt, and Keynes, *Essays*, pp. 324–47.

305. McWilliams Tullberg, *Women at Cambridge*, p. 85.

306. Annan, *The Dons*, p. 21.

307. Soffer, "Authority in the University: Balliol, Newnham and the New Mythology," in *Myths of the English*, ed. R. Porter (Oxford: Polity Press, 1992), p. 210.

308. There is, however, some question of whether Sidgwick talked too much: "Mrs. Marshall visited her friend in the evening too, and brought her difficulties to be talked over at the Newnham fireside. Nora Sidgwick talked more freely, she tells us, after Henry's death; much of her silence had come from the need of listening, or of directing attention, to him. But with students she was less happy in establishing terms: many were shy, some really rebuffed. Unaware she damped enthusiasm by a dry answer. Her brief 'yes' or 'no', in response to an untold effort to open talk at the dinner-table, were disheartening to a new student. That she also was disheartened by her social shortcomings, was the last thing they would suspect. Once, she wished aloud to a friend that she could be like other people. 'I am afraid you never will be', replied the friend." (*Mrs. Henry Sidgwick*, pp. 168–69). Again, Mary, a Newnham success, sacrificed her career as an economist to advance her husband Alfred's.

309. Phillips, ed., *A Newnham Anthology*, p. 4.

310. Ethel Sidgwick, *Mrs. Henry Sidgwick*, p. 27.

311. Ibid., pp. 169–70. This is a testament to Eleanor's tact, since, as her correspondence reveals, she shared many of Henry's reservations about orthodoxy.

312. Ibid., p. 132.

313. This fact, along with much else concerning the Sidgwicks' feminism, rather vitiates the critique advanced by Walker in *Moral Understandings*; again, see my "Sidgwick's Feminism" for some more specific commentary on her reading of Sidgwick as advancing a masculinist and exclusionary "theoretical-juridical" model of moral theory.

Chapter 7. Colors

1. In R. L. Stevenson, *Essays and Poems*, ed. C. Harman (London: J. M. Dent, 1992), pp. 161–62. Stevenson was of course a friendly rival to Symonds, as well as his neighbor in Davos; *Treasure Island* was composed at Symonds's Am Hof.

2. *Principia Ethica*, p. 258. As Shaw observes, "many of Moore's readers found his *Principia Ethica* fresh and exciting back in 1903 because they saw it as breaking with established morality by giving so much moral freedom to the individual." But Shaw, like so many others, suggests that Moore "was less taken with the glories of ordinary morality than Sidgwick" – a judgment hardly vindicated by any comparison of the two on the subject of sexual purity. See Shaw, *Contemporary Ethics*, p. 155.

3. Quoted in Holroyd, *Lytton Strachey, the New Biography*, p. 92.

4. Sidgwick to Symonds, August 13, 1883. (CWC)

5. Here and throughout this chapter the reference is to more standard interpretations of Bentham; Sidgwick apparently did not have any real understanding of Bentham's subtler arguments concerning human irrationality.

6. The original of this letter is in the Sidgwick Papers, Wren Library, Trinity College, Cambridge University, Add.Ms.c.94.

7. See Dicey, *Lectures on the Relation between Law and Public Opinion in England during the Nineteenth Century* (London: Transaction Books, 1981; 1st ed. 1905), pp. 429–30. Although Dicey was another of Sidgwick's longstanding Oxford friends, he appears to have had little real understanding of Sidgwick's political and economic views; Dicey was a prime example of how reactionary the old Benthamite defense of individualism had become, and he grew quite hysterical about the Home Rule issue.

8. To appreciate how prescient Sidgwick was on the problem of such global economic measures, compare A. Sen, *Development as Freedom* (New York: Knopf, 1999), a recent critique of the limitations of neoclassical economic theory on questions of development, though not one very appreciative of Sidgwick's contributions. Peter Singer's *One World: The Ethics of Globalization* (New Haven, CT: Yale University Press, 2002), especially Chapter 3, also provides a clear account of many of these dilemmas, though in many respects the judicious approach of Charles Lindblom, in *The Market System* (New Haven, CT: Yale University Press, 2001) better reflects a Sidgwickian cognizance of how much economists do not know.

9. See the letters from Spencer in the Sidgwick Papers, Wren Library, Trinity College, Cambridge University, Add.Ms.c.95.89–91; Sidgwick's letters are in the

Spencer Papers, University of London Library. Again, for a close comparison of Sidgwick and Spencer, see Weinstein, "The Anxiety of Influence."

10. For the full horror of twentieth-century Marxian socialism, recounted by someone with decidedly Sidgwickian sensibilities, see Jonathan Glover, *Humanity: A Moral History of the Twentieth Century* (New Haven, CT: Yale University Press, 2000).

11. See Feuchtwanger, *Democracy and Empire: Britain 1865–1914* (Baltimore: Edward Arnold, 1985), p. 112.

12. Included in CWC. Sidgwick actually developed a very considerable expertise in devising and assessing taxation schemes. His correspondence with Edgeworth, for example, has the latter expressing warm appreciation for Sidgwick's insights into the possible advantages of taxing luxury goods or other commodities, as opposed to imposing rates of a more general nature. See the letter from Edgeworth in the Sidgwick Papers, Wren Library, Trinity College, Cambridge University, Add.Ms.c.93.109.

13. There are scattered bits of correspondence between Sidgwick and the representative of various cooperatives (M 205, n1). As for his efforts to help the university with its finances, which the depresssion rendered precarious given the dependence of the colleges on agriculture, Sidgwick's schemes were apparently a failure because of their "excessive subtlety and elaboration," according to his colleague and sympathizer Henry Jackson. See Jackson's remarks (M 374–76), which may suggest part of what Marshall had in mind when he criticized his friend's mania for overregulation. See also Keynes, *Essays*, pp. 125–217.

14. *The New Palgrave: A Dictionary of Economics*, ed. J. Eatwell, M. Milgate, and P. Newman (London: Macmillan, 1987), vol. 4, p. 329.

15. Mark Blaug, *Economic Theory in Retrospect* (Cambridge: Cambridge University Press, 1985), p. 300.

16. Richard Howey, *The Rise of the Marginal Utility School* (New York: Columbia University Press, 1965), p. 95.

17. Scott Gordon, *The History and Philosophy of Social Science* (London: Routledge, 1991), p. 258

18. Blaug, *Retrospect*, p. 479. Blaug also describes Sidgwick's critical dissection of the "mixed static-dynamic" character of Ricardo's famous rent theory as "outstanding."

19. *The Athenaeum*, June 16, 1883, p. 757.

20. Ronald Coase, *Essays on Economics and Economists* (Chicago: University of Chicago Press, 1994), p. 171. Coase does not discuss Sidgwick much, but he does bring out the conflicts Marshall had with such figures as Foxwell and Keynes (J. M. Keynes's father, and a very good friend of Sidgwick's). Sidgwick's correspondence with Foxwell (in CWC) is illuminating on these controversies.

21. J. S. Nicholson, "The Vagaries of Recent Political Economy," *The Quarterly Review* 219 (July and October 1913), p. 420.

22. For some relevant discussion, see Lewis Feuer's Introduction to J. S. Mill, *On Socialism* (Amherst, NY: Prometheus Books, 1976), especially p. 49, note 72.

23. For a full acount of the snarled relationships between Widgwick, Marshall, and Cambridge, as well as much background material on Sidgwick and economics,

see Peter Groenewegen, *A Soaring Eagle: Alfred Marshall, 1842–1924* (Aldershot: Edward Elgar, 1995), especially pp. 663–70; such Sidgwick–Marshall correspondence as survives is available in *The Correspondence of Alfred Marshall, Economist* (New York: Cambridge University Press, 1996), though once again, much material has been lost.

24. See Riley's helpful introduction to J. S. Mill, *Principles of Political Economy* (New York: Oxford University Press, 1994), especially p. xlvii, note 85.

25. See also his slightly more spirited statement in "Bi-Metallism," *The Fortnightly Review*, new series 40 (July–December 1886), pp. 473–80.

26. As Sidgwick put it to Lady Welby, in 1891: "It is a difficult matter to persuade a plain man to go through the process necessary to attain precision of thought: it requires great literary skill in presenting the process. I tried to do something of this sort in my *Principles of Political Economy* but I fear I bored the reader horribly." Sidgwick Papers, Wren Library, Trinity College, Cambridge University, Add.Ms.c.98.64.

27. Eric Hobsbawm, *The Age of Empire, 1875–1914* (New York: Pantheon Books, 1987), pp. 87–88.

28. That is to say, there is little reason to suppose that there is a "Henry Sidgwick Problem" – akin to the "Adam Smith Problem" – arising from the contrasting methods, historical versus analytic, of his various works. The Smith problem was merely a concocted one anyway, and the same is true in the case of Sidgwick, despite Collini's remarks in "Ordinary Experience" (in Schultz, *Essays*, pp. 352–53).

29. W. A. Dunning, review in *The Political Science Quarterly* 7 (1892), p. 537.

30. Woodrow Wilson, review in *The Dial*, 12 (May 1891–April 1892), p. 216.

31. D. G. Ritchie, review in the *International Journal of Ethics* 2 (1891–92), pp. 254–55.

32. As I will suggest below, Sidgwick's correspondence with Bryce is a crucial resource for understanding the *Elements* and Sidgwick's political views generally; the original correspondence is in Bryce MSS 15, Bodleian Library, Oxford University.

33. Sidgwick's correspondence with Browning – many of the originals of which are held in the archives at Kings College, Cambridge University – provides another rich source for exploring his views on political theory and political history, though he was frequently rather frustrated with Browning's less-than-rigorous approach (see CWC). Still, Browning, Seeley, and Sidgwick formed a united front.

34. Sidgwick Papers, Wren Library, Trinity College, Cambridge University, Add.Ms.b.71.1.44. See Collini, "My Roles and Their Duties," for an engaging account of Sidgwick's possible candidacies, and a superb account of Sidgwick's work on various royal commissions.

35. The Greek term means "beliefs." This remark seems rather remarkable, given Sidgwick's early steeping in Plato and apparent aspirations to being a "superior" man. But see the revealing "A Discussion between Professor Henry Sidgwick and the Late Professor John Grote on the Utilitarian Basis of Plato's Republic," *Classical Review* 3 (March 1889), pp. 97–102.

36. Collini, "My Roles and Their Duties," p. 48. Collini's valuable work on the Victorian "Public Moralists" certainly provides a necessary context for considering

Sidgwick's relationship to Mill, though he is right to insist that Sidgwick was much more the academic, however painful he often found that role.

37. Harvie, *Lights*, p. 221.
38. Max Egremont, *Balfour: A Life of Arthur James Balfour* (London: Collins, 1980), p. 84.
39. Ibid., pp. 86–87.
40. Hastings Rashdall, review in the *Economic Review* 2 (1892).
41. *The Letters of Frederic William Maitland*, ed. C. H. S. Fifoot (Cambridge, MA: Harvard University Press, 1965), p. 58. p. 38.
42. James Bryce, "Henry Sidgwick," *Proceedings of the British Academy* (1903–4), p. 274.
43. F. Hayek, *The Constitution of Liberty* (Chicago: Regnery, 1960), p. 419, note 2. He was right.
44. For a comprehensive assessment of the social conditions Sidgwick analyzed, see *The Cambridge Social History of Britain 1750–1950*, ed. F. M. L. Thompson, 3 vols. (Cambridge: Cambridge University Press, 1990).
45. The originals of these lectures are in the Sidgwick Papers, Wren Library, Trinity College, Cambridge University, Add.Ms.c.98.52–53.
46. Karl Polanyi, *The Great Transformation* (Boston: Beacon Hill, 1944), p. 102.
47. Perhaps he had been thinking of Sidgwick's views on the Irish landlords.
48. See Walter Lippmann, *Public Opinion* (New York: Free Press, 1997; first edition 1922). In many respects, of course, Lippmann was the one who, along with his arch-critic (albeit a very respectful one) Dewey, brought these debates into their modern form, with a confrontation with the propagandistic potential of the mass media.
49. This position, also set out in a letter to the *Spectator* for May 31, 1884, marks a considerable change from his youthful opinions, as noted in the previous chapter.
50. A long-standing dissenting view of his; even in 1861, he had found Mill's views on this score hard to swallow (M 66).
51. As Mill famously explained in his *Autobiography*; an excellent account of Mill's socialism is given in Jonathan Riley's "J. S. Mill's Liberal Utilitarian Assessment of Capitalism Versus Socialism," *Utilitas* 8 (March 1996), pp. 39–71.
52. See *The American Commonwealth*, ed. G. McDowell, two vols. (Indianapolis: Liberty Fund, 1995). Sidgwick's close connection to Bryce, another Old Mortality man, will be discussed later.
53. Sidgwick wrote in his journal that Maine's essays – eventually published as *Popular Democracy* – were "the best antidemocratic writing that we have had" (M 392), but Bryce soon disabused him of any such view.
54. This further confirms the argument set out in Chapter 4, Part II, concerning how the dualism of practical reason marked, in Sidgwick's eyes, a potentially explosive development for the social order, given the religious content of ordinary morality.
55. Though of course, given the fate of the great "sciences" of society – Marx's, Weber's, Durkheim's – Sidgwick looks rather intelligent on this score.
56. Which is undoubtedly why he tends to be overlooked in discussions of the growth of the public sphere that invoke Mill and Dewey, such as Jürgen Habermas's

Between Facts and Norms, trans. W. Rehg (Cambridge, MA: MIT Press, 1996), p. 171. Needless to say, Sidgwick's version of "publicity" is highly qualified, being so subject to consequentialist constraint, and many will think it perverse to place the defender of an esoteric morality in this context, associating him more with the collapse of the public sphere than with its defense. But this is no more problematic than situating Mill in this way, given how Sidgwick was so clearly a continuation of the Millian project. Habermas appears not to recognize that Mill was a utilitarian – and a largely consistent one.

57. He wrote in his journal: "As regards 'law and order' in London, there is an idea that the lawless and disorderly party have got the worst of it for the present, and know it; nor can I learn from any one whose opinion I regard that the problem of 'distress of unemployed' is really formidable at present; but there is an uneasy feeling that it may soon become so, and that 'something must be done' – something, I suppose, in the direction of recognising the 'Right to Labour,' or rather the right to get wages. I have always thought myself that our system of poor relief required development in this direction" (M 480–81).

58. Again, contrast the accounts in Collini, Kloppenberg, and Harvie, cited in previous notes.

59. Walt Whitman, "Democratic Vistas" in *Whitman: Poetry and Prose* (New York: Library of America, 1982), pp. 985–86.

60. Quoted in Elshtain, *Jane Addams*, p. 92.

61. Again, the best recent treatment of Mill on India is Zastoupil's *John Stuart Mill and India*, though Eric Stokes's *The English Utilitarians and India* is virtually a classic on the subject.

62. Rothblatt, *Revolution*, p. 155. Shannon, in *The Crisis of Imperialism, 1865–1915* (London: Paladin Books, 1974), also observes that "Jowett at Oxford and Seeley at Cambridge thought in terms of a very deliberate and calculated teaching programme to prepare an intelligent ruling class for the tasks of government. Theirs was an educational theory of legitimacy and morality, merit and service, just as Gladstone's politics was a public theory of the same" (p. 82).

63. See his Introduction to Seeley's *The Growth of British Policy* (Cambridge: Cambridge University Press, 1922), pp. xii–xiii.

64. Ibid., pp. xiv–xv.

65. Ibid., p. xx.

66. Quoted in Sir John Seeley, *Introduction to Political Science*, ed. H. Sidgwick, (London: Macmillan, 1896), pp. v–vi.

67. Ibid., pp. x–xi.

68. Of course, not everyone was impressed with this approach, and Sidgwick had his usual reservations; Maitland wrote to H. A. L. Fisher about "a discussion with Sidgwick in which I endeavoured to convince him that 'inductive political science' is rubbish, and I had far more success than I expected." See *The Letters of Frederic William Maitland*, ed. C. H. S. Fifoot (Cambridge: Cambridge University Press, 1965), p. 28. Contrast Browning, *Memories of Sixty Years*, p. 235.

69. Seeley, *Introduction*, pp. 340–41.

70. Ibid., pp. 341–42.

71. Ibid., pp. 346–47.
72. Sidgwick was one of the electors; see George Feaver, *From Status to Contract: A Biography of Sir Henry Sumner Maine, 1822–1888* (London: Longmans, 1969), pp. 255–56.
73. Indeed, Sidgwick never tired of citing Maine on the historical development of land tenure.
74. Maine, *Popular Government*, p. 190.
75. Shannon, *Crisis*, p. 187.
76. Seeley, *Expansion*, p. 196.
77. Which is to say, it is rather worse than the "enabling violations" described by Gayatri Chakravorty Spivak, in *A Critique of Postcolonial Reason* (Cambridge, MA: Harvard University Press, 1999), p. 371. Spivak's work has surprisingly little to say about the utilitarian side of philosophical reason as a subject for her critique.
78. Seeley, *Expansion*, p. 214.
79. Ibid., p. 205.
80. Ibid., pp. 304–5.
81. Ibid., p. 396.
82. Ibid., pp. 50–51.
83. Ibid., p. 13.
84. Again, the brutal ongoing reality of British imperialism at this time is better depicted in such works as Kiernan's *Lords of Humankind*.
85. Woodcock, *Who Killed the British Empire? An Inquest* (London: Jonathan Cape, 1974), p. 202.
86. Ensor, *England*, p. 163.
87. Shannon, *Crisis*, p. 252.
88. Quoted in Stocking, *Victorian Anthropology* (New York: The Free Press, 1987), p. 124.
89. Quoted in Gauri Viswanathan, *Masks of Conquest: Literary Study and British Rule in India* (New York: Columbia University Press, 1989), pp. 156–57.
90. It was in some ways already behind the times, given how Canada and other parts of the empire had come to regard dominion status as a step toward self-sufficiency rather than confederation within some grand imperial parliament. Still, as Ensor records, the League "formed the chief nursery of imperialist thought at this early stage. W. E. Forster had been its first head; Lord Rosebery, W. H. Smith, Froude, J. R. Seeley, and James Bryce were among its supporters; and it enrolled some of the best-known colonial statesmen. But its members could never agree on a positive policy; and in 1893 it broke up" (p. 178).
91. These are the words of a descendant, Humphrey Trevelyan, in *The India We Left* (London: Macmillan, 1972), p. 103. Sidgwick admired his friend's book *Cawnpore* (M 128), a work betraying considerable racial prejudice.
92. The original of this letter (which is reproduced in CWC) is in the Lytton Papers, Knebworth House Collection, Hertfordshire Record Office.
93. For example, Peter Singer. See his recent *One World*, a work that also makes an interesting concession to Sidgwick's case for esoteric morality: "If it is true that advocating a highly demanding morality will lead to worse consequences than

advocating a less demanding morality, then indeed we ought to advocate a less demanding morality. We could do this, while still knowing that, at the level of critical thinking, impartialism is sound" (p. 192). This is indeed a more truly Sidgwickian perspective than that of Singer's previous works.

94. In H. A. L. Fisher, *F. W. Maitland: A Biographical Sketch* (Cambridge: Cambridge University Press, 1910), pp. 47–48.

95. By "State" Sidgwick generally means "a political society or community; i.e. a body of human beings deriving its corporate unity from the fact that its members acknowledge permanent obedience to the same government, which represents the society in any transactions that it may carry on as a body with other political societies. And I shall assume this government to be independent, in the sense that it is not in habitual obedience to any foreign individual or body or to the government of a larger whole" (EP 221). He also assumes a certain "degree of civilisation" and "supreme dominion over a particular portion of the earth's surface." Interestingly, against the identification of "State" with "Nation," "attempts to give definiteness to the implications of this latter term are liable to obscure its real meaning: since I can find no particular bond of union among those that chiefly contribute to the internal cohesion of a strongly-united society – belief in a common origin, possession of a common language and literature, pride in common historic traditions, community of social customs, community of religion – which is really essential to our conception of a Nation-State" (p. 223).

96. *National and International Right and Wrong*, eds. J. Bryce and E. M. Sidgwick (London: George Allen and Unwin, 1919), pp. 12–13.

97. E. M. Sidgwick, *The International Crisis in its Ethical and Psychological Aspects* (London: Oxford University Press, 1915), p. 15.

98. Singer, in *One World*, ingeniously uses this very passage to turn the tables on Williams, challenging the latter's critique of Sidgwick's indirect utilitarianism (see Chapter 4). Although many of the narrower attachments that Sidgwick listed are justifiable on impartial grounds – and would have been seen as such even by Bentham and William Godwin – taking "an impartial perspective shows that partialism along racial lines is something that we can and should oppose, because our opposition can be effective in preventing great harm to innocent people. . . . Thus we can turn Williams' aphorism against him: philosophers who take his view have one thought too few. To be sure, to think *always* as a philosopher would mean that, in our roles as parent, spouse, lover and friend, we would indeed have one thought too many. But if we *are* philosophers, there should be times when we reflect critically on our intuitions – indeed not only philosophers, but all thoughtful people, should do this" (p. 163).

99. On this, see Eric J. Hobsbawm, *Nations and Nationalism since 1780* (Cambridge: Cambridge University Press, 1990).

100. This review originally appeared in the *Spectator* (November 1873).

101. See Shannon, *Crisis*, p. 301.

102. Bryce, *American Commonwealth*, p. 1148.

103. Ibid., pp. 1150–51.

104. Ibid., pp. 1152–53.

105. Ibid., pp. 1161–62.

106. Ibid., p. 1164.

107. Ibid., p. 1166.

108. Ibid., pp. 1165–66.

109. The chief thesis of *Orientalism* and *Culture and Imperialism*. See also *Orientalism: A Reader*, ed. A. L. Macfie (New York: New York University Press, 2000), for an excellent overview of the issues. To my mind , the evident racism of such figures as Bryce, Pearson, Seeley, Rashdall, Sidgwick, and so many others powerfully supports Said's basic thesis.

110. Bryce, *Studies in History and Jurisprudence* (New York: Oxford University Press, 1901), pp. 475–76.

111. Unfortunately, I have been unable to determine precisely which article Sidgwick sent Bryce.

112. On this, see Georgios Varouxakis, *Mill on Nationality*, especially Chapter 3, and his contributions to *Classical Utilitarianism and the Question of Race*, ed. Schultz and Varouxakis.

113. See Chapter 3; that the familial cotton interests did so as well might seem a plausible suspicion, if it were anyone other than Sidgwick.

114. Interestingly, he always seems to use the word with reference to blacks, never in the larger (and at the time common) sense as applying to all people of color. For a cogent exploration of the history of the "n word," see Randall Kennedy, *Nigger: The Strange Career of a Troublesome Word* (New York: Pantheon Books, 2002). For a broader historical perspective, see George M. Frederickson *Racism: A Short History* (Princeton, NJ: Princeton University Press, 2002).

115. Whitman himself wrote, "As if we had not strained the voting and digestive calibre of American Democracy to the utmost for the last fifty years with the millions of ignorant foreigners, we have now infused a powerful percentage of blacks, with about as much intellect and calibre (in the mass) as so many baboons" (Reynolds, *Whitman*, p. 470). Apparently his notion of sympathetic comradeship really was quite Greek.

116. Symonds, *Papers*, pp. 1–2. To be sure, there were many, many possible sources for Sidgwick's racist pronouncements, including even Kant. As Robert Bernasconi has pointed out, "Kant saw race mixing as leading to a degradation or pollution of whites, as loss of some of their talents and dispositions" ("Kant as an Unfamiliar Source of Racism," in *Philosophers on Race*, eds. J. K. Ward and T. L. Lott [Oxford: Blackwell, 2002] p. 159). And this is not to mention the infamous Carlyle–Mill exchange, "On the Nigger Question," for a trenchant account of which see David Theo Goldberg, "Liberalism's Limits," in *Philosophers on Race*, pp. 195–204.

117. In fact, as Hobsbawm has observed, "the pressure to ban coloured immigrants, which established the 'White California' and 'White Australia' policies between 1880s and 1914, came primarily from the working class, and Lancashire unions joined with Lancashire cotton-masters to insist that India must remain deindustrialized. Internationally, socialism before 1914 remained overwhelmingly a movement of Europeans and white emigrants or their descendants" (*Age of Empire*, p. 72).

118. Pearson, *Character*, pp. 337–38.
119. Ibid., p. 342.
120. Ibid., pp. 343–44.
121. Ibid., p. 31.
122. Ibid., pp. 84–85.
123. Ibid., p. 28.
124. Harvie, *Lights*, p. 234.
125. Pearson, *Character*, pp. 16–17.
126. *Charles Henry Pearson: Memorials by Himself, His Wife, and His Friends*, ed. William Stebbing (London: Longmans, Green, 1900), p. 186.
127. Ibid., p. 184.
128. Ibid., pp. 168–69.
129. Sidgwick to Pearson, Feb. 8, 1893, Bodleian MS.Eng.Lett.d.190,175.
130. Bryce, *American Commonwealth*, p. 1424.
131. Included in *The Mind of Arthur James Balfour*, ed. Wilfrid Short (New York: George H. Doran, 1918), p. 92. Bryce would also go on to give an inaugural talk for the new Eugenics Society.
132. Ibid.
133. These paragraphs are highly indebted to Young, *Arthur James Balfour*, especially pp. 274–84.
134. Young, *Balfour*, p. 281.
135. Ibid.
136. Ibid.
137. The essay as reprinted in MEA was unchanged from its original published version, in *The National Review* 24 (December 1894), pp. 563–76. For some further remarks on the significance of this piece, see my "The *Methods* of J. B. Schneewind," with the "Response" by Schneewind. Clearly, Sidgwick, for his part, regarded Pearson's work as philosophically and epistemologically loaded, much to the discomfort of his later scholarly commentators.
138. Indeed, they clearly did not – see Stocking, *Victorian Anthropology*, and Richard Lewontin, *Biology as Ideology* (New York: HarperCollins, 1991).
139. Bryce, "Relations" (Oxford: Clarendon Press, 1902), pp. 15–16, p. 44.
140. Bryce, *American Commonwealth*, p. 1179.
141. Dicey to Bryce, Bryce MSS, Bodleian Library, Oxford University.
142. See the correspondence concerning this contained in the Sidgwick Papers, Wren Library, Add.Ms.c.104.26. Leslie Stephen also found nothing to which to object, and Dicey in fact praised the book as the only kind of historical work worth doing.

Chapter 8. Last Words?

1. Quoted in Jones, *Victorian Political Thought*, p. x.
2. Kiernan, *Lords of Human Kind*, pp. 235–36. Kiernan's work is an antidote to such nostalgic visions of empire as Cannadine's *Ornamentalism*.
3. Rayleigh, "Some Recollections of Henry Sidgwick."

4. Ibid. Indeed, Sidgwick was apt to say that since he had no "physical" courage, he hoped he at least had "moral" courage.

5. T. O. Lloyd, *The British Empire, 1558–1983* (Oxford: Oxford University Press, 1984), p. 253.

6. James Bryce, *Impressions of South Africa* (New York: Century, 1900), p. 485. The first edition of this work appeared in 1897, and Sidgwick must have known it.

7. Another tragic upshot of such notions came when Prime Minister Balfour countenanced Milner's schemes for the importation of Chinese laborers to work the Rand mines in the Transvaal: "Merely in itself it was a horror; for to ship tens of thousands of Chinese young men overseas to perform for long years the hardest underground toil, and coop them up for their leisure in horde-compounds with no society but each other's, meant deliberately creating, as in the sequel it did create, moral sinks of indescribable human beastliness" (Ensor, *England*, p. 377). Milner was of course a Balliol believer in "social service."

8. Kiernan insightfully analyzes Curzon's erudition: "Curzon's book on Persia came out in 1892, a few years before he was made Viceroy of India. He saw Persia in Churchillian fashion, as an arena where the mastery of Asia was to be decided; he prepared for his tour with Churchillian thoroughness, turning over all the two or three hundred books in European languages. Probably none of them did more to fix his ideas than *Hajji Baba*; in 1895 he wrote a foreword to a new edition of the novel, recommending it as a still faithful inventory of the 'unchanging characteristics of a singularly unchanging Oriental people.' His concern as he rode about the country filling his notebooks was with facts about Persia's trade, resources, politics, just as later on he was passionately interested in India, but not much in Indians, mere clay to be moulded on the potter's wheel of empire" (*Lords of Human Kind*, p. 131). And Said rightly stresses Curzon's "almost pedagogical view of empire"–captured in his remark that "we train here and we send out to you your governors and administrators and judges, your teachers and preachers and lawyers," and his comparison of the "Imperial fabric" to Tennyson's "Palace of Art," with English foundations and colonial pillars supporting "the vastness of an Asiatic dome" (*Orientalism*, p. 213). See also Gilmour, *Curzon*, Chapter 22.

9. Sidgwick to Balfour, April 16, 1897, Balfour Collection, British Library. Again, see Collini, "My Roles and Their Duties," for a knowledgeable account of Sidgwick's advisory work.

10. Quoted in Hobsbawn, *The Age of Empire*, p. 303.

11. Kiernan, *Lords of Human Kind*, p. 247.

12. Clearly, Sidgwick himself had always worried about the temptation to inaction, to being antipractical.

13. Dr. Talbot, too, was appreciative of Sidgwick's efforts: the Society "benefited greatly by the quiet way in which [Sidgwick] introduced order into our rather rambling discussions, and, along with the quality of his own contributions, by his earnest and hopeful desire to draw some result out of our work, which should in some degree correspond with its object of helping men of different kinds to some joint constructive thought" (M 576).

14. Sidgwick to Balfour, April 9, 1897, Balfour Collection, British Library.

15. Attached to a letter of 1895, Balfour Collection, British Library.

16. Sidgwick to Ward, May 18, 1895 (CWC). The originals of this correspondence are in the Wilfrid Ward Papers, St. Andrews University.

17. Sidgwick to Ward, December 19, 1898.

18. Sidgwick to Ward, March 4, 1898.

19. See James Ward's singularly helpful Preface to this work, which nicely traces the overlap between Sidgwick's ethics, politics, and metaphysics.

20. The passage continues: "For there can be no doubt that one of the most important sources of human error lies in the acceptance of traditions and suggestions incapable of being supported on adequate evidence."

21. Sidgwick to Ward, March 4, 1898.

22. Sidgwick to Ward, May 10, 1899.

23. On this, see F. Beiser, *The Fate of Reason: German Philosophy from Kant to Fichte* (Cambridge, MA: Harvard University Press, 1987), a fairly exhaustive account of the religious anxieties behind Kant's philosophizing. And as a construction of the dualism, the passage cited here lends weight to Schneewind's account, discussed in Chapter 4. Again, Mackie, in *The Miracle of Theism*, has also given a lucid summation of Sidgwick's dualism as a simple conflict between different accounts of what one has "most reason to do" that arises absent the moral well-orderedness of the universe.

24. Eleanor Sidgwick to Wilfrid Ward, July 3, 1906, Wilfrid Ward Papers, St. Andrews University.

25. Oppenheim, *Other World*, p. 150.

26. Sidgwick to Bryce, Aug. 8, 1894.

27. It should be duly recorded that Sidgwick also gave a great deal of money to support Hodgson in his work in the U.S., and largely paid for his travels to India and to England. See Gauld, *Founders*, p. 258. Luckhurst, in *The Invention of Telepathy*, also has much to say about Hodgson, who appears to have been a Victorian version of Joe Nickels, the brilliant debunker of more recent parapsychological pretensions.

28. Oppenheim, *Other World*, p. 150.

29. Broad, *Lectures on Psychical Research*, p. 259. According to Broad, "although instructed opinion is almost unanimous in holding that trance-mediumship supplies data which require a paranormal explanation of *some* kind, there is no consensus of experts in favour of any one suggested paranormal explanation." Broad also noted that the "interest of these phenomena to the psychical researcher depends, of course, primarily on their containing this nucleus of something *para*normal, as distinct from merely *ab*normal. But he would be most unwise to confine his attention to this, and to ignore the question of the psychological processes at the back of the phenomena of trance-mediumship in general. For any particular view that one may take as to the nature of those processes will inevitably be relevant, favourably or unfavourably, to any particular type of proposed explanation of the paranormal features which characterize some of these phenomena."

30. Quoted in Oppenheim, *Other World*, p. 376.

31. Ibid., p. 374.

32. Quoted in ibid., p. 258.
33. Almeder, *Death and Personal Survival: The Evidence for Life after Death* (Lanham, MD: Rowman and Littlefield, 1992), pp. 216–17. See also Tom Shroder, *Old Souls: The Scientific Evidence for Past Lives* (New York: Simon and Schuster, 1999).
34. Quoted in Almeder, *Death and Personal Survival*, p. 229.
35. Eleanor Sidgwick, "Different Types of Evidence for Survival," *Proceedings of the Society for Psychical Research* 29 (December 1917), pp. 250–51.
36. Oppenheim, *Other World*, p. 260.
37. Symonds, *Letters*, vol. 3, p. 671.
38. Gauld, *Founders*, p. 275.
39. Ibid., p. 326.
40. Myers, *Human Personality and Its Survival of Bodily Death*, p. 122. Needless to say, this work includes an exhaustive and very enthusiastic account of the Piper sittings, providing all the details of the reports by Lodge, Hodgson, and others.
41. Broad, "Henry Sidgwick and Psychical Research," pp. 147–48.
42. It is this vanguardism that one finds missing from such otherwise valuable accounts as Reba Soffer's "The Modern University and National Values, 1850–1910," *Historical Research* 60 (June 1987), pp. 166–87.
43. Lubenow, *The Cambridge Apostles*, p. 35.
44. Quoted in ibid., pp. 40–41.
45. Ibid., pp. 41–42.
46. Brown, *Metaphysical Society*, p. 17.
47. Allen, *The Cambridge Apostles*, p. 213.
48. Lubenow, *The Cambridge Apostles*, p. 234.
49. Ibid., p. 233.
50. Ibid., pp. 228–29.
51. Brown, *Metaphysical Society*, p. 9.
52. In Maisie Ward, *The Wilfrid Wards and the Transition* (London: Sheed and Ward, 1934), p. 419.
53. See Michael Foldy's *The Trials of Oscar Wilde* (New Haven, CT: Yale University Press, 1997), p. 30 and p. 58; George Wyndham had written to his father that "I know on the authority of Arthur Balfour, who has been told the case by the lawyers who had all the papers, that Wilde is sure to be condemned, and that the case is in every way a very serious one, involving the systematic ruin of a number of young men."
54. Sheffield Archives, ref. Carpenter MSS 386/52. This altogether remarkable letter continues with Brown explaining that in his view "men understand men & women women better than men understand women or women men" and that in "carnal connection . . . a man with a woman thinks most of his own sensation; a man with a man thinks quite as much of his companion as of himself," views that Symonds may well have shared.
55. Sheffield Archives, ref. Carpenter MSS 386/53.
56. For a somewhat fuller account of this and other exchanges between Sidgwick and Brown, see my "Eye of the Universe: Henry Sidgwick and the Problem Public," *Utilitas* 14 (July 2002), pp. 155–88.

57. Ibid., pp. 177–78. See also Schultz et al., *Strange Audacious Life*, especially on Gosse's role in constructing Symonds's reputation.
58. Brown to Carpenter, Sheffield Archives, ref. Carpenter MSS 386.
59. Sheffield Archives, ref. Carpenter MSS 386/76. This letter revealingly remarks that: "I should like to say a word on the charge of having acted unfairly to J.A.S. The question was, for me, one of great difficulty; I should like to point out that as far as J.A.S.'s place in the history of the controversy is concerned that is secured by the German book which contains all he had to say, and more than Mr. Ellis was prepared to publish in English. . . . J.A.S. had all this matter by him for years, most of it in print; the Problem in Greek Ethics was finished & printed more than ten years before his death and yet he never published it, never even put his name to the few copies he printed – this proves to me he had at least grave doubts about publishing – of course in view of his wife and family."
60. Phyllis Grosskurth, *Havelock Ellis, A Biography* (New York: Knopf, 1980), pp. 181–82. Grosskurth, along with Timothy D'Arch Smith, has been emphatic in condemning Sidgwick's efforts, albeit in a confused fashion.
61. The London specialist was Dr. Allingham.
62. I am grateful to Andrew Belsey (who enjoys the distinction of having Sidgwick as a great great uncle) for making this letter available to me.
63. Arthur Sidgwick was quite incensed when he thought that Brown might be featuring his letters in the Symonds biography, and he in fact was not particularly cooperative in supplying them.
64. Quoted in Lubenow, *The Cambridge Apostles, 1820–1914*, p. 307.
65. These details are recounted in a letter from Dakyns to his son Henry, dated August 21, 1900; my thanks to Andrew Dakyns for providing me with a copy of it, as part of our work on the unpublished manuscript *Strange Audacious Life*.
66. See Lubenow, *The Cambridge Apostles, 1820–1914*, pp. 36–38.
67. Curiously, however, Russell would often go on record as holding that it was important to treat the religious impulse with respect; see, e.g., "A Free Man's Worship." Even in this he was often the disciple of Sidgwick. And to his credit, Sidgwick was impressed with Russell's philosophical talents, writing a very enthusiastic letter of recommendation for him. It is mildly amusing, and suggestive of how little the younger set knew about Sidgwick, that, at the very time when the latter was overseeing the Symonds biography, Russell would discuss one of his Apostolic performances thus: "I was very glad, as it turned out, that they had chosen Mr. Bennet for me to write on, as [Henry] Sidgwick and two other angels turned up, and the other subjects were too intimate to read about before an old man like Sidgwick" (*Collected Papers of Bertrand Russell*, vol. I, p. 77).
68. Sidgwick Papers, Wren Library, Trinity College, Cambridge University, Add.Ms.c.100.174.
69. Myers, *Fragments*, pp, 112–13.
70. Sidgwick, "Prayer," p. 9.
71. Myers, *Fragments*, p. 113.
72. Ibid., p. 108.

73. The report of the wickerware coffin was made directly to me by the Rt. Hon. Guy Strutt, who as a boy attended Eleanor's funeral. Apparently it was when Eleanor was finally laid to rest, in 1936, that the inscription on the monument was changed to "In Thy Light Shall We See Light." The cemetary and surrounding area remain as tranquil and beautiful as in Sidgwick's day.
74. Quoted in Gauld, *Founders*, p. 316.
75. Though it should be noted that Podmore's death in 1910 may have been a suicide. See Oppenheim, *Other World*, p. 149.
76. Ethel Sidgwick, *Mrs Henry Sidgwick*, pp. 153–54.
77. Sidgwick Papers, Wren Library, Trinity College, Cambridge University, Add.Ms.c.103.
78. Myers had joined James at Dr. Baldwin's clinic in Rome, to be treated with a "serum, concocted from the testicles and other glands of goats, injections of which were alleged to relieve atheromatous conditions of the arteries." He suffered an inexplicable reaction, marked by Cheyne-Stokes breathing, and seemed, according to James, to evince an "eagerness to go." See Gauld, *Founders*, p. 333. For a very full, recent account, see Luckhurst, *The Invention of Telepathy*, pp. 253–54.
79. This letter is from the Houghton Library, Harvard University, "Sidgwick, Eleanor," 612–14.
80. Broad, *Lectures on Psychical Research*, pp. 290–91.
81. This is included in *Presidential Addresses to the Society for Psychical Research 1882–1911* (Glasgow: Robert Maclehose for the SPR, 1912), pp. 290–91.
82. This is included as an Appendix to Ethel Sidgwick, *Mrs Henry Sidgwick*, pp. 309–10.
83. E. M. Sidgwick, "The Society for Psychical Research, A Short Account of Its History and Work on the Occasion of the Society's Jubilee, 1932," *Proceedings of the Society for Psychical Research* 41 (1931–33), p. 26.
84. Barrett, *Psychical Research*, p. 237.
85. Gerald Balfour, "Psychological Aspects of Mrs. Willett's Mediumship," *Proceedings of the Society for Psychical Research* 43 (1935), p. 318.

Index